HISTORICAL DICTIONARY

The historical dictionaries present essential information on a broad range of subjects, including American and world history, art, business, cities, countries, cultures, customs, film, global conflicts, international relations, literature, music, philosophy, religion, sports, and theater. Written by experts, all contain highly informative introductory essays of the topic and detailed chronologies that, in some cases, cover vast historical time periods but still manage to heavily feature more recent events.

Brief A–Z entries describe the main people, events, politics, social issues, institutions, and policies that make the topic unique, and entries are cross-referenced for ease of browsing. Extensive bibliographies are divided into several general subject areas, providing excellent access points for students, researchers, and anyone wanting to know more. Additionally, maps, photographs, and appendixes of supplemental information aid high school and college students doing term papers or introductory research projects. In short, the historical dictionaries are the perfect starting point for anyone looking to research in these fields.

HISTORICAL DICTIONARIES OF EUROPE

Jon Woronoff, Series Editor

Greece, by Thanos M. Veremis and Mark Dragoumis. 1995.

Romania, by Kurt W. Treptow and Marcel Popa. 1996.

United Kingdom: Volume 1, England and the United Kingdom, by Kenneth J. Panton and Keith A. Cowlard. 1997.

United Kingdom: Volume 2, Scotland, Wales, and Northern Ireland, by Kenneth J. Panton and Keith A. Cowlard. 1998.

Hungary, by Steven Béla Várdy. 1997.

Ireland, by Colin Thomas and Avril Thomas. 1997.

Russia, by Boris Raymond and Paul Duffy. 1998.

Federal Republic of Yugoslavia, by Zeljan Suster. 1999.

Belgium, by Robert Stallaerts. 1999.

Poland, 2nd edition, by George Sanford. 2003.

Estonia, by Toivo Miljan. 2004.

Bulgaria, 2nd edition, by Raymond Detrez. 2006.

Sweden, 2nd edition, by Irene Scobbie. 2006.

Finland, 2nd edition, by George Maude. 2007.

Georgia, by Alexander Mikaberidze. 2007.

Belgium, 2nd edition, by Robert Stallaerts. 2007.

Moldova, 2nd edition, by Andrei Brezianu and Vlad Spânu. 2007.

Switzerland, by Leo Schelbert. 2007.

Contemporary Germany, by Derek Lewis with Ulrike Zitzlsperger. 2007.

Netherlands, 2nd edition, by Joop W. Koopmans and Arend H. Huussen Jr. 2007.

Slovenia, 2nd edition, by Leopoldina Plut-Pregelj and Carole Rogel. 2007.

Bosnia and Herzegovina, 2nd edition, by Ante Čuvalo. 2007.

Modern Italy, 2nd edition, by Mark F. Gilbert and K. Robert Nilsson. 2007.

Belarus, 2nd edition, by Vitali Silitski and Jan Zaprudnik. 2007.

Latvia, 2nd edition, by Andrejs Plakans. 2008.

Contemporary United Kingdom, by Kenneth J. Panton and Keith A. Cowlard. 2008.

Norway, by Jan Sjåvik. 2008.

Denmark, 2nd edition, by Alastair H. Thomas. 2009.

France, 2nd edition, by Gino Raymond. 2008.

Spain, 2nd edition, by Angel Smith. 2008.

Iceland, 2nd edition, by Guđmunder Hálfdanarson. 2009.

Turkey, 3rd edition, by Metin Heper and Nur Bilge Criss. 2009.

Republic of Macedonia, by Dimitar Bechev. 2009.

Cyprus, by Farid Mirbagheri. 2010.

Austria, 2nd edition, by Paula Sutter Fichtner. 2009.

Modern Greece, by Dimitris Keridis. 2009.

Czech State, 2nd edition, by Rick Fawn and Jiří Hochman. 2010.

Portugal, 3rd edition, by Douglas L. Wheeler and Walter C. Opello Jr. 2010.

Croatia, 3rd edition, by Robert Stallaerts. 2010.

Albania, 2nd edition, by Robert Elsie. 2010.

Malta, 2nd edition, by Uwe Jens Rudolf and Warren G. Berg. 2010.

Armenia, 2nd edition, by Rouben Paul Adalian. 2010.

Russian Federation, by Robert A. Saunders and Vlad Strukov. 2010.

Kosovo, 2nd edition, by Robert Elsie. 2011.

Lithuania, 2nd edition, by Saulius Sužiedėlis. 2011.

Ukraine, 2nd edition, by Ivan Katchanovski, Zenon E. Kohut, Bohdan Y. Nebesio, and Myroslav Yurkevich. 2013.

Ireland, new edition, by Frank A. Biletz. 2014.

Slovakia, 3rd edition, by Stanislav J. Kirschbaum. 2014.

Switzerland, 2nd edition, by Leo Schelbert. 2014.

Bulgaria, 3rd edition, by Raymond Detrez. 2015.

Georgia, 2nd edition, by Alexander Mikaberidze. 2015.

Estonia, 2nd edition, by Toivo Miljan. 2015.

Sweden, 3rd edition, by Elisabeth Elgán and Irene Scobbie. 2015.

Netherlands, 3rd edition, by J. W. Koopmans. 2015.

Iceland, 2nd edition, by Sverrir Jakobsson and Guðmunder Hálfdanarson. 2016.

Denmark, 3rd edition, by Alastair H. Thomas. 2016.

Contemporary Germany, 2nd edition, by Derek Lewis and Ulrike Zitzlsperger. 2016.

Historical Dictionary of Contemporary Germany

Second Edition

Derek Lewis and Ulrike Zitzlsperger

ROWMAN & LITTLEFIELD
Lanham • Boulder • New York • Toronto • Plymouth, UK

Published by Rowman & Littlefield
4501 Forbes Boulevard, Suite 200, Lanham, Maryland 20706
http://www.rowman.com

10 Thornbury Road, Plymouth PL6 7PP, United Kingdom

British Library Cataloguing in Publication Information Available

Library of Congress Cataloging-in-Publication Data

Names: Lewis, Derek (Derek R.), author. | Zitzlsperger, Ulrike, author.
Title: Historical dictionary of contemporary Germany / Derek Lewis and Ulrike Zitzlsperger.
Description: Second edition. | Lanham, Maryland : Rowman & Littlefield, 2016. | Series: Historical dictionaries of Europe | Includes bibliographical references.
Identifiers: LCCN 2016011958 (print) | LCCN 2016014451 (ebook) | ISBN 9781442269569 (hardcover : alk. paper) | ISBN 9781442269576 (electronic)
Subjects: LCSH: Germany—History—1945—Dictionaries. | Germany—History—1945—Chronology.
Classification: LCC DD237 .L395 2016 (print) | LCC DD237 (ebook) | DDC 943.08703—dc23
LC record available at http://lccn.loc.gov/2016011958

Printed in the United States of America

Contents

Editor's Foreword

Germany is again at the center of Europe physically, partly because Europe itself has expanded to the east and partly because the country has become an indispensable partner in virtually all European undertakings, to say nothing of a leader of the European Union. Indeed, Germany's chancellor, Angela Merkel, is generally regarded as setting the agenda not only for economy and trade but even for foreign policy. Obviously this new Germany is different from the old one that collapsed in 1945 and different from the divided Germany that was reunified in 1990. Indeed, it has even changed measurably since the first edition of this book, which explains the need for a second edition. This is essential to show just what has been accomplished by the "new" Germany, which for our purposes is dated back to 1961 and the building of the Berlin Wall.

Like the other country volumes, this second edition of the *Historical Dictionary of Contemporary Germany* starts with a chronology that traces events through the years. This is followed by a list of acronyms. Of particular interest is the introduction, which provides an excellent overview of the country and its progress in multiple fields. But this is overshadowed, and further explained, by a growing dictionary section with entries on significant persons, places, institutions, events, and issues. Important figures are mentioned in the appendixes. Finally, no matter how big the dictionary—and it has certainly expanded substantially since last time—the bibliography again directs readers to thousands of other sources in English and German.

Summing up such a large, important, and varied country as Germany was certainly not easy, and fortunately it has been done by the same team that wrote the first edition. Derek Lewis was senior lecturer in German at Exeter University in the United Kingdom until 2005 and also a visiting lecturer at the University of Würzburg. He has published extensively, including two books: *The New Germany* and *Contemporary Germany: A Handbook*. While Dr. Lewis handled the political, economic, and social aspects, the cultural side was covered by Professor Ulrike Zitzlsperger, director of education for modern languages at Exeter University since 2014. Between them they have provided a very insightful look at what is clearly again a key—if not *the* key—player in contemporary Europe.

Jon Woronoff
Series Editor

Preface

This *Historical Dictionary of Contemporary Germany* addresses the main historical, cultural, and social developments of the Federal Republic of Germany (FRG), with some additional information about the former German Democratic Republic (GDR). It covers the period from the building of the Berlin Wall (1961) to the present day. West Germany remained remarkably stable following the foundation of the FRG in 1949 and became something of a model state in many respects. It is still widely admired for the "social partnership" between industry and government, which has promoted economic success alongside democratic structures; for its role of quiet leadership within Europe; and for its pioneering measures to improve and sustain the environment. Although many aspects of the "German model" of the 1970s no longer apply as the nation confronts new social, economic, and political challenges that have emerged, especially since reunification, Germany is still regarded as a cornerstone of a greatly expanded European Union (EU), as a reliable but still somewhat cautious partner in the North Atlantic Treaty Organization (NATO), and as a democracy in which civil and human rights are respected. This revised edition also considers Germany's responses to more recent issues, such as the eurozone financial crisis and the challenges of a global foreign policy. In addition, more attention has been given to the country's ethnic minorities, its evolving policy toward immigration, and the issues raised by increasing numbers of asylum seekers.

Contemporary Germany cannot, however, be properly understood without reference to its historical background. The postwar constitution, or Basic Law (Grundgesetz), both reflects Germany's tradition of federalism and has provided the foundation for a modern democratic state embedded in multilateral international structures. Despite shifts in physical boundaries and profound demographic changes, the federal states have retained many of their traditions and identities reaching back to the Middle Ages. Similar considerations apply to aspects of human and economic geography. Many of Germany's leading companies originated in the industrial revolution of the 19th century, a factor that is reflected in the selected accounts of their corporate evolution included in this volume and which makes current developments in a global market all the more interesting.

Germany's political culture, in which federal structures play a key role alongside central institutions, and where it is traditional for political leaders to first make their mark at the regional level before moving onto the national stage, provides a wide range of personalities—probably much more so than in "centrist" states such as France or Great Britain. This book presents the leading figures at both the national and regional levels, although some gaps in coverage are inevitable.

Finally, this book attempts to provide overviews of and insights into aspects of contemporary German culture, with entries on literature, the theater, cinema, and architecture and references to important contemporary institutions, personalities, and movements. The entries include a cross-section of topical debates and terms that are frequently mentioned in relevant cultural histories. Few are subject specific; instead, they relate to general aspects of the arts, media, sociology, architecture, and other facets of culture that influence the working of society and establish a narrative trend closely linked to issues that preoccupy the wider public.

To facilitate the rapid and efficient location of information and make this book as useful a reference tool as possible, extensive cross-references have been provided in the dictionary section. Within individual entries, terms that have their own entries are in boldface type the first time they appear. Related terms that are not discussed in a particular entry but have their own entries are provided as *See also* cross-references. *See* references take the reader from topics that do not have their own annotations to related entries that deal with those topics.

Acronyms and Abbreviations

Items marked with an asterisk are translations/descriptions provided by the author. In other cases, the English translations have been found in authoritative sources. For abbreviations of government ministries, see the entry FEDERAL GOVERNMENT.

AA	Auswärtiges Amt (Federal Foreign Office)
AdK	Akademie der Künste (Academy of Arts)
AfD	Alternative für Deutschland (Alternative for Germany*)
AfNS	Amt für Nationale Sicherheit (Office for National Security*)
AG	Aktiengesellschaft (joint stock corporation)
AGIL	Alternative-Grünen-Initiativen-Liste (Alternative Greens Initiative List*)
AI	Amnesty International
AKA	Ausfuhrkredit-Gesellschaft mbH
AL	Alternative Liste für Demokratie und Umweltschutz (Alternative List for Democracy and Environmental Protection [Berlin])
ALFA	Allianz für Fortschritt und Aufbruch (Alliance for Progress and Awakening*)
AMCF	Association of Management Consulting Firms
ANOG	Arbeitsgemeinschaft für naturnahen Obst-, Gemüse- und Feldfruchtanbau (Federation for Natural Methods in Fruit and Vegetable Farming*)
AOK	Allgemeine Ortskrankenkasse
APO	Außerparlamentarische Opposition (Extra-Parliamentary Opposition)
ARD	Arbeitsgemeinschaft öffentlich-rechtlicher Rundfunkanstalten der Bundesrepublik Deutschland (Association of Public Broadcasting Corporations in the Federal Republic of Germany)

ARGUS — Arbeitsgemeinschaft für Umweltschutz und Stadtgestaltung (Assocation for Environmental Protection and Urban Design*)

ASB — Arbeiter-Samariter-Bund (Workers' Samaritan Association*)

ASHIP — Association of Statutory Health Insurance Physicians (kassenärztliche Vereinigung)

ASKI — Arbeitskreis Selbständiger Kulturinstitute e.V. (Work Group of Independent Cultural Institutes*)

ASR — Akademie für Staats- und Rechtswissenschaften (Academy for Political and Law Sciences,* GDR)

AStA — Allgemeiner Studentenausschuss/Studierendenausschuss (German Students' Association*)

ATD — Anti-Terror-Datei (Antiterror Database)

AWO — Arbeiterwohlfahrtsorganisaton (Workers' Welfare Organization*)

AZR — Ausländerzentralregister (Central Register of Foreigners*)

BA — Bundesagentur für Arbeit (Federal Employment Agency; formerly Bundesanstalt für Arbeit, Federal Labor Office)

BAF — Bundesaufsichtsamt für Flugsicherung

BaFöG — Bundesausbildungsförderungsgesetz (law regulating student grants*)

BAK — Bundesarchitektenkammer (Federal Chamber of Architects)

B.A.U.M. — Bundesdeutsche Arbeitskreis für Umweltbewusstes Management (German Environmental Management Association)

BBU — Bundesverband Bürgerinitiativen Umweltschutz (Federation of Citizens' Initiatives for Environmental Protection*)

BDA — Bund Deutscher Architekten (Association of German Architects)

BDA — Bundesvereinigung der Deutschen Arbeitgeberverbände (Confederation of German Employers' Associations)

BDI — Bundesverband der Deutschen Industrie (Federation of German Industries)

BDL — Bank Deutscher Länder (Bank of German Federal States*)

BdV	Bund der Vertriebenen (Federation of Expellees*)
BfA	Bundesversicherungsanstalt für Angestellte
BFB	Bund Freier Bürger (Federation of Free Citizens*)
BFD	Bund Freier Demokraten (Federation of Free Democrats*)
BfN	Bundesamt für Naturschutz (Federal Office for the Protection of Nature)
BfV	Bundesamt für Verfassungsschutz (Federal Office for the Protection of the Constitution)
BGA	Bundesverband des Deutschen Groß- und Außenhandels e. V. (Federation of German Wholesale and Foreign Trade)
BHE	Bund der Heimatvertriebenen und Entrechteten (Federation of Refugees, Schleswig-Holstein*)
BIBB	Bundesinstitut für Berufsbildung (Federal Institute for Vocational Education*)
BITS	Berliner Institut für Transnationale Sicherheit (Berlin Institute for Transnational Security*)
BKA	Bundeskriminalamt (Federal Criminal Police Office)
BL	Basic Law (Grundgesetz, GG)
BLK	Bund-Länder-Kommission (joint government/federal state commission*)
BMBF	Bundesministerium für Bildung und Forschung (Federal Ministry of Education and Research)
BMEL	Bundesministerium für Ernährung und Landwirtschaft (Federal Ministry of Food and Agriculture)
BMF	Bundesministerium der Finanzen (Federal Ministry of Finance)
BMFSFJ	Bundesministerium für Familie, Senioren, Frauen und Jugend (Federal Ministry of Family Affairs, Senior Citizens, Women and Youth)
BMG	Bertelsmann Music Group
BMI	Bundesministerium des Innern (Federal Ministry of the Interior)
BMJV	Bundesministerium der Justiz und Verbraucherschutz (Federal Ministry of Justice and Consumer Protection)

BMUB	Bundesministerium für Umwelt, Naturschutz, Bau und Reaktorsicherheit (Federal Ministry for the Environment, Nature Conservation, Building and Nuclear Safety)
BMVg	Bundesministerium der Verteidigung (Federal Ministry of Defense)
BMVI	Bundesministerium für Verkehr und digitale Infrastruktur (Federal Ministry of Transport and Digital Infrastructure)
BMWi	Bundesministerium für Wirtschaft und Energie (Federal Ministry for Economic Affairs and Energie)
BMZ	Bundesministerium für wirtschaftliche Zusammenarbeit und Entwicklung (Federal Ministry for Economic Cooperation and Development.
BND	Bundesnachrichtendienst (Federal Intelligence Service)
BNetzA	Bundesnetzagentur für Elektrizität, Gas, Telekommunikation, Post und Eisenbahnen (Federal Agency for Electricity, Gas, Telecommunications, Post and Railways*)
BÖLW	Bund der Ökologischen Lebensmittelwirtschaft (Federation of the Organic Food Industry*)
BP	Bayernpartei (Bavaria Party)
BRIC	Brazil, India, China (countries)
BStU	Bundesbeauftragte(r) für die Unterlagen des Staatssicherheitsdienstes der ehemaligen Deutschen Demokratischen Republik (Federal Commissioner for the Records of the State Security Service of the Former German Democratic Republic)
BVS	Bundesanstalt für vereinigungsbedingte Sonderaufgaben (successor to the Trust Agency)
BVV	Bezirksverordnetenversammlung (a local district council or assembly in Berlin)
BVVG	Bodenverwertungs- und verwaltungs GmbH (company set up in 1992 to privatize state-land, property, and other assets in eastern Germany)
CAP	Common Agricultural Policy (German: *gemeinsame Agrarpolitik*)
CASTOR	Cask for storage and transport of radioactive material

CDA	Christlich-Demokratische Arbeitnehmerschaft (Christian Democratic Employees' Association*)
CDU	Christlich Demokratische Union (Christian Democratic Union)
CETA	Comprehensive Economic and Trade Agreement
CFE	Treaty on Conventional Armed Forces in Europe
CFSP	Common Foreign and Security Policy
CIA	Central Intelligence Agency (U.S.)
CSCE	Conference on Security and Cooperation in Europe
CSDP	Common Security and Defense Policy
CSU	Christlich-Soziale Union (Christian Social Union)
DA	Demokratischer Aufbruch (Democratic Awakening)
DAAD	Deutscher Akademischer Austauschdienst (German Academic Exchange Service)
DAM	Deutsches Architekturmuseum (German Museum of Architecture*)
DAZ	Deutsches Zentrum für Architektur, Planungs- und Bauwesen (German Museum for Architecture, Planning, and Building*)
DBD	Demokratische Bauernpartei Deutschlands (Democratic Farmworkers' Party of Germany*)
DBU	Deutsche Bundesstiftung Umwelt (German Federal Environmental Foundation)
DDfE	Direkte Demokratie für Europa (Direct Democracy for Europe*)
DDP	Deutsche Demokratische Partei
DEK	Deutscher Evangelischer Kirchentag (Conference of German Evangelical Churches*)
DFB	Deutscher Fußballbund (German Soccer Association)
dffb	Deutsche Film- und Fernsehakademie Berlin (German Film and Television Academy Berlin*)
DFG	Deutsche Forschungsgemeinschaft (German Research Association*)
DFS	Deutsche Flugsicherung GmbH (organization responsible for air navigation services*)

DGB	Deutscher Gewerkschaftsbund (German Federation of Trade Unions)
DIF	Deutsches Filminstitut
DIHK	Deutsche Industrie- und Handelskammer (Association of German Chambers of Industry and Commerce)
DKP	Deutsche Kommunistische Partei (German Communist Party)
DLM	Direktorenkonferenz der Landesmedienanstalten (Conference of Directors of State Media Authorities*)
DM	Deutsche Mark (currency of the FRG until 2002)
DOSB	Deutscher Olympischer Sportbund (German Olympic Sports Federation)
DPG	Deutsche Postgewerkschaft (German Postal Trade Union*)
DPS	Deutsche Partei Saar (German Saarland Party*)
DRP	Deutsche Reichspartei
DSB	Deutscher Sportbund (German Sports Federation)
DSU	Deutsche Soziale Union (German Social Union)
DSW	Deutsches Studentenwerk (German National Association for Student Affairs)
DVP	Deutsche Volkspartei (German People's Party*)
DVU	Deutsche Volksunion (German People's Union*)
DW	Deutsche Welle (German world broadcasting service*)
EAEC	European Atomic Energy Community
EC	European Community or European Communities
ECB	European Central Bank (Europäische Zentralbank, EZB)
ECHR	European Court of Human Rights (Europäischer Gerichtshof für Menschenrechte)
ECJ	European Court of Justice (Europäischer Gerichtshof)
ECOFIN	Economic and Financial Affairs Council of Ministers
ECSC	European Community for Coal and Steel
EDU	European Democratic Union
EEC	European Economic Community
EEG	Erneuerbare-Energien-Gesetz (law on renewable energy*)
EFGP	European Federation of Green Parties

EFiD	Evangelische Frauen in Deutschland e.V.
eG	Eingetragene Genossenschaft (registered cooperative*)
EK	Ersatzkrankenkasse
EKD	Evangelische Kirche in Deutschland (Evangelical Church in Germany)
EKU	Evangelische Kirche der Union (Evangelical Church of the Union)
EMAS	Environmental Management and Audit Scheme
EMI	European Monetary Institute
EMS	European Monetary System
EMU	European Monetary Union
EOS	Erweiterte Oberschule (extended upper school, GDR)
EPP	European People's Party
ERM	European Exchange Rate Mechanism
ERP	European Recovery Program
ESCB	European System of Central Banks
ESDP	European Security and Defense Policy
ESS	European Security Strategy
EU	European Union
EURATOM	European Atomic Energy Community
EVG	Eisenbahn- und Verkehrsgewerkschaft (rail workers' trade union)
EVZ	Stiftung Erinnerung, Verantwortung, und Zukunft (Foundation Remembrance, Responsibility and Future)
FAZ	*Frankfurter Allgemeine Zeitung*
FCC	Federal Constitutional Court (Bundesverfassungsgericht, or BVerfG)
FDGB	Freier Deutscher Gewerkschaftsbund (Free German Trade Union Federation, GDR)
FDJ	Freie Deutsche Jugend (Free German Youth, GDR)
FDK	Familienbund der Deutschen Katholiken (Federation of German Catholic Families*)
FDP	Freie Demokratische Partei (Free Democratic Party)

FRG	Federal Republic of Germany (Bundesrepublik Deutschland, BRD)
GAL	Grün-Alternative Liste (Green Alternative List*)
GASIM	Gemeinsames Analyse- und Strategiezentrum illegale Migration (Joint Center for Illegal Migration Analysis and Policy)
GAZ	Grüne Aktion Zukunft (Green Action Future*)
GDBA	Gewerkschaft Deutscher Reichsbahnbeamten und Anwärter (rail and transport workers' union, renamed in 1994 the Verkehrsgewerkschaft GDBA)
GDP	gross domestic product
GDR	German Democratic Republic (Deutsche Demokratische Republik, DDR)
GETZ	Gemeinsames Extremismus- und Terrorismusabwehrzentrum (Joint Center for Countering Extremism and Terrorism)
GfdS	Gesellschaft für deutsche Sprache (Society for German Language)
GG	Grundgesetz (Basic Law)
GKV	Gesetzliche Krankenversicherung (statutory health insurance)
GM	genetically modified
GMF	German Marshall Fund of the United States
GMP	Gerkan Marg and Partners
GTAZ	Gemeinsames Terrorismusabwehrzentrum (Joint Counterterrorism Center)
GUE/NGL	Confederal Group of the European United Left/Nordic Green Left (in the European Parliament)
GVP	Gesamtdeutsche Volkspartei (All-German People's Party)
HDW	Howaldswerke Deutsche Werft AG
HFF	Hochschule für Fernsehen und Film (University for Television and Film*)
HHG	Helsinki Headline Goal
HRG	Hochschulrahmengesetz (Higher Education Framework Law*)

HRK	Hochschulrektorenkonferenz (Conference of University Rectors)
HVB	Hypo- und Vereinsbank AG
HVK	Hauptverteidigungskräfte (Main Defense Forces*)
IAB	Institut für Arbeitsmarkt- und Berufsforschung (Institute for Employment Research)
IBA	Internationale Bauausstellung (International Building Exhibition)
IBD	Identitäre Bewegung Deutschland (Identitarian Movement for Germany*)
ICC	International Congress Center (Berlin)
ICPR	International Commission for the Protection of the Rhine/ Internationale Kommission zum Schutz des Rheins (IKSR)
IDA-NRW	Informations- und Dokumentationszentrum für Antirassismusarbeit in Nordrhein-Westfalen (Information and Documentation Center for Anti-Racism in North Rhine-Westfalia*)
IDS	Institut für deutsche Sprache (Institute for German Language*)
IFS	Internationale Filmschule Cologne GmbH (International Film College Cologne GmbH*)
IKSR	See ICPR
IMF	International Monetary Fund
INF	Intermediate Range Nuclear Forces
IR	Islamrat (Council of Islam*)
IS	Islamic State
ISAF	International Security Force in Afghanistan
ITUC	International Trade Union Federation (German: Internationaler Gewerkschaftsbund, IGB)
ITWF	International Transport Workers' Federation
IUB	International University of Bremen
JFB	Jüdischer Frauenbund in Deutschland (Jewish Women's Federation in Germany*)
JN	Junge Nationaldemokraten (Young National Democrats*)

JU	Junge Union (Young Union, the youth wing of the CDU/CSU*)
JUSO	Jungsozialisten (Young Socialists, the youth wing of the SPD*)
KEK	Kommission zur Ermittlung der Konzentration im Medienbereich (Commission on Concentration in the Media)
KFOR	Kosovo Force
KfW	Kreditanstalt für Wiederaufbau (Bank for Reconstruction*)
KJVD	Kommunistischer Jugendverband Deutschlands (Communist Youth Federation of Germany*)
KMK	Kultusministerkonferenz (Standing Conference of State Ministers of Education)
KPD	Kommunistische Partei Deutschlands (Communist Party of Germany)
KRK	Krisenreaktionskräfte (Crisis Response Forces*)
LDP	Liberal-Demokratische Partei (Liberal Democratic Party*)
LDPD	Liberal-Demokratische Partei Deutschlands (Liberal-Democratic Party of Germany)
L-E-R	Lebensgestaltung-Ethik-Religionskunde (Education in Lifestyle, Ethics, and Religion*)
LPG	Landwirtschaftliche Produktionsgenossenschaft (agricultural cooperative, GDR*)
LSG	Landschaftsschutzgebiet (Landscape Protection Area*)
MBFR	Mutual Balanced Forces Reduction
MfS	Ministerium für Nationale Sicherheit (see Stasi)
MINUSMA	United Nations Multidimensional Integrated Stabilization Mission in Mali
MLPD	Marxistisch-Leninistische Partei Deutschlands (Marxist-Leninist Party of Germany)
NACC	North Atlantic Cooperation Council
NASHIP	National Association of Statutory Health Insurance Physicians
NATO	North Atlantic Treaty Organization

NÖSPL	Neues Ökonomisches System der Planung und Leitung (New Economic System of Planning and Management, GDR)
NOK	Nationales Olympisches Komitee (National Olympic Committee)
NPD	Nationaldemokratische Partei Deutschlands (National Democratic Party of Germany)
NPDP	National-Demokratische Partei Deutschlands (National-Democratic Party of Germany, GDR*)
NRC	NATO–Russia Council
NRW	Nordrhein-Westfalen (North Rhine-Westfalia)
NSA	National Security Agency (U.S.)
NSG	Naturschutzgebiet (Nature Protection Reserve*)
NSU	Nationalsozialistische Untergrund (Nazi terror group)
NSWE	Deutsche NordseeWerke, Emden
NVA	Nationale Volksarmee (National People's Army, GDR)
OA	Ost-Ausschuss der deutschen Wirtschaft (Committee on Eastern European Economic Relations)
OECD	Organisation for Economic Co-operation and Development
ÖLG	Öko-Landbaugesetz (law on ecological farming*)
OMT	Outright Monetary Transactions
OPEC	Organization of the Petroleum Exporting Countries
ÖSS	Ökonomisches System des Sozialismus (Economic System of Socialism*)
ÖTV	Öffentliche Dienste, Transport und Verkehr (public service transport workers union*)
PCA	Partnership and Cooperation Agreement
PDS	Partei des Demokratischen Sozialismus (Party of Democratic Socialism)
PISA	OECD Programme for International Student Assessment
PJC	Permanent Joint Council
PKK	Partiya Karkerên Kurdistanê (Kurdistan Workers' Party)
PKV	Private Krankenversicherung (private health insurance)
POS	Polytechnische Oberschule (General Polytechnical Upper School, GDR)

PPR	personalized proportional representation
PRC	People's Republic of China
PRO	Partei Rechtsstaatliche Offensive (Law and Order Offensive Party)
PSI	Public Services International
QE	quantitative easing
RAF	Rote Armee Fraktion (Red Army Faction)
RCC	Regional Cooperation Council
RegTP	Regulierungsbehörde für Telekommunikation und Post (Regulatory Body for Telecommunications and Post*)
REP	Die Republikaner (The Republicans)
RIB	Rüstungsinformationsbüro (Arms Information Bureau*)
RLP	Rheinland-Pfalz (Rhineland-Palatinate)
RSBK	Rudolf Scharping Strategie Beratung Kommunikation GmbH
RuDEA	Russian–German Energy Agency
SALT	Strategic Arms Limitation Talks
SAP	Sozialistische Arbeiterpartei (Socialist Workers' Party*)
S&D	Progressive Alliance of Socialists and Democrats
SDP	Sozial Demokratische Partei in der DDR (Social Democratic Party in the GDR)
SDS	Sozialistischer Deutscher Studentenbund (Federation of Socialist German Students)
SED	Sozialistische Einheitspartei Deutschlands (Socialist Unity Party of Germany)
SFVV	Stiftung Flucht, Vertreibung, Versöhnung (Federal Foundation Flight, Expulsion, Reconciliation)
SGB	Sozialgesetzbuch (social security law codex*)
SME	small to medium-sized enterprise
SÖL	Stiftung Ökologie und Landbau (Foundation for Ecology and Agriculture*)
SPD	Sozial-Demokratische Partei Deutschlands (Social Democratic Party of Germany)
SPSEE	Stability Pact for South Eastern Europe

SRP	Sozialistische Reichspartei Deutschlands
SRU	Sachverständigenrat für Umweltfragen (The German Advisory Council on the Environment)
SSW	Südschleswigscher Wählerverband (South Schleswig Electoral Association*)
START	Strategic Arms Reduction Talks
Stasi	Staatssicherheitsamt (East German secret police)
SWP	Stiftung Wissenschaft und Politik
TEEC	Treaty establishing the European Economic Community
TSCG	Treaty on Stability, Coordination and Governance
TTIP	Trans-Atlantic Trade and Investment Partnership
UEFA	Union of European Football Associations
UEK	Union Evangelischer Kirchen in Deutschland (Union of Evangelical Churches in Germany*)
UN	United Nations
UNEF	United Nations Emergency Force
UNESCO	United Nations Educational, Scientific and Cultural Organization
UNIFIL	United Nations Interim Force in Lebanon
UNTAC	United Nations Transitional Authority in Cambodia
U.S.	United States of America
USSR	Union of Soviet Socialist Republics
VCI	Verband der Chemischen Industrie (Association of Chemical Industries)
VDA	Verband der Automobilindustrie (Automobile Industry Association*)
VDE	Verband der Elektrotechnik, Elektronik und Informationstechnik (Association for Electrical, Electronic and Information Technologies; also Verkehrsprojekte Deutsche Einheit, German Unity Transport Project)
VDMA	Verband Deutscher Maschinen- und Anlagebau (Federation of German Machine and Plant Production)
VDZ	Verband Deutscher Zeitschriftenverleger (Association of German Magazine Publishers*)
VEB	Volkseigener Betrieb (state-owned concern in the GDR)

VELKD	Vereinigte Evangelisch-Lutherische Kirche Deutschlands (United Evangelical-Lutheran Church in Germany)
VFA	Verband Forschender Arzneimittelhersteller (Association of Research-Based Pharmaceutical Companies)
WASG	Wahlalternative Arbeit und Soziale Gerechtigkeit (Election Alternative for Labor and Social Justice*)
WDA	Weltverband Deutscher Auslandsschulen (Association of German Schools Abroad*)
WEU	Western European Union
WHO	World Health Organization
WIZO	Women's International Zionist Organization (Germany)
WR	Wissenschaftsrat (Research Council)
WTO	World Trade Organization
ZfA	Zentrum für Antisemitismusforschung (Center for Research into Anti-Semitism*)
ZIB	Zentrum für internationale Bildungsvergleichsstudien (Center for International Student Assessment)
ZKM	Zentrum für Kunst- und Medientechnologie (Center for Art and Media, Karlsruhe)
ZMD	Zentralrat der Muslime in Deutschland (Central Council of Muslims in Germany*)
ZVEI	Zentralverband Elektrotechnik- und Elektronikindustrie (German Electrical and Electronic Manufacturers' Association)
ZVS	Zentralstelle für die Vergabe von Studienplätzen (Central Student Admissions Office*)
ZWST	Zentralwohlfahrtsstelle der Juden in Deutschland (Central Welfare Office for Jews in Germany).

Map

Chronology

The following chronology lists key events in German politics and society from 1961 to 2015. The main focus is the FRG, although events in the former GDR are also covered. Material is drawn from a variety of printed chronicles, including *Die Fischer Chronik Deutschland* (the latest edition covers 1949–2014) and the *Fischer Weltalmanach*, which appears annually. Of Internet sources and news archives, FAZ (from 2001) offers accessible monthly summaries of main events. Online annual chronicles up to 2008 are available from the Lebendiges Museum Online project at the Haus der Deutschen Geschichte; a yearly index is available at http://www.dhm.de/lemo/home.html (for direct access, a sample address is http://www.hdg.de/lemo/html/2008/).

1961 1 January: Trade between the GDR and the FRG, regulated under the terms of a treaty from 1951 but suspended by West Germany in 1960 in response to restrictions imposed by the East Germans on West Berliners visiting East Berlin, is resumed. **18 March:** Franz-Josef Strauß is elected leader of the Christian Social Union (CSU). **3 April:** The first civilian service volunteers start work instead of military conscription. **3–4 June:** Soviet and U.S. leaders Nikita Khrushchev and John F. Kennedy meet in Vienna to discuss disarmament and Berlin, but fail to reach agreement; the Western powers later turn down a Russian proposal for a neutral and demilitarized Berlin. **6 June:** The FRG launches a second German television channel (ZDF), which begins broadcasting on 1 April 1963. **15 June:** East German leader Walter Ulbricht denies plans to erect a wall in Berlin separating the eastern and western sectors. **17 June:** The FRG's first nuclear power station begins operating in Kahl, Bavaria. **30 June:** The FRG sets up a new pillar of social welfare support. **25 July:** John F. Kennedy declares his determination to defend West Berlin and maintain a military presence there. **13 August:** The East Germans start erecting the Berlin Wall. **30 October:** The FRG and Turkey conclude an agreement for Turkish guest workers to work in Germany. **7 November:** Konrad Adenauer (CDU) is reelected federal chancellor and a coalition government of the CDU, CSU, and FDP is formed on 14 November. **30 November:** In a letter to Adenauer, GDR minister president Otto Grotewohl proposes normalizing relations between East and West Germany, but the FRG government refuses to receive it. **15 December:** The trial of former SS officer Adolf Eichmann starts in Jerusalem. **30 December:** GDR leader Walter Ulbricht claims that the mass exodus of East Germans to the West has cost the economy 30 billion Marks.

1962 15–18 January: U.S. and Soviet tanks withdraw from positions at checkpoints. **24 January:** The GDR People's Chamber introduces military conscription. **16–17 February:** Severe floods hit northern Germany. **22 February:** East Germany introduces a visa requirement for West Germans entering the GDR. **5 April:** The Bundestag introduces state funding for political parties. **1 June:** Adolf Eichmann is executed in Tel Aviv. **2–8 July:** Chancellor Konrad Adenauer's state visit to France heralds postwar Franco-German reconciliation. **17 August:** The shooting by East German guards of 18-year-old Paul Fechter while he is attempting to flee over the Berlin Wall provokes violent demonstrations in West Berlin. **22 August:** The USSR announces the closure of its garrison headquarters in East Berlin. **23 August:** News emerges that the drug thalidomide (Contergan), produced by Chemie-Grünenthal and released in 1957 to counter the effects of morning sickness in pregnant mothers, has led to thousands of birth deformities; the trial of Grünenthal employees is shut down in December 1970, with evidence uncovered by the UK Thalidomide Trust in August 2014 of government intervention (Harold Evans, "Thalidomide: How Men Who Blighted Lives of Thousands Evaded Justice," *Guardian*, 15 November 2014). **4–9 September:** French president Charles de Gaulle pays a state visit to the FRG. **26 October:** Start of the "*Spiegel* affair," in which police raid *Der Spiegel* magazine after it criticizes government defense policy, and its editors are arrested on suspicion of treason. **19 November:** In the wake of the *Spiegel* affair, FDP ministers withdraw from the coalition, demanding the immediate resignation of defense minister Franz-Josef Strauß and, within the current legislative period, of Chancellor Konrad Adenauer; Strauß resigns on 30 November, and the coalition continues on 11 December.

1963 15–21 January: The ruling SED party in the GDR adopts its first manifesto program and statutes and confirms Walter Ulbricht's leadership and policies of Soviet-oriented communism. **22 January:** Chancellor Konrad Adenauer and President Charles de Gaulle sign the landmark Elysée Treaty of Franco-German cooperation in political, economic, and cultural affairs. **7 March:** Germany and Poland sign a trade agreement. **14 April:** The first Easter marches take place in West German cities, protesting against military uses of nuclear power; these become an annual event. **23–26 June:** U.S. president John F. Kennedy visits the FRG and West Berlin, where he makes his famous "Ich bin ein Berliner" speech, in which he stresses that all free people, wherever they live, are citizens of Berlin. **24–25 June:** The GDR introduces its "New Economic System of Planning and Control." **17 July:** Speaking in Tützingen, Egon Bahr (SPD) introduces his vision of a new German Ostpolitik based on "change through rapprochement." **5 August:** The USA, UK, and USSR sign a treaty limiting nuclear weapons testing; the FRG joins the agreement on 19 August. **15 October:** Chancellor Konrad Adenauer resigns. **16 October:** Ludwig Erhard (CDU) is elected federal chancellor, continuing the CDU/CSU–FDP coalition. **8 December:** East German leader Walter Ulbricht declares his willingness to negotiate with Erhard's government. **17 December:** For the first time since the erection of the Berlin Wall, West Berliners are permitted to visit East Berlin during Christmas and the New Year. **20 December:** Twenty-one former guards from the Auschwitz concentration camp go on trial in Frankfurt/Main (the trial ends in August 1965).

1964 2 January: Identity cards in the GDR now include the designation "citizen of the German Democratic Republic." **14 February:** The five-member independent economic Council of Experts is constituted. **15–16 February:** Willy Brandt is elected SPD party leader and chancellor candidate. **17 March:** The FRG and Portugal conclude an agreement on guest workers for Germany. **19 March:** Several federal states agree to build new universities, marking a significant expansion of the higher education system. **22 March:** Chancellor Erhard rejects the Oder–Neiße line as the boundary between Germany and Poland. **3 May:** Opening of the first direct air link between the FRG and the USSR. **12 June:** The GDR and USSR sign a 20-year friendship treaty, which refers for the first time to two separate sovereign German states and to West Berlin as an independent political entity; the FRG and Western powers reject the "three-state theory." **10 September:** The number of foreign guest workers in the FRG reaches one million. **6 October:** The GDR amnesties 10,000 prisoners, including political detainees. **2 November:** For the first time since the Berlin Wall was built, pensioners are allowed to visit the West. **28 November:** The neo-Nazi National Democratic Party of Germany (NPD) is founded in Hanover. **1 December:** The GDR requires Western visitors to convert a minimum amount of Western currency into East German marks.

1965 27 January: The Bundestag passes a law on assistance for refugees from the GDR. **12 February:** Responding to the increasing number of foreigners in the FRG, the Bundestag passes a new law giving rights equal to those of German citizens. **24 February:** East German leader Walter Ulbricht visits Cairo, the first time he has visited a non–Warsaw Pact state; in response the FRG suspends economic aid to Egypt on 7 March. **25 February:** The GDR People's Chamber agrees on a reform of the national education system. **25 March:** The Bundestag sets the limitation period on war crimes prosecutions at 1969. **6 April:** The Russians protest at the holding of plenary sessions of the Bundestag in West Berlin by overflying them with jet aircraft and blocking overland routes to the city. **6 May:** Leading assemblies and councils of the GDR declare that a reunited Germany must be socialist. **12 May:** Nine Arab states break off links with the FRG after it opens diplomatic relations with Israel. **19 August:** Verdicts are announced in the Auschwitz trials. **20 October:** Following national elections held on 19 September, Ludwig Erhard is elected federal chancellor, heading a grand coalition of CDU, CSU, and FPD.

1966 2 February: More than 2,000 students in West Berlin clash with police in demonstrations against the Vietnam War as the city becomes the focus of a growing student protest movement. **19 March:** For the first time, the leadership of the SPD publicly responds to an "open letter" from the ruling SED in the GDR. **27 March:** The right-wing NPD wins a surprising 3.9 percent of the vote in elections to the Hamburg parliament. **9 May:** The GDR opens its first nuclear power station (in Rheinsberg) and continues to develop its chemical and electronics industries (Leuna II/Schwedt). **1–6 July:** France withdraws from the North Atlantic Treaty Organization (NATO) and pulls its air force out of the FRG; it later agrees to meet all military commitments to West Germany (21 December). **6 July:** Warsaw Pact states demand that NATO halt the creation of a multinational nuclear force and propose a conference on security and cooperation in Europe (the Bucharest Declaration). **19 July:** Regional elections in North Rhine-Westfalia return a CDU/FDP coalition with a narrow majority; this is replaced by an SPD/FDP coalition with Heinz Kuhn (SPD) as minister president (9 December). **27 July:** The European Economic Community (EEC) establishes a common agricultural market, effective 1 July 1967. **16 September:** Relatively mild sentences given by a Frankfurt court to three former Auschwitz concentration camp guards are criticized. **27 October:** The CDU/CSU–FDP national coalition breaks up after failing to agree on tax increases to control a budget deficit; Ludwig Erhard forms a minority CDU cabinet but fails to win public and party support. **6 November:** After gaining 7.9 percent of the vote in elections in Hessen, the NPD enters a regional state parliament for the first time; the SPD retains its absolute majority, and Georg August Zinn continues as minister president. **20 November:** In elections in Bavaria, the CSU retains control, but the NPD, with 7.4 percent of the vote, enters its second regional assembly. **28 November:** After its 65th crash, the F-104-G fighter jet ("starfighter") is grounded amid strong criticisms of government policy toward the German air force. **1–2 December:** The CDU/CSU and SPD form a grand coalition government, with Kurt Georg Kiesinger (CDU) as chancellor and Willy Brandt (SPD) as vice-chancellor and foreign minister; Kiesinger announces his priorities as passing national emergency laws (*Notstandsgesetze*), improving relations with the eastern bloc (including the GDR), regaining control of the budget, and regenerating the economy. **12 December:** In Baden-Württemberg, the CDU and SPD form a coalition, and Hans Filbinger (CDU) succeeds Kurt Georg Kiesinger as minister president. **14 December:** Heinrich Albertz (SPD) replaces Willy Brandt as governing mayor of West Berlin. **December:** Unemployment rises as the German economy enters a recession.

1967 1 January: As the recession takes hold, a 40-hour week is introduced in the engineering industry. **31 January:** The FRG's assumption of diplomatic relations with Romania marks the de facto end of the Hallstein doctrine, by which West Germany tried to discourage other states from recognizing the GDR. **14 February:** Economics Minister Karl Schiller's "concerted action" initiative to regenerate the economy begins with a meeting of leaders from business, labor, politics, and science; this is followed by a series of laws and measures designed to increase government investment, coordinate public spending, and monitor economic performance. **20 February:** The GDR passes a law that marks the introduction of separate citizenship for East and West Germans. **17–22 April:** The 7th Party Congress of the SED announces the transition from the New Economic System of Planning and Management (NÖSPL) to the Economic System of Socialism (ÖSS). **19 April:** Former chancellor Konrad Adenauer dies at age 91. **23 April:** In regional elections in Rhineland-Palatinate and Schleswig-Holstein, the NPD enters both assemblies; Peter Altmeier (CDU) and Helmut Lemke (CDU) continue CDU/FDP coalitions in both states. **7 May:** Large loans for the Friedrich Krupp concern indicate a deep crisis in the coal and steel industry; by the end of the year, 57,000 workers have lost their jobs in the sector, despite government subsidies and mergers. **10 May:** Adolf von Thadden becomes chairman of the NPD. **22–23 May:** Kurt Georg Kiesinger succeeds Ludwig Erhard as chairman of the CDU. **25 May–4 June:** Violent demonstrations accompany the visit of the Shah of Persia to West Berlin. The killing of a student, Benno Ohnesorg, by a police officer (2 June) further radicalizes the student movement and prompts mass protests in universities throughout the FRG; the governing mayor of West Berlin, Heinrich Albertz, resigns over the affair (29 September). **4 June:** Regional elections in Lower Saxony confirm the SPD/CDU coalition, with Georg Diederichs (SPD) as minister president, but the NPD enters parliament with 7 percent of the vote. **26 June:** The Bundestag agrees to a new law on the financing of political parties. **1 October:** The SPD loses overall control of Bremen, and the NPD enters the assembly with 8.8 percent of the vote; Hans Koschnick (SPD) heads an SPD/FDP coalition (28 November). **19 October:** Klaus Schütz (SPD) succeeds Heinrich Albertz as mayor of West Berlin. **13–14 December:** NATO presents the Harmel Report on the future strategy of the alliance.

1968 30 January: Walter Scheel is elected chairman of the FDP. **17 February:** Some 3,000 people attend an international conference in West Berlin organized by the Federation of Socialist German Students (SDS) to protest the U.S. war in Vietnam. **27 March:** Controversial limits on university places (*numerus clausus*) are introduced. **3 April:** Andreas Baader, Gudrun Ensslin, Thorwald Proll, and Horst Söhnlein mount arson attacks on two Frankfurt department stores; they are arrested on 12 April and receive three-year sentences (31 October). The attacks, a protest against the political and social establishment in the FRG, mark the beginning of violent political terrorism in West Germany. **9 April:** A new constitution for the GDR comes into force, defining East Germany as a socialist state and giving the ruling SED a preeminent role. **11–17 April:** Student demonstrators and police clash in several German cities following an attack by a 23-year-old worker on student leader Rudi Dutschke that leaves him severely injured. **28 April:** Regional elections in Hessen confirm Hans Filbinger (CDU) as minister president, leading a CDU/SPD coalition. **22 May:** A government commission recommends curbs on press monopolies. **30 May:** Despite protests, the Bundestag incorporates an "emergency constitution" (Notstandsverfassung) in the Basic Law of the FRG, suspending certain civil rights in times of national catastrophe; it comes into effect on 28 June. **13 June:** Following an exchange of letters between Chancellor Kurt Georg Kiesinger and GDR minister president Willi Stoph, the former expresses his readiness to meet East German leaders; the GDR insists on West Germany recognizing "both German states" and requires visas for journeys from the FRG to West Berlin. **20–21 August:** GDR forces join the USSR in invading Czechoslovakia to suppress a democratic reform movement. **22 September:** The German Communist Party (DKP) is founded in the FRG as the successor party to the banned Communist Party of Germany (KPD). **September:** Unemployment falls to 0.9 percent as the FRG's economy recovers following the success of Economics Minister Karl Schiller's program of "concerted action."

1969 5 March: Gustav Heinemann is the first SPD member to be elected president of the FRG. **18 March:** The federal government agrees on measures to curb rapid economic growth (almost 12 percent) and head off inflation. **8 May–11 July:** Seven states, mainly in Asia and the Middle East, establish diplomatic relations with the GDR. **9 May:** As the FRG reforms its penal system, homosexuality, adultery, and blasphemy are no longer punishable offenses (effective in September). **12 May:** A major reform of the FRG's financial system comes into force, redistributing tax revenue between the Bund and federal states and giving regions more access to federal funds. **19 May:** Helmut Kohl becomes minister president of Rhineland-Palatinate. **10 June:** The creation of the Federation of Evangelical Churches (BEK) in the GDR marks the end of the eastern Protestant church's independence from the state and of its unity with the FRG. **12 June:** A new law guarantees employees sick pay during illness. **13 June:** Particularly violent clashes occur between student demonstrators and police in Göttingen. **3 July–27 November:** The Ministry of Education and Culture agrees to introduce *Gesamtschulen* (comprehensive schools) on a trial basis. **3 September:** The newly established federal office to promote aid for developing countries starts work in Frankfurt/Main. **9 September:** The statute of limitations on crimes of genocide committed during the Third Reich is lifted. **28 September:** A national election gives the CDU/CSU 46.1 percent of votes, the SPD

42.7 percent, and the FDP 5.8 percent; the extreme right-wing NPD fails to clear the 5 percent hurdle. Willy Brandt (SPD) forms a coalition with the FDP and promises to introduce "more democracy" (*mehr Demokratie wagen*) in West German society and improve relations with the GDR. **3 October:** Albert Osswald (SPD) is elected minister president of Hessen. **25 October:** After divisions in the grand coalition (CDU/CSU-SPD) and turbulence on international money markets, the West German Mark (DM) is revalued 8.5 percent upward against the U.S. dollar.

1970 17 February: The SPD/CDU coalition in Lower Saxony collapses as the SPD accepts a defector from the NPD; regional elections (14 June) return an SPD administration under Alfred Kubel with a majority of one seat. **24 February:** Economics Minister Karl Schiller presents a four-stage plan for the creation of a single European currency. **19 March:** A historic first meeting between leaders of the FRG (Chancellor Willy Brandt) and the GDR (Minister President Willi Stoph) takes place in Erfurt, where Brandt is hailed as a hero by East Germans; both leaders meet again in Kassel (FRG) on 25 May. **22 March:** Regional elections in Hamburg result in a coalition between SPD and FDP headed by Herbert Weichmann (SPD). **26 March:** The western Allies and USSR start negotiations, which lead to the Four Power Treaty on Berlin. **29 March:** For the first time, the ARD and ZDF television stations use a weather map of Europe without national boundaries; up to now, the map of Germany had always shown the borders of 1937. **14 May:** The Baader-Meinhof/Red Army Faction (RAF) terrorist organization is formed as the imprisoned Andreas Baader is freed by a group including Ulrike Meinhof. **14 June:** Regional elections in North Rhine-Westfalia return an SPD/FDP coalition with Heinz Kühn (SPD) as minister president; the CDU/FDP coalition holds onto power in the Saarland. **18 June:** The FRG lowers the voting age from 21 to 18. **12 August:** The FRG and USSR conclude the Moscow Treaty, which renounces the use of force and acknowledges Germany's existing borders. **8 November:** Regional elections in Hessen confirm the SPD/FDP coalition, led by Albert Osswald (SPD). **22 November:** Alfons Goppel becomes minister president in Bavaria, where regional elections give the CSU an absolute majority. **7 December:** The FRG and Poland sign the Warsaw Treaty, which acknowledges the Oder–Neisse border between the GDR and Poland; Chancellor Willy Brandt, kneeling before a memorial to the victims of the Warsaw Ghetto, reinforces the positive image of a changed postwar Germany.

1971 21 January: It is reported that the GDR has laid over two million mines and 80,000 kilometers of barbed wire along its border with West Germany; begun in August 1961, the 3.6-meter-high concrete Berlin Wall around West Berlin eventually extends 155 kilometers, with 302 watchtowers and 20 bunkers. **24 January:** Under the terms of the Warsaw Treaty, the first ethnic Germans (Aussiedler) from eastern Europe arrive in the FRG. **31**

January: For the first time since 1952, telephone links are restored between East and West Berlin, although making calls is usually difficult. **12 February:** Thirteen members of the Baader-Meinhof/RAF group are arrested. **10 March:** The FRG formally abandons the Hallstein doctrine. **14 March:** City elections in West Berlin confirm the SPD in power. **21 March:** Regional elections in Rhineland-Palatinate give the CDU an absolute majority, with Helmut Kohl as minister president. **30 March:** West Germany's first law on environmental protection, restricting aircraft flight paths and designating noise-free zones for schools and hospitals, comes into force. **25 April:** The CDU wins an overall majority in regional elections in Schleswig-Holstein; Gerhard Stoltenberg succeeds Helmut Lemke as minister president. **3 May:** Walter Ulbricht, leader and general secretary of the ruling SED in the GDR, steps down; he is succeeded by Erich Honecker. **6 June:** *Stern* magazine publishes an article in which 374 women, many well-known, admit to having had an abortion; the article is initiated by the feminist Alice Schwarzer and triggers a groundbreaking debate. **2 August:** The television magazine program *Kennzeichen D* is launched; it aims to improve relations between and provide information on both German states. **3 September:** The U.S., USSR, UK, and France sign the Four Power Agreement on Berlin. **10 October:** Following the collapse of the SPD/FDP coalition in Bremen, regional elections give the SPD an absolute majority; the FDP had quit in opposition to the "left-wing" orientation of the newly founded University of Bremen. **25–27 October:** The FDP passes its Freiburg Theses, marking the transition from nationalist-conservative to social liberal policies. **10 December:** Willy Brandt receives the Nobel Peace Prize in Oslo in acknowledgment of his efforts to improve East–West relations. **17 December:** The FRG and GDR sign a transit agreement; the first inter-German treaty, it regulates transport between the two states and makes travel easier.

1972 6 January: In a speech to the East German army, Erich Honecker condemns the FRG as a foreign and imperialistic country. **28 January:** The chancellor and leaders of the federal states agree on the "radicals decree" (*Radikalenerlass*), which aims to exclude political extremists from public service and generates controversy for many years. **4 February:** Scheduled flights resume between the FRG and the Soviet Union. **9 March:** The GDR parliament legalizes abortion within the first three months of pregnancy; 22 members either vote against or abstain, the first time that the assembly has not unanimously approved a government measure. **29 March:** For the first time since 1966, West Berliners are permitted to visit East Berlin; around 1.2 million do so during Easter. **23 April:** The CDU gains absolute control in regional elections in Baden-Württemberg; as a result, the national SPD/FDP coalition loses its majority in the Bundesrat. **24 April:** Following weeks of intense debate in the Bundestag over Willy Brandt's Ostpolitik, the CDU/CSU opposition fails to bring down the government in a vote of no confidence. **17 May:** After a fierce debate, the Bundestag ratifies the Ostpolitik treaties; the Bundesrat follows suit two days later. **1–15 June:** In an intensive operation, the police arrest the core of the Baader-Meinhof/RAF group. **23 June:** The Bundestag approves the reduction of compulsory military service from 18 to 15 months (effective 1 January 1973). **5–6 September:** Arab terrorists kill 11 members of Israel's team during the Olympic Games in Munich. **5 October:** Artists critical of the GDR are allowed for the first time to exhibit at the VII Arts exhibition in Dresden. **6 October:** The GDR announces an amnesty for political and other prisoners and allows those released to move to the FRG. **19 November:** A national election returns the SPD/FDP coalition to power with an increased majority (SPD 45.8 percent of votes, CDU 35.2 percent, CSU 9.7 percent, FDP 8.4 percent). **10 December:** Heinrich Böll receives the Nobel Prize for Literature; since January he has been under attack after criticizing the popular newspaper *Bild* for one-sided reporting on the Baader-Meinhof/RAF group. **13 December:** Annemarie Renger becomes West Germany's first female president of the Bundestag.

1973 7–8 February: The UK and France officially recognize the GDR, which by the end of the year has established diplomatic relations with 100 foreign states and has been admitted to several international organizations; opponents of the regime hope for liberalization and a relaxation of censorship. **11 May:** The Bundestag ratifies the Basic Treaty; after initially voting against it (2 May), the Bundesrat follows suit on 25 May. **29 May:** In a ruling that is seen as a setback for student reformers who had campaigned in the 1960s for more democracy in higher education, the Federal Constitutional Court (FCC) gives more powers to university professors. **16 June:** The FRG and GDR apply to join the United Nations (UN) and are admitted on 18 September. **26 June:** The West German DM is revalued by 5.5 percent; this is the fifth revaluation since 1961 and follows continued speculation against a weak U.S. dollar (devalued by 10 percent on 12 February); six European currencies eventually decouple themselves from the U.S. currency in a linked currency exchange called "the snake" (11–12 March). **1 July:** The FRG acknowledges community service for conscientious objectors as equivalent to military service. **1 August:** Former East German leader Walter Ulbricht dies. **October–November:** Following the Yom Kippur War in the Middle East and a sharp rise in oil prices, the FRG experiences the worst economic crisis in its history; over a million people are unemployed. The government prohibits private motoring on four Sundays during November and December and imposes speed limits on main highways (*Autobahnen*). **5 November:** Despite the provisions of the Four Power Agreement on Berlin, the GDR doubles the amount of West German currency that must be exchanged upon entering East Berlin; the number of visitors from West Berlin/FRG drops by 50 percent. **23 November:** The FRG halts recruitment of foreign workers (*Gastarbeiter*) from states outside the European Community (EC).

1974 1 January: The FRG abolishes retail price fixing. **18 January:** The Bundestag introduces the "polluter pays principle" in environmental protection. **3 March:** In elections in Hamburg, the SPD loses its overall majority but continues in coalition with the FDP; Hans-Ulrich Klose (SPD) becomes governing mayor on 21 November. **6 March:** North Rhine-Westfalia decides to create an "open university" (*Fernuniversität*) to relieve pressure on student numbers. **14 March:** The FRG and GDR agree to exchange "permanent representatives." Günter Gaus represents the FRG in East Berlin and Michael Kohl the GDR in Bonn; their offices open on 2 May. **22 March:** The Bundestag lowers the age of adulthood from 21 to 18 and raises the age of consent to marriage for women from 16 to 18. **1 April:** Hamburg is the first federal state to introduce "educational holidays," which allow employees two weeks' extra holiday every two years to undertake further education. **24 April:** Willy Brandt's adviser, Günter Guillaume, is arrested as a GDR spy; Brandt steps down (6 May), and Helmut Schmidt (SPD) forms a new government. **26 April:** The Bundestag agrees to changes in the abortion law (paragraph 218), legalizing termination in the first 12 weeks of pregnancy if the mother undergoes medical counseling; the law is referred to the FCC on the day it is due to come into force (21 June). **15 May:** Walter Scheel (FDP) is elected president of the FRG. **9 June:** In regional elections in Lower Saxony, the SPD loses its absolute majority but forms a coalition with the FDP, with Alfred Kubel (SPD) as minister president. **26 June:** The collapse of the Cologne-based Herstatt Bank leads to the biggest banking insolvency since the Wall Street crash of 1929. **19 July:** The Treaty of Prague comes into force; agreed upon between the FRG and the CSSR in December 1973, the treaty, which formally nullifies the Munich agreement of 1938, normalizes relations and establishes full diplomatic relations. **7 October:** The GDR revises its constitution to remove all references to German reunification. **27 October:** The CSU increases its majority in regional elections in Bavaria. In elections in Hessen, the CDU emerges as the strongest party, although the SPD/FDP coalition continues. **9 November:** Imprisoned Baader-Meinhof/RAF group member Holger Meins dies after a hunger strike; 10 other prisoners are also on hunger strike, and Meins's death provokes demonstrations in several German cities. Verdicts are delivered against fellow terrorists Ulrike Meinhof and Horst Mahler. **10 November:** Günter von Drenkmann, president of the Berlin supreme court, is murdered following a terrorist kidnapping attempt; the fight against terrorism is stepped up. **12 December:** The Bundestag approves a new higher education framework law, effective from 26 January 1976, which regulates university entry requirements, introduces recommended maximum periods of study and limited codetermination for staff, and endorses the comprehensive university (*Gesamthochschule*) as a new type of institution.

1975 1 January: The FRG concludes a financial and economic agreement with Yugoslavia; similar agreements follow with CSSR (22 January), Bulgaria (14 May), and Poland (9 October). **12–25 January:** CSU leader Franz Josef Strauß visits the People's Republic of China, where he meets Mao Tse Tung. **17 February:** Protesters halt the construction of a nuclear power station at Whyl (Baden-Württemberg); mass demonstrations and protests take place at other sites in Germany. **27 February:** Members of the "Movement 2 June" kidnap Berlin CDU leader Peter Lorenz; he is later released (5 March) after the government allows five imprisoned terrorists to go to Yemen. **2 March:** Elections to the West Berlin assembly return the CDU as the strongest party, but the SPD/FDP coalition continues in office. **9 March:** The CDU gains an absolute majority in regional elections in Rhineland-Palatinate. **13 April:** The CDU retains its majority after regional elections in Schleswig-Holstein. **24 April:** Seven self-styled anarchists ("Kommando Holger Meins") occupy the West German embassy in Stockholm to force the release of imprisoned members of the Baader-Meinhof/RAF group; two hostages are murdered before Swedish authorities kill two terrorists and overpower the others. The relationship that develops between captors and captives is an example of the "Stockholm syndrome." **4 May:** Regional elections in North Rhine-Westfalia confirm the SPD/FDP coalition, while elections in the Saarland result in a CDU minority government. **6 May:** The GDR allows West German banks to open branches in East Berlin. **21 May:** The trial begins of core members of the Baader-Meinhof/RAF group. **22 May:** A ruling by the FCC strengthens the 1972 radicals' decree; from now on mere membership in a nonprohibited organization that is considered hostile to the constitution can lead to exclusion from public service. The decree provokes battles between the Bundestag and the CDU/CSU–dominated Bundesrat. **29 May:** As national unemployment exceeds one million, Baden-Württemberg is the first federal state to offer foreign workers financial incentives to leave Germany. **19 June:** The GDR introduces a new civil legal codex that unifies earlier laws and defines socialist and private property; it comes into effect in January 1976. **30 July–1 August:** Helmut Schmidt (FRG) and Erich Honecker (GDR) meet for talks during the signing of the final acts of the Conference on Security and Cooperation in Europe (CSCE) in Helsinki. **25 September:** The FRG government presents a revised law that permits abortion only for medical, ethical, and social reasons; the move follows a rejection by the FCC on 25 February of the original abortion law passed in April 1974. **29 October–2 November:** Chancellor Helmut Schmidt visits the People's Republic of China, the first West German head of state to do so; both countries agree to intensify economic links.

1976 12 February: The Bundestag revises the law on abortion (paragraph 218); this comes into effect on 18 May but is criticized by the Roman Catholic Church for legalizing abortions during the first three months of pregnancy if the mother is in social need. **16 March:** A reform of the penal system in the FRG places greater stress on resocialization. **30 March:** The FRG and GDR sign an agreement to improve joint mail and telecommunication systems. **5 April:** Campaigning under the slogan "freedom instead of socialism," the CDU gains a resounding victory in regional elections in Baden-Württemberg. **9 May:** The terrorist Ulrike Meinhof is found hanged in her cell, triggering demonstrations in several West German cities. **14 June:** The Bundestag approves new marital laws that make husband and wife equal in all legal respects. **24 June:** The Bundestag passes new antiterrorism legislation (in force from 18 August) making the formation of terrorist associations punishable by up to 10 years in prison and giving the authorities powers to monitor meetings between terrorists and their lawyers; the CDU/CSU opposition demands even stricter measures. **24 July:** Despite increasing economic cooperation, tensions rise between the West and East German governments following stricter border controls by the GDR authorities and the shooting of people attempting to escape. **18 August:** Oskar Brüsewitz, a vicar from Zeitz (GDR), burns himself alive in protest of the regime and state restrictions on the church; his death is widely reported in the West. **3 October:** In a national election, the SPD gains 42.5 percent of the vote, the CDU/CSU 48.6 percent, and the FDP 7.95 percent. The SPD/FDP coalition government continues in office, and Helmut Kohl leads the CDU/CSU opposition. **30 October:** Antinuclear protestors and police clash at Brokdorf (Schleswig-Holstein). **16 November:** In a move seen as a turning point in cultural policy, the GDR expatriates the dissident singer/songwriter Wolf Biermann.

1977 13 January: The German ambassador to the UN, Rüdiger von Wechmar, is the first German to attend a meeting of the UN Security Council. **19 January:** Following a prolonged crisis precipitated by the resignation of Minister President Alfred Kubel in Lower Saxony (January 1976), the CDU and FDP form a coalition led by Ernst Albrecht (CDU). **19 February:** Twenty thousand demonstrate against the building of the nuclear power station at Brokdorf; this is followed by a 15,000-strong protest at Gorleben (Lower Saxony), where a nuclear reprocessing facility is planned (22 February). Violent clashes occur between demonstrators and police at a projected facility in Grohnde (13 June). **24 March:** The GDR concludes a friendship treaty with Hungary; similar treaties follow with Mongolia (6 May), Poland (28 May), Romania (8–10 June), Bulgaria (14 September), CSSR (3 October), and Vietnam (4 December). **7 April:** The murder of the FRG's chief federal prosecutor, Siegfried Buback, in Karlsruhe marks the start of a series of terrorist crimes in what comes to be known as the "German autumn." These include the murder of the banking executive Jürgen Ponto (30 July) and the kidnapping of employers' leader Hanns-Martin Schleyer, who is found dead on 19 October; a rocket attack by the Baader-Meinhof/RAF group on federal prosecution headquarters in Karlsruhe fails (25 August), although the regional court in Karlsruhe is later bombed (31 October). A Palestinian commando group hijacks a Lufthansa aircraft, forcing it to land in Mogadishu in Somalia (13 October). **28 April:** The terrorists Andreas Baader, Gudrun Ensslin, and Jan-Carl Raspe receive life prison sentences; all three commit suicide in Stuttgart-Stammheim prison (18 October), generating a fierce debate over the causes and handling of terrorism. **4 May:** A secretary is arrested in the West German chancellor's office on suspicion of spying for the GDR; several other East German agents in government ministries are arrested during the year. **5 May:** Ludwig Erhard (CDU), regarded as the father of the social market economy and the postwar West German economic miracle, dies. **21–25 May:** Chancellor Helmut Schmidt visits Poland; he is criticized by refugee organizations and conservative politicians for acknowledging Germany's crimes against the Polish people during World War II. **26 June:** GDR Politburo member Werner Lamberz visits Africa, offering development aid in return for the importation of East German goods. **28 August:** Rudolf Bahro is arrested in the GDR after the West German magazine *Der Spiegel* publishes a chapter of his book.

1978 6–7 January: Helmut Schmidt becomes the first West German Chancellor to visit Romania, which agrees to allow ethnic Germans to emigrate to the FRG in return for economic aid. **10 January:** The GDR authorities close the East Berlin office of *Der Spiegel* after it publishes a dissident group's manifesto. **16 February:** The Bundestag passes new antiterror laws providing for physical barriers between terror suspects and their lawyers, increased police powers of search, and faster legal procedures. **March:** Disputes between engineering unions and employers that began in December 1977 result in strikes and lockouts involving 200,000 workers; normal work is resumed in April. **29 March:** The Third International Russell Tribunal convenes in Frankfurt/Main and criticizes the FRG for its 1972 radicals' decree. **4 June:** The CDU wins an overall majority in regional elections in Lower Saxony; the SPD retains power in elections in Hamburg, where Hans-Ulrich Klose is confirmed as governing mayor. **13 July:** Former CSU politician Herbert Gruhl founds Germany's first national political party for environmental issues, the Green Action Future (Grüne Aktion Zukunft, GAZ), in Bonn; similar groups begin contesting regional elections. **7 August:** Hans Filbinger (CDU) resigns as minister president of Baden-Württemberg following revelations of his past involvement with the Nazi Party; he is succeeded by Lothar Späth (CDU). **26 August:** The GDR cosmonaut Sigmund Jähn is the first German to take part in a space mission. **1 September:** The GDR introduces military education in the school curriculum. **20 September:** Johannes Rau (SPD) becomes minister president of North Rhine-Westfalia. **8 October:** Regional elections in Hessen confirm the SPD/FDP coalition led by Holger Börner (SPD). **15 October:** The CSU wins a large majority in regional elections in Bavaria, and Franz Josef Strauß becomes minister president (6 November). **25 October:** The CDU agrees to a "program of basic principles" (*Grundsatzprogramm*) at a party conference in Ludwigshafen; entitled "freedom, solidarity, and justice," the program is the first since the party was founded in 1945. **26 October:** A joint FRG–GDR border commission created in 1973 produces a report on the 1,400-kilometer intra-German frontier; despite disagreement over a stretch along the Elbe River, the document is signed on 29 November. **16 November:** The FRG and GDR agree to a comprehensive transport treaty that includes building a new highway link between Hamburg and Berlin. **12 December:** The FRG, France, and other EC states agree to set up the European Monetary System (EMS), which is introduced on 13 March 1979.

1979 17 January: North Rhine-Westfalia declares the first "smog alarm" in the Ruhr area when sulfur dioxide levels reach harmful levels. **21 January:** German television broadcasts the U.S. film *Holocaust*, triggering a new debate on German identity and how to deal with the past. **17 March:** Citizens and environmental groups form the Greens (Green Party) in Frankfurt/Main. **18 March:** The SPD/FDP coalition led by Dietrich Stobbe (SPD) is confirmed in elections to the West Berlin city assembly; the CDU holds onto its majority in elections in Rhineland-Palatinate. **21 March:** The FRG eases restrictions on foreign workers (from outside the EC) by allowing their children and spouses to join them. **1 April:** In a relaxation of the 1972 radicals' decree, applicants for public service jobs at the national level are no longer subject to routine tests for loyalty to the constitution; several federal states adopt the new guidelines, which are strongly opposed by the CDU/CSU. **14 April:** The GDR obliges Western journalists to obtain approval to conduct interviews. **28 April:** The CDU retains power in regional elections in Schleswig-Holstein. **23 May:** Karl Carstens is elected president of the FRG. **10 June:** In the first elections to the European Parliament, the SPD gains 40.8 percent of the seats in Germany, the CDU 39.1 percent, the FDP 6 percent, and the Greens 3.2 percent. **2 July:** The CDU/CSU selects Franz Josef Strauß as its chancellor candidate for the 1980 Bundestag elections. **16 September:** Two GDR families flee to West Germany in a hot air balloon, attracting worldwide attention. **6 October:** Soviet leader Leonid Brezhnev announces that 20,000 Soviet soldiers and 1,000 tanks will be withdrawn from East German soil. **7 October:** In elections to the Bremen assembly, the SPD retains its majority, and the Greens pass the electoral hurdle for the first time. **11 October:** The GDR releases the dissident Rudolf Bahro as part of an amnesty on the occasion of its 30th anniversary. **14 October:** In Bonn, 100,000 protesters stage the largest demonstration against nuclear power seen so far. **12 December:** In a move supported by Chancellor Helmut Schmidt, NATO foreign and defense ministers agree to a "dual track" decision on arms control: unless the USSR agrees to negotiate on withdrawing its intermediate-range nuclear SS20 missiles in Europe, NATO will deploy similar weapons in Germany starting in 1983. **15 December:** The Vatican withdraws permission to teach from the Tübingen-based theology professor Hans Küng; in 1970 Küng had published a book questioning papal infallibility, allegedly deviating from Catholic doctrine. **24 December:** Rudi Dutschke, leader of the radical students' movement during the 1960s, dies in Denmark from the effects of the assassination attempt on him in 1968.

1980 13 January: Over 1,000 delegates from various groups constitute the national Green Party in Karlsruhe; a manifesto is published at a congress in Saarbrücken on 23 March. **30 January:** As a reform movement threatens the communist leadership in Poland, the GDR calls off a planned meeting between Erich Honecker and Helmut Schmidt. **16 March:** In regional elections in Baden-Württemberg, the CDU retains its majority and the Greens gain six seats. **27 April:** In regional elections in the Saarland, the SPD emerges as the strongest party, but the CDU and FDP continue their governing coalition. **3 May:** Some 5,000 antinuclear protesters occupy the planned storage facility at Gorleben and declare the "free republic of Wendland"; they are peacefully removed by police on 4 June. **11 May:** The SPD retains power in regional elections in North Rhine-Westfalia. **2 July:** The FRG introduces restrictions on asylum seekers and speeds up the processing of applications. **19 July–3 August:** Following a Bundestag recommendation (23 April), the FRG joins 30 other countries in boycotting the Olympic summer games in Moscow in response to the Soviet invasion of Afghanistan (December 1979). **2 September:** SED Politburo member Hermann Axen attacks the reform movement in Poland as "anti-socialist" and "contra-revolutionary." **26 September:** A right-wing extremist kills 13 people and injures 219 in a bomb attack during the October festival in Munich. **5 October:** National elections confirm the CDU/CSU as the strongest party, with 44.5 percent of the vote; the SPD (42.9 percent) and FDP (10.6 percent) agree to continue their ruling coalition under Chancellor Helmut Schmidt (5 November). **9 October:** The GDR raises the compulsory daily exchange rate for West German visitors to the GDR to 25 DM. **13 October:** Erich Honecker lists five demands for normalizing relations between East and West Germany, including the FRG's recognition of GDR nationality. **10 November:** Honecker's visit to Austria is his first official trip to a Western country.

1981 15 January: A financial scandal forces West Berlin's mayor, Dietrich Stobbe, and the senate to resign; Hans-Jochen Vogel (SPD) takes over, leading an SPD/FDP coalition. **29 January:** Violent clashes mark a long-running conflict between squatter groups and the police in West Berlin, where around 80,000 need homes and 9,700 apartments are unoccupied; an 18-year-old dies after police forcibly remove squatters on 22 September. **12 February:** Education ministers of the federal states agree that German schoolbooks should depict Germany in the boundaries of 1937; the use of the acronym BRD (= FRG) is discouraged because it allegedly emulates East

German usage. **28 February:** Some 100,000 people demonstrate against the construction of a nuclear power station in Brokdorf. **2–3 April:** FRG Foreign Minister Hans-Dietrich Genscher meets Soviet leaders in Moscow to discuss the deployment of intermediate-range nuclear force (INF) missiles; SPD leader Willy Brandt visits the USSR (29 June-3 July). **10 May:** After the CDU gains seats in elections in West Berlin, Richard von Weizsäcker (CDU) becomes governing mayor, leading a minority administration tolerated by the FDP (11 June). **23 May:** The world's first museum on women and their history opens in Bonn. **25 May:** Hans-Ulrich Klose (SPD), governing mayor of Hamburg, announces his resignation as his party leadership fails to support his plans to phase out nuclear energy; he is succeeded by Klaus von Dohnanyi (24 June). **30 June:** The trial of Majdanek concentration camp guards, which began in 1975, ends with several convictions. **20 August:** A letter from Hans-Dietrich Genscher to the FDP leadership marks the beginning of the party's shift of support from the SPD to the CDU; Genscher argues for stricter fiscal policies in order to control the budget deficit, although he supports the coalition's policy on nuclear weapons, which deeply divides the SPD. **31 August:** The terrorist bombing of a base in Ramstein marks the start of a series of violent attacks on U.S. military installations and personnel. **9 September:** Most asylum-seekers are no longer permitted to work during their first two years in the FRG. **10 October:** Some 300,000 people demonstrate in Bonn for peace and disarmament. **20 October:** A gun battle takes place between West German police and neo-Nazis in North Germany; arms and explosive caches are found in October and December. **26 October:** The ruling coalition agrees on Operation '82, a program of spending cuts designed to overcome the acute budget deficit; the measures come into effect on 1 January 1982. **3–14 December:** Over 100 East German writers meet in East Berlin and criticize the GDR government, especially over peace and arms issues; supported by the church, the peace movement gathers momentum in the east. **11 December:** Helmut Schmidt's visit to the GDR is the first by a West German chancellor since 1970, but is overshadowed by growing tension between East and West as the reform movement in Poland gains ground.

1982 8 February: *Der Spiegel* reveals a financial scandal surrounding the trade-union-owned housing association Neue Heimat, shattering public trust in the organization. **24 February:** West German authorities investigate the Flick concern for tax evasion; in what comes to be known as the Flick affair, it emerges that political parties and leading figures, including government ministers, are involved in providing favors for donations; the affair lasts until 1987 and is regarded as the greatest political scandal in the FRG's history. **9 March:** The Palestine Liberation Organization (PLO) opens an embassy in the GDR. **18 March:** Members of the Bundestag and GDR parliament meet officially for the first time in East Berlin. **23 March:** In regional elections in

Lower Saxony, the CDU retains its overall majority as the SPD loses votes and the Greens enter parliament for the first time. **6 June:** Following elections to the Hamburg assembly, Klaus von Dohnanyi governs with a minority SPD administration until further elections (19 December) give the SPD an overall majority. **10 June:** A NATO summit conference is held in Bonn; up to 500,000 demonstrate against U.S. arms policies, while U.S. president Ronald Reagan's visit to West Berlin (11 June) triggers demonstrations and clashes with the police. **18 June:** The FRG agrees to continue interest-free ("swing") credit for intra-German trade as the GDR enters its worst ever recession. **17 September:** As the FDP defects to the CDU/CSU following disputes over economic policy, Chancellor Helmut Schmidt forms a minority SPD government; Schmidt is brought down by a constructive vote of no confidence (1 October), which returns Helmut Kohl (CDU) as chancellor. Kohl promises an economic and political sea change. **26 September:** After regional elections in Hessen, Holger Börner (SPD) heads a minority government; with 8 percent of the vote, the Greens enter the assembly for the first time. **10 October:** The CSU is confirmed in power following regional elections in Bavaria. **14 October:** Uwe Barschel (CDU) replaces Gerhard Stoltenberg as minister president of Schleswig-Holstein. **30 October:** Some 10,000 people demonstrate against a new runway for Frankfurt/Main airport. **11–16 November:** Police capture leading members of the Baader-Meinhof/ RAF terrorist group (Brigitte Mohnhaupt, Adelheid Schulz, and Christian Klar). **15–16 December:** The Bundestag agrees to a revised budget for 1983; presented by the new coalition government (CDU/CSU-FDP), it combines cuts in social provision with increased contributions and provides incentives for business.

1983 7 January: Federal president Karl Carstens dissolves the Bundestag and sets 6 March as the date for a national election; this gives a clear majority to the CDU/CSU–FDP coalition (55.8 percent of votes) and sees the Greens enter parliament with 27 seats (5.6 percent), while the SPD slips to 38.2 percent. The new government makes immediate cuts in social welfare in order to regain control of the national budget. **February:** Unemployment reaches a historic high of 2.53 million. **6 March:** Regional elections confirm the CDU as the governing party in Rhineland-Palatinate. **13 March:** The CDU continues in office following regional elections in Schleswig-Holstein. **3–4 April:** Thousands demonstrate on Easter peace marches and throughout the year against the stationing of medium range Pershing II nuclear missiles; 1.3 million people take part in protest actions in October, including a 300,000-strong demonstration in Bonn and a human chain linking Ulm and Stuttgart. On 22 November, the Bundestag votes to support deployment, which begins later that month and is completed in early 1984. **25 September:** Following regional elections in Hessen, Holger Börner (SPD) continues to head a minority government. The SPD retains control of Bremen. **5 Octo-**

ber: Erich Honecker undertakes to dismantle self-triggering weapons along the intra-German border. **26–27 November:** Former CSU deputies Franz Handlos and Ekkehard Voigt, together with the journalist Franz Schönhuber, found the ultra-right-wing party The Republicans (Die Republikaner, REP) in Munich. **30 November:** Around 12,000 foreign workers receive financial aid to return to their home countries; the scheme, which is designed to reduce pressure on the labor market, continues until 30 June 1984.

1984 1 January: Cable television is launched in the FRG with a pilot project in Ludwigsburg. East German peace activists Bärbel Bohley and Ulrike Poppe, arrested on 12 December 1983, begin a hunger strike. **24 January:** East Germans seeking refuge in the FRG's permanent representation in East Berlin are allowed to go to the West; more East Germans seek asylum in Western embassies in East Berlin and Prague and demand the right to emigrate. **9 February:** Eberhard Diepgen (CDU) is elected governing mayor of West Berlin. **13 February:** Visiting Moscow for the funeral of Soviet leader Yuri Andropov, Helmut Kohl and Erich Honecker meet face to face for the first time. **11 March:** At the Leipzig Trade Fair, GDR leader Erich Honecker announces his intention to visit the FRG. **25 March:** The CDU retains control of Baden-Württemberg in regional elections. **1 May:** The GDR halts emigration, which had been increasing in previous months; an estimated 400,000 people want to leave. **10 May:** West German engineering workers begin strike action that wins them a 38.5-hour workweek (effective 1 April 1985); a similar deal is struck with striking print workers on 6 July. **23 May:** Richard von Weizsäcker, a popular cross-party figure, is elected president of the FRG. **17 June:** In the second elections to the European Parliament, the CDU gains 37.5 percent of the seats in Germany, the SPD 37.4 percent, the CSU 8.5 percent, the Greens 8.2 percent, and the FDP 4.8 percent. **26 June:** In Hessen, the SPD and Greens agree to create a workable administration, but the alliance breaks down over nuclear energy policy (20 November). **27 June:** FDP economics minister Otto Graf Lambsdorff resigns over the Flick affair. **22 September:** On the World War I battlefield of Verdun, Chancellor Helmut Kohl and French President François Mitterrand confirm, hand in hand, the reconciliation between the countries.

1985 1 January: The launch of SAT 1, the FRG's first private satellite television station, marks a new era in broadcasting. **23 January:** The West German government approves the construction of an atomic fuel reprocessing plant at Wackersdorf (Bavaria); building begins in November with heavy police protection. **25 January:** The FRG revokes all convictions of the "people's court" (*Volksgerichtshof*) during the Third Reich. **1 February:** Terrorists murder the businessman Ernst Zimmermann in Munich. **February:** The joint East–West German border commission resumes its work but fails to agree on the frontier along the Elbe River. **10 March:** Elections to the Berlin city assembly confirm the CDU/FDP coalition. In regional elections in the Saarland, the SPD, led by Oskar Lafontaine, takes power from the CDU/FDP. **12 March:** At the funeral of Soviet leader Constantin Chernenko in Moscow, Chancellor Kohl and Erich Honecker declare that war must never again emanate from German soil. **2 April:** Leading members of the Baader-Meinhof/RAF group, Christian Klar and Brigitte Mohnhaupt, receive life sentences for multiple and attempted murder. **16 April:** The GDR allows *Der Spiegel* to reopen its East Berlin office, which had been closed in 1978. **23–24 April:** Erich Honecker pays a state visit to Italy, his first to a NATO country, and is received by Pope John Paul II. **1–6 May:** A visit by U.S. president Ronald Reagan is meant to cement the close relationship with the FRG, but it generates controversy when Reagan and Kohl visit the Bitburg war cemetery, where SS soldiers are buried. **8 May:** Federal president Richard von Weizsäcker's speech on the 40th anniversary of the end of World War II, in which he openly refers to the German defeat as "liberation" and stresses the need to remember the Third Reich's crimes against humanity, is internationally acclaimed. **12 May:** The SPD retains control of North Rhine-Westfalia in regional elections. **11 June:** In the largest spy exchange since 1945, 25 Western agents are exchanged for four East Germans on the Glienicke Bridge in Berlin. **19 June:** Three are killed and 42 injured in a bomb attack at Frankfurt/Main airport, where two people are also killed and several injured in an attack on the U.S. base (8 August). **25 June:** The Saarland is the first federal state to rescind the 1972 radicals' decree. **28 June:** The Bundestag makes it an offense for demonstrators to cover their faces or to carry protective equipment against teargas. **5 July:** The FRG raises the "swing" credit to the GDR (from 600 to 850 million DM) for five years. **1 August:** Following a Bundestag decision (25 April), it becomes a crime to deny Nazi crimes against humanity (the "Auschwitz lie"). **1 September:** Franz Josef Strauß and Erich Honecker meet at the Leipzig Trade Fair. **16 October:** The SPD and Greens finally form a ruling coalition in Hessen. **13 November:** Oskar Lafontaine, SPD minister president of the Saarland, controversially suggests that recognition of GDR citizenship could be a precondition for normalizing travel for East Germans. **6 December:** The SPD and the SED meet in East Berlin to discuss the creation of a nuclear-free arms zone in central Europe. **18 December:** The Bundestag rejects direct participation in the U.S. Strategic Defense Initiative (SDI), despite supporting it politically. **21 December:** The fatal beating of a young Turk by skinheads in Hamburg fuels concern over an increase in attacks on foreigners.

1986 7 January: Police forcibly remove protesters from the site of the Wackersdorf atomic reprocessing plant; demonstrations, often violent, continue here and in Brokdorf (6 June), Hamburg (8 June), and Hanau (9 November). The nuclear power station at Brokdorf becomes operational on 7 October. **5 April:** A terrorist attack on a West Berlin discothèque frequented by U.S. soldiers leaves 4 dead and 200 injured; Libyan involvement is suspected. **17 April:** National service is lengthened from 15 to 18 months (from 1 June 1986). **26 April:** An explosion in a nuclear reactor in Chernobyl (Ukraine) disperses radioactivity over much of northern Europe, including Germany; the FRG introduces emergency measures to reduce the effects on the food chain (1–4 May) and creates the Ministry for Environmental Protection and Atomic Safety (3 June), although thousands demonstrate against nuclear power. The SPD demands its phased reduction and the Green Party its immediate cessation, while the CDU, CSU, and FDP insist on continuing Germany's atomic energy program. **6 May:** After 12 years of negotiations, a cultural agreement between the GDR and FRG resolves disputes over art collections in Berlin. **15 June:** The CDU loses votes in regional elections in Lower Saxony but forms a ruling coalition with the FDP. **9 July:** Terrorists kill a senior Siemens executive and his driver in a bomb attack. **19 September:** The first partnership between towns in the FRG (Saarlouis) and GDR (Eisenhüttenstadt) is launched. **12 October:** The CSU retains its majority in regional elections in Bavaria, and the Greens enter the assembly for the first time. **15 October:** German–Soviet relations are strained after Chancellor Helmut Kohl compares Mikhail Gorbachev with the Nazi propaganda minister Josef Goebbels. **9 November:** In elections in Hamburg, the CDU emerges as the strongest party, although the SPD continues a minority administration. **13 November:** The Bundestag tightens restrictions on asylum seekers, especially on rejected applicants and those from Eastern Europe; asylum for economic reasons is rejected out of hand, and airlines face fines for bringing foreigners to the country without entry papers. **21 November–4 December:** The Rhine River is severely polluted by a chemical accident at the BASF plant in Ludwigshafen.

1987 January: Throughout the year, Berlin's 750th anniversary is celebrated separately in both parts of the divided city. **25 January:** National elections produce losses for the SPD (37 percent of the vote) and CDU/CSU (44.3 percent) and gains for the FDP (9.1 percent) and the Greens (8.3 percent); the CDU/FDP coalition continues with Helmut Kohl as chancellor and Hans-Dietrich Genscher as foreign minister. **5 April:** Following the collapse of the SPD/Green coalition in Hessen over nuclear power (9 February), regional elections end 40 years of SPD domination. The CDU, with Walter Wallmann as minister president, forms a coalition with the FDP. **17 May:** After the SPD and CDU fail to agree on a coalition, fresh elections in Hamburg lead to an SPD/FDP administration, with Klaus von Dohnanyi (SPD) as governing mayor. Following elections in Rhineland-Palatinate, the CDU loses its absolute majority and enters into coalition with the FDP. **12 June:** U.S. president Ronald Reagan visits Berlin and challenges Gorbachev to "tear down this wall"; the GDR government rejects Gorbachev's reform policies, despite growing opposition from within the ruling Socialist Unity

Party of Germany and the population. **17 July:** The GDR abolishes the death penalty (last used in 1981) and declares a general amnesty for 24,600 convicted criminals. **17 August:** Rudolf Hess (93), the last surviving Nazi leader, commits suicide in Spandau prison; the USSR had rejected all appeals to free him. **26 August:** Chancellor Kohl agrees not to upgrade 72 U.S. medium-range Pershing missiles on German soil; the move supports the "double global zero strategy" agreed to by the U.S. and USSR, which aims to eliminate INF missiles in Europe and Asia and all short-range missiles worldwide. President Reagan and Mikhail Gorbachev formally agree to the INF treaty on 8 December, and the removal of Pershing II missiles from Germany begins on 1 September 1988. **27 August:** The SPD and SED publish a joint paper, strongly criticized by West German conservatives, which argues for peaceful competition between the political systems of East and West Germany and stresses that each is capable of reform. **7–11 September:** GDR leader Erich Honecker visits the FRG. **12 September:** *Der Spiegel* reveals electoral dirty tricks used by Uwe Barschel, minister president of Schleswig-Holstein, who is later found dead in a Geneva hotel (11 October); the so-called Barschel affair is seen as the FRG's Watergate. **13 September:** The SPD retains its absolute majority in elections in Bremen; elections in Schleswig-Holstein result in a CDU/FDP coalition, although the result is overshadowed by the Barschel affair. **3 December:** Following smog alarms in urban areas of northern Germany in February, the Bundestag bans leaded fuel, effective from February 1988.

1988 17 January: Police arrest civil rights activists during demonstrations commemorating the deaths of communist leaders Rosa Luxemburg and Karl Liebknecht in East Berlin. **8 May:** Fresh elections in Schleswig-Holstein, called in the wake of the Barschel affair, give the SPD an absolute majority and end 38 years of CDU rule; Björn Engholm becomes minister president on 31 May. **8 June:** Henning Voscherau (SPD) succeeds Klaus von Dohnanyi as governing mayor of West Berlin. **19 June:** During a Michael Jackson concert in West Berlin, young East Germans are brutally dispersed as they try to listen from the other side of the Berlin Wall. **24 June:** After a long political battle, the Bundestag passes a tax reform that is designed to relieve middle and higher earners; the measures, which are further revised in 1989, come into effect on 1 January 1990. **15 August:** The GDR establishes diplomatic relations with the European Community (EC). **30 August–2 September:** The SPD decides that by 1994, 40 percent of its members of parliament and committees will be women. **1 September:** The 38th Berlin Festival begins as West Berlin is designated the "culture capital" of Europe. **7–9 October:** Otto Graf Lambsdorff succeeds Martin Bangemann as chairman of the FDP. **19 October:** Max Streibl (CSU) is elected minister president of Bavaria following the death of Franz Josef Strauß (3 October). **24–27 October:** Chancellor Helmut Kohl and Foreign Minister Hans-Dietrich Genscher, with leading industrialists, visit the USSR; an agreement is signed for German companies to build a nuclear reactor in Russia. **11 November:** The GDR bans the Soviet magazine *Sputnik*, which contains an article on the Hitler–Stalin pact; Mikhail Gorbachev is increasingly seen as a symbol of hope for East German opposition groups, who are working with the tacit support of the church. **25 November:** The Bundestag agrees to controversial health-care reform designed to control costs; it comes into effect on 1 January 1989. **7 December:** The FRG creates a national office for protection against radiation following serious irregularities in the handling of radioactive waste at the Hanau nuclear power station in Hessen; reports also emerge of safety problems with the Biblis A and B reactors (Hessen), and the nuclear power station at Mülheim-Kärlich (Rhineland-Palatinate) is shut down following a court decision highlighting irregularities in the approval procedure (9 September). Biblis A and B resume operation in February 1989.

1989 1 January: With the easing of restrictions on foreign travel (announced by the GDR authorities on 30 November 1988), many East Germans register to leave the country; around 160,000 have applied by 30 September. **18 January:** Several thousand students protest against study conditions in West Germany, including overcrowded lecture theaters, accommodation shortages, and poor academic support. **29 January:** In a surprise result, West Berlin elects its first SPD/Green Party government, displacing the CDU/FDP coalition. The right-wing Republicans gain 7.5 percent of votes, and Walter Momper (SPD) becomes governing mayor. **12 March:** Around 600 East Germans demonstrate in Leipzig, demanding unrestricted travel. **20 April:** Despite opposition from the SPD and the Greens, the Bundestag agrees to legislation to split the federal postal services into separate operations for mail, banking, and telecommunications in preparation for privatization. **7 May:** GDR opposition groups demonstrate that the official results for local elections are falsified. **23 May:** Richard von Weizsäcker is reelected president of the FRG. **2 June:** The Bundestag passes legislation allowing shops and businesses to extend opening hours on Thursdays. **18 June:** In the third elections to the European Parliament, the SPD gains 37.3 percent of the seats in Germany, the CDU 29.5 percent, the Greens 8.4 percent, and the CSU 8.2 percent; the Republicans achieve 7.1 percent, more than the FDP (5.6 percent). **August–September:** Large numbers of East Germans wanting to emigrate occupy West German embassies in Prague, Budapest, and Warsaw; the regime comes under increasing pressure as various political parties and groups are founded. **4 September:** The first of the "Monday demonstrations" takes place in Leipzig; these grow in size and include demands for freedom of expression, the lifting of travel restrictions, and the right to free assembly. **11 September:** Suspending agreements with the GDR, Hungary opens its frontier with Austria, allowing several thousand East Germans to escape to the West. **1–4 October:** The GDR leadership attempts to control the exodus by allowing trainloads of East Germans to leave from Prague and Warsaw. **7 October:** The Social Democratic Party (SDP) of the GDR is founded; it is later renamed SPD (13 January 1990) and eventually merges with its West German sister party (26–27 September 1990). **9 October:** As the GDR celebrates its 40th anniversary, Mikhail Gorbachev warns the East Germans not to be overtaken by events ("Wer zu spät kommt, den bestraft das Leben"). **19 October:** Erich Honecker is forced to resign all offices and is succeeded by the Communist hard-liner Egon Krenz. **3 November:** The GDR opens the border with the CSSR, leading to a further mass exodus. **4 November:** Mass demonstrations (over one million) on the Alexanderplatz in East Berlin are believed to be the largest peaceful mass gatherings ever held in Germany. **7 November:** The entire GDR government steps down. **8 November:** The GDR Politburo resigns and is replaced by a smaller one led by Egon Krenz. **9 November:** Politburo member Günter Schabowski prematurely announces the opening of the Berlin Wall and other borders; East Germans are euphoric and there are mass celebrations in Berlin. **9 November/12 December:** The Bundestag/Bundesrat approve a pension reform (in force from 1992) that is designed to control annual pension increases and will progressively raise the retirement age to 65. **10 November:** The CDU (GDR) elects Lothar de Maizière as leader and reconstitutes itself at a special congress on 15–16 December; it merges with the West German CDU on 1 October 1990. **13 November:** The GDR parliament elects the reform Communist Hans Modrow chairman of the Council of Ministers and charges him to form an interim cabinet; his government experiences several political crises and acts largely as an administrative instrument until elections are held in March 1990. **28 November:** Chancellor Kohl presents a 10-point plan for reuniting Germany. **30 November:** The Baader-Meinhof/RAF group murders senior banking executive Alfred Herrhausen in a bomb attack. **1 December:** The GDR parliament removes the SED's claim to leadership from the constitution; the following day, there is an uproar as a report reveals the scale of the party's corrupt practices. **3 December:** The SED disintegrates as its entire Politburo and Central Committee resign; at emergency congresses (8–9, 16–17 December), members reject dissolution, appoint Gregor Gysi as leader, and rename the party SED-PDS; "SED" is dropped from the title in February. **7 December:** The Round Table, a forum for dialogue between reformers and the East German government, is formed and meets until 12 March 1990. **11 December:** Representatives of the wartime Allies meet in Berlin and agree to monitor developments in East Germany. **18 December:** In the "Berlin declaration," the SPD proposes a confederation of the two German states; two days later, it publishes its "Berlin program," which supersedes the 1959 Godesberg program.

1990 15 January: Hans Modrow's refusal to dismantle the secret police (Stasi) prompts demonstrators to storm the organization's Berlin headquarters. **28 January:** Following regional elections in the Saarland, Oskar Lafontaine is reelected minister president and is also confirmed as the SPD's chancellor candidate for the national election; national elections in the GDR are set for 18 March. **4 February:** The FDP is founded in the GDR; it merges with its West German sister party on 11 August. **5 February:** The conservative Alliance for Germany is founded in the GDR. **7 February:** The Alliance 90 (Bündnis 90) is formed in the GDR. **10 February:** Mikhail Gorbachev informs Helmut Kohl in Moscow that the USSR will not oppose German reunification. **8 March:** The Bundestag guarantees the existing border (Oder–Neiße line) with Poland. **18 March:** The Alliance for Germany wins a convincing victory in the first free national elections in East Germany since 1933. **14 April:** Lothar de Maizière (CDU) becomes GDR premier; his broad-based coalition experiences many setbacks, but its main task is to prepare the way for reunification with the FRG in response to increasing pressure from East Germans. **13 May:** The SPD retains control of North Rhine-Westfalia in regional elections. Elections in Lower Saxony bring an SPD/Green coalition to power, with Gerhard Schröder (SPD) as minister president. **16 May:** The FRG sets up the German Unity Fund to provide financial support for the GDR and prepare for economic union. **18 May:** The FRG and GDR agree to the Treaty on Economic, Monetary, and Social Union. **7 June:** Susanne Albrecht, a member of the Baader-Meinhof/RAF group, is arrested in the GDR, which harbored and supported several members of the organization; more arrests follow. **17 June:** The GDR parliament sets up the Trust Agency for the privatization of state-owned businesses and organizations. **19 June:** Germany, France, and the Benelux states sign the Schengen Agreement, removing border controls for persons and goods. **1 July:** The West German DM replaces the East German mark in the former GDR as the Treaty on Economic, Monetary, and Social Union comes into force. **22 July:** The GDR parliament passes a law reestablishing the historical federal states in the east. **23 August:** The GDR parliament votes to accede to the territory of the FRG. **31 August:** The FRG and GDR conclude the Treaty on Unification, which establishes the legal basis for political reunification and extends the Basic Law to East Germany. **12 September:** Following the 2 + 4 talks between the former Allies and the FRG/GDR, a treaty is agreed upon that settles external aspects of reunification, including Germany's border with Poland; the treaty removes all residual allied rights over Germany and designates 3 October as the day of reunification. **22 September:** The Greens/Alliance 90 is formed in the GDR to campaign for the all-German national election on 2 December. **24 September:** The GDR signs a treaty with the USSR abrogating its membership in the Warsaw Pact. **1 October:** Compulsory military service is reduced from 15 to 12 months. **3**

October: East and West Germany are formally reunited. **12 October:** An attack on Interior Minister Wolfgang Schäuble leaves him paralyzed. **14 October:** Regional elections are held in the new east German states: the CDU wins an absolute majority in Saxony and forms ruling coalitions in Mecklenburg-West Pomerania, Saxony-Anhalt, and Thuringia; the SPD enters into coalition with the FDP and Alliance 90 in Brandenburg. In elections in Bavaria, the CSU successfully defends its absolute majority. **2 December:** Helmut Kohl wins a resounding victory at the first all-German national election: the CDU/CSU gains 43.8 percent of the seats, the SPD 33.5 percent, the FDP 11 percent, and the Green Party 4.2 percent; in elections in (united) Berlin, the CDU emerges as the strongest party, although Walter Momper (SPD) continues as governing mayor.

1991 13 January: Lothar Späth (CDU) resigns as minister president of Baden-Württemberg and is succeeded by Erwin Teufel (CDU, 22 January). **17 January:** As a U.S.-led coalition attacks Iraq in response to the latter's invasion of Kuwait, the German government promises financial support in place of military participation. **18 January:** Chancellor Helmut Kohl (CDU), the "unity chancellor," forms his fourth cabinet; the vice-chancellor and foreign minister is Hans-Dietrich Genscher (FDP). **20 January:** The SPD and Greens form a ruling coalition with Hans Eichel (SPD) as minister president following regional elections in Hessen. **24 January:** Eberhard Diepgen (CDU) is elected governing mayor of Berlin. **20 February:** Some 50,000 eastern German shipyard workers demonstrate against closures and job losses; in the following months, several thousand protest against rising unemployment and the dismantling of the welfare state as Chancellor Kohl's promised economic miracle fails to materialize. **25 February:** The nuclear waste storage facility in Morsleben (Saxony-Anhalt) is shut down on safety grounds; the government also orders the dismantling of the atomic power station in Greifswald (10 September). **13 March:** Erich Honecker flies to Moscow to avoid arrest for his role in the shoot-to-kill policy at the border between East and West Germany. **1 April:** Baader-Meinhof/RAF terrorists murder Detlev Karsten Rohwedder, president of the Trust Agency. **23 April:** Following a decision by the FCC confirming the legality of the postwar land reform undertaken in the Soviet-occupied zone after 1945, Germans cannot reclaim lost land and property there, although they may claim compensation. **24 April:** Rudolf Scharping (SPD) leads his party to victory in regional elections in Rhineland-Palatinate, giving the SPD a majority in the Bundesrat. **14 May:** The Bundestag introduces a solidarity surcharge on income tax from 1 July to help finance reunification. **25 May:** GDR minister president Willi Stoph and defense minister Heinz Kessler are arrested for complicity in the shoot-to-kill policy at the German border. **2 June:** The SPD takes control of Hamburg in city elections; Henning Voscherau continues as governing mayor. **6 June:** Former trade union leader Harry Tisch is the first member of the East German leadership to be tried for and convicted of corruption. **17 June:** Poland and Germany sign a treaty of friendship and cooperation. **20 June:** The Bundestag votes narrowly to move the seat of government from Bonn to Berlin. **28–30 June:** German Protestant churches reunite in Coburg as members of the EKD. **5 July:** The Bundesrat votes to remain in Bonn. **2 September:** The first trials of East German border guards begin in Berlin. **6 September:** Lothar de Maizière, interim GDR premier during 1990, resigns all offices following allegations that he was a Stasi informer. **17–22 September:** Attacks on foreigners in Hoyerswerda (Saxony) and elsewhere fuel concerns over mounting xenophobia. **21 September:** Alliance 90 is formally created as a party from elements of East German opposition groups. **29 September:** In elections in Bremen, the SPD loses its absolute majority and forms a coalition with the FDP and the Greens; the extreme right-wing German People's Union (DVU) gains votes. **16 October:** François Mitterrand and Helmut Kohl present a 50,000-strong joint Franco-German army brigade. **30 October:** A ban on environmentally harmful fluoro-hydrocarbon gases comes into effect; by 1995 these will be prohibited in all marketed products. **7 and 29 November:** The Bundestag and Bundesrat ratify the agreement reached between NATO and the Warsaw Pact in November 1990 to reduce conventional forces in Europe; the FRG had announced plans to cut the number of Bundeswehr bases on 24 May. **14 November:** The Bundestag passes a law regulating access to the files of the East German Stasi (effective 1 January 1992); Joachim Gauck heads the office entrusted with managing the archives.

1992 19 January: The "House on Lake Wannsee" near Berlin, where leading Nazis agreed on the extermination of Jews, opens as a memorial. **20 January:** A Berlin court convicts the first border guard in connection with the GDR's shoot-to-kill policy. **5 February:** Bernhard Vogel (CDU) becomes minister president of Thuringia. **7 February:** Germany signs the Maastricht Treaty, which formally establishes the European Union (EU). **27 February:** Germany and the Czech and Slovak Federation conclude a treaty on friendship and cooperation. **5 April:** Regional elections in Baden-Württemberg result in a CDU/SPD coalition headed by Erwin Teufel (CDU). Elections in Schleswig-Holstein confirm the SPD in power. **24 April:** A strike over pay by the transport workers' union ÖTV, the first by German public service workers in 18 years, brings traffic and public services to a halt. **5 June:** Against a background of mounting attacks on asylum seekers and a backlog of 360,000 requests for asylum (many from eastern Europe), the Bundestag approves a faster application-processing procedure. **26 June–10 July:** The Bundestag and Bundesrat agree to a unified abortion law for the whole of Germany, but the changes are suspended following an appeal to the FCC by CDU/CSU members and the state of Bavaria (4 August). **17 July:** Germany agrees to send naval vessels to the Adriatic as part of the UN sanctions against former Yugoslavia; the Bundestag confirms the move five days later. **29 July:** After spending eight months in the Chilean embassy in Moscow, Erich Honecker is forced to return to Berlin, where he is arrested. **23–25 August:** Foreigners and asylum seekers are attacked in Rostock. **24 September:** Germany and Romania sign an agreement to return asylum seekers. **8 October:** Willy Brandt dies. **19 October:** Petra Kelly, an early influential figure in the Green Party, and her partner, Gert Bastian, are found dead in their apartment. **8 November:** Some 300,000 people demonstrate in Berlin against xenophobia; in the weeks before Christmas, mass demonstrations in support of foreigners are held in several German cities. **12 November:** The trial of senior figures in the East German SED (Erich Mielke, Willi Stoph, and Erich Honecker) begins; Honecker acknowledges political responsibility for building the Berlin Wall but denies personal guilt for those killed along it. **23 November:** Three Turkish women are killed in arson attacks in Mölln (Schleswig-Holstein); two perpetrators receive life sentences for the crime (8 December). **27 November:** The German interior minister bans the extreme right-wing organization Nationalistische Front; bans on similar groups follow, and the authorities place the Republicans under observation. **9 December:** The Bundestag approves a law about the health-care system that is designed to cut spiraling costs. **28 December:** The author Günter Grass quits the SPD in protest against the party's policy on asylum seekers.

1993 13 January: The trial of Erich Honecker is halted on health grounds; the following day he flies to Chile, where he dies (29 May). **30 January:** Lothar Bisky succeeds Gregor Gysi as leader of the PDS. **17 February:** More than 27,000 workers demonstrate against closures in the steel industry; during the year, several large companies (Krupp-Hoesch AG, Saarstahl AG, Thyssen, Daimler-Benz, Ruhrkohle AG) announce cuts and job losses. **2–4 April:** The government approves Bundeswehr participation in a UN/NATO protection force in Bosnia; the move is challenged by the FDP but authorized by the FCC (8 April). This is Germany's first engagement in armed conflict since World War II. The government also agrees to send troops to join the UNOSOM peacekeeping force in Somalia (21 April). **3 May:** The engineering employers' refusal to implement wage agreements leads to Germany's first major industrial dispute for 60 years. **11–16 May:** The western German Greens and the eastern German Alliance 90 merge to form Alliance 90/The Greens. **19 May:** Heide Simonis (SPD) succeeds Björn Engholm as minister president of Schleswig-Holstein, making her Germany's first female regional head of state. **26 May:** Under police protection, the Bundestag approves changes to article 16 of the Basic Law, restricting the categories of persons who may apply for asylum. **27 May:** After months of conflict between the central government and the federal states, the Bundestag agrees to the federal consolidation program (Solidarity Pact) for financing reunification. Edmund

Stoiber (CSU) becomes minister president of Bavaria. **30 May:** In Solingen (North Rhine-Westfalia), five Turkish women and girls die in an arson attack that shocks the nation and prompts renewed demonstrations against xenophobia. **11 June:** Klaus Kinkel succeeds Otto Graf Lambsdorff as leader of the FDP. **25 June:** Rudolf Scharping is elected leader of the SPD. **27 June:** The arrest of presumed Baader-Meinhof/RAF terrorists in Bad Kleinen leaves two dead; blunders in the action lead to the resignations of the interior minister and the attorney general. **19 September:** Following elections in Hamburg, the SPD forms a ruling coalition with the Instead Party (Statt-Partei). **12 October:** The Bundestag ratifies the Maastricht Treaty after the FCC rules that the latter does not violate the Basic Law; Germany is the last EU state to do so. **25 October:** Thuringia is the last of the new federal states to agree a constitution. **26 October:** Erich Mielke, former head of the Stasi, is convicted for the murder of two policemen in Berlin in 1931; he faces further charges. **24 November:** Volkswagen becomes the first German company to introduce a four-day week with wage cuts (from January 1994); many large engineering and steel manufacturers announce substantial job losses.

1994 January: Deutsche Bahn AG is established in preparation for privatization of the railway system. **March:** Violent demonstrations in German cities by Kurds protesting against oppression in Turkey provoke a debate on what to do with law-breaking asylum seekers. **11 March:** The Bundestag introduces nursing care insurance (effective in 1995). **13 March:** The SPD retains control of Lower Saxony in regional elections. **25 March:** Arsonists attack a synagogue in Brandenburg; foreigners are assaulted in Magdeburg (12 May), and skinheads desecrate the Buchenwald concentration camp memorial (23 July). **15 April:** The bankruptcy of property developer Jürgen Schneider is the biggest of its kind in the history of the FRG and uncovers a major financial scandal; Schneider receives a prison sentence (December 1997), and banks are criticized for negligence. **26 April:** The FCC confirms that denial of the mass killings in concentration camps (the "Auschwitz lie") is illegal. **23 May:** Roman Herzog is elected president of the FRG. **June–August:** Russian troops depart from German soil; the last forces of the Western Allies officially leave on 8 September. **12 June:** In the fourth elections to the European Parliament, the SPD gains 32.2 percent of the seats in Germany, the CDU 32 percent, the Greens 10.1 percent, the CSU 6.8 percent, the PDS 4.7 percent, the FDP 4.1 percent, and the Republicans 3.9 percent. **26 June:** As the CDU loses votes in regional elections in Saxony-Anhalt, the SPD–Alliance 90/The Greens form a minority ruling coalition under Reinhard Höppner (SPD), which is partly dependent on PDS support. **12 July:** The FCC rules that Bundeswehr operations outside the NATO area are compatible with the Basic Law if they have Bundestag approval. **26 July:** Former members of the GDR leadership (Heinz Kessler, Fritz Streletz, and Hans Albrecht) are convicted for their involvement in the shoot-to-kill policy at the border with the FRG. **30 August:** The Basic Law is changed to enable the privatization and restructuring of the national postal and telecommunications system. **11 September:** In regional elections in Brandenburg, Manfred Stolpe leads the SPD to an overall majority. **23 September:** The Bundestag/Bundesrat agree on a reform of the Basic Law that includes environmental protection, new rights for the disabled, and gender equality as objectives of the state. **25 September:** In regional elections in Bavaria, the CSU retains its absolute majority. **16 October:** A national election returns Helmut Kohl for a fifth term. The CDU gains 41.5 percent of the seats, the SPD 36.4 percent, and the FDP 6.9 percent; the Greens (7.3 percent) make gains at the expense of the main parties; and the PDS (4.4 percent) falls below the 5 percent hurdle but enters the Bundestag via direct mandates in East Berlin. Regional elections are held in Mecklenburg-West Pomerania (resulting in a CDU/SPD coalition), the Saarland (SPD confirmed in office), and Thuringia (CDU/SPD coalition). **26 October:** Kurt Beck (SPD) succeeds Rudolf Scharping as minister president of Rhineland-Palatinate. **31 December:** The Trust Agency is wound up, with large debts.

1995 7 February: In Bremen the coalition government of SPD, Alliance 90/The Greens, and FDP collapses over environmental policy. **24 February:** The interior minister bans the neo-Nazi parties Freiheitliche Arbeiterpartei (FAP) and Nationale Liste (NL). **25 April:** Amid high security and demonstrations, the first CASTOR transport of nuclear waste leaves the Philippsburg power station (Baden-Württemberg) for storage in Gorleben (Lower Saxony). **April–May:** Germany commemorates the end of World War II, emphasizing the victims (especially in concentration camps) and the need to avoid a repetition of war. **14 May:** In regional elections in North Rhine-Westfalia, the SPD loses its 15-year absolute majority and forms a ruling coalition with Alliance 90/The Greens. **10 June:** Wolfgang Gerhardt takes over from Klaus Kinkel as leader of the FDP; after a series of regional election defeats, the party is represented in only five states. **29 June–14 July:** The Bundestag/Bundesrat agree to changes in the abortion law: abortions remain illegal, but are not punishable offenses if the mother accepts counseling within 12 weeks of conception. **30 June:** The Bundestag sanctions the sending of German forces to the former Yugoslavia, which is torn by civil war; this is the first time the Bundeswehr has been used in combat operations outside the NATO area. **13 November:** The trial begins of Egon Krenz and six other members of the SED-Politburo, who are accused of manslaughter/attempted manslaughter in connection with the shoot-to-kill policy at the intra-German border. **16 November:** Oskar Lafontaine defeats Rudolf Scharping in a battle for the leadership of the SPD. **14 December:** The federal states agree to a controversial spelling reform, to be introduced in schools beginning 1 August 1998.

1996 21 January: Germany and the Czech Republic sign a joint declaration regretting injustices associated with World War II; these include abuses by the German army and the deportation of Germans from the Sudetenland. **22 January:** The Berlin prosecution service reports that since reunification it has processed 15,000 cases involving violations of human rights in the former GDR. **30 January:** The government presents a package of spending cuts ("action program for investment and jobs"); the Bundestag eventually approves parts of the package, although this requires the "chancellor's majority" (13 September), and there are fierce protests from the SPD opposition, trade unions, churches, and other groups. **31 January:** Alexander Schalck-Golodkowski, head of the "department of commercial coordination" (Koko) in the former GDR, is convicted of arms smuggling. **15 February:** Talks among government, business, and trade unions intended to create an "alliance for work" collapse. **24 March:** Regional elections in Baden-Württemberg produce losses for the SPD and gains for Alliance 90/The Greens and FDP; the CDU forms a ruling coalition with the FDP. Following elections in Schleswig-Holstein, Heide Simonis (SPD) leads a coalition with the Alliance 90/The Greens. **27 March:** After riots by Kurds, the government strengthens deportation laws. **5 May:** The inhabitants of Berlin and Brandenburg vote by referendum against merging the two states; a merger had been agreed upon by both regional assemblies (April 1995) for implementation in 1999–2002. **8 May:** CASTOR containers transport reprocessed nuclear waste from France to Gorleben (Lower Saxony) in an operation accompanied by demonstrations and the largest police presence in the FRG's history. **31 July:** Bavaria introduces its own, more restrictive abortion laws. **23 October:** A four-year investigation into the alleged involvement with the Stasi of Manfred Stolpe, minister president of Brandenburg, is finally dropped. **1 November:** Shops are permitted to open from 6:00 am to 8:00 pm on weekdays and from 6:00 am to 4:00 pm on Saturdays. **18 November:** Deutsche Telekom enters the stock exchange in the largest share auction in European history. **13 December:** The Bundestag approves Bundeswehr participation in the Stabilization Force (SFOR) in Bosnia-Herzegovina.

1997 23 January: The government presents to the Bundestag a taxation reform package that is eventually defeated by SPD-led opposition in the Bundesrat (17 October); the Bundestag later agrees to a cost-cutting pension reform that does not require Bundesrat approval (10 October). **27 May:** Former GDR spy chief Markus Wolf receives a suspended prison sentence for depriving citizens of their liberty. **17 June:** EU states, including Germany, agree to the Treaty of Amsterdam, which lays down the rules for the single European currency and new decision-making powers in preparation for EU enlargement. **23–27 July:** The Oder River floods after heavy rainfall, causing widespread damage along the German–Polish border. **23 July:** The government presents its first "report on the status of German unity," including details on financial transfers to the eastern states. **25 August:** Former SED-politburo members Egon Krenz and Günter Schabowski receive prison sentences. **21 September:** After elections in Hamburg, Ortwin Runde (SPD) leads a coalition with Alliance 90/The Greens.

1998 1 January: The German post office's monopoly on telecommunications services ends. **16 January:** The Bundestag agrees to controversial changes in the Basic Law permitting electronic surveillance of members of the public in the fight against major and organized crime; Bundesrat assent follows (6 February). **5 February:** News that unemployment is over 12 percent leads to demonstrations in several German cities. **1 March:** In regional elections in Lower Saxony, the SPD retains control; Gerhard Glogowski succeeds Gerhard Schröder as minister president (28 October). **15 April:** The Russian parliament passes a law (called "the booty art law" in Germany) that all artwork captured in Germany by the Soviet Union during World War II will remain in its possession. **20 April:** In a letter to Reuters, the Baader-Meinhof/RAF terrorist group announces its self-dissolution. **23 April:** The Bundestag votes to introduce the European currency. **26 April:** Following regional elections in Saxony-Anhalt, the SPD forms a minority government led by Reinhard Höppner, which is tolerated by the PDS; the extreme right-wing DVU enters a regional assembly in the eastern states for the first time, with 12.9 percent of the vote. **6 May:** The Federal Office for the Protection of the Constitution estimates that there are 48,500 supporters of extreme right-wing organizations in Germany. **20 May:** CASTOR transports are suspended following revelations of safety lapses. The Bundestag passes a law rehabilitating 100,000 victims of the Nazis' legal system, including homosexuals and deserters. **27 May:** Wolfgang Clement (SPD) succeeds Johannes Rau as minister president of North Rhine-Westfalia. **13 September:** Regional elections in Bavaria confirm the CSU in power. **27 September:** A national election brings to power an SPD/Green Party coalition led by Chancellor Gerhard Schröder (SPD), with Joschka Fischer (Greens) as vice-chancellor and foreign minister; the election ends 16 years of CDU/CSU rule and is the first time in the FRG's history that an incumbent government has been voted out. The SPD gains 40.9 percent of the vote, the CDU/CSU 35.2 percent, the Alliance 90/Greens 6.7 percent, and the FDP 6.2 percent; the PDS wins 19.5 percent of the vote in the eastern states but only 1 percent in the west. The coalition, which is formed on 27 October, undertakes to reduce unemployment, reform taxation, and phase out nuclear power. **26 October:** Wolfgang Thierse (SPD) is elected president of the Bundestag. **3 November:** Following regional elections in Mecklenburg-West Pomerania (27 September), the SPD forms a coalition with the PDS, with Harald Ringstorff (SPD) as minister president; this is the first time the PDS has joined a regional government. **7 November:** Wolfgang Schäuble replaces Helmut Kohl as CDU leader; Kohl is elected honorary chairman, and Angela Merkel becomes general secretary. **10 November:** Reinhard Klimmt (SPD) succeeds Oskar Lafontaine as minister president of the Saarland. **14 November:** After a long legal battle, the Bavarian government deports, without his parents, a 14-year-old Turkish boy who had grown up in Munich and committed more than 60 criminal acts; the case had provoked a national debate about the treatment of foreign juvenile criminals.

1999 7 February: Regional elections in Hessen result in a CDU/FDP coalition led by Roland Koch (CDU). **24 February:** Bundeswehr forces take part in NATO operations in Yugoslavia; although the Bundestag approves the mission as necessary humanitarian intervention in order to prevent genocide, there is widespread unease over NATO's unilateral action. German forces also join the UN-approved Kosovo Force (KFOR) in June. **4–18 March:** The Bundestag/Bundesrat agree upon a three-stage tax reform, to be implemented in 1999, 2000, and 2002. **11 March:** Following policy disputes with Chancellor Gerhard Schröder, Oskar Lafontaine (SPD) announces his resignation as finance minister and party chairman; Schröder is elected chairman and Hans Eichel becomes finance minister (13/15 April). **1 April:** The "eco-tax," levied on fuel oil, gas, and electricity, comes into force. **19 April:** The Bundestag convenes officially for the first time in the restored Reichstag. **7 May:** The Bundestag passes a law on nationality that permits children of foreign nationals who have lived in Germany for eight years to choose dual citizenship; the option is available to children up to the age of 23. **24 May:** Johannes Rau is elected president of the FRG. **13 June:** In elections to the European Parliament, the CDU/CSU gains 48.7 percent of the seats in Germany, the SPD 30.7 percent, the Alliance 90/The Greens 6.4 percent, and the PDS 5.8 percent; the FDP fails to clear the 5 percent hurdle. **5 September:** Regional elections in the Saarland end 15 years of SPD rule; Peter Müller (CDU) becomes minister president (29 September). The SPD loses seats in elections in Brandenburg. Franz Müntefering is elected general secretary of the SPD, a newly created post. **12 September:** Regional elections in Thuringia return the CDU with an absolute majority and Bernhard Vogel as minister president. **19 September:** Regional elections in Saxony confirm the CDU's overall majority and Kurt Biedenkopf as minister president. **20–23 September:** Following instructions from Pope John Paul II, the German Roman Catholic Church withdraws from the official system of abortion counseling. **30 September:** The department of the Berlin court set up to prosecute injustices perpetrated by the GDR regime is wound up; it has initiated 22,854 cases and prosecuted 1,065 individuals, of whom 335 have been convicted so far. **11 November:** The FCC requires the government to revise (by December 2002) the system of financial equalization for distributing funds to the federal states. **30 November:** The CDU is hit by the biggest financial scandal of its history when former chancellor Helmut Kohl admits to accepting illegal donations between 1993 and 1998. **15 December:** Sigmar Gabriel (SPD) is elected minister president of Lower Saxony. **16 December:** The Bundestag agrees to a reform of the health-care system that aims to control medical costs negotiated among doctors, hospitals, and health insurance funds. **17 December:** The German and U.S. governments agree to set up a foundation to compensate victims of forced labor policies during the Third Reich.

2000 14 January: It emerges that the CDU in Hessen has maintained illegal bank accounts in Switzerland; Minister President Roland Koch is later implicated. **18 January:** After refusing to reveal the sources of illegal donations to the CDU, Helmut Kohl is forced to resign as honorary chairman; in a comprehensive leadership shake-up, Angela Merkel is elected party chairman (10 April). **4 February:** Vodafone and Mannesmann announce a merger agreement that will create the world's fourth largest company; this move by the British company Vodafone creates controversy in a country unaccustomed to shareholder-driven takeovers. **16 February:** Federal president Johannes Rau is the first German president to address the Israeli parliament (in German); he asks for forgiveness for the persecution of Jews during the Third Reich. **27 February:** Following regional elections in Schleswig-Holstein, Heide Simonis (SPD) continues the coalition government (SPD–Alliance 90/The Greens). **29 March:** The renewable energy law (*Erneuerbare-Energien-Gesetz*) comes into force. **17 April:** Deutsche Telekom launches T-Online on the stock exchange. **14 May:** Regional elections in North Rhine-Westfalia result in a coalition of SPD–Alliance90/Greens, with Wolfgang Clement (SPD) as minister president. **25 May:** A government commission proposes structural reforms to the Bundeswehr; the government agrees to measures to create a smaller, more professional army (14 June). **31 May:** The government approves a "green card" scheme (effective 1 August) to attract foreign workers with computer skills to Germany. **15 June:** The government and the power industry agree on a 32-year timetable for withdrawal from nuclear energy. **23–24 June:** The Alliance 90/The Greens elect Fritz Kuhn and Renate Künast as leaders. **17 July:** An agreement is signed in Berlin to compensate victims of slave labor during the Third Reich; financed by government and business, a special fund is set up to pay restitution and promote future projects. **31 July–17 August:** As part of its telecommunications deregulation program, the German government sells Universal Mobile Telecommunications System licenses to six mobile phone operators/consortia. **12 August:** Legislation comes into force creating a foundation to compensate victims of forced labor during the Third Reich (Stiftung Erinnerung, Verantwortung, und Zukunft). **11 October:** Marianne Birthler succeeds Joachim Gauck as head of the office responsible for managing the Stasi files. **14 October:** The PDS elects Gabriele Zimmer as leader. **27 October:** The Bundestag alters the Basic Law to permit women in the armed forces to carry weapons and take part in combat operations. **31 October:** The EXPO 2000 exhibition, held in Hanover, closes with a deficit of over a billion euros; of the planned 40 million visitors, only 18.1 million came. **17 November:** The Bundestag passes the first stage of what the government plans to be a comprehensive reform of the pension system; the long-term aim is to stabilize contributions and even out the funding gap created by an aging population and a shrinking workforce. **24 November:** The first case of bovine spongiform encephalopathy (BSE) is found in Schleswig-Holstein; the total reaches 94 by August 2001.

2001 9 January: Health minister Andrea Fischer and agricultural minister Karl-Heinz Funke resign over the spread of BSE to Germany. **31 January:** The government applies to the FCC to ban the right-wing NPD; the application collapses when it emerges (in 2002) that 14 party members were working undercover for the authorities. **2 March:** Proceedings against former chancellor Helmut Kohl over his involvement in the CDU donations scandal are dropped after he pays 300,000 DM. **10 March:** The Greens elect Claudia Roth as coleader alongside Fritz Kuhn. **25 March:** Regional elections in Baden-Württemberg confirm the CDU/FDP coalition led by Erwin Teufel (CDU). Following elections in Rhineland-Palatinate, Kurt Beck (SPD) continues as minister president of an SPD/FDP coalition. **May/June:** The Bundestag and Bundesrat agree to changes to the pension system that will promote an element of private insurance; they also approve an increase in student grants (April) and higher subsidies for families with children (July). **5 May:** Guido Westerwelle succeeds Wolfgang Gerhardt as leader of the FDP. **1 June:** The Bundestag extends the Bundeswehr's mandate in Kosovo and later approves German forces' participation in NATO missions in Macedonia (29 August and 27 September). **16 June:** Eberhard Diepgen (CDU), governing mayor of Berlin, resigns following a financial scandal; Klaus Wowereit (SPD) takes over as head of an interim administration and later forms a coalition with the PDS. **5–13 July:** The Bundestag/Bundesrat agree to changes to the system of financial equalization between federal states; a second Solidarity Pact for transfers to the eastern states is also approved. **1 August:** A new law giving same-sex relationships similar rights to marriages comes into effect. **3 August:** The government accepts recommendations of a commission chaired by Rita Süssmuth (CDU) proposing orienting immigration policy toward the labor market. **19 September:** Following terrorist attacks in New York City (11 September), the Bundestag passes antiterror laws and increases internal security. **23 September:** Ronald Schill and his ultraconservative party (PRO) achieve a surprise electoral success in Hamburg, a traditional SPD stronghold; Schill becomes interior senator (minister) in a CDU/FDP–PRO coalition under Ole von Beust (CDU). **16 November:** Chancellor Schröder uses a vote of confidence to secure a Bundestag majority to approve Bundeswehr operations in Afghanistan. **22 December:** The

Bundestag agrees to send up to 1,200 soldiers as a contribution to ISAF in Afghanistan; this is the first time Bundeswehr soldiers have faced combat outside of Europe.

2002 1 January: The single European currency (euro) enters circulation, replacing the DM in Germany; the new "Job-Aqtiv" law, which is designed to reduce the numbers of long-term unemployed, comes into effect. **8 April:** The Kirch media concern declares insolvency. **21 April:** Following regional elections in Saxony-Anhalt, Wolfgang Böhmer (CDU) forms a coalition government with the FDP. **18 July:** Chancellor Gerhard Schröder sacks Defense Minister Rudolf Scharping for accepting payments from a parliamentary lobbyist; Scharping is replaced by Peter Struck. **3 August:** Gerhard Schröder rejects German participation in a possible war against Iraq. **7 August:** Unemployment passes four million as economic recession deepens. **11–17 August:** The Elbe River floods and causes immense damage in eastern Germany; the disaster prompts the government to postpone the 2003 tax reform. **22 September:** A national election brings losses for the SPD and gains for the CDU/CSU: the SPD and CDU/CSU each win 38.5 percent of the vote, the Greens 8.6 percent, and the FDP 7.4 percent. The PDS (4 percent) fails to clear the 5 percent hurdle but retains two direct mandates in the Bundestag. The SPD/Green coalition is confirmed on 16 October. Regional elections in Mecklenburg-West Pomerania return the country's first coalition between the SPD and PDS, with Harald Ringstorff (SPD) as minister president. **5 November:** The Berlin senate declares a financial emergency, with debts of over 46 billion euros. **6 November:** The North Rhine-Westfalia parliament elects Peer Steinbrück (SPD) as minister president. **17 December:** From April 2003, "mini-jobs" (paying up to 400 euros a month) will no longer attract income tax/national insurance contributions.

2003 1 January: The "drinks can deposit," a levy on all one-way drink packaging containing mineral water, beer, and carbonated soft drinks, comes into effect. **24 January:** The government and the Central Council of Jews in Germany agree on funding for Jewish communities in Germany and for integrating Jewish immigrants from the east. **2 February:** Roland Koch leads a CDU government after regional elections in Hessen. The SPD loses control of Lower Saxony, where Christian Wulff (CDU) forms a coalition with the FDP. **10 February:** Alongside the Netherlands, Germany assumes joint leadership of ISAF in Afghanistan; six months later a Bundeswehr general leads ISAF on behalf of NATO. **13 March:** The Bundestag changes the law to allow shops to open until 8:00 pm on Saturdays. **14 March:** Against strong opposition from trade unions and left-wingers in the SPD, Chancellor Gerhard Schröder presents a program of major structural, economic, and social welfare reform (Agenda 2010). **17 March:** Jürgen Möllemann (FDP) resigns from his party and later commits suicide after facing investigation over illegal donations (5 June). **18 March:** The FCC rejects the government's application to ban the NPD. **20 March:** A U.S.-led coalition attacks Iraq; thousands of Germans (including 500,000 in Berlin) demonstrate against the war. The U.S. defense minister, Donald Rumsfeld, calls Germany and France "old Europe" for refusing to join the war, although a reconciliatory meeting between Schröder and U.S. president George W. Bush takes place in September. **25 May:** Following elections in Bremen, the CDU/SPD grand coalition, led by Henning Scherf (SPD), continues in office. **5 June:** Dieter Althaus (CDU) succeeds Bernhard Vogel as minister president of Thuringia. **29 June:** IG Metall abandons its strike in eastern Germany over parity with workers in the west, producing a split in the union's leadership. **August:** The Rürup Commission, set up to recommend ways of sustaining Germany's social and health-care provision, submits its final report. **19 August:** Hamburg senator Ronald Schill is forced from office. **21 September:** In regional elections in Bavaria, the CSU wins a historic two-thirds majority. **26 September and 17 October:** The Bundestag and Bundesrat approve a major health-care reform package. **3 October:** After making anti-Semitic remarks, Hessen politician Martin Hohmann (CDU) is forced to resign from his party. **1 November:** Some 100,000 people demonstrate in Berlin against the dismantling of the social welfare system; large-scale protests continue in 2004, mainly in eastern Germany. **15 November:** The Bundestag agrees to a controversial "savings package" for the health-care sector. **19 December:** As the first stage of Agenda 2010, the Bundestag/Bundesrat agree to far-reaching changes to the health insurance system; the package of 15 measures, effective 1 January 2004, is the most extensive in the history of the FRG. **December:** Over 4.3 million people (10.4 percent of the civilian labor force) are registered as unemployed; 67,000 under age 20 are jobless.

2004 1 January: The second stage of the tax reform comes into effect and is rolled up with parts of the (brought forward) third stage. The Federal Employment Office is restructured and renamed the Federal Employment Agency; its head is dismissed over irregularities in distributing contracts (24 January). **22 January:** The EU Court of Human Rights supports compensation claims by Germans dispossessed of land and property in eastern Germany before 1990. **5 February:** Courts in Hamburg release a suspected Al Qaida member for lack of evidence; the conviction of a second member is quashed on 4 March. **6 February:** Gerhard Schröder resigns as leader of the SPD; Franz Müntefering is elected chairman and Klaus-Uwe Benneter general secretary (21 March). **16 February:** Maatwerk GmbH, the largest provider of personal service agencies, declares insolvency. **27 February:** Chancellor Schröder meets with President George W. Bush to improve U.S.–German relations, which had deteriorated over the war against Iraq. **29 February:** The CDU wins an overall majority in regional elections in Hamburg; the minister president is Ole von Beust. **18–28 May:** Germany passes new security laws relating to air traffic and the exchange of information with other EU states on suspected terrorists. **23 May:** Horst Köhler is elected federal president. **13 June:** The CDU retains control of Thuringia as the SPD's share of the vote plummets; in the European Parliament elections, the CDU/CSU gain 44.5 percent of the seats, the SPD 21.5 percent, Alliance 90/The Greens 11.9 percent, and the PDS and FDP 6.1 percent each; the SPD loses votes in district elections in six federal states. **23 June:** After journalists try to open up the Stasi's files on former chancellor Helmut Kohl, German courts limit public access to information in the archives. **1–9 July:** After four years of debate, the Bundestag/Bundesrat agree to a new immigration law. **2–9 July:** The Bundestag/Bundesrat pass the final stage (IV) of the Hartz recommendations on restructuring and reducing unemployment benefits; the measures will be phased in from January 2005. **22 July:** In what is seen as a test of shareholder-driven management in Germany, a Düsseldorf court dismisses charges of corruption against senior executives of Mannesmann; a new trial begins but is abandoned in November 2006 following payment of collective fines of 5.8 million euros. **10–15 September:** Federal president Johannes Rau pays a state visit to China as the latter replaces Japan as Germany's main trading partner in Asia. **16 September and 11 December:** The publication of two Pisa Reports indicating a fall in educational standards in Germany sparks a national debate.

2005 26 January: The FCC rules that student tuition fees are no longer illegal. **27 January:** The 60th anniversary of the liberation of Auschwitz concentration camp is commemorated; various events marking the end of World War II are held during the year. **2 February:** Unemployment reaches a historic five million. **20 February:** Following elections in Schleswig-Holstein, the CDU and SPD agree in April to a grand coalition, with Peter Harry Carstensen (CDU) as minister president. **22 March:** Lufthansa takes over Swiss Air. **25 April:** Foreign Minister Joschka Fischer admits mistakes in the issuing of entry permits to eastern Europeans in the "visa affair." **19 April:** After the death of Pope John Paul II (2 April), the German cardinal Joseph Ratzinger is elected his successor and becomes Pope Benedict XVI. **4 May:** Around 350 obsolete laws, some dating from before World War I, are removed from the statute books. **10 May:** The Holocaust Memorial is dedicated in Berlin; the memorial marks the end of 16 years of planning and coincides with debates on how to commemorate the Berlin Wall. **30 May:** The CDU/CSU nominate Angela Merkel as their chancellor candidate. **3 June:** Regional education ministers decide to make the spelling reform mandatory in schools. **10 June:** The PDS and WASG agree to an electoral alliance, the Left Party. **16 June:** The EU formally shelves its proposed constitution. **1 July:** Chancellor Gerhard Schröder engineers a vote of no confidence in the Bundestag to trigger a national election. **8 July:** A corruption scandal at Volkswagen forces the resignation of personnel chief Peter Hartz, architect of the Hartz reforms. **August:** Around 10,000 hospital doctors strike over pay and working conditions; the dispute continues until May/June 2006. **4 September:** Chancellor Gerhard Schröder and his electoral challenger, Angela Merkel, engage in a public television debate. **8 September:** Germany and Russia agree to build a gas pipeline across the Baltic. **18 September:** In national elections, the CDU/CSU win 35.2 percent of votes, the SPD 34.2 percent, the FDP 9.8 percent, the Left Party 8.7 percent, and the Greens 8.1 percent; the inconclusive result leads to intensive interparty negotiations to form a ruling coalition. **20 September:** Green Party politician Joschka Fischer resigns from all parliamentary and party offices. **28 September:** Henning Scherf, mayor of Bremen, announces his resignation and is succeeded by Jens Böhrnsen in November. **10 October:** The CDU/CSU and SPD agree on a coalition, with Angela Merkel as chancellor and a majority of SPD cabinet ministers. After 60 years, the U.S. air force closes its Rhine-Main base at Frankfurt/Main airport. **18 October:** Norbert Lammert (CDU) is elected president (speaker) of the Bundestag. **10 November:** The CDU and SPD agree to raise the turnover tax from 16 to 19 percent, effective in January 2007. **15 November:** Matthias Platzeck is elected as SPD chairman, replacing Franz Müntefering. **22 November:** The Bundestag elects Angela Merkel (CDU) as Germany's first female chancellor.

2006 January: The Federal Intelligence Agency (BND) pays for CDs providing details about German tax evaders maintaining foreign accounts; the issues surrounding this and future purchases persist for several years. **1 February:**Adherents of Islam protest the publication in the German press of caricatures of the prophet Mohammed, which had originally appeared in Denmark. **6 February:** The largest public sector strike in 14 years begins; the dispute ends with agreement between ver.di and the federal states on 19 May. **17 February:** The Bundestag raises unemployment benefits (*Arbeitslosengeld II*) in the eastern states to western levels (effective 1 July). **1 March:** The EU moves to increase penalties against Germany for breaching the European Stability and Growth Pact for the fifth year running, but withdraws them in October as Germany announces a public spending deficit below the 3 percent limit. **10 April:** Kurt Beck, minister president of Rhineland-Palatinate, succeeds Matthias Platzeck as leader of the SPD. **29 May:** The longest strike in the history of the public sector in Germany ends when hospital doctors agree on a compromise pay deal. **1 June:** The Bundestag passes measures penalizing recipients of unemployment benefits (*Arbeitslosengeld II*) who refuse more than three offers of work during a year. The Bundeswehr takes over command of ISAF in northern Afghanistan. **30 June and 7 July:** The Bundestag and Bundesrat approve the most comprehensive reform of the German federal system since 1949; the reforms come into effect on 1 September. **25 August:** Germany's largest intermediate storage facility for nuclear waste begins operation at Gundremmingen (Bavaria). **12 September:** Muslims protest critical remarks about Islam made by Pope

Benedict XVI during a lecture in Regensburg; the pope visits Turkey in November and prays with the Mufti of Istanbul in a sign of reconciliation. **20 September:** The Bundestag approves the sending of a German naval force to Lebanon as part of the EU's commitment to maintaining a truce between Israel and Hizbollah. **25 September:** Fearing protests by Islamists, the Deutsche Oper Berlin temporarily removes Mozart's opera Idomeneo from the program. **19 October:** The FCC rejects the city of Berlin's attempt to force the government to provide extra assistance to help it out of its financial crisis. **5 October:** The coalition parties agree on a health-care system reform, which is passed by the Bundestag and Bundesrat on 2 and 16 February 2007. **30 October:** The visit by Polish prime minister Jaroslaw Kaczynski to Germany is overshadowed by a dispute over the Russo-German gas pipeline in the Baltic, which will bypass Poland, raising Polish fears of a political axis between Berlin and Moscow. **9 November:** Berlin removes controls on shop opening hours during workdays; other federal states follow. **29 November:** The federal government agrees to a bill to progressively increase the retirement age from 65 to 67 between 2012 and 2029. **30 November:** The jobless total falls below four million for the first time in four years.

2007 1 January: Chancellor Angela Merkel assumes the six-month presidency of the EU Council and the chair of the G8. Romania and Bulgaria join the EU, which now has 27 member states. **12 January:** The Bundestag extends Germany's ISAF mandate in Afghanistan for another year. **25 March:** EU leaders in Berlin agree to implement by 2009 a new treaty on the Union's general political objectives. **3 April:** The FCC approves the construction of a controversial nuclear waste repository, Schacht Konrad, near Salzgitter. **19 May:** Three German soldiers are killed in a suicide attack in Afghanistan. **11 May–20 June:** Deutsche Telekom workers strike over outsourcing plans that will bring inferior employment conditions and job losses. **13 May:** Following regional elections in Bremen, The Left Party enters a Landtag in western Germany for the first time. **6 June:** The G8 summit begins in Heiligendamm on the Baltic. **11 June:** Final compensation sums for victims of forced labor during the Third Reich are agreed upon. **13 June:** The Bundestag approves a special pension for victims of the East German Stasi. **16 June:** The PDS and WASG formally merge to create Die Linke (The Left), led jointly by Lothar Bisky and Oskar Lafontaine. **1 July:** Foreigners who have lived and worked in Germany for eight years (six, with children) acquire a right to long-term residency. **4 July:** The FCC approves requirements for Bundestag deputies to declare subsidiary earnings. **1 August:** The spelling reform (*Rechtschreibreform*) comes into force in all German schools. **9 August:** The European Central Bank increases the money supply as shares plummet in the wake of the crash in the U.S. mortgage market. **27 August:** Chancellor Angela Merkel pays a three-day state visit to China. **1 September:** Smoking is banned in government offices, public transport, and rail stations. **19 September:** The government establishes a 100 million euro fund to compensate Jewish victims of Nazi forced labor policies. **23 September:** Chancellor Merkel's reception of the Tibetan Dalai Lama in Berlin creates diplomatic friction with China. **29 September:** Erwin Huber is elected leader of the CSU. **17 October:** Culture ministers of the federal states agree to standardize the higher school-leaving certificate (*Abitur*) from 2010 to 2012. **27 October:** Kurt Beck is reelected leader of the SPD. **9 November:** The Bundestag agrees to a controversial law enabling phone tapping, with limited exemptions for doctors, lawyers, and journalists. **14 November:** Rail locomotive drivers begin the longest strike in their history, lasting into December. **16 November:** The Bundestag lowers unemployment contributions, extends unemployment benefits for workers aged 58 or over, and raises salaries of its deputies by almost 10 percent. **13 December:** Leaders of the EU sign the Treaty of Lisbon, which comes into force in 2009. **12 December:** Border controls between Germany, Poland, and the Czech Republic are removed as the latter join the Schengen Agreement. **31 December:** Deutsche Post's monopoly on letter handling ends.

2008 1 January: Eleven federal states ban smoking in pubs, bars, and restaurants. **15 January:** With tax receipts exceeding expenditure, the national budget has a surplus for the first time since 1969. **27 January:** Following regional elections in Hessen, an SPD/Green Party coalition collapses before Andrea Ypsilanti (SPD) can take office as minister president. After elections in Lower Saxony, the CDU/FDP coalition continues and The Left Party enters the assembly for the first time. **14 February:** The head of Deutsche Post, Klaus Zumwinkel, resigns following government pressure over alleged tax evasion. **24 February:** Elections in Hamburg result in the first regional CDU/Green Party coalition. **5 April:** Following failure to form a government, Hessen sets new elections for 18 January 2009. **11 April:** The Bundestag relaxes the law on research using embryonic stem cells. **14 April:** Georg Milbradt (CDU) steps down as minister president of Saxony and is succeeded by Stanislaw Tillich (CDU) on 28 May. **24 April:** The Bundestag ratifies the Lisbon Treaty. **24 May:** Prosecutors initiate action against Deutsche Telekom, which admits monitoring contacts between business leaders and journalists. **5 June:** Visiting Germany, Russian president Medvedjev warns NATO not to expand in eastern Europe. **6 June:** The Bundestag approves new renewable energy targets. **16 July:** At 3.3 percent, inflation in Germany is the highest since 1993. **7 September:** Frank-Walter Steinmeier takes over as acting chairman of the SPD following the surprise resignation of Kurt Beck. **17 September:** The Bundestag extends the Bundeswehr's operations off the Lebanese coast and agrees to its participation in a peacekeeping mission in Sudan. **28 September:** In regional elections in Bavaria, the CSU loses its overall majority for the first time since 1962; Horst Seehofer (CSU) leads a coalition with the FDP. **3 October:** As the financial crisis deepens, Chancellor Merkel announces a state guarantee for all private savings and giro accounts. **6 October:** Erwin Sellering (SPD) is elected minister president of Mecklenburg-West Pomerania after Harald Ringstorff resigns. **9 October:** Deutsche Bahn postpones entry into the stock market. **12 October:** European leaders in Paris agree on a "protective umbrella" for banks as the global financial crisis deepens. **15 October:** The Bundestag/Bundesrat agree to a 500 billion euro emergency rescue package. **16 October:** The Bundestag extends the Bundeswehr's mandate in Afghanistan. **3 November:** The Commerzbank is the first major German bank to receive support (8,200 million euros) from the government rescue fund, alongside a 15 billion euro guarantee. **12 November:** The Bundestag approves a controversial law extending the powers of the Federal Criminal Police Office (BKA) to combat terrorism, but it is rejected in the Bundesrat and passed over to the mediating committee. **15 November:** The Green Party elects Cem Özdemir as co-chairman. **1 December:** Angela Merkel is reelected CDU leader. **4 December:** The Bundestag approves its first economic stimulus package (23 billion euros) to combat the downturn caused by the financial crisis.

2009 12 January: The Bundestag approves a second economic stimulus package. **18 January:** Regional elections in Hessen give a CDU/FDP coalition a majority, and Roland Koch (CDU) continues as minister president. **9 February:** Karl-Theodor zu Guttenberg (CSU) replaces Michael Glos (CSU) as economics minister. **12 February:** Government and federal states agree on a long-term debt brake to curb the national deficit. **18 June:** The Bundestag passes a law blocking child pornography Internet sites. **22 April:** Four members of the Islamist terrorist "Sauerland group" go on trial in Düsseldorf for planning bombing attacks; they are convicted on 4 March 2010. **21 May:** Forty years after fatally shooting the student Benno Ohnesorg in Berlin, retired policeman Karl-Heinz Kurras is revealed as a Stasi spy and member of the SED; a Berlin court convicts him of possessing illegal weapons. **28 May:** The Bundestag agrees to measures giving addicts easier access to artificial heroin. **7 June:** In elections to the European Parliament, the CDU wins 30.7 percent of the vote, the SPD 20.8 percent, the Greens 12.1 percent, the FDP 11 percent, The Left Party 7.5 percent, and the CSU 7.2 percent. **12 June:** The Bundestag/Bundesrat approve new measures for budgetary control proposed by the second commission on federalism reform (including a "debt brake"), which had been set up starting in 2007. **18 June:** Advanced health-care directives for patients are ruled to be binding, even when they involve death (effective 1 September). **3 August:** Arms lobbyist Karlheinz Schreiber is repatriated to Germany to face charges of tax evasion; he is convicted on 5 May 2010. **30 August:** The CDU loses heavily in regional elections in Thüringia, where it enters into coalition with the SPD under Christine Lieberknecht (CDU), and in the Saarland, where Annegret Kramp-

Karrenbauer (CDU) forms a government with the FDP and the Greens. **4 September:** In Afghanistan, dozens of people, including civilians, are killed or injured in an air attack ordered by the Bundeswehr; this will eventually lead to the resignation of a minister, a state secretary, and a military general inspector. **27 September:** In national elections the FDP achieves the best results in its history (14.6 percent of the vote) and enters into a governing coalition with the CDU/CSU (33.8 percent) under Chancellor Angela Merkel. The SPD's performance (23 percent) is the worst since 1949; the Greens gain 10.7 percent of the vote and The Left Party 11.9 percent. Regional elections are held in Brandenburg, where the SPD, under minister president Matthias Platzeck, forms a coalition with The Left Party, which beats the CDU into third place, and in Schleswig-Holstein, where Peter Harry Carstensen (CDU) leads a coalition with the FDP. **9 November:** The Bundestag agrees to a third economic stimulus package; the following day, the chancellor presents a five-point plan to lead Germany out of the crisis. **13 November:** The SPD elects Sigmar Gabriel party chairman and Andrea Nahles general secretary. **27 November:** Labor minister Franz Josef Jung resigns after 31 days in office, the shortest ever period in the FRG's history. **8 December:** The FDP is fined 3.5 million euros for illegal party donations involving one of its leading figures, Jürgen Möllemann. **16 December:** The government agrees to a budget that includes a record debt level of 85,500 million euros.

2010 2 March: The Federal Constitutional Court rules the mass storage of telephone and Internet data illegal. **24 March:** The government sets up a roundtable to investigate the sexual abuse of children in public, private, and religious institutions; its final report and recommendations appear in November 2011. **25 March:** Eurozone members agree to the first rescue package for Greece, which is threatened with bankruptcy. **6 May:** The "Topography of Terror," Germany's first permanent exhibition and documentation center for Nazi crimes, re-opens in Berlin. **9 May:** Following regional elections in North Rhine-Westfalia, the SPD and Green Party form (on 14 July) a ruling coalition led by Hannelore Kraft (SPD); with the defeat of the CDU, the government loses its majority in the Bundesrat. **10 May:** The EU agrees to a 750 billion euro rescue package to restore financial stability to the eurozone. **15 May:** Gesine Lötzsch and Klaus Ernst succeed Oskar Lafontaine and Lothar Bisky as coleaders of The Left Party. **17 May:** The Second German Islam Conference begins, following months of disagreement over its participants and agenda. **31 May:** Federal president Horst Köhler announces his resignation following controversial remarks he made linking Germany's mission in Afghanistan to national economic interests. **7 June:** In the largest austerity package in the FRG's history, the government agrees to an 80 billion euro program of budget cuts, especially in social welfare; the "consolidation program" will run from 2011 to 2015 and reduce the national structural deficit. **23 June:** The federal labor court removes the principle of "one firm, one collective labor agreement." **25 June:** The Federal High Court allows patients to refuse life-prolonging treatment. **28 June:** German forces end their antiterrorism mission in the Horn of Africa. **30 June:** Christian Wulff is elected president of the FRG. **31 August:** Volker Bouffier (CDU) succeeds Roland Koch as minister president of Hessen. **15 December:** The government ends peacetime national conscription from July 2011, replacing it with voluntary military or community service. **7 July:** Germany accepts two detainees from the U.S. prison camp in Guantanamo Bay. **25 August:** Christoph Ahlhaus (CDU) succeeds Ole von Beust as first mayor of Hamburg. **18 September:** Some 100,000 people demonstrate in Berlin against plans to prolong the operation of nuclear power stations; the plans are included in the government's energy program on 28 September. **30 September:** Hundreds of protestors against the Stuttgart 21 transport project are injured in clashes with the police. **12 October:** Germany is elected a nonpermanent member of the UN Security Council for 2011–2012. **28 October:** Unemployment falls below three million (7 percent) for the first time since 2008.

2011 2 February: Hessen is the first federal state to ban the wearing of the burka by public service employees. **15 February:** The German and New York stock exchanges decide to merge, but this is eventually blocked by the EU. **20 February:** Led by Olaf Scholz, the SPD wins an absolute majority in Hamburg city elections. **2 March:** Thomas de Maizière (CDU) replaces defense minister Karl-Theodor zu Guttenberg (CSU), who resigns when his doctorate is withdrawn for plagiarism; Hans-Peter Friedrich (CSU) becomes interior minister. **14 March:** Roland Jahn takes over from Marianne Birthler as head of the organization managing the Stasi archives. The government reviews its decision to continue operating nuclear power stations following the catastrophe in Fukushima. **17 March:** Germany abstains in the UN vote to apply a no-fly zone over Libya. **21 March:** Finance ministers of the EU agree on a permanent rescue fund for the euro (ESM). **26 March:** Some 250,000 demonstrators in several cities demand an immediate withdrawal from nuclear energy. **27 March:** After elections in Baden-Württemberg, a coalition between the Greens and SPD, headed by Winfried Kretschmann (Green Party), is agreed to on 12 May. **19 April:** Reiner Haseloff (CDU) heads a coalition with the SPD following regional elections in Saxony-Anhalt (20 March). **29 April:** Jens Weidmann is appointed head of the German Federal Bank. **12 May:** Philip Rösler (FDP) becomes economics minister and, on 18 May, vice-chancellor; on 13 May he succeeds Guido Westerwelle as party leader. **18 May:** Defense minister Lothar de Maizière announces reforms to the Bundeswehr. In Rhineland-Palatinate, Kurt Beck (SPD) heads an SPD/Green Party coalition following elections on 27 March. **22 May:** After elections in Bremen, Jens Böhrnsen (SPD) continues the coalition with the Greens. **7 June:** President Barack Obama awards Chancellor Angela Merkel the American Freedom Medal. **9 June:** The Bundestag approves a simplification of the tax system. **20 June:** Eurozone finance ministers agree to stiffer rules for budget deficits. **28 June:** On a state visit by China to Berlin, Germany and China deepen economic cooperation. **10 August:** Following elections in the Saarland (25 March), Annegret Kramp-Karrenbauer (CDU) heads a coalition of CDU/SPD. **4 September:** After regional elections in Mecklenburg-West Pomerania, the SPD and CDU agree in October to continue their coalition under Erwin Sellering (SPD). **18 September:** In city elections in Berlin, the Pirate Party enters the assembly; SPD and CDU agree to a coalition under Klaus Wowereit (SPD) in November. **22 September:** Pope Benedict XVI pays a state visit to Germany. **4 November:** Police in Zwickau (Thuringia) uncover the underground Nazi terror group NSU, responsible for several murders between 2000 and 2007; failings in the police and security organizations later lead to resignations. **9 November:** The FCC declares the 5 percent hurdle for elections to the European Parliament unconstitutional. **December:** The accumulated national public debt reaches a record 2,065 billion euros (the figures for 1980 and 1990 were 238 billion and 538 billion).

2012 6 January: Saarland minister president Annegret Kramp-Karrenbauer (CDU) ends the coalition with the FDP and Green Party, the first "Jamaica coalition" (black/yellow/green) in a federal state. **26 January:** The Bundestag agrees to start withdrawing the Bundeswehr from Afghanistan; the number of soldiers there is reduced. **30 January:** Leaders of the EU agree to a fiscal pact to stabilize the Eurozone; the provisions include a debt brake to curb national budget deficits. **17 February:** Christian Wulff resigns as president of the FRG as federal prosecutors pursue allegations that he provided favors to business and media interests when minister president of Lower Saxony. **27 February:** The Bundestag approves its contribution to a second financial rescue package for Greece. **18 March:** Joachim Gauck is elected president of the FRG. **25 March:** Following (brought forward) regional elections in the Saarland, Annegret Kramp-Karrenbauer (CDU) forms a coalition with the SPD. **4 April:** Author Günter Grass is accused of anti-Semitism for claiming that Israeli policy in the Middle East endangers world peace. **11 April:** Gesine Lötzsch resigns as leader of The Left Party. **29 April:** Bernd Schlömer is elected leader of the Pirate Party. **3 May:** The trial begins of members of the "Düsseldorf Group" of Islamist terrorists. **5 May:** During violent demonstrations against the neo-Nazi group Pro NRW in Bonn, a radical Salafist seriously injures two police officers. **6 May:** Following regional elections in Schleswig-Holstein, Torsten Albig (SPD) forms a coalition with the Greens and the Danish minority party SSW. **13 May:** The CDU loses seats in regional elections in North Rhine-Westfalia, and the SDP/Green Party coalition under Hannelore Kraft (SPD) continues. **16 May:**

In what is seen as punishment for the CDU's poor performance in the North Rhine-Westfalia regional election, Chancellor Angela Merkel controversially forces the dismissal of environment minister Norbert Röttgen (CDU), who was party chairman and lead candidate in the state; Röttgen is succeeded by Peter Altmaier. **25 May:** The Bundestag passes a new organ donation law requiring health insurance funds to ask all members over 16 if they wish to offer a transplant. **29 June:** The Bundestag approves the European Stability Mechanism (ESM). **30 June:** Formerly Germany's largest regional bank, WestLB is broken up after facing bankruptcy in 2008. **2 July:** The president of the Federal Office for the Protection of the Constitution resigns over failures in investigating the NSU terror group. **12 August:** At the London Olympic Games, Germany ranks sixth, with 11 gold, 19 silver, and 14 bronze medals. **22 August:** North Rhine-Westfalia is the first federal state to introduce Islam as a regular school subject. **18 September:** The extreme right-wing party The Right is founded in Dortmund. **9 November:** The government agrees to scrap the 10 euro fee to visit a doctor, first introduced in 2004, effective from January 2013. **9 November:** The Bundestag introduces financial support for parents who stay at home to care for preschool children (*Betreuungsgeld*) from 2013. **4 December:** Angela Merkel is reelected leader of the CDU. **5 December:** Interior ministers of the federal states recommend applying to the FCC to ban the extreme right-wing NPD. **30 December:** The accumulated national public debt is 2,030 billion euros, slightly lower than the previous record year.

2013 6 January: The opening of Berlin's new airport is postponed for the fourth time; Brandenburg's minister president Matthias Platzeck (SPD) takes over from Berlin's mayor, Klaus Wowereit (SPD), as chair of the supervisory board. **7 January:** Franz Kuhn is elected the first Green Party governing mayor of a regional capital (Stuttgart). **16 January:** Malu Dreyer (SPD) replaces Kurt Beck as minister president of Rhineland-Palatinate. **20 January:** Following elections in Lower Saxony, Stephan Weil (SPD) leads a coalition with the Green Party (19 February). **13 February:** Federal education minister Annette Schavan (CDU) resigns after her doctorate is withdrawn for plagiarism; she is succeeded by Johanna Wanka (CDU). **18 February:** The Bundestag agrees to a change to the electoral law that balances the number of overhang mandates among parties. **9 April:** The government and federal states undertake to find a permanent nuclear storage facility by 2031; in the meantime, further transports to the temporary facility at Gorleben will cease. **14 April:** The anti-euro party AfD decides to participate in the forthcoming national election. **15 April:** A nepotism scandal hits the Bavarian regional parliament. **6 May:** The trial begins in Munich of members of the neo-Nazi terror group NSU; the principal defendant is Beate Zschäpe. **18 June:** President Barack Obama visits Berlin. **22 August:** A Bundestag committee reports serious failures by the police and security authorities regarding the NSU terror group. **28 August:** Dietmar Woidke (SPD) succeeds Matthias Platzeck (SPD) as minister president of Brandenburg. **11 September:** The first of 5,000 refugees from the Syrian civil war arrive in Germany. **15 September:** In regional elections in Bavaria, the CSU wins an absolute majority; Horst Seehofer continues as minister president. **22 September:** In the national election the CDU/CSU fall just short of an absolute majority, while their former coalition partner (FDP) fails the 5 percent entry hurdle. After regional elections in Hessen, the CDU under Volker Bouffier concludes a coalition with the Greens (December). **6 October:** The Bundeswehr ends its mission in the north Afghanistan province of Kundus. **19 October:** The Green Party elects Simone Peter as coleader alongside Cem Özdemir. **23 October:** After it emerges that the U.S. security organization NSA has been monitoring Chancellor Angela Merkel's cell phone, she protests personally to President Obama. **31 October:** After meeting Green Bundestag member Hans-Christian Ströbele, the U.S. whistleblower Edward Snowden announces he is prepared to assist Germany in investigating the NSA's spying activities. **5 November:** It emerges that the British intelligence authority GHCQ maintains a listening post on the UK embassy roof in Berlin. **14 November:** The trial begins of former federal president Christian Wulff; he is accused of accepting hospitality from a film producer and promoting his film. **27 November:** The CDU, CSU, and SPD agree to a national coalition government under Chancellor Angela Merkel.

2014 14 March: The Federal Office for the Protection of the Constitution stops monitoring Bundestag members of The Left Party but continues surveillance of extremist groups within the party. **24 August:** Federal interior minister Thomas de Maizière estimates that the number of asylum seekers will rise to 200,000 in 2014, the highest since 1990. **31 August:** Regional elections in Saxony produce losses for most parties (the FDP fails to clear the 5 percent hurdle), while the AfD enters parliament with 14 seats. Stanislaw Tillich (CDU) forms a coalition with the SPD in November. **14 September:** Following regional elections in Brandenburg, Dietmar Woidke (SPD) heads a coalition with The Left Party; the AfD attracts disillusioned voters from other parties and enters parliament with 11 seats. Elections in Thuringia return a coalition of The Left Party/SPD/Greens led by Bodo Ramelow (The Left Party); this is the first time The Left Party has headed a regional government. **21 September:** The Bundestag and Bundesrat compromise on a reform of the asylum law. **1 October:** Renewable energies surpass brown coal as the prime source of electricity generation. **7/8 October:** Street battles between Kurds and Islamist groups take place in Celle and Hamburg. **12 October:** Arson attacks are made on an asylum seekers' hostel near Rostock; similar incidents follow in Verra (Bavaria) on 2 December. **22 October:** Pegida begin weekly demonstrations in Dresden against the Islamization of Germany. **27 October:** Forty-four police officers are injured during a violent demonstration by 4,000 right-wing extremists in Cologne. **11 December:** The government agrees to introduce a minimum quota for women in leading positions of large companies. Klaus Wowereit (SPD) steps down as governing mayor of Berlin and is succeeded by Michael Müller (SPD). **15 December:** Finance Minister Wolfgang Schäuble predicts annual structural budget surpluses until 2018, although some federal states face problems meeting the debt brake. **28 December:** After 13 years, NATO formally ends ISAF operations in Afghanistan; since 2002 the Bundeswehr has been involved in several hundred combat operations in the region.

2015 18 January: Police in Saxony ban a planned demonstration by Pegida following death threats against its leader, Lutz Bachmann. **11 February:** Following an initiative by Chancellor Angela Merkel and French president François Hollande, a new packet of measures (Minsk II) is agreed to for a cease-fire between warring government and pro-Russian separatists in eastern Ukraine. **15 February:** The AfD enters the Hamburg senate in city elections; the CDU suffers a historic defeat, and on 8 April governing mayor Olaf Scholz (SPD) agrees to a ruling coalition with the Greens. **1 March:** Despite objections from environmentalists, a new coal-fired power station in Hamburg goes online. **23 March:** Public service workers in most federal states strike as state authorities negotiate to make savings. **4 April:** Right-wing extremists stage an arson attack on a home earmarked for 40 asylum seekers in Tröglitz (Saxony-Anhalt), whose mayor had already resigned over demonstrations against the incomers. **25 April:** In a statement supported by the Bundestag, Federal president Joachim Gauck enrages Turkey by referring to its genocidal massacre of 1.5 million Armenians during World War I. Several thousand brown coal miners demonstrate in Berlin against plans by economics minister Sigmar Gabriel (SPD) to impose an environmental tax on older mines; opponents of coal mining demonstrate in Garzweiler (North Rhine-Westfalia). **20 May:** Railway locomotive drivers end strikes, which began in September 2014 over tariff agreements, the longest dispute in the history of Deutsche Bahn. **22 May:** To curb the influence of smaller trade unions, the Bundestag legislates to reestablish the principle of "one firm—one union"; opponents plan to challenge the law in the FCC. **7–8 June:** Germany hosts the annual G7 summit in Bavaria. **1 July:** The federal government introduces a "bureaucracy brake": for each new regulation, an existing one must be abolished within a year. **11–13 July:** At a marathon summit, and facing the prospect of Greece's enforced exit from the euro, EU leaders thrash out the basis for negotiating a third emergency bailout; its terms are harsher than those rejected in a national referendum in Greece a week earlier. The Greek parliament agrees to the terms, and the Bundestag approves the bailout by a large majority on 18 August (60 CDU members had voted against negotiations on 17 July). **31 July:** Germany's chief prosecutor suspends an investigation into two journalists suspected of treason for revealing government plans to increase Internet surveillance; this would be the first time since the *Spiegel* affair of 1962 that German journalists would face treason charges. **8 September:** Chancellor Merkel opens Germany's borders to mainly Syrian refugees, but reinstates controls after more 19,000 arrive in Munich on 13/14 September. Germany and France propose mandatory refugee quotas for EU states. **9 September:** EU Commission president Jean-Claude Juncker proposes that member states accept the mandatory distribution of 160,000 refugees. The EU leaders had rejected a similar plan for 40,000 in May. **24 September:** The government agrees with the federal states to a package of financial support to meet the costs of an estimated 800,000 asylum seekers, as Merkel faces growing opposition, even within her own party, to her open-door policy. **15/16 October:** The Bundestag/ Bundesrat approve legislation expediting asylum procedures and the deportation of rejected applicants. **3 December:** The Bundestag votes to provide support for, but not to engage actively in, air strikes against Syria.

2016 13 March: Regional elections in Baden-Württemberg, Rhineland-Palatinate, and Saxony-Anhalt return losses for the CDU and gains for the anti-immigration AfD as voters punish Angela Merkel for her open-door refugee policy. New coalition governments are eventually formed in all three. states. **20 March:** An agreement between the EU and Turkey comes into effect: migrants arriving in Greece will be returned to Turkey if they do not apply for asylum or their claim is rejected.

Introduction

With an area of 357,022 square kilometers, Germany is one of Europe's largest countries, after Ukraine (603,550 sq. km), France (551,500 sq. km), Spain (505,370 sq. km), and Sweden (450,295 sq. km). It has the largest population (around 81 million), followed by Great Britain (63.4 million) and metropolitan France (62.8 million). Politically and administratively, the country is organized as a federation of states (Länder) around a political center (the so-called Bund, or federation). Within this system of federalism, the relationship between the center and the federal states is laid down in the Basic Law (BL), which, among other things, defines areas of relative political authority or competence and the institutions and processes of legislation, government, and law.

From 1949 until 1990, Germany existed as two separate states, the Federal Republic of Germany (FRG) and the German Democratic Republic (GDR), with different political, economic, and social institutions. For the FRG, a milestone event was the General Treaty, concluded in 1952 between West Germany and the Western Allies (United States [U.S.], Great Britain, and France), but for various reasons effective from 1955. The treaty formally ended the occupation following the country's defeat in World War II and assigned, with some restrictions, the rights of a sovereign state to the FRG. Also in 1952, the GDR established a formal "demarcation line" with West Germany, with official controls on exit and entry. The erection of the Berlin Wall in August 1961, accompanied by East Germany's consolidation of the entire inner German border (1,378 km long) into an almost insuperable barrier, became a potent symbol of the divergence between the two states. Although the process of separation had been long under way, most Germans were surprised when it became practically impossible to meet relatives or friends on the other side of the border. While West Germany continued to develop as a social market economy, pursuing integration in Western economic, political, and military alliances, East Germany became in all but name a one-party state, functioning with a centrally managed command economy as a member of the Warsaw Pact and the bloc of Soviet-controlled states of Eastern Europe.

The demise of the GDR and its eventual incorporation into the West German political system—a process that began in the fall of 1989 and culminated in reunification on 3 October 1990—created a new Germany at the heart of central Europe, at times referred to as the "Berlin Republic" to reflect the shift of the capital from Bonn to Berlin. Reunification itself was achieved by

1

a series of treaties that were negotiated with remarkable speed within a single year. They set the framework for merging the economies and social systems of the two states (Treaty on Monetary, Economic, and Social Union), the internal political aspects (Treaty on Unification), and—following the so-called 2 + 4 talks between the two Germanies and the former Allied powers, who had effectively been in charge of foreign relations since 1945—and external security issues (the Treaty on the Final Settlement with Respect to Germany). The formal processes of reunification were, however, only part of the picture. The privatization of eastern Germany's industries and the sudden switch from a centrally controlled to a market-oriented economy involved huge financial and human costs, whose effects are still felt, especially among older generations who had grown up and lived with the Wall, and could persist for decades. While western Germans for the most part experienced these costs as a financial burden, for many in the east, despite the greater opportunities for travel and personal and political freedom, they involved at least short-term deindustrialization, hitherto unknown unemployment, migration, and considerable psychological adaptation.

Reunification also coincided with an ongoing domestic debate about Germany's industrial competitiveness in a changing global economy. The parameters of this debate ranged from the status of German corporatism, shareholder value, and the burden on businesses of state regulations and taxation to managerial competence, entrepreneurship, and the need for more flexibility in industrial relations. The five new federal states also brought the potential for changes to the political balance between the regions and the center within the constitutional framework of German federalism. In international terms, reunification confirmed Germany's integration in the North Atlantic Treaty Organization (NATO) and the European Union (EU). As a founding member in 1957, Germany accompanied the EU's sometimes tortuous evolution from a small economic community into an expanded organization of states with a significant and still deepening degree of political and social union. At the same time, the international community looked to united Germany for signs of changes in direction with respect to its policy on Europe and on security and defense issues. The European dimension of German foreign policy became even more important as the EU attempted to work out structures for enlargement that would, on the one hand, integrate new members from eastern Europe anxious to join the "club" of prosperous western states and, on the other hand, manage budgets, streamline internal decision making, and harmonize the historical treaties of the EU within the framework of a new constitution or its equivalent.

As a member of NATO and the Western system of alliances, Germany was also expected to expand its role in international peacekeeping military operations. This provoked a constitutional debate during the 1990s following pressure to intervene in a civil war in the then Yugoslavia. In the light of the end of the Cold War, which arguably coincided with the fall of the Berlin Wall, and changing defense/security needs, the German armed forces began to reassess their role and capabilities, partly within the context of plans to develop a European defense capability. While German foreign policy underwent no fundamental shifts, the transatlantic relationship came under severe strain over the U.S.-led attack on Iraq in 2003, when Germany and France reaffirmed their traditional alliance by uniting in opposition to what many Europeans regarded as a highly dubious war. Upon reunification some observers wondered whether Germany would become more assertive and revert to behaving as a historical nation-state. In fact, the Germans have continued to achieve their goals by working through existing multilateral alliances and networks, although certain shifts in emphasis can be detected.

LAND AND PEOPLE

After the upheavals of World War II and their aftermath (which included large movements of evacuees, an influx of refugees and expellees from the east, and the return of prisoners of war over a period of at least 15 years), the populations of the FRG and the GDR stabilized around 1950 at 50 and 18 million, respectively. Thereafter, the population of East Germany stagnated, falling to 16 million before reunification, while that of West Germany rose as the country underwent far-reaching economic and social changes. Following sharp increases during the 1950s and 1960s, the population of the FRG fluctuated at between 61 and 61.5 million during the 1970s and 1980s. With the incorporation of the former GDR, united Germany was home to over 79 million people in 1990, rising steadily to 82 million in 1999, where it has more or less remained. At the same time, the general picture of national demographic growth masks a range of trends and influences, not least a current popular perception that Germans are actually declining in numbers.

Geographically, Germany lies in the temperate climate zone of northern Europe and experiences changeable weather (the following statistics are from Wehling and Sattler, *Der Fischer Atlas Deutschland* [2001]). The prevailing winds are from the west, and rainfall is high, ranging from an annual 500 to 800 millimeters in the North German Lowland Plain to 1,000–2,000 millimeters in the Central Uplands and between 700 millimeters along the Danube and 1,500 millimeters at the fringes of the Alps. The oceanic climate of the northwest, with its cool summers and mild winters, is gradually displaced by continental conditions with more extreme variations (hot summers and cold winters) toward the east and south. Average temperatures in January (the coldest month) range from –2/+2 degrees Celsius in the north, to –2 degrees in Munich, to –8 degrees or lower in the Bavarian Alps. The warmest month is July, when average temperatures lie, for most of the country, in the range of 14–18 degrees Celsius, with higher temperatures in, for example, Berlin and the Rhine basin. With the exception of mountain regions such as the Harz, Black Forest, Sauerland, and Alps, more rain falls in summer than in winter. The east of the country is drier (the Thuringian Basin and the loess areas of Magdeburg typically experience annual rainfall levels below 500 mm), as are sheltered parts of the west, such as the Rhine valley. Areas enjoying the most hours of sunshine lie south of Frankfurt/Main and Nuremberg and to the east around Berlin, Magdeburg, and the Baltic coast. In the summer months Germany is typically influenced by cool airstreams from the north (the Atlantic and polar regions) and by subtropical air from the south. During the winter the tropical air mass in the south retreats so that Europe is dominated by air from the north, producing rain and snow, although cold and dry air occasionally intrudes from the large continental landmass to the east.

Germany can be divided into the following geographical areas according to its main physical features. The main feature in the north of the country is the North German Lowland Plain (Norddeutsches Tiefland), which is part of the great North European Plain stretching from France to Russia and is crossed by major rivers (the Rhine, Weser, Elbe, and the Oder) flowing northward into the North Sea and Baltic. Between the mainland and North Sea islands (the East and North Frisians) lies the Wattenmeer, an area of mudflat stretches and sandbanks cut through by sea channels. Salt marshes have formed around the mouths of the Weser and Elbe rivers and farther along the coast. The Baltic coast, an area of outstanding natural beauty, has long and narrow sea inlets (Förden) to the west (Schleswig-Holstein) and lagoons (Bodden) to the east (Mecklenburg-West Pomerania). Offshore lie the islands of Rügen, Usedom, and Fehmann. Farther inland, the landscape ranges from flat and sandy plains (Geest) in the west and north of Hamburg to clay hills, heathland (the Lüneburger Heide, north of Hanover), and in the east, the lakes, moors, hills, and forests of Mecklenburg-West Pomerania.

South of the North German Lowland Plain are the Central Uplands (Mittelgebirge), a range of hills and mountains running west to east and rising to between 200 and 1,500 meters Parallel to the northern foothills of the Uplands are wide, fertile stretches of loess (Börden). Fertile basins cut into the Uplands, examples being the Lower Rhenish Basin, the Westfalian Basin, and the Saxon-Thuringian Basin. The oldest rocks in the Upland range are slate, granite, and gneiss, and some of the highest peaks are volcanic in origin. The landscape is varied and includes the Rhenish Slate Mountains (Rheinisches Schiefergebirge), which span the Rhine River between Cologne/Bonn and Bingen and encompass the lower mountain ranges of the Eifel (up to 746.9 m), Hunsrück (816 m), Taunus (881 m), Westerwald (657.3 m), Siegerland (677.7 m), Bergisches Land (519.2 m), Sauerland (843.2 m), and the Rothaar Mountains (Rothaargebirge, 843.2 m). To the

Uplands also belong the Hessisches Bergland (950 m) and the Weser and Leine mountain ranges (Weser- und Leinebergland), which are named after the rivers that flow through them. To the east are situated the Harz Mountains, which rise to 1141.2 meters at their highest point (peak Brocken). Farther south are the mountains of the Rhön (950 m), the Bavarian Forest (Bayerischer Wald, 1,455.5 m), the Upper Palatinate Forest (Oberpfälzer Wald, 1,042 m), the Fichtel Mountains (Fichtelgebirge, 1,051 m), the Franconian Forest (Frankenwald, 794 m), and the Thuringian Forest (Thüringer Wald, 982.9 m). The Ore Mountains (Erzgebirge) in the east constitute the border with the Czech Republic. The highest peak on the German side of this range is the 1,215-meter-high Fichtelberg.

To the south and west of the Central Uplands lie the South or Southwest German Central Upland Scarps (Südwestdeutsches Mittelgebirgs-Stufenland). To the west of the range runs the Upper Rhine valley. This extends from the Black Forest (Schwarzwald), whose highest point is the Feldberg (1,493 m) in the far south, to the forest of the Oden (Odenwald) and the Spessart further north. The Uplands also include the Palatinate Forest (Pfälzer Wald) west of the Rhine and, stretching from the eastern Danube right across southern Germany, the line of the Swabian-Franconian Scarpland, comprising the Schwäbische Alb, the 1,015.3-meter-high Lemberg Mountain, and the Fränkische Alb.

To the south and east of the Central Upland Scarps lies the 100-kilometer-wide belt of the Alpine Foreland (Alpenvorland). Rising north to south from 400 to 600 meters to meet the Alps, the Foreland encompasses the Swabian-Bavarian Plateau, with hills and large lakes (Starnberger See, Chiemsee) in the south, and the hills of Lower Bavaria (Unterbayerisches Hügelland) to the east. It is crossed by several rivers, including the Iller, Wertach, Lech, and Isar, which flow mainly northward from the Alps to enter the Danube.

The German Alps, stretching from Lake Constance (Bodensee) in the west to Salzburg (Austria) in the east, constitute a small and narrow section of the European Alps, a range of limestone fold mountains extending west–east from France to Yugoslavia. At the foot of the high mountain range of the Alps lies a belt of sandstone hills with characteristic alpine pastures and moorland. From west to east, the German High Alps comprise the Allgäuer Alps (with the peaks Hochfrottspitze, 2,649 m; Mädelegabel, 2,645 m; and Hochvogel, 2,592 m), the Bavarian Alps (with the peak Zugspitze, 2,962 m), the Karwendel Mountains (with the peak Östliche Karwendelspitze, 2,537 m; and the lakes Walchensee and Eibsee), and the Berchtesgaden Alps (with the peak Watzmann, 2,713 m; and the lake Königssee). Ancient glaciers formed during the last ice age are found on the highest mountains.

Germany's major river systems (including tributaries) are the Ems, Weser, Elbe, Oder, Rhine, and Danube. With the exception of the Danube, which rises in the Black Forest in southwestern Germany and flows eastward before leaving Germany near Passau and eventually entering the Black Sea, these rivers all discharge into the North Sea or Baltic. Germany's longest river is the Rhine (total length 1,320 km, of which 865 km flows across Germany), followed by the Elbe (700 km) and the Danube (647 km). The Rhine also carries the largest volume of water, at a rate of 2,260 cubic meters per second, compared to 1,430 cubic meters for the Danube and 750 cubic meters for the Elbe. The Rhine and the Elbe move almost two-thirds of the country's volume of surface water (Wehling and Sattler 2001). The rivers have important functions as transport highways and sources of energy and food, not to mention irrigation, waste discharge, and leisure activities. Between 1970 and 2000, a total of 36,000 kilometers of waterway was straightened and channeled. Many of the larger rivers were narrowed and deepened, while dikes and channels were built to reclaim natural floodplains for farming and settlement. The drawback of this work has been that river flows have become much faster, increasing the danger of flooding during extreme weather conditions and where building and agriculture have reduced the ability of land to absorb rain and melted snow and ice. Climatic change in the form of hotter and drier summers and milder, wetter winters has contributed to more frequent flooding in recent times. Catastrophic floods occurred in recent years on the Rhine and Mosel (1993–1994 and 1995), the Oder (1997), and the Elbe and Danube (2002). In 2002 in Germany alone, the costs of the floods amounted to 11,500 million euros, and further severe flooding occurred again in 2009, 2010, and in particular in 2013 in the south and east. In 1996, the German government passed a new law (Wasserhaushaltsgesetz) requiring the federal states (Länder) to improve provisions for combating floods; measures include retaining and protecting natural floodplains and creating new ones. Germany has extensive polderland (along the Rhine and Elbe between Magdeburg and Hamburg) and many dams (e.g., in the Saale/Elbe, the Ruhr/Maas, Upper Rhine, and Eder-Fulda/Weser regions).

HISTORICAL SURVEY

Historiography

A major theme in studies of 20th-century Germany—even after the milestones of the "historians' quarrel" of the 1980s and reunification, continuing to account for a quarter of publications—remains the rise, course, and nature of the National Socialist regime (Schildt 2012). For Germans, the process of recalling, interpreting, and coming to terms with this period (encapsulated in the terms Vergangenheitsbewältigung and Aufarbeitung) has persisted well into the post-Nazi era and gained renewed momentum after 1990. In German academic circles, the process began seriously with the founding of an institute for contemporary historical study (Institut für Zeitgeschichte, Munich) in 1949 and a journal (*Vierteljahrshefte für Zeitgeschichte*), which appeared in 1953 and to this day publishes articles on National Socialism and the Holocaust. From the voluminous literature on the period, various perspectives have emerged. In trying to understand the origins and the nature of the totalitarian regime, early studies during the 1950s pinpointed the collapse of the party system during the Weimar Republic and investigated the relationship between Adolf Hitler's personal authoritarianism and the confused structures of his party. Combining his experiences as a journalist in 1930s Germany with a historical perspective, William Shirer (1960) saw National Socialism as the grotesque, deterministic finale of a tradition of nationalism and militarism dating back well before the 20th century (the so-called special path or Sonderweg). Others, such as Hitler's biographer John Toland (1976), attempted to penetrate beyond the conventional view of the Nazi leader as simply evil incarnate and reach a deeper understanding of his attributes and motivation. Following on from Martin Broszat's (1969) landmark study of the domestic and foreign policy of the National Socialist regime (albeit only up to 1939, but one of the first of its kind), two interpretive schools of thought emerged, later categorized as "intentionalism" and "functionalism" (or "structuralism"). Intentionalists, who focus on the ability of powerful individuals to influence historical events, saw Hitler as a single-minded autocrat, formulating his war aims and genocidal policies at an early stage and executing them according to a consistent plan. Functionalists/structuralists, on the other hand, identify the broader political or economic circumstances that condition historical development. Thus, concentrating less on the leader figure and more on the decision-making structures of the National Socialist state, they regard Hitler as an opportunist who operated within a general ideological framework and proved unable to dominate events (especially during World War II) as they unfolded. Rivalries and competing factions within the party, alongside Hitler's own suspicions about potential opposition, resulted in policy improvisation and confused governance, a feature that is sometimes labeled "polycratic" (as opposed to "monocratic") rule. Intentionalists include Karl Dietrich Bracher, Eberhard Jäckel, Saul Friedländer, Klaus Hildebrand, Gerald Fleming, and Ino Arndt. Functionalist approaches are found in the works of Hans Mommsen and Uwe Dietrich Adam, and in those of the British historian Ian Kershaw (1987), who argued that Hitler's leadership qualities owed more to myth nurtured by propaganda than to political reality. A synthesis of the two schools is also possible; Kershaw, for example, suggests that Hitler's intentions created a climate that unleashed structural forces in the state that made his prophesies self-fulfilling. Historians have also addressed the question of whether the National Socialists represented a throwback to conservatism or succeeded in creating a genuinely new and revolutionary social community (Volksgemeinschaft) with resonances into the present. Another issue is the relationship between the ostensible modernism of society under the National Socialists—for instance, in terms of its industry, social welfare system, and exploitation of communication tools and the media—and its pursuit of genocidal racial and foreign policies. Both the historians' quarrel of the 1980s and the fall of the GDR in 1990 specifically rekindled comparisons between the nature of dictatorships, in particular with regard to the methods of social control and the levels of overt violence employed in the Nazi and Soviet states. The complexity of issues confronted here is further reflected in the investigation of Germans as both victims (e.g., of Nazi persecution, wartime bombing campaigns, atrocities of occupying armies, and forced expulsion) and perpetrators (demonstrated through publications, memorials, and exhibitions). The particular difficulty for Germans of integrating the Holocaust into a conventional historical narrative—a discontinuity that Dan Diner (1990) described as a "civilization break"—has led to the suggestion that all the debates about the genocide share one common denominator: the desire to move away from victim-centered memories to somehow contain the National Socialist legacy and enable the German people to normalize its relationship with the past (Schmitz 2006). More recent cultural assimilations of the National Socialist period include the numerous, sometimes trivialized representations of Hitler in films, and the emergence of counterfactual speculations on how the Holocaust might have been averted or scenarios following a German victory in World War II (Rosenfeld 2014).

Overall, Germany's engagement with its recent history is both thorough and multifaceted. Teaching about the National Socialist regime—as yet less so about the GDR—is integral to the school curriculum, and there are regular exhibitions and lectures, for instance in the German Historical Museum in Berlin, although there are similar museums in Bonn and Leipzig. The provision of numerous memorials that serve as a reminder of past atrocities is exemplary in Germany: prominent is the Memorial to the Murdered Jews of Europe (Denkmal für die ermordeten Juden Europas) in Berlin, not to mention the sites of former concentration camps elsewhere in the country. The commemoration of the Berlin Wall still provokes discussion, but memorial foundations and museums engage with both daily life and political developments in the former GDR. In 1993, the Neue Wache memorial in Berlin was rededicated to the memory of "war and tyranny," which at the time struck many as too vague to be appropriate.

For the postwar FRG, the dominant historiographical theme is that of a "success story" (Erfolgsgeschichte)—in other words, of a country rising from the ashes of destruction to achieve economic prosperity, democratic pluralism, civil stability, and international legitimacy through integration into Western multilateral structures. Germany's ability to weather social and economic changes from the late 1960s onward and meet the political, financial, and social demands of incorporating the new federal states (1990) has reinforced the success narrative. Nevertheless, German historians have not glorified these achievements in a nationalistic sense and have not been afraid to draw attention to negative aspects of the old FRG, such as the long-term implications of expanding the welfare state and subsidy policies that arguably promoted social inequalities. After Germany entered the new, post-1990 era, fresh issues emerged, including debt management, east–west internal migration, alienation between eastern and western Germans, the importation of west German elites into the new federal states, and the exploitation of fears about the numbers of asylum seekers; foreign policy (in particular, more recently, the relationship with Russia), internal security, and responses to terrorism can be added to the list. Studies of the parallel history of the GDR also underwent significant shifts, notably the move away from the "system immanent" approach adopted during the 1970s and 1980s, which aimed to assess the country "objectively" according to its own measures and yardsticks, in favor of empirical and more critical methods available with the hindsights and also distance of reunification. In fact, 25 years after the fall of the Wall, a whole generation has no experience of German history prior to 1989.

German historiography underwent a paradigmatic shift during the 1950s. Moving away from a focus on history as political events and the actions of leading figures (using evidence drawn from official documents and apparently objective happenings), researchers in Bielefeld and Frankfurt widened the sources and areas of investigation to encompass social classes, families, and even personal recollections and family histories. The aim was to offer a more holistic, total history or "history of society" (Gesellschaftsgeschichte), integrating economics, politics, sociology, and even ideas and culture. In the process, regional history attracted more attention, and laypeople became actively involved alongside academics. The following account, while touching on social issues, makes no attempt to present a rounded, comprehensive picture of German history in these terms, but focuses on the main political stages and events in the development of Germany after 1949.

The German Democratic Republic (GDR)

The history of the GDR can be divided into two main periods: from 1949 until the erection of the Berlin Wall in 1961 and from 1961 to the fall of the regime in late 1989. Under the tutelage of the Union of Soviet Socialist Republics (USSR) and the leadership of Walter Ulbricht, the GDR, which was founded in October 1949 shortly after the creation of the FRG, developed as a communist/socialist state ruled by the Sozialistische Einheitspartei Deutschlands (SED). The early years of the GDR were characterized by the transfer of industries and agriculture into state ownership and the development of a central planning mechanism for managing the economy. During this period, the SED party apparatus expanded to several hundred thousand functionaries and employees, with much of the population organized in socialist institutions, including trade unions, youth movements, and cultural organizations. Initially, many East Germans embraced the socialist experiment, hoping for genuine and positive change, but the pace and nature of transformation—in particular the development of heavy industry at the expense of consumer goods while meeting the demands of reparations to the Soviet Union and rising military expenditure—led the state into an economic crisis, which culminated in the so-called Workers' Uprising of June 1953, which is now seen as a socially much broader expression of discontent against the regime. As economic problems—exacerbated by the enforced collectivization of agricultural land, supply bottlenecks, and rising national debt—continued, emigration of East Germans to the west (totaling 2.5 million between 1949 and 1961, with 200,000 crossing to West Berlin in 1960) was halted only by the erection of the Berlin Wall in August 1961. The wall, which divided Berlin and left the western part of the city an island in East German territory, sealed off the last remaining and most popular escape route to the FRG.

From 1961 onward, the GDR consolidated itself as the population stabilized (emigration to the west was no longer an option), and the economy began to recover from the damage of enforced collectivization. The party tightened its control and enshrined its monopoly of power in a revised national constitution of 1968. When East German troops appeared alongside those of the USSR in the 1968 invasion of Czechoslovakia, the GDR, of all the eastern bloc states, appeared as the Soviet Union's most trusted and loyal ally. However, in May 1971 Ulbricht, the political architect of East Germany, was forced to stand down as leader in favor of Erich Honecker, who had organized the building of the Berlin Wall. At the time it was felt that Ulbricht had fallen afoul of his Soviet masters by presenting the GDR as a model for other Eastern European states and by resisting rapprochement with the west, although it is also possible that he was the victim of internal conspiracies within the SED. Under the banner of "unity of economic and social policy," Honecker attempted, on the one hand, to boost industrial production through modernization and, on the other hand, to raise the standard of living by increasing pensions, lowering working hours, providing more consumer goods, and tackling the chronic housing shortage. At the same time, he reinforced ideological control and strengthened the political role of the SED and its apparatus at all levels. Further revisions to the constitution (1974) emphasized the national identity of the GDR as a permanent state that was distinct from the FRG and irrevocably bound to the USSR.

Honecker's political and diplomatic successes include improved relations with the FRG and the acceptance of East Germany into the international community. Following the achievements of Ostpolitik, the GDR was admitted to the UN (1973), was officially recognized by over 130 states (although not by West Germany), and concluded around 500 international agreements. Although those who hoped for a thaw in cultural censorship were disappointed after 1976, East Germany's political understanding with the FRG weathered a general deterioration in East–West relations during the 1980s. Increasing numbers of East Germans were permitted to visit relatives in the FRG, and several thousand were allowed to emigrate. At the 11th party congress in 1986, the political leadership expressed confidence about the achievements of socialism in the economy, welfare provision, education, and East Germany's contribution to international peace.

Between 1985 and 1989, when the Soviet leader Mikhail Gorbachev embraced policies of openness and relaxed the Soviet grip on its satellite states (glasnost and perestroika), the East German leadership became increasingly isolated as it insisted on adhering to "socialism in the colors of the GDR" (a formula unofficially adopted during the 1970s as an analogy with the French Communist Party's notion of "communism in the colors of France"). Although Honecker and his aging colleagues in the Politburo welcomed Gorbachev's initiatives to relax international tension and end the arms race, they rejected moves toward greater internal democracy, including open discussions about communism under Stalin, and ignored or suppressed calls for domestic reform. The regime came under massive internal pressure, as citizens either demonstrated for liberalization and reforms or simply left the country via bordering socialist states. Unable to draw on the external support of the Soviet Union, it collapsed in the autumn of 1989, leaving the road open to democratization and eventual reunification with the FRG.

The Federal Republic of Germany (FRG): From 1949 to 1966

Following the foundation of the FRG in 1949 and the election of a series of coalition governments dominated by the Christian Democratic Union (CDU) and led by Federal Chancellor Konrad Adenauer until 1963, the main themes of West German society and politics were the consolidation of democratic institutions, the reconstruction of the economy according to social-market principles (the "economic miracle" of the 1950s and 1960s), and integration into the political and military structures of Western Europe and the North Atlantic Treaty Organization (NATO). In his later years, however, Adenauer lost the confidence of the public and his party, and he eventually resigned in 1963. Attempts by the defense minister, Franz Josef Strauß, leader of the CDU's sister party in Bavaria, the Christian Social Union (CSU), to silence a respected news magazine that had exposed failings in military policy led to a national scandal that threatened the coalition with the Free Democratic Party (FDP), although the government survived when Strauß withdrew from the cabinet. Adenauer's successor was Ludwig Erhard (CDU), a popular economics minister and considered the father of Germany's economic recovery. Faced, however, with the FRG's first economic recession (slowing growth, rising unemployment, and a collapsing market for coal and steel), Erhard was unable to provide the necessary leadership, and the coalition broke up after failing to agree on measures to correct a budget deficit (while Erhard planned tax increases, the FDP insisted on spending cuts). Erhard resigned in October 1966.

The Conservative/Social Democrat Grand Coalition under Kurt Georg Kiesinger: 1966–1969

The grand coalition of 1966–1969 gave the Social Democratic Party of Germany (SPD) its first chance to participate in government. Led by Kurt Georg Kiesinger (CDU), with Willy Brandt (SPD) as vice-chancellor and foreign minister, the coalition regained control of the economy by coordinating economic, financial, and social policy and promoting jointly financed projects between the federal government and the states. It passed the controversial "emergency laws" (Notstandsgesetze, 1968), which defined the powers of the executive in times of national emergency, thereby removing certain remaining rights of the Allied powers over Germany's sovereignty, and weathered the social unrest and political polarization that accompanied the student demonstrations of 1967–1968. Although the coalition took tentative steps toward improving relationships with the Soviet-dominated eastern bloc, its unwillingness to concede diplomatic recognition to the GDR and the invasion of Czechoslovakia in August 1968 by the USSR blocked progress on concluding a nonaggression treaty with the Soviets. The CDU/CSU was also in principle less inclined than the SPD to conduct a dialogue with the east.

The period from 1949 to the late 1960s saw profound social and economic changes in Germany. Waves of immigrants from the East and guest workers from southern Europe provided a reservoir of labor for the postwar economic recovery and significantly altered the national demographic profile. Germany also began to address more openly the legacy of National Socialism as reparations to Israel were agreed (1952), a center for investigating war crimes was established (in 1958 in Ludwigsburg), and the first trials by the German authorities of ex-Nazis were held (in 1958 in Ulm and 1963 in Frankfurt). Finally, a radical, student-led protest movement, opposing nuclear arms, challenging the establishment, and demanding reforms to higher education, emerged during the late 1960s, eventually crystallizing into violent street demonstrations during 1967–1968 and reinforcing the sense that German society was facing serious challenges to its social and political fabric.

The Social/Liberal Coalition under Willy Brandt: 1969–1974

In 1969, the SPD formed a ruling coalition with the FDP, the first time it had led a government in the FRG. Despite its slim majority in the Bundestag, the coalition, led by Chancellor Willy Brandt, introduced a variety of measures designed to democratize German society and substantially widen welfare provision. It lowered the voting age, encouraged citizens' initiatives, extended health care and pensions, and drew up plans to expand and modernize education and to improve infrastructure, administration, and the environment. Proposals to extend codetermination in industry and to liberalize abortion and divorce laws were either abandoned after opposition from the FDP or delayed by a Bundesrat dominated by the conservative opposition parties, the CDU/CSU. Unable to control a budgetary crisis induced by a combination of economic downturn and the high costs of the social program, Brandt resigned in May 1974. The immediate reason for the resignation was the discovery of an East German spy, Günter Guillaume, in his circle of close advisers.

Brandt is remembered less for his domestic reforms than for the success of his policy on Eastern Europe (Ostpolitik), which contributed significantly to East–West détente and placed the FRG's relationship with the GDR on a more pragmatic footing. The seeds of Ostpolitik were sown in a lecture given in 1963 by Brandt's adviser, Egon Bahr, who proposed that West Germany enter into dialogue with the GDR authorities to reduce international tension and improve conditions for ordinary East Germans. The aim was to achieve a gradual change in East Germany through reconciliation (Wandel durch Annäherung). The opportunity to follow up the proposal came in 1967–1968 when NATO, through the publication of the Harmel Report (December 1967) and a meeting of foreign ministers in Reykjavik (June 1968), indicated its readiness to negotiate a reduction in troops (mutual balanced forces reduction, MBFR) with the USSR. As part of the "Reykjavik signal," NATO explicitly acknowledged the need to resolve the German question as a basis for a lasting peace in Europe. Subsequent developments now took place against a background of talks between NATO and the Warsaw Pact that were aimed at reducing East–West tension and fostering cooperation on arms limitation (the Strategic Arms Limitation Talks, or SALT I, started in Helsinki in November 1969).

As German chancellor, and freed from the constraints of working with the CDU, Brandt concluded a series of landmark treaties with the USSR and other Eastern European countries, including the GDR. In a nonaggression

pact with the USSR (Treaty of Moscow, August 1970), the FRG acknowledged the existing borders in Europe (notably those to the east) and agreed to
respect the territorial integrity of its eastern neighbors. In practice, this
amounted to acceptance of the line of the Rivers Oder and Neiße (the so-
called Oder–Neiße line), which had emerged as a de facto border at the end
of World War II and represented a substantial transfer to Poland of land that
had once been German. The FRG reinforced these commitments in a parallel
agreement with Poland (Treaty of Warsaw, December 1970), although a key
undertaking—the formal recognition of the Polish–German border—was not
binding on a future reunited Germany (the issue was not resolved until 1990).
The treaties came into force after the Bundestag ratified the Four Power
Agreement on Berlin, concluded among the wartime allies (the U.S., USSR,
Great Britain, and France) in September 1971. This complex accord settled
the precarious status of West Berlin, which, although not a constituent part of
the FRG, was now guaranteed its overland links—the strictly guarded transit
routes across GDR territory—with the Federal Republic. While the Western
powers stressed West Berlin's ties with West Germany, all four signatories
specifically granted the FRG the right to represent West Berlin and its citizens abroad and to extend international agreements to its territory. The USSR
promised humanitarian improvements for West Berliners, in particular the
opportunity to visit relatives in the eastern part of the city. Although West
Germans greeted the Four Power Agreement on Berlin with enthusiasm, it
had little to say about East Berlin, which had in effect been incorporated into
the GDR, and it did not resolve fundamental differences between the FRG
and the GDR over the legal status of the city as a whole. Nevertheless, it
removed the threat of military or similar action against West Berlin, improved some conditions for its citizens, and eliminated a major source of
international tension.

Specific negotiations between the FRG and the GDR had been conducted
since the early 1970s between Egon Bahr (for the FRG) and Michael Kohl
(GDR). Following an agreement on travel (the Verkehrsvertrag of May 1972,
the first state treaty between East and West Germany), the leaders of both
states concluded the fourth major treaty, the Basic Treaty on Relations between the FRG and the GDR (Grundlagenvertrag), the following December.
Amid fierce debates and accusations by conservative politicians that the
agreement had sold the goal of German reunification down the river, the
general election victory for the SPD in November 1972 was seen as a public
endorsement of Brandt's Ostpolitik, and the Bundestag ratified the treaty in
May 1973. An attempt by Bavarian conservatives to have the Basic Treaty
thrown out as unconstitutional was rejected by the Federal Constitutional
Court (FCC), which in July 1973 ruled that the treaty did not contravene the
BL's commitment to reunification or undermine the FRG's legal claim to
represent the whole of Germany. As its full title implied, the Basic Treaty

provided a constructive foundation for inter-German relations; these would be based on equality, nonaggression, and mutual respect for territorial boundaries and would lead to links in areas such as the economy, technology, travel, and humanitarian concerns, as normally cultivated between sovereign states. The FRG stopped short of full diplomatic recognition of the GDR and, in a separate letter, reaffirmed its commitment to reunification and free elections for the whole of Germany. To East Germany's annoyance, the FRG also continued to claim that the GDR was not a foreign state and that there was no such thing as GDR nationality: in terms of international law, the FRG saw itself as the sole successor state to Germany as it existed at the end of World War II.

As an outcome of the Basic Treaty, East and West Germany exchanged "permanent representatives" instead of full ambassadors, although the distinction meant little in practice. A major advantage for the GDR was that it gained favorable terms for intra-German trade and, in certain areas, backdoor membership in the European Community (EC). While the treaty normalized relations between the two Germanies in many respects, the West German objective of improving conditions for ordinary East Germans would always remain subject to the whim of the GDR regime, which, for example, linked concessions on human rights to transfers of hard currency (such as payments in return for freeing jailed dissidents). Nevertheless, Ostpolitik opened the door to a new chapter in intra-German relations, enabled the FRG and GDR to join the United Nations (September 1973), and ensured their participation in the Conference on Security and Cooperation in Europe (CSCE, 1973–1975), which the USSR saw as a means to gain Western endorsement of its domination of Eastern Europe. In the long run, even conservative opponents of Ostpolitik came to recognize that it furthered West German interests by exposing the GDR's economic dependency on the FRG and highlighting human rights concerns, and successive CDU/CSU–led governments after 1982 maintained the policy, even during periods of East–West tension.

The Social/Liberal Coalition under Helmut Schmidt: 1974–1982

The Social Democrat Chancellor Helmut Schmidt took over during Germany's severest economic downturn since World War II, triggered by a dramatic rise in oil prices associated with the Arab–Israeli conflict in the Middle East. Economic instability came to a head again in 1978–1979, when a global recession, a devalued U.S. dollar, energy shortages, and the collapse of the international monetary system prompted EC states, led by France and Germany, to protect their currencies from fluctuations by linking them within the European Monetary System (EMS). Through positive leadership at a time of American weakness, Schmidt enhanced Germany's standing on the world stage and developed an international reputation as an effective crisis manager. At home, he introduced measures to overcome structural problems in the German economy (e.g., in coal, steel, and shipbuilding) and to stimulate domestic demand. However, his period in office was dogged by persistent high unemployment and budget deficits when Germany was attempting to steer a middle course between the traditional model of the social market economy (consensus between employers and labor) and neoliberal demands to reduce welfare spending, stop subsidizing traditional industries, and deregulate markets. The SPD/FDP coalition eventually collapsed when the junior partner withdrew its support after demanding deeper budget cuts, especially in welfare provision, alongside the introduction of a more business-friendly economic policy in order to stimulate growth (October 1982). At the same time, the country weathered a wave of attacks by the extremist Red Army Faction (RAF), which reached their climax in the autumn of 1977 with a series of murders and kidnappings of leading figures in politics and business and the hijacking of an aircraft intended to force the release of imprisoned terrorists. When it became clear that the government, backed by the opposition CDU/CSU, would not accede to these demands and was prepared to adopt firm internal security measures to combat terrorism, a number of the group's leaders committed suicide in captivity. Violent attacks under the name of the RAF continued into the 1980s and 1990s, until the group announced its dissolution in 1998.

Despite the achievements of Ostpolitik, East–West relations deteriorated markedly during the second half of the 1970s. Negotiations to control and limit nuclear weapons (Strategic Arms Limitation Talks I, 1969–1972) had culminated in the SALT I treaty, which was signed in May 1972 in Moscow. A second round of talks (SALT II) started in 1973 and in 1979 produced an agreement that the U.S. Congress failed to ratify. The main cause of renewed international tension was the stationing by the USSR of medium-range SS20 missiles that directly threatened West Germany and its European allies and were regarded by the West as destabilizing the existing balance of military power. In the teeth of opposition from his own party and from an increasingly vigorous peace movement in Germany, Helmut Schmidt supported NATO's response to the Soviet move. Presented in December 1979, the "dual-track decision" committed NATO to deploying similar weapons (U.S. Pershing II missiles) on German soil if, by the end of 1983, the USSR had not agreed to remove the SS20s. Schmidt's strategy deeply split German society and also the SPD, many of whose senior figures sympathized with the peace lobby. A public petition against deployment, the Krefeld Appeal, collected 2.7 million signatures between November 1980 and April 1982, while mass protests accompanied a NATO summit in Bonn and a state visit by U.S. president Ronald Reagan in West Berlin (June 1982).

Schmidt's isolation within a divided SPD was an important factor in his subsequent parliamentary defeat (see below). The party notably failed to absorb and integrate the ecological- and peace-oriented protest movements of the 1970s and 1980s, and when these emerged as a fourth force in German politics in the form of the Greens (the Green Party constituted itself at the federal level in 1980), it faced a serious electoral challenge.

The Conservative/Liberal Coalition under Helmut Kohl: 1982–1989

From 1976, as leader of the CDU parliamentary group in opposition, Helmut Kohl successfully modernized his party. He overhauled its organization, increased membership, and raised electoral appeal by orienting it toward the political center, overcoming a challenge from the right-wing Franz Josef Strauß (CSU) in the process. In October 1982, Kohl was appointed federal chancellor following a parliamentary vote of no confidence in Helmut Schmidt (SPD), which had been triggered by the defection of FDP members from the ruling coalition. The following December, in a maneuver that disturbed some constitutionalists, Kohl engineered his own defeat in another vote of confidence designed to force the dissolution of the Bundestag and a national election. When this was held in March 1983, the electorate endorsed Kohl's chancellorship, giving the CDU/CSU a resounding 49 percent of the vote, the party's best result since 1957. Once in power, Kohl promised a political sea change, although he initiated no radical shifts in economic and foreign policy. Aided by an upturn in the global economy, which boosted growth and exports, Kohl's government regained control of the domestic budget by reducing the state contribution to welfare, social care, health services, and education (student grants), although the cuts were moderate compared to, say, the neoconservative policies of Margaret Thatcher in Great Britain. At the same time, unemployment in Germany continued to rise, exceeding 2.5 million in February 1983 and averaging 9.3 percent for the year, the highest in the history of the FRG.

In foreign policy, Kohl continued his predecessor's strategy in taking a strong line against the Soviet military threat, in particular by supporting the dual track policy adopted by NATO on medium-range nuclear weapons. Because negotiations since 1981 between the U.S. and the USSR on reducing intermediate-range nuclear forces (INF) had hit a wall, the Bundestag finally agreed in November 1983 to the stationing of Pershing II missiles in West Germany. These began arriving later that month and were fully deployed by the turn of the year. At the same time, public protests and demonstrations outside U.S. bases in Germany continued until the weapons were finally withdrawn in the autumn of 1988, following the successful conclusion of an INF treaty in December 1987. The START I talks, which had begun in June

1982 and were aimed at reducing (not just limiting) nuclear weapons, were concluded in July 1991 when the U.S. and USSR agreed to cut their atomic arsenals by one-third. In January 1993, the superpowers agreed to a second phase of reductions, to be implemented by 2003 (START II), although the treaty was not ratified by the U.S. until 1996 and, following U.S. action against Iraq (1998) and the conflict in Kosovo (1999), was not ratified by the USSR until 2002. As a result of Kohl's steadfastness on nuclear weapons, the U.S. and West Germany developed a close relationship during the 1980s and early 1990s, overcoming the differences in economic policy of the late 1970s. While cementing the transatlantic relationship, Kohl, together with French President François Mitterrand, vigorously promoted the development of the EC/EU. During the 1980s and 1990s, Kohl was a driving force behind milestone treaties (the Single European Act and the Treaty of Maastricht) that deepened European political, economic, and social integration.

Against the background of controversy surrounding NATO's dual-track decision on nuclear weapons, the conservative–liberal coalition continued links with the GDR, aiming to improve conditions for East Germans and win concessions from East Germany on visits, human rights, and border controls, mainly in return for economic aid. Throughout the 1980s, East and West Germany quietly concluded a series of agreements on cross-border travel, family visits, transit traffic, postal services, cultural exchanges, cooperation in scientific projects, and the dismantling of mines and automatic guns along the border (1983–1984). In June 1983, the FRG renewed its interest-free "swing" credit for inter-German trade (increased in 1985 and extended for five years) and granted the GDR large credits (1,000 million DM in June 1983, arranged by the CSU leader Franz Josef Strauß, and 950 million DM in July 1984). The credits, which the USSR condemned as Western ploys designed to undermine the socialist order, were used to alleviate an economic crisis in the GDR that was triggered by poor harvests, a shortage of hard currency combined with a dependence on Western imports, and a credit embargo imposed by Western banks on the debt-ridden states of Eastern Europe. Critics of the credits argued that they in fact stabilized the GDR regime.

A projected visit to the FRG by the East German leader Erich Honecker, planned for 1983 in return for Helmut Schmidt's trip to the GDR in December 1981 (the first by a West German leader since 1970), was called off in April following pressure from a Soviet Union ostensibly irritated over negative comments in Western newspapers on deaths at East–West border crossings. Kohl and Honecker met in Moscow in February 1984, but Soviet disapproval led to Honecker's visit to West Germany being postponed again in September. The following year, the two leaders, meeting on the occasion of the funeral of Soviet leader Konstantin Chernenko in Moscow, issued a joint declaration reaffirming the integrity of existing borders and the commitment to peace. High-level contacts also took place between politicians from East and West Germany, for example, with Federal president Karl Carstens, Franz Josef Strauß (CSU), Egon Bahr (SPD), and Oskar Lafontaine (SPD). From 1985 onward, the SPD developed particularly close links with the Socialist Unity Party of Germany (SED), East Germany's ruling communist party. In October 1986 both parties issued joint proposals for a nuclear-free zone around the inner-German border, and the following August they published a controversial paper arguing for dialogue and open competition between the two social and political systems, which, it was claimed, were both capable of reform. The document was fiercely attacked by conservative and liberal politicians in the FRG as an endorsement of the GDR regime. A third paper followed in April 1988, and in July the SED and SPD formally proposed establishing a "zone of confidence" in central Europe encompassing the FRG, GDR, and Czechoslovakia.

Erich Honecker's visit to the FRG finally took place on 7–11 September 1987, the first time an East German head of state had set foot on West German soil. By this time, however, protest voices, encouraged by the reform policies of a new Soviet leader, Mikhail Gorbachev (elected 1985), were already being raised in the GDR. In June 1987, around 3,000 demonstrators in East Berlin defied a heavy police presence to express their support for Gorbachev and to demand political freedoms and the removal of the Berlin Wall. The same year saw celebrations for the 750th anniversary of Berlin—held separately in both parts of the city. In a public speech in front of the Brandenburg Gate, U.S. president Ronald Reagan's demand—"Mr. Gorbachev, tear down this Wall"— sparked some interest, although the eastern bloc was already facing challenges that were to help pave the way to democratization.

Reunification: 1989–1990

The FRG had always maintained a consistent stance on the goal of eventual reunification, which was embodied in the BL, even if there seemed no practical prospect of achieving it. The East German regime, on the other hand, while initially asserting the existence of two distinctive German states while advocating the eventual re-creation of a single (socialist) German nation, went on to reject reunification altogether in view of what it saw as the irreconcilable identities of a socialist country and a capitalist one. The shift had become clear by at least 1967, when the GDR introduced a law creating a separate East German citizenship. As far as the USSR and the Western powers were concerned, the division of Germany appeared to be a price worth paying for maintaining the geopolitical equilibrium in Europe.

During the 1980s, the dissident movement in the GDR—a disparate collection of individuals and citizens' groups who were partly supported by the Protestant church—grew in strength. There were several reasons for East Germans' growing dissatisfaction. Politically, the ruling SED and its geriatric leadership continued to preach the virtues of egalitarian socialism but had lost touch with the needs and aspirations of ordinary citizens, who resented the privileges of party functionaries. Economically, East Germans, who compared their own circumstances with images of West German prosperity broadcast by cross-border television stations (which they watched in the face of official prohibition), were forced to accept a relatively low standard of living, inadequate housing, poor infrastructure, censorship, and restrictive travel laws. In addition, the state maintained a barrage of propaganda, stifled dissidence, and deployed an extensive secret service apparatus (the Stasi) to secure its hold on power. Dissidence strengthened as the Soviet Union relaxed its grip on the satellite states of Eastern Europe. Throughout the 1980s, record numbers of East German citizens applied for exit visas for the FRG; according to Western sources, applications averaged 22,600 annually between 1980 and 1988 and peaked at almost 41,000 in 1984. During the eventful summer of 1989, many thousands left for Hungary (which dismantled its border with Austria between May and August) in order to reach the West, while others occupied West German embassies in Prague and Warsaw. At home, peaceful protests in Leipzig, Magdeburg, and Dresden in early October were suppressed by the authorities.

Following the first "Monday demonstration" in Leipzig on 4 September 1989, which was repeated in many other towns throughout East Germany, protests reached a climax on 9 October, when 70,000 demonstrated in Leipzig. This time the authorities did not intervene, and further demonstrations followed on 23 October (300,000 in Leipzig) and 4 November (over one million in Berlin, the largest demonstration in German history). Stunned by the scale of public opposition and lacking Soviet backing for a military crackdown, the regime entered into dialogue with the protesters. The move, however, came too late. On 18 October, after another official celebration of the 40th anniversary of the founding of the GDR, Erich Honecker stepped down, and the regime's attempt to ease the pressure on itself by lifting travel restrictions turned, almost accidentally, into the opening of the Berlin Wall (9 November). Finally, on 1 December, the People's Chamber stripped the SED of its constitutionally enshrined monopoly on power. From then on, the SED rapidly disintegrated and lost its influence, although it subsequently reemerged as the Party of Democratic Socialism (PDS). In place of the former SED-led regime, the chamber elected an interim administration under Hans Modrow, which ruled as a "government of national responsibility" from 11 November until the national election of 18 March 1990.

As the dead hand of the SED was lifted in East Germany, various democratic organizations and parties were formed, from dissident groups such as Democratic Awakening to the reconstituted Social Democratic Party in the GDR. The March election was a contest between a CDU-led alliance of conservative and liberal parties (Alliance for Germany) headed by Lothar de Maizière, which campaigned for swift reunification, and the social democrats, who favored a gradualist approach. Although Chancellor Kohl, sensing an opportunity to bring the two Germanies together, had already (on 28 November 1989) proposed a 10-point plan for reunification, his subsequent fast-track path was based on the particular application of article 23 of the BL, which would allow the GDR simply to accede to the constitution's jurisdiction. The SPD, on the other hand, favored the staged process provided by article 146, according to which a new constitution for the whole of Germany would first be drawn up and then approved by its people. The citizens of the GDR, where, despite some dissenting voices, pressure for reunification—and the much-longed-for introduction of the West German DM—began to build up after November 1989, returned the conservative alliance as the single largest group, although just short of an overall majority (192 of 400 seats). The result enabled de Maizière, faced with a collapsing economy and a continuing exodus to the west, to form an all-party grand coalition to press ahead with reunification. In May 1990, the governments of the GDR and FRG agreed on a treaty that (from 1 July) provided for the introduction into East Germany of the West German mark (DM), the social market economy, and the West German system of social security (Treaty on Monetary, Economic, and Social Union). On 31 August, the FRG and GDR concluded the Treaty on Unification, which created the legal basis for political reunification. This treaty extended the existing BL (and West German law in general) to the territory of the GDR, designated Berlin as the capital of the new united Germany (with a decision on the seat of government to be reached later), harmonized financial systems, and settled various issues of property (including that owned by the GDR state and its organs). The formal date for reunification was set for 3 October 1990. While some argued for 9 November as the date, this was rejected on account of its negative historical associations (anti-Jewish pogroms in 1938, Adolf Hitler's march on Berlin in 1923, and possibly also the abdication of the Kaiser amid revolutionary developments in 1918 following defeat in World War I).

Since the Allied powers of World War II retained a residual responsibility for Germany as a whole, their approval for reunification was also required. Consultations among the Allies and with the two Germanies (the so-called 2 + 4 talks) took place between May and September 1990. The principal issues at stake were the status of Berlin, the German–Polish border, and above all, Germany's membership in NATO. Although the USSR had already signaled its acknowledgment of the Germans' right to live in a unified state (January

1990), the breakthrough came in July 1990, when Gorbachev gave the go-ahead for a united Germany to conclude foreign alliances (in other words, to remain in NATO). The Treaty on the Final Settlement of Germany (agreed on 12 September 1990) affirmed Germany's national borders, which included the Oder–Neisse boundary with Poland (since this did not correspond to the 1937 frontier of the former German Reich, the country was technically unified, not reunified). The treaty also removed all residual Allied rights over German territory, including Berlin. Germany committed itself to international peace and membership in NATO; renounced atomic, biological, and chemical weapons; and limited the size of its army to 370,000; Soviet troops would withdraw from German territory over four years in return for financial aid. This historic treaty formally concluded the end of World War II, ended the postwar division of Germany, and paved the way for an eastward enlargement of the EU. Taken as a whole, the three treaties on reunification represented the total demise of the former GDR, whose government, legal system, social institutions, and economy were simply swept aside and replaced by those of West Germany.

The final stages of the political process were completed after 3 October 1990. In July, the People's Chamber had passed a law that dissolved the administrative districts (Bezirke) of the former GDR and replaced them with five new federal states (the "neue Bundesländer") following the West German model. The law came into effect on 14 October, when elections were held in the east to create full regional assemblies. The electorate returned CDU majorities in most of the new Länder, rewarding Chancellor Kohl for his determined pursuit of reunification. Following the first free election for the whole country since 1933, on 2 December, the SPD paid a further heavy price for its halfhearted support for reunification when the CDU/CSU–FDP coalition gained an absolute majority (54.8 percent of votes) in an enlarged parliament of 662 seats (the CDU/CSU won 319 seats and the FDP 79). Reunification was seen as a personal triumph for Kohl, who was dubbed the "unity chancellor." In June 1991, the Bundestag decided by a narrow majority to move parliament and the seat of government to Berlin, leaving some administrative functions in Bonn. The debate in the Bundestag about the move was in fact a discussion of the German status quo: while some argued that the historical promise to move to Berlin as soon as possible must be upheld, others countered that Bonn stood for over 40 years of functioning democracy alongside partners in Europe and beyond. The new home of the Bundestag, the restored Reichstag building, was eventually opened in April 1999. The last Allied forces stationed on German soil (around 400,000 former Soviet and 6,000 Western troops) left between June and September 1994.

The terms *unification* (Vereinigung) and *reunification* (Wiedervereinigung) were both widely used in public discourse relating to the events of 1989–1990, and they continued to be employed almost interchangeably. However, they could imply quite different things—a fact that official circles in Germany tried to circumvent by using another term entirely; the government favored the phrase "reestablishment of German unity" (Wiederherstellung der deutschen Einheit), on the grounds that it made it clear (at least in official eyes) that the unity of 1990 did not amount to a restoration of the historical and political boundaries of the German Reich as they had existed before World War II. Those boundaries would have included the eastern territories of Pomerania, Silesia, and East and West Prussia, which, after 1945, were incorporated into Poland and the Soviet Union. Such a reunification was not on offer in 1989–1990, and to emphasize it would have sent negative signals to Germany's eastern neighbors, rekindling unpleasant historical memories. The national Day of German Unity (Tag der deutschen Einheit), which is celebrated on 3 October, implicitly stresses the sense of being unified rather than the process of (re)unification, with all its historical baggage. In line with a common perception that the outcome of the events of 1990 represented at least a partial restoration of what Germany had been before 1945, this book standardizes by using the term "reunification."

The Postreunification Conservative/Liberal Coalition under Helmut Kohl: 1990–1998

In the run-up to the 1990 election, Chancellor Helmut Kohl had rashly promised "flourishing landscapes" of prosperity to eastern Germany. By 1992, however, it was clear that the costs of reunification had been greatly underestimated. Huge transfers were required to finance the economic transition in the east, renew the infrastructure, support social welfare programs (necessitated by consistently high unemployment, which climbed on average from 10 percent in 1991 to 16 percent in 1994), and raise standards of living to west German levels. Between 1990 and 1997, one trillion DM flowed from west to east within the framework of various funds (including the German Unity Fund and financial equalization). Throughout the 1990s, Germany had to work hard to overcome social tensions and to bridge a gulf between westerners, who had come to regard the eastern states as a financial and economic burden, and easterners, who had grown disillusioned with the absent fruits of reunification. The terms "Ossi" and "Wessi" were long indicative of this "wall in people's minds" (Peter Schneider), with westerners perceived as know-it-alls and easterners as unable to cope with the realities of a market economy. The 1990s saw a rise in neo-Nazi extremism and a wave of violence against foreigners in both west and east Germany. The attacks began with the murder of an Angolan in Eberswalde (Brandenburg,

1990) and reached a peak with the death of 10 immigrants and asylum seekers in an arson attack in Lübeck (1996). Thousands of Germans demonstrated in support of foreigners, and a number of extremist organizations were banned.

In the national election of 1994, the CDU/CSU–FDP coalition was returned with a reduced majority (of 672 seats, 295 went to the CDU/CSU and 47 to the FDP). The CDU/CSU fared well in regional elections, although the success of the PDS added a new dimension to the political landscape in the east. Despite public protests (and memories of the Chernobyl disaster of April 1986, when a Ukrainian nuclear reactor dispersed radioactive material over large parts of northern Europe), the government continued to support the nuclear energy program (subsequent governments modified this policy, and a complete withdrawal from atomic energy was decided on after the Fukushima disaster in 2011). Faced with rising public expenditure, the government attempted, with limited success, to initiate structural reforms in health-care provision, taxation, and the pension system and also pursued a more restrictive policy on asylum seekers. Under Kohl's leadership, Germany began to assume greater responsibilities as a foreign power. The German navy and air force helped monitor UN sanctions in the former Yugoslavia (1992), and in 1993–1994, the government gained approval from the Bundestag and the FCC for the Bundeswehr to take part in peacekeeping missions outside the NATO area.

The national election of September 1998 exposed the scale of popular disenchantment with a long-serving chancellor who had presided over continuing high unemployment. There was a widespread perception that Germany was stagnating through the inability of its political structures to pass badly needed reforms in its economy and welfare systems. For the first time in the history of the FRG, a ruling government was voted out of power. The CDU/CSU, with 35.2 percent of the votes (245 seats in a Bundestag of 669), suffered its worst electoral result since 1953 and fared especially badly in the east. Its coalition partner, the FDP, gained 43 seats (a loss of 4 compared with 1994). Led by chancellor-candidate Gerhard Schröder, the SPD was the overall winner (with 298 seats), while the Green Party (47 seats), as in 1994, emerged as the third-strongest party. The PDS consolidated its position in the eastern states (36 seats, a gain of 6 from 1994).

The Red/Green Coalition under Gerhard Schröder: 1998–2005

The SPD/Green Party coalition was elected on a broad platform of pledges, including restructuring Germany's complex and crippling taxation system, controlling the burgeoning health-care budget, and phasing out nuclear energy. In order to compensate for its planned tax cuts, the coalition proposed reducing additional labor costs and promoting energy saving through an "ecological tax" to be levied on electricity and fossil fuels. The measures were watered down following fierce protests from energy interests and industry, although levies on fuel, heating oils, gas, and electricity (including concessions for industrial consumers) were introduced in April 1999, with annual increases planned through 2003. Although cuts in business taxes for joint-stock companies were announced in 1999, there was little change in the overall tax burden for small businesses and employees, while consumer taxes actually rose.

One of the main targets for the incoming coalition was to reduce unemployment. However, an economic global downturn meant that the jobless total for 2002 remained at a similar level to the election year, when it approached four million. The Alliance for Work, which was originally set up in 1995 following a proposal by the trade union leader Klaus Zwickel and was resurrected by Schröder in 1998, had little practical effect. The Job-Aktiv-Gesetz, a package of measures scheduled to come into force in January 2002 and designed to head off long-term unemployment by broadening opportunities and creating more flexibility in the labor market, was expected to founder over the basic shortage of jobs. The eastern states, where the rate of bankruptcies rose and the number of businesses remained well below the national average, continued their passage through the economic doldrums and registered unemployment rates of almost 18 percent. The government and the Länder agreed to renew the solidarity pact (Solidarpakt II), guaranteeing the east large subsidies between 2005 and 2019.

Social change and liberalization was high on the coalition's agenda in 1998, with the Greens often pushing harder than the SPD. The government made some progress in introducing a new citizenship law, although the conservative opposition successfully resisted the proposal for a dual passport. In July 2002, the FCC rejected objections from the CDU/CSU to a new law legitimizing homosexual marriages and giving them similar legal rights as heterosexual relationships. Although the Green Party pledged before the election to reduce the role of the security services in national life, the terrorist attacks of 11 September 2001 in the U.S. prompted the German government, with the help of Green interior minister Otto Schily, to introduce new laws (later circumscribed by the courts) giving the state greater powers of surveillance, in particular to monitor citizens' bank accounts and telephone calls. Moves were also made to introduce a controversial profiling procedure (Rasterfahndung) designed to identify potential terrorists by collecting and analyzing large amounts of data on citizens.

Following the closely fought national election campaign of September 2002, the SPD/Green coalition was returned to power. The composition of the Bundestag (603 seats) was as follows: SPD, 251 seats (38.5 percent of the votes); CDU/CSU, 248 seats (38.5 percent); Green Party, 55 seats (8.6 percent); FDP 47 seats (7.4 percent), and PDS 2 seats (4 percent). Chancellor

Schröder, who had campaigned on a platform of labor market reform and increased spending on education and child care, struggled to maintain his reformist agenda as the government was forced almost immediately to take emergency measures to control a huge budget deficit exacerbated by an economic downturn, possibly the worst in the country's history. The key point of the government's strategy to overhaul economic, health-care, and welfare structures was embodied in Schröder's Agenda 2010 program, although the chancellor had a tough battle persuading party and parliament to adopt it. In 2005, when unemployment reached a record 5.2 million, Schröder unveiled a further package of emergency measures to stimulate the economy. Following a series of regional election defeats and tensions with the coalition partner, an increasingly unpopular Schröder surprised the nation in July 2005 by engineering a parliamentary vote of no confidence in his chancellorship, thus forcing a national election, which took place in September. In a narrow result, the SPD failed to gain a clear mandate, and Schröder resigned.

Within the CDU, its leader Angela Merkel managed to retain her stature within the party after the 2002 election, her position continued to be challenged by Edmund Stoiber (CSU), who consolidated his Bavarian power base. To some extent, the two figures personified the two sides of the internal debate that the CDU began after 2002: whether to adopt a more liberal stance on many issues (Merkel) or to swing further to the right (Stoiber). The FDP's disappointing election result was compounded by a funding scandal and anti-Israeli activities involving its former deputy leader, Jürgen Möllemann. Observers questioned whether the party leader, Guido Westerwelle, had the authority to reestablish the FDP as a credible force for liberal politics in Germany. Neither were prospects for the PDS favorable. The party's share of the votes fell from 36 seats in 1998 to just 2 in 2002, and it elected a hard-line left-wing leadership.

The Conservative/Social Democrat Grand Coalition under Angela Merkel: 2005–2009

The inconclusive national election of September 2005 reflected the nation's uncertainty over the pace and scale of social and economic reform. Although Gerhard Schröder (SPD) failed to win a strong mandate for his Agenda 2010 program, Angela Merkel (CDU) lost electoral support for even more radical change. In a virtually hung parliament, in which the CDU/CSU gained fractionally more seats (226, 35.2 percent of votes) than the SPD (222, 34.2 percent), Merkel was forced into a grand coalition with the SPD, with herself as chancellor. Responding to demands for budgetary control, the government raised both the turnover tax (from 16 to 19 percent) and tax on annual incomes over 250,000 euros (from 42 to 45 percent). Moving away from conservative notions of the family and addressing concerns over the declining birthrate, the coalition approved financial incentives for unmarried parents and paid parental leave, and created a legal right to publicly funded day-care facilities. Immigration and the integration of foreigners were promoted, and Merkel moved ecological policies forward, persuading the U.S. to endorse a framework for combating climate change at the 2007 G8 summit and leading the EU to agree on concrete measures. At home the health-care system underwent modernization, and some progress was made on federalism reform. In foreign policy Merkel indicated that, in contrast to her predecessor, she would distance herself from Moscow (Gerhard Schröder was a personal friend of Russian leader Vladimir Putin) and develop a new relationship with the U.S., which had deteriorated over the war against Iraq. She also suggested that the close relationship with France would give way to a new balancing and mediating role in Europe, with the emphasis on developing relations with the new EU states, especially Poland. As Germany took over the EU presidency in 2007, Merkel took up the issue of the EU constitution, which had been on ice since 2005 and was finally resolved through the Treaty of Lisbon (agreed in 2007). Challenged by the global financial crisis of 2008–2009, the coalition successfully negotiated recovery from Germany's worst ever economic recession, rescued a number of banks, and reduced unemployment levels through state-subsidized work programs.

The Conservative/Liberal Coalition under Angela Merkel: 2009–2013

In a historically low voter turnout, both main parties lost votes in the 2009 national election, although the SPD (with 23 percent of votes) was hardest hit, and the CDU/CSU (33.8 percent) was able to form a coalition with the FDP, which achieved its best ever result (14.6 percent). However, the coalition was beset by fierce policy conflicts, especially over health care and taxation, and failed to meet several of its election commitments. Taxation reform was again shelved, and the supervision of banks, originally planned to reside with the German Federal Bank, was eventually handed over to the European Central Bank. An initial decision to extend the life of nuclear power stations (2010) was reversed after the Fukushima disaster (2011), although the government and federal states failed to agree on changes to the rising costs of promoting renewable energy through electricity tariffs. An election promise to finally bring pension levels in eastern Germany up to those in the west could not be kept, and plans to introduce a special pension to combat poverty in retirement were postponed. The Bundesrat also refused to approve a bill on preventive health measures, which would have increased costs to health insurance funds (2013). In foreign policy, Germany demonstrated its reluctance to join unconditionally its allies' military adventures by abstaining on the UN vote to intervene in Libya (2011). It also began relaxing its visa entry policy for foreign workers, especially from non-EU trading partners. At the European level, Germany assumed a leading role during the eurozone crisis, cofinancing rescue packages while acting as a policy driver in negotiating long-term strategies for fiscal discipline with the EU. The crisis led to particular tensions with Greece, which at times demanded reparations for the German occupation during World War II.

The Conservative/Social Democrat Grand Coalition under Angela Merkel: 2013–

With 41.5 percent of votes in the 2013 national election, the CDU/CSU emerged as the strongest party, increasing its lead over the SPD (25.7 percent), which only marginally improved its performance over 2009. The Greens (8.4 percent) and the Left Party (8.6 percent) also lost ground, and the FDP (4.8 percent) failed to clear the entry hurdle, leaving Merkel free to continue in coalition this time with the social democrats and a stronger majority. A largely unadventurous coalition agreement made concessions to the SPD, largely over welfare issues, including the introduction of a minimum wage (from 2017), rent controls in major cities, dual citizenship for those born in Germany, the option of early retirement for employees with 45 years of insurance contributions, and increases in the minimum pension for low earners. Other measures were higher pensions for older mothers with children born before 1992 (a long-standing demand of the CSU); extra finance for higher education, research and development, and transport infrastructure; tighter regulations on labor leasing; and extensions to the toll system on major roads. The program's welfare provisions suggested a certain pulling back on Gerhard Schröder's Agenda 2010 reforms and contrasted with the level of cuts Germany was demanding of its partners hit by the eurozone crisis.

Although Germany successfully hosted the annual G7 summit in Elmau (Bavaria, 7–8 June 2015), the results were largely symbolic. The dispute over the surveillance activities of the U.S. National Security Agency was simply ignored. The determination to conclude free trade deals between the EU and Canada (CETA) and the U.S. (TTIP), however, was reinforced by a commitment to reach an agreement by the end of the year. On the other hand, Greece's financial problems remained unresolved, with the EU, and Germany in particular, resisting the notion of any write-down of its debt, although some compromise on this appeared likely following pressure from the International Monetary Fund during negotiations for a third bailout in 2015. The distance between the West and Russia (which was absent at the summit) over the conflict in Ukraine if anything increased as Europe and the U.S. affirmed their united stance and threatened deeper sanctions unless Russia fully implemented the peace accord. Pressure from Merkel, a strong proponent of measures to combat climate change, did achieve a consensus on limiting global warming to 2 degrees (Celsius) and on phasing out fossil fuel consumption altogether by 2050. The agreement was praised by environmental groups and raised hopes that the UN climate conference in December in Paris might move to legally binding commitments. A sharp increase in the number of asylum seekers, especially from the Balkan states and countries affected by conflict in the Middle East, became a serious issue for the EU and Germany in particular (as a favored destination) in 2015 and 2016.

A referendum vote in Great Britain in June 2016 to leave the EU not only raised the prospect of complex negotiations over the terms of future economic and political relationships between Britain and EU countries, but also threatened to challenge the future cohesion of the EU itself.

ABITUR. Also called the Allgemeine Hochschulreife, the Abitur is the highest level school graduation certificate in Germany, entitling the school leaver to enter university or higher **education**. Studied over three years (a preparation year in school year 10 or 11, followed by two intensive "qualification years"), it is traditionally, but not exclusively, offered by the Gymnasium, the secondary level school that is attended by the academically most able pupils in the German education system. The syllabus for the Abitur was radically reformed in 1972 with the launch of a more flexible, modular course structure, known as the "reformierte Oberstufe" (or Kollegstufe in **Bavaria**), which aimed to widen choices for pupils: the number of compulsory subjects was reduced from 15 to around 10; new subjects, alongside modernized curricula, appeared and were grouped into basic courses (Grundkurse, two to three hours per week) and intensive courses (Leistungskurse, four or more hours); and a revised, more differentiated assessment regime incorporating coursework was introduced. While smaller teaching groups adapted to individual needs made the system more expensive, there eventually emerged a common model of four or five subjects (at least three assessed by written examination and one orally), comprising two Leistungskurse and a core of German, mathematics, and a foreign language. By 2000, all the **federal states** except **Rhineland-Palatinate** had adopted a central examination (Zentralabitur), which means that a single authority, usually the regional ministry of culture, sets the written examination papers for most subjects. The final grade, which is made up of weighted assessments from the qualification years and the examination, is on a scale from 1.0 (the highest score) to 4.0 (pass); finer differentiations are possible (e.g., 1.1 descending to 1.9).

After 1972, the system was repeatedly modified, although the trend was toward reducing the wide breadth of student choice and retaining traditional core subjects. Especially after reunification, almost all Gymnasien shortened the total school study period from nine to eight years (G9 to G8), although some have since reverted to the older model. After 2006, when the regional education ministers recommended a national system for calculating Abitur grades but required the **Länder** to implement it, each state produced its own scheme, resulting in significant discrepancies across the country. The established model of Grund-/Leistungskurse gave way to a range of variations, with some states adopting a rigid system of four main subjects, while others introduced main and subsidiary subjects. As a result, the composition and balance of subjects now vary widely across states, as do the assessment weightings (e.g., for half-yearly reports) and even the designation of the subject level (profile, core, extended, advanced, extended, intensive, seminar, elective, and so on). It is also generally acknowledged that pupils of similar ability get different grades in different states. At the same time, since 1950, when just 10 percent of pupils achieved the Abitur, access has been progressively widened to a larger proportion of the school population, with around 20 percent qualifying in 1970; the current figure is 60 percent in the higher level school types. To counter criticisms that the Abitur is too academically oriented, business leaders and educationalists have also called for the introduction of the "vocational Abitur" (Berufsabitur), designed to open up higher education to, for example, skilled workers or apprentices.

ABORTION. Since 1871, abortion in Germany has been a punishable offense (according to § 218 of the German penal code), although the law was modified in 1927 to permit termination for medical reasons. The situation did not fundamentally change until 1974, when the **Social Democratic Party of Germany/Free Democratic Party (SPD/FDP)** coalition (1969–1982), by a narrow **Bundestag** majority, legalized abortions during the "termination period" (the first 12 weeks of pregnancy). Following a successful complaint by the opposition **Christian Democratic Union/Christian Social Union (CDU/CSU)** to the **Federal Constitutional Court (FCC)** on the grounds that abortion violated the right to life enshrined in the first two articles of the constitution (**Basic Law, BL**; the FCC's judgment BVerfG 39,1 of 25.02.1975: Schwangerschaftsabbruch I is relevant here), the law was modified to permit abortions if certain "indications" were met; these were medical (serious danger to the mother's health and with no time limit), embryopathic (up to 22 weeks), criminal or ethical (e.g., pregnancy as a result of rape, up to 12 weeks), or social (exceptional domestic or economic conditions, up to 12 weeks). Radicals in the feminist movement, however, continued to argue for the complete abolition of § 218, and the debate remained strongly polarized, with the Roman Catholic Church leading the anti-abortion lobby.

The issue came to a head again after reunification (3 October 1990), when the practice of the former **German Democratic Republic (GDR)** was continued as an interim measure in the new **eastern federal states** only. In East Germany, where mothers had in 1972 acquired the unconditional right to terminate within the first 12 weeks of pregnancy, abortions became so commonplace that one in three pregnancies was terminated during the 1980s. At the same time, the Treaty on Unification required new legislation for the whole of Germany to be in place by 1992, when a cross-party majority of the Bundestag agreed on a revised law for the whole of Germany that fully legalized abortion during the 12-week termination period, subject to the mother receiving counseling from an officially recognized body. The FCC, however, ruled that abortions within 12 weeks, while still in principle illegal (rechtswidrig), should not be punishable (straffrei), although mandatory counseling should be made substantially more rigorous (involving making the mother aware that the developing unborn child is an independent human life); while health-care funds would not be not required to pay for terminations, doctors and hospitals were not obliged to perform them (BVerfG 88,203, Schwangerschaftsabbruch II of 28.5.1993). The judgment was widely seen as opening up fresh controversies and as disadvantaging **women**, especially in the east, who lacked the resources to fund abortions privately. In 1995, the Bundestag approved a further revision to § 218, later modified in 2010, which, with no time limit and no requirement for mandatory counseling, removed the threat of punishment from a mother undergoing an abortion for medical or social reasons, if this was carried out by a different doctor from the one who previously advised her (a 12-week limit still applied, however, to abortions for criminological reasons); abortions on demand, although permitted within 12 weeks, remained subject to counseling and did not attract social funding. The Catholic Church in particular criticized the revision as ambiguous, but despite differences with the state over objectives, it participated in the preabortion counseling program until 1998–1999, when Pope John Paul II forced the German bishops, led by Cardinal **Karl Lehmann**, to withdraw (a specially founded lay organization, Donum Vitae, stepped in to take over the role).

The 1995 law governs terminations to this day, although details have been revised, for instance, to clarify state funding for abortions and the position of counseling. To sum up: German law, perhaps unusually by international standards, regards all abortions as illegal but as permitted (i.e., not judicially pursued) in certain circumstances. After increasing from 130,899 in 1996 to a peak of 134,964 in 2002 (possibly reflecting changes in statistics gathering), the annual total of recorded abortions fell steadily, to 102,800 in 2013; of these, 4 percent were for medical or criminological reasons.

ABS, HERMANN JOSEF (1901–1994). Banker. Born in Bonn, Hermann Abs trained at the Louis David private bank in Bonn, where he also briefly studied law and economics until 1921. During the 1920s, he worked for various **banks** in Germany, Amsterdam, Great Britain, the United States, and Latin America and became a fluent linguist before returning to Germany (1935). In 1937/1938, Abs joined the executive board of the **Deutsche Bank**, retaining the position until 1945. He was a member of the advisory council

(Beirat) of the Deutsche Reichsbank and from 1944 was involved in a working group that advised on external economic affairs and armaments. Although he never joined the National Socialist Party, Abs was suspended from all posts in 1945 and briefly interned by the Allies, before acting as a financial adviser to the British occupation authorities. From January 1949, he chaired the Frankfurt-based banking organization charged with financial reconstruction (Kreditanstalt für Wiederaufbau, KfW) in preparation for the establishment of the Federal German Republic (FRG) in October 1949. In 1952, he joined the executive board of the Deutsche Bank and was appointed chairman of the board of the Süddeutsche Bank AG in Munich. From 1957 until 1967, Abs was board spokesman for the reconstituted Deutsche Bank AG (Frankfurt) before taking over the chairmanship of the supervisory board. After 1949, Abs acted as a financial adviser to the German government under Chancellor **Konrad Adenauer** and played a key role in negotiations with the U.S. over frozen prewar financial credits. He headed the German delegation on the London Debt Conference (1952) and in 1955 negotiated terms for the American release of German property confiscated during World War II. A member of over 20 executive boards at the height of his career during the 1960s, Abs came to be regarded as Germany's most successful and influential banker. He never joined a political party and maintained a low public profile.

ACADEMY OF ARTS (AKADEMIE DER KÜNSTE, AdK). This is an independent public body that promotes the arts in Germany, provides advice and support in cultural matters for both the **Bund** and the **federal states**, fosters interdisciplinary dialogue, and acts as a representative of German arts and culture abroad. Found in 1696 in **Berlin** by electoral prince Friedrich III of **Brandenburg**, the academy was the first of its kind in the German-speaking countries and the third in Europe. In 1918, it was renamed the Prussian Academy of Arts (Preußische Akademie der Künste).

After World War II, the AdK, like many other institutions, reflected the reality of German division: the Academy of Arts (East) was established in 1950, its Western counterpart in 1954. Both merged in 1993, after a difficult debate that was characterized by the former ideological divide and the challenges of reunification. Today there are about 400 members; new members are elected in a secret ballot. The founding members in the **German Democratic Republic (GDR)** included the poet Johannes R. Becher, the playwright Bertolt Brecht, the composer Hanns Eisler, and the authors Anna Seghers and Arnold Zweig. Initially driven by the desire to further "humanism" and the "progress of society," the ruling **Socialist Unity Party of Germany (SED)** increased its influence on the institution over the years. During the Cold War years, the AdK (West) was based at Hanseatenweg, Berlin, in a building designed by the architect Werner Düttmann. The academy now has a new home on the Pariser Platz in Berlin, in the immediate vicinity of the Brandenburg Gate. The building's architects were Günter Behnisch, Manfred Sabatke, and Werner Durth. The academy curates exhibitions and organizes debates, offers a wide range of publications, and houses a renowned and substantial archive.

Presidents of the Akademie der Künste (East Germany) were Heinrich Mann (1950), Arnold Zweig (1950–1953), Johannes R. Becher (1953–1956), Otto Nagel (1956–1962), Willi Bredel (1962–1964), Konrad Wolf (1965–1982), Manfred Wekwerth (1982–1990), and Heiner Müller (1990). Presidents of the Akademie der Künste (West Germany) were Hans Scharoun (1955–1968), Boris Blacher (1968–1977), Werner Düttmann (1977–1983), **Günter Grass** (1983–86), Giselher Klebe (1986–1989), and Walter Jens (1989). Presidents of the reunified academy have been Gyögy Konrád (1997–2003), Adolf Muschg (2003–2006), Klaus Staeck (2006–2015), and Jeanine Meerapfel (2015–), a German Argentinian filmmaker who became the first female president in the academy's 300-year history. International members include the artist Ai Weiwei, the architect Lord Norman Foster, and the writer Cees Nooteboom. The academy is responsible for a number of prestigious awards, including the Heinrich Mann Prize and Alfred Döblin Prize.

In all, Germany now has seven large academies of science and five academies with a focus on arts and **literature**; the largest is the Berlin Academy of Arts, with specialist sections such as art and **architecture**, music, literature, **cinema**, and visual culture. The Bayerische Akademie der Schönen Künste was founded in Munich in 1948, the Deutsche Akademie für Sprache und Dichtung in Darmstadt in 1949, and the Sächsische Akademie der Künste (Dresden) in 1996. The smallest academy is the Akademie der Wissenschaften und der Literatur (Mainz), founded in 1949.

ACADEMY OF SCIENCES (AKADEMIE DER WISSENSCHAFTEN). Founded in 1700 by Gottfried Wilhelm Leibnitz as the Sozietät der Wissenschaften (and later working under various titles), the Prussian Academy of Sciences (Preußische Akademie der Wissenschaften) was fundamentally reorganized by Alexander von Humboldt between 1806 and 1812. In 1838, it was formally charged with the promotion of the sciences, although there was no commitment to **education** or teaching. The academy was closely involved in most aspects of scientific research in Germany (including the natural sciences, medicine, and **literature**) and worked with regional, national, and international organizations. In 1899, it took a leading role in the creation of the International Association of Academies and from 1901 was involved in awarding the Nobel Prizes for physics, chemistry, medicine, and literature. It was on the academy's initiative that the Kaiser-Wilhelm-Gesellschaft, which was to become the Max Planck Society, was set up in 1911. The academy was subjected to state influence during the Third Reich (1933–1945), and **Jewish** members were expelled. In 1946, the Soviet occupation authorities reconstituted the former Prussian Academy of Sciences as the German Academy of Sciences in **Berlin** (Deutsche Akademie der Wissenschaften zu Berlin). From 1954, the East German organization came under direct state control. After reunification (1990) it was dissolved, although its constituent institutes and activities were "evaluated." In 1992, it was reestablished (by means of an interstate treaty between the **federal states** of Berlin and **Brandenburg**), with 48 founding members, as the Berlin-Brandenburg Academy (Berlin-Brandenburgische Akademie). Its members are organized into five "classes" (arts, social sciences, mathematics/natural sciences, biosciences/ medicine, technology) and follow the model of similar academies in London and Paris in promoting the sciences and providing a forum for the discussion of scientific issues. The academy maintains a large archive of material and library resources (www.bbaw.de).

Today Germany has eight larger academies of sciences: in **Hamburg**, Göttingen, the Academy of Sciences and Literature in Mainz, in Munich, the Berlin-Brandenburgische Akademie der Wissenschaften in Berlin, in Heidelberg, the Nordrhein-westfälische Akademie der Wissenschaften in Düsseldorf, and the Sächsische Akademie der Wissenschaften in Leipzig. In 2008, after prolonged debated, the Leopoldina was declared the main base of the national Academy of Sciences in Germany.

ACKERMANN, JOSEF (1948–). Banker. Josef Ackermann was born in Mels (Switzerland) and studied economics and social sciences at the University of St. Gallen, specializing in banking. After working as a research assistant at the Institut für Nationalökonomie, the university's institute for national economics, he earned a doctorate in economics (1977) and lectured in financial policy and economic theory (until 1989). From 1977, he worked in senior capacities for the Swiss bank SKA (Schweizerische Kreditanstalt, Credit Suisse from 1996) in Lausanne, New York, and London before becoming its president (1993); he left in 1996 over differences of opinion with its management board. After joining the executive board of the **Deutsche Bank AG** in Frankfurt/Main (1996), he directed the bank's takeover of the U.S. investment bank Bankers Trust (1998), but vetoed a planned merger with the **Dresdner Bank**. In May 2002, he was appointed the bank's spokesman and chief executive, a move that represented an unusual concentration of power in one person. After introducing a transatlantic business culture based on rewarding performance into the largely conservative world of German banking, he was widely credited with turning the Deutsche Bank into Germany's first global bank. He was also a member of the supervisory board of Mannesmann AG (1999–2000) and, in February 2004, along with other former senior Mannesmann executives, appeared before a court in

Düsseldorf to face charges of breaching shareholders' trust after approving large bonuses to directors when the concern was taken over by the British mobile phone company Vodafone (2000). Although the court acquitted the defendants (July 2004), the case fueled a national debate about business competitiveness, and a federal court ruled in December 2005 that he should be retried. The case was dropped in November 2006 when Ackermann paid a fine of 3.2 million euros. While Ackermann claimed that Germany should be moving toward an Anglo-American model of incentive-driven performance, opponents argued that such huge payments endangered the traditional "Rhineland model" of corporate consensus among management, **banks**, **trade unions**, and the state. He was also criticized by Federal Chancellor **Gerhard Schröder** in 2005 when Deutsche Bank announced record profits alongside a program of job cuts. In 2004, Ackermann attracted further criticism for receiving the highest executive salary in Germany: 11 million euros. After leaving Deutsche Bank in 2012, he became chief executive of Zurich Insurance Group, but resigned the following year after the company's head of finance committed suicide. In 2013, he also left the supervisory board of Siemens following a battle with the board's chairman, Gerhard Cromme.

ADENAUER, KONRAD (1876–1967). Christian Democratic Union (CDU) politician and **federal chancellor**, 1949–1963. Born in Cologne, Konrad Adenauer studied law and economics in Freiburg, Munich, and Bonn (1894–1901) before working as a lawyer and auxiliary judge in Cologne (1901–1906). A member of the conservative Catholic Deutsche Zentrumspartei (from 1905), he was senior mayor of Cologne from 1917 until 1933. During the Weimar Republic, he served in the first (from 1918) and second (1921–1933) chambers of the Prussian parliament. During the French occupation of the Rhineland (1919–1930), he suggested negotiating with France over a possible secession from Germany. Removed from office by the National Socialists in 1933, Adenauer lived in seclusion in Rhöndorf during World War II, but was reinstated as mayor of Cologne by the U.S. military authorities in May 1945, only to be dismissed again in October by the British ("for incompetence"). Elected chairman of the newly founded CDU in 1946, he served as a deputy in the **Bundestag** from 1949 until 1966 and was chancellor of the Federal Republic of Germany (FRG) in five successive coalition cabinets (with the **Free Democratic Party, FDP**), until his resignation in 1963. As chancellor and concurrently foreign minister (1951–1955), Adenauer rejected Russian overtures apparently directed at establishing a neutral, reunited Germany, championing instead the FRG's integration into Western political, economic, and military institutions, in particular the precursors to the **European Union (EU)** and **NATO** (which West Germany joined in 1955). From an early stage, he considered reconciliation with France an overriding priority. In maintaining firm control over his cabinet, binding members of his party and the Bundestag to government policy, carefully managing the dissemination of information, and insisting on the prerogatives of the "chancellor principle" as laid down in the **Basic Law (BL)**, Adenauer established a stable and efficient parliamentary system, in stark contrast to the later years of the Weimar Republic. He also fully exploited his position as intermediary with the Allied powers and as the voice of German interests to further his foreign policy aims within the context of his country's limited sovereignty. Under Adenauer, West Germany experienced an economic boom, largely due to the social market policies of his economics minister, **Ludwig Erhard**, who succeeded him as chancellor in 1963. In his final years of office, Adenauer lost the confidence of his party, parliament, and the country. Contributory factors were his refusal to countenance a successor (in particular Erhard), inept attempts to establish a second television station under state control (1960), criticism of West Berlin's mayor **Willy Brandt** and delay in visiting the city during the crisis of 1961, and involvement in the *Spiegel* affair (1962).

AGENDA 2010. In March 2003, Federal Chancellor **Gerhard Schröder** announced a wide-ranging program of long-term reforms in labor policy and in Germany's systems of **health care**, social welfare, and **pensions**, to which he gave the title Agenda 2010. The object of the reforms, some of which were already under way, was to reduce health-care and welfare costs by increasing citizens' contributions, stimulate economic growth, free up the labor market, improve opportunities for training, and simplify government.

In health care, the current range of services provided by the public health insurance funds (Krankenkassen) faced cutbacks in order to reduce average contributions to below 13 percent (in practice, they rose to over 15 percent by 2013). The automatic entitlement to sick pay (Krankengeld) would be removed unless privately funded (the government quickly retreated on this measure; it is currently financed for six weeks by the employer and thereafter by the health insurance fund), and the maternity benefit would be paid for from income tax (available for employed mothers only; it is now paid for by joint contributions from the employer and insurance fund). Patients would pay a consultation fee (implemented in 2004 but withdrawn in 2013) and be required to fund more services (such as spectacle frames and funerals) themselves, with exceptions made for children, the chronically ill, and the socially disadvantaged. The insurance funds' monopoly of contracts with doctors would be removed, and new technology, including an electronic identity card for patients, would be introduced to streamline record keeping.

Reforms in the labor market were linked to the recommendations of the **Hartz Commission**. Unemployment benefits would be limited to a maximum of 12 months, extended to 18 months for older workers (aged over 55). Unemployment and social welfare benefits, hitherto separate, would be combined and capped, although those with children would receive more, and there would be an incentive to take work without a reduction in state benefits. Small businesses with up to five employees would be allowed to employ additional temporary staff, with reduced rights to contest dismissal and special provisions made for job losses incurred for business reasons. Although the principle of sectoral collective bargaining remained unchallenged, local wage agreements were permitted if the parties concerned agreed. Companies engaging apprentices could qualify for financial credit (of up to 100,000 euros for each trainee), and regulations would be relaxed in order to make it easier for individuals to set up their own businesses. New rules on low-paid, part-time jobs below the income tax threshold (so-called mini-jobs, paying up to 400 euros a month) had already been introduced in April 2003. The rules were intended to remove low-paid employees from the black market and streamline employers' contributions to the national insurance fund. Moves were also made to make the pension system more affordable. Apart from bringing forward the third stage of the **taxation** reform (from 2005 to 2004), Agenda 2010 further aimed to direct more tax revenue to local councils and finance the expansion of all-day schools.

Although it was widely accepted that Germany urgently needed to overhaul its generous social budget and inflexible labor market, Agenda 2010 attracted criticism from **trade unions** and left-wingers anxious about cuts in employment protection and welfare. After Schröder threatened to resign unless his party and the coalition adopted the main parts of the program (October 2003), the **Bundestag** duly approved it, although opposition in the **Bundesrat** resulted in the proposed legislation going to mediation between the two assemblies. Schröder finally won cross-party support in December 2003, although only after making concessions. He reduced the volume of tax cuts planned for 2004 (now to be spread over two years, with immediate requirements to be financed through one-off privatizations and new debt), tightened conditions on job seekers (who would have to accept lower pay than local rates), and removed the protection against dismissal (for new employees in companies with fewer than 10 workers, instead of 5 as before).

The conservative opposition parties welcomed the privatization measures of Agenda 2010, but criticized the planned increase in debt. Trade unions regretted the diminution of job protection, and the program as a whole was coolly received in the **eastern federal states**. In 2004, the proposals led to major divisions within the **Social Democratic Party of Germany (SPD)** and to fears of a damaging split between the party and the trade unions. While observers generally considered that the program contributed to Germany's longer term economic stability, SPD leaders after Schröder remained skeptical and consistently distanced themselves from its measures.

AGRICULTURE. While 52 percent of Germany's land area is used for agriculture and a further 30 percent is commercially forested, primary production agriculture made up barely 1 percent of GDP in 2013 (2.2 percent in 1984); at the same time, the sector contributes significantly to downstream activities in the food industry, and Germany ranks as the world's fourth largest food exporter. Most agricultural land is arable (70.5 percent), with the rest used for grazing (28 percent). The most fertile areas are the flat, loess-covered belts bordering the northern Central Uplands and stretching from the Dutch border to Görlitz and Zittau in the east. Other productive regions include the Rhein-Neckar plain, the marshes and fenlands of the **North Sea** coast, the moraines of **Schleswig-Holstein**, western **Mecklenburg-West Pomerania** and northern **Brandenburg**, and large parts of the **Alpine** Foreland. In terms of total arable land area, the main crops are cereals, made up of wheat (over 50 percent), barley (25 percent, also for animal feed and beer production), maize (15 percent, for animal/poultry feed), rye (10 percent, increasingly for fodder), and a small volume of oats (around 1 percent). Green crops, primarily maize, harvested unripe for fodder or industry, account for 24 percent of land area, followed by oil seed (12 percent) and root crops (5 percent, with potatoes and sugar beets). The main vegetable products, ranked in terms of land area, are asparagus, carrots, onions, white cabbage, cauliflower, and bush beans. The area north of Nuremberg is famous for garlic, while hops are grown to the south and west of Regensburg and in the Hallertau region between Ingolstadt and Landshut. Fruit cultivation is centered on **Baden-Württemberg**, **Lower Saxony**, and **Rhineland-Palatinate**. Apples constitute 80 percent of production, followed by pears, plums, and cherries. Livestock farming, much of it intensive, includes pigs (27 million), cattle (13 million, of which 5 million are dairy cows), sheep (2.1 million), and over 128 million poultry birds. Dairy farming predominates on the **North Sea** coast, high sections of the Central Uplands, and the Alpine Foreland and river valleys. Cattle are reared across the whole country, although **Bavaria** and Lower Saxony account for nearly half the total, and numbers declined significantly after 1998 owing to cuts in **European Union** (**EU**) subsidies and reduced exports. Pig farming is concentrated in Lower Saxony and **North Rhine-Westfalia** and in Lower Saxony. Some 44 percent of poultry (egg-laying hens and broilers for chicken meat) is reared in Lower Saxony, where Osnabrück is a center of egg production. Effective in 2009, the use of large cages with heavy concentrations of battery chickens was prohibited. Germany has 13 wine-growing areas (the largest of which is the economic region of Rheinhessen), totaling 100,000 hectares and with an estimated 80,000 growers; after France, Italy, and Spain, Germany contributes around 5 percent of EU production and exports 20 percent to Great Britain, the United States, and the Netherlands. Germany is the EU's leading producer of milk, pork, potatoes, and oil-seed rape, importing mainly meat, fish, butter, eggs, fruit, vegetables, and coffee; while Germans have increased their consumption of milk and fruit in recent years, they have eaten less meat, especially beef. A major world trader in food, Germany exports milk and dairy products, meat, cereals, and baked products, mainly to other EU states (its principal trading partner is the Netherlands) and the U.S., but increasingly to eastern Europe (Russia and Poland), South America, and Asia. Germany is also the EU's leading importer of products from developing countries.

Before reunification, agriculture in the FRG underwent significant structural changes that, from the late 1950s onward, were driven largely at European level by the so-called Common Agricultural Policy (CAP). Designed initially as part of the postwar recovery to create a single protected and self-sufficient market, in which subsidies stimulated output and provided secure incomes for farmers and stable prices for consumers, by the 1970s the policy had become a complex, bureaucratic, and expensive mechanism generating huge surpluses of unwanted products (especially cereals, dairy products, and meat) and supporting farmers through artificially high prices above world market levels. During the 1980s, the focus of CAP shifted to curbing overproduction by applying quotas and paying farmers premiums (e.g., to produce certain items only or to withdraw farmland from use); ecological farming was also promoted. More recently, as a net contributor to the EU budget, Germany has been concerned to limit spending, although its position has been complicated by the needs of the eastern German states and the accession of 12 new EU states in 2004, many of which have significant agricultural interests. Within the framework of CAP reform, the number of farming units in the FRG declined from over one million in 1970 to just 648,000 in 1989; at the same time the number of small concerns (under 20 hectares) fell as the figure for larger units rose. A feature of western German farms is that most smallholdings are now run as secondary activities to their owners' principal source of income. Partly as the result of inheritance laws and the viability of specialist cash crops, there are more smallholdings in southern Germany than in the north. Since the 1950s, the number of agricultural workers in western Germany has declined steadily, from 3.6 million in 1960 to around 1 million in 2010, half of whom are family members.

After reunification, the state-run agricultural sector of the former **German Democratic Republic (GDR)** underwent major restructuring. Largely completed by the end of the 1990s, the process involved converting more than 4,000 large-scale agro-units to smaller, private concerns, resulting in around 28,000 smallholdings and over 1,200 large cooperatives or limited companies. Compared with the west, agriculture in the eastern states is now characterized by a relatively small number of large farming units, especially in Mecklenburg-West Pomerania and **Saxony-Anhalt**. The human cost of the changes was enormous: of the GDR's 915,000 farmworkers, only 187,000 remained by 1993. Landowners (ranging from politically stigmatized Junkers to smallholders) who had been expropriated before the GDR's foundation (1949) were excluded from compensation in the 1990 Treaty of Unification, although Chancellor **Helmut Kohl**'s claim that this was a condition of Soviet agreement was repeatedly denied by the USSR's last president, Mikhail Gorbachev. After 1992, the Bodenverwertungs- und Verwaltungs GmbH (BVVG) began privatizing state-owned land in eastern Germany and by 2015 had sold off 1.6 million hectares (an area about half the size of Brandenburg), with 200,000 hectares remaining. In 2005, the European Court of Human Rights rejected restitution claims from former owners on the grounds that the FRG could not be held responsible for the actions of the Soviet occupation authorities, although owners can buy back their land at a reduced rate. In many cases, it was the managers of the large agricultural collectives created by the GDR regime who benefited from reunification, as they forced out rivals, took over land, and transformed the collectives into profitable limited liability companies. Compared with the west, significantly more farmed land in the east is leased, and family participation is lower. Germany as a whole has seen the number of farming units decline (to less than 300,000 in 2010), although the total farmed area has remained constant since 2007, at 16.7 million hectares.

Organic farming, which includes arable crops, animal husbandry, and grazing land and has enjoyed state subsidies in Germany since 1989, is now governed by EU regulation, which sets standards for producers, consumer protection, and competition, as well as providing a kitemark (the Bio-Siegel, or Bio-Seal). Associated landmark legislation in Germany (the Öko-Land-baugesetz, ÖLG) was announced in 2002 and came into force in 2009. In 2012, 7.7 percent of farms in Germany employed organic methods on 6.2 percent of the land (compared with 2.1 percent in 1996). Leaders in ecological farming are the eastern states of Mecklenburg-West Pomerania and Brandenburg, which benefited from financial incentives for restructuring after reunification, but also Bavaria, which has the highest number of organic farms (5,700). There are numerous organizations for organic producers, of which Demeter (founded in Germany in 1954, but with roots dating back to 1928) and ANOG (founded in 1962) were probably the first. Others include the ecological foundation Ökologie und Stiftung Landbau (SÖL, 1975), Bio-kreis (1979), Bioland (1971), Naturland (1982), Ecoland (1997) Gäa (1989 in Dresden), Ecovin (for wine, 1985), and Biopark (1994). BÖLW (Bund Ökologische Lebensmittelwirtschaft), established in 2002, is the national federation for producers and distributors. Several universities also have chairs and research centers for ecological farming. A new development is the emergence of "energy managers" (Energiewirte), farmers who have diversified into wind farms, biomass plants and, especially, solar technology.

Attracted by favorable feed-in tariffs, they numbered 37,400 in 2010. The first "biosupermarket" opened in 1993 in Münster, and the sector now turns over more than 800 million euros annually.

Germany started testing genetically modified (GM) crops (sugar beets, potatoes, rape, and maize) in 1995, but fierce public resistance from the outset, led by the **Green Party** and also taking the form of sabotage of test sites by radical groups, prompted companies such as Sygenta (2004) and BASF (2012) to relocate their agricultural biotech activities abroad (in particular to the United States). A variety of maize, developed by Monsanto and cultivated between 2006 (947 hectares) and 2008 (3,170 hectares), remains the only commercially grown GM crop in Germany, although new sowings were prohibited starting in 2009 following concerns over effects on insect life. Legislation regulating GM technology in Germany has existed since 1990. The latest version of the Genetic Engineering Law (Gentechnikgesetz, in force 2008) provides for the "coexistence" of GM and GM-free crops (based on minimum distances), a semipublic register of test and field release sites, and measures, including labeling, to protect the integrity of GM-free products. In practice, applications for open test sites dwindled to virtually zero in 2013, and several federal states are aiming for GM-free status, at least for publicly owned land, as members of the Charter of Florence group, established in 2005. In 2013, only Mecklenburg-West Pomerania was listed in the register as having land (1,800 sq. m) earmarked for experimental release, but it was not actually cultivated.

Germany's forests represent a significant and expanding natural resource (of annually newly planted woodland, only two-thirds is commercially exploited). The most densely wooded states are Rhineland-Palatinate and **Hessen** (over 40 percent), while Schleswig-Holstein has 10 percent. Following the large-scale cutting back of forests, most recently during the two world wars, areas have been replanted and are now ecologically managed, with habitats for game animals (deer and boar) alongside rare birds and diverse flora and fauna, and controlled recreational activities, including hunting. Current woodland composition is 60 percent coniferous and 40 percent deciduous, the principal species being spruce (28 percent, mainly in the south), pine (23 percent, widespread in the north), beech (15 percent), and oak (10 percent). Some 44 percent of forested land is in private hands (largely smallholdings in Bavaria and northwestern Germany), while 33 percent is owned by the state (mainly the federal states, notably the **Saarland**), and around 20 percent is controlled by communal bodies (Rhineland-Palatinate and Hessen). The public has general recreational access to woodland anywhere and at any time. The German forest and timber industry, including processing, furniture production, paper, and printing, employs around 1.3 million workers and has an annual turnover of 170,000 million euros, although significant volumes of raw material (such as sulphate wood pulp) and wood products are imported, and the sector faces stiff competition from Scandinavia and eastern Europe.

See also ENVIRONMENT.

AHLHAUS, CHRISTOPH (1969–). Christian Democratic Union (CDU) politician. Born in Heidelberg (**Baden-Württemberg**), Christoph Ahlhaus trained in banking (1988–1990) and studied law in Heidelberg, **Berlin**, and Munich, then public administration in Speyer (1998), before qualifying as a practicing lawyer (1999). He joined the **Christian Democratic Union (CDU)** in 1985 and was active at the local and district levels in the Heidelberg area until 2001, before moving to **Hamburg**, where he was regional business manager for the party (2001–2006) and sat in the city assembly (2004–2006), acting as spokesman and specializing in internal and legal affairs. He was also party leader of north Hamburg district until 2012 and state councilor (Staatsrat) for the interior authority (2006–2008), which he chaired from 2008. Despite political wrangles in the Hamburg senate, Ahlhaus succeeded **Ole von Beust** as first mayor in August 2010. However, elections in the following February brought record losses for the CDU, with the **Social Democratic Party of Germany (SPD)** forming a coalition led by governing mayor **Olaf Scholz.**

ALBIG, TORSTEN (1963–). Social Democratic Party of Germany (SPD) politician. Born in **Bremen**, Torsten Albig studied history and social sciences (from 1982), then law at the University of Bielefeld, qualifying as a legal assessor (1991). After joining the revenue and **taxation** department of **Schleswig-Holstein** (1992), he became deputy head of the regional financial college (1993–1994) and adviser for finance and tax in the state's representation in Bonn (from 1994). A member of the SPD since 1982, he worked in the office of party chairman **Oskar Lafontaine** and was seconded to its strategic planning section (1996–1998). After the national election (1998), Albig served as spokesman and head of communication for three SPD finance ministers: Lafontaine (1998–1999), **Hans Eichel** (1999–2001), and **Peer Steinbrück** (2006–2009). He resigned from the civil service (2001) to become spokesman for the **Dresdner Bank** and in 2002 returned to Schleswig-Holstein to sit on the city council of the regional capital, Kiel, where he was elected mayor (2009–2012). In 2012, he entered the **Landtag**; following regional elections in which his party gained a fractionally lower share of votes than the governing **Christian Democratic Union (CDU)**, he became **minister president**, leading an alliance of SPD, **Alliance 90/The Greens**, and the Danish minority party (SSW).

ALBRECHT, ERNST (1930–2014). Christian Democratic Union (CDU) politician. Born in Heidelberg (**Baden-Württemberg**), Albrecht studied philosophy and theology at the universities of Tübingen (Germany) and Cornell (United States) from 1948 to 1951, then law and economics at universities in Tübingen and Bonn, earning a doctorate in 1953. He was appointed attaché to the council of ministers of the Coal and Steel Union (Montanunion, 1954), precursor of the **European Union (EU)**, and between 1958 and 1970 held several senior posts with the European Economic Community (EEC), including cabinet head of the EEC Commission (from 1958) and general director (1967–1970). He represented the CDU in the regional assembly for **Lower Saxony** (1970–1990), during which time he also worked as financial director for the Hanover-based biscuit factory Bahlsen Keksfabrik (1971–1976). In 1976, Albrecht was elected **minister president** of Lower Saxony (reelected 1982, 1986) and stood unsuccessfully as CDU/**Christian Social Union (CSU)** chancellor candidate against **Franz Josef Strauß** (1979). Other positions he held included president of the **Bundesrat** (1985–1986) and deputy chairman of the national CDU (1979–1990). A popular minister president, his vote supporting the **Ostpolitik** treaties in the Bundesrat in 1976 was crucial for ratification, and he offered **asylum** to 1,000 Vietnamese refugees in 1978. In 1990, after 14 years as minister president, he was ousted by **Gerhard Schröder** (SPD). During Albrecht's premiership, Lower Saxony agreed that Gorleben could be used as a location for nuclear waste and a reprocessing plant. The decision proved highly controversial, and when transports of reprocessed waste from France to Gorleben started in 1996, they were halted in the face of protests, before resuming in 2001. His published work on contemporary politics includes *Der Staat, Idee und Wirklichkeit* (1976).

ALBRECHT, THEODOR (1922–2010) AND KARL (1920–2014). Retail business entrepreneurs. The Albrecht brothers were born in the industrial town of Essen (now in **North Rhine-Westfalia**). Their father worked as a coal miner and later in a bread factory. After completing his basic school **education**, Theodor (Theo) trained in his mother's grocery shop in the working-class district of Schonnebeck (Essen). His brother Karl completed an apprenticeship in a delicatessen. In 1946, after military service during World War II, the brothers took over the family business, which was rapidly expanded after the 1948 **currency** reform into a chain of 13 grocery stores covering the Ruhr area and operating under the name of Albrecht (1955); a key innovation was the principle of customer self-service. In 1961, the brothers divided the group into two separate organizations: Aldi Süd, based in Mülheim on the Ruhr and controlled by Karl Albrecht, and Aldi Nord in Essen, managed by Theo. Distinct spheres of operation were agreed upon (and also later applied to the foreign acquisitions), and the brand name ALDI was adopted (1962), although the discount strategy remained the same: basically furnished stores offering good-quality goods at low prices with no service frills. After 1967, expansion followed into other European countries, the United States (1976), and Australia (2001). In 1971, Theo Albrecht was kidnapped; he was released after 17 days upon payment of a record 7 million DM ransom, an event that increased the family's avoidance of publicity. Starting in 1993, both Theo and Karl Albrecht withdrew from operational management, although the family continues to control the company though a complex network of foundations. The brothers were long considered to be among the wealthiest people in Germany. Aldi Nord maintains over 5,400 branches worldwide (Belgium, Denmark, France, Luxembourg, the Netherlands, Poland, Portugal, Spain, and the United States), including 2,500 in northern and eastern Germany. Aldi Süd has over 1,800 branches in western and southern Germany and 4,700 in Australia, Great Britain, Ireland, Austria, Switzerland, Slovenia, Hungary, and the United States. The combined turnover of the Aldi companies is estimated at 63,000 million euros (2014).

ALLIANCE 90/THE GREENS (BÜNDNIS 90/DIE GRÜNEN). Alliance 90/The Greens originated in various preunification opposition groups in the **German Democratic Republic (GDR)** that later merged with the western German **Green Party**. On 3 January 1990, **Democratic Awakening (DA)** and the **United Left**, together with what later became the **Social Democratic Party of the GDR**, formed the Electoral Alliance 90: Citizens for Citizens (Wahlbündnis 90: Bürger für Bürger). On 7 February 1990, and with a slightly different grouping, this became the Alliance 90 (Bündnis 90), which campaigned for entry into the **People's Chamber** in the elections of 18 March. Its members were **New Forum, Democracy Now**, and the **Initiative Peace and Human Rights**. On 22 September 1990, the Alliance 90/The Greens was formed in East Germany to campaign for the all-German national election (2 December). At a congress in Leipzig, the alliance formally merged with the Green Party in the western states (15 May 1993).

See also GREEN PARTY (DIE GRÜNEN).

ALLIANCE FOR GERMANY (ALLIANZ FÜR DEUTSCHLAND). The Alliance for Germany was an electoral alliance of conservative parties and political groups in the former **German Democratic Republic (GDR)** that was established in 7 February 1990 to campaign for a swift merger with the Federal Republic of Germany (FRG). Supported by the West German **Christian Democratic Union (CDU)**, its members were the CDU (GDR), **Democratic Awakening (DA),** and **German Social Union (DSU)**. In the elections for the **People's Chamber** of 18 March, the alliance won 172 seats out of 400 and emerged as the strongest group, although it lacked an overall majority. It formed a governing coalition with the **Social Democratic Party of Germany** and a grouping of East German liberal parties (the Bund Freier Demokraten [BFD], comprising the Liberal-Demokratische Partei [LDP], the Deutsche Forumpartei [DFP], which had split from **New Forum**, and the Freie Demokratische Partei [FDP]). The alliance was dissolved upon reunification (3 October 1990).

ALLIANCE FOR WORK (BÜNDNIS FÜR ARBEIT). The Alliance for Work originated in an initiative by Federal Chancellor **Gerhard Schröder** who, after his election in 1998, called on **trade unions** and employers to work together in combating unemployment. The alliance first met in December 1998, with Sunday "summit meetings" prepared by a steering group and attended by government ministers and representatives of labor and **employers' organizations**. Working parties researched topics such as **taxation**, employment policy, and the **Aufbau Ost** program for supporting the eastern **federal states**. A group of experts collected statistics and prepared technical reports.

The alliance continued the tradition of consensual German economic policy planning, typified by the "concerted action" initiative of former economics and finance Minister **Karl Schiller**. This took the form of a high-level forum of experts, ministers, and economic interest groups set up in 1967 to counter Germany's first postwar recession, but it broke up in 1977 when trade unions walked out after employers protested to the **Federal Constitutional Court (FCC)** over an extension to the laws on **codetermination**. The Alliance for Work deliberated against the background of a renewed national debate about Germany's rigid labor laws, which discouraged companies from applying Anglo-Saxon policies of hiring and firing workers in response to global market conditions (only very large concerns, for instance, could master the complex and time-consuming paperwork for engaging temporary workers). Criticized as more of a talk-shop than a motor for effective action, the alliance failed to meet for eight months (August 2000–March 2001), just when Germany entered a period of low economic growth. Employers argued that, alongside already burdensome government regulations, an increase in trade unions' influence on industry would increase bureaucracy, reduce Germany's international competitiveness, and harm domestic job prospects, especially if businesses shifted production to cheaper labor markets in eastern Europe. Keen to encourage companies to hire new workers, employees' organizations were also unhappy at the level of overtime worked by Germans, which reached a record 1,900 million hours in 2001.

Ten years after reunification, calls for structural economic changes focused on a number of areas. The system of collective bargaining, whereby unions and employers fixed wages and conditions for whole sectors and regions, and which had served postwar western Germany so well, was hindering the structural changes required to meet the challenges of foreign competition and of an internally imbalanced, postreunification economy. In particular, small businesses and parts of the poorer east needed the freedom to negotiate agreements at plant and local level in order to survive. Some also argued that unemployment and social welfare benefits should be cut for those who refused to accept jobs, and that there should be incentives for retraining or relocation. Paradoxically, while unemployment remained high in eastern Germany, the **tourism** and information technology industries in the prosperous south were experiencing labor shortages, and even when unemployment soared to over four million (January 2002), the number of unfilled job vacancies rose sharply. After several efforts to regain momentum, the alliance was finally abandoned in 2003, when Schröder announced his **Agenda 2010** reform package.

See also ECONOMIC DEVELOPMENT (FRG) AFTER 2000; ECONOMIC DEVELOPMENT 1990–1999.

ALLIANZ DEUTSCHLAND AG. The Allianz Versicherungs-AG was founded in 1890 in **Berlin**. Three years later, it opened a branch in London and by 1913 was generating 20 percent of its income from foreign premiums. In the 1920s, it expanded by merging with and taking over a number of **banks** and insurance companies. During World War II, the concern's headquarters were destroyed by bombing (1943), and in 1949 it relocated to Munich (accident and property insurance) and Stuttgart (life insurance). In 1959, Allianz began to rebuild its foreign network. A branch in Paris was followed by offices in Italy (1966); Great Britain, the Netherlands, Spain, and Brazil (1974); and the United States (1976). From the mid-1980s onward, Allianz steered a steady course of global expansion through buy-ups, acquisitions, and joint ventures. Upon reunification (3 October 1990), the concern took over the state-run insurance organization of the former **German Democratic Republic (GDR)**, the Staatliche Versicherung der DDR.

Under the leadership of Henning Schulte-Noelle, chief executive of the holding company from 1991 to 2003, Allianz embarked on a cost-cutting program while continuing its foreign acquisitions in Europe, the U.S., and Asia. It took over and integrated its operations with the **Dresdner Bank** (2001), which provided the resources for it to become a general purpose financial and investment company, although the bank was sold off in 2009. In 2003, Allianz recast itself as a Societas Europaea (SE), a new legal form of shareholder company in the **European Union (EU)**, with streamlined structures and better equipped to effect cross-border mergers. The German operation continued under the title Allianz Deutschland AG. Its works council (Aufsichtsrat) also admitted members from across the EU. Allianz in Germany is now a huge concern, with around 20 million customers, 9,000 representatives, and 30,000 staff members, contributing one-quarter (28,000 million euros) of the parent group's turnover. Core businesses are insurance (life, **health**, property, and accident) and banking. Oliver Bäte became chief executive in 2015.

ALPS. The narrow fringe of the German Alps in the far south of the country is—from west to east—made up of the Allgäuer Alps between Lake Constance and the Lech River (the highest peak is the Hochfrottenspitze, 2,649 m); the Bavarian Alps between the Lech and Inn Rivers (including the Zugspitze, 2,962 m, Germany's highest mountain); and the Berchtesgadener Alps (peak Watzmann, 2,713 m), which are in turn part of the Salzburger Alps. Of the entire European alpine mountain range, which extends for 1,200 kilometers, from France in the west to Austria and Slovenia in the east, only around 3 percent (part of the eastern Alps) is on German territory. The Alps are a major north–south transit route, although 70 percent of freight traffic is routed via passes at Brenner (road and rail link between Austria and Italy), Gotthard (road/rail, in Switzerland), and Mont Blanc (road only, France–Italy). Two new rail tunnels under the existing Gotthard tunnel, started in 1996, are due for completion around 2017 and will create the longest rail tunnel (57 km) in the world and form the main transit route across the Alps. Of several passes for road traffic on or near German territory, the highest is at Riedberg (1,420 m).

At the colline level (up to 600 m) of the Alps' foothills and in fertile valleys and basins, fruit and arable farming predominate. Above this are found deciduous forests (the montane level, up to 1,200 m), coniferous woodland (the subalpine level, up to 2,000 m), and meadowland used by dairy farmers for summer grazing (the alpine level, up to 3,300 m). Beyond the snowline at 3,300–4,000 meters, with maximum temperatures of around –3 degrees Celsius, the landscape consists of ice and rock. Where agriculture used to be the primary source of income, tourism and skiing now often generate over 80 percent of wealth. As winter and summer tourism expanded between the 1950s and 1980s, with some areas also undergoing significant industrialization and urbanization, the German alpine population expanded (from 1 to 1.2 million), although emigration continued from the more remote localities. Despite the end of the industrial boom between 1975 and 1980 and stagnation in alpine tourism (as a result of new holiday destinations, competition from southern and eastern Europe, trends toward shorter stays, and the declining popularity of mountain walking among younger people), the population reached 1.4 million in 2000. Some ski resorts have responded to the decline in tourist numbers with improved infrastructure, new activities, and marketing initiatives. To counter the dangers that intensive tourism and transit routes present to the area's fragile ecology, the eight alpine countries (Germany, Austria, France, Italy, Slovenia, Switzerland, Liechtenstein, and

Monaco) agreed to a treaty (the Alpine Convention, in force from 1995) to promote sustainable development and protect the interests of its 14 million inhabitants.

ALTERNATIVE FOR GERMANY (ALTERNATIVE FÜR DEUTSCH-LAND, AfD). Founded in February 2013 and growing rapidly to reach a membership of over 20,000 by the end of 2014, the AfD is a conservative populist party that campaigns principally for the abolition of the **eurozone**, which it regards as a failed economic model, and for a decentralized, less bureaucratic **European Union (EU)**. In its brief manifesto for the 2013 national election, the party, which fell just short of the 5 percent entry hurdle to enter the **Bundestag**, also argued for promoting the family and **education**, regulating **immigration** according to economic needs, and using public referenda to deliver more democratic government. Despite its recent foundation, the party narrowly failed (with 4.1 percent of votes) to clear the entry hurdle in state elections in **Hessen** (2013), but won seats in several regional assemblies in 2014 and 2015. A "political academy" undertakes training and holds seminars for campaigning and education. The party leadership was shared by Bernd Lucke (economics professor and former member of the **Christian Democratic Union [CDU]**), Frauke Petry (a chemist and entrepreneur), and Konrad Adam (journalist). In 2015, damaging internal divisions emerged as many supporters of the party's economic agenda felt alienated by its attraction for right-wing extremists. Lucke withdrew from the leadership at a party congress in Essen in July 2015, claiming that the AfD was moving toward more antiforeigner and anti-Western positions. He was succeeded by Petry, who had led a long and bitter campaign against him (Jörg Meuthen was elected coleader, or "speaker"). Lucke promptly cofounded a rival party, the Allianz für Fortschritt und Aufbruch (ALFA), in Kassel, taking many former AfD supporters with him. In 2016, the AfD achieved dramatic electoral successes in **Baden-Württemberg**, the **Rhineland-Palatinate**, and **Saxony-Anhalt**, gaining 15.1, 12.6, and 24.2 percent of votes to regional assemblies. Popular concern over the government's **asylum policy** and **immigration** was a major factor. During 2015–2016 in **Saxony** and **Brandenburg**, the party became the target of numerous violent attacks by left-wing **extremists**.

ALTERNATIVE MOVEMENTS (ALTERNATIVE BEWEGUNGEN). From the 1970s onward, many (but not exclusively) younger people in Germany tired of the often highly theoretical debates of the **students' movement** of the 1960s, but equally disenchanted with what was perceived as dated mainstream culture, sought new and potentially more effective life concepts. This development was in part also influenced by the worldwide impact of the beatnik and hippie movement in the United States (U.S.).

Seeing self-fulfillment as an aim, these individuals and groups were often antihierarchical and democratic in nature. Rejecting what they perceived as the traditional and dated consumerism of the modern industrial society, they were usually involved in groups or movements engaged in issues such as the **environment**, peace, and **women**'s rights. These groups tended to be associated with a left-wing political agenda, though this is an inappropriate simplification, and in reality the main focus was and remains either to form an opposition against the establishment or to foster alternative approaches.

In this context the first "Frauenverlag" (publishing house for and run by women) was set up in Munich (1974). A "Frauenhaus" (house for women) was established in West **Berlin** (1976) and provided a home for women trying to escape violent men. The concept of cooperatives in the commercial sector became widespread, in particular with regard to **publishers**, print shops, bookshops, pubs, and ecologically managed farms. There are still a number of thriving culture- and lifestyle-oriented cooperatives, such as the UFA Fabrik in Berlin. Some of these ideas were institutionalized (the fair trade model is one example) and changed people's way of thinking in many areas.

Alternative movements are also labeled new social movements (Neue Soziale Bewegungen), with a distinct sense of political and institutional opposition, forming the basis for the so-called citizens' movements (Bürgerbewegungen) that concerned themselves with a vast array of short- and long-term issues, be they local, regional, or international in scope. Apart from those mentioned above, topics also include the developing world and the national census. In terms of organization, these movements were and are still either localized, responding to particular regional concerns, or form part of—increasingly—international networks.

Some of these movements engaged and continue to influence the public. An example is the squatter movement (Hausbesetzerbewegung) in the cities of **Hamburg** and Berlin, which led at times to violent confrontations with the police. However, parts of the squatter movement were also responsible for restoring buildings that would—for example in Berlin—have been pulled down. Other cities where similar activities took place include Düsseldorf, Cologne, Tübingen, and Leipzig. Today, concerns about the impact of widespread gentrification, in particular in large cities such as Berlin, are widely discussed. Key issues are the attempt to maintain old buildings against the ambitions of an increasing number of foreign investors, the need for cheap accommodations, and the requirement for a sound infrastructure in housing settlements. These movements experienced a new impetus after reunification, when social structures, in particular in the former **German Democratic Republic (GDR)**, underwent considerable change.

ALTHAUS, DIETER (1958–). Christian Democratic Union (CDU) politician. Born in Heiligenstadt (**Thuringia**), Dieter Althaus studied physics and mathematics in Erfurt (1979–1983) before working as a schoolteacher in Geismar (1983–1989). In 1987, he was appointed his school's deputy director. In 1989, he was nominated for a medal for outstanding work in the Communist youth organization of the **German Democratic Republic (GDR)**, the Pionierorganisation Ernst Thälmann. His claim that he turned down the award was disputed by political opponents. Althaus joined the CDU of the GDR (1985) and took part in the protest movement of October 1989, helping to organize demonstrations in Heiligenstadt. In January 1990, he took over the organization of **education** in Heiligenstadt, prohibiting further activities by the Communist youth in schools. In May 1990, he was elected councilor for the newly constituted district of Heiligenstadt and the following September entered the regional parliament (**Landtag**), where he took a special interest in educational policy.

During 1992–1999, Althaus served as regional minister of education and culture under minister president **Bernhard Vogel** (CDU), playing a key role in restructuring the school system in the post-GDR years: he introduced the three-tiered model of primary school (Grundschule), comprehensive secondary (Regelschule), and higher secondary school (Gymnasium), and also worked to ensure that teachers' qualifications in his federal state were recognized nationally. Deputy leader (1993–2000), then leader (2000–2009), of the regional CDU, he served on the party's national executive committee (2000–2010) and the presidium (2006–2010).

Following Vogel's resignation in 2003, Althaus succeeded him as **minister president** and was reelected in June 2004, leading a CDU government with a ruling majority. In 2009, he suffered a serious skiing injury and, following the CDU's loss of its overall majority in the state elections the same year, stepped down as minister president and leader of the regional party. In 2010, he resigned his parliamentary mandate when he was appointed vice president of the automobile supplier Magna International. A mainstream conservative politician, Althaus developed a reputation as a forthright critic of the **federal government** and for introducing modern methods of communication in the Thuringian state bureaucracy.

ALTMAIER, PETER (1958–). Christian Democratic Union (CDU) politician. Peter Altmaier was born in Ensdorf (**Saarland**) and studied law at the University of the Saarland (from 1980) before qualifying as a practicing lawyer (1985, 1988). After working for the Europa Institute at the university (1985–1990), he joined the Commission of the **European Union (EU)** as a civil servant (1990–1994), where he served as general secretary for the Administrative Commission on Social Security for Migrant Workers (1993–1994). A member of the youth wing (**Junge Union**) of the CDU from

1974 and of the main party from 1976, Altmaier joined the regional party executive committee of the Saarland in 1991 and chaired the Saarlouis district association from 2000 to 2008. He entered the **Bundestag** in 1994, where he represented the party on various committees for legal and EU affairs and was **state secretary** (Staatssekretär) for the interior minister (2005–2009) and business manager for the parliamentary party group (2009–2012). He was also elected president of the nonparty Europa-Union Deutschland (2006–2011) and its honorary president from 2011. During 2012–2013, Altmaier was federal minister for the **environment**, nature protection, and nuclear safety before being appointed federal minister for special tasks and head of the **Office of the German Chancellor** (2013). He is a close confidant of Federal Chancellor **Angela Merkel** and is valued for his frankness and ability to negotiate compromises between the government and the parliamentary party. Considered a modernizer in the CDU, Altmaier supported a reform of **immigration** law in the 1990s, criticized **Roland Koch**'s antiforeigner campaign, and distanced himself from the Vatican's opposition to homosexual marriages.

ANTI-SEMITISM. Despite the small numbers of Jews in the former Federal Republic of Germany (FRG) and the **German Democratic Republic (GDR)**, occasional acts of anti-Semitism, including attacks on synagogues perpetrated by extreme right-wing groups and individuals, were reported in West Germany before reunification. Although similar actions in East Germany were not officially acknowledged, the author **Stefan Heym** drew attention to anti-Semitic undercurrents in 1982, as did church leaders. During Christmas and New Year 1959–1960, 470 incidents (including an attack on a Cologne synagogue) involving around 230 mainly young people were registered in the FRG, leading to international concerns over a resurgence of National Socialism and to the banning of the neo-Nazi Deutsche Reichspartei (DRP) in the **Rhineland-Palatinate**. Extremists also damaged facilities of the state **radio and television** network ARD before it began broadcasting a series on the Holocaust in January 1979.

Reunification heralded a dramatic increase in neo-Nazi violence, especially in eastern Germany, targeting mainly **foreigners** and **asylum** seekers, but also Jewish communities. This sudden upsurge was partly linked to social alienation (especially among unemployed young people) arising from the economic problems of reunification and the legacy of the authoritarian structures of the former GDR. In the country as a whole, the incidence of reported anti-Jewish criminal violence (including physical attacks and arson) reached an unprecedented peak (22) in 1992, after which it died down (5 in 1994), before rising again to 45 in 2013. The number of other forms of anti-Semitic crime (insults, incitement, desecration of synagogues and cemeteries) varied from 1,515 in 2002 to more than 1,200 in 2013. As a proportion of politically motivated right-wing violence, anti-Semitic acts represented a relatively small element (around 3 percent in 2013). The **Federal Office for the Protection of the Constitution** (Bundesamt für Verfassungsschutz, BfV), which monitors extremist groups and produces annual reports, related the increases in criminality after 2000 to the onset of the Second Intifada in the Occupied Territories of Palestine, although it acknowledged that the perpetrators could not be identified in many cases. In its 2011 report, the BfV noted 29 Islamist organizations with around 37,400 supporters, which shared anti-Jewish sentiments. Members of other right-wing groups for whom anti-Semitism was a binding ideology numbered 26,000.

In 2008, the **Bundestag** initiated an expert commission to report regularly on anti-Semitism in Germany and recommend measures to counter it. Presented in November 2011, the first report concluded that latent anti-Semitism, based on deeply rooted stereotypes and ignorance about Jews, permeated most levels of German society and had for many years remained constantly present in 15 to 20 percent of the general population. Manifestations ranged from anti-Jewish chants at football matches, to the use of "Jew" as an insult in school playgrounds and elsewhere, distortions of historical fact, and accusations that Jews have instrumentalized the Holocaust in order to hold Germans in "guilt bondage" (Schuldknechtschaft). Alongside other media, the **Internet** in particular was exploited by right-wing and Islamist extremists to target and mobilize young people, including those of Arab and Turkish origin, although the report also pointed to anti-Semitism in leftist ideologies and examined suggestions of anti-Jewish stereotypes evoked by some critics of financial globalization.

A member of the expert commission, Juliana Wetzel, concluded that, apart from the banning of extremist groups in general, there was currently no general strategy for combating anti-Semitism in Germany, and that measures would need to be long-term and sustained. Individual politicians in the FRG have also attracted attention for anti-Semitic speeches or remarks, usually resulting in their resignation or expulsion from office. Examples are the former president of the Bundestag, Philipp Jenninger (November 1988); **Hessen** politician Martin Hohmann (**Christian Democratic Union, CDU**, in 2003); and the **Free Democratic Party** (**FDP**) politician **Martin Möllemann (2003)**. Although distinct from racially based anti-Semitism, criticism of the state of Israel has proved controversial for intellectuals such as the author **Günter Grass**, who called the policies toward Iran of the "atomic power Israel" a danger to world peace (2012), and the journalist **Rudolf Augstein**, whom the Simon Wiesenthal Center included in a list of leading anti-Semites following his condemnation of Israeli policies in the Occupied Territories (2013). The writer **Martin Walser** was similarly condemned for arguing that Auschwitz should no longer be used as a "moral cudgel" against present-day Germans (1998).

Founded in 1982, the Center for Research into Anti-Semitism (Zentrum für Antisemitismusforschung, ZfA) at the Technical University of **Berlin** is a leading organization of its kind. Its main publication is a yearbook on anti-Semitism research (*Jahrbuch für Antisemitismusforschung*), which has appeared annually since 1992. The Information and Documentation Center for Anti-Racism in **North-Rhine Westfalia** (Informations- und Dokumentationszentrum für Antirassismusarbeit in Nordrhein-Westfalen, IDA-NRW) collects data, research studies, and educational material dedicated to combating all forms of racism. The Holocaust features prominently in German education, and academics in a number of institutions engage with the lives of Jews in Germany through the centuries. Despite anti-Semitic incidents, Berlin has also become a popular destination for young Jewish immigrants.

See also CENTRAL COUNCIL OF JEWS IN GERMANY (ZENTRALRAT DER JUDEN IN DEUTSCHLAND); EXTREMISM; JEWS IN GERMANY.

APPEL, FRANK (1961–). Business executive. Frank Appel was born in **Hamburg** and studied chemistry at the University of Munich (from 1983), graduating with a diploma (1988), before earning a doctorate in neurobiology at the ETH in Zurich (1993). After working for the business consultancy firm McKinsey (1993), joining its management board in 1993, he moved to **Deutsche Post AG** (1994), where, as a member of the executive board (from 2002), he developed global business operations and organized the takeover of the British logistics company Excel (2005). In 2008, he succeeded **Klaus Zumwinkel** as chief executive of Deutsche Post.

ARBEITSKREIS SELBSTÄNDIGER KULTURINSTITUTE E.V. (ASKI). The ASKI (Work Group of Independent Cultural Institutes) was set up in 1967 as an initiative of the Federal Ministry of the Interior. It links around 36 renowned and independent culture and research institutes that are considered to represent cultural life in Germany. This includes museums, art halls, archives, libraries, and documentation centers on art, music, **literature**, **language**, **architecture**, design, printing, the preservation of cemeteries and historical monuments, **cinema**, and **radio**. The work group aims to maintain the plurality of culture and promote the interests of its members vis-à-vis the general public and the **federal states**. (The website www.aski.org/ provides up-to date information about it activities.) Members include the Bach Archive (Leipzig), the Bauhaus Archive, the German Academy for Language and Literature (Deutsche Akademie für Sprache und Dichtung, Darmstadt), the Film Museum (**Berlin**), the Germanic National Museum (Germanisches Nationalmuseum, Nuremberg), and the Goethe Museum/Kippenberg Foundation (Düsseldorf). Among its high profile activities are, for example, events relating to the "decade of Martin Luther" (Lutherdekade), which will culminate in October 2017 on the occasion of the 500th anniversary of the German Reformation.

ARCHITECTURE IN GERMANY. The heyday of German architecture is still associated with the avant-garde and modernist movements of the early 20th century. Outstanding representatives of the time include Mies van der Rohe, Walter Gropius, and Hans Scharoun, who like many others, sooner or later were forced under the National Socialist regime to emigrate, in the process taking some of their concepts into other cultures. Gropius (1883–1969), founder and first director of the Bauhaus (1919), is considered one of the most formative architects of the last century. Although the Bauhaus was—by then based in **Berlin**—forced to close in 1933, it exerts considerable influence even today and also left its mark in the United States (U.S.) and Israel. For the Bauhaus, which also emphasized the importance of economic factors and the value of training, architecture was just one aspect of a range of specialist areas, many of which took the form of cooperative projects. Gropius himself designed the Bauhaus building in Dessau (1927), which exemplifies several features specific to the movement. Today it is open for visitors, as are the so-called Meisterhäuser, which exemplify the thinking of the movement in their use of building materials, color, and design. Mies van der Rohe (1886–1969), also a Bauhaus director, is acknowledged as one of the fathers of architectural modernism. The Mies van der Rohe Award for European Architecture was established in 1981. Hans Scharoun (1893–1972) was Berlin's first director of buildings (Stadtbaurat) after World War II and the first president of the West Berlin Academy of Arts (1955–1968). Scharoun was the leading architect of the Berlin Kulturforum, a complex of museums, art galleries, and cultural institutions close to the Potsdamer Platz, and maintained a strong influence on Berlin after World War II.

The sheer scale of destruction of World War II and 12 years of building according to National Socialist ideology—including Hitler's and Speer's aspirations to rebuild Berlin as Germania—necessitated a functional approach to rebuilding the country. The pressure of having to rebuild whole cities went hand in hand with utopian ideas that ignored social realities, in the process fostering the "autogerechte Stadt," a city dominated by automobile users. A primary example is the building of motorways in West Berlin during the Cold War that went hand in glove with new buildings such as Tegel Airport and the International Congress Center (ICC). At the same time, city and town planners sought to provide easier access to more green spaces, in particular in quarters dedicated to large housing projects; one example is the Gartenstadt Vahr in **Bremen**, built in response to postwar housing needs by Ernst May, Max Säume, Günther Hafermann, and Hans Bernhard Reichow.

The move from an industrial to an information-based society, concerns over the **environment**, and globalization eventually fostered a new, post-modern approach to architecture in the late 1960s that continues into the 21st century. Fed by a demand for apartments and houses, the concept of "new cities," with their own infrastructures, long remained popular in both the Federal Republic of Germany (FRG) and the **German Democratic Republic (GDR)**. West German examples include the Nordweststadt (Frankfurt/Main) and the Märkisches Viertel (Berlin); East Germany adopted the approach in most of its larger towns and cities, including Berlin (Mahlsdorf, Hellersdorf). The latter proved popular in that local provisions often mirrored the infrastructure representative of villages, including well-organized child care.

While National Socialist architecture—in particular that of its main proponent, Albert Speer—had promoted monumental building and structured settlements such as Prora on the island of Rügen or the Reichssportfeld in Nuremberg, the GDR attempted a new beginning according to its own ideological guidelines. Although the East Berlin showpiece Stalinallee (completed between 1952 and 1958 and renamed Karl Marx-Allee in 1961) was planned largely in the monumental style characteristic of socialist realism, new guidelines and a more pragmatic approach emerged after the death of Josef Stalin. East German architects were obliged to work in collectives following strict party directives and therefore were rarely able to leave an individual mark. Exceptions include Hermann Henselmann (1905–1995), Heinz Graffunder (1926–1994), and Edmund Collein (1906–1992). The legacy of Richard Paulick (1903–1979), chief architect in Hoyerswerda (1956–1961), Schwedt (1962–1964), and Halle-Neustadt (1963–1968), was the industrial serial production of apartments. Eisenhüttenstadt (1951–1961, Stalinstadt), close to the Polish border, is an example of a city consciously designed following socialist guidelines. After reunification, many towns and cities in eastern Germany began an extensive process of renovation that focused on buildings and central precincts neglected under the old regime. The reason for the neglect was partly economic and partly ideological: mansions and large private houses in particular were associated with bourgeois rule. A primary example was the Berlin City Palace (Stadtschloss) in East Berlin, which was demolished in 1950 despite international, including Soviet, attempts to halt the process. After prolonged debates and thanks to the initiative of the **Hamburg** businessman Wilhelm von Boddien, the palace is now being rebuilt (completion is anticipated for 2019) and will house museums. Termed "Humboldtforum," the Forum's first artistic director is Neil McGregor (formerly of the British Museum, London).

In the 1990s, debates about architecture were often concerned in one way or another with eastern Germany. Issues included the problem of shrinking cities (many East Germans, seeking new beginnings, had moved to other parts of the country), reassessment of the architecture and production methods of the former GDR, and the treatment of East Germany's architectural and artistic legacy.

Influential postwar architects in the FRG include Egon Eiermann (1904–1970) who, together with the Munich-based Sepp Ruf (1908–1982), built a pavilion for the World Exhibition in Brussels in 1958 that was architecturally representative of the new Germany. As a teacher Eiermann was particularly instrumental in shaping postwar developments. Helmut Hentrich's (1905–2001) and Hubert Petschnigg's high-rise Thyssen building in Düsseldorf came to epitomize the era of the so-called economic miracle. Hentrich contributed significantly to the rebuilding of Düsseldorf and belongs to the "second generation" of modern architects. Founded in 1972, HPP (Hentrich, Petschnigg, and Partner) is now one of Germany's largest architectural concerns. Designed by Bernhard Hermkes (1903–1995), the Grindel-Towers in Hamburg-Harvestehude (1956) are considered the first programmatic manifestation of postwar modernism in Hamburg.

Benchmark buildings of the 1970s include the Olympic facilities in Munich (1972), whose tent-like structures symbolize a light, modern approach that contrasted vividly with the Olympic Games of 1936. The architect Günther Behnisch (1922–2010) was a member of the Stuttgart School, which significantly shaped West German architecture. His work, which is characterized as antimonumentalist and often incorporates improvised building materials in order to provide transparency, includes the **Bundestag** building (Bonn, 1964) and the **Academy of Arts** (Berlin, 2005). Frei Otto (1925–2015), also associated with facilities for the 1972 Olympic Games and renowned for his lightweight constructions, is regarded as a catalyst for ecological building; Otto received the Pritzker Prize posthumously in 2015. Other influential architects include Rolf Gutbrod (1910–1999); Heinz Bienefeld (1926–1995), who specialized in church buildings; Gottfried Böhm (1920–), the first German to be awarded the Pritzker Architectural Prize (1986); Fritz Bornemann (1912–2007); Alexander Freiherr von Branca (1919–2011); Werner Düttmann (1921–1983); Peter Busmann (1933–); and Karljosef Schattner (1924–2012), who made his name developing an "architectural dialogue" between the old and the new in Eichstätt (**Bavaria**).

By the 1980s, the concept of urban renewal was gaining ground in Germany. Originating in the West Berlin quarter of Luisenstadt, the approach rejected the 1960s policy of demolition and new building and promoted a more sensitive style of town planning. In 1983, the Berlin regional assembly adopted 12 new planning and development guidelines that attached primacy to what was compatible with social needs (soziale Verträglichkeit). In accordance with the new policy, the 1984/1987 International Building Exhibition (Internationale Bauausstellung, IBA) created an umbrella for a variety of projects in the western part of the city. Led by J. P. Kleihues (1933–2004), IBA

Neu (new building) presented postmodern developments, while IBA Alt (rehabilitation) under Hardt-Waltherr Hämer (1922–2012) focused on the careful renovation of residential quarters. "Critical reconstruction" (kritische Rekonstruktion) became a watchword for thoughtful urban rebuilding that aimed to take account of the 19th-century city outline. This approach proved crucial in planning policy after the fall of the **Berlin Wall** and was at the center of a fierce architectural debate (Architekturstreit). IBA 1984/1987 set a national and international benchmark for such projects and their impact.

In more general terms, the IBA exhibitions aim to promote change within a defined regional remit and emphasize the social, cultural, and ecological effects of town and landscape planning. Financial backing for the exhibitions is usually provided by local communities and the government. IBA Emscher Park (1989–1999, **North-Rhine Westfalia**) presented around 120 individual projects. IBA Stadtumbau (urban redevelopment), held in **Saxony-Anhalt**, continued until 2010. Meanwhile, green issues are taken up by the biennial Federal Garden Exhibition (Bundesgartenschau), which was established in 1951. The exhibition provides models for future changes, fosters communication between experts and citizens, and sets the agenda for regional development.

Ever since reunification Berlin, despite major projects elsewhere in Germany (such as the Elbphilharmonie in Hamburg, the new railway station complex in Stuttgart [Stuttgart 21], the City Tunnel in Leipzig, and the North-South-"Stadtbahn" in Cologne) has garnered particular national and international interest in its architecture, not least thanks to the large-scale rebuilding that took place during the 1990s and early 2000s (e.g., on Potsdamer Platz, the new government quarter, restoration work on the Museum Island, large-scale development of the transport infrastructure, and also new housing developments outside the city center). These changes also reflect an ongoing preoccupation with gentrification in Berlin and other large German cities; the development of the tourist sector, including new hotels; and the comparison between the former distinct political entities of East and West.

International influences have had a profound effect on postwar German architecture. Following the construction boom after the fall of the Berlin Wall, architecture also became a matter of public interest. This was due to the enormous scale of work undertaken, such as Berlin's Potsdamer Platz, which from 1995 to 2000 was Europe's biggest inner-city building site. Potsdamer Platz captured the public's and tourists' imagination, since the investors (both the government and private contractors) made a conscious attempt to promote the building process by means of so-called Architainment (combining building work with cultural events) and a temporary museum explaining developments (Infobox).

Several international architects were involved in projects in reunified Germany—Lord Norman Foster, for example, designed the renovations for the Reichstag building in Berlin; a first renovation had been initiated in the 1960s and was led by Paul Baumgarten [1900–1984]). Building schemes in Germany that impact the public sphere are competition based. Exhibitions are frequently held in order to display the results of these open competitions. Foreign architects, such as Richard Meier, Charles Moore, Frank Gehry, Jean Nouvel, Philip Johnson, Hans Hollein, Gustav Peichl, Alvar Aalto, Arne Jacobsen, Giorgio Grassi, and Foster, were therefore able to contribute to developments.

Established architects who have played a role in reunified Germany include Peter Kulka (1937–), Arno Lederer (1947–), the Austrian brothers Manfred and Laurids Ortner, Jürgen Sawade (1937–2015), Rob Krier (Luxembourg, 1938–), Peter P. Schweger (1935–), Max Dudler (Switzerland, 1949–), Auer und Weber, Hascher + Jehle, Jochem Jourdan (1937–), and Chicago-based Helmut Jahn (1940–). Josef Paul Kleihues (1933–2004) initiated the Dortmund Architectural Days in 1974. Hans Kollhoff (1946–), who succeeded Kleihues as president of the Academy of Architecture (Bauakademie) in Berlin in 2004, is considered to be a member of the "Berlin School" and favors American-style high-rise buildings. Along with Charlotte Frank, Axel Schultes (1943–) became more widely known to the public for his design of the **Office of the Federal Chancellor** (Bundeskanzleramt) in Berlin, part of the government building complex, the so-called Band des Bundes (completed in 2001). The main feature of Schultes' design was that it established an architectural bridge between the former East and West in Berlin by spanning the Spree River. The work of Otto Steidle (1943–2004) is characterized by functionality and prefabricated segments that lend an "unfinished" touch to his work. Arguing that form should not be reduced solely to function, Oswald Mathias Ungers (1926–2007) searched instead for basic typologies that could take diverse shapes. One of his most famous buildings is the Museum of German Architecture (Deutsches Architekturmuseum, DAM) in Frankfurt/Main (1984). The museum, which works closely with architectural associations in Germany and abroad, hosts exhibitions and discussions on national and international architecture and maintains a collection of architectural drawings, plans, and models; its library of over 25,000 books and magazines provides material on architectural history and theory since 1800. Meinhard von Gerkan (1935–) and Gerkan Marg and Partners (GMP) are regarded as one of the leading architectural partnerships in contemporary Germany. Gerkan, who stated that architecture is "art in social context" designed Berlin's Tegel airport (1974) and main railway station (2006). His Berlin-**Brandenburg** Airport Willy Brandt, originally due to open in 2010, was delayed for technical difficulties, which eventually contributed to the resignation of Berlin's governing mayor **Klaus Wowereit** (in office from

2001 until 2014). Heinz Hilmer (1936–) and Christoph Sattler (1938–) became known to the wider public through their master plan for the redevelopment of inner-city Berlin (Potsdamer Platz, 1994).

Other leading architects, especially of the younger generation, include Helge Bofinger (1940–); the firm of Bothe, Richter, Teherani (Teherani took part in the 1994 Next Modern exhibition that was to reshape Hamburg); Stephan Braunfels (1950–), whose new building for the Neue Pinakothek museums in Munich won particular acclaim; Thomas Herzog (1940–); Ingenhoven, Overdiek, and Partner; Krüger, Schubert, and Vandreike; KSP Engel und Zimmermann Architekten; Hilde Léon und Konrad Wohlhage; Matthias Sauerbruch (1955–, with Louisa Hutton), whose building for the Office of the **president of the Federal Republic** of Germany (Bundespräsidialamt) in Berlin won acclaim (1994); Paul Kahlfeldt (1956–); and Werner Sobek (1953–).

In recent years, public attention has focused on the building of memorials in Germany. Some major sites have been developed by international architects such as Peter Eisenman (Holocaust Memorial, Berlin) and Daniel Liebeskind (Jewish Museum, Berlin). German architects have also played a role, however, including the Saarbrücken-based firm of Wandel Hoefer Lorch + Hirsch, which designed the Frankfurt Shoah Wall and platform A of the Grunewald railway station, used for the deportation of Berlin Jews during the National Socialist regime. Günter Domenig's (1934–2012) documentation center (2001), at the location where the National Socialists celebrated their annual rallies, is considered exemplary for a deconstructivist approach to architecture.

The at times controversial reconstruction or redevelopment of individual buildings, such as the Frauenkirche in Dresden or the palace in Berlin, and whole town centers, such as Frankfurt's old city, has continued well into the 21st century.

Each of the **federal states** has its own chamber of architects (Architektenkammer). The Federal Chamber of Architects (Bundesarchitektenkammer, BAK), whose main office is in Berlin, is a corporate body in public law and represents 118,000 architects at the national and international levels. The Association of German Architects (Bund Deutscher Architekten, BDA), founded in 1903, represents freelance architects and has regional associations in all the federal states. Like many other sectors of the German economy, architecture in recent years has been severely affected by the downturn in work and projects. The highest density of architects is found in Berlin, **Baden-Württemberg,** and Hamburg, with Saxony-Anhalt and Brandenburg at the lower end. Overall, more than 80 percent work as construction architects, about 5 percent as landscape architects, 4 percent as interior designers, and 3 percent as urban planners. The German Museum for Architecture, Planning, and Building (Deutsches Zentrum für Architektur, Planungs- und Bauwesen,

DAZ), founded in 1995, provides a meeting place for architects, builders, investors, engineers, and related professionals. Germany's leading architectural prize is the Deutscher Architekturpreis, which is awarded every two years.

See also TOWN PLANNING LAW (RAUMORDNUNGSGESETZ).

ASYLUM POLICY. Mindful of those who fled or attempted to flee Germany during the National Socialist dictatorship and of the many refugees who entered the country after 1945, the Federal Republic of Germany (FRG) operated a liberal asylum policy in its early years, based on a straightforward commitment in the **Basic Law (BL)**: "Persons persecuted on political grounds shall have the right of asylum" (BL, article 16). At the same time, asylum seekers are considered differently from ethnic Germans and their descendants (**Aussiedler/Übersiedler**), who have a legal right of return (BL, article 116). Asylum policy was politically uncontroversial as long as numbers of refugees, mainly from eastern bloc states and totaling 70,400 from 1952 to 1968, remained low. However, between 1972 and 1980 annual figures rose sharply, from 5,289 to 107,818 and, after fluctuations, peaked at 438,191 in 1992, although this figure included multiple and repeated applications. Restrictions, primarily on eligibility to take work and on social welfare benefits, were introduced inconsistently during the 1970s and 1980s, but had little effect on numbers applying for asylum. Following a highly polarized political debate, accompanied by violent and often fatal attacks on asylum seekers and migrants (most notoriously in Rostock-Lichtenhagen and Mölln in 1992 and Solingen in 1993), the **Bundestag** agreed to new legislation (1993), which attached stringent conditions to article 16. In particular, applicants could not enter Germany through a safe third country (effectively eliminating entry overland); in addition, social benefits were restricted and asylum seekers, housed in communal centers, could not as a rule work for one year (this was reduced to nine months in 2013). The new laws coincided with the end of the war in Yugoslavia, and applications fell sharply, from almost 128,000 first-time applications in 1995 to just over 19,000 in 2007 (the figures including subsequent or renewed applications were 166,951 and 30,303). After this, numbers rose again, to reach 173,072 (202,834) in 2014 and a record 231,302 (256,938) between January and August 2015.

Aside from the BL, asylum status is governed by international agreements—such as the post–World War II Geneva Convention (agreed to in 1951; effective from 1954), the **United Nations (UN)** Convention against Torture (1984/1987), and the European Convention on Human Rights (1950/1953)—and is implemented through a complex asylum procedure law (Asylverfahrensgesetz), which grants different categories of protection, usually depending on the reason for asylum, and accords distinct privileges (such as length of stay and the right to be joined by family members). The categories include the right of asylum (Asylberechtigung), refugee protection (Flüchtlingsschutz), "subsidiary protection" (subsidärer Schutz, applicable where the situation in the country of origin renders return impossible), and non-refoulement or prohibition of deportation (Abschiebungsverbot; e.g., to a country that routinely practices torture). In 2014, relatively few applications for asylum were granted through the BL (1.8 percent). War-torn Syria accounted for 30 percent of applicants (mainly granted), while 30 percent (mainly rejected) came from the Balkans (Serbia, Kosovo, Macedonia, Bosnia-Herzegovina, Albania). Despite the high rejection rates, political and practical obstacles meant that only around 15 percent of rejected asylum applicants were actually deported or returned home.

Since the first Dublin Convention (agreed to in 1990; effective in 1997), efforts—largely unsuccessful—have been under way to harmonize asylum policy at **European Union (EU)** level, and the system came under severe strain in the crisis year of 2015, as large numbers of refugees fled civil war in North Africa and the Middle East. To the disappointment of Interior Minister **Thomas de Maizière**, EU leaders failed in 2015 to adopt a proposal by Germany (a favorite destination for refugees and expected to receive 800,000 by the end of the year) to distribute significant volumes of asylum seekers across EU countries according to their population and economic strength. In addition, 50,000 refugees were expected to use Germany as a transit country to other parts of the EU, not to mention thousands of EU citizens (Roma from Romania, young Greeks and Spaniards seeking work) not recorded as refugees. Many incomers enter Germany as tourists before claiming asylum, although most such applications are rejected. In any case, the influx of 2015 imposed a heavy burden of accommodation, housing, and (for children) **education** on the German state, in particular the local districts (Kommunen), which are not necessarily reimbursed by regional government. While most Germans are sympathetic to the plight of refugees, violent attacks on foreigners and their places of accommodation became commonplace in 2015, especially in eastern Germany.

As Germany opened its borders to asylum seekers in 2015, Chancellor **Angela Merkel (Christian Democratic Union, CDU)** appointed Frank-Jürgen Weise, the head of the Federal Employment Agency (Bundesagentur für Arbeit), to head the Federal Office for Migration and Refugees (Bundesamt für Migration und Flüchtlinge), which had been swiftly expanded to process asylum applications more rapidly and integrate successful applicants into education and work. Merkel's personal "welcome" for refugees, in particular Syrians, which circumvented the normal procedures of entry, was accompanied by an emergency program of financial aid to the **federal states**, but it was also criticized by some conservative politicians, notably from the **Christian Social Union (CSU)**, the CDU's sister party.

See also FOREIGNERS; IMMIGRATION; POPULATION AND PEO-PLE; SCHENGEN AGREEMENT.

AUDI AG. Audi AG, with headquarters in Ingolstadt/**Bavaria** and owned by **Volkswagen AG**, is one of Germany's leading automobile manufacturers. The company originated in 1899 when August Horch (1868–1951) founded A. Horch & Cie in Cologne-Ehrenfeld and built his first motor vehicle (1901). The following year he relocated to eastern Germany, eventually moving to Zwickau, where he established the A. Horch & Cie. Motorwagen-Werke AG (1904). In 1909, following a dispute with the supervisory board, he left the company to set up a rival concern. A disagreement over the title was settled by translating his name (Horch) into Latin, resulting in the founding of the Audiwerke GmbH (1910). During the 1920s and 1930s the Audi works, whose headquarters were relocated to Chemnitz (1936), became the world's largest manufacturer of motorcycles, producing the famous DKW model. Audi also launched a successful small automobile with innovative front-wheel drive and won a world record in motor racing (1937). During World War II, production was redirected exclusively to meet the demands of the Wehrmacht. In 1945, the Soviet occupation authorities dismantled the entire Audi plant as reparations; hitherto known as Auto Union AG, Chemnitz, it ceased to exist by 1948.

With financial aid from the Bavarian government and the postwar **Marshall Plan** fund, the Auto Union GmbH was refounded in Ingolstadt (1949). Production of motorcycles and automobiles resumed, and the following year a subsidiary plant was opened on the premises of Rheinmetall-Borsig AG in Düsseldorf, where DKWs continued to be made until 1961. In the late 1950s, at the instigation of **Friedrich Karl Flick**, Audi became a fully owned subsidiary of Daimler-Benz AG, which offloaded it in 1966 after it had become a successful competitor. In 1969, the concern merged with the Neckarsulmer Strickmaschinen Union (NSU) to create Audi-NSU. NSU was founded in 1873 as a manufacturer of knitting machines before moving in 1880 to Neckarsulm (now in **Baden-Württemberg**), where it began producing motorcycles and, under the NSU brand name from 1905, motor vehicles. In 1965, Audi passed into the control of Volkswagen and in 1985 was renamed Audi AG. In 2015, the company reported a turnover of more than 58,400 million euros and produced 1.8 million vehicles with a workforce of around 82,800 (more than 58,300 in Germany). Rupert Stadler became chief executive in 2010.

See also AUTOMOBILE INDUSTRY.

AUFBAU OST. The term Aufbau Ost (literally "construction east") refers to the program for the economic and social reconstruction of the **eastern federal states** of the former **German Democratic Republic (GDR)**. The program consists primarily of the **German Unity Fund** (1990–1994) and **Solidarity Pacts I** and **II** (1995–2004 and 2005–2019). The need for a large-scale project of rebuilding and regeneration arose from the poor state of the economy and infrastructure in eastern Germany after reunification (3 October 1990). Seen as a national government priority, the program was coordinated by the Federal Ministry of Transport, Building, and Housing, which in 2002 set up a special Aufbau Ost department (Aufbau Ost, Raumordnung, und Strukturpolitik). In July 1997, the **federal government** presented its first report on the status of German unity (*Bericht zum Stand der Deutschen Einheit*), and from 2002 progress reports were submitted annually to the **Bundestag.** In June 2004, Economics Minister **Wolfgang Clement** and Transport Minister **Manfred Stolpe** commissioned a study by the GO group (Gesprächskreis Ost, discussion group east), which involved 16 experts from politics, labor, and industry led by the former governing mayor of **Hamburg, Klaus von Dohnanyi.** The study argued for improved government coordination of the Aufbau Ost program and, more controversially, a shift away from subventions in favor of creating a more competitive manufacturing base by facilitating access to investment, credit, and capital. Some members of the group distanced themselves from the report, and its recommendations were largely ignored. Despite expansion in manufacturing and processing, by 2013 continuing high unemployment rates in the new **Länder** indicated that economic convergence between eastern and western Germany was still a long way off. The total costs of Aufbau Ost are estimated at 82,200 million euros (for the Unity Fund), 94,500 million euros (for Solidarity Pact I), and 156,000 million euros (for Solidarity Pact II).

See also SOLIDARITY SURCHARGE (SOLIDARITÄTSZUSCHLAG); UPSWING EAST (AUFSCHWUNG OST).

AUGSTEIN, RUDOLF (1923–2002). Journalist and publisher. Rudolf Augstein was born in Hanover (**Lower Saxony**), the son of a photographic equipment dealer. After leaving school, he worked briefly in a local newspaper before serving in the German army during World War II. Wounded at the eastern front, he ended the war in U.S. captivity before returning to Hanover, where, as a journalist, he wrote reports that were critical of the British occupation authorities. In 1946, he cofounded and edited the weekly news magazine *Die Woche*, which appeared under license in the British zone. Renamed *Der Spiegel* (1947), the Hamburg-based magazine acquired a reputation for independent, analytical journalism. It became a national institution and key political opinion former in the postwar Federal Republic of Germany

(FRG), and its circulation climbed from 65,000 to over five million at the end of the 1990s, with Augstein publishing weekly commentaries on political and social events.

In 1962, the police occupied *Der Spiegel*'s premises and arrested Augstein and fellow journalists on suspicion of treason after the magazine published a critical report on Fallex 62, a military exercise by the **North Atlantic Treaty Organization** (**NATO**). The article's author, Conrad Ahlers (who later became a government spokesman), was arrested in Spain at the behest of the German authorities. Augstein himself spent three months in prison, but was released following a public outcry and cross-party outrage. Defense Minister **Franz Josef Strauß**, against whom the magazine had conducted a long campaign and who later admitted responsibility for the actions, was forced to resign, along with five ministers of the **Free Democratic Party** (**FDP**). A new government was formed, and the affair marked the beginning of the end of **Konrad Adenauer**'s chancellorship. The "*Spiegel* affair" became ingrained in the national collective memory as a watershed in consolidating press freedom and democracy.

Although it later emerged that *Der Spiegel* had engaged former members of the National Socialist Party in its early years, the magazine was regarded as a bastion of probity, free speech, and democracy. In 1984, it uncovered the payments-for-favors scandal involving FDP politicians and the industrialist **Friedrich Karl Flick.** It supported **Willy Brandt**'s policy of reconciliation toward Eastern Europe during the 1970s, and in 1989–1990 it backed German reunification. Augstein briefly entered the **Bundestag** as a member of the FDP, but resigned his mandate after just 44 days. *Der Spiegel* was also the first major news magazine to create its own website (beating *Time* magazine by one day). Not until 1993, with the launch of *Focus* in Munich, did a rival format publication emerge. In 2000, Augstein was elected "journalist of the century." A self-confessed cynic, Augstein published widely on politics, but he also wrote poems and compiled a history of Prussia. Following his death in November 2002, Chancellor **Gerhard Schröder** paid tribute to him at a special press conference.

AUSSIEDLER/SPÄTAUSSIEDLER. Aussiedler (literally "outsettlers") are persons of German nationality or ethnicity who lived beyond the eastern boundaries of present-day Germany (i.e., in Poland; beyond the Oder–Neiße rivers; or in the former Soviet Union, Czechoslovakia, Hungary, or Romania) before the end of World War II and who either left these areas or who were forcibly expelled as a result of the conflict. Legally entitled to return to the Federal Republic of Germany (FRG) as German citizens, many returnees were descendants of Germans who had emigrated to the east as early as the 18th century. In the first, and largest, wave of migration between 1945 and 1949/1950, 12–14 million German refugees (estimates vary) moved westward to settle within the boundaries of what in 1949 became the FRG and the **German Democratic Republic (GDR)**. The influx amounted to 20 percent of the total population (45 percent in the case of **Mecklenburg-West Pomerania**) and permanently changed the national demography in terms of social balance, religion, and the labor force. While the incomers initially encountered widespread hostility in a time of postwar hardship, they were eventually integrated into existing structures and, in West Germany, boosted the workforce in the early stages of the economic recovery.

The term "Aussiedler" originated in a 1953 law on expellees (Bundesvertriebenengesetz) but gained currency following the **Ostpolitik** treaties that were concluded between West Germany and eastern bloc states in the 1970s and, among other things, facilitated the return of disadvantaged German minorities. By 1987, a further 1.4 million ethnic Germans had entered the FRG on this basis, and with the end of the Cold War the annual influx rose sharply, to 200,000 (1988) and 400,000 (1990). The legislation on expellees was originally based on the presumption of persecution of ethnic Germans, but with the liberalization of Eastern Europe and in the face of increasing numbers, the government introduced annual quota limits (220,000 in 1993, reduced to around 100,000 in 2000), alongside a language test (from 1996) and a lengthy questionnaire. Between 1991 and 2006, a total of 1.9 million Aussiedler and their relatives entered Germany (mainly from the Soviet Union), although the annual figure fell to below 6,000 in 2007. Since 1950, a total of 4.5 million returnees, including family members, have been repatriated.

From January 1993, returnees were officially referred to as Spätaussiedler ("late outsettlers"), and in 2010 the law was changed to restrict the right to return to persons born before the end of 1992. Often with little or no German, returnees received state assistance on integration, including accommodation, language courses, education, and vocational retraining. Alone among immigrant groups, they enjoyed from the very beginning a legal status fully equivalent to that of existing German nationals. East German nationals who moved to the FRG before reunification (1990) were referred to as Übersiedler ("resettlers") and automatically received West German citizenship.

See also IMMIGRATION.

AUTOMOBILE INDUSTRY. Alongside **chemicals** and **engineering**, motor vehicle manufacturing has been a key **industry** in Germany for several decades and accounts for 25 percent of industrial turnover. Of around 790,000 workers employed in the sector, more than 390,000 are directly involved in manufacturing, while the rest are engaged in subsidiary businesses, ranging from components, accessories, chemicals, and textiles to sales, servicing, and fuel. More recently, automobile manufacturing in Germany has undergone far-reaching structural changes in response to international competition, with companies cutting production costs, relocating production abroad, sourcing materials and components globally, reducing the number of suppliers, forming strategic alliances with competitors, and introducing advanced technologies in production and assembly. Although traditional centers of domestic manufacturing, such as Wolfsburg (**Volkswagen AG**), Cologne and Saarlouis (Ford), the Stuttgart area (**Daimler AG**/Mercedes-Benz and **Porsche**), Rüsselsheim (Opel), and **Bavaria** (**AUDI AG, BMW AG**), remain intact, modern new plants have opened up in eastern Germany, for example in Leipzig (BMW), Eisenach (Opel), Zwickau, Chemnitz, and Dresden (VW). Manufacturing and supply have also transferred to eastern/central Europe and Asia. In 2015, German companies manufactured more than 15 million automobiles worldwide, of which 5.7 million were built in Germany. Domestic plants have focused on niche markets and on developing variants of existing models, such as all-terrain vehicles and convertibles. Germany currently ranks fourth in automobile production, behind China, the United States, and Japan. The umbrella organization for the industry is the VDA (Verband der Automobilindustrie), which has existed under its current name since 1946.

See also ENGINEERING; PIËCH, FERDINAND (1937–); QUANDT FAMILY.

AWARDS AND PRIZES. Germany offers several hundred different prizes and awards for cultural contributions at the municipal, federal, and national levels. Cultural areas covered are **literature**, **architecture**, the arts, **television and radio**, peace initiatives, **theater**, music, and **cinema**. Literary prizes are often named after famous 19th- and 20th-century writers (e.g., Alfred Döblin, Erich Maria Remarque, Friedrich Hölderlin, and Theodor Fontane). One of the most renowned is the Georg Büchner Prize. There are also special awards for particular subject areas, such as the spoken word (Deutscher Hörbuch-Preis) and youth literature. The Echo, established in 1992, is now considered the world's second most important award for musical achievements after the U.S. Grammys. First celebrated in **Hamburg**, the award event is now held in **Berlin** on the grounds that the city was home to five of Germany's leading music companies. The Adolf Grimme Award is considered the highest award for contributions to television. Its categories cover information and culture, fiction entertainment, and "special"; it is awarded in Marl, in the northern part of the Ruhr. Award winners include Dieter Zimmer, Ulrich Tukur, Katharina Thalbach, Lea Rosh, Jürgen Flimm, Herbert Grönemeyer, and Peter Hamm.

Traditionally, German scientists and scholars measured their reputation primarily in terms of publications and the acquisition of a second doctorate (Habilitation). During the 1990s, however, in response to the internationalization of scientific research and a growing interest in technological innovation, the number of new awards, prizes, scholarships, and fellowships available to academics and researchers in Germany increased dramatically. To some extent, the trend reflected a convergence with Anglo-Saxon academic traditions. By 2005, around 2,400 prizes and research scholarships were being regularly awarded by 600 sponsors, mainly for medicine, natural sciences, and technology, followed by arts, humanities, and social sciences. For a full directory of prizes and scholarships, see Hermann and Späth (2005).

AXEL SPRINGER SE. Founded by **Axel Springer** in 1946 as the Axel Springer Verlag GmbH, this concern went on to become Germany's largest single newspaper publishing house. It is now a leading international **media** concern, with centers in **Hamburg** and Munich, and headquarters in **Berlin**, a city that Springer, a fierce anticommunist, supported throughout his life on ideological grounds. Core activities are (for the German and foreign markets) printed newspapers (including the national daily *Die Welt* and the tabloid *BILD*, earlier, *Bild-Zeitung*), journals, and magazines (e.g., *Computer Bild, Auto BIL+D*); domestic and foreign digital media, including holdings in **television** production and radio; and a services/holding segment, which includes newspaper printing, logistics, and distribution. The concern is present in 34 countries, with the main foreign markets being France, Spain, Switzerland, and eastern Europe (including Poland, Hungary, the Czech and Slovak Republics, Serbia, and Russia), and expansion is under way in India. Overall, Springer produces more than 230 newspapers and magazines, over 140 offline offerings, and 120 apps. Turnover in 2015 was more than 3,300 million euros, and its workforce numbered more than 15,000.

During the social tensions in Germany during the 1960s and 1970s, the antiliberal policies of the company's founder—reflected in his opposition to **Ostpolitik** and in the fierce criticism of the students' movement by the flagship tabloid, now *BILD*—made it a target of violent attacks by extremists. A notorious incident was the bombing of the Hamburg publishing house in 1972, which injured 17 staff members. Responding to the findings of a government commission on press concentration, the company, which controlled 39 percent of newspapers and 18 percent of magazines in Germany, sold off some popular magazines (1968). Although unsuccessful in buying the television channel Zweites Deutsches Fernsehen (ZDF) in 1965, Springer moved into regional newspapers and specialist journals in the 1970s. When Axel Springer died in 1985, fierce battles erupted over control of the company, involving his family heirs and the major shareholders, the **Burda** brothers and later, **Leo Kirch**. After a brief truce between 1990 and 1994, Springer, led by chief executive Jürgen Richter (1994–1997), acquired a 40 percent share of the Kirch-owned Sat.1 television channel, but Richter was eventually forced to resign, and the conflict did not end until the Kirch concern collapsed in 2002. From the mid-1980s, the company produced new variations of its popular *Bild-Zeitung* (*Bild der Frau*, *Sport Bild*, *Auto Bild*, *Computer Bild*); invested abroad; expanded its television holdings; and moved into studio production and, most recently, digital media. The **Internet** bookshop Booxtra was launched in 1999. In slimming down its portfolio during 2002–2003, Axel Springer AG offloaded its book publishing operations (Ullstein Heyne List and Weltkunst Verlag GmbH) and a number of television production companies. An attempt to take over the ProSiebenSat.1 television group (in which Springer acquired a 11.5 percent stake in 2000) was vetoed by the Federal Cartel Office in 2006 following a renewed public debate over pluralism in media ownership. In 2014, the office approved the planned sale of several printed publications (including the news dailies *Berliner Morgenpost* and *Hamburger Abendblatt*, the women's magazine *Bild der Frau*, and TV magazines *Hörzu* [*Hör zu* up until 1972] and *TV Digital*) to the Funke media group in order to develop the digital side of the business. In 2013, Springer completed its transformation into a European registered company (Societas Europaea, or SE).

The concern's chief executive (appointed in 2002) is Mathias Döpfner. Born in 1963, Döpfner studied music, German literature, and theater in Frankfurt and Boston. He worked as a journalist for the *Frankfurter Allgemeine Zeitung* (from 1982) and managed a public relations agency (1988–1990) before joining the staff of the executive board of the publishers Gruner + Jahr in Paris (1992). He was chief editor for the *Berliner Wochenpost* (1994–1996), the *Hamburger Morgenpost* (1996–1998), and Springer's *Die Welt* (from 1998), before moving to the executive board in 2000. Controlling shareholders remain the Springer family.

AXEN, HERMANN (1916–1992). German Democratic Republic (GDR) politician. Born in Leipzig, Hermann Axen joined the youth wing of the Communist Party of Germany (KPD, 1932) at age 16 and worked underground for the party after the National Socialist takeover (1933). He fled to France (1938), was arrested by the Gestapo (1940), and returned to Germany, where he spent the remainder of World War II in prisons and concentration camps. After the war, he became secretary of the central council of the communist youth organization in eastern Germany, the Free German Youth (Freie Deutsche Jugend, FDJ), which he cofounded alongside **Erich Honecker**. As a veteran Communist in the postwar GDR, he joined the Central Committee of the **Socialist Unity Party of Germany** (**SED**, 1950) and headed the party's propaganda department (1949–1953). He was also a member of the **People's Chamber** (from 1950). From 1953 until 1956, he was deputy leader of the East Berlin regional SED, before becoming chief editor of the party's newspaper, *Neues Deutschland* (1966). He was also Central Committee secretary for international relations and headed the parliamentary committee of the People's Chamber responsible for foreign affairs (from

1971). Appointed a candidate member of the Politburo of the SED in 1963 and a full member in 1970, Axen was one of the party's most powerful and influential figures. After the regime collapsed in 1989, he was dismissed from the Politburo (8 November) and fled to Moscow. Returning in January 1990, he was imprisoned, charged with misuse of office and corruption, but was released in February on health grounds. An autobiographical account of his life and work in the SED (*Ich war ein Diener der Partei*) appeared in 1996.

B

BADEN-WÜRTTEMBERG. Germany's third largest **federal state** in terms of area (35,751 sq. km), population (10.6 million), and contribution to national GDP (15 percent in 2015), Baden-Württemberg lies in the southwest of the country. The valley of the **Rhine** River marks the border with France to the west, while Lake Constance (Bodensee), Germany's largest lake, separates the region from Switzerland and Austria in the south; to the east lies **Bavaria**. The landscape is varied, with the Black Forest (Schwarzwald) in the southwest (including Baden-Württemberg's highest peak, the 1,494-m-high Feldberg) and the low mountain chain of the Schwäbische Alb (highest peak: Lemberg, 1,015 m). To the north and east are hills and farmland, the Hohenlohe Plain and the forested areas of the Central Uplands (the Swabian Forest). The landscape is interrupted by fertile regions, called Gaue. Apart from the Rhine and the Danube, which rises near Donaueschingen in the Black Forest, the region's main rivers include the Neckar and its tributaries. Baden-Württemberg enjoys some of the warmest temperatures in Germany, and its **agriculture** supports fruit, wine, and specialist horticulture, including hops, cabbage, and asparagus.

Until the early 19th century, the region was fragmented into petty states, which are still reflected in a dense network of churches, monasteries, castles, residences, towns, and villages. A complex history has produced a juxtaposition of Protestant/Calvinist spheres of influence (such as Württemberg) alongside Roman Catholic areas to the south (Upper Swabia). The confessional division still manifests itself in voting patterns. Perceived cultural differences between the more liberal, easygoing inhabitants of Baden (along the Rhine) and the hardworking, thrifty, and devout citizens of Protestant north Württemberg (commonly referred to as "Swabians") have persisted into modern times. Surrounded by hills and mountains, Württemberg, with its capital, Stuttgart, nurtured a powerful middle class, while Roman Catholic peasant farmers farther south (Upper Swabia) developed traditions of independence and self-sufficiency. The combination of a lack of natural raw materials and the late development of **transport** infrastructure proved the perfect crucible for a mixture of political conservatism, self-determination, and economic innovation, for which the region's inhabitants are still known.

Reflecting past territorial divisions, the cities of Stuttgart (north Württemberg), Tübingen (south Württemberg and Hohenzollern), Karlsruhe (north Baden), and Freiburg (south Baden) became main administrative centers when the federal state of Baden-Württemberg was created in 1952. Reforms during the 1970s reduced the number of smaller districts (Kreise and Gemeinden), blurring many of the historical distinctions. Nevertheless, Baden-Württemberg remains a region of small communities, of which 80 percent have fewer than 10,000 inhabitants. The decentralized tradition is reflected in a duplication of cultural services, such as state libraries, museums, art galleries, theaters, and opera houses (e.g., in Stuttgart and Karlsruhe, both of which were former capital cities). Stuttgart has an international opera and ballet, while Mannheim is renowned for its theater house (Nationaltheater Mannheim).

Industry is decentralized, diversified, and export oriented and relies heavily on technical expertise and innovation. The main activities are **engineering**, motor vehicle manufacturing (**Daimler, Audi**, and **Porsche**), and electronics, followed by finishing and processing industries (textiles, wood, and synthetic materials). Service industries are relatively weak, and the region lacked a major bank until the creation, through mergers, of the Landesbank Baden-Württemberg (LBW, 1999). Small to medium-sized businesses, often family owned, predominate. Unemployment is among the lowest in the federal states (3.8 percent in 2015, compared with the national average of 6.4 percent), and the proportion of **foreigners**, especially in Stuttgart and other major cities, is high, at 14.3 percent (national average: 11.2 percent in 2015). Baden-Württemberg's reputation for leading-edge industry is underpinned by an **educational** system known for its excellence. There are several universities, including the historic foundations of Heidelberg, Freiburg, and Tübingen, and numerous colleges and institutions of higher and further education. In 1998, the broadcasting stations Süddeutscher Rundfunk (SDR) and the Südwestfunk (SWF) merged to form the Südwestrundfunk (SWR), which broadcasts across both Baden-Württemberg and neighboring **Rhineland-Palatinate** and is the second largest station in the ARD **television and radio** network. The region, especially around Karlsruhe, is also a center for publishing (books and specialist magazines) and multimedia.

Baden-Württemberg's constitution provides for a parliament (**Landtag**) with, following the election of 2016, 143 members (the number may vary with so-called overhang mandates). In 2008, the Landtag agreed to reforms designed to improve its public image: deputies' salaries were raised and expenses regulated to increase the proportion of full-time politicians and provide financial transparency, and members could no longer combine public employment with parliamentary office. Parliamentary business was also changed to allow greater questioning of ministers, and constituency boundaries were drawn more fairly. In parliament, so-called **state secretaries** (Staatssekretäre) and Staatsräte act as ministerial advisers. These may be members of the regional government, although they may not exceed one-third of the complement of ministers and do not necessarily have voting rights. Over the years, the constitution has been modified to enhance the right of petition, increase the power of investigative committees, and give the Landtag a voice in **European Union (EU)** issues where regional interests are at stake. The constitution provides for elements of direct democracy (plebiscites), although these have rarely taken place.

For most of the region's postwar history, the dominant political party has been the **Christian Democratic Union (CDU)**, which provided minister presidents from 1953 until 2011: Gebhard Müller (1953–1958), **Kurt Georg Kiesinger** (1958–1966), **Hans Filbinger** (1966–1978), **Lothar Späth** (1978–1991), **Erwin Teufel** (1991–2005), **Günther Oettinger** (2005–2010), and **Stefan Mappus** (2010–2011). During 1966–1972 and 1992–1996, the CDU ruled in a **grand coalition** with the **Social Democratic Party of Germany (SPD)**, although it commanded an absolute majority in the intervening period. Between 1996 and 2011, the party governed in coalition with the **Free Democratic Party (FDP)** and in 2006 fell one seat short of an absolute majority. The 2011 election saw a historic result for the **Alliance 90/The Greens**, which drove the SPD into third place. Key factors were public anxiety over the implications of the Fukushima atomic reactor catastrophe and the party's opposition to the controversial Stuttgart 21 railway expansion project (started in 2010, this costly undertaking involves a major rebuilding of Stuttgart's main railway station, the construction of nine tunnels up to 55 km, and 57 km in new rail links in and around the city). Although the CDU remained the strongest party, it was forced into opposition for the first time in 58 years, and the FDP barely cleared the 5 percent hurdle. The outcome was a Greens/SPD coalition, with the Green candidate, **Winfried Kretschmann**, as minister president. The SPD's long-standing weakness has been attributed to religious factors, distrust of centralist parties, and the value attached to local personal networks; even working-class voters tend to define themselves in terms of their local village or community and eschew social change. In local politics, the mayor (Bürgermeister) is a powerful figure: he or she is directly elected by constituents for eight years and tends to have at best a loose link to a political party (other states have since followed the model of direct election, which for many years existed only in Baden-Württemberg and Bavaria). Mayoral office is often a springboard to a political career at the regional (Land) level. Regional elections in 2016 resulted in unprecedented losses for the CDU (from 39 to 27 percent of votes), with the populist **Alternative for Germany (AfD)** entering parliament (15.1 percent). The

Greens (30.3 percent) won most votes and formed a green-black "Kiwi coalition" with the CDU, the first in the history of the FRG. Kretschmann continued as minister president.

BAHR, EGON KARL-HEINZ (1922–2015). Journalist and **Social Democratic Party of Germany (SPD)** politician. Born in Treffurt/Werra **(Thuringia)**, in 1940 Egon Bahr was prevented from studying music because his grandmother was Jewish. After completing commercial training in industry, he served as a soldier in the German army (1942–1944), then worked briefly for the armaments manufacturer Rheinmetall-Borsig. After 1945, he began a career as a journalist in **Berlin** and from 1948 to 1950 was correspondent for the *Tagesspiegel* newspaper in **Hamburg** and Bonn, before joining Radio in the American Sector (RIAS) as chief commentator. Between 1953 and 1954, he led the RIAS office in Bonn. He joined the SPD in 1956 and was appointed by **Willy Brandt**, mayor of West Berlin, as head of the city's press and information office (1960).

After the low point of the erection of the **Berlin Wall** in August 1961, Bahr worked closely with Brandt to develop a new foreign policy that aimed to improve relations with the **German Democratic Republic (GDR)** and the eastern bloc. Bahr announced the new thinking in a landmark speech to the Evangelical Academy in Tutzing (July 1963), arguing for a gradual change in international relations through rapprochement (Wandel durch Annäherung). Later known as "the new eastern policy" (die Neue Ostpolitik, or simply **Ostpolitik**), the tangible fruits of the strategy were a series of treaties concluded with member states of the Soviet bloc during the 1970s that reduced the political and military tensions of the Cold War and promoted trade and cooperation between Eastern and Western Europe. Bahr played a key role in both formulating the strategy for détente and conducting the complex and exhausting negotiations that accompanied the process. He held the position of ministerial director (Ministerialdirektor), a politically appointed senior civil servant, in the Federal Ministry for Foreign Affairs, where he also led the strategic planning department and served as a special envoy (1966–1969).

From 1969 until his resignation in 1990, Bahr represented the SPD in the **Bundestag**. With responsibility for Berlin (Bundesbevollmächtigter) and as federal minister for special tasks (1972–1974), Bahr was prominent as Brandt's key adviser in all aspects of Ostpolitik. With Michael Kohl, GDR state secretary, he signed two important treaties on behalf of the FRG in 1972. The first was the Treaty on Traffic (Verkehrsvertrag), which regulated traffic and transport arrangements between East and West Germany, including West Berlin. The second, the Treaty on Basic Relations (Grundlagenvertrag), pledged both states to respect each other's frontiers, exchange permanent representatives (ambassadors in all but name), and promote intra-German trade. To set the formal seal on the normalization of relations, the FRG and GDR would both apply for membership in the **United Nations (UN)**. In recognition of his services to détente, Bahr received Germany's highest honor, the Federal Cross of Merit (1973 and, with additional honors, 1975).

After the achievements of Ostpolitik and following Brandt's resignation (1974), Bahr shifted the focus of his political activities. As minister for economic cooperation under Chancellor **Helmut Schmidt** (1974–1976), he worked to improve aid for developing nations, believing that a fair global economy was the best basis for world peace. As SPD party manager (1976–1981), he fended off attacks from the party's radical left wing but distanced himself from the chancellor's support for the "dual track" decision (1979). This decision, by which the **North Atlantic Treaty Organization (NATO)** undertook to deploy American intermediate-range nuclear forces (INF) in Western Europe by 1983 unless the Soviet Union negotiated the removal of similar SS20 missiles, triggered widespread protests and boosted the West German peace movement. Bahr himself became increasingly committed to disarmament and reducing the nuclear threat. He chaired a parliamentary subcommittee on disarmament and arms control (1980–1990) and consistently argued for a greater German say on the nuclear issue. On a visit to Moscow (June 1981), he publicly expressed doubts about U.S. readiness to limit the spread of atomic weapons in Europe. As a member of the Independent Commission on Disarmament and Security Issues (the Palme Commission, chaired by the then Swedish premier Olaf Palme), Bahr supported its final report (1982), which advocated a nuclear weapon-free zone in Europe. On meeting the GDR leader, **Erich Honecker** (1983), Bahr declared that the stationing of U.S. medium-range nuclear weapons in West Germany would provoke countermeasures by the Soviet Union on East German soil.

As director of the Institute for Peace Research at the University of Hamburg (1984–1994), Bahr published widely on peace and security issues. As adviser to **Rainer Eppelmann**, the minister for disarmament and defense in the interim GDR government (from July 1990), he argued that it would not be in a united Germany's best interests to join NATO. After reunification, Bahr proposed the establishment of a "German peace corps," in which citizens would be able to serve in place of national military service in the **Bundeswehr** (1991). When the Yugoslav federation began to disintegrate, Bahr advocated an economic boycott of the region (1991), supported the deployment of Bundeswehr troops on active peacekeeping missions within the framework of the UN (1992), and argued for an expansion of the **European Union (EU)** to include eastern European states. Despite his commitment to peace and disarmament, Bahr, in a controversial speech in 1999, supported the setting up of a European security system in which Germany would play its full part and, if necessary, intervene militarily to protect minorities. He also opposed the expansion of NATO. In 1996, Bahr published his memoirs under the title *Zu meiner Zeit* (In My Time).

BAHRO, RUDOLF (1935–1997). German Democratic Republic (GDR) dissident and social scientist. Bahro was born the son of a farmer in Bad Flinsberg (Silesia, now in Poland). At the end of World War II, he fled to eastern Germany and grew up in the GDR, where he became a candidate member of the ruling **Socialist Unity Party of Germany (SED,** 1952) and later a full member (1954). He studied philosophy at Humboldt University in **Berlin** (1954–1959), worked for a newspaper in Oderbruch (**Brandenburg**) writing propaganda material for the collectivization of **agriculture** (1959–1960), and edited the Greifswald University newspaper (1960–1962). He also worked for the executive board of a **trade union** for academics and scientists in Berlin (Gewerkschaft Wissenschaft, 1962–1965) and was deputy chief editor of a student magazine (*Forum*) published by the national youth organization Freie Deutsche Jugend (FDJ, 1965–1967). For 10 years (1967–1977), he headed a department organizing work in a large Berlin rubber factory.

From 1972 to 1975, Bahro worked on a doctoral dissertation for the Technical University for Chemistry in Leuna-Merseburg on the role of the SED in higher **education** and state-run industrial concerns, but it was rejected for lack of ideological conformity. Between 1973 and 1976, he also worked on a manuscript for a book, *Die Alternative. Zur Kritik des real existierenden Sozialismus*, which criticized the political and economic system of the GDR from a Marxist perspective. When the book appeared in the Federal Republic of Germany (FRG) in 1977 and Bahro publicly commented on it on West German television, he was arrested, expelled from the SED, and sentenced to eight years' imprisonment for treasonable activities and collecting secret information (1978). The defense lawyer at his trial was **Gregor Gysi,** whom Bahro later defended against charges of working against his own client's interests (1995–1996). Bahro's book was widely distributed among dissident groups in the GDR; translated into several languages; and became a key text for advocates of the "third way," which aimed to combine the economic advantages of socialism with the democratic principles of a liberal political system. A number of leading figures, including the author **Heinrich Böll,** campaigned for his release, and he received several international honors, including the Carl von Ossietzky medal of the International League for **Human Rights** and membership in the Swedish and Danish **PEN** Club.

Amnestied and exiled to West Germany in 1979, Bahro cofounded the **Green Party** (1980) and was a member of its national executive committee (1982–1984), but left the party in 1985. In the West, he completed his doctorate on work conditions under "real existing socialism" ("real existierender

Sozialismus," University of Hanover, 1980) and held academic posts at the universities of Hanover, **Bremen**, and Berlin. He argued for a new policy based on the relationship between the **environment** and socialism; spent four weeks with members of the Bhagwan movement in Oregon, U.S. (1983); and published a book setting out the need for industrial societies to avoid ecological disaster by adopting environmentally friendly policies (1987).

After the fall of the GDR, Bahro returned to East Berlin (1989), where he was officially rehabilitated (1990). In **Saxony**, he founded a group dedicated to leading an alternative lifestyle through ecological farming, which he hoped would lead to reform of society as a whole. He continued to publish articles arguing for environmental policies to head off global destruction. From 1990 until his death, Bahro held a personal chair as professor for social ecology at Humboldt University in Berlin.

BALANCE OF PAYMENTS. The balance of payments (Zahlungsbilanz) is the balance of all financial transactions between Germany and the rest of the world. It is made up of the current account (Leistungsbilanz), the capital or financial account (Kapitalbilanz), and the foreign exchange account (Devisenbilanz). The current account includes the balance of foreign **trade** (Handelsbilanz), the balance on services (Dienstleistungsbilanz, mainly "invisible" services related to the **tourism**/travel **industry** and **transport**), and the transfers account (Übertragungsbilanz, including development aid, contributions to international organizations, and transfers made by migrant workers). While the capital account records the inward/outward flows of capital and investments, the foreign exchange account registers the status of gold and foreign **currency** holdings of the **German Federal Bank**. Germany's exporting success has contributed to consistent surpluses in its current account and overall balance of payments, even during challenging international conditions between 2007 and 2012. Negative figures traditionally occur for invisible services (for instance in 2001 and 2002) and for capital transfers when German companies are investing heavily abroad. Updates on and analyses of the balance of payments are available from the German Federal Bank and the World Bank.

BALTIC SEA (OSTSEE). The German Baltic Sea coast stretches for 2,247 kilometers (including the coasts of offshore islands), of which 535 kilometers are in **Schleswig-Holstein** and 1,712 are in **Mecklenburg-West Pomerania**. About 70 percent of the area is made up of inner coastal waters, that is, inlets, spits, lagoons (so-called Haffs or Bodden, depending on origin), river estuaries, and narrow channels between islands. In contrast to the **North Sea**, and owing to the proximity of neighboring states, the exclusive economic zone off the Baltic coast (where Germany has rights of scientific research and economic exploitation as well as obligations of environmental protection) extends only marginally beyond the 12-sea-mile limit of national territorial waters. The largest of the offshore islands is Rügen (926 sq. km), followed by Usedom (445 sq. km, part of which belongs to Poland), and Fehmarn (185.4 sq. km). With its mixture of cliffs and broad, sandy beaches, Mecklenburg-West Pomerania's coast became a popular tourist destination during the 19th century. Of the area's numerous seaside resorts and spas, the oldest is Heiligendamm, founded in 1793, and the first town in Germany to host the G8 summit (2007). Alongside fine villas, many coastal towns have piers, often equipped with restaurants, cafés, and leisure facilities.

The Baltic is linked to the North Sea by a canal running for 100 kilometers between Kiel in the east and Brunsbüttel in the west. Busier, in numbers of ships handled, than even the Panama and Suez Canals, the North Sea–Baltic Canal (formerly the Kaiser-Wilhelm Canal and renamed in 1948) provides a vital transport link for the port of **Hamburg** and the states bordering the Baltic (Denmark, Sweden, Finland, Estonia, Latvia, Lithuania, Poland, and Russia); for these countries the canal is also the fastest and shortest sea link to world markets. With the canal's enlargement in 2004, the **European Union** (**EU**) acquired in the Baltic virtually its own inland sea. Following an initiative supported by the Federal Ministry for Foreign Affairs and Hamburg, a "Baltic Network" (Ostsee-Netzwerk) was established as part of an EU strategy agreed to in 2009 to develop the region's economic potential, while preserving its environmental balance and diversity.

BANGEMANN, MARTIN (1934–). Free Democratic Party (FDP) politician and former civil servant. Martin Bangemann was born in Wanzleben (**Saxony-Anhalt**). After studying law and earning a doctorate at the University of Munich, he practiced as a lawyer in Metzingen (**Baden-Württemberg**). He joined the FDP in 1963 and took a leading role in the so-called Freiburg Program, in which the party set out its democratic, liberal-social, and political agenda (1971). Deputy chairman (1969–1974), later chairman (1974–1878), of the regional party in Baden-Württemberg, he represented the FDP in the **Bundestag** (1972–1980, 1984–1989) and also sat in the European Parliament (1973–1983). In 1974, he succeeded Karl Hermann Flach as FDP general secretary, but resigned a year later over policy differences with the government coalition partner, the **Social Democratic Party of Germany** (**SPD**), and after advocating links with the **Christian Democratic Union/Christian Social Union** (**CDU/CSU**). In 1984, he succeeded **Otto Graf Lambsdorff** as federal economics minister, a post he held until 1988. In 1985, he took over from **Hans-Dietrich Genscher** as party chairman, but resigned three years later to become **European Union** (**EU**) commissioner for industrial policy and, from 1993, information technologies and **telecommunications**. As commissioner, he sponsored a report (*Europe and the Glo-*

bal Information Society, 1994) that marked the start of a major transnational initiative to bring the information society to the EU. All commissioners resigned in 1999 following allegations of fraud and mismanagement, and Bangemann subsequently joined the board of the Spanish telecommunications company Telefónica (2000–2001), then formed his own company, MB Consultants.

BANKS. Germany's 2,000 or so banks are structured into three tiers or "pillars." The first pillar, of around 300 private and commercial banks, accounts for 36 percent of the sector (measured in terms of assets) and includes the large group of universal, retail, and corporate banks, as well as investment banks and branches of foreign operations. To this tier belong the centrally organized big banks (Großbanken), of which the largest are the **Deutsche Bank AG** (Frankfurt/Main), **Commerzbank AG** (Frankfurt/Main), UniCredit Bank AG (Munich), and Deutsche Postbank AG (Bonn). The number of fully independent, often family-owned private banks has fallen sharply in recent times, as they have gone under, merged, or been taken over by larger commercial operations; the Hamburg-based M. M. Warburg & Co., with 2,000 employees, is one of the last and probably largest survivors in this sector. The second pillar comprises the public banks (31 percent), in particular the 400 or so savings banks (Sparkassen) and regional banks (Landesbanken), which are state owned and regulated by public law. These are subject to the standards and regulations of state institutions and constitute a uniquely large sector. To the third pillar belong the 1,140 or so regional credit cooperatives (Genossenschaftsbanken, recognizable by the suffix eG in the title), which are privately owned by their members, who are as a rule their customers. Although relatively small, the cooperatives have by far the largest number of branches (around 1,000). The titles of these banks vary, but are commonly Volksbanken in the cities and Raiffeisenbanken in rural areas. Other cooperatives include the Sparda and PSD banking groups, as well as institutions for churches and the professions. Regional cooperatives can also be members of central (national) banks such as WGZ and DZ. In addition, the third pillar embraces special function banks (Spezialbanken), such as mortgage banks (Hypothekenbanken, Pfandbriefbanken) and building and loan associations (Darlehen-/Bausparkassen), central securities depositories (Wertpapiersammelbanken), institutions for financing exports to economically weak regions and developing countries (Ausfuhrkredit-Gesellschaft mbH, AKA, and Kreditanstalt für Wiederaufbau, KfW), and guarantee banks for small to medium-sized companies (Bürgschaftsbanken and Kreditgarantiegemeinschaften). The KfW, which is owned 80 percent by the **federal government** and 20 percent by the federal states, also handles financial transactions, including privatizations, for the government. So-called Realkreditinstitute are specialist banks that provide long-term loans to public bodies, businesses, and private clients and manage credit for the central government, regions, and municipalities. Full-service banks are known as universal banks (Universalbanken), among which are not only the big banks, but increasingly also the cooperatives.

German banks historically invested capital in large domestic concerns (especially coal, steel, and electrical **engineering**), developing close, long-term investment relations with businesses or even owning them (many firms have bank directors on their executive boards). They played a major role in the development of Germany's **industry** during the 19th century, when regional governments lacked the resources and structures needed for large-scale finance, and were vital for economic reconstruction after World War II. While the historical "house bank" (Hausbank) system contributed to Germany's successful corporate culture, the dependency relationship has come under criticism for inhibiting competitiveness and for exposing businesses to increased risk, especially at times of economic crisis.

During the 1990s, the Commission of the **European Union (EU)** applied pressure on the German government to modify the liability structure of its large public banking sector, which enjoyed indirect subsidies through state guarantees that contravened EU rules on competitiveness. Attention focused on the expansion of Germany's largest regional public bank, the Westdeutsche Landesbank (WestLB) in 1992, which was partly financed by the state of **North-Rhine Westfalia**. After Germany accepted modifications to the subsidy system in 2002, state guarantees for public savings and regional banks were finally abolished in July 2005.

German banks, especially regional banks and those that were heavily exposed to risky U.S investments or loans to heavily indebted EU states, were hit hard by the **eurozone crisis**, which broke in 2009, and most needed state help to stave off bankruptcy, with restructuring often accompanied by shrinking workforces. Although banks have shifted their focus to the domestic market, competition here is fierce, and the regional banks in particular have had to work hard to attract new private clients. In 2009, a "bad bank law" came into effect, which isolated toxic debt from main operations in return for state guarantees. In the mid-2000s, the Deutsche Bank in particular was hit by large fines (imposed by British and U.S. authorities) for the manipulation of LIBOR benchmark interest rates, although the exemplary severe sentences imposed on, say, the British trader Tom Hayes, were not matched in Germany, where the justice system does not traditionally punish individuals for acting within a corporate culture.

See also ABS, HERMANN JOSEF (1901–1994); ACKERMANN, JOSEF (1948–); ALLIANZ DEUTSCHLAND AG; BREUER, ROLF E. (1937–); HERRHAUSEN, ALFRED (1930–1989); KÖHLER, HORST (1943–); PÖHL, KARL OTTO (1929–2014).

BARSCHEL, UWE (1944–1987). Christian Democratic Union (CDU) politician. Born in Glienicke (**Berlin**), Uwe Barschel studied law, economics, political science, and pedagogy at the Pedagogical University (Pädagogische Hochschule, PH) in Kiel (1969–1971), earning doctorates in law and philosophy. He taught briefly at the PH (1969–1970) before entering practice as a lawyer. An activist in the youth wing (**Junge Union, JU**) of the CDU from 1960, he joined the main party in 1962 and enjoyed a swift rise to political prominence. He served as regional chairman of the JU in **Schleswig-Holstein** (1967–1971), was appointed regional deputy party chairman (1969), and was elected a member of the regional state parliament (**Landtag**, from 1971), where he led the parliamentary group (1973–1979) before entering the **Bundestag** (1979). In the same year, he became regional finance minister and subsequently interior minister, gaining a reputation as an effective opponent of federal interior minister Gerhart Baum. Barschel chaired the standing committee of regional interior ministers (1981–1982) and the standing committee of regional minister presidents (1982–1983).

In 1982, Barschel succeeded **Gerhard Stoltenberg** as **minister president** of Schleswig-Holstein, leading his party to an absolute majority in the regional elections the following year. Barschel's promising career came to an abrupt end when, on the eve of the next regional election (1987), *Der Spiegel* published allegations about his media adviser, Rainer Pfeffer, who had been recruited from the **Springer** concern to advise on campaign strategy. Although he was reelected, Barschel became the focus of a major scandal, which two parliamentary investigations never fully resolved. What is known is that Barschel engaged Pfeiffer to conduct a smear campaign against his rival, **Björn Engholm**, leader of the opposition **Social Democratic Party of Germany** (**SPD**). It also emerged that Engholm knew about the campaign at an early stage and exploited it for political advantage. Shortly after the election, Barschel was forced to announce his resignation (25 September 1987) and was later found dead in a Geneva hotel from an overdose of sleeping tablets and tranquilizers (11 October). Files compiled by the **Stasi**, which became available after reunification, suggested possible involvement in international arms dealing. Barschel published extensively on public law and political science, and especially regional politics.

BARZEL, RAINER (1924–2006). Christian Democratic Union (CDU) politician. Rainer Barzel was born in Braunsberg (East Prussia, now in Poland). He grew up in **Berlin** and completed national service (1941–1945) during World War II, reaching the rank of flight lieutenant. After the war, he studied law and economics at the University of Cologne (1945–1948), qualifying with a doctorate (1949). A member of the CDU, Barzel served in the state government of **North Rhine-Westfalia** (1949–1956) and on the regional party presidium (1956–1957), before entering the **Bundestag**

(1957–1987). In 1962–1963, he was minister for all-German affairs in **Konrad Adenauer**'s last cabinet. From 1964 until he resigned in 1973, he chaired the joint parliamentary group of the CDU and **Christian Social Union (CSU)** in the Bundestag. During the **grand coalition** (1966–1969), he worked closely with **Helmut Schmidt**, his counterpart in the **Social Democratic Party of Germany (SPD)**. In 1972 Barzel, who had succeeded **Kurt Georg Kiesinger** as party leader the year before, led an unsuccessful vote of no confidence against Chancellor **Willy Brandt** (SPD), whom he accused of selling out German national interests and abandoning any prospect of reunification through his **Ostpolitik**. (It later emerged that at least one of his own party members who had voted against the motion had been bribed by the East Germans.) The motion, which alienated many Germans, was the first of its kind in the history of the Federal Republic of Germany (FRG). The CDU/CSU, with Barzel as chancellor candidate, went on to lose the national election the following November, and he eventually resigned as party chairman and leader of the parliamentary group in order to practice as a lawyer (1973).

When the CDU/CSU returned to power (1982), Barzel became minister for intra-German relations (Minister für Innerdeutsche Beziehungen) in the first cabinet of **Helmut Kohl**, preparing the groundwork for payments to the **German Democratic Republic (GDR)** in return for the release of political prisoners. In 1983, he succeeded Richard Stücklen (CSU) as president of the Bundestag, but he resigned the following year following allegations, later proved to be unfounded, of his involvement in the financial scandal over donations made to the **Free Democratic Party (FDP)** in return for tax concessions. Barzel published widely on contemporary politics (his memoirs appeared in 2001), and he received numerous awards.

See also FLICK, FRIEDRICH KARL (1927–2006).

BASELITZ, GEORG (1938–). Artist. Baselitz is among Germany's eminent contemporary painters, sculptors, draftsmen, and printmakers. Born Hans-Georg Kern, he changed his name based on his place of birth, Deutschbaselitz. From 1956, he studied art at the Hochschule für bildende und angewandte Kunst in East Berlin, and from 1957 at the Hochschule der Künste in West **Berlin**. From 1984 until 1992, he was a member of the Academy of Arts (Berlin). Starting in 1969, Baselitz presented his subjects upside-down to highlight the importance of form but also the artifice of painting. He became particularly influential for the neo-Expressionist painters (Neue Wilde) in Germany. Solo museum exhibitions of his work are indicative of his eminence in the art world; they appeared at, for example, the Salomon Guggenheim Museum (New York), the Smithsonian (Washington, D.C.), the Albertina in Vienna, the Royal Academy of Arts (London), the Pinakothek der Moderne (Munich), Musée d'Art Moderne de la Ville de Paris, and the Victoria and Albert Museum (London). In 2014, the British Museum in

London presented the exhibition "Germany Divided: Baselitz and his Generation," including works by A. R. Penck, Sigmar Polke, and Gerhard Richter. Baselitz has lived in Germany, Switzerland, and Italy.

BASF SE. In 1865, Friedrich Engelhorn founded a factory (Badische Analin-& Soda-Fabrik AG, BASF) in Ludwigshafen for the manufacture of tar-based dying materials. The business expanded rapidly, developing fertilizers and products for the textile **industry**, and in 1925 merged with **Hoechst, Bayer**, Agfa, and two other concerns to form I. G. Farbenindustrie AG (I. G. Farben), with headquarters in Frankfurt/Main. In the 1920s and 1930s, the new company expanded into fuels, synthetic rubber, and paints to become one of the largest **chemical** manufacturing enterprises in the world. After 1945, its directors were placed on trial for war crimes for using slave labor from National Socialist–occupied countries (in 1999, BASF contributed 100 million DM to a compensation fund created jointly by German industry and the state). The company itself was placed under Allied control and dismembered, with BASF eventually reemerging with two other concerns (1952) to form an independent company based in Ludwigshafen. Exploiting the huge increase in demand for synthetic materials during the 1950s, BASF once again expanded, manufacturing nylon, polythene, and polyester products and increasingly using petrochemicals instead of coal as raw material. The 1960s saw the construction of manufacturing plants abroad (throughout Europe, India, Japan, Australia, and North and South America), and the plant in Antwerp (Belgium) was developed into BASF's second largest production base in Europe. BASF also acquired and established new companies marketing finished products, including **pharmaceuticals**. Overseas expansion, especially in Asia, continued during the 1980s and 1990s.

After reunification (1990), BASF bought up and invested heavily in the Schwarzheide (Lausitz) plant in eastern Germany. Between 1998 and 2001, in conjunction with PetroFina, it built the world's largest steamcracker at Port Arthur in the United States, its largest single investment outside Europe. In July 2001, BASF underwent restructuring, creating 38 regional and 10 global operational units, designed to improve marketing and customer relations. Since its early years, the company has stressed the so-called Verbundprinzip, which networks its six major bases (in Ludwigshafen, Antwerp, Freeport and Geismar [U.S.], Kuantan [Malaysia], and Nanjing [China]) and 390 production locations (170 in Germany). In 2015, BASF SE turned over 70,000 million euros and employed more than 113,000 people. The largest chemical concern in Germany and one of the biggest in the world, BASF's principal markets include chemicals (domestic and industrial), **agricultural** products, and **energy** (oil and gas). Kurt Bock, who joined the company in 1985, became chief executive in May 2011.

BASIC LAW (BL). The Basic Law, or Grundgesetz (GG), came into force on 23 May 1949 as the founding constitution of the Federal Republic of Germany (FRG). It was drawn up in eight months by a Parliamentary Council (Parlamentarischer Rat) of delegates of 11 German states under the supervision of the postwar western Allied powers of occupation (United States, Great Britain, and France). As reflected in its title, the BL was intended to be provisional as long as Germany remained divided. However, since the five reconstituted **federal states** of the former **German Democratic Republic (GDR)** simply adopted the existing BL in October 1990, it became the constitutional basis of the new reunited Germany, with agreed transitional arrangements for the law on **abortion** and on extending the West German **legal system** to the east. While the BL owed much to the historical tradition of German **federalism**, its founding fathers tried to avoid the constitutional flaws of the Weimar Republic (1919–1933). Following the experiences of the National Socialist period (1933–1945), the BL was intended to provide a secure basis for a peaceful, democratic, and socially balanced state.

The BL emphasizes the primacy of **human rights**, catalogs the rights and freedoms of the individual, defines the relationship between the political center (the **Bund**) and the federal states (Länder), describes the role of the organs and institutions of government (**Bundestag, Bundesrat**, the **federal government**, and the offices of the **federal chancellor** and the **president of the Federal Republic**), the legislative process (Gesetzgebung), the legal system (Rechtsprechung), and finance within the federal framework (Finanzwesen). It also describes and defines the role of the **Federal Assembly** (Bundesversammlung) and the joint committee of the Bundestag/Bundesrat (Gemeinsamer Ausschuss). The unalterable core of the constitution (Verfassungskern), as laid down in article 79(3), includes the guarantee of human dignity (article 1); the principles of democratic, constitutional order (article 20); the division into federal states; and the latter's participation in the legislative process. The BL also lays down the composition and function of Germany's Supreme Court, the **Federal Constitutional Court (FCC**, the Bundesverfassungsgericht). As the only body empowered to interpret the BL, the FCC safeguards the law's integrity, arbitrates in disputes between the organs of government (such as the Bund and the Länder or among the Länder themselves), and may be called on by individuals and other bodies to defend constitutional rights. The court tests legislation for compatibility with the BL and may ban political parties that it regards as a danger to the constitution. No legal code or statute is valid unless it can be interpreted in accordance with the BL.

Although the BL has served Germany well, it was changed or extended by 45 laws (comprising 69 articles) between 1951 and 1998 (alterations require a two-thirds majority of both Bundestag and Bundesrat). The first major and controversial changes were laws that paved the way for conscription and the establishment of the **Bundeswehr** (1955–1956) and emergency laws that suspended civil rights in times of national crisis (the Notstandsgesetze of 1968, articles 115a-l). Following the 1968 student protests and a widespread perception that Germany needed social and political reform, a commission of inquiry on constitutional reform (Enquête-Kommission zur Verfassungsreform) was set up in 1973, although there proved to be little enthusiasm for radical change, and the debate died down. The overall trend has been to transfer competencies away from the Länder to the political center (the Bund) or to give the center responsibilities in hitherto unregulated areas (such as nuclear **energy**, **health**, the **environment**, higher **education**, and finance). Taken as a whole, the creeping moves toward a unitary state represent a significant shift away from the original concept of the BL, with its concern to preserve the tradition of federalism. The law on the Treaty of Unification (Gesetz zum Einigungsvertrag), passed on 23 September 1990, revised the BL in the light of Germany's new political situation. Apart from technical adjustments, changes included the removal of the formal pledge to reunification from the preamble (Wiedervereinigungsgebot), altering the voting relationship in the Bundestag to take account of the new **eastern federal states**, and providing a transitional period for the implementation of west German law. Germans whose property was appropriated by the authorities in the east between 1945 and 1949, when the area was under Soviet military occupation, would not have a right to restitution (this did not apply to the period after 1949).

Following a recommendation in the Treaty on Unification, a Joint Constitutional Commission of 32 members each from the Bundestag and Bundestag met between 1992 and autumn 1993 to consider reforms to the BL. The agenda for change included recasting the balance of powers between Bund and Länder, merging **Berlin** and **Brandenburg**, incorporating "aims of the state" (Staatsziele) in the BL, and holding a plebiscite for the people to approve a (possibly new) constitution for the whole of Germany. Although no substantial revisions of the BL emerged from the exercise, some changes were introduced in 1994. The state was charged with specific aims, including promoting equal rights for men and **women**, removing discrimination against the disabled, and protecting the environment. Länder could also in future agree on territorial reorganization by interstate treaty (although a proposed merger of Berlin and Brandenburg was rejected by plebiscite in 1996), and more financial powers were accorded to local communities (Kommunen). The legislative rights of the Länder were extended in some areas. Demands for the BL to include opportunities for plebiscites in issues of national importance were rejected.

After a commission was created in 2003 to review the workings of the federal system, the BL was further revised in two stages: the first stage rebalanced the competencies of the Bund and Länder (2006), while the second stage introduced a debt brake and aimed to modernize financial relations between the two tiers.

See also BUDGET; FEDERALISM REFORM; LEGAL SYSTEM.

BAUER, HEINZ HEINRICH (1939–). Publisher. Heinz Heinrich Bauer was born in **Hamburg**, where his father, Alfred Bauer, owned a **publishing** house. The business was partially destroyed during World War II, but was rebuilt after 1945 to become West Germany's second largest publisher. After training in the firm as a typesetter and book printer, Bauer worked in various departments. In 1972, he became a partner in the company Heinrich Bauer KG, with a 10 percent holding, which rose to 96 percent when his father died in 1984. As the new owner, Bauer consolidated the company by shedding a stake in the private television station SAT 1, although he acquired an interest in Radio Hamburg (1986). He developed operations abroad, mainly in the United States (U.S.), Great Britain, and France, where he founded magazines such as *First for Women* (U.S.), *Bella* (Britain), and *Marie France* (France). During the first half of the 1990s, the Heinrich Bauer Verlag made a series of acquisitions (Verlagsunion Pabel-Moewig, Hestia, Diana, Neff) and expanded in eastern Germany, taking over the newspaper *Magdeburger Volksstimme* and launching a magazine, *Unsere Illustrierte* (1991). Bauer returned to private television by taking a shareholding in RTL2, although he discontinued the long-standing popular magazine *Quick* (1992) and was unsuccessful in launching some new titles in a highly competitive market. Nevertheless, the Bauer concern continued to dominate the domestic market, with a range of popular magazines aimed at **women**, young people, **television and radio** audiences, leisure activities, and special interest groups (popular titles include *Neue Revue, Praline,* and *Das Neue Blatt*). More recently, Bauer has, through acquisitions, extended its interests in eastern Europe, Great Britain (where it owns 80 magazine titles and more than 40 commercial radio stations), and Australasia (taking over ACP magazines in 2012).

In 2015, the Bauer Media Group reported a turnover of 2,300 million euros with a workforce of 11,000 in 20 countries, including the U.S. and China, across four continents. Since 2009, foreign operations have generated over half of gross revenue. The group publishes around 600 journal/magazine titles and more than 400 digital products and runs 100 radio and television stations worldwide. With control of the company passing in 2011 to Bauer's daughter, Yvonne, who is chief executive and majority shareholder, it remains a family concern.

See also MEDIA; PRESS.

BAVARIA (BAYERN). Bavaria is the largest of Germany's **federal states** in terms of geographical area (70,550 sq. km) and is second only to **North Rhine-Westfalia** in population (12.6 million) and GDP (18 percent of the national total in 2015). It borders the Austrian **Alps** in the south and the Czech Republic in the east. To the north lie the states of **Thuringia** and **Hessen** and to the west **Baden-Württemberg**. North of the Alps (including Germany's highest peak, the 2,962-m Zugspitze) lies the Alpine Foreland (Alpenvorland), a picturesque area of undulating hills and lakes that is a popular leisure destination, especially for the inhabitants of the state capital, Munich (population 1,250,000). The region is divided by the Danube River, which flows from west to east. North of the river lies Franconia (Franken-land), which is oriented to the Rhein-Main economic region to the west and the forested mountain area of the Upper Palatinate (Oberpfalz) to the east. Along the eastern border with the Czech Republic lies the Bavarian Forest (Bayerischer Wald).

Historically, the three main ethnic groups of Bavaria were the Bavarians (or Altbayern) in the south and east, the Alemannic Swabians in the southwest, and the Franks in the north and northwest. After World War II, over one million refugees from the Sudetenland (now part of the Czech Republic) settled in Bavaria, constituting what is commonly regarded as the region's fourth ancestral Germanic group. Alongside Munich, the main cities are Nuremberg (505,600), Augsburg (272,700), Regensburg (152,000), and Würzburg (126,800). These and other cities still show their origin as medieval royal residences and cities of the Holy Roman Empire (Reichsstädte). The bishoprics of Bamberg, Würzburg, and Augsburg were centers of medieval power, as was the trading and manufacturing city of Nuremberg, which became a major trading link connecting northern, eastern, and southern Europe (Italy) and was the home of the Reichstag, the assembly of leading princes and free cities of the empire. Although Bavaria has always been regarded as a hub of Roman Catholicism, a strong Protestant tradition established itself during the Reformation among Franconians and Swabians (in 2011, the ratio was 6.8 million Roman Catholics to 2.6 million Protestants).

During the 19th century, Bavaria became a relatively liberal modern state, and after the creation of the German Empire (1871) it retained a strong regional identity. Given the low level of industrialization, politics were dominated by Catholic-oriented landowners and farmers, despite the presence of a middle class and a small stratum of nobility. After civil unrest at the end of World War I and brief rule by radical socialists, Bavaria was governed by center-right administrations that pursued conservative policies. In 1949, the Bavarian state parliament (**Landtag**) voted against adoption of the **Basic Law (BL)** on the grounds that it did not go far enough in devolving powers from the center. Nevertheless, the Landtag recognized the BL's binding legality and went on to become both a consistent advocate of regional interests and, partly in response to its powerful refugee lobby, a vocal promoter of reunification. Since the late 1970s, Bavaria has worked hard to place regionalism and subsidiarity at the heart of **European Union (EU)** politics and to promote **federalism**. During the 1980s, it established its own representation in Brussels and was instrumental in setting up the EU's "committee of the regions." Bavaria is a member of the community of Alpine States (Arbeitsgemeinschaft Alpenländer, founded in 1972) and cooperates in similar organizations with other countries and cross-border regions (often called Euroregions).

Bavaria's main political party, the **Christian Social Union (CSU)**, overcame internal divisions during the 1950s to dominate regional state politics after 1957. Since 1962, with a brief interruption during 2008–2013, when it formed a coalition with the **Free Democratic Party (FDP)**, the CSU has ruled with an unchallenged majority in the Landtag (the FDP failed to reenter parliament in 2013). The CSU's most formative leader was **Franz Josef Strauß**, who served as **minister president** from 1978 to 1988. His successors in both posts were **Max Streibl** (1988–1993), **Edmund Stoiber** (1993–2007), **Günther Beckstein** (2007), and **Horst Seehofer** (2008–). The CSU's success has been attributed to its communication skills and close network of personal links with businesses (large and small) and public organizations. Even revelations in 2013 that 56 deputies in the CSU (alongside representatives of other parties) had been illegally misappropriating public funds since 2000 in order to employ family members in state jobs inflicted little electoral damage on the party. Conservative in outlook, the party campaigns on traditional family values and is a strong supporter of the social policies that underpin these.

Traditionally a rural **agricultural** area, Bavaria did not undergo the industrialization of other regions (such as the Ruhr valley and **Saxony**) during the 19th and early 20th centuries. Notable exceptions were the cities of Nuremberg and Augsburg (centers of mechanical and electrical **engineering**), Munich (locomotive construction), and Schweinfurt (bearings); parts of the **Alps** were home to the production of porcelain, **chemicals**, and hydroelectric power. During the postwar economic boom, the absence of heavy **industry** proved an advantage as Bavaria developed new, modern businesses from the 1960s onward. Key factors were a skilled and motivated refugee workforce, the relocation of businesses from the east (including **Siemens**), improvements in infrastructure (especially motorway links and nuclear power stations), and the construction of an oil refinery at Ingolstadt. In 1992, a canal linking the rivers Main and Danube (Main-Donau Kanal) and a second airport at Munich, which also attracted young professionals seeking work in a congenial **environment**, were opened.

The main industrial activities, which are concentrated in the south, are **automobile** manufacturing (Munich, Ingolstadt, Regensburg), electronics and computers (Munich, Erlangen), chemicals, aeronautics, and more recently, biotechnology. Leading companies are Siemens, **BMW**, and **Audi**, while service industries (insurance and banking), **publishing**, **cinema**, and the **media** are also strongly represented. The north of the region, the home of traditional metal-processing industries, has suffered from international competition, and unemployment rates are relatively high there, although Bavaria as a whole has one of the lowest jobless levels of all the federal states (3.6 percent in 2014, compared with the national average of 6.7 percent). **Foreigners** constitute 11.2 percent of the population.

Bavarians are extremely proud of their **educational** system. The state has five major universities, of which the largest, Munich, was founded in 1472 and currently has around 49,000 students; Würzburg, founded in 1402, has over 25,000 students. The region also boasts numerous technical colleges and several research institutes. The regional state government has been especially proactive in attracting high-technology inward investment, using money from privatization during the 1990s to subsidize education and research as well as cultural facilities (art galleries and museums). Despite the decline of agriculture, farmers remain a powerful political lobby. Exports include beef, milk and other dairy products, sugar, and cereals. Bavaria is a favorite **tourist** destination, registering the highest number of overnight stays of all the federal states (a main attraction is the annual beer festival, Oktoberfest).

Bavaria's comprehensive constitution assigns special value to the "dignity of the human personality" ("Würde der menschlichen Persönlichkeit") and stresses the cultural identity of the Bavarian state. There is also a constitutional commitment to building a socially and economically just society and protecting the environment. The preamble specifically rejects National Socialism as godless and without conscience or respect for human dignity. The state parliament (Landtag) consisted of 204 members until 2003, when the number was reduced to 180, and is elected for four years (effective 1998). Constitutional changes in 1998 strengthened the role of parliament vis-à-vis the executive and improved facilities available to the opposition. Until 1999, the Landtag was unique in having a second chamber or senate, a 60-member assembly of representatives of business, church, farmers, and **trade unions** that advised parliament and could present laws, although it had only a suspensory veto on legislation. Never popular with the people, the senate was wound up after a plebiscite in 1998. Plebiscites have often been held on important issues; these include the introduction of cross-denominational Christian schools (1968), the reduction of the voting age (1970), broadcasting (1973), the adoption of environmental protection as a constitutional aim (1984), waste disposal (1991), and a ban on smoking in restaurants (2010). In 1998, a majority voted to extend the constitution to include a commitment to a united Europe that respected the independence of its regions. At the same time, new objectives for the state (Staatsziele) were adopted, notably rights for the disabled, equality of gender, the protection of animals, and the promotion of **sport**. The regional government comprises a minister president and up to 17 **state ministers** and **state secretaries**. A recent development is the strengthening of executive government in the form of a powerful state chancellery that, under the minister president's control, implements and oversees policy.

BAYER AG. The Bayer AG group (Leverkusen) dates from 1863, when the businessman Friedrich Bayer and the master dyer Johann Friedrich Weskott founded a dyestuffs factory in Barman (Wuppertal). It expanded rapidly abroad, buying a part interest in a coal tar dye factory in the United States (1865) and a factory in Moscow (1876) and producing from a plant in northern France (1883). A **pharmaceuticals** division was established in 1881. The company's scientists made several major discoveries, including the painkilling drug aspirin (patented in 1899). In 1912, the headquarters transferred to its current site at Leverkusen. In 1925, Bayer merged with other companies to form I. G. Farbenindustrie AG. After World War II, this concern was appropriated and broken up by the Allies, although the company soon reestablished itself as Farbenfabriken Bayer AG (1951).

After changing its name to Bayer AG (1972), the company entered a phase of vigorous international expansion. From 2002, following the withdrawal of the drug Libopay/Baycol and manufacturing problems with another key product (Kogenate), the group restructured into operationally separate divisions under the umbrella of a holding company. The divisions that eventually emerged were (from 2013): Bayer HealthCare AG (including pharmaceuticals), Bayer CropScience AG (agrochemicals), Bayer Material Science (polycarbonates, polyurethanes, coatings and adhesives), and three subconcerns providing service functions for the group. Acquisitions during this period included the health arm of Roche (2005) and Schering AG (2006). Bayer's principal market is Europe, followed by North America, Asia, South America, Africa, and the Middle East. Turnover was more than 46,000 million euros in 2015, with a total workforce of 116,800 (36,700 in Germany). The chief executive (since 2010) is Dutch-born Marijn Dekkers, who worked for 25 years in the U.S.

See also CHEMICAL INDUSTRY.

BAYREUTH FESTIVAL (BAYREUTHER FESTSPIELE). In 1862, the composer Richard Wagner worked out the first detailed plan for an opera festival, which took place in Bayreuth in 1876 with a performance of the *Ring der Nibelungen*. Ever since, the annual festival has taken place in a specially designed theater, and performances are considered to be among the highlights of the German cultural calendar. Since the 1980s, producers have included Wolfgang Wagner (1981, 1985, 1989, 1996), Götz Friedrich (1982), Werner Herzog (1987), Harry Kupfer (1988), Heiner Müller (1993), Keith Warner (1999), Jürgen Flimm (2000), Christoph Schlingensief (2004), and Frank Castorf (2014)—more experimental directors triggering lively debates that seek to rekindle public interest beyond music enthusiasts.

BECHER, BERND (1931–2007) AND HILLA (1934–2015). Conceptual artists. Bernd and Hilla Becher, born in Siegen and Potsdam, respectively, were collaborative conceptual artists who became famous for their photography, which focused on industrial buildings and structures, following the objectives of the new topographic movement. Today their work is held in collections worldwide, including the Tate Gallery (London), the Museum of Modern Art (New York), the Guggenheim Museum (New York), the Getty Museum (Los Angeles), and the Museum of Contemporary Art Chicago. The Bechers' influence on documentary photographers and artists—including Andreas Gursky, Thomas Ruff, and Thomas Struth—has been fundamental.

The Bechers met during their studies at the Art Academy in Düsseldorf, where both later also taught. They identified early on what became their photographic leitmotiv: the disappearance of industrial architecture (from 1959), for example in the Ruhr valley. Their participation in the Documenta (a leading exhibition of contemporary art held periodically in Kassel since 1955) in 1972 brought wider recognition of their art. Furthermore, their work highlighted the need for the preservation of industrial architecture, a need that became obvious well beyond Germany once they widened their photographic remit to include visits to Great Britain, France, Belgium, and the United States (New Jersey, Michigan, Pennsylvania, and Ontario), triggering a renewed interest in neglected structures such as water towers and gasholders. Their work coincided with principal changes in the industrial landscape during the 1970s and 1980s, and their documentary style in the tradition of new objectivity depicted a culture that was soon gone for good.

The Bechers mounted numerous exhibitions. In 1990, they were awarded the Golden Lion at the Biennale in Venice; in 1994, the Goslar Kaiserring; and in 2004, the Hasselblad Award.

BECK, KURT (1949–). Social Democratic Party of Germany (SPD) politician. Kurt Beck trained as an electrical engineer (1963–1968) and worked as a radio technician (1969–1972) before joining the SPD in 1972. A member of the transport and public service workers' **trade union** Öffentliche Dienste, Transport, und Verkehr (ÖTV) since 1969, he chaired a staff association at local and district levels from 1972 to 1985. In 1979, Beck entered the state parliament (**Landtag**) of **Rhineland-Palatinate**, where he was manager of the SPD parliamentary group (1985–1991) and subsequently its leader (1991–1994). He also served as local mayor for Steinfeld (1989–1994) and was elected leader of the regional party (1993). In October 1994, he succeeded **Rudolf Scharping** as **minister president** for Rhineland-Palatinate and became first vice president of the **Bundesrat** (November 2001). In state elections (1996, 2001), Beck maintained the SPD's parliamentary majority, continuing the coalition with the **Free Democratic Party (FDP)**. As regional premier, he faced problems of unemployment, declining industries, budget deficits, and economic and social issues as a result of the withdrawal of the United States and Allied troops after the end of the Cold War (the **Bundeswehr** drastically reduced its own presence in the region); the area was also hit by severe flooding in 1995. In 2000, Beck oversaw a major restructuring of local government. When the SPD gained an absolute majority in the 2006 state election, it was largely attributed to his energy and personal popularity, and between 2006 and 2008 he led the national SPD following the resignation of **Matthias Platzeck**. He was chairman of the interstate broadcasting commission (Rundfunkkommission der Bundesländer, 1994–2013), served on the administrative council (Verwaltungsrat) of the ZDF television station (from 1999), chaired the social democratically oriented Friedrich-Ebert Stiftung (Friedrich Ebert Foundation, from 2013), and represented Germany in Franco-German cultural affairs. In early 2013, Beck resigned as minister president and in the same year became an adviser for the **pharmaceutical** concern **Boehringer** Ingelheim.

See also TELEVISION AND RADIO.

BECK, ULRICH (1944–2015). Sociologist. One of the world's most renowned sociologists and intellectuals, Beck was born in Stolp in Pomerania (now Poland) and grew up in Hanover. He worked on modernization, ecological issues, individualization, and globalization. In 1986, he published *Risk Society: Towards a New Modernity*, which proved to be groundbreaking and has been translated into 35 languages; it is today considered to be among the 20 most influential sociology-based books of the 20th century. Beck perceived the approach of a risk society as "a systematic way of dealing with hazards and insecurities induced and introduced by modernization itself." He also established the term "second modernity": if modernity was characterized by the move from an agricultural to an industrial society, then second modernity describes the development of the industrial society toward a network and information society.

Beck started his university career at the Universities of Münster (1979–1981) and Bamberg (1981–1982) before teaching at Munich University, at the Fondation Maison des Sciences de l'Homme in Paris, and at the London School of Economics. He was a member of the board of trustees at the Jewish Center in Munich and of the German branch of **Pen International**. He held numerous honorary doctorates and awards, among the latter the Lifetime Achievement Award for his distinguished contribution to futures research of the International Sociological Association (2014). His books include *German Europe* (first published in 2012, translated in 2013) and *What Is Globalization* (first published in 1997 and translated into English in 1999).

BECKSTEIN, GÜNTHER (1943–). Christian Social Union (CSU) politician. Born in Hersbruck **(Bavaria)**, Günther Beckstein studied law in Erlangen and Munich (from 1962), ran a legal practice from 1971, and earned a doctorate in 1975. Chairman of the Nuremberg branch of the conservative **Junge Union (JU**, 1973–1978), later deputy leader and leader (1991–2008) of the district CSU, he was a member of the regional parliament **(Landtag)** from 1974 to 2013. Briefly deputy leader of the parliamentary group (1988), Beckstein served as **state secretary** (Staatssekretär) in the Bavarian interior ministry (1988–1993), before becoming **state minister** (1993–2007) and deputy **minister president** (2001–2007) under **Edmund Stoiber**. As chairman (1980–1992) and subsequently honorary chairman of the CSU regional police working group, he had a special interest in home security affairs. He briefly succeeded Stoiber as minister president (October 2007–October 2008), but withdrew from reelection after the CSU lost its overall majority in the regional election of September 2008. Beckstein generally adopted conservative positions on **immigration** (urging restrictions) and internal **security** (supporting more surveillance measures) and also criticized the proliferation of violent computer games. He was appointed deputy president of the synod of the Evangelical Church in Germany in 2009.

BEER, ANGELIKA (1957–). Green Party politician. Angelika Beer was born in Kiel, **Schleswig-Holstein**, where her father represented the **Christian Democratic Union (CDU)** in the **Landtag**. After training and working as an assistant to a doctor, lawyer, and solicitor, she worked as a **human rights** researcher and was active in peace and **environmental** groups in Schleswig-Holstein. She was also a founding member of the Green Party (1980), which she represented in the **Bundestag** (1987–1990, 1994–2002). When the Greens failed to clear the 5 percent hurdle for entry into the first all-German parliament after reunification, she worked as a coordinator for an organization campaigning to outlaw land mines (Medico International, 1990–1994). She also joined the Arms Information Bureau (Rüstungsinformationsbüro, RIB) in **Baden-Württemberg**, the **Berlin** Institute for Transnational Security (Berliner Institut für Transnationale Sicherheit, BITS), and the Institute for International Politics (Institut für Internationale Politik, IIP), also in Berlin.

A member of the national executive of **Alliance 90/The Greens** (1991–1994), Beer served as party spokeswoman on defense when the Greens reentered parliament (1994), specializing in disarmament and weapons control. As a member of a European human rights delegation visiting Turkey (August 1996), she had to leave prematurely after opposing German arms supplies to the country. A committed antimilitarist and pacifist, she opposed Germany's armed intervention in Bosnia, although she was later criticized by members of her own party for defending Foreign Minister **Joschka Fischer** when he backed air attacks against Serbia mounted by the **North Atlantic Treaty Organization** (**NATO**, 1998) and military action in Afghanistan. In December 2002, she was elected, alongside **Reinhard Bütikofer**, coleader of the Green Party, succeeding **Claudia Roth** and **Fritz Kuhn** (until 2004). She also served as a member of the European Parliament (2004–2009), specializing in foreign affairs, **security**, and defense. In 2009, Beer surprised her colleagues by announcing her resignation from the Green Party over its failure to engage with the German government's peace policies on Kosovo, Afghanistan, and Iraq. In the same year, she joined **The Pirates/** Pirate Party, which she represented in the Schleswig-Holstein regional parliament following the election of 2012.

BEISHEIM, OTTO (1924–2013). Retail entrepreneur. Born in Vossnacken/ Essen (**North Rhine-Westfalia**), the son of an estate manager, Beisheim trained as a leather goods salesman. A member of the Waffen-SS and a prisoner of the British during the war, he then trained with an electrical wholesale company in Mülheim, eventually becoming a director. In 1964, after seeing the self-service cash-and-carry concept at work during a visit to the United States, he set up his own business, the Metro Cash & Carry Market. Joined by the brothers Michael and Reiner Schmidt-Ruthenbeck, who supplied business expertise from their own wholesale concern in the industrial Ruhr, and in 1967 by the Haniel family, whose wealth was derived from a coal and steel empire founded in the late 19th century, the concern grew rapidly during the postwar German economic miracle. Düsseldorf-based Metro (rebranded as Metro Group in 2002) is now one of the world's largest multinational trading organizations, with a turnover of around 59,200 million euros (2014/2015), much of which is generated abroad; the total workforce numbers around 250,000. During the 1970s, Beisheim handed over operational control of the business to his associate, Erwin Conradi, and his holdings were progressively reduced as new partners came on board and the concern entered the stock exchange (in 1996). Although marginalized by 2007, he remained one of Germany's richest men, with an estimated personal fortune of 3,400 million euros, and was considered a pioneer of postwar retailing, alongside Dieter Schwarz (founder of Lidl) and the **Albrecht** brothers (ALDI), who led the way in discounting.

Beisheim supported charitable foundations in Munich and Switzerland; was a major donor to the Otto Beisheim School of Management (WHU, from 1983) in Koblenz; and after reunification (3 October 1990), financed the creation of the Otto-Beisheim Foundation at the Technical University of Dresden, which awarded him an honorary doctorate (1993). In 2005, he spectacularly withdrew a 10 million euro donation to a school in Tegernsee (**Bavaria**) when teachers demanded clarification of his role in the SS.

Beisheim, who acquired Swiss citizenship in 1988, avoided public appearances, although his friendship with the former Bavarian **media** mogul **Leo Kirch** attracted attention, notably in 1990, when he purchased 2,500 films from Kirch in order to save the latter from financial difficulties (the films were sold to private broadcasters). In 2004, he financed the hitherto largest private development in Berlin, the Beisheim Center on the Potsdamer Platz. Following an illness, Beisheim took his own life in 2013.

See also DISTRIBUTION AND RETAIL.

BEITZ, BERTHOLD (1913–2013). Business executive. Born in Demmin (now in Poland), Beitz trained in commerce with Shell AG in **Hamburg** (from 1939). In 1941, he moved to the oil company Karpaten-Öl AG in Borislaw (Poland), where he saved many Jewish workers from deportation to National Socialist concentration camps and for which Israel later officially honored him. After serving in the German army (1944–1945), he returned to Hamburg to become vice president of an agency responsible for insurance in the British zone of occupation. Appointed general director of the Iduna-Germania insurance company (1949), he joined the **Krupp** concern for the then sensational annual salary of one million DM (1953). After the death of Alfried Krupp von Bohlen und Halbach (1967), Beitz, as chairman of the majority shareholding Krupp foundation, restructured and expanded the company. As the concern ran into financial trouble, he moved to the supervisory board, which he chaired from 1970 until 1989, and remained a powerful influence on the company's development until its merger with **Thyssen** (1999). A strong promoter of science, **education**, and **sport** in **North Rhine-Westfalia** through the Krupp foundation, Beitz was awarded the Federal Cross of Merit and honorary doctorates from the University of Greifswald (1983) and the University of the Ruhr (1999). From 1984 until 1988, he served as vice president of the International Olympic Committee (IOC), which also made him an honorary life member.

See also INDUSTRY.

BENDA, ERNST (1925–2009). Constitutional judge. Born in **Berlin**, Ernst Benda completed his school **education** during World War II, but was unable to attend university because his grandfather was a Jew. At the age of 18,

Benda volunteered for naval service and spent World War II on a speedboat operating off the coast of occupied Norway. After the war he returned to Berlin, where he worked as a building laborer before studying law, first at Humboldt University in East Berlin (1946–1948) and then, after falling afoul of the Communist authorities, at the newly founded Free University in West Berlin (1948–1951). He won a scholarship to study political science and journalism at the University of Wisconsin in Madison, in the United States (1949–1950), where he concentrated on American constitutional law. After passing his state law examinations (1951, 1955), he practiced as a lawyer in Berlin (1955–1971).

Benda joined the **Christian Democratic Union (CDU**, 1946) and was elected to the (West) Berlin city assembly (1955–1957) before entering the **Bundestag**, where he represented the city from 1957 until 1971. He joined the CDU national executive committee (1966) and served on the executive committee of the CDU/**Christian Social Union (CSU)** parliamentary group (from 1969), heading a working group on legal issues. In 1967, he became a parliamentary **state secretary** under Interior Minister Paul Lücke before himself becoming minister (1968–1969) in the **grand coalition** led by Chancellor **Kurt Georg Kiesinger**. His post made him the target of protesters opposing the controversial emergency laws (Notstandsgesetze), which the coalition eventually introduced in June 1968. (Previous attempts in 1960 and 1962 to introduce similar legislation, designed to give the government special powers in times of national emergency and mark the final stage of West Germany's progression to sovereignty from the Western Allies, had failed because of opposition from the **Social Democratic Party of Germany** [SPD] and fears of misuse by an authoritarian state.)

In 1971, following a tug-of-war between the political parties, Benda was appointed president of the **Federal Constitutional Court (FCC)**. During his period of office (until 1983), the FCC ruled on a number of hotly debated issues at a time of major political and social change in West Germany, including the **Ostpolitik** treaties, a new **abortion** law, limits on university places (*numerus clausus*), the **radicals decree** (Radikalenerlaß), military conscription, and the national census. Although Benda was a potential candidate to be **president of the Federal Republic** and mayor of West Berlin (a post he coveted), the CDU was unwilling to wait until the end of his term of office in the FCC, and he quit politics to take up a professorship in public law at the University of Freiburg (1984–1996). He was president of the German-Israel Society (1967–1970) and of the Conference of German Evangelical Churches (Deutscher Evangelischer Kirchentag, DEK, 1993–1995) and chaired the **media** council (Medienrat) of Berlin-**Brandenburg** (1992–2008).

Benda published and coedited a number of books, mainly on constitutional law. His honors include an honorary professorship (University of Trier, 1978), an honorary doctorate (Würzburg, 1974), the Federal Cross of Merit (1969, 1983), and the Moses-Mendelssohn Medal (1995).

See also BASIC LAW (BL).

BENNETER, KLAUS UWE (1947–). Social Democratic Party of Germany (SPD) politician. Born in Karlsruhe (**Baden-Württemberg**), Klaus Uwe Benneter studied law at the Free University of **Berlin** (1966–1971). After training at the superior court of justice (Kammergericht) in Berlin (1971–1974), he practiced law in the city (from 1975) and worked as a notary (from 1985). In 1974, Benneter became deputy leader (chairman) of the **Young Socialists (JUSOS)** wing of the SPD and in 1977 its leader. In the same year, he was thrown out of the party for advocating alliances with the German Communist Party (DKP). Readmitted in 1983, he resumed his political career in Berlin and occupied various positions in the local party and government. These included treasurer of the Berlin SPD (1990–1996); deputy regional party chairman (1996–2000); and member of the Berlin assembly, where he specialized in legal and constitutional issues (1999–2002). A member of the **Bundestag** (2002–2009), he also headed the commission of inquiry that investigated the scandal surrounding undeclared donations to the **Christian Democratic Union (CDU)** in Berlin.

Regarded as a left-wing rebel, Benneter often criticized the **grand coalition** of SPD and CDU that ruled Berlin between December 1990 and October 2001. Upon election to the Bundestag (September 2002), however, he supported Chancellor **Gerhard Schröder** and defended the latter's **Agenda 2010** reform program when it threatened to split the party. Although he failed in a bid to be elected to the national SPD party executive (November 2003), he succeeded **Olaf Scholz** as general secretary (March 2004) at a time when the SPD membership was heavily demoralized following a decline in electoral popularity and the replacement of Schröder as party leader by **Franz Müntefering**. During the leadership crisis that gripped the SPD following the lost national election of September 2005, Benneter was succeeded by **Hubertus Heil.**

BERLIN. Spanning the Spree River, Berlin, Germany's capital and largest city, has the status of a **federal state**. Its 3.5 million inhabitants (2015) include more than 620,000 **foreigners** (16.4 percent and rising) and almost 950,000 **immigrants** and their descendants (27.4 percent). Of the 186 states representing foreign incomers, 73.7 percent are from Europe, 14.2 percent from Asia, and 5.6 percent from America. The largest single immigrant group is Turkish (101,000), although there were increases in residents from Romania, Spain, and Bulgaria in 2012.

The geographical area of the city (888 sq. km) equals those of Munich, Stuttgart, and Frankfurt/Main combined, with a quarter of this taken up by lakes, waterways, parks, and greenery. Located midway between the **Baltic** coast and the Ore Mountains (Erzgebirge) in the east, Berlin is at the geographical periphery of western Europe, a position that was emphasized by the city's political isolation after World War II. Partly due to Germany's federalist structure, Berlin even before the war never dominated national life or became a political and cultural center to the extent that Paris, London, or Rome did. West Germans' lack of identification with Berlin as "their" capital was reflected in the postreunification debate over whether the seat of government and parliament should move there from Bonn. Opponents of the move argued that Bonn represented the new, peaceful, democratic and federalist state and that Berlin stood for Prussian centralism and the darker side of German history. When the **Bundestag** eventually voted on relocating the government to Berlin (June 1991), the majority for Berlin was narrow (338 votes to 320). Once decided, however, the move itself was largely completed by 1999–2000. The major ministries, including those for the interior, justice, finance, and the economy, transferred to Berlin, although Bonn remained an administrative center. The terms of the move were agreed to in a treaty among the **federal government**, the Berlin assembly, and the state of **Brandenburg** (Hauptstadtvertrag, 1992). The then federal president, Richard von Weizsäcker, moved in January 1994. In March 1994, the Bundestag passed the Berlin/Bonn law, which settled legal aspects of the transfer, and in the same year agreement was reached on financial compensation for Bonn and subventions for Berlin (Hauptstadtfinanzierungsvertrag). Bonn was officially called a "federal city" (Bundesstadt) in recognition of its special status. The Bundestag took possession of the renovated Reichstag building in Berlin in April 1999, and the **Bundesrat**, which in July 1991 had provisionally voted to stay in Bonn (38 votes out of 68), opted in September 1996 to move to the capital, where it held its first meeting in 2000.

Founded in the 12th century as Germans settled Slav territories east of the Elbe, Berlin developed during the 17th and 18th centuries as the capital of the small but powerful state of Brandenburg-Prussia. Immigrants and refugees contributed significantly to the city's cultural, economic, and public life, while its physical center was shaped by baroque and neoclassical architecture. During the 19th century, industrialization attracted further waves of immigrants from the eastern provinces and Poland. As the capital of the unified German Reich from 1871, Berlin grew rapidly and by 1914 comprised two million inhabitants (compared with 500,000 in 1850). When Greater Berlin was created in the 1920s, the figure rose to 3.7 million, by which time the city had acquired its characteristic layout of a large working-class quarter in the east and north, an elegant "west end," and well-to-do suburbs with villas and lakes to the southwest. Unter den Linden, a wide boulevard stretching eastward from the Brandenburg Gate to the historic center (the Mitte district), is the city's central axis; during the 19th and early 20th centuries, it was extended westward as the Kurfürstendamm, an elegant thoroughfare that developed as the commercial center of West Berlin during the postwar division.

Berlin has been and still is renowned for its thriving subculture, which has moved between districts over the years (during the Cold War period, it was located mainly in the West Berlin districts of Kreuzberg and Schöneberg). The biggest industrial city in continental Europe, Berlin was also Germany's financial center and, until the National Socialist period, was home to the largest **Jewish** population (175,000) of any Western European city. During the turbulent years of the Weimar Republic (1919–1933), Berlin became a mecca for artists experimenting with new forms and ideas, giving it an enduring reputation as a city of tolerance, international flair, and culture. At the same time the city, like the rest of the country, saw street fighting between political extremists, economic depression in 1923 and again in 1929–1930, and the rise of Adolf Hitler. Under the National Socialist dictatorship, Hitler's architect, Albert Speer, planned to replace large parts of the inner city with "Germania." However, during World War II much of the city was reduced to rubble by Allied bombing and, as the Soviet army invaded in April 1945, artillery action.

After the war, Berlin was divided into four sectors, three controlled by the Western Allies (the United States, Great Britain, and France) and an eastern sector (controlled by the Soviet Union). East Berlin became the capital of the **German Democratic Republic (GDR)**. West Berlin, which survived a Soviet land blockade (June 1948 to May 1949) and the erection of the **Berlin Wall** (August 1961), became an island showcase of Western prosperity inside Communist Eastern Europe. Nevertheless, the city, once mainland Europe's largest manufacturing center and home to Germany's oldest corporate empires, never regained its prewar economic status.

Although the immediate military and political threat to its existence receded after **Ostpolitik,** West Berlin retained something of a siege mentality. Heavily dependent on subsidies from West Germany, it attracted immigrants (especially guest workers from Turkey) and developed a lively cultural scene. The fall of the Wall in November 1989 and reunification the following year heralded a radical alteration of the face of the city. After a massive building and reconstruction program, the epicenter shifted eastward toward the historical hub of the city (Bezirk Mitte). In 1996, a projected merger between Berlin and the surrounding federal state of Brandenburg (agreed to in both parliaments) was rejected by referendum, although the two **Länder** continue to cooperate. Historically, Berlin comprised a large number of administrative districts or boroughs (Bezirke), which enjoyed considerable independence and even had their own mayors. In an attempt to rationalize this system and avoid conflicts between the center and the districts, the number of boroughs was reduced to 12 in 1998 (effective in 2001).

Berlin's postreunification constitution came into effect in 1995, although it was in many respects a continuation of the constitution that had been adopted for West Berlin in October 1950. With the cessation of Allied responsibility for the city, Berlin became a full-fledged Land within the German system of **federalism**. Its parliament, called the house of deputies (Abgeordnetenhaus), elects an executive government (senate), which consists of a governing mayor (Regierender Bürgermeister), a deputy mayor (Bürgermeister), and since 1998, eight senators, who function as ministers. In practice, parliamentary party groups exert considerable influence on government and are often represented at cabinet (senate) meetings. Members of the assembly (149 in 2012) are not necessarily full-time politicians and are not obliged to give up their jobs. The constitution contains a catalog of basic rights (including the right to resist and the right to strike), emphasizes social services (including the right to social welfare and housing), and gives citizens opportunities to influence the legislative process through plebiscites. It also accords unmarried partners similar rights as married couples and families.

Despite subsidies and inducements, the former West Berlin, disadvantaged by its lack of a hinterland and by the absence of opportunities for employers and employees, failed to attract the businesses it needed to become economically self-sufficient—a large proportion of the workforce worked for the state—and the situation did not change immediately after 1990. Fewer people than expected moved to the city, which further suffered from the sudden withdrawal of subsidies and job losses in the east as the political and bureaucratic apparatus of the former GDR was dismantled. Between 1996 and 2000, Berlin registered a net loss of population. At the same time, the foreign population rose steadily, partly because of the city's location between eastern and western Europe and partly because existing networks of foreigners attracted newcomers. After 2000, the overall population stabilized, with a tendency to small annual increases, and it has also proved attractive to people from English-speaking countries.

Although several large concerns established branches or headquarters in Berlin after reunification (including **Daimler**, Sony, and Deutsche Bahn AG), the centers of corporate decision making remained in western Germany. Even the construction boom benefited foreign and other **European Union (EU)** contractors more than Berlin's own building firms. Compared with the national average (6.4 percent in 2015), unemployment remained high (10.7 percent), with a rise only in the number of service sector jobs. In 1996, the city government introduced a program of cuts and privatization of assets to offset a mounting budget deficit caused, among other things, by an oversized bureaucracy and the high costs of upgrading housing in the east of the city. The duplication of educational and cultural facilities in east and west meant that closures were inevitable. The collapse of the regional public-sector bank BGB amid a property scandal in 2000 also cost the city millions of euros. The city was tarnished by a series of corruption scandals from the 1970s through the 2000s, which forced the resignation of leading politicians from all parties, including the governing mayor, **Eherhard Diepgen**, in 2001, and came to be known as "Berliner Filz" (Berliner sleaze). Despite these setbacks, the long-term aim is to establish Berlin as a focus for East–West commerce, services, and technology, and the city, with its extensive unused capacity in office and business accommodation, not to mention low costs and welfare benefits, has attracted large numbers of entrepreneurs, mainly in **media**, information technology/communications, and the creative industries. In 2015, Berlin contributed 4 percent of the national GDP, with the main contributors being financial and property services (32 percent); public services (31 percent); and trade, transport, tourism and information, and communications (20 percent). The city has 4 universities, 7 higher technical colleges (Fachhochschulen), 4 higher colleges of art (Kunsthochschulen), 26 private higher education colleges (Privathochschulen), and more than 60 research institutes. In 2014/2015, over 166,000 students were enrolled, of whom an estimated 16 percent were from abroad. Berlin's cultural institutions include 3 opera houses, several major orchestras and choirs, more than 50 theaters, 175 museums, around 300 art galleries, and 300 cinemas. In 1999, the city's "island of museums" (Museumsinsel) was admitted to the list of centers of cultural heritage compiled by the **United Nations (UN)** Educational, Scientific, and Cultural Organization (UNESCO); other UNESCO sites are the landscape of palaces and gardens between Berlin and Potsdam and six modernist housing estates. Berlin, which hosts a major annual international film festival, the Berlinale, is especially strong in media and publishing, and the **television** broadcasters ARD, RTL, Pro7/Sat1, and ZDF each maintain a studio in the city center. By 2015, the distribution of cultural institutions between east and west was settled following controversy in the 1990s, when each part of the city had felt disadvantaged after reunification.

Until the early 1960s, when West Berlin was openly threatened by the Soviet Union and placed a high priority on internal political unity, the city was governed by a consensus of the main parties, the **Social Democratic Party of Germany (SPD)**, **Christian Democratic Union (CDU)**, and **Free Democratic Party (FDP)**. For many years the SPD, respected for its history of resistance to communism and later for its advocacy of rapprochement with Eastern Europe, was the strongest party and provided distinguished mayors such as Ernst Reuter (1948–1953) and **Willy Brandt** (1957–1966). The party governed alone from 1967 until 1975, then in coalition with the FDP from

1975 until 1981. Having finally endorsed Ostpolitik and capitalizing on internal divisions in the SPD, the CDU returned after decades in opposition to lead, first a minority administration (1981–1983) and then a coalition with the FDP (1983–1989). Governing mayors from the CDU were **Richard von Weizsäcker** (1981–1984) and Eberhard Diepgen (1984–1989 and 1991–2001). The Alternative Liste für Demokratie und Umweltschutz (Alternative List for Democracy and Environmental Protection, AL), founded in 1979 by groups of **environmentalists** and citizens' rights groups, established a brief coalition with the SPD from January 1989 until December 1990 (after reunification, the AL joined **Alliance 90/The Greens**). From reunification until 1999, the CDU led a coalition with the SPD, with the CDU deriving its electoral support from the west of the city. The **Party of Democratic Socialism (PDS)** maintained a strong base in the east. The legacy of division during the communist years was reflected in the difficult negotiations that preceded the formation of coalitions: a partnership with the PDS (the successor party to the **Socialist Unity Party of Germany, SED**) remained taboo for the CDU, and it was not until 2002, following elections the year before, that the SPD agreed to a coalition with the PDS, with **Klaus Wowereit** (SPD) as governing mayor. The coalition was reelected in 2006, with **The Left Party** providing three of the eight senators. After elections in 2011, this was replaced by a **grand coalition** of SPD and CDU, with Wowereit as mayor. The FDP failed to clear the entry hurdle, and **The Pirates** entered a regional assembly for the first time. In 2014, Wowereit stepped down as mayor and was succeeded by Michael Müller (SPD). In the same year, Berlin celebrated the 25th anniversary of the fall of the Berlin Wall, demonstrating that it had regained a sense of normality and stability and looked forward to a positive future.

See also BERLIN WALL; CINEMA; CULTURAL METROPOLIS (KULTURMETROPOLE); FEDERALISM.

BERLIN WALL. The **Berlin** Wall was erected during the night of 12–13 August 1961, although the process of the city's demarcation had in fact been under way since the early 1950s. While the Wall garnered worldwide attention owing to Berlin's role as an arena of Cold War conflict, in reality the whole of Germany was divided over a length of more than a 1,000 kilometers, with nearly impenetrable fortifications, disrupting communities and ways of life for good.

The immediate purpose of the Wall was to create a physical barrier between the western and eastern sectors of the city of Berlin and stem the exodus of citizens of the **German Democratic Republic (GDR)** to the west, which reached 200,000 in 1960 and exceeded 207,000 between January and August 1961. Up until this point, Berlin was still a single entity, with many of its inhabitants living and working in both parts of the city (the

"Grenzgänger"). Eventually 4 meters high and 165 kilometers long, the concrete wall completely sealed off West Berlin from the East German hinterland—effectively isolating the western part and making it heavily dependent on subsidies from the Federal Republic. There were in due course two walls—one facing to the West and, linked by the death-strip and its numerous devices seeking to make the Wall impenetrable, the "Hinterlandmauer," which was what GDR citizens saw on the rare occasions they got close enough. East Germans were not allowed to take photographs of the Wall, and attempts to escape often failed for the very reason that refugees did not know about the death-strip. Maps produced in East Berlin only reproduced details for the eastern part of the city, thereby increasingly undermining any sense of the reality of the West.

Passage was possible only through heavily guarded checkpoints that distinguished representatives of the Allied forces, Berliners, visitors from West Germany, and foreigners. At least 138 East Germans were killed attempting to cross to the West, and the Checkpoint Charlie Museum (Museum Haus am Checkpoint Charlie) records the numerous attempts to flee the GDR. The Wall, which GDR propaganda termed an antifascist protection barrier, became a potent symbol of East–West division and brought international shame on the GDR regime, which pursued a shoot-to-kill policy toward would-be escapees.

The Berlin Wall fell after some miscommunication resulting from an announcement by Politburo member **Günter Schabowski** during a press conference on 9 November 1989. This followed the virtual collapse of the regime after months of a mass exodus of its citizens via other eastern bloc countries and a growing number of very public protests, in particular in the cities of Leipzig (the "Montagsdemonstrationen") and Berlin. After initial enthusiasm in East and West, the reality of the challenges of reunification produced a sense of schism that was termed the "wall in the head" (Mauer im Kopf) mentality, a phrase made famous by the author Peter Schneider in his essay on the effects of the division of the city on the mentalities of East and West Berliners (*Der Mauerspringer*, 1982). The terms "Ossi" and "Wessi," referring to East and West Germans, also became indicative of tensions and prejudices that developed during the existence of the Berlin Wall.

Although most physical evidence of the wall has vanished, the visitor can still gain some impression of what the barrier looked like and what it represented. A 70-meter-long reconstruction of the Wall can be viewed in the Bernauer Straße (the Wall ran down the middle of the street), which also houses a documentation center and is close to one of the former so-called ghost-stations, the underground railway stations that no longer served as stops after the physical division of the city. Possibly the most famous of the Wall's crossing points was Checkpoint Charlie, which was the exit/entry point between East Berlin and the American sector in the West and was used by non-Germans, diplomats, and military personnel. At Friedrichstraße there is also an open-air exhibition with 175 photos and brief commentaries about the history of the Wall. At the "palace of tears" (Tränenpalast) at Friedrichstraße railway station—so named for the relatives of families split up by the Wall bidding tearful good-byes to each other there after reunions— the Haus der Geschichte der Bundesrepublik Deutschland now houses a bilingual (German and English) exhibition (GrenzErfahrungen) that explores not only the reality of these border crossings but also aspects of daily life and the fall of the Wall. The reception camp for refugees and escapees to West Berlin, Notaufnahme Marienfelde e.V., which eventually closed in 1990, is a designated site of historical interest and showcases the brutal reality of life for those who left the GDR and had to stay there, sometimes for years. Among the numerous smaller memorials in Berlin and elsewhere is the "parliament of trees" (Parlament der Bäume). A 1.3-kilometer section of the original wall ("Hinterlandmauer") between the Ostbahnhof und Oberbaumbrücke is the so-called East Side Gallery. Dubbed the "largest open-air art gallery of the world," its surface offered a "canvas" to 118 artists from 21 countries, who painted their impressions, memories, and interpretations of the barrier. Opened in September 1990, the "gallery" was restored in 2000, but its status has been repeatedly under threat, not least since its location hampers building work planned along the nearby Spree River. The East Side Gallery also triggered controversy among the artists themselves, with some keen to restore their own work on a regular basis. The decades since the fall of the Wall and German reunification have been marked by numerous debates, events, and literature about Germany's memory culture, including the Berlin Wall and the memory of the GDR, both as a political system and in terms of its culture. Accordingly, the spectrum of memorials is wide ranging. One other location that plays an important role here is the Stasimuseum, the former headquarters of the secret police (**Stasi**). It now serves as a research center and a memorial of the GDR's political system in the widest sense.

In over a quarter of a century, Berlin has seen a good number of large-scale events commemorating particular anniversaries, be it the building of the Berlin Wall in 1961 or its demise in 1989. The most recent anniversary in 2014, on the occasion of the 25th anniversary of the fall of the Wall, served yet again, and possibly for the last time, as an assessment of the state of reunification. The **media** left no doubt that, despite the emotions involved and the fact that the impact of the former Wall may still be felt, it has also become a matter of history. How exactly this aspect of history is to be taught in German schools remains another issue for debate.

See also OSTPOLITIK.

BERTELSMANN SE. Bertelsmann SE & Co. KGaA, founded and built up by **Reinhard Mohn**, is a global **media** concern with a presence throughout the world, whose core divisions (since 2013) are the RTL Group (**television and radio**), Penguin Random House (book **publishing**), **Gruner + Jahr** (magazines), Arvato (services), and Be Printers (print). Based in Gütersloh, the company's main shareholders are the Bertelsmann and Reinhard Mohn Foundations (89.9 percent) and the Mohn family (19.1 percent). The Bertelsmann conglomerate comprises around 1,200 individual firms or shareholdings in over 50 countries, with more than 112,000 employees worldwide. Principal markets are in western Europe (Germany, France, Great Britain, and Spain) and the United States (U.S.), with an increasing engagement in China, India, and Brazil. Of the total annual turnover of 17,000 million euros, RTL accounted for 35.1 percent, Arvato 28.2 percent, Penguin Random House 21.6 percent, and Gruner + Jahr 8.9 percent.

RTL has a stake in 57 television and 31 radio stations in various countries (2014) and is the largest private broadcaster in Europe; its channels include the flagship RTL Television in Germany, the Netherlands, Belgium, Luxembourg, Croatia, and Hungary; M6 in France; and Antena 3 in Spain. RTL's subsidiary, Fremantle Media, is one of the largest media concerns outside the United States and is involved in television production, licensing, and distribution. Penguin Random House claims to be the world's biggest publisher, with 250 individual publishers producing over 15,000 new titles and selling over 800 million print, audio, and e-books every year. The outsourcing division Arvato offers business services ranging from data management, customer service, and distribution to digital/print production and storage. Core markets for Be Printers, whose 11 production centers provide paper and digital services to the printing industry, are in Europe (Germany, Britain, Italy, Spain) and America (the U.S. and Colombia). Under Thomas Rabe, who became chief executive in January 2012, Bertelsmann launched a 5- to 10-year strategy of strengthening core activities and expansion in promising international markets. The management team was restructured, a new division for printing services (Be Printers) was created, and the company changed from an AG to an SE & Co. KGaA. Random House was also merged with Penguin (part of the Pearson Group).

BEUST, OLE VON (1955–). Christian Democratic Union (CDU) politician. Born in **Hamburg**, Ole von Beust joined the youth wing (**Junge Union, JU**) of the CDU in 1971 and worked as an assistant to the CDU parliamentary group in the Hamburg regional assembly (1973–1975). After studying law at the University of Hamburg (1975–1980) and qualifying in 1983, he set up his own legal practice in the city. Elected to the Hamburg assembly (1978), he joined the CDU regional executive (1992) and the national executive (1998) and led the Hamburg party parliamentary group (from 1993).

Following regional elections in September 2001, he became governing mayor of Hamburg, leading a coalition "citizens' bloc" (Bürgerblock) of CDU, the Schill Party, and **Free Democratic Party (FDP)** with a slim majority over the **Social Democratic Party of Germany (SPD)**. Within a year, Beust increased his cross-party popularity and was undisputed leader of the coalition. However, the 2001 election was remarkable for the strong performance of the newly founded Schill Party, led by the populist **Ronald Schill**, who campaigned on a law-and-order, antiforeigner platform and was appointed deputy mayor and interior senator. The coalition weathered attacks by Schill, but eventually collapsed in December 2003. Elections in February 2004 returned Beust as mayor, with an absolute majority for the CDU and heavy losses for the SPD. The FDP and Schill's former party failed to clear the electoral hurdle. Reelected as mayor after the 2008 city election, Beust led a coalition of CDU (which had lost votes) and the **Green Party** (under the name Grün-Alternative Liste, GAL), the first at the regional level. During his three periods of office, Beust carried out several controversial privatizations, and his proposed reform of the school system also attracted criticism. Although he was for many years a popular figure and long-standing ally of Chancellor **Angela Merkel**, he failed to enter her cabinet (2009) after distancing himself from her austerity program, and he resigned all political posts in 2010.

BEUYS, JOSEPH (1921–1986). Artist. A happening and performance artist and also a theorist of art who triggered important debates in Germany and beyond by questioning established definitions of art, Beuys was born in Krefeld and served as a fighter pilot during World War II. In March 1944, his plane was shot down at the Crimean front. He later claimed that local Tatars had saved his life by applying fat to his wounds, although he was known for conscious myth making. After the war, in 1946, he enrolled at the Düsseldorf Academy of Fine Arts and graduated in 1953. He engaged early on with unconventional materials, including fat. In 1961, he became a professor at the Art Academy; among his students were Jörg Immendorff and Katharina Sieverding. In the 1960s, Beuys became known to the wider public, not least due to institutional frictions that led to his dismissal in 1972. Among other things, Beuys criticized the restrictive policies of admissions of students to the Art Academy, and he became increasingly involved in German politics. Between 1980 and 1985, he worked as a visiting professor for a number of institutions.

Beuys was renowned for his nontraditional performances; his 1965 happening "How to Explain Pictures to a Dead Hare" became one of his most famous contributions. He also saw a close link between art and its therapeutic effects. An exhibition at the Guggenheim Museum in New York in 1979 triggered lively debates and critical responses, and in 1982 Beuys used his contribution to the Documenta in Kassel to showcase his "social sculptures." As ever accompanied by controversy, he nevertheless triggered the planting of 7,000 oak trees.

Beuys has been exhibited worldwide, including at the Venice Biennale (Italy, 1976), the Seibu Museum of Art in Tokyo (Japan, 1984), the Tate Modern (London, 2005), and the Hamburger Bahnhof/Museum für Gegenwart in Berlin (Germany). Major collection holders of Beuys's work are the Pinakothek der Moderne in Munich (Germany); the Harvard University Art Museum in Cambridge, Massachusetts; the Walker Art Center in Minneapolis; the Kunstmuseum in Bonn (Germany); and, among the most complete collections, the Borad Art Foundation in Los Angeles.

BIEDENKOPF, KURT H. (1930–). Lawyer and **Christian Democratic Union (CDU)** politician. Kurt Biedenkopf was born in Ludwigshafen (**Rhineland-Palatinate**). In 1938, his family moved to Schkopau near Merseburg in eastern Germany, but they were later evacuated to **Hessen**. He studied political science in the United States (1949–1950) and law and economics in Munich and Frankfurt (1950–1954), earning a doctorate in law (1958) and qualifying to practice in 1960. He made repeated visits to the U.S., where he obtained a master's degree in law (1962) and in 1963 earned a postdoctoral qualification (Habilitation) at Frankfurt, before becoming professor of commercial and labor law at the Ruhr-University of Bochum (1964–1970), where he also served as vice-chancellor/rector (1967–1969). Between 1968 and 1970, he chaired the commission for industrial **codetermination** set up by Chancellor **Kurt Georg Kiesinger**. In 1971, Biedenkopf left academic life to become managing director of Henkel GmbH, where he worked until 1973. From 1977 until 1990, he practiced as a lawyer.

Although a member of the CDU from 1966, Biedenkopf held no official position in the party until **Helmut Kohl** appointed him general secretary (1973–1977). He represented the CDU in the **Bundestag** (1976–1980) and chaired the district organization in Westfalia-Lippe (1977–1986) before taking over the regional party for **North Rhine-Westfalia** (NRW, 1986). He played a major role in drawing up the CDU's program of basic principles (Grundsatzprogramm, 1978) and represented the party in the NRW's state parliament (**Landtag**, 1980–1988), where he led the parliamentary group (1980–1983). Following power struggles within the party, Biedenkopf handed over his regional functions to **Norbert Blüm** in order to return to the Bundestag (1987–1990).

After the collapse of the **German Democratic Republic (GDR)**, Biedenkopf became a visiting professor of economic policy at the University of Leipzig (April 1990), but soon returned to politics as **minister president** of the federal state of **Saxony** (27 October 1990), where he also headed the regional CDU (1991–1995). Hailed as "King Kurt of Saxony," he led the

CDU to repeated electoral victories and, as a staunch defender of eastern German interests, became popular, even among opposition party supporters. In 2002, he resigned as minister president following a series of controversies. The first of these involved the sale (at an unusually low price) in 1992 of state-owned land in Paunsdorf/Leipzig to a property developer friend. He and his wife were also criticized for living in subsidized accommodation in a government guesthouse, using state employees for private purposes, and negotiating a special rebate for domestic furniture purchased from the Swedish company Ikea. In April 2002, he was succeeded as minister president by the former regional finance minister, **Georg Milbradt**. Subsequent activities include the founding presidency of Dresden International University (2003–2006) and a professorship at the social science research center WZB (Wissenschaftszentrum Berlin für Sozialforschung, 2011–).

BIERMANN, WOLF (1936–). Poet and songwriter. Wolf Biermann was born in **Hamburg** to a working-class family. His father was murdered in Auschwitz in 1943. In 1953, Biermann moved to the **German Democratic Republic (GDR)**, where he studied political economy at Humboldt University in **Berlin**. After meeting the composer Hanns Eisler (1898–1962) in 1960, Biermann began writing poetry and songs. In 1961, he founded a **theater** for workers and students in Berlin, although the authorities blocked a performance on the subject of the **Berlin Wall** and closed the theater in 1963. In the same year, his application to become a full member of the **Socialist Unity Party of Germany** (SED) was rejected. In 1965, the appearance in West Germany of his collection of poems (*Die Drahtharfe*) and recorded songs (*Wolf Biermann [Ost] zu Gast bei Wolfgang Neuss [West]*) earned Biermann the official censure of the East German regime, which banned him from publishing in the GDR. Among his international supporters at the time was Joan Baez, who invited him to the World Youth Festival in 1972. After the ban was lifted in 1976, Biermann began a tour of the Federal Republic of Germany (FRG), but was promptly expatriated by the SED for being antisocialist and anti-GDR. The move marked an end to expectations of a more liberal policy on the part of the East German leader **Erich Honecker** and resulted in 13 leading East German intellectuals (including **Stefan Heym** and **Christa Wolf**) signing an unprecedented petition of protest (November 1976). Between 1976 and 1982, Biermann toured in Western Europe. His songs reflected his critical stance toward the GDR regime, although he always maintained his loyalty to socialism and a strong sense of having lost his real home once he was forced to leave.

Biermann took part in the occupation of the headquarters of the **Stasi** in January 1990, dismissed opposition groups in the former GDR as being infiltrated by Stasi agents, and cofounded an organization to help victims of political injustice (Bürgerbüro e.V., 1996). He attacked the **Party of Demo-**

cratic Socialism (PDS) politician Gregor Gysi and publicly accused the author Stefan Heym of cowardice (1994). Dismissive of the peace movement, he supported the involvement of the North Atlantic Treaty Organization (NATO) in Kosovo in 1999 and the United States (U.S.) in its response to the terror attacks of September 2001 and its invasion of Iraq. After reunification, Biermann continued to publish poetry and songs and received several awards, including the Georg Büchner Prize (1991) and the national prize of the Deutsche Nationalstiftung (1998).

See also LITERARY QUARREL (LITERATURSTREIT); LITERATURE.

BIRTHLER, MARIANNE (1948–). Alliance 90/The Greens politician. Marianne Birthler was born in East **Berlin** in the former **German Democratic Republic (GDR)**, qualifying and working as an export and foreign trade consultant. From 1976 to 1981, she trained as a religious catechist, before working as a teacher and assistant for the Elias parish/community of the Protestant Church in the Prenzlauer Berg district of Berlin (1981–1986) and advising the church on youth issues (1987–1990). In 1986, Birthler cofounded a church-based opposition group (Arbeitskreis Solidarische Kirche) and in 1988 joined the group **Initiative Peace and Human Rights**. After the fall of the East German regime (1989), she served on a working group for youth and **education** of the **Round Table**. Following the national election of March 1990, she represented the Alliance 90/The Greens in the **People's Chamber** of the GDR, where she was spokeswoman for the parliamentary group until October 1990. She also cofounded a group proposing a federation of all German **federal states** (Bund Deutscher Länder).

From reunification until the all-German elections of December 1990, Birthler represented the Alliance 90/The Greens in the **Bundestag**, where she was also party spokeswoman and regarded as a member of its "realist" wing. In regional elections (October 1990), she was elected to the **Brandenburg** state parliament (**Landtag**). As the state's first minister for education, youth, and **sport**, she piloted through parliament a controversial measure that introduced religious education in schools, with general ethics training for all pupils. In 1992, she resigned her ministerial post in protest against links between Minister President **Manfred Stolpe** and the East German secret police, the **Stasi**. Birthler also served on the **Bundesrat** committee on constitutional affairs and on the joint Bundesrat/Bundestag commission for the constitution. Her other positions included membership in the national executive of the Alliance 90/The Greens (1992–1993), party spokeswoman (1993–1994), and head of the Berlin office of the parliamentary group (1995–1999).

Succeeding **Joachim Gauck** as **federal commissioner for the records of the State Security Service of the former German Democratic Republic (BStU)** from 2000 to 2011, Birthler almost immediately became involved in legal disputes over the release of files allegedly shedding light on the involvement of former chancellor **Helmut Kohl** in the scandal over undeclared donations to the **Christian Democratic Union (CDU)**. Emphasizing the need to treat western and eastern German citizens equally, she argued that restrictions on access to files should not impede political education or the legitimate requirements of the **media** acting in the public interest. In 2005–2006, Birthler and the BStU also came under pressure for delaying revelations about the extent to which the Stasi were able to target and even infiltrate Bundestag members during the social–liberal **grand coalition** (1969–1972). Birthler has been active in various organizations, trusts, and foundations, including the presidium of the Conference of German Evangelical Churches (Deutscher Evangelischer Kirchentag, DEK, 1993–2005), the German commission for the **United Nations (UN)** Educational, Scientific, and Cultural Organization (UNESCO, 1993–1996), and a commission researching recent relations between Germany and Russia (2001–2011). Along with other former East German dissidents, she was awarded the Federal Cross of Merit (1995).

BISKY, LOTHAR (1941–2013). PDS/**The Left Party** politician. Born in Zollbrück (now in Poland), Lothar Bisky fled to **Schleswig-Holstein** at the end of World War II but returned to the former **German Democratic Republic (GDR)** in 1959, where he studied philosophy in **Berlin** (1962–1963) and cultural sciences in Leipzig (1963–1966), earning a doctorate in 1969. Appointed honorary professor at Humboldt University in Berlin (1979), he also lectured at the Academy of Social Sciences (Akademie für Gesellschaftswissenschaften), attached to the Central Committee of the **Socialist Unity Party of Germany (SED**, 1980–1986), which he joined in 1963, and was vice-chancellor/rector of the Film and Television Academy (Hochschule für Film und Fernsehen) at Potsdam-Babelsberg (1986–1990). After the fall of the regime, Bisky represented the **Party of Democratic Socialism (PDS)** in the **People's Chamber** (1990); was elected to the **Landtag** for **Brandenburg**, where he led the regional party (1991–1993); and chaired a committee of inquiry investigating alleged links between **Manfred Stolpe** and the GDR secret police, the **Stasi** (1992–1994). A member of the presidium of the PDS (1989–1991), he succeeded **Gregor Gysi** as party leader (1993–2000, reelected 2003–2007). During this period, the party emerged from an electoral alliance with the **Election Alternative for Labor and Justice** (WASG) under **Oskar Lafontaine** as **The Left Party**, which Bisky cochaired with Lafontaine (2007–2010).

In December 1994, together with Gysi (leader of the PDS parliamentary group), Bisky went on a weeklong hunger strike in protest against proposals to levy 67 million DM in taxes from the PDS (a court eventually decided that the sum should be taken from assets of the former SED). In 1995, allegations surfaced that Bisky had spied for the Stasi, although he denied being an informant and continued to do so following the release in July 2003 of the "Rosenholz" files. Held by the U.S. Central Intelligence Agency (CIA) since 1990, the files suggested that the Stasi had registered Bisky as a spy since 1966. The allegations prompted the main parties to block Bisky's appointment as vice president of the **Bundestag** (October 2005), where he served as a deputy (2005–2009). He led The Left Party in the European Parliament from 2007 to 2010 and during 2007–2009 was listed as editor of the left-wing news daily *Neues Deutschland*. During its leadership dispute in 2012, The Left Party considered recalling Bisky, but he refused, arguing that his time had passed.

BITTERFELD WAY. In April 1967, the **Socialist Unity Party of Germany (SED)** in the **German Democratic Republic (GDR)** affirmed the Bitterfeld Way (Bitterfelder Weg) at its eighth party conference as a strategy for advancing the socialist counterrevolution. The term was coined in 1959 at a conference held in the industrial town of Bitterfeld and organized by the publisher Mitteldeutscher Verlag. It was intended to convey a programmatic approach to the arts, in which the workforce (the "Werktätige," embracing agricultural and industrial workers) was actively integrated in the process of producing and enjoying art and culture. The aim was to overcome the traditional divide between the arts and the people. A second resolution (1964) stipulated that education should encourage the development of the socialist personality. One of the authors considered representative of this type of literature is Brigitte Reimann, whose novel *Ankunft im Alltag* (Arrival in everyday life) appeared in 1961. The novel's title led to the term "Ankunftsliteratur" (arrival literature) to denote the portrayal of a figure who is finally led to see the merits of the socialist system. The Bitterfeld Way is an excellent example of the alignment of culture and politics in the GDR.
See also LITERATURE.

BLÜM, NORBERT (1935–). Christian Democratic Union (CDU) politician. Norbert Blüm was born in Rüsselsheim (**Hessen**), trained as a toolmaker, and worked for the motor car manufacturer Opel AG (1952–1957). After attending evening classes to earn his higher school certificate, he went on to study philosophy, German, history, and theology, graduating with a doctorate in philosophy (1967). Between 1966 and 1968, he edited *Soziale Ordnung*, a magazine published by the workers' organization Christlich-Demokratische

Arbeitnehmerschaft Deutschlands (CDA), which is oriented to the CDU. He was also executive manager of the CDA's social affairs committees (1968–1975).

A member of the Roman Catholic workers' movement and of the metal workers' **trade union** IG Metall, Blüm became a prominent member of the CDU and a leading representative of its workers' wing. He joined the CDU national executive (1969); headed the CDA's social affairs committee in **Rhineland-Palatinate** (1974–1977) and at the national level (1977–1987); was elected to the party presidium (1981); and led the regional CDU in **North Rhine-Westfalia** (1987–1999), where he succeeded in uniting a deeply divided and politically enfeebled party. Initially elected to the **Bundestag** via the CDU party list for Rhineland-Palatinate, he served as a member of parliament during 1972–1981 (including a brief period as deputy leader of the CDU/**Christian Social Union [CSU]** parliamentary group, 1980–1981) and also from 1983 until 2002. In 1981, he moved to West **Berlin**, where the newly elected governing mayor, **Richard von Weizsäcker**, appointed him minister (senator) for federal affairs, and where he also sat on the city assembly (until 1982). In 1982, Blüm returned to the Bundestag as federal minister for labor and social affairs under Chancellor **Helmut Kohl**, a post he retained for 16 years, until the coalition of the **Social Democratic Party of Germany (SPD)** and the **Green Party** took over government in 1998. Toward the end of his tenure, he presided over rising unemployment, but continued to defend the principle of the social state as Germany's ability to maintain its provision on **pensions** was called into question. From 1992 until 2000, he was deputy leader of the CDU. He has published widely on politics, **trade unions**, and social affairs (including *Das Sommerloch. Links und rechts der Politik*, 2001); is a consistent defender of **human rights** (he is a member of Amnesty International); and has received a number of awards.

BMW AG. BMW (Bayerische Motorenwerke) AG is the parent company of the Munich-based BMW Group, which is one of Germany's largest **automobile** and motorcycle manufacturers. Alongside other famous brands such as MINI and Rolls-Royce, BMW maintains 12 production and assembly plants in several countries across the world, including Great Britain, Austria, China (Tiexi), South Africa (Rosslyn), and, since 2014, Brazil (Araquari). Its main markets are Europe, Asia, and the United States. The company is owned by the **Quandt family**. Founded in 1929 and renowned for its record-breaking motorcycles and sports cars, BMW built prototype jet aircraft engines during World War II. The firm recovered from severe war damage, but efforts to compete against **Volkswagen** and establish itself in the domestic small car market during the boom years of the economic miracle brought it to the edge of bankruptcy (1959). With new managers and funding from the state government of **Bavaria**, Herbert Quandt restored the company to profitability by 1962, and it went on to become one of Germany's most successful motor manufacturers, extending its interests into financial services (BMW Financial Services), insurance (Bavaria Wirtschaftsagentur), and information technology (Softlab GmbH, 1992–2008). In 2015, BMW employed more than 122,200 people worldwide, produced more than 2.2 million vehicles, and reported a turnover of 92,200 million euros. The chairman of the executive board (from 2006) is Dr. Harald Krüger.

See also AUTOMOBILE INDUSTRY; INDUSTRY.

BOEHRINGER INGELHEIM. Continuing a family tradition of manufacturing **chemicals** that began in Stuttgart in 1817, Albert Boehringer (1861–1939) set up a factory in Ingelheim, near Mainz, in 1885 to produce tartaric acid salts. The popularity of carbonated lemonade and baking powder fueled the company's expansion, and by the end of the century it had become the world's largest producer of lactic acid for the leather, dyeing, and food industries—an activity that, interrupted only by World War II, continued until 1972. A new facility at Biberach on the Riss (**Baden-Württemberg**) opened in 1946 and is now the center for research and development, while the main plant at Ingelheim focuses on production and distribution; a plant in Dortmund produces microsystems technology for biomedicines. During the 1950s, with the postwar economic boom under way and new drugs emerging, Boehringer became a major producer of **pharmaceuticals** for human and veterinary use. The founder's younger son, Ernst Boehringer (1896–1965), expanded interests in Western Europe (Austria, Switzerland, Spain, Italy, France, and Great Britain). In 1991, operational management passed out of the hands of the Boehringer/Baumbach family, which, however, retains ownership. In recent years, Boehringer Ingelheim (the name was adopted in the 1960s to distinguish the company from Boehringer Mannheim, which originated with the family concern but was eventually taken over by La Roche in 1997) has invested heavily in research in Germany. In 2014, the company's global workforce totaled more than 47,500 in 145 countries throughout the world. Turnover was 14,800 million euros (mainly from prescription medicines), 28 percent of which was derived from European sales and 47 percent from North and South America. Among the 20 largest concerns of its kind in the world, Boehringer is rivaled within Germany only by **Bayer AG**. Andreas Barner was appointed chairman of the board of managing directors in 2012.

See also INDUSTRY.

BOHLEY, BÄRBEL (1945–2010). Artist and **human rights** activist. Born in **Berlin** immediately after the end of World War II and later inspired to become a pacifist by her father's memories of fighting on the eastern front,

Bärbel Bohley studied at the East **Berlin** Academy of Art (Kunsthochschule) and, from 1974, worked as an independent painter and graphics artist. A leading figure in the peace movement in the **German Democratic Republic (GDR)** and cofounder of the **Women** for Peace group, which maintained contacts with the **Green Party** in West Germany, she was arrested by the East German authorities in 1983–1984. Undaunted, she became a prominent member of the citizens' group **Initiative Peace and Human Rights** and was again arrested after taking part in a protest march held in 1988 in memory of the early communist martyrs Rosa Luxemburg and Karl Liebknecht. Expelled from the GDR, she was allowed to return after six months following the intervention of the Protestant Church. A committed Christian, Bohley cofounded the opposition group **New Forum** and led the occupation of the former **Stasi** headquarters in Berlin, but her advocacy of a gradual approach to reunification failed to resonate with the majority of East Germans. After viewing her own Stasi file in 1992, she accused **Gregor Gysi**, leader of the **Party of Democratic Socialism (PDS)**, of informing for the Stasi, for which a court later fined her. Between 1995 and 1996, she hosted a discussion group of intellectuals from eastern and western Germany who were committed to promoting the development of democracy in the new **federal states**. After working in the Office of the High Representative in Sarajevo (1996–1999) on reconstruction and refugee assistance, she cofounded the Seestern e.V. project to provide holidays for disadvantaged children in Bosnia and eastern Europe (2001). She returned to Germany in 2008 after being diagnosed with lung cancer.

BÖHME, IBRAHIM (1944–1999). Social Democratic Party of Germany (SPD) politician. Born Manfred Böhme in Bad Dürrenberg (**Saxony-Anhalt**), Böhme spent part of his childhood in an orphanage following the early death of his mother and estrangement from his father. Claiming (falsely) that his parents were Jewish, he later adopted the name Ibrahim. Reconstructing his biography is complicated by his lifelong propensity to fabricate identities and details of his background (as revealed by biographer Christiane Baumann in 2009). After leaving school (1961) and training as a bricklayer at the state-run Leuna oil refinery in eastern Germany, he worked in a children's home attached to the Leuna works (1964–1965). A member of the ruling **Socialist Unity Party of Germany (SED)** in the **German Democratic Republic (GDR)** since 1961, he earned its disapproval by expressing support for the dissident Robert Havemann in 1965. Leaving Leuna, he worked as an assistant librarian in Greitz (from 1965, also studying to qualify after 1967), but was questioned and disciplined by the authorities for criticizing the Soviet invasion of Czechoslovakia (1968). After this, he worked briefly for the East German postal service, but was rehabilitated in 1970 and became local secretary for a local youth cultural group, where he met artists and intellectuals and organized lectures and events while also feeding information—on, among others, the poet Reiner Kunze—to the **Stasi**, for which he spied from 1969 onward. When the Stasi began to doubt Böhme's reports on Kunze, he was placed in detention and expelled from the SED against his wishes (1978), although he resumed his spying activities upon his release. After moving to Neustrelitz, where he worked in a theater, he was dismissed in 1981 for sympathizing with the Polish Solidarity movement and took various casual jobs. In 1989, he joined the citizens' rights group **Initiative for Peace and Human Rights** and in October cofounded the **Social Democratic Party in the GDR**, which he led from February to March 1990. He also represented the party at the **Round Table** forum from December 1990. A member of the **People's Chamber** (March–August 1990), Böhme was appointed police commissioner for the East German mayor's office (September 1990) and joined the national executive of the all-German SPD. In December 1990, Böhme resigned all offices and positions following the publication by Kunze of evidence of his complicity with the Stasi (Böhme had denied similar reports previously published in *Der Spiegel*). Expelled from the SPD in 1992, he lived quietly in eastern **Berlin** and continued to deny any involvement with the Stasi.

BÖHMER, MARIA (1950–). Christian Democratic Union (CDU) politician. Born in Mainz, Maria Böhmer studied mathematics, physics, politics, and pedagogy; completed her state examination (1971); earned a doctorate (1974); and qualified as a professor (Habilitation, 1982). She also undertook research in Augsburg and Cambridge, England, and in 1975 won an international award for her contribution to contemporary pedagogy. After lecturing at Mainz, she worked for the state of **Rhineland-Palatinate** (RLP), specializing in **women**'s issues (as Landesfrauenbeauftragte, 1982–1990), before becoming professor for pedagogy in Heidelberg (from 2001). A member of the CDU from 1986, she was deputy leader of the regional party in RLP and entered the **Bundestag** in 1990, where she served as deputy chairwoman of the basic policy commission (Grundsatzkommission) of the CDU (1991–1993) and headed a party commission on ecology and the **social market economy**. In 1994, she initiated a campaign against violence on **television** and chaired a committee of the television channel ZDF for the protection of families and young people. A member of the CDU national executive (from 1994), Böhmer served as deputy leader of the CDU/**Christian Social Union** (CSU) parliamentary group (2000–2005) and as chairwoman of the women's union of the CDU (Frauenunion, from 2001). From 2005 until 2013, she was appointed **state minister** for Federal Chancellor **Angela Merkel** and government commissioner for migration, refugees, and integration. In Merkel's third cabinet (2013–), she moved (also as state minister) to the foreign ministry, with responsibility for cultural and **education**al policy.

During her career, Böhmer has focused on social questions, including women, the family (advocating measures to help families affected by bereavement and to help women balance work and family life), the church, education, and youth. She has also published on the ethical and political implications of advances in genetic science, opposing, for example, the use of embryos in genetic research.

BÖHMER, WOLFGANG (1936–). Gynecologist and **Christian Democratic Union (CDU)** politician. Born in Dürrhennersdorf in the Oberlausitz (**Saxony**), Wolfgang Böhmer studied medicine at the Karl-Marx University of Leipzig, earned a doctorate (1959), and was appointed professor (1983). After working as a gynecologist in Görlitz (1960–1973), he moved to Wittenberg, where he was a senior hospital doctor until 1991. Böhmer's political career began after reunification, when he entered the state parliament (**Landtag**) of **Saxony-Anhalt** as a member for the CDU (1990). He served as finance minister in the regional cabinet (1991–1993) and as minister of labor and social affairs (1993–1994), resigning in the wake of allegations of excessive salary payments to western politicians. However, he went on to lead the regional CDU (1998–2004) and its parliamentary group (July 2001–April 2002) and was vice president of the Landtag (1998–2002), with responsibilities for labor, health care, social affairs, and finance. When Böhmer took over the CDU leadership, he consolidated a deeply divided party reeling from its catastrophic performance in regional elections (its 22 percent share of the voters was only just ahead of that of the **Party of Democratic Socialism [PDS]**) and became a reluctant candidate for the post of **minister president** in the election of April 2002, standing only when no other contenders presented themselves. Hitherto not considered a high profile politician in the CDU, Böhmer won respect for a pragmatic and well-conducted electoral campaign (unlike the national party, he firmly rejected **immigration** as an election issue) and went on to gain a convincing victory. In May 2002, he succeeded **Reinhard Höppner (Social Democratic Party, SPD)** as minister president and formed a ruling coalition with the **Free Democratic Party (FDP)**. This marked the end of the so-called **Magdeburg Model**, under which the SPD had governed Saxony-Anhalt since 1994–1995 with the tacit support of the PDS. Following the state elections of March 2006, Böhmer led a **grand coalition** of the CDU and SPD until the election of 2011, when he retired from politics. He also served as president of the **Bundesrat** (2003). Böhmer is an active Christian and served in the social affairs chamber (Sozialkammer) of the **Evangelical Church in Germany (EKD)**.

BÖHRNSEN, JENS (1949–). Lawyer and **Social Democratic Party of Germany (SPD)** politician. Jens Böhrnsen was born in **Bremen** and studied law at the University of Kiel (1968–1973). After qualifying as a practicing lawyer (1973, 1977), he went on to become a judge in Bremen (1978–1995), specializing in administrative law. A member of the SPD from 1967, he joined the ver.di **trade union** in 1969 and the workers' welfare organization AWO (Arbeiterwohlfahrtsorganisation) in 1979. He represented the SPD in the Bremen regional assembly (1995–2005), where he also led the party parliamentary group (1999–2005) and sat on a committee investigating the collapse of the Vulkan shipbuilders (1996). In 2005, Böhrnsen succeeded **Henning Scherf** (SPD) as governing mayor and president of the Bremen senate, winning assembly elections in 2007 and 2011 and heading coalitions with the **Green Party**. From 2005 to 2007, he served as senator for justice and constitutional affairs and for church affairs (the latter also from 2007). As mayor, he rejected a proposal for Bremen to merge with neighboring **Lower Saxony** to solve the city's acute financial problems (2005).

BÖLL, HEINRICH (1917–1985). Writer. Heinrich Böll was born in Cologne and served as an infantry soldier in World War II. His short story, "Der Zug war pünktlich" (1949), reflected the immediate impact of the war and set the tone of much of his future work, which included further short stories and novels exploring moral, religious, and social values in the Federal Republic of Germany (FRG). He joined the **Group 47** of writers and poets in 1951 and was president of the (West) German **PEN** Club (1970–1972) and of the international PEN Club (1972–1974). In 1972, Böll won the Nobel Prize for Literature, the first German recipient in 43 years. In the same year, he published a controversial article warning the state against overreacting in its handling of **Ulrike Meinhof,** a member of the **Red Army Faction** terrorist group. During the 1970s, he accused the **Springer**-owned **press** of whipping up mass public hysteria through one-sided reporting. In 1972, Böll became actively involved with the **Social Democratic Party of Germany (SPD)** and during the 1980s was engaged in the German peace movement. He also housed the Soviet writer Aleksandr Solzhenitsyn when he first came to the West. In 1983, Böll was made an honorary citizen of the city of Cologne; his cottage in Ireland has served as a residence for writers since 1992. Like **Günther Grass,** Böll is representative of a generation of German writers and public figures who considered their active involvement in and criticism of politics an obligation that resulted from the experience of the National Socialist regime (1933–1945).

BÖRNER, HOLGER (1931–2006). Social Democratic Party of Germany (SPD) politician. Holger Börner was born in Kassel (**Hessen**). His father was persecuted by the National Socialists and, during the family's economic deprivation after World War II, the son was compelled to break off his schooling and train as a builder (1947). An activist in the **trade unions**, he joined the SPD in 1948 and was national chairman of its **Young Socialists (JUSOS)** wing (1961–1964). In 1957, he entered the **Bundestag** (its youngest member), where he chaired the parliamentary committee on **transport** (from 1965). In 1967, he joined the Federal Ministry of Transport as parliamentary **state secretary** to **Georg Leber** in the **grand coalition** led by Chancellor **Kurt Georg Kiesinger**. Following the 1972 national election, he served as SPD parliamentary business manager under **Willy Brandt** (until 1976). In October 1976, after the resignation of Albert Osswald (SPD), he became **minister president** of Hessen, continuing the long-standing coalition of the SPD with the **Free Democratic Party (FDP)**. He was also regional party leader (1977–1985). Börner's premiership was marked by political turbulence and fierce controversies over nuclear **energy** and the construction of the new Frankfurt international airport. When the FDP fell short of the 5 percent hurdle in the September 1982 regional election, Börner led a minority administration until further elections (September 1983), although these too failed to produce a working majority. In June 1984, he was reelected minister president. Although his government was tolerated by the **Green Party**, a formal alliance—the first red/green coalition in Germany—was agreed upon only in October 1985, and it collapsed in February 1987 over opposition to a proposed nuclear reactor in Hanau. Börner dismissed his **environment** minister, **Joschka Fischer**, resigned as regional party leader, and announced that he would not be seeking reelection to the **Landtag**. Under his premiership, Hessen pioneered the introduction of **health**-care insurance (Pflegeversicherung), passed measures on environmental protection and **energy** saving, and appointed a cabinet representative for **women**. He was under constant threat from the **Red Army Faction (RAF)** terrorist group. Following elections in April 1987, Börner was succeeded by **Walter Wallmann** of the **Christian Democratic Union (CDU)**, who led a coalition with the FDP. From 1987 until 2003, Börner was chairman of the Friedrich Ebert Foundation.

BOSCH. The foundations of the Bosch concern were laid in 1886, when Robert Bosch (1861–1942) founded a workshop for precision and electrical **engineering** in Stuttgart. Profiting from the boom in **automobile** manufacturing, the business grew rapidly in Germany and abroad, including France and the United States, and by 1914 it was exporting 88 percent of its output. During the 1930s, the range of products expanded to include electrical tools, radio, and refrigerators. Bosch became a household name for the quality of German **industry** and developed a reputation for good labor relations, introducing the eight-hour day in 1906 and paying its workers generously.

After World War II, the company lost its factories in the east, while those in the west were temporarily confiscated by the Allies. The founder's son, Robert, briefly took over the running of the concern in 1954 before handing over management to Hans Walz (1883–1974), who, in conjunction with other senior managers, had effectively run the company since 1942. In 1963, Walz was succeeded by Hans L. Merkle (1913–2000), under whose stewardship Bosch became a leading global player. Subsequent chief executive officers were Marcus Bierich (1926–2000) and Hermann Scholl (b. 1935). While Bierich introduced a less formal style of management and improved consultation with staff, Scholl, who took over in 1993, vigorously pursued a policy of acquisitions that by 2002 had established Bosch as the world's second largest supplier to the automotive industry. In July 2003, Scholl was succeeded by Franz Fehrenbach, an engineer who joined Bosch in 1975 and moved to the board in 1999. Fehrenbach took over at a time when the company was experiencing a downturn in demand for motor vehicle products (which accounted for two-thirds of turnover) and was regarded as suffering from old-fashioned, hierarchical management and bureaucratic procedures. He was succeeded by Volkmar Denner in 2012.

The parent company, Robert Bosch GmbH (Stuttgart), belongs largely (92 percent) to the Robert-Bosch Stiftung (Robert Bosch Foundation), which is one of Germany's biggest private foundations; the remaining interest is held by the Bosch family. Decision making is in the hands of the Robert Bosch Industrietreuhand KG, which includes representatives of management and the family, in particular the latter's spokesman, Christof Bosch. In 2015, Robert Bosch GmbH turned over around 70,100 million euros, of which 80 percent was outside Germany, and employed 375,000 workers worldwide (132,000 in Germany). The group has around 360 subsidiaries in 150 countries. Its principal business sectors are automotive technology, drive/control systems and packaging, consumer goods (power tools and household appliances), and **energy** and building technology (including thermal/solar energy and security systems, although Bosch announced its withdrawal from solar power in 2013).

BOUFFIER, VOLKER (1951–). Christian Democratic Union (CDU) politician. Volker Bouffier was born in Gießen (**Hessen**), where he studied law at the university (1970–1975) and worked as a research assistant (1975–1978) before qualifying as a practicing lawyer and notary (1978/ 1987). After leading the **Junge Union (JU)**, the youth organization of the CDU between 1978 and 1984 in Hessen, he represented the main party on the councils for Gießen town (1979–1993) and district (1979–1999). He also joined the regional executive committee (1978) and was regional deputy leader (1992–2010). His other positions include regional party leader (from June 2010) and deputy chairman of the national CDU (from November 2010). As a member of the Hessen parliament (**Landtag**) during 1982–1987 and from 1991, he served as **state secretary** (Staatssekretär) in the Ministry of Justice (1987–1991), then as minister for internal affairs and sport (1999–2010). As interior minister, Bouffier reformed the regional police service, which pioneered measures against **Internet** crime; showed strong support for increased security surveillance on citizens, including computer-based profiling (Rasterfahndung); and promoted the repatriation of refugees. A close colleague of **Roland Koch**, he succeeded the latter as **minister president** of Hessen in August 2010 and went on to lead a coalition between the CDU and the **Green Party** following the regional election of 2013.

BRANDENBURG. In terms of area, Brandenburg is the largest of the eastern **federal states** (29,483 sq. km). It surrounds the city-state and national capital, **Berlin**, and shares a border with Poland in the east. To the north is the state of **Mecklenburg-West Pomerania**, while **Saxony-Anhalt** lies to the west and **Saxony** to the south; for a short stretch of the River Elbe, it also adjoins eastern **Lower Saxony**. Situated in the North German Plain, Brandenburg's landscape is generally flat, with undulating hills (its highest points are the 200-meter Hagelberg and the 200.7-meter Kutschenberg) and many lakes, rivers, and forests. Major rivers are the Oder (on the eastern border) and the Havel, which also runs through Berlin. After Mecklenburg-West Pomerania, Brandenburg has the lowest population density (85 persons per sq. km) of all the German federal states. Although one-third of the population of 2.5 million lives in the area of Berlin/Potsdam, where the postreunification exodus from Berlin to its Brandenburg outskirts led to a population bulge, most inhabitants are found in small communities in rural areas. The overall population level in 2014, of which **foreigners** accounted for 2.8 percent, was one of the lowest since unification and continued a downward trend evident since 2001. A slight rise in 2015 was put down to an influx of mainly foreigners (now 3.6 percent of the population), although the rate of births continued to decline. The largest cities are the state capital, Potsdam (over 158,000 inhabitants), and Cottbus (over 99,000), followed by Brandenburg on the Havel (over 71,000) and Frankfurt on the Oder (58,700).

Established in the 12th century during the German colonization of Slav territories, Brandenburg and its history are synonymous with the rise of the Hohenzollern dynasty. From the 15th to the 18th centuries, the Hohenzollerns developed and extended the province as the core of the Kingdom of Prussia (established in 1701). In the 17th and 18th centuries, Brandenburg-Prussia reclaimed marshes and fenland and built up a powerful army, a sound economy, excellent transportation links, and an efficient civil service. An example of "enlightened absolutism," the Prussian state also welcomed **immigrants** and refugees, who contributed to business, manufacturing, science, and culture. The unification of Germany, in the form of the German Reich of 1871, came about under Prussian leadership. After World War II, German territory east of the Oder River was incorporated into Poland, and the German population, which had lived there for many centuries, was expelled. When Prussia was officially dissolved in 1947, the historic province of Brandenburg was briefly resurrected. In 1952, however, as part of the **German Democratic Republic (GDR)**, it was replaced by the administrative districts (Bezirke) of Potsdam, Frankfurt/Oder, and Cottbus. Not until October 1990 was the federal state (Land) of Brandenburg reconstituted as part of reunited Germany.

Brandenburg's constitution, adopted in 1992, was heavily influenced by the citizens' groups that brought about the "peaceful revolution" of 1989–1990. The constitution includes a powerful plebiscitary element, which requires the lowest quorum levels of all the federal states (from 1 to 4 percent of the population) to trigger a full referendum and also allows all residents (not just German citizens) to participate. Other features include not only the "right to life" but also a guarantee of "dignity in death," respect for an individual's sexual identity, and statements of policy objectives that commit the state to meet social needs (including adequate housing and full employment) and to support a balanced ecology. The constitution explicitly commits Brandenburg to working for peaceful relations with other nations, especially neighboring Poland (Polish is taught in some schools). The regional assembly consists of 88 members who are elected for five years. Significant roles are assigned to parliament and its recognized party groupings.

Despite its relatively low membership in the region, the dominant political party is the **Social Democratic Party of Germany (SPD)**. The party leader after reunification was **Manfred Stolpe**, who also served as **minister president** (1990–2002) until he was succeeded by **Matthias Platzeck**. From 1990 to 1994, Stolpe led a "traffic light coalition" of the SPD, **Free Democratic Party (FDP)**, and **Alliance 90/The Greens** that established a reputation for consensus-based politics (the term "traffic light" refers to the colors of the parties). Following regional elections in 1998, the SPD formed a coalition with the **Christian Democratic Union (CDU)**. Despite its high membership and good election performance, the **Party of Democratic Socialism (PDS)** was consistently rejected as a coalition partner by the main parties. The Alliance 90/The Greens were hampered by internal disunity, and in 1998 the FDP failed to clear the 5 percent hurdle. Also in 1998, the extreme right-wing **German People's Union (DVU)** entered parliament for the first time, gaining five seats. The DVU went on in 2004 to increase its share of the vote (to 6.1 percent), while the SPD (31.9 percent) and CDU (19.4 percent) suffered losses. Although the SPD entered into negotiations with the PDS, which came in third with 28 percent of votes, it continued the coalition with the CDU. However, following regional elections in 2009 and losses for the CDU, this was replaced by a ("red/red") coalition with **The Left Party**, headed by Platzeck. The DVU failed to clear the 5 percent hurdle and gained no seats. Platzeck stepped down in August 2013 for health reasons and was succeeded by **Dietmar Woidke** (SPD), who continued the coalition upon reelection in 2014, pledging investment in **education** and highways.

Brandenburg has always had a special relationship with Berlin, and although the city was formerly detached from the surrounding province in 1881, both continued to cooperate in areas such as town planning and housing. Following a recommendation in the Treaty of Unification (1990) to create a unitary state of Berlin-Brandenburg, the governments and major political parties (not, however, the PDS), agreed on a merger, but the plan was rejected in a referendum held in 1996 (reasons include Brandenburgers' fear of financial disadvantages and the reluctance of Berliners employed by the state to be redeployed anywhere in the region). Nevertheless, both Länder continued to coordinate their policies, especially in areas of **transport**, the economy, education, and culture, and a merger remains a long-term objective.

Brandenburg's traditional sectors of **industry** included brown coal (lignite) extraction in the south (Cottbus/Niederlausitz), metal processing (Brandenburg/Havel), optics (Rathenow), and mechanical **engineering** (Eberswalde). During the GDR era, a large steel production facility was established at Eisenhüttenstadt, and motor vehicles were manufactured in Ludwigsfelde. After reunification, however, lignite production was cut by 80 percent for **environmental** reasons, while many other industries closed down. The region was also hit by the loss of its eastern European markets. Although some older industries survive, the sectors contributing most to GDP are now food, **chemicals**, and engineering (including electronics). The area around Potsdam has become a national center for biotechnology research. **Agriculture** predominates, although the closure of large collective farms after 1990 meant that the structure of the farming economy did not stabilize until after 1993. Even so, in 2010 Brandenburg had 5,566 farming units, around 64 percent of which were over 20 hectares (the European average) and accounted for 98 percent of agricultural land. The state contributes 2 percent of national GDP (2015) and has an unemployment rate of 8.7 percent (national average: 6.4 percent).

Tourism is important to the region. Its many attractions include places of cultural and historical significance (such as the palaces in and around Potsdam) and areas of natural beauty. Brandenburg has three universities (Potsdam, a technical university in Cottbus, and the Europa-University Viadrina in Frankfurt/Oder, with close links to Poland). There is also an academy of **cinema** and **television** studies in Potsdam-Babelsberg, which has become a renowned international center for film production. The educational system is progressive, having adopted the comprehensive school as standard, although many schools, especially at the primary level, are threatened with closure in rural areas. **Religion** was not encouraged in the GDR, which is reflected in the fact that only around 20 percent of the population in this historically Protestant region are now church members. During 1992–1995, the state piloted a new school subject (now called Lebensgestaltung-Ethik-Religions-kunde, L-E-R), which combined religious education with general ethics for all pupils, regardless of confession. Although criticized by church groups as marginalizing traditional religious education, L-E-R was being taught throughout the region in 2015.

BRANDT, WILLY (1913–1992). Social Democratic Party of Germany (SPD) politician and **federal chancellor**, 1969–1974. Willy Brandt was born in Lübeck as Herbert Ernst Karl Frahm. His mother was a sales assistant, but he never knew his father, a teacher and member of the SPD, and the boy, who was raised by his grandfather, also a party member, joined a socialist workers' youth organization (Sozialistische Arbeiterjugend, 1929) and the SPD (1930). The following year, he switched to the Socialist Workers' Party (SAP), a left-wing splinter group of the SPD, and was elected leader of its youth wing. On leaving school (1932), he began training at a maritime bro-kers' firm in Lübeck, but fled to Norway when the National Socialists came to power (1933) and changed his name to Willy Brandt. Brandt became stateless in 1938 after the National Socialists withdrew his German national-ity. In Oslo, he studied history and worked as a journalist, before returning to **Berlin** in 1936 to work underground for the SAP. In 1937, he visited Spain to observe and report on the civil war for the Republicans. Briefly taken prison-er of war by German forces when they occupied Norway (1940), Brandt escaped recognition before fleeing to Stockholm, where he worked as a journalist. In Sweden, the Norwegian government in exile conferred on him Norwegian citizenship. In 1942, Brandt rejoined the SPD. After the war, he reported for Scandinavian newspapers on the Nuremberg war trials (1945–1946) and worked as press attaché for the Norwegian military mission in Berlin (1947).

Upon regaining German citizenship (July 1948), Brandt joined the SPD executive committee in Berlin. During the Berlin blockade and airlift (June 1948–May 1949), he worked closely with Ernst Reuter (1889–1953), whose appointment as elected SPD governing mayor of West Berlin was initially vetoed by the Union of Soviet Socialist Republics (USSR) in June 1947. Brandt represented the SPD in the **Bundestag** (1949–1957, 1965–1992) and was president of the West Berlin city parliament (1955–1957) before suc-ceeding Otto Suhr as mayor (1957–1966). In 1958, he was elected leader of the Berlin SPD and a member of the national party executive. He was a strong supporter of the Godesberg Program (1959), which marked the SPD's reorientation away from Marxism toward a genuine "people's party" with a broad electoral appeal. In 1964, Brandt succeeded the veteran Erich Ollenhauer as party leader, retaining the post until 1987, and in the national elections of 1961 and 1965 was the SPD's chancellor candidate against **Konrad Adenauer** and **Ludwig Erhard**, both members of the **Christian Democratic Union (CDU)**.

As mayor of Berlin during the erection of the **Berlin Wall** (August 1961) and its tense aftermath, Brandt won international respect and developed a profound interest in East–West relations. Between 1961 and 1963, he worked closely with **Egon Bahr** (SPD), head of Berlin's press and information office, to develop the basis for what came to be known as **Ostpolitik**: the policy of improving relations with the **German Democratic Republic (GDR)** and other eastern bloc states.

As foreign minister and deputy chancellor in the CDU/SPD **grand coalition** (1966–1969) under Chancellor **Kurt Georg Kiesinger**, Brandt negotiated a Franco-German agreement on troops and supported limitations on nuclear arms. Ignoring the Hallstein doctrine, according to which the FRG maintained the sole right to represent the German nation internationally and refused diplomatic links with states that recognized the GDR, he opened relations with Romania and Yugoslavia and set up West German trade representatives in Poland, Czechoslovakia, and Hungary. Following national elections in 1969, the SPD and **Free Democratic Party (FDP)** formed a ruling coalition, with Brandt as chancellor and **Walter Scheel** (FDP) as his deputy and foreign minister. This was the first time the SPD had headed a government since 1930. Although it was constrained by a narrow majority, the distrust of right-wing members of the FDP, and a **Bundesrat** controlled by the opposition CDU/**Christian Social Union (CSU)**, Brandt pledged his government to an ambitious program of domestic reforms, which included expanding and modernizing the **education**al system and improving social welfare benefits.

Although Brandt had campaigned on the slogan "risking more democracy" ("mehr Demokratie wagen") in reforming Germany's domestic institutions, his greatest achievement was undoubtedly détente with the East. A historic moment occurred in March 1970, when he visited the GDR and met the latter's head of state, **Willi Stoph**, in Erfurt. To the consternation of the leadership of the **Socialist Unity Party of Germany (SED)**, Brandt was feted as a hero by the East German people. On a visit to Warsaw in December, his kneeling before the memorial to the Jewish ghetto was widely appreciated as a poignant gesture of German atonement for the atrocities committed under the National Socialists. The Ostpolitik treaties were bitterly opposed by the conservative opposition in the Bundestag, and although Brandt survived a constructive vote of no confidence mounted by the CDU leader

Rainer Barzel (April 1972), he engineered a further vote in order to trigger national elections (November 1972) and resolve the parliamentary stalemate. For the first time in the history of the Federal Republic of Germany (FRG), the SPD gained more seats than the CDU, and the SPD/FDP coalition was returned with an increased majority. The result was a personal victory for Brandt, who had campaigned on the slogan "Germans, you can be proud of your country" ("Deutsche, Ihr könnt stolz sein auf Euer Land"). In 1973, Brandt was at the height of his popularity: he was the first West German leader to visit Israel (June) and to address the general assembly of the **United Nations (UN)** in New York (September).

In May 1974, Brandt suddenly resigned as chancellor, ostensibly over the unmasking of his adviser, **Günter Guillaume**, as an East German spy. In reality, Brandt was exhausted by years of government crises, not only over Ostpolitik but following his failure to manage Germany's worsening finances, as a turndown in the economy and increases in welfare spending had produced large debts at the national and regional levels. Brandt was succeeded as chancellor by **Helmut Schmidt**.

Despite retiring from frontline German politics, Brandt remained active in the cause of international peace and Third World development. A member of parliament in what later became the **European Union (EU**, 1979–1983), he was president of the Socialist International (1976–1992) and founding chairman of the North-South Commission, which, established in 1977 by a group of developing nations to promote a fairer balance in world trade between industrial and poorer states, issued what became known as the Brandt Report in 1980. Brandt supported efforts by the Austrian chancellor, Bruno Kreisky, to resolve differences between Israel and the Palestinians (1978) and met the Soviet leader Leonid Brezhnev in Moscow to discuss arms control (1981). He was also one of the first Western politicians to meet Mikhail Gorbachev (1985) and personally negotiated with President Saddam Hussein to obtain the release of 193 foreigners held hostage in Iraq during the Gulf War (1990). For his contribution to international peace, Brandt received "man of the year" recognition from *Time* magazine (1970) and the Nobel Peace Prize (1971). He was also awarded the Third World Prize in New York (1984) and the Albert Einstein Peace Prize in Washington (1985). In 1986, he set up the Stiftung Entwicklung und Frieden, a foundation for the promotion of peace and development. In 1987, he resigned as leader of the SPD after internal party disputes over his proposal to appoint Margarita Mathiopoulos as press spokesperson. In the same year, he was elected honorary chairman of the SPD.

After the fall of the Berlin Wall, Brandt gave a speech in West Berlin in which he anticipated Germans from the FRG and the GDR coming together in unity (10 November 1989). His famous statement that "what belongs together will now grow together" ("jetzt wächst zusammen, was zusammen gehört") became a motto of the German people's need to achieve a genuine sense of commonality beyond political union. In December 1990, as "father" (Alterspräsident) of the Bundestag, he opened the first session of the new all-German parliament in the historic Reichstag building in Berlin. The following year, he proposed the motion to move the seat of government from Bonn to Berlin, which was passed by 338 votes to 320. Brandt died in October 1992 and was buried in Berlin, where over a thousand guests from all over the world, including several heads of states, attended his funeral. His political memoirs (*Erinnerungen*) appeared in 1989. More successful on the international stage than in domestic politics, Brandt is remembered primarily for the achievements of Ostpolitik and for representing the new generation of postwar German politicians.

BRAUN, LUDWIG GEORG (1943–). Business executive. Ludwig Georg Braun was born in the north of **Hessen**, the fifth generation of the founding family of the B. Braun group in Melsungen. The group, which manufactures medical and surgical products, originated in a small apothecary in Melsungen, acquired by Julius Wilhelm Braun in 1839. The company opened its first branch in **Berlin** (1889), expanded abroad during the 1890s, and built its first foreign production plant in Milan (1925). Although it failed to exploit the postwar economic boom during the 1950s and 1960s and had to fight for survival, the company's fortunes had recovered by 1969, and during the following decade new products were developed to accommodate advances in surgical techniques. A production facility opened in Penang, Malaysia (1973), and a U.S. subsidiary, B. Braun of America, was set up in partnership with Burron Medical Inc., Bethlehem (1979). The 1990s and first decade of the 2000s saw rapid expansion, with two new plants opening in Germany (including the Benchmark-Factory in Tüttlingen), the creation of a center in Great Britain, and the purchase of McGaw Inc. (California; the largest acquisition in the firm's history). Some restructuring took place in 2000, including a withdrawal from biotechnology and the formation of a logistical alliance with Paul Hartmann AG.

In 1993, *Der Spiegel* published reports that the company had illegally acquired brain tissue in order to manufacture a plaster-type medical product that was used in skin transplant operations but was subsequently linked to the deaths of 40 patients in Japan between 1985 and 1996. B. Braun withdrew the product and settled out of court for damages of over a million euros. The affair had little effect on the firm's commercial success, however, which reported a worldwide turnover of around 5,430 million euros in 2015 and employed 54,000 workers worldwide (13,600 in Germany). The company's main divisions are Hospital Care (including supplies for infusions and injections) and Aesculap (products and services for surgery and cardiology), followed by Out Patient Market (nursing care and the chronically ill) and Avitum (haemodialysis). Its largest markets are Europe and North America, and the company has more than 200 subsidiaries and holdings in 57 countries.

In 2011, Georg Ludwig Braun, chief executive since 1977, was succeeded by Heinz-Walter Große, the first non-family member to occupy the position. Nevertheless, the concern remains family owned, and with the entry of Otto Philipp Braun on the management board (2012), is represented there by its sixth generation. The "Rothschild principle," which enables family members to run foreign subsidiaries, has helped prevent the discord that has dogged other business "clans" in Germany. The company prides itself on its product quality and democratic working practices, including measures to keep jobs in Germany. On the other hand, when G. L. Braun, a supporter of the **Free Democratic Party** (**FDP**), served as president of the German Chamber of Industry and Trade (DIHK, 2001–2009), he was viewed as less politically aware than his predecessor, Peter Stihl, and was criticized after tactlessly calling for zero raises for employees in a round of pay talks. He also raised eyebrows after announcing that he would not attend meetings of the national forum, the **Alliance for Work**, if they continued to be held on Sundays. As president, he supported an increase in working hours (without additional pay) and the lowering of taxes.

See also CHEMICAL INDUSTRY; PHARMACEUTICALS.

BREMEN. The maritime and trading city-state of Bremen (official title: the Free Hanseatic City of Bremen) is the smallest of Germany's **federal states**: its area is only 419 square kilometers and its population around 658,000. The state is made up of two cities: Bremerhaven and the larger Bremen, which lies 54 kilometers farther inland on the Weser River (the cities are separated by the territory of **Lower Saxony**). From 1358 until 1810, Bremen was a member of the Hanseatic League (or Hanse), an association of free trading cities. The separation of the cities originates from Bremen's decision in 1827 to build a coastal harbor that would preserve access to the open sea. During the 19th century, Bremen handled coffee, cotton, wool, and tobacco and became a departure point for many emigrants to North America. After World War II, the main activities were trade, fishing, shipbuilding, aircraft construction, **automobile** manufacturing, and steel. Although the city authorities invested heavily in social services, **education**, cultural facilities, and infrastructure, the measures failed to stem the outward flow of population, and the state lost **taxation** revenues as commuters preferred to live in neighboring Lower Saxony. Controversy surrounded the founding of a university in 1971, which some criticized as a breeding ground for left-wing activists, and which rapidly became a center for campaigners for the **environment** and opponents of nuclear **energy**.

With a decline in motor manufacturing in the early 1960s, West German unemployment rose to record levels, and the city slipped deeper into debt. Economic fortunes improved with the return of motor vehicle production (in the form of Mercedes-Benz in 1978) and aeronautics (Airbus), although the closure of the large Weser shipyard (owned by **Krupp**) in 1983 was a serious blow. During the 1980s, Bremen worked hard to attract new industries (aviation, microelectronics, environmental technology), and the university established itself as a center for research in geophysics, science, and **engineering**. Bremen's last major shipyard, the Vulcan, closed in 1995, and unemployment reached 16.8 percent in 1997. The founding of the International University Bremen (IUB) in 1999 marked the first attempt to establish a private university in Germany offering a wide range of subjects, based on the U.S. model. Bremen contributes 1 percent of national GDP (2015) and continues to have a high unemployment rate of 10.9 percent (national average: 6.4 percent in 2015). **Foreigners** represent 16.1 percent of the population, compared with the national average of 11.2 percent.

Bremen's parliament (Bremische Bürgerschaft) plays a twin role as the elected City Council of Bremen (Stadtbürgerschaft) and the parliament of the state of Bremen (**Landtag**). Elected for four years, it is made up of 83 members (67 from Bremen and, since 2003, 15 from Bremerhaven), who choose the cabinet (senate); the 5 percent hurdle applies separately to the city and the state. The senate in turn elects two mayors, one of whom is elected as the head of the government (called president of the senate). At the same time that they enter the Bürgerschaft, members also constitute local or district assemblies. Bremen was the first state to reduce the voting age to 16 (May 2011). Historically, the strongest political party is the **Social Democratic Party of Germany** (SPD), which led various coalitions from 1947 until 1971, after which it ruled alone until 1991. Leading figures were senate presidents Hans Koschnick (1967–1985) and Klaus Wedemeier (1985–1995). Following electoral disaster for the SPD in May 1995, Bremen was governed by a **grand coalition** of the SPD and **Christian Democratic Union (CDU)**. Led by **Henning Scherf** (SPD), the coalition, which worked hard to bring public finance under control, was endorsed by the electorate in 1999, when only the **Green Party** was left in parliament to oppose the SPD/ CDU alliance, and again in May 2003. In November 2005, Scherf was succeeded as mayor by the SPD parliamentary group leader **Jens Böhrnsen**, who continued the grand coalition until the elections of 2007 and 2011, when the CDU fell both times into third place behind the Greens, who entered into coalition with the SPD. Extreme right-wing parties entered parliament in 1967 (the **National Democratic Party of Germany, NPD**) and 1987 (the **German People's Union, DVU**). High unemployment, poor educational performance, and ongoing budget deficits continue to challenge the city-state, and both the Greens and the SPD sustained losses in the 2015 regional election. Despite a narrow majority, the coalition continued, with Carsten Sieling (SPD) succeeding Böhrnsen as governing mayor.

BRENNINKMEYER, DOMINIC (1959–). Business executive. Dominic Brenninkmeyer (also spelled Brenninkmeijer) is a member of the Brenninkmeyer family that owns and controls the multinational C&A textile retail group (German branch: C&A Mode GmbH & Co. KG). The business was originally founded by the brothers Clemens and August Brenninkmeyer (hence C&A) in 1841 in Sneek (Holland), where they had emigrated 20 years earlier from Mettingen, near Osnabrück (**North Rhine-Westfalia**). Under National Socialist influence during the 1930s, the famously reclusive Brenninkmeyer family appeared to react positively to anti-Jewish policies and, after World War II, fought a long battle to avoid publishing annual reports. Nevertheless, by mass producing clothing for a broad market at affordable prices, C&A developed into one of Europe's leading fashion retailers, with a store in virtually every German city in the 1960s. Responding to a downturn during the 1990s, the company, led by Lucas Brenninkmeyer, head of European operations (1998–2008), and his cousin Dominic, chief executive in Germany (2000–2005), turned itself around in two years by cutting costs, withdrawing from Great Britain and Denmark (2000–2001), and reducing the number of its German branches and distribution centers. C&A invested heavily in remodeling and updating its outlets and expanded into Poland, the Czech Republic, and Russia; special outlets for children (Kids Stores) were also developed.

Dominic Brenninkmeyer's father was head of C&A in Britain, where the son grew up and studied business, economics, and languages. He trained entirely within the company, learning trade and commerce in C&A Holland and purchasing in C&A in Great Britain, where he became head of buying children's clothing (1985). In 1988, he moved to the United States (U.S.), where he eventually became vice president of marketing and chief executive of the subsidiaries Miller's Outpost (Los Angeles) and Woman's World (San Diego). Brenninkmeyer's success is attributed to the more open style of management he acquired in the U.S. and to his drive to modernize fashion lines and revitalize marketing strategy. His successors as chief executive of C&A in Germany were Bart Brenninkmeyer (2006–2012) and Benedikt Spangenberg (2012–). The family-controlled company does not publish full figures, but currently operates an estimated 450 outlets in Europe and turns over around 6,800 million euros (around 50 percent in Germany), with a workforce of 37,000. The holding company for C&A's operations is the Swiss-based COFRA Holding AG.

See also DISTRIBUTION AND RETAIL.

BREUEL, BIRGIT (1937–). Christian Democratic Union (CDU) politician. The daughter of a **Hamburg** banker, Breuel trained in banking, and studied political science at the universities of Hamburg, Oxford, and Geneva. In 1959 she married Ernst-Jürgen Breuel, who worked for a publishing house. After qualifying in retail commerce, she worked for an economics history archive in Hamburg and in 1961–1962 in New York. As a member of the parents' council in a Hamburg school, she opposed the **education**al policy of the city government, which was controlled by the **Social Democratic Party of Germany (SPD)**. After joining the CDU in 1966, she was elected to the Hamburg city parliament (1970) and became party spokeswoman on economic affairs. She failed to win a direct seat in the **Bundestag** (1976), but was appointed economics minister in the cabinet of Minister President **Ernst Albrecht** following his regional election victory in **North Rhine-Westfalia (NRW)** in 1978—the first time a woman had held a major ministerial post in Germany. A strong advocate of the free market economy, Breuel criticized the culture of subsidies and developed a reputation as a strong-minded, conservative politician. She set up a special department promoting privatization and established the first privately owned water purification plant in Germany. After the CDU lost its absolute majority in NRW (1986), she moved to the finance ministry, where she remained until 1990.

A member of the national CDU executive and protégée of Chancellor **Helmut Kohl**, Breuel joined the executive board of the **Trust Agency** (October 1990), which had been created to privatize the state-run assets of the former **German Democratic Republic (GDR)**. She took over as head of the agency a few days after the murder of Detlev Carsten Rohwedder (April 1991). When the agency was closed (December 1994), she represented the **federal government** during the preparations for the international millennium exhibition in Hanover, Expo 2000. As the exhibition's executive manager (from April 1997), she attracted criticism as head of a loss-making event that swallowed up large public subsidies. Breuel, who retired from public life after 2000, received the Hanns-Martin-Schleyer-Prize for services to the community (1992) and has published several books on contemporary politics and current affairs.

BREUER, ROLF E. (1937–). Banker. Born in Bonn, Rolf Breuer qualified in banking (1956) before studying law at the universities of Lausanne, Munich, and Bonn, where he gained a doctorate (1967). In 1966, he began his career with the **Deutsche Bank AG** in Karlsruhe before moving to the bank's headquarters in Frankfurt/Main (1969), where he moved swiftly up the promotional ladder to become chairman and spokesman of the executive board (1997–2002) and head of the supervisory board (2002–2006). He was also president and chairman of the supervisory board of the **German Stock Exchange** (1993–2005). A keen modernizer of banking practices, he pioneered the introduction of the Ibis electronic share trading system and was particularly active in restructuring the bank and developing its investment business, for example in the United States through the purchase of Bankers Trust. To his disappointment, a planned merger with the **Dresdner Bank** fell through (2000), and hedge funds thwarted a union of the German and London stock exchanges, although these did deepen their cooperation. In April 2006, Breuer resigned from Deutsche Bank when the German Federal Court of Justice found against him over a **television** interview given in 2002, in which he made indiscreet remarks considered harmful to companies trying to raise credit, in particular the **media** concern owned by **Leo Kirch**. Until his resignation, Breuer was considered one of Germany's top bankers and, as a member of the **Christian Democratic Union** (**CDU**), continued to be active in local politics in the Frankfurt area.

See also BANKS.

BSIRSKE, FRANK (1952–). **Trade union** leader and **Green Party** politician. Bsirske was born in Helmstedt (**Lower Saxony**) into a working-class family. He joined the **Social Democratic Party of Germany** (**SPD**) at the age of 15, but was expelled two years later for collecting signatures in support of a Communist candidate at a regional election. Upon leaving school in 1971, he took casual work at the postal service, where he joined a trade union. After studying political science (1971–1978) in West **Berlin** with a scholarship from the Böckler Foundation, he worked as an educational officer for the Hanover district of a socialist youth group (1978–1987) and for the parliamentary group of the Green Party on the Hanover city council (1978–1989). He became secretary to the local headquarters of the public service and transport workers' union Öffentliche Dienste, Transport, und Verkehr (ÖTV), serving as deputy managing executive (1990–1991). During 1991–1997, he was deputy district chairman of the ÖTV in Lower Saxony and, after an interlude in the personnel and administrative department of the city of Hanover (1997–2000), was elected the union's national leader. In March 2001, he became the inaugural head of the ver.di (Vereinte Dienstleistungsgesell- schaft) trade union, reelected for a fourth period in 2011. The second largest union in Germany after IG Metall, ver.di emerged from an amalgamation of four service sector unions and the salaried employees' union DAG. Bsirske implemented a program of savings and restructuring in the union, although membership fell from 2.8 million in 2001 to 2.1 million in 2013 as the number of jobs in public sector services declined. Bsirske joined the left wing of the SPD in opposing welfare cuts proposed by Chancellor **Gerhard Schröder** in his **Agenda 2010** program, clashed with **Baden-Württemberg**'s minister president **Roland Koch** over revelations of Germany's richest persons (2002), and has led the union in numerous rounds of negotiations and strikes involving public and private services. In 2008, he attracted criticism for flying first class to Los Angeles on Lufthansa while the airline, on whose supervisory board he sat, was engaged in a strike with ver.di members. Bsirske has served on the supervisory boards of various companies (RWE AG, Lufthansa AG, Postbank) and joined the board of **Deutsche Bank AG** in 2013.

BUBIS, IGNATZ (1927–1999). Jewish community leader. Born in Breslau (Silesia, now in Poland), Bubis and his family fled National Socialist persecution to settle in the Polish town of Deblin on the Vistula River (1935), although Bubis himself only narrowly escaped death during the Holocaust. In 1945, he moved to eastern Germany, fleeing to West Germany in 1949 after being accused of black marketing by the Soviet secret police. In the Federal Republic of Germany (FRG), he ran a precious metals trading business based in Stuttgart and Pforzheim and later imported gold jewelry from Italy. After moving to Frankfurt/Main (1956), he built up a property company and was later elected to the council of the Jewish community (1965). In 1969, he joined the **Free Democratic Party (FDP)**, working actively at the local and then regional levels.

During the late 1960s and early 1970s, Bubis became involved in a controversial project to pull down and redevelop property in Frankfurt that was occupied by student tenants. Although the buildings were finally cleared (1974), Bubis withdrew from the development with heavy financial losses and attacked the campaign against him as left-wing and anti-Semitic. Although he temporarily resigned all offices in the Jewish community, Bubis later took a more active role in the FDP, joining its regional executive. Resuming his work for the community, he was elected chairman of the Frankfurt Jewish council (1978) and joined the directorate of the **Central Council of Jews in Germany**, helping set up a Jewish center and welfare facilities in Frankfurt. In 1989, he became the council's deputy chairman. In 1979, he had argued strongly that no time limit should apply to the war crimes committed during the National Socialist period and in 1985 joined other Jews in occupying the stage of the Frankfurt Schaubühne theater to protest a performance of Rainer Werner Fassbinder's play *Der Müll, die Stadt und der Tod* (The rubbish, the city, and death), in which, according to Bubis, the main figure, a Jewish speculator, was portrayed as an anti-Semitic stereotype; the play was subsequently banned from Frankfurt.

In 1992, Bubis succeeded **Heinz Galinski** as leader (and in 1997 as president) of the Central Council of Jews in Germany. He took over at a challenging time for Jews in Germany, when racism and **anti-Semitism** were on the rise after reunification, and many Russian Jews of German descent were entering the country. Bubis developed a reputation for compromise and dialogue with opponents and helped Jewish issues gain a high profile in the **media**. Repeatedly the target of personal threats, he took part in public demonstrations and argued for the law to be applied rigorously against racist activities. At the same time, he worked to improve the image of Germany in Israel and accompanied various delegations to the Middle East. In 1993, he was mentioned as a potential candidate for the post of **president of the Federal Republic**, but he believed that Germany was not ready for a Jewish leader. In 1997, he stood as FDP candidate in the Frankfurt local elections and helped the party win seats on the city council.

In 1998, Bubis engaged in a public debate with the author **Martin Walser** on the issue of individual and collective guilt for the Holocaust. Bubis accused Walser of encouraging the "culture of looking away," which he regarded as a contemporary form of covert anti-Semitism. Shortly before he died in August 1999, Bubis gave a pessimistic interview to *stern* magazine in which he claimed to have achieved little as president of the Central Council of Jews and asserted that Jewish and non-Jewish Germans were as alienated as ever. He was buried in Israel because he did not want his grave in Germany to be desecrated (as had happened to that of his predecessor, Galinski). Leading German politicians, including the president of the FRG and a government minister, attended the funeral in Tel Aviv. Bubis was succeeded as council president by **Paul Spiegel**.

Bubis received several honors, including the Federal Cross of Merit (1992, 1996) and the Goldstein Prize from Israel for his services to Jews in Germany (1998). He was elected president of the European Jewish Congress (1998) and also headed the governing council of the regional radio station, Hessischer Rundfunk (1987–1993). A biography appeared in 1993 and an autobiography in 1996.

BUCERIUS, GERD (1906–1995). Newspaper publisher. Born in Hamm (near **Hamburg**), Gerd Bucerius graduated as a doctor of law and worked as a judge in Kiel and Flensburg. When the Nazis came to power, he was excluded from the judiciary because his first wife was Jewish (he himself had Jewish ancestry). Practicing law in Hamburg, he helped **Jews** and others being persecuted by the Nazis before he was called up for work service. Immediately after World War II, he served as a senator (Bausenator) for the city of Hamburg (1945), a member of the Advisory Council for the British occupation zone, and a representative for Hamburg in the Economic Council based in Frankfurt/Main (1947–1949). From 1949 until 1962, he represented the **Christian Democratic Union (CDU)** in the **Bundestag**, before quitting the party over policy disagreements. A liberal conservative, Bucerius was the only CDU member of parliament to vehemently oppose readopting **Konrad Adenauer** as chancellor candidate.

Bucerius is best known as the cofounder of the weekly *Die Zeit* (1946), which became one of the most respected liberal newspapers in Europe, and in which he published regular and often controversial commentaries on political and social issues. The paper operated at a commercial loss from 1946 until 1975 and was financed only through profits from the *stern* magazine, in which Bucerius acquired a majority stake in 1951. In 1957, Bucerius became the sole publisher of *Die Zeit*, handing over editorial management to former chancellor **Helmut Schmidt** in 1985. In 1971, Bucerius set up a foundation (the Zeit-Stiftung Ebelin und Gerd Bucerius) to promote new initiatives and support promising individuals in the social sciences, **education**, art, and culture; its particular mission is to contribute to the development of a civil society. The foundation also established the Bucerius Law School (Hamburg), which admitted its first students in October 2000 and offers programs in international commercial law, with study abroad.

See also PRESS.

BUDGET. In accordance with the requirements of the **Basic Law** (**BL**, article 110), the **Bundestag** considers and approves a draft domestic budget (Bundeshaushaltsplan). Drawn up for one or more years and set annually by the federal finance office (Bundesfinanzamt), the draft is presented by the federal government and, after detailed consideration, approved by the Bundestag after consultation with the **Bundesrat**. The calculation of the budget, especially the national debt, is complex and depends on accounting methods and exclusions. Specific areas and types of debt or expenditure can be identified, including the core public budget (öffentlicher Kernhaushalt) of direct expenditure by **Bund, Länder**, and local government, and the total or overall public budget (öffentlicher Gesamthaushalt), which in addition to the core, encompasses extra items (Extrahaushalte) such as universities, road building, and state-sector public bodies to which over 80 percent of core budget activities are privately outsourced. A third budgetary layer takes in outsourced market-sector bodies (e.g., hospitals, waste disposal, and **transport** services) with a 50 percent or more public holding. Total debt may also be split between a cyclical element, which rises or falls according to the economic cycle and is considered neutral in the longer term, and a structural part, from which cyclical factors have been removed, although how the division is reached is a subject of technical debate. Structural new debt (strukturelle Neuverschuldung) refers to the additional structural debt accumulated within a certain period, usually one year.

Germany's total accumulated or gross public debt (Staatsverschuldung), which was just 19.3 percent in 1950, climbed rapidly from 130,000 million euros in 1975 to reach a historic peak of more than 2,011,000 million (two trillion) euros in 2010 (over 80 percent of annual GDP), falling slightly thereafter. Structural new debt during this period varied widely, but for the Bund it peaked at just less than 2,000 million in 2004 and 2010. The debt reference levels of the Maastricht Treaty (1993) require a eurozone member state's annual deficit (generally corresponding to Germany's total public budget deficit, as defined above) not to exceed 3 percent of its GDP, while gross or accumulated debt must not go beyond 60 percent of GDP. Germany exceeded the former limit during 2001–2005 and 2009–2010, and the latter annually after 2003. Beginning in 2009, the BL incorporated a "debt brake" (Schuldenbremse, articles 109 and 115) to control new structural debt by setting the borrowing limit for the Bund at 0.35 percent of GDP (effective in 2016); for the states the limit was zero (effective in 2020). The measures were recommended by the second commission on **federalism reform**; adopted by the Bundestag in May/June 2009; and in conjunction with a four-year austerity package ("consolidation program"), which was implemented in 2011 and included cuts in **social welfare** and unemployment benefits alongside increased investment in **education** and economic growth, were claimed by the federal finance ministry in 2014 to be on target, at least for the Bund. The Bund's expenditure in 2015 was around 300,000 million euros, mainly for social welfare (42 percent), followed by defense (11 percent) and debt repayments (9 percent); transportation and digital infrastructure accounted for 7.8 percent, education and research 5.1 percent, and health 4 percent. While many **federal states** were on their way to conforming to the debt brake, the most heavily indebted Länder were the city-states of **Hamburg**, **Bremen**, and **Berlin**, followed by the **Saarland** and **North Rhine-Westfalia.** The Bund aimed to reduce its own structural new debt to zero by around 2015, and in 2014 announced that it had balanced the budget for that year.

BULMAHN, EDELGARD (1951–). Social Democratic Party of Germany (SPD) politician. Born in Petershagen (**North Rhine-Westfalia**), Edelgard Bulmahn spent a year in an Israeli kibbutz (1972–1973) before studying English and political science in Hanover (1973–1979) and working as an English teacher (1979–1987). A member of the SPD from the age of 18, she was active in the party's **Young Socialists (JUSOS)** youth wing before serving as a district councilor for Hanover-Linden (1981–1986) and in 1987 entered the **Bundestag** as a directly elected member for a city constituency. Bulmahn's political star rose swiftly, and she occupied senior positions on committees on **education** and research (1987–1996) before becoming a spokesperson in these areas for the SPD parliamentary party (1996–). In October 1998, she took over from **Gerhard Schröder** as leader of the regional party in **Lower Saxony** (until 2003) and was appointed federal minister of education and research, a post she retained in Schröder's second cabinet (2002–2005). Between 2005 and 2009, she chaired the Bundestag committee for economics and technology.

As education minister, Bulmahn saw her department reduced in size when its responsibilities for technology were transferred to the Ministry of Economics (renamed Ministry of Economics and Technology). Her plans to introduce a more generous student grant system by extending entitlement to every student regardless of parental support were trimmed by the chancellor, although the new law, when it came into force in April 2001, significantly increased overall spending on grants (a reported 50 percent rise over the 1998 level) and was claimed to open the door to higher education to an additional 80,000 young people. Her proposals to link professorial salaries to performance rather than length of service and to introduce the post of junior professor attracted criticism from conservative circles in German higher education. She was an early supporter of the green card scheme for **immigrant** workers, and her enthusiasm for biotechnology and support for importing stem cells for medical research led to open conflict with the justice minister, **Herta Däubler-Gmelin**. Bulmahn played an important role in a government committed to technological progress and educational reform. A member of the SPD executive (1993–2011), she became party spokesperson on a subcommittee for "civilian conflict prevention and cross-linked security" (2009) and on a commission studying "growth, wellbeing and the quality of life" (2011). In 2013, she was elected deputy president of the Bundestag.

BUND. In the contemporary political context of the Federal Republic of Germany (FRG), this term, which means "federation," is widely used to refer to the central aspects and institutions of legislation and government within the German federal system.

See also BUNDESRAT; BUNDESTAG; FEDERAL STATES (LÄNDER); FEDERALISM.

BUND FREIER BÜRGER (BFB). *See* FEDERATION OF FREE CITIZENS (BUND FREIER BÜRGER, BFB).

BUNDESKANZLERAMT. *See* OFFICE OF THE FEDERAL CHANCELLOR (BUNDESKANZLERAMT).

BUNDESRAT. The 69-member Bundestag, which since 2000 has convened in **Berlin**, is the national assembly of the 16 **federal states** (Länder) of the Federal Republic of Germany (FRG). Each state parliament (**Landtag**) sends delegates (between three and six) to the assembly in approximate relation to the size of its population. Upon reunification (1990), the allocation of seats was as follows: six each for **North Rhine-Westfalia** (NRW), **Bavaria, Baden-Württemberg**, and **Lower Saxony**, four for **Hessen, Saxony, Saxony-Anhalt, Thuringia, Brandenburg, Rhineland-Palatinate, Schleswig-Holstein**, and **Berlin**; and three for **Saarland, Bremen, Hamburg**, and **Mecklenburg-West Pomerania**. Following a population census, Hessen gained an additional fifth seat in 1995. The system is designed to ensure that large states (e.g., NRW has more inhabitants than the eastern states combined) do not marginalize smaller ones, which in turn cannot outvote the rest. Decisions must be reached by absolute or, for constitutional changes, two-thirds majority (i.e., 35 or 45 votes, respectively). The delegates are members of the government of their home states (Landesregierung), to whose directives they are bound, and they change only with a new regional cabinet; there are no direct elections to the Bundesrat. Since votes are counted unanimously for a state, the Landesregierung usually determines beforehand how its delegates will vote, entrusting the vote itself to a single member or "vote-leader" (Stimmführer); if another deputy of the same state disagrees with the vote, the vote for the state becomes invalid, following a decision by the **Federal Constitutional Court (FCC)** in 2002. Political differences between coalition partners in the home state can lead to tensions in the assembly. Abstentions count in practice as no votes.

Bundesrat members conduct most of their work in their home states. Even more so than in the **Bundestag**, most of the assembly's day-to-day work is carried out in standing committees, which are supported by a 200-member secretariat. Technical experts from the **Bund** and Länder also work together in areas such as social, labor, or financial legislation and tend to form close-knit networks (informally referred to as Fachbrüderschaften). The "ministerial bureaucracy" (Ministeralbürokratie) may be seen, on the one hand, as vital for efficient decision making and enabling politicians, whose technical expertise is often limited, to focus on main issues, or on the other hand, as undermining democratic accountability. The presidency of the Bundesrat rotates annually among the minister presidents of the states and is largely uncontroversial.

The main organs of the Bundestag are the presidium (Präsidium), the plenary assembly (Plenum), the committees (Ausschüsse), and the European Chamber (Europakammer). The presidium, which comprises the president and his three deputies, draws up and presents the budget for approval by the assembly and implements decisions (Beschlüsse). The plenary assembly, which meets, normally in public, around 11 times a year at three- to four-week intervals, functions rather like that of the Bundestag, as do the committees. A sign of the institutional linkage between regional and central government is the offices or standing representations (ständige Vertretungen), which the Länder maintain in Berlin. These exist to promote regular contact among the Bundesrat, the Bundestag, and the **federal government**, as well as among the member states themselves. A regional minister or senior civil servant normally heads each office.

Although the Länder have little direct policy influence at **European Union (EU)** level, Germany was instrumental in creating the Committee of Regions; established by the Treaty of Maastricht in 1992 and active from 1994, it advises on EU legislation. Of its maximum 350 members, Germany has 24 seats, with 21 reserved for the Länder. The Treaty of Lisbon (2009) went so far as to give the regions of member states the right to object to EU legislation if it impinges on their competencies (so-called subsidiarity control). The regions are also represented in some 300 Bund-Länder delegations, which lobby the Commission and the Council of the EU. Aside from these provisions, the BL specifies that the federal states must be represented (in practice through Bundesrat delegates) in forming EU legislation on school **education**, broadcasting, and culture. Moreover, the FCC, considering the Lisbon Treaty, ruled in 2009 that the Bundesrat must approve changes in EU treaties and any transfer of powers to the Union. Finally, the European Chamber itself was set up (in 1992) to enable its representatives (Bundesrat delegates) to react swiftly to EU initiatives and reach decisions without convening the full assembly.

See also FEDERALISM.

BUNDESTAG. The German federal parliament or Bundestag represents the German people and is the main legislative body of the Federal Republic of Germany (FRG). Since April 1999, it has convened in the renovated Reichstag building in **Berlin**. At the time of reunification, the assembly had 656 members, reduced to 598 in 2002, although more seats can be created by "overhang mandates." Members are elected by secret ballot, are not bound by directives from their party or an interest group, and are expected to vote according to conscience—at least in theory, since the threat by **Volker Kauder**, leader of the parliamentary group of the **Christian Democratic Union (CDU)**, to remove from Bundestag committees any party member who voted against the Greek bailout in 2015 raised the question of what exactly constitutes an issue of conscience. The assembly is elected for four years, but following a change to the **Basic Law (BL)** in 1998, this period can be extended by a month to avoid holding elections during the summer vacation, when voter turnout may be low. Mindful of the experiences of the Weimar Republic (1919–1933), the BL's founding fathers did not give the Bundestag a general right to dissolve itself. The assembly may pass a vote of no confidence in the **federal chancellor** only if it also elects, by majority, a successor (BL, article 67: the "constructive vote of no confidence"). On the other hand, the chancellor may ask the assembly for a vote of confidence which, if he or she loses, may trigger dissolution and fresh elections, unless members elect another chancellor within 20 days (BL, article 68: the "vote of confidence"; see below). Although the BL states the precise circumstances under which the Bundestag may be disbanded, the manipulation of parliamentary votes of confidence by a chancellor to engineer the assembly's dissolution and force elections has generated constitutional controversy: **Willy Brandt** did so in 1972, **Helmut Kohl** in 1982, and **Gerhard Schröder** in 2005. In February 1983, the **Federal Constitutional Court (FCC)** clarified the conditions governing dissolution. In this respect, the German parliamentary system contrasts with that of Great Britain or France, where government leaders have much greater freedom to dissolve parliament and call elections. Germany has also changed its leaders much less frequently than most other established European democracies.

The Bundestag has sole powers of legislation, with the exception of laws requiring approval of the **federal states** and tightly circumscribed situations of constitutional emergency (BL, article 81). It approves the domestic **budget**, controls the level of credit taken on by the executive, and ratifies international treaties. The Bundestag elects (and removes from office) the chancellor, which, in a parliamentary system in which interparty coalitions are common, gives the assembly considerable influence over how the government is formed and what program it adopts. Although the chancellor has the constitutional right to set policy guidelines, the government must take account of views expressed in the Bundestag. At the same time, the government is not obliged to seek the assembly's permission for its every decision, and until the mid-1980s, **foreign policy** (aside from the ratification of treaties) was largely left to the executive. Although the FCC endorsed the government's right to decide on the stationing of medium-range nuclear weapons in Germany (1984), it later ruled that the Bundestag's explicit permission was required for German armed forces to conduct missions outside the area of the **North Atlantic Treaty Organization** (**NATO**, 1994).

The Bundestag controls and monitors the activities of government and the administration, mainly through the right of its members to question ministers and receive information. In practice, this right is exercised in various forms: a weekly session of written questions during plenary sessions, which can last up to three hours (Fragestunde); 35 minutes of questions following the Wednesday cabinet meeting (Regierungsbefragung); and a 60-minute "topical hour" (aktuelle Stunde), allowing individual members to address the assembly for a maximum of five minutes. Responses in the Fragestunde and Regierungsbefragung are usually delivered by parliamentary state secretaries, who read from a prepared text, but an attempt in 2010 by the president of the Bundestag, **Norbert Lammert** of the **Christian Democratic Union** (**CDU**), to liven up the sessions according to the British model, in which government ministers engage directly in exchanges with the opposition, was overruled. A group of members may also submit a "small question" (kleine Anfrage) to the government, which responds in writing, or an interpellation/ "large question" (große Anfrage), which is included in the order of business and often leads to a full-scale plenary debate. Plenary sessions are transmitted by the Phoenix broadcasting station and can be viewed in the Mediathek section of the Bundestag website.

As part of its budget monitoring role, the Bundestag receives an annual report from the finance minister on income and expenditure, assets, and deficits. In addition, the assembly appoints a parliamentary commissioner for defense (Wehrbeauftragte[r]) for five years, who reports annually on morale and the protection of basic rights in the armed forces. Through committees and/or commissioners, it also monitors defense, data protection, and the secret services and has powers to constitute parliamentary committees of investigation (Untersuchungsausschüsse). A committee of investigation can be called by 25 percent of Bundestag members (BL, article 44) and it can apply to the courts for powers of search or even to fine or detain individuals in order to gather evidence (its powers were extended in 2001). Such committees have been constituted to investigate numerous improprieties, including the *Spiegel* affair (1962), the financial and political scandal surrounding **Karl Friedrich Flick** (1983), and anonymous donations to the CDU involving the former chancellor, Helmut Kohl (2000).

Although a constructive vote of no confidence in the chancellor effectively topples the whole government, it places the government in a strong position vis-à-vis parliament while ensuring that the assembly takes responsibility for continuity of the executive. The vote was called unsuccessfully in April 1972 by opposition parties to try to bring down Willy Brandt over his **Ostpolitik**, and again (successfully) in September 1982 when Helmut Kohl formed a coalition among the CDU, the **Christian Social Union (CSU)**, and the **Free Democratic Party (FDP)** to overthrow **Helmut Schmidt (Social Democratic Party of Germany, SPD)**.

The Bundestag has full autonomy in organizing and conducting its business. Debates are held and votes taken in the plenary session (Plenum), which is the public forum for debates, speeches, and votes. The first act of a newly formed parliament is to elect the presidium (Präsidium), whose principal members are the president of the Bundestag (Bundestagspräsident) and his deputies. The president represents the **president of the Federal Republic**; plays an advisory role in all committees; and chairs the joint committee (Gemeinsamer Ausschuss), which is constituted from members of the Bundestag/**Bundesrat** and acts as an emergency parliament in the event of military attack. His main function is to formally call, manage, and conclude parliamentary sessions and to ensure their orderly conduct. The Council of Elders (Ältestenrat) comprises members of the presidium and other Bundestag members nominated by the parliamentary groups (Fraktionen). The council supports the president of the Bundestag in managing plenary sessions, draws up the order of business, sets the number of speakers and the times allotted for their speeches, and agrees with the parliamentary groups on the composition and chairs of the various Bundestag committees. Parliamentary business managers (Geschäftsführer) are Bundestag members whose responsibility it is to manage the day-to-day business of their parliamentary group and ensure that members are present in plenary sessions when a vote is taken.

Most parliamentary business is conducted in the committees (Ausschüsse), which are the backbone of the assembly. A small number of committees (foreign affairs, defense, petitions, and **European Union [EU]** affairs) are prescribed by the BL. Numerous standing (or technical) committees (Fachausschüsse) handle issues ranging from the budget, transport, housing, economics, technology, labor, **education**, and the **environment** to culture, **sport**, and **human rights**. Other committees include the **mediation committee** (Vermittlungsausschuss), committees for electing members of the FCC (BL, article 94), senior judges (article 95), and the joint committee (article 53a). In addition, the Bundestag sets up ad hoc committees (including committees of investigation) for particular tasks and constitutes so-called commissions of inquiry (Enquête-Kommissionen), comprising members of parliament and external experts charged with drawing up recommendations on specific issues. Such commissions have reported on constitutional reform, **women** in society, nuclear **energy**, and the regime of the **Socialist Unity Party of Germany** (**SED**) in the former **German Democratic Republic** (**GDR**).

Although parliamentary groups (Fraktionen) are not explicitly mentioned in the BL, an FCC ruling assigns them a central constitutional role in parliamentary life (based on article 21 of the BL). Such groups are recognized associations of Bundestag members and belong either to a single party (the normal case) or to different parties sharing political goals. They act as a filter and coordinator of parliamentary business, enable decisions to be reached in committee and in working parties, and facilitate the smooth running of the assembly. Groups, which must constitute at least 5 percent of Bundestag members, are represented proportionally in committees, the presidium, and the Council of Elders and are allocated staff and financial resources. Since 1960, it has also been customary for leaders of the parliamentary group(s) of the government party/parties to take part in cabinet meetings from time to time and, in particular where a governing party does not enjoy a large majority, they play an important role in ensuring party support for Bundestag votes. Responding to an appeal by smaller parties (mainly the Greens and the **Party of Democratic Socialism, PDS**) in the first all-German parliament of 1990, the FCC ruled that, although these failed to qualify as full parliamentary groups, they were entitled to a somewhat lesser, group-like status (called a "Gruppe"). The Gruppe may not present motions for business, is not entitled to chair committee meetings, and receives less financial support, although it may bring forward draft bills and questions in the plenary session. Membership in a group (Fraktion or Gruppe) gives an individual deputy more influence than he or she could possibly command individually. Bundestag members enjoy immunity from prosecution for the duration of their mandate (although this can be revoked by the assembly) and legal indemnity (for their utterances in parliament and beyond the period of their mandate), and receive generous salaries (pegged to those of senior judges following recommendations of a 1995 commission) and fringe benefits.

See also ELECTORAL SYSTEM; FEDERALISM.

BUNDESWEHR. The Bundeswehr (literally: federal defense force) comprises the army, navy, and air force of the Federal Republic of Germany (FRG), although the term is often used to refer to the army alone. Ten years after the end of World War II, the Bundeswehr was reconstituted as part of the **North Atlantic Treaty Organization (NATO,** May 1955). Controversial at the time, the decision to rearm Germany was eventually accepted as an inevitable consequence of the developing Cold War. At the same time, the **German Democratic Republic (GDR)** built up its own national army (the Nationale Volksarmee, NVA) under the auspices of the Soviet-led **Warsaw Pact**.

The **Basic Law (BL,** articles 26 and 87a) prohibits the use of the Bundeswehr for wars of aggression. The armed forces may be deployed only in national defense or as part of the defense of NATO, in which case NATO also assumes operational command of Bundeswehr units. Other forms of military deployment are permitted only within the terms of the BL. The Bundeswehr also makes a significant contribution to humanitarian and peacekeeping missions. Overall command of the forces is in the hands of the federal defense minister during peacetime and of the **federal chancellor** in times of national emergency. During the Bundeswehr's early years, General Wolf Graf von Baudissin (1907–1993) developed the concept of soldiers as "citizens in uniform" (Bürger in Uniform), integrated into society and imbued with democratic values ("inner leadership" or "innere Führung"). From 1956 the Bundeswehr was a conscription army, with a core of full-time professional servicemen. The length of peacetime national service (Wehrpflicht) varied and lasted at most nine months, although it fell to six before it was ended in 2011 (provision for its reintroduction remains in the BL, article 12a). From 1961, conscientious objectors could opt for civilian community service (Zivildienst), which around 90,000 young men did annually. When the service ended, many hospitals and care homes, which had come to rely heavily on it as a source of cheap labor, expressed serious concerns.

Every five years, the **Bundestag** elects a defense commissioner (Wehrbeauftragter), who is wholly responsible to parliament and whose role is constitutionally defined (BL, article 45b). Members of the armed forces have the right to directly petition the commissioner, who also presents an annual report (Wehrbericht) to the Bundestag. The report reviews the state and moral of the armed forces, including any complaints raised by serving personnel. In 2015, Hans-Peter Bartels (**Social Democratic Party of Germany, SPD**) succeeded Hellmut Königshaus (**Freie Demokratische Partei Deutschlands, FDP**) in the post of commissioner.

In the decade after reunification (3 October 1990), the Bundeswehr underwent major structural changes. In 1990, it took over 51,000 members of the NVA, which comprised 103,000 before its dissolution, not to mention over 2,000 east German tanks, 1.2 million hand weapons, 300,000 tons of munitions, 400 fighter aircraft, 57 warships, and over 3,300 items of real estate; most of these assets were disposed of. Eventually all NVA generals were dismissed, and 8,000 full officers received a two-year contract, after which only 2,500 were integrated into the army and a few hundred remained in the air force and navy; 7,600 junior officers were retained. In order to comply with the 2 + 4 treaty, the Bundeswehr reduced its size to 370,000 between 1990 and 1994.

Following a decision by the **Federal Constitutional Court (FCC)** in July 1994 to allow the Bundeswehr, subject to the approval of the Bundestag, to participate in international peacekeeping missions (mounted by NATO, the West European Union [WEU], or the **United Nations [UN]**), German forces increased their global military involvement in areas such as the former Yugoslavia, Africa, parts of the former Soviet Union (including Georgia in 1994 and Chechnya in 1995–1996), and Afghanistan. At the same time, in the light of changing security needs, the Bundeswehr was reorganized into a crisis response force (Krisenreaktionskräfte, KRK), a main defense force (Hauptverteidigungskräfte, HVK), and a basic force (Grundorganisation), although funding cuts forced further troop reductions to 340,000. Experience of foreign missions prompted further reforms in 2004. Intervention forces (numbering 35,000) were earmarked to execute peacemaking operations against militarily organized opponents, while a similar number performed longer term peacekeeping functions. A third pillar provided 147,000 support personnel for operations, as well as assisting in civilian emergencies at home. Reservists complemented professional soldiers in all spheres.

In 2010, partly in response to the need for government spending cuts, but also to meet national defense guidelines drawn up in 2011 that stressed the need for a flexible force able to respond to international crises, defense ministers **Karl-Theodor zu Guttenberg (Christlich-Soziale Union Deutschlands [CDU]**, 2009–2011) and **Thomas de Maizière (Christlich-Demokratische Union Deutschlands [CDU]**, 2011–2013) embarked on the most far-reaching and complex structural changes in the Bundeswehr's history. This so-called reorientation (Neuausrichtung) provided for ending conscription (implemented in 2011); reducing troop numbers to a maximum of 185,000, comprising 170,000 professional servicemen, 12,500 volunteers, and 2,500 reservists; a wide-ranging reorganization and streamlining of management, personnel, training, recruitment, inspection, and base locations within Germany; and a review of procurement. In 2015, the Bundeswehr's peacetime strength (including all three services) stood at around 180,000 active military personnel, including 60,700 in the army, 28,800 in the air force, 15,900 in the navy, 910 in the ministry of defense, 19,000 medics, and nearly 19,000 women, for whom all restrictions on an army career were lifted in 2001. By 2015, the Bundeswehr had engaged in over 130 operations in various parts of the world.

See also FOREIGN POLICY AFTER 1990; SECURITY POLICY, EXTERNAL.

BURDA FAMILY. Publishers. Born a printer's son in 1903 in Philippsburg (**Baden-Württemberg**), Franz Burda studied economics and earned a doctorate before taking over the family printing business in 1929, which expanded rapidly. Although he had published some magazines during the 1940s, his breakthrough came after World War II with the launch of the illustrated *Das Ufer* (1948). In the same year, he initiated the first Bambi film award, now an international honor. In 1949, Franz Burda cofounded, with his wife Aenne, *Burda-Moden*, which rapidly became Germany's most popular fashion magazine. The *Bunte Illustrierte* (*Das Ufer* renamed) followed in 1954; with photo series in color, it enjoyed similar success. In 1971, Burda acquired a stake in the U.S. printing company Meredith (Lynchburg), later renamed Meredith-Burda. By the early 1980s, Burda had grown into one of the largest publishers in Europe, producing over 30 titles, although a projected merger with the **Axel Springer** group was vetoed by the Bundeskartellamt (Federal Cartel Office). During the 1980s, the company established its own **television** production company, PAN-TV. After Franz Burda's death (1986), the interests in the family business passed to his three sons, Franz, Frieder, and Hubert. The following year Hubert, the youngest son, became sole partner and chairman of the executive board.

Aenne Burda (née Lemminger, 1909–2005) trained in commerce before marrying Franz Burda (1931). She played an active role in her husband's business. By including cut-out patterns and designs, *Burda-Moden*, which she managed, opened up the fashion world to women, and by 1965 its circulation had reached one million. When a Russian edition appeared (1985), *Burda-Moden* became the first Western magazine to be published and distributed regularly in the Soviet Union. By 2002, with a circulation of over two million, it was being published in 16 languages in 90 countries. In 1994, Aenne Burda handed control of *Burda-Moden* to her son, Hubert. She was ranked as one of Germany's leading female publishers (her biography appeared in 1999).

Hubert Burda, born in 1940 in Heidelberg, studied art history, archaeology, and sociology in Munich, Rome, London, and Paris (1960–1965), graduating with a doctorate in archaeology and art. After training in New York with *Time* magazine, *TV Guide*, and an advertising agency, he returned in 1966 to the family business in Germany to take over management of the radio/television magazine *Bild und Funk*, whose circulation he boosted by over 20 percent within a few months. Hubert Burda became an executive partner of the company and was chief editor for *Bunte* (1965–1975). When his father died (1986), Hubert took over management of the company, which he renamed Hubert Burda Medien. Hubert Burda expanded the business and made it into an international multimedia **publishing** house, producing titles such as *Bunte* (popular light entertainment), *Playboy*, *SUPERillu* (eastern Germany's most popular illustrated magazine), and *Focus* (news and current affairs). Launched in 1993 and combining information with graphics, *Focus* was the first publication to challenge the long-established *Der Spiegel* (edited by **Rudolf Augstein**) and confirmed Burda as a serious news publisher. Digital offerings included an **Internet** portal (Europe Online, 1994), bundled Internet services (Focus Digital, from 2000), and BurdaNet (providing integrated Internet solutions for businesses in Russia from 2000). A web-based service, Computer Knowledge for All (Computerwissen für alle), offering news, advice, articles, reviews on hardware and software, and an online forum, was launched in 2001.

The Offenburg-based Hubert Media Group's main divisions are Burda International (some 240 magazines and numerous digital media products in central/eastern Europe, Russia, the United States, and Asia), Digital (including business networking [Xing], holidays [HolidayCheck], online dating [Elitepartner], a news portal [Focus Online], and other digital services), Verlage Inland (lifestyle and entertainment magazines), and Druck (printing services). Advertising for all the company's magazines and online services is centrally handled by the Burda Advertising Center/Burda Community Network (BNC). In 2014, the group turned over 2,456 million euros, with a workforce of 10,300 in 241 subsidiaries (149 in Germany and 92 abroad). Its global publishing portfolio included 500 print and digital products. Main foreign markets were in eastern Europe, with the strongest growth in Asia and Turkey, and plans were under way for entry into South America. Paul-Bernhard Kallen succeeded Hubert Burda as chief executive in 2010. The Burda family remain the majority shareholders.

In 1997, Hubert Burda was elected president of the Association of German Magazine Publishers (Verband Deutscher Zeitschriftenverleger, VDZ). The Burda group also trains 25 journalists a year at its two colleges, in Munich and Offenburg (the Burda Journalistenschule). In 1999, Burda established the Hubert-Burda Stiftung (Hubert Burda Foundation) for the promotion of culture and the sciences. Since 2001, the Felix Burda Foundation has supported work for the prevention of bowel cancer. The following year saw the opening of the Burda Media Park in Offenburg, an architectural showpiece. Hubert Burda himself worked actively to promote German–**Jewish** relations, supported the Shoah Foundation, and founded the Petrarca Prize for literature. His other awards include the Federal Cross of Merit for his contribution to society, the Print Media Prize from the **Bavarian** state government (2000), an honorary doctorate from the Ben-Gurion University in Israel (2001), and an honorary professorship (2002).

Born in 1936, Frieder Burda is best known as the owner of one of the world's leading collections of modern classical and contemporary art. In order to promote art and make his collection more accessible to the public, he established the Frieder Burda Foundation (1998). The Frieder Burda Museum opened in Baden-Baden in 2004.

See also MEDIA; PRESS.

BÜTIKOFER, REINHARD (1953–). Green Party politician. Reinhard Bütikofer was born in Mannheim (**Baden-Württemberg**) and grew up in Speyer. He interrupted his studies of philosophy, history, and sinology at the University of Heidelberg (from 1971) to undertake two years of civilian service, as an alternative to conscription. At Heidelberg, he was a student representative, joined a Maoist student group (1974–1980), and was active in the Green Alternative List (GAL, from 1982). Elected to Heidelberg city council (1984), he joined the Green Party shortly afterward. After his election to the state parliament (**Landtag**) of Baden-Württemberg (1988), he established a reputation for expertise in financial affairs and the domestic budget. He left parliament in 1996 to devote time to his family, but returned to active politics and was elected coleader of **Alliance 90/The Greens** in Baden-Württemberg (1997). He was later criticized for his handling of policy over Bosnia at a national conference in 1998, when the Greens opposed sending German armed forces on peacekeeping missions, and over the electorally unpopular decision to campaign for an increase in motor fuel prices. Although he helped draw up the Greens' manifesto for elections to the European Parliament (1994, 1999), the party did not adopt him as a candidate, but he was a member of the European Federation of Green Parties (EFGP).

When the Greens entered government in coalition with the **Social Democratic Party of Germany** (**SPD**, 1998), Bütikofer was elected national party manager and joined the national executive and the recently established party council. A member of the "realist" wing of the party, he proved to be a skilled tactician and mediator between pragmatists and radicals, notably in 1999, when the party was split over the timing of a withdrawal from nuclear energy. In 2000–2001, he chaired a committee drawing up a new program of basic principles that would carry the party forward to 2020. In 2002, he was elected, alongside **Angelika Beer**, coleader of the Green Party, succeeding **Claudia Roth** and **Fritz Kuhn** and holding the position until 2008. He entered the European Parliament in 2009 and became coleader of the European Green Party in 2012.

C

CARSTENS, KARL (1914–1992). Christian Democratic Union (CDU) politician and **president of the Federal Republic,** 1979–1984. Karl Carstens was born in **Bremen**. From 1933, he studied law and politics and attended universities in Germany (Frankfurt/Main, Munich, Königsberg [Kaliningrad from 1946], and **Hamburg**) and France (Dijon) before passing his state law exams (1936, 1939) and earning a doctorate (1938). During World War II, he served in an antiaircraft artillery regiment and in 1940 joined the National Socialist Party for professional reasons, but was never an active member. In 1945, Carstens practiced as a lawyer in Bremen, subsequently working for the Bremen senate and representing the city-state in Bonn (1949–1954). In 1948–1949, he obtained a scholarship to study law at Yale University in the U.S., where he graduated with a master's degree. Between 1950 and 1954, Carstens pursued an academic career, teaching constitutional and international law at the University of Cologne, where he was appointed professor (1960).

Between 1954 and 1966, Carstens worked in the Federal Ministry for Foreign Affairs, specializing in European affairs and representing the FRG at the European Council in Strasbourg (1954–1955). In 1955, the year in which he joined the CDU, he returned to Bonn and was later appointed a **state secretary** (1960). In 1961, Carstens became deputy to Foreign Minister Heinrich von Brentano and then to his successor, Gerhard Schröder (both CDU). When Schröder moved to the Ministry of Defense, Carstens followed him (1967). In 1968–1969, during the **grand coalition**, he headed the **Office of the Federal Chancellor** under **Kurt Georg Kiesinger** (CDU) and was state secretary to the **federal government**. After the social–liberal coalition came to power in 1969, Carstens left the civil service to head the research institute of the Deutsche Gesellschaft für Auswärtige Politik (German Society for Foreign Policy in Bonn, 1969–1972). He represented the CDU in the **Bundestag** (1972–1979), sat on the parliamentary committee for **foreign policy**, and chaired the CDU/**Christian Social Union** (**CSU**) parliamentary group (1972–1976), succeeding **Rainer Barzel**, who resigned after mounting an unsuccessful vote of no confidence against **Willy Brandt** over the **Ost-politik** treaties. Following the social–liberal coalition's 1976 election victory, Carstens was elected president of the Bundestag.

In 1979, after a fierce campaign in which opponents brought up his former membership in the National Socialist Party, Carstens defeated the **Social Democratic Party of Germany** (**SPD**) candidate, **Annemarie Renger**, to become president of the Federal Republic, a post he held until 1984. While in office, Carstens traveled extensively and won respect for his objectivity, political sensibility, sense of tradition, and engagement with young people (major youth events were staged in his official residence, the Villa Hammerschmidt). When East–West relations became strained during the 1980s and the prospect of medium-range nuclear missiles on German soil inspired a popular peace movement, Carstens spoke publicly against unilateral disarmament. In January 1983, when an alliance of CDU/CSU and the **Free Democratic Party** (**FDP**) mounted a constructive vote of no confidence that removed Chancellor **Helmut Schmidt** from office, Carsten's controversial decision to dissolve the Bundestag was later confirmed by the **Federal Constitutional Court** (**FCC**). Carstens retired from active politics in 1984 and died in 1992 in Bonn.

Carstens received many honors, including the gold medal of the Jean Monnet Foundation for Europe (1990). His publications include works on constitutional and European law and an autobiographical account (1993). The Karl und Veronika Carstens Stiftung (co-named after his wife, a doctor) is a private foundation, established in 1982 and dedicated to the promotion and support of complementary medicine.

CARSTENSEN, PETER HARRY (1947–). Christian Democratic Union (**CDU**) politician. Peter Harry Carstensen was born in Nordstrand (**Schleswig-Holstein**). He studied **agricultural** sciences and after graduating (1973, 1976) worked as a lecturer and consultant at an agricultural college (Landwirtschaftsschule und Wirtschaftsberatungsstelle Bredstedt, 1976–1983). A member of the CDU from 1971, he represented the party in the **Bundestag** (1983–2005), specializing in food, agriculture, forestry, and consumer issues. After serving as deputy leader of the CDU in Schleswig-Holstein (from July 2000), he became leader (2002). In the regional election of February 2005, in which the CDU and the **Social Democratic Party of Germany** (**SPD**) gained 30 and 29 seats, respectively, Carstensen, following protracted negotiations, was narrowly elected **minister president** of a **grand coalition** government of the two parties (April 2005), ending 17 years of CDU opposition in the state. Carstensen proposed tackling Schleswig-Holstein's mounting debt (20,000 million euros in 2005) by cutting back state bureaucracy, closing government departments, and reducing the public sector payroll. He declared **education** a priority by filling over 3,000 vacant teachers' posts and planned to invest in growth industries such as **health**-care services, maritime activities, microelectronics, and renewable **energy**. In 2010, he withdrew as leader of the CDU in Schleswig-Holstein and, following brought-forward elections in 2012, was succeeded as minister president by **Torsten Albig** (SPD).

CENTER FOR ART AND MEDIA TECHNOLOGY (ZENTRUM FÜR KUNST- UND MEDIENTECHNOLOGIE, ZKM.). Since the 1980s, when it was initiated by Heinrich Klotz, the ZKM has been concerned with the relationship between digital technology and the traditional arts. Officially founded in 1989, its work is pursued on an international scale, and it caters to both contemporary developments and the conservation of culture. Klotz defined as one of the principles of the ZKM that it was to explore "the creative possibilities between the traditional art and media technologies for the purpose of achieving innovative results." ZKM attaches great importance to communication and puts on numerous exhibitions. Born in 1935 in Worms, Heinrich Klotz, a professor of art history, was also actively involved in setting up the architectural museum in Frankfurt/Main (from 1979) and published widely on **architecture** and design. Since 2004/2005, ZKM also houses the Museum of Contemporary Art.

CENTRAL COUNCIL OF JEWS IN GERMANY (ZENTRALRAT DER JUDEN IN DEUTSCHLAND). Founded on 19 July 1950 in Frankfurt/Main, at a meeting of delegates from all zones of occupation, the council is the umbrella organization of Jewish communities in the Federal Republic of Germany (FRG). At the time of its founding, only 15,000 Jews remained in the country following the persecutions of the National Socialists (1933–1945). The council later moved its headquarters to Düsseldorf and then Bonn before settling in **Berlin** (1999). In 1990, it incorporated the new **eastern federal states** and has now grown to around 120,000 members organized into 23 regional associations with 108 communities. The council encompasses all denominations, ranging from strict orthodox to reform, conservative, and liberal, and its activities include publishing a weekly newspaper for Jewish affairs, the *Jüdische Allgemeine*, and integrating **immigrants** from the former Soviet Union under the auspices of its welfare organization, the Zentralwohlfahrtsstelle der Juden in Deutschland (ZWST). Since 1957, it has awarded the Leo Baeck Prize in memory of the former rabbi who, from 1933 until his deportation to Theresienstadt concentration camp in 1943 (which he survived), was president of the Reichsvertretung deutscher Juden (Reich Representation of German Jews), refusing offers to emigrate in order to remain in Germany and support his community (he died in London in 1956). In 2009, the Paul Spiegel Prize for civil courage was inaugurated. In

2003, the council concluded an agreement with the FRG, which undertook to provide an annual 3 million euros to preserve Jewish culture, build up the Jewish community in Germany, and support the council's activities. Support was also earmarked for two institutions in Heidelberg: a college for Jewish studies (Hochschule für Jüdische Studien) and a central archive for research into the history of **Jews in Germany** (Zentralarchiv zur Erforschung der Geschichte der Juden in Deutschland). Its presidents have been **Heinz Galinski** (1954–1963, 1988–1992), Herbert Lewin (1963–1969), Werner Nachmann (1969–1988), **Ignatz Bubis** (1992–1999), **Paul Spiegel** (2000–2006), **Charlotte Knobloch** (2006–2010), **Dieter Graumann** (2010–2014), and **Josef Schuster** (2014–).

See also ANTI-SEMITISM; EXTREMISM; RELIGION; TERRORISM.

CHEMICAL INDUSTRY. The foundations of Germany's chemical industry were laid in the mid-19th century; many household corporate names date from that period. Chemicals production currently accounts for around 10 percent of the nation's manufacturing and processing industry GDP and, after engineering, is the second largest contribution to the foreign trade surplus (two-thirds of production is exported). Germany is the **European Union (EU)**'s largest producer of chemicals and ranks fourth in global terms, with some of the world's largest chemical concerns. In 2013, the total production value of the chemical industry was over 143,000 million euros, with pharmaceuticals accounting for a further 29,000 million euros. Of the country's 2,000 or so chemical companies employing a total of 428,000 people, over 90 percent are small to medium-sized enterprises with fewer than 500 employees. The industry is concentrated along the **Rhine River** (in **North Rhine-Westfalia, Hessen, Rhineland-Palatinate**), and is also present in **Baden-Württemberg** (with a wide spectrum of small concerns), **Lower Saxony**, and **Bavaria**. Postreunification restructuring led to many closures of polluting and outdated plants in the "chemical triangle" (Bitterfeld, Buna, and Leuna, now in **Saxony-Anhalt**) of the former **German Democratic Republic (GDR)**, where the focus is now on modern "chemical parks," in which businesses share facilities and infrastructure, a concept that has been copied throughout Germany. The sector, 20 percent of which is made up of pharmaceuticals, is the basis for several key, expanding technologies, some of which are directly integrated into chemical concerns; they include microelectronics and semiconductors, laser technology, and biotechnology. While some of these client industries continue to be served by domestic chemical manufacturers, others, such as textiles and synthetic fibers, have moved to low cost regions in eastern Europe and Asia. During the 1990s, large concerns restructured themselves in order to concentrate on core activities, such as pharmaceuticals, although basic chemicals, especially organics and primary synthetics, still account for 50 percent of total production.

Challenges faced by the domestic German chemical industry include the rising costs of energy and of measures to protect the **environment** since the 1980s (Lake Constance and the Rhine River were very badly affected); the application of gene-changing technologies to plants and animals; and the need to undertake long-term investment in research and development, much of which is increasingly done abroad, where centers of production and demand are also now located. Turnover and profit margins in pharmaceuticals have been depressed by the expiration of patents, the growth of generic drugs, and government efforts to cut the costs of prescribed medicines, for instance through encouraging health insurance funds to negotiate discounts and rebate agreements. The total workforce of the combined chemical and pharmaceutical sector has fallen steadily, from over 716,700 in 1991 to around 438,000 in 2013.

The leading German chemical concerns in terms of turnover and number of employees are **BASF SE** (Ludwigshafen), **Bayer AG** (Leverkusen), Fresenius SE & Co. KGaA (Bad-Homburg), Linde AG (Munich), Henkel AG & Co. KGaA (Düsseldorf), Boehringer Ingelheim GmBH, Evonik Industries AG (Essen), and Merck KGaA (Darmstadt). The largest German subsidiary of a foreign concern is currently Sandoz International GmBH (Holzkirchen). *See also* INDUSTRY

CHRISTIAN DEMOCRATIC UNION (CHRISTLICH-DEMOKRA-TISCHE UNION, CDU). The CDU has its historical roots in the Catholic Center Party (Zentrumspartei), founded in 1871. After the experiences of the National Socialist period, Roman Catholic and Protestant political leaders in postwar Germany overcame confessional differences to establish a broad-based, Christian-oriented, conservative party. Originally formed at regional level in 1945, the CDU became a national party in 1950. Following a brief period in which it embraced economic dirigisme (the Ahlen Program of 1947), the party, led by **Konrad Adenauer** (1876–1967), campaigned on an electoral platform of a socially responsible capitalism. Known as the **social market economy**, this policy was formally adopted in the Düsseldorf Guidelines (July 1949). The CDU went on to dominate the **Bundestag** in successive elections from 1949 to 1966, until the government passed to a grand coalition with the **Social Democratic Party of Germany (SPD)**. Chancellors from the CDU directly after Adenauer were **Ludwig Erhard** (1963–1966) and **Kurt Georg Kiesinger** (1966–1969). After a period in opposition (1969–1982), during which it regenerated its leadership and overcame its reservations over rapprochement with the East (**Ostpolitik**), the CDU reentered government in coalition with the **Free Democratic Party (FDP)**. Led by **Helmut Kohl**, federal chancellor from 1982 to 1998, the CDU campaigned for "freedom, solidarity, and justice" (Freiheit, Solidarität, und Gerechtigkeit) and supported the conservative social values of family, marriage, state, and church. The CDU's sister party in **Bavaria** is the **Christian Social Union (CSU)**.

In its first program of basic principles (Grundsatzprogramm, 1978), the CDU reaffirmed its traditional identity as a conservative party of mass appeal, or Volkspartei ("people's party"). A second program (1994) broadened the commitment to a social market economy to take account of ecological issues. While continuing to emphasize the primacy of marriage, a mini party congress in 1999 extended the definition of family to include partnerships outside marriage. The party also outlined its vision of a federally organized **European Union (EU)** with devolved powers of subsidiarity. During the 1980s, successive CDU/FDP administrations presided over a flourishing economy and began privatizing public sector activities. Party membership rose from around 300,000 in the late 1960s to 734,555 in 1983. Following the political triumph of reunification (1990), rising domestic budgets and unemployment undermined Kohl's leadership, and the CDU lost its majority in the **Bundesrat** (1997) and in the 1998 national election. In opposition and with a new leader, **Angela Merkel** (from 2000), the party embarked on a process of renewal, although it was undermined by internal disputes, debt, and financial scandals surrounding Kohl's acceptance of illegal donations (see below). At a party congress in Erfurt (April 1999), the CDU adopted the "Erfurt guidelines," which were intended to overcome the recent past and modernize the party's image and organization. A commission was set up to work out new policies on the family, the social state, and **education** and on creating a leaner, more efficient state. To counter the problems of a declining and aging membership, the CDU resolved to introduce more internal democracy in decision making and to involve outsiders in projects. While defining the CDU as a "people's party of the center," the third basic principles program (2007) committed the party to improving child-care facilities and extending **taxation** concessions to include partnerships with children.

When the CDU in the **German Democratic Republic (GDR)** regained its independence from the government-controlled block of parties in 1989–1990, it swiftly established its claim to leadership in eastern Germany by virtue of its efficient organization and experience in local politics. Led by **Lothar de Maizière**, the party reaffirmed its Christian values and advocated a socially responsible and ecologically sensitive capitalism. In the national election to the **People's Chamber** (March 1990), the GDR/CDU emerged as the strongest party, although its church-oriented leaders, whose roots lay in the socialist bloc of aligned parties, were eventually replaced by new figures. In October 1990, the East German CDU amalgamated with its sister party in the west.

Between 1999 and 2001, the CDU was rocked by a series of financial scandals, involving tax evasion by its national treasurer, **Walther Leisler Kiep**; admissions by ex-chancellor Kohl that he had accepted secret, anonymous donations; and revelations of hidden Swiss bank accounts maintained by the party in **Hessen**. These violations of party finance laws not only triggered a committee of inquiry and sanctions by the Bundestag, they also deeply demoralized the CDU and reinforced public cynicism about **political parties** in general. Kohl was forced to resign as honorary party chairman (January 2000), and **Wolfgang Schäuble** withdrew as leader of the party and its parliamentary group (February 2000). General Secretary Angela Merkel, who had called in an open letter in December 1999 for the CDU to distance itself from Kohl, was elected the party's first female leader in April 2000. In opposition, at a party congress in Leipzig in 2003, Merkel championed the most radical neoliberal program in the CDU's history, which included drastically simplifying the taxation system, replacing graduated contributions to **health** insurance by a flat-rate premium, and raising the retirement age to 67. Although some of these proposals were eventually implemented (the health premium, over and above standard graduated contribution, came into force in 2009, and the Bundestag approved the new pension age in 2007), fears of voter alienation provoked a change in the tone of the 2011 party congress in Leipzig, with Merkel now talking of minimum wage thresholds and controlling market forces. Under Merkel's stewardship, the CDU improved its performance in regional elections, and despite losing seats at the national election of 2005, it was able to form a grand coalition with the SPD. Despite garnering a disappointing share of seats in the 2009 election, the party continued to govern, this time with the FDP. In the election of 2013, the CDU emerged as the strongest party, just falling short of an absolute majority.

An interesting feature of recent CDU-led governments under Merkel is the "Protestantization" of the cabinet: of ministers appointed in or after 2013, Protestants, many of whom were actively engaged in their church, were in the majority. While this may be simply due to regional factors, most ministers were CDU members, and when **Annette Schavan** resigned in 2013, **Peter Altmaier** was left as the sole Roman Catholic at ministerial level. Although ministerial appointments are not made on confessional grounds, the development may reflect features of modern German Protestantism that appeal to contemporary Germans in general and to Merkel's style of modest restraint and careful, deliberative decision making in particular. In the SPD, on the other hand, Protestants have always been well represented, especially since the left-wing politicization of the German Evangelical Church during the 1970s and 1980s.

The CDU is organized at the national and regional levels, from 17 Landesverbände (regional associations) down to 10,000 Ortsverbände (local branches) and nearly 500,000 members. A national/federal executive committee (Bundesvorstand) bases its day-to-day work on the party's guideline program of basic principles; the decisions of a national party congress (Bundesparteitag), which convenes at least every two years; and a federal committee (Bundesausschuss), otherwise known as the "mini party congress" (kleiner Parteitag). In practice, the party's main power base is in western states, with the eastern regional associations exerting little influence at national party congresses. The executive committee, which includes the chairman and general secretary, reports to the national congress, although in practice much of its work is carried out by the presidium (Präsidium), comprising the party leader/chairman and deputies, the general secretary, the treasurer, and seven senior persons elected by members of parliament. Associated with the party are numerous interest groups and associations (e.g., for **women**, workers, **trade unions**, small businesses, and refugees), not to mention the conservative Konrad-Adenauer-Stiftung (Konrad Adenauer Foundation), which undertakes research and educational activities and awards grants and scholarships. Party leaders in the postwar period have been Konrad Adenauer (1950–1966), Ludwig Erhard (1966–1967), Kurt Georg Kiesinger (1967–1971), **Rainer Barzel** (1971–1973), Helmut Kohl (1973–1998), Wolfgang Schäuble (1998–2000), and Angela Merkel (2000–). Recent general secretaries include **Laurenz Meyer** (2000–2004), **Volker Kauder** (2005), **Ronald Pofalla** (2005–2009), **Hermann Gröhe** (2009–2013), and **Peter Tauber** (2013–). The party's youth wing is the **Junge Union (JU)**.

CHRISTIAN SOCIAL UNION (CHRISTLICH-SOZIALE UNION, CSU). The CSU was founded in 1945/1946 in **Bavaria** as the sister party of the **Christian Democratic Union (CDU)**. Both **political parties** work together in the **Bundestag** and maintain a joint parliamentary group alongside their individual ones. By agreement, the CDU does not campaign in Bavaria, and the CSU does not campaign nationally, although the latter does provide cabinet ministers. The CSU is predominantly, but not exclusively, Roman Catholic and is more conservative and regional than the CDU in its outlook. At the same time, it tends to show a greater concern with social issues than its sister party. Apart from a three-year period (1954–1957) when the **Social Democratic Party of Germany (SPD)** led a coalition government in Bavaria, the CSU has ruled continuously in its home state, from 1996 without a coalition partner. Following bitter disputes in the 1950s, the CSU succeeded in marginalizing its rival, the Bayernpartei (BP), with whom it formed a "little coalition" between 1962/1963 and 1966, in which the BP provided no cabinet minister. The BP, which campaigns for independence from the Federal Republic of Germany (FRG), currently has around 6,000 members and at every election since 1966 has failed to clear the 5 percent hurdle for entry to the regional assembly. Between 1970 and 2008, the CSU enjoyed an absolute majority in the assembly, although the situation changed dramatically in the election of 2008, when the party lost seats to the **Free Voters** party, the **Alliance 90/The Greens**, and the FDP, with which it formed a ruling coalition. The CSU regained its majority in 2013, with the FDP failing to clear the 5 percent hurdle.

For a long period (1961–1988), the CSU was led by the charismatic but controversial **Franz Josef Strauß**, who established the party as a symbol of Bavaria itself while also developing its profile at the national level, although suggestions of campaigning beyond the region came to nothing. **Edmund Stoiber** was elected leader in 1999. After reunification, the party attempted to establish a presence in the eastern states of **Thuringia** and **Saxony** by supporting the **German Social Union (Deutsche Soziale Union, DSU)**, but despite initial successes, the DSU proved unable to sustain itself, and the CSU leadership dropped the plan. In 1993, the party reaffirmed its commitment to Christian politics, supported nuclear **energy**, and saw the **European Union (EU)** ideally developing as a group of nation-states. Its 2007 statement of basic policy principles reiterated its traditional conservative values, based on regional identity, family, **education**, social welfare, ecology, and the promotion of local **agriculture**—all within a European framework.

Although the CSU long retained a stable membership, it steadily lost members between 2001 (177,852) and 2014 (about 147,000), in particular to smaller parties owing to demographic developments, disappointments at the party's political direction, and problems of identifying members at the local level. Its leading organs are a party congress (Parteitag), party committee (Parteiausschuss), executive committee (Parteivorstand), and presidium (Präsidium). The presidium is the main executive organ, managing day-to-day business, controlling financial affairs, and exerting a powerful political influence. Associated with the CSU is the Hanns-Seidel Stiftung (Hanns Seidel Foundation), which carries out research and consultancy and promotes political education. In 2007, the party founded its own academy to train and promote future politicians. Its youth wing is the **Junge Union** Bayern. Party leaders in the postwar period have been Josef Müller (1946–1949), Hans Ehard (1949–1955), Hanns Seidel (1955–1961), Franz Josef Strauß (1961–1988), **Theo Waigel** (1988–1999), Edmund Stoiber (1999–2007), **Günther Beckstein** (2007–2008), and **Horst Seehofer** (2008–).

CHURCHES. *See* RELIGION.

CINEMA. The 1960s marked the beginning of a highly prolific period for cinema in the Federal Republic of Germany (FRG). In 1962, during the Obershausen Short Film Festival (Oberhausener Kurzfilmtage), a group of young German film directors announced their criticism of traditional German cinema, which they declared to be dead. In proposing a "new German cinema" (the so-called Oberhausen Manifesto), they argued for new aesthetic standards in film that would reflect society. They also demanded a halt to the established system of funding and patronage from interest groups and commercial partners. Representatives of the group included Rainer Werner Fassbinder, Alexander Kluge, Peter Schamoni, Edgar Reitz, and Volker Schlöndorff—all of whom were and remain of great influence on contemporary German cinema history. Their films aimed to confront society with its shortcomings and restored Germany's reputation in international cinema. They adopted themes such as **abortion**, divorce, intergenerational conflict, and social outsiders, and employed experimental techniques, such as montage, the inclusion of documentary material, and the use of lay actors. Because directors at times wrote their own scripts, these films are also called "auteristic films" or "Autorenfilme" (an example is the director, writer, and producer Wim Wenders). The New German Film movement marked the end of a crisis period for West German cinema and represented Germany's answer to developments that had started much earlier in France. It also marked the end of the inward-looking period that had characterized productions in the 1950s.

From January 1968 onward, the German state financially supported directors' work with a law on the promotion of film (Filmfördergesetz). In 1971, the directors themselves set up the Filmverlag der Autoren, a publishing house handling production rights and marketing. On the downside, it must be acknowledged that the anti-aesthetic ethos of some of the "new wave" films and their disregard for narrative and composition cost them a wider public audience. The generation after Oberhausen relied rather on the methods of the American off-off film, which were used with great success, for example, by May Spils in *Zur Sache Schätzchen* (1968) to portray the "attitude to life of a whole generation" (Hilmar Hoffmann).

Cinema in the **German Democratic Republic (GDR)** focused on fairy tales, literary adaptations, antifascist films, and documentary dramas. Although subjected to censorship, some films contained veiled criticism of the state. As in **literature**, the replacement of **Walter Ulbricht** by **Erich Honecker** (1971) initially offered hope for a more liberal approach. Eminent directors working in the GDR included Frank Beyer (*Jakob der Lügner*, 1974), Heiner Carow (*Die Legende von Paul und Paula*, 1973), Kurt Maetzig, Wolfgang Staudte, and Konrad Wolf. DEFA (Deutsche Film AG), East Germany's only film studio, had been set up in 1946 in the Soviet-occupied sector and was a state-owned company from 1952 to 1990. Until 1990, DEFA produced about 680 films for cinema and 620 for **television**. After being administered by the **Trust Agency**, DEFA entered private ownership as the Babelsberg Studios GmbH in 1992. The DEFA Foundation was set up in 1999 to preserve the historic cinematic legacy of the GDR.

During the 1990s and early 2000s, German cinema achieved fresh prominence. Alongside comical and lighthearted works (e.g., *Run, Lola, Run*, directed by Tom Tykwer), films on historical topics and periods (especially the Third Reich and the Weimar Republic) became popular, with some even breaking into the international market (e.g., Oliver Hirschbiegel's *Downfall* and Florian Henckel von Donnersmarck's *The Lives of Others*). The company X-Filme Creative Pool (founded by Stefan Arndt, Tom Tykwer, Dani Levy, and Wolfgang Becker in 1994) has been among the most successful in establishing German cinema internationally, combining commercial with artistic film production. With *Good Bye, Lenin* (2003), Becker created a fresh look at the impact of the fall of the **Berlin Wall** and the way of life in East Germany that, more than a decade after the fall of the Wall, was lost for good. Among recent films with Berlin as a location, Jan-Ole Gerster's *Oh Boy* (2012) has been well received, while *The People vs. Fritz Bauer* (Lars Kraume, 2015) shows the renewed engagement with West Germany's postwar history.

Other influential filmmakers to make an impact in recent years include Detlev Buck, Doris Dörrie, Andreas Dresen, Caroline Link, Rosa von Praunheim, and Sönke Wortmann. Significant contributions have come from young non-German filmmakers whose works have attracted attention (*Kanak Attack* [2000], *Gegen die Wand* [2004]). While films about **immigrants** appeared as early as the 1970s and 1980s, productions since the 1990s have made an impression through their fresh, unsentimental take on the issues. An example is Yasemin Şamdereli's very successful *Almanya—Willkommen in Deutschland* (2011), which looked at all immigrant generations to Germany since the first wave of guest workers arrived and the ensuing different challenges they faced.

As in many other countries today, multiplex cinemas in Germany predominate in cities, although some traditional and specialist cinemas are able to maintain their appeal. Since 2009, overall income has increased due to large numbers of visitors, and the trend is expected to continue in future years. Compared with the rest of the world, Germany ranks 10th in terms of number of visits to the cinema per inhabitant.

Although the international success of German film remains limited—some notable exceptions aside—Germany has a well-established filmmaking industry. Film funding is regionally based, with organizations such as Filmboard Berlin-**Brandenburg**, FilmFörderung **Hamburg**, Mitteldeutsche Medienförderung, and Nord Media playing a key role. At the national level, funding is provided by the Filmförderungsanstalt and the Kuratorium junger deutscher Film. Among film academies in Germany, the following are worth mentioning: the Deutsche Film- und Fernsehakademie Berlin (dffb), the Hochschule für Fernsehen und Film (HFF), the Hochschule für Film und Fernsehen "Konrad Wolf," the IFS Internationale Filmschule Cologne

GmbH, and the Kunsthochschule Kassel. The following archives and film museums provide material on the history of—among other things—German film: Bundesarchiv/Filmarchiv, Defa Stiftung, Deutsches Filminstitut-DIF & Filmarchiv, Deutsches Filmmuseum Frankfurt a.M., Filmmuseum Düsseldorf, Filmmuseum Potsdam, Friedrich-Wilhelm-Murnau-Stiftung, and the Stiftung Deutsche Kinemathek. The Deutsche Filmakademie (German Film Academy) was founded in September 2003 and since 2005 has awarded prizes to the best German films, after the model of the Oscars.

Germany has a number of prestigious and regular film festivals. The first Berlinale—the Berlin Film Festival—took place in 1951 and ranks in importance for the European market next to Cannes and Venice. It presents world premieres and provided a forum for the early work of directors such as Roman Polanski, Werner Herzog, Jean-Luc Godard, and Martin Scorsese. To be included in the festival, films must meet the criteria of aesthetic innovation, cultural difference, and social reality. In 2015, the Berlinale was attended by more than half a million visitors from 82 countries. Recent honorary awards have gone to Wolfgang Kohlhaase and Hanna Schygulla, Armin Mueller-Stahl, Meryl Streep, Claude Lanzmann, Ken Loach, and Wim Wenders. Other German cities with regular film festivals include Mannheim, Oberhausen, and Leipzig.

See also MEDIA.

CLEMENT, WOLFGANG (1940–). Social Democratic Party of Germany (SPD) politician. Wolfgang Clement was born in Bochum (**North Rhine-Westfalia**, NRW). After graduating in law from the University of Münster (1960–1965), he completed a legal traineeship at the Oberlandesgericht (higher regional court) in Hamm (1965–1967) before briefly joining the law institute of the University of Marburg as a research assistant. In 1968, he joined the newspaper *Westfälische Rundschau* as political editor (he had already done occasional work for the paper during his student years) and served as deputy chief editor from 1973 to 1981. An SPD member from 1970, his active political career began when he became spokesman for the party's national executive committee in Bonn (1981); in 1985 he was appointed deputy parliamentary business manager (Bundesgeschäftsführer). In 1986, after disastrous local election results and disagreements with **Johannes Rau**, the party's chancellor candidate, over national election strategy, Clement resigned and returned to journalism, to become chief editor of the **Hamburg**-based daily *Hamburger Morgenpost*. In 1989, he returned to NRW to head the state chancellery under Rau and manage European affairs, before becoming regional minister for special tasks (Minister für besondere Aufgaben, 1990–1995). In 1993, he joined the election team of chancellor candidate **Rudolf Scharping** (SPD). Elected to the NRW state parliament (1993–2002), he became a member of the SPD's regional executive (1994).

Under the red/green coalition elected in the NRW regional elections of 1995, Clement was the minister responsible for economics, small to medium-sized industries, technology, and **transport** (1995–1998), where he raised left-wing eyebrows by advocating privatization and lowering wages to reduce unemployment. In May 1998, he succeeded Rau as **minister president** of NRW and the following year was elected deputy chairman of the national party. After the reelection of the red/green coalition in NRW in June 2000, he declared the creation of jobs and economic modernization as his main political objectives. A strong supporter of **Gerhard Schröder** and with a reputation as a technocrat and **media** specialist, he was regarded as a center-right modernizer keen to overhaul Germany's costly social welfare system and restructure the economy in order to meet the challenges of globalization. As "super minister" of a merged economics and labor department in Schröder's new cabinet between 2002 and 2005 (**Peer Steinbrück** succeeded him in NRW), Clement vigorously pursued implementation of the reforms proposed by the **Hartz Commission**, although policy failures amid rising unemployment and his public branding of welfare recipients as "parasites" in the summer of 2005 rendered him a political liability. Seen by environmentalists as too business-friendly, Clement had also openly opposed the plan by **environment** minister **Jürgen Trittin** (**Green Party**) to introduce a deposit on drink cans (2001) and was widely seen as a lobbyist for the **energy** industry. Following the election of the SPD/**Christian Democratic Union** (**CDU**) coalition in 2005, Clement attacked the demerger of his department, withdrew from politics, and became increasingly distanced from the SPD, which he criticized for moving too close to **The Left Party**. In contravention of SPD policy, he argued for postponing the exit from nuclear energy and reducing targets for carbon emissions from coal-fired power stations. His intervention in the regional election campaign in **Hessen** in early 2008, when he warned voters not to support the SPD candidate, **Andrea Ypsilanti**, on account of her antinuclear and anticoal energy policies, brought him into open conflict with his party, which, amid moves for his expulsion, he finally quit in November. After this, he began to cultivate links with the **Free Democratic Party** (**FDP**), supporting the party in the NRW regional election campaign of 2012.

COAL. *See* ENERGY: COAL.

CODETERMINATION (MITBESTIMMUNG). The legal foundations of industrial codetermination in Germany were laid in the late 19th and early 20th centuries, when works councils, made up of representatives of the workforce, at first voluntary and with very limited powers, were permitted in the mining **industry**. After World War I, the Weimar constitution explicitly called for the creation of works councils (Betriebsräte, article 165), and between 1920 and 1922 legislation was passed requiring their formation in private and state-run businesses. Significantly, council members were also entitled to be represented on the supervisory boards of capital-financed companies, which gave rise to the distinction between codetermination at works and at board level. While the councils were largely concerned with social and personnel issues at plant level, representatives on the supervisory board exerted some influence on policy making. Under the National Socialists (1933–1945), all forms of worker democracy were abolished, but after World War II the British authorities, believing that employee representation at company board level would prevent the emergence of monopolistic industrial conglomerates, which had bolstered the National Socialist regime, actively promoted codetermination at works and management level in their occupation zone. German business leaders, anxious to fend off foreign control of the coal and steel industry, were initially sympathetic to the idea, and supervisory boards with 50 percent worker representation appeared in this sector from 1947. After the foundation of the Federal Republic of Germany (FRG) in 1949 the government, obliged to intervene to resolve bitter disputes between workers and employers over codetermination, introduced Works Constitution Laws (Betriebsverfassungsgesetze) for the iron, steel, and coal sectors (1951 and 1952). The laws provided for virtual parity of representation between the employers and workforce on the 11-member supervisory boards (Aufsichtsrat) of concerns with over 1,000 employees (boards included up to three noncompany trade unionists and one "neutral" member). A unique feature of the legislation was that the personnel director (Arbeitsdirektor) of the executive board (Vorstand) could be elected only by a majority of the workforce (dating back to the 19th century, the two-tier supervisory/executive board system has been a traditional feature of German corporate governance).

Under Chancellor **Willy Brandt (Social Democratic Party of Germany, SPD)**, and after much controversy, parity of representation on the supervisory board, which had long applied to the iron, steel, and coal sector, was extended to companies employing over 2,000 workers, although the chairman, usually representing management, had a casting vote (1976). The new provision affected larger companies in the important **chemical, engineering**, and **automobile** industries. Employers' objections to the new law were overruled by the **Federal Constitution Court (FCC**, 1979), although today only about 40 companies are wholly subject to the original coal and steel codetermination laws. Legislation was extended in 2001 to include all private and public concerns with at least five permanent employees, to facilitate the creation of works councils in smaller firms (between 5 and 100 employees) and require councils to reflect the gender composition of the workforce in their composition. In 2004, the One-Third Participation Act (Drittelbeteiligungsgesetz) ruled that one-third of the supervisory boards of joint stock companies (AGs) and limited liability companies (GmbHs) employing between 500 and 2,000 people should be electable by the workforce, thus reducing the parity principle for smaller companies. From 2015, at least 30 percent of supervisory board members had to be either men or women, in practice, to improve representation for the latter.

Although there is no legal obligation to set up works councils, companies must take account of and provide facilities for them if the workforce opts for them. Politically neutral and unable to take part in industrial action (although its members can be members of a trade union), the council represents the general interests of the workforce, for example, with regard to pay, working conditions, hours, and training, and has rights of information and consultation on issues of personnel and management strategy. The council's views must also be heard in cases of dismissal, and special provisions on its role and powers apply to organizations such as churches and the **media**. The size of a council, which is elected by the workforce for four years, is linked to that of the company. Provision also exists for other forms of councils at the local, European, and even world levels, depending on the structure of the company.

In 2013, 43 percent of workers in Germany were represented by a works council. Representation was highest (79 percent) in the waste disposal, water, energy, and mining industries and lowest in building and catering (17–15 percent). While 91 percent of larger companies (over 500 employees) maintained a council, the figure fell to just 9 percent for concerns employing between 5 and 50. For most industries, representation was higher in the western federal states than in the east.

Although codetermination was for many years seen as promoting a consensual system of industrial relations within a legal framework, critics such as employers' leader Michael Rogowski (2004) called it an "error of history," arguing that it stifled entrepreneurial flexibility. A commission under **Kurt Biedenkopf** set up by Chancellor **Gerhard Schröder** to propose reforms failed in 2006 to reach a consensus among employers, trade unionists, and academics (Biedenkopf had chaired a similar commission, which had led to the 1976 revisions), and the main political parties continued on the whole to endorse the existing system. The Hans-Böckler Stiftung (Hans Böckler Foundation) monitors and researches issues of corporate governance and codetermination and provides up-to-date information. The Institut für Arbeitsmarkt- und Berufsforschung (Institute for Employment Research, IAB) provides similar data in relation to the broader labor market.

See also TRADE UNIONS.

COHN-BENDIT, DANIEL (1945–). Green Party politician and student leader. Born in Montauban in France (his father had emigrated from **Berlin** in 1933 when the National Socialists came to power), Daniel Cohn-Bendit completed his school **education** in Germany (Oberhambach/**Rhineland-Pa-**

latinate). He studied sociology at the universities of Nanterre, Paris, and Frankfurt/Main and played a leading role in the student revolution in Paris during May 1968. The French government expelled him from the country and did not lift the ban until 1978, although he then chose to remain in Germany. During his exile, he worked in a bookstore in Frankfurt where, along with **Joschka Fischer**, he was prominent in the Sponti-Szene, an informal movement of militant left-wingers who attempted to trigger a street revolution through political agitation, house occupations, and demonstrations. From 1978 until 1990, he edited the alternative magazine *Pflasterstrand*, which acted as a platform for the movement's ideas. In 1978, the movement committed itself to participating in the parliamentary system, in particular through involvement with the Green Party, which Cohn-Bendit joined in 1984. Cohn-Bendit belonged to the "realist" section of the party and vigorously opposed its fundamentalist wing, which resisted formal structures and cooperation with the political establishment. His support for military intervention during the Bosnian war in the mid-1990s alienated the pacifist wing of his party, and he advocated German participation in similar action during the Syrian civil war (2013).

Between 1989 and 1997, Cohn-Bendit represented the Greens in the Frankfurt city council, heading a newly created department for multicultural affairs. He argued against a hardening of Germany's **asylum** laws, for clear legislation on **immigration**, and for a liberalization of the laws on citizenship. In 1994, he was elected to the European Parliament, where, since 2002, he has cochaired the parliamentary group of the Greens/European Free Alliance. In the parliament, he chaired the delegation of the joint **European Union (EU)**–Turkey committee (from 2002) and has been involved in various committees, ranging from culture, youth, education, and **media** to foreign affairs, **human rights**, defense and **security**, economics, and constitutional issues. In 2013, he announced his intention not to stand in the 2014 election.

In 1997, the University of Tilburg (Netherlands) awarded Cohn-Bendit an honorary doctorate for services to politics; he also received the Hannah Arendt Prize for political thought (2001), the Cicero Rednerpreis (Cicero Prize for Rhetoric, 2009), and the Theodor Heuss Prize (2013) for civic courage (2013). A gifted and committed speaker, he has published numerous essays and books on political issues, addressed **anti-Semitism**, and made frequent appearances in the broadcasting media, including moderating a literary program on Swiss television (1994–2003).

See also STUDENTS' MOVEMENT.

COMMERZBANK AG. The Commerzbank AG (Frankfurt/Main) is one of Germany's largest universal **banks**. The bank was founded in 1870 in **Hamburg** as the Commerz- und Disconto-Bank by businessmen, traders, and merchant bankers. A London branch was established three years later and flourished until the outbreak of World War I. With the opening of further branches in Frankfurt/Main and **Berlin** (1897) and the acquisition of the Berliner Bank (1905), the center of the bank's business moved from Hamburg to the capital. Following further expansion and takeovers during the 1920s and 1930s, the bank officially adopted the title Commerzbank AG. After World War II, the bank lost almost half of its branch network, which was located in Soviet-occupied eastern Germany. The Western Allies split up the big banks in 1947–1948, but the elements of the Commerzbank were able to reconstitute themselves in 1958. After 1970, the bank moved its activities from Düsseldorf to Frankfurt, where its headquarters have been based since 1990. In common with other banks, the Commerzbank helped finance the economic recovery in the Federal Republic of Germany (FRG) during the 1950s and 1960s and enjoyed rapid growth. It opened new branches at home and abroad, including in Luxembourg (1969) and New York City (1971), where it was the first German bank to open in the United States. It merged with the **Dresdner Bank** in 2009 and maintains a strong presence in Poland. Operating profit in 2015 was 1,062 million euros, with a total workforce of around 51,000 (almost 39,000 in Germany). The Commerzbank currently has 1,200 branches and offices in Germany and is present in 50 countries. The executive chairman is Martin Zielke (appointed 2016).

COMMITTEE ON EASTERN EUROPEAN ECONOMIC RELATIONS (OST-AUSSCHUSS DER DEUTSCHEN WIRTSCHAFT, OA). Founded in 1952, the committee promotes and represents the interests of German business in eastern Europe. It currently oversees 21 states (Russia, Belarus, Ukraine, Moldova, and Albania; the **European Union [EU]** members Romania and Bulgaria; EU candidate members Croatia, Macedonia, and Montenegro, as well as Serbia, Bosnia-Herzegovina, Kosovo; and the countries of the South Caucasus and Central Asia). With around 180 member businesses—ranging from small to medium-sized companies to those quoted on the German stock-exchange—it is supported by the leading German business organizations and maintains a network of links at diplomatic and commercial levels in Germany and its partner states. In July 2011, the OA argued for the abolition of visas between eastern Europe (especially Russia) and the EU in order to promote trade and business activity.

COMMON AGRICULTURAL POLICY (CAP). *See* AGRICULTURE.

COUNCIL OF EUROPE. Founded in 1949, the council is Europe's leading human rights organization. It includes 47 member states, 28 of which are also members of the **European Union (EU)**. All Council of Europe member states have signed the European Convention on Human Rights, a treaty designed to protect **human rights**, democracy, and the rule of law. Founding members include Great Britain and West Germany. Based in Strasburg (France), the organization is not to be confused with the Council of the EU, which is a body of governance within the EU itself.

COUNCIL OF EXPERTS (SACHVERSTÄNDIGENRAT). Since 1963, a Council of Experts for Monitoring National Economic Development (Sachverständigenrat zur Begutachtung der gesamtwirtschaftlichen Entwicklung, often referred to as the Sachverständigenrat) has been tasked with providing objective annual assessments of the state of the national economy and making independent policy recommendations. The council is made up of five economics experts, commonly known as the "five wise men," who are nominated by the **federal government** and appointed by the **president of the Federal Republic**; one council member is replaced each year. The council presents its assessment by 15 November, although it can also be charged with providing further reports. Its main task is to make recommendations for ensuring price stability, employment, and external economic stability alongside domestic growth, but it is also expected to point out negative economic developments and recommend policy alternatives. The council is supported by a team of 11 economists under a secretary general and maintains an administrative liaison office, which is part of the Statistisches Bundesamt (Federal Statistical Office).

CRAFT ASSOCIATION. The association (Deutscher Werkbund, or German Craft Association) has traditionally sought to achieve a synthesis between art and industrial production methods and hence also a partnership between creative forces and product manufacturers. Founded in Munich in 1907 as an association of architects, designers, and industrialists (and shaped not least by the approach of the British arts and crafts movement), it was dissolved under the National Socialist Regime. Up until then one of its focal aims had been to improve Germany's standing as an exporter in the global world. Founding members included Hermann Muthesius, Peter Behrens, Heinrich Tessenow, Fritz Schumacher, and Theodor Fischer. When it was refounded in 1950, its first presidents were Hans Schwippert and Otto Bartning.

The Werkbund fosters interdisciplinary discourse on **architecture**, design, graphic art, photography, urban development, landscape, and the crafts. Together with a college of design (Hochschule für Gestaltung) in Ulm during the 1960s, the association contributed significantly to raising aesthetic awareness in West Germany. At first the association was concerned with the transition from craftsmanship to industrial production, but from the 1950s onward it focused on the challenges posed by ecology and the shift from industry to the public service sector. In line with its aim of promoting discourse, the organization also holds "craft association days" (Werkbundtage). Themes for these events (which began in 1998) include "Urban culture in dialogue: Experiences in East and West" (1999); "City development—Who is involved?" (2002); "One must take a stand—The work and influence of Julius Posener" (2004); "The future as provocation" (2005); "The city as a laboratory—the future of living in the city" (2009); and "Industrial Culture" (2014). The Werkbund offers lectures and organizes exhibitions and roundtable discussions.

The Werkbund's structure reflects Germany's system of **federalism**: Werkbund Nord comprises **Bremen, Hamburg, Mecklenburg-West Pomerania, Saxony-Anhalt,** and **Schleswig-Holstein**; other federal representations are to be found in **Saxony, Saarland, Rhineland-Palatinate, North-Rhine Westfalia, Hessen, Berlin, Bavaria,** and **Baden-Württemberg.** Overall there are about 1,500 members. The Museum der Dinge in Berlin houses the organization's collections and archive.

CULTURAL AND MEDIA POLICY. In 1998, the government of the Federal Republic of Germany (FRG) created the office of Representative for Culture and **Media** (Beauftragte[r] für Kultur und Medien), based in Bonn and **Berlin**. The position has been held by Michael Naumann, Julian Nida-Rümelin, Christina Weiss, Bernd Neumann, and Monika Grütters.

The representative's tasks include the promotion and fostering of cultural institutions and projects and the preservation of Germany's free and pluralistic **media** landscape. Wide-ranging reforms for culture and the media have provided a new legal framework, in which key elements include the promotion of **Deutsche Welle**; a treaty for supporting culture in the capital, Berlin; a foundation for funding cultural projects (Kulturstiftung des Bundes); support for filmmaking; and cooperation with Europe. Cultural and media politics (Kultur- und Medienpolitik) in Germany are based on the belief that both are the expression and the result of an ongoing critical debate in the **Bundestag** and in society. At the same time, cultural policy remains largely the responsibility of the **federal states** and the communities. The **Bund** concentrates on aspects of national and international relevance, including memorials in relation to the National Socialist terror regime and the **German Democratic Republic (GDR)**. Topics and projects include diverse activities such as the participation in celebrations of the 500th anniversary of the German Reformation in 2017 and art looted by either the National Socialists or the Allied forces ("Raub- and Beutekunst").

CULTURAL METROPOLIS (KULTURMETROPOLE). This term is widely used in Germany to refer to **Berlin** as a cultural center, even though the country's federal structure allows all the **federal states** to maintain a strong cultural profile. After World War II, cultural activities in the city, which had thrived as a center of the arts in the 1920s, enjoyed a revival and at the same time mirrored the political conflict between East and West. The creation of two German states (1949) and the erection of the **Berlin Wall** (1961) profoundly affected the city's **museums** and collections. Nevertheless, by the 1960s West Berlin had reestablished itself—not least thanks to substantial subsidies from the Federal Republic of Germany (FRG)—as a flourishing venue for festivals, exhibitions, and musical and **theater** performances, as well as for alternative culture, with the accent on the contemporary. By the 1980s, the sheer density of these events was second to none in the cultural landscape of West Germany. At the same time, the **German Democratic Republic (GDR)** had concentrated most of its cultural institutions in East Berlin, not least because cultural policy was considered to be an integral aspect of politics. Unofficially, there was a lively exchange of ideas between the two parts of the city.

The status of culture and levels of activity, although still unique for Germany as a whole, have changed in the course of reunification. Alternative projects are still featured, but within Berlin there have been numerous topographical shifts, and the once exceptionally accessible market for renting and buying flats and houses has become more restrictive even though prices are well below New York's, London's, or Paris's standards. The perception of Berlin as a cultural metropolis also played a major role during the debate in 1991 on moving the seat of government from Bonn, which was perceived as a provincial location, to Berlin.

CURRENCY. The Deutsche Mark (DM), which served as the currency of the Federal Republic of Germany (FRG) from June 1948 until January 2002, became a symbol of West Germany's economic recovery and continuing prosperity after World War II. The prehistory of the DM dates back to 1871, when the Reichstag introduced the mark (and its subunit, the pfennig) as the currency of the newly founded German Empire. Hitherto used only as a unit of weight, the mark superseded seven other currencies in circulation in the German states (one of these, the Taler, was the etymological precursor of the U.S. dollar). The so-called Reichsmark (RM), which remained the standard currency of the territory of the German Empire until 1948, underwent two periods of hyperinflation, 1919–1923 and 1945–1948. These experiences, which impoverished many Germans, made a lasting impression on the national psyche and implanted in the general public a desire for sound money and financial stability, which would become an important factor in the monetary policy of the FRG. When the military government of the Western Allies introduced the DM on 21 June 1948 (the "currency reform"), the aim was to remove the volume of inflated RM in circulation and create a new currency as a basis for economic recovery. The decision to retain some link with the past by keeping the nomenclature of the "old mark" was deliberate. The reform was implemented in a series of laws that came into effect between June and October 1948. These introduced the new coins and notes, fixed the rates and amounts at which old RM were converted to DM, and regulated savings accounts. The move also triggered a blockade of West Berlin by the Soviet Union, which was not lifted until 12 May 1949.

The new currency contributed significantly to the restoration of business and fiscal confidence in the postwar economy. Its introduction went hand in hand with landmark legislation initiated by **Ludwig Erhard**, the FRG's first economics minister, in 1948, which effectively threw out the mass of controls and regulations accumulated from the war. The minting of the currency passed into the hands of a central bank (Bank Deutscher Länder, BDL), and the total volume in circulation was restricted to 10,000 million DM until July 1957, when the money supply became the statutory responsibility of the newly created **German Federal Bank** (Bundesbank). The bank saw its primary role as protecting the currency from inflation and, indeed, from the 1970s until the mid-1990s Germany maintained the lowest rate of inflation of any advanced industrial country. From 19 September 1949 until the FRG's entry into the International Monetary Fund (IMF) in 1952, the DM was exchanged at a rate of $0.24 (U.S.). It became freely convertible in 1958 and, as the "economic miracle" steamed ahead, developed into one of Western Europe's strongest currencies. Revalued upward in 1961 and 1969, it continued to rise when the Bretton Woods system of fixed parities was abandoned in 1973 in favor of freely floating exchange rates. However, instability in rates, including appreciation of the DM in relation to other European currencies and the U.S. dollar during the 1980s and 1990s, eventually led to moves toward **European Currency Union (EMU)**.

In response to the moves in West Germany, a similar currency reform took place in the eastern zones of occupation (22–28 June 1948). Eventually officially named "Mark der DDR" (1967), the East German mark was never freely convertible or exchanged in international money markets and was worthless outside the **German Democratic Republic (GDR)**, which set its own arbitrary conversion rates or reached special arrangements with trade partners. As the DM established itself as a hard currency in the east, the regime eventually legalized its possession (on 1 February 1974) and even licensed special shops where it could be used to purchase Western goods.

The next major development in the history of the DM was its extension to the former GDR in July 1990 as part of the economic, currency, and social union agreed upon by the East German parliament and the FRG in May/June. Wages, salaries, and pensions were exchanged at a rate of 1:1, with different rates applying to larger savings accounts. These highly favorable terms for the practically worthless East German currency were criticized by some economists but seen as politically essential to ensure popular support for union in the east. The final stage in the history of the DM saw its replacement by a single European currency as the process of EMU came to fruition. First introduced as a "bankers'" currency on 1 January 1999, the euro, issued by the European Central Bank, became the official circulating currency of the 12 states making up the so-called eurozone, including Germany, in January 2002.

See also BALANCE OF PAYMENTS; EUROZONE CRISIS.

D

DAAD (Deutscher Akademischer Austauschdienst/German Academic exchange service). Today the world's largest funding organization for the exchange of students and researchers on an international scale, the DAAD offers a host of academic related activities, including the development of cooperation, help with study in Germany, the organization of so-called lektors to promote German language learning (21 in North America, 31 in South America, overall 53 in Africa and the Middle East, 70 in the Asian-Pacific region, and 307 in the whole of Europe), and, among other services, a scholarship database.

Founded in Heidelberg in 1925 and based on an initiative in cooperation with the New York City–based Institute of International Education, the main headquarters is situated in Bonn, with an office also in Berlin. Worldwide, the DAAD has 15 regional offices (including London, New York, Rio de Janeiro, Tokyo, and Beijing) and 56 information centers (including Toronto, San Francisco, Sydney, and Shanghai). Between 1950 and 2015, the DAAD supported over two million academics. The documents based on the first two decades of the organization's work were destroyed in November 1943. The new foundation was established in 1950, following Allied initiatives to bring Germany's academic postwar isolation to a close. A first agreement with the **German Democratic Republic (GDR)** was signed in 1986. By 2014, the list of future initiatives included a plan for 350,000 foreign students to have studied at a German university by 2020. With 287,353 students from abroad in 2012, Germany ranks internationally in third place, behind the United States (U.S.) and Great Britain and ahead of France, Australia, and Canada. The DAAD's budget is based mainly on funds from various government ministries. Of particular importance are the Foreign Office (Auswärtiges Amt) and the Federal Ministry of Education and Research (Bundesministerium für Bildung und Forschung). (An English-language web page with links is available at http://www.daad.de/en/.)

DAHRENDORF, RALF (1929–2009). Sociologist. Ralf Dahrendorf was born in **Hamburg**, the son of a **Social Democratic Party of Germany (SPD)** deputy in the city senate. During the National Socialist period (1933–1945), he was imprisoned for joining an "illegal" school organization (1944). After World War II, he studied philosophy, classical philology, and sociology in Hamburg and London (1947–1952), graduating with a doctorate on Karl Marx. He went to study under Karl Popper at the London School of Economics (1952–1954), where he earned a Ph.D. on unskilled labor in British industry (1957). In 1957, he worked as a professorial assistant at the University of the **Saarland** before becoming professor of sociology in Hamburg (1958–1960), Tübingen (1960–1966), and the newly founded University of Constance (from 1967). He also paid several visits to the United States as a guest professor (1959, 1960, 1962, 1968); served as director of the London School of Economics (1974–1984); and served as warden of St. Anthony's College, University of Oxford (1987–1997). A British citizen from 1991, he became a member of the British House of Lords (1993) and briefly chaired the Independent News and Media group (1993).

Although a long-standing member of the SPD (1947–1960), Dahrendorf joined the **Free Democratic Party** (**FDP,** 1967–1988), which he represented in the **Landtag** of **Baden-Württemberg** (from 1967) before becoming parliamentary **state secretary** in the Federal Ministry for Foreign Affairs under **Walter Scheel** (1969–1970). In 1970, he was elected to the party's national executive and was chairman of the Friedrich-Naumann Stiftung (Friedrich Naumann Foundation) in Bonn (1982–1984), a liberal foundation created in 1958 that had close links to the FDP. As a member of the commission of the **European Union** (**EU,** 1970–1974), he was responsible for external relations and **trade**.

Alongside honorary doctorates from numerous countries, Dahrendorf was awarded several prizes, including the Theodor Heuss Prize for promoting reform and innovation in **education**, culture, and European politics (1997). He published widely on sociology, education, and politics (more than 25 books), but achieved particular prominence in 1966 for *Bildung ist Bürgerrecht* (education is a civil right), in which he argued that access to education was a universal human right. Responding to this and similar calls, the German government invested large sums of money in expanding its schools and university system. In the "year of revolution" (1968), Dahrendorf famously conducted a public discussion with the radical student leader **Rudi Dutschke** on an automobile roof. He also published on Karl Marx, the sociology of **industry**, class conflict, globalization, and liberalism, and many of his works have been translated.

DAIMLER AG. With its origins in the pioneering motorized carriages of Gottlieb Daimler and Carl Benz in the 1880s, the Stuttgart-based, tradition-rich Daimler company manufactures a full range of motor vehicles, including the quality Mercedes-Benz brand. It produces 2.8 million passenger and utility vehicles in Europe, North and South America, Asia, and Africa, and distributes throughout the world. The main shareholders are in Europe and the United States (U.S.). For 2015, the company reported a turnover of more than 149,000 million euros and employed around 274,000 people. The chief executive is Dieter Zetsche, who in 2006 succeeded Jürgen Schrempp, the prime mover in Daimler-Benz's takeover of the crisis-ridden Chrysler concern in the U.S. in 1998, which resulted in the creation of DaimlerChrysler AG. The takeover was not a success, however, and following the demerger in 2007 and the ending of cooperation with Mitsubishi Motors and the Hyundai Motor Company, the company name reverted to Daimler AG. In 2010, the U.S. Department of Justice initiated a court action against the company, alleging that it paid bribes to win government contracts in Russia, Turkey, Egypt, and China between 1998 and 2008, when it was struggling financially after its takeover of Chrysler. The company admitted the charges and was fined $185 million; it also disciplined and dismissed a number of staff members.

See also AUTOMOBILE INDUSTRY; INDUSTRY.

DANES. *See* ETHNIC MINORITIES: DANES.

DÄUBLER-GMELIN, HERTA (1943–). Social Democratic Party of Germany (SPD) politician and lawyer. Born in Pressburg (now Bratislava, capital of Slovakia), Herta Däubler-Gmelin studied history, law, economics, and politics at the universities of Tübingen and **Berlin** before practicing law in Berlin. A member of the SPD, which she represented in the **Bundestag** (1972–2009), she served as deputy leader of the parliamentary group (1983–1993) and of the national party (1988–1997). She also chaired various committees on legal policy; **human rights** and humanitarian aid; and consumer protection, food, and **agriculture**. As federal minister of justice in the SPD/**Green Party** coalition government led by Chancellor **Gerhard Schröder** (1998–2002), she supported judicial reform, the legalization of same-sex partnerships (in the teeth of fierce opposition from the **Christian Democratic Union [CDU]**), a European charter of human rights, and the creation of an international court of justice. She was forced to resign, however, after drawing a comparison between U.S. president George W. Bush and Adolf Hitler over U.S. policy on Iraq. Further setbacks included being beaten by Hans-Ulrich Kloser to lead the SPD parliamentary party (1994) and the intervention by **Wolfgang Schäuble** (CDU) to block her appointment as vice president of the **Federal Constitutional Court** (**FCC**), on the grounds that she was "too political" (1993). Däubler-Gmelin holds an honorary chair at the Free University of Berlin (since 1996) and worked for many years to promote human rights and constitutional reform in Africa. She is a visiting professor in Shanghai, actively promotes dialogue between China and Germany, and has also engaged in the defense of human rights at home (e.g., in data protection scandals involving **Deutsche Telekom** and the U.S. National Security Agency [NSA]).

DEBT BRAKE. *See* BUDGET.

DEFA (DEUTSCHE FILM AG). After World War II, DEFA became the successor concern to the original Babelsberg Film Studios, founded in 1911. The studios had flourished during the Weimar Republic (1919–1933) and went on to produce films under the National Socialist regime (1933–1945), many of which were propagandistic. Reestablished in 1946 in the Soviet-occupied sector and considered a means of reeducating the Germans, DEFA was a state-owned concern (VEB) in the **German Democratic Republic** (**GDR**) from 1952 until 1990 and came under strong political influence from the regime. By 1990, DEFA had produced about 900 feature films, 5,800 documentaries and newsreels, and over 4,000 synchronizations for foreign-language films. Many of the films dealt with historical drama, antifascism, and literary adaptation. Feature films were produced in Babelsberg near Potsdam, animated films in Dresden, and newsreels and documentaries in Berlin. After reunification, DEFA was sold by the **Trust Agency** to the French company CGE, which restored and modernized its premises (1993–1997). In 2004, the premises were bought by a private consortium.

The DEFA foundation was established in 1998 and promotes film in general, but it also preserves the heritage of the studios. Famous productions include Wolfgang Staudte's *The Kaiser's Lackey* (*Der Untertan*, 1951), Frank Beyer's *Jacob the Liar* (Jakob der Lügner, 1975), and *Traces of Stone* (*Spur der Steine*, 1966).

See also CINEMA; MEDIA.

DEFENSE. *See* BUNDESWEHR.

DEMOCRACY NOW (DEMOKRATIE JETZT). Established in September 1989, Democracy Now was a citizens' group in the former **German Democratic Republic** (**GDR**) with around 3,000 members. Its cofounder, Wolfgang Ullmann (1929–2004), played an important role in the **Round Table** forum and was a member of the interim cabinet of **Hans Modrow**, which governed from 18 November 1989 until 14 April 1990 after the fall of the ruling **Socialist Unity Party of Germany (SED)**. In its manifesto, which was distributed throughout the GDR, the group advocated reforming the system of state socialism as practiced by the previous regime and introducing a genuine form of "democratic socialism." During October/November 1989, the movement shifted its stance, abandoning calls to retain socialism and advocating gradual reunification with West Germany. For the national election of 18 March 1990, it campaigned as a member of the **Alliance 90** group.

DEMOCRATIC AWAKENING (DEMOKRATISCHER AUFBRUCH, DA). An opposition group in the former **German Democratic Republic (GDR)**, Democratic Awakening (DA) originated in late August 1989 following a meeting in Dresden of dissidents, including **Rainer Eppelmann**, Wolfgang Schnur, and Friedrich Schorlemmer. It was formally constituted in East **Berlin** in October, when Schnur was elected leader. The group argued for reunification with the Federal Republic of Germany (FRG) in the contexts of a European framework for peace and of a **social market economy** that respected the **environment** and social needs. After members of its socially and ecologically oriented wing (including Schorlemmer) left in January 1990, the group realigned itself as a conservative party and subsequently joined the **Alliance for Germany**.

DEMOCRATIC BLOCK (DEMOKRATISCHER BLOCK). The Democratic Block was an umbrella forum of approved **political parties** and mass organizations in the former **German Democratic Republic (GDR)** under the control of the ruling **Socialist Unity Party of Germany (SED)**. Its origins lay in a block of antifascist, democratic parties, created in Soviet-occupied Germany in July 1945 in order to facilitate cooperation in the postwar reconstruction. It later incorporated the so-called mass organizations (including **trade unions**, youth, and **women**) and was named the Democratic Block of Parties and Mass Organizations in June 1949, shortly before the establishment of an East German state. October 1949 also saw the formal creation of the National Front of Democratic Germany/Socialist Unity Party of Germany (renamed National Front of the German Democratic Republic in 1973). This arose out of the Deutscher Volkskongress (German People's Congress), which was set up in East Germany in 1947 as precursor to a parliament for an all-German state. While the block's function was mainly political, the Front, whose members included around 350,000 citizens not in political parties or organizations, acted as a link between the state and society. The block held its last meeting on 28 November 1989. The **Christian Democratic Union (CDU)** of the GDR was the first party to quit the block (4 December) and was soon followed by the others.

See also GERMAN DEMOCRATIC REPUBLIC (GDR): POLITICAL INSTITUTIONS.

DEMOCRATIC PEOPLE'S PARTY (DEMOKRATISCHE VOLK-SPARTEI, DVP). Historically a right-wing liberal party during the period of the Weimar Republic (1918–1933), the tradition of the DVP is preserved in the federal state of **Baden-Württemberg**, where it merged with the **Free Democratic Party** (**FDP**) in 1948. The FDP in Baden-Württemberg still goes under the title FDP/DVP.

DEUTSCHE BANK AG. Deutsche Bank AG is the largest of Germany's universal **banks**, with a strong global presence. Founded in 1870 in **Berlin**, the bank's London branch, which opened three years later, became the focus of international expansion and remained the bank's most important foreign branch until World War I, when it was forced to close. From the late 19th century onward, the bank was closely involved in the development of German **industry**. Before 1914, it cofinanced numerous business ventures, both in Germany and abroad. Examples are the Northern Pacific Railway in the United States (U.S.), railways in Turkey and the Middle East, and the conversion of the **Siemens** concern to a shareholding company. During the interwar period, it played a role in the founding of Deutsche Lufthansa and the merger of motor manufacturers **Daimler** and Benz to create Daimler-Benz AG (1926). The National Socialist dictatorship (1933–1945) saw the expulsion of Jewish members of the board. When its Berlin headquarters and branches in the Soviet-occupied zone were closed down in 1945, the bank relocated to **Hamburg**, where, in occupied western Germany, it was split up into 10 independent regional banks (1947–1948). In 1949, the Berliner Disconto Bank AG was founded as the successor to the old Deutsche Bank, and in 1952 the regional banks were combined to form three shareholding companies, which were finally merged in 1957 to create the Deutsche Bank AG, with registered headquarters in Frankfurt/Main. In 1997, the bank initiated an independent historical commission to investigate its dealings in goods belonging to victims of National Socialist persecution. The commission's report was followed by similar studies.

From the 1960s onward, the Deutsche Bank AG steadily expanded its domestic and foreign operations. These include the privatization of the **Volkswagen** concern (1961), the establishment of consortia in partnership with other European and U.S. banks, and setting up an investment bank in New York (1978–1979). Branches or offices were also opened in London, Moscow, Paris, Milan, Luxembourg, Australia, South America, Japan, and the Far East. As part of its globalization strategy from the late 1980s onward, Deutsche Bank took over the Morgan Grenfell group (1989) and began investing heavily in e-commerce (2000). A planned merger with the **Dresdner Bank**, however, was abandoned (2002). In 2001, the bank restructured its operations into two new areas: corporate and investment banking for firms and institutional clients, and private clients and asset management for both private and institutional investors. In November 2001, the three big German banks—Deutsche Bank, **Dresdner Bank**, and **Commerzbank**—merged their mortgage lending subsidiaries into a single concern, the Eurohypo AG. The largest of its kind in Germany, Eurohypo was wound up in 2012 in the wake of the global financial crisis. In 2002, as part of an ongoing restructuring of management, the bank announced a slimming down of its executive board and the separation of strategic and operative functions; two years later it embarked on a program to shed jobs at home. Between 2008 and 2012, the bank acquired a majority shareholding in the Postbank, the former subsidiary of the Federal German Post Office (Deutsche Bundespost), which at that time had 14 million customers, although this was later acknowledged to be a strategic mistake. Following the departure of **Josef Ackermann** (chief executive 2002–2012), Jürgen Fitschen and Anshuman Jain cochaired the management board and in 2015 launched another new strategy in response to regulatory demands to reduce debt, increase capitalization, and raise profitability. In a move that marked a distinct shift away from its earlier ambitions to become a leading global bank, the strategy involved shrinking the bank's size and operations, closing 200 of its 700 branches in Germany, reducing its stake in the Postbank to under 50 percent by 2016 with a view to a total divestment by 2018, saving an additional 3,500 million euros annually, and partly or totally pulling out of between seven and ten countries outside Europe; at the same time the bank planned to retain customers through increased digitalization.

Starting in 2002, the bank and its executives, including Ackermann, **Rolf Breuer**, and Fitschen, became involved in a long-running legal dispute with the **Kirch** concern over allegations that it had helped push the latter toward bankruptcy; although the bank settled with Kirch's heirs in 2014, further actions by the public prosecutor were likely. The bank was further hit by fines totaling 5,763 million euros for assisting tax evasion (2010) and conducting controversial mortgage dealings (2010) in the U.S., and manipulating LIBOR and TIBOR benchmark interest rates (2013), not to mention interest rates in the U.S. and Great Britain (2015). Following the fines and the bank's troubled history, it announced in June 2015 the resignation of Jain, with Fitschen to follow in 2016. John Cryan, a British national and member of the supervisory board since 2013, took over as executive chairman. Cyran rigorously pursued the restructuring strategy, which included replacing virtually the entire management board in 2015.

Deutsche Bank currently has 2,790 branches worldwide (1,800 in Germany), employs around 101,000 people (45,000 in Germany), and has a reported total income of nearly 48,000 million euros (2015). In the same year, however, the bank registered a historic loss of more than 6,700 million euros. Its activities are divided into corporate banking and securities, global transaction banking, asset and wealth management, private and business clients, and noncore operations.

DEUTSCHE POST AG. As part of a complex program of gradual privatization that took place in three legislative stages between 1989 and 1995, the state-owned German postal and **telecommunications** service, the Deutsche Bundespost (Federal German Post Office), was split into the Deutsche Bundespost (postal services, renamed Deutsche Post AG in 1995), the Deutsche Postbank AG (retail **banking** and giro services, and a subsidiary of **Deutsche Bank** from 2010), and Deutsche Telekom AG (telecommunications). The "postal reform," which was driven by the need to modernize and comply with the market liberalization policy of the **European Union (EU)**'s Single European Act (1987), was initiated by the coalition of the **Christian-Democratic Union (CDU)** and **Free Democratic Party (FDP)** despite opposition from the **Social Democratic Party of Germany (SPD)**, the **Green Party**, and the German post office workers' **trade union**. A government minister for post and telecommunications retained overall control until 1998, when a national regulatory body (RegTP) was set up; in 2005 this was renamed BNetzA, which also became responsible for gas, electricity, and railways. In practice, the deregulation of postal services progressed much more slowly than for telecommunications, with the final monopoly—on letters—ending in 2008.

Klaus Zumwinkel, chief executive from 1995 until 2008, developed Deutsche Post AG into a general logistics company. The concern, which entered the **German Stock Exchange** in 2000, completed a takeover of the parcel delivery service DHL in 2002, bought Great Britain–based Excel in 2005, and was restructured and relaunched under the brand name Deutsche Post DHL in 2009. After taking over the Postbank operations (1999), it sold most of its stake to Deutsche Bank (2008–2010). Based in Bonn and the largest postal service in Europe, the group delivers more than 64 million letters a year in Germany, employs around 497,700 workers globally (189,000 in Germany), and turns over more than 59,230 million euros (2015). **Frank Appel** took over from Zumwinkel in 2008. Recent developments have seen a reduction in the post office branch network and prolonged strikes over the introduction of 50 regional parcel delivery companies employing workers at rates below the agreed-upon trade union tariff.

DEUTSCHE TELEKOM AG. Deutsche Telekom AG, with headquarters in Bonn, is one of Germany's largest companies and the biggest **telecommunications** concern in Europe. Formerly state owned, Telekom entered the **German Stock Exchange** in stages from 1996 and acquired interests and partnerships in the rest of Europe and the United States (U.S.). Under chief executives Ron Sommer (1995–2002), Kai-Uwe Ricke (2002–2006), and René Obermann (2006–2013), the company underwent successive changes, including the creation of four strategic divisions in 2000 (T-Com [fixed links], T-Mobile [cell phones], T-Online [**Internet**] and T-Systems); a new brand identity in 2007 (T-Home for home-based services and T-Mobile for cell phone users); the merger of T-Mobile UK and Orange UK (2010); and the amalgamation of mobile and fixed networks alongside the launch of new products, including TelekomCloud (2011) and a smartphone equipped with the Firefox Mozilla operating system (2013).

Although prepared for privatization from 1989/1990, the principal single stakeholder in Telekom before 2006 was the state (in the form of the **federal government** and the state-owned, Frankfurt-based bank Kreditanstalt für Wiederaufbau), which forced Ron Sommer's resignation as share values plummeted. Chief executive Karl-Uwe Ricke focused on reducing the company's debts, which involved large job losses, although he also quit as share values continued to disappoint and the fixed link network lost customers. René Obermann steered the concern through a prolonged strike over the transfer of 50,000 jobs to service companies (2007) and scandals over eavesdropping on journalists and trade unionists on supervisory boards (2008). In 2015, Telekom employed 226,000 people (66,600 in Germany), turned over 69,200 million euros, and boasted 156.4 million cell (mobile) phone customers (40.4 million in Germany). The company's main business segments are in the U.S., Germany, and the rest of Europe. It also runs a systems service division for corporate customers and a "shared services" operation for central and strategic operations.

DEUTSCHE WELLE (DW). Deutsche Welle is Germany's global broadcaster, transmitting news, information, and programs via **television and radio** and the **Internet** throughout the world. The content focus is on Germany and German affairs, and the station broadcasts in 30 languages (in German and English around the clock) to around 28 million listeners. The station, which began operations in 1953 and was originally housed in Cologne, is now based in Bonn. Its stated objective is the promotion of "intercultural dialogue." The Deutsche Welle television service, registered in Berlin, was launched in 1992. DW employs 1,500 workers from over 60 countries and is exclusively funded by **tax** revenue (over 270 million euros annually). Since

1965, journalists from developing countries and more recently also from eastern Europe have received advanced training at the Deutsche Welle Akademie (renamed in 2004).

See also MEDIA.

DIEPGEN, EBERHARD (1941–). Christian Democratic Union (CDU) politician. Born in **Berlin**, Eberhard Diepgen studied law at the Free University of (West) Berlin, where he was active in the student union (Asta) and practiced as a lawyer (from 1972). He joined the CDU in 1962, represented the party in the West Berlin assembly (Abgeordnetenhaus, 1971–2001), and occupied various positions in the party hierarchy, including as a member of the Berlin regional executive (1971–2001), regional/deputy chairman (1975–1981/1981–1983), and parliamentary group leader (1980–1984, 1989–1991). From 1983 until 2002, he served as leader of the Berlin CDU (succeeding **Richard von Weizsäcker**) and was a member of the national party executive. During the 1970s, Diepgen, together with Klaus Landowsky, an old university friend and leader of the parliamentary party group in the West Berlin assembly, modernized the local CDU organization, and in 1984, when elected governing mayor of West Berlin, succeeded in breaking 30 years of domination of the city by the **Social Democratic Party of Germany (SPD)**. With a brief interruption (1989–1990), he went on to become the first mayor of the reunited city (elected in January 1991), a position he held until 2001, when he lost a vote of no confidence following the collapse of the uneasy coalition with the SPD. The following year, Diepgen resigned as leader of the Berlin CDU after losing the support of his local party, which had become embroiled in a financial scandal involving Landowsky and undeclared payments to party funds by the Berlin Hypobank, which had also made poor investments that had to be borne by a city already in financial crisis. Before October 1990, Diepgen, who had grown up in divided Berlin during the Cold War, consistently argued for an end to the **German Democratic Republic (GDR)** and for reunification. At heart a local politician, he never cultivated a close relationship with the national party and retired from political life in early 2002. He chaired the supervisory board of the airport managing company Berlin Brandenburg Flughafen Holding GmbH (1996–2001) and was elected honorary chairman of the Berlin CDU in 2004.

DISTRIBUTION AND RETAIL. Germany's extensive retail and wholesale industry includes 514,000 businesses, employs 4.8 million people (in 2014), and contributes between 8 and 15 percent of GDP (statistics vary). Over half of the workers are in retail, although wholesale generates most of the revenue and—excluding the repair and servicing of **automobiles** and motor vehicles—involves over 159,000 companies. While retailers are the largest employers in Germany, 50 percent of the workforce are only marginally or partially engaged. Important segments of the retail economy are food, information technology, household goods, print **media**, **sports** items, and toys, as well as street stalls and markets. In a highly competitive market—illustrated by the failure of the U.S.–based Walmart concern to penetrate it between 1998 and 2006—growth in **Internet** sales and e-commerce has proved spectacular in recent years, especially in clothing, consumer electronics, and books. For furniture, do-it-yourself home improvements, and food, most Germans prefer more traditional, store-based shopping. While showrooming (viewing items in one store but buying online in another) has adversely affected companies like Media-Saturn (IT and electronics), fashion retailers such as Esprit and H&M have profited through seamlessly integrating shop-based and Internet services. Despite major restructuring and consolidation, leading to a decrease in the number of companies (2012 saw the bankruptcy of the drugs and pharmacy chain Schlecker), once leading universal department stores such as Karstadt (which took over Hertie in 1994 and merged with Quelle in 1999) and Galeria Kaufhof (now owned by the Metro Group) continue to lose market share to specialty stores (C&A, H&M, Media-Saturn) and to e-commerce. Leading retailers are the Metro-Group (Metro, Real, Media-Saturn [electronics and appliances], and Kaufhof [general]), followed by the Schwarz Group (Lidl [food], Kaufland [mainly food]). Alongside Lidl, other food discount chains, such as Aldi, Edeka, and Rewe, are also major players. Convenience stores and retail outlets in filling and railway stations have enjoyed higher traffic in recent years.

The German wholesale industry is the largest in the **European Union (EU)** and includes suppliers who specialize in specific goods (Spezialgroßhandel) or deliver a complete range to retailers (Sortimentsgroßhandel), cash and carry firms (retailers select goods and collect), and rack jobbers (the wholesaler provides racks of merchandise for a retailer, splitting the profits obtained from sales). The period immediately after reunification saw a retail boom, fueled by the sudden emergence of a new consumer market of 16 million east Germans, but the sector entered a difficult phase after the recession of 1993. The wholesale industry also faced declining revenues after 1995 as the EU moved to extend the open market, and competition increased through globalization and Internet commerce, which enhanced market transparency and enabled consumers to deal directly with producers. Restructuring, mergers, and insolvencies affected smaller concerns and the **Mittelstand** in particular. The principal market segment for general wholesalers remains foodstuffs, drink, and tobacco, while specialty wholesalers focus on household and consumer goods (including textiles and clothing, electrical goods, **pharmaceuticals**, paper, printed material, and office items), and also handle more imports. Heightened competition has led to a growth in both cash and carry wholesaling, which is no longer restricted to foodstuffs, and rack jobbers, which are now used routinely by many retailers.

Distribution is either direct (manufacturers supply goods directly to the end-user) or indirect (via intermediary organizations). Since Germany is regarded as a high-cost country for entry, foreign importers tend to use independent traders or sales agents. Special trading companies exist to handle imports and sell goods on to domestic dealers and retailers. An umbrella organization is the Bundesverband des Deutschen Groß- und Außenhandels (Federation of German Wholesale and Foreign Trade, BGA). Wholesalers and retailers are active importers, especially of consumer items. Imported consumer goods, including foodstuffs, textiles, and furniture, are retailed via supermarkets, mail-order companies, and department stores, although other types of purchasing associations and cooperatives also play a role.

See also ALBRECHT, THEODOR (1922–2010) AND KARL (1920–2014); BEISHEIM, OTTO (1924–2013); BRENNINKMEYER, DOMINIC (1959–); OTTO FAMILY; SCHICKEDANZ FAMILY; TRADE.

DOBRINDT, ALEXANDER (1970–). Christian Social Union (CSU) politician. Born in Peißenberg (**Bavaria**), Alexander Dobrindt studied sociology at the university in Munich (1989–1995), qualifying with a diploma. He worked as a manager in a small **engineering** firm in Peißenberg (1996–2001), in which he was also a silent partner (2001–2005). After joining the **Junge Union (JU)** youth wing of the CSU in 1986 and the main party in 1990, he was active in the JU (1990–1997) and a local councilor (from 1996). Dobrindt entered the **Bundestag** in 2002, where he served as an advisory member on small to medium-sized businesses (the **Mittelstand**) to the **Christian Democratic Union (CDU)**/CSU parliamentary group (from 2005), deputy chairman of the parliamentary committee for the economy and labor (2005), and CSU spokesman on economic affairs (2005–2008), and chaired a CDU/CSU working party on **education** and **research** (2008–2009). From 2009 until 2013, he was general secretary of the CSU, before being appointed federal minister for **transport** and digital infrastructure in Chancellor **Angela Merkel**'s third coalition cabinet. On the right wing of the CDU, Dobrindt consistently criticized the **Green Party** and advocated not just removing state finance for **The Left Party** but also banning it. He resisted giving more powers to the **European Union (EU)** and granting equal legal status to same-sex partnerships and opposed dual citizenship for **immigrants**.

DOHNANYI, KLAUS VON (1928–). Social Democratic Party of Germany (SPD) politician. Klaus von Dohnanyi was born in **Hamburg**. His father was executed for resisting the National Socialists. Dohnanyi studied law at the University of Munich, where he earned a doctorate (1949), and also at Columbia, Stanford, and Yale in the U.S., graduating with a law degree. After practicing law in New York and working at the Max Planck Institute in private law, Dohnanyi joined the Ford Motor Co., where he was employed in Detroit and later in Cologne as head of the planning department. From 1960 until 1968, he was a cofounder and managing partner of the Munich-based Infratest institute for market research and management consultancy. A member of the SPD from 1957, he worked as **state secretary** to **Karl Schiller** and SPD minister of economics in the **grand coalition** government of Chancellor **Kurt Georg Kiesinger** between 1968 and 1969. Dohnanyi also served as a member of the **Bundestag** (1969–1981) and as state secretary in the Federal Ministry of **Education** and Science under Hans Leussink (1969–1972), whom he succeeded as minister (1972–1974). As education minister, Dohnanyi prepared the draft of a new framework law for higher education (Hochschulrahmengesetz), which came into force in 1976 and set national guidelines for regulating universities in Germany. He was also a parliamentary state secretary in the Federal Ministry for Foreign Affairs (1976–1981). In 1979, he was elected SPD party chairman for **Rhineland-Palatinate** and in 1981 succeeded **Hans-Ulrich Klose** as first governing mayor of **Hamburg**, a post he held until his resignation in 1988. Dohnanyi's period of office was marked by conflicts with antinuclear power demonstrators and a six-year battle with illegal squatters in houses in the city's Hafenstraße.

After 1988, Dohnanyi worked as a publicist and economics consultant. He took a special interest in the reconstruction of eastern Germany after reunification and worked for the **Trust Agency** and its successor organization as a special representative (1993–1996). When his contract with the agency ended, he continued to work in the east as a government consultant. He was a member of the Gesprächskreis Ost der Bundesregierung (Discussion Circle East of the Federal Government, GO) working group of experts charged by **Manfred Stolpe (Christian Democratic Union [CDU]** minister responsible for eastern reconstruction) and **Wolfgang Clement** (SPD economics minister) to make recommendations on the regeneration of eastern Germany. Although the report, which appeared in 2004, was shelved, Dohnanyi publicly criticized economic aspects of the reunification process. He annoyed **trade unions** by proposing a 42-hour workweek in the east, and in an interview with *Der Spiegel* magazine in 2012 argued that the eastern states had become a drain on resources and required a new investment model. A fluent English speaker and sought-after lecturer on world and European affairs, Dohnanyi received many honors and is a member of the Club of Rome.

See also ENERGY: NUCLEAR POWER/ELECTRICITY.

DÖRING, WALTER (1954–). Free Democratic Party (FDP) politician.
Born in Stuttgart (**Baden-Württemberg**), Walter Döring studied history and English at the University of Tübingen (1974–1979), earning a doctorate in 1981, and worked at various schools/colleges before leaving the teaching profession in 1988. Chairman of the local branch of the FDP/**Democratic People's Party (DVP)** in Schwäbisch Hall (1981–1998), he served at the regional level on the party's executive (1983–2004) and as leader (1985–1988, 1995–2004); he also led the FDP/DVP parliamentary group in the **Landtag** (1988–1996), where he was a member from 1988 until 2006. In 1996, he was appointed regional economics minister and deputy **minister president** for Baden-Württemberg and was credited with increasing his party's share of the vote in the 1996 regional election. From 1996, he was also regional delegate to the **Bundesrat**. Despite his criticisms of the national leadership, Döring became deputy leader of the national FDP in May 1999. In 2004, he resigned all offices following a corruption scandal involving undeclared donations to the party by the lobbyist Moritz Hunzinger. Thereafter he pursued a career in business.

DREGGER, ALFRED (1920–2002). Christian Democratic Union (CDU) politician. Born in Münster (**North Rhine-Westfalia**), Alfred Dregger performed military service in World War II before studying law and public administration at the University of Marburg (1946–1949), earning a doctorate (1950) and qualifying as a practicing lawyer (1953). He worked as a researcher for the Bundesverband der Deutschen Industrie (Federation of German Industries, 1954–1956) and was a board member of an association of German towns (Deutscher Städtetag, 1956–1970; also president from 1965 and vice president from 1967). In 1956, he was elected mayor of Fulda, the youngest person ever to hold such a position in the Federal Republic of Germany (FRG). As mayor (until 1970), he presided over an extensive modernization program, which gave the town new schools, buildings, housing, and an improved **transport** infrastructure.

Dregger represented the CDU in the state parliament (**Landtag**) of **Hessen** (1962–1972, also briefly in 1972 and 1978), where he led the parliamentary group (1969–1972) and was party chairman (1967–1982). Under Dregger's leadership, the CDU in Hessen dramatically increased its electoral appeal and was a credible rival to the **Social Democratic Party of Germany (SPD)**. Although Dregger was four times the CDU's leading candidate at regional elections, the post of **minister president** eluded him. He joined the CDU national executive (1969) and presidium (1977), served as deputy leader (1977–1983), and succeeded **Helmut Kohl** as chairman of the CDU parliamentary group in the **Bundestag** (1982–1991). A long-standing deputy in the

Bundestag (1972–1998), he won a direct mandate eight times in a row. Although he wanted to continue for a ninth term, pressure for change and protracted internal party squabbles forced him to step down.

A conservative with an abrasive, combative style (his nicknames included Django Dregger and Don Alfredo), Dregger remained a fierce critic of the Soviet Union and argued consistently for German reunification and for the restoration of the honor of the German army, despite its role under the National Socialists. He originated the controversial slogan "freedom, not socialism" for the election campaign of 1976, when the CDU again lost to the SPD. Although a committed democrat and an influential figure in the CDU during the postwar years, he failed to develop a power base at the political center. When the CDU took a more liberal direction in 1991, he was replaced by **Wolfgang Schäuble** as leader of the parliamentary party. He wrote several books on law and contemporary politics and was awarded the Federal Cross of Merit (1977, 1984, 1985).

DRESDNER BANK. Until 2009, when it was merged with the **Commerzbank**, the Dresdner was one of Germany's leading universal **banks**. Originating in a small private bank founded in 1771 in Dresden, it was established in 1872 to provide capital for local **industry** during the economic boom that followed the creation of the German Reich after the Franco-Prussian War (1870–1871). It soon became the second largest bank in the Reich, moving its management headquarters to **Berlin** (1881), where it remained until 1945. During the 1890s, the bank extended its branch network throughout Germany and abroad and retained its tradition of financing small to medium-sized enterprises (the **Mittelstand**) well into the 20th century. World War I cost the Dresdner its foreign network, and it was also badly hit by the hyperinflation of the early 1920s and the collapse of the world economy in 1929–1930. A director of the bank, Hjalmar Schacht, helped stabilize the **currency** in late 1923 and went on to serve as president of the Reichsbank (1924–1930). In the boom of 1925–1929, the bank again expanded rapidly both at home and abroad. The National Socialists, who ruled from 1933 to 1945, controlled the bank through a minority of party members on its board of directors. Jewish employees were forced out and, although the bank helped some to escape and reestablish themselves abroad, it managed the accounts of several Nazi organizations.

After World War II, the Soviet Union closed or confiscated the bank's assets in Berlin and the east, although the fact that not all of its directors were members of the National Socialist Party enabled them to contribute to the establishment of the state-owned bank of **Saxony** in the **German Democratic Republic (GDR)**. In western Germany, normal banking business was resumed with the currency reform of 1948, and the Dresdner Bank was refounded (1952), with headquarters in Frankfurt/Main and centers in

Düsseldorf and **Hamburg**. Benefiting from the economic miracle of the 1950s, it grew to become one of the largest banks in the Federal Republic of Germany (FRG). When the GDR collapsed in 1989, it was the first West German bank to open a branch in Dresden (January 1990), a historic return to its origins. Taken over by the **Allianz** insurance group in 2001—a process that involved large job losses—it was sold to the Commerzbank in 2009, and the original name survives only in a branch opened in Dresden in 2010.

DREYER, MALU (1961–). Social Democratic Party of Germany (SPD) politician. Born in Neustadt (**Rhineland-Palatinate**, RLP), Malu Dreyer studied English and theology at the University of Mainz (from 1980) before switching to law. After qualifying as a practicing lawyer (1987, 1990), she worked as a research assistant at Mainz (1989–1991) and subsequently as a state prosecutor in Bad Kreuznach. Following a spell in the research and documentation service of the RLP state parliament (1992–1995), Dreyer was elected full-time mayor of Bad Kreuznach (from 1995). After heading the regional department for social affairs, family, and health (from 1997), she held three ministerial positions for social and related affairs between 2002 and 2012 before being elected **minister president** (2013), leading a coalition between the SPD and the **Green Party**. Dreyer has chaired the Trier branch of the SPD district since 2005. Diagnosed with multiple sclerosis in 1994, she undertakes longer journeys in a wheelchair.

DUAL SYSTEM. *See* EDUCATION: VOCATIONAL; ENVIRONMENT: WASTE MANAGEMENT.

DUTSCHKE, RUDI (1940–1979). Student leader. Rudi Dutschke was born in Schönfeld/Mark in **Brandenburg**, the son of a post office official. Although he completed his higher school certificate (1958), the authorities of the **German Democratic Republic (GDR)** refused to allow him to attend university because of his critical views. After training in **industry** and commerce in a state-owned factory, he moved to West **Berlin** in 1960, where he studied sociology at the Free University (from 1961) and became involved in left-wing student politics, cofounding the group Subversive Aktion (1963), which affiliated with the militant **Federation of Socialist German Students (SDS)** in 1964.

As West Berlin became a center for the student protest movement during the 1960s, Dutschke took part in demonstrations against the Vietnam War and the introduction of the emergency laws by the first **grand coalition** (1966–1969). A charismatic speaker, he called for the formation of an active opposition movement outside parliament and the replacement of established political structures. During a demonstration against a state visit by the shah of Iran (June 1967), a student, Benno Ohnesorg, was shot and killed in Berlin by a police officer, unleashing further unrest (after reunification it emerged that the officer in fact worked for the GDR authorities). Dutschke rapidly emerged as a leading figure in the SDS, although he distanced himself from violence, preferring to take part in hunger strikes, open discussions with the prominent left-wing social scientist Herbert Marcuse, and interviews with the **media**. He also demanded the breaking up of the publishing empire of **Axel Springer**, whose newspapers campaigned fiercely against the protesters. When Dutschke was shot and badly injured by a young decorator in April 1968, the Springer press was blamed for indirectly inciting the crime through its inflammatory headlines. The incident marked the end of Dutschke's active participation in the student movement. After a series of operations, he recuperated abroad before going to live in a commune in London (1969). In 1970, he studied at the University of Cambridge before being deported from Great Britain for subversive activities. The following year, he moved to Denmark, where he lectured at the University of Aarhus. He visited the Federal Republic of Germany (FRG) and West Berlin several times, speaking for the first time since his injury at an anti–Vietnam War demonstration in Bonn (1973).

In 1973, Dutschke earned a doctorate in sociology at the Free University of (West) Berlin on the differences between western European and Asiatic forms of socialism. He also published a study of the Hungarian socialist Georg Lukács (1974); worked on research projects on sociology and politics; lectured in Norway, Italy, the Netherlands, and Germany; and visited the Soviet Union and the GDR, where he met the dissidents **Wolf Biermann** and Robert Havemann. Between 1978 and 1979, he took part in the Russell Tribunal on **human rights** in West Germany and actively supported the **Green Party**. In 1979, he died from the delayed aftereffects of the attempt on his life. Three biographies of him have appeared, including one by his wife, Gretchen, in 1996.

E

EASTERN FEDERAL STATES AFTER REUNIFICATION. Since 1997, the interior ministry of the **federal government** has issued reports (annually from 2002) on the state of German unity, indicating the extent to which the eastern **federal states** have become economically, financially, socially, and demographically aligned to the western Länder. The report for 2013 presented an overview of various aspects of the status in the east almost a generation after reunification (1990). Thanks to an internationally more competitive economy, a modern **transport** and **energy** infrastructure, and high-quality **educational** and research facilities, the standard of living of easterners was greatly improved, if still not equal to that of westerners, whose average wages were higher and who paid more **tax**es. At the same time, because eastern Germans—including **women**—started work earlier in life, their pensions, pegged to the length of employment, were higher. Life expectancy in east and west had virtually equalized, although the east, especially in rural areas, had a dramatically aging population. Despite the fact that the heavy population drain to the west had—for the first time since reunification—been largely halted, and the birth rate after 2008 actually exceeded that in the west, the overall population continued to decline (by 13.5 percent during 1990–2012) and was expected to fall by a further 14 percent by 2030. A stubbornly negative statistic was unemployment, which, although down from 18.7 percent in 2005 to 10.2 percent in 2014, has consistently remained about twice the level of the western states since unification. A less clear picture emerged for educational achievement, with some states (**Saxony, Thuringia, Mecklenburg-West Pomerania**) leading the nation in terms of school-leavers with **Abitur**, while others performed less well, and the east as a whole presented the highest proportion of children leaving school with no qualification at all. Encouraging for a nation committed to participatory democracy was the steady increase in political engagement in elections, citizens' groups, and associations, although it still failed to match western levels.

Launched in the mid-1990s and jointly financed by the **European Union (EU)** and German government, the German Unity Transport Project (Verkehrsprojekte Deutsche Einheit [VDE]) is a series of large-scale, ongoing improvements to transportation links within eastern Germany, including links to the west. A total of 34,000 million euros had been invested by 2012, resulting in the eastern states developing into a vital north–south and east–west transport hub. Relative to the west, however, the rollout of the latest high-speed broadband technology in the east had progressed more slowly. Although the east's central geographical position, relatively cheap land, and lower wages, not to mention its (largely state-financed) world-class **research and development** facilities, offered powerful incentives for external investors, very few large businesses had located their headquarters there; not one company listed on the **German stock exchange** (DAX) was to be found, with negative consequences for research-oriented, high-technology activities. In its 2013 report, the federal government listed more than 80 ongoing initiatives to support and promote employment, investment, science, education, the **environment**, society, culture, and **sport** in the east, including elements of the **Aufbau Ost** program and the **Solidarity Pact**.

Apart from clear economic disparities—westerners have more personal wealth and own relatively more automobiles, televisions, and telephones— the legacy of different historical development since 1945/1949 and postreunification uncertainties have produced a range of sociocultural and lifestyle differences between east and west. For example, in the east, more women work outside the home and occupy leading positions at management level, more children are born out of wedlock, and people are generally less content with their lives. When supplementary financial support for parents who stay at home to care for preschool children (Betreuungsgeld) was introduced in 2013, the uptake was strong in the western states of **Bavaria**, **North Rhine-Westfalia** and **Baden-Württemberg**, but negligible in the east, partly reflecting suspicion there that the allowance reinforced the traditional role of the nonworking mother. Traditionally, the working day begins and ends earlier in the east. Easterners also still prefer to take holidays close to home, for instance on the **Baltic** coast, while westerners (who, incidentally, engage more readily in sporting activities) travel farther afield. Unsurprisingly, children whose parents lived during the era of the **German Democratic Republic (GDR)** are more knowledgeable about life in the communist era than their western counterparts. Less seriously, more easterners would prefer to be buried in their garden, and men apparently wear tighter swimming costumes (or even less).

Although eastern Germany has relatively few resident **foreigners** (2.4 percent, compared with 10.5 percent in the west in 2013), the level of xenophobia remains disturbingly high (38.7 percent in the east, 21.7 percent in the west) and is increasing, especially in the younger generation and non-naturalized migrants, a group in which **anti-Semitism** is also more pronounced than in German nationals. Explanations for such deeply rooted antagonism toward foreigners range from a sense of marginalization during economic downturns (unemployment, a lower standard of living) to the legacy of communist rule, during which contact with foreigners and knowledge of the wider world were limited, and even the failure of a swift de-Nazification program after 1945 to address fundamental issues. In addition, the regime nurtured ideological assumptions of a socialist patriotism based on an imagined GDR identity, which actively discouraged self-critical confrontation with Germany's nationalistic past and with right-wing extremism in East Germany itself. Whatever the reasons, violent attacks on foreign workers and **asylum** seekers peaked with pogroms in Hoyerswerda (1991) and Rostock/Lichtenhagen (1992). By 2009, 23 fatalities (mainly of foreigners) had taken place, proportionally more than in the west (24). While such incidents have decreased nationally since the early 2000s, statistics vary, partly because of uncertainty over the perpetrators. Following the physical violence of young skinheads and neo-Nazis during the early 1990s, organized political parties such as **The Republicans (REP)**, the **National Democratic Party of Germany (NPD)**, and the **German People's Union (DVU**, which was the first to enter a regional parliament, in **Saxony-Anhalt** in April 1998) played a significant role in fostering xenophobia in the east.

ECOFIN COUNCIL. The Economic and Financial Affairs (ECOFIN) Council is made up of the economics and finance ministers of the member states of the **European Union (EU)**. It meets monthly to monitor economic and budgetary policy, review financial markets and capital movements, and examine economic relations with non-EU countries. It also considers legal, practical, and international issues involving the EU's single currency, the euro. Together with the European Parliament, it prepares and approves the budget of the EU, which is currently about 100,000 million euros. Non-eurozone members abstain in votes of the council on matters unrelated to the **currency** union. The Eurogroup, an informal group of eurozone members, normally meets the day before the ECOFIN meeting.

ECONOMIC DEVELOPMENT (FRG) 1949–1969. Following West Germany's incorporation into the western economic bloc after World War II, various factors contributed to the rapid growth of the economy of the Federal Republic of Germany (FRG) during the 1950s. These included capital injections from the Marshall Plan (from April 1948), a **currency** reform (June 1948), the writing off/restructuring of debt accumulated by Germany before the war and immediately after it (the London Debt Agreement, 1953), and the introduction of a **social market economy**. Fueled by a large labor force and the demand for rapid reconstruction of war-damaged cities and plants, the FRG's economy expanded at a startling rate, with annual growth levels reaching 10 and even 12 percent (1951/1955). The boom period, which lasted until the mid-1960s, is commonly known as the German "economic miracle" (Wirtschaftswunder).

Beneficiaries of the postwar expansion included the traditional industrial centers of the Ruhr, the **Rhine**-Main, and Rhine-Neckar regions, as well as the cities and conurbations of **Hamburg**, Munich, Hanover, **Bremen**, Stuttgart, and the Nuremberg-Fürth-Erlangen area. From 1957 until 1963, growth slowed as inflation and prices rose within the context of full employment and improvements in working conditions, including a shorter workweek; many businesses moved into more rural areas, where cheaper labor was still available. At the same time, heavy **industry** in the Ruhr area (coal, iron, and steel) declined in the face of increased competition and cheaper oil. Light and service industries expanded in less industrialized regions such as **Baden-Württemberg**, **Hessen**, and **Bavaria**. A combination of relatively low growth and high inflation produced a minor recession in 1966, and the economy contracted in 1967. Falling **taxation** revenues alongside rising government expenditure resulted in a budgetary crisis, which a **grand coalition** (1966–1969) overcame by introducing elements of government intervention and fiscal planning (called "medium-term financial planning" and "global control") into the postwar model of the social market economy. Unemployment fell (from 680,000 in 1967 to 150,000 by 1970) and wages rose as production and exports recovered.

See also ECONOMIC DEVELOPMENT (FRG) AFTER 2000; ECONOMIC DEVELOPMENT (FRG) 1970–1989; ECONOMIC DEVELOPMENT 1990–1999; GERMAN MARSHALL FUND OF THE UNITED STATES (GMF).

ECONOMIC DEVELOPMENT (FRG) 1970–1989. After the boom period of the 1950s and 1960s, **industry** in the Federal Republic of Germany (FRG) entered a period of structural change that continued through the end of the century and significantly transformed the economic landscape. Factors in this dynamic process were globalization, the emergence of new technologies and markets, and the transfer of manufacturing facilities to foreign countries with lower labor costs. With full employment and rising wages, the FRG's economy performed well by international standards during the 1960s and early 1970s, although a weak U.S. dollar alongside an undervalued German **currency** (DM) attracted large-scale inflows of capital in volatile world monetary markets. As a result, inflation climbed steeply by West German standards, exceeding 6 percent in 1973–1974. An oil embargo imposed by Arab states in protest against Western support for Israel during the Yom Kippur War of October–November 1973 triggered the FRG's first major recession. A second oil crisis followed in June 1979, when the Organization of the Petroleum Exporting Countries (OPEC) raised oil prices by 42 percent. During 1974–1975, domestic production stagnated, and unemployment, which had stood at under 149,000 in 1970 (0.7 percent), passed the politically sensitive one million threshold (4.8 percent) in 1975.

The 1974–1975 recession marked the end of full employment in postwar Germany. Investment programs stimulated a recovery in growth from 1976 onward, although at the price of government debt that proved impossible to clear. By this time, it was evident that the German economy, long held up as a model for other industrial nations, was coming under pressure for systemic change. Consumer demand stagnated as the population ceased to grow, and profits fell as businesses, facing higher **energy** costs and stiffer foreign competition, invested less; at the same time, taxes rose to meet increased state expenditure. Despite efforts in the early 1980s to implement cuts and reduce state spending, the **Social Democratic Party of Germany (SPD)/Free Democratic Party (FDP)** coalition led by Chancellor **Helmut Schmidt** collapsed, largely because of its failure to manage the economy and control the **budget** deficit. The contraction of the traditional industries of coal, steel, shipbuilding, textiles, and clothing continued.

Under the conservative–liberal coalition led by **Helmut Kohl**, who was elected chancellor in 1982, state spending stabilized, although government debt continued to rise during the 1980s and by 1990 was 55 percent higher than in the previous decade. Growth remained moderate, at between 1.7 percent (1987) and 5.5 percent (1990), with low inflation and large, export-generated **trade** surpluses. Unemployment remained stubbornly high, reaching 2.3 million in 1985, although it fell to 1.9 million in 1990. From the 1980s onward, the number of bankruptcies registered by large corporations rose steadily, with one of the most spectacular being the dramatic failure of the **Kirch** Media Group in 2002. The largest insolvency in the history of the FRG, the collapse of Kirch (owing 7,000 million euros) dwarfed that of other concerns, notably the Philipp Holzmann building concern (2002, 1,300 million euros), the household **engineering** name Babcock-Borsig (2002), the drilling specialists Flowtex (2000, 820 million euros), the sports surface suppliers Balsam AG (1994, 1,080 million euros), the property company Jürgen Schneider (1994, 1,020 million euros), AEG (1982, 920 million euros), and the Coop retailing group (1989, 870 million euros). For some economists, these bankruptcies marked the end of the success of the traditional networks of business practice in Germany, in which comfortable relationships among politicians, **banks**, and industrialists had prevented large corporate failures. Nevertheless, the West German economy was considered to be in sound overall shape to absorb the costs of reunification in October 1990.

See also ECONOMIC DEVELOPMENT (FRG) AFTER 2000; ECO-
NOMIC DEVELOPMENT (FRG) 1949–1969; ECONOMIC DEVELOP-
MENT 1990–1999.

ECONOMIC DEVELOPMENT 1990–1999. The merging of the economic
and monetary systems of the FRG and the former **German Democratic
Republic (GDR)** in 1990 brought a short-lived economic boom in the west,
fueled by industrial expansion, an increase in **trade** and services, and orders
for the construction **industry** in the east. For the **eastern federal states**,
however, the transition to a market economy was traumatic. Their infrastructure (**energy, transport, telecommunications**) was inadequate, and the industries left over from the central planning regime of the **Socialist Unity
Party of Germany (SED)**, with their outdated plants and, by western standards, unproductive labor forces, could not compete. The **Trust Agency**,
formed in 1990 to privatize the former state-owned enterprises, wound up its
activities in 1994 after limited success. Huge transfers were required to finance the economic transition in the eastern **federal states**, support social
welfare programs, and raise standards of living to western levels, not to
mention to cover the costs of repairing damage to the **environment**. Unemployment in the east rose alarmingly, continued at high levels throughout the
1990s, and contributed to a widespread sense of disillusionment with reunification. Between 1992 and 1998, unemployment climbed from 14.8 to 19.5
percent (falling to 19 percent in 1999), with figures of 20–21 percent in some
states (**Mecklenburg-West Pomerania, Saxony-Anhalt**). While the western
states fared better, unemployment continued at relatively high rates, ranging
from 6.6 percent in 1992 to 11 percent in 1997 and 9.9 percent for 1999;
states such as **Bremen**, the **Saarland**, and **Berlin** were hit noticeably harder
than, for example, **Bavaria** or **Baden-Württemberg**. For Germany as a
whole, unemployment continued to be a problem into the next decade: it rose
from 7.7 percent in 1992 to 11.4 percent in 1997; after falling to 9.4 percent
in 2001, it increased again, to 10.8 percent in 2002. In mid-2004, the jobless
total was running at an absolute figure of around 4.4 million, the highest
since reunification.

As the postreunification boom leveled off in 1992, Germany was hit by a
global recession. Growth declined between 1994 and 1996 (from 2.3 to 0.8
percent), although it recovered during the second half of the decade, returning to 2.9 percent in 2000. A striking feature of the economy during this
decade was the result of structural shifts that had been under way since the
1960s. While services accounted for 13.6 percent of GDP in 1960, the proportion had risen to 29.5 percent in 1990, and if public and private services
are included, exceeded 50 percent in 2000. Manufacturing and industry,
which contributed 53.2 percent in 1960, had shrunk progressively, to around
41 percent in 1984, 34 percent in 1994, and just 29 percent in 2003. The shift

from a manufacturing to a service economy was reflected in the **German Stock Exchange** by the creation of a so-called **New Market**. Although this functioned only from 1997 to 2003, it was aimed specifically at companies developing and exploiting new technologies where Germany's economic future was felt to lie. By 2003, services accounted for over 69 percent of GDP (57 percent in 1984).

See also ECONOMIC DEVELOPMENT (FRG) AFTER 2000; ECONOMIC DEVELOPMENT (FRG) 1949–1969; ECONOMIC DEVELOPMENT (FRG) 1970–1989.

ECONOMY. See AGRICULTURE; AUTOMOBILE INDUSTRY; BANKS; BUDGET; CODETERMINATION (MITBESTIMMUNG); CURRENCY; DISTRIBUTION AND RETAIL; ECONOMIC DEVELOPMENT (FRG) AFTER 2000; ECONOMIC DEVELOPMENT (FRG) 1949–1969; ECONOMIC DEVELOPMENT (FRG) 1970–1989; ECONOMIC DEVELOPMENT 1990–1999; EDUCATION: VOCATIONAL; ENERGY; ENERGY: COAL; ENERGY: NUCLEAR POWER/ELECTRICITY; ENERGY: OIL AND GAS; EUROZONE CRISIS; GERMAN DEMOCRATIC REPUBLIC (GDR): ECONOMY; INDUSTRY; MEDIA; MITTELSTAND; PHARMACEUTICALS; PUBLISHING; TAXATION; TRADE; TRADE UNIONS.

ECONOMIC DEVELOPMENT (FRG) AFTER 2000. The terror attacks of 11 September 2001 in the United States (U.S.) accelerated an already marked decline in global economic activity as the world's three largest economies (Europe, North America, and Japan) experienced their first simultaneous contraction since the 1970s. After the autumn of 2000, German exports fell sharply, and overall growth fell from 3 percent (for 2000) to just 0.6 percent in 2001 and 0.2 percent in 2002; by the summer of 2003 it had ground to a halt, marking the economy's technical entry into recession. At the same time, the **budget** deficit continued to grow as the state grappled with high social welfare costs exacerbated by rising unemployment, which peaked at 11.7 percent (almost 4.9 million) in 2005 (18.7 percent/1.6 million in the **eastern federal states** and 9.9 percent/3.2 million in the west). The rise was especially disappointing for a government whose electoral victory in 1998 owed much to its pledge to reduce unemployment (from 4.4 million in 1997). At 3.6 percent of GDP in 2002, the level of government debt remained well above the **European Union (EU)**'s approved 3 percent ceiling, which, at Germany's insistence, had been included in the Maastricht Treaty and formed part of the subsequent **Stability and Growth Pact**. Agreed to in July 1997, the pact set out the convergence criteria for the introduction of the single **currency** and was intended to enforce monetary discipline on members of the planned eurozone. Germany overshot the 3 percent barrier in its annual budgets for 2003, 2004, and 2005.

In 2003, Germany's economic difficulties were further exacerbated by the war in Iraq, appreciation of the euro, and strikes in the manufacturing sector in eastern Germany. Static **taxation** revenues and rising government expenditure produced a deficit of 79,000 million euros in the domestic budget, and worried taxpayers in **Berlin** erected a "national debt clock" on the city's Friedrichstraße. These factors, together with concern over Germany's medium-term growth prospects, increased pressure on Chancellor **Gerhard Schröder** to implement his **Agenda 2010** policy in order to ease labor markets, tighten fiscal policy, and stimulate the economy, although his ability to push through structural reforms was undermined by his weak domestic political position. Despite its unusual historical circumstances, the city of **Berlin** became a focal point of Germany's economic malaise, plunging heavily into debt as the government withdrew subsidies. Reflecting a pattern that was repeated across eastern Germany in the late 1990s, the capital experienced a crash in property prices as the postreunification building boom ended. The **European Central Bank (ECB)**, concerned as ever to dampen inflation and preserve the stability of the currency, was reluctant to lower interest rates, which might have stimulated borrowing and hence growth. The ECB's policy of preserving the value of money was inherited from the **German Federal Bank** (on which it was closely modeled) and ran counter to the style of the U.S. Federal Reserve, which had always been more prepared to lower interest rates in an effort to reinvigorate demand. As a result, the EU's largest economy continued to be squeezed by "stagflation" (rising prices and low growth) as it passed through the deadline for the introduction of the euro.

The creation of the eurozone on 1 January 2002 did little to reverse the underlying economic trends, and in some respects the global downturn hit Germany harder than its European neighbors. Not only was its construction sector still suffering from overcapacity after the postreunification boom, but unlike the situation in France, German exports depended heavily on capital goods, such as machine tools, **engineering** products, and manufacturing equipment. These were also adversely affected by the decline in business investment as confidence in the information technology industries, which had been buoyant throughout the 1980s and 1990s, faded. The picture was complicated by the fact that the economies of the single-currency eurozone countries failed to converge. As growth rates, consumer behavior, and labor costs differed, Germany looked to be a high-cost country and unattractive to inward investors looking to transfer technology and resources to new operational sites. The productivity gap between the western and eastern states seemed set to continue, as did the high labor costs, which were due less to actual wage levels than to social insurance on-costs that also made employers reluctant to create new jobs. Following low growth (+1.2/0.7 percent) in Germany during 2004–2005 and a recovery (+3.7 percent) in 2006, the global financial crisis produced a dramatic downturn (-5.1 percent) in 2009, although a remarkable upswing (+4 percent) the following year demonstrated the German economy's capacity to invest for recovery during a period of adversity. During 2012–2013, growth tailed off to 0.7–0.4 percent, while public debt rose (to 80 percent of GDP in 2012) in order to finance state-funded rescue programs. At the same time unemployment, which had been falling since the peak of 11.7 million in 2005, stabilized at around 6.9 percent (about three million during 2011–2015). Overall, the service sector continued to employ 73 percent of the workforce and generate 70 percent of GDP (63 percent in 1991), with **industry** making up the rest (26 percent, compared with 30 percent in 1991) and **agriculture** of little significance (under 1 percent). A remarkable feature of the economy toward the middle of the decade was the steady rise of people in work (from 34.9 million in 2005 to 38.3 million in 2014), which, through tax revenue and a decrease in outgoings for unemployment benefit, resulted in a record 66,000 million euros income to the exchequer, enabling the government, unlike other major European states focusing more on austerity programs than on structural reforms, to balance its annual budget. As for foreign **trade**, Germany led the world for exports between 2003 and 2008. Although displaced by China in 2009 and falling to third place behind the U.S. in 2010, it also maintained a healthy trade **balance of payments** surplus (247,900 million euros in 2015).

See BANKS; ECONOMIC DEVELOPMENT (FRG) 1949–1969; ECONOMIC DEVELOPMENT (FRG) 1970–1989; ECONOMIC DEVELOPMENT 1990–1999; EUROZONE CRISIS; INDUSTRY; MITTELSTAND; TRADE.

EDUCATION: PRIVATE SCHOOLS. Compared with other European countries, the private school sector in Germany is small, although it has grown steadily in recent years. Some 3,500 schools provide general private education (10 percent of the national total in 2013), alongside over 2,100 vocational schools (24 percent); the total private school population is around 11.3 million, with relatively high numbers in **North Rhine-Westfalia** (213,000), **Bavaria** (187,000), and **Baden-Württemberg** (over 154,000). Although most school types are represented, private general schools are found mainly at the primary level (23.5 percent), followed by Gymnasien (15 percent) and Realschulen (10 percent). The right to found private schools is anchored in the **Basic Law** (article 6.4), although those which function as substitutes for state schools (Ersatzschulen, or regular schools), offering equivalent leaving qualifications (either internally or externally examined), must be approved by the **federal state** and are subject to its laws. Ersatzschulen also receive local government funding, on average two-thirds of equivalent costs per pupil at a state school. So-called supplementary schools (Ergänzungsschulen) offer mainly vocational qualifications in areas where state training is not available, such as theater, languages, or cosmetics. Although these schools do not require federal state approval, they must be registered with the regional cultural ministry and are entirely privately funded. Well-known regular private schools that offer a specific pedagogic methodology include the Waldorf network (234 schools with over 85,000 pupils) and the Montessori schools (over 1,000 establishments, mainly at preschool and primary levels).

EDUCATION: SCHOOLS. After the experiences of the National Socialist regime (1933–1945), the newly founded Federal Republic of Germany (FRG) restored an educational system whose origins lay in the humanistic tradition of the 19th century and from which are derived the traditional school types of the Volksschule (elementary school for the majority of children), the Gymnasium (preparation for university), and the Realschule (vocationally oriented secondary school, called the Mittelschule until 1964). Following a reform in 1959, the Volksschule was divided into a Grundschule (primary school from ages six to nine) and Hauptschule (secondary school from age 10); adjustments were also made to the other school types, but these did not change fundamentally. To ensure democratic structures and counter the dangers of centralism, the **Basic Law** (**BL**) also affirmed the Kulturhoheit (cultural sovereignty) of the **federal states** by granting them autonomy in educational affairs. Although autonomy has produced one of the most complex school systems in the world, with considerable regional variations in provision, curricula, and school types, the **Länder** do coordinate policy making through interstate bodies, of which the most important is the Kultusministerkonferenz (Standing Conference of State Ministers of Education, KMK), established in 1948. Coordinating organizations at other levels include the Hochschulrektorenkonferenz (Conference of University Rectors, HRK), the Bund-Länder-Kommission für Bildungsplanung und Forschungsförderung (Joint Commission for Educational Planning and the Promotion of Research, established in 1979), the Planungsausschuss für Hochschulbau (Planning Committee for University Building), and the Wissenschaftsrat (Research Council, WR), a forum of academics and representatives from government, business, and public life set up in 1957 to formulate strategic policy for higher education and research at the regional and national levels. The federal states' financial independence from the **Bund** and the resulting ban on cooperation (Kooperationsverbot), reinforced by the process of **federalism reform**, has most recently created problems for the Länder, which, under pressure themselves from the so-called debt brake, are unable to receive any financial help for schools and only exceptionally for higher education.

By contrast, the **German Democratic Republic (GDR)** radically transformed its schools and universities to create a universally available education system along socialist lines. By 1959, traditional German secondary schools had been replaced by a single, 10-year Polytechnische Oberschule (General Polytechnical Upper School, POS), providing a standard comprehensive education from ages 7 to 16, with a two-year sixth grade or Erweiterte Oberschule (extended upper school, EOS) for progression to university. Although the policy extended opportunity and removed class barriers, it resulted in a rigid and highly centralized system that valued ideological and political conformity and stifled individual development. Moreover, entry to higher level schooling, not to mention university education, was dependent on toeing the party line. A further mark of the ideological and political differences between East and West was that the first foreign language in the GDR was Russian, in contrast to English in the FRG. While the GDR produced relatively more school-leavers with a university-entrance certificate than West Germany, its moribund economy could not absorb the highly educated workforce. This system did not essentially change until 1989.

During the 1960s the FRG, responding to an urgent need to expand and reform its education provision in order to widen participation and meet social and economic demands (Bildungskatastrophe, or "catastrophe in education" was a common slogan of the time), built more schools and universities, raised the graduation age, and restructured the curriculum. Many of the changes were embodied in the interstate Hamburg Agreement (Hamburger Abkommen) of 1964, which the **eastern federal states** adopted after reunification. The agreement regulates school types, the criteria for transferring between schools, the duration of compulsory schooling, the school calendar and holidays, and forms and standards of assessment (including graduation certificates). In the following decade, a national structural framework for education was agreed upon, establishing a pattern of schooling provided by the main school types: school years 1 to 4 (ages 6 to 9) for the Grundschule (primary school); years 5 to 10 (ages 10 to 15) for secondary stage I (Gymnasium, Realschule, Gesamtschule, Hauptschule), and years 11 to 13 (ages 16 to 18) for secondary stage II (sixth grade). The framework also introduced a unified curriculum for years five to six that acted as an "orientation stage" for entry into the appropriate secondary stage. The stage can be integrated into one of the existing secondary school types or be offered in a separate school. In 1969, a government-Länder advisory body, the Deutscher Bildungsrat (German Educational Council), which existed from 1965 until 1975, recommended the creation of a new school type, the Gesamtschule (comprehensive school), which would combine the traditional school types under one roof (integrierte Gesamtschule), facilitate transfer from one to the other, and offer a wider curriculum. Introduced experimentally from 1972 and agreed to nationally by the federal states in 1982, comprehensive schools were actively promoted in **Hessen** and **North Rhine-Westfalia** (NRW) but did not prove universally popular; **Saxony** and **Bavaria** have none. The reforms ran out of steam during the 1980s, when Germany continued with its vertical school structure based on separate school types, and despite increasing flexibility within the system following the introduction of new school types, most pupils remain in their chosen secondary school type, which is also generally closest to their homes, in years five and six until graduation.

Minimum compulsory education comprises nine years full time at school (from the age of six) plus, if applicable, three years part-time vocational training. Basic educational materials are in principle free (Lernmittelfreiheit, also Lehrmittelfreiheit), although this is being undermined in many states. Demand for private schools, which are attended by about 8 percent of schoolchildren, is rising. The private sector is best represented in the special needs sector (Förderschulen) and is entitled to some financial support from the state. Between 1996 and 1999, every child aged between three and six gained the right to a preschool education. In August 2013, nursery care for one- to three-year-olds also became available, largely in order to help parents combine work with raising a family. As a result, the number of preschool centers catering for both age ranges has risen. These are maintained privately (by the churches, associations, parents' groups, and commercial organizations) or by the state, with parents contributing means-tested fees whose levels are set locally. Children generally attend primary school (Grundschule) for between four and six years, although most federal states have made four the rule. As in other countries, there are often debates about early education, for example, how writing/spelling should be taught and when to introduce keyboard skills.

Of the main post-primary-school types, the Gymnasium traditionally prepares pupils for the higher or university entrance certificate (**Abitur** or Allgemeine Hochschulreife). It currently accounts for more than 34 percent at secondary level I (2014), and the proportion is rising. Up to 70 percent of Gymnasium pupils come from the middle and professional classes. Although access for working-class children has improved as a result of reforms to the educational system, many such children prefer to study for Abitur or its equivalent at a vocationally oriented school, without going on to university. The Gymnasium has also become a popular school type in the **eastern federal states**, where it was reintroduced after reunification, and of all the school types, it is the only one to have retained its name and function throughout Germany. At the same time, the Gymnasium can take a variety of forms, reflecting specialization in natural sciences, ancient or modern languages, vocational subjects, sports, music, and so forth.

The six-year Realschule (so named in 1964 but originally established in the 19th century to educate middle-level staff for German **industry**) gained popularity during the 1980s and 1990s and is attended by 23 percent of pupils (2014). Providing a compulsory 10th year (age 15), it offers a wide range of subjects, often with an applied slant, and prepares pupils for technical and managerial professions. The leaving certificate (mittlerer Bildungsabschluss, Mittlere Reife or Realschulabschluss) is the minimum requirement for an apprenticeship and also qualifies for admission to secondary stage II. Plans for a national standard certificate, even after school year 10 in the Gymnasium, were proposed in 1970, but have proved difficult to implement.

The Hauptschule is aimed at nonacademic pupils for whom the preferred route is to leave full-time education at 15 before entering part-time vocational training (usually three years). A foreign language, usually English, is obligatory. There are opportunities to transfer to Realschule or Fachoberschule, which increase options for further vocational education. Despite efforts to enhance the range of subjects taught, the poorly regarded Hauptschule accounts for just 12 percent of the school population and faces problems of discipline, gender imbalance (boys predominate), and a high proportion of **immigrant** children. Some 25 percent of its pupils failed to graduate (with Hauptschulabschluss), and in general they experience difficulties finding apprenticeships. With falling roles the Hauptschule, which was never reestablished in the eastern federal states after reunification, has an uncertain future, and in several western states it has already been incorporated into other school types, with a wide variety of qualifications for this level. After 2012 in **Bavaria**, for instance, Hauptschulen could rename themselves Mittelschulen if they offered whole-day schooling and a qualification equivalent to the Realschulabschluss.

The Gesamtschule (integrated comprehensive school), which accounts for almost 16 percent of pupils at secondary stage I, combines all three tiers (Hauptschule, Realschule, Gymnasium), although pupils can be segregated according to either school type (in the so-called cooperative comprehensive school) or by ability from subject to subject (the integrated comprehensive school).

After reunification, some people wished to retain the egalitarian aspects of the GDR's school system, and although the POS's were dissolved and replaced by western German school types, the eastern states took advantage of their "cultural sovereignty" to introduce variations, which have in some cases spread to the west. With the exception of the Gymnasium, much of the traditional secondary school system has undergone radical structural change. The bewildering array of new school titles includes Sekundarschule (introduced experimentally in **North Rhine-Westfalia** from 2013/2014 for years 5 to 10, with options for cooperating with a Gymnasium or Gesamtschule), the integrierte Sekundarschule (replacing all secondary school types except Gymnasium in **Berlin** from 2011), the Werkrealschule (formerly Hauptschule and offering the mittlere Reife and vocationally oriented education in **Baden-Württemberg** from 2011), the Gemeinschaftsschule (also in Baden-

Württemberg from 2013 for years 5 to 10, and planned for the **Saarland** as the sole school type alongside the Gymnasium after 2017), the Oberschule (in **Saxony**, formerly Mittelschule, to exist alone alongside the Gymnasium), the Regionalschule (in **Schleswig-Holstein**, alongside Gemeinschaftsschule and Gymnasium), the Regelschule (in **Thuringia**, for years 5 to 10, alongside Gesamtschule and Gymnasium), and the Stadtteilschule (from 2010 in **Hamburg**, the main school type alongside the Gymnasium). Children with special needs or severe learning difficulties are admitted to special schools (Förderschulen or Sonderschulen), where teachers are specially trained for each school type.

In order to rationalize what many see as an overly long school education, most states have also introduced—not without controversy—an accelerated eight-year program (G8) for the Abitur. School mergers, the disappearance of the Hauptschule, and a declining birthrate, especially in western states, are major issues confronting the German school system. Reviews of Germany's educational performance in key subjects are provided every three years by PISA (Programme for International Student Assessment) under the auspices of the OECD (Organisation for Economic Co-operation and Development). Starting no later than 2016, the PISA reviews are to be undertaken by the Centre for International Student Assessment (Zentrum für internationale Bildungsvergleichsstudien, ZIB, created in 2010), which is located at the Technical University of Munich. The umbrella organization for German schools abroad is the Weltverband Deutscher Auslandsschulen (WDA).

Debates about school education, often triggered by specific cases, include violence among pupils and the integration of children with a **migration background** (sparked, for example, by demands by teachers in 2005/2006 to close the **Berlin** Rütli-school), the wearing of headscarves by Muslim teachers (subject to rulings by the **Federal Constitutional Court** in 2003 and 2015), and proposals to promote teaching in local and regional dialects (following evidence from a 2005 PISA study that pupils from dialect areas display greater linguistic competence).

Preschool education normally takes place in a Kindertagesstätte (Kita), although the titles vary regionally: while a Kindergarten generally takes children between three and six years old, a Kita (also Kinderkrippe, Schulhort) caters for infants under three, and a single facility may combine both age groups, with options for children staying beyond midday. The legal right to a place in a Kita was introduced in 1996, with full effect from 1999: in August 2013 this was extended to every child from age one, and in 2014 more than 660,000 children under age three (30 percent of the national group) were accommodated. The scheme is financed by the state, which provides one third of preschool facilities (e.g., in larger towns or local districts); the rest are provided by churches, charities, associations, parents' groups, and commercial organizations. In the former GDR, the state established extensive preschool services (often all-day and attached to the workplace), partly to free mothers for work and alleviate the labor shortage, and partly to reinforce the nurturing of a socialist personality loyal to the regime.

See EDUCATION: PRIVATE SCHOOLS; EDUCATION: UNIVERSITIES AND HIGHER EDUCATION; EDUCATION: VOCATIONAL; STUDENTS' MOVEMENT.

EDUCATION: UNIVERSITIES AND HIGHER EDUCATION. Drawing on a tradition established by Wilhelm von Humboldt in the 19th century, German universities enjoy autonomy in an integrated system of teaching and research (Freiheit und Einheit von Forschung und Lehre). As a result, universities have considerable managerial independence and are generally free to make decisions about and direct their own programs. While historic universities (such as Heidelberg, Cologne, Leipzig, and Erfurt) date from the Middle Ages, very large institutions emerged during the 19th century to meet the needs of industry and applied science (e.g., in **Berlin**, Munich, and **Hamburg**). To satisfy the huge increase in demand during the 1960s and early 1970s, a period that also saw widespread student discontent with an aging teaching cohort, many new universities (including Essen, Dortmund, and Regensburg) were founded. At the same time, a higher education framework law (Hochschulrahmengesetz, HRG) was agreed to in 1976. Implemented by the individual **federal states** (Länder), this set national guidelines on provision, admissions, internal democracy, and periods of study (called Regelstudienzeiten, these depended on a subject area studied under ideal conditions, although many students took longer). The result was a system that aimed to combine diversity with homogeneity and enable students to move smoothly from one university to another while following similar degree programs. Much later, in 2007, as part of **federalism reform**, the **federal government** decided to remove the HRG and give universities even greater autonomy (e.g., to be entrepreneurial and adapt to **European Union [EU]** requirements), although by 2015 this had not been fully agreed upon.

The 1980s and 1990s saw several technical colleges gain university status and an increase in the number of institutions (Fachhochschulen) offering applied and vocational programs, mainly in **engineering**, applied sciences, business, and social sciences. As early as 1973, the government had also proposed creating "comprehensive universities" (Gesamthochschulen), integrating traditional universities and technical colleges under a single roof, but only **Hessen** and **North Rhine-Westfalia** introduced these, and the designation was abandoned in 2003. Despite the expansion program, rising student numbers forced the government and federal states to abandon the principle of universal entry for holders of the high school certificate (**Abitur**) in popular subjects. In 1974, a central office (the Zentralstelle für die Vergabe von Studienplätzen, ZVS) was created n Dortmund to set entry quotas (the so-called *numerus clausus*), although its role declined during the 1990s as universities themselves assumed direct control over most admissions. Since public higher education institutions are funded primarily (90 percent) by the **Bund** and the federal states, with the latter contributing the lion's share (80 percent), and the remainder from private sources (research contracts, sponsors, student fees), the government and states have agreed to joint financial pacts since 2007, which have been successively revised in order to manage a growing student demand (between 2005 and 2015, the total number of students rose from 1.9 to 2.7 million). A number of universities, such as the Goethe University in Frankfurt/Oder and Georg-August University in Göttingen, are public or private foundations, with freedom to appoint their own professors and directly raise funds from private sources—areas normally in the hands of the state or Land.

Germany has 392 institutions of higher education, of which 121 are universities, 215 are Fachhochschulen, and 56 are colleges for music and art (2013). The largest universities are in Munich (50,500 students, with a further 36,000 at the Technical University), Cologne (45,600), Berlin (34,500 at the Free University, 35,000 at Humboldt University, and 31,000 at the Technical University), Münster (42,500), Bochum (41,500), and Hamburg and Frankfurt/Main (41,000 each). Many universities, such as Kiel, Gießen, Dortmund, Leipzig, and Würzburg, cater for between 20,000 and 30,000 students. A special case is Hagen in North Rhine-Westfalia, which specializes in distance learning for 88,000, although there are also 15 private institutions offering correspondence-type courses.

Students traditionally graduate with a diploma (Diplom, which is somewhere between a bachelor's and a master's degree), a master's degree (Magister), or a doctorate (Promotion); a second doctorate (Habilitation) is normally required for a professorial post. Following agreement by EU states in 1999 to integrate and standardize structures of study by 2010 (the so-called Bologna process), Germany began revising its higher education system, in particular introducing the six-semester, modularized bachelor's degree for undergraduates alongside applications- or research-based master's programs. Although the bachelor's qualification was intended to shorten study times and enable graduates to enter the job market sooner, many institutions found the transition difficult, and it has been subject to criticism. For selected students, a few universities (e.g., Technical University of Dortmund and the Humboldt University in Berlin) have also begun implementing a fast-track, parallel four-year master's and doctoral program.

Students planning on a teaching career at the secondary level traditionally completed a state examination (Staatsexamen or Lehramtsprüfung) and practical training (Praktikum/Referendariat), although several states have begun introducing a combined bachelor's/master's program in education. The universally most popular subject was business studies, followed by (for men) mechanical/electrical engineering and information technology, and (for **women**) German **language/literature**, medicine, and law. While German universities tend to develop strengths in specific areas, there is less overt grading of institutions than in Great Britain or the United States, although the Gütersloh-based CHE (Centrum für Hochschulentwicklung) claims to provide the most detailed rankings, which are published in the weekly newspaper *Die Zeit*.

German students (and school pupils) may apply for state-funded scholarships via the BaFöG (Bundesausbildungsförderungsgesetz, the "law on support for training and education") scheme, which was introduced in 1971 to expand access to education for lower income groups. BaFöG is currently means-tested and is evenly split into a straightforward grant and an interest-free loan. For students in tertiary education, the loan element is repayable up to a limit of 10,000 euros, from five years after the final BaFöG installment and over a period of up to 20 years; levels of repayment are income dependent. In 2014, 925,000 students received BaFöG funding; of these, 647,000 were in higher education (rising) and 278,000 attended school (falling). School pupils and students can also apply for support through the education credit program (Bildungskreditprogramm), which unlike BAFöG is a finite fund. The Berlin-based Deutsches Studentenwerk (German National Association for Student Affairs, DSW), originally founded in 1919/1920, is an umbrella organization of 58 independent student unions throughout Germany, providing social, financial, and cultural support services to students. The Allgemeiner Studierendenausschuss or Allgemeiner Studentenausschuss (AStA), present at most universities, provides similar services and generally elects delegates to a "students' parliament," which assigns roles and responsibilities to representatives.

Although the red/green coalition under **Gerhard Schröder** modified the HRG in 2002 to rule out general tuition fees for first degrees completed within the standard period of study, the **Federal Constitutional Court (FCC)** in 2005 gave federal states the freedom to levy them. Several states, mainly in the west, went on to apply fees (generally from 300 to 500 euros a semester) for first degrees, but such fees remained politically controversial, and in 2013 **Lower Saxony** was the last regional parliament to announce their removal.

See also EDUCATION: SCHOOLS; EDUCATION: VOCATIONAL; RESEARCH AND DEVELOPMENT (R&D); STUDENTS' MOVEMENT.

EDUCATION: VOCATIONAL. Vocational education in Germany is organized as a "dual system" (Duales System), which combines paid training at work with compulsory part-time attendance at a vocational school (Berufsschule) up to the age of 18. Around two-thirds of Germany's workforce are estimated to have undertaken some form of training within the dual system.

The type of vocational school depends on whether the trainee is full or part time, the length and type of training, and regional conditions. Although there are no formal prerequisites for entry, employers are selective, especially for popular jobs, for which a school leaving certificate may be required. In some cases, trainees can qualify for admission to university. The system, which is much admired abroad, is historically well established in Germany and widely considered to have produced a highly qualified workforce that has sustained the needs of the nation's **industry** and commerce. The scheme is heavily financed by employers—although state funding increased during the unemployment-burdened 1990s—and is managed by **employers' organizations** (chambers of commerce), **trade unions**, and educational providers.

The Bundesinstitut für Berufsbildung (Federal Institute for Vocational Training, BIBB) was established in 1970 as a central coordinating authority. Based in Bonn and **Berlin**, BIBB acts as a think tank attached to the Federal Ministry of Education and **Research**. It carries out research in vocational development to identify the requirements of companies, commercial developments, and the state of the job market. Working with experts from trade unions, the **federal states**, and employers, it monitors and analyzes vocational education and training in companies, tries out new approaches, and works to modernize company regulations. It also maintains a list of recognized trades/occupations, supports in-company vocational education and training practice, develops and evaluates new concepts for training, supports international training programs, and provides information and statistics.

The legal basis for the dual system is the law on vocational educational (Berufsbildungsgesetz, 1969), which lays out mutual obligations, conditions, provisions for assessment, and so forth. The most sought-after occupations are in office and retail commerce (Kaufmann/Kauffrau), sales, motor vehicle repair and maintenance (since 2003 designated KFZ-Mechatroniker on account of the electronics component), industrial commerce (Industriekaufmann/Industriekauffrau), wholesale trade and exports (Kaufmann im Groß/Außenhandel), and the **health** sector. There are 330 approved occupations.

Although often seen as a model for other countries, the dual system faces challenges, including a decline in traineeships in traditional industries that is not matched by an increase in the service sector; the lack of traineeships for lower qualified school-leavers as employers look more to graduates (e.g., with a bachelor's degree); and the trend for employers to focus on fast-track, business-specific training or, notably in industry and construction, to rely increasingly on unqualified workers. At the same time, the number of actual trainees fell in 2013 to a record low (530,000), partly due to the increased popularity of the **Abitur** as a gateway to higher academic education. New schemes try to make training more interesting, such as by including periods abroad.

See also EDUCATION: SCHOOLS; EDUCATION: UNIVERSITIES AND HIGHER EDUCATION.

EICHEL, HANS (1941–). Social Democratic Party of Germany (SPD) politician. Born in Kassel (**Hessen**), Hans Eichel studied German language and **literature**, philosophy, politics, and history at the universities of Marburg and **Berlin** and qualified as a schoolteacher (1970). After joining the SPD (1964), he was active as deputy leader of the party's **Young Socialists (JUSOS)** wing (1969–1972). While working as a schoolteacher (1970–1975), he also chaired the SPD group in the Kassel city council and served as mayor (Oberbürgermeister, 1975–1991). He argued for ecologically sound policies, opposed the civil and military use of nuclear power, and worked for the integration of **women** in the workforce. In 1981, he became the first mayor of a major German city to cooperate with the **Green Party**. Elected regional party chairman (1989), he led the SPD to electoral victory in Hessen (1991) and was **minister president** of an SPD/Green Party coalition government until 1999, when a **Christian Democratic Union (CDU)** government was returned under **Roland Koch**. In 1997, he became financial coordinator for the national SPD. As chair of the **mediation committee** of the **Bundestag** and **Bundesrat** (1997), he developed a reputation for financial competence in handling negotiations on **taxation** reform.

When the SPD and Green Party formed a national government (1998), Eichel was appointed president of the Bundesrat before succeeding **Oskar Lafontaine** as federal minister of finance (April 1999), a post he held until 2005. From 1999 until 2002, he presided over one of the most comprehensive and far-reaching reviews ever undertaken of the German domestic **budget**. Nicknamed "Iron Hans" (Eisenhans), he announced wide-ranging cuts and tax reforms designed to control deficits at a time of falling revenues and rising social welfare costs. Eichel's declared aim was to balance the federal budget by 2006, although the cost-cutting measures were criticized by left-wingers in the SPD, especially in eastern Germany, and the deficit rose as the economic situation worsened.

In June 2004, Eichel announced plans to use 12,000 million euros left over from the postwar Marshall Plan reconstruction fund to allow the government's own public sector development bank to buy government shares in **Deutsche Telekom AG** and **Deutsche Post AG**. Along with other measures, this backdoor form of privatization was intended to take pressure off the domestic budget and enable the minister to claim that the national deficit would not exceed the limits agreed to by the **European Union (EU)** in its **Stability and Growth Pact**. In fact, the deficit rose to 3.6 percent of GDP in 2005.

See also BANKS.

ELECTION ALTERNATIVE FOR LABOR AND JUSTICE (WAH-LALTERNATIVE ARBEIT UND GERECHTIGKET, WASG). The WASG was founded in January 2005 by disaffected left-wing **trade unionists** and members of the **Social Democratic Party of Germany (SPD)** led by **Oskar Lafontaine**, who resigned as SPD finance minister (March 1999) following policy disagreements with Chancellor **Gerhard Schröder**. In 2006, WASG had around 12,000 members, mainly in western Germany. In July/August it entered into an electoral alliance and de facto merger with the **Party of Democratic Socialism (PDS)** to form **The Left Party**. The move was opposed by regional WASG associations in **Berlin** and **Mecklenburg-West Pomerania**.

ELECTORAL SYSTEM. While Germany's **Basic Law (BL,** article 38) specifies that members of the **Bundestag** are directly elected in a free, universal, and secret ballot (voters must be at least age 18); represent the whole people; and are not tied to party directions, further details are left to federal legislation, which was last significantly amended in 2012–2013. Elections are held every four years using a complex system of modified (or "personalized") proportional representation (plans in 1966 to move to a first-past-the-post system by 1973, motivated by fears that minority parties could destabilize the Bundestag, were quickly abandoned). The current model is in part a response to the experience of the Weimar Republic (1919–1933), when too many parties destabilized parliament. A voter casts two votes: the first for an individual candidate in his or her constituency (the direct personal mandate or Grundmandat), the second for a party (the list mandate or Listenmandat). The second vote is used to work out the overall proportion of seats in the Bundestag for each party: thus, if a party gains 25 percent of the second votes nationally, it receives 25 percent of the seats in parliament (the total of constituencies/nominal seats was settled at 299/598 in 2002). Half of the total number of seats is allocated to the directly elected candidates by simple majority and the other half proportionally to candidates on lists (Landeslisten) drawn up by the parties in each of the **federal states**. A feature of the system is that a party can win more direct seats (by the first vote) than it is entitled to by proportional representation (the second vote). If this happens, the party keeps the extra "overhang" seats (Überhangmandate). Because the **Federal Constitutional Court (FCC)** ruled it unfair that overhang seats could alter the proportional balance of total seats arrived at through second list votes, they have been offset since 2013 by the creation of as many additional "equalization" seats (Ausgleichsmandate) for the parties as are required to restore the original balance. This system is more equitable, but can increase considerably the number of seats in the Bundestag. The 2013 national election produced 4 additional overhang and 29 equalization seats, giving a total of 631 members. To enter parliament, a party must win at least

5 percent of votes nationally or at least three constituency seats by the first, direct vote. **European Union (EU)** citizens may stand as candidates and vote in local and European Parliament elections.

Elections to the regional **Landtag** parliaments are governed by individual state constitutions. There are considerable variations. The size of the assemblies varies from around 180 (**Bavaria, North Rhine-Westfalia,** and **Lower Saxony**) to 51 (**Saarland**), and electoral periods are either four or five years. Some assemblies allow voters a single vote only, others two. The ratio of direct to list mandates differs (some parliaments having only direct mandates), while overhang mandates may or may not be allowed. Slightly different methods are used to calculate the proportional allocation of seats, although a 5 percent entry hurdle (alternatively one or two direct mandates in some cases) is standard. Local government elections to the so-called Kommunen, which include town/city councils, districts (Kreise), and municipalities (Gemeinden), also vary according to local electoral law and conditions, although they all operate variations of a proportional system of representation. In certain cases, voters cast up to three votes for a council, often headed by a mayor.

Elections every five years to the European Parliament began in 1979. These are governed by the electoral system of each member state. The 5 percent hurdle that Germany applied was overruled in 2011 by the FCC, which also rejected a 3 percent barrier agreed to by the Bundestag in 2013. Consequently, for the 2014 European election, a system-immanent default hurdle of about 0.5 percent applied, favoring very small parties, such as **The Pirates** and the **National Democratic Party of Germany (NPD)**, which each gained one seat. Following extensions to the powers of the parliament and a redistribution of member states' seats agreed to in the Treaty of Lisbon (2009), Germany's allocated mandates fell from 99 to 96. In the 2014 election, the **Christian Democratic Union (CDU)** won 29 seats, the **Social Democratic Party of Germany (SPD)** 27, the **Green Party** 11, the **Free Democratic Party (FDP)** 3, and **The Left Party** 7. The 766-member assembly convenes in Brussels and Strasburg.

Since Germany has 16 federal states, the country is in a more or less permanent state of electioneering. Regional (federal state) elections are often taken as a barometer of a government's popularity. Because they affect the balance of power in the **Bundesrat**, they also have an indirect influence on central government and legislation. Since the mid-1970s, **political parties** have been concerned about steadily falling electoral turnouts, especially for regional assemblies and in the **eastern federal states**. Turnout for national elections varied from just over 91 percent in 1972 to around 70 percent in 2009 and 2013, while for the European Parliament it fell steadily, from 65.7 percent in 1979 to 43.5 percent in 2009. Participation in regional elections is particularly low, ranging from 67 percent (**Brandenburg** 2009) to 44 percent

(**Saxony-Anhalt** 2006). Concerns have also been expressed about the representativeness of the Bundestag, whose members serve for three or more periods and do not reflect the population in terms of age, gender, or occupation.

See also LOCAL GOVERNMENT.

EMPLOYERS' ORGANIZATIONS. The two leading employers' organizations are the Bundesvereinigung der Deutschen Arbeitgeberverbände (Confederation of German Employers' Associations, BDA) and the Bundesverband der Deutschen Industrie (Federation of German Industries, BDI). While the BDA claims to represent all sectors of the German economy, including **industry**, **agriculture**, and services, the BDI technically speaks for **industry** alone. In practice, the BDI's members range from motor vehicle manufacturing to food retailers. Through its 38 branch or sector associations, the BDI indirectly represents over 100,000 small, medium-sized, and large businesses employing eight million. Although its general aim is to ensure a favorable environment for German industry and jobs, the BDI focuses on the **Mittelstand** and on services with close links to industry. Its main organs are a presidium and executive board. Ulrich Grillo was elected president in 2013. BDA members are not individual companies, but rather regional or national sector associations. Privately financed through voluntary membership fees, the BDA, which is based in **Berlin**, currently has 6,500 member associations representing one million companies employing 20 million people. A general assembly of association members meets annually to elect a president, presidium, and executive board. The BDA's president is Ingo Kramer (elected 2013).

Alongside the BDI and BDA are numerous associations for nonindustrial activities, including **banks** and insurance companies, wholesalers, exporters, newspaper **publishers**, hoteliers and restaurateurs, shipowners, and farmers. Wage negotiations and collective bargaining with **trade unions** are conducted, not by the BDI or BDA, but by the individual employers' associations. All businesses, including trades, farms, and the self-employed, are obliged to join a guild or a local chamber of commerce (Handelskammer), of which there are around 80. The national organization for these is the Deutsche Industrie- und Handelskammer e.V. (Association of German Chambers of Industry and Commerce, DIHK), with 16 specialist committees, whose members are drawn from all sectors of the economy. Among other things, the DIHK registers companies and provides training.

A national forum of around 15 leading business associations is the Gemeinschaftsausschuss der Deutschen Gewerblichen Wirt- schaft (Joint Committee of German Associations in Trade and Industry), which was founded in Bonn in 1951 to enable the associations to coordinate policy on strategic political and economic issues. It is located in the Haus der Deutschen Wirtschaft in Berlin, which also houses the BDA, BDI, and DIHK. In 2000, it called on industry to support the initiative to set up a trust fund to compensate the victims of forced labor during the National Socialist period.

ENERGY. From 1949 to 1957, government-subsidized hard coal extraction met energy demands during Germany's rapid postwar reconstruction (the "economic miracle"). Between 1958 and 1972, the demand for domestic coal fell, and mines closed in the face of cheaper oil imports and the opening up of Dutch natural gas fields; the first official **environmental** program also emerged at this time (1971). Responding to the oil price shocks of 1973–1974 and 1979–1980, the government sponsored its first energy research program (1974), leading to the strategy of a balanced energy mix that incorporated nuclear power. Recent policy landmarks include laws to liberalize energy markets in the **European Union (EU**, the Law on Electricity and Gas Supply, 1998) and promote renewable energies (Renewable Energies Law, 2000), the decision to withdraw from nuclear power (2002), the EU Emission Trading System (from 2005), measures to import large volumes of gas from Russia (2005), and a fresh hike in crude oil prices (2008). In its ambitious "energy concept" of 2010, the government pledged to reduce greenhouse gas emissions by 80 percent over 1990 levels by 2050, phase out nuclear power stations by 2022, and progressively meet Germany's energy needs through renewable sources while also reducing overall consumption. As a bridging measure, modern gas- and coal-fired power stations would be built.

Germany remains a high consumer of energy. With limited natural resources, the country imports around two-thirds of its necessary primary energy and is heavily dependent on other countries for raw materials, including oil, gas, coal, and nuclear power. In 2014, Germany imported 87 percent of its anthracite (20 percent in 1995), more than 99 percent of its mineral oil (95 percent), and around 88 percent of its natural gas (79 percent) needs. Overall, the country has increased its reliance on imports, despite the lessons of sudden oil price rises imposed by oil-producing countries. For environmental and economic reasons, coal consumption is declining, although there remain significant domestic coal reserves, and coal continues to be the single largest contributor to electricity generation (over 40 percent, although renewables [25.8 percent] overtook brown coal [25.6 percent] as the single main source of energy in 2014). Primary energy usage (before conversion to secondary energy carriers, such as electricity) is dominated by oil (35 percent in 2014) and natural gas (20.5 percent), followed by anthracite (12.6 percent), brown coal (12 percent), and nuclear power (8.1 percent); the contribution of renewable domestic sources (11 percent) is rising. Unlike in other countries, technological improvements and conservation measures have kept Germany's energy usage static during the last approximately 15 years, despite economic growth, and variations in consumption are now largely weather-related (around 29 percent of energy is devoted to room heating). The number of people employed in the energy sector has progressively fallen, from around 560,000 in 1991 to 235,000 in 2014, mainly in electricity generation (176,000).

See also ENERGY: COAL; ENERGY: NUCLEAR POWER/ELECTRICITY; ENERGY: OIL AND GAS; ENERGY: RENEWABLE.

ENERGY: COAL. Germany is estimated to possess around 2,500 million metric tons of hard coal (anthracite) and 40,500 million tons of brown coal (lignite) of recoverable reserves, at an average seam depth of 920 meters (in the Ruhr area). Total probable resources, at 82,900 and 77,000 tonnes, are much greater, although the cost of extracting deep hard coal makes it less economical than imported coal (mainly from Russia and Colombia), which contributes 77 percent of national consumption. While hard coal met 88 percent of primary energy needs in 1950, this had fallen to 30 percent in 1980 and under 13 percent by 2014. Under the terms of the government's long-term "energy concept" (2010), power generation from hard coal (and gas) will act as a technological bridge and reserve supplier, at least until subsidized production is phased out by 2018, in line with **European Union (EU)** agreements. Currently operating deep mines—all run by RAG Deutsche Steinkohle AG with a workforce of 23,000—include three in the Ruhr (75 percent of production), one in the Saar coalfield (10 percent), and one near Ibbenbüren (north of the Ruhr, 15 percent). In 2007, the RAG Stiftung (RAG Foundation) was created to manage the gradual shutdown of the industry in a socially acceptable manner. Its current chairman is former economics minister Werner Müller (appointed in 2012).

Most opencast lignite extraction takes place in the Rhineland. Here, the area around Cologne, Aachen and Mönchengladbach is the largest single lignite mining field in Europe, covering 2,500 square kilometers, and accounts for around 70 percent of German production. Other areas are found in the eastern German Lausitz (around Dresden), in central Germany (between Leipzig and Halle), and near Helmstedt (in southeastern **Lower Saxony**). An environmentally dirty fuel, emitting twice as much carbon dioxide as gas, lignite is nevertheless abundant and cheap to extract, and is used mainly for generating electricity in power stations contiguous to the coalfields (no transport costs are involved). Several companies are engaged in this industry (RWE, Vattenfall, MIBRAG, ROMANTA, and E.ON), and it is the only fuel that does not rely on state subsidies. Although lignite use is scheduled to be phased out by 2050, the fall in electricity prices as a result of an increase in supply from renewable energies has actually led to a renaissance in lignite production, which now accounts for over a quarter of electricity generation— more than anthracite, nuclear, or gas. Lignite's resurgence has also been helped by the fact that more modern and fuel-efficient gas power stations either cannot meet their operating costs or even fail to come online when built. Although many lignite fields in eastern Germany were closed upon reunification for **environmental** reasons, with large job losses, some have reopened and contribute significantly to the economy. Restoring the landscape is now an important aspect of any mining project, with about 20 artificial lakes, some linked by canals, being created by flooding former opencast mines to produce a spectacular water landscape.

See also ENERGY; ENERGY: NUCLEAR POWER/ELECTRICITY; ENERGY: OIL AND GAS; ENERGY: RENEWABLE.

ENERGY: NUCLEAR POWER/ELECTRICITY. Nuclear power accounts for around 8 percent of primary energy production in Germany and 15 percent of electricity generation (2014). However, it has a checkered history. During the postwar economic boom, which saw a wave of enthusiasm for the exploitation of peaceful atomic energy, the first commercial nuclear power station opened in 1960 in Kahl on the River Main (**Bavaria**) and was linked to the national electricity grid the following year. Tests to store radioactive waste in old salt mines began in 1967. Despite growing opposition over safety concerns and disasters at Three Mile Island in Harrisburg (United States) in 1979 and Chernobyl (Ukraine) in 1986 (when large volumes of radioactivity fell on Germany), further plants were built, including a fast breeder reactor at Kalkar that was technically in operation between 1985 and 1991 but was never used. Mass protests took place at Wyhl (1975, where the plant was never built), Kalkar (1977), and Brokdorf (1976). From the mid-1970s onward, protests also focused on the storage of nuclear waste at sites in Germany (long-term at Gorleben and short-term at Ahaus) and on its transport by rail in CASTOR containers. The transports, which began in 1995, were halted in 1998 and resumed in 2001, though they were disrupted by hundreds of demonstrators.

In 2000, the **Social Democratic Party (SPD)/Green Party** coalition under **Gerhard Schröder** negotiated with the power industry a phased withdrawal from nuclear energy by 2021, although a new government of the **Christian Democratic Union (CDU)/Free Democratic Party (FDP)** led by **Angela Merkel** agreed in 2009 to postpone the wind-down. After numerous disputes and uncertainties, the Fukushima incident in Japan in 2011 prompted Merkel to announce safety checks of all 17 German plants, the temporary closure of 7 reactors built before 1980, and the formation of commissions to review technical and ethical issues. Combining its long-term national plan for energy (the "energy concept," presented in 2010) with a turnaround in energy policy (Energiewende) the following year, the government proposed retaining nuclear power as a bridging technology on the way to providing a new energy mix, phasing out all nuclear plants by 2022. By

2014, the industry had closed 19 plants dating from the 1960s and 1970s, retained 8 as nonoperational, and was still running 9. At the same time, the costs of storing nuclear waste (conservatively estimated at between 30,000 and 70,000 million euros) presented a serious problem for an industry facing fierce competition from subsidized eco-energy sources. Government plans to make companies (E.ON, RWE, EnBW, and Swedish-owned Vattenfall) wholly and perpetually responsible for these costs were criticized by some as unrealistic. An estimated 40,000 employees are currently engaged in nuclear power generation.

See also ENERGY; ENERGY: COAL; ENERGY: OIL AND GAS; ENERGY: RENEWABLE.

ENERGY: OIL AND GAS. Germany's reserves (both certain and probable) of crude oil were estimated at 31.5 million metric tons in 2013). Total annual production is 2.4 million tonnes (2015), mostly from the Mittelplatte oil field in western **Schleswig-Holstein** (55 percent), followed by **Lower Saxony** (Dieksand, Emlichheim, and Georgsdorf, 34 percent) and **Rhineland-Palatinate** (Römerberg, 8 percent); this represents a small upward trend since 2010. Germany has over 97,000 million cubic meters of certain reserves of natural gas, although potential reserves are estimated to be much higher (150 million cubic meters in conventional deposits, 450 million in coal seams, and up to 2,300 million in shale). Most (96.7 percent) is extracted in Lower Saxony—over half from the Weser-Ems region. Production, which accounted for just 7 percent of national consumption in 2015, has decreased substantially in recent years, owing largely to a fall in investment and a decline in exploring new fields (fracking was banned starting in 2012). Both industries are estimated to employ over 10,000 highly qualified workers.

Production levels are insufficient to meet national needs, and following price increases introduced by the Organization of Petroleum Exporting Countries (OPEC) in the 1970s, Germany sought new suppliers of oil and gas. Total energy imports now exceed 70 percent of current consumption, with a heavy reliance on Russia for oil (34 percent) and natural gas (38 percent). In 2005, Germany and Russia concluded an agreement to build a double pipeline under the **Baltic Sea** directly linking Vyborg (near St. Petersburg) and Greifswald. Completed in 2011–2012 and operated by Nord Stream AG, the link was projected to meet around 40 percent of Germany's gas needs, raising concerns over the country's dependence on Russian supplies.

See also ENERGY; ENERGY: COAL; ENERGY: NUCLEAR POWER/ ELECTRICITY; ENERGY: RENEWABLE; TRADE.

ENERGY: RENEWABLE. In 1990, the German government passed an act (the Stromeinspeisegesetz)—later copied across the **European Union (EU)**—obliging the big power companies to offer small suppliers a fixed feed-in tariff. The first to take advantage of this were hydroelectric generators in **Bavaria**. Since then, the Renewable Energy Law (Erneuerbare-Energien-Gesetz, EEG), in force from 2000 and periodically revised, has played a decisive role in promoting the proportion of energy generated from renewable sources (over 11 percent in 2014). Its principle is simple: suppliers receive a guaranteed remuneration (rate per kilowatt-hour) over 20 years or so and have priority in being linked to the network. The law, which is seen as balancing decades of subsidies for coal and nuclear power generation, is designed to open up the energy supply market, stimulate investment in renewables, and reduce **environmental** pollution. The main renewables, which contribute to fuel, heating, and electricity, are wind and solar power and biogas, followed by geothermal and hydroelectric sources. Within an overall target of increasing the contribution of renewable energy by 40–45 percent by 2025 and by 55–60 percent by 2035, solar power and land-based power generation would each rise annually by 2.5 gigawatts (GW) and biomass by 100 megawatts (MW); 6.5 GW of offshore wind power would be installed by 2020 and a further 15 GW by 2030. Revisions to the EEG in 2014, however, were criticized for their complexity and for increasing the cost of electricity from renewable sources. Geography significantly influences the distribution of energy source types; while wind contributes most to flatter, northern Germany (21.6 percent in Lower Saxony), it falls dramatically in more mountainous areas of the south (4 percent in **Bavaria** and 1.4 percent in **Baden-Württemberg**). Political factors also play a role, such as the Bavarian government's decision to increase the distance between housing and higher, more modern wind turbines (2014) and local resistance by environmental groups.

See also ENERGY; ENERGY: COAL; ENERGY: NUCLEAR POWER/ELECTRICITY; ENERGY: OIL AND GAS; NORTH SEA (NORDSEE).

ENGHOLM, BJÖRN (1939–). Social Democratic Party of Germany (SPD) politician. Born in Lübeck (**Schleswig-Holstein**), Björn Engholm trained as a typesetter (1959–1962) and joined the print workers' **trade union**, IG Druck und Papier. After attending evening classes in **Hamburg** (from 1962), he went on to study politics, economics, and sociology at the University of Hamburg, graduating with a diploma (1972). While studying, he worked as a journalist and as a tutor for a trade union educational program. A member of the SPD from 1962, he led the Lübeck branch of the party's **Young Socialists (JUSOS)** wing (1965–1969) and represented the SPD in the **Bundestag** (1969–1983). After specializing in **education, sport,** and the **media,** he became parliamentary **state secretary** in the Federal Ministry of Education and Science (1977–1981), which he headed as minister under Chancellor **Helmut Schmidt** (1981–1982). While in office, he combated youth unemployment, improved measures for special needs children, and resisted cuts in students' grants. When the SPD/**Free Democratic Party** (**FDP**) coalition collapsed in 1982, he served for 14 days as interim minister for food, **agriculture**, and forestry. In 1983, Engholm was the SPD's **minister president** candidate in the Schleswig-Holstein state elections, but was defeated by **Uwe Barschel** of the **Christian Democratic Union** (**CDU**). A deputy in Schleswig-Holstein's state parliament (**Landtag**, 1983–1994), Engholm led the SPD parliamentary group (1983–1988) and joined the national executive (1994).

In the wake of the scandal surrounding **Uwe Barschel** in the September 1987 regional election campaign, an inquiry commission found that Engholm had been a victim of serious malpractice and misuse of power during the campaign. Fresh elections (May 1988) returned the SPD to office with an absolute majority and Engholm as minister president. Engholm included four **women** in his cabinet, one of whom was the first minister for women in Germany. Under his stewardship, Schleswig-Holstein revised its regional constitution, lifted the so-called **radicals decree** (introduced during the 1970s to exclude suspected extremists from public service jobs), extended **codetermination** for public service workers, and enhanced **women**'s rights. Other measures included reforms and expansion in education (e.g., the introduction of comprehensive schools [Gesamtschulen] and widening university entrance criteria). Well regarded as premier of a modernizing state, Engholm became a prominent figure in the SPD, joining the party presidium (1988–1993) and succeeding **Hans-Jochen Vogel** as party leader (1991). He was instrumental in persuading the SPD to accept the Treaty of Maastricht, stricter **asylum** laws, and the deployment of **Bundeswehr** forces in **United Nations** (**UN**)–approved out-of-area operations. Reelected minister president in 1992, he resigned the following year and withdrew from politics after admitting that he had lied to the Barschel commission and had known about the intrigues against him before the election.

ENGINEERING. Germany's heterogeneous mechanical engineering **industry**, not counting electronics, **automobiles**, **chemicals**, and manufacturing, comprises 6,400 companies and employs more than one million (around 20 percent are higher **education** graduates); turnover is 218,000 million euros (2015). The range of products is extremely diverse, although leading sectors include power transmission systems, construction equipment, materials and air-handling technologies, machine tools, **agricultural**/food processing/packaging machinery, valves, and pumps. Exports totaled more than 155,500 million euros, accounting for 77 percent of production and directed mainly at Europe and Asia, especially China. The sector includes a large number of small to medium-sized enterprises (the so-called **Mittelstand**). Although German companies are considered to have high labor costs, they compete successfully in specialist areas in which technical know-how and customer service are paramount. The umbrella association for engineering and machine tools is the Verband Deutscher Maschinen- und Anlagebau (Federation of German Machine and Plant Production, VDMA).

Considered separately, the electrical/electronics industry turns over 179,000 million euros with a workforce of 848,000 (2015); exports in 2014 reached a record 166,000 million euros. A very wide product range covers equipment for the automobile and **energy** industries, **transport**ation, **telecommunications**, information technology, and **health**, as well as household goods and entertainment. Around 50 percent of production goes for export, increasingly to eastern Europe since 1990. Depending on the nature of the product, market volume, and degree of specialization, companies differ widely in size, although many are concentrated in **Bavaria, Baden-Württemberg**, and **North Rhine-Westfalia**, often close to urban areas, universities, and centers of highly qualified personnel. Umbrella organizations of the electrical engineering industry are the Zentralverband Elektrotechnik- und Elektronikindustrie (German Electrical and Electronic Manufacturers' Association, ZVEI) and the Verband der Elektrotechnik, Elektronik und Informationstechnik (Association for Electrical, Electronic, and Information Technologies, VDE).

See also TRADE.

ENVIRONMENT. After Chancellor **Willy Brandt** included protection of the **environment** as a government objective in 1969, there followed an "emergency program" (Sofortprogramm, 1970) and legislation to curb noise, pollution, and toxic emissions (1971–1974). A federal office for the environment (Umweltbundesamt) was created (1974), although a full-blown ministry (responsible for the environment, nature protection, and nuclear reactor safety) was not established until after the Chernobyl disaster (1986). Three key principles—that "the polluter pays"; that environmental protection is a cooperative task involving the state, citizens, and business; and that damage to the environment should be prevented before it occurs—eventually became **European Union** (**EU**) policy. Although the oil crisis of 1974 and subsequent economic downturn put a brake on further initiatives, a new government under Chancellor **Helmut Kohl**, responding to the emerging green movement and public concern over deforestation through acid rain and the pollution of rivers and lakes, introduced controls on large-scale combustion emissions from power stations and **industry** (Großfeuerungsanlagenverordnung, 1983) and catalyzers in new motor vehicles (1984). As a result, by 1993 harmful gas and particle emissions had fallen in western Germany by between 72 and 89 percent. These measures, alongside laws promoting waste recycling (1994) and renewable **energy** (1990), made Germany, which was also confronted by the shocking legacy of pollution in the former **German Democratic Republic (GDR)**, a pioneer in environmental protection. Although postreunification economic problems, as well as opposition to a tax on carbon-generating energy, prompted the government to pull back on environmental issues during the 1990s, a new administration under **Gerhard Schröder** (from 1998) decided to phase out nuclear power; initiated a series of eco-taxes (from 1999); and passed a sustainability strategy for protecting land, forest, and fisheries (Nachhaltig-keitsstrategie, 2000). Resisting lobbying from industry groups, Chancellor **Angela Merkel** also committed Germany to meeting international targets for reducing climate-changing emissions, and in 2007 she played a key role in encouraging the EU to adopt ambitious policy measures and persuading the United States (U.S.) to join the post-Kyoto process at Heiligendamm in 2007, although the success proved short-lived after American and Chinese leaders bilaterally negotiated a "minimal consensus" at the 2009 world climate summit in Copenhagen. In response to the disappointment of Copenhagen, Merkel initiated an international forum, the Petersberg Climate Dialog (Peters-berger Klimadialog), in an effort to translate negotiation into action. The forum first met in Bonn in 2010, subsequently annually in **Berlin**, but achieved few tangible results. In 2015, hoping for greater cooperation from the U.S. and China, Merkel hosted the G7 summit in Elmau in the Bavarian **Alps** in June and was scheduled to cohost the **United Nations (UN)** conference on climate change in Paris in December. She also announced a doubling of Germany's contribution to climate change measures in developing countries until 2020. In Germany, successive governments and the **federal states** have, despite prolonged efforts, failed to integrate existing legislation into a single environmental code (Umweltgesetzbuch).

Established in 1990, the Deutsche Bundesstiftung Umwelt (German Federal Environmental Foundation, DBU) supports research and projects contributing to improvements in the environment. Since 1993, it has also awarded Europe's largest prize (500,000 euros) to individuals and organizations in this field. In 1995, the EU (then the European Community) also began operating a scheme encouraging businesses to undergo an ecological audit (Environmental Management and Audit Scheme, EMAS); some 1,200 German concerns, mainly in **Baden-Württemberg** and **Bavaria**, participated in 2014.

See also ENVIRONMENT: EMISSIONS; ENVIRONMENT: FAUNA AND FLORA; ENVIRONMENT: FORESTS; ENVIRONMENT: PROTECTED SITES; ENVIRONMENT: WASTE MANAGEMENT; ENVIRONMENT: WATER.

ENVIRONMENT: EMISSIONS. Although Germany is the biggest producer of greenhouse gases in the **European Union (EU)**, its government has resisted demands from economic lobbying groups to compromise ambitious targets on emissions reductions agreed to originally at the world climate conference in Kyoto in 1997. As part of the EU's commitment to reduce its emissions between 2008 and 2012 by 8 percent over 1990 levels, Germany set itself a 21 percent target, and by the end of 2012 it had achieved more than a 25 percent reduction, with the largest decreases in carbon monoxide (produced mainly by auto emissions) and sulfur dioxide (solid fuel combustion). For carbon dioxide, which contributes 87 percent of emissions, the reduction has been continual, largely because of industrial restructuring in the **eastern federal states** after reunification (1990), antipollution measures by the state, and the economic downturn during 2009–2011. Other gases include nitrous oxide (generated by farming fertilizers, animal husbandry, and the **chemicals** industry), methane (farm animals, coal mining, gas distribution, burning processes, and waste disposal), and fluorocarbons (**agriculture**). An important element in Germany's concept of mixed **energy** is the EU-Emissions Trading Scheme, in which energy-intensive companies, including airlines since 2012, receive certificates that entitle them to emit a fixed amount of carbon dioxide and can be traded with other businesses. The aim since 2005 has been to move away from allocating free certificates toward phasing in a market-based system of auctioning.

See also ENVIRONMENT.

ENVIRONMENT: FAUNA AND FLORA. Germany is estimated to have around 45,000–48,000 species of animals and 28,000 types of plants, although not all are native to the country; many migratory birds, for instance, pass through or overwinter in Germany. The Bundesamt für Naturschutz (Federal Agency for Nature Conservation, BfN) publishes detailed and extensive "red lists" (Rote Listen) of endangered fauna and flora. A positive legacy of the border between West and East Germany—a prohibited corridor ("death strip") of up to 200 meters wide and about 1,400 kilometers long—was the undisturbed protection it offered for over 40 years to 1,200 species of endangered plant and animal life. To preserve these ecological features, the "Green Belt" (Grünes Band) was launched in 1989 as part of a pan-European project encompassing the former "Iron Curtain" countries from the North Sea to the Adriatic and the Black Sea. The initiative was supported by the BfN, Friends of the Earth Germany (BUND), and the **Greens**. Germany is also a signatory to a number of international and European agreements to sustain wildlife and reverse the effects of decades of industrial pollution, intensive farming, and urban development. These agreements include the **European**

Union (EU) convention on the conservation of wildlife and natural habitats (Bern Convention) of 1979, the EU fauna flora habitat guideline of 1992, and the 1992 convention of Rio.

See also ENVIRONMENT.

ENVIRONMENT: FORESTS. A third of Germany's land area is forested, of which 29 percent is owned by the **federal states** and 4 percent (mainly alongside water routes and highways or used by the military) by the central government (the **Bund**); 44 percent is in private hands, public corporations (Körperschaften) own 20 percent, and trusts own 4 percent. Around half of the woodland is concentrated in **Bavaria** (2.6 million hectares), **Baden-Württemberg** (1.4 million ha), **Lower Saxony** (1.2 million ha), and **Brandenburg/Berlin** (1.1 million ha). The most common trees are spruce (28 percent) and pine (23 percent), followed by beech (15 percent) and oak (10 percent). Although concerns during the early 1980s that Germany's forests would be wiped out by acid rain proved unfounded, 23 percent of trees were considered in 2013 to be severely damaged, that is, with over 26 percent defoliation; least at risk in this category were pine (12 percent), compared with spruce (28 percent), beech (48 percent), and oak (36 percent). Annual reports on the state of woodlands are issued by the Federal Ministry of Food and Agriculture. Overall forestation is increasing annually by around 10,000 hectares, with more wood being produced than is harvested. In 2004, the **federal government** launched a "charter for wood" (Charta für Holz), designed to promote the economic exploitation of Germany's extensive forestry resources and to increase the per capita population's consumption of wood products from sustainable sources by 20 percent within 10 years.

Forestry and wood processing employ 1.2 million workers and turn over 170,000 million euros annually. Some 21 percent of felled timber is destined for wood fuel and energy, and Germany's wood materials and products industry (mainly chipboard, destined for building and furniture) is the largest in Europe (2014). In 2012, Germany imported significantly more raw timber than it exported, mainly from Poland, the Czech Republic, and Latvia. Austria was a leading export destination.

See also ENVIRONMENT.

ENVIRONMENT: PROTECTED SITES. Approximately one-third of Germany's natural **environment** is under some form of graded protection. The highest level of protection is accorded to so-called nature protection reserves (Naturschutzgebiete, NSGs). The 8,480 or so NSGs in Germany cover 3.6 percent of total land area (up to 8 percent in **Hamburg, Brandenburg** and **North-Rhine Westfalia**) and protect fauna, flora, and landscapes from any form of human activity for reasons of special scientific interest, rarity, or outstanding beauty. Although some NSGs, such as the Ammerge-birge Mountains in **Bavaria** (38,876 hectares) and the Lüneburg Heath in **Lower Saxony** (23,437 ha), are very large, most are small and unlikely to protect endangered species in the long term. For this reason, between 1970 and 2004 the German authorities created 14 large national parks (National-parke), which may incorporate NSGs and include the Bavarian Forest (24,217 ha), the coastal mudflats (Wattenmeere) of **Schleswig-Holstein** (441,500 ha) and Lower Saxony (345,000 ha), and the lagoon landscape (Boddenlandschaft) of **Mecklenburg-West Pomerania** (78,600 ha). The na-tional parks are largely state owned and are typically divided into zones, with a prohibited central zone (Kernzone) providing maximum protection for plants and wildlife, and controlled pedestrian access and commercial and leisure activities in the surrounding zones. Not counting offshore areas, na-tional parks cover 0.5 percent of Germany's land surface. A much larger area (around 28 percent) is given over to around 7,400 landscape protection areas (Landschaftsschutzgebiete, LSGs). Often areas of outstanding natural beauty, these are open to farming and recreation, although building and industrial activities are strictly prohibited. Nature parks (Naturparke) number over 100 and cover 27 percent of the land. Usually privately owned, they often sustain sizable communities engaged in **agriculture** and **tourism**. In over 700 desig-nated nature forest reserves (Naturwaldreservate) across Germany, plants and trees are allowed to grow without human intervention and harvesting, and the results contribute to scientific study, **education**, and conservation of the gene pool. Sixteen large-scale biospheres (Biosphärenreservate) were created after 1979 as part of a global initiative by the **United Nations (UN)** Educational, Scientific, and Cultural Organization (UNESCO) to promote conservation and develop new ways in which human beings could live and work ecologi-cally with nature. The biospheres cover less than 4 percent of Germany's land area. Introduced in 2010, national nature monuments (Nationale Natur-monumente) are a new designation for sites, many of which are already covered in the above categories but are also considered to be of cultural or historical significance. Although the protection of the natural environment is the responsibility of the **federal states**, effective measures demand national consultation and coordination. For this purpose a supra-regional body, EU-ROPARC DEUTSCHLAND, was established (1991), and the most valuable reserves were brought together under the "national natural landscapes" (Nationale Naturlandschaften) initiative (2005).

ENVIRONMENT: WASTE MANAGEMENT. Germany's comprehen-sive and efficient system of collecting, separating, and recycling waste mate-rial employs around 160,000 in 6,000 businesses and has a turnover of 36,800 million euros (2013), which is expected to grow steadily by over 4 percent and reach 41,100 million by 2016. Waste is processed at 15,000 plants across the country, with 14 percent of raw materials used by industry now derived from recycled material. It is also estimated that recycling has contributed 20 percent of the reduction in harmful emissions that Germany has achieved as part of its Kyoto targets. From 2004 to 2012, the number of landfill sites throughout the country fell from 2,005 to 1,146. Germany's largest waste disposal company is Remondis. Founded in its present form in 2005 and based in Lünen (**North Rhine-Westfalia**), it has repeatedly won the Deutscher Nachhaltigkeitspreis (National German Sustainability Award) for modern and efficient recycling processes and for developing new energy sources. Another leading concern is the Alba Group, which was founded in 1968 in Berlin and introduced the "Berlin Model" of separating categories of waste material that was adopted as the basis of effective recycling throughout Germany.

Legislation on waste management evolved historically from prescribing how waste should be disposed of satisfactorily (the 1970s), to reducing the quantity of waste through recycling (1980s), to most recently maintaining overall levels of resources and materials for as long as possible in a so-called consumption/recycling loop (Kreislaufwirtschaft) or "sustainable substance flow" (Stoffstromwirtschaft). In particular, Germany pioneered a parallel scheme alongside existing waste disposal facilities in the form of the Dual System. Progressively extended since 1990, when it was first managed by Der Grüne Punkt-Duales System Deutschland GmbH (The Green Dot company), the system now requires all producers and distributors to license end-user retail packaging for recycling, with Green Dot competing alongside several other operators.

Since the first packaging ordinance (Verpackungsverordnung) of 1991, German producers and retailers have been obliged to take back packaging, according to its use and recyclability, and contribute to its disposal. Since 2003, producers/importers of drinks in nonreusable packaging have levied a deposit (Pfand) for each item sold to the retailer, who in turn levied the same amount on the end user/customer. The process was repeated in reverse, with the levy refunded at each stage as the item was eventually returned to the retailer/producer. The aim was to discourage the discarding of wrappings and containers and promote reusable packaging, on which no deposit was levied. In 2006, the system was extended to include some reusable packaging (with lower levies), although it was not obligatory and relied on suppliers to apply it in their own interests. Repeatedly revised and strengthened, the law is scheduled to be replaced by new legislation (Wertstoffgesetz), which would extend household recycling facilities to include nonpackaging items. Given its sophistication and legal foundation, the system is probably unique to Germany.

See also ENERGY.

ENVIRONMENT: WATER. Germany has extensive natural water resources, totaling 188,000 million cubic meters. Of the total volume, only around 17 percent are exploited, principally by **energy** suppliers (mainly for cooling, 66 percent) and the **chemicals** industry (11 percent); the public water supply accounts for 2.7 percent. Some 62 percent of drinking water is extracted from ground sources, the rest from surface water (30 percent) and springs (8 percent). Average daily per capita consumption is 122 liters, compared with 147 liters in 1990. Over 13,000 water protection areas (Wasserschutzgebiete)—nearly 14 percent of Germany's land surface—prohibit activities that can pollute natural water sources. By the 1970s, the **Rhine** at Düsseldorf, which is not only Europe's busiest river but also provides water for consumers and **industry**, had become very heavily polluted, as had the Main and Neckar rivers. Following the installation of purification plants, the introduction of phosphate-free detergents, and controls on chemicals in farming, the river system has now largely recovered, although **agricultural** pollutants have prevented Germany meeting **European Union** (**EU**) standards, in the form of the European Water Framework Directive, for surface and groundwater quality. To restore the **environment** in the former **German Democratic Republic** (**GDR**), where 46 percent of the river system had become too contaminated even for industrial use, Germany closed polluting industries and invested heavily in purification plants. Since 1990, industrial and household water consumption across Germany has fallen sharply owing to conservation and the rising costs of extraction and purification.

Alongside waste disposal, the supply and protection of natural water sources is governed by legislation (Wasserhaushaltsgesetz), first passed in 1957 and revised in 2009–2010 as part of the process of **federalism reform** to enable the central government (the **Bund**) to frame nationwide directives within the context of concurrent legislation. Public and private utilities coexist in supplying water, and charges to consumers are regulated by public authorities and legislation.

ENZENSBERGER, HANS MAGNUS (1929–). Writer, editor, and translator. Hans Magnus Enzensberger was born in Kaufbeuren (**Bavaria**) and studied German literature and philosophy. He lived in **Hamburg, Berlin**, and Munich and in the United States (U.S.), Mexico, and Cuba. A member of **Group 47**, he made his debut as a lyricist in the 1950s and 1960s before writing political essays, short stories, radio plays, and children's books. A driving force of the intellectual and cultural scene in the Federal Republic of Germany (FRG) and one of the last eminent intellectuals to have experienced the Third Reich firshand, he declared the "death of literature" in 1968 and told writers to move from their desks onto the streets. An advocate of the author's duty to politicize the readership, he founded the influential left-wing journal *Kursbuch* in 1965. During the 1980s and 1990s, he wrote several political essays in which he confronted issues of the time. His numerous works also include operas and plays, and he worked as a translator and college teacher. In 1980, he cofounded *TransAtlantik*, which aspired to be comparable to the *New Yorker* magazine, and from 1985 edited *Die Andere Bibliothek*, which currently lists 367 volumes. His awards include the Georg Büchner Prize (1963), the Heinrich Böll Prize (1985), the Heinrich Heine Prize (1998), and Pour le mérite (2000). His works include *Verteidigung der Wölfe* (a collection of lyric poetry, 1957), the play *Der Untergang der Titanic* (1980), the essay "Die Große Wanderung" (1992), and the book *The Silences of Hammerstein* (2008). In 2010, *The Guardian* newspaper described Enzensberger, together with **Grass** and **Walser**, as "one of the holy trinity of German postwar literature."

EPPELMANN, RAINER (1943–). Theologian and politician. Born in **Berlin**, Rainer Eppelmann attended school in the west of the city after World War II, although the erection of the **Berlin Wall** (1961) prevented him from completing his higher school certificate (**Abitur**), and he worked in east Berlin as a roofer. After training as a bricklayer (1962–1965), he continued in the trade until 1966, when he was sentenced to eight months in prison for refusing to do national service and take an oath as a noncombatant soldier. He went on to study theology at a Protestant college in East Berlin (1969–1974) before working as a priest in the Samaritans community and performing youth work in the city's Friedrichshain district. Eppelmann's insistence on combining his role as a priest with an active commitment to political reform soon led to conflict with the authorities of the **German Democratic Republic (GDR)**. In September 1981, he published a letter to the East German leader, **Erich Honecker**, demanding a ban on toy guns for children and an end to military training as a compulsory subject in schools. The following January, Eppelmann was briefly arrested after publishing a call for "peace, not arms" (the so-called Berliner Appell). In 1985, with 34 others, he signed a protest calling for freedom of expression, the right to travel and to form associations, and equality of educational opportunity, regardless of religion or belief. He later complained to the East German secret service, the **Stasi**, about eavesdropping equipment he had found in his apartment (1988) and registered a protest that the ruling **Socialist Unity Party of Germany (SED)** had falsified electoral results in local elections in Friedrichshain (May 1989). In October 1989, he cofounded and was spokesman for the dissident group **Democratic Awakening (DA)**. After the fall of the regime, he joined the interim government of **Hans Modrow** as minister without portfolio (February 1990). When Wolfgang Schnur resigned as the DA's leader, Eppelmann took over and, following national elections in March, was one of four party members elected to the **People's Chamber**. A month later, the party merged with the East German **Christian Democratic**

Union (CDU). Between April and October 1990, he served as minister for disarmament and defense in the cabinet of **Lothar de Maizière**, where he worked for the dissolution of the **Warsaw Pact**.

After reunification, Eppelmann was elected deputy chairman of the CDU in **Brandenburg** and deputy in the **Bundestag** (1990–2005), where he led a commission investigating the SED dictatorship (Enquête-Kommission zur Aufarbeitung und Folgen der SED-Diktatur), which presented its final report in 1994. He chaired the CDU's **trade union** association, the Christlich-Demokratische Arbeitnehmerschaft (CDA, 1994–2001), and served on the CDU presidium (1998–2000). In 1998, he became honorary chairman of the Bundesstiftung zur Aufarbeitung der SED-Diktatur, a foundation to reappraise the SED regime, retaining the position after leaving the Bundestag. As well as maintaining an extensive archive for researchers and publishing its findings, the foundation—in collaboration with the daily newspapers *Die Welt* and *BILD*—mounted in 2011 a major exhibition on the border between East and West Germany to commemorate the 50th anniversary of the erection of the Berlin Wall.

EPPLER, ERHARD (1926–). Social Democratic Party of Germany (**SPD**) politician. Erhard Eppler was born in Ulm, studied German **language**, **literature**, and history, and worked for eight years as a schoolteacher. He opposed postwar German rearmament and, alongside **Gustav Heinemann**, cofounded the All-German People's Party (Gesamtdeutsche Volkspartei, GVP) in 1952, which advocated German neutrality as a necessary precondition of reunification. He left the GVP in 1955 and the following year joined the SPD, which he later represented in the **Bundestag** (1961–1976). Eppler held various offices, including parliamentary spokesman on **foreign policy** (1967–1968) and leader of the **Baden-Württemberg** SPD (1973–1981), and he was recruited by **Willy Brandt**, who had a special interest in Third World development, as federal minister for economic cooperation (1968–1974), but resigned when **Helmut Schmidt** succeeded Brandt as **federal chancellor** (1974).

Eppler became active in the peace and ecology movement that emerged during the 1980s, although he remained on the national SPD executive (1970–1991) and presidium (1973–1989, with an interruption during 1982–1984), chaired the party's commission on basic policy values (Grundwertekommission, 1973–1992), represented his party in the Baden-Württemberg regional parliament (1976–1982), and served as deputy chairman on policy commissions (1985–1989). With **Hans-Jochen Vogel**, Eppler was an architect of the Berlin Program. Adopted in December 1989, this represented the SPD's most significant statement of basic policy since the 1959 Godesberg Program and was notable for reorienting the party toward the new social movements of the 1980s, including **women's** rights, concerns for the **environment**, global peace, and economic justice. A political moderate, Eppler was regarded as one of the SPD's leading thinkers and policy makers. A committed Christian, he served on the synod of the organization of German evangelical churches (EKD, 1968–1984) and played a leading role in the Deutscher Evangelischer Kirchentag (German Evangelical Conference, DEK), where, among other offices, he was president (1989–1991). In 1985, he was elected to the **PEN** Club and has published widely on contemporary politics. In 1991, he withdrew from all political posts.

ERHARD, LUDWIG (1897–1977). Christian Democratic Union (CDU) politician and **federal chancellor**, 1963–1966. Ludwig Erhard was born in Fürth (**Bavaria**) and trained in commerce (1913–1916) before serving in World War I (1916–1919), where he was severely wounded. After studying business and economics in Nuremberg (1919–1922) and Frankfurt (1922–1925), where he earned a doctorate, he managed the family textile business (1925–1928), worked for a consumer research institute in Nuremberg (1928–1942), and supervised glass manufacture in Lorraine (1940–1945). In 1942, he founded his own institute for consumer research and in 1943–1944 wrote a pamphlet on financing war and debt consolidation, in which he outlined a strategy for rebuilding the postwar economy. In occupied postwar Germany, Erhard was appointed economics minister in Bavaria (1945–1946) and, from 1948, director of the combined economic area of the western zones, where he laid the groundwork for **currency** reform and the introduction of the Deutsche Mark (DM). As economics minister under Chancellor **Konrad Adenauer** in the newly founded Federal Republic of Germany (FRG, 1949–1963), Erhard was credited with masterminding national economic recovery according to the principles of a **social market economy**. After Adenauer's resignation, he served as federal chancellor from 1963, although differences over financial and economic policy between the ruling CDU and the **Free Democratic Party (FDP)** eventually led to the coalition's collapse. Economic recession; crisis in the coal industry; unemployment; and demands from U.S. president Lyndon B. Johnson to increase reparations as a contribution to the U.S. war effort in Vietnam (which began seriously in 1965) further undermined Erhard's standing, and he resigned in 1966. During the oil crisis of 1973, Erhard, seeing the basis of the social market threatened, argued for moderate government expenditure to counter unemployment and inflation. A member of the **Bundestag** from 1949, Erhard chaired the CDU briefly during 1966–1967. His book on German economic policy, *Deutsche Wirtschaftspolitik*, appeared in 1962.

ETHNIC MINORITIES. Although the **Basic Law** (**BL**, article 3) prohibits discrimination against individuals on grounds of gender, origin, race, language, and political or religious beliefs, it does not mention specific national or ethnic minorities. In practice, however, Germany explicitly recognizes four such minorities: Sorbs, Frisians, Danes, and Sinti/Roma, whose rights and privileges are generally enshrined in the constitutions of the **federal states** in which they live. In addition, the European Charter for Regional or Minority Languages entered German law in 1998–1999. Apart from reinforcing the protection of general human rights for minorities, the charter specifically encourages signatory states to promote minority languages in all areas of public life. In 2005, a minorities secretariat was set up in Berlin to coordinate the exchange of information among the **Bundestag**, the government, and the minorities, and to monitor and report on their concerns and circumstances. The secretariat also informs the minorities and their associations about developments at government level, helps them broaden their public profile, and acts as a conduit between the minorities and other national and international organizations. Other numerically significant minorities are Turks, Poles, and Italians.

ETHNIC MINORITIES: DANES. From the 15th century onward, the areas of Schleswig (in the north) and Holstein (to the south) in the Jutland peninsula maintained a complex territorial relationship with neighboring Denmark, being partly under Danish and partly under German rule. Following the expulsion of the Danish army (1864), both became a Prussian province and subsequently part of the German Empire (1871). The population in the north maintained strong links with Denmark, and after the German defeat in World War I and a controversial referendum (1920), northern Schleswig was ceded to the Danes. After World War II, the Danes turned down an offer by the postwar British occupation authorities to reincorporate all or part of southern Schleswig into Denmark (including the option of a plebiscite); despite doubts about its long-term economic and political viability, **Schleswig-Holstein** joined the Federal Republic of Germany (FRG) as a federal state in 1949. The Danish minority in the far north of the state, in southern Schleswig, numbers around 50,000 people, almost all German nationals. The umbrella organization for cultural activities and fostering the Danish language, which is commonly used in the region, is the Flensburg-based SSF (Sydslesvigsk Forening), with which 24 associations are affiliated. The Dänischer Schulverein (Danish School Association) maintains a large network of schools, ranging from nurseries to high schools, vocational schools, and boarding facilities. Both the German and Danish states contribute generously to these and other amenities, including political activities, **sport**, hospitals, care for the aged, churches, and a Danish-language newspaper. A political party, the SSW (Südschleswigscher Wählerverband), founded in 1948, has been exempt from the 5 percent entry hurdle to the Bundestag since 1953; since 1955 the exemption has also applied to the **Landtag**. In the 2012 regional election, the SSW returned three deputies, making it the third strongest party. Politically it stands between the two main national parties, the **Christian Democratic Union (CDU)** and the **Social Democratic Party (SPD)**, and orients itself closely to Scandinavian values. Rights for the Danish minority are anchored in the state constitution for Schleswig-Holstein and in the Treaty on Unification.

ETHNIC MINORITIES: FRISIANS. The descendants of a Germanic or Germanicized tribe inhabiting the **North Sea** coasts of the Netherlands, Denmark, and Germany, the German Frisians (or Friesians) now inhabit the coastal areas and islands of northern **Lower Saxony** (where they are known as east Frisians) and western **Schleswig-Holstein** (north Frisians). Their tradition of dyke building and coastal protection stretches back several centuries. Most Frisians (around 500,000) actually live in the neighboring Netherlands (the west Frisians), where their language enjoys a special status. Lower Saxony is home to about 350,000 Frisians, although their language is extinct there, with the exception of a tiny pocket of 1,500 speakers farther inland in the Saterland community of Cloppenburg. Of 50,000 estimated north Frisians in Schleswig-Holstein, up to 10,000 actively speak the north Frisian variety of the language, which is protected under the terms of the European Charter for Regional or Minority Languages, with perhaps as many more having a passive knowledge of it. North Frisian is taught in 27 schools (in 2006–2007), mainly at the primary level, and can be studied at the universities of Kiel and Flensburg. The Frisian language, which has several dialects—some under threat of extinction—also has a tradition of written dictionaries, teaching materials, and literature. Umbrella organizations include the Interfriesischer Rat (Interfrisian Council) or Friesenrat (Frisian Council), founded in 1998 to promote cooperation among the west, east, and north Frisian communities, and the Nordfriisk Institut (North Frisian Institute, founded 1948), which is dedicated to fostering research into and the teaching of north Frisian language, history, and culture.

ETHNIC MINORITIES: ITALIANS. Of around 784,000 citizens with an Italian **migration background**, 529,000 are registered Italian nationals. Significant numbers of (male) Italians were recruited to work temporarily in Germany under the first intergovernmental agreement in 1955, with migration reaching a peak during the 1960s and early 1970s, although most of the 3.6 million "guest workers" and their dependents eventually returned home. Many settled in **Baden-Württemberg**, which now claims to have the largest single Italian migrant community—extending into the second and third generations—outside Buenos Aires and Rio de Janeiro: they number 165,000, with 40,000 concentrated in the Stuttgart industrial area. The region proved especially attractive because of its proximity to Italy. This contributed to a "transnational migration," wherein migrants maintain close links with their homeland, which they frequently visit and never definitively leave.

Coming largely from poor, rural backgrounds in southern Italy, with low levels of **education** and no foreign-language skills or preparation for work abroad, Italian migrants were not always sympathetically regarded by Germans in the early years, and they relied heavily on pastoral assistance from Roman Catholic church missions (Missione Cattolica Italiana). Catholic centers, often covering very large communities, sprang up in major cities of the industrial Ruhr to provide extensive support facilities, especially for incoming families. German attitudes to the **immigrants** were initially rooted in a complex mixture of distrust and prejudice (partly fueled by resentment at Italy's role in World War II), coupled with romantic notions nurtured by popular Italian films and music (several singers were big hits in the 1950s). Gradually, however, perceptions shifted toward an appreciation of the country's cuisine (many Italians set up restaurants, introducing Germans to new foods), its natural beauty (accessible to Germans through mass tourism), stylish fashion products, and the industry and inventiveness of the workforce. Nevertheless, long after the guest worker era, studies indicated relatively low levels of educational achievement among Italian children, who, coming from poor educational backgrounds, found themselves disadvantaged when entering the selective German school system. Despite achieving economic prosperity and assimilation in the workplace (aided by the integrative policies of the **European Union [EU]**), Italians failed to penetrate senior management and the upper- and middle-class professions to the extent that they were able to in other European countries and the United States. Reasons for this may lie in the rural origins and enduring conservative values of the community, alongside its insistence on retaining close physical links with the homeland.

ETHNIC MINORITIES: POLES. After Turks, Poles constitute the second largest ethnic minority in Germany. Around 1.5 million Poles have a **migration background**, over half of whom entered Germany as descendants of ethnic Germans in eastern Europe (**Aussiedler**) during the 1980s and early 1990s. Between 400,000 and 500,000 are registered **foreigners**, often on time-limited work contracts. Although Poles, as citizens of the **European Union (EU)**, have moved to Germany in increasing numbers since 2011, **immigration** dates back 200 years. Waves of politically motivated immigrants entered, for example, in the 18th century (when Poland was partitioned), the 19th century (following failed uprisings), and the 20th century (during and following the world wars, after the uprisings of 1956 and 1968, and in response to the declaration of a state of emergency in 1981). In the late

1800s, many also came to work in the coal and steel industries of **North Rhine-Westfalia** (**NRW**), which, of all the **federal states**, still has the largest population with a Polish background (567,000), followed by Berlin (with up to 200,000). In 2011–2012, NRW mounted a festival celebrating links with Poland (Poland-North Rhine-Westfalia Year), and it has 60 schools offering Polish-language courses and 2,000 Polish students in higher **education**. Sizable communities are also found in **Baden-Württemberg** (182,000) and **Bavaria** (161,000).

Despite the large numbers of immigrant Poles and their descendants, integration for a community that refers to itself as "Polonia" has never presented the same problems that the Turkish minority has had. The Konvent der polnischen Organisationen in Deutschland (Convention of Polish Organizations in Germany), founded in 1998 as an umbrella organization for groups and associations, is recognized by the German government as representing the interests of Polish residents. Other groups, which are equally invisible to the wider German public, include Oświata (for Polish schools), the Deutsch-Polnisches Jugendwerk (for youth), and the Verein Polnischer Frauen in Wirtschaft und Kultur (for **women**). Attitudinal differences can be drawn between older-generation Poles concerned to preserve traditional national customs and younger, German-speaking migrants keen to interact with incomers from other backgrounds.

ETHNIC MINORITIES: SINTI AND ROMA. According to Roma and Sinti tradition, this minority has been established in the German-speaking area for 2,000 years, with a presence documented since the 14th century. Although widely associated with itinerant gypsies, Sinti and Roma came to be represented in most occupations and professions and were fully assimilated in their home countries of eastern and western Europe. Over 500,000 racially stigmatized Sinti/Roma from Germany and occupied territories perished in National Socialist concentration camps, however, and it is estimated that the surviving German community currently numbers no more than 70,000 (although the Sinti Alliance Germany claims 150,000). Although not as geographically delimited as Sorbs, Frisians, and Danes, Sinti/Roma now live mostly in the **eastern federal states** and the conurbations of **Berlin**, **Hamburg**, the **Rhine**-Ruhr and Rhine-Main areas, and Kiel. As well as the German **language**, Sinti/Roma in Germany speak a particular variety of Romany (derived from ancient Sanskrit), although National Socialist persecutions have greatly undermined the continuity of linguistic and cultural traditions in individual communities. The Zentralrat Deutscher Sinti und Roma (Central Council of German Sinti and Roma), with 15 regional associations, was founded in 1982 and liaises with national and regional governments to combat discrimination and protect the rights of the minority. It has negotiated compensation for victims of the National Socialists, ended discriminatory practices of the police and judiciary, and campaigned against negative portrayals of Sinti in the **media**. In 1997, the council opened a national documentation and cultural center in Heidelberg, and in 2012 a memorial to victims of persecution was officially dedicated in Berlin. The Sinti Allianz Deutschland (Sinti Alliance Germany, since 2013 based in Hildesheim) was founded in 2000 by 20 representatives of Sinti tribes. Independent and self-financing, the alliance focuses on protecting and nurturing cultural customs that are specific to the Sinti, as opposed to Roma.

ETHNIC MINORITES: SORBS. Of an estimated 60,000 western Slav Sorbs in Germany, the remnants of an influx of western Slav tribes in the migrations of the sixth century, two-thirds, mainly Roman Catholic, live around the southern reaches of the Spree River in eastern **Saxony** (the Spree forest and Oberlausitz/Upper Lusatia region), and the remainder, largely Protestant, in **Brandenburg** (Niederlausitz/Lower Lusatia). There is also a small Sorb presence across the border in Poland, in an area that belonged to Germany before 1945 and from which many German citizens were expelled at the end of World War II. The Soviet Union's designation of Saxony as a settlement area for German expellees in general diluted the Sorbian presence in the region. Although the **German Democratic Republic (GDR)** recognized the Sorbs as a national minority (article 40 of the 1968 constitution), set up cultural institutions, and—at least in the early years—officially promoted their language, the priorities of integration into a socialist political and economic system, which involved the collectivization of **agriculture** and the destruction of communities by opencast coal mining, undermined the minority's linguistic and family traditions in the longer term. It is estimated that the Sorbian population fell by 50 percent during this period. The Domowina, founded in 1912 as an independent umbrella organization for Sorbs and suppressed by the National Socialists, reemerged in 1945, but was exploited as a vehicle for policies of the **Socialist Unity Party of Germany** (SED) and was regarded with suspicion by Catholic Sorbs in particular. In 1990–1991, the Domowina reconstituted itself as an independent organization, widened its membership to include individuals and regional associations, and adopted a new program; it currently has around 7,300 members.

The Sorbs' cultural "capital" is the city of Bautzen in Saxony, although Cottbus (Brandenburg) is also a center. The language and customs of the Sorbs, who have their own **radio/television** stations and publishing house (the Domowina-Verlag, Bautzen), are protected in the state constitutions of Brandenburg and Saxony. In practice, unemployment and increased mobility since reunification present greater threats to their cultural identity than historical attempts at Germanicization. The main Sorb cultural organizations include the Institut für Sobrastik (Institute for Sorbian Studies) at the University of Leipzig, which trains Sorb teachers and scholars, and the Sorbisches

Institut (Sorbian Institute) in Bautzen, which, founded in 1991 and jointly supported by the **Bund** and the states of Brandenburg and Saxony, fosters Sorbian language, culture, and traditions; produces media material; and maintains premises for various activities. A political party, the Wendische Volkspartei, founded in 2005 in Brandenburg and renamed the Lausitzer Allianz (Lusatia Alliance) in 2010, lobbies for Sorb interests, although it has enjoyed only marginal electoral success at the municipal level. In May 2008, **Stanislaw Tillich**, in Saxony, became the first Sorb to head a regional government.

ETHNIC MINORITIES: TURKS. Almost a quarter of registered **foreigners** in Germany are Turks (1.7 million), followed by Poles (530,000) and Italians (529,000). Also counting **immigrants**, descendants with a **migration background**, and 471,000 children born in Germany to Turkish parents (revealed in 2013 following a change in statistical collection), the total—which includes 800,000 or so Kurds—is almost three million, making them the country's largest ethnic minority. Although economic and military links between Germany and Turkey date from the 19th century, Turks did not begin to enter the country in significant numbers until after 1961, when Turkey agreed to provide short-term "guest workers" for Germany's industries experiencing labor shortages during its economic boom. Many of these workers were joined by their families and stayed to set up homes and businesses, with subsequent generations entering all areas of occupational, professional, cultural, and political life. Guest-worker recruitment was halted during the recession of 1973, but Turks, especially Kurds, continued to enter the country as refugees. After a military Putsch in Turkey in 1980, intellectuals and professionals also sought **asylum** in the Federal Republic. **Berlin** is home to the largest single Turkish community (176,000 or 5 percent of the city's population), and between 1962 and 2010 around one million settled in the towns and cities of **North Rhine-Westfalia**, which has a current Turkish population of 821,000 (taking account of returnees and other changes).

Turks are predominantly Sunni Muslims, with a much smaller proportion of Alevites. There are an estimated 3,000 mosques and prayer houses in Germany, but a project to erect a large central mosque in Cologne, launched in 1996, was dogged by disputes over its size and design (by German architects), and it had still not been completed by 2016. With a capacity for 1,200 and financed wholly by private donations and the Muslim community, the building was projected to cost over 30 million euros. There are also numerous German-Turkish institutions and foundations for promoting intercommunity relations, as well as political and cultural organizations. Of religiously oriented associations, the Cologne-based DITIB (Türkisch-Islamische Union der Anstalt für Religion), founded in 1984, claims to represent the religious and cultural interests of the majority of Turks in Germany. The IGMG (Islamische Gemeinschaft Milli Görüs), with roots dating back to 1976 in Cologne, has a religious and social outlook that the **Federal Office for the Protection of the Constitution** regards as a potential threat to the German democratic system. The VIKZ (Verband der Islamischen Kulturzentren), also based in Cologne, is the oldest Turkish-Islamist organization active in Germany and aims to foster Islamic values among young people. The AABF (Alevitische Gemeinde Deutschland) was founded in 1990 (renamed in 1994) to meet the needs of the expatriate Alevite community.

Turks are served by several daily newspapers, many of which maintained editorial branches in Frankfurt/Main until falling circulations (the result of competition from digital media and the emergence of a German-speaking younger generation only marginally interested in domestic Turkish issues) forced some closures. Leading titles include *Hürriyet* (the oldest and best known, and produced in Frankfurt from 1969 until 2013), *Zaman* (the only subscription newspaper and with a fairly stable readership), *Milliyet*, *Sabah*, and *Türkiye*. Although Turks can now access dozens of Turkish-language cable and satellite **television** channels, Kanal Avrup (founded in Duisburg in 2005) broadcasts specifically to expatriate Turks in Germany and the rest of Europe, while the Westdeutscher Rundfunk (WDR) has been transmitting news and reportage in Turkish on its popular evening **radio** program, *Köln Radyosu*, since 1964. Leading contributors to literature and theater include the Turkish-born Ermine Sergi Özdamar and Aras Ören, both former guest workers.

A long-standing debate about the difficulties of integrating Turkish immigrants into German society has focused on combating the low levels of educational achievement in schools and colleges compared with other migrant groups and on the lack of contact with Germans (e.g., lack of intermarriage). The language barrier and the cultural isolation of **women** have also been highlighted. At the same time Turks, who may be entitled to vote either in Germany or Turkey, are a significant group for politicians, both in the Federal Republic, where the **Green Party** and the **Social Democratic Party of Germany** (**SPD**) have traditionally relied on their votes, and for Turkish leaders such as President Erdogan, who in 2010 called for the creation of Turkish-language high schools (Gymnasien) in Germany. The failed coup in Turkey in July 2016 also had repercussions for the Turkish community in Germany.

EU. *See* EUROPEAN UNION (EU).

EURO PLUS PACT. Promoted in particular by the German government to help stabilize the Greek economy during the **eurozone crisis**, which broke in 2009, and to deepen financial and economic unity throughout the single

currency area, the pact was adopted in March/June 2011 by the 17 eurozone states, although it was open to all **European Union (EU)** members and was subsequently joined by Bulgaria, Denmark, Latvia, Lithuania, Poland, and Romania (hence the "plus" in the title). The pact aims to improve competitiveness (e.g., through a more favorable business environment, **education** and research, and greater competition in the service sector), raise employment (by lowering wage costs and creating a flexible labor market), foster sustainable public finances (by adjusting **pensions** to meet changing demographic trends, bringing older persons back into work, and applying national rules on debt control), reinforce financial stability (through systems of national bank regulation), and coordinate **taxation** policy across member states. The pact is integrated into the **European Semester**, and heads of state meet annually to determine objectives and review progress. At the same time, each country is free to determine how the pact is implemented, and it has been criticized as being too broadly formulated.

EUROPEAN CENTRAL BANK (ECB). Created in 1998 as part of the process of monetary union and the creation of a single **currency** (the euro) for the **European Union (EU)**, the ECB controls monetary policy for those member states that have joined the eurozone. Since the Treaty of Lisbon (2007), it has been a formal institution of the EU. The bank's main purpose is to maintain stable prices by controlling inflation, which it achieves by setting interest rates that apply uniformly across the zone. Based in Frankfurt/Main and closely modeled on the **German Federal Bank**, it is headed by an executive board comprising a president, vice president, and four members nominated by eurozone member states. Strategic decisions are led by a governing council, which includes a five-person executive board and the 19 heads of the central banks of the eurozone countries. A general council liaises with non-eurozone EU states, which are free to determine their own monetary policies. The bank's first president was Wim Duisenberg, followed by Jean-Claude Trichet (2003), and Mario Draghi (2011). Almost 50 percent of its reserves (10,800 million euros) come from the German Federal Bank, the French Banque de National, and the Italian Banca d'Italia.

The **eurozone crisis**, which broke in October 2009, exposed the dangers and limitations of applying a single monetary policy, largely based on interest rates, to member states with different economies, growth patterns, and debt levels. Unable even to negotiate with a single finance minister (the EU does not have one), the ECB must juggle the interests of all eurozone member states. In practice, although nominally independent and above national politics, the bank is dominated by the zone's economically most powerful countries, especially Germany. Since financial transfers in the eurozone are not vertical (from the center to areas of need within a state) but primarily horizontal (from state to state), Germany was able during the crisis to impose austerity on Spain or Greece without direct electoral backlash. Moreover, while central banks in the United States and Great Britain can negotiate directly with their governments to influence wider economic policy beyond the purely fiscal (e.g., to influence labor and employment), the restricted mandate of the ECB prevents this within the EU. European Union treaties also prohibit the ECB from bailing out or financing governments, for example through buying their sovereign bonds (i.e., government national debt)—a constraint that was strongly upheld by Germany as the eurozone states negotiated to combat the emergency.

As fears grew during the crisis that high borrowing costs might force some states out of the eurozone, Draghi dramatically announced that "the ECB is ready to do whatever it takes to preserve the euro" (July 2012), which was interpreted to mean that the bank might indeed purchase sovereign bonds, underwritten by the bank, in unlimited quantities. In August 2012, the ECB went on to draw up a mechanism for the purchase of such bonds (the Outright Monetary Transactions, OMT), although the governor of the German Federal Bank, Jens Weidmann, voted against it at the meeting of the governing council in September. In the event, these preparations alone were enough to relieve speculators' pressure on the euro, and by 2015 no bonds had actually been purchased through OMT, whose legality was challenged in Germany by a group of German politicians and economists in an appeal to the **Federal Constitutional Court (FCC)**. Although the FCC reserved the right to rule independently in the future, both it and the European Court of Justice (ECJ) eventually endorsed OMT (2015/2016). While a negative ruling by the FCC would not be binding on the ECB, the German Federal Bank's withdrawal from the OMT program could lead to its collapse.

Despite progress on structural reforms in Spain and Italy, by 2013 it was clear that the focus of the eurozone's problems was shifting away from simply meeting the costs of borrowing needed to service government debt toward the twin threats of deflation and recession (in 2013/2014, inflation fell below zero, for the first time since 2009, while real GDP growth was below 1 percent). The ECB therefore decided to intervene more directly in order to stimulate growth by using newly created money to purchase, each month starting in March 2015, 60,000 million euros of sovereign debt from national and supranational institutions, mostly held in banks and pension/insurance funds. Otherwise known as quantitative easing (QE), the purchases would hopefully release cash in affected countries for genuine investment and would continue until at least the end of September 2016 or until inflation approached 2 percent. German dissenters, including Weidmann and Sabine Lautenschläger, the German member of the ECB's executive board, fiercely opposed the program, and while they were unable to veto it, their pressure ensured that national banks, not the euro system as a whole, would meet 80 percent of purchases and possible losses—a measure that could help avoid the claim that the ECB had exceeded its mandate by bailing out governments and issuing fully mutualized eurobonds (where the risk would be met entirely by the central bank and its eurozone underwriters). Nevertheless, Federal Chancellor **Angela Merkel**, without criticizing the ECB directly, expressed concern that QE might induce governments to pull back on structural economic and fiscal reform. Others felt that the purchases by the national banks and the failure to fully mutualize the debt signaled that the eurozone was failing to move toward a genuine single-currency union.

EUROPEAN (ECONOMIC) COMMUNITY. *See* EUROPEAN UNION (EU).

EUROPEAN FINANCIAL STABILITY FACILITY (EFSF). Following a meeting of the **ECOFIN Council** in May 2010, the EFSF was created by member states of the single **currency** (euro) area of the **European Union (EU)** to provide financial assistance to countries experiencing acute budgetary problems in the wake of the **eurozone crisis**. A temporary mechanism, the EFSF was intended to issue bonds or other debt instruments on the capital markets and lend the proceeds to target countries, mainly Greece, but also Portugal and Ireland. It would further provide loans to governments to recapitalize banks. The fund of 440,000 million euros was guaranteed up to a total of 780,000 million euros by member states in proportion to their national share of the capital of the **European Central Bank (ECB)**, which in the case of Germany, the largest contributor (211,000 million euros), was 27 percent. Payouts were linked to fiscal and economic reforms in the receiving countries and monitored by the troika of the European Commission, the ECB, and the International Monetary Fund (IMF). Following her reelection in September 2009, German chancellor **Angela Merkel**'s popularity nosedived (Germany was the largest contributor to the fund), and her party experienced a series of defeats in elections in the **federal states**. In the face of the unrelenting financial crisis, it was realized that the EFSF, scheduled to run out in 2013, was inadequate, and it was replaced on 8 October 2012 by a permanent scheme, the **European Stability Mechanism (ESM)**. During the interim period, Merkel steadfastly resisted proposals to issue eurobonds, whereby the eurozone as a whole would guarantee loans to indebted states at favorable rates, and insisted on binding members to common budget rules in the new rescue package.

EUROPEAN FINANCIAL STABILITY MECHANISM (EFSM). Created in May 2010 alongside the **European Financial Stability Facility (EFSF)**, the EFSM was a temporary fund contributing 60,000 million euros for the financial stabilization of **European Union (EU)** member states hit by the **eurozone crisis**. Its beneficiaries were Ireland and Portugal. Germany contributed 20 percent of the total fund, in proportion to its share of the EU budget. The fund was superseded by the **European Stability Mechanism (ESM)**, inaugurated in October 2012.

EUROPEAN MONETARY UNION (EMU). Governments of the European Economic Community (EEC) agreed to make monetary union a goal at a conference at the Hague in 1969, and the project of full European economic and monetary union was placed on the agenda of the European Council by German foreign minister **Hans-Dietrich Genscher** in 1988. Despite skepticism and indifference on the part of many Germans and **industry**, EMU was actively promoted by Chancellor **Helmut Kohl** as part of his "Europeanization" of Germany, in which cooperation with France was a key element. The EMU represented a decisive move beyond earlier attempts to harmonize **currencies** of member states of the EEC/**European Union (EU)**, notably through the "snake": an agreement in 1972 to limit currency exchange rates to 2.25 percent. In 1979, the snake was replaced by the European Exchange Rate Mechanism (ERM) within the framework of the European Monetary System (EMS), which was the brainchild of Chancellor **Helmut Schmidt** and French president Valéry Giscard d'Estaing. The aim was to stabilize exchange rates, control inflation, and stimulate trade. Member states linked their currencies to a central European Currency Unit (ECU), which was calculated daily from the weighted average of the "basket" of EMS currencies. Although the ECU was never a circulated **currency**, it was used in some financial transactions. If a currency fluctuated beyond an agreed upon, narrow margin, national central banks and the European Monetary Cooperation Fund (EMCF) intervened to support it. The system, in which the West German mark (DM) acted as an anchor, partly disintegrated in 1992–1993 as some currencies proved unable to sustain these limits, especially when the **German Federal Bank** maintained high interest rates in response to the domestic economic strains of reunification. The Spanish peseta was devalued, and the British pound and Italian lira quit the ERM altogether.

As part of a major initiative to deepen European integration, European Community leaders agreed on a roadmap for EMU at a summit in Maastricht (February 1992). The Treaty of Maastricht, which emerged from the summit, laid down criteria for the convergence of national economies in the areas of price stability and inflation, government debt, interest rates, and exchange rates. In January 1994, the European Monetary Institute (EMI) was established to promote cooperation between the EU national central banks and prepare the ground for full monetary union. This process included the creation of a **European Central Bank (ECB)** and the European System of Central Banks (ESCB), and the EMI submitted annual reports on progress between 1994 and 1997. An EU summit in Madrid (1995) agreed to a timetable for union and, following a suggestion by German finance minister **Theo Waigel**, gave the new currency its name: the euro. Finally, in May 1998, the Council of the EU declared that 11 member states, including Germany, had qualified for participation in the EMU. The ECB began functioning on 1 June 1998 (the EMI was dissolved) and in January the following year assumed responsibility for monetary policy in the so-called eurozone. At the same time, participating countries locked their exchange rates and adopted the euro as the single European currency, which replaced the ECU. In addition, stock markets and non-cash money transfers were transacted in euros, and the old ERM was superseded by ERM II, which linked the currencies of some states outside the main eurozone to the euro. Euro coins and notes were introduced on 1 January 2002, and national currencies of participating states were withdrawn from circulation on 30 June. European Union countries that had not adopted the euro were obliged to participate in the ERM II for at least two years before joining the eurozone.

The projected economic benefits of the EMU included lower interstate transaction costs, reduced exchange rate risks, increased competition, and the integration and expansion of European financial markets. Upon its introduction, the euro became a global currency alongside the dollar, and by 2016 it had been adopted in 19 of the 28 states of the EU. The new currency is estimated to have raised the level of trade both within the eurozone itself and with outside countries, although there is some uncertainty over the scale of the increase. In 2009, the eurozone entered a prolonged crisis as the global economy contracted and as banks and several member states incurred dangerous levels of debt.

See also BALANCE OF PAYMENTS; EUROZONE CRISIS.

EUROPEAN PARLIAMENT. *See* ELECTORAL SYSTEM; EUROPEAN UNION (EU).

EUROPEAN SEMESTER. Partly in response to the **eurozone crisis**, the Council of the **European Union** (**EU**) agreed in June 2010 on a system of biannual reporting by member states, including those in the euro area, in order to monitor progress toward achieving the economic and social targets set out in the 10-year Europe 2020 reform program. Called the European Semester, the program aimed to establish a long-term model of economic growth and stability for the EU that also covered employment, **education**, research and innovation, social inclusion, poverty reduction, and climate/ **energy**. The semester starts when the EU Commission adopts its Annual Growth Survey, usually toward the end of the year, which sets out EU priorities for the coming year to boost growth and job creation. The EU Commission assesses these programs and provides country-specific recommendations, which are considered and endorsed by the EU Council before member states are issued with policy advice on their national **budgets**. Provisions exist for warnings, incentives, and sanctions in the case of persisting budgetary imbalances, notably under the terms of the **Treaty on Stability, Coordination and Governance (TSCG)**, which is linked to the semester. The member states vary in their implementation of the process, but responsibility in Germany lies with the **Bundestag** and **Bundesrat**, with the involvement of finance ministers of the **federal states** and the Stability Council (Stabilitätsrat), which was set up as part of the national **federalism reform** process in order to forestall budgetary crises.

EUROPEAN STABILITY MECHANISM (ESM). Replacing previous mechanisms—the **European Financial Stability Facility (EFSF)** and the **European Financial Stability Mechanism (EFSM)**, which had been set up to stabilize the economies of the eurozone within the **European Union (EU)** in the wake of the financial crisis that struck in 2009/2010—the ESM was agreed to by the 17 eurozone finance ministers in January 2012 and was inaugurated in October (Treaty on the European Stability Mechanism). The aim was to provide long-term stability for the euro area and, linked with the **Treaty on Stability, Coordination and Governance (TSCG)**, to overhaul its economic and fiscal structures. The ESM is essentially a large fund providing bailouts, subject to the conditions of the TSCG, to restore the creditworthiness of embattled eurozone economies running unsustainable public debt levels. With a capital of over 700,000 million euros, made up of member states' contributions of 80,000 million euros (21,700 million from Germany) and a further 620,000 million euros of guarantees (168,300 million from Germany, representing its 27 percent share of capital in the ECB), the fund is able to disburse up to 500,000 million in loans, bond purchases, precautionary credit lines, and facilities for recapitalizing banks. The main beneficiaries—including those inherited from the EFSF—were Cyprus, Ireland, Portugal, Spain, and (until 2014) Greece. Between December 2013 and May 2014, Spain, Ireland, and Portugal successfully exited their programs as investor confidence in their financial markets returned, but problems remained with Greece. The ESM applies no single interest rate to loans, although these are made at substantially lower costs than comparable borrowing on financial markets.

Although the German **Bundestag** and **Bundesrat** approved the ESM Treaty in June 2012, ratification was held up by appeals to the **Federal Constitutional Court (FCC)** by Bundestag member Peter Gauweiler (**Christian Socialist Union, CSU**) and others, who argued that the financial credits to be offered by the ESM via the ECB were beyond the control of parliament. The court rejected the appeals, but stipulated that German liability be limited to 190,000 million euros, with a right to veto any increase.

EUROPEAN UNION (EU). The **Basic Law** (**BL**) not only refers to the Federal Republic of Germany (FRG) as an equal member of a united Europe committed to world peace (preamble and article 24), but specifically permits Germany to surrender sovereign powers to supranational systems of security that promote a common European order and global harmony. Accordingly, from its foundation in 1949, the FRG consistently promoted the goal of wider European integration. The first treaties in this process, to which the founding six states of Belgium, France, Germany, Italy, Luxembourg, and the Netherlands were signatories, merged the member states' coal and steel industries (Treaty Establishing the European Coal and Steel Community [ECSC], in force from 1952) and coordinated research programs for the peaceful use of nuclear **energy** (Treaty Establishing the European Atomic Energy Community [EURATOM], 1958). A third, landmark treaty (Treaty Establishing the European Economic Community (TEEC, signed in 1957, effective in 1958) aimed to create a common market by eliminating **trade** barriers and to establish a shared **agricultural** policy. Also known as the Treaty of Rome, the TEEC technically expired in 2002, but was superseded by further agreements. The three treaties constituted what was commonly referred to as the European Communities or, simply, European Community (EC). Since the EEC was the principal component of the EC, the term "Common Market" was also widely used. In 1967, the governing bodies of the EEC, ECSC, and EURATOM were merged.

From these founding moves, further treaties were concluded, each deepening integration and clarifying decision making. The Single European Act (agreed to in 1986, effective in 1987) introduced limited majority voting in order to reduce an individual state's veto power and extended the prerogatives of a (since 1979) directly elected European Parliament. It also prepared the groundwork for creating a genuinely competitive single internal European market of goods and services by aiming to remove barriers that still protected many national enterprises and to open up sectors such as energy and **telecommunications**.

The Treaty on European Union (or Maastricht Treaty, agreed to in 1992, effective in 1993) formally renamed the EEC the European Union (a term that had been used as a declaration of objectives since 1972), introduced elements of a political union (EU citizenship, a common **foreign** and **security policy**, and coordination on justice and home affairs), and took the first steps toward monetary union and a single **currency**. It also introduced the codecision procedure, enabling the European Parliament to colegislate in certain areas alongside the EU Council (see below).

The Treaty of Amsterdam (agreed to in 1997, effective in 1999) revised Maastricht by setting rules for the introduction of the euro (the European Central Bank would be located in Frankfurt/Main) and allowed groups of member states to share certain powers ("integrated differentiation"). Codecision was extended to prepare for enlargement from 15 to 25 states in 2004.

After a lengthy consultation process, the member states signed an agreement to replace all existing treaties by a single constitution (Treaty for Establishing a Constitution of Europe, 2004). Although this ambitious project was shelved when the proposed constitution was rejected in national referenda in France and the Netherlands, its basic elements were subsequently incorporated into the Treaty of Lisbon (agreed to in 2007, effective in 2009), which gave more power to the European Parliament, extended codecision (renamed the "ordinary legislative procedure") to most key areas, created a single representative for foreign affairs, and clarified power competencies between the EU and national governments.

Initially, the FRG supported European integration in order to regain national sovereignty and legitimacy after World War II and to develop export markets that would sustain its economic recovery. As a front-line state during the Cold War, it also benefited from being embedded within a multinational security framework. Added bonuses were the special status that the EEC accorded to the **German Democratic Republic (GDR)** as a trading partner of the FRG and the inclusion of West **Berlin** in the Treaty of Rome. Successive federal chancellors cultivated a close relationship with France, and the two countries determined the extent and pace of integration. In return for acting as the community's paymaster, Germany reaped economic and political benefits, while the linkage with the EU helped achieve international agreement on reunification. From 1991, the EU also invested heavily in eastern Germany, with the best part of 21.7 million euros also transferred in the period 1994–1999 and 15,000 million euros earmarked for 2007–2013, after which the amount was expected to decrease.

During the 1980s and 1990s, **Helmut Kohl** (federal chancellor 1982–1998) worked closely with François Mitterrand (French president 1981–1995) to agree on and promote the pre-Lisbon treaties. Even when EU expansion was complicated by residual problems left over from World War II—in particular the legacy of the expulsion of ethnic Germans from Czechoslovakia between 1945 and 1947—Kohl did not link the issue with enlargement, and the two states concluded a friendship treaty in 1992. Although France and Germany continued to champion integration, Kohl's successor, **Gerhard Schröder** (chancellor 1998–2005), and his French counterparts, Lionel Jospin (prime minister 1997–2002) and Jacques Chirac (president 1995–2007), did not develop the close personal relationship that had existed between Kohl and Mitterrand. As a result, the Franco–German partnership lost some of its driving force as EU politics became characterized by shifting patterns of national positions and alliances. On the other hand, Germany's leadership role in the EU was enhanced when **Angela Merkel** (chancellor from 2005) used the German presidency of the European Council in 2007 to relaunch the issue of the EU constitution, forge compromises, and see its provisions eventually included in the Treaty of Lisbon. It was also Germany that called the tune during the **eurozone crisis** that erupted in 2009.

Since the 1970s, the EEC/EU has been progressively enlarged, reaching 28 members when Croatia joined in 2013. In that year a number of countries were also on the road to joining the EU, with so-called candidate countries, such as Turkey, in the process of integrating their legislation into EU law alongside potential candidates yet to fulfill membership requirements.

The main political institutions of the EU are as follows. The European Council (German: Europäischer Rat) is made up of the heads of government of the member states and sets the general political direction and priorities of the EU. The current president is former Polish prime minister Donald Tusk, who succeeded the Belgian Herman von Rompuy in December 2014. The European Council has no power to pass laws, but its meetings (four times a year) are equivalent to government summits. The Council of the European Union (Rat der Europäischen Union), also known as the Council of Ministers, is where national ministers (or their representatives) from each EU country meet to adopt laws and coordinate policies; its presidency rotates every six months among the member states. The European Commission initiates and drafts new laws, implements policies, and spends funds. The body's 28 commissioners, one from each EU state, are appointed for a five-year term and are assigned specific policy areas by its president, former Luxembourg premier Jean-Claude Juncker since 2014. The appointment of all commissioners, including the president, is subject to the approval of the European Parliament, to whom they remain accountable. The conservative Juncker, who beat the rival candidate German social democrat Martin Schulz for the post, aimed to streamline the commission's operations by enhancing the role of its vice presidents, who would coordinate priorities and could even veto initiatives by individual commissioners.

While decision making in the European Parliament tended traditionally to be reached through ad hoc majorities formed by shifting constellations of factions that changed according to policy area, the two major groupings (the conservative European People's Party [EPP] and the Progressive Alliance of Socialists and Democrats [S&D]) began to cooperate more effectively after the 2014 election, notably coshaping policy responses to the 2015 refugee crisis in conjunction with the European Commission. The EU's governance system, however, remains highly complex, with interlocking treaty provisions and considerable overlap of functions. Strategy is also determined informally by a "G5" group—comprising the commission president, his deputy, the president, and leaders of the two largest factions in the European

Parliament—who meet at least every four weeks and set priorities for the following two years. In practice, the formal decision-making structures can also be easily undermined by political realities such as the eurozone crisis, during which rescue packages were drawn up by a small number of individual national states (in this case led by Germany), largely bypassing the commission and parliament.

See also FEDERALISM; FOREIGN POLICY AFTER 1990; FOREIGN POLICY: 1949–1969; FOREIGN POLICY: 1970–1990; SCHENGEN AGREEMENT; SECURITY POLICY, EXTERNAL; TRADE.

EUROZONE CRISIS. In October 2009, the eurozone entered a prolonged period of fiscal uncertainty as Greece disclosed total public debt and annual borrowing that were twice as high as previously thought and well above prescribed limits for eurozone members. The crisis deepened as similarly unsustainable debts emerged for France, Spain, and the Irish Republic in the wake of the global financial emergency that had broken in 2007–2008. Even as the commission of the **European Union (EU)**, the **European Central Bank (ECB)**, and the International Monetary Fund (IMF), referred to as the "Troika," settled on a staged 110,000 million euro rescue package for Greece (the first stage was agreed in May 2010 and a second came into effect in March 2012), the eurozone economy continued to shrink. Bailouts followed for Ireland (November 2010), Portugal (May 2011), Hungary (2008, although not yet a eurozone member), Cyprus (March 2013), and Spanish banks (November 2012). Credit ratings agencies downgraded the larger economies of Italy (September 2011, July 2013) and France (November 2012), as they also struggled with structural deficits. Austerity measures coupled with programs to reschedule the liability and bail out indebted banks provoked extreme social and political turbulence in Greece and, to a lesser extent, in Spain and Italy, with considerable pressure on Germany to finance the rescue packages. The EU responded to the crisis with a range of instruments and mechanisms. The principal ones were the **European Financial Stability Mechanism (EFSM)** and **European Financial Stability Facility (EFSF**, both 2010), the **European Semester** (2010), a revised **Stability and Growth Pact** (2011), a **Euro Plus Pact** (2011), and the **European Stability Mechanism (ESM**, 2012). The political outcome of these measures was the intergovernment **Treaty on Stability, Coordination and Governance (TSCG**, 2011). In addition to these schemes, which were largely designed to buy private debt and provide millions of euros in cheap loans to banks, the ECB agreed in January 2015 to print money to buy sovereign bonds (i.e., government debt) directly from governments ("quantitative easing"). Despite opposition from Germany, which was concerned that the plan would encourage spendthrift countries to relax their economic reforms, it was adopted and scheduled to run until at least September 2016.

Although the eurozone's immediate crisis was triggered by high public debt levels, the underlying causes were more complex. Apart from Greece and Portugal, both Ireland and Spain had until 2007 (and unlike Germany) actually adhered to the annual **budget** deficit limit of 3 percent of government spending laid down by the original Stability and Growth Pact (in force from 1999). However, gross national or public debt (budget deficits accumulated over the years, also below 60 percent for Ireland and Spain until 2008) became unmanageable when the private sector global debt bubble burst, ending an era of easy credit (low interest rates) and cross-border lending that had also fueled a property boom in some countries. At the same time, interest rates soared, making borrowing more expensive and depressing tax receipts as economies contracted. When Germany indicated that even eurozone states could default on national debt and insisted that they should bear the responsibility to restore budgetary discipline through austerity measures, the crisis deepened. Federal Chancellor **Angela Merkel**, in particular, came under fire for failing to react promptly as EU leaders took several months to agree upon and implement a series of rescue programs. The Germans, who were also creditors to indebted states and had profited from increased markets in neighboring countries that were unable to increase the competitiveness of their own exports through **currency** devaluation, remained unmoved by arguments that their own export surpluses had been partly paid for through imports into these countries and saw little point in sending good money after bad. The moralist notion of prudent northern European economies versus profligate southerners gained ground and proved politically convenient before domestic audiences. Some observers even pointed out that Germany had evidently forgotten what its own postwar economic recovery owed to the writing off and restructuring of accumulated debt. The political resistance to austerity measures proved especially strong in Greece, where some circles claimed that Germany owed them 11,000 million euros derived from a forced loan imposed during the National Socialist occupation in 1942. By early 2015, however, the reluctance of Greece to implement structural reforms within an EU framework had alienated a number of eurozone states, including smaller countries such as Portugal, Malta, and the Baltic states, which had weathered their own financial crises.

The budget imbalances between exporting and importing countries in the single-currency area originated in the disparities between member economies when the euro was launched in 1999. Not only were convergence criteria overlooked for political reasons (e.g., economic statistics on the status of Greece were either falsified or ignored), but importing countries such as Greece, Portugal, Spain, and Ireland were encouraged to borrow beyond their means by eurozone-wide low interest rates and easy access to money by banks eager to invest. When the private financial sector collapsed, these economies could not, in a currency area controlled by the ECB, rebalance

EXTRA-PARLIAMENTARY OPPOSITION • 245

themselves by using fiscal instruments, such as devaluation, quantitative easing, interest rate adjustment, and inflation control, which were available to noneuro states. Although the eurozone began to move toward coordinating members' economic systems after the peak of the crisis, it remains a long way from true fiscal union, which would include a single **taxation** regime, common loans (called eurobonds or stability bonds), and direct transfers from richer to poorer states (as occurs internally in countries and in Germany's own system of **financial equalization**). Even after weathering the immediate threats to financial stability (Ireland and Portugal completed their emergency bailout programs in 2014, enabling them to reenter the markets and access normal financial mechanisms to meet their longer term needs), eurozone members continue to face the long-term challenges of economic recovery and the social implications of austerity.

As the danger of an exit from the eurozone by Greece, which experienced particular difficulties in meeting the terms of its bailouts, loomed ever larger in 2015, the basis of negotiating a third emergency rescue package, coupled with even more severe conditions and subject to agreement by national parliaments, was hammered out in July. Although the Bundestag voted to support further negotiations, the issue exposed differences within Germany's political parties. Sixty **Christian Democratic Union (CDU)** deputies voted against the deal, with **Wolfgang Schäuble**, CDU finance minister and head negotiator of the German delegation, openly contemplating a Greek exit from the eurozone. Left-wing members and politicians of the **Social Democratic Party of Germany (SPD)**, by contrast, were less willing to accept a possible "Grexit," and the **Greens** were unanimous in accusing the government—and Schäuble in particular—of betraying former chancellor **Helmut Kohl**'s legacy of a commitment to a united Europe. The crisis also triggered a wider European debate about the wisdom of an austerity-focused response to Greece's debt problems that did not include major write-downs.

See also SOCIAL MARKET ECONOMY (SOZIALE MARKTWIRTS-CHAFT).

EXTRA-PARLIAMENTARY OPPOSITION (AUßERPARLAMEN-TARISCHE OPPOSITION, APO). The APO emerged during the second half of the 1960s from a generation of young protesters, mainly students, demanding radical reforms to the postwar political, economic, and educational structures of German society. The formation of the **grand coalition** between the two main political parties in 1966 and the disappearance of an effective opposition in the **Bundestag** fueled their conviction that changes could only be achieved outside the institutional parliamentary framework. A loosely organized movement of various groups, the APO came to be dominated by the Marxist-oriented **Federation of Socialist German Students (SDS)**, and its activities reached a peak during widespread and often violent demonstrations in 1968 that alienated most citizens and moderate left-wing parties. As the coalition proved unexpectedly capable of genuine reform, the APO lost its impetus. The SDS dissolved itself in 1970, and the movement rapidly fragmented into cadre groups (K-Gruppen) inspired by Maoism and Latin American revolutionaries. Its legacy was also taken over by extremist terrorist groups such as the **Red Army Faction (RAF)**.

See also STUDENTS' MOVEMENT.

EXTREMISM. Extremist political movements and groups considered a threat to Germany's democratic order or to "the concept of international understanding" as laid down in the **Basic Law** (**BL**, article 9, on freedom of association) are monitored by the **Federal Office for the Protection of the Constitution** (Bundesamt für Verfassungsschutz, BfV) and its counterparts in the **federal states**. The BfV issues annual reports on extremist activities of various kinds (including neo-Nazi, left-wing, anti-Semitic and Islamist, as well violent and nonviolent groups' actions) and on measures to combat them. Of particular concern are activities of extremists who perpetrate acts of violent **terrorism**. For 2014, the BfV recorded 32,700 politically motivated criminal offenses (31,645 in 2013), of which 38 percent were propaganda related and 10 percent acts of violence (mainly bodily harm but also including arson, robbery, and attacks on infrastructure). Neo-Nazis accounted for 16,559 (including 990 violent) criminal attacks, increasingly directed at **foreigners**, **immigrants**, and **asylum** seekers, but also against **Jews** and upholders of the democratic order, including political opponents, police officers, and journalists. While membership in potentially violent leftist groups has been variable (falling from 29,400 in 2012 to 27,770 in 2013 and 27,200 in 2014), the readiness to commit violent offenses—targeted mainly at the police/security authorities and right-wing opponents—remained high: 2014 saw 4,424 criminal offenses (4,491 in 2013), including 995 acts of violence (1,220 in 2013) and seven murder attempts (six directed at police officers). Figures for what the BfV terms the "human potential" for Islamist extremists in Germany are less certain, but were given at 43,890 in 2014, representing a slight but steady rise over previous years (43,190 in 2013 and 42,550 in 2012), largely owing to the dynamic growth of militant Salafist movements (5,500 adherents in 2013, compared to 7,000 in 2014). For 2014, the BfV specifically listed 13 active Islamist organizations in Germany, although not all of these were committed to violence. Although no organized structures for the Islamic State (IS) movement are known to exist in Germany, a number of adherents were prosecuted during 2014, and the interior minister formally banned IS in September.

The BfV also distinguishes a heterogeneous category of extremism involving non-Islamist foreigners motivated by left-wing ideologies (Marxism-Leninism, Maoism), nationalism, and separatism. These groups can overlap ideologically, but radical leftists of mainly Turkish origin aim for a revolution and the creation of a socialist/communist state in their home country. The membership potential of this category totaled 29,330 in 2014 (28,810 in 2013). Of those in leftist parties, about 14,000 belonged to the PKK (Kurdistan Workers Party) and its subgroups, which were banned and driven underground in 1993 following violent attacks on Turkish institutions, and 1,300 to the TKP/ML (Turkish Communist Party/Marxist-Leninists). Separatists included 1,000 adherents of the LTTE (Liberation Tigers of Tamil Ealam) and 790 members of Sikh groups. Extreme nationalists accounted for 10,000. For 2014, the BfV reported 2,014 instances of politically motivated criminal acts by foreigners (544 in 2013), including 259 involving violence (76 in 2013). The dramatic increase was partly attributed to protests against the rise of IS in Syria and Iraq.

Prohibition of extremist groups deemed hostile to the principles of the BL is an established instrument of the German state. Before legislation regulating the formation (and banning) of associations (Vereine) was passed in 1964, 327 prohibition orders were enacted by the **federal states**, involving 191 organizations and largely targeting communist and, to a lesser extent, neo-Nazi groups. Between 1964 and reunification (1990), the number fell to just 17, and no German left-wing group has been banned since the Heidelberg branch of the **Federation of Socialist German Students** (**SDS**) in 1970. Significantly, the basis for banning shifted from political orientation to violent criminal activity. Since 1990, however, prohibitions have undergone a renaissance, including 15 against right-wing groups and several applied to left-wing, foreign, and (since 2001) Islamist associations. Bans can be imposed by the federal interior minister, interior ministers of the federal states, and the **Federal Constitutional Court** (**FCC**), and are generally considered effective in undermining extremist activities.

See ANTI-SEMITISM; EXTREMISM: ISLAMIST; EXTREMISM: LEFT-WING; EXTREMISM: RIGHT-WING; SECURITY POLICY, INTERNAL.

EXTREMISM: ISLAMIST. The wide spectrum of Islamist extremism in Germany ranges from self-motivated individuals to groups with close links to organizations abroad and smaller groups or independent cells inspired by foreign jihadist networks. Systematic links with al-Qaeda, whose numbers are unknown and which appears to have no organization in Germany, are not thought to play a significant role. Al-Qaeda's ideology has, however, radicalized increasing numbers of second- and third-generation **immigrant** Muslims and converts, especially through the **Internet**. Events in the Middle East (Iraq, Israel, Lebanon, Egypt, Syria) and Afghanistan are also triggers for recruitment, prompting young radicals to attend terrorist training centers abroad and present a security risk upon their return to Germany. More than

600 German Islamists are thought to have left the country to support fighting in Syria and Iraq in 2014, in particular to join the Islamic State (IS) and train in terrorist activities—a significant increase over 2013 (270). Within Germany, Salafism, whose leaders advocate displacing all forms of civil and state law by sharia rule, remains the fastest growing movement, with 7,000 adherents. While most recruits are men, women are becoming increasingly involved, especially through Internet-based support networks ("cyber mobilization"). The highly organized Salafists recruit through sophisticated campaigns and appeals to a clear-cut personal lifestyle, using seminars, lectures, literature, and other **media**. Active in Germany since the late 1990s, their first use of street violence occurred at counterdemonstrations against an extreme right-wing group in Solingen and Bonn in May 2012. In 2014, Salafists "patroled" the center of Wuppertal as "sharia police," distributing leaflets and urging young people to conform to Islamic law. Anti-Semitism is an integral part of their ideology. Such incidents, and open threats of retaliation against Germans abroad by a Salafist preacher, prompted the German interior minister to ban one subgroup and take legal proceedings against others. Violent anti-Salafist protests by Yazidis and Kurds took place in Herford, Celle, and Hamburg in 2014.

The largest Islamist organization in Germany is the IGMG (Islamische Gemeinschaft Millî Görüş e.V.), with 31,000 members, mainly Turks. Although it rejects violence and publicly promotes moderation and integration, the IGMG is considered extremist because it represents a specific form of Turkish nationalism and aims to replace Western civilization with a universal Islamic political and economic order based on sharia law. It maintains a comprehensive network of religious, social, cultural, and support institutions in Germany, using educational, sporting, and outdoor activities to win over to its values youths of Turkish origin. Just three months after al-Qaeda's attack on the United States in September 2001, Germany applied its first ever ban on an Islamist organization, the Kalifatsstaat (Califate State) and its 35 subgroups, founded in Cologne in 1984/1985 and led by Metin Kaplan, the so-called Calif of Cologne. After this, further groups were banned, for reasons that included Holocaust denial, disseminating anti-Semitic and anti-Western propaganda (e.g., Yeni Akit GmbH, 2005), and providing financial support for HAMAS (Al-Aqsa e.V., 2003). Several Salafist groups were outlawed from 2012 onward.

See also ANTI-SEMITISM; EXTREMISM; SECURITY POLICY, INTERNAL; TERRORISM.

EXTREMISM: LEFT-WING. Left-wing extremism in postwar Germany may be divided into a Marxist-Leninist camp, which is dedicated to the replacement of the capitalist social order by a socialist or communist dictatorship, and underground bands of anarchists. Loosely organized and going under many names, the anarchist cells are considered the most committed to using violence to destabilize or overthrow the state. An important historical aspect of left-wing extremism in Germany was the emergence of the **students' movement** and an **extra-parliamentary opposition** during the second half of the 1960s.

For many years, the strongest representative of Marxist-Leninist orthodoxy in the Federal Republic of Germany (FRG) was the German Communist Party (DKP). The DKP was founded in 1968 as the successor to the prewar Communist Party of Germany (KPD), which was banned in West Germany in 1956. Pro-Soviet and pro–East Germany, the DKP enjoyed the financial and organizational support of the ruling **Socialist Unity Party of Germany (SED)** in the **German Democratic Republic (GDR)**. Led by Kurt Bachmann (1969–1973), Herbert Mies (1973–1990), and Heinz Stehr (1990–2010), the party maintained several sister organizations and recruited mainly among workers, students, and young people. More recent leaders are Bettina Jürgensen (2010–2013), and Patrik Köbele (2013–). Between 1969 and 1987, its membership fluctuated from around 30,000 to 42,000. A major stronghold was working-class **North Rhine-Westfalia**, where it had 14,000 or so members during the 1970s and 1980s, although even there the party gained seats only in local elections. In the wake of the 1968 student protest movement, the DKP faced competition from numerous Maoist groups, although these had even less of an electoral impact. The reforms in the Soviet Union and the collapse of the GDR in 1989 plunged the DKP into crisis, as internal divisions arose over how to respond to the changes. The party also lost its sponsorship from the SED, but it stuck to its Marxist-Leninist principles, even as its membership plummeted from around 35,000 (1989) to 6,500 (1998) and supporters migrated to the SED's successor, the **Party of Democratic Socialism (PDS)**. Owing to its declining and aging membership (3,500), not to mention financial difficulties and internal disputes, the party's external activities are usually undertaken in conjunction with other movements. Membership in a rival party founded in 1982, the Maoist-Stalinist–oriented Marxistisch-Leninistische Partei Deutschlands (Marxist-Leninist Party of Germany, MLPD), was estimated at 1,800 in 2014. Of a handful of Trotskyist groups, the **Federal Office for the Protection of the Constitution** (Bundesamt für Verfassungsschutz, BfV) considered the "marx21" network, founded in 2007 as a section of the London-based International Socialist Tendency, to be the most active in recent years. The 350-strong Sozialistische Alternative (Socialist Alternative, SAV) was similarly part of the British-based Committee for a Workers International. Rote Hilfe e.V., with 6,500 members, focuses on providing support to criminals and violent offenders from the left-wing spectrum. Following a decision by the **Federal Constitutional Court (FCC)** in October 2013, the government announced in February 2014 that the BfV no longer monitored individual parliamentary members of the PDS/**The Left Party**, although the agency would continue to regard its extremist factions as a potential constitutional threat.

Of 27,200 estimated supporters of extreme left-wing views in 2014, about 7,600 were regarded as confrontationally violent. Cells are found mainly in urban areas (notably **Berlin**, **Hamburg**, the Rhine-Main region, and around Dresden/Leipzig and Nuremberg), but also in smaller university cities such as Göttingen and Freiburg. The biggest and most aggressive subgroups (sometimes called "Autonome" or "the autonomous") typically mobilize violent street riots; blockades; and attacks on buildings, the police, and other symbols of state authority, as well as on right-wing opponents. A recent development is the readiness of a new generation of activists to overcome the fragmentation of the movement by forming alliances with other groups.

For extremists of various degrees, the **Internet** functions as a tool of communication, propagation, recruitment, and research for targets, while music, in the form of concerts, songs, and "mobilization videos," attracts younger supporters and generates finance. A new development is computer hacking and cyber attacks, including the "defacement" of an opponent's Internet presence. Between 1990 and 2013, no leftist extremist groups were officially banned in Germany, although individuals were prosecuted for criminal offenses (e.g., three members of the group Militante Gruppe [MG], who were convicted in 2009 for attacks on army trucks; the group itself was responsible for several arson attacks in Berlin and **Brandenburg**). In October 2011, the government introduced a program (the Aussteigerprogramm) providing anonymity and support (including housing and **education**) for those wishing to leave the extremist scene.

See also ANTI-SEMITISM; EXTREMISM; SECURITY POLICY, INTERNAL; TERRORISM.

EXTREMISM: RIGHT-WING. Extreme right-wing parties emerged in three phases in the postwar Federal Republic of Germany (FRG). Until it was banned in 1952, the Sozialistische Reichspartei (SRP) attracted former National Socialists. Its successor, the Deutsche Reichspartei (DRP), was prohibited in 1960. The second phase was marked by the founding of the **National Democratic Party of Germany** (NPD, 1964), and the third by the appearance of the **German People's Union** (DVU, 1971) and **The Republicans** (REP, 1987). Common ideological themes of organized right-wing extremism in Germany are advocacy of a strong state (with echoes of National Socialism), a rejection of Germany as a multicultural nation (with undercurrents of racism and **anti-Semitism**), contempt for liberal values and democratic institutions, and a populist appeal to issues of "law and order." Specific targets of violence are **foreigners**, **asylum** seekers, the homeless, and **homosexuals**, as well as political opponents and representatives of the democratic state. Stances on economic policy range from support for the free market economy to socialist-type protectionism. The electoral impact of organized extremism has been restricted to the **federal states**, where its effects, although disturbing, have not destabilized the political system.

The **Federal Office for the Protection of the Constitution** (Bundesamt für Verfassungsschutz, BfV) recorded a "human potential" of 21,000 right-wing extremists in 2014, of whom 10,500 were violently oriented. Around 7,200 belonged to a subculture of loosely organized, mainly locally based skinheads, who shunned political parties and formal structures (the only nationally active skinhead group in Germany were the Hammerskins, founded in the United States in 1988). The largest neo-Nazi party in 2014 was the NPD, with 5,200 members, followed by the Citizens Movement for NRW (Bürger Bewegung pro NRW), with roots dating back to 1996 and 950 members. A third party, Die Rechte (The Right), which was founded in May 2012 and attracted around 150 members of the dissolved DVU, steadily increased its regional associations and membership to 500 in 2013/2014. Some 2,500 belong to other groups. The coming to light in November 2011 of the long-standing neo-Nazi group Nationalsozialistische Untergrund (NSU), whose extreme violence was typical of such groups' affinity with weapons and explosives, exposed serious defects in the authorities' effectiveness in combating extremism and resulted in a number of official resignations. The trial against NSU leaders began in May 2013. Organizations to support jailed extremists have also emerged, using mainly the **Internet** to maintain communication, promote solidarity events and concerts, and even create groups within prison.

Skinhead subculture emerged in the FRG during the 1970s and in the **German Democratic Republic (GDR)** in the following decade, gaining ground during the 1980s and 1990s, after which its appeal to young people steadily declined. Focusing on bands, music, and festivals, skinheads constituted a potential recruiting ground for the more organized groupings—in particular the NPD—and membership in extreme right-wing groups increased dramatically in the **eastern federal states** after reunification (1990). Following a sharp rise in acts of **terrorism** in the early 1990s, the interior ministry had banned 15 groups by 2014, with federal states (mainly **Brandenburg** and **North Rhine-Westfalia**) prohibiting many more. Although adherents responded by developing informal, largely anonymous networks of communication and disseminating propaganda through cell phones, e-mail, and the Internet (including music, **radio**/video portals, and social networks), their public activities were considerably curtailed and their leaders forced from the scene In 2014, a leading organization for youth protection on the Internet registered 1,417 German-language extremist websites and 4,755 social content items, only 7 percent of which were hosted in Germany.

Most incidents of politically motivated and organized right-wing violence in 2014 were registered in North Rhine-Westfalia (370, compared to 192 in 2013) and **Berlin** (111/81), although, in relation to the population, figures were much higher in the eastern states, where racially motivated violence remained especially high. At the same time, the dramatic increase in asylum seekers from the Middle East and North Africa in 2015 was accompanied by a sharp increase in violence, in particular attacks on hostels and accommodations for refugees (but also on police, aid workers, and groups working for peace)—again most notably in eastern Germany. Nationally, less than half of the estimated perpetrators were identified and prosecuted. In view of official prohibitions and closures of meeting places for extremists, the NPD was suspected of providing the organizational infrastructure for many demonstrations against foreigners. In line with similar measures against adherents of other types of extremism, the government provided an exit program (Aussteigerprogramm) from 2011, offering support for those wishing to leave the scene.

In 2012, a new right-wing group emerged after the model of the "bloc identitaire" in France. The so-called Identitarian Movement (Identitäre Bewegung Deutschland, IBD) aimed to win over young people and students to a cultural racism based on national ethnic identity. Initially more successful in Austria than Germany, it gained traction during the asylum-seekers crisis of 2014 and cultivated links with **Pegida**.

See also EASTERN FEDERAL STATES AFTER REUNIFICATION; EXTREMISM; SECURITY POLICY, INTERNAL; TERRORISM.

F

FEDERAL ASSEMBLY (BUNDESVERSAMMLUNG). The Federal Assembly is the largest parliamentary assembly of the **Bundestag**. It is convened by the president of the Bundestag solely to elect by secret ballot the **president of the Federal Republic (FRG)**, after which it dissolves itself. The procedures for the election are laid down in the **Basic Law (BL**, article 54). The assembly is made up of all Bundestag members and an equal number of delegates from the parliaments of the **federal states**. These delegates do not have to be members of their parliaments, and their number varies according to the size of the populations of their home states and party representation in the **Landtag**. The purpose of such a large assembly is to ensure the broadest possible base of political support from both the states and the center. Although the assembly's members are not bound to directives, in practice they tend to vote according to party allegiances. After its first meeting in Bonn in 1949, the assembly convened until 1969 in West **Berlin**, despite protests from the Soviet Union and the **German Democratic Republic (GDR)**. Following the agreements associated with **Ostpolitik**, the assembly met in Bonn (1974–1989), but returned to Berlin after reunification.

FEDERAL CHANCELLOR (BUNDESKANZLER[IN]). The federal chancellor and his or her ministers constitute the **federal government** of Germany (article 62 of the **Basic Law, BL**). The chancellor is elected after a national election, normally by an absolute majority of the **Bundestag** (BL, article 63), and may be replaced at any time by a constructive vote of no confidence (BL, article 67). In practice, chancellors who lose the confidence of parliament and their party resign before a formal vote is taken (as did **Konrad Adenauer** in 1963, **Ludwig Erhard** in 1966, and **Willy Brandt** in 1974). Because the BL assigns the chancellor a preeminent position, Germany is often referred to as a "chancellor's democracy" (Kanzlerdemokratie). According to the "chancellor principle" (Kanzlerprinzip) or "principle of chancellor policy guidelines" (Richtlinienkompetenz), as derived from the BL (article 65), the chancellor is responsible for setting the cornerstones of policy guidelines and ensuring that these are followed.

The first act of a newly elected chancellor is to form a cabinet of ministers, who are usually elected Bundestag members. Although the chancellor may select his or her own ministers, in practice he or she is circumscribed by the demands of coalition parties, not to mention the status of individuals in his or her party and the need to represent the interests of the **federal states**. (Coalition governments have been the rule in German politics, and it is customary during the election campaign for the smaller parties to declare which of the main parties they propose to ally themselves with.) Ministers who are proposed by the chancellor are formally appointed by the **president of the Federal Republic (FRG)**. The chancellor also selects a deputy. Since the first **grand coalition** (1966–1969), this post has been traditionally held by a leading member of the junior coalition, who is also the foreign minister (the importance attached to defense and finance is considered to rule out ministers of these departments). At the same time, Germany's position in Europe, especially since reunification, means that chancellors have become more directly involved in **foreign policy**, enjoy a high personal prestige, and are exposed to extensive **media** coverage. An unwritten convention of government is that certain ministers have a working or professional link to their area of responsibility. Thus, the justice minister is normally a lawyer, the minister for **agriculture** has a farming background, and the minister for labor has links with the **trade unions** or **industry** (for this reason, **Gerhard Schröder** in 1998 appointed the nonparty Werner Müller, a former industrial manager, as economics minister).

Federal chancellors since 1949 have been Konrad Adenauer (**Christian Democratic Union, CDU**, 1949–1963), Ludwig Erhard (CDU, 1963–1966), **Kurt Georg Kiesinger** (CDU, 1966–1969), Willy Brandt (**Social Democratic Party of Germany, SPD**, 1969–1974), **Helmut Schmidt** (SPD, 1974–1982), **Helmut Kohl** (CDU, 1982–1998), Gerhard Schröder (SPD, 1998–2005), and **Angela Merkel** (CDU, 2005–).

Before national elections, the main parties nominate a "chancellor candidate" (Kanzlerkandidat)—normally the incumbent chancellor for a party in power—to run for office. A party candidate is often **minister president** of a federal state (examples include Kurt-Georg Kiesinger, **Johannes Rau**, **Oskar Lafontaine**, Gerhard Schröder, and **Edmund Stoiber**) or a national politician with a career as minister president behind him or her (such as Helmut Kohl, **Hans-Jochen Vogel**, and **Rudolf Scharping**). A notable exception is, of course, Angela Merkel. Although the party leader is generally selected as the chancellor candidate, this is not always the case: the SPD was led by Willy Brandt, for instance, during Helmut Schmidt's chancellorship (1974–1982), and by Oskar Lafontaine when Gerhard Schröder became chancellor in 1998. The rules and procedures for nominating the chancellor candidate vary from party to party and from election to election. While Helmut Kohl was selected by the national executives of the CDU and **Chris-**

tian Social Union (CSU) in 1975, the parliamentary groups put forward Franz Josef Strauß in 1980. In 1993, the SPD established a provision for direct nomination by a ballot of party members, but in practice it has left the choice to the party executive, whose decision is confirmed by a party conference.

From the BL (article 65) is derived the "principle of joint cabinet decision-making" (Kollegialprinzip), which ensures that ministers agree on decisions as a unit and as a rule support them in public. The "principle of ministerial autonomy" (Ressortprinzip) assigns ministers considerable independence within their areas, and depending on their personal competence and parliamentary backing, can render them powerful figures. The potential tension over competencies between a chancellor and minister, especially over crucial issues, is largely theoretical in view of the former's power of dismissal. Cabinet meetings, which are the main forum for policy decisions, are held in private; voting patterns are secret; and deliberations are (in theory) confidential, although individuals, either for personal or party-political reasons, have not always adhered to these conventions. Since the BL names only the ministers of finance, defense, and justice (articles 114, 65a and 96), these ministries are assumed to be constitutionally required, leaving the chancellor free to propose ministers for other areas (Ressorts). Chancellors have also appointed ministers for special tasks (including five for the period between reunification and the first all-German elections). Following the election of 1990, Chancellor Helmut Kohl split the ministry of youth, family, **women**, and **health** into three separate ministries in order to bring more women into the cabinet: Hannelore Rönsch (family and senior citizens), Angela Merkel (women and youth), and **Gerda Hasselfeldt** (health). The ministries of family, women, and youth (plus senior citizens) were later remerged (1994). When Gerhard Schröder formed his SPD/**Green Party** coalition in 1998, he greatly extended the responsibilities of the Federal Ministry of Finance, headed by the influential Oskar Lafontaine. A minister is supported by one or more senior advisers who hold the rank of **state secretary**. Although not prescribed by the BL, a key institution of government, created by Konrad Adenauer directly after his election in 1949, is the **Office of the Federal Chancellor** (Bundeskanzleramt). This acts as a mini-ministry, coordinating and managing the work of the government with the ministries, the Bundestag and **Bundesrat**, the political parties, and the federal states.

Successive German chancellors have also made use of informal mechanisms and committees outside the cabinet to coordinate policy with coalition partners, the parliamentary party, and other interest groups. Examples include the Kressbonner Circle (during the first grand coalition), the Clover Group (Kleeblatt, named after its four members, Helmut Schmidt and his three advisers), and the "elephants' round" (Elefantenrunde) of party leaders during the early years of the coalition between the CDU/CSU and the **Free**

Democratic Party (FDP) after 1983. The tradition was continued by the SPD/Green Party coalition (1998–2005). Although such informal committees are not constitutionally required and in theory undermine the authority of the cabinet, they oil the wheels of the political machinery and maintain links between the government and influential politicians, including those from the federal states, who are not at the political center.

FEDERAL COMMISSIONER FOR THE RECORDS OF THE STATE SECURITY SERVICE OF THE FORMER GERMAN DEMOCRATIC REPUBLIC.

The office of the commissioner (German title: Bundesbeauftragte[r] für die Unterlagen des Staatssicherheitsdienstes der ehemaligen Deutschen Demokratischen Republik, BStU) was established after the fall of the Communist regime in the German Democratic Republic (GDR) to manage the huge archive of files assembled by the East German secret service, the Stasi. The files, which comprise over 111 kilometers of documents, 1.7 million items of photographic material, 2,800 films and videos, 27,600 tapes, and thousands of sacks of material rescued from destruction, are particularly sensitive because they not only expose the workings of the service's internal apparatus, but also contain personal information on individuals and reveal the extent to which the Stasi coerced East German citizens to spy on each other. The ratio of spies to citizens in the GDR (1:180) was lower even than in the Soviet Union (1:595). The BStU's role is to regulate access to the files and to support initiatives for education and research on how the GDR regime functioned. Originally appointed by the post-Communist GDR government in June 1990 to oversee the Stasi's dissolution, Joachim Gauck was confirmed as the first commissioner on reunification (3 October 1990). His successors were Marianne Birthler (2000–2011) and Roland Jahn (2011–). Based in the former Stasi headquarters in Berlin, the office comprises the commissioner, a director, and various departments that administer and control access to the archives; 12 regional offices are dispersed throughout eastern Germany, although staffing levels were reduced in the second decade after reunification.

The legal basis for the management of the archives is the Stasi records law (Stasiunterlagengesetz), first passed by the Bundestag in December 1991 and modified in 2006 to extend its time limit. Anyone has the right to inspect his or her personal files and determine the extent to which the Stasi influenced his or her life. Access was extended in 2012 to the children of deceased parents and grandparents (the Stasi's recruitment of minors to inform on parents and vice versa was particularly disturbing), and subject to the protection of the rights of those affected, the records are also open to researchers and representatives of the media. Since 2006, access to files on civil servants and politicians has been restricted to those in senior positions.

From its creation until the end of 2014, the BStU received 3.05 million requests from citizens for access to their personal files, and although interest peaked in the mid-1990s, 67,763 people applied in 2014. Other applicants included public service personnel (1,755,406) and journalists and researchers (30,456), while others (496,895) related to claims for rehabilitation, restitution, or criminal proceedings. In 2008, the BStU joined a network of similar organizations from the Czech and Slovak Republics, Bulgaria, Hungary, Poland, and Romania (European Network of Official Authorities in Charge of the Secret-Police Files).

Against the background of attempts by the BStU to release the contents of files that were claimed to shed light on the involvement of former chancellor **Helmut Kohl** in accepting illegal financial donations to the **Christian Democratic Union** (**CDU**), a protracted legal battle between Kohl and the office took place between 2001 and 2004. The final outcome was a court ruling that placed considerable restrictions on the disclosure of personal information (including intercepted and recorded telephone conversations). The ruling was welcomed by Kohl's lawyers and interior minister **Otto Schily**, but criticized by Birthler and some journalists.

FEDERAL CONSTITUTIONAL COURT (BUNDESVERFASSUNGS-GERICHT, BVerfG). The Federal Constitutional Court (FCC) is Germany's Supreme Court. The functions and responsibilities of the court, which is highly respected and regarded as the "guardian of the constitution" (Hüter der Verfassung), are set out in the **Basic Law** (**BL**, articles 93 and 94). The FCC interprets and applies the BL, settles disputes between state organs and institutions (including those between the **Bund** and the **federal states**), rules on complaints from individuals alleging an infringement of their constitutional rights, and also receives referrals from other courts and the parliamentary assemblies and their members on the compatibility of proposed laws and measures with the BL.

The FCC is made up two senates (first and second senate) of eight judges each. For each senate, four judges are elected by a two-thirds majority of the **Bundesrat** and four by a 12–member committee of the **Bundestag**. From the 16 judges, the Bundestag and Bundesrat take turns electing a president and vice president. In 1994, Jutta Limbach was elected the first female president of the FCC. As **Social Democratic Party of Germany** (**SPD**) senator for justice in **Berlin** (1989–1994), Limbach reorganized the city's judiciary and legal system after the collapse of the **German Democratic Republic** (**GDR**) and was responsible for the arrest and subsequent release of **Erich Honecker**. Subsequent presidents were Dr. Hans-Jürgen Papier (appointed 2002) and Prof. Dr. Andreas Voßkuhle (2010). Unlike other judges, an FCC judge serves for a maximum of 12 years, must be at least 40 years old, and is obliged to retire at age 68. The judge may not be a member of the Bundestag,

Bundesrat, or any government organ and must not hold any other post (with the exception of a university lectureship) for the duration of the appointment. The first senate is primarily responsible for basic rights, while the second senate focuses on disputes between state organs and parliaments. In cases of doubt, a six-member committee made up of the president, vice president, and two judges from each senate determines where a case should be heard. Special cases can be heard in a plenary session of both senates. The judges deliberate in secret, although hearings may be broadcast by **television and radio**, subject to certain limitations. How judges vote on a ruling can be made public, and a dissenting judge may express a personal position.

To cope with the flood of complaints, mainly from individuals alleging infringements of constitutional rights, in 1993 the FCC introduced a series of vetting procedures designed to filter out unjustified or inappropriate cases. Although over 90 percent of appeals fail to pass these hurdles, Germans readily have recourse to the court, which is overloaded with cases. Concern has been expressed over how Germany's political institutions have drawn the FCC into making decisions on issues that should be settled through the normal political process. It has also been suggested that its decisions should be subject to periodic review in the light of changing social circumstances.

On the basis of the BL, the FCC in the 1950s informed the development of a codex of general and basic personal rights in Germany (Allgemeines Persönlichkeitsrecht), which were distilled during the 1980s into individual rights to informal determination (Recht auf informelle Selbsbestimmung) and, more recently, extended to include rights of privacy for computer users (Computergrundrecht, 2008), with the possibility of further rulings on personal data protection on the **Internet**. The court has also ruled on the **media** and broadcasting, party finance, freedom of protest, **taxation** law, **abortion**, the right to strike, social welfare, electoral law, anti**terrorism** measures, and the right to display and wear religious symbols in schools. Following Chancellor **Gerhard Schröder**'s engineering of a vote of no confidence to force national elections in 2005, the **president of the Federal Republic** referred a decision on the legality of the move to the court. The range of issues handled by the FCC and its occasionally controversial involvement in political and social issues of the day is evident from an overview of some of its rulings.

Reviewing the constitutional commitment to freedom of broadcasting (Rundfunkfreiheit), the court developed the legal framework for the establishment of a complex network of public and private television/radio stations from 1961 onward (BVerfG 12, 205 of 28.1.1961, Rundfunkentscheidung). In its so-called *Spiegel* ruling of 1966, the court strengthened the position of investigative journalism by affirming press freedom as a bulwark of the free and democratic state (BVerfG 20, 162 of 5.8.1966).

The court has ruled on various constitutional issues relating to reunification, **foreign** policy, the transference of powers to the **European Union (EU**, formerly EEC), and the state's obligation to provide social justice and equality (the Sozialstaat). In a landmark ruling of 1994, the second senate gave the go-ahead for armed missions on foreign soil by the **Bundeswehr** if approved beforehand by the Bundestag. Although the FCC rejected claims that the introduction of the euro was unconstitutional (BVerfG, 2 BvR 1877/97 of 31.3.1998), its rulings on European integration have proved far-reaching. In the so-called Solange I judgment ("so lange" = "as long as," BVerfG 37, 271 of 29. 5. 1974), the FCC asserted the right to test European law against the BL, a move that spurred the European Court of Justice (ECJ) to develop its own body of **human rights** legislation. As a result the FCC, in its Solange II decision (BVerfG 73, 339 of 22.10.1986), felt able to declare that European laws no longer *as a rule* needed its seal of approval. On the other hand, while EU member states have generally upheld the principles of direct effect (individuals' rights under EU law must be upheld by national courts) and supremacy (EU law overrides member states' law where the ECJ has jurisdiction), the FCC's rulings on, for example, the Treaties of Maastricht and Lisbon (BVerfG 89, 155 of 12.10.1993 and BVerfG 123, 267 of 30.6.2009) led the way in resisting centralist tendencies in the EU to override the national prerogative. The court not only retained the overall right to determine which competencies may or may not be transferred to the EU (the "competency-competency question"), but also indicated particular competencies that cannot be unconditionally transferred (including aspects of criminal law, policing, military coercion, taxation, public expenditure, welfare provision, family law, and **education**). Deeper EU integration may require fundamental changes to the BL that can be achieved only through a referendum.

Landmark rulings on the Sozialstaat include requiring the state to provide uniform, nationwide criteria for allocating university places in oversubscribed subjects (the *numerus clausus* judgment, BVerfG 33, 303 of 18.7.1972); equalize **pensions** for widowed partners and their dependents (Hinterbliebenenrente BVerfG 39, 169 of 12.3.1975); ensure that tax relief and welfare benefits provide a minimum standard of living for claimants, their dependents, and **asylum** seekers (Existenzminimum GE 87, 153 of 25.9.1992; Hartz-IV Regelsätze BVerfG 1 BvL 1/09 of 9.1.2009; Asylbewerberleistungsgesetz BVerfG, 1 BvL 10/10 of 18.7.2012); and extend tax relief from heterosexual couples to registered single-sex partnerships (BVerfG, 2 BvR 909/06 of 7.5.2013). Beginning in 1975, the court also often delivered controversial rulings on abortion. On issues of religious and personal freedoms in a multicultural society, the FCC declared unconstitutional the requirement for Bavarian schools to display the crucifix in their classrooms (BVerfG 93, 1, Kruzifixurteil of 16.5.1995). In 2003, the court found no constitutional grounds for prohibiting Muslim schoolteachers from wearing headscarves in schools, but handed the decision over to the individual federal states; following outright bans almost immediately imposed by **Baden-Württemberg**, **Bavaria**, and **North Rhine-Westfalia** and years of controversy (other states either acted neutrally or did not legislate), the FCC in 2015 finally ruled such blanket measures unconstitutional and required the states to revise their laws (BVerfG, 2 BvR 1436/02 of 3.6.2003, and 1 BvR 471/10, 1 BvR 1181/10 of 27.1.2015). The FFC has also ruled on university fees (BVerfG, 1 BvL 1/08 of 8.5.2013) and professorial salaries (BVerfG, 2 BvL 4/10 of 14.2.2012).

See also EDUCATION: SCHOOLS; LEGAL SYSTEM; RELIGION.

FEDERAL FOUNDATION FLIGHT, EXPULSION, RECONCILIATION (BUNDESSTIFTUNG FLUCHT, VERTREIBUNG, VERSÖHNUNG, SFVV). Sponsored and administered by the German Historical Museum, this Berlin-based foundation was established by the **Bundestag** in 2008 to research, document, and maintain public awareness of ethnic expulsions and the experiences of refugees in the context of World War II. Its main, but not exclusive, focus is the displacement of Germans in Europe, and it maintains a permanent exhibition. The foundation, however, has faced accusations of historical revisionism (especially from Poland) and disputes over who should be its director. In 2010, objections from Poland prevented the **Christian Democratic Union** (CDU) politician **Erika Steinbach** from joining its governing council as a representative of Germany's national association for expellees, the Bund der Vertriebenen (BdV).

FEDERAL GOVERNMENT (BUNDESREGIERUNG). The executive government of the Federal Republic of Germany (FRG) comprises the **federal chancellor** and his or her ministers, who make up the cabinet. Although the **Basic Law** (**BL**) does not explicitly describe the functions of the government, the latter enjoys a constitutional status equivalent to parliament and is not regarded as simply a subsidiary organ or "executive committee" of the **Bundestag**. Current ministries are (in 2015 and with their official English titles): Federal Ministry for Foreign Affairs (Auswärtiges Amt, AA); Federal Ministry of **Education** and Research (Bundesministerium für Bildung und Forschung, BMBF); Federal Ministry for Family Affairs, Senior Citizens, **Women**, and Youth (Bundesministerium für Familie, Senioren, Frauen und Jugend, BMFSFJ); Federal Ministry of Finance (Bundesministerium der Finanzen, BMF); the Federal Ministry of **Health** (Bundesministerium für Gesundheit, BfG); Federal Ministry of the Interior (Bundesministerium des Innern, BMI); Federal Ministry of Justice and Consumer Protection (Bundesministerium der Justiz und Verbraucherschutz, BMJV); Federal Ministry of Food and **Agriculture** (Bundesministerium für Ernährung und Landwirtschaft, BMEL); Federal Ministry for the **Environment**, Nature Conservation, Building, and Nuclear Safety (Bundesministerium für Umwelt, Naturschutz, Bau und Reaktorsicherheit, BMUB); Federal Ministry of **Transport** and Digital Infrastructure (Bundesministerium für Verkehr und digitale Infrastruktur, BMVI); Federal Ministry for Economic Affairs and **Energy** (Bundesministerium für Wirtschaft und Energie, BMWi); Federal Ministry for Economic Cooperation and Development (Bundesministerium für wirtschaftliche Zusammenarbeit und Entwicklung, BMZ); Federal Ministry of **Defence** (Bundesministerium der Verteidigung, BMVg); and Federal Ministry of Labour and Social Affairs (Bundesministerium für Arbeit und Soziales, BMAS). The minister for special tasks (Minister für besondere Aufgaben) is as a rule not associated with any department and is appointed for specific purposes. The position may have more than one incumbent, and during 1990–1991 five ministers were appointed to handle issues arising from reunification. Owing to mergers and the inclusion or reassignment of new competencies over the years, several departments have been renamed.

Special mention should be made of the Ministry for Pan-German Affairs (Ministerium für Gesamtdeutsche Fragen), which from 1949 until 1969 was responsible for nurturing awareness of the lost eastern territories after World War II, although it was largely an adjunct of the **Office of the Federal Chancellor**, especially under **Konrad Adenauer**, and achieved little public prominence. In 1969, in the wake of the new policy of **Ostpolitik** and rapprochement with the **German Democratic Republic (GDR)**, it was renamed Ministry for Intra-German Relations (Ministerium für Innerdeutsche Beziehungen), and it was wound up in 1991.

See also FEDERALISM.

FEDERAL INTELLIGENCE AGENCY (BUNDESNACHRICHTEN-DIENST, BND). Established in April 1956 and incorporating the Organisation Gehlen—which had been set up by the U.S. occupation authorities in 1946 under the leadership of former National Socialist spymaster and Soviet expert Major General Reinhard Gehlen—the BND, with Gehlen as its first president (until 1968), is Germany's foreign counterespionage and intelligence agency. Gehlen's past and the agency's links with former National Socialists remained controversial, and a commission of historians (Historikerkommission), convened in 2011 to investigate the BND's early years, revealed that the agency had destroyed documents relating to former Nazi party members. With no brief for operations on German territory, the BND's main targets were originally the Soviet Union and **Warsaw Pact** states. Following the attack on Israeli athletes during the summer Olympics in Munich in 1972, and especially since the end of the Cold War, it has concentrated on combating global **terrorism**, the international drug and arms trade, and the smuggling of nuclear weapons. In 2003, the BND moved its central functions and over 1,000 staff members from Pullach (Munich) to Berlin-Lichterfelde, although it maintains several outstations in Germany and abroad. The same year saw the creation of a new post of deputy president responsible for military affairs. In 2006, building began on new premises near the seat of government and the **Bundestag**. Following restructuring between 2008 and 2009, the agency comprised a president, two vice presidents (responsible for military affairs and modernization), and 12 departments covering areas such as reconnaissance, geographical regions, terrorism, arms proliferation, and information technology. The BND employs around 6,000 people, split equally between soldiers and civilians. For many years the BND's role was determined solely by the **federal government**. In May 1989, it became directly responsible to the **Office of the Federal Chancellor**, and in December 1990, the Bundestag agreed to legislation regulating its structure and functions.

See also INTELLIGENCE AGENCIES.

FEDERAL OFFICE FOR THE PROTECTION OF THE CONSTITUTION (BUNDESAMT FÜR VERFASSUNGSSCHUTZ, BfV). Founded in 1950 and subject to Allied supervision until 1955, this office—one of Germany's three national **intelligence agencies**—is responsible for monitoring threats to the democratic order of the Federal Republic of Germany (FRG), as embodied in the **Basic Law** (**BL**). Subject to the interior ministry and with 2,700 staff members, the BfV collects and analyzes information about **extremist**, terrorist, and other potential security threats, including the activities of foreign intelligence services. The agency's main purpose is to inform the federal government about the domestic security situation, and it has no police powers (e.g., of detention or arrest). Based in Cologne and headed by a president (Hans-Georg Maaßen since 2012) and vice president, the BfV comprises six departments, most of which are responsible for dealing with various forms of extremism, terrorism, and espionage. Its comprehensive annual reports include statistics on terrorist activities and the status of extremist groups and organizations. Over time, the **federal states** have established their own agencies that are independent of the national BfV. In 2015, the BfV presented the results of an investigation conducted by a commission between 2011 and 2014 into the involvement of former National Socialists and members of the Gestapo in the agency's work between 1950 and 1975. Interim results published in 2013 revealed that 13 percent of the agency's staff during this period had a Gestapo or National Socialist background.

The extensive use of undercover agents, which the agency regards as an essential tool in the fight against violent extremism, has attracted criticism in recent years. Attempts by the authorities to ban the extreme right-wing **National Democratic Party** (**NPD**) in 2001 were rejected by the **Federal Con-**

stitutional Court (FCC) in 2003 on the grounds that BfV agents were active in the party leadership. Suspicions also surfaced that agents were involved in the neo-Nazi NSU terror group, whose activities began in 2000, although the authorities did not appear to be aware of its existence until 2011. In 2015, the **Bundestag** passed legislation regulating the use of undercover agents and requiring the national BfV and regional agencies to improve the exchange of information.

In 2015, Hans-Georg Maaßen instigated legal action against journalists who had published secret information about the internal budget and plans of the BfV, possibly leading to charges of treason. Following a storm of protest from the **media**, public, and politicians, the chief prosecutor, Harald Range, who had pursued the action, was dismissed by Justice Minister **Heiko Maas**, and Maaßen, despite his concerns over a history of security leaks, was widely seen as having damaged his relationship with the government.

FEDERAL STATES (LÄNDER). Germany is made up of 16 federal states (Länder; singular Land). The 13 so-called area states (Flächenländer) are **Baden-Württemberg, Bavaria, Brandenburg, Hessen, Mecklenburg-West Pomerania, Lower Saxony, North Rhine-Westfalia, Rhineland-Palatinate, Saarland, Saxony, Saxony-Anhalt, Schleswig-Holstein,** and **Thuringia. Berlin** (the federal capital), **Hamburg,** and **Bremen** are city-states. The states vary in terms of geographical size, population, and economy, not to mention cultural diversity. Bavaria, Lower Saxony, and Baden-Württemberg have the largest surface areas, while North Rhine-Westfalia is the most populous, followed by Bavaria and Baden-Württemberg. Of the 13 states, 11 made up the old Federal Republic of Germany (FRG, 1949–1990). The five **eastern federal states**, which were established through legislation (the Ländereinführungsgesetz) passed by the **People's Chamber** of the **German Democratic Republic (GDR)** on 22 July 1990, are Brandenburg, Mecklenburg-West Pomerania, Saxony, Saxony-Anhalt, and Thuringia. These formally joined the West German federation of states when the Treaty of Unification came into force and the GDR ceased to exist (3 October 1990). Soon afterward (14 October), elections were held in all the accession states, enabling them to constitute their first parliaments (**Landtage**) and regional governments. In the following decade the eastern states progressively restructured their administrative units (Bezirke and Kreise), which were left over from the GDR years. From 1949 until 1990, Bonn and (East) Berlin had been the capitals of the FRG and GDR, respectively. Upon reunification, Berlin regained its historical position as the capital of Germany and subsequently became the seat of government, although some administrative functions remained in Bonn. The imbalance in the size and population of some states has prompted proposals for mergers, especially in eastern Germany. The national assembly of the federal states is the **Bundesrat.**

See also BUND; FEDERALISM; FEDERALISM REFORM.

FEDERALISM. Between the foundation of the Federal Republic of Germany (FRG) in 1949 and reunification in 1990, the federal system, based on a division of powers between a central legislature (the **Bund**) and the regions or **federal states** (the Länder), was widely and positively acknowledged as a structural pillar of the West German political and social order. Federalism distributed power and responsibility between the regions and the political center, encouraged citizens to engage in local democracy, protected minorities and other social groups, evened out economic imbalances, and promoted social and cultural heterogeneity. The framework for the current federal system is laid out in the **Basic Law (BL)** of 1949, although German federalism has a long cultural history extending from the Middle Ages to the Second Empire (1871–1918) and the Weimar Republic (1919–1933). In the FRG, each federal state has a regional or state parliament (usually called a **Landtag**), which sends delegates to the national regional assembly, the **Bundesrat**.

The BL defines the areas in which the Bundestag and the Bundesrat have legislative powers (articles 70–74). As a general principle, the BL catalogs the spheres in which the center has primacy, giving the federal states authority over any areas that may remain. Areas in which the Bund has "exclusive" powers to legislate (ausschließliche Gesetzgebung) include **foreign policy**, defense, nationality, rail and air **transport**, combating **terrorism**, currency, and customs/border control (article 73). The federal states may legislate here only if the Bund explicitly gives them the powers to do so (article 71). For "concurrent legislation" (konkurrierende Gesetzgebung), the Bundesrat is empowered to make laws except where there is a legislative requirement to preserve the legal and economic unity of the nation (article 72). Since the **federalism reform** of 2006, 33 areas of concurrent legislation are listed and include most aspects of law (civil, criminal, commercial, labor, and social welfare), the right of residence for **foreigners**, transportation, and the **environment**. Where states may deviate from federal legislation passed under concurrent powers (article 72), the law, unless otherwise agreed to by the Bundesrat, does not come into force for six months; this gives the states time to consider the extent of any deviation and prevents draft laws being shuttled backward and forward between the Bund and the Länder.

Procedurally, the BL also distinguishes laws that the Bundesrat may delay but not veto (called "objection laws" or Einspruchsgesetze) from those that require the specific assent of the Bundesrat and cannot be overruled by the Bundestag (called "consent laws" or Zustimmungsgesetze). Consent laws include changes to the constitution, legislation affecting specific rights of the Länder in finance and **taxation**, and the administration of federal laws. To prevent obstructionism, the Bundesrat must raise objections within time limits. Areas or competencies that the BL does not explicitly identify as requiring Bundesrat approval are considered objection laws.

Legislation is formally initiated by the Bundestag, the Bundesrat, or the **federal government** (Bundesregierung). If a draft law (bill) emanates from the government, it is first sent to the Bundesrat (first passage), which normally has six weeks to consider its constitutional status, possible implications for the assembly's administrative practices, and whether it is an objection or consent law. Since the first passage stage is not required for a bill brought by the Bundestag, the government, using its majority there, often employs this faster path, especially for urgent legislation. In the Bundestag, a bill undergoes three debates or readings, including consideration by the Council of Elders, faction groups, standing expert committees, and open sessions of members. If a bill finds a majority in the Bundestag, it is passed to the Bundesrat. Bundesrat approval is always needed for consent laws, but if it refuses an objection bill, the Bundestag can override the veto by an equivalent majority. To avoid friction between the assemblies—or in most cases a consent bill failing because the Bundesrat rejects it—a **mediation committee** can be invoked. For objection laws, this can be initiated by the Bundestag, the Bundesrat, or the federal government, and for consent laws, by the Bundesrat alone, in which case the Bundesrat must act within three weeks and provide justification. The committee can propose confirming a bill or amending it, or it can fail to agree on a compromise. In any case, the bill must be passed back to the Bundestag and/or Bundesrat to be approved. Clearly, the success of many government or Bundestag bills depends greatly on the ruling parties' having a majority in the Bundesrat, which has not often been the case in postwar Germany. Disputes about whether laws require Bundesrat agreement may ultimately be referred to the **Federal Constitutional Court** (**FCC**), but the historical tendency of the Bund to extend its powers at the expense of the states—by invoking article 72 of the BL or through so-called guideline or framework legislation (Rahmengesetzgebung)—was a driver in the federalism reform measures of 2006, which redefined competencies and removed framework legislation altogether.

The number of consent laws (averaging 51 percent between 1949 and 2013, increasing to over 60 percent during 1983–1987) proved to be higher than the BL's founding fathers envisioned, fueling disputes over the "blocking" capability of the Bundestag, especially when the government fails to command an absolute majority in the latter assembly. In practice, and especially since reunification, the Bundesrat has tended to form interstate coalitions across party lines in order to further regional interests, regardless of national political majorities. Following the first tranche of federalism reform, the proportion of consent laws fell (to 39 percent between 2006 and 2013). Most referrals to the mediation committee are initiated by the Bundesrat (88 percent since 1949).

The need for the federal states to coordinate their activities with one another and the Bund has led over the years to a system of "cooperative federalism" (kooperativer Föderalismus), a complex, institutionalized network of committees and decision-making interests involving politicians, administrators, and experts at all levels. During the 1990s, the question arose as to whether the system of German federalism was meeting national needs or impeding political and economic structural reform. Cooperative federalism was largely shaped by the 1969 finance reform bill, a package of measures passed by the first **grand coalition** (1966–1969) and designed to regenerate the economy by easing cooperation between regions and the center. The measures introduced a framework that, among other things, enabled the Bund and Länder to undertake joint projects (Gemeinschaftsaufgaben) and share tax revenue (the Steuerverbund). Although the changes lifted from the Länder the burden of, for example, building universities and hospitals or modernizing **agriculture** and regional economic infrastructure, the "financial strings" (goldener Zügel) reinforced the trend away from a federal toward a unitary state, as the states concentrated more on influencing policy at the center (and later in Europe) and at the same time became its executive agents ("executive federalism"). The federalism reform of 2006 reduced the center's capacity for financial support and introduced a new form of legislation, "alternative legislation" (Abweichungsgesetzgebung), which gave the Länder more opportunities to frame their own laws, for example about nature protection or university admissions.

FEDERALISM REFORM. Following its enlargement upon reunification, Germany established three cross-party, joint **Bundestag/Bundesrat** commissions to restructure the country's system of **federal government**. The task of the first commission, the Independent Federalism Commission (Unabhängige Föderalismuskommission), which met between 1991 and 1992, was to recommend which federal institutions should be relocated in the new **eastern federal states**. The aim was to achieve a fair distribution of bodies and to strengthen both the federalist idea and the new states' sense of identity with the **Bund**. As a result, three federal courts, one ministry, and various agencies transferred to the east. Two subsequent commissions addressed more fundamental issues, in particular the need for greater transparency in the relationship between the Bund and the **Länder** (who is responsible for what) and for a legislative structure that would help disentangle the dense and complex network of mechanisms and committees linking the two parliaments. The goal was a streamlined decision-making process no longer subject to blocking vetoes or prolonged negotiations over overlapping competencies. The first of these commissions, the Kommission von Bundestag und Bundesrat zur Modernisierung der bundesstaatlichen Ordnung (Commission of the Bundestag and Bundesrat for the Modernization of the Federal Order), or simply Federalism Commission I, sat between November 2003 and December 2004. Although the commission reached agreement on several areas, **education** remained a stumbling block, and it was only under a new government, elected in 2005, that a package of reforms (so-called Federalism I), the most extensive in the country's history, was approved by both parliaments in June/July 2006 and incorporated into the **Basic Law (BL)**. The measures, which aimed to reduce the number of consent laws (from 60 to 35–40 percent), eliminated framework legislation altogether (existing competencies were either assigned to consent or concurrent legislation or left to the Länder). The federal states gained greater roles in education (to include universities, although the Bund retained responsibility for admissions and final qualifications) and **environmental** legislation, and also assumed responsibility for the salaries and working conditions of civil servants. At the European level, the states would represent Germany in the areas of education, broadcasting, and culture only if their regional interests were affected. Although the complex instrument of joint financing (Mischfinanzierung) would be phased out (e.g., the Länder took over responsibility for building universities), reform of the wider system of **financial equalization** was passed over, to be addressed by the next commission, the Gemeinsame Kommission der Bund-Länder-Finanz-Beziehungen (Joint Commission on the Modernization of Bund-Länder Financial Relations), or Federalism Commission II, which sat between March 2007 and March 2009 and whose recommendations came into force in August 2009 as Federalism II. After the introduction of laws ending joint financing in university building, educational planning, local transportation, and social housing (Entflechtungsgesetze, 2006), the number of consent laws during the 2009–2013 legislative period fell markedly, from 53 to 38.9 percent.

Although Federalism Commission II was meant to tackle structural financial issues within the federal system (relations between Bund and Länder, **taxation**, disparities between rich and poor states, economic growth, and public debt reduction), it rapidly focused on the debt question, especially when its work was interrupted by the global financial crisis of 2008–2009. The commission's principal recommendation was to balance the annual budgets of Bund and Länder through eliminating borrowing and applying a "debt brake" or limit (Schuldenbremse). For the Bund, the deficit limit (and borrowing level) was set at an annual 0.35 percent of GDP (effective in 2016), while the Länder were permitted no credit at all (effective in 2020). The brake could be adjusted for natural catastrophes, emergencies, or "deviations from the normal business cycle" (a controversial formula that was not further defined). In the transitional period, the five poorest Länder (**Bremen, Saar-**

land, Berlin, Saxony-Anhalt, and Schleswig-Holstein) would receive aid from a joint "consolidation fund." An early warning system operated by a joint Stabilitätsrat (Stability Council) would monitor progress and preempt future budgetary crises. Established in 2010, the council was designed to be smaller and more effective than the old Finanzplanungsrat (Financial Planning Council) of 1969, which it replaced, although it had no power to implement sanctions. Minor administrative measures included improving and coordinating IT services, introducing benchmarking (e.g., to facilitate comparisons of budgets across Bund and Länder), setting up a national cancer data bank, and downgrading some national road routes (with financial implications for the Länder).

Federalism I was widely criticized for simply reallocating "mini-competencies" between Bund and Länder, while failing to achieve any significant disentanglement of powers and decision making. Objections to Federalism II referred to the irrationality of applying a debt brake to the Länder without also reviewing the much larger issues of fiscal equalization between rich and poor states and the future of the current Solidarity Pact, both of which topics were bracketed out of the discussion. Yet another reform package in the near future appeared inevitable, with the current system of cooperative debt management, with all its controversies and complexities, continuing in the meantime.

See also BUDGET.

FEDERATION OF FREE CITIZENS (BUND FREIER BÜRGER, BFB). This populist right-wing group, inspired and supported by the Austrian nationalist Jörg Haider, was founded in 1994 in Wiesbaden by the lawyer and former **Free Democratic Party** (**FDP**) member Manfred Brunner. The party opposed the Treaty of Maastricht and the introduction of the euro and campaigned for the denationalization of state-run industries, a liberalization of the economy, and traditional German family values (e.g., advocating that large families should be exempt from **taxation**). At the height of its activity, it boasted 2,800 members, mainly older academics in **Bavaria** and **Hessen**. In January 1998, it merged with another right-wing group, the Offensive für Deutschland (Offensive for Germany), led by former FDP member Heiner Kappel, to form BFB-Die Offensive. Electorally, the party proved a failure, and it disintegrated in the face of disputes over leanings toward right-wing extremist groups such as The **Republicans** (**REP**). Upon its dissolution in Fulda in August 2000, the party had around 1,500 members. Brunner briefly rejoined the FDP in Saxony (1999–2001). In 2002, he was convicted for tax fraud.

FEDERATION OF SOCIALIST GERMAN STUDENTS (SOZIALIS-TISCHER DEUTSCHER STUDENTENBUND, SDS). Founded in 1946 as an independent organization, the SDS's links with the **Social Democratic Party of Germany (SPD)** were severed in 1960 when the latter distanced itself from Marxism and radical socialism in the Godesberger Program (1959), expelling SDS members the following year. The SDS went on to become a tightly organized, Marxist-oriented student group, which campaigned during the 1960s for full-scale reforms of the German higher **education** system (parity of representation for students in decision making, the right of student associations to adopt political positions, and an overhaul of courses and examinations). Following models taken from the United States, the SDS organized sit-ins, disruptions, and other forms of protests, which after 1965 evolved into a full-scale student revolt demanding a radical transformation of German society. Drawing its theoretical roots from the works of the philosopher Herbert Marcuse and the Frankfurt School social scientists Theodor W. Adorno and Max Horkheimer, the SDS became the leading group of the Extra-Parliamentary Opposition (APO), whose activities culminated in violent student clashes with the authorities in 1968. The APO failed to capture the support of the public at large, and the internally divided SDS dissolved itself as a national organization in 1970. At its height, its membership reached 2,500, with power bases at the universities of Cologne, Marburg, and Munich. Prominent members included **Helmut Schmidt, Rudi Dutschke, Ulrike Meinhof,** and the lawyer Horst Mahler.

See also EXTREMISM: LEFT-WING; RED ARMY FACTION (ROTE ARMEE FRAKTION, RAF); STUDENTS' MOVEMENT.

FILBINGER, HANS KARL (1913–2007). Christian Democratic Union (CDU) politician. Born in Mannheim (**Baden-Württemberg**), Hans Filbinger studied law and economics at the universities of Freiburg and Munich, graduating with a doctorate in law (1939). He also studied in Paris (1938–1939) before returning to Freiburg University to work as a research assistant and tutor. During World War II, he was enlisted in the German navy (1940) and from 1943 served in the military judiciary. The group of army officers around Colonel Graf von Stauffenberg, who attempted to assassinate Adolf Hitler in 1944, planned a role for Filbinger after the coup, although the Gestapo's failure to discover his involvement probably saved his life. After the war, he returned to Freiburg University, where he worked as a lawyer (from 1946) and cultivated links with the Freiburg school of economists, which laid the theoretical foundations for the postwar **social market economy.** He joined an international commission charged with breaking up Germany's industrial cartels (1947), was elected to the Freiburg city council

(1953), and entered the regional government of Baden-Württemberg (1958). In 1960, he was appointed interior minister and elected to the regional state parliament (**Landtag**), where he represented Freiburg city until 1980.

In 1966, Filbinger succeeded **Kurt Georg Kiesinger** as **minister president** of Baden-Württemberg, heading a **grand coalition** of the CDU and **Social Democratic Party of Germany** (**SPD**) until 1972, when the CDU gained a record absolute majority, repeated in 1976. Under Filbinger's leadership, Baden was incorporated into the state of Baden-Württemberg (confirmed by a plebiscite majority of 82 percent in 1970), denominational schools were replaced by Christian "community schools" (Gemeinschaftsschulen), and a university for medicine and natural sciences was founded at Ulm (1967). Baden-Württemberg remained largely untouched by the **students' movement** and social unrest of 1968, although regional elections in that year saw the neo-Nazi **National Democratic Party of Germany** (**NPD**) enter the Landtag with 9.8 percent of the vote. During this period, local government was reformed (the number of administrative districts was drastically reduced), and Baden-Württemberg became one of Germany's most prosperous regions. From 1970 until 1974, Filbinger represented Germany within the framework of the Franco–German Treaty of Friendship, deepening cultural links between the two countries at the national and regional levels; schoolteaching in French was introduced for some subjects, and progress was made in the mutual recognition of vocational qualifications. Filbinger also served as president of the **Bundesrat** (1973–1974).

In 1978, Filbinger retired from all political offices following reports of his activities as a military judge during World War II, although it emerged that the revelations were orchestrated by the East German secret police, the **Stasi**. When the author Rolf Hochhut, writing in *Die Zeit*, revealed that Filbinger had been involved in four death sentences passed by National Socialist courts, the latter infamously responded by declaring that what was legal then could not be illegal now ("Was damals Recht war, kann heute nicht Unrecht sein!"). Firmly on the right wing of the CDU, Filbinger founded the Christian and conservative Hans Filbinger Foundation (1979), which also supports a study center for young people (Studienzentrum Weikersheim). In May 2004, Filbinger's nomination for membership in the **Federal Assembly**, which was constituted to elect a new federal president, reignited protests over his judicial career under the National Socialists. The recipient of honors from the German and French governments and of numerous international awards, he also published on contemporary politics and society.

FINANCE, PUBLIC. *See* BUDGET.

FINANCIAL EQUALIZATION (LÄNDERFINANZAUSGLEICH). The complex system of financial equalization for redistributing **taxation** revenues from rich **federal states** to poorer ones in order to ensure a uniform standard of living and services across the country is both a cornerstone of German **federalism** and a constant source of political dispute and referrals to the **Federal Constitutional Court (FCC)**. The scheme, which allocates transfers between **Bund** and **Länder** (vertical equalization) and from state to state (horizontal equalization), came to involve huge sums of money and raised political tensions that came to a head after reunification, when the ratio of donor states (mainly **Bavaria, Hessen, Baden-Württemberg**) to recipients (**Berlin** and all the eastern states, especially **Saxony**) fell sharply. Disputes focus on the need for transparency in calculating transfers, which **taxation** revenues to include, weightings for special factors, and the need to provide incentives for beneficiary states to improve their finances. In 1999, the FCC required the legislature to reform the system in two stages: first, to draw up a "standards act" (Maßstäbegesetz) clarifying the criteria for transfers, and second, to ensure that transfers did not unduly penalize donor states. In the event, the Bund and Länder postponed a standards act until the expiration of a compromise equalization budget agreed for 2005–2019. The budget, did, however, limit transfers of sales tax revenues from richer to poorer states to 25 percent and increased the per-inhabitant weighting of transfers from city-states (Berlin, **Hamburg, Bremen**) on the basis that their residents also use the facilities of surrounding states; furthermore, contributions by donor states would not reduce their own financial strength below the national state average. An additional element of vertical equalization is the **Solidarity Pact**, providing central government support to the eastern states after reunification.

See LOCAL GOVERNMENT; SOLIDARITY SURCHARGE (SOLIDARITÄTSZUSCHLAG).

FISCAL COMPACT. *See* STABILITY AND GROWTH PACT.

FISCHER, ANDREA (1960–). Green Party politician. Born in Arnsberg (**North Rhine-Westfalia**), Andrea Fischer trained and worked as an offset printer before studying economics in **Berlin** (from 1985). She subsequently worked as a research assistant at the European Parliament, at the WZB Berlin social science center in Berlin, and at the Bundesversicherungsanstalt für Angestellte (BfA, an independent organization representing the interests of pensioners and members of the national social security system). After entering the **Bundestag** as an **Alliance 90/The Greens** member (1994), she specialized in social policy and, following the national election of 1998, became **health** minister in the cabinet of Chancellor **Gerhard Schröder**, the first

Green minister at federal level. In January 2001, together with Agriculture Minister Karl-Heinz Funke (**Social Democratic Party of Germany, SPD**), she resigned over the mad cow (or BSE) crisis, acknowledging that mistakes had been made in allowing the use of prohibited animal feed in German beef cattle. Withdrawing from active politics, Fischer worked as a journalist and health-care lobbyist, although she briefly represented the Greens in a central Berlin district council (September 2011 to October 2012).

FISCHER, JOSCHKA (1948–). Green Party politician. Born in Gerabronn (**Baden-Württemberg**), the son of an ethnic German expellee from Hungary, Joseph (Joshcka) Fischer left school before graduating in order to train as a photographer (1965), but did not complete his apprenticeship and in 1966 traveled in Europe, Turkey, and Kuwait before returning to Germany to work as a toy salesman. In 1967, he married his first wife in Gretna Green in Great Britain, and the couple took an active part in the **students' movement** in Stuttgart before moving to Frankfurt/Main (they divorced in 1984). Between 1968 and 1975, Fischer mixed with left-wing figures such as the student leader **Daniel Cohn-Bendit** and, as a member of a militant group (Revolutionärer Kampf), he took part in often violent demonstrations and street battles and was sentenced to three days in Stuttgart-Stammheim prison for a breach of the peace. In 1971, he was briefly employed at the Opel AG motor vehicle factory (Rüsselsheim) before being dismissed for political agitation, and eventually worked as a taxi driver in Frankfurt. Years later, as a government minister, Fischer's radical past returned to haunt him when he admitted assaulting a policeman during a 1973 street demonstration, although he rejected accusations that he had harbored the **Red Army Faction** (**RAF**) terrorist Margrit Schiller. In 2001, he was called as a witness at the trial of his former friend, Hans-Joachim Klein, who was charged with taking part in a 1975 attack on a meeting of ministers from the Organization of the Petroleum Exporting Countries (OPEC) in which three people died. Fischer vehemently denied claims by Bettina Röhl, the journalist daughter of the terrorist **Ulrike Meinhof**, that he had advocated the use of Molotov cocktails at a 1976 demonstration (held in protest against Meinhof's suicide) at which a policeman almost died in a fire-bombed car. Fischer also claimed to have distanced himself from political extremism when the RAF group kidnapped and murdered the leader of the German employers' federation, Hanns Martin Schleyer (1977).

Fischer joined the Green Party in 1982 and was one of its first members to enter the **Bundestag** (1983). He acted as the party's parliamentary business manager, proved an effective speaker, and led the "realist" wing of the Greens before resigning his mandate in accordance with the party's principle of rotation (1985). From 1985 to 1987, Fischer was minister for the **environment** and **energy** in the **Social Democratic Party of Germany (SPD)**/Green

Party coalition in the state of **Hessen**, the first Green to achieve government office. Although Fischer introduced measures to control industrial pollution, the unstable coalition broke up in 1987, when the Greens demanded that the state government withdraw approval for a nuclear plant at Hanau. Fischer was dismissed as minister but headed a Green parliamentary group in a reelected state assembly led by a coalition of the **Christian Democratic Union (CDU)** and **Free Democratic Party (FDP)**.

When the Greens failed to clear the 5 percent hurdle in the 1990 national election, Fischer initiated major changes in the party, including scrapping the rotation principle, electing a party leader, and allowing members to sit in both regional and national parliaments. The restructured party gained enough seats in the Hessen state election of 1991 to form a new coalition with the SPD, with Fischer as deputy **minister president** and minister for **energy** and the environment. He introduced a levy on dangerous industrial waste and halted the production of fuel rods and uranium processing at the Hanau plant. Resigning as minister to focus on the 1994 national election, Fischer mooted the possibility of forming a government coalition with the SPD, on condition that it would phase out nuclear energy and not support military action in war-torn former Yugoslavia. After the election Fischer, alongside Kerstin Müller, was elected spokesman for the **Alliance 90/The Greens** parliamentary grouping in the Bundestag. Between 1995 and 1998, Fischer attempted, with limited success, to unite his party in backing **United Nations**-sponsored military intervention in Yugoslavia and adopting a less antibusiness approach. In the election year of 1998, he argued for the extension of the **North Atlantic Treaty Organization (NATO)** to eastern Europe and Germany's role as a key partner in the Western alliance.

Following the Greens' best ever national election results (October 1998), Fischer served as deputy chancellor and foreign minister in an SPD/Green Party coalition under Chancellor **Gerhard Schröder** (1998–2005). Although his call (in November 1998) for NATO to renounce the first use of nuclear weapons embarrassed the government and provoked a crisis within the coalition, Fischer supported sending an 8,500-member German peacekeeping force under UN mandate to Kosovo (1999), a move that alienated the Green Party's mainstream pacifist wing, and he suffered a burst ear drum when he was hit by a bag of paint thrown at him by an irate party member. As foreign minister, Fischer supported Turkey's entry into the **European Union (EU)**, argued for an end to the automatic right of veto in the UN Security Council, and ensured that German soldiers were sent to East Timor to provide humanitarian and medical aid. More controversially, at a secret meeting of the Bundessicherheitsrat (Federal Security Council), he voted against supplying Turkey with Leopard II tanks, although the council approved the move. He also led Germany's opposition to the U.S.-led war on Iraq in 2003. Fischer was a prime mover in pushing the SPD toward phasing out nuclear energy, although, alongside environment minister **Jürgen Trittin**, he ran into problems with his party over proposals, which were eventually dropped, to build a nuclear power station in Finland and export the mothballed facility at Hanau/Frankfurt to China.

In 2001, Fischer provoked debate by proposing a European government that would downgrade the status of nation-states. Schröder's proposal in early 2002 to establish a separate ministry for Europe after the autumn election was, however, widely taken as a move to sideline the well-liked Fischer. Because of his high profile and influence within the Green Party, which does not allow cabinet office holders to hold party positions, Fischer was long regarded as its "secret leader." Arguably Germany's most popular and colorful politician, Fischer succeeded in taming the chaotic fundamentalist wing of the Greens and enabling the party to participate in credible government. In 2005, he commissioned a report by independent historians on the role of the German foreign ministry during the National Socialist period, which, when published in 2010, revealed the extent to which German diplomats connived in the persecution of Jews and covered up their activities in the postwar Federal Republic. In the same year, Fischer's popularity fell when he was questioned by a parliamentary committee investigating allegations that he had failed to prevent citizens from the former Soviet Union entering Germany on improperly issued visas. Following the national election of September 2005, he resigned all parliamentary and party offices, visited the University of Princeton (U.S.) as a guest professor (2006–2007), and founded an international business consultancy (2007). He was also a founding member and trustee of the Arab Democracy Foundation (from 2007), worked for the consulting firm Albright Group in Washington, D.C. (from 2008), and was an adviser to the Nabucco/Turkey–Austria gas pipeline project (from 2009).

FLICK, FRIEDRICH KARL (1927–2006). Businessman and industrialist. Friedrich Karl Flick was born in **Berlin**, the third and youngest son of Friedrich Flick (1883–1972), who founded a coal and steel empire during the Weimar Republic. After supporting the bourgeois political parties, Flick Sr. became a generous benefactor (and, from 1937, member) of the National Socialist Party, playing a leading role in the armaments **industry** during World War II. A close friend of Heinrich Himmler, he was jailed for seven years in 1947 for war crimes, including profiteering from slave labor. Despite showing no remorse and refusing to compensate those who had worked in his factories, he was released early (1950) and forced to sell his coal and steel interests, although he reinvested shrewdly in the booming postwar economy and established a large concern with diverse interests that included a 40 percent share of Daimler-Benz. By the late 1960s, he was one of the richest men in the world. His son, Friedrich Karl, entered the family business in 1957 and by the time of his father's death (1972) virtually controlled the company, removing all remaining relatives by 1975. Flick restructured the shareholdings (retaining just 10 percent of Daimler-Benz) and redirected resources to a number of profitable industrial ventures, eventually making him one of Germany's wealthiest men. Like his father, Flick financially supported political parties, in particular the **Free Democratic Party** (**FDP**).

In the early 1980s, Flick and his organization became embroiled in a political and financial scandal, the "Flick affair," which came to court in 1986–1987. After the group had sold a shareholding in Daimler-Benz for reinvestment abroad (1975), it was alleged that two FDP economics ministers, Hans Friderichs and his successor, **Otto Graf Lambsdorff**, had exempted the transaction from **tax** in return for political donations. Charges of corruption against the former ministers and a Flick executive, Eberhard von Brauchitsch, were dropped for lack of evidence, although all three were fined heavily for tax evasion. At one point, Chancellor **Helmut Kohl** faced accusations that he had lied to an investigating parliamentary committee, but he escaped having to resign when the scandal died down. Flick himself appeared before the committee in 1983. Although the scandal focused on the Flick concern and its relationship to the FDP, it damaged the standing of all the major **political parties** in Germany, which had been receiving donations from Flick and other businesses since the 1950s. Perhaps prompted by the adverse publicity, Flick sold his entire interest in his group to **Deutsche Bank** (1985), which broke it up and sold it off. Flick himself retired and in 1994 settled in Austria, where he had acquired citizenship several years previously. What remained of the original Flick concern was converted into a holding company. Retirement, however, did not spare Flick from his father's National Socialist past. He personally refused to contribute to a compensation fund for former slave workers, negotiated in 1999 by the government and industry, although a contribution on "humanitarian grounds," agreed between the Deutsche Bank and a former Flick subsidiary, Dynamit Nobel, eventually emerged.

FOREIGN POLICY: 1949–1969. During the founding years of postwar West Germany, **Konrad Adenauer**, the country's first **federal chancellor** (1949–1963) and foreign minister (1951–1955), pursued a policy of integrating the Federal Republic of Germany (FRG) into Western political, military, and economic structures, notably the **North Atlantic Treaty Organization** (**NATO**) and the precursor organizations of the **European Union** (**EU**). Despite the misgivings of some contemporaries, Adenauer maintained that only a strong, united Western bloc, with the FRG firmly embedded within it, could persuade the Union of Soviet Socialist Republics (USSR) to negotiate meaningfully on German reunification. He was above all determined not to provoke the same international distrust that had accompanied German foreign policy during the prewar Weimar period, when Germany had tried to maintain a balance of interests (so-called Schaukelpolitik) between the Western powers and the USSR. Between 1952 and 1954, the USSR sent a series of notes offering to negotiate the creation of a reunited, neutral German state that would be disengaged from the West. Considering this a dangerous path to follow, Adenauer refused to follow up on these offers. His position, the "policy of strength" (Politik der Stärke), was in line with the U.S. intention to contain and roll back communism in Europe during the late 1940s and 1950s. A key aspect of West German policy at this time was the threat that the FRG would break off diplomatic relations with any state that recognized the **German Democratic Republic (GDR)**. Known as the Hallstein doctrine, this policy was in line with the "magnet theory," which maintained that the economic and political achievements of the West would prove to be an irresistible model for a future reunified Germany.

See also FOREIGN POLICY AFTER 1990; FOREIGN POLICY: 1970–1990.

FOREIGN POLICY: 1970–1990. As a result of the **Ostpolitik** pursued by the coalition of the **Social Democratic Party of Germany (SPD)** and the **Free Democratic Party (FDP)** led by **Willy Brandt (federal chancellor,** 1969–1974), **Konrad Adenauer**'s "policy of strength" was superseded by a series of treaties and agreements with the Union of Soviet Socialist Republics (USSR) and its satellites, including the **German Democratic Republic (GDR)**. These agreements reduced tension with the eastern bloc, secured the position of the isolated enclave of West **Berlin**, and went a long way toward normalizing relations between East and West Germany. Although the policy was denounced as a sellout by the conservative opposition and refugee organizations, subsequent German governments, including those led by the **Christian Democratic Union (CDU)/Christian Social Union (CSU)**, continued to maintain a pragmatic relationship with the GDR, even during periods of international tension.

Although Ostpolitik appeared to be a fairly sudden and radical departure from the previous "policy of strength," its roots predate 1969. The era of peaceful coexistence between the two Germanies may be seen as beginning soon after the erection of the **Berlin Wall** (1961), when the GDR halted the outflow of its population and stabilized itself internally. It is also arguably unfair to regard Adenauer as an inveterate warrior of the Cold War, because in June 1962 he secretly offered the USSR a 10-year truce, in which the FRG agreed not to challenge the status of the GDR in return for greater freedoms and improved living conditions for East Germans (the offer was made under the influence of his close adviser, Hans Globke, and under pressure from the newly elected U.S. president, John F. Kennedy, who was actively pursuing a "strategy of peace" toward the USSR). Moreover, Willy Brandt, the future architect of Ostpolitik and governing mayor of West Berlin (1957–1966), had, with U.S. support, defied official government policy from at least 1963 onward by negotiating directly with the East German authorities. Such open disregard of the Hallstein doctrine was justified on the grounds that confrontation was not bringing Germans together, but rather leading them into a political dead end. Despite the disputed origins of Ostpolitik, the policy of improving the relationship with the USSR and establishing working links with the GDR is widely credited with easing the path to reunification when the opportunity eventually arose. At the same time, proponents of the "policy of strength" were able to argue that it was the Western powers' uncompromising resolve over several decades that finally undermined the social, political, and economic viability of the eastern bloc. Thus, while **Helmut Kohl**, federal chancellor from 1982 to 1998, declared that Adenauer's policy of strength was the very foundation of reunification, others were able to claim precisely that role for more conciliatory approaches.

See also FOREIGN POLICY AFTER 1990; FOREIGN POLICY: 1949–1969.

FOREIGN POLICY AFTER 1990. Before reunification and during the following decade, Germany was regarded as an example of a "civilian power" (Zivilmacht), achieving its foreign policy goals through peaceful, diplomatic means and projecting its national identity "normatively," that is, by presenting a model of liberal democracy, respect for **human rights**, and cultural values. To these ends, Germany participated in building democratic, transnational economic and political structures (the **European Union, EU**), contributed generous aid for global development, and invariably acted as a compliant partner in its alliances. Military activity abroad was confined to providing logistical assistance and supporting humanitarian missions (the first was in 1960 in response to an earthquake in Morocco, and many more followed). Germany's postunification emergence as a European leader, especially during the **eurozone crisis**, and foreign policy decisions since the early 2000s have, however, brought the traditional paradigm into question. While on the one hand, German responses to external events appear more often to reflect internal domestic concerns, on the other hand, observers sense a lack of clear strategic direction alongside a growing sense of independence. Economic factors, such as **trade** and **energy**, have emerged as a priority driver.

In general terms, Germany continues to base its nonmilitary foreign policy on European integration (via the EU) and on strategic partnerships both within Europe and beyond. Thus, in response to the **eurozone crisis**, the Germans declared their long-term aim as the creation of a financial "stability union," in which the European Fiscal Compact (**Treaty on Stability, Coordination and Governance** in the Economic and Monetary Union, TSCG), which came into force in January 2013, represented a milestone. Germany has also been deepening its relationship with Poland and has strengthened the

Weimar Triangle as a vehicle for trilateral cooperation with Poland and Russia (Berlin also sees itself as a bridge between the West and Moscow). Examples of partnerships include the "neighborhood partnerships" linking the EU with states of eastern Europe and of the southern Mediterranean and a "transformation partnership" between the EU and north Africa (initially Egypt and Tunisia); Germany and the Russian Federation concluded a bilateral "modernization partnership" in 2008. Beyond Europe and North America, where the long-term ambition is to create a transatlantic internal market, Germany announced its intention to forge links with countries of Latin America and the Caribbean (2010) and with the emergent BRIC states (Brazil, India, and China, 2012). Within Germany, the high number of residents of Turkish origin (three million) has generated close political, economic, and cultural links between the two countries, although German center-right parties remain lukewarm toward Turkey's application for full membership in the EU; following the failed coup against President Recep Tayyip Erdogan and the subsequent crackdown in 2016, which strained relations with the EU, Germany was also concerned that tensions would spill over into its own Turkish community. Also, to stimulate its economy, in 2011 Germany began liberalizing its visa entry policy for foreign workers, especially those from major trading partners outside the EU (the so-called EU blue card).

Militarily and politically, Germany remains anchored within the **North Atlantic Treaty Organization** (**NATO**) and the defense and **security** institutions of the EU, although the extent of its participation in operations in Afghanistan, its refusal to join the invasion force in Iraq (2003), and its abstention on the **United Nations** (**UN**) vote to intervene in Libya (March 2011) to depose Mu'ammar al-Gaddhafi, demonstrated that it would no longer unconditionally support military operations by its allies. Critics such as former foreign minister **Joschka Fischer** went so far as to attack the country's abstention on Libya as a foreign policy debacle that isolated Germany from its Western partners. In fact, Germany's cautious approach to active **Bundeswehr** involvements was driven by a shortage of resources and, more potently, public skepticism at home that was rooted both in a historical reluctance to engage militarily and in the questionable outcomes of the involvements in Afghanistan and Iraq. On balance, foreign policy came to be seen as motivated more by economic interests than by security or defense considerations, with Germans preferring to mediate between East and West (e.g., in the Ukraine crisis of 2014) rather than simply copromote Western interests. Ultimately, German reservations about even the limited intervention in Libya—led largely by France and Great Britain—appeared vindicated as the region imploded into chaos and civil war. At the same time, however, other events contributed to project Germany onto central stage in international affairs, especially in Europe. While France was distracted with internal economic reforms and Britain contemplated leaving the EU, it fell to Germany to undertake initiatives in Ukraine and in the eurozone crisis. Ironically, the introduction of the euro, conceived initially in order to bind the Germans closer to Europe, resulted in rendering its weaker states more dependent on an increasingly powerful and influential Germany.

Most notably under **Angela Merkel**, the center of foreign policy formulation and decision making has shifted from the Federal Ministry for Foreign Affairs to the **Office of the Federal Chancellor**. To regain the initiative for his ministry and to foster a more proactive German stance on new challenges to the international security order, Foreign Minister **Frank Walter Steinmeier** supported a joint working group of the Stiftung Wissenschaft und Politik (German Institute for International and Security Affairs, SWP) and the German Marshall Fund of the United States (GMF), which met between 2012 and 2013 and produced the outline of a new strategy on foreign and security policy (2014). This move was accompanied by supporting speeches from the **president of the Federal Republic, Joachim Gauck** (3 October 2013), and the defense minister, **Ursula von der Leyen** (at the 50th Munich Security Conference, January 2014).

See also FOREIGN POLICY: 1949–1969; FOREIGN POLICY: 1970–1990; FOREIGN POLICY: CENTRAL ASIA; FOREIGN POLICY: FRANCE; FOREIGN POLICY: GREAT BRITAIN; FOREIGN POLICY: PEOPLE'S REPUBLIC OF CHINA (PRC); FOREIGN POLICY: THE RUSSIAN FEDERATION; FOREIGN POLICY: UNITED STATES.

FOREIGN POLICY: CENTRAL ASIA. During its presidency of the Council of the **European Union (EU**, January–June 2007), Germany initiated the adoption of the EU Strategy for Central Asia (comprising the republics of Kazakhstan, Kyrgyzstan, Tajikistan, Turkmenistan, and Uzbekistan). Reflecting its close engagement with the region, Germany was one of the first countries to establish diplomatic relations with the new republics following independence in 1991, and in 2013 it was the only EU member state with embassies in all of them. The strategy aims to provide support for political, administrative, and economic modernization; to develop functioning social markets in the region; and to promote areas such as **education** and the preservation of cultural heritage. While 239,000 ethnic Germans still live in the central Asian states, over one million, including spouses, children, and other family members, have settled in Germany since the 1990s. As part of its program to promote German minorities in eastern, southeastern, and central Europe, the **federal government** has also provided resources to improve the living conditions of people of German descent in central Asia. **Goethe-Institutes** for the promotion of German language and culture were opened in Almaty (1994) and Tashkent (1998), and reading rooms and language centers were set up throughout the region.

FOREIGN POLICY: FRANCE. Arising out of a recognition of the need for reconciliation after World War II, the Franco–German relationship developed into the closest bilateral partnership of all the founding members of the emerging **European Union (EU)**, with the two countries working together to deepen institutional integration at all levels. The relationship was characterized by unusually close, even personal, friendships between heads of state from different political camps: **Konrad Adenauer** and Charles de Gaulle (during the early, foundation years of reconciliation), **Helmut Schmidt** and Valéry d'Estaing (weathering the economic difficulties of the 1970s), **Helmut Kohl** and François Mitterrand (driving forward integration during the 1980s and early 1990s), and **Gerhard Schröder** and Jacques Chirac (navigating Europe through the wars in the Balkans, Afghanistan, and Iraq). The significance of the Franco–German partnership at the core of the EU declined when the Cold War ended and as the Union expanded its membership and revised its institutions and decision-making processes, which reduced the influence of individual member states. At the same time, France and Germany still counted for around 48 percent of the EU's GDP, when, crucially, **Angela Merkel** and Nicolas Sarkozy (the "Merkozy" duo) assumed a leadership role in steering the member states through the **eurozone crisis** (2009–), although some criticized the partnership as high-handed in its actions. While France did not persuade Germany to approve the issue of eurobonds, it argued successfully for financial support for the weakest countries, especially Greece; the creation of a European rescue and stability fund (EFSF/ESM); and empowering the European Central Bank to buy up state loans. On the other hand, Germany, which was widely seen as the "paymaster" of the financial rescue packages, especially as the French economy weakened, refused to be rushed into swift action to calm the financial markets and prevailed in insisting on long-term fiscal discipline. In fact, France and Germany had already begun to diverge when Chancellor Schröder embarked on his **Agenda 2010** reform program, which Merkel continued. While Germany pledged to curb its own welfare state and strengthen its export-oriented economy, France, under Sarkozy's successor, François Hollande (from 2012), faced weak growth, factory closures, job losses, and strains on public finances, not to mention an electorate reluctant to implement structural economic reform.

The closeness of the Franco–German relationship beyond the joint commitment to European economic integration is less obvious. France is a nuclear power (Germany is not), has a permanent seat on the **United Nations (UN)** Security Council (Germany does not), and—at least in name—was not fully integrated into **NATO** during 1966–2009; it has also engaged militarily in North Africa and initiated the Euro-Mediterranean Partnership (1995), while Germany has focused—at least economically—on eastern Europe and China. At a very early stage, de Gaulle's Fouchet Plans (1961–1962) envisaged, alongside the European Economic Community, the creation of a political confederation of European states, in all likelihood led by France and conceived of as a counterpart to NATO. Much later, soon after the fall of the **Berlin Wall**, Mitterrand called for a "European confederation" along similar lines, although this also failed because the eastern European countries, with German support, were more interested in direct integration into the existing structures of the West (in particular the EU and the Atlantic alliance). While the Europeans have deepened security policy cooperation within the framework of a Common Foreign and Security Policy (CFSP, in effect from 1993) and the European Security and Defense Policy (ESDP, 1999), mutually shared Franco–German positions on external operations have not always emerged, with France generally taking the proactive stance. Although both countries refused to join the U.S.-led invasion of Iraq in 2003, they diverged over intervention in Libya, with Germany abstaining from a UN Security Council vote in 2011 to establish a no-fly zone, and only unwillingly did Germany lead the EUFOR RD Congo mission in 2006. The inconsistencies lie in the different strategic outlooks of France and Germany, with the latter remaining hesitant to use military force and regarding itself as a bridge builder between North America and Europe. In 2014, the German and French foreign ministers, **Frank-Walter Steinmeier** and Laurent Fabius, agreed on closer cooperation, with the potential to enable the EU to move toward a more coordinated foreign/security policy and to overcome the unilateralist approaches often adopted by its leading members. The relationship was also revived by the Franco–German initiative to broker a second cease-fire between Russia/separatist forces and the government in eastern Ukraine: the so-called Minsk II protocol, agreed upon in February 2015, replaced the previous protocol, which had broken down the year before.

FOREIGN POLICY: GREAT BRITAIN. Between 1949 and 1990, German foreign policy was finely balanced between a European orientation (toward France and the emerging **European Union [EU]**) and Atlanticism (United States [U.S.] and Great Britain). From the early 1970s, Germany also pursued East–West détente (**Ostpolitik**) and the longer term goal of reunification. Within this framework, Germany's relationship with Britain, while never as close as with France, developed positively as both countries quietly cooperated as the leading European members of the **North Atlantic Treaty Organization** (**NATO**). Large British forces stationed on German soil reinforced the partnership. At the same time, the British government viewed certain events as challenges to what it saw as its own historically preeminent role, in particular the so-called special relationship with the U.S.: Germany's reunification, which was opposed by Prime Minister Margaret Thatcher but supported by her foreign secretary; its intention to seek a permanent seat on the **United Nations** (**UN**) Security Council; and George H. W. Bush's call for Germans and Americans to act as "partners in leadership" (1990). The British were also skeptical about Germany's enthusiasm for reinforcing European security structures, which might include Russia and possibly develop at the expense of NATO's transatlantic component.

Although the political climate improved with Thatcher's departure (1990), Chancellor **Helmut Kohl**'s vigorous pursuit of closer European integration fueled euro-skepticism within Britain's ruling Conservative Party. The election of center-left governments in both Britain and Germany (1997/1998) heralded a fresh start, however, with Premier Tony Blair signaling a more constructive approach to Europe and agreeing with France at St. Malo in 1998 to develop a common European Security and Defense Policy (ESDP); cooperation with NATO was subsequently formalized within the terms of the **Berlin** Plus Agreement (2003). Germany's active involvement with military missions in the Balkans (Kosovo, 1999) further demonstrated how closely the policy objectives of both countries, which also supported the enlargement of NATO (1999) and the EU (from 2004), were now aligned. In any case, the U.S.-led attacks on Afghanistan (2001) and Iraq (2003) abruptly exposed fundamental divergences in the British and German approaches, with the former unconditionally supporting the Americans and the Germans either opposed to armed intervention (in Iraq) or, at best, reserved in its support (Afghanistan). To a large extent, these divergences echoed the historical anchoring of Great Britain within the Atlanticist camp and Germany's need to assess and rebalance its interests after reunification. Although the **euro-zone crisis** (which broke in 2009) was never an issue of foreign or security policy, the reactions of Britain and Germany exposed clear differences in national culture: while the British regarded the entire euro model (with diverging economies and no central treasury) as flawed and felt reinforced in their euro-skepticism, Germany saw the main causes of the crisis as spend-thrift Mediterranean states requiring greater financial integration and regulation within the broader European project, to which it remained politically and economically committed. The referendum vote by Britain in 2016 to leave the EU altogether raised a number of questions over the country's future relationship with both the EU and Germany.

FOREIGN POLICY: PEOPLE'S REPUBLIC OF CHINA (PRC). Sino–German relations are encumbered with little historical baggage: a small and short-lived German colonial presence in China ended in 1914, after which contacts were limited to military advisers in the 1930s (withdrawn after the outbreak of the First Sino–Japanese War in 1937) and links between the Chinese Communist Party and German communists after 1927 through the Moscow-based Communist International (Comintern). During the Cold War, the **German Democratic Republic (GDR)** officially recognized the PRC (1949), and both countries concluded trade and friendship agreements

(1950, 1955). Links stagnated, however, when the GDR leadership backed the Soviet Union during the Sino–Soviet rift (from 1960), although the PRC unreservedly supported the erection of the **Berlin Wall** (1961). Eventually, in 1985, the GDR and China concluded an agreement on long-term economic and technical cooperation (for 1986–1990) while the East German government—to the horror of the West German **Bundestag**—supported the Chinese in their crackdown on the student protest movement in the summer of 1989. Talks in 1964 about a possible trade agreement between China and the Federal Republic of Germany (FRG) failed, and West Germany did not diplomatically recognize the PRC until 1972, in the wake of rapprochement between the Chinese and the United States (U.S.). There followed a bilateral trade treaty (1973), and **Volkswagen** opened a plant in Shanghai after an investment agreement came into force (1985). Although the Chinese government criticized Chancellor **Helmut Kohl**'s 10-point plan for an all-German confederation in November 1989, it welcomed reunification in October 1990.

Since the 1980s, (West) German foreign policy has focused primarily on trade and investment links with the PRC and the latter's integration into the European economic system (the then European Economic Community reached a comprehensive trade agreement with the PRC as early as 1978). The promotion of German exports and the creation of an economic presence in China underpin the German government's Asia Concept policy document of 1993 and the foreign ministry's regional concept for East Asia, published in 2002. German political leaders actively promote this policy and are accompanied by very large trade delegations on their visits to the country. Defense and security issues (e.g., Taiwan's and China's military ambitions in Asia), which encumber Sino–U.S. relations, are less of a problem for European countries than economic piracy or even progress on human rights. Since 1972, (West) Germany has acknowledged the "one China policy," and in 1992 halted the delivery of submarines to Taiwan, where it maintains a diplomatic presence short of full recognition.

As leading exporters, Germany and the PRC are major partners in their respective regions. In 2004, the two countries concluded a Strategic Partnership in Global Responsibility, which has furthered political and economic cooperation within existing international frameworks, notably the **United Nations (UN)** and the **European Union (EU)**. Following a meeting between Chancellor **Angela Merkel** and Premier Wen Jiabao in July 2010, the partnership was upgraded to include annual high level intergovernmental consultations. At a summit of the two leaders in 2012, more than 40 agreements were reached between ministerial departments. Of the many dialogue mechanisms that now exist between the two countries, the annual symposium on the rule of law (Deutsch-chinesischer Rechtsstaatsdialog), inspired by an initiative of former chancellor **Gerhard Schröder** in 1999, brings experts together to address issues such as civil rights, copyright protection, and state control of the Internet, all of which remain areas of fundamental difference. While China views Germany as an economic and political gateway into Europe, most of the traffic has been one way, with Chinese investment in Germany still small compared with the volume of German companies investing and producing in China. Like banks and financial services, foreign investment in China is strictly controlled by the state and always involves a joint venture, with the Chinese partner taking the larger profit share (German companies are increasingly concerned about the long-term implications of this). Alongside motor vehicles and **chemicals** (Volkswagen, **Audi, BMW, Daimler**, and **Bayer** have large presences in China), German involvement encompasses **energy**, high-technology industries, and health care. In 2005, an agreement on promoting and protecting mutual investment came into force, although it noted continuing Chinese discrimination against foreign investors. With its leading track record on green issues, Germany is also keen to contribute to China's efforts to develop clean energy and address climate change. In 2009, a bilateral Common Strategic Development Partnership was agreed on, which replaced all former developmental aid with new programs of cooperation and investment, notably in the areas of the **environment**, energy, and economic and civic reform. Institutional cooperation also embraces scientific research, cultural exchanges, and **education**. Details of the organizations and programs involved can be found at the Federal Ministry for Foreign Affairs website (www.auswaertiges-amt.de). Regular reports on the state of economic and technological links are available from the Federal Ministry for Economic Affairs and Energy. In 2012, a "direct" rail freight link was inaugurated between Duisburg in Germany and Chongqing in China: the Trans-Eurasia-Express.

FOREIGN POLICY: THE RUSSIAN FEDERATION. During the long period of the Cold War, from the aftermath of World War II until the collapse of the USSR (which was replaced by the Russian Federation in December 1991), the "foreign policies" of both the FRG and the **German Democratic Republic (GDR)**—inasmuch as they were able to pursue them independently—were determined by their positions with the East–West power blocs. The GDR remained a client state of the Soviet Union, plundered for reparations until the uprising of 1953 and hemorrhaging its population to West Germany before the erection of the **Berlin Wall** in 1961, after which it began to make progress toward economic and social stability. The FRG, although firmly embedded in the postwar economic and military structures of Western Europe and the United States (U.S.), was freer to shape its foreign policy in response to changing agendas. While the GDR adhered to the "two states" solution of a permanently divided Germany, the FRG consistently argued for reunification, claiming at the same time to speak for the disenfranchised East Germans—much to the irritation of Moscow, which was in constant fear of

West German revanchism. Beginning in 1969, however, West Germans came to see their strategy as counterproductive: not only was it isolating them from their allies at a time when the latter were prepared to negotiate with the eastern bloc, but their alienation of the GDR was actually cementing the latter's development as a separate state. The fruits of this realization were ultimately **Ostpolitik**—primarily a West German initiative—and détente, which was embodied in a series of treaties between the FRG and eastern bloc states between 1970 and 1973. The thaw in relations between the USSR and FRG was, however, ruptured during the 1980s by the dispute over the stationing of Soviet and U.S. medium-range nuclear missiles on German soil. Although the issue divided West Germans and fueled a powerful peace movement (which involved a lot of Soviet appeals to the people over Western leaders' heads), Moscow's intransigence simply reinforced the FRG government's decision to support deployment (the last U.S. missiles were not withdrawn until 1991). In any case, détente between the two Germanies survived, largely because it was in neither's economic, political, or security interest to abandon it (it also helped that GDR leader **Erich Honecker** was not pleased at having to pay for the Soviet missiles on East German territory).

The accession of Mikhail Gorbachev as Russian leader in 1985 heralded—for various reasons but principally to remove the drain of its military policies on state resources—a new approach to Germany. In short, the USSR was prepared to replace bloc-based military confrontation with negotiation and cooperation. While Gorbachev at first almost certainly never envisaged the dissolution of the Soviet Union or a reunited Germany within the **North Atlantic Treaty Organization** (**NATO**), these were the eventual—and accepted—outcomes. Honecker finally visited the FRG (1987), Chancellor **Helmut Kohl** visited the USSR (July 1990), and as part of the package of reunification, Germany subsidized the withdrawal of Soviet forces from East Germany and extended 3,000 million DM credit to the Russian economy. Anxious not to delay the withdrawal of 540,000 troops and dependents (completed by 1994), Germany further agreed to repeated Soviet requests for additional financial support. Financial aid and economic cooperation soon became major features of bilateral relations, as Russia sought to develop its industries and Germany looked to expand export markets. Most assistance for civic and economic transformation in Russia originated from Germany, which also contributed to American programs for nuclear disarmament. Germany thus became the main creditor of Russia, although in contrast to the U.S., it was not prepared to write off debts for loans. At the same time, the chaotic nature of the Russian state under Gorbachev's successor, Boris Yeltsin (president 1991–1999), discouraged many German firms from investing there, despite Chancellor Helmut Kohl's personal friendship with the new leader.

The security vacuum that followed the dissolution of the **Warsaw Pact** led several former communist states in Europe to seek closer association with or even membership in NATO, prompting Moscow to accuse Germany of reneging on an alleged commitment that the alliance would not be enlarged. NATO's (and Germany's) involvement in the Kosovo conflict (from 1999) further soured relations, as Russia refused to recognize the area's independence from Serbia. The accession of Vladimir Putin as president (2000–2008)—and his close personal relationship with Chancellor **Gerhard Schröder**—marked a succession of changes in the bilateral relationship. Initially—alongside disagreements with the U.S. over an American missile system and Russian support for states such as Iran and North Korea that were partially offset by Putin's expression of solidarity with the U.S. following the terror attacks of September 2001—the Russian leader aimed to cultivate positive links with the **European Union (EU)** and with Germany in particular. As a result, the period between 2001 and 2005 marked a deepening of consultations (the **Petersburg Dialog**); an increase in cultural, social, and educational contacts; and commitments by Germany to promote Russia's integration into European structures. By this time, however, Schröder's personal relationship with Putin at the same time that Russia appeared to retreat from progress toward a civil, democratic society attracted criticism at home.

A framework factor in recent German foreign policy toward the Russian Federation is the Partnership and Cooperation Agreement (PCA) between Russia and the **European Union (EU)**, which provides for political dialogue, **trade**, investment, and cooperation in a wide range of economic, scientific, and cultural areas. In force from December 1997, the PCA has been renewed annually since 2007, and negotiations for a revised agreement began in 2008, when, at a meeting with Dmitry Medvedev (president 2008–2012) at Yekaterinburg, German foreign minister **Frank-Walter Steinmeier (Social Democratic Party of Germany, SPD)** presented his government's plan to deepen links with Russia through a bilateral modernization partnership. In fact, the German coalition government was divided on its approach to Russia. While Steinmeier headed the Federal Ministry for Foreign Affairs, which pursued closer integration, the increasingly influential **Office of the Federal Chancellor** under **Angela Merkel (Christian Democratic Union, CDU)** remained more skeptical, especially toward Putin (reelected president in 2012). During its presidency of the EU Council (January–June 2007), Germany had hoped to revitalize the PCA, but Putin, preoccupied with enhancing national sovereign status, showed little interest. Alleged Russian involvement in a cyberattack on Estonia in 2007; the Russian–Georgian war (August 2008); recurrent gas transit disputes between Russia and Ukraine between 2005 and 2009; and concerns over **human rights**, governance, and authoritarianism in the Federation further strained relations with the EU as a whole, while systemic obstacles hindered business cooperation with Germany in particular.

Nevertheless, Germany concluded a number of bilateral agreements in areas such as the **environment** (2008, under the auspices of the environment minister, **Sigmar Gabriel** [SPD]) and **energy** (in the form of the Munich-based Russian–German Energy Agency [RuDEA], set up in 2009 to improve energy efficiency in Russia with German know-how). By 2012, several projects on legal training, health care, **transport**ation, and **education** were under way. Germany's initiatives coincided with a summit in Rostov-on-Don in May/June 2010, when the EU and Russia set the foundations for a modernization partnership focusing on economic cooperation, technological innovation, and the development of civil and judicial institutions. Germany further agreed to support Russia's long-standing bid to join the World Trade Organization (WTO), to which it was admitted in August 2012. Since the early days of the PCA, which saw more rhetoric than concrete progress, the German approach has become more pragmatic and focused on economic links. On a visit by the chancellor to one of the regular intergovernmental forums (in Moscow in November 2012), several agreements were signed between German and Russian companies, while Merkel and Putin openly disagreed over progress on human and political rights in Russia.

The pragmatic approach has enabled the Russo–German relationship to survive political setbacks, such as a resolution in the **Bundestag** strongly criticizing the Russian judicial system and the trials of political activists (November 2012) and Germany's perceived targeting of Russian financial assets in Cyprus during the **eurozone crisis** (2013). Most enthusiastic about economic cooperation are large German concerns (e.g., **Siemens**, **BMW**, **Volkswagen**, MAN, and **BASF** have built factories or invested in Russia), although corruption, legal uncertainties, and bureaucracy continue to deter smaller businesses. Large-scale strategic partnerships, such as Nord Stream, are rare. As Russia's increasing desire for German economic and technological investment outweighs its willingness to reform its civil institutions, the Federation has fallen down the list of both foreign policy and economic priorities for Germany, where expertise on east European policy has diminished within the government apparatus and in academia. Russia's annexation of Crimea and support for separatists in eastern Ukraine (2014) marked a serious downturn in relations with both the EU, which applied economic sanctions, and NATO, which moved to increase its presence in eastern Europe. Although supporting the measures agreed to by the EU and NATO, Germany, in contrast to the Baltic states and Poland, which saw themselves as the most immediately threatened by Russian territorial ambitions, proved more reluctant during the decision-making process to abandon its traditional policies of détente and political dialogue.

See also COMMITTEE ON EASTERN EUROPEAN ECONOMIC RELATIONS (OST-AUSSCHUSS DER DEUTSCHEN WIRTSCHAFT, OA).

FOREIGN POLICY: UNITED STATES. Ever since Chancellor **Konrad Adenauer** adopted his policy of integrating the postwar Federal Republic into Western political and economic structures (in particular the **North Atlantic Treaty Organization [NATO]** and the emerging **European Union [EU]**), Germany has maintained a close relationship with the U.S., which acted as a protecting power and security guarantor throughout the Cold War. Through the Berlin Airlift (1948–1949) and the Marshall Plan (1948–1952), the U.S. progressed from being an occupying power to a valued partner in **security, trade**, scientific development, **education**, and culture, with numerous links and exchanges at all levels. Although U.S. support for reunification was especially welcome, President George W. Bush's call for a bilateral partnership of leaders (1990) in a post–Cold War world failed to materialize, as Germany, led by Chancellor **Gerhard Schröder**, proved reluctant to endorse unconditionally Anglo-American military interventions in Iraq (2003) and, to some extent, in Afghanistan (from 2001). While Schröder's successor, **Angela Merkel**, rebuilt diplomatic bridges with the U.S., she did not significantly deviate from Germany's restrained approach to military adventures. A diplomatic downturn followed the revelations in 2013 of mass surveillance by the U.S. National Security Agency (NSA), which was also discovered to have tapped the chancellor's cell phone. In response, Germany canceled the 1968 intelligence agreement with the United States (U.S.) and Great Britain, although this had been practically defunct since 1990. German efforts to be included in the nonspying pact among the U.S., Britain, New Zealand, Australia, and Canada were rebuffed. In July 2014, two members of the Bundesnachrichtendienst (German Federal Intelligence Agency) were arrested for allegedly spying for the CIA, while *Der Spiegel* magazine reported the following month that Germany had monitored telephone calls between senior U.S. politicians. Despite these setbacks, both sides emphasized the underlying continuity of a solid and stable relationship, with the Americans, on the one hand, tending to view official German reactions to spying issues as responses to domestic opinion, and on the other hand, unsure of their long-term significance at the same time that younger generations of Germans were emerging without a historical sense of the value of the transatlantic alliance. Speeches by senior German politicians in 2014 (Foreign Minister **Frank-Walter Steinmeier**, Federal President **Joachim Gauck**, and Defense Minister **Ursula von der Leyen**) calling for greater German engagement in foreign affairs were welcomed in the U.S., although it remained to be seen what the material results might be.

FOREIGN TRADE. *See* TRADE.

FOREIGNERS. The first and most significant wave of foreigners—considered here to be those holding foreign passports and distinct from **asylum** seekers, refugees, expellees, and ethnic Germans returning to Germany—to enter the Federal Republic of Germany (FRG) was made up of foreign guest workers (Gastarbeiter) recruited between 1955 and 1973 from Mediterranean countries on time-limited permits to augment the domestic labor force during the postwar economic boom. The recruits, generally young and male, worked primarily in **industry**, especially where employers found it difficult to engage native Germans. As a result of intergovernmental agreements signed with Italy (1955), Spain, Greece (1960), Turkey (1961), Morocco (1963), Portugal (1964), Tunisia (1965), and Yugoslavia (1968), the number of guest workers rose from 500,000 in 1962 to around 2.6 million (4.2 percent of the population) in 1973. Although a "rotation principle" was meant to ensure that individual workers would return home to be replaced by others, many remained on extended permits, and a halt to recruitment in 1973 simply prompted a further influx of family members entitled to enter Germany under existing residency laws; by the end of the decade, they accounted for 60 percent of new **immigrants**. The contrast between the reality of a large, settled, and progressively integrated foreign population and the political fiction that Germany was not a country of immigration fueled decades of controversy over the need for appropriate legislation governing inward migration. A new immigration law in 2005 went some way toward settling the issue.

Between 1975 and 1980, the total foreign population (including guest workers) hovered at between 4 and 4.5 million (7.2 percent of the total population), but rose sharply after reunification to reach 7.4 million in 1997 (almost 9 percent); after remaining at around 8.9 percent, it reached a record 7.6 million in 2013. Almost a quarter of foreign residents were Turks (1.6 million), followed by Poles (530,000) and Italians (529,000); other nationalities included Greeks (298,000), Croats (225,000), Romanians (205,000), Serbs (202,000), and citizens of the Russian Federation (202,000). Of foreign immigrants to Germany in 2013, 75 percent originated in the **European Union** (**EU**), principally from the 10 accession states since 2004 (especially Poland and Hungary). The **eurozone crisis** prompted an increase in immigrants from southern Europe (Greece, Italy, and Spain), while relaxations in entry restrictions for qualified professionals also drew increasing numbers from India, Croatia, the United States, and China (27,000 in 2012).

Foreigners have settled mainly in more densely populated parts of western Germany, following established, often work-related, patterns of migration. Statistics on the number of foreign residents in Germany vary significantly according to whether they are derived from the national central register for foreigners (Ausländerzentralregister, AZR) or calculated from census figures. Other factors that may underpin the figures are the inclusion of children and the creation in 2005 of a wider category of persons with a so-called **migration background**. According to the AZR, the **federal states** with the highest numbers of foreigners (in 2014) were **North Rhine-Westfalia** (over 2 million, 11.7 percent of the population), **Baden-Württemberg** (1.4 million, 13.2 percent), **Bavaria** (1.4 million, 11.2 percent), and **Hessen** (861,000, 14.2 percent); the city-states of **Berlin, Hamburg**, and **Bremen** have the highest densities (14.5, 14.9, and 14.7 percent, respectively). Eastern Germany has relatively few foreigners and by far the lowest densities (at most 3 percent).

In 1978, the German government appointed a special representative for affairs concerning foreigners (Beauftragte[r] der Bundesregierung für Ausländerfragen) to report on and tackle issues of integration. In 2005, the office was superseded by a representative for migration, refugees, and integration (Beauftragte[r] für Migration, Flüchtlinge und Integration) within the Federal Ministry for Family Affairs, Senior Citizens, Women, and Youth.

Like the FRG, the former **German Democratic Republic (GDR)** recruited foreign workers to supplement a labor shortage in industry, although in far smaller numbers. The total rose from around 3,500 in 1966 to 14,000 the following year and reached 93,500 in 1989. Most workers came from Vietnam (59,000 in 1989) and Mozambique (15,000). Unlike western Germany, the GDR strictly applied the rotation principle; working conditions were often tough, with shift work in the least popular industries; and families were not permitted to join the migrants. Quartered in segregated accommodations, workers enjoyed little social contact with Germans, and marriages with GDR citizens were rare. Of the total 190,000 foreign residents in the GDR in 1989, the Vietnamese constituted the largest contingent (31.4 percent), followed by Poles (51,700, 27 percent), although most of the former returned home after reunification owing to uncertainty about their status.

FORESTRY. *See* AGRICULTURE; ENVIRONMENT: FORESTS.

FREE DEMOCRATIC PARTY (FREIE DEMOKRATISCHE PARTEI, FDP). The FDP was founded in a merger of regional liberal parties in western Germany in December 1948. The party's heterogeneous membership ranged from left-wing liberals to nationalists and conservatives, although it became a strong supporter of the **social market economy** and appealed to professional people and owners of small businesses. Despite its small size, the party formed ruling national coalitions with the **Christian Democratic Union (CDU)/Christian Social Union (CSU)** during 1949–1956 and 1961–1966 before governing jointly with the **Social Democratic Party of Germany (SPD)** from 1969 until 1982. The party adopted the abbreviation F.D.P in 1968–1969, although the initialism FDP is commonly used.

The FDP has traditionally regarded itself as a "third force" in German politics and a maker of national coalitions, moderating the influence of the larger parties. Under the leadership of **Walter Scheel** (1968–1974), the FDP shifted to the left, advocating greater rights for workers, the social responsibilities of property ownership, and protection of the **environment**. The leftward swing and commitment to the social state were embodied in the so-called Freiburg (1971) and Kiel Theses (1977). In 1982, however, the FDP switched its support back to the CDU/CSU, with which it governed until 1998. **Hans-Dietrich Genscher**, party leader from 1974 to 1985, served for many years as foreign minister under Chancellors **Helmut Schmidt** (SPD, 1974–1982) and **Helmut Kohl** (CDU, 1982–1992). In 1985, the party adopted a "liberal manifesto" (*Liberales Manifest*), which retained the social and ecological commitment of the Freiburg program while also arguing for a reduced role on the part of the state and advocating greater protection for individuals from the misuse of data and from the **media**. The theme of less government and more room for individual incentive was reinforced in the Wiesbaden Principles (1996), although the party found it increasingly difficult to convert its message into votes. Recent leaders such as **Klaus Klinkel** (1993–1995), **Wolfgang Gerhardt** (1995–2001), **Guido Westerwelle** (2001–2011), and **Philipp Rösler** (2011–2013) have struggled against a series of problems: a sharply declining membership (and income) after reunification (57,000 in 2013 compared to 170,000 in 1991); virtual disappearance from the national electoral map between 1998 and 2009 (it obtained only 6.4 percent of seats in the **Bundestag** in the 1998 election, rising to 7.4 percent in 2002 and 9.8 percent in 2005, although it made some gains in regional elections); failure to gain a following in the **eastern federal states** (in August 1990, the FDP merged with the two liberal parties in the **German Democratic Republic [GDR]**, the Bund Freier Demokraten and the Deutsche Forumpartei); and financial and political scandals surrounding its (former) deputy leader, **Jürgen Möllemann**. The party's fortunes improved dramatically when it gained 14.6 percent of seats in the national election of 2009, after which it entered into government with the CDU; the FDP was also well represented in virtually all regional parliaments, where it formed several ruling coalitions. However, punished by the electorate for failing to deliver its election promises vis-à-vis the CDU, the FDP failed in 2013, for the first time in its history, to clear the 5 percent entry hurdle for the Bundestag. As a result, the entire leadership resigned, and the party resolved to rebuild itself from the grass roots. In particular, it faced the need to broaden its electoral appeal beyond professionals, civil servants, and higher wage earners.

The FDP's main organs are a 662-member national party congress (Bundesparteitag), the national executive (Vorstand) with 34 elected delegates, and a 9-member presidium (Präsidium). Research and educational activities are supported by the Friedrich-Naumann Stiftung (Friedrich Naumann Foundation). Unlike the main parties, the FDP has relatively few associated organizations.

Party leaders in the postwar period have been Theodor Heuss (1948–1949), Franz Blücher (1949–1954), Thomas Dehler (1954–1957), Reinhold Maier (1957–1960), Erich Mende (1960–1968), Walter Scheel (1968–1974), Hans-Dietrich Genscher (1974–1985), **Martin Bangemann** (1985–1988), **Otto Graf Lambsdorff** (1988–1993), **Klaus Kinkel** (1993–1995), Wolfgang Gerhardt (1995–2001), Guido Westerwelle (2001–2011), Philipp Rösler (2011–2013), and **Christian Lindner** (2013–). The party's youth wing, the Deutsche Jungdemokraten (German Young Democrats), split from the main party in protest at the rightward move after 1982 and was officially replaced by the Junge Liberale or JuLis (Young Liberals).

See also POLITICAL PARTIES.

FRISIANS. *See* ETHNIC MINORITIES: FRISIANS.

G

GABRIEL, SIGMAR (1959–). Social Democratic Party of Germany (SPD) politician. Sigmar Gabriel was born in Goslar (Lower Saxony) and studied politics, sociology, and German at the University of Göttingen (1982–1987) before qualifying as a schoolteacher in Goslar (1989). After lecturing in political education for trade union organizations (Arbeit und Leben, the transport and public service workers union ÖTV, and the metal workers union IG Metall, 1983–1988), he worked as an adult education tutor in Lower Saxony (1989–1990). A member of various left-wing youth organizations (1976–1989), Gabriel joined the SPD (1977) and the ÖTV (1979), going on to represent the SPD in Goslar as a district (1987–1998) and town councilor (1991–1999). As a deputy in the Lower Saxony state parliament (Landtag, 1990–2005), he served on various committees and rose rapidly in the SPD parliamentary group, first as speaker on internal affairs (1994–1997), then as deputy leader (1997–1998), and finally leader (1998–1999, 2003–2005). In December 1999, Gabriel succeeded Gerhard Glogowski (SPD) as minister president of the state. Glogowski had taken over from Gerhard Schröder when the latter became federal chancellor (October 1998), but was forced to step down after 13 months following allegations of financial corruption. Against a background of high unemployment and declining revenues, Gabriel focused on educational reform after the Pisa report highlighted the poor performance of children in Lower Saxony's schools, but his proposal to raise taxes to finance improvements in education lost him the regional election in early 2003. The SPD suffered dramatic losses throughout the region (the worst in its history), paving the way for the Christian Democratic Union (CDU) to end 13 years in opposition and form a coalition government with the Free Democratic Party (FDP) under Christian Wulff (CDU). Gabriel openly criticized the SPD for its moribund structures and condemned the government's economic and financial policies, including the introduction of a levy on nonrecyclable containers. Despite disagreements with the SPD leadership, Gabriel was respected by Chancellor Schröder and regarded as a talented modernizer and possible future party leader. He served as minister for the environment in the coalition cabinet of

Angela Merkel (2005–2009), taking a leading role in the precoalition negotiations over environmental policy and arguing strongly to retain the commitment to abandon nuclear **energy**. He joined the SPD national executive in
2007, was elected party leader in 2009, and in 2013 was appointed economics and energy minister and vice-chancellor in Merkel's third coalition cabinet. Together with **Andrea Nahles**, general secretary from 2009 to 2013,
Gabriel was credited with helping restore some of the divided party's political fortunes after the election defeat of 2009. Despite this, Gabriel looked
increasingly improbable as a potential chancellor-candidate to challenge
Merkel in the 2017 national election, as electoral support for the SPD stagnated, a regional court reversed his decision to promote a fusion between
retailers Edeka and Tengelmann (2016), and backing within the party for
trade agreements with Canada (CETA) and the United States (TTIP), in
negotiations for which he took a leading role, diminished. In August 2016, he
surprised observers by declaring the TTIP negotiations as effectively failed.

GALINSKI, HEINZ (1912–1992). Jewish community leader. Heinz Galinski was born in Marienburg (West Prussia, now Malbork in Poland), the
son of a businessman. After completing commercial training, he worked as a
textile salesman from 1933 before moving to **Berlin** in the late 1930s in the
hope of escaping the worst of the National Socialist persecutions of **Jews**.
Sometime between 1940 and 1945, his father died in police hands, and his
wife and mother perished in Auschwitz. Galinski himself worked in forced
labor camps until he was liberated from Bergen-Belsen concentration camp
in 1945. Unlike many of his Jewish contemporaries, Galinski resolved to stay
in Germany. Adopting the slogan "integration, not assimilation," he helped
to reestablish the Jewish community in Berlin, where, as the community's
leader (1949–1992), he set up youth and welfare facilities and in 1957 laid
the foundation stone for a Jewish center on the site of a synagogue destroyed
in the pogrom of November 1938. The center soon developed into an important meeting place for Jews and gentiles. Galinski played an important role in
devising legislation for compensating Jewish and non-Jewish victims of National Socialism.

As chairman of the **Central Council of Jews in Germany** (1954–1963,
1988–1992), Galinski became a prominent spokesman on Jewish affairs and
worked hard to preserve the memory of the Holocaust and its lessons. Rejecting the notion of an amnesty for National Socialists, he consistently spoke
out against the dangers of racism and right-wing **extremism**. In 1975, he
himself became a target of the left-wing terrorist group **Red Army Faction
(RAF)**, narrowly escaping a bombing attempt on his life. He remained critical of German and European policy on the Middle East, which in his view
was overly conciliatory toward the Palestine Liberation Organization (PLO),
although he defended Chancellor **Helmut Schmidt** in 1981, when the latter

was criticized by the Israeli prime minister, Menachem Begin. Galinski was made an honorary citizen of Berlin (1987), where he died. Since 1985, an annual Heinz-Galinski-Prize has been awarded in his name; in 1995 the Heinz Galinski Elementary School opened in Berlin. His successors as chairman of the Central Council of Jews in Germany were **Ignatz Bubis, Paul Spiegel, Charlotte Knobloch, Dieter Graumann**, and **Josef Schuster**. The web page www.zentralratjuden.de provides details about Galinski's work and that of the organization.

See also ANTI-SEMITISM; JEWS IN GERMANY; TERRORISM.

GAUCK, JOACHIM (1940–). President of the Federal Republic, 2011–. Joachim Gauck was born in Rostock. His father, a seaman, was deported from the **German Democratic Republic (GDR)** to Siberia (1951–1955); at school, Gauck expressed his opposition to the **Socialist Unity Party of Germany (SED)**, after which he was refused admission to study German **language** and **literature** at university. Turning to theology, he studied at Rostock (1958–1965), was ordained (1967), and worked for the Evangelical-Lutheran Church in Mecklenburg, serving as a pastor in Lüssow (near Güstrow) and, from 1970, in Rostock. His support for **human rights**, peace, and the protection of the **environment** during the 1980s attracted the attention of the GDR secret police, the **Stasi**. In the 1989 revolution, he led weekly church services in Rostock, took part in public demonstrations against the regime, and became a cofounder and spokesman for the local opposition group **New Forum**. Following elections in March 1990, he represented New Forum in the **People's Chamber**, where he headed a special commission to oversee the disbanding of the Stasi. In August 1990, he co-initiated legislation establishing the framework for preserving the Stasi's archives and, in the interests of coming to terms with the GDR's past, making their contents more widely available. In October 1990, the People's Chamber gave Gauck responsibility for the archives, and in December 1991 he was formally confirmed as head of what informally came to be known as the Gauck Office, the agency that administered and controlled access to the files (his official title was the **Federal Commissioner for the Records of the State Security Service of the Former German Democratic Republic**, BStU). He held the post until 2000.

As commissioner for the files, Gauck presented a series of reports detailing the numbers of requests for access (between 1991 and 1997, around 1.3 million applications from private persons and 2.3 million requests from government authorities and organizations) and revealing that between 20,000 and 30,000 agents had been active in the Federal Republic of Germany (FRG) until 1989, either spying or attempting to influence West Germany's political system. Gauck resisted calls to close the files, arguing repeatedly that the GDR's past should not be forgotten and that perpetrators of even lesser crimes against human rights should not be allowed to escape justice. Following his recommendation, the government agreed in 1997 to extend the statute of limitations on such crimes to October 2002. Although he earned cross-party respect for his role, Gauck displeased the West German political elite by refusing to accept that the revelations in the Stasi's files should apply only to east Germans. In particular, he angered former chancellor **Helmut Kohl** by offering to make available Stasi tape recordings that appeared to support allegations that Kohl had accepted illegal donations to the **Christian Democratic Union (CDU)**. Alongside other opponents of the GDR regime, including **Ulrike Poppe** and **Jens Reich**, Gauck was awarded the Theodor-Heuss Medal in 1991. His other awards include the Federal Cross of Merit (1995), the Hannah Arendt Prize for political thought (1997), and an honorary doctorate of the University of Rostock (2000). A gifted public speaker, he received the Dolf-Sternberger prize for his speech to the **Bundestag** on the 10th anniversary of the fall of the **Berlin Wall** and was awarded the Cicero Prize for rhetoric. In 2010, Gauck was nominated by the **Social Democratic Party of Germany (SPD)** and the Green Party for the position of president of the Federal Republic, but was defeated by **Christian Wulff (CDU)**. He eventually succeeded, however, following Wulff's resignation in 2012. The only one of 11 presidents not to be a member of a political party, Gauck urged his country to adopt a more self-confident foreign policy (2014) and welcomed refugees to Germany while expressing sympathy for those who argued for limitations on numbers. He also provoked controversy after criticizing the possible formation of a regional coalition in Thuringia led by **The Left Party** politician **Bodo Ramelow** (2014). In 2016, he announced his intention not to seek a second term of office.

GAUS, GÜNTER (1929–2004). Social Democratic Party of Germany (SPD) politician and journalist. Born in Braunschweig (**Lower Saxony**), Günter Gaus studied history and German **language** and **literature** at the University of Munich, but left his studies to work as a journalist for the news magazine *Der Spiegel* (1953–1961) and the daily *Süddeutsche Zeitung* (1961–1965). Even before he became director of programs and deputy director (Intendant) at the SWF (Südwestfunk) radio and broadcasting station (1965–1969), he had acquired celebrity status for his interviews with leading politicians and figures from the arts and sciences. His first broadcast interview, with Economics Minister **Ludwig Erhard (Christian Democratic Union, CDU)**, marked the launch of the *Zur Person* series in April 1963. The series, which was noted for Gaus's intelligent interviewing style and original use of camera techniques, was first shown by the **Zweites Deutsches Fernsehen (ZDF)** and, with interruptions and under different titles, was continued by four other stations (including the private broadcaster SAT 1) until 2003. In 1969, Gaus returned to *Der Spiegel* as chief editor, appearing regularly on

television as a commentator on politics and current affairs and endorsing the **Ostpolitik** pursued by Chancellor **Willy Brandt**. In 1973, Brandt appointed him **state secretary** in the **Office of the Federal Chancellor** and, when the Basic Treaty of Relations came into force, head of the permanent representation of the Federal Republic of Germany (FRG) in East **Berlin** (1974–1981). The representation was in all but name West Germany's embassy to the **German Democratic Republic (GDR)**, and Gaus effectively became Bonn's chief negotiator, successfully concluding 17 inter-German treaties and agreements. In January 1981, following differences with Chancellor **Helmut Schmidt**, Gaus was replaced by Klaus Bölling as head of the Berlin office. A member of the SPD from 1976, Gaus moved to West Berlin to become senator for science and research under governing mayor **Hans-Jochen Vogel**, although he vacated the post in May following the success of the CDU in city elections.

After 1981, Gaus resumed his career in journalism and television, conducting interviews with well-known personalities from East and West Germany and publishing several books in which he analyzed and commented on society and politics. He also ventured into **literature** (his short story, "Wendewut," appeared in 1990), and from 1990 onward he coedited the left-wing weekly *Freitag*. In 1998–1999, his five-volume collection of interviews with authors, **minister president**s, artists, prominent **women**, and witnesses to history reappeared in a revised and extended edition (under the title *Zur Person*). Gaus was awarded the Adolf-Grimme Prize for services to German television (1988) and the German Critics' Prize (Deutscher Kritikerpreis, 1991). In 1991, he served on the newly created broadcasting advisory council (Rundfunkbeirat) of the five new **eastern federal states**.

GEIßLER, HEINER (1930–). Christian Democratic Union (CDU) politician. Heiner Geißler was born in Oberndorf on the Neckar River (**Baden-Württemberg**) and attended a Jesuit college in St. Blasien before studying philosophy and law at the universities of Munich and Tübingen, earning a doctorate in 1960 and qualifying as a practicing lawyer the following year. After his appointment as a judge (1962), he headed the office of the minister for labor and social affairs in Baden-Württemberg (1962–1965) before representing the CDU in the **Bundestag** (1965–1967, 1980–2002). Between 1967 and 1977, he served as minister for social affairs, **health**, and **sport** in **Rhineland-Palatinate**, where he also sat in the regional **Landtag** (1971–1979). In 1977, he succeeded **Kurt Biedenkopf** as general secretary of the CDU when it was developing a new program and **foreign policy** and establishing the foundations for its future coalition with the **Free Democratic Party (FDP)**, a partnership that lasted from 1982 until 1998. Geißler was instrumental in reorganizing the CDU and transforming it into a powerful electoral force and political machine. As federal minister for youth, family, and health under Chancellor **Helmut Kohl** (1982–1985), he introduced legislation on conscientious objectors, children's benefits, **pensions**, and **welfare**. Following a power struggle with Kohl, in which he attempted to move the CDU to the left, he lost his post as party general secretary to **Volker Rühe** in 1989. Geißler remained on the CDU national executive (1989–2000) and party presidium (1989–1994) and was deputy leader of the CDU/**Christian Social Union (CSU)** parliamentary group (1991–1998). In 2002, he served on parliamentary committees for **human rights** and humanitarian aid and for foreign affairs. Geißler has published numerous books on contemporary politics, social affairs, and the relevance of Christianity to modern society. In 2007, he joined ATTAC, which opposes neoliberal globalization (in particular through financial markets and tax havens) and campaigns for fair trade and the cancellation of the debts of developing countries.

GEMEINDE. *See* LOCAL GOVERNMENT.

GENSCHER, HANS-DIETRICH (1927–2016). Free Democratic Party (FDP) politician. Hans-Dietrich Genscher was born in Halle-Reideburg (**Saxony-Anhalt**), where his father worked for a farmers' association near Halle. In the final months of World War II, Genscher was enlisted in the German army, ending up in American, then British, captivity. After the war, he completed his school **education** in Halle and in the same year (1946) joined the Liberal-Demokratische Partei Deutschlands (Liberal-Democratic Party of Germany, LDPD) in eastern Germany. He studied law and economics in Halle and Leipzig (1946–1949) before qualifying as a lawyer (1949) and working for the regional court in Halle (until 1952). In 1952, Genscher left the **German Democratic Republic (GDR)** to settle in **Bremen**, where he joined the FDP. Continuing his law career, he worked for the Bremen regional court and took his final law exams in **Hamburg** (1954) before practicing in Bremen. In 1956, Genscher moved to Bonn, where he was first a research assistant (1956–1959) and then manager (1959–1965) for the FDP parliamentary group. In 1962, he became FDP party manager. Elected to the **Bundestag** in 1965, he served as a member of parliament until 1998. During this long period, he occupied various senior positions in the FDP, including deputy chairman (1968–1974) and chairman (1974–1985). He was interior minister in the **Social Democratic Party of Germany (SPD)**/FDP coalition under Chancellor **Willy Brandt** (1969–1974) and, following the latter's resignation, foreign minister and vice-chancellor under **Helmut Schmidt** (1974–1982). Despite protests from his party's left wing, Genscher supported the constructive vote of no confidence in Chancellor Schmidt that brought down the government in 1982, leading to the formation of a coalition with the **Christian Democratic Union (CDU)**/**Christian Social Union (CSU)**.

From 1982 until 1992, when he stepped down of his own accord, Genscher served as foreign minister and deputy chancellor under three CDU/FDP coalitions led by **Helmut Kohl**.

As foreign minister in Brandt's government, Genscher played a leading role in the policy of **Ostpolitik**, which eased relations with the Union of Soviet Socialist Republics (USSR) and the GDR. He also took part in the final stage of the negotiations surrounding the 1972–1975 Conference on Security and Cooperation in Europe (CSCE), in which the **North Atlantic Treaty Organization** (**NATO**) and the USSR agreed to a common framework for resolving postwar issues of military security and cooperating in economic, social, technical, and humanitarian fields. Genscher continued to work for dialogue and détente during the ups and downs of East–West relations during the late 1970s and 1980s. Following his visit to Moscow with Helmut Schmidt (June 1980), the Russians signaled their readiness to negotiate with the United States over the deployment of intermediate-range nuclear forces (INF) in Europe. Genscher also supported closer integration within the **European Union** (**EU**) and, from 1987 onward, encouraged the reform movement in the USSR by urging the Western powers to respond positively to it (his policy, occasionally disparaged as appeasement, came to be known as Genscherism). In 1989, he met with Polish opposition leader Lech Walesa and supported moves toward democracy in Poland and Hungary. In 1990, Genscher represented the Federal Republic of Germany (FRG) at the crucial 2 + 4 negotiations, which settled the external aspects of German reunification. Under Genscher's leadership, Germany was the first state to recognize Slovenia and Croatia in 1991, a move that was widely criticized.

A foreign minister for 18 years, Genscher received a standing ovation from all parties when he left the Bundestag in 1998 to resume a career in law and business. During his political career, he had also been instrumental in establishing a **United Nations** (**UN**) convention on anti**terrorism** (1976), demanded a worldwide ban on chemical weapons (1988), and was the first West European foreign minister to visit Iran (1984) following the Islamic Revolution of 1979.

Genscher received many national and international honors. He was president of the NATO Council and the Council of Ministers of the West European Union (1984–1985), president of the European Movement in Germany (1992–), and honorary professor in political science at the Free University of Berlin (1994–1995). In 1992, he was elected honorary chairman of the FDP. In the 1980s, the satirical magazine *Titanic* created the comic figure "Genschman," the savior of the world, in the mold of Batman.

See also FOREIGN POLICY AFTER 1990; FOREIGN POLICY: 1949–1969; FOREIGN POLICY: 1970–1990.

GERHARDT, WOLFGANG (1943–). Free Democratic Party (FDP) politician. Wolfgang Gerhardt was born in Ulrichstein-Helpershain (**Hessen**) and studied pedagogy, German, and politics at the University of Marburg (1964–1969), earning a doctorate (1970). After heading the regional office of the Friedrich-Naumann Stiftung (Friedrich Naumann Foundation) in Hanover (1969–1970), he became personal assistant and adviser to the interior minister of the federal state of Hessen (1971–1978), before taking over management of the ministerial office (1978). A member of the FDP from 1965, he was elected leader of the regional party association (1982–1995) and its national executive (1983–) and served as deputy leader of the national party (1985–1995), which he represented in the regional state parliament (**Landtag**, 1978–1982, 1983–1987, 1991–1994). Gerhardt held various positions at Land level, including minister for science and the arts and deputy minister (both 1987–1991), president of the standing conference of cultural/**education** ministers (KMK), and member of the **Bundesrat** (1987–1991). A deputy in the **Bundestag** (1994–2013), he led the national FDP (1995–2001, when he was succeeded by **Guido Westerwelle** following an internal party struggle) and its parliamentary group (1998–2006). In 2010, Gerhardt joined the commission that drew up the FDP's manifesto for the 2013 election, at which he, along with all other party members, lost his Bundestag seat. Other positions he held include chairman of the Friedrich Naumann Foundation (from 2006) and honorary chairman of the Hessen party association (from 2012).

GERMAN ADVISORY COUNCIL ON THE ENVIRONMENT (SACHVERSTÄNDIGENRAT FÜR UMWELTFRAGEN, SRU). Established in 1972, the SRU was one of the first institutions to be set up by the German government to provide advice on **environmental** policy. It consists of seven professors from various disciplines, each nominated by the government every four years, and publishes regular assessments of the state of the environment and of official policy. Working under the auspices of the Federal Ministry for the Environment, Nature Conservation, Building and Nuclear Safety, the council is also expected to contribute to policy formation and implementation.

GERMAN CULTURAL COUNCIL (DEUTSCHER KULTURRAT). The German Cultural Council is the umbrella organization of 200 cultural organizations in the Federal Republic of Germany (FRG). The council covers the entire cultural spectrum, and its members include the Deutscher Musikrat (for music), the Rat für Darstellende Künste (fine arts), the Deutsche Literaturkonferenz (**literature**), the Kunstrat (art), the Rat für Baukultur (architecture), the Sektion Design (design), the Sektion Film und Medien (**cinema**

and **media**), and the Rat für Soziokultur und kulturelle Bildung (sociocultural issues and **education**). The council maintains a "red list" of endangered cultural institutions in Germany, including libraries, **museums,** and **theaters**. A comprehensive overview of current activities and debates can be found at www.deutscher-kulturrat.de.

See also CULTURAL AND MEDIA POLICY.

GERMAN DEMOCRATIC REPUBLIC (GDR): ECONOMY. While the postwar Federal Republic of Germany (FRG) prospered as a Western, **social market economy**, eastern Germany (the GDR after 1949) adopted a Soviet-style model based on the wholesale transfer of land, **agriculture, banks,** and **industry** to state ownership. Although all **energy** production and major industries were in the hands of the state by 1955, the transfer process was carried out in phases and was finally completed between 1972 and 1976, leaving only a handful of small, privately run businesses that accounted for just 3 percent of production. From then until reunification, the structure of the GDR's economy was characterized by large-scale industrial plants (Kombinate) covering entire sectors that encompassed raw material extraction through to final processing. Farming was carried out by large collectives or cooperatives (Landwirtschaftliche Produktionsgenossenschaften, LPGs) specializing in animal or arable production. The GDR became deeply integrated into the economic bloc of the Union of Soviet Socialist Republics (USSR), on which it depended for **trade** and raw materials. Although trade with the FRG earned significant amounts of hard **currency**, this was never allowed to develop fully. The emphasis on currency-generating exports was satisfied at the expense of domestic needs, and consumer goods remained in short supply.

Production targets and priorities were set and implemented according to medium-term economic plans drawn up by the state. Following the first half-year plan for July–December 1948, plans were drawn up for the following two years (1949–1950), then for five years (1951–1955, 1956–1960), and then for seven years (1959–1965). A "perspective plan" for 1964–1970, which replaced the failed seven-year plan, was not agreed upon until 1967 and was replaced by a series of annual interim plans. Further plans were set for 1966–1970, 1967–1970, 1971–1975, 1976–1980, 1981–1985, and 1986–1990. Up until the 1960s, the plans focused on basic resources and heavy industry, leading to severe imbalances in the economy and consumer shortages. Some plans (notably those for 1951–1955 and 1959–1965) spectacularly failed to achieve their targets and triggered social unrest that seriously threatened the regime. Arguably the two most extreme indicators—with political consequences—of economic failure were the workers' uprising of 1953 and, following an enforced program of collectivization that produced food shortages and expropriated many small business owners, an exodus of around 2.5 million to West Germany between 1949 and 1961 that was stemmed only by the erection of the **Berlin Wall**.

In June 1963, the GDR government responded to the 1961–1962 crisis by introducing an economic reform program, the Neues Ökonomisches System der Planung und Leitung (New Economic System of Planning and Management, NÖSPL), which incorporated limited market-oriented mechanisms into the framework of central planning. These included interest rates, incentive payments, more flexible pricing, and a measure of independence for individual plants, which were encouraged to introduce quality measures and to merge into larger, sector-wide units of production. After years of economic stagnation, NÖSPL succeeded in raising the general standard of living. However, although state-owned concerns retained some autonomy in policy implementation, key industries were again subjected to central control and ideologically motivated planning after 1967. Known as the Ökonomisches System des Sozialismus (Economic System of Socialism, ÖSS), the new strategy aimed to promote science and technology in industry, especially electronics, **chemicals**, and **engineering**. The focus on growth industries and new technology was intended to close the gap with the West and was applied once again at the expense of the consumer sector. Combined with severe weather toward the end of 1970, the result was a supply crisis that contributed to the downfall of the East German leader **Walter Ulbricht** and his replacement by **Erich Honecker** in May 1971.

Under Honecker, economic targets became more realistic, and in the early 1970s, standards of living improved as more resources were directed to raising wages and **pensions**, providing better housing, and producing consumer goods. Production and incomes rose, and the GDR economy was held up as a model of efficiency by Eastern European standards. This positive perception coincided with the rise of a less critical "system-immanent" approach to GDR studies in West Germany that aimed to assess the East German economy and political system on its own terms, rather than judging it through Western eyes. In practice, economic central planning in the GDR intensified, placing an overwhelming emphasis on industrial production (70 percent of GDP), followed by agriculture (11 percent), with only a tiny service sector. The system was underpinned by an extensive but unproductive bureaucracy, employing 400,000 persons or 3 percent of the adult population (1989). At the same time, failure to renew or modernize plants and infrastructure hindered the development of both industry and agriculture, and toward the end of the 1970s, the economy stagnated again, partly as a result of the global energy crisis and partly through structural weaknesses. Despite limited travel opportunities, increased contacts with West Germans in the wake of the **Ostpolitik** treaties sharpened East Germans' realization that their economy was failing them. During the 1980s, the GDR generated alarming levels of foreign debt that were only partly controlled by reducing imports (and the domestic standard of living) and through credit infusions from the FRG. Nevertheless, Honecker and the GDR leadership proclaimed the superiority of the socialist economic system to the very end, and the true levels of economic underperformance, infrastructural decay, and ecological pollution emerged only after the collapse of the regime in 1989, when it became clear that the country had reached only one-third of Western productivity levels and was effectively broke. After 1989, the scale on which senior SED figures had misappropriated scarce resources, including luxury goods from the West, in order to maintain a lifestyle of personal material privilege also became apparent. For the general public, the disparity had been evident in the so-called Intershops, in which Western consumer items could be purchased only with "hard" Western currency.

See also EASTERN FEDERAL STATES AFTER REUNIFICATION.

GERMAN DEMOCRATIC REPUBLIC (GDR): POLITICAL INSTI-TUTIONS. For all intents and purposes, the GDR was a single-party state. Unlike in the Union of Soviet Socialist Republics (USSR), other political parties were permitted, but they were organized into a **Democratic Block** (also known as the National Front), and their leaders and activities were closely monitored and controlled by the **Socialist Unity Party of Germany** (**SED**). The purpose of the block was to transmit socialism to all sections of the population, such as **trade unions, women**, and youth (the so-called mass organizations), as well as to groups that were historically anticommunist. Thus, the **Christian Democratic Union** (**CDU**) in the GDR appealed to Christian conservatism, the Liberal-Demokratische Partei Deutschlands (Liberal-Democratic Party of Germany, LDPD) to small tradesmen and the former bourgeoisie, the National-Demokratische Partei Deutschlands (National Democratic Party of Germany, NPDP) to nationalists, and the Demokratische Bauernpartei Deutschlands (Democratic Farmworkers' Party of Germany, DBD) to **agricultural** workers. The National Front and "block parties" were controlled by the Democratic Block, which drew up lists of approved candidates and coordinated election campaigns.

The SED and its party apparatus exerted strict control over state institutions. The distribution of seats in the national parliament, the 500-member **People's Chamber** (Volkskammer), remained unchanged between 1963 and 1989 and ensured a permanent majority for the SED. Although the SED had only 127 seats, representatives of the mass organizations were nearly always party members. Almost never dissenting or conducting genuine parliamentary debates, the chamber met only four or five times a year, to rubber-stamp SED policies. The chamber also elected the 44-member Council of Ministers (Ministerrat), which was chaired by a minister president (Ministerpräsident); the 20-member Council of State (Staatsrat); the chairman of the Nationaler

Verteidigungsrat (National Defense Council); and senior judges. The councils acted as ministerial cabinets running the economy, implementing defense and **foreign policy**, and administering elections and the legal system. Not until the SED fell from power in October/November 1989 did the People's Chamber begin to function as a genuinely democratic forum and legislative body.

The center of decision making in the GDR was the Politburo of the SED, which was chaired by party leader **Erich Honecker** from 1971 until October 1989. In 1989, the Politburo comprised 21 full members and 5 candidate members, although actual power lay in the hands of an inner circle of veteran communists who held key political and ministerial posts. The principal figures in the Politburo were **Erich Mielke**, minister for state security; **Willi Stoph**, chairman of the Council of Ministers; **Günter Mittag**, who controlled economic policy; and **Hermann Axen**, head of propaganda (termed "agitation") and foreign policy. Other leading Politburo members included **Werner Krolikowski, Heinz Keßler, Harry Tisch, Kurt Hager, Joachim Herrmann, Horst Sindermann, Egon Krenz**, and **Günter Schabowski**. The Politburo was appointed by the Zentralkomitee (Central Committee) of the SED, which was in turn elected by around 2,500 delegates at the party congress (Parteitag). The congress was a carefully stage-managed event held every five years, traditionally serving as the leadership's platform for announcing policy initiatives. Between 1950 and 1986, the Central Committee, which replaced the former party executive (Vorstand), grew from 51 full members (30 candidates) to 165 (57 candidates), partly because of the expansion of its responsibilities and partly because inactive veteran members simply retained their seats. The Central Committee represented the SED political elite and maintained strict loyalty and party discipline. It appointed a secretariat to ensure that Politburo rulings were implemented and to supervise the activities of the People's Chamber, the Council of Ministers, and the Council of State. It drew on a large bureaucracy of over 2,000 staff members in 40 departments to manage and direct all aspects of life in the GDR, from administration to the economy, infrastructure, **education**, and cultural affairs. Public positions in the GDR were allocated according to the nomenclatura, a largely secret system in which trusted party members rose up through the hierarchy to be rewarded with posts of responsibility, more through their political and ideological reliability than their technical expertise.

The SED's most feared instrument of political and social control was the secret police, or **Stasi**. The scale of the Stasi and its operations emerged only after reunification, and the issue of how to handle its extensive archives posed questions for both the interim GDR government and reunited Germany. Before it lost power, the SED had almost 2.3 million members (August

1989), but within 10 months, that figure had shrunk by 85 percent. Many SED loyalists moved to its successor party, the **Party of Democratic Socialism (PDS)**.

The character of the GDR regime's control and its effect on citizens have led researchers to question the use of simple labels such as "totalitarian dictatorship." Although the SED's policy making was strongly centralized and undemocratic, the state provided an extensive welfare system, opportunities for education, new roles for women, and generous rewards for conformity. Apart from the ability to retreat into "niches" of personal privacy, there were also elements of participatory democracy at the level of local politics, in lower management, and on the factory floor. These more benign features suggest that East Germany in its later years was a "modern dictatorship," in which physical terror largely gave way to more subtle forms of social control. Despite widespread disillusionment over economic progress, the state achieved a high level of self-censorship and acceptance on the part of its citizens, which goes some way to explaining post-1990 nostalgia for the preunification era. Some researchers reject outright the label of a "totalitarian state," which suggests a fixed, static society and fails to capture the changes that the GDR underwent from the Stalin era through Honecker's tenure. At the same time, the fact that the GDR followed on almost immediately from the National Socialist period has led to direct comparisons with the Nazi dictatorship. Proposed similarities include domination by a monopolistic mass party, the assertion of an all-embracing ideology (focusing on youth and the need to defend the state against a hostile, capitalist West), government control over the judiciary and other areas of life, a secret police, a centrally controlled economy, and an anti-Western, antiliberal worldview. There were, however, significant differences between the SED and the National Socialists. While the SED claimed to be international and utopian in outlook, the National Socialists were unashamedly nationalistic and racist and regarded military aggression and genocide as legitimate ways of achieving their aims. Although the SED's authority rested largely on external support (from the USSR), it was able to mold German society over a much longer period (40 years) than the National Socialist dictatorship had. It should also be noted that the GDR was subjected to immediate scrutiny and analysis after 1990, especially by Westerners, whereas Germans took much longer to even begin the process of critically examining and coming to terms with National Socialism. At the same time, the fall of the GDR encouraged historians to consider some aspects of preunification West Germany, including the struggle between the secret services of East and West; the role of the "eastern bureaus" (Ostbüros) of the West German political parties; and the numerous, well-funded research institutes in the FRG. To this list can be added the activities of refugee associations and the hitherto largely ignored phenomenon of migration from West to East Germany, which has been less well documented than movement from East to West.

See also EASTERN FEDERAL STATES AFTER REUNIFICATION; GERMAN DEMOCRATIC REPUBLIC (GDR): ECONOMY.

GERMAN FEDERAL BANK (DEUTSCHE BUNDESBANK). The German Federal (or Central) Bank was established by legislation in 1957 to protect the value of the German **currency**, ensure price stability, manage national financial reserves, and provide for the smooth running of interbanking and international transactions. Although technically owned by the government, the bank consistently maintained that its responsibility for the currency was distinct from economic and fiscal policy, which was the executive's domain. The bank's independence of government, which earned it widespread respect, was demonstrated on several occasions and led to conflict with chancellors (**Ludwig Erhard** in 1966) and ministers (**Karl Schiller** in 1972). Similar disputes arose with the governing **Social Democratic Party of Germany** (**SPD**) during the 1980s, when the bank resisted pressure from other European states and the United States to raise interest rates. After the fall of the **German Democratic Republic** (**GDR**) and during the negotiations for reunification in 1990, the bank opposed the one-to-one exchange rate of the old East German currency for the West German mark on the grounds that it was inflationary. It also criticized the government for its reluctance to control the costs of reunification and openly defied plans to revalue gold reserves in the run-up to the **European Monetary Union** (1997). After 1974, the bank set and published annual money supply targets, which it achieved between 1979 and 1985, although subsequent policies became more flexible in response to large currency inflows.

Based in Frankfurt/Main and with a full-time staff of over 9,500 people (3,800 in Frankfurt), the Federal Bank maintains nine regional centers in the **federal states**, which control 41 branches in main towns and cities. The bank is managed by an executive board, appointed by the **president of the Federal Republic** and comprising a president, vice president, and four other members. The president, vice president, and one ordinary member are proposed by the **federal government** and the remaining members by the **Bundesrat** after consultation with the government. After the progressive introduction of the euro (from 1999), the bank saw its functions greatly reduced and integrated with those of the European Central Bank (ECB), for which it acted as a model. The Federal Bank continues, however, to exercise a supervisory role over the German banking system, and its president (governor) has a seat on the ECB governing council. The bank provides German **banks** with money for refinancing and manages currency and gold reserves (held in Germany, Great Britain, and the United States). Prominent recent presidents have been

Karl Otto Pöhl (1988–1991) and Karl Tietmeyer (1993–1999), who was succeeded by Ernst Welteke (1999–2004). The current president is Jens Weidmann (2011–).

GERMAN MARSHALL FUND OF THE UNITED STATES (GMF). The fund was set up in 1972 when Chancellor Willy Brandt, in an act of gratitude on behalf of the German people, donated 150 million DM to provide a permanent memorial to the original Marshall Plan (official title: European Recovery Program, ERP), which provided around $160,000 million between 1948 and 1952 (1957 in the case of West Berlin) to rebuild European economies devastated by World War II. Alongside the humanitarian goals of alleviating poverty and unemployment, the ERP aimed to halt the spread of communism in Europe and create future export markets for the United States (U.S.). Named after U.S. foreign minister George C. Marshall, who announced the project in 1947, the program was instrumental in triggering the postwar economic boom in West Germany, which received some 11 percent of the fund. The ERP is also credited with creating the foundations for the eventual economic integration of Western Europe and the creation of the European Union (EU). The independent GMF, which received further endowments from the German government in 1986 and 2001, is dedicated to furthering transatlantic cooperation through grants, research, and bringing together political and business leaders. Based in Washington, D.C., it maintains offices throughout eastern and western Europe. After the fall of the Berlin Wall (1989), the GMF expanded its activities in central and eastern Europe, where it assisted in the transition to democracy.

GERMAN PEOPLE'S UNION (DEUTSCHE VOLKSUNION, DVU). In 1971, when the extreme right-wing National Democratic Party of Germany (NPD) appeared close to breaking up, the Munich-based publisher Gerhard Frey (1933–2013) founded the DVU as a loose network of subscribers to his newspaper, the *Deutsche National-Zeitung* (renamed *National-Zeitung*, 1985). During its career, the party and its parliamentary representatives remained financially and politically dependent on Frey and, on the basis of his network, membership rose from 5,000 in 1976 to 22,000 in 1990, after which it fell to 1,000 in 2012, when it dissolved itself and merged with the NPD. The DVU held annual rallies in Passau, rejected German responsibility for World War II, argued for extending Germany's national borders eastward, and linked foreigners with rising crime figures. Formally constituted as a party under the name DVU-Liste D in 1987, it worked closely with the NPD. In 1987, an alliance of both parties gained seats in the Bremen city parliament (repeated in 1991, 1999, and 2003), and in 1992 the DVU succeeded in sending five members to the Schleswig-Holstein regional assembly (**Land-**

tag) with 6.3 percent of the vote. Spectacularly gaining 16 seats in **Saxony-Anhalt** in 1998, it became to the first extreme right-wing party to enter a regional parliament in eastern Germany. In **Brandenburg**, after clearing the 5 percent hurdle in the 1999 election, the DVU raised its share of the vote to 6.1 percent in 2004 to become the fourth largest party, behind the **Social Democratic Party of Germany (SPD)**, **the Christian Democratic Union (CDU)**, and the **Party of Democratic Socialism (PDS)**.

See also ANTI-SEMITISM; EXTREMISM; POLITICAL PARTIES; REPUBLICANS, THE (DIE REPUBLIKANER, REP).

GERMAN PRESS COUNCIL (DEUTSCHER PRESSERAT). In 1956, **media** organizations in Germany, anticipating a move by the **federal government**, formed their own body to act as a control and regulator. Its members include representatives from journalists' organizations, **trade unions**, and publishers (the Bundesverband Deutscher Zeitungsverleger, Deutscher Journalistenverband, Deutsche Journalistinnen- und Journalisten Union within ver.di, and the Verband Deutscher Zeitschriftenverlage). As a body, the German Press Council may be compared with the British Press Council. Since 2009, the council is based in **Berlin**, after moving there from Bonn.

At first the council concentrated on defending the freedom of the **press**, but now it is more concerned with ensuring that its own recommendations of best practice are observed. A codex for online publications is under negotiation. The council issues three levels of criticism, the "Hinweis" (notice), the "Missbilligung" (censure), and, the highest form of disapproval, the "Rüge" (reprimand). Papers that have been subjected to criticism include *Bild*, *BZ*, *Stern*, and *Dresdner Morgenpost*. An overview of the council's work past and present is available online at www.presserat.de.

See also PUBLISHING; TELEVISION AND RADIO.

GERMAN SOCIAL UNION (DEUTSCHE SOZIALE UNION, DSU). The German Social Union was created on 20 January 1990, in the former **German Democratic Republic (GDR)**, following a merger of conservative Christian groups. The DSU saw itself as a sister party to the Bavarian **Christian Social Union (CSU)**, which tried to establish itself in the GDR during 1990. Led by Hans-Wilhelm Ebeling and his deputy, Hans-Joachim Walther, the DSU called for swift reunification and the immediate adoption of the legal and constitutional system of the Federal Republic of Germany (FRG) in East Germany. In the March 1990 elections to the **People's Chamber**, the party did well in certain states (**Saxony** and **Thuringia**), but it performed badly in regional elections the following October and disappeared during the all-German elections to the **Bundestag** in December, when its voters shifted their support to the **Christian Democratic Union (CDU)**.

GERMAN STOCK EXCHANGE (DEUTSCHE BÖRSE AG). The German Stock Exchange, based in Frankfurt/Main and operating under its current name since 1992, has branches throughout the world, including Luxembourg, Zurich, London, Prague, Moscow, New York, Chicago, and Singapore. The exchange functions as a trading organization for shares and securities and provides transaction services and market information through its subsidiaries, cooperating with other exchanges to offer access to global capital markets. In December 1996, Deutsche Börse AG, in partnership with the Swiss stock exchange, set up Eurex, then the world's largest futures exchange. Its Xetra® platform, introduced in 1997, claims to be one of the world's fastest and most efficient electronic trading systems. In 2002, it became the sole owner of Clearstream, a supplier of international securities services. Under Werner Seifert, chief executive from 1993 to 2005, Deutsche Börse developed into one of Europe's most dynamic and highly valued exchanges, well ahead of smaller exchanges in **Hamburg**, Düsseldorf, Munich, and Stuttgart. Despite the demise of its **New Market** (Neuer Markt) venture (1997–2003), the Frankfurt exchange grew from a medium-sized organization trading cash equities into a profitable, international operation handling 90 percent of equity trading in Germany; it also trades derivatives and is engaged in clearing and settlement. Negotiations to amalgamate with the London stock exchange collapsed in 2001 and 2005, and a merger with the New York stock exchange was vetoed by the commission of the **European Union (EU)** in 2012. With a workforce of 4,540, the group turned over 2,043 million euros in 2014. Reto Francioni was appointed chief executive officer in 2005. In March 2016, the London and Frankfurt exchanges finally agreed terms for a merger.

GERMAN UNITY FUND (FONDS DEUTSCHE EINHEIT). The German Unity Fund was established in May 1990 to offset the pressures on the economy of the new **eastern federal states** as they adjusted to the merger with the Federal Republic of Germany (FRG). Financed by the **Bund**, the western federal states, and credit, the fund was initially intended to underpin the new Länder with a total subsidy of 115,000 million DM until they could be incorporated into the national system of **financial equalization** in 1995. Some 85 percent of the subsidy would be transferred directly to the eastern states and 15 percent provided by the Bund in the form of centrally financed projects and public works. The fund, which supported numerous large-scale projects, mainly for infrastructure, services, and communications, was topped up by a further 45,700 million DM between 1992 and 1994. Between 1990 and 1993, a special fund (Kreditabwicklungsfonds) also managed debts inherited from the former **German Democratic Republic (GDR)**. Payments to the east through the fund ceased in 1995, when it was turned into an amortization fund and superseded by the first **Solidarity Pact**.

GERSTENMAIER, EUGEN KARL (1906–1986). Christian Democratic Union (CDU) politician and president of the **Bundestag** (1954–1969). Eugen Karl Gerstenmaier was born in Kirchheim/Teck (**Baden-Württemberg**), one of seven children of a manager in a piano factory. After qualifying in commerce (1921), he studied philosophy, German, and Protestant theology at the universities of Tübingen, Rostock, and Zurich, earning a doctorate in theology in 1935. A member of the underground Protestant "confessing church" (Bekennende Kirche) from 1934, he was arrested and briefly detained by the National Socialists, although he continued his activities for the church until 1944, when he narrowly escaped execution for his involvement in the attempted assassination of Adolf Hitler (20 July 1944). Sentenced to seven years' imprisonment, he was freed in 1945. After the war, he cofounded the charitable relief arm of the organization of the Evangelical Church in Germany (EKD), although he was compelled to resign as its head in 1951 over **taxation** problems. From 1948 onward, he was a member of the governing synod of the EKD.

Gerstenmaier represented the CDU in the Bundestag (1949–1969), chairing the parliamentary committee for foreign affairs (from 1951 onward). He became deputy chairman of the CDU (1956) and was also cofounder and head of the German Africa Society. In 1954 he was elected president of the Bundestag, a post he held until 1969 and which he used to undertake several major building projects; the deputies' building (Abgeordnetenhaus) in Bonn was nicknamed "Tall Eugen" after him. In 1969, he resigned as president over allegations that he had received excessively high compensation for the National Socialists' refusal in 1938 to recognize his theological thesis as a qualification to teach at university. After the national election of 1980, he chaired an all-party refereeing committee. His autobiography appeared in 1981.

GERSTER, FLORIAN (1949–). Social Democratic Party of Germany (SPD) politician. Florian Gerster was born in Worms (**Rhineland-Palatinate**, RLP). After national service (he later rose to the rank of senior lieutenant in the reserve), he studied psychology and business administration at the University of Mannheim, qualifying with a diploma in psychology (1970–1975). A member of the SPD from 1966, Gerster represented the party on the Worms city council (1974–1990) and in the RLP **Landtag** (1977–1987, 1996–2002), specializing in social policy, **health**, and **Bundeswehr** issues. He entered the **Bundestag** in 1987, but returned to Mainz in 1991 to become Staatsminister für Bundes- und Europaangelegenheiten (Regional Minister for Federal and European Affairs) in the newly elected SPD/FDP coalition led by **Rudolf Scharping** (SPD). Under Scharping, Gerster played a prominent role in security and **foreign policy**. He was a member of the German delegation to the North Atlantic Assembly (1990–2002), the forum of the **North Atlantic Treaty Organization (NATO)** for parliamentarians from member and associate states. In view of concerns over the rising number of objections to military service, he proposed, contrary to SPD policy, replacing conscription (Wehrpflicht) with a more general form of compulsory service (allgemeine Dienstpflicht). He also supported Bundeswehr participation in international peacekeeping operations.

When Scharping was elected party chairman and moved to Bonn (1993), Gerster was a favorite to succeed him as **minister president**, although the position eventually went to **Kurt Beck** (October 1994), in whose government Gerster took over the regional ministry of labor, social affairs, and health and rapidly developed a national profile. Widely regarded as an up-and-coming politician and modernizer in the SPD, he became leader of the regional party and a member of the national council (Parteirat). He was credited with adopting measures for helping reduce unemployment and modernizing the labor market in RLP by increasing the role of private agencies and promoting working at home. He also argued for greater incentives for the unemployed to take work, including the requirement to accept job offers, and for widening the gap between state benefits and paid work. In March 2002, the "Mainz model," which Gerster had pioneered and tested in RLP and **Brandenburg**, was introduced nationally and planned to be in effect until the end of 2003. Designed to lift the unemployed out of social welfare, the model provided for a combined wage that included a state-subsidized "top-top" for an unemployed person taking a low-paid job; critics condemned the scheme as complex and failing to create new jobs in a harsh labor market. Regarded as an independent thinker in the right wing of the SPD, Gerster was an early supporter of raising the compulsory retirement age, spoke out on the need to curb health costs, and argued for a 12-month limit on unemployment pay and for merging welfare and unemployment benefits.

In February 2002, Gerster was appointed president of the Nuremberg-based Bundesanstalt für Arbeit (Federal Labour Office, BA), heading a three-member executive board. The BA, which had been criticized for inefficiency and falsifying statistics, employed more than 90,000 people in 840 offices and managed a huge unemployment budget as well as acting as an employment agency. Gerster announced plans for a radical restructuring (July 2003) to transform the organization from a state-run bureaucracy into a modern, market-oriented service provider, subject also to stricter financial controls. A renamed agency (Bundesagentur für Arbeit) emerged in January 2004. In the same month, however, Gerster was dismissed following revelations that he had bypassed the official tendering process in approving consultants' contracts. There was also concern over the agency's lack of success in job placements. Crucially, Gerster's reforms, the pace of change, and his aggressive style had also encountered resistance within the German bureaucracy. He was succeeded by his former deputy, Frank-Jürgen Weise, and pursued a career in business and health sector personnel recruitment.

GLOS, MICHAEL (1944–). Christian Social Union (CSU) politician. Michael Glos was born in Brünnau (Lower Franconia/**Bavaria**). After qualifying as a master miller (1968), he took over the family farming and corn milling business following the premature death of his father. Disillusioned with the performance of the first **grand coalition** (1966–1969), he joined the CSU in 1970 and became active in local politics in his hometown of Prichsenstadt and the district of Kitzingen (1972–1993). After 1976, he occupied various positions in the organization of the Lower Franconia district CSU before joining the party presidium and executive (1993). In 1976, he entered the **Bundestag** as a directly elected member for Schweinfurt-Kitzingen, the youngest CSU representative in the house. In parliament, his posts included chairman of CSU working parties on finance, the budget, and **taxation**; spokesman for the **Christian Democratic Union (CDU)**/CSU parliamentary group on taxation (1987–1990); and deputy leader of the group with responsibility for the economy, **transport**, small to medium-sized businesses (the **Mittelstand**), and **agriculture** (1990–1992). From 1993 to 2005, he led the CSU in the Bundestag and was also deputy chairman of the joint CDU/CSU group. Glos was instrumental in promoting fellow Bavarian **Edmund Stoiber** as chancellor candidate in the autumn 2002 national election, in preference to **Angela Merkel**. He served as minister for economics and technology in Merkel's first coalition cabinet (2005–2009), although he later claimed that he did not feel equipped for the task. A leading figure in the CSU, Glos retained close links with his home district and strongly promoted Bavarian interests in **Berlin**.

GOETHE INSTITUTE. Founded in 1951 as successor to the Deutsche Akademie, the Goethe Institute aims to promote German **language** and culture as an autonomous and politically independent institution. By 1953, there were three German towns offering the institute's language courses: Bad Reichenhall, Murnau, and Kronau. These towns were deliberately chosen for their rural setting in order to present a peaceful, positive, and traditional view of Germany. The **students' revolution** of 1968 prompted the institute to modernize its approach, and it now concentrates on topics relevant to society and avant-garde art. The new approach was strengthened by a greater understanding of culture, as redefined by **Ralf Dahrendorf** in 1970 and commissioned by the Federal Foreign Office. By 1989–1990, the Goethe Institute had begun to focus its activities on the former eastern bloc countries. In 2001, it merged with its sister organization Inter Nationes to create Goethe-

Institut Inter Nationes e.V., although it reverted to its former title in 2003. Today the so-called cultural institutes (Kulturinstitute) of the organization work within a worldwide network and are financed by the Federal Foreign Office and the Federal Press Office (Bundespresseamt), but also by sponsors and self-generated income. They promote the German language abroad, foster international cooperation, host exhibitions and readings, show films, and cultivate a positive image of Germany in other countries. German as a foreign language is taught and assessed on several levels (A1 to C2), and the institutes also support teachers of German abroad. Cultural activities cover all relevant areas, with a strong focus on retrospective activities and current affairs, including **architecture, education, literature, cinema**, music, dance, and **media**. To date there are 160 Goethe Institutes in 84 countries, whose activities are coordinated from Munich. Past presidents of the organization are Kurt Magnus (1951–1962), Max Grasmann (1962–1963), Peter H. Pfeiffer (1963–1971), Hans von Herwarth (1971–1977), Klaus von Bismarck (1977–1989), Hans Heigert (1989–1993), and Hilmar Hoffmann (1993–2001). Jutta Limbach, former president of the **Federal Constitutional Court (FCC)** and author of the essay "Hat Deutsch eine Zukunft?" ("Does the German language have a future?", 2010), was president from 2002 until 2008, when Klaus-Dieter Lehmann took over. The institute maintains a web page that both covers its history and provides up-to-date information worldwide (www.goethe.de).

GRAND COALITION. In the parliamentary system of the Federal Republic of Germany (FRG), this term traditionally refers to a governing alliance of the electorally strongest parties, that is, the **Christian Democratic Union (CDU)/Christian Social Union (CSU)** and the **Social Democratic Party of Germany (SPD)**. At the national level (the **Bundestag**), the first grand coalition governed from December 1966 until October 1969. Led by Federal Chancellor **Kurt Georg Kiesinger** (CDU) and Deputy Chancellor and Foreign Minister **Willy Brandt** (SPD) and formed primarily to overcome problems in the economy, the coalition restored financial stability, passed the controversial emergency laws (Notstandsgesetze) enabling West Germany to realize full national sovereignty, and established diplomatic relations with a number of Eastern European states as a precursor to **Ostpolitik**. Representing a transition between the postwar years of CDU-led governments and the coming to power of the SPD, the coalition broke up as a result of interparty differences over the nuclear deterrent and economic policy (in particular, revaluation of the DM), and faced mounting social unrest, which culminated in the **students' movement** of 1967–1968. While the preunification FRG saw only one national grand coalition, the more recent fragmentation of electoral behavior and the emergence of new parties, in particular the **Green Party** and **The Left Party**, have encouraged their formation. The grand coalition under **Angela Merkel** (CDU, 2005–2009) similarly confronted big issues such as budget control and **federalism reform**, although her second grand coalition (2013–) emerged largely through the failure of its natural junior political partner, the **Free Democratic Party (FDP)**, to enter the Bundestag. Although grand coalitions with large majorities are often viewed as undemocratic stopgaps that sideline effective opposition, they can be electorally popular when major structural reforms are needed. At federal state level, grand coalitions in the preunification FRG did occur, but were relatively uncommon. A quite different situation emerged in the new **eastern federal states**, however, where the two main parties were more often prepared to join forces rather than admit the **Party of Democratic Socialism (PDS)** and its successor, The Left Party, to government. Even so, as they lost their traditional electoral appeal in the face of the minority party challenge, they could not always command the large majorities historically associated with grand coalitions.

GRASS, GÜNTER (1927–2015). Writer. Born in Danzig of German Polish parents, Günter Grass served in World War II, was wounded, and was held in U.S. captivity until 1946. His belated revelation in 2006 that as a teenager he had served in the Waffen-SS for a brief period in 1945 attracted some criticism given his influential role in postwar West Germany. After the war, he trained as a stonemason and sculptor in Düsseldorf and **Berlin**. Grass began writing lyric poetry and drama in the 1950s. In 1958, he received an award from **Group 47** for the manuscript of his novel *Die Blechtrommel (The Tin Drum)*, which appeared in 1959 and brought him international acclaim. The novella *Katz und Maus (Cat and Mouse*, 1961) and the novels *Hundejahre (Dog Years*, 1963) and *Der Butt (The Flounder*, 1977) confirmed his reputation as a socially and politically engaged writer. In 1965, 1969, and 1972, he took part in the election campaigns of the **Social Democratic Party of Germany (SPD)**, criticizing from 1966 onward what he referred to as "reactionary" politics in the Federal Republic of Germany (FRG) and the suppression of freedom in the **German Democratic Republic (GDR)**. Grass's involvement in politics is representative of a generation of artists, publicists, and writers who saw **Willy Brandt** as a symbol of political renewal. Grass adopted a critical stance on reunification, proposing a gradual process that would enable both parts of the country to develop a federalist national culture (Kulturnation). Although he joined the SPD in the 1980s and was engaged in the peace movement, he left the party in 1993 in protest against its hardening of policy toward **asylum** seekers. His novel *Ein weites Feld (Too Far Afield*, 1995) dealt with reunification in a historical context. In recent years Grass was critical of **European Union (EU)** policies. His negative comments on Israel's nuclear policy and its threats to Iran generated accusations of **anti-Semitism** in 2012. His views alienated many and made him persona non grata in Israel. Nevertheless, Grass remains one of Germany's most important intellectual voices in the 20th and 21st centuries. In 1999, he was awarded the Nobel Prize for Literature. The city of Lübeck opened a museum and exhibition center, the Günter Grass House, in 2002. At a memorial service in May 2015, the writer John Irving delivered the eulogy.

GRAUMANN, DIETER (1950–). Jewish community leader. Born in Ramat Gan (Israel), Dieter (formerly David) Graumann was taken to live in Frankfurt/Main at the age of 18 months. He studied economics at Frankfurt University and King's College, London, graduating in 1979 with a doctorate on European monetary union. After working for **Deutsche Bank**, he became president, later honorary president, of Makkabi Deutschland, a Jewish sports association in Germany, and also runs a real estate/property management business. In 1995, he joined the executive board of the Jüdische Gemeinschaft Frankfurt am Main (Jewish Community in Frankfurt), with responsibility for finances, education, and cultural work. From 2010 until 2014, he served as president of the **Central Council of Jews in Germany**. In office Graumann praised Germany's efforts to preserve the memory of the Holocaust but condemned a visit by a three-man delegation from the German national football team to Auschwitz as too small (2012). In the same year, he rejected a ruling by a Cologne court that circumcision of infants constituted bodily harm, and he joined other leading Jews in attacking the author **Günter Grass** for criticizing Israel's policy toward Iran.

GREEN PARTY (DIE GRÜNEN). The roots of the Green Party lie in the extra-parliamentary opposition groups, student protests, and environmentally oriented citizens' initiatives of the late 1960s and early 1970s. These eventually organized themselves, first at the regional and then at the federal level, as the "Greens," formally constituting a national party on 13 January 1980 in Karlsruhe. Founding members were the peace activist **Petra Kelly**, the former **Christian Democratic Union (CDU)** speaker on **environmental** affairs Herbert Gruhl (1921–1993), and the artist **Joseph Beuys** (1921–1986). At a defining party congress in Saarbrücken (1980), the Greens described their orientation as "ecological, social, grass-roots, democratic, and non-violent." Campaigning principally on the environment, especially against nuclear **energy**, but also for social justice, rights for **women**, and against the arms buildup, the Greens epitomized citizens' democracy and nonviolent civil activism.

The Greens gained seats in state parliaments in **Bremen** (1979), **Baden-Württemberg** (1980), and **Hessen** (1982) before entering the **Bundestag** with 27 deputies in March 1983 (increasing to 68 in 2009, 60 in 2013). Its first ruling coalition at Land level, with the **Social Democratic Party of**

Germany (SPD), governed Hessen from 1985 to 1987, although a coalition with the CDU, in **Hamburg**, did not materialize until 2008–2010. Despite electoral successes during the 1980s, the party was torn by internal disputes between fundamentalists, who rejected cooperation with the main parties, and pragmatic realists, who were willing to work within the parliamentary system and enter into political alliances; conservative-minded members either remained in the minority or left the party. Prominent representatives of these wings were the fundamentalist **Jutta Ditfurth** and the realists **Otto Schily** (who defected to the SPD in 1989) and **Joschka Fischer**. After failing to enter the Bundestag in 1990, the Greens' fortunes recovered as the pragmatists within the party gained ascendance following the Neumünster Party Congress of 1991.

After the fall of the regime in the **German Democratic Republic (GDR)**, the west German Greens and east German citizens' groups merged to create the **Alliance 90/The Greens** (Bündnis 90/Die Grünen); the merger was agreed to in principle by eastern Germans in 1990 and finalized in 1993. Campaigning separately from the western Greens, the new grouping won six seats in eastern states in the postreunification Bundestag (1990), although the party never made much headway in the new **Länder**, which lacked the ecologically aware, middle-class basis that fostered its development in the west. In the 1998 election the Greens, arguing for a price increase in gasoline and against German participation in operations in Bosnia, garnered a disappointing 6.7 percent of the vote, but it was enough to enable them to form, for the first time, a national coalition with the SPD and to secure three ministerial posts (held by Joschka Fischer, **Andrea Fischer**, and **Jürgen Trittin**). While many Greens continued to oppose Germany's involvement in military operations in Yugoslavia (1998) and later in Afghanistan (2001), they successfully promoted ecological taxes (1999) and the commitment to phase out nuclear energy (2001). The Greens increased their share of votes in the 2002 national election (8.6 percent), continued in coalition with the SPD (until 2005), and performed well in regional and European elections. Although excluded from national government after 2005, the Greens achieved a dramatic 13.7 percent share of votes in the Hessen regional election of 2009 and did well in the national election the same year (10.7 percent). For the first time, they also entered into coalition with the CDU and **Free Democratic Party (FDP)** in the **Saarland** (2009–2012). In early 2014, they were coalition partners in several **federal states**. However, after what they regarded as a serious defeat in the general election of September 2013, when their share of the vote fell from 10.7 to 8.4 percent (68/63 seats), and the breaking off of coalition negotiations with the **Christian Democratic Union (CDU)**, they replaced the leaders of their parliamentary group and elected a new national cochairperson.

Despite the existence of a national structure, local and regional organizations within the Green Party enjoy considerable autonomy, campaigning under various titles that reflect specific policy concerns. Thus the so-called Green Lists (Grüne Listen) focus on ecological/antinuclear issues, while Alternative Lists (Alternative Listen) tend to campaign on social and gender-related topics, world peace, or the arms race. After the merger with the eastern groups, citizens' rights came to the fore, and the agenda moved away from ecological radicalism and pacifism. The legacy of early leaders such as Petra Kelly, who saw the Greens as an "anti-party party," was reflected in the rotation principle, which obliged members of parliament to stand down and be replaced at regular intervals in order to retain the link with the grass roots. The rotation principle proved constitutionally controversial since, according to the **Basic Law** (**BL**, article 38), Bundestag members are not bound to party directives, and after 1980 the party began moving away from both the principle of and the absolute prohibition on elected deputies holding government office. It also set up national structures resembling those of the established parties. In 2003, the party decided that one-third of members of the executive could also be members of parliament, although members could not lead the Bundestag parliamentary group or be government ministers. The supreme organ of the Green Party is a 750-member federal assembly (Bundesversammlung) or annual conference of delegates (Bundesdelegiertenkonferenz), half of whose members must be women and which elects national party committees and, for two years, the federal executive committee (Bundesvorstand). The executive represents the party both to its members and externally and, unlike the main political parties, has two chairpersons. Other organs are the party council (Parteirat), whose 16 members coordinate and develop policy; a council of states (Länderrat), which decides on general policy guidelines and coordinates business among the various party bodies; and a national council for women's issues (Bundesfrauenrat). The Heinrich-Böll Stiftung (Heinrich Böll Foundation), with offices in 30 countries of the world, acts independently to develop "green ideas," projects, and strategic partnerships. After hovering at around 44,000 from 2001 to 2008, party membership rose steadily to reach a historic 61,000 in 2013. Current party leaders are **Simone Peter** (elected 2013) and **Cem Özdemir** (since 2008).

GRÖHE, HERMANN (1961–). Christian Democratic Union (CDU) politician. Born in Uedem (**North Rhine-Westfalia**), Hermann Gröhe studied law at the University of Cologne (1980–1987), where he also worked as a research assistant (1987–1993) before qualifying as a practicing lawyer (1987, 1993). Gröhe joined the CDU in 1977 and was active in the party youth organization, the **Junge Union** (**JU**), initially at district level (1983–1983) and subsequently as national chairman (1989–1994). He represented the main party as a district councilor for Neuss (1984–1989,

1993–1994) and was a member of the CDU's commission that drew up its program of basic principles (*Grundsatzprogramm*) before entering the **Bundestag** in 1994. Between 1994 and 1998, Gröhe served as spokesman for the so-called Junge Gruppe (Young Group) of conservative deputies, which was founded in 1990 for CDU parliamentarians under 35 years old, and also on **human rights** for the party parliamentary group (1998–2005). During 2008–2009, he was **state minister** in the **Office of the Federal Chancellor**, responsible for coordination between the **Bund** and the **federal states**, reducing bureaucracy, and links with the Bundestag. After serving as general secretary of the CDU (2009–2013), Gröhe was appointed **health** minister in **Angela Merkel**'s third cabinet in 2013. Since 1997, he has also been active in the **Evangelical Church in Germany** (**EKD**) and in 2001 joined the executive board of the conservative Konrad-Adenauer Stiftung (Konrad Adenauer Foundation).

GROUP 47 (GRUPPE 47). Group 47 was an influential literary forum formed after World War II, which aimed to promote the development of a new German **literature** that responded to the lessons learned during 12 years of a totalitarian regime. The group met first in 1947 and convened for the last time in Saulgau in 1977, when it officially dissolved itself. Membership fluctuated, and there was always a keen political involvement. One of the main initiators was Hans Werner Richter (1908–1993), who by the mid-1950s had observed a change in the membership, inasmuch as "a new generation—the children of the war" were making themselves heard. While pressure from conservative groups actually strengthened the group, in 1967 it came into open confrontation with students who wanted now to actively change, no longer interpret, the world. For many the group's activities embodied the new postwar Germany, in which **language** and culture acted as more of a binding and potentially promising factor than politics. Members included Alfred Andersch, **Heinrich Böll**, Heinz Friedrich, **Günter Grass**, Wolfgang Hildesheimer, Wolfdietrich Schnurre, and **Martin Walser**.

GRUNER + JAHR AG. Based in **Hamburg**, Gruner + Jahr AG is one of Europe's largest magazine **publishers**, engaged in 500 **media** publishing activities in more than 20 countries. It employs 8,100 people worldwide and maintains modern printing plants in Europe and the United States (including its subsidiary Brown Printing, purchased in 1979). Turnover in 2015 was 1,538 million euros (45 percent outside of Germany). Well-known magazine titles include *stern*, *Brigitte*, *Focus* (in Germany), and *National Geographic* (also published in other languages). The economics newspaper *Financial Times Deutschland,* a co-venture with the Pearson Group that appeared in 2000 and was fully acquired by G + J in 2008, was the first new national daily to be launched in Germany for several decades, but was never profitable and ceased publication in 2012. Following the decision in 2014 by the founding **Jahr family** to sell off its 25 percent shareholding, G + J became a wholly owned subsidiary of **Bertelsmann SE**.

Stern was originally founded as a youth magazine in 1948 by the journalist Henri Nannen (1913–1996) and rapidly became Germany's most popular weekly magazine, containing articles on issues of general interest, society, and politics, and also specializing in photography. In 1951, Nannen sold most of his *stern* holdings to **Gerd Bucerius** (1906–1995), publisher of the respected weekly *Die Zeit*, although he remained as chief editor. Nannen retired in 1983 after the magazine published diaries by Adolf Hitler that proved to be forged. In 1965, Bucerius joined forces with **John Jahr** (1900–1991), who published *Constanze, Brigitte, Schöner Wohnen*, and *Capital*, and with the printer Richard Gruner to establish Gruner + Jahr GmbH & Co. In 1969, Gruner sold all his shares, enabling **Reinhard Mohn** of **Bertelsmann** to acquire a 25 percent holding, which increased to 75 percent by 1976. In 1971, the firm bought a 24.75 percent stake in the Spiegel Verlag, which publishes the weekly news magazine *Der Spiegel*. John Jahr and Gerd Bucerius withdrew from operational management, and the company changed its name to Gruner + Jahr AG & Co the following year (1972). By this time the firm was producing, alongside *stern* (which reached a record circulation of over two million in 1980), titles for the youth market (*Jasmin, Eltern, Twen*); Europe's most popular magazine for **women**, *Brigitte*; and the monthly food and drink magazine *Essen & Trinken*. After establishing itself firmly in Germany, G + J became the first German publisher to enter the international magazine market, in the late 1970s. Expansion followed in Spain (1978) and Western Europe, the United States (1979), Poland (1993) and eastern Europe, Russia (1998), China (2006), and India (2011), although in 2014 it announced, alongside increased investment in digital content, a program of cuts and job losses following a downturn in turnover and its print market operations. The three-member executive board is chaired by Julia Jäkel (appointed 2013), whose areas of responsibility include the Henri Nannen school of journalism, which was founded in 1979 and trains journalists for G + J, *Der Spiegel*, and *Die Zeit*.

See also PRESS.

GUILLAUME, GÜNTER (1927–1995). East German spy. Born in 1927 in **Berlin**, Günter Guillaume worked as an editor for an East German publishing house (Volk und Welt) in East Berlin before moving to the Federal Republic of Germany (FRG) in 1956. He joined the **Social Democratic Party of Germany (SPD)** a year later and rose to become business manager for the party group in the Frankfurt/Main city council. After cultivating contacts with the party leadership, he became a researcher in the **Office of the Feder-**

al Chancellor in 1972 and a close confidant of **Willy Brandt**. Although the **Federal Office for the Protection of the Constitution** (Bundesamt für Verfassungsschutz, BfV) was already suspicious of his background, it was not until 1974 that it emerged that Guillaume had been trained in the **German Democratic Republic (GDR)** to infiltrate and spy on West Germany's political leadership. He was arrested on 24 April 1974 and admitted to being an agent and officer of the National People's Army of the GDR. The affair led to Brandt's resignation and the setting up of a parliamentary committee of investigation. Sentenced to 15 years' imprisonment for treason (1975), Guillaume was amnestied and returned to the GDR in exchange for Western agents (1981).

GUTTENBERG, KARL-THEODOR ZU (1971–). Christian Social Union (CSU) politician. Born in Munich, Karl-Theodor zu Guttenberg studied law and politics in Bayreuth and Munich (1992–1999), earning a doctorate in 2007. A member of the CSU, he entered the **Bundestag** in 2002, specializing in defense, **foreign policy**, and Anglo-German and European affairs before joining the party executive committee and becoming general secretary (2008–2009). Between February and October 2009, at the height of the global financial crisis, Guttenberg succeeded **Michael Glos** (CSU) as federal minister for economics and technology in **Angela Merkel**'s first cabinet, where he took a leading role in negotiations with General Motors in efforts to save the Opel **automobile** company from closure. In Merkel's second cabinet (from October 2010), he was appointed the youngest ever defense minister, but resigned all political posts the following year following claims that his doctorate was plagiarized (the degree was later withdrawn). A popular minister, Guttenberg presented in 2010 various models for restructuring the armed forces, including the end of national conscription (which was later adopted). His taboo-breaking acknowledgment in April 2010, following the deaths of German soldiers in Afghanistan, that German troops were in reality engaged in a war that had officially been referred to only as "armed conflict," provoked a public debate.

GYSI, GREGOR (1948–). Party of Democratic Socialism (PDS) politician. Gregor Gysi was born in **Berlin** to a long-established Jewish family. His father served as cultural minister, ambassador, and state secretary for church affairs in the former **German Democratic Republic (GDR)**. After graduating from school with a vocational qualification in animal husbandry (1996), Gysi studied law at Humboldt University in East Berlin (1966–1970), trained in Berlin, and was admitted as a lawyer in 1971. In 1976, he earned a doctorate on the subject of the implementation of law in a socialist society and chaired two leading lawyers' organizations in the GDR (1988–1989). He joined the national youth movement Freie Deutsche Jugend (Free German Youth, FDJ, 1962) and the state-approved trade union organization Freie Deutsche Gewerkschaftsbund (Free German Trade Union Association, FDGB, 1963) and was admitted to the ruling **Socialist Unity Party of Germany (SED)** in 1967.

Although a member of the GDR's privileged elite, Gysi, in his role as a lawyer, defended several prominent East German dissidents, including **Rudolf Bahro**, Robert Havemann, **Ulrike Poppe**, and **Bärbel Bohley**. Believing in a just, non-Stalinist socialist society, he worked to improve justice and **human rights** in the GDR. During the dying days of the regime in the autumn of 1989, he helped draft a bill to counter the inept law proposed by the government on easing foreign travel restrictions for East German citizens and was instrumental in gaining government permission for the mass demonstration on 4 November 1989, at which he was one of the speakers. He was later appointed a member of the working group that prepared the emergency congress of the SED and chaired a subcommittee investigating corruption and misuse of power in the party.

From 1989 until 1993, Gysi chaired the successor party to the SED, the SED/PDS, later renamed the PDS, which he represented at the **Round Table** discussions between opposition groups and the government (December 1989–March 1990). Between March and October 1990, he represented the PDS in the **People's Chamber** and chaired its parliamentary group. In 1990, he opposed the swift takeover of the GDR by the Federal Republic of Germany (FRG) and argued for reunification under article 146 of the **Basic Law (BL)**, which envisaged reunification after agreement on a new constitution. In December 1990, Gysi entered the new all-German **Bundestag**, representing the PDS and leading the PDS/Left List group (1990–1998). Although the PDS gained 17 seats in the assembly and worked hard during the rest of the decade to establish a significant presence in the western and eastern **federal states**, it was marginalized by the establishment.

In 1991, Gysi was accused of spying for the East German secret police, the **Stasi**. In 1997, the authority responsible for administering the Stasi's files **(Federal Commissioner for the Records of the State Security Service of the Former German Democratic Republic, BStU)** supported the accusations and stated that Gysi had indeed acted as an informer between 1978 and 1989. The following year, the charges were also upheld by the all-party Immunity Committee of the Bundestag, although the PDS and **Free Democratic Party (FDP)** dissented. Gysi himself vigorously denied the allegations. In 1993, along with the author **Stefan Heym**, he cofounded the Komitee für Gerechtigkeit (Committee for Justice), which campaigned for justice for citizens of the former GDR in the new, united Germany. With **Lothar Bisky** (party leader 1993–2000), he embarked (in December 1994) on a weeklong hunger strike as a protest against proposals to extract from the PDS

67 million DM in taxes owed by the former SED. In 1996, the Bundestag removed Gysi's parliamentary immunity so that he could be tried for offenses relating to the occupation of the Berlin offices of a government commission charged with investigating the SED's concealment of party funds and property. Found guilty, he was fined 8,000 DM (1998). In 1997, he quit the executive of the PDS, but in the national election the following year, he entered the Bundestag as chair of the PDS parliamentary group, only to resign the position in 2000.

Thereafter, Gysi focused on local politics in his home city of Berlin. In the 2001 city elections, he conducted a strong campaign, appealing to Berliners' pride in their city (which had been hit by corruption scandals and faced bankruptcy) and promoting the PDS as a party of peace following the terrorist attacks of 11 September and the U.S. military campaign in Afghanistan. When the PDS emerged as the second strongest party after the **Social Democratic Party of Germany** (**SPD**), and after the latter failed to reach agreement with the FDP and the **Greens**, SPD leader **Klaus Wowereit** concluded a coalition with the PDS, with Wowereit as mayor and Gysi as deputy mayor and minister (senator) for economic affairs. Gysi resigned his office and mandate after only a few months (August 2002) to resume his career as a lawyer, amid claims that he lacked technical expertise and the confidence of business interests; he also faced allegations over the misuse of fringe benefits.

Despite serious illness, Gysi returned to politics to stand as the PDS's lead candidate in the national election of 18 September 2005. A gifted speaker and the only figure in the party to enjoy a national profile, he promoted the merger with the **Election Alternative Labor and Social Justice (WASG)** to form the new **Left Party** and was elected to the Bundestag (reelected 2007, 2009, 2013). In 2015, he was succeeded as leader of the parliamentary group by Sahra Wagenknecht. His books, *Was nun? Über Deutschlands Zustand und meinen eigenen* and *Wie weiter? Nachdenken über Deutschland*, appeared in 2003 and 2013.

H

HABERMAS, JÜRGEN (1929–). Düsseldorf-born Jürgen Habermas is a renowned intellectual and contemporary philosopher and sociologist. He studied between 1949 and 1954 in Göttingen, Zurich, and Bonn. From 1956 onward, he worked with the critical theorists Max Horkheimer and Theodor Adorno, but finished his dissertation in Marburg under Wolfgang Abendroth. Although he was critical of the Frankfurt School—an interwar foundation based in the Institute for Social Research at the Goethe University Frankfurt—he remains strongly associated with it. In outlook, members of the school have always been critical of both capitalism and of Soviet-style socialism, emphasizing instead the importance of social development. Habermas's habilitation on the *Strukturwandel der Öffentlichkeit* ("The Structural Transformation of the Public Sphere," 1962; the book appeared in English in 1989), which traces how the once clear distinction between the state (as representative of the public realm) and society (in the widest sense of the private) disappeared from the end of the 19th century onward, remains among his most influential contributions. Habermas taught in Marburg and Heidelberg and returned to Frankfurt in 1964, eventually retiring in 1993. Between 1971 and 1985, he was also director of the Max Planck Institute for the Study of the Scientific-Technical World in Starnberg. In 1981, he published another highly influential study, *The Theory of Communicative Action*. Habermas became involved in Germany's **historians' quarrel** in 1986 when he positioned himself against Ernst Nolte and others. In turn, he was attacked by Joachim Fest and Hagen Schulze, while Hans Mommsen and Hans-Ulrich Wehler supported his views. In 1983, Habermas became a foreign honorary member of the American Academy of Arts and Sciences, and he is also a permanent visiting professor at Northwestern University and Evanston and Theodor Heuss professor at The New School, New York.

HAGER, KURT (1912–1998). German Democratic Republic (GDR) politician. Kurt Hager was born in Bietigheim (**Baden-Württemberg**) to a working-class family. A member of the youth wing of the Communist Party of Germany (KPD) from 1929 and of the parent party from 1930, he worked as a journalist after leaving school in 1931. Arrested by the National Socialists in 1933, he spent several months in a concentration camp (Heuberg). After his release, he worked underground for the KPD and was arrested briefly in Switzerland (1936) before moving to Paris. He took part in the Spanish Civil War (1937–1939), where he ran radio stations; at the outbreak of World War II, he emigrated to France and then to Great Britain. In Britain he was briefly interned (1940–1941), but later worked as a forester, welder, and journalist, writing under the pseudonym Felix Albin. Returning to (eastern) Germany in 1946, Hager rapidly developed a career in the ruling **Socialist Unity Party of Germany** (**SED**) as its leading specialist on propaganda and ideology. In 1949, he was appointed professor in philosophy at Humboldt University in East Berlin. Other positions included culture and science secretary to the Central Committee of the SED (from 1955), member of the Politburo (candidate from 1958, full member from 1963), member of the Staatsrat (Council of State, from 1976), and deputy in the **People's Chamber** (from 1958).

After 1985, Hager opposed the reform policies of Soviet leader Mikhail Gorbachev, famously declaring in an interview with the West German *stern* magazine that he saw no need for the GDR to "replace its apartment wallpaper" simply because a neighbor was doing so (1987). During the 1989 revolution, he was removed from all official positions and in January 1990 was expelled from the SED/**Party of Democratic Socialism** (**PDS**). With other members of the former Politburo of the SED, he faced a court trial in 1995, although proceedings against him were suspended on health grounds (May 1996). Unrepentant to the end, Hager rejected any notion of personal guilt for the GDR regime and complained that the GDR leadership was being subjected to "victors' justice."

HAMBURG. Situated on the lower reaches of the Elbe River, the city-state of Hamburg covers an area of 755 square kilometers and has an increasing population of over 1.7 million, which is expected to approach two million by 2030; 15.6 percent of residents are **foreigners** (2015), the highest proportion of the **federal states** (national average: 11.2 percent). During the Middle Ages, Hamburg developed as a port and center of brewing. The granting of the status of a free city (by Emperor Friedrich Barbarossa in 1189) and membership in the Hanseatic League (from 1321) are still commemorated in the city's official title, the Freie und Hansestadt Hamburg (Free and Hanseatic City of Hamburg). Following the Black Death (1350), Hamburg's citizens won major freedoms, and during the 15th century, it became the most powerful city of the league, trading with England, France, and Spain and subsequently North America and the Far East. By the early 17th century, Hamburg had become Germany's largest city. It took in Protestant refugees during the Reformation, welcomed wealthy **Jews**, and maintained its independence during the Thirty Years' War (1618–1648), through defenses and financial payments. By the end of the 18th century Hamburg, alongside London and Amsterdam, was one of Europe's richest trading centers. In 1937, the city's boundaries were extended to encompass surrounding industrial areas, transforming its economy, which now contributes 4 percent of national GDP (2015). Devastated by heavy bombing in 1943, Hamburg recovered after World War II to become Germany's largest port and, after **Berlin**, its second largest city. Sea defenses were reinforced following severe flooding in 1962.

In this maritime city, 10,000 people and 80 companies are still directly engaged in shipbuilding and offshore supply activities, although key industries now include **media**, advertising, and **publishing** (many national newspapers and magazines are produced in Hamburg). Despite its wealth, Hamburg loses sizable **taxation** revenue by virtue of its large commuter population. The reason for this is that Germans pay taxes to the federal state of their residence, not their place of work; around 32 percent of the workforce travels in from the surrounding regions, and the draw of the city extends into neighboring **Lower Saxony** and **Schleswig-Holstein** and even farther afield, to **Mecklenburg-West Pomerania**. Many young, professional families have also preferred to move out of the city. Unemployment stands at 7.4 percent (2015). Hamburg boasts a world-famous opera house and two symphony orchestras and has a lively **theater** and music scene. A prestigious waterfront concert hall, the Elbphilharmonie, with a seating capacity of 2,100, is projected to open in 2017. The glass structure is built on the massive red brick construction of a former warehouse and rises up to a height of 110 meters. The city also has a high number of foreign consulates.

Since 1996, the 121-member Hamburg parliament (Bürgerschaft) has elected the first mayor (erster Bürgermeister), who is also the head or president of the senate (cabinet), for a four-year legislative period. The president appoints a deputy (the second mayor) and a further 10 or so senators (ministers), who must be approved by parliament. Around 14 state councilors (Staatsräte)—political civil servants—support the senators in their work. The constitution explicitly states that membership in the assembly is compatible with an external job or profession (indeed, many meetings used to be held outside working hours). It also accords a special role to the opposition as a public forum for criticism of the administration, and the city is a leader in holding referenda on civic issues. From 1957 until 2001, the **Social Democratic Party of Germany** (**SPD**), ruling either alone or in partnership with the **Free Democratic Party** (**FDP**), dominated government. During the 1990s, the city's politics became less stable as a divided SPD faced rising social problems, including a financial deficit and public perceptions of a law-and-order problem. In 1993, the SPD formed a coalition with the **Instead Party (Statt Partei)** and in 1997 with the **Green Party**. Over 40 years of SPD rule finally ended with elections in September 2001, when the **Chris-**

tian-Democratic Union (CDU), led by Ole von Beust, formed a coalition cabinet with the FDP and the controversial Law and Order Offensive Party under Ronald Schill. The coalition broke up in 2003, and Beust was returned with an overall majority in the election of February 2004. Reelected in 2008, Beust continued as mayor, this time in coalition with the Greens (Grüne Alternative Liste, GAL), but resigned in August 2010 to be replaced by Christoph Ahlhaus (CDU). The coalition was the first regional CDU/Green partnership in Germany. Under Beust, a large number of ambitious civic projects were planned, although not all came to fruition. Disagreements between GAL and the CDU over undertakings such as deepening of the River Elbe and the rebuilding of a coal-fired power station plagued the short-lived coalition, until the Greens withdrew in November 2010. The following February, new elections returned the SPD with a small majority, and Olaf Scholz became first mayor. After a collapse of support for the CDU in the 2015 elections, Scholz formed a ruling coalition with the Greens/GAL; the AfD entered the assembly with 8 seats and the Left Party increased its share of the vote to gain 11 seats. The government won a plan to bid (against Berlin) to host the 2024 Olympic Games (although the bid was dropped after the population voted against it) and pledged to improve housing, education, transportation, and climate protection. Past SPD mayors include Hans-Ulrich Klose (1974–1981), Klaus von Dohnanyi (1981–1988), Heinrich Voscherau (1988–1997), and Ortwin Runde (1997–2001).

HARTZ COMMISSION. This government commission (official title: Moderne Dienstleistungen am Arbeitsmarkt/Modern Services in the Labor Market) was charged with drawing up recommendations for reforming Germany's labor market and overhauling the functions of the national employment bureau in Nuremberg. Chaired by Peter Hartz, then personnel director of Volkswagen AG, its members included representatives of business, management, trade unions, and local politicians. Hartz, who had introduced innovative models for combating unemployment at Volkswagen, was directly recruited by Chancellor Gerhard Schröder. The recommendations were presented in August 2002, and in the national election campaign of the same year, Schröder promised to implement them in full. The measures were incorporated in the chancellor's Agenda 2010 program and were phased in as four packages of legislation (Hartz I to IV) between January 2003 and 2005.

While Hartz I (in force from January 2003) promoted new forms of part-time working and vocational training, Hartz II (also 2003) aimed to broaden the lower paid sector by regulating "mini-jobs," which had hitherto been part of the black market. In addition, Hartz II enabled jobless people who registered as self-employed (the "Ich AG") to receive graded subsidies in return for being hired out by personal service agencies (PSAs), hopefully leading to permanent employment (within two and a half years of its introduction, the number of businesses founded had risen from 125,000 to 250,000, and in 2006 the scheme was discontinued in its original form). Under Hartz III (January 2004), the Bundesanstalt für Arbeit (Federal Labour Office) was restructured and renamed the Bundesagentur für Arbeit (Federal Employment Agency, BA). Most controversially, Hartz IV (January 2005) reorganized unemployment benefits. The existing allowance, renamed Arbeitslosengeld I (unemployment benefit I), could now be paid for a maximum of one year instead of two, after which it was merged with the social welfare benefit (Sozialhilfe) to form a new allowance. Called Arbeitslosengeld II (unemployment benefit II), this would progressively fall from 60 percent of former salary to a flat, basic welfare rate for the long-term unemployed, although it was later pegged to **pension** levels. The unemployed were obligated to accept job offers, received reduced benefits if a partner was employed, and saw benefits tied to space restrictions on living accommodations. Between 2005 and 2016, the standard rate rose from 345 euros a month (in the west) to 404 euros throughout Germany.

Hartz IV, which represented a fundamental change in managing the unemployed, was designed to simplify the payment system, reduce overall unemployment support, and increase pressure on recipients to reenter the job market. Its introduction was accompanied by protests from the political left, trade unions, and social welfare organizations, although these benefited from the "one euro jobs"—low-paid, state-subsidized, short-term jobs, mainly in the care or civic sectors, that were designed to reintegrate Hart IV recipients into the employment market. In 2010, the **Federal Constitutional Court (FCC)** obliged the government to clarify its calculations of benefit rates, in particular as they affected children.

See also GERSTER, FLORIAN (1949–); SOCIAL SECURITY SYSTEM.

HASELOFF, REINER (1954–). Christian Democratic Union (CDU) politician. Reiner Haseloff was born in Bülzig (**Saxony-Anhalt**) in the former **German Democratic Republic of Germany (GDR)** and studied physics at the Technical University of Dresden and Humboldt University in **Berlin** (1973–1978), before working at an institute for **environmental** protection in Wittenberg (1978–1990). He was awarded a doctorate by Humboldt University in 1991 and from 1992 to 2002 was director of the Wittenberg employment office. A member of the CDU since 1976, Haseloff joined the regional executive committee in 1990 and represented the party at the local level (1990–1992) before becoming regional vice chairman (2004–2012) and a member of the national executive (2008). He served as **state secretary** (Staatssekretär) in the Saxony-Anhalt ministry for economics and labor (2002–2006), then as minister (2006–2011). In 2011, he was elected **minister president**, heading a **grand coalition** between the CDU and the **Social**

Democratic Party of Germany (SPD). Haseloff continued as premier in 2016 after the **Greens** joined the coalition following electoral losses by both main parties and major gains by the **Alternative for Germany (AfD)**.

HASSELFELDT, GERDA (1950–). Christian Social Union (CSU) politician. Gerda Hasselfeldt was born in Straubing (**Bavaria**). Her father was town mayor and a member of the **Bundestag**. She studied economics in Munich and Regensburg and from 1975 until 1987 worked for the Federal Labor Office (Bundesanstalt für Arbeit), where she rose to become head of the career advisory department of the Deggendorf branch. A member of the CSU from 1969, she entered the Bundestag in 1987 and served in the cabinet of Chancellor **Helmut Kohl** as federal minister for planning, building, and urban development (1989–1991) and as minister for **health** (1991–1992). She was also regional chairwoman of the CSU **women**'s union (Frauen-Union, 1991–1995) and spokeswoman on financial affairs for the national **Christian Democratic Union (CDU)**/CSU parliamentary group in the Bundestag (1995–2002). From October 2002 until November 2005, she served as the group's deputy leader, responsible for consumer protection, food, and **agriculture**; local government policy; and **tourism**. Other posts she held include vice president of the Bundestag (2005–2011), member of the CSU executive (from 2009), and leader of the CSU Bundestag parliamentary group (from 2011).

HEALTH SYSTEM. Around 87 percent (70.8 million) of German citizens are either contributory or noncontributory members of a statutory health insurance fund (Gesetzliche Krankenversicherungskasse, GKV). In contrast to fully private insurance funds (Private Krankenversicherungskassen, PKVs), the GKVs are self-governing organizations that finance and administer health care according to the services and entitlements set out in the social welfare codex (Sozialgesetzbuch). The historical diversity of the statutory funds has been greatly reduced; while more than 1,800 were listed in 1970, the number had fallen to 118 by 2016, more recently through a wave of mergers as a result of the 1993 health-care system reform. The main funds are currently the Ersatzkassen (EKs, six funds whose origins lie in self-help organizations, accounting for 37.7 percent of the insured population), the Allgemeine Ortskrankenkasse (AOK, an umbrella body of 13 regional funds, 35 percent), and 118 work-based funds (Betriebskrankenkassen, BKKs, 16 percent); a small number of minor funds cater to **agricultural** workers, miners, seafarers, and guilds (Innungskassen or Knappschaften). There are 45 private funds, the largest of which is the Debeka group. Health insurance, alongside that for **pensions** and unemployment, is obligatory for employees, who contribute a graduated portion of their income (above around 400 euros per month up to a certain limit, the Beitragsbemessungsgrenze). The contribution (reduced from 15.5 to 14.6 percent from January 2015, although most funds maintained the higher rate for better services) is shared more or less equally between employee and employer, and the limit is adjusted annually in line with average national earnings. Since the wage continuation law (Lohnfortzahlungsgesetz) of 1969, both state and nonstate employees continue to receive wages from their employers in the event of illness, currently for up to six weeks, after which their health insurance fund pays sickness benefits (Krankengeld).

During the 1970s, Germany's economic performance financed improvements to both treatments and benefits, and health insurance was extended to groups such as students, independent farmers, the disabled, and artists. In response to concerns over spiraling overheads, the first cost-cutting law (Krankenversicherungskostendämpfungsgesetz, 1977) introduced modest savings, including supplementary prescription charges. In 1989, a series of complex, far-reaching, and often controversial health reform laws was initiated (Gesundheitsreformgesetze), designed to reduce costs, improve efficiency, and make the system more flexible. Many of the reforms were determined by the recommendations of the **Rürup Commission** and the goals set by **Agenda 2010** in 2003. Measures taken included requiring patients to make direct contributions (e.g., for dental work, spectacles, medicines, dressings, and transportation); implementing a national risk equalization scheme across funds to minimize profit-oriented risk selection (1994); introducing compulsory additional private insurance for nursing care (1995); increasing competition among the insurance funds by enabling members to switch providers (from 1997); reducing sickness benefit (1997); pegging increases in doctors' fees to national incomes (2000); cutting funeral grants (2004); setting prices for prescribed drugs and negotiating rebates from **pharmaceutical** companies (2004, 2011); and requiring private funds to offer a base tariff, with services in line with the statutory funds (2009). A major change was the creation in 2009 of a single national health fund (Gesundsheitsfonds) and the introduction of a uniform contribution rate of 15.5 percent (hitherto negotiated separately by representatives of employers and employees with the insurance funds); any additional services would be financed by flat-rate contributions from members (referred to as the "health premium"). In a final stage of the reforms, beginning in 2011 the health fund would collect (from members) and pool (to insurance funds) all contributions in the statutory health system.

Doctors (and dentists) are organized into 17 regional associations (kassenärztliche Vereinigungen, associations of statutory health insurance physicians, ASHIPs), which have a monopoly on negotiating regional contracts with the statutory funds on behalf of their members. In return, the associations guarantee a national network of medical coverage for patients. The national umbrella body for the associations (NASHIP) agrees on the doctors' fee schedule with the insurance funds and is involved in determining the benefits catalog. A national committee (Gemeinsamer Bundesausschuss, or federal joint committee) is the highest decision-making body responsible for the joint self-government of physicians, dentists, hospitals, and health insurance funds. Recent calls for ending the contract system (e.g., through expanding the model of direct contacts between service supplier and insurance fund) on the grounds that it is uncompetitive are countered by the ASHIPs with concerns over quality control. In 2004, the Berlin-based Barmer EK (Barmer GEK) became the first statutory fund to introduce the cost-effective house-doctor model, in which the general practitioner acts as the first port of call for medical, including specialist, services (from 2016, however, patients have been able to book urgent appointments directly with specialists via regional appointments service centers). Doctors, especially in urban areas, derive up to one-third of their income from private patients, while those in rural areas, especially in the east, are more likely to be sustained by patients on statutory health insurance. At the same time, Germany suffers from a shortage of general practitioners, especially outside urban areas. The German Medical Association (Bundesärztekammer) is the joint association of the state chambers of physicians (Landesärztekammer), representing the interests of more than 485,000 physicians (2015) in matters relating to professional policy, and plays an active role in opinion-forming processes with regard to health and social policy and in legislative procedures.

See also SOCIAL SECURITY SYSTEM.

HEIL, HUBERTUS (1972–). Social Democratic Party of Germany (SPD) politician. Born in Hildesheim (**Lower Saxony**), Hubertus Heil performed community/national service before studying politics and sociology at the universities of Potsdam and Hagen (from 1995). At school he was active in the **Young Socialists (JUSOS)** wing of the SPD, which he joined in 1988. After chairing the Braunschweig district branch of the youth wing (1991–1995) and working for the party in the **Brandenburg** regional assembly (**Landtag**, 1994–1998), he entered the **Bundestag** in 1999, where he specialized in the economy, labor, **industry**, and **telecommunications**. He served as general secretary of the SPD (2005–2009) and deputy leader of the party parliamentary group (from 2009) and joined the national executive in 2011.

HEIMAT. The term "Heimat," which translates roughly as "homeland," remains for many Germans a problematic expression because of its abuse by the National Socialist regime (1933–1945). In the late 1970s, the term enjoyed a marked revival, which was best epitomized by Edgar Reitz's film trilogy *Heimat* and the novel *Herbstmilch* by Anna Wimschneider. It also appeared in other **literature** (e.g., in the works of **Heinrich Böll, Günter Grass**, and Erwin Strittmatter) as writers attempted to deal with the links between past and present in their subjects' immediate surroundings. In tear-jerking films of the 1950s, Heimat often stood for "typical German regions," such as the Black Forest and associated traditional lifestyles. However, its association with dialect songs (by groups such as the Cologne-based BAP or the Munich-based Münchner Freiheit) and major exhibitions (e.g., in 1977 on the 12th-century Staufer dynasty and in 1981 on Prussia) demonstrated that it had a much wider cultural significance and contributed to a reassessment of wider German history. Approaches to the concept of Heimat have remained critical, but are now more relaxed. On the one hand, there are political and social concerns in light of ultraconservative movements such as **Pegida**, while on the other hand, recent football world cups such as the event hosted in Germany in 2006 and the national team's successful participation in Brazil 2014 show that a new generation of Germans is far more ready to see a unified and multicultural Germany as a country with a functioning democracy. Abroad, evaluations of German history over the longer term have further contributed to such development: a notable example is an exhibition on German culture and history (Germany—Memories of a Nation) in the British Museum in London in 2014/2015, curated by Neil McGregor.

HEINEMANN, GUSTAV (1899–1976). Social Democratic Party of Germany (SPD) politician and **president of the Federal Republic**, 1969–1974. Gustav Heinemann was born in Schwelm (**North Rhine-Westfalia**), the son of a health insurance fund director. He served as a soldier in World War I; studied law, economics, and history at the universities of Münster, Marburg, Munich, Göttingen, and **Berlin**; and was an active student member of the Deutsche Demokratische Partei (German Democratic Party, DDP) during the Weimar Republic. In 1929, he earned a doctorate in law at Münster. After qualifying as a lawyer (1926), he practiced in Essen and worked for the steel company Rheinische Stahlwerke (1928–1936), where he became a director of mining operations (1936–1949). He also taught mining and commercial law at the University of Cologne (1933–1939). Shortly after the National Socialists came to power (1933), he joined the underground Protestant "Bekennende Kirche" ("confessing church") and chaired the Essen branch of the Young Men's Christian Association (1936–1950).

Heinemann cofounded the **Christian Democratic Union (CDU)** in Essen in 1945, where he was mayor from 1945 to 1949. A committed Christian and pacifist, he was a member of the council of the Evangelical Church in Germany (EKD, 1945–1967) and served on the international affairs commission of the World Council of Churches (1948–1961). He represented the CDU in the regional assembly of North Rhine-Westfalia (1947–1950), where he was also justice minister (1947–1948). Joining **Konrad Adenauer**'s first cabinet as interior minister in 1949, Heinemann resigned one year later over German rearmament, which he saw as an obstacle to reunification. He later regarded the erection of the **Berlin Wall** (1961) as a direct consequence of Adenauer's **foreign policy**. After resigning from the CDU (1952), he founded the Gesamtdeutsche Volkspartei (All-German People's Party, GVP), which held German neutrality to be a prerequisite for reunification. When the party was dissolved following poor election results (1957), Heinemann joined the SPD, which he represented in the **Bundestag** until he was appointed justice minister in the **grand coalition** (1966–1969), where he piloted a major reform of criminal law and removed the statute of limitations for murder and National Socialist war crimes. As a lawyer, he represented the news magazine *Der Spiegel* in the so-called *Spiegel* affair (1962). In 1969, Heinemann was elected president of the Federal Republic, actively supporting **Willy Brandt's Ostpolitik** and developing a reputation for objectivity, moderation, and probity that earned him international respect. As a national figurehead, he visited many countries before retiring in 1974 and helped launch the "history workshop" movement, which inspired young people to uncover and investigate historical evidence beyond what was normally found in school textbooks. Heinemann died in Essen.

HENDRICKS, BARBARA (1952–). Social Democratic Party of Germany (SPD) politician. Born in Kleve (1952), Barbara Hendricks studied history and social sciences at the University of Bonn (1970–1976), qualified as a schoolteacher in 1976, and earned a doctorate in 1980. From 1976 until 1978, she performed voluntary work for the Deutsches Studentenwerk (German National Association for Student Affairs, DSW). A member of the SPD from 1972, she was a researcher for the press office of the main party parliamentary group (1978–1981), speaker for the finance minister of North Rhine-Westfalia (1981–1990), and leader of the Kleve local SPD district (1989–2014), and served on the Parteirat (party council, 1990–2001). From 1991 until 1994, she worked as a senior civil servant (Ministerialrätin) for the regional ministry of the **environment**, with responsibility for cross-border planning. Elected to the **Bundestag** in 1994, Hendricks occupied various posts (parliamentary **state secretary** to the federal finance minister [1998–2007], member of the SPD executive council [2001–2013], and party treasurer [2007–2013]), before being appointed federal minister for the environment, nature conservation, and nuclear safety in Chancellor **Angela Merkel's** third coalition cabinet in December 2013. In 2014, she joined the executive committee of the social democratically oriented Friedrich-Ebert Stiftung (Friedrich Ebert Foundation). She is an active Roman Catholic, serving in various church organizations.

HERRHAUSEN, ALFRED (1930–1989). Banker. Alfred Herrhausen was born in Essen (**North Rhine-Westfalia**). He studied business administration at the University of Cologne, earning a diploma (1952) and a doctorate (1955). After working at the management headquarters of the Essen-based gas utility company Ruhrgas AG (from 1952), he moved to the electricity supplier, Vereinigte Elektrizitätswerke Westfalen (VEW), in Dortmund (1955). Closely involved in the partial privatization of VEW in 1966, he joined the company's executive board a year later, with responsibility for finance. In 1970–1971, he became a deputy member, then full member of the board of the **Deutsche Bank**, where his responsibilities included the Essen region and operations in North and South America, Australasia, and South Africa. In 1974, he joined a government commission charged with drawing up proposals for restructuring the German credit industry; in 1983, he was appointed one of three independent consultants for reorganizing the steel sector. In 1985, he was elected joint spokesman for the board of Deutsche Bank (sole spokesman from 1988). A personal friend of former chancellor **Helmut Kohl** and regarded as one of the most powerful men in Germany, Herrhausen was murdered by the left-wing terrorist **Red Army Faction** (**RAF**) in a carefully planned car-bomb attack at his home in Bad Homburg (30 November 1989).

See also BANKS.

HERRMANN, JOACHIM (1928–1992). German Democratic Republic (**GDR**) politician. Joachim Herrmann was born in **Berlin** to a working-class family. After 1945, he worked as a messenger boy before becoming a trainee journalist and finally editor for the *Berliner Zeitung* (until 1949). A member of the ruling **Socialist Unity Party of Germany** (**SED**) and the youth movement (Freie Deutsche Jugend/Free German youth, FDJ) of the GDR from 1946, he attended the Soviet Communist Party college for youth (Komsomol) in Moscow (1953–1954). He became a candidate member of the SED Central Committee in 1967 (full member in 1971) and of the party's Politburo in 1973 (full member in 1978). Responsible for agitation, propaganda, and the **press**, Herrmann edited or controlled various socialist journals and newspapers in the GDR, including the youth journal *Junge Welt* (deputy editor 1949–1952, chief editor 1954–1960), the *Berliner Zeitung* (chief editor 1962–1965), and the SED party organ *Neues Deutschland* (succeeding Rudolf Singer as chief editor, 1971–1978). He was also a senior functionary (Staatssekretär/state secretary), responsible for pan-German affairs (from 1965), and a deputy in the **People's Chamber** (from 1976). Along with other figures in the GDR leadership, Herrmann was removed from the Politburo and Central Committee on 18 October 1989 and expelled from the SED/ **Party of Democratic Socialism** (**PDS**) the following January.

HERZOG, ROMAN (1934–). Christian Democratic Union (CDU) politician and **president of the Federal Republic**, 1994–1999. Roman Herzog was born in Landshut (**Bavaria**), the son of an archivist. After studying law at the University of Munich (1953–1957), he passed his state law examinations (1957, 1961) and earned a doctorate with a dissertation on the **Basic Law (BL)** and the European Convention on **Human Rights** (1958). After working as an assistant at the University of Munich (1958–1964), he was appointed lecturer (1964–1965), then professor for national law and politics at the Free University of **Berlin** (1965–1969), and coedited a commentary on the BL (from 1964). From 1969 until 1972, he was professor, and from 1971 rector, at the Hochschule für Verwaltungswissenschaften (University of Administrative Sciences) in Speyer.

An active Christian and a member of the CDU from 1970, Herzog coedited a Protestant lexicon of political and state terminology (from 1966) and the weekly newspaper *Christ und Welt—Rheinischer Merkur* (1981–1994). He occupied various positions in the Evangelical Church in Germany (EKD), chaired the national Evangelischer Arbeitskreis (Evangelical Work Group) of the CDU/**Christian Social Union (CSU**, 1978–1983), and was a member of the CDU national executive (1979–1983). After serving as minister for culture and **sport** in **Baden-Württemberg** (1978–1980), he attracted attention as regional interior minister (1980–1983) when he oversaw the introduction of a levy on nonapproved demonstrations (to pay for the costs of policing) and proposed (in 1982) that police should be equipped with rubber-bullet guns.

In 1983, Herzog was appointed vice-president of the **Federal Constitutional Court (FCC)**, and later president (1987–1994). Under his stewardship, the court reached several landmark decisions. It revoked the ban on demonstrations against the nuclear power station in Brokdorf in northern Germany, ruling that violent or illegal actions by a minority could be used to remove the constitutional right of freedom of assembly. In a ruling that went against the views of some members of the **Free Democratic Party (FDP)** and **Social Democratic Party of Germany (SPD)**, the court also confirmed in 1990 that, since the German Reich had not ceased to exist as a legal entity in 1945, its frontiers (in particular the border with Poland) could be fixed only after the conclusion of a peace treaty that formally reunited Germany. He urged a revision of Germany's outdated citizenship laws to promote integration of **asylum** seekers and **immigrants** and argued for changes to the BL, including giving more powers to the **federal states**, overhauling the financial provisions of the constitution, and consulting the people directly via national referenda. He also criticized the growing tendency of politicians to use the FCC to settle political issues that should be resolved in Bonn/Berlin.

In 1994, Herzog succeeded **Richard von Weizsäcker** as seventh president of the Federal Republic, a post he held until 1999. Visiting Poland on the 50th anniversary of the Warsaw uprising, he delivered a widely praised speech. During his period of office, Herzog supported the introduction of a single European **currency** (1995), opposed a general amnesty for perpetrators of the communist dictatorship in the **German Democratic Republic** (**GDR**, 1996), and advised Germans who had been expelled from the former Czechoslovakia after World War II to regard united Germany as their home and not to pursue claims for the restitution of property. In 1996, he proclaimed an annual day of remembrance for victims of the National Socialist dictatorship, with a different group to be commemorated each year. In 1997, Herzog became the first German head of state to visit the Russian Federation after reunification, although in an otherwise successful five-day tour, his address to the Russian parliament was canceled after the latter objected to the conviction in Germany of **Egon Krenz**, the last leader of the **Socialist Unity Party of Germany** (**SED**). As federal president, Herzog paid many state visits and received numerous national and international honors, including an honorary doctorate of the University of Oxford (1996) and the Leo Baeck Prize of the **Central Council of Jews in Germany** (1998). In 2003, he chaired a CDU commission on social policy reform that had been constituted as a counterweight to the government's own **Rürup Commission**. Herzog has published widely on politics and constitutional law, and he spoke repeatedly on the need to reform **education** in Germany, advocating market-orientated approaches that combined reward for achievement with conservative values.

HESSEN. Bounded by six other **federal states**, Hessen, with an area of 21,114 square kilometers, is situated at the geographical heart of Germany. The diverse landscape, which is dominated by the Central Uplands, includes the wooded hills of the Taunus in the west; the Odenwald and Spessart forests to the south; and to the north the Vogelsberg, a range of hills, forests, and moorland, rising to 773 meters. In the east are broad, partly forested plateaus. The main cities are Frankfurt/Main (population 691,000); the state capital, Wiesbaden (279,000); Kassel (196,000); Darmstadt (149,000); and Offenbach (123,000). Apart from Kassel, the centers of population are in the south, where they form part of the prosperous Rhine-Main region. Around 40 percent of Hessen's six million inhabitants are concentrated in 9 percent of the total geographical area. More than 40 percent are Protestant and 25 percent Roman Catholic. The proportion of **foreigners** is high (15.2 percent), compared with the national average of 11.2 percent.

Celts, Germanic tribes, and Romans first settled in the area, which became a power center for the Carolingian Empire under the Franconian ruler Charles the Great (742–814). The seeds of Frankfurt's future prosperity were sown in the 12th and 13th centuries, when German emperors were crowned in the city and it acquired trading privileges. During the 16th-century Reformation, Protestant princes formed an alliance in Hessen, although territorial unity evaporated as the region fragmented into petty dukedoms and was devastated during the Thirty Years' War (1618–1648). The region's internal and external boundaries changed frequently during the following centuries. In the 18th century, Hessen was a focus for baroque culture, when several fine castles and residences were built. Its absolutist rulers hired out troops to the British in the American Revolutionary War, and many citizens emigrated to Hungary and Russia. Three territorial principalities emerged in the early 19th century: Hessen-Kassel in the north, Hessen-Darmstadt in the south, and Hessen-Nassau around Frankfurt. Industrialization, social unrest, and opposition to absolutist governments resulted in the ill-fated revolution of 1848–1849, when the short-lived Frankfurt Parliament drew up a democratic framework for a united Germany. Hessen owes its current unity and boundaries to the U.S. authorities after World War II, who made Frankfurt their headquarters; the city housed key administrative, economic, and financial institutions of the Western zones of occupation.

The regional constitution, which predates the **Basic Law (BL)**, emphasizes social factors such as protection for workers, the right to strike (lockouts are outlawed), and **codetermination**. Soon after the war, sectors of **industry** (mining, **energy**, steel, and railways) were declared state-owned for the common good, although Allied takeovers, reprivatization, and federal law rendered the policy irrelevant. The constitution contains a provision for plebiscites, although these have been little used. A notable exception was the petition by 220,000 citizens in 1981 to hold a plebiscite on the proposed construction of a new takeoff runway at Frankfurt Airport (Startbahn 18 West). The Hessen courts later rejected the petition on the grounds that the regional government lacked the legislative powers to block the development. The 100-member (or more) regional state parliament (**Landtag**) elects by absolute majority a **minister president**, who determines government policy and appoints a cabinet of ministers that is approved by the assembly.

From 1946 until 1974, regional politics were dominated by the **Social Democratic Party of Germany (SPD)**, which commanded outright majorities in 1950–1954, 1962–1966, and 1966–1970. Led by Georg August Zinn (minister president 1950–1969), Hessen implemented programs to house and integrate over one million refugees, improve social infrastructure (especially in rural areas), reform **education** (by providing free schoolbooks, introducing the comprehensive school model, and raising numbers of students), and attract new industries (including **Volkswagen** in Braunatal and the **chemical company Hoechst** in Bad Hersfeld). The state was also an early supporter of nuclear energy, with power stations built at Hanau and Biblis, before the policy became politically controversial. By the 1960s, Hessen had been transformed into one of Germany's most prosperous regions. Between 1970 and 1982, the SPD governed in coalition with the **Free Democratic Party (FDP)**, although the social democrats' monopoly was undermined by a controversial merger of local districts, rising budgetary costs, financial scandals, and rising discontent over the **environment**. Environmental issues came to a head over atomic power, in particular proposals to extend the Biblis facility, construct a new plant in Borken, and reprocess spent nuclear fuel in the region.

The **Green Party** entered the Landtag in 1982, marking the onset of a long period of shifting coalitions and political instability. The Greens tolerated a minority SPD government until 1985 (the FDP had switched allegiance to the **Christian Democratic Union [CDU]**, which had steadily increased its electoral base under the leadership of **Alfred Dregger**). There followed SPD-led coalitions with the Greens (1985–1987, the first red–green government at the federal state level), the FDP (1987–1991), the Greens again (1991–1995), and then **Alliance 90/The Greens** (1995–1999). Minister presidents during this period were Holger Börner (SPD, 1976–1987), **Walter Wallmann** (1987–1991), and, with **Joschka Fischer** as deputy, **Hans Eichel** (1991–1999). While Börner contended with the issues of atomic energy and environmental objections to the extension of Frankfurt Airport, Wallmann promoted aid for eastern Germany, especially neighboring **Thuringia**, and laid the foundations for the location of the European Central Bank (ECB) in Frankfurt. In 1999, after decades in opposition, the CDU, led by the right-wing **Roland Koch**, formed a governing coalition with the FDP after conducting a controversial campaign that questioned the place of foreigners in German society and was later marred by allegations of illegal funding. The CDU was reelected in 2003 with an absolute majority, but in 2008 lost seats, emerging neck and neck with the SPD, which negotiated a coalition with the Green Party that collapsed before the candidate minister president, Andrea Ypsilanti (SPD), could take office. A new election (January 2009), dominated by issues of education (university fees and improvements to school facilities) and the economy (including the extension of Frankfurt airport), returned a CDU/FDP coalition led by Koch. Following Koch's sudden resignation, **Volker Bouffier** (CDU) took over as minister president in August 2010. In the regional election of September 2013, heavy losses by the FDP, which only just cleared the 5 percent entry, eliminated it as a potential coalition partner with the CDU, which went on to form a government with the Greens (led by Tarek Al-Wazir), who gained 11.1 percent of votes.

The hub of Hessen's economy lies in the south (Rhein-Main region). Frankfurt, nicknamed Mainhattan, is home to the **German Federal Bank**, the ECB, and the **German Stock Exchange** and employs more than 70,000 workers in **banks** and insurance and financial services. The city hosts international fairs and exhibitions and is a center of **publishing** (newspapers, books, and magazines) and **telecommunications**. The main employer is Frankfurt Airport (Fraport AG), with around 21,000 employees at various locations and a turnover of more than 2,580 million euros (2015). Leading companies in the Rhein-Main region include Hoechst AG, the Merck group (Darmstadt), Opel (Rüsselsheim), and Heraeus (Hanau). Hessen has several universities (Frankfurt, Darmstadt, Gießen, Marburg, and Kassel), with centers of research and development in micro-structures and optical electronics (Wetzlar), software (Marburg), and environmental science (Kassel). Unemployment (5.5 percent) is below the national average (5.7 percent in 2014), and the state contributes 9 percent of national GDP (2015).

HEYM, STEFAN (1913–2001). Writer and journalist. Stefan Heym was born Hellmuth Flieg in Chemnitz (**Saxony**). His father was a Jewish businessman. Compelled to leave school in Chemnitz after composing an antimilitary poem (1931), he completed his higher school certificate in **Berlin** (1932), where he studied philosophy, German, and journalism and wrote occasional articles. When the National Socialists came to power in 1933, he changed his name to Stefan Heym and fled to Prague, where he worked as a journalist. During the Third Reich, his father committed suicide, and many members of his family perished in concentration camps. In 1935, Heym emigrated to the United States (U.S.), where he completed a master's degree at the University of Chicago (1936) and edited an antifascist German-language newspaper in New York (1937–1939). A member of the German-American Writers' Association (1938–1940), he published his first novel (*Hostages*) in 1942 (this appeared in German under the title *Der Fall Glasenapp* in 1958). During World War II, he enlisted (1943) in the U.S. army and took part as a sergeant in the Normandy invasion (1944), specializing in psychological warfare. In 1945, he founded a newspaper (*Neue Zeit*) in Munich but was sent back to the U.S. and dismissed from the army for his procommunist views. His war novel *The Crusaders* (1948) became a best seller. In 1951–1952, in protest against the Korean war, Heym returned his U.S. military medals and moved to East Berlin in the **German Democratic Republic (GDR)**.

In the GDR Heym, who never joined a political party, understood himself as a "critical Marxist" and was often at odds with the regime and its leaders. Most of his novels, which often dealt critically with the GDR and its Stalinist past, were printed in West Germany, where he became the most widely read East German author. A member of the Schriftstellerverband of the GDR, the official East German writers' association, from 1954, he was expelled from the organization in 1979. Following the collapse of the regime in November 1989, Heym called for a socialist alternative to West Germany. Among other GDR intellectuals, he had spoken at the decisive demonstration against the GDR regime on 4 November 1989, when he articulated what many felt: that after years of intellectual, economic, and political stagnation, recent events felt as if "someone had opened a window." Between 1994 and 1998, he represented the **Party of Democratic Socialism (PDS)** in the **Bundestag** and advocated an alliance of left-wing parties (1997).

Heym's many awards included honorary doctorates from the universities of Bern and Cambridge (1990–1991) and the honorary presidency of the East German **PEN** Club (1993). He was the first German author to receive the Jerusalem Prize for Literature (1993). His novels include *Lasalle* (1969), *5 Tage in Juni* (1971), *Der König David Bericht* (1972), and *Collin* (1979). An autobiography (*Nachruf*) appeared in 1988.

HISTORIANS' QUARREL (HISTORIKERSTREIT). The "historians' quarrel" arose during the late 1980s when two conservative historians, Ernst Nolte and Andreas Hillgruber, argued that the National Socialist genocide, viewed in the context of Soviet atrocities in the Stalin era, was not a uniquely evil historical event and should not prevent West Germans from recognizing the positive aspects of their own history or national identity. Although Nolte had published similar ideas in 1980 and 1985, it was his article in the *Frankfurter Allgemeine Zeitung* in June 1986 that sparked public and often acrimonious debate. The challenge to the conservatives (who did not present a single, united view) was led by the left-wing philosopher **Jürgen Habermas**. Responding in *Die Zeit* in July 1986, Habermas maintained that the position adopted by Nolte, Hillgruber, Joachim Fest, Hagen Schulze, and others (notably chancellor **Helmut Kohl**'s adviser, Michael Stürmer, and speechwriter, Klaus Hildbrand) undermined a true understanding of the Holocaust and the National Socialist period. Habermas's position was shared by Hans-Ulrich Wehler, Jürgen Kocka, Hans Mommsen, and Heinrich August Winkler. The controversy drew attention to issues that had been exercising historians for some time, in particular whether the Holocaust was an inevitable product of Adolf Hitler's **anti-Semitism** and whether the National Socialist regime and its genocidal policies represented a "special path" (Sonderweg) in German history, perhaps even an irrational upheaval unrelated to past and subsequent events in Germany itself. The dispute was in parts so bitter because it touched on the question of the historical and political self-confidence of Germans after World War II. While some saw the controversy as symptomatic of a lack of such confidence, others interpreted it as proof of a robust and fully functioning political culture in the Federal Republic of Germany (FRG). The quarrel also highlighted a distinct difference from how history was perceived in the **German Democratic Republic (GDR)**, where, true to the Marxist dialectic, forces of old were considered to have been overcome by the socialist good. Historians outside Germany who became involved included, for example, Richard Evans, Ian Kershaw, and Gordon Craig. Similar debates have meanwhile taken place in other countries of the former eastern bloc.

HOECHST AG. Hoechst AG originated in 1863 when a small group of partners established a factory in the town of Höchst on the Main River to manufacture dyes from coal tar. The company expanded steadily and in 1883 moved into **pharmaceutical** and **chemical** production. During the 1890s, several famous chemists, including Nobel Prize winners Emil von Behring, Robert Koch, and Paul Ehrlich, worked with Hoechst, and by the outbreak of World War I, the company had established subsidiaries in Moscow, Paris, and Manchester. During the industrial consolidation of the interwar period, Höchst became part of the I. G. Farbenindustrie AG group. After World War II, I. G. Farben was placed under U.S. administration and broken up, although Hoechst reemerged in 1951 as a separate concern, Farbwerke Hoechst AG. During the 1950s and 1960s, the new company shifted its raw material base from coal to oil and was soon mass producing synthetic fibers, plastics, and films alongside its traditional range of dyes, pharmaceuticals, and agrochemical products for the international market. In 1965, it built its first large-scale biological treatment plan for industrial wastewater. In 1968, the group entered into a partnership with the Paris-based pharmaceutical company Roussel Uclaf S.A., in which it acquired a majority shareholding. The 1990s saw further restructuring and expansion in the U.S., with the acquisition of Celanese Corporation (1994) and the drug company Marion Merrell Dow (1995). In July 1997, following more acquisitions and mergers, Hoechst AG became a holding concern for a number of companies operating independently throughout the world. The following September, it entered the New York Stock Exchange. Under the leadership of Jürgen Dormann (appointed board chairman in 1994), Hoechst underwent a major realignment. In 1998, it sold off its industrial chemicals interests (including polyester, synthetics resin, polyethylene, and coatings) to concentrate on pharmaceuticals and life sciences, and in 1999, it merged with the French company Rhône-Poulenc S.A. to create a new concern, Aventis. By 2004–2005, Hoechst had been broken up to become a holding company within the Sanofi-Aventis group (Sanofi from 2010), with no shareholdings or operational activities of its own.
See also INDUSTRY.

HOLTZBRINCK PUBLISHING GROUP. The group's origins lie with Georg von Holtzbrinck (1909–1983), who began selling subscriptions to books and periodicals during the 1930s. During the postwar period, he developed the book club business to acquire stakes in **publishing** and newspaper companies, including S. Fischer, Rowohlt, and *Handelsblatt*. In 1971, the business was reconstituted under the aegis of a holding company, the Georg von Holtzbrinck GmbH publishing group. After Holtzbrinck's son, Georg-Dieter (born in 1941), took over the concern in 1980, the company expanded into newspapers (acquiring *Die Zeit*), the international book market (taking over Henry Holt), and science and **education** (with the acquisition of *Scientific American*, W. H. Freeman, and the Macmillan group). The book club segment was wound up in 1989, and in 2001 management passed to Dieter's brother, Stefan (born in 1963), who realigned the business toward the **Internet** and digital publishing. Newspapers were sold off by 2013, although a stake in *Die Zeit* was retained, and international markets were further developed. The group's three divisions comprise Macmillan Science and Education (generating 49 percent of revenue), Macmillan Publishers (fiction and nonfiction, 42 percent), and Holtzbrinck Digital Information and Services (including news media, 7 percent). It has outlets in 120 countries, mainly in North America, Germany, and Great Britain. Turnover in 2014 was 1,727 million euros (39 percent in North America and 20 percent in Germany).

See also PRESS.

HOMOSEXUALITY. In 1935, the National Socialists sharpened existing German laws against male homosexuality (since 1871 **women** had been exempt from criminal conviction) and incarcerated and murdered several thousand in concentration camps and prisons. After World War II, the laws, paragraphs 175/175a of the German penal codex (Bundesstrafgesetzbuch), were retained in the Federal Republic of Germany (FRG), and between 1945 and 1969, of 100,000 males accused, 50,000 were convicted and imprisoned for offenses. Controversy accompanied a wave of arrests and trials in Frankfurt/Main in 1950–1951, although a 1957 ruling of the **Federal Constitutional Court (FCC)** confirmed that the 1935 laws could not be regarded as invalid simply on the grounds that they were passed by the National Socialists. Neither were homosexual victims of National Socialist persecution entitled to compensation or rehabilitation, a position confirmed by federal German courts until the 1970s. The **German Democratic Republic (GDR)** also retained the 1935 laws and prohibited homosexual organizations and publications, although it reduced the maximum penalty to five years' imprisonment. During the 1960s, the GDR effectively decriminalized homosexuality between males aged over 18, although the situation was not formalized until 1968, and many prejudices remained. In 1988, East Germany removed all laws against homosexuality.

In the FRG, following a liberalization of the law by the first **grand coalition** (1969), homosexual sex between males over 21 was legalized, although male prostitution remained outlawed. In 1973, a further relaxation took place, and the age of consent was lowered to 18. Finally, in 1994, paragraph

175 was removed altogether. Following pressure to acknowledge homosexual victims of the National Socialists, the **Bundestag** included them in a rehabilitation law of 1998. In August 2001, a new law came into effect that acknowledged "registered life partnerships" (eingetragene Lebenspartnerschaften, EL), popularly referred to as "Homo-Ehen," with marriage-like rights and obligations. The law had been resisted by the **Christian Democratic Union (CDU)/Christian Social Union (CSU)** and **Free Democratic Party (FDP)**, although an attempt by some **federal states (Bavaria, Saxony,** and **Thuringia)** to have it declared unconstitutional was rejected by the FCC (18 July 2001).

HONECKER, ERICH (1912–1994). German Democratic Republic (GDR) leader, 1971–1989. Born in Wiebelskirchen **(Saarland)**, Erich Honecker trained as a roofer. In 1926 he joined a communist youth group, and in 1929 the Communist Party of Germany (KPD). After training at the Lenin Communist Party School in Moscow, he became a senior party official in 1930. When the National Socialists came to power (1933), he worked underground for the KPD in southern Germany, but was arrested in 1935 and sentenced two years later to 10 years' imprisonment for high treason. After his release (1945), he joined a group of leading communists under **Walter Ulbricht**, who returned from Moscow to reconstruct eastern Germany under the direction of the Union of Soviet Socialist Republics (USSR). As youth secretary to the Central Committee of the KPD (1945–1946), Honecker built up the communist youth organization in the eastern zone. In 1946, this became the Free German Youth (Freie Deutsche Jugend, FDJ), which he headed until 1955. In 1950, he became a candidate member of the Politburo of the **Socialist Unity Party of Germany (SED)** and a member of the Central Committee. After training at the USSR's Communist Party school for senior functionaries in Moscow (1955–1956), Honecker returned to the GDR, where he supported Ulbricht's purge of opponents in the SED leadership. In 1958, he was appointed to the secretariat of the Central Committee with responsibilities for party organization and security. In the same year, he became a full member of the Politburo and succeeded Ulbricht as secretary (head) of the Central Committee. In 1961, on Ulbricht's instructions, he coordinated the erection of the **Berlin Wall**.

When Ulbricht resigned (May 1971), Honecker succeeded him as leader, taking over all major offices (first secretary of the Zentralkomitee [Central Committee], chairman of the Nationaler Verteidigungsrat [National Defense Council] from June 1971, general secretary of the SED from May 1976, and chairman of the Staatsrat [Council of State] from October 1976). As state leader, Honecker strengthened links with the USSR, attempted to coordinate economic development with an increase in living standards, and presided over improvements in relations with the Federal Republic of Germany

(FRG). At the same time, he reinforced ideological and political control and in the second half of the 1980s refused to follow the reformist policies of the Soviet Union and democratize the GDR. During the 1989 revolution, he was forced to resign all offices (18 October), ostensibly on health grounds, and was expelled from the SED (3 December) before fleeing to Moscow (13 March 1991), where he found refuge in the Chilean embassy (many South Americans had found refuge in the GDR after a right-wing putsch in Chile in the early 1970s). Following pressure from Germany, he was returned to **Berlin** (July 1992), where, alongside other members of the GDR leadership (**Erich Mielke, Willi Stoph, Heinz Keßler**, Fritz Streletz, and Hans Albrecht), he was placed on trial for crimes committed against would-be escapees at the border/Berlin Wall. After making a brief statement in which he acknowledged his responsibility for building the Wall but demonstrated no sense of moral guilt, Honecker refused to participate in the proceedings; he was eventually discharged on grounds of ill health (January 1993). He flew to Santiago (Chile) to join his wife, Margot, and their daughter, and died in exile there on 29 May 1994.

HÖPPNER, REINHARD (1948–). Social Democratic Party of Germany (SPD) politician. Reinhard Höppner was born in Haldensleben (**Saxony-Anhalt**), in eastern Germany. While studying at high school (1963–1967), he worked as an electrical fitter, then went on to study mathematics at the Technical University of Dresden, graduating with a diploma (1971) and a doctorate (1976). He also chaired the synod of the Evangelical Church in **Saxony**. From 1971 to 1990, he worked as a lector for an East **Berlin** publisher (Akademie Verlag). Following the collapse of the regime in the **German Democratic Republic (GDR)**, he joined the **Social Democratic Party in the GDR** (1989) and became vice president of the **People's Chamber** (1990). Elected to the state parliament (**Landtag**) of **Saxony-Anhalt** in October 1990, he led the opposition parliamentary group of the SPD. The state had been governed by a **Christian Democratic Union (CDU)/Free Democratic Party (FDP)** coalition since 1990, but after the 1994 elections, Höppner took over as **minister president**, leading a minority coalition of SPD and **Alliance 90/The Greens** that relied on the support of the **Party of Democratic Socialism (PDS)** to command a majority in the Landtag. The controversial arrangement, which was the first time that a regional government had cooperated with the PDS, came to be known as the **Magdeburg model** and required Höppner to perform a delicate political balancing act. When the Greens failed to clear the 5 percent hurdle in the 1994 elections, the SPD governed alone, again relying on PDS votes.

Saxony-Anhalt was severely affected by rapid deindustrialization and unemployment after reunification. Although Höppner became a well-known advocate of the interests of the **eastern federal states** and was closely involved in the negotiations of transfers to the east for the second phase of the so-called **Solidarity Pact** (agreed in June 2001), his popularity waned, and the SPD suffered a crushing defeat in the 2002 regional elections, after which **Wolfgang Böhmer** took over as minister president, leading a CDU/FDP coalition. Höppner joined the presidium of the Deutscher Evangelischer Kirchentag (Conference of German Evangelical Churches, DEK) in 1994 and served on its executive board 2001–2007; in 2007, he was also elected president.

HUMAN RIGHTS. Fundamental human rights are the first to be cataloged in the **Basic Law** (**BL**) and are at the heart of Germany's self-perception as a Western, liberal, and democratic state. A number of organizations within Germany monitor human rights in practice and promote their observance.

The Institut für Menschenrechte (Institute for Human Rights) was established in March 2001 on the recommendation of the **Bundestag** with a mandate to research, report on, and support human rights both in Germany and internationally. Although funded by federal ministries, the organization is politically independent and is managed by an executive board, which is overseen by a 16-member board of trustees made up of representatives of German society, academia, the **media**, and politics. Early in 2003, conservative members of the board of trustees forced out the director for allegedly pursuing domestic political issues outside the remit of international human rights. These issues included the rights of **foreigners**, **asylum** seekers, and the unemployed, and the institute suffered a serious loss of prestige in the ensuing public debate.

ProAsyl, which describes itself as an independent human rights organization, was created in 1986 following a meeting between the **United Nations** (**UN**) High Commissioner for Refugees in Germany and Jürgen Miksch of the Evangelische Akademie Tutzing (Evangelical Academy Tutzing). Miksch went on to become chairman of ProAsyl, which was founded in response to a hardening of government policy toward asylum seekers. The organization currently focuses on campaigning against what it regards as Europe's inhumane policies on refugees and supporting and representing individual asylum seekers. Its current chairman is Andreas Lipsch.

The Humanistische Union (Humanist Union) claims to be Germany's oldest human rights organization. Founded in 1961, it has campaigned against the emergency laws (Notstandsgesetze, 1968), inhuman conditions in prisons and psychiatric wards, and laws banning the employment of left-wingers in state positions (**radicals decree**, 1972); it also opposes restrictive asylum legislation. Since 1997, the union has published an annual report on basic human rights in Germany (*Grundrechte-Report*). Now produced in conjunction with other human rights organizations, recent issues have drawn attention to civil rights issues raised by heightened security and increased surveillance; the detention of suspects in response to terror attacks; and the rights of refugees, children, and **women**.

Many of the concerns expressed in the *Grundrechte* reports have been echoed by Amnesty International (AI), which also publishes, country by country, an annual review of human rights across the world. The group's more recent concerns about Germany have centered on the authorities' return of vulnerable refugees, asylum seekers, and members of ethnic minorities to countries of origin; the failure to establish an independent police complaints body and ensure that all police officers on duty wear identity badges; and the under-resourcing of the Nationale Stelle zur Verhütung von Folter (National Agency for the Prevention of Torture).

See also INITIATIVE PEACE AND HUMAN RIGHTS (INITIATIVE FRIEDEN UND MENSCHENRECHTE).

HYPOVEREINSBANK (HVB). The HVB banking group was formed in January 1998 following a merger of two regional **banks** in **Bavaria**, the Bayerische Hypotheken- und Wechsel-Bank AG and the Bayerische Vereinsbank AG. The merger was the largest in German banking history and created the country's second largest bank after the **Deutsche Bank**. The Vereinsbank was originally founded in 1869 as a private bank. The roots of the Bayerische Hypotheken- und Wechsel-Bank go back to the 18th century, although it was closely involved in the region's economic and industrial development during the 19th century and later functioned as the Bayerische Staatsbank (Bavarian State Bank). Proposals for amalgamating the three Bavarian regional banks (the Vereinsbank, the Staatsbank, and the Hypo) were debated during the 1960s, and in 1971 the Bayerische Vereinsbank and the Bayerische Staatsbank merged. In 2005, HVB was taken over by the Italian bank UniCredit and in 2009 changed its legal name to UniCreditBank AG, although it continues to trade under the title HypoVereinsbank. The larger UniCredit group has around 144,000 employees and maintains 7,900 outlets in 17 European countries, including Russia. Turnover was 4,390 million euros.

I

IMMIGRATION. The definition of German citizenship by blood descent/ ethnic origin (Abstammungsprinzip) as opposed to place of birth (Territorialprinzip or Geburtsortprinzip) was established in law in 1913 and remained in effect in the Federal Republic of Germany (FRG) until 2000. Despite abuses of the old law by the National Socialists, the FRG retained it in order to preserve the notion of a "community of descent" (Abstammungsgemeinschaft) and provide a right of return for ethnic Germans and their descendants displaced after World War II (**Aussiedler**); it also afforded those fleeing East Germany (**Übersiedler**) automatic citizenship. The first law regulating the admission of expellees (Bundesvertriebenengesetz) was passed in 1953, and descendants of ethnic Germans entered the country fairly easily. The residency status for non-Germans, on the other hand, was regulated by the so-called law on **foreigners** (Ausländergesetz), introduced in 1965 to formalize the legal status of foreign workers (guest workers) and in force until 2005, when it was superseded by new legislation governing immigration (Zuwanderungsgesetz). After 1957, with the creation of the European Economic Community (EEC), the precursor to the **European Union (EU)**, citizens of member states were freely entitled to live and work in the FRG. Liberal provision was also made for **asylum** seekers and **Jews.** Guest worker recruitment ceased in 1973, but during the 1980s economic demands and changes in Germany's demographic structure prompted calls for new legislation to promote and regulate immigration (including time-limited residency) and provide paths to citizenship. A modified law on foreigners in 1991 relaxed restrictions and established new forms of residency, notably for relatives, female spouses, young people, pensioners, and families of asylum seekers, but immigration from outside the EU was still not permitted, and residency for foreigners remained time limited. The law was criticized as complex and as failing to address the issues of citizenship by birth and dual nationality. A hotly debated reform of citizenship law, in force from January 2000, finally broke free of the Abstammungsprinzip by offering citizenship to children born in Germany to foreign residents of at least eight years, and for other categories, reducing the 15-year residency requirement to eight.

Although various factors (transitional laws for children and applications made under old or new legislation) affected naturalizations before and after 2000, they peaked at almost 187,000 at the end of 2000, falling to around 94,500 by 2008, after which they began to climb again. Turks have traditionally constituted the largest single group acquiring citizenship (44 percent in 2000), although the level has since declined. While multiple passports are officially discouraged, around 50 percent of naturalized citizens retain their original nationality, although the proportion varies widely according to the country of origin.

Officially, Germany distinguishes between what might be termed "inward migration" (Zuwanderung) and immigration (Einwanderung). While most people use the terms interchangeably, German law and bureaucracy recognize only "inward migrants," implying that Germany is not a land of true immigration, such as the United States or Canada, which actively admit and absorb foreign settlers in large numbers. However, even before the law of 2000, the official fiction that Germany was not a country of immigration appeared both absurd in view of its large and long-standing foreign population and also ill-advised in the face of a national skills shortage, especially in information technology. To counter the latter, Chancellor **Gerhard Schröder** launched a green card scheme, which between 2000 and 2004 admitted around 18,000 foreigners with computer skills for five-year residency. The scheme provided fresh impetus for an immigration law (Zuwanderungsgesetz), which after a tortuous legislative passage came into force in 2005. Replacing the old Ausländergesetz (and green card) and incorporating provisions on residency (Aufenthaltsgesetz), the law facilitated immigration for highly qualified persons and simplified the previously complex list of categories of residence to two: time-limited permission to stay (Aufenthaltserlaubnis) and indefinite right of settlement (Niederlassungserlaubnis), with the prospect of eventual citizenship after a number of years. The new law also promoted the integration of both immigrants and foreigners already living in Germany, while foreigners considered dangerous to the state would be more easily deported. In 2012, in line with EU objectives, Germany agreed to an EU blue card scheme, which offered highly qualified, non-EU citizens residency, subject to earning at least 46,000 euros a year in a skills shortage area (science, technology, or medicine); residency was initially for four years and renewable. In 2013, 1,193 qualified for the card in Germany, most of whom (1,367) were already living in the country, with considerably more acquiring residency outside the scheme. More recent evidence suggests that regulating immigration through purely economic criteria is unrealistic, and the debate about how to revise the law continues.

In 2005, the term **"migration background"** (Migrationshintergrund) was introduced to reflect circumstances beyond the narrow distinction between persons with or without German nationality (as defined by the **Basic Law**

[**BL**], article 116). A person with a migration background was defined as having first- or second-generation foreign roots. It therefore included foreigners (without German nationality and irrespective of whether or not they were born in Germany), all immigrants (regardless of nationality), Aussiedler, and anyone descended from at least one parent who had entered Germany after 1949. Of the total population, 20.3 percent (16.4 million) fell into this category in 2014, and 7.2 percent (less than six million) were foreigners (the official figure for foreigners for 2015 is 11.2 percent [9.1 million], possibly reflecting differences in how statistics are gathered and a large influx of refugees). They include the single largest group of true immigrants, about 3.1 million Aussiedler from the former eastern bloc and Soviet Union. Overall, Germany is increasingly a land of true immigration, with more than 1.5 million people entering in 2014 (and that number is rising), compared with 914,200 emigrants. At the same time, overall flows indicate a very high mobility. Around 60 percent of incomers in 2014 were from the EU, led by Poland (198,000 entering and 139,000 leaving, leaving a net balance of 59,000), Romania (192,000/117,000/75,000), Bulgaria (78,000/44,000/34,000), Italy (73,000/36,000/37,000), Syria (65,000/2,800/62,200), and Greece (35,000/15,000/20,000).

In contrast to the first generation of guest workers, immigrants are now much better qualified, with 47 percent of southern Europeans possessing a university degree; Poles, with 45 percent having a vocational qualification, integrate well with German working life and customs, while 40 percent of Bulgarians and Romanians arrive with no occupational training. The difference in educational and skill levels accounts for the fact that integration problems are found more with the historical immigration population than with newcomers.

See also POPULATION AND PEOPLE.

INDUSTRY. During the postwar phase of economic expansion (from 1950 to the early 1960s), the main industrial areas of activity of the Federal Republic of Germany (FRG) were coal mining and steel production (in the Ruhr valley, lower Rhine, and Salzgitter/eastern **Lower Saxony**), **chemical** production (Düsseldorf, Leverkusen, Cologne, Frankfurt/Main, Ludwigshafen, **Hamburg**, and parts of **Bavaria**), **engineering** (the Ruhr valley, Rhineland, and around Stuttgart), **automobile** manufacturing (the Rhineland, Stuttgart, Hanover, Wolfsburg, Hamburg, **Bremen**, and southern Bavaria), and electrical goods (Stuttgart, Nuremberg, Munich, the Rhineland, and **Berlin**), followed by clothing and textiles, timber and paper manufacturing, and food. During the 1960s and 1970s, the **automobile industry** enjoyed strong growth, while building and construction, after meeting the immediate demands of postwar reconstruction, continued to expand as the **population** increased, cities grew, and the road network was extended. At the same time, the traditional industries of coal and steel entered a series of crises with changes in the **energy** market and falling demand. Export-led foreign **trade** became a pillar of the economy and remained so during the following decades.

In the 1970s, Germany's economy was challenged by rising energy prices, cheaper imports, and increased foreign competition. While some older industries (coal and steel, textiles, clothing, and shipbuilding) declined, others (engineering, automobile manufacturing, and chemicals) expanded. Although electrical engineering remained a growth area, its product range was transformed. As cheaper Asian imports displaced home electrical goods, German producers such as **Siemens AG** focused on **telecommunications**, computers, and information technology. These developments, which continued into the 1980s and 1990s, affected employment patterns, with coal, steel, and textiles shedding large numbers of workers. At the same time, overall unemployment rose as growth companies, such as motor vehicle producers, shifted manufacturing to countries with lower labor costs and increased their per capita production through automatization. The service sector, often integrated with manufacturing and offering complete business solutions, is increasingly important.

The structural transformation of German industry is reflected in a geographical shift of activity away from its historical urban centers in the north and northwest (the Ruhr and the **Saarland**) in favor of the south, where southern **Hessen**, **Baden-Württemberg**, and Bavaria now enjoy higher growth rates and lower unemployment and have become centers of new investment-led, high-technology industries such as electronics, biomedicine, and **pharmaceuticals**. Around 98 percent of German companies are small to medium-sized (the **Mittelstand**). The four key sectors of German industry by revenue are (excluding **health**) automobiles, engineering, chemicals, and electrical/electronic engineering. In 2014, Germany ranked fifth in the world in terms of International Monetary Fund statistics on GDP. The main umbrella organization for German industry is the Berlin-based BDI (Bundesverband der Deutschen Industrie, Federation of German Industries).

See also ECONOMIC DEVELOPMENT (FRG) AFTER 2000; ECONOMIC DEVELOPMENT (FRG) 1949–1969; ECONOMIC DEVELOPMENT (FRG) 1970–1989; ECONOMIC DEVELOPMENT 1990–1999; EMPLOYERS' ORGANIZATIONS.

INITIATIVE PEACE AND HUMAN RIGHTS (INITIATIVE FRIEDEN UND MENSCHENRECHTE). The Initiative Peace and Human Rights originated in 1985–1986 as a dissident group responding to the prohibition by the authorities in the **German Democratic Republic (GDR)** of a peace seminar in East **Berlin**. The 200-member group monitored the state's observance of **human rights** as laid down in the Helsinki Final Act (1975) and was constantly harassed by the authorities. It produced a magazine (*Grenz-fall*) between 1986 and 1988, issued manifestos between March and October 1989, and recorded arrests and abuses by the security forces during the demonstrations of September–October 1989, campaigning for the release of protesters. Its leading members were Martin Böttger, **Bärbel Bohley** (who later joined the **New Forum** group), Werner Fischer, Peter Grimm, Ralf Hirsch, Gerd Poppe, **Ulrike Poppe** (who later joined the **Democracy Now** group), Lotte Templin, Wolfgang Templin, **Ibrahim Böhme** (who went over to the **Social Democratic Party of Germany, SPD**), Reinhard Weißhuhn, and **Marianne Birthler**. For the elections to the **People's Chamber** (18 March 1990), it entered into a common list with other groups under the title **Alliance 90**. The group did not see itself primarily as a political organization and supported a "third-way" solution to the GDR's economic crisis.

INSTEAD PARTY (STATT PARTEI). Founded in 1993 by Markus Wegner in **Hamburg**, the party (full name: Statt Partei—die Unabhängigen/Instead Party—the Independents) emerged from disaffected members of the regional **Christian Democratic Union (CDU)** over the selection of candidates for the national election of 1990 and the Hamburg city election of 1991. Campaigning on a right-wing platform for greater responsibility for citizens and a more open democracy, it entered the Hamburg parliament in 1991 and governed in cooperation with the **Social Democratic Party of Germany (SPD)**, although electoral success beyond the municipal level in other regions (it won some seats in **Schleswig-Holstein** in 1994) eluded it. Following internal divisions and Wegner's resignation (1995), the party failed to clear the 5 percent hurdle in the 1997 Hamburg election and faded into obscurity, losing many of its members to the **Schill** Party.

INTELLIGENCE AGENCIES. Germany maintains three intelligence agencies: the **Federal Intelligence Agency** (Bundesnachrichtendienst, BND), the Office for the Protection of the Constitution (Bundesamt für Verfassungsschutz, BfV), and the Militärischer Abschirmdienst (Military Counter-Espionage Service, MAD). While the BND manages intelligence operations outside Germany, the BfV monitors internal threats to security, and MAD is responsible for maintaining the security of the **Bundeswehr** and its personnel. Characteristic of the German security system is the strict application of the "separation rule" (Trennungsgebot), which has its origins in a note (the "Polizeibrief" of April 1949) from the postwar occupation authorities to the founding fathers of the **Basic Law (BL)**, requiring them to separate the functions of the intelligence services (information gathering) from those of the police (law enforcement). Designed to prevent the misuse of powers by the agencies, as occurred with the Gestapo during the National Socialist period, the rule means that, while the BfV might, for instance, uncover an arms cache held by an extremist group, it remains the role of the police to take action and arrest the perpetrators. The rule, which does not apply to the FBI in the United States, for example, not only physically separates the services in terms of organization and personnel, but also controls the sharing of information.

See also EXTREMISM; SECURITY POLICY, EXTERNAL; SECURITY POLICY, INTERNAL; TERRORISM.

INTERNET. Germany's Internet originated in computer centers at the universities of Karlsruhe—with the first e-mail links via CSNet to centers in the United States (U.S.) and other countries from 1984—and Dortmund (using a Datex-P link with Amsterdam in 1988). Between 1987 and 1989, the federal state of **Baden-Württemberg** became the first region outside the United States to link up its major universities and scientific institutions, using the BelWü network and a prototype Internet protocol (IP). When, in 1990, the Deutsche Forschungsnetz (German National Research and Education Network, DFN) promoted the TCP (Transmission Control Protocol) IP standard over the rival OSI (Operating Systems Interconnection), the basis was laid for Internet connectivity between Germany and the rest of the world. During the 1990s the Internet expanded vigorously, largely thanks to private, commercial service providers. A milestone was the creation in 1995 of DE-CIX (German Commercial Internet Exchange) in Frankfurt/Main, a large, neutral data exchange point (so-called peering platform), to which all German providers could directly link, without going first via the United States. This now claims to be one of the largest Internet exchanges in the world. Technically, the Internet consists of a core "backbone" of fast, high-capacity satellite or fiber optic cable links maintained by network service providers (NSPs). These provide points of access to local exchanges run by Internet service providers (ISPs), who supply "last mile" links to end users typically connecting to a telephone line; here, DSL (digital subscriber line) technology transmits data digitally via a local telephone network, which uses the public switched telephone network. There are 100 NSPs in Germany, although, despite the liberalization of the telephone/**telecommunications** market in Germany during the 1990s and criticism of its tariff structures, **Deut- sche Telekom** remains the largest provider; others include the Spanish concern Telefonica and British-owned Vodafone. The ISPs offer hosting (registration of domains, renting of web servers, e-mail) and access (dial-up and broadband services), as well as content management. Examples of ISPs in Germany are T-Online, Arcor, Hansenet, and AOL. Between 2007 and 2012, the national turnover of cell phone Internet usage rose from 1,700 million to 5,500 million euros, and it was expected to reach 9,400 million in 2017.

Apart from a solitary link between the Free University in West **Berlin** and Humboldt University in East Berlin, the Internet was unknown in the **German Democratic Republic (GDR)**, where the telephone network was anyhow very limited. After reunification, the federal German post office (**Deutsche Post**) and subsequently **Deutsche Telekom** embarked on an accelerated infrastructure construction program.

Around 31 percent of the population in 2014 were estimated to be regular Internet users, mainly in the 14–64 age range (2014), compared with 6 percent in 2003. Concerns over Internet data security did little to dampen usage. While more than 95 percent of Google users felt that their personal information was not protected, a similar number had few reservations over the issue; the figures for users of online banking were between 51 and 54 percent.

J

JAHN, ROLAND (1953–). East German dissident. Born in Jena in the former **German Democratic Republic (GDR)**, Jahn began studying economics at Jena University (1975), but joined the Carl-Zeiss factory as a transport worker after he was dematriculated for opposing the expatriation of the singer **Wolf Biermann** (1977). Continuing his protests against the regime, he was imprisoned for eight months during 1982–1983, and upon his release cofounded a dissident peace group (the Friedensgemeinschaft Jena); in June 1983 he was forcibly expelled from the GDR. From West Berlin, Jahn maintained his contacts with opposition groups, building up an East–West information network and reporting for Western media on **human rights** violations and **environmental** damage in the GDR. During this time the East German secret police, the **Stasi**, continued to spy on him and, among other things, tapped his telephone line. Jahn was instrumental in encouraging Radio Glasnost, a dissident (and illegal) radio station, which began broadcasting from East Berlin during the 1980s. After the fall of the **Berlin Wall**, Jahn, by now author and editor of a west German television magazine (ARD's *Kontraste*), took an active role in organizations exploring the GDR dictatorship, including the Bundesstiftung zur Aufarbeitung der SED-Diktatur, a foundation for reappraising its legacy (from 1999), and the Stiftung Berliner Mauer, a foundation for preserving the memory of the Berlin Wall (2006–2010), for which he was awarded several prizes. In 2011, he was appointed **Federal Commissioner for the Records of the State Security Service of the Former German Democratic Republic, BStU**).

JAHR FAMILY. Publishers. John Jahr was born in 1900 in **Hamburg**. He trained in commerce (1916–1918) and served as a soldier in the final hostilities of World War I, before returning to Hamburg to train as a journalist with a **sports** newspaper (1919). After working for the *Hamburger Nachrichten* as sports editor (1920–1924), he founded his own sports magazine, *Sport-Chronik*. He also cofounded a publishing company before being contracted by the left-wing Münzenberg Verlag to handle advertising for two of its magazines (*Arbeiter-Illustrierte Zeitung/AIZ* and *Weg der Frau*). When the National

Socialists closed down Münzenberg (1933), Jahr moved to **Berlin**, where he established a book publishing firm, bought a weekly **women**'s magazine, and managed a bookstore. In 1944, at the height of World War II, his businesses were confiscated by the National Socialists, and he returned to Hamburg. After the war Jahr, together with **Axel Springer**, received a license from the occupation authorities in Hamburg to publish the women's magazine *Constanze*. As the business expanded, he founded new titles, including *Brigitte* and *Schöner Wohnen*, and from 1950 until 1962 held a stake in the news weekly *Der Spiegel*, which was edited by **Rudolf Augstein**. Other publications he owned included the business magazine *Capital* and the women's illustrated *Petra* (1964). In 1965, with **Gerd Bucerius** and the printer Richard Gruner, he cofounded **Gruner + Jahr** GmbH, which went on to become one of Germany's leading publishers of magazines, including *stern*. Soon after Gruner sold his shares to **Bertelsmann** (1969), both Jahr and Bucerius withdrew from operational management to join the supervisory board (1971). In 1987, Jahr became deputy chairman of the supervisory board of the newly constituted Gruner + Jahr AG, which became a subsidiary of the Bertelsmann concern, although the Jahr family retained a 25.1-percent stake until they sold out completely to Bertelsmann in November 2014 following uneven financial performance as the company managed the transition from printed media to digitally managed content. At the time of John Jahr's death in 1991, the company's portfolio included publishers, hotels, booksellers, and property, as well as holdings in **banks** and casinos. Until 2014 his four children, sons John Jahr Jr. (1933–2006), Michael (1938–), and Alexander (1940–2006), and daughter Angelika Jahr-Stilcken (1941–), continued to run the various branches of the concern, although the third generation—with the exception of granddaughter Alexandra (1964–), owner of the Jahr Top Special publishing house, which was originally cofounded in partnership with the **Axel Springer** group in 1971—were less closely involved.

See also MEDIA; PRESS.

JEWS IN GERMANY. Of the 500,000 Jews who lived in Germany in 1933, only around 15,000 had survived in Germany by the end of World War II. The Jewish community in **Berlin**, which had grown to 172,000 during the 1920s, although few were observant, numbered 7,000 in late 1945. Despite these losses, postwar communities quickly reestablished themselves in Berlin, Frankfurt/Main, and Munich. Between 1945 and 1950, about 200,000 Jews, mainly from Eastern Europe, entered Allied-controlled Germany as displaced persons. Housed in transit camps, most emigrated to Palestine (Israel from 1948) or the United States (U.S.) until the last of the camps closed in 1952. The 1950s saw further **immigration** from Hungary and Poland and an influx of Jews from the **German Democratic Republic (GDR)** to West Berlin following anti-Jewish measures by the Soviet leader Josef

Stalin in 1952–1953. In eastern Germany, the Jewish community progressively declined, from 3,500 (1945) to 1,200 (1967), numbering just 350 in eight communities in 1989, although the figures do not include nonreligious Jews. In its unequivocal support of the Palestinians in the Middle East, the GDR government became a consistent critic of Israel and "Zionism," and only toward the end of the regime did the ruling **Socialist Unity Party of Germany (SED)** make tentative moves toward a dialogue with Israel and its own small Jewish community. By contrast, the Jewish population in the Federal Republic of Germany (FRG) remained fairly constant, at between 26,000 and 30,000 in 50 registered communities until 1989. Between 1989 and 2009, 219,000 Jews from territories of the former Soviet Union entered Germany fairly freely, mainly under special measures (the Kontingentflüchtlingsgesetz) that were agreed to in 1991 and remained in force until a more restrictive immigration law was applied beginning in 2005. Entrants were distributed throughout the **federal states** according to a quota system. After such rapid growth, the registered Jewish population stabilized after 2005 (108,289) at around 102,000, although the total, including nonorganized Jews, is estimated at 200,000, making Germany the home of the third largest east European diaspora after Israel and the United States. Ironically, the preference of so many immigrant Jews for Germany over Israel prompted the Jewish Agency for Israel in 2002 to press the German government—unsuccessfully—to sharpen entry requirements. At the same time, the entry of large numbers of nonobservant Jews (especially where Jewish ancestry is claimed through the father alone) has led to nonacceptance by some established Jewish communities. Distinguished Jews in German public life include regional politicians, actors and cultural figures, **television** personalities, and the community leaders **Heinz Galinski**, **Ignatz Bubis**, and **Paul Spiegel**.

After the founding of the FRG in 1949 and its close alliance with the U.S. in the Cold War, dialogue among the German government, Jewish organizations, and Israel deepened, resulting in high-level political contacts and exchange programs. Restitution for war crimes remained high on the political agenda, and in the Luxembourg Treaty of September 1952, the FRG agreed to a package of continuing reparations and payments to Israel and to the Conference of Jewish Material Claims against Germany (claiming that it was an "antifascist" state, the GDR refused to take part). Between 2000 and 2007, the Stiftung Erinnerung, Verantwortung, und Zukunft (Foundation Remembrance, Responsibility and Future, EVZ) administered a fund financed jointly by the German government and **industry** to recompense victims of National Socialist forced labor policies. By 2013, the FRG had paid out a total of 75,000 million euros to casualties of National Socialist persecution.

Over the years, German–Jewish dialogue has been extended to cover areas such as the statute of limitations for war criminals, support for Israel, Holocaust awareness, **education**, combating **anti-Semitism**, and the emigration of Soviet Jews. Its course has been marked by visits to Israel by leading German politicians and by speeches, notably by Federal President **Richard von Weizsäcker** in 1985 and, on the anniversary of the liberation of Auschwitz in 2005, by Chancellor **Gerhard Schröder** (2005). Public interest in **theater**, films, and television programs, including the first dramatization of the diaries of Anne Frank in Berlin in 1956; NBC's series on the Holocaust, which was broadcast in 1979; and Steven Spielberg's *Schindler's List*, released in 1993, has also played a part. The controversial question of German guilt over the historical persecutions can still arise in public discourse. Examples include the so-called **historians' quarrel** (1986–1987); books such as Michael Wolffsohn's *Ewige Schuld* (Eternal Guilt, 1988) and Daniel Goldhagen's *Hitler's Willing Executioners* (1996); and a speech by the author and peace prize winner **Martin Walser** calling for a considered end to Germans' preoccupation with war guilt (1998). The Holocaust Memorial, officially opened in Berlin in 2005 after a long public debate, is one of many commemorative memorials established in former concentration camps and other sites throughout Germany.

Despite the shadow of the Holocaust and fairly isolated incidents of anti-Semitism, the fact that many Israelis of German descent (possibly around 100,000) hold a German passport, although they do not necessarily live in Germany, reflects Jewish confidence in the German state. Although the Jewish community in the FRG is now relatively small and largely eastern European (not German) in origin, Jewish life flourishes in several cities. In Berlin, Jewish restaurants, theaters, clubs, and schools have appeared, and the Jewish Museum has become a major tourist attraction since opening in 1999. The city has in fact numerous memorials to remind visitors of its past, including engraved brass plates mounted in the pavement (so-called Stolpersteine) and marking locations where Jews were kept awaiting deportation. A rabbinical seminary (Abraham Geiger College) opened in 2002 in Potsdam, and universities have seen a renewed interest in Jewish studies. The community itself is divided between conservative Orthodox Judaism and Reform Judaism, a liberal movement that originated in Germany in the early 19th century and has reemerged as an influential force among immigrants estranged from their religious roots. The main Jewish organization in Germany, the **Central Council of Jews in Germany**, is unitary in outlook but espouses orthodoxy. Others include the Zentralwohlfahrtsstelle der Juden in Deutschland (Central Welfare Office for Jews in Germany, ZWST), founded in 1917 and reestablished in 1951. The weekly newspaper *Jüdische Allgemeine*, founded in 1946 in the British zone of occupation, and has been based in Berlin since 1999.

See also EXTREMISM; GRAUMANN, DIETER (1950–); KNOBLOCH, CHARLOTTE (1932–); RELIGION.

JUNG, FRANZ JOSEF (1949–). Christian Democratic Union (CDU) politician. Born in Erbach (**Hessen**), Franz Josef Jung studied law at the University of Mainz (1970–1974) and began practicing as a lawyer in 1976. In 1978, he earned a doctorate in regional planning in Hessen. Active in the youth wing (**Junge Union, JU**) of the CDU from 1973, he represented the main party in the Hessen regional parliament (**Landtag**) between 1983 and 2005, where he was business manager (1987–1999), and later leader (2003–2005), of the parliamentary group; he was also minister for federal and European affairs and head of the state chancellery (1999–2000). Other positions that he held within the party include deputy regional party leader (1998–2014) and member of the national executive (from 1998). As regional general secretary (1987–1991), Jung also shared responsibility for a scandal that broke in 2000, when it emerged that the CDU in Hessen had maintained secret accounts to finance election campaigns. A member of the **Bundestag** from 2005, Jung went on to serve as federal defense minister (2005–2009) in Angela Merkel's first cabinet. Appointed minister for work and social affairs in October 2009, he resigned after just 33 days, the shortest ever period of ministerial office, after taking responsibility for an air attack in Kunduz (Afghanistan), ordered in 2009, while he was still defense minister; the attack, ordered by a German officer, killed or wounded 142 civilians, including children.

JUNGE UNION (JU). Founded in 1947, the youth wing of the **Christian Democratic Union (CDU)** and the **Christian Social Union (CSU)** (full title: Junge Union Deutschland) is open to nonparty members aged between 14 and 35 and has a total membership of around 120,000. This figure is the largest of the **political parties**, although it has not regained the peak of over 250,000, reached in the early 1980s. Not until the 1970s, when the conservatives were in opposition, did the JU exert a significant influence on the parent organization, for which it acts as a training ground, in particular by building networks and gaining positions of influence. Through its program of basic principles, *Für eine humane Gesellschaft* ("For a human society," 1973) and alliances with other party associations, the union contributed to the process of internal reform and modernization in which the CDU was engaged. The JU's long-standing chairman, Philipp Mißfelder (from 2002), was succeeded by Paul Ziemiak in 2014.

K

KANT, HERMANN (1926–2016). Writer. Born in **Hamburg**, the son of a gardener, Hermann Kant trained as an electrician. Conscripted toward the end of World War II, he was captured by the Soviet Army and, as a prisoner in Poland, cofounded an antifascist committee. He returned to the **German Democratic Republic (GDR)** in 1949 and joined the **Socialist Unity Party of Germany (SED)**. After completing his higher school **education** (1949–1952), he studied German at Humboldt University in East **Berlin** (1952–1956), earning a doctorate (1957).

Kant began his writing career with a collection of short stories (*Ein bißchen Südsee*) in 1962 and established his reputation in both East and West Germany with the novel *Die Aula* (1965). Vice president (from 1969) and president (1978–1989) of the Schriftstellerverband of the GDR, the official East German writers' organization, Kant was an active supporter of the regime and played a role in the expulsion of several authors. He served in the **People's Chamber** (1981–1990) and was a member of the Central Committee of the SED (1986–1989). He received several literary awards (including the Heinrich Heine Prize of the East German Academy of Arts [1963], the Heinrich Mann Prize [1967], and the GDR National Prize for Art and Literature [1983]) and was honored by the GDR and the Soviet Union. During the GDR period, he also wrote the novels *Das Impressum* (1972) and *Der Aufenthalt* (1976, filmed in 1983), and the short story collection *Der dritte Nagel* (1981). From 1959 to 1962, he edited the literary journal *Neue Deutsche Literatur*, which alongside *Sinn und Form* was the GDR's most important journal of its kind. First established in 1952, its publication after reunification in 1990 was taken over from the then dissolved Schriftstellerverband by the Aufbau publishing house.

After reunification, Kant refused to regard artists expelled from the Schriftstellerverband as victims and successfully prosecuted allegations that he was an agent of the GDR secret police, the **Stasi**. He resigned from the East German **PEN** Club (1991) and the **Academy of Arts** (1992), but continued to publish. His later works include his autobiography (*Abspann*, 1991) and the novels *Komoran* (1994), *Okarina* (2002), and *Kino* (2005), and in

2015, the narrative *Ein strenges Spiel*. Kant is representative of the ongoing debates about individuals' involvement with the state and issues of retrospective assessments.

KAUDER, VOLKER (1949–). Lawyer and **Christian Democratic Union (CDU)** politician. Born in Sinsheim **(Baden-Württemberg)**, the son of expellees from Serbia in the former Yugoslavia and a member of the youth wing **(Junge Union, JU)** of the CDU from 1966, Volker Kauder studied law and political science at the University of Freiburg (1971–1975) and worked in the internal administration section of the state of Baden-Württemberg (1975–1980) before becoming a deputy regional councilor (Landrat) for the district of Tuttlingen (1980–1990). After occupying various positions in the local CDU, Kauder entered the **Bundestag** (1990) and served as honorary general secretary of the regional party (1991–2005). A close confidant of **Erwin Teufel, minister president** of Baden-Württemberg, Kauder was highly regarded as an organizer of electoral campaigns. In the Bundestag, he specialized in social and labor issues and was particularly interested in the care of the mentally ill. Although Kauder supported **Edmund Stoiber** as chancellor candidate in the latter's contest with **Angela Merkel** (2002), he gained Merkel's trust as the party's parliamentary business manager (2002–2005), notably in coordinating the CDU/**Christian Social Union (CSU)**–ruled **federal states** in the **Bundesrat**. In January 2005, he succeeded **Laurenz Meyer** as general secretary of the national CDU (until December 2005) and in November 2005 took over from Merkel as leader of the CDU/CSU parliamentary group, a position he has retained (2015) longer than any other CDU politician since 1949. A traditional conservative (he opposed the right of adoption for homosexual couples, the equality of traditionally married and same sex partnerships for **tax** benefits, and recognition of Islam as an integral part of German culture), he is credited with having considerable influence with Chancellor Merkel on ethical issues.

KELLY, PETRA (1947–2002). Green Party politician. Petra Kelly was born Petra Karin Lehmann in 1947 in Günzburg **(Bavaria)**. After her mother married a U.S. army officer (John E. Kelly), the family moved to the United States (1960), where Petra completed her schooling. She studied political science and world politics at the American University in Washington, graduating with a bachelor's degree (1966–1970), and subsequently taught at the university. As a student, she organized political seminars, demonstrated against racial discrimination and the Vietnam War, and worked in the offices of Senators Robert Kennedy and Hubert Humphrey during their presidential election campaigns (1968). In 1970–1971, she returned to Europe and completed a master's degree in politics at the University of Amsterdam. At the same time, she worked as a research assistant at the Europa Institute before becoming a civil servant at the Commission of the **European Union (EU)** in Brussels.

Kelly joined the ecologically oriented citizens' rights group Bundesverband Bürgerinitiativen Umweltschutz (Federation of Citizens' Initiatives for Environmental Protection, BBU) and between 1972 and 1979 was active in various political groups in Germany, Europe, and the United States, campaigning on the **environment**, civil rights, **women**'s issues, and world peace. Following her stepsister's death from cancer in 1973, she founded an association supporting research into cancer in children (G. P. Kelly-Vereinigung zur Unterstützung der Krebsforschung für Kinder e.V./G. P. Kelly Foundation for the Support of Research into Child Cancer). In 1979, she left the **Social Democratic Party of Germany (SPD)** and joined the executive board of the BBU, with responsibility for international links. In 1979–1980, she cofounded the German Green Party and in 1980 was elected coleader (speaker) alongside August Haußleiter and Norbert Mann, a position she held until 1982, when she withdrew in accordance with the party's rotation principle. Kelly was the most prominent of the 27 Green members to enter the **Bundestag** following the national election of March 1983. Reelected in 1987, she held the seat until 1990. During this period, she was a member of the parliamentary party's Sprecherrat (speakers' council) from 1983, served on committees for **foreign policy**, and took part in public demonstrations for international peace. Her maiden speech in the Bundestag was on **human rights** violations in Tibet (October 1987). In February 1987, she attended the Moscow Peace Forum, where she met Andrei Sakharov and the Soviet leader Mikhail Gorbachev.

In 1985, Kelly moved to Bonn with her partner and colleague Gert Bastian, a former **Bundeswehr** general. By this time her position in the party had weakened, and she received only 30 votes when standing as party leader (speaker) in April 1991. Although she campaigned vigorously against division within the party and for it to retain its grassroots orientation to fundamental green and human rights issues (she was especially concerned about the aborigines in Australia, the North American Indians, and Tibet), she was seen increasingly as a lone idealist. In February 1992, she began moderating the **television** program *Fünf vor Zwölf*, which dealt with environmental affairs. On 1 October 1992 in Bonn, Bastian apparently shot the sleeping Petra Kelly before committing suicide (the bodies were discovered three weeks later). In 1993, the author and feminist **Alice Schwarzer**, who knew the couple well, published a book (*Eine tödliche Liebe: Petra Kelly und Gert Bastian*) suggesting that Petra Kelly might not have wished to die. Kelly received the Alternative Nobel Peace Prize (1982) and the Woman of the Year award from the U.S. group Women Strike for Peace (1983). The Petra-

Kelly Stiftung (Petra Kelly Foundation), based in Munich and with an office in northern **Bavaria**, was established in 1997 to preserve her ideas and political legacy.

KEßLER, HEINZ (1920–). German Democratic Republic of Germany (GDR) politician. Born in 1920 in Lauban (Silesia, now in Poland), Heinz Keßler trained and worked as a toolmaker (1934–1940) before serving in World War II. A young communist, he deserted to the Soviet Army in 1941 and trained in the Soviet Antifaschule (Anti-Fascist School) before serving as a political officer on the eastern front. Returning to (eastern) Germany after the war, he joined the Communist Party of Germany (KPD) in 1945 and in 1946 cofounded the youth organization Freie Deutsche Jugend (Free German Youth, FDJ), where he become a close associate of its future leader, **Erich Honecker**. From 1946, he was a member of the party executive and Central Committee of the **Socialist Unity Party of Germany (SED)**, and from 1950 to 1989, sat in the **People's Chamber** of the GDR. After training at the Soviet Air Force Academy (1955–1956), he was appointed deputy to the minister of defense (1957–1967), chief of the air force and later also deputy to the minister in charge of the Nationale Volksarmee (National People's Army, NVA), and a member of the Nationaler Verteidigungsrat (National Defense Council). From 1976 until 1979, he served as deputy commander in chief of the combined forces of the **Warsaw Pact**. In 1985, Keßler succeeded Heinz Hoffmann (1910–1985) as defense minister and was appointed a general in the NVA. The following year, he became a full member of the Politburo of the SED.

In November 1989, Keßler resigned all posts and was investigated by a parliamentary committee for misuse of office, corruption, and personal enrichment, although no charges ensued. In January 1990, he was expelled from the SED/**Party of Democratic Socialism (PDS)**. Detained in 1991 pending investigation for complicity in the shoot-to-kill policy at the border between the GDR and the Federal Republic of Germany (FRG), he was sentenced in 1993 to seven and one-half years' imprisonment but released after four and one-half years on grounds of age, health, and good conduct.

KIEP, WALTHER LEISLER (1926–2016). Christian Democratic Union (CDU) politician. Born in **Hamburg**, Walther Leisler Kiep studied history and economics, trained in business and commerce with the Frankfurt-based Metallgesellschaft AG, and worked in the United States for the Insurance Company of North America (1948–1955) before joining the insurance brokers Gradmann & Haller in Frankfurt/Main as executive partner (1955). A member of the CDU from 1961, he represented the party in the **Bundestag** (1965–1976, 1980–1982). An independent-minded parliamentarian, he supported **Ostpolitik** and defied the majority of his own party in voting to ratify the Basic Treaty on Relations (Grundlagenvertrag). Kiep held various positions in the CDU, including membership in the **Hessen** presidium and treasurer (1967–1976), national treasurer and presidium member (1971–1992), and economics spokesman for the parliamentary group. He was regional finance minister for **Lower Saxony** under **Ernst Albrecht** (CDU, 1976–1980) and in 1980 served in the shadow cabinet of chancellor candidate **Franz Josef Strauß**. In the Hamburg regional election of June 1982, Kiep led the CDU to a historic electoral success, forcing the **Social Democratic Party of Germany** (**SPD**) into second place, although he was unable to form a ruling coalition.

As party treasurer, Kiep attracted negative headlines over the financial scandal surrounding **Friedrich Karl Flick** during the 1980s. Accused of aiding and abetting **tax** evasion (May 1990), he was fined 650,000 DM, although his conviction was rescinded on appeal (October 1992), and he resigned as party treasurer, a post he had held for 21 years. Despite the affair, Kiep enjoyed a high standing in the CDU and was respected for his negotiating skills and for his political and financial contacts with the United States. He continued to be responsible for U.S.–German relations within the CDU, served as president of the private European Business School (1994–2000), and was engaged by Chancellor **Gerhard Schröder** as a special envoy on foreign missions (from July 1999). Disclosure of Kiep's involvement in tax evasion and the subsequent legal proceedings (November 1999) marked the beginning of a series of revelations that plunged the CDU and its leadership into the most serious financial scandal of its history.

Kiep published several books, such as *Goodbye America: Was dann?* (1972), *A New Challenge for Western Europe* (1974), and *Was bleibt ist große Zuversicht* (1999), and his awards include an honorary doctorate from the Freiberg Technical University of Mining (1997) and the Federal Cross of Merit. In the 1980s and 1990s, he sat on the boards of various companies and organizations and was chairman of Atlantik-Brücke (1984–2000), an association dedicated to improving U.S.–German links.

KIESINGER, KURT GEORG (1904–1988). Christian Democratic Union (CDU) politician and **federal chancellor**, 1966–1969. Kurt Georg Kiesinger was born in Ebingen (**Baden-Württemberg**). His mother died soon after he was born, and he grew up with six children from his father's previous marriage. With the financial support of a friend of his father, Kiesinger studied philosophy and history at the University of Tübingen (1925) before changing to law and politics in **Berlin** (1926–1931), where he subsequently worked as a lawyer (from 1935). A member of the National Socialist Party from 1933 to 1945, Kiesinger worked as a research assistant in the radio broadcasting department of the foreign ministry (from 1940) and later as its deputy head (from 1943). Evidence later emerged that he had attempted to block anti-**Jewish** measures. On release from Allied internment (1945–1946), Kiesinger ran a revision school for law students at the University of Würzburg. After being cleared of complicity in the National Socialist regime (1948), he worked as a lawyer in Tübingen and Würzburg.

A member of the CDU from 1946, Kiesinger represented the party in the **Bundestag** (1949–1959), successfully chairing the **mediation committee** of the Bundestag/**Bundesrat** (1950–1957) and developing a reputation as a gifted speaker. He was a member of the parliamentary executive committee of the CDU (from 1950) and chaired the Bundestag foreign affairs committee (1954–1958). Although widely regarded as ministerial material (he himself coveted the post of foreign minister and strongly supported Germany's integration into Western Europe), he was repeatedly passed over by **Konrad Adenauer**. Neither was he successful in two candidacies for the presidency of the Bundestag (1951 and 1954).

Kiesinger's political fortunes improved as **minister president** of **Baden-Württemberg** (1958–1966), where he concentrated on cultural policy, founded a number of new universities (Constance, Ulm, and Mannheim), and staged lavish receptions for foreign visitors, including Queen Elizabeth II. In December 1966, he took over from **Ludwig Erhard** as federal chancellor to form a **grand coalition** with the **Social Democratic Party of Germany** (**SPD**), which lasted until October 1969.

Although the CDU emerged as the strongest party in the 1969 election, the SPD and **Free Democratic Party** (**FDP**) formed a ruling coalition with **Willy Brandt** as chancellor. Thereafter Kiesinger, who was elected CDU chairman in 1967, lost influence in his party. During his period of office, he was repeatedly attacked over his membership in the National Socialist Party and activities during the Nazi regime. He resigned as CDU chairman in 1971 but remained in the Bundestag until 1980.

KINKEL, KLAUS (1936–). Free Democratic Party (FDP) politician. Born in Metzingen (**Baden-Württemberg**), Klaus Kinkel studied law at the universities of Tübingen, Bonn, and Cologne (1956–1960), passing his state law examinations (1960, 1965) and earning a doctorate in 1964. After working in various federal offices (1965–1970), he became personal assistant to and subsequently head of the staff office of Interior Minister **Hans-Dietrich Genscher** (1970–1974). In 1974, Kinkel moved to the Federal Ministry for Foreign Affairs, where he was responsible for management (until 1977) and planning (until 1979). From 1979 until 1982, he was president of the **Federal Intelligence Service** (Bundesnachrichtendienst) before being appointed **state secretary** in the federal justice ministry (until 1991). A member of the FDP from 1991 and of the **Bundestag** from 1994, Kinkel was briefly minister of justice (1991–1992), then was elected national chairman of the executive committee of the FDP. He also served as foreign minister under Chancellor **Helmut Kohl** (May 1992–October 1998) and as vice-chancellor (1993–1998). As deputy chancellor and also leader (1993–1995) of the FDP, Kinkel was widely regarded as the public face of the party, which he saw as primarily representing the interests of business. Although Kinkel enjoyed broad respect for his ability and liberal views, the FDP suffered catastrophic regional electoral results during the 1990s, and he was compelled to take a back seat under the coalition of **Social Democratic Party of Germany (SPD)** and the **Green Party**, which came to power in 1998. Kinkel led the FDP parliamentary group from 1998 until 2002, when he left the Bundestag to practice law.

KIRCH, LEO (1926–2011). Media entrepreneur. Born in 1926, the son of a wine producer, Leo Kirch grew up in the Franconian village of Fahr near Volkach (**Bavaria**). After studying business administration and mathematics in Würzburg and Munich, Kirch earned a doctorate on the influence of geography on transport in 1952 before working as a research assistant at the University of Munich. During the 1950s, he began to buy up films, selling the performance rights to cinemas. In 1956, he founded his first company, Sirius-Film GmbH. Kirch's film collection steadily expanded over the years and formed the basis of what became one of the largest and most comprehensive **cinema** and **television** film libraries in the world. Housed in the Munich suburb of Unterföhring, it held an estimated 15,000 television films and 50,000 television series productions.

Kirch achieved his first major business coup in Rome in 1956, when he acquired the rights to Fellini's *La Strada*, which became a European cinema classic. Rights to the Howard Hughes/RKO film library followed in 1969. To market his collection, he founded Beta Film (1959), which became the largest film licensing concern outside the United States. In 1963, he created TaurusFilm as the center of his operations, which included producing films for cinema and television after 1968. Subsequently rebranded as KirchMedia, the organization established itself as a global leader in providing free-from-air television, trading film rights, and making and distributing new films; it also became deeply involved in all aspects of new media, including technology and software. In 1966, he founded Unitel, dedicated to the production of high-quality classical music programs.

During the 1980s, Kirch took advantage of personal links with a conservative administration committed to the deregulation of broadcasting to extend his interests in television. He pioneered private free-from-air services (financed through advertising) and pay-TV (financed by viewers' subscriptions) and transformed the German media landscape into the most varied in Europe. By the middle of the decade, the Munich-based Kirch Group (Kirch-Gruppe) dominated private television in Germany. In 2000, the channels

ProSieben (launched in 1989 and now often written as Pro7) and Sat 1 merged to form the largest private television concern in Germany. Known as ProSiebenSat.1 Media AG, this comprised the four channels Sat 1, ProSieben, Kabel 1, and N24 (all financed via advertising revenue), with KirchMedia as the major shareholder. The **sports** channel Premiere World, the successor to Premiere (launched in 1990), led the digital pay-TV market. In 2001, the group acquired the European broadcasting rights for the Fédération International de Football Association (FIFA) soccer championships in 2002 (Canada) and 2006 (Italy). It also had a majority shareholding in SLEC Holding, which owned the rights to run Formula One racing for 99 years. Premiere World became the major funder and broadcaster of the German national soccer league, whose first division players enjoyed generous transfer fees. In 1996, Kirch was honored in Cannes as the most outstanding media personality of the previous 40 years.

In 2002, the structure of the Kirch Group (KirchGruppe) was highly complex, comprising some 65 separate operations, companies, and major shareholdings. Overarching everything was the Kirch Unternehmensstiftung (Kirch Foundation), owned and controlled by the Kirch family. Such a complex network of mergers and cross-ownership fueled concerns about very large, monopolistic "mediamulti" corporations. Kirch, however, proved adept at exploiting partnerships and holdings and in using family members to circumvent fairly lax state media laws designed to counter excessive concentration. Moreover, the state of Bavaria was keen to house and finance the group's operation in order to reap the economic and political benefits of providing a home to a global commercial media corporation. By late 2001, however, it was clear that the Kirch Group was in serious financial difficulties. As the world economy entered recession and advertising revenue fell, the huge investments made in sports broadcasting rights failed to deliver the anticipated returns, and the concern ran up large debts. In April 2002, the core concern (KirchMedia) was declared bankrupt. In the run-up to the 2002 national election, various aspects of the Kirch concern became political issues, including the close relationship between Kirch and the Bavarian state government, the prospect of large job losses, and the implications of half of Germany's commercial television ending up in foreign ownership as the group was broken up. To maintain his empire, Kirch had relied heavily on a network of connections and personal friendships with conservative politicians, including **Edmund Stoiber** and **Helmut Kohl**. In August 2004, the creditors' committee of the insolvent ProSiebenSat.1 agreed to sell to the American Israeli Haim Saban, who also purchased the film library. The deal, which cost Saban and his partners $1,300 million, represented the largest ever foreign investment in German media. Although the group itself ceased to exist, many of its operations (film, sport, television, and media services) were incorporated into Constantin Medien AG, also based in Munich. Until his death, Kirch engaged in a fierce legal battle with the **Deutsche Bank**, whose former chief executive, **Rolf Breuer**, he accused of bringing about his bankruptcy and the collapse of his concern; the dispute dragged on until 2014, when the bank reached a settlement with Kirch's heirs.

KLOSE, HANS-ULRICH (1937–). Social Democratic Party of Germany (SPD) politician. Hans-Ulrich Klose was born in Breslau, in a family that was expelled from Silesia after World War II and resettled in Bielefeld (**Lower Saxony**). After studying law in Freiburg and **Hamburg**, Klose qualified in 1965 and worked as a state lawyer in Hamburg until 1968. After joining the SPD (1964) and engaging in local politics, he entered the Hamburg parliament (1970), where he chaired the SPD parliamentary group (from 1972), served as minister (senator) for internal affairs (1973), and was elected city mayor (1974–1981). In the regional election of 1978 the SPD, led by Klose, gained an absolute majority in the assembly. Its former coalition partner, the **Free Democratic Party (FDP)**, failed to pass the 5 percent hurdle.

Politically left of center in a city parliament traditionally dominated by the right wing of the SPD, Klose attracted criticism in 1978 by arguing for a relaxation of the so-called **radicals decree** (Radikalenerlass), which had been passed in 1972 to exclude political extremists from public service. As mayor, he oversaw a scandal involving the discovery of a large quantity of poisons and explosive material at the Hamburg company Stoltzenberg (1979). He also handled a long-running dispute over the future of the broadcasting station Norddeutscher Rundfunk (NDR), which was finally settled when the states of Hamburg, **Schleswig-Holstein**, and Lower Saxony agreed to a joint treaty that secured its continuation (1980). During 1980–1981, Klose was forced to reconsider his policy on nuclear **energy** when mass protests over the building of an atomic power station at Brokdorf prompted the Hamburg SPD to oppose the regional party's decision to support the project. Klose resigned as mayor, but retained his seat in the assembly until he entered the **Bundestag** in the 1983 national election. He joined the executive committee of the SPD parliamentary group (1983) and was elected to the national committee (1984). A specialist in Latin American issues, he served on the parliamentary committee for economic cooperation. Supported by **Oskar Lafontaine**, Klose became party treasurer in 1987 and did much to place the SPD on a sound financial footing.

Regarded as an independent thinker in the SPD, Klose was one of the first senior party members to condemn the Sandinistas in Nicaragua and to support military action by the western allies during the Gulf War (1990–1991); he also came out more strongly for German reunification than many of his colleagues. As chairman of the SPD's parliamentary group (1991–1994), he improved its efficiency by reducing the number of working groups. Occasionally at odds with his own party, he was widely censured for calling for a ballot of all party members in order to choose the chancellor candidate (1991) and for supporting more flexible working hours and practices (1992). Many saw him as too accommodating when he led interparty negotiations over changes to the **asylum** law. He also found himself in a minority over his willingness to allow German forces to take part in any **United Nations** (**UN**)–approved operations, including those requiring the use of arms, when the SPD challenged the government's decision to commit German troops to Somalia in the **Federal Constitutional Court** (**FCC**) in 1993 (the party subsequently moved closer to Klose's position). Neither did his party welcome his declaration of support for nuclear energy if a demonstrably safe reactor could be developed or his call for restructuring the social welfare state. As vice president of the Bundestag (1994–1998), Klose argued for a reform of parliament, including a reduction of its size and a review of members' salary levels. He served as chairman, then deputy chairman, of the Bundestag parliamentary committee on foreign affairs (1998–2002, 2002–2013) and led the assembly's German-American group (2003–2013); he was also coordinator of transatlantic cooperation at the foreign ministry (2010–2011). Klose has published on political and social issues.

KLUNCKER, HEINZ (1925–2005). Trade union leader. Heinz Kluncker was born in Wuppertal (**North Rhine-Westfalia**), the son of a locksmith/ metalworker, and developed an early sympathy for social democracy. After training as a textile wholesaler (1942), he was conscripted into the German army (1943) and spent two years in British and U.S. captivity. He returned to Germany in 1946, joined the **Social Democratic Party of Germany** (**SPD**) in Wuppertal, and worked for the local party until October 1949, when he moved to **Hamburg** to study economics, sociology, and law at a trade union–sponsored academy (the Akademie für Gemeinwirtschaft/Academy for Social Economy, later incorporated into the University of Hamburg). He graduated in 1951 and the following year began working for the public service and transport union Öffentliche Dienste, Transport, und Verkehr (ÖTV).

Specializing in collective bargaining and wage negotiations, Kluncker rose rapidly in the ÖTV, joining the executive board (1961) and chairing it from 1964 to 1982. In 1964, he became a member of the national executive board of the Deutscher Gewerkschaftsbund (German Federation of Trade Unions, DGB). Not widely known outside trade union circles in the early years, Kluncker restructured the ÖTV, modernized its internal decision-making processes, and improved its public image. Under his leadership, the ÖTV became one of the first unions to develop contacts with workers' organizations in the eastern bloc during the 1960s, despite the friction this caused with fellow labor leaders in the United States. One of Kluncker's achievements was the agreement in 1965 by the federal defense ministry that professional and part-time soldiers could join a trade union. In 1973–1974, the ÖTV fought a bitter struggle with government and public sector employers, finally settling for an 11 percent wage increase after demanding a 15 percent rise and holding a brief strike (February 1974). Kluncker's victory was widely perceived as contributing to the downfall of Chancellor **Willy Brandt**, who had argued strongly against inflationary wage increases. Further milestones in Kluncker's career included agreements on a 40–hour week (reduced from 42) in 1972 and on 13 months' annual pay (from September 1973).

Regarded as one of Germany's most powerful union leaders during the 1970s, Kluncker occupied prominent positions in international labor organizations, including vice president of the International Transport Workers' Federation (ITWF, 1971–1978) and president of the international trade union federation Public Services International (PSI, 1971, 1977, 1981). At home, he argued vigorously for structural reforms in the German labor movement, stressing the need to consolidate through mergers. His final major success, achieved in April 1982 in the teeth of political and **media** hostility, was a wage increase (of 3.6 percent) for his membership at a time when public sector **budgets** were in crisis and employers were threatening a reduction in pay. Two months later, Kluncker unexpectedly resigned as ÖTV leader and from the DGB national executive for health reasons, although he continued to chair the PSI until November 1985 (the PSI subsequently elected him honorary life president). During his retirement, Kluncker helped establish trade unions in developing countries and campaigned for workers' freedoms and rights throughout the world. He lectured regularly in the United States and in 1988 spent four months as a fellow at the institute of politics at Harvard University. He served on the program commission for the SPD in **Baden-Württemberg** (1985) and chaired the party's council of seniors (1990–1995), which entitled him to an advisory seat on the national executive board.

KNOBLOCH, CHARLOTTE (1932–). Jewish community leader. Born the daughter of Fritz Neumann, a lawyer in Munich, Charlotte Knobloch survived the National Socialist regime when she was adopted as the "illegitimate daughter" of a farming family in Herrieden (Franconia). Her grandmother perished in Auschwitz, although her father survived as a forced laborer and returned to Munich in 1945, where he was elected president of the small Jewish community. After training in commerce in Munich, Charlotte married the businessman Samuel Knobloch. The couple, who planned to emigrate to the United States, stayed in Germany after the birth of their son (two more children followed). She became active in local Jewish affairs, looking after older members and taking an interest in social issues, and was elected president of the Munich community in 1985. Under her energetic 20-

year leadership, the community expanded to around 9,000 (2005), built a new Jewish center (the largest of its kind in Europe), and integrated many incomers from the former Soviet Union. She was also treasurer of the Jüdischer Frauenbund in Deutschland (Jewish Women's Federation in Germany, JFB) and cofounded the Women's International Zionist Organization (WIZO) in Germany. Elected the first woman president of the **Central Council of Jews in Germany** in June 2006, Knobloch declared her priorities as strengthening Jews' sense of identity in Germany, combating **anti-Semitism**, and integrating Jewish **immigrants**. When her presidency of the council expired, she did not stand for reelection, which was widely attributed to her having lost the confidence of other council members and having undermined the body's political stature during her tenure. She was forced, for example, to withdraw demands in 2006 to include National Socialism as a separate subject in German schools, while the council had argued for it to be integrated into the range of existing subjects. Her friendly relationship with **Guido Westerwelle** of the **Free Democratic Party** (**FDP**) on an official visit to Israel in November 2009 also angered **Jews** who recalled that Westerwelle had not apologized for his deputy, **Jürgen Möllemann**, for making remarks critical of Israel during the 2002 national election campaign.

KOCH, ROLAND (1958–). Lawyer and **Christian Democratic Union** (**CDU**) politician. Roland Koch was born in Frankfurt/Main and grew up in Eschborn/**Hessen** (where he still lives). His father, Karl-Heinz Koch, was a lawyer, deputy in the Hessen state parliament (**Landtag**), and justice minister under **Walter Wallmann**, **minister president** of Hessen (1987–1991). Roland Koch studied law, qualified in 1985, and ran a commercial law practice in Eschborn (1985–1999). At age 14, he founded a branch of the youth wing (**Junge Union, JU**) of the CDU in Eschborn and, after joining the main party (1974), became the youngest district party leader (for Taunus-Main, 1979–1991). Rising swiftly in the regional party, he served as deputy leader of the national JU (1983–1987) before entering the Hessen regional assembly in 1987. He also chaired the party group in the district assembly (1989–1997), led the CDU group in the Hessen Landtag (1990–1991, 1993–99), and was elected regional party chairman and a member of the national party presidium (1998).

Following regional elections in February 1999, Koch became minister president for Hessen, heading a coalition of the CDU and **Free Democratic Party** (**FDP**) with a parliamentary majority of just two seats. His campaign call for a public petition opposing the proposals by the **federal government** to allow dual citizenship as part of a new law on **immigration** was endorsed by the national CDU, but it made race an election issue and was widely seen as an appeal to populist nationalistic elements. In 2000, he survived a financial scandal involving undeclared donations to the party, partly because it was overshadowed by revelations of corruption in the CDU at the national level and partly because his predecessor, Manfred Kanther, absolved Koch of any knowledge of the affair. In 2001, Koch was accused of misusing his position when he arranged for the judiciary to search the office and private rooms of the biographer of Foreign Minister **Joschka Fischer** in the hope of finding material incriminating Fischer in extremist activities during the 1960s. As minister president, Koch maintained links with big business and claimed to have reduced the number of crimes in the state by introducing part-time policemen and greater security surveillance. Compared with national levels, unemployment in Hessen fell after he combined social and unemployment benefits and withdrew benefits from unemployed persons who refused work from the regional job centers. He also increased the number of teachers to counter a crisis in lost class hours in schools.

In the 2003 regional election campaign, Koch campaigned for law and order and a stronger role for a better armed Germany in European and world politics, and opposed admitting Turkey or Russia into the **European Union (EU)** on the grounds that Europe should remain a community of Western Christian nations. Despite making controversial remarks two months before the election, in which he compared criticism of wealthy Germans with persecution of the **Jews** under the National Socialists, Koch led the CDU to an overall majority in the regional state parliament, enabling his party to rule without a coalition. Koch pledged to employ more teachers, shorten the period of study for the higher school certificate from 13 to 12 years, and introduce standard examinations across the state. He also promised measures to strengthen Frankfurt's position as an international financial center and in 2003 criticized opponents of plans to sell the mothballed Hanau nuclear power station to China, describing the decision to close the plant in the 1980s as "madness." The CDU lost its overall majority in the 2008 election, but formed a ruling coalition with the FDP as minister president after fresh elections the following year, called after the failure of the SPD and **Green Party** to agree on a government (during the interim period, Koch continued as caretaker minister president, although the university tuition fees he had introduced were abolished). In 2010, Koch suddenly withdrew from politics to head the building and services company Bilfinger (from July 2011), although he resigned in August 2014 following a dramatic fall in profits and share values. Regarded as a staunchly provincial politician, Koch also served as deputy leader of the CDU (2006–2011) and has published books on his conservative values (*Gemeinsam Chancen nutzen* and *Beim Wort genommen*, 2002; *Konservativ: Ohne Werte und Prinzipien ist kein Staat zu machen*, 2010).

KOHL, HELMUT (1930–). Christian Democratic Union (CDU) politician and **federal chancellor**, 1982–1998. Helmut Kohl was born in Ludwigshafen (**Baden-Württemberg**), the youngest of three children, into a middle-class, Roman Catholic family. Kohl was 15 when World War II ended and was deeply affected by the death of his 19-year-old brother, who was killed on the western front. He studied law, social sciences, politics, and history at the universities of Frankfurt/Main and Heidelberg (1950–1956) before working as an assistant at the Alfred Weber Institute for political science at Heidelberg (1956–1958) and completing a doctorate (1958). After a brief spell as management assistant at an iron smelting works in Ludwigshafen (1958–1959), he worked as a consultant for the association of **chemical** industries in Ludwigshafen (1959–1969). Kohl joined the CDU in 1946 and cofounded its youth wing in Ludwigshafen (1947). Rising through the party ranks, he served as a member of the state parliament (**Landtag**) for **Rhineland-Palatinate** (1959–1976), where he was deputy leader (from 1961) and then leader of the CDU parliamentary group (from 1963) before becoming **minister president** (1969–1976).

As regional premier, Kohl, who ruled with an absolute majority after 1971, initiated a comprehensive reform of administrative districts and, with **Heiner Geißler**, restructured the state's social welfare and **health** systems. After unsuccessfully challenging **Rainer Barzel** for the CDU leadership in 1971, he was elected party chairman in 1973 (until 1998) and chancellor candidate in 1975. In 1976, Kohl resigned as minister president of Rhineland-Palatinate to enter the **Bundestag** and take over leadership of the CDU/**Christian Social Union (CSU)** parliamentary group in opposition. During these early years, Kohl was a powerful modernizing and unifying force in his party. One of his first tasks after the lost election of 1976 was to prevent the CSU, led by **Franz Josef Strauß**, splitting from the CDU. After the CDU lost the 1980 election, this time heavily and with Strauß as its chancellor candidate, Kohl cultivated links with the government coalition partner, the **Free Democratic Party (FDP)**.

In October 1982, the CDU, together with members of the FDP, brought down Chancellor **Helmut Schmidt** in a controversial constructive vote of no confidence that resulted in Kohl leading a new conservative–liberal coalition. Two months later, Kohl engineered a constitutionally dubious vote of no confidence in his own chancellorship, in which his supporters abstained in order to force the dissolution of parliament and fresh elections. The electoral victory that followed (March 1983), together with further wins in 1997, 1990, and 1994, resulted in Kohl becoming the longest serving federal chancellor since Otto von Bismarck (Reichskanzler from 1871 until 1890). Between 1982 and 1990, his government regained control of the domestic budget, reduced inflation, and revived a faltering economy. Opposing the peace movement and supporting a firm stance by the **North Atlantic Treaty Or-**

ganization (**NATO**) against the Union of Soviet Socialist Republics (USSR), Kohl succeeded in maintaining friendly but pragmatic relations with the **German Democratic Republic (GDR)**. He also used his personal relationship with French President François Mitterrand to deepen integration of the **European Union (EU)**. While Kohl focused more on domestic issues, his deputy and foreign minister, **Hans-Dietrich Genscher** (FDP), became a respected figure on the international stage.

The crowning point of Kohl's political career occurred in the fall of the GDR regime in late 1989, when he seized the opportunity to reunite East and West Germany. Sensing the mood of the people, especially in the east, and overcoming reservations about the speed and terms of economic and political union, he expedited the key treaties that merged the systems of both states and secured a united Germany within the framework of the EU and NATO. In the postreunification decade, Germany reinstated **Berlin** as its capital—a move Kohl supported—contributed to international peacekeeping operations in the former Yugoslavia and Somalia, set up a 50,000-strong combined army brigade with France, and committed to European monetary union. But despite the "chancellor's bonus" of reunification, Kohl's popularity declined after 1994 as the true costs of taking over the GDR emerged, the eastern German economy failed to prosper, and unemployment (especially in the east) rose to record levels (over four million in 1995). A combination of social and economic problems resulted in the CDU losing the national election of 1998.

Helmut Kohl was widely honored, both nationally and internationally, for his contribution to European integration and German reunification. In addition to receiving several honorary doctorates, he was made an honorary citizen of the EU (1998, a distinction shared only with Jean Monnet) and was awarded the Grand Cross of the Federal Republic with laurel wreath, an honor hitherto bestowed only on **Konrad Adenauer**. Low points during Kohl's period of office included a dispute with Israel over proposed arms sales to Saudi Arabia (1984); controversy surrounding his laying a wreath at the military cemetery in Bitburg, where SS soldiers were buried (1985); and accusations that he withheld information from parliamentary committees investigating illegal political donations (involving the industrialist **Friedrich Karl Flick**). At one point, he also drew an unfortunate parallel between the Soviet leader Mikhail Gorbachev and the National Socialist propaganda minister Josef Goebbels (1986).

Most damagingly of all, Kohl finally admitted in late 1999 that between 1993 and 1998 he had accepted illegal party donations totaling two million DM. It was further alleged that he was involved in providing political and commercial favors when the government approved the sale of armored vehicles to Saudi Arabia and of an eastern German oil refinery to the French concern Elf Aquitaine. In 2000, public prosecutors began an investigation.

Although Kohl acknowledged personal mistakes in the management of his party's accounts and apologized for lack of transparency, he refused to reveal the sources of anonymous donations and was obliged to resign as honorary party chairman in early 2000. From 2001 onward, he was also engaged in a legal battle to prevent the release of files which the East German **Stasi** had compiled on him. The 7,000 pages, based partly on illegal phone taps, were believed to shed light on his role in the corruption scandal. In June 2004, a Leipzig court ruled that files relating to his private life should remain classified but granted limited access to information on his political activities (Kohl himself had accessed his files in September 2000).

As federal chancellor and party leader, Kohl built up over many years a network based on personal links and patronage that, combined with his strict control over the party machinery, excluded potential rivals. As a result, the demise of the "Kohl system" in 1998 left a political vacuum, which the CDU found difficult to fill, although he provided the springboard for **Angela Merkel**'s career. His memoirs (*Erinnerungen 1930–1982* and *Erinnerungen 1982–1990*) appeared in 2004–2005.

KÖHLER, HORST (1943–). Economist, banker, and **President of the Federal Republic**, 2004–2010. Horst Köhler was born in Skierbieszów (Poland), the son of a landworker. His family, who originated in Romania and moved to Poland during World War II, fled with their eight children from the advancing Soviet Army to Leipzig. They moved again in 1953 to settle in Ludwigsburg (**Baden-Württemberg**). Köhler studied economics and political science at the University of Tübingen (1965–1969), earning a doctorate (1977). After working as a research assistant at the Institute for Applied Economic Research at the university (1969–1976), he occupied various civil service and government posts (1976–1989) in economics and finance, at both the national and (in **Schleswig-Holstein**) regional levels. A member of the **Christian Democratic Union (CDU)** since 1981, Köhler worked under finance minister **Gerhard Stoltenberg** (1982–1987) and succeeded **Hans Tietmeyer** as **state secretary** in the Federal Ministry of Finance, with responsibility for monetary relations and international financial aid (1990–1993). He was lead negotiator for Germany on the Maastricht Treaty (which created the single European **currency**), was closely involved in the economic and financial aspects of reunification (including agreeing on payments to Russia in return for the withdrawal of troops from German soil), and acted as "sherpa" (adviser) to Chancellor **Helmut Kohl** at a series of G7 summits (Houston 1990, London 1991, Munich 1992, and Tokyo 1993).

In 1993, Köhler left government to become president of the Deutsche Sparkassen- und Giroverband (German Savings Bank Association). In 1998, Finance Minister **Theo Waigel (Christian Social Union, CSU)** appointed him president of the London-based European Bank for Reconstruction and

Development. Köhler was credited with turning around the fortunes of the bank following its record of poor investments in the economic regeneration of eastern Europe. As director of the International Monetary Fund (IMF, 2000–2004), he moved the organization away from forcing developing countries to adopt damaging funding strategies designed for advanced economies.

Largely unknown outside financial circles, Köhler surprised the nation in March 2004 when he was nominated by the CDU/CSU and **Free Democratic Party (FDP)** to succeed **Johannes Rau** as president of the Federal Republic. He was elected by the **Federal Assembly** (Bundesversammlung) in May 2004 with a narrow majority. Köhler was Germany's first president not to have a strong background in politics, and his appointment was welcomed in business and financial circles, although less so by **trade unions**, especially after he declared that Germans should accept longer working hours. In the run-up to his election, he argued for a faster pace of economic reform and political decision making and was critical of the lack of direction in U.S. policy in post-invasion Iraq. His veto of bills passed by parliament in 2006— one privatizing Germany's air safety authority, Deutsche Flugsicherung, and another on consumer safety law—was the first in the history of important legislation in the FRG. He also criticized the minimum wage, arguing that it destroyed jobs, and urged the government to press ahead with market and labor reforms. In 2010, he resigned following criticism of his remarks suggesting that Germany's operations in Afghanistan were necessary to protect national economic interests.

See also BANKS.

KRAFT, HANNELORE (1961–). Social Democratic Party of Germany (SPD) politician. Born in Mühlheim on the Ruhr (**North Rhine-Westfalia, NRW**), Hannelore Kraft trained in banking (1980–1982) and studied economics in Duisburg (1982–1998) and at King's College in London (1986–1987) before graduating with a diploma (1989). Between 1989 and 2001, she worked as a business consultant and project leader. She joined the SPD in 1994 and entered the NRW regional parliament (**Landtag**) in 2000, where she was minister for federal and European affairs (2001–2002) and then for science and **research** (2002–2005). Her positions in the party include leader of the regional parliamentary group (2005–2010), regional party leader (2007–), member of the national presidium (2007–), and deputy national leader (2009–). In July 2010, she was elected **minister president** of NRW, heading a minority coalition with the **Green Party**. The coalition continued after elections brought forward in 2012 because of budgetary disputes. As minister president, Kraft argued for the primacy of social welfare policies over **budget** cuts and, in **education**, for replacing the tripartite school system and abolishing fees for nurseries and university students. For the 2013 national election, she was also considered by observers as a possible chancellor candidate, but vehemently rejected the possibility. During 2010–2011, she became the first female president of the **Bundesrat**.

KRAMP-KARRENBAUER, ANNEGRET (1962–). Christian Democratic Union (CDU) politician. Born in Völklingen (**Saarland**), Annegret Kramp-Karrenbauer studied law and politics at the universities of Trier and Saarbrücken (from 1982), graduating with a master's degree (1990). A member of the CDU from 1981 and of the regional **Junge Union (JU)** executive (1985–1988), she represented the main party at the local level before briefly entering the **Bundestag** (March–October 1998). After working in the policy planning unit of the regional CDU (1991–1998), she was elected to the state assembly (**Landtag**), where she was personal assistant and business manager to the parliamentary party (1999–2000). Between 2000 and 2011, she served four times as minister, covering internal affairs, **sports**, family, culture, and work. Her other positions include chair of the regional CDU **women**'s union (Frauenunion, from 1999), vice chair of the national organization (from 2001), member of the national party presidium (from 2010), and regional CDU leader (from 2011). In 2011, she took over from **Peter Müller** as **minister president** of the Saarland, heading a coalition of the CDU, the **Free Democratic Party (FDP)**, and the **Green Party**; she was also justice minister (2011–2012). Following elections in 2012, she concluded a governing coalition with the **Social Democratic Party (SPD)**.

KRENZ, EGON (1937–). German Democratic Republic of Germany (GDR) politician. Egon Krenz was born in Kolberg (now in Poland). In 1944, he moved to Damgarten (**Mecklenburg-West Pomerania**) near the **Baltic** coast. After World War II, he trained as a toolmaker and qualified as a schoolteacher (1953–1957). A member of the East German youth organization Freie Deutsche Jugend (Free German Youth, FDJ) from 1953 and of the **Socialist Unity Party of Germany (SED)** of the GDR from 1955, he rose rapidly in the party hierarchy before becoming secretary of the FDJ's central council, with responsibility for youth work in universities and higher **education**. He studied social sciences in Moscow at the university maintained by the Communist Party of the Soviet Union (1964–1967) and graduated with a diploma (1967) before returning to the FDJ central council, where he was responsible for agitation and propaganda. In 1971, he became head of the Ernst Thälmann organization for young communists. His other offices included membership in the **People's Chamber** of the GDR (1971–1990), the Zentralkomitee (Central Committee) of the SED (from 1973), and the Politburo (from 1983). After serving as a member of the Staatsrat (Council of State, 1981–1984), he took over as deputy chairman (1984–1989).

Krenz's open support for the brutal suppression of the Chinese students' protests in Peking in June 1989 confirmed his reputation as a party hard-liner. Following the fall of his mentor **Erich Honecker** (18 October 1989), he served briefly as general secretary of the SED and as head of the Council of State and the Nationaler Verteidigungsrat (National Defense Council). The last leader of a discredited regime, he was forced to withdraw from all offices in December 1989. He resigned from the People's Chamber and was expelled from the renamed SED/**Party of Democratic Socialism** (**PDS**) the following January. In 1995, along with other leading members of the SED, he stood trial for his role in the shoot-to-kill policy at the East–West German border and was sentenced to six and one-half years in prison (August 1997). His sentence was interrupted by a series of appeals, including one to the European Court of Human Rights (which confirmed the original judgment in March 2001), and he was finally released in December 2003. Krenz criticized the sentences passed on him and on other officials and border guards as "victors' justice." His publications include a biography (*Egon Krenz: Wenn Mauern fallen*, 1990) and an account of the 1989 revolution (*Herbst '89*, 1999).

KRETSCHMANN, WINFRIED (1948–). Green Party politician. Win-fried Kretschmann was born in Spaichingen (**Baden-Württemberg**); studied biology, chemistry, and ethics at the University of Hohenheim (from 1970); and qualified as a schoolteacher (1977) before working in various schools. Owing to his involvement with a communist student movement at Hohen-heim, he was initially barred under the **radicals decree** from teaching at state schools, although the ban was later lifted. A cofounder of the Green Party in Baden-Württemberg (1979–1980), he represented the Greens at local council (Kreistag) level in 1982–1984 and in the regional parliament (**Landtag**) during 1980–1984, 1988–1992, and from 1996, taking a special interest in **environment** and **transport**. His other positions included parliamentary speaker for the Greens (1983–1984) and deputy parliamentary group leader (2001–2002), then leader (from 2002). He also served on the national com-mission for the second stage of **federalism reform** (from 2007) and on a mediation committee for the controversial Stuttgart 21 transport project (2010). In 2011, he was elected the first Green **minister president** of Baden-Württemberg, leading a governing coalition with the **Social Democratic Party of Germany** (**SPD**). In September 2014, Kretschmann angered his party leadership by voting in the **Bundesrat** in favor of a compromise pack-age on **asylum** provision that included relaxing conditions for refugees in Germany, allowing them to take work after three months and move freely throughout the country, and providing them with money in place of vouch-ers. While not in principle opposed to these provisions, the main party re-sisted the inclusion of Serbia, Macedonia, and Bosnia-Herzegovina as safe countries of origin, which was also part of the package. Respected for his economic competence, Kretschmann continued in office after the regional election of 2016—when the Greens beat the CDU into second place—as leader of an unprecedented "Kiwi coalition" alongside the **Christian Democratic Union (CDU)**.

KRUPP FAMILY. The Krupp concern developed as a large steel manufacturer and **engineering** firm between 1850 and 1945. Founding members were Friedrich Krupp (1787–1826) and the brothers Alfred and Hermann Krupp (1812–1987, 1814–1979). During World War I, Krupp AG was a major arms producer, and between 1933 and 1945 the Krupp family name became inextricably linked to the military economy of the National Socialist regime; at the height of World War II the concern's workforce reached a peak of 243,000 (1943). Chief executive from 1909 to 1943 was Gustav Krupp (Gustav von Bohlen and Halbach, 1870–1950). Although he did not support Adolf Hitler before 1933, Krupp joined the National Socialist Party in 1940 and received high honors from it. He was accused of war crimes at the Nuremberg trials in 1945, but proceedings were suspended because he had become an invalid after an automobile accident in 1944.

Gustav Krupp's eldest son, Alfried Krupp von Bohlen and Halbach (1907–1967), joined the company in 1936, succeeding his father as chair of the executive board in 1943. Arrested with other senior colleagues by the Allies in 1945, he was sentenced to 12 years' imprisonment for plundering occupied territories and exploiting slave labor. It was decided to expropriate and split up the concern, with coal production separated from steel manufacture (the so-called Mehlemer Agreement), but owing to a lack of buyers, the diversification order remained largely unfulfilled. After he was released by general amnesty (1951), Alfried returned in 1953 to rebuild the firm.

Helped by his close aid and representative, **Berthold Beitz**, Alfried Krupp built new plants, opened up foreign markets, and by 1958 had reestablished the company as a major employer (105,200 staff), achieving record turnovers. A subsidiary in Brazil was opened to manufacture parts for engines and vehicles (1961). Krupp donated part of the library of the family home, the Villa Hügel in Essen—built by Alfred Krupp in 1870 and now run by the nonprofit foundation the Alfried Krupp von Bohlen und Halbach Stiftung—to Bochum University (1966) and bequeathed his extensive collection of records to the Folkwang College of Music. After Alfried's death (1967), since his son Arndt (1938–1986) had renounced the inheritance, the business was turned into a limited liability company (Fried. Krupp GmbH), and the remaining family shares passed to the foundation. This marked the end of the Krupp family's active involvement in one of Germany's best known and longest standing industrial concerns.

See also INDUSTRY; THYSSENKRUPP AG.

KUHN, FRITZ (1955–). **Green Party** politician and linguist. Fritz Kuhn studied German and philosophy at the universities of Munich and Tübingen. He represented the Green Party in the **Baden-Württemberg** state parliament (**Landtag**, 1984–1988), where he led the party parliamentary group. Appointed professor for language communication at the Merz Academy in Stuttgart in 1989, he returned to parliament in 1992, chairing the party grouping (until 2000) and focusing on economic and financial policy. After the national election of 1998, he served on the delegation of Greens who negotiated with the **Social Democratic Party of Germany** (**SPD**) to form the red/green ruling coalition. Between 2000 and 2002, he cochaired the national Green Party alongside **Renate Künast** and **Claudia Roth** (from 2001). Elected to the **Bundestag** (2002–2013), he led the party parliamentary group (2005–2009), specializing in economic and technological affairs. As mayor of Stuttgart from 2013, he criticized the lack of transparency about the controversial Stuttgart 21 project to rebuild the city's main railway station.

KUHNT, DIETMAR (1937–). Industrial executive. Born in Breslau (now in Poland), Dietmar Kuhnt moved with his parents to Neuss on the **Rhine** River (**North Rhine-Westphlia**) during World War II. He studied law at the universities of Cologne and Freiburg (1957–1961), passing his state examinations (1961, 1966) and earning a doctorate in criminal law (1966). Between 1966 and 1968, he worked as an assistant in an auditing office (the Rheinisch-Westphälische Wirtschaftsprüfungsgesellschaft mbH) in Essen before joining the Rheinisch-Westphälische Elektrizitätswerk (RWE) AG electricity company as a legal adviser and eventually heading its legal department (1977–1989). He occupied various senior positions within the RWE group, including board chairman (1995–2003) and member of the supervisory board (2003–2006). Under his stewardship, RWE AG merged with VEW AG (Dortmund) to create Germany's largest electricity company (2000) and took over Great Britain's leading electricity provider (Innogy Holdings PLC, 2002) and American Water Works in the United States (2003). In the 1980s, Kuhnt was a strong advocate of Germany's controversial nuclear **energy** program, in which his company was heavily involved, although it experienced a setback after shutting down its Mühlheim-Karlich reactor near Koblenz after barely two years' operation (1987–1988). During tough negotiations with the government coalition of the **Social Democratic Party of Germany** (**SPD**) and the **Green Party**, which had been elected in 1998 on a platform of total withdrawal from atomic power, Kuhnt extracted generous terms for Germany's nuclear **industry**, with long periods of phased closures for existing plants.

KULTURABKOMMEN (CULTURAL AGREEMENT). After it expatriated the songwriter **Wolf Biermann** in 1976, the **German Democratic Republic (GDR)** experienced a considerable loss of international prestige as it tightened censorship and increased state influence on cultural activities. As part of an attempt to restore its reputation during the following decade, the regime pursued a cultural agreement (Kulturabkommen) with the FRG on 6 May 1986, which had been planned since 1972. The agreement aimed to promote exchanges in **education**, science, the arts, and culture, areas that were often tightly controlled by the East German state. Nevertheless, the agreement helped to make GDR authors such as **Christa Wolf** and Ulrich Plenzdorf and painters such as Bernhard Heisig, Willi Sitte, and Wolfgang Mattheuer more widely known. As early as 1986, an exhibition of contemporary artists from West Germany was held in the GDR. It included works by Horst Antes, Raimund Girke, Gotthard Graubner, Anselm Kiefer, Siegmar Polke, Gerhard Richter, and Guenter Uecker. In 1987 alone, about 100 proposals for such exchanges were put forward.

The GDR stressed the existence of its own socialist German national culture, which was derived from communist/socialist ideology. As a result, the GDR maintained a massive and heavily centralized apparatus for the control of cultural activities, including several ministries (e.g., for culture and national education), mass organizations (such as the Kulturbund), and societies for specific groups (including the Schriftstellerverband for writers and the Komponistenverband for composers). In the FRG, cultural policy is the responsibility of the individual **federal states** and their cultural ministries (Kultusministerien), with no ideological guidelines. The 1990 Treaty on Unification stipulated that culture constituted an essential part of the process of reunification both for eastern and western Germany and for Germany's role in Europe. The treaty also stated that the culture of the former GDR should not be disadvantaged. A cultural fund (Kulturfonds) was set up to ease the process of adaptation at a time when cuts threatened the cultural landscape of the **eastern federal states**.

Today the FRG maintains cultural agreements with 94 countries that are coordinated by the Federal Foreign Office. Their aims are to foster communication across the **European Union (EU)**, to promote culture in an attempt to minimize conflict between different countries, and to safeguard education in the widest sense and preserve cultural interests. Apart from furthering cooperation among institutions of higher education, the FRG is also committed to the repatriation of cultural objects (Kulturgüterrückführung), not only items stolen by the National Socialists (NS-Raubkunst) or private individuals from occupied countries, but also those appropriated from Germany itself by Allied forces (Beutekunst).

KÜNAST, RENATE (1955–). Lawyer and **Green Party** politician. Born in Recklinghausen (**North Rhine-Westfalia**), Renate Künast studied social work at a technical college in Düsseldorf (Fachhochschule für Sozialwesen, 1973–1976) before joining the **Berlin**-Tegel district judiciary as a social worker, where she worked with male drug addicts (1977–1979). She studied law at the Technical University in Berlin (from 1979), qualifying as a practicing lawyer (1985) and specializing in criminal law and cases involving **foreigners**. An active member of the antinuclear movement during the 1980s, she demonstrated against the storage of nuclear waste at Gorleben and joined the "Free Republic of Wendland," a commune of several hundred protesters who occupied a proposed nuclear waste storage site at Trebel/Lüchow-Dannenberg (**Lower Saxony**) for one month in 1980, until they were forcibly dispersed by police.

In 1979, Künast joined the West Berlin Alternative Liste, a grouping of locally organized political activists with links to the Green Party, and in 1982 became a member of the management committee of the Greens. Elected to the Berlin assembly (1989–2000), she led the Green Party group in a short-lived governing coalition with the **Social Democratic Party of Germany (SPD)** in the city senate (1989–1990), chairing the **Alliance 90/The Greens** group (1990–1993, 1998–2000) and acting as its spokesperson on legal affairs (1993–1998). After the national election in 1998, she took part in coalition discussions with the SPD and was considered a potential minister of justice. Alongside **Fritz Kuhn**, she co-led the national party between 2000 and 2001 and is regarded as an expert on civil and **human rights**, internal **security**, sexual equality, and the protection of minorities. Elected to the **Bundestag** in 2002, she was minister for consumer protection, food, and **agriculture** (2001–2005) in the red/green coalition of Chancellor **Gerhard Schröder**. Künast was not only the first woman and Green politician to hold the post; she was also unusual in not being a lobbyist for the farming community. Fearful of her ideological commitment to ecological issues, both opposition politicians and farming interests criticized her for lack of competence. Her first policy statements indicated a commitment to enhancing consumer protection (especially in the light of the bovine spongiform encephalopathy crisis) and to promoting ecological methods in arable and animal farming, and she displayed little sympathy for a return to high subsidies for farmers. Leader of the Greens' parliamentary group (2005–2013), she is considered a pragmatist in her party, with a reputation for energy and ambition. She has also published on ecological and consumer issues and received awards for her work on the **environment** and animal protection.

L

LAFONTAINE, OSKAR (1943–). Former **Social Democratic Party of Germany (SPD)** politician. Born in Saarlouis (**Saarland**), Oskar Lafontaine studied physics at the universities of Bonn and Saarbrücken (1962–1969) with a stipend from an organization of German bishops (Cusanuswerk), graduating with a diploma. He worked for a transport and utilities concern (Versorgungs- und Verkehrsgesellschaft Saarbrücken GmbH, 1969–1974) and was a member of the executive board of a tram operating company in the Saar valley (1971–1974). After joining the SPD in 1966, he was active in the party's **Young Socialists (JUSOS)** wing and in local politics before entering the regional state parliament (**Landtag**) as a deputy (1970–1975). In 1974, Lafontaine was elected mayor of the city of Saarbrücken, serving as Oberbürgermeister (senior governing mayor) from 1976 until 1985. As regional SPD party chairman (1977–1996), he tried unsuccessfully to engage the **Free Democratic Party (FDP)** as a ruling coalition partner until the social democrats gained an overall majority in the 1985 regional elections. He was also a long-standing member of the SPD national executive (1979–1999).

Lafontaine's opposition to any form of nuclear armament and to the **North Atlantic Treaty Organization (NATO)**, from which he demanded Germany's withdrawal, brought him into direct conflict with Chancellor **Helmut Schmidt**. During a visit to the **German Democratic Republic (GDR)** in 1985, Lafontaine, in contravention of long-standing national policy, called for the Federal Republic of Germany (FRG) to recognize East German citizenship in order to normalize cross-border travel. In 1987, he also received GDR leader **Erich Honecker**, who was born in the Saarland, in his home region.

As **minister president** for the Saarland (1985–1998), Lafontaine preserved the local steel **industry** from total closure and provided social welfare benefits for its declining workforce. He also oversaw the introduction of the comprehensive school as the standard form of **education**, possibly the only German federal state to do so. In 1987 he, alongside **Johannes Rau**, was appointed deputy party chairman and headed a commission on policy formulation. After the fall of the **Berlin Wall** in November 1989, he advocated a cautious approach to reunification. His opposition on financial grounds to a common German nationality for citizens of the FRG and GDR and his proposal to restrict east–west migration contrasted sharply with Chancellor **Helmut Kohl**'s promise of swift and unconditional merger and contributed to the SPD's poor showing in the eastern German election of March 1990. After reunification, Lafontaine became a vocal critic of government policy in eastern Germany.

Recovering from a knife attack at a local election address (April 1990), Lafontaine was adopted as SPD chancellor candidate for the all-German national election of December 1990. However, after the SPD returned its worst electoral performance since 1957, he deferred to **Hans-Jochen Vogel** as candidate for party leader. In 1992, a regional court ruled that Lafontaine had been illegally receiving a pension for his period as mayor of Saarbrücken since 1986 and ordered him to repay 228,000 DM.

In 1992–1993 Lafontaine, along with **Björn Engholm,** oversaw a radical shift in SPD policy at a conference in Petersberg near Bonn. Here the party accepted changes to the **Basic Law** (**BL**) that tightened up Germany's hitherto liberal **asylum** laws and allowed its armed forces to take part in **United Nations** (**UN**) military operations outside the NATO area. After **Rudolf Scharping** took over as party chairman (1993), Lafontaine headed a commission charged with devising a strategy for achieving economic growth and combating unemployment. He was also earmarked as finance minister in a future SPD government. His 20-point program (1994) envisaged a large-scale redistribution of the national **taxation** burden from rich to poor.

In 1995, Lafontaine defeated Scharping in a party leadership contest and went on to take over a commission (Fortschritt 2000) to work out future policy for the economy, finance, and ecology. When the SPD/**Green Party** coalition assumed government in October 1998, Lafontaine was appointed finance minister under Chancellor **Gerhard Schröder**, with whom, however, he had major differences, resulting in his resignation only a few months later (in March 1999) and his stepping down as party leader. While in office, he criticized the policies of the **German Federal Bank** and called for a more open debate on monetary policy.

In a book published in October 1999 (*Das Herz schlägt links*/The heart beats on the left), Lafontaine savagely attacked Schröder and other senior SPD politicians for abandoning traditional socialist values in favor of neoliberalism ("third-way socialism") and criticized the party leadership for favoring closer links with the United States and Great Britain at the expense of the relationship with France. Condemned inside and outside the SPD, the personally framed attack was regarded as a serious political error. Although he apologized to party colleagues (April 2000), "Red Oskar" (also known as the "Napoleon of the Saar") stuck to his calls for curbs on international capital movements and for more dirigiste economic policies aimed at ensuring social justice. Effectively in political exile after 1999, Lafontaine was openly critical of Schröder's **Agenda 2010** reform program, and at the Saarland regional party conference of June 2004, he accused the government of concealing from the German people the implications of its plans for dismantling the social state. He took part in the "Monday demonstrations" in eastern Germany against proposals by the **Hartz Commission** to restrict unemployment benefits and publicly reflected on the possibility of a left-wing breakaway party from the SPD. His stance undermined the SPD's candidate in the Saarland regional election of September 2004 and contributed to the party's worst ever result there in 44 years (Chancellor Schröder did not even visit the region during the election campaign). In 2005, Lafontaine turned his back on the SPD, then joined the newly founded **Election Alternative for Labor and Social Justice** (Wahlalternative Arbeit und soziale Gerechtigkeit, WASG) and, soon afterward, its political ally the Linkspartei.PDS, which later became **The Left Party** and went on to win 54 seats in the 2005 **Bundestag** election, increasing to 76 seats in 2009. In 2007, The Left Party elected Lafontaine its coleader, alongside **Lothar Bisky**. In 2010, Lafontaine announced his withdrawal from the Bundestag and the leadership of The Left Party, but he continued to head the parliamentary group in Saarland. Lafontaine has publicized his political views in a number of books and publications.

LAMBSDORFF, OTTO GRAF (1926–2009). Free Democratic Party (FDP) politician. Born in Aachen, Otto Graf Lambsdorff was severely injured as a soldier in World War II (from 1944) and became a prisoner of war. After the war, he studied law and politics at the universities of Bonn and Cologne (1947–1950), earning a doctorate in law (1952). He worked in banking and insurance (1955–1977) and joined the executive board of the Victoria Versicherung insurance group (1972). In 1951, Lambsdorff joined the FDP, which he later represented in the **Bundestag** (1972–1998) and for whose parliamentary group he was spokesman (1977–1984). From 1977 until 1982, he served as economics minister under Chancellor **Helmut Schmidt** in the government coalition between the FDP and the **Social Democratic Party of Germany (SPD)**. Policy differences between the FDP and SPD, however, came to a head over Lambsdorff's widely publicized paper of September 1982, in which he argued for concessions to businesses and cuts in social welfare to stimulate economic growth. The eventual outcome was a coalition between the FDP and the **Christian Democratic Union (CDU)/Christian Social Union (CSU)** under Chancellor **Helmut Kohl**, in whose cabinet Lambsdorff continued as economics minister.

In 1984, Lambsdorff resigned as minister after being implicated in a scandal in which the Flick group received tax concessions in return for party donations. After the affair had blown over, Lambsdorff became chairman (1988–1993), then honorary chairman (1993–), of the FDP, returning to the public eye as negotiator on behalf of the German government of a $5,000 million settlement for former victims of the National Socialists' forced labor program during World War II (1999–2002).

A strong advocate of business-friendly government, Lambsdorff sat on the supervisory boards of a number of German and foreign companies and chaired the board of the Friedrich-Naumann Stiftung (Friedrich Naumann Foundation), which has close links with the FDP (1995–2006). He also chaired Liberal International (1991–1994) and the European region of the Trilateral Commission, a forum of political and business leaders from Europe, North America, and Japan (1991–2001).

LAMMERT, NORBERT (1948–). Christian Democratic Union (CDU) politician. Born in Bochum (**North Rhine-Westfalia**), Norbert Lammert studied politics, sociology, and history at the universities of Bochum and Oxford (1969–1975), graduating with a diploma (1972) and a doctorate (1975). He subsequently worked as a freelance lecturer in adult **education** at various academies, institutions, and companies and was appointed honorary professor at Bochum (2008) and vice chairman of the **Konrad Adenauer** Foundation (from 2001). A member of the CDU from 1966, he entered the **Bundestag** in 1980, where his positions included **state secretary** to three ministers: education and science (1989–1994), economics (1994–1997), and **transport** (1997–1998). During 1995–1998, he was government coordinator for aviation and space travel. Leader of the regional CDU in North Rhine-Westfalia (1996–2006), he was culture and media spokesman for the party parliamentary group in the Bundestag (1998–2002). He was vice president of the Bundestag from 2002 and elected its president in 2005.

LAND (PLURAL LÄNDER). *See* FEDERAL STATES (LÄNDER).

LANDTAG (PLURAL LANDTAGE). Each of Germany's **federal states** (Länder) is governed by a directly elected regional state parliament, or Landtag (called Bürgerschaft in the city-states of **Bremen** and **Hamburg**, or Abgeordnetenhaus, house of deputies, in **Berlin**). The relationship between the regional assemblies and the national parliament (**Bundestag**) is constitutionally regulated by the **Basic Law (BL)**. Although the assemblies have progressively (and voluntarily) ceded executive powers to the center during the course of the history of the Federal Republic of Germany (FRG), they can still pass laws in areas where the states have exclusive legislative competence. The Landtag chooses a **minister president** (Ministerpräsident) as regional head of state, elects or approves members of the regional government (Landesregierung), monitors policy, reflects the views of citizens, and sends delegates to the national assembly of federal states, the **Bundesrat**. Each Landtag also elects a president, who, supported by a presidium including representatives from the assembly, chairs plenary sessions and is responsible for the general management of parliamentary business. The Landtage are represented in the **Federal Assembly** (Bundesversammlung), which elects the **president of the Federal Republic** (Bundespräsident). The size of the Landtag varies from around 180 in **Bavaria** and **Lower Saxony** to 51 in the **Saarland**.

The composition and role of a Landtag is governed by the constitution (Landesverfassung) of the federal state. While the constitutions of the 16 Länder do not vary fundamentally from the BL, there are some differences. Some states, for example, explicitly acknowledge the right to strike (**Hessen**, **Rhineland-Palatinate**, Saarland, and **Brandenburg**) or to resist central state power if basic rights are infringed (Berlin, Bremen, Hessen, **Saxony-Anhalt**). Certain Länder constitutions (Bavaria, Hessen, Bremen, Rhineland-Palatinate) actually predate the BL, although differences in provision are settled by the principle that federal law (Bundesrecht) overrides regional law (Landesrecht; article 31 of the BL).

By 1993, all the new federal states from the former **German Democratic Republic (GDR)** had adopted new constitutions. Although broadly similar to those of the western states, they tended to place greater stress on the responsibilities of the state toward society (in terms of basic rights, the economy, welfare, and culture) and include elements of direct democracy (referenda or plebiscites). While the western states refer in general terms to the BL for a catalog of fundamental **human rights**, the constitutions of the eastern states, with experiences of the GDR era, list them explicitly. Most interstate differences arise in electoral law, notably in the number of votes that each voter may cast, how the votes are weighted, and the method used to calculate the final number of seats according to the proportional system. A 5 percent entry hurdle applies to all state elections, with exceptions for minorities (Sorbs in Brandenburg and Danes in **Schleswig-Holstein**). Greater variation occurs in district and local elections (Kommunalwahlen).

Most Landtage are elected using personalized proportional representation (PPR), the exceptions being Bremen, Hamburg, and Saarland, which operate a pure PR system. Using PPR means that some seats, so-called direct seats, are directly allocated to members elected on a first-past-the-post system (the personalized element), and the remaining seats go to candidates on party lists according to the overall proportions of votes cast (the proportional element); in most Länder, the lists are closed (the party determines the order in which listed candidates are elected) as opposed to open (voters influence the order).

Voters generally cast two votes (one for each element), although two Länder (**Baden-Württemberg** and the Saarland) operate PPR with a single vote (also **North Rhine-Westfalia** until 2005), while Hamburg and Bremen use 10 and 5 votes, respectively, with open lists. The ratio of direct to proportional seats varies from, for instance, 60 to 60 seats in Saxony to 128/53 in North-Rhine Westfalia. Used in Bundestag elections since 1949 (the double vote was introduced in 1953), PPR was gradually extended to most western federal states between 1947 and 1958 (Rhineland-Palatinate adopted it in 1989 for the 1991 regional election). Landtag members may sit for the Land as a whole or for constituencies (Wahlkreise) within the Land; they may also have to stand in a constituency in order to gain a seat (Baden-Württemberg). At Land level, PPR helps small parties enter parliament and create a working opposition, although it is more common in Landtag elections than in the Bundestag for a party to win an overall majority, possibly because of the nature of regional politics. The minimum voting age is generally 18, reduced to 16 in Bremen (from 2009), Brandenburg (from 2012), and Hamburg (from 2013). Normally legislatures sit for five or, in Bremen, four years; in 2013 Hamburg voted to extend the period from four to five years.

See also FEDERALISM.

LANGUAGE. German is the mother tongue of around 100 million people in Europe, with a further 15 million learning it as a foreign language, mainly in Poland, Russia, and France, although statistics vary widely and are complicated by emigration, political factors, concepts of dialect, and the distinction between first and second languages. Apart from being the main language in Germany and Austria, German is strongly represented in Switzerland (4.2 million speakers), Luxembourg (370,000), Liechtenstein (33,000), France (Alsace, 1.2 million), eastern Belgium (67,000–75,000), Denmark (20,000–50,000), and Italy (South Tyrol, 280,000). German-speaking minorities are also found in the United States (1.6 million); Brazil (over 500,000); Argentina (up to 500,000); Paraguay (100,000); and various states of eastern Europe, such as Poland (700,000), Hungary (250,000), the Czech Republic (150,000), and European Russia (78,000). Numbers in Romania fell dramatically between 1992 (almost 120,000) and 2012 (36,000). Other regions where German is spoken are South Africa (39,500), Namibia (25,000), and Israel (96,000). Through its global network of **Goethe Institutes**, Germany has also invested heavily in promoting its culture and language in central, eastern, and southeastern Europe, where it has developed strong economic interests. In addition, the government and **federal states** continue to lobby for greater use of the German language within the bureaucracy of the **European Union** (**EU**), where it ranks far behind English and French, despite the fact that the languages of all member states officially have equal status.

The German language can be viewed in terms of its local or regional dialects, regional or supra-regional colloquial German (Umgangssprache), and a national written and spoken standard (Standardsprache). Dialects, especially in urban areas, progressively lost their importance as a means of communication during the 19th century and were increasingly supplanted by the Umgangssprache, which is made up of varieties of colloquial German that occupy an intermediary position between local dialects and the national standard. Although dialects are receding, especially in northern Germany, major dialect borders (such as the east–west "Appel-Apfel" line) are still present, and new forms of larger regional dialects are emerging in conurbations such as Cologne, Frankfurt/Main, Munich, and beyond. These appear to be regionally colored forms of the Umgangssprache and represent part of the continuum with the national standard. The Umgangssprache emerged as a useful lingua franca for lower social classes (and **immigrants**) in towns and cities during the 19th century and now tends to span relatively large geographical areas (e.g., **Berlin** and surrounding **Brandenburg**). The Umgangssprache has also influenced the standard written and spoken language: its forms appear in **literature** (realism and naturalism); journalistic texts; and other linguistic genres such as political debates, group jargons, and advertising.

The standard language (Standardsprache), established in schools, **education**, and the **media**, is documented by convention through a series of reference works on grammar, style, and lexis produced, among others, by the Duden publishing house in Mannheim. At the same time, the standard language displays a rich variety of functional styles and text types, leading to variations in orthography, grammar, vocabulary, and word formation, some of which are conditioned by regional factors (e.g., south German "Samstag" versus north German "Sonnabend," for Saturday, and different forms for verb tenses). Standard German has also exerted a powerful influence on Swiss and Austrian German. The Mannheim-based Institut für deutsche Sprache (IDS) collects data, maintains archives of written and spoken German (also in electronic form), and conducts and promotes linguistic research.

The division of Germany after 1949 ignited a debate over whether the divergence of the political, economic, and social systems of the Federal Republic of Germany (FRG) and the **German Democratic Republic (GDR)** would lead to two distinct national varieties of the German language. During the 1960s and early 1970s, the debate was strongly colored by political standpoints, although by the 1980s a more objective view of German as a "pluricentric" language with different national standards, rather like English, had established itself. It was also acknowledged that the monopoly on public discourse and the media in the GDR by the party-political speak of the regime could not be taken as a reliable indicator of language usage by the population at large. Although most differences between east and west were found in lexis, actual estimates of differences in words/terms and their meanings varied widely (from between 800 to 24,000). German in the GDR lent itself to adopting cultural terms relating to Russian, while the FRG was heavily influenced by English.

Following the wholesale takeover of eastern German institutions and structures by the FRG after reunification, the debate largely dried up, especially since fundamental problems of communication between east and west Germans never really existed. There has, however, been interest in how easterners have adapted to western styles of discourse and language behavior after 1990. After reunification, it was also noted that far more Berliners in the east of the city, for example, used the regional dialect.

Although they continued to be used in informal situations (at home and with friends), German dialects continued their overall decline after 1945. Reasons for the decline include postwar migrations of refugees, increasing social and economic mobility, the growth of the media, and the expansion of general education. However, the process has not been uniform. Dialect usage in northern and central areas of the FRG has receded to a greater extent than in the south and southwest, while in parts of eastern Germany, such as Mecklenburg (north), the Ore Mountains (Erzgebirge), and Thuringia (south), dialects have retained their identity. In some areas, dialects have enjoyed a mini-renaissance as cultural groups have attempted to revive their usage through songs, courses, and literature, and dialect forms have occasionally entered popular songs. Dialect is also less of a marker of social status than, for instance, in Great Britain, and it was/is present in the speech of leading politicians such as **Helmut Schmidt**, **Franz Josef Strauß**, **Edmund Stoiber**, and **Lothar Späth**. At the same time, political associations have in the past had an impact on perceptions: the Saxon dialect, for instance, acquired negative overtones since it was used by the East German leader **Walter Ulbricht**, who was responsible for the building of the **Berlin Wall** in 1961. Amid some controversy, the threatened Low German dialect was adopted in 1998 as a minority language by the EU through the European Charter for Regional and Minority Languages. The relationship between dialect and colloquial German (Umgangssprache) varies from region to region. In the south, colloquial everyday German is much closer in its sounds and vocabulary to the dialect than it is in the north, where the influence of the standard written and spoken language has historically been much stronger (paradoxically, perhaps, through the need of dialect speakers to consciously adopt a different standard). At the same time, intrusions by colloquial language into the national standard, especially in the media, have attracted critical comments from purists, as has the widespread adoption of Anglo-American words, phrases, and idioms (sometimes referred to as "Denglisch," a mixture of "Deutsch" and "Englisch"). While teacher training in Germany promotes the standard form (also known as High German), regional peculiarities are recognized as a means of expression in the spoken language.

Like all natural languages, German is subject to constant change and evolution in phonetics, morphology, syntax, and lexis. Examples of changes to the phonetic system include the spread of uvular "r" at the expense of the trilled "r," while morphology has seen the spread of weak verb forms as strong verbs have ceased to be productive, as well as shifts in the use of genitive and dative forms. Modern German syntax tends to prefer shorter, less complex sentence structures alongside longer and more complex noun phrases (nominalization). Lexis is naturally the most dynamic area, as it responds to a variety of influences reflecting changes in lifestyle and communication ([social] media, advertising), the impact of new subject domains (such as information technology), and the trend toward internationalization ("television" [for "Fernsehen"], "terminal," "chip"). The feminist movement has resulted in efforts to avoid what is perceived as sexist-, male-dominated language, as shown in the avoidance of words displaying overt masculine grammatical gender ("Studierende/Lehrperson" for "Studenten/Lehrer"), the creation of new feminine forms ("Bankkauffrau," the personal pronoun "frau/jedefrau"), the use of pairs denoting both genders ("Liebe Bürger und Bürgerinnen"), and the highlighting of the infix letter I ("BürgerInnen"). A wide variety of social, economic, and linguistic influences is at work here. Some recent developments not only reflect German's social and cultural status quo, but also have implications for teaching and education in general. One such development is *Kiezdeutsch*, an urban youth language characterized by simplification (shortening sentences; contraction of words) and innovation (integration of foreign, including Turkish and Arabic, terms, and also technological terms). *Kiezdeutsch* is closely related to the so-called Kanak Sprak, a sociolect that was put on the map by the Turkish German writer Feridun Zaimoğlu.

The issue and debates about **spelling reform** also highlighted the German public's concern with language in general, an awareness that is not least influenced by the lessons learned from the National Socialist period. Annually since 1991, a "jury" of mainly linguists has nominated the "Unwort des Jahres" (inappropriate word of the year), reflecting either antidemocratic or discriminatory terms used by the mass media. In 2011, for example, the word was "Döner-Morde" (Döner-killings), which reflected insensitivity toward the right-wing dimension of racially motivated murders over many years.

The Gesellschaft für deutsche Sprache (GfdS) in Wiesbaden is dedicated to promoting interest and research in the German language and runs an advisory service. The society conducts an annual review of the most popular (widely used) words and terms, which culminates in a Word of the Year competition that is reported in the national press and sums up national preoccupations for that period: in 1990, for example, "die neuen Bundesländer" (the new **federal states**) in response to unification; in 2002, "Teuro," following the transition from the Deutsche Mark to the euro, which was accompanied by price increases; and "Bundeskanzlerin" in 2005, reflecting the election of Merkel as Germany's first female chancellor.

LAW AND ORDER OFFENSIVE PARTY (PARTEI RECHTSSTAAT-LICHER OFFENSIVE). *See* SCHILL, RONALD B. (1958–).

LEBER, GEORG (1920–2012). Social Democratic Party of Germany (SPD) politician. Georg Leber was born in Obertiefenbach (**Rhineland-Palatinate**) on the Lahn River. He trained in commerce, served during World War II, and was wounded in 1945. After working as a bricklayer, he joined the SPD in 1947, and in 1949, joined the newly founded building industry **trade union** IG Bau, Steine, Erden, which he led from 1957 to 1966. After entering the **Bundestag** (1957), Leber joined the SPD party executive and parliamentary group (1961) and was a member of the presidium (1968–1973).

Leber was one of the architects of the first **grand coalition** under Chancellor **Kurt Georg Kiesinger** (1966–1969) and served as minister of **transport** (1966–1972, extended in 1969 to include post and communications) and defense minister (1972–1978). As transport minister, he was responsible for the so-called Leber Plan (Verkehrspolitisches Programm für die Jahre 1968 bis 1972/Transport Plan for the Years 1968–1972), a blueprint for national transport reform which, among other things, attempted to shift freight traffic from road to rail. Leber proved a popular and successful defense minister, earning the sobriquet "the soldiers' father" ("Soldatenvater"). He expanded the **Bundeswehr**, modernized its armory, improved training and **education**, and established the two military universities in **Hamburg** and Munich (1973). At the same time, his mounting defense budget and support for the **North Atlantic Treaty Organization (NATO)**, including its firm line on the nuclear deterrent and close links with the United States, alienated the left wing of the SPD. Leber resigned as minister in February 1978, taking responsibility for illegal bugging conducted by Germany's Militärischer Abschirmdienst (Military Counter-Espionage Service, MAD). Briefly a member of the European Parliament (1958–1959), Leber received several honors, including an honorary doctorate from the University of Tübingen (1980), the Federal Cross of Merit (1969, with additional awards thereafter), a commander of the French Foreign Legion (1980), and the Theodor Heuss Prize (1985). His book (*Vom Frieden*) appeared in 1980.

LEFT PARTY, THE (DIE LINKSPARTEI/DIE LINKE). The Left Party was formed, first at the regional level and then nationally, in July/August 2005 as an electoral alliance between the **Party of Democratic Socialism**

(PDS), led by **Lothar Bisky**, and the **Election Alternative for Labor and Justice (WASG)** under **Oskar Lafontaine**. The PDS also adopted the new title Linkspartei.PDS and offered electoral list positions to WASG members for the election to the **Bundestag** in 2005. Discussion over whether to include the suffix PDS in the name reflected internal divisions about the need to retain electoral appeal in the east (the PDS's stronghold) while avoiding alienating western voters (where WASG members were most active). Despite rivalry between the two groups in some **federal states**, the prospective merger enabled the PDS to appeal to voters throughout Germany and cross the 5 percent hurdle required to gain 54 seats in the national parliament. In June 2007, the PDS and WASG formally merged under the name Die Linke (The Left), chaired jointly by Bisky and Lafontaine. During 2008 and 2009, the new party won seats in regional, national, and European elections; despite a damaging leadership struggle in May 2012, it emerged in the 2013 Bundestag election as the third strongest party, with 8.6 percent of the vote (64 seats). Party coleaders following Bisky and Lafontaine after 2010 have been Gesine Lötzsch (2010–2014), Klaus Ernst (2010–2012), Katja Kipping (2012–), and Bernd Riexinger (2010–). In 2009 in **Brandenburg**, The Left Party formed a coalition government led by the SPD; following elections in **Thuringia** in 2014, in which The Left Party beat the SPD into third place, **Bodo Ramelow**, leader of the party group in the regional parliament, emerged as **minister president** of a governing coalition with the social democrats and the **Green** Party. Ramelow was the first member of The Left Party to become a regional premier.

The Left Party campaigns on a left-wing platform of overcoming capitalism through a system of democratic socialism. Although it is present in all the **federal states**, it is strongest in the east, and also the **Saarland**. Its main organs are a national congress (Bundesparteitag), which elects an executive (Vorstand), comprising 44 members including the two coleaders. Constituted in 2008, a six-member national committee (Bundesausschuss) promotes coordination between the party's regional associations (Landesverbände) in the eastern and western federal states and undertakes initiatives to bring the two closer together. Membership in 2015 stood at around 59,000, concentrated in **Saxony** (more than 8,600), **Berlin** (7,400), and Brandenburg (more than 6,600).

See also GYSI, GREGOR (1948–); POLITICAL PARTIES.

LEGAL SYSTEM. The framework for the legal system of the Federal Republic of Germany (FRG) is laid down in the **Basic Law (BL**, articles 92–104), which places the application of law in the hands of an independent judiciary, specifies the role and composition of the **Federal Constitutional Court (FCC)**, and names the federal courts (Bundesgerichte) and their areas of jurisdiction. Although the **Bund** can issue framework regulations (Rahmenvorschriften) governing the judicial system in the **federal states**, these appoint and manage their own courts and judges. German law distinguishes between civil (or private) law (Zivilrecht or bürgerliches Recht) and public law (öffentliches Recht). Civil law, which dates from 1900 and is laid down in the Civil Codex (Bürgerliches Gesetzbuch), regulates relations between individual citizens, including legal entities, and embraces family and children's law, inheritance law, intellectual property, and, with some exceptions, commercial and labor law. Public law governs relations between citizens and the state and between the state and its organs. It encompasses constitutional and international law, criminal law, and the specialist areas of administrative law, which includes law on roads, building, **taxation**, and the **environment**, as well as fiscal and social welfare law. All codes and statutes have to be interpreted in accordance with the BL.

The FCC is not a general court of final appeal. It deals primarily with constitutional issues and rules on cases involving the possible infringement of an individual's fundamental rights as laid down in the BL. Nevertheless, if a lower court believes that a regulation or a statute violates the constitution, it must halt its proceedings and refer the issue to the FCC. Outside the specific area of constitutional law, the supreme federal civil and criminal court in the FRG is the Federal Court of Justice (Bundesgerichtshof). Based in Karlsruhe and with an office in Leipzig, this court constitutes the highest level of appeal in civil law (Revisionsgericht). Handling appeals from higher regional courts (Oberlandesgerichte), it acts through 28 senates, grouped according to areas of law (for civil matters) or region (for criminal law). Leave to appeal to the court is usually reserved for issues of great importance and where a unitary interpretation of an item of law is required. Appeals are based solely on points of law, and the court will not hear witnesses or assess evidence.

Under the auspices of the Federal Court of Justice, each state has at least one higher regional court, or Oberlandesgericht (called Kammergericht in **Berlin**). This is the highest court for general civil and criminal cases at Land level and normally handles appeals. Below this exists a second level of court, the regional court (Landgericht), followed by the local or district court (Amtsgericht), which is as a rule the court of first instance and is chaired by a single judge. The term Landesgericht (as opposed to Landgericht) refers more widely to any kind of regional court. For historical reasons, these courts are all referred to as courts of general jurisdiction (ordentliche Gerichte). A court over which more than one judge presides, known as a Kollegialgericht (or as a chamber [Kammer] in the case of a Landgericht or a senate in a higher court), handles cases requiring detailed judicial discussion. The Amtsgericht does not require parties to be represented by a lawyer, and its jurisdiction covers minor disagreements (e.g., in which the amount in dispute is not over 5,000 euros), residential leases, family issues, and the enforcement of judgments. Other matters are referred to the Landgericht.

The structure of the national Bundesgerichtshof, with its regional and sub-regional courts, is paralleled for the four other main areas of law in Germany, albeit with fewer courts and judges. Thus the Bundesarbeitsgericht (Federal Labor Court, based in Erfurt), with regional Landesarbeitsgerichte and district Arbeitsgerichte, rules typically on disputes between employers and employees (including **trade unions**) and the law on **codetermination**. The Bundesverwaltungsgericht (Federal Administrative Court, Leipzig), with regional Oberverwaltungsgerichte and district Verwaltungsgerichte, settles disputes between citizens and public institutions (in the sense of öffentlich-rechtliche Institutionen, which have a special legal status in German law). The Federal Social Court (Bundessozialgericht, Kassel), with regional Landessozialgerichte and district Sozialgerichte, handles all aspects of social security provisions (**pensions, health** insurance, nursing care, welfare benefit), which are regarded as a special branch of administrative law. The Bundesfinanzhof (Federal Fiscal Court, Munich), whose name is derived from the prewar Reichsfinanzhof and which, unusually, maintains only regional courts, considers cases involving taxation and other government levies.

Disagreements over the jurisdiction of a court are settled by a joint senate (Gemeinsamer Senat) constituted from presidents and senior judges from the five federal courts (Bundesgerichte). Since the regional (Land) courts implement both national and state law, the vast majority of cases are settled at this level, with the federal courts hearing appeals and acting as a unifying influence in the interpretation and application of legislation.

The German judicial system is integrated into that of the **European Union (EU)**. The Luxembourg-based European Court of Justice (ECJ) checks whether instruments of the European institutions and governments are compatible with EU treaties, settles disputes between organs of the EU and between member states, and, at the request of national courts, interprets EU law. German issues on which the ECJ has ruled include gender parity in public service jobs during the 1980s and 1990s, appeals against conscription (2003), government promotion of "green electricity" (2001), the banning of cigarette advertising (2001), and women as combat soldiers (2000). The European Court of Human Rights (ECHR) in Strasbourg, founded in 1959, has been open since 1998 to direct appeals from citizens of signatory countries of the **Council of Europe** (not to be confused with the EU's European Council) pursuing possible violations of basic freedoms and **human rights**.

German judges are wholly independent and can be removed from office only by judicial decision (i.e., not by politicians or governments). Federal judges are appointed by a government minister in conjunction with a selection committee comprising Land ministers and an equal number of representatives elected by the **Bundestag** (the Richterwahlausschuss). There are currently over 500 federal judges and around 15,500 judges in regional (Land) service, mainly engaged in general jurisdiction. Judges are free to join **political parties** or **trade unions**, although they cannot sit in a regional state parliament (**Landtag**) or the Bundestag.

Legal training in Germany follows distinct pathways. So-called jurists (Juristen) study law as an academic subject at university for at least eight semesters (four years), taking a further year to pass their "first law state examination" (erste juristische Staatsprüfung). To become a fully qualified practicing lawyer (Volljurist or Rechtsassessor), the candidate then undergoes two years of training at a college in a federal state, coupled with work placements at court and a law firm (Referendariat) before passing the second or final state examination (zweite juristische Staatsprüfung or Staatsexamen). In order to provide a route for the large numbers of students in Germany who have completed their first law examination and plan a career in business or **industry**, new qualifications and study pathways have been introduced. These are the master's degree (Magister) and diploma (Diplomjurist), which give their holders a recognized academic title. Law diplomas with a business orientation have been offered by higher technical colleges (Fachhochschulen) for some time. German universities have also started introducing bachelor's degrees in law.

The second state examination is a prerequisite for admission to the state prosecution service (as Staatsanwalt) and the judiciary (as judge, or Richter). Professional training and appointments are the responsibility of the justice ministries of the federal states. Provision also exists for the appointment of lay or honorary judges (Laienrichter or Schöffen), who do not require law qualifications, sit in most types of courts, and number around 60,000. A qualified lawyer may also acquire a license to practice as a notary (Notar). Full-time notaries, who are employed by the federal state judicial authority and are assigned a geographical area or district, perform a variety of legal services, including registering and certifying documents, authenticating transactions, forming a company, handling property purchase contracts and divorce settlements, and providing objective advice for clients. A notary is regarded as an impartial counsel or representative of the state, and his or her services are mandatory for certain contracts and transactions. A company lawyer (Syndikusanwalt or Firmenanwalt) is employed by a business concern or a foundation.

Lawyers are organized into chambers (Rechtsanwaltskammern), which are self-regulating associations recognized in public law and financed exclusively from members' contributions. A newly qualified lawyer automatically joins a chamber, which provides advice, monitoring, and professional support for its members. There are currently 28 chambers throughout Germany.

LEHMANN, KARL (1936–). Roman Catholic leader. Born in Sigmaringen (**Baden-Württemberg**), Karl Lehmann studied in Freiburg and Rome (1956–1964), earning doctorates in philosophy (on Martin Heidegger, 1962) and theology (1967). A formative tutor during his studies was Karl Rahner (1904–1984), a Jesuit and one of Germany's most influential Catholic theologians. Following ordination by Cardinal **Julius Döpfner** (1963) and professorships in Mainz (from 1968) and Freiburg (1971), Lehmann rose rapidly in the church hierarchy. He was appointed bishop of Mainz (1983) and served as elected chairman of the Conference of German Catholic Bishops (Bischofskonferenz, 1987–2008). In 2001, he was raised to the cardinalship by Pope John Paul II.

Lehmann became one of Germany's best known and most popular clergymen, developing a reputation for seeking compromise and promoting ecumenical dialogue. Under his leadership, the Roman Catholic Church in Germany avoided the damaging internal splits that beset sister churches in other European countries during times of social and spiritual change. Although he has never considered himself a rebel and fiercely maintained church unity, Lehmann occasionally attracted the disapproval of the Vatican, which he regarded as exerting too much power, by suggesting that the church should admit married men as priests, rethink the role of **women**, and show more tolerance toward remarried divorcees. He engaged in public debate with the Catholic dissident Hans Küng, who lost official approval to teach doctrine at the University of Tübingen (1979) and argued (in vain) for the church to participate in the state-run **abortion** counseling service in Germany. Universally respected for his diplomatic and leadership skills, Lehmann is considered a member of the liberal wing of the church, in contrast to the conservative cardinal **Joachim Meisner** of Cologne, with whom he has publicly disagreed. Lehmann was also a long-standing friend of former chancellor **Helmut Kohl**.

See also RELIGION.

LEYEN, URSULA VON DER (1958–). Christian Democratic Union (**CDU**) politician. Ursula von der Leyen was born in Brussels, the daughter of **Ernst Albrecht, minister president** of **Lower Saxony** (1976–1990). After attending the European School in Brussels (1964–1971), she studied economics at the universities of Göttingen and Münster (1977–1980) and went on to qualify in medicine at the Medizinische Hochschule in Hanover (MHH, 1980–1987), where she worked in a **women**'s clinic (1988–1992) and earned a doctorate (1991). After a period at Stanford University (California, 1992–1996), she returned to work at the MMH, researching social medicine and **health** systems (1998–2002) and completing a master's degree in public health (2001). A member of the CDU (from 1990), she was a local councilor in Hanover (2001–2004) and a member of the CDU parliamentary group in the regional assembly (**Landtag**) for Lower Saxony (2003–2005), where she became regional minister for social affairs, women, family, and health (2003–2005). She went on to serve in successive ministerial positions under **Angela Merkel**, responsible for family, senior citizens, women, and youth (2005–2009); labor and social affairs (2009–2013); and (the first woman to hold this post) defense (2013–). A member of the CDU presidium from 2004, she became deputy party leader in 2010. As minister, she argued in 2007 for a massive expansion of nursery places (eventually set at 230,000 by 2010) and a law on the filtering of **Internet** child pornography (enacted in 2010 but dropped in 2011). One of her first acts as defense minister was to instigate a major independent review of procurement and monitoring of large-scale projects following cost overruns and delays in delivery (examples include the Eurofighter, the Tiger helicopter, air-defense systems, and transport aircraft); the review was accompanied by personnel changes at **state secretary** level.

LIEBERKNECHT, CHRISTINE (1958–). Christian Democratic Union (**CDU**) politician. Born in Weimar (**Thuringia**) in the former **German Democratic Republic of Germany** (**GDR**), Christine Lieberknecht studied theology at the University of Jena (1976–1982) and trained for the clergy in Thuringia (1982–1984) before working as a pastor near Weimar until 1990. A member of the CDU of the GDR from 1981, she was active in the Christian Peace Conference, an international movement based in Prague, which included churches from communist countries. In September 1989, Lieberknecht cosigned an appeal to the East German CDU to sever links with the ruling **Socialist Unity Party of Germany** (**SED**). During 1989–1990, in the final months of the GDR, she was elected a member of the national party executive committee and deputy leader of the CDU in Thuringia. She also cofounded the first group of Young European Federalists and worked on an advisory committee to create the new federal state of Thuringia. Following the CDU's victory in the first free regional elections in East Germany (14 October 1990), Lieberknecht became culture minister in the new regional government—a coalition of the CDU and the **Free Democratic Party** (**FDP**)—and moved swiftly to restructure the **education** system; she held the post until 1992. Elected to the regional assembly (**Landtag**) in 1991, she served as minister for federal and European affairs (1992–1994); for federal affairs in the state chancellery (1994–1999); and also for social affairs, the family, and **health** (May 2008–October 2009). From July 2004 to May 2008, she led the CDU parliamentary group in the Landtag. Following regional elections in 2009, in which the CDU lost its overall majority but the **Social Democratic Party of Germany** (**SPD**) declined to form a coalition with **The Left Party** and the **Green Party**, Lieberknecht succeeded **Dieter Althaus**

(CDU) as **minister president** of Thuringia, leading a **grand coalition** with the social democrats. She also won the respect of opposition parties while she was president of the assembly between 1999 and 2004.

LINDNER, CHRISTIAN (1979–). Free Democratic Party (FDP) politician. Christian Lindner was born in Wuppertal (**North Rhine-Westfalia, NRW**) and studied politics, law, and philosophy at the University of Bonn (from 1996), graduating with a master's degree in 2006. During 1997–2004, he ran an advertising agency, cofounded an **Internet** business, and published two books on investment and digital marketing. A member of the FDP from 1995, he represented the party in the regional assembly (**Landtag**) of NRW (2000–2009), where he served as deputy leader of the parliamentary group (from 2005). During 2004–2010, he was also general secretary of the regional party. Moving to the **Bundestag** in 2009, he was elected general secretary of the national FDP until 2011, but left the Bundestag the following year to lead the parliamentary group in the NRW assembly. Following the party's failure to enter the Bundestag in 2013 and the resignation of its entire national leadership, Lindner was elected the youngest ever party chairman, pledging to rebuild the FDP from the bottom up.

LITERARY QUARREL (LITERATURSTREIT). This debate, which arose almost immediately after German reunification in 1990, centered on the question of the role of the intellectual in relation to the state and whether writers had an obligation, where necessary, to publicly oppose political policies. At first the debate focused on criticism directed from the West toward the East and targeted authors who had stayed in the **German Democratic Republic (GDR)**. One such author was **Christa Wolf**, whose short novel *Was bleibt?* attracted particular censure. Written in 1979 but not published until 1990, the novel was attacked by Frank Schirrmacher in the *Frankfurter Allgemeine Zeitung* and by the leading West German literary critic, Marcel Reich-Ranicki (1990), partly on the basis that the author had failed to use her privileged position to protest against the regime. The argument essentially mirrored questions of responsibility and the political/cultural impact of reunification in the early 1990s. Although some authors (such as Lew Kopelew, **Günter Grass**, and Walter Jens) came to Wolf's defense, the dispute took a particularly bitter turn after **Wolf Biermann** outed the author Sascha Anderson as an informant for the GDR secret police, the **Stasi**, in 1992. Also relevant in this context is the term "state-artist" (Staatskünstler) and the questions of how much artists' cooperation with state-imposed guidelines was acceptable and what role they should play in postreunification Germany.

The more general question of the function of the writer remained topical throughout the 1990s, although its precise concerns shifted. Another writer who triggered a heated literary debate was Botho Strauß, who in his essay "Anschwellender Bockgesang" argued for a return to an unpolitical domain of pure art and aesthetics in order to preserve society. By contrast, **Martin Walser** provoked controversy when, in a speech delivered after receiving the Peace Prize of the German Book Trade (Friedenspreis des Deutschen Buchhandels) in 1998, he suggested calling an end to Germans' preoccupation with the country's Nazi past. All in all, the decade after reunification clearly represented a major shift: after years of ideological debates and confrontations, the postreunification years afforded a reassessment of the role of the writer and the intellectual in society more generally.

See also LITERATURE.

LITERATURE. Reunification in 1990 had a major impact on literature and the literary scene in Germany. The first decade was characterized by reflections on the image of the **eastern federal states** (often described in female terms) and the west (the male, more dominant counterpart). While some authors, such as Thomas Brussig, satirized the events, others, such as Volker Braun, expressed a sense of loss. Even well into the second decade of reunification, German literature displayed marked differences between east and west. At the same time, a generational shift could be observed. While in the early 1990s, established writers such as **Günter Grass**, **Martin Walser**, **Christa Wolf**, Friedrich Christian Delius, Uwe Timm, and **Stefan Heym** maintained their prominent role, a new generation came to the fore, including Julia Franck, Jana Hensel, Florian Illies, Judith Hermann, Tim Staffel, Tanja Dückers, and André Kubiczek, to name but a few. Their writing is at times characterized by a rather apolitical and autobiographical approach. The term "Popliteratur" refers to literature that concentrates on daily and personal issues (exponents include Benjamin von Stuckrad-Barre, Christian Kracht, and Alexander von Schönburg). Another and ongoing trend concentrates on reevaluating Germany's past and its long-term impact, in particular the Third Reich (e.g., Bernhard Schlink, Michael Wildenhain, and Friedrich Christian Delius); writers exploring this theme occasionally do so in the context of a debate about a new German identity. Crime writing has become an increasingly popular genre in Germany. It includes so-called regional crime writing, which is firmly embedded in certain areas, cities, or **federal states** (e.g., Jakob Arjouni, Manfred Bomm, Horst Bosetzky, Jan Eik, and Klaus Wanninger), and can also embrace a feminist agenda (Doris Gercke) or be based on a historical period (e.g., Volker Kutscher).

Unlike in the 1970s, when authors such as **Heinrich Böll**, **Hans Magnus Enzenzsberger**, and above all Grass played an important role in German society, the political impact of literature today is more marginal. Nevertheless, the reassessment of, for instance, German law in fiction (by Ferdinand von Schirach, among others) has touched upon principal issues in society. This goes hand in glove with a desire to reassess the postwar years and to document lives in historical context. The **Berlin** author Annett Gröschner is a prime example, while Eugen Ruge's novel *In Times of Fading Light* (2013) depicts the experiences of several generations of communists in Germany, in emigration, and in Soviet camps. Ursula Krechel (1947–) has traced the fate of a Jewish emigrant who returned to postwar West Germany (*Landgericht*, 2012).

In contrast to the 1960s, 1970s, and 1980s, during which Berlin attracted only a relatively small number of authors for prolonged periods of time, the city is now the focus of a thriving literary scene. This includes so-called Vorlesebühnen (public readings from stage), in which authors present short pieces of literature and interact with the audience. Most of the participants in such events publish their works in the form of collected stories or as part of anthologies (examples are Jochen Schmidt and Wladimir Kaminer).

Immediately after the fall of the **Berlin Wall**, a particular theme emerged in the form of the so-called Wenderoman, a novel depicting the events of November 1989 and their aftermath. Proponents of this trend include Thomas Brussig, Günter Grass, Ingo Schulze, and Jens Sparschuh. Others were concerned with the big city novel in the tradition of Alfred Döblin's *Berlin Alexanderplatz*—one of many novels that enjoyed a revived interest after conditions changed so dramatically. It can be seen as indicative of the transitional quality of the 1990s that the Feuilleton, a section in German newspapers devoted to the observation of daily or special events in literary terms, found renewed popularity (a notable contributor is Alexander Osang, but there are also numerous reprints from the 1920s and early 1930s). The **press** and **media** also provided the initial forum for some of the conflicts between the eastern and western German literary scene in the years immediately following reunification. The **literary quarrel** is a good example of this.

The divide between literature in the Federal Republic of Germany (FRG) and the **German Democratic Republic (GDR)** had become obvious in the 1950s, even before the building of the Berlin Wall in 1961. The wall then featured in German literature over several decades, most famously in Peter Schneider's novel *Der Mauerspringer* (1982). His narrative exemplified differences and similarities between East and West, be they political, linguistic, or biographical, with a focus on the former capital. However, it also showed that there were strong links between the artistic and literary scenes in both countries, which after all, shared the same **language**. These links were especially important for writers such as **Wolf Biermann** and Jurek Becker (there are many more), who did not agree with the party line and were forced to publish in the FRG—and in some cases left East Germany for good.

The GDR, proceeding from a communist ideological background, promoted an all-inclusive "society of literature" ("Literaturgesellschaft"—the term originates from the author Johannes R. Becher, who was an influential figure in the GDR's early years). This was a society characterized by a literature accessible to everyone and with a wide spectrum of writers. The term "Literaturgesellschaft" can be contrasted with "Literaturbetrieb" ("literature as business"), with its negative, commercial connotations of the more market- and production-oriented situation in West Germany. In 1967 at its seventh party conference, the **Socialist Unity Party of Germany** (**SED**) confirmed the **Bitterfeld Way** as the way forward to promote the socialist counterrevolution. From 1959, when a first conference in Bitterfeld had coined the term to describe the programmatic approach to the arts, all workers (Werktätige) were included in the literary process, while writers were encouraged to experience work in factories or the mines. A second resolution in 1964 stipulated that **education** had to foster the notion of the socialist personality. This rather affirmative approach to culture was stifling for those who were not in agreement with party politics. The East German writers' association, the Schriftstellerverband der DDR, had been set up in 1950. Headed by the authors Anna Seghers from 1952 to 1978, **Hermann Kant** (1978–1990), and Rainer Kirsch (until its dissolution on 31 December 1990), membership in the association was essential. Censorship and care of its members went hand in hand.

Distinctive trends in the literature of the GDR included discussion of the interaction between state and individual, the individual's pursuit of happiness, documentary forms of literature (Maxi Wander), the depiction of **women** (Brigitte Reimann, Helga Königsdorf, Irmtraud Morgner), the literary figure of the jester (Christa Wolf, Ulrich Plenzdorf, Irmtraud Morgner, Thomas Brasch, Adolf Endler), and a new subjectivity (Günter Kunert, Günter Endler, Rainer Kunze, Sarah Kirsch, Elke Erb). Aside from these themes, writers adopted positions that varied between acceptance of the state (Hermann Kant) and criticism that was either subtle (Günter de Bruyn, Christoph Hein, Christa Wolf) or open (Wolf Biermann).

Any hopes that had been raised by the SED's eighth party conference in 1971, when **Erich Honecker**'s promise of "no taboos" appeared to herald a more liberal approach in cultural policy, were undermined by the expatriation of the songwriter Wolf Biermann in 1976. This became a benchmark event that was to shape the years to come. By the 1980s, a distinctive subculture associated with the East Berlin district of Prenzlauer Berg had established itself. Representatives of this culture included Peter Wawerzinek, Adolf Endler, Bert Papenfuß, and Durs Grünbein, whose work was not limited to writing novels or poetry but also included meetings, concerts, readings, exhibitions, and the production of underground newspapers ("subkulturelle Zeitungen" and Samsidat). When after reunification one of the circle's main contributors, Sascha Anderson, was outed as an informant for the GDR secret police (**Stasi**), the entire scene seemed to be temporarily undermined. Today the writers of the former GDR can be divided into those who were too young to be shaped by the regime but are characterized by their experiences in the years after 1989 and, with various literary results, those with a long-term familiarity with East Germany.

In the FRG, the late 1960s marked a significant change, in that new topics came to the fore. The certainties—such as the perceived need to rebuild one's life—that seemed to have characterized the 1950s were lost as the more recent past and contemporary issues that had culminated in the **students' movement** exerted an immediate impact on literature (an example being the work of **Hans Magnus Enzensberger**). While **Group 47** had stressed the need for a fresh understanding of the author in society, Group 61 developed a new focus that encouraged involving workers in literature (Max von der Grün). This type of social realism was, however, not to be compared with the ideological and state-driven socialist realism of the GDR. Instead, writers such as Günter Wallraff experimented with different styles, such as symbolic representation and report-style contributions. Wallraff (1942–) worked as undercover journalist to explore working conditions and, most famously, the approaches of the tabloid press to then highlight wide-ranging issues.

The 1970s and 1980s were characterized in turn by a new interest in the subjective and individuality as a basis for fictional writing. Concerns of the 1970s, such as the **environment** or the women's movement, were mirrored in the narratives, while more experimental approaches left their mark in poetry ("concrete poetry"). As part of the innovative and alternative trends of the 1970s, women founded their own **publishing** houses (e.g., Frauenoffensive in Munich, 1976), while traditional publishing houses began to develop sections with a focus on **women's literature**. A number of authors who had come to Germany as guest workers established the genre of migrants' literature (Migrantenliteratur), dealing with the immigrants' concerns of the time. Although the term has lost some of its popularity, writings by authors with German as a second language enjoy particular popularity (e.g., those by the Turkish writer Emine Sevgi Özdamar; the German Turkish writer Feridun Zaimoglu, who put the sociolect "Kanak Sprak" on the map; and the Russian author of popular short stories, Wladimir Kaminer).

Throughout these years, a number of established writers, such as Grass, Böll, Walser, and Uwe Johnson, continued to dominate the literary scene. One of the most eminent literary critics in Germany was Marcel Reich-Ranicki (1920–1913), who was acclaimed the "pope of literature" and until 2004 led the controversial television show *Das literarische Quartett*, a vehicle intended to draw attention to new publications. As a young man, Reich-Raniscki had escaped from the Warsaw Ghetto, a memory he shared with the wider public in his memoir *The Author of Himself* (1999). The German feuilletonist, essayist, and biographer Fritz J. Raddatz (1931–2015) was part of a similar tradition of German intellectuals, whose observations assessed individual authors within a wider contemporary context.

A huge variety of grants and awards fosters literary activities in Germany. Examples are the Berliner Literaturpreis, the Deutscher Buchpreis, the Deutscher Krimi Preis, the Deutscher Jugendliteraturpreis, and the Georg-Büchner-Preis. So-called houses of literature (Literaturhäuser) act as meeting places for authors, audiences/readerships, and **publishers**, providing rooms for readings, discussions, and workshops. Such places can be found in Berlin, **Hamburg**, Frankfurt/Main, Munich, Cologne, and Stuttgart. Some cities appoint a resident writer (Stadtschreiber) for a year. Important literary archives include the national literary archive at Marbach (Deutsches Literaturarchiv Marbach), the Stiftung Weimarer Klassik, the Staatsbibliothek zu Berlin, and the archive of the Berlin Academy of Arts (Archiv der Berliner Akademie der Künste). The publishers of German newspapers also maintain thematic "libraries," for example, SZ-Bibliothek, the BILD Bestseller Bibliothek, and the Zeit Vorlesebibliothek. Two annual book fairs not only serve as national and international platforms for publishing houses but are also important indicators of trends, whether the increasing popularity of e-books on the German market, the importance of youth literature and regional literature, or current translations from other countries. Both the Frankfurt and Leipzig book fairs have a centuries-long tradition that was revived after World War II. Topical lists of authors and the opportunity to listen to literature read by the writers themselves are available at http://www.literaturport.de.

Germany has had its fair share of Nobel Prize laureates, including Heinrich Böll (1972), Elias Canetti (1981), Günter Grass (1999), and Herta Müller (2009). Müller's work is concerned with violence and terror and also reflects life in Romania during the Communist regime. Many critics considered the writer and academic W. G. Sebald (1944–2001) a potential future winner; among his most notable writings are *Austerlitz* (2001) and *On the Natural History of Destruction* (1999).

LOCAL GOVERNMENT. The smallest unit of local government in Germany is the Gemeinde (plural: Gemeinden) or Kommune (Kommunen), of which there were 11,100 in 2014. These communities or municipalities are roughly equivalent to parishes in Great Britain. Many of the smaller communities also form larger single groups at the next higher administrative tier, the Kreis, or district. Gemeinden tend to be very small, but those that stand on their own elect representatives to a local council (the Gemeinderat or Stadtrat). Most have between 200 and 20,000 inhabitants. Gemeinden that are grouped together under a Kreis send councilors both to their local municipal council, the Gemeinderat, and to a district council, the Kreistag, which is headed by a chief councilor (Landrat). A district may be either rural (Landkreis) or urban (Stadtkreis). Larger cities such as Cologne, Bonn, and Munich constitute their own Kreis, usually with a mayor (Bürgermeister) and city council (Stadtrat) and are also known as kreisfreie Städte: around 100 German cities have this status. Some big cities maintain representatives of districts or neighborhoods (Bezirksvertreter), who advise the city council on issues such as the local **environment**, street lighting, and pathways.

The role of Gemeinden is vaguely defined in the **Basic Law** (**BL**, article 28). In practice, they are obliged to maintain certain services such as schools, local police, and fire services and to perform administrative functions on behalf of the national or regional government, for example organizing elections, running local **immigration** services, issuing visas, and providing social welfare benefits. They also have the freedom to undertake local initiatives, such as building **sports** centers. Although they control their own budgets, they receive the lowest proportion of **taxation** revenue, and the imposition of more tasks from the political center has placed them under increasing financial strain. Both the established parties and local citizens' groups are represented on local and district councils, which are politicized to a degree.

Between the late 1960s and reunification, the number of Gemeinden in the Federal Republic of Germany (FRG) fell from around 24,000 to 8,500, with some combining to form larger administrative units (Gemeindeverbände) in order to coordinate services such as **education** and water supply. Some **federal states** have an extra, nonelected layer of administration between region (Land) and district (Kreis), the so-called Regierungsbezirk. Others, where such a layer is present, have renamed, restructured, or even abolished it altogether. The financial arrangements underpinning local government in Germany are highly complex.

See also ELECTORAL SYSTEM.

LOVE PARADE. The first Love Parade took place in 1989 in **Berlin** with 150 participants; 15,000 took part in 1992, 500,000 in 1995 (under the motto "peace on earth"), 1 million in 1997 ("let the sun shine in your heart"), and over 1.3 million in 2000 ("one world, one love parade"). During its heyday, the Love Parade epitomized youth and club culture, putting Berlin on the map as a capital of techno music and reflecting the energy and vibrancy of the reunified city in transition. Originally described as a political demonstration—which in German law means the state has to pay for security—a court had ruled by 2001 that this was in fact a commercial event, so that thereafter the organizers were responsible for the provision of security. After 2002, the event increasingly struggled to find sponsors and lost its status. The enthusiasm and optimism of the early 1990s evaporated at the same time that interest in techno music declined, and it reverted to being housed in clubs and special locations. Between 2007 and 2010, events were held in the Ruhr region, until on 24 July 2010 the event in Duisburg ended in tragedy, with at least 21 killed and 500 injured. The ultimate responsibility for the disaster, whether it was due to mistakes on behalf of the organizers or the police, could never be clarified. As a concept the love parade has meanwhile been adopted worldwide.

LOWER SAXONY (NIEDERSACHSEN). In medieval times, the area broadly covered by Lower Saxony today (47,618 sq. km) was the home of Saxon and Frisian tribes before it was incorporated into the Franconian empire of Charles the Great (known also as Charlemagne) in the late eighth century. During the 18th century the kingdom of Hanover, which had links with the British crown, became the leading power in northwestern Germany, until it was annexed by Prussia (1866), while Braunschweig (in the southeast), Oldenburg (in the north), and Schaumburg-Lippe remained independent states. After World War II, all four provinces were merged to create the state of Lower Saxony. The second largest of the **federal states**, Lower Saxony now stretches from the Dutch border in the west to the Elbe River in the east and from the **North Sea** coast to **North Rhine-Westfalia** and **Hessen** in the south and also adjoins **Mecklenburg-West Pomerania**, **Brandenburg**, **Saxony-Anhalt**, and **Thuringia** and encloses the city-states of **Bremen** and **Hamburg**. Lower Saxony's main geographical regions are the northern coast with the East Frisian Islands; the flat, treeless marsh landscape along the lower reaches of the rivers Ems, Weser, and Elbe; the sandy belt of the Geest; and the foothills of the Central Uplands, from which rise the Harz Mountains in the southeastern corner, whose highest point is the Wurmberg (971 m). The Harz also included the border with the former **German Democratic Republic (GDR)**. In common with other former border zones (Zonenrandgebiete), the area—a prohibited zone on the East German side—became largely deserted after the erection of the **Berlin Wall** (1961) and is now part of the Green Belt (Grünes Band) initiative to preserve the natural environment, which flourished during this period. The narrow strip of land bordering the Central Uplands includes fertile areas of loess and black earth as well as natural raw materials such as coal, iron ore, oil, and natural gas.

Lower Saxony's geographical diversity has produced sparsely populated rural areas alongside centers of **industry**. Of the total **population** (7.8 million, or 9.7 percent of the national population), the main concentrations are in the south and include the state capital Hanover (526,000), Braunschweig (251,000), Osnabrück (165,000), Wolfsburg (123,000), Göttingen (121,000), Hildesheim (103,000), and Salzgitter (102,000). After World War II, Lower Saxony absorbed two million refugees and expellees from the east, although its border with the former **German Democratic Republic (GDR)** remained an economic backwater from which many emigrated. Further influxes of population occurred during the 1960s, as foreign guest workers were recruited into industry and again after reunification. Currently, 8.4 percent of the population are **foreigners**.

After the war, Lower Saxony was faced with reorienting its economy away from its traditional industries, while also severing links in the east and forming new ones in western Germany. A further transformation took place during the 1970s and 1980s, as the economy shifted its historical dependence on **agriculture** to developing industry and services. Today agriculture and fisheries account for just around 1.8 percent of GDP, compared with 5 percent for building and construction, 26 percent for manufacturing and industry, and almost 67 percent for services. With **Volkswagen** (at Wolfsburg, Emden, Braunschweig, Salzgitter, and Osnabrück) and the truck/bus builder MAN (Hanover and Osnabrück), the main industry is **automobile** and motor manufacturing, employing 116,000 workers and contributing 41 percent of the region's industrial turnover. Also important are food (14 percent of regional GDP and employing almost 65,000 workers), mechanical **engineering** (6 percent, over 57,000), **chemicals** (5 percent, over 23,000), and rubber/synthetics (5 percent, 43,000). Niche industries are aviation (employing around 30,000 and including the Airbus works in Stade), advanced optical engineering, and medical technology, while more traditional mining (mainly of materials for the building industry) continues alongside the exploitation of oil and natural gas from reserves. Lower Saxony contributes 9 percent of national GDP, and unemployment (6.1 percent) is close to the national average (6.4 percent in 2015).

Despite its significance for the food industry, the number of workers directly engaged in agriculture has fallen steadily, to around 150,700 (including family members). Alongside arable farming, cattle, pigs, and poultry are reared, and the area around the Elbe River has extensive fruit orchards. Centers of **tourism** include the coast, the Harz Mountains, and the Lüneburg Heath; the region boasts around 40 **health** spas and several coastal resorts. Hanover is a major communications hub for traffic between the south and the north (Scandinavia) and between east and west. The city, which was home to Expo 2000, has an international airport and hosts numerous trade fairs (including CeBIT). Lower Saxony has several universities and institutions of higher **education**, the largest of which is the University of Hanover. **Research** focuses on the **environment** (Braunschweig, Clausthal) and **energy** (Oldenburg and Wilhemshaven). The region is predominantly Protestant (over 50 percent), with a sizable Roman Catholic population (18 percent), mainly in the southwest.

In 1997, the regional constitution extended its catalog of objectives for the state to include an entitlement to adequate housing and **sports** facilities, rights for animals, and a prohibition on discrimination against the disabled. The constitution also contains plebiscitary elements. The regional assembly

(**Landtag**), whose minimal number of members is legally set at 135, elects a **minister president** for five years. The minister president appoints a cabinet of ministers, which is in turn approved by the assembly. From 1957 until 1976, the political landscape was dominated by the **Social Democratic Party of Germany** (**SPD**), which, led by Alfred Kubel, ruled either alone (1970–1974) or in coalition, either with the **Christian Democratic Union** (**CDU**) or the **Free Democratic Party** (**FDP**). The CDU gained control in 1976 and, under Minister President **Ernst Albrecht**, governed alone (1977–1986) or in alliance with the FDP until 1990. Albrecht's decision in 1977 to store nuclear waste at Gorleben triggered nationwide controversy and continued to influence the regional elections until at least 2013. In May 1990, the SPD, which had gained a relative majority of seats at the 1986 election, returned to power when it formed a coalition with the **Green Party** under **Gerhard Schröder**, who continued as minister president until he was elected **federal chancellor** in 1998. His successors were Gerhard Glogowski (briefly) and **Sigmar Gabriel**. In 2003 the CDU, led by **Christian Wulff**, ended 13 years of opposition to reenter government in coalition with the FDP. Reelected in 2008, Wulff continued the coalition until he resigned in 2010 to become **president of the Federal Republic. David McAllister** (CDU) took over as minister president, but lost the 2013 election to a coalition of SPD and Greens led by **Stephan Weil** (SPD). The election also saw **The Left Party**, which entered parliament in 2008 with 11 seats, fail to clear the 5 percent entry hurdle. The CDU traditionally derives its support from the rural northwest of the region, while the SPD has strongholds in the industrial southeast.

M

MAAS, HEIKO (1966–). Social Democratic Party of Germany (SPD) politician. Born in Saarlouis (**Saarland**), Heiko Maas worked briefly on the production line of the Ford motor works in Saarlouis (1988) before studying law at the University of the Saarland and qualifying as a practicing lawyer (1989–1996). A member of the SPD from 1989 and regional party chairman from 2000, he was elected to the Saarland regional assembly (**Landtag,** 1994–1996, 1999–2013), where he also led the party parliamentary group (1999–2013, in opposition until 2012). In the regional assembly, he was **state secretary** (1996–1998) and then minister for the **environment, energy,** and **transport** (1998–1999). During 2012–2013, he served both as regional minister for economics, labor, energy, and transport and as deputy **minister president**. A member of the national presidium of the SPD from 2001, Haas was appointed federal minister for justice and consumer protection in Chancellor **Angela Merkel**'s third coalition government (2013–).

MAGDEBURG MODEL. The Magdeburg model was a minority coalition of the **Social Democratic Party of Germany** (**SPD**) and the **Green Party** in the federal state (Land) of **Saxony-Anhalt**, which governed from 1994 until 1998. The coalition, led by Minister President **Reinhard Höppner** (SPD), could be overturned only by a combined majority of the opposition **Christian Democratic Union** (**CDU**) and the **Party of Democratic Socialism** (**PDS**), the successor party to the **Socialist Unity Party of Germany** (**SED**) in the former **German Democratic Republic** (**GDR**). Conservative politicians attacked the SPD and Greens for relying on PDS support, although it functioned well at the regional level. The SPD continued to rely on PDS support following the 1998 regional election, when the Greens failed to enter parliament.

See also FEDERAL STATES (LÄNDER); FEDERALISM.

MAIHOFER, WERNER (1918–2009). Lawyer and **Free Democratic Party** (**FDP**) politician. Born in Konstanz (**Baden-Württemberg**), Werner Maihofer studied law at the University of Freiburg (1946–1950), gained a doctorate in 1950, and taught law at various universities in Germany after 1953. His academic career included being professor of criminal law at the University of Saarbrücken (1955–1970), where he was also rector (1967–1969); rector of the University of Bielefeld (from 1970); and vice president of the conference of university rectors of the Federal Republic of Germany (FRG, 1968–1971). A member of the FDP from 1969, he joined the party presidium the following year (until 1978) and was a deputy in the **Bundestag** from 1972 until 1980. He served as federal minister for special tasks under Chancellor **Willy Brandt** (1972–1974) and as interior minister (1974–1978). Maihofer resigned in June 1978, following the release of a report highlighting failures in the handling of the search for Hanns Martin Schleyer, president of the Bundesvereinigung der Deutschen Arbeitgeberverbände (Confederation of German Employers' Associations, BDA) and the Bundesverband der Deutschen Industrie (Federation of German Industries, BDI), who was kidnapped and murdered by left-wing **terrorists** (1977). Maihofer played an important role in drafting changes to the German codex of criminal law during the 1970s and chaired the FDP commission that drew up the Freiburg Theses (1971). He published widely on law and politics, was elected to the West German **PEN** Club (1971), held honorary doctorates at the universities of Nancy (1968) and Dublin (1987), and was awarded the Federal Cross of Merit (1975).

MAIZIÈRE, LOTHAR DE (1940–). Lawyer and **German Democratic Republic of Germany (GDR)** premier (1990). Born in Nordhausen (now in **Thuringia**), Lothar de Maizière studied the viola and then law as an external student at Humboldt University in East **Berlin** (1969–1975), playing in theaters and orchestras, including the Berlin Symphony Radio Orchestra. From 1976 he practiced law, and he was elected deputy chairman of the association (Kollegium) of lawyers in East Berlin (1987). Although specializing in tax and commercial law, he also defended Christians who had fallen afoul of the authorities, as well as conscientious objectors and young people involved in the peace movement. In 1985, he became a member of the synod of the Federation of Protestant Churches of the GDR and served as co–vice president (1987–1990). Much of his work with the church involved social and political issues that were not openly discussed in the GDR. After joining the **Christian Democratic Union (CDU)** in the GDR at the age of 16, de Maizière became increasingly disillusioned over the control exerted on the party by the state. On 10 November 1989, one day after the fall of the **Berlin Wall**, he was elected leader (chairman) of the East German CDU, and on 17 November he was appointed minister for church affairs in the interim government of **Hans Modrow**.

After the GDR national election of March 1990, de Maizière was elected premier (minister president) of the **grand coalition** government between the CDU, the **Social Democratic Party of Germany (SPD)**, and the Liberals, which negotiated reunification with the Federal Republic of Germany (FRG). In an interview held on the 50th anniversary of the FRG, he declared his signing of the 2 + 4 treaty with the Allies, which marked the final conclusion of World War II, to be the crowning moment of his career. After reunification (3 October 1990), he was elected party deputy to Chancellor **Helmut Kohl** at the first all-German congress of the CDU in **Hamburg** and was appointed federal minister for special tasks. Following the all-German elections of December 1990, de Maizière, who had chaired the **Brandenburg** regional party association of the CDU since November, was elected to the enlarged **Bundestag.**

In August/September 1991, following claims that he had spied for the GDR secret police (**Stasi**), de Maizière resigned his parliamentary mandate and as deputy party leader and regional chairman in order to resume his career as a lawyer in Berlin. His cousin, **Thomas de Maizière**, become defense minister in 2005.

See also PETERSBURG DIALOG.

MAIZIÈRE, THOMAS DE (1954–). Christian Democratic Union (CDU) politician. Born in Bonn, Thomas de Maizière studied law and history in Münster and Freiburg (1974–1979), qualifying as an assessor (1982) and earning a doctorate in law (1986). A member of the CDU from 1971, he worked for two governing mayors of West **Berlin, Richard von Weizsäcker** and **Erberhard Diepgen** (1983), before heading the policy section (Grundsatzreferat) of the Berlin senate chancellery and acting as speaker for the CDU parliamentary party in the city assembly (1985–1989). In the final months of the **German Democratic Republic (GDR)** in 1990, he assisted in restructuring the office of the minister president of the GDR and was a member of the delegation committee negotiating the Treaty of Unification. In the new federal state of **Mecklenburg-West Pomerania**, he became **state secretary** (Staatssekretär, 1990–1994) and chief of the state chancellery (1994–1998) under **Minister President** Berndt Seite before moving to **Saxony**, where, under Minister President **Kurt Biedenkopf**, he was head of the chancellery (1999) and, under **Georg Milbradt**, state secretary for finance (2001–2002), justice (2002–2004), and internal affairs (2004–2005). From 2005 to 2009, during **Angela Merkel**'s first coalition, he served as chief of the **Office of the Federal Chancellor** and federal minister for special tasks (representing the government in intelligence matters) and was subsequently federal minister of the interior (2009–2011, 2013–) and also of defense (2011–2013). In 2010, he took part in the negotiations over the **European Stability Mechanism (ESM)** and, as defense minister, continued the restructuring of the **Bundeswehr**. As interior minister, he was engaged in developing Germany's policy on internal **security** and was Merkel's most valuable assistant in managing the influx of **asylum** seekers in the summer of 2015. A deputy in the regional assembly (**Landtag**) of Saxony during 2004–2005, he entered the **Bundestag** in 2009 and joined the national executive committee of the CDU in April 2012. He is a cousin of the CDU politician **Lothar de Maizière**.

MANN, GOLO (1909–1994). Historian and writer. Born in Munich, the son of the writer Thomas Mann, Golo Mann studied philosophy and history at the universities of Munich, Berlin, and Heidelberg (1927–1932), where he earned a doctorate on the philosopher Gottfried Hegel (1933). When the National Socialists gained power in 1933, Mann left Germany with his family for France, teaching German history and literature at the Ecole Normale Supérieure in St. Cloud (near Paris) and lecturing at the University of Rennes (1933–1937). After coediting an antifascist journal in Zurich (1937–1940), he moved to the United States, where he taught history at various universities (1942–1958). Returning to Europe in 1958, he was a visiting professor at Münster (1958–1959) before being appointed professor of political sciences in Stuttgart (1960), a post he held until he retired on health grounds in 1964. During the 1960s, Mann built up an international reputation as one of Germany's leading historians and political scientists, although he was also celebrated as a literary historian. He joined the **PEN** Club in 1964 and was awarded the Georg Büchner Prize in 1968. His biography of General Albrecht von Wallenstein (*Wallenstein: Sein Leben erzählt von Golo Mann*, 1971) was hailed as a masterpiece. A respected political and historical commentator in the founding years of the Federal Republic of Germany (FRG), Mann supported the **Ostpolitik** of **Willy Brandt**, attacked the efforts of terrorists to undermine civil order during the 1970s, and during the **historians' quarrel** of the 1980s argued that the crimes of the National Socialists should be viewed as unique. Awards he received include honorary doctorates from the universities of Nantes (1973) and Bath (Great Britain, 1987), Pour le Mérite (1973), the Federal Cross of Merit (1972), and the Goethe Prize of the city of Frankfurt/Main (1985).

MAPPUS, STEFAN (1966–). Christian Democratic Union (CDU) politician. Born in Pforzheim (**Baden-Württemberg**), Stefan Mappus trained as an industrial clerk (Industriekaufmann) before studying economics and social sciences at the University of Hohenheim (from 1988), where he graduated with a diploma (1993) and worked as a research assistant in political science (1993–1995). He also worked part time for **Siemens AG** (1995–1997) and was later briefly employed by the **pharmaceutical** and **chemical** concern

Merck (2011). A member of the **Junge Union (JU)** of the CDU from 1983 and of the main party from 1985, Mappus entered the regional **Landtag** (1996) and was active in local politics before becoming political **state secretary** (Staatssekretär, 1998–2004), and subsequently minister (2004–2005), in the Baden-Württemberg ministry of **environment** and **transport**. He also led the regional parliamentary group (from 2005) and served as party vice chairman (2005–2009) and chairman (2009–2011). In February 2010, Mappus succeeded **Günther Oettinger** as **minister president** of Baden-Württemberg, leading a coalition of the CDU and the **Free Democratic Party (FDP)**, but following his party's worst ever performance in the 2011 regional election, resigned the party leadership and his parliamentary mandate. During his political career, Mappus was criticized for misuse of power when he applied pressure to close down a local exhibition on neofascism in Germany highlighting the role of leading CDU figures under the National Socialists (2002). On the right wing of the party, Mappus also attacked a well-established festival for **homosexuals** and lesbians (Christopher Street Day, 2005) and refused to purchase data exposing **tax** avoiders in the region (2010). He was further involved in the region's controversial purchase of foreign shares in a regional **energy** company (EnBW), undertaken secretly and designed to deliver cheaper energy, but allegedly without due diligence (2010).

MARSHALL FUND. *See* GERMAN MARSHALL FUND OF THE UNITED STATES (GMF).

MARSHALL PLAN. *See* GERMAN MARSHALL FUND OF THE UNITED STATES (GMF).

MCALLISTER, DAVID (1971–). Christian Democratic Union (CDU) politician. Born in West **Berlin**, David McAllister studied law at the University of Hanover (1991–1996) and qualified as a practicing lawyer (1996, 1998). A member of the CDU from 1988, he led the Cuxhaven district association of the youth organization (**Junge Union [JU]**, 1991–1994) before becoming mayor of the town of Bad Bederkesa in the state of **Lower Saxony** (2001–2002), a district councilor for Cuxhaven (1996–2010), and a deputy in the regional parliament (**Landtag**, 1998–2014). His positions in the CDU include general secretary (2002–2004) and chairman (from 2008) of the regional party and leader of the regional parliamentary group (2003–2010). In 2005, he declined an offer from **Angela Merkel** to become general secretary of the national CDU. From 2010 until 2013, he was **minister president** of Lower Saxony, leading a coalition of the CDU and the **Free**

Democratic Party (FDP). McAlllister has dual German and British nationality. He was elected to the European Parliament in 2014, where he leads the Group of the European People's Party.

MECKLENBURG-WEST POMERANIA (MECKLENBURG-VOR-POMMERN). Situated in northeastern Germany, Mecklenburg-West Pomerania (MWP, area 23,210 sq. km) shares a land border with Poland to the east and faces the **Baltic Sea** to the north. Off its coast lie many islands, of which Rügen and Usedom are the largest. The land rises to just 179 meters at the highest point (the Helpter Hill in Mecklenburg-Strelitz) and is characterized by undulating plains, hills, basins, forests, and over 2,000 lakes, the largest being Lake Müritz. Already the most sparsely inhabited of the **federal states**, the **population** of MWP (currently 1.6 million) has faced a steady decline since 1990 (around 1.9 million), largely owing to emigration, especially of young people, and to deaths overtaking childbirths; that trend is expected to continue. All the main cities—Rostock (204,000); the state capital, Schwerin (96,000); Neubrandenburg (65,000); Stralsund (58,000); Greifswald (55,000); and Wismar (44,000)—have registered declines in population, most of which is concentrated on the Baltic coast. Just 4.1 percent of the population are **foreigners** (2015), among the lowest of the federal states.

The origins of MWP lie in the German colonization of Slav territory during the 12th century. West of the Oder River lies Mecklenburg, with historical Pomerania to the east. By the 15th century, the area had gained its independence from the rulers of **Saxony**, while the northern cities (Rostock, Wismar, Stralsund, Greifswald, Wolgast, and Anklam) had joined the powerful Hanseatic trading league. The rural economy was characterized by large feudal estates owned by aristocrats and worked by a bonded peasantry (feudal bondage was not lifted until 1820). The Thirty Years' War (1614–1648) and the Napoleonic Wars in the early 19th century devastated and depopulated the land. Although some modernization occurred after Pomerania became a province of Prussia in 1815, social conditions and patterns of land ownership hindered economic development, as land workers emigrated to the towns and overseas to North America, and seasonal laborers from Poland came in to replace them. At the end of World War II and under Soviet occupation, the land east of the Oder River (East Pomerania) became Polish territory, leaving Germany/the **German Democratic Republic (GDR)** with a rump of West Pomerania (Vorpommern). In 1952, the province was dissolved into the administrative districts (Bezirke) of Rostock, Schwerin, and Neubrandenburg. Reunification (1990) saw the creation of the current state of MWP, although some argued for merging with **Brandenburg**. MWP was the first eastern German state to hold elections (14 October 1990) and constitute a regional government (27 October).

Once regarded as the "corn basket" of Germany, MWP is mainly **agricultural** (in the 19th century, Stettin/Szczezin was the only city to undergo industrialization). During the GDR years, farmland was collectivized and converted to large cooperatives. Following privatization after reunification, many farmworkers left agriculture, and the workforce fell from 180,000 in 1989 to just 71,400 in mid-1991, although the average size of the modernized and restructured farming units remained higher than in western Germany, and the region's dairy farms are among the most modern in the **European Union (EU)**. At the same time, the area has few raw materials, a poor infrastructure, and little **industry**. Before 1989, the Baltic seaports supported a thriving shipbuilding industry, constructing and repairing vessels for the Soviet and eastern European fishing and merchant fleets, and by 1989 maritime activities accounted for around 40 percent of the region's industrial production and workforce. When this market disappeared and the yards were exposed to Western competition, strikes and protests broke out as the shipyards were scheduled for privatization or shutdown (in 1992 and 1996). Closures and takeovers during the 1990s resulted in a sharp decline in the workforce (from 34,000 in 1990 to 9,500 in 1995). The **energy** sector also suffered, as the old Soviet-built nuclear power station near Greifswald was dismantled for safety reasons (1990). Unemployment continues to be very high (at 10.4 percent, the highest of the federal states, compared with 6.4 percent for Germany as a whole in 2015). On the positive side, **transportation** links have been improved, and main highways linking **Berlin** with Rostock and **Hamburg** pass through the south of the region. Food production remains the region's largest industry, followed by **engineering, chemicals**, and wood products. Also important is **tourism**, based on the attractions of the Baltic coast, with its many islands, bathing/health resorts, sandy beaches, and lagoons. The area boasts many national parks and areas of outstanding natural beauty. Other economic sectors include health care, building, and services, and the region contributes 1 percent of national GDP (2015).

MWP has two ancient and small universities: Rostock, with 15,000 students, and Greifswald, with around 12,000. In 1992, the region joined the interstate broadcasting station Norddeutscher Rundfunk (NDR), which covers **Lower Saxony, Schleswig-Holstein**, and Hamburg. The move contradicted earlier assumptions that it would join forces with other eastern **Länder** (Berlin and **Brandenburg**) and was motivated partly by historical resentment over political control from (East) Berlin. At the same time, the decision was criticized for passing up the chance to establish a distinctive "east German" broadcasting identity.

The regional constitution, agreed upon in 1993 and modeled partly on that of neighboring Schleswig-Holstein, sets out a number of objectives for the state, including European integration, cooperation with Poland and the Baltic states, safeguarding the **environment**, promotion of gender equality, the protection of children, and the creation and preservation of jobs; it also contains plebiscitary elements. The regional assembly (**Landtag**), elected for five years (from 1994 onward), comprises at least 71 members, making it the smallest of the **eastern federal states**. The first government after reunification was a coalition of the **Christian Democratic Union** (**CDU**) and the **Free Democratic Party** (**FDP**, 1990–1994) led by CDU minister presidents Alfred Gomolka (1990–1992), who resigned after protests over shipyard closures, and Berndt Seite (1992–1994). Lengthy negotiations following the 1994 election resulted in a **grand coalition** of the CDU and the **Social Democratic Party of Germany** (**SPD**), headed again by Seite. In 1998 the SPD, under **Harald Ringstorff,** concluded Germany's first regional ("red/ red") coalition with the **Party of Democratic Socialism** (**PDS**), which was renewed in 2002. Following the election of September 2006, Ringstorff governed in partnership with the CDU. The same election, in which voter participation was at a record low (59.2 percent), saw the extreme right-wing **National Democratic Party of Germany** (**NPD**) enter the assembly with 7.3 percent of the vote. In 2008, Ringstorff retired and was succeeded by **Erwin Sellering** (SPD), who, following the election of 2011, entered into a coalition with the CDU. The **Left Party** increased its share of the vote, with slight losses for the NPD, which retained five seats.

MEDIA. The overarching legal framework for German media is derived from the sovereignty of the **federal states** in cultural matters (hence the regional basis of the public broadcasting service, ARD) and the constitutional guarantee of freedom of the **press**, broadcasting, and other sources of information (**Basic Law [BL]**, article 5). Until the 1980s, the main organs of mass media (and sources of information for the public) in the Federal Republic of Germany (FRG) were the press and the state-run **television and radio** stations. The sector has since been transformed by the emergence of private broadcasters (leading to a dual private/state-run system) and new digital technologies (telemedia). Despite the diversity of media output, the process of mergers and takeovers, which started in newspaper **publishing** in the 1950s, has continued, resulting in very large "mediamultis" engaged in press, broadcasting, book/digital publishing, and related services, and exhibiting shifting patterns of activity and corporate ownership. The commercial media concerns in Germany included in this entry all rely heavily on income from advertising revenue, which stood at over 15 million euros annually between 2012 and 2015, with the lion's share going to television (29 percent); daily newspapers (17 percent) and other print media, except specialist journals and weekly news titles, face consistently falling revenue levels.

In 2015, the largest ranked media organization in Germany was the Gütersloh-based **Bertelsmann** group (books, print and digital services, television, and radio), followed by the ARD (state-owned radio and television),

Axel Springer (newspapers, journals, print and distribution services, television, and radio), Hubert **Burda** Media (journals, printing, and direct marketing), the ProSiebenSat.1 group (television, radio, and **Internet**), **Bauer** Media (journals and digital publishing), ZDF (state-owned television), Verlagsgruppe Georg von **Holtzbrinck** (journals, newspapers, television production, Internet services, and market research), and the Funke media group (formerly WAZ and involved in newspapers, journals, radio, Internet services, and press distribution). Other concerns include Südwestdeutsche Medienholding (SWMH, mainly newspapers, including Verlagsgruppe Stuttgarter Zeitung), M. DuMontSchauberg (MDS, regional newspapers), Madsack (regional newspapers), and Ippen (digital portals for regional newspapers).

The Kommission zur Ermittlung der Konzentration im Medienbereich (Commission on Concentration in the Media, KEK) was established in 1997 as an official, independent body to monitor both the terms of commercial broadcasting licenses and the content of television programs; the aim is to prevent excessive media concentration, which is regarded as a danger to freedom of information. Between 2000 and 2015, the commission, which records data on audience share, companies' holdings, and market structures, produced five reports on media concentration. In its 2015 report, the commission highlighted the inadequacy of existing legislation to counter the convergence of media genres and providers resulting from the increasing use of Internet and digital technology; it also questioned the justification of focusing on television in the longer term as a major former of public opinion. At the regional level, 14 Landesmedienanstalten (state media authorities) issue licenses for commercial broadcasters; the authorities also coordinate oversight of national providers.

See also BUCERIUS, GERD (1906–1995); CINEMA; MOHN, REINHARD (1921–2009).

MEDIATION COMMITTEE. The mediation committee (full title: Vermittlungsausschuss von **Bundestag** und **Bundesrat**) is convened to negotiate compromises between the Bundestag and Bundesrat over bills for legislation that fail to pass both assemblies, especially where the political majorities diverge. The committee, whose function is laid down in the **Basic Law** (**BL**, article 77,2) and plays an important role in German **federalism**, comprises 16 members from each assembly, drawn in proportion to the size of parliamentary groups (the number was raised from 22 to 32 in 1990). The members are usually experienced parliamentarians and include the **minister presi**dents or finance ministers of the **federal states** (since the committee is often called by the Bundesrat) and those government ministers whose laws are involved. Although the **federal chancellor** has the right to participate in the committee's meetings, this has not happened in practice. The chairman of the committee, which reaches its decisions by consensus (no side may outvote the other), is obliged to act neutrally and propose procedures for resolving differences. The committee has no legislative powers: once a compromise is reached, the bill is passed back to the assemblies for the required majorities.

MEHDORN, HARTMUT (1942–). Industrial executive. Born in Warsaw, Hartmut Mehdorn studied mechanical **engineering** in **Berlin** and graduated with a diploma (1965) before joining the **Bremen**-based aircraft company VFW (Vereinigte Flugtechnische Werke Fokker GmbH, 1966), rising to become head of production (1978). After holding various senior positions at companies such as Airbus, Messerschmitt-Bölkow-Blohm, and Heidelberger Druckmaschinen, he took over as chairman of the loss-making national rail carrier Deutsche Bahn AG at the instigation of Federal Chancellor **Gerhard Schröder** (1999–2009). Mehdorn embarked on a major program of structural reforms, including cost-cutting, changes in management, and tariff revisions, although moves toward full privatization failed to materialize (plans to join the stock exchange were postponed in 2008 owing to the global financial crisis), and industrial relations were poor. Following allegations that the concern had violated data protection laws involving its employees, Mehdorn resigned in 2009. As chief executive of Air Berlin (2011–2013), he was appointed chairman of the company managing Berlin's projected new airport (Flughafen Berlin Brandenburg GmbH) in 2013, but stepped down in 2015 following a series of delays and setbacks in its completion (now scheduled for 2017).

See also TRANSPORT: AIR TRAFFIC.

MEINHOF, ULRIKE (1934–1976). Journalist and **terrorist** leader. Ulrike Meinhof was born in Oldenburg (**Lower Saxony**). Her father, the director of the Jena city museum, died when she was five years old. After World War II, the family moved to Oldenburg in western Germany, where, after the death of her mother in 1948, Ulrike and her elder sister were raised by a history professor, Renate Riemeck, who introduced her to socialist ideas. While studying philosophy, pedagogy, sociology, and German at the universities of Marburg and Münster from 1955, she joined the **Federation of Socialist German Students** (SDS) in 1958, allying herself with radical members who displaced the organization's moderate wing in 1959. Meinhof wrote articles, took part in antinuclear demonstrations, and organized protest petitions. She contributed to the **Hamburg**-based journal *konkret*, whose editor she married in 1961, and subsequently to the **television** magazine program *Panorama* in **Berlin**. In 1965, she was fined 600 DM for describing **Franz Josef Strauß** as "the most infamous of German politicians" in an article published in *konkret*.

After teaching journalism at the Free University of **Berlin** (1969–1970), Meinhof achieved notoriety when in May 1970 she played a leading role in helping the terrorist Andreas Baader escape from a library in West Berlin. The incident marked the birth of the Baader-Meinhof underground terrorist group, which later called itself the **Red Army Faction (RAF)**. In a taped message one month after Baader's liberation, Meinhof unequivocally declared her personal commitment to violence in what she saw as a struggle designed to mobilize the proletariat and provoke armed conflict with the authorities. After paramilitary training in Jordan with the Palestinian El Fatah organization (June–August 1970), Meinhof and other members of the group returned to the Federal Republic of Germany (FRG) to wage a campaign of guerrilla warfare against the political establishment. In June 1972, along with Baader and others, Meinhof was arrested and held under a strict prison regime in Cologne-Ossendorf. She embarked on two hunger strikes (1973, 1974) before she was sentenced to eight years' imprisonment for her part in freeing Baader (November 1974). Later moved to the high-security wing at the detention facility of Stuttgart-Stammheim, she was found hanged in her cell on 4 May 1975. Although the authorities maintained that she had committed suicide, rumors that she had been murdered provoked protests and violent actions by RAF members in Germany and abroad. Her funeral in West Berlin attracted a large demonstration by sympathizers.

See also EXTREMISM.

MEISNER, JOACHIM (1933–). Roman Catholic leader. Born in Breslau-Lissa (Polish Wrocław, formerly in German Silesia), Joachim Meisner left Silesia as a refugee in 1945 to settle in **Thuringia** and trained in **banking** before entering a late vocation seminary in Magdeburg in 1951. He studied philosophy and theology in Erfurt (1959–1962), where he was ordained (1962). After earning a doctorate in theology in Rome (1969), he was appointed bishop of Erfurt-Meiningen (1975) and later of the divided city of **Berlin** (1980–1989), where he encountered numerous political problems. A cardinal from 1983, he served as archbishop of Cologne, Germany's largest Catholic diocese, from 1989 until his resignation in 2014. A conservative counterpart to the liberal cardinal **Karl Lehmann** in Mainz and instrumental in the election of **Joseph Ratzinger** as Pope Benedict XVI, Meisner frequently attracted controversy, for instance by comparing **abortion** to the crimes of the National Socialists (2011) and accusing Chancellor **Angela Merkel** of wanting to solve Germany's demographic problems by promoting **immigration** instead of encouraging **women** to stay at home and have children (2013).

See also RELIGION.

MERCKLE FAMILY. Pharmaceutical entrepreneurs. Born in 1935, Adolf Merckle founded Ratiopharm in 1974 in Ulm as a subsidiary of Merckle GmbH, a traditional, medium-sized pharmaceutical concern, which specialized in drugs for rheumatism, osteoporosis, and bowel disease. Following up on an idea that had originated in the United States and the first to implement it in Germany, Ratiopharm concentrated on producing generic forms of drugs whose patents had lapsed. At first the company faced stiff competition from the original producers, but it was helped during the 1980s by increasing financial pressure on **health**-care providers to cut costs. By 2000, Ratiopharm, whose commercial success lay in the volume production of paracetamol and nasal drops sold with small profit margins, dominated a rapidly expanding domestic market at a time when the demand for patented drugs was shrinking, and Merckle became one of Germany's richest men. Expanding rapidly, the group acquired stakes in several companies (including VEM [electrical motors], Zollern, Kässbohrer [**engineering**], Phoenix [pharmaceutical wholesalers], Blauwald [forestry], and HeidelbergCement). It overreached itself, however, during the economic crisis of 2008 through credit-financed investments in **Volkswagen** (Adolf Merckle took his own life in 2009) and was forced to reduce its holdings and sell off Ratiopharm (2010). Management of the group passed to Adolf's sons, Philipp Daniel and, in particular, Ludwig, who restored the concern to stability and growth. In 2014–2015, the group reported a turnover of 22,000 million euros.

MERKEL, ANGELA (1954–). Christian Democratic Union (CDU) politician and **federal chancellor**, 2005–. Angela Merkel was born Angela Dorothea Kasner in **Hamburg**, the eldest of three children of a Protestant theology student and a schoolteacher. In 1954, her parents moved to the **German Democratic Republic (GDR)**, where her father worked as a pastor. Angela Kasner studied physics at the University of Leipzig (1973–1978) before working as a **research** assistant at the Institute of Physical Chemistry at the Academy of Sciences in (East) **Berlin** (1978–1990), where she specialized in quantum chemistry and gained a doctorate in 1986. After the collapse of the communist regime, Merkel joined the reform group **Democratic Awakening** in December 1989, serving as its **press** spokeswoman from February 1990. Following the national election of 18 March 1990, she became deputy spokeswoman for the interim government of **Lothar de Maizière**.

A member of the CDU from August 1990 and elected to the all-German **Bundestag** the following December, Merkel began a promising ministerial career under Chancellor **Helmut Kohl**, first as minister for **women** and youth (1991–1994) and then as minister for the **environment**, nature, and nuclear reactor security (1994–1998). In her first international appearance, she represented Germany at the first United Nations Conference of the Parties (COP 1) in Berlin in 1995 (the COP is the supreme decision-making body of the United Nations [UN] Framework Convention on Climate Change), leading the meeting to positive agreements prior to the adoption of the Kyoto Protocol in 1997 and signaling a long-term interest in environmental issues. As minister for nuclear safety, she survived pressure to resign over excessive levels of radioactivity in CASTOR transports, which she halted. Her progress within the CDU was equally impressive: she rose from deputy leader of the national party (1991–1998) and regional leader for **Mecklenburg-West Pomerania** (1993–2000) to national general secretary (1998–2000). At the party conference in Essen in April 2000, she took over from her mentor, **Wolfgang Schäuble**, as leader (elected by a 60 percent majority) and in 2002–2003 succeeded **Friedrich Merz** as leader of the CDU/**Christian Social Union (CSU)** parliamentary group. Merkel took over a demoralized party, which had lost the 1998 election and faced a falling membership, large debts, and the scandal of Helmut Kohl's acceptance of illegal donations. Writing in the *Frankfurter Allgemeine Zeitung* in December 1999, Merkel publicly distanced herself from Kohl and offered the prospect of a younger, fresher leadership.

Although Merkel had maintained a low-key profile under Kohl, she acquired as Schäuble's protégée the image of a left-of-center conservative. She publicly met with homosexuals and lesbians and advocated a liberal policy on family issues. On the grounds that it would foster racial hatred, she openly rejected the tactic adopted by **Roland Koch** in the 1999 **Hessen** regional election of mounting a public petition against the government's proposed introduction of a dual passport. Merkel's first serious political defeat occurred in July 2000, when she failed to muster the CDU-ruled federal states in the **Bundesrat** in opposition to the **taxation** reforms proposed by the government coalition of the **Social Democratic Party of Germany (SPD)** and the **Green Party**. Despite the high hopes and genuine grassroots support that accompanied her election as leader, she struggled in the early years to establish her personal authority in the party and was passed over for **Edmund Stoiber** as chancellor candidate in the 2002 election. In supporting U.S. president George W. Bush in the invasion of Iraq in 2003, she ran against the national feeling and ignored warnings from within her own party.

A key issue for Merkel and her party remained reform of the social welfare system, especially since the claims of former chancellor Kohl that **pensions** were safe had long been exposed as untenable (the "pension lie"). In what was seen as an astute tactical move, Merkel appointed (in February 2003) the respected former **president of the Federal Republic, Roman Herzog**, as head of a CDU commission to draw up recommendations for reform, which were adopted at a party conference in Leipzig (December 2003). The election of her preferred candidate, **Horst Köhler**, as federal president in May 2004 further strengthened her standing in the CDU. As chancellor candidate in the run-up to the national election of September 2005, Merkel advocated large-scale taxation reform, measures to improve labor market flexibility, and a reduction of bureaucracy; in **foreign policy**, she signaled a willingness to improve relations with the United States and to promote enlargement of the **European Union (EU)** at the expense of closer integration of core member states, such as France. She has also been instrumental in asserting the influence of the **Office of the Federal Chancellor** in determining foreign policy, to some extent undermining the traditional roles of the Federal Ministry for Foreign Affairs and its head, provided by the junior coalition partner. In the election campaign, she performed poorly in a face-to-face **television** debate with **Gerhard Schröder** (SPD) and made a serious error in appointing Paul Kirchhof, a former constitutional judge, as her finance shadow minister when he advocated a radical 25 percent flat rate tax that was not part of the party manifesto. Nevertheless, in a close-run election, she emerged as **federal chancellor** of a **grand coalition** with the SPD (November 2005), the first woman and eastern German to hold the office. Although the first year of her chancellorship was regarded as lacking direction, Merkel went on to head two further coalition governments, with the **Free Democratic Party (FDP)** in 2009 and again with the SPD in 2013. Firmly established as Europe's strongest head of state, she took a leading role in determining fiscal policy in the response to the **eurozone crisis**, although her naturally cautious approach to decision making and sensitivity to domestic politics attracted some criticism in the early stages of the crisis. During 2015, she personally asserted an open door policy toward **asylum** seekers from the Middle East, which proved controversial in view of the size of the influx, revealed differences with more conservative elements of the government coalition, and undermined her popularity among the electorate. In September of that year, she overtook **Konrad Adenauer** as the CDU's longest serving leader.

Merkel makes few efforts to cultivate an image, reveals little of her private life, and maintains a small circle of key advisers, some of whom are close confidants. Of these, Eva Christiansen, born in 1970 in Cologne, was appointed CDU parliamentary group speaker in 2002 and has worked alongside Merkel in the Office of the Federal Chancellor since 2005. As head of the **media** and political planning section, she approves important speeches and advises Merkel on her public appearances. Steffen Seibert, born in 1960 in Munich and a former journalist for the ZDF **television** channel, was appointed government spokesman and head of its **press** and information office in 2010 with the rank of **state secretary**. In this capacity, he works closely with the chancellor to convey her responses to domestic and foreign political events. Former business manager of the parliamentary party (2009–2012) **Peter Altmaier** developed a reputation for managing good relations between the CDU/**Christian Social Union (CSU)** and government and is considered a key figure in maintaining Merkel's power base within the party. Beate Baumann, born in 1963 in Osnabrück (**Lower Saxony**), is Merkel's personal office manager in the Konrad Adenauer Haus (Konrad Adenauer House, the administrative headquarters of the CDU in Berlin) and works directly with Christiansen. A personal friend of the chancellor, Baumann also exerts considerable powers of access to her. While Merkel regards CDU general secretary **Peter Tauber** as an important ally in modernizing the party organization, **Volker Kauder**, leader of the parliamentary group, is useful for his traditionally conservative views. Since 1998, Merkel has lived with her husband, Joachim Sauer, a chemistry professor, in Berlin.

See also ENERGY: NUCLEAR POWER/ELECTRICITY; STEINMEIER, FRANK-WALTER (1956–).

MERZ, FRIEDRICH (1955–). Christian Democratic Union (CDU) politician. Born in Brilon (**North Rhine-Westfalia**), Friedrich Merz studied law and political science at the University of Bonn (1976–1981), qualifying as a lawyer in Saarbrücken (1985), where he served as a judge (1985–1986), before setting up his own legal practice and working for the Verband der Chemischen Industrie (German Association of Chemical Industries, VCI) in Bonn and Frankfurt/Main. In 1990, he joined the law partnership Leinen & Dietrichs at the higher regional court in Cologne. He also represented the Sauerland/Siegerland district in the European Parliament (1989–1994).

Merz entered the **Bundestag**, representing the CDU, in 1994. As an active member of the finance committee of the CDU/**Christian Social Union (CSU)** parliamentary group (1996–1998), he served as the group's reporter on the introduction of the euro and developed a solid reputation for financial competence. In January 1997, he joined the CDU regional executive in **North Rhine-Westfalia**. When the CDU lost the national election of 1998, Merz, along with other, younger conservative politicians, including **Angela Merkel**, came to the forefront as the party reviewed its future and rejuvenated its leadership. Merz joined the national executive (November 1998) and served as deputy chairman (November 1998–February 2000, October 2002–November 2004) and chairman (February 2000–September 2002) of the CDU/CSU parliamentary group.

Merz's rapid rise in the party was followed by an equally swift fall. At the height of the scandal over illegal party donations that engulfed former chancellor **Helmut Kohl** in early 2000, many hoped that Merz, with his acknowledged financial expertise and probity, would lead the party out of its funding crisis. He was briefly regarded as a potential successor to **Wolfgang Schäuble** and played an important role in the 2002 national election campaign, but was forced to cede leadership of the parliamentary party to Merkel when the CDU/CSU failed to dislodge the coalition of the **Social Democratic Party of Germany (SPD)** and **Green Party**. Nevertheless, as deputy leader of the group (from 2002), Merz led the CDU's attack on the government's reform program, arguing in 2003 for a simplification of Germany's complex **taxation** system and the removal of many tax breaks. Following his long-standing rivalry with Merkel, he resigned as deputy leader of the parliamentary party (2004), but failed in an appeal to the **Federal Constitutional Court (FCC)** to prevent disclosure of ancillary income for Bundestag members (2007). In his book, *Mehr Kapitalismus wagen* (2008), he advocated an increased role for economic neoliberalism—controversially just when the global financial crisis broke. Merz withdrew from the Bundestag in 2009 and became chairman of the Atlantik-Brücke association for promoting links between the United States and Germany. During 2010–2011, he was responsible for the privatization and sale of the WestLB regional **bank**.

MEYER, LAURENZ (1948–). Christian Democratic Union (CDU) politician. Born in Salzkotten (**North Rhine-Westfalia**), Laurenz Meyer studied economics at the University of Münster, qualified with a diploma (1975), and started work at the **energy** supply company VEW AG in Dortmund (later part of the REWE group). A member of the CDU from 1968, he served on the Hamm town council (1975–1995), led the CDU parliamentary group on the council (1989–1995), and was candidate mayor (1994). Elected to the state parliament (**Landtag**) for North Rhine-Westfalia in 1990, he was economics spokesman for the CDU (1990–1999) and then deputy leader (1997–1999) and leader (1999–2000) of the parliamentary group. He also served as regional party treasurer (1995–2001) and as first vice president of the assembly (2000). In 2000, he was elected to the CDU national executive and in November became general secretary during the renewal of party leadership that followed the election defeat of 1998 and the financial scandals that engulfed the CDU in 2000. He entered the **Bundestag** in October 2002, but resigned as general secretary (December 2004) when it emerged that he had continued to receive payments from RWE AG after taking up his CDU post (in which he was succeeded by **Volker Kauder**). The feeling within the party was especially sensitive following the donations scandal surrounding **Helmut Kohl**, and the affairs once again raised questions about Bundestag members accepting external payments alongside their parliamentary salaries. Meyer failed to enter the Bundestag in 2009.

MIELKE, ERICH (1907–2000). German Democratic Republic (GDR) politician. Born in **Berlin**, the son of a cartwright, Erich Mielke trained and worked as a forwarding agent (1924–1927). He joined the youth wing of the Communist Party of Germany (KPD) in 1921 and the main party in 1927. Until 1931, he also worked as a reporter for the party newspaper, *Rote Fahne*. During this turbulent period in German politics, Mielke belonged to a paramilitary group defending the party against attacks by right-wing extremists. Involved in the murder of two policemen during a demonstration in

Berlin (1931), he fled via Belgium to the Soviet Union and was sentenced to death by a German court in absentia. In Moscow he trained at the Lenin School (1934–1935), and he served with the international brigades during the Spanish Civil War (1936–1939). After a brief spell in Belgium (March 1939–May 1940), he was interned in France (May 1940–April 1941).

After World War II, Mielke emerged again in Berlin, where as a member of the KPD (**Socialist Unity Party of Germany [SED]** from 1946) he rose rapidly in the party, taking charge of denazification in the Soviet occupation zone and building up the police and security apparatus in eastern Germany (the GDR from 1949). He joined the Central Committee of the SED (1950) and became a leading functionary in the ministry for state security, where he occupied various positions before succeeding Ernst Wollweber as minister (1957). From 1958, he sat as a deputy in the **People's Chamber**. When **Erich Honecker** took over as party leader and head of state (1971), Mielke joined the SED Politburo as candidate member (full member from 1976). From 1980 he held the rank of army general.

With the fall of the regime in November 1989, Mielke resigned as minister (17 November) and was expelled from the People's Chamber and the SED. In December 1989, he was taken into investigative detention and later charged with various offenses, including abuse of office, corruption, and complicity in the shoot-to-kill policy at the border with the Federal Republic of Germany (FRG). In October 1993, he was sentenced to six years' imprisonment for the murder of the policemen in Berlin in 1931, although he was released on health grounds (July 1995), and all legal proceedings against him were dropped in 1998. After his release, Mielke lived quietly until his death as a pensioner in Berlin-Hohenschönhausen. A veteran communist, Mielke was known primarily as the architect of the GDR's secret police, the **Stasi**, and its vast apparatus. He also kept a "red case" containing files and information on Erich Honecker dating back to the 1930s. In 2004, the box passed into the keeping of the **Federal Commissioner for the Records of the State Security Service of the Former German Democratic Republic**. The former Stasi headquarters is now a museum and memorial. A biography of Mielke, by Jochen von Lange, appeared in 1991 (*Erich Mielke: Eine deutsche Karriere*).

MIGRATION BACKGROUND. A term (German: Migrationshintergrund) introduced in 2005 to denote residents in Germany who have, either directly or indirectly, a foreign background.

See also IMMIGRATION.

MILBRADT, GEORG (1945–). Christian Democratic Union (CDU) politician. Georg Milbradt was born in Eslohe in the Sauerland (**North Rhine-Westfalia**), where his parents had settled after fleeing Posen in the east, and grew up in Dortmund. After obtaining a doctorate (1973) in finance at the University of Münster, where he studied business, law, and mathematics and was also active in Asta, the student union, he qualified as a professor (Habilitation) and took up a teaching post at the University of Osnabrück (1982). From 1983 until 1990, he headed the financial department of the city of Münster, helping it to gain a reputation for being well managed and business friendly.

A member of the CDU from 1973, Milbradt moved east to serve as finance minister under Minister President **Kurt Biedenkopf** (CDU) in the newly established federal state of **Saxony** (1990–2001). Milbradt's declared policy of cost-cutting and strict budgetary control in order to finance investment won him widespread respect and was instrumental in taking the CDU to an outright majority in the 1994 regional election, when he also gained a seat in the assembly (**Landtag**). Although often unpopular with his colleagues for maintaining a tight rein on spending, Milbradt, who had led the regional CDU since 2001, was already regarded as Biedenkopf's likeliest successor and took over as **minister president** when the latter announced his resignation in January 2002. Although Milbradt's management of the flooding that hit the region in the summer of 2002 won praise, his party lost its overall majority in the 2004 regional election and formed a government with the **Social Democratic Party of Germany (SPD)**, with Milbradt as leader. This was the first coalition in the state's history. Following his involvement in the liquidity crisis of the Saxony regional **bank** (SachsenLB), which was subsequently sold off to the regional bank of **Baden-Württemberg**, Milbradt resigned all political posts in 2008 and quit the Landtag the following year.

MINISTER PRESIDENT (MINISTERPRÄSIDENT). The minister president is the head of government of a federal state (Land). Since 1954, the minister presidents of the **federal states** have convened a standing conference (the Ministerpräsidentenkonferenz, MPK), which meets at least four times a year and is hosted and chaired by each state in annual rotation. The conference is chiefly concerned with concluding treaties and agreements, either between the states or with the **Bund**. Recent items on its agenda have also included European policy, reform of the federal system, and **financial equalization**. The title of minister president was also held by the nominal head of state of the former **German Democratic Republic of Germany (GDR)** until 1990.

See also FEDERALISM; LANDTAG (PLURAL LANDTAGE).

MINISTRY OF CULTURE (KULTUSMINISTERIUM). Although Germany has no national ministry of culture, each of the **federal states** is responsible for schools, universities (in part), further **education**, and cultural provision (e.g., **theater**) in its region and may also concern itself with the relationship between **religion** and the state. For these functions, several states have a ministry of culture (a historical term), while others assign them to one or more administrative bodies. At the national level, activities are coordinated by a standing conference of regional cultural ministers (Kultusministerkonferenz) based in **Berlin** and Bonn.

MISCHNICK, WOLFGANG (1921–2002). Free Democratic Party (FDP) politician. Born in Dresden (**Saxony**), Wolfgang Mischnick served in the German army during World War II, rising to the rank of lieutenant. In 1945, he cofounded in Dresden the Liberal-Demokratische Partei (Liberal Democratic Party, LDP), which in 1952 was renamed the Liberal-Demokratische Partei Deutschlands (Liberal Democratic Party of Germany, LDPD) to emphasize its pan-German claim. He represented the party in local elections and on the city council (1946). A member of the party's central executive committee for the Soviet occupation zone, he stood as a candidate for the regional elections but was forced by the Soviet authorities to withdraw. Politically neutralized and threatened with arrest, he fled via West **Berlin** to **Hessen** in western Germany (April 1948). In Frankfurt/Main, he immediately joined the LDP/FDP, working for the party and its newspaper (the *LDP-Kurier*, later renamed *Deutscher Kurier*). He sat on the FDP national executive (1954–1991) and was party deputy leader (1964–1998). He also led the national youth wing of the FDP (1954–1957) and represented the party in the Hessen state parliament (**Landtag**). During the 1960s, he occupied various positions on the Frankfurt city council and in 1960 gave one of the first speeches on the **environment**.

A member of the **Bundestag** from 1957 until 1994, Mischnick served as minister for refugees, expellees, and war victims (Bundesminister für Vertriebene, Flüchtlinge, und Kriegsbeschädigte, 1961–1963); business manager for the FDP parliamentary group (1959–1961); and subsequently deputy leader (1963–1968) and leader (1968–1991). He was honorary chairman from 1991. In 1982, he argued for continuing the coalition with the **Social Democratic Party of Germany (SPD)** but, to preserve party unity, supported the shift of support to the **Christian Democratic Union (CDU)/ Christian Social Union (CSU)**. After reunification (1990), he worked for the reconstruction of the **eastern federal states**. As a senior FDP politician and one of the longest-serving members of the Bundestag, Mischnick held a variety of parliamentary offices. Outside parliament, he also served on numerous boards and councils, including the broadcasting council of the news-

and culture-oriented radio station Deutschlandfunk, which he chaired from 1982 to 1991. Mischnick received numerous awards from Germany and abroad and contributed more than 300 articles to newspapers.

MITSCHERLICH, ALEXANDER (1908–1982). Psychoanalyst. Mitscherlich was born in Munich in 1908. He studied history, art history, and philosophy in Munich before he moved to **Berlin**, where he opened a bookshop supporting ideas that brought him into conflict with the National Socialists. To escape further spells of imprisonment, he temporarily moved to Switzerland, but returned to Germany and concluded a degree in neurology in 1941. After World War II, Mitscherlich served as an observer at the Nuremberg Trials. He established a clinic of psychosomatic medicine at Heidelberg University and became its chair in 1953. In 1960, together with his wife Margarete Mitscherlich, he founded the Sigmund Freud Institute in Frankfurt. Together with the political theorist Hannah Ahrendt (1906–1975) and the members of the Frankfurt School—who, based on sociological, psychoanalytical, and philosophical approaches were critical of capitalism and Soviet-style socialism—Mitscherlich shaped intellectual debates in West Germany and formulated a range of concerns in the postwar years. His engagement with the impact of National Socialism on the Germans led to the publication, with Margarete Mitscherlich, of *The Inability to Mourn: Principles of Collective Behaviour* (1967), an analysis of the Holocaust, the war crimes, and the public's response to these. His book *Inhospitality of Our Cities. A Deliberate Provocation* (1965) considered the implications of postwar urban planning and **architecture** and reflected concerns about how the urban environment was being dealt with. Mitscherlich won numerous awards and recognitions for his work.

MITTAG, GÜNTER (1926–1994). German Democratic Republic (GDR) politician. Günter Mittag was born into a working-class family in Stettin (now Szczecin in Poland). During World War II, he worked for the German air force and trained on the railways. He joined the Communist Party of Germany (KPD) in 1945 (**Socialist Unity Party of Germany [SED]** from 1946) and during 1950–1951 occupied various positions in the party apparatus, including the Central Committee of the SED. In 1958, as an external student, he graduated with a diploma in economics at the Hochschule für Verkehrswissenschaften (College of Transport Sciences) in Dresden; two years later, he earned a doctorate on the development of **transport** systems under socialism. A full member of the SED Central Committee (from 1962) and of the Politburo (from 1996), and a deputy of the **People's Chamber** (from 1963), Mittag became primarily responsible for economic development and policy under party leader **Walter Ulbricht** and in 1963 helped implement the Neues Ökonomisches System der Planung und Leitung (New Economic System, NÖSPL). His other positions included being a member of the Staatsrat (State Council, 1963–1971, and from 1979) and of the Nationaler Verteidigungsrat (National Defense Council, 1982–1989); deputy chairman of the Ministerrat (Council of Ministers, 1973–1976); and deputy to the head of the State Council, **Erich Honecker** (from 1984). During the regime change of 1989, Mittag was removed from all offices, expelled from the SED and Central Committee (23 November 1989), and placed in investigative detention (December 1989–August 1990). In 1991, he faced charges of misappropriation of funds for his private homes, but was declared unfit to stand trial for these and other charges. He was released from detention in May 1993 and died in Berlin in March 1994. A biography (*Günter Mittag: Um jeden Preis; Im Spannungsfeld zweier Systeme*) appeared in 1991.

MITTELSTAND. Owing partly to geographical factors and historical traditions dating from the early modern period, over 98 percent of German firms are small to medium-sized enterprises (SMEs), the so-called Mittelstand. Although originally possessing much wider social connotations (distinguishing, for instance, the middle classes from business elites or the proletariat) the term is now largely used in an economic sense. The category includes firms that either employ fewer than 500 people or have a maximum annual turnover of 50 million euros. The sector is highly diverse, embracing **research** and development, financial services, **transport**, information technology, **media**, **publishing**, and many branches of **engineering** and **industry**; it is especially strong in catering, building, recycling, motor services, and the timber industry. Most firms are owned and run by families who are closely involved in all aspects of decision making and operational management. Despite their fragmentation, German SMEs employ 60 percent of the nation's workforce and 84 percent of trainees/apprentices. Depending on the measure applied, they contribute around one-third of national economic activity and gross national product.

Because SMEs hardly existed in the former **German Democratic Republic (GDR)**, both **Bund** and **Länder** directed considerable resources to promoting a new Mittelstand in the **eastern federal states** after 1990, largely through the mechanism of a joint program (the Gemeinschaftsaufgabe Verbesserung der regionalen Wirtschaftsstruktur, GRW). Although this succeeded in establishing a larger number of SMEs in the east by 2012, the sector there had a relatively lower number of concerns than in the west; developed fewer partnerships with larger businesses; and enjoyed less access to investment capital for innovation, marketing, and growth in the start-up phases.

Although they are considered to be the backbone of the national economy and are electorally important, SMEs face particular problems compared with big companies. They operate within tighter financial margins, have less scope for weathering unfavorable commercial conditions, and are especially vulnerable to changes and downturns in the economic cycle. A significant proportion of new businesses also fail within five years. Unlike large concerns, SMEs are unable to disperse profits to foreign subsidiaries, benefit less from government subsidies, and cannot generally relocate abroad to take advantage of lower labor costs (this is particularly true, for example, of tradesmen, hairdressers, and small retailers who depend on a local customer base). The Institut für Mittelstandsforschung (IfM) is a research institute for SMEs based at the University of Mannheim and supplies information and statistics on the sector.

MODROW, HANS (1928–). Politician and premier of the **German Democratic Republic** (**GDR,** 1989–1990). Hans Modrow was born in Jasenitz/ Ueckermünde (now in **Mecklenburg-West Pomerania**) into a working-class family. He trained as a toolmaker/engineer (1942–1945) and served in the civilian army (Volkssturm), which was hastily recruited to defend German cities in the last days of World War II. During his captivity in the Soviet Union (1945–1949), he attended a school for antifascism and on his return to eastern Germany joined the **Socialist Unity Party of Germany** (**SED**); the state-run youth movement, Freie Deutsche Jugend (Free German Youth, FDJ); and the Freier Deutscher Gerwerkschaftsbund (Federation of **Trade Unions,** FDGB). After working briefly as a toolmaker, he enrolled as an external student at the Karl Marx party school (1954–1957) and earned a diploma at the Bruno Leuschner college of economics in **Berlin** (1959–1961). In 1966, he graduated with a doctorate in economics from Humboldt University in (East) Berlin, presenting a thesis on the sociological problems of economic planning. As a highly educated, ideologically sound, and capable member of the political elite, Modrow rose steadily in the party hierarchy. After attending the communist youth college (Komsomol) in Moscow (1952–1953), he joined the FDJ's central council (1953–1961), served as local SED party secretary for Berlin-Köpenick (1961–1967), and was a member of the Berlin district executive (1954–1971). A candidate member of the Central Committee of the SED (from 1958), he became a full member in 1967. Appointed secretary for agitation and propaganda in the Berlin area (1967), he headed the department of propaganda of the Central Committee (from 1971) and was a long-standing member of the **People's Chamber** (1958–1990).

Although he was first party district secretary in Dresden (from 1973), Modrow maintained a modest, low-key lifestyle and distanced himself from the Berlin political center. When the regime came under threat in October

1989, he initiated dialogue with opposition groups—notably the "Group of 20" citizens in Dresden—and was the first to set up formal contacts between the authorities and their opponents to avoid violent confrontation. During the crisis months of November/December 1989, he served in the embattled SED Politburo before his election as deputy chairman of the reformed SED/**Party of Democratic Socialism** (**PDS**). He became honorary chairman of the PDS in February 1990.

As a reform communist and interim premier of the GDR between the collapse of the SED in November 1989 and the national elections of March 1990, Modrow attempted to ensure an orderly transition to democracy. He fought (in vain) to preserve the identity and political independence of the GDR, arguing for a confederation with the Federal Republic of Germany (FRG). After reunification, he represented the PDS in the all-German **Bundestag** (1990–1994), serving on the parliamentary committee for external political affairs. In May 1993, the Dresden district court found Modrow guilty of electoral fraud during the GDR period, and he was cautioned and fined. In February 1994, he lost his immunity from prosecution as a Bundestag deputy and the following year received a 10-month suspended sentence for giving false testimony to a special committee charged with investigating misuse of office and power in the former GDR. In June 1999, he was among six PDS members elected to the European Parliament, where he served (until 2004) on a committee for development aid and was responsible for negotiations with the Czech Republic on accession to the **European Union** (**EU**). In 2007, Modrow was quietly removed as honorary chairman of the successor party to the PDS, **The Left Party,** as he became increasingly estranged from its leadership, arguing openly against its reformist direction and against cooperation with the **Social Democratic Party of Germany** (**SPD**). The differences were laid out in a disputation with **Gregor Gysi,** leader of the Left Party's parliamentary group (2005–2015), which appeared in 2013 (*Ostdeutsch oder angepasst: Gysi und Modrow im Streitgespräch*).

MOHN, REINHARD (1921–2009). Publisher. Born in Gütersloh (**North Rhine-Westfalia**), Reinhard Mohn served in the German air force in North Africa during World War II. Returning from captivity in the United States, he trained as a bookseller in 1946 and, the following year, aged 26, took over the management of his father's business, the small printing and **publishing** firm of Carl **Bertelsmann**, which the Mohn family had acquired in 1887. After branching out into light fiction in the 1920s, the business expanded vigorously.

After the war, Reinhard Mohn developed the company into one of the largest **media** groups in the world. It was also one of the first German companies to confront its role during the National Socialist regime, publishing documentation in 2002. A highly successful innovation was the direct distribution of books to readers via the so-called Bertelsmann Readers' Ring, later called "The Club." Founded in 1950, the club now maintains 160 shops throughout Germany and sells printed and digital media online. From 1952, Bertelsmann built up a reputation for reference books and lexica, and in 1962 the concern went international, extending its operations to Spain, followed by the rest of Europe (1970). The acquisition of book publishers Bantam Books (1980) and Doubleday (1986), as well as the music labels Arista (1979) and RCA (1986), established Bertelsmann firmly in the U.S. book and media markets; the creation of the New York–based Bertelsmann Music Group (BMG) in 1987 consolidated the process. The launch of private **television** in Germany in 1984 saw **Gruner + Jahr** and Bertelsmann merge their electronic media operations into the Ufa Film- und Fernseh-GmbH (**Hamburg**), whose stake in Germany's first private TV channel, RTL, heralded the emergence of what is now the country's most successful privately financed television and media group (RTL Deutschland). The period 1990–2000 saw strong expansion in eastern Europe, including a temporary excursion into printed daily newspapers, and also entry into the Chinese market, with a book club in Shanghai (1997). Although the Shanghai club was wound up in 2008, growth continued in the region. The acquisition of U.S.-based Random House in 1998, the largest investment in its history, turned Bertelsmann into the largest book publisher in the English-speaking world and shifted its principal market to North America. In 1999, the specialist academic and scientific publisher Springer joined the group to become BertelsmannSpringer, although the operation was sold off in 2003. Under chief executive Thomas Middelhoff (1998–2002), Bertelsmann unsuccessfully experimented with e-commerce and Internet services. Middelhoff's successor, Gunter Thielen (2002–2008), thoroughly reorganized the company, and operations were decentralized or sold off, preparing the ground for a new phase of expansion, including a joint venture with Sony, Sony BMG (2004), the third largest music concern in the world. As part of a new strategy of organic growth and concentration on core growth activities—driven by chief executive Hartmut Ostrowski (appointed 2008)—Bertelsmann withdrew from music recording and sold off Sony BMG to focus on musical rights management.

Mohn's Christian ethics and social principles earned him the sobriquet "Red Mohn" (Mohn also being the German word for poppy). He introduced profit sharing (1970) and converted the business into a share capital company, in which he remained a majority shareholder (1971). After this, Bertelsmann AG became less of a family concern than a large management-led organization, with centers in Gütersloh, Hamburg, and Munich. Mohn established the Bertelsmann Stiftung (Bertelsmann Foundation) in 1977 as the concern's owner and majority shareholder and retired as chief executive in 1981, moving to head the supervisory board. The foundation works for social, political, and cultural reforms in all areas of life, including **education,** the media, and the wider business community. Although Mohn renounced his remaining shareholder voting rights in 1999, the family's involvement continued through his second wife, Elisabeth ("Liz," born in 1942), and son Christoph (born in 1965), who became chairman of the supervisory board in 2013.

MÖLLEMANN, JÜRGEN W. (1945–2003). Free Democratic Party (FDP) politician. Born in Augsburg (**Bavaria**), Jürgen Möllemann trained as a parachute jumper during his national service (in later years, he would often parachute into party rallies); studied history, German, and **sports** at the Pedagogical University in Münster (1966–1969), where he chaired the students' association (AStA); and worked as a schoolteacher in Beckum (1969–1972). A member of the **Christian Democratic Union (CDU)** from his schooldays, he left the party in 1969 to join the FDP. In 1972, he entered the **Bundestag**, where he represented the FDP until 2000 and served as spokesman on **education** (until 1975) and security (until 1982) for the parliamentary group. During this period, he comanaged a public relations agency in Munich (1981–1982) and briefly edited the teenage magazine *twen* (1982). Möllemann aroused controversy with his blunt criticism of Israel's treatment of the Palestinians, whose leader, Yassar Arafat, he met in 1979.

Appointed parliamentary **state secretary** in the Federal Ministry for Foreign Affairs under Chancellor **Helmut Kohl** (CDU) in 1982, Möllemann was elected leader of the regional FDP in **North Rhine-Westfalia** (NRW) the following year, but declined to stand as **minister president** in the state elections of 1985, preferring instead to become an adviser on eastern and security policy to Foreign Minister **Hans-Dietrich Genscher** (FDP). From 1987, he was federal minister of education and science and from 1991, federal minister for economic affairs, where he faced the problems of financing reunification, in particular the large transfers required to support the eastern **federal states** as part of the **Upswing East** program. In January 1993, he resigned his ministerial post over the "letterhead affair," in which he had used official writing paper to promote a company run by a family member. Later that year, he founded WEB/TEC, a business consultancy, in Düsseldorf.

A vocal critic of government policy, Möllemann was forced to resign as leader of the FDP in NRW in 1994, although he was recalled in early 1996. When the coalition of the **Social Democratic Party of Germany (SPD)** and the **Green Party** assumed government in 1998, he joined the FDP presidium (1999), but resigned the following year. Following the 2000 regional election in NRW, he led the FDP parliamentary group in the **Landtag**. A close ally of **Guido Westerwelle**, who was elected leader of the national FDP in May 2001, Möllemann served as shadow spokesman on **health** during the 2002 national election campaign, but came under fire for his support of Jamal

Karsli, a member of the FDP since 2002 and an outspoken critic of Israel. Möllemann was increasingly seen as a political liability for trying to steer the FDP single-handedly into a right-wing populist course and for revelations that he had contravened German laws on the funding of political parties by maintaining a secret account for anonymous donors between 1996 and 2002 (for this a **Berlin** court fined the party 3.5 million euros in 2009). When in November 2002 the FDP considered expelling him, the flamboyant Möllemann responded by threatening to found his own party, but he eventually resigned in March 2003, declaring that he would continue to sit in the regional and national parliaments as an independent member. Two months later, he died when his parachute failed to open during a jump. The incident, which occurred shortly after parliament refused to lift his parliamentary immunity and while police were raiding his home in Münster for evidence of **tax** evasion and fraud, was widely considered to be suicide. Möllemann also served as president of the German-Arab Society (Deutsch-Arabische Gesellschaft, 1981–1991 and 1993–2003).

MÜLLER, GERD (1955–). Christian Social Union (CSU) politician. Gerd Müller was born in Krumbach (**Bavaria**) and studied pedagogy, political science, and economics (1975–1980), graduating with a diploma and a doctorate. A member of the CSU from 1976, he taught at a technical college (Fachoberschule) and was a senior councilor (Oberregierungsrat) in the Bavarian ministry of economics (1980–1989). He sat in the European Parliament (1989–1994) and entered the **Bundestag** in 1994, where he served as **state secretary** in the Federal Ministry for Food, **Agriculture** and Consumer Protection (2005–2013). In 2013, he joined Chancellor **Angela Merkel**'s third cabinet as federal minister for economic cooperation and development.

MÜLLER, MICHAEL (1964–). Social Democratic Party of Germany (SPD) politician and governing mayor of **Berlin** (2014–). Born in Berlin, Michael Müller studied economics and administration at college (Fachoberschule, from 1983), trained in commerce (qualifying in 1986), and worked as a self-employed printer from 1986 until 2011. A member of the SPD since 1981, he served as chairman of a local (Berlin) party association (Abteilungsvorsitzender, 1991–2000) and occupied various positions in the district council for Berlin-Tempelhof (Bezirksverordnetenversammlung, BVV, 1989–1996) before being elected to the Berlin city assembly (Abgeordnetenhaus) in 1996. His other positions in the SPD include chairman/leader of the Tempelhof-Schöneberg association (2000–2004), leader of the parliamentary group in the city assembly (2001–2011), and chairman of the Berlin regional/city association (2004–2012). After serving as mayor (deputy to the governing mayor) and senator for city development and the **environment**

(2011–2014), he succeeded **Klaus Wowereit** as governing mayor of Berlin in December 2014. At the same time, he took over the chair of the supervisory board of the much-delayed Berlin Brandenburg airport.

MÜLLER, PETER (1955–). Former **Christian Democratic Union (CDU)** politician. Born in Illingen (**Saarland**), Peter Müller studied law and political science in Bonn and Saarbrücken (1975–1983) and worked as a legal trainee and an assistant in state and administrative law at the University of the Saarland, where he also later took up a teaching post. In 1986, he was appointed a judge, eventually working for the regional court in Saarbrücken. An active member of the CDU from 1971 and leader of its regional youth wing (**Junge Union [JU]**, 1983–1987), Müller entered the Saarland state parliament (**Landtag**) in 1990. He joined the national party presidium (1990), served as parliamentary business manager (1990–1994), and chaired the parliamentary group (1994–1999) before taking over leadership of the regional CDU (1995). In the regional elections of September 1999, Müller led his party to an overall majority, the first in 14 years, to become **minister president** of the Saarland. Regarded as a modernizer, he acted decisively to reduce the state's dependence on steel and coal and to introduce high-technology and service industries. He presided over an economic revival of the region, which, despite large debts and the legacy of economic restructuring, registered significant growth and unemployment below the national average. He also argued for changes to the proposals drawn up by the **Hartz Commission** to soften their effect on unemployed persons who had made social security contributions over several years. Although reelected with an absolute majority in 2004, his party entered into coalition with the **Free Democratic Party (FDP)** and **Alliance 90/The Greens** following the election of 2009 (the so-called Jamaica coalition, named after the similarity of the colors of the parties to the Jamaican flag, was the first in Germany). In 2011, Müller resigned as minister president to become a judge at the **Federal Constitutional Court (FCC)**. The move was criticized for undermining the stability of the coalition government, and many regarded Müller as unqualified for the judicial post. During his political career, Müller enjoyed a reputation as a lively debater and as a "young Turk" in the CDU, keen to modernize the economy and administration of his home region (he also advocated the repatriation of foreign nationals convicted of criminal offenses).

MÜNTEFERING, FRANZ (1940–). Social Democratic Party of Germany (**SPD**) politician. Born in Neheim-Hüsten (**North Rhine-Westfalia, NRW**) into a working-class family, Franz Müntefering trained as an industrial clerk (Industriekaufmann, 1954–1957) and worked in the **engineering** industry (1957–1975). A member of the SPD (from 1966) and of the metalworkers' **trade union** IG Metall (from 1967), he occupied various positions in local and regional politics before entering the **Bundestag** (1975–1992), where he specialized in housing policy and was business manager for the SPD parliamentary party (1990–1992). He joined the SPD national executive in 1991, but returned to regional politics as minister for labor, **health**, and social affairs in NRW's government under Minister President **Johannes Rau** (1992–1995). In 1995, he was appointed party manager and played a key role in the organization of the 1998 national election campaign, gaining credit for setting up an effective coordination center and communications infrastructure. In May 1998, he succeeded Rau as leader of the SPD in NRW, but almost immediately joined the shadow cabinet of chancellor candidate **Gerhard Schröder**.

Müntefering returned to the Bundestag after the 1998 national election, which brought the SPD/**Green Party** coalition to power. As federal minister for transport, building, and housing (1998–1999), he organized the government's relocation to **Berlin** and was involved in restructuring the national railway operator, Deutsche Bahn AG, appointing **Hartmut Mehdorn** chief executive. During the second half of the 1990s, Müntefering belonged, alongside Schröder, **Oskar Lafontaine**, and **Rudolf Scharping**, to the senior leadership of the SPD, and in September 1999 he resigned as minister to become general secretary of the party (until 2002). This was a new position, created to coordinate the activities of the **Office of the Federal Chancellor**, the parliamentary group, and the main party following devastating electoral defeats in European and local elections. After the 2002 national election, Müntefering assumed leadership of the parliamentary group and in March 2004 succeeded Schröder as party chairman, but resigned in November 2005 when his preferred candidate for the post of party general secretary was beaten by the left-winger **Andrea Nahles**; the move precipitated a leadership crisis, although he later briefly returned as leader (October 2008–November 2009). After the 2005 national election, he was instrumental in negotiating a ruling coalition with the **Christian Democratic Union** (**CDU**) and served as vice-chancellor and federal minister for labor and social affairs in the cabinet of **Angela Merkel** (2005–2007).

The outspoken Müntefering developed a strong reputation as the SPD's troubleshooter and for combining the image of a modernizer with traditionalist roots in the working-class Ruhr region. In the run-up to the regional election in NRW in May 2005, he attracted controversy when he condemned "anonymous investors" as "locusts" of international capitalism and released a list of 12 leading German industrialists who, he claimed, were destroying German society. His criticism of **tax** havens provoked indignation in Luxembourg and Switzerland (2009). He did not offer himself for reelection to the Bundestag in 2013, and in the same year he became president of the Arbeiter-Samariter-Bund (Workers' Samaritan Association, ASB).

MUSEUMS. The 1970s and 1980s saw a boom in museums in the Federal Republic of Germany (FRG) that was unparalleled since the end of the 19th century. Many of Germany's museums originated in royal, church, and civic collections, while others owe their existence to generous donations. Since the immediate priority after World War II had been to rebuild the country, the creation of new premises for museum collections and exhibitions had taken longer than other projects, although many cities eventually invested in architecturally progressive new buildings that became cultural centerpieces. Examples include the Museum Battenberg in Mönchengladbach, by Vienna-born Hans Hollein (1934–2014), and the Neue Staatsgalerie in Stuttgart, by the Glasgow-born James Stirling (1926–1992).

Reunification had a major impact on collections, especially in **Berlin**. Some were "reunited" (brought together from former East and West Germany/Berlin), while others were relocated to new premises. Berlin has today about 175 museums. Some of these form part of memorials, while others either specialize in or include sections on the country's National Socialist past—for example, the German Historical Museum, Berlin—or the communist years of the **German Democratic Republic (GDR)**—such as the **Stasi** Museum and the DDR Museum, both in Berlin. However, as a tourist destination, the Museums Island, which comprises five significant collections that all belong to the Berlin State Museums, remains the principal focus. In 1999, the complex was listed as a UNESCO World Heritage site, and the museums have undergone a long process of renovation and redesign. The Jewish Museum in Berlin, designed by Daniel Libeskind and opened in 2001, demonstrates how **architecture** can enhance content: the museum is essentially divided into three pathways, representing those murdered in the Holocaust, those forced into emigration, and finally the continuity of Jewish history. The **Berlin Wall** is commemorated at a variety of locations, but the broader history of the Wall is presented at Bernauer Straße, Friedrichstraße station (Palace of Tears/Tränenpalast), and the House at Checkpoint Charlie. During the redevelopment of Berlin's city center following reunification, a temporary museum (Infobox) caught the public's imagination. Among the most noteworthy new projects is the development of the Humboldt Forum along Unter den Linden, where the City Palace (the Hohenzollern residence) was situated until its postwar ruin was destroyed at the behest of the government of the GDR. The Forum will have three users: the Prussian Cultural Heritage Foundation, which will display its collections of non-European cultures; the Humboldt University Berlin; and the Federal State of Berlin. A "Workshop of Knowledge" will form part of the attempt to foster cultural debates there.

German history is presented in three main museums: the German Historical Museum (Deutsches Historisches Museum) in Berlin, which houses a permanent exhibition alongside temporary and topical ones; the Foundation

Haus der Geschichte der Bundesrepublik in Bonn; and the Zeitgeschichtliches Forum in Leipzig, which focuses on the division of Germany and the GDR.

Most visitors in Germany frequent local museums, followed by art museums; natural science museums; and museums devoted to history, archaeology, and specialist areas (such as art history). On average, 106 million people visit exhibitions and museums throughout the country, which has around 6,250 museums in all. Some of these museums have engaged in new ways of participation with the public, including the highly successful, so-called Long Night of the Museums. The following list includes some of the leading state-held and private collections, some of which are also housed in buildings of interest: Internationales Zeitungsmuseum (Aachen); Fuggerei-Museum (Augsburg); Bode-Museum, Pergamon-Museum, Neues Museum, Altes Museum, Jüdisches Museum, Deutsches Historisches Museum, Topographie des Terrors, Kupferstichkabinett, Gemäldegalerie, Bauhaus-Archiv, Neue Nationalgalerie, Hamburger Bahnhof, Sammlung Berggruen, and Museumszentrum Dahlem (Berlin); Worpsweder Kunsthalle (**Bremen**); Haus der Geschichte; Kunstmuseum Bonn (Bonn); Römisch-Germanisches Museum, Museum Ludwig, and Wallraff-Richartz-Museum (Cologne); Bauhaus-Museum (Dessau); Albertinum, Gemäldegalerie Alte Meister (Dresden); Kunstsammlung North Rhine-Westfalia (Düsseldorf); Museum Folkwang (Essen); Goethe-Museum, Jüdisches Museum, Kunsthalle Schirn, Museum für Moderne Kunst, Deutsches Architekturmuseum, Museum für Angewandte Kunst, and Städelsches Kunstinstitut (Frankfurt/Main); Bergbaumuseum Rammelsberg (Goslar); Kunsthalle (**Hamburg**); Sprengel-Museum (Hanover); Universitätsbibliothek (Heidelberg); Museum für Neue Kunst (Karlsruhe); Ludwig-Museum (Koblenz); Deutsches Buch- und Schriftmuseum, Bacharchive, and Bach-Museum (Lutherstadt Wittenberg); Lutherhaus (Eisenach); Gutenberg-Museum (Mainz); Städtische Kunsthalle (Mannheim); Schiller-Nationalmuseum (Marbach); Alte Pinakothek, Neue Pinakothek, Lenbachhaus, Deutsches Museum, and Staatsbibliothek (Munich); Spielzeugmuseum, Dokumentationszentrum Reichsparteitagsgelände, and Germanisches Nationalmuseum (Nuremberg); Mercedes-Benz-Museum, Porsche-Museum, and Staatsgalerie (Stuttgart); Kunsthalle (Tübingen); Bauhaus-Museum, Schillerhaus, and Goethe-Museum (Weimar); and Herzog-August Bibliothek (Wolffenbüttel). A complete list for the whole of Germany may be found at http://www.deutsche-museen.de.

N

NAHLES, ANDREA (1970–). Social Democratic Party of Germany **(SPD)** politician. Born in Mendig **(Rhineland-Palatinate)**, Andrea Nahles studied German literature/**language** and politics at the University of Bonn (from 1989), graduating with a master's degree. A member of the SPD from 1988, she was active in the **Young Socialists (JUSOS)** and elected national leader (1995–1999). She served on the main party national executive (1997–2013) and was a member of the **Bundestag** during 1999–2002, re-elected in 2005. On the left wing of the party, she was a leading critic of Chancellor **Gerhard Schröder**'s **Agenda 2010** program of social welfare reform. Her other roles in the party include deputy leader (2007–2009) and general secretary (2009–2013). Together with **Sigmar Gabriel**, who was elected party leader in 2009, Nahles was credited with repairing the divided party's image after the election defeat of 2009 and as driving the left-wing agenda (minimum wage, **pensions** at age 63, more child benefit for parents working part time, quotas for **women** in company supervisory boards), which brought it back into coalition with the **Christian Democratic Union (CDU)** in 2013. In 2013, Nahles was appointed federal minister for labor and social affairs in **Angela Merkel**'s third coalition cabinet. The following year, she presented a new law to parliament designed to restore the long-standing principle of tariff unity (which means that a firm concludes a collective wage agreement for a particular sector with a single **trade union**), which had been undermined by a decision of the federal labor court in July 2010.

NATIONAL DEMOCRATIC PARTY OF GERMANY (NATIONAL-DEMOKRATISCHE PARTEI DEUTSCHLANDS, NPD). Founded in November 1964 in Hanover by Adolf von Thadden and members of prohibited or defunct extreme right-wing parties and groupings, the NPD exploited the popular uncertainty generated by West Germany's economic crisis of 1966–1967 to gain seats in 7 out of 11 state parliaments (**Baden-Württemberg, Bavaria, Bremen, Hessen, Lower Saxony, Rhineland-Palatinate**, and **Schleswig-Holstein**). After narrowly missing entering the **Bundestag** in the 1969 national election, the party was racked by internal disputes over policy direction, and Thadden resigned in 1971. In the 1980 national election, the NPD registered the worst result in its history (0.2 percent of the vote). Although the NPD attracted renewed public attention by adopting a strong anti**foreigner** stance in the early 1990s, the choice of Günther Deckert as leader (1991) provoked further internal division and membership plummeted from 28,000 (1969) to an all-time low of 3,500 in 1996 (in 2014, it was around 5,200). Led by Udo Voigt (1996–2011), the NPD cultivated the image of a national protest movement, consciously attracting neo-Nazis and skinheads and calling itself the National Extra-Parliamentary Opposition (NAPO).

In early 2001 the German government, represented by Interior Minister **Otto Schily**, and the Bundestag/**Bundesrat** applied to the **Federal Constitutional Court (FCC)** to ban the NPD as undemocratic and hence unconstitutional. In its history, the court had banned only two political parties on the grounds that they posed a danger to the democratic order: the neo-Nazi Sozialistische Reichspartei Deutschlands (SR) in 1952 and the Communist Party of Germany (KPD) in 1956. In March 2003, the FCC ruled that it could not proceed with the application because the infiltration of so many government agents in the party's leadership made it impossible to discount the state's influence on its behavior.

In 2004, the NPD's electoral fortunes improved. The party made deep inroads in the local/district elections (Kommunalwahlen) of June 2004, notably in **Saxony**, where in some areas it gained between 8 and 11.8 percent of the vote. In the **Saarland** regional election (September 2004), it narrowly missed the 5 percent hurdle for entering the **Landtag**, the best result for a far-right party in western Germany for several years. The NPD won considerable support from younger voters who felt marginalized by the government's reform agenda, **Agenda 2010**. In the Saxony regional election (also September 2004), the NPD astonished observers by entering parliament with 9.2 percent of votes, just behind the **Social Democratic Party of Germany (SPD)** with 9.8 percent. This was the first time since 1968 in Baden-Württemberg that it had entered a regional assembly. In its campaign, the NPD attacked the government's plans to cut **social welfare** benefits, nurtured skepticism toward foreigners and **immigrants**, and argued for measures to force German companies to invest in Germany. As part of its strategy of bringing together right-wing parties (under the slogan of a "German people's front"), the party also agreed not to run in parallel with the **German People's Union (DVU)**, which made gains in the **Brandenburg** election held at the same time. In October 2004, the NPD and DVU agreed on a formal alliance to share electoral lists, and in the September 2006 election in Mecklenburg-West Pomerania, the NDP entered the assembly for the first time, with 7.3 percent of the vote. A merger of the parties agreed upon in 2010 failed, however, over the NPD's reluctance to assume the DVU's debts.

During internal party disputes over strategic direction, Voigt was replaced as leader in November 2011 by Holger Apfel, who had been a member of the regional parliament of Saxony since 2004 and advocated a new "serious radicalism." The public debate over prohibiting the party simmered on, however, and membership continued to fall. Following disappointing regional election results during 2009–2010 and a long-standing financial crisis (exacerbated by the misappropriation of 750,000 euros by former treasurer Erwin Kemma and by government fines for filing false financial reports), Udo Pastörs took over leadership in 2014, but was replaced by Frank Franz later in the year. The NPD's youth wing, the Young National Democrats (Junge Nationaldemokraten, JN), founded in 1969, acts as a link between the main party, radical youth elements and other neo-Nazi organizations, and has an estimated 350 members.

See also ANTI-SEMITISM; EXTREMISM; POLITICAL PARTIES; REPUBLICANS, THE (DIE REPUBLIKANER, REP).

NATO. *See* NORTH ATLANTIC TREATY ORGANIZATION (NATO).

NEW FORUM (NEUES FORUM). A citizens' dissident group in the former **German Democratic Republic (GDR)**, New Forum was founded at a meeting in **Berlin** in the apartment of Katja Havemann, widow of the dissident Robert Havemann, on 9 September 1989. The following day, it published a manifesto (*Aufbruch 89*) calling for political change, democracy, and dialogue with the regime. The manifesto, which was one of the first open challenges to the regime and attracted much attention in the Western **media**, was signed by leading dissidents and endorsed during the following weeks by around 200,000 East Germans. New Forum saw itself as a nonparty group and adopted a nonconfrontational stance vis-à-vis the authorities, which refused to recognize it (19–21 September). The Forum supported the Monday demonstrations in Leipzig, which led to the downfall of the regime; took part in the **Round Table** discussions; and joined the **Alliance 90/The Greens** in the run-up to the election of March 1990. As the political revolution developed in the GDR, the Forum failed to organize itself into a coherent force and lost members to various political parties, although it remained active for a few years after reunification.

NEW MARKET (NEUER MARKT). The New Market was a segment of the **German Stock Exchange** established on 10 March 1997 to generate financing for companies in the so-called New Economy. Based on information technology, digital media, **telecommunications**, and biotechnology, this sector experienced rapid growth in the dot.com boom of the 1990s. The New Market provided easy access to the stock exchange for start-up companies by not requiring evidence of past performance. The Nemax (later Nemax All Share) index listed all companies in the sector (over 300 initially), while Nemax 50 comprised the top 50 performers. After reaching a historic peak on 10 March 2000, share values fell as it emerged that companies could not sustain such growth rates or meet projected targets. The **Internet** and telecommunications concern Gigabell AG was the first to announce insolvency (September 2000). Others followed, while financial irregularities and criminal manipulations (falsification of balance sheets and insider trading) led to a number of exclusions. In particular, the **terrorist** attacks on the World Trade Center (11 September 2001) fueled a worldwide loss of business confidence. Trading ceased on 21 March 2003, and the New Market was closed on 5 June. In December 2004, 30 blue-chip companies transferred from the defunct Nemax 50 to the TecDax index.

NOELLE-NEUMANN, ELISABETH (1916–2010). Elisabeth Noelle-Neumann studied at universities in Berlin, Königsberg, and in 1937 and 1938, at the University of Missouri, United States. Her doctorate was on public opinion research in the United States. In 1947, together with her husband, Peter Neumann, she founded the Institute für Demoskopie Allensbach, a public opinion research organization that became one of the most influential of its kind in West Germany. Between 1964 and 1983, she held a professorship at the Johannes Gutenberg University in Mainz; she held a guest professorship at Chicago University from 1978 until 1991. There were considerable protests against her planned return to the United States in 1992 because of a number of **anti-Semitic** comments she had made under the National Socialist regime and her refusal to explain herself in the matter.

NORTH ATLANTIC TREATY ORGANIZATION (NATO). NATO was created in April 1949 in Washington, D.C., as a collective security pact to defend states of North America and Western Europe against military aggression by the Union of Soviet Socialist Republics (USSR). The Federal Republic of Germany (FRG) joined in 1955. NATO's members integrated their military commands, promised mutual assistance in the event of an attack, and promoted economic and cultural cooperation. When the **Warsaw Pact** was disbanded in 1991, NATO established the North Atlantic Cooperation Council (NACC, renamed Euro-Atlantic Partnership Council in 1997) as a joint consultation forum for North American, central and east European, and central Asian neighbors on security matters; the council also offered a platform for states to apply to join NATO itself. With the end of the Cold War, NATO, which has now expanded to 28 member states and maintains headquarters in Brussels, began adjusting to a new global role. After reunification, Germany in particular was widely expected to take a more proactive role in international affairs and defense commitments within the NATO framework, and its defense minister, **Volker Rühe**, took a leading role in persuading NATO to admit its first wave of eastern European states, including Poland and Hungary, in 1999.

The main issues that confronted NATO in the aftermath of the Cold War were its role in relation to the **European Union** (**EU**) and its response to the disintegration of the former Yugoslavia. After Germany committed its forces to Kosovo in 1999 and went on to provide support troops for operations in Afghanistan, the government of Chancellor **Gerhard Schröder** argued for a formal EU framework for political and military decision making that would recognize and manage international crises. Following deficiencies in the EU's military response to the conflict in the former Yugoslavia, the Treaty of Nice (agreed to in 2000) introduced a new common foreign and security policy (CFSP), focusing on humanitarian, rescue, crisis management, and peacekeeping tasks, including the deployment of combat forces (the so-called Petersberg tasks). The EU decided that it "must have the capacity for autonomous action, backed up by credible military forces, the means to decide to use them, and a readiness to do so in order to respond to international crises without prejudice to actions by NATO." However, the EU stressed that it was not creating a European army and that the commitment and deployment of national troops would depend on decisions of sovereign member states, many of whom were NATO members. Practical progress on implementing the plan proved slow and was hindered among other things by pressure on budgets strained by the economic downturn. In 2003 Germany and France, supported by Belgium and Luxembourg, called more directly for the EU to plan and mount its own military operations, independently of NATO. In February 2004, Great Britain, Germany, and France moved directly to establish joint battle groups (each of 1,500 troops and able to be deployed by air, sea, or land under UN mandate to areas of crisis within 15 days). The groups reached operational readiness in 2007. The EU's move was also partly seen as a response to the U.S./British–led invasion of Iraq in 2003, which went ahead despite Franco-German requests for **United Nations** (**UN**) weapons inspectors to have more time to complete their assessment of Iraq's alleged possession of weapons of mass destruction. The attack would complicate Germany's political relationship with the United States and raised questions about the organization's role as a global alliance.

In June 1999, following an EU initiative in late 1998, the Stability Pact for Southeastern Europe (SPSEE) was adopted in Cologne. More than 40 partner countries (including Germany) and organizations (including NATO, the UN, the G8, and the International Monetary Fund) undertook to strengthen the countries of southeastern Europe "in their efforts to foster peace, democracy, respect for **human rights** and economic prosperity in order to achieve stability in the whole region." All countries in the region were given the prospect of integration into the European–North American geopolitical and economic system, and the EU was expected to be the major donor for economic aid. The SPSEE, in which Germany had a strong interest, represented the first serious attempt by the international community to replace the earlier policy of reaction to crises in southeastern Europe by a long-term strategy of conflict prevention. The initiative also represented a continuation of Germany's traditional policy of avoiding crises through nonmilitary multilateral involvement. The SPSEE was replaced by the Regional Cooperation Council (RCC) in 2008. In 2002, the NATO–Russia Council (NRC) replaced the Permanent Joint Council (PJC), a forum for consultation and cooperation created by the 1997 NATO–Russia Founding Act on Mutual Relations, Cooperation and Security, which remains the formal basis for NATO–Russia relations. The NRC suspended civilian and military cooperation in 2014 in the wake of the Ukrainian crisis.

While NATO in recent years has been engaged in more missions than ever, including, in 2014, peacekeeping in Kosovo, anti**terrorism** patrols in the Mediterranean, antipiracy in the Gulf of Aden and off the Horn of Africa, assistance to the African Union in Somalia, and the ISAF operation in Afghanistan (the only operation in which all 28 partners participated), internal differences in commitment that emerged over Iraq (2003) and Libya (2011) may limit the organization's ability to develop united responses to global challenges. It also remains to be seen whether Germany (and the EU in general) can back up its strategic ambitions with actual resources, in particular as countries such as Germany cut defense budgets in the wake of the 2008–2009 financial crisis. Germany resisted pressure from the United States to raise its defense spending from its current 1.3 to 2 percent of GDP, arguing that it was more important for NATO to collectively agree and implement specific arms projects.

New challenges arose for NATO during the second half of the 2000s, as Russia adopted more aggressive policies aimed at extending its influence in the area of the former Soviet Union. The new self-assertiveness was marked by President Putin's criticism of U.S. "uni-polarism" at the Munich security conference (2007), Russia's withdrawal from the Treaty on Conventional Armed Forces in Europe (CFE), the invasion of Georgia (2008), military maneuvers rehearsing encirclement of the Baltic states and movements into other eastern European countries (ZAPAD, 2013), the annexation of Crimea, and support for Russian separatists in the eastern Ukraine (2014). Responding to the threat of territorial violations, NATO ended military cooperation with Russia (2014) and drew up plans to establish, for the first time, a visible presence in eastern Europe, and to create a rapid deployment force headquartered in Stettin/Szczecin (the Readiness Action Plan). Although Germany, among others, was forced to abandon the notion of partnership with Russia, Chancellor **Angela Merkel**, keen to continue political dialogue and avoid a descent into another Cold War, held out longest in arguing that NATO should adhere strictly to the terms of the NATO–Russia Founding Act. Concluded in 1997, the act committed NATO to avoiding the "additional permanent stationing of substantial combat forces" in eastern Europe "in the current and foreseeable security environment"; it has also led to the creation of joint consultative bodies and mechanisms. At the NATO summit in Great Britain (August 2014), Merkel nevertheless accepted the Readiness Action Plan, in which the **Bundeswehr**, numbered among the few European armies with the resources to supply sizable troop numbers, would play a key role. A speech by the Russian general chief of staff in 2013 suggested that Russia would be pursuing a new strategy of "non-linear" or "hybrid warfare," targeting information systems and deploying special troops under the guise of peacekeeping operations before resorting to more conventional forms of attack.

See FOREIGN POLICY AFTER 1990; FOREIGN POLICY: 1949–1969; FOREIGN POLICY: 1970–1990; SECURITY POLICY, EXTERNAL.

NORTH RHINE-WESTFALIA (NORDRHEIN-WESTFALEN, NRW). North Rhine-Westfalia has a total area of 34,084 square kilometers; with 17.6 million inhabitants, it is the most populous of Germany's **federal states**. It shares borders with the Netherlands and Belgium in the west and with **Lower Saxony** (north and east) and **Hessen** and **Rhineland-Palatinate** (east and south). Its has 29 cities with over 100,000 inhabitants, the largest of which are Cologne (over one million), the state capital Düsseldorf (595,000), Dortmund (573,000), and Essen (567,000). It is also the most densely settled of the (noncity) federal states, although the bulk of the population is concentrated in the west, where the earliest settlements were founded and industrialization began in the early 19th century following the discovery of rich coal deposits around the Ruhr River. The state's modern boundaries were drawn up in 1946 under British military occupation; they encompassed the northern regions of the **Rhine** and former Westfalia, both one-time provinces of Prussia, with Lippe-Detmold added in 1947. The aim was to create an economically strong region in which the industrial Ruhr would counterbalance the rural east and contribute to the recovery of postwar western Germany. Between 1945 and 1970, the population expanded from 11 to 17 million, as refugees and subsequently foreign guest workers settled there. **Foreigners** currently make up 12.8 percent of the population and live almost entirely in urban areas.

The Ruhr, with its heavy coal and steel **industry**, was the traditional industrial heartland of Germany. During the 1960s, coal and steel production began to decline as falling demand and a series of crises led to mergers, closures, and unemployment, although government subsidies and special initiatives prevented the worst social consequences. Jobs were also lost in the textile and clothing industry, based in the Rhine and Münster regions. As part of a long-term (and ongoing) restructuring process, the economic focus shifted to precision mechanical **engineering** and metal products, **automobile** manufacture, electrical engineering/electronics, synthetic materials, **chemicals**, and waste management. An international building exhibition—IBA Emscher Park, 1989–1999—showcased the region and its plans for economic and environmental regeneration.

While 56 percent of the region's GDP was based on manufacturing and **energy** in 1970, that figure had fallen to 29 percent by 2012, while service providers, many of which are partnered with industry, rose from 42 percent to over 70 percent. Although NRW is home to many large concerns, notably **Bayer (pharmaceuticals** and chemicals), **Bertelsmann (media** and **publishing), Deutsche Post** DHL, Deutsche Telekom (**telecommunications**), E.ON and RWE (energy), Metro (retail and trading), Rewe (food) and **ThyssenKrupp** (steel production and engineering), the region's 761,000 small to medium-sized businesses (the **Mittelstand**), which employ 80 percent of the workforce, constitute its economic backbone. Since 1970, the number employed in services has risen by over a million, to 6.6 million. Overall unemployment (8 percent in 2015) is slightly above the national average (6.4 percent), although it is highest in the Ruhr area. The state is home to the public **television and radio** station Westdeutscher Rundfunk (WDR) and to the commercial stations RTL, VOX, and VIVA, which are based in Cologne. Despite its historical structural problems, the NRW economy contributes 21 percent to the national GDP (2015) and ranks as the 13th largest in the world. A cultural center, the region has numerous **theaters** and **museums**, stages several film festivals, and is known for innovative **architecture** (awarding a prize every five years since 2000); avant-garde artists such as Pina Bausch, Max Ernst, Emil Schumacher, Joseph Beuys, and Bernd and Hilla Becher, not to mention attractions such as the medieval cathedrals of Cologne and Aachen. Although not renowned for **tourism**, the Sauerland region and the Teutoburger Forest attract many visitors, especially on short breaks.

The regional state parliament or **Landtag** (237 members in 2012) is elected for five years and chooses a **minister president**, who appoints a cabinet of ministers. The constitution assigns the minister president and his government a relatively strong position, although the assembly agrees on the **budget**, reflects public opinion, and monitors the executive. Despite a constitutional provision for plebiscites, the requirement that at least 20 percent of eligible voters must petition for a referendum long represented a major hurdle; such a petition has only once been successfully applied, when in 1978 the government was persuaded to withdraw plans to introduce a comprehensive-type school. In 2002, however, the threshold was reduced (to 15 percent), and other forms of participation, including "people's initiatives" (Volksinitiativen) were introduced. The constitution, which affirms the right to work and guarantees **codetermination**, was modified to promote the introduction of mixed religion schools (1968), provide a basic right to data protection (1978), and include protection of the **environment** as an objective of the state (1985).

Politically, NRW has seen very stable administrations. Under Minister President Franz Meyers, the **Christian Democratic Union (CDU)** governed from 1958 until 1966 (from 1962 in coalition with the **Free Democratic Party, FDP**). In 1966, the **Social Democratic Party of Germany (SPD)** assumed power and provided a succession of minister presidents: the former editor of the *Rheinische Zeitung*, Heinz Kühn (1977–1978); **Johannes Rau** (1978–1998); **Wolfgang Clement** (1998–2002); and **Peer Steinbrück** (2002–2005). After a long-running coalition with the FDP between 1966 and 1980, during which the CDU had a relative majority (1970–1975), the SPD defended an overall majority until 1995, when it formed an alliance with the **Alliance 90/The Greens**. The Greens had entered the assembly in 1990, but doubled their share of the votes at the following election, breaking the SPD's monopoly. The red/green coalition was widely regarded as a test run for the eventual partnership (from 1998) between the two parties at national level (similarly, the regional SPD/FDP coalition in 1966 prefigured the **grand coalition** of 1969). During the 1980s and 1990s, the CDU reduced its electoral chances by changing candidates (these included **Norbert Blüm** and **Kurt Biedenkopf**). However, in the regional election of May 2005, the CDU capitalized on the unpopularity of the national SPD to form a ruling coalition with the FDP, headed by **Jürgen Rüttgers** (CDU) as **minister president**. In 2010 the SPD, led by **Hannelore Kraft**, returned to power in a minority coalition with the Greens, which was reelected in elections brought forward to 2012 after successive budgets had been challenged by the regional constitutional court for allowing borrowing to exceed investment. In 2010–2011, the parties agreed, after a long-running dispute, on a consensus on the structure of the **educational** system, in which a number of Gemeinschaftsschulen (integrating all school streams from years 1 to 10), as advocated by the SPD and Greens, would be introduced on a six-year trial basis and the traditional Realschule and Gymnasium, favored by the CDU, retained. Traditional SPD voters are found in the industrial Ruhr area and the Protestant cities of the Rhineland, while CDU strongholds lie in rural districts. In relation to its large population, NRW is underrepresented in the **Bundesrat**. Nevertheless, it is politically one of the most important of the federal states and, during the years of conservative-liberal government (1982–1998), was widely regarded as the SPD in opposition. Minister President Johannes Rau was chancellor candidate in the national election of 1987, and NRW led the way in resisting the government's commitment to nuclear **energy**. The economic restructuring and modernization that NRW undertook during the 1970s was paralleled by reforms in local and district authorities. These later began replacing their traditional model of a council-elected mayor and an appointed chief executive officer as administrative head by a U.S.-type system of directly elected executive mayors.

There are several leading universities and institutions of higher education in NRW, including Cologne, Bochum, Dortmund, Aachen, Münster, Bielefeld, and Bonn. The total student population exceeded 600,000 in 2012–2013. The largest single university, with a record 80,000 students (2014), is the Fernuniversität Hagen, which specializes in distance learning.

NORTH SEA (NORDSEE). Germany's North Sea coast stretches 13,000 kilometers, from just west of the Ems River to the border with western Denmark in the Jutland peninsula. The coastline thus follows **Lower Saxony** (750 km), Bremerhaven at the mouth of the Weser River, and the western part of **Schleswig-Holstein** (550 km). German territorial waters extend 12 sea miles offshore, while the so-called exclusive economic zone, where Germany has rights of scientific **research** and economic exploitation as well as obligations of **environmental** protection, reaches 200 sea miles at its farthest point. The economic significance of the North Sea and its coastal zone is based on shipping (via **Hamburg**), fishing (3.5 million tons annually and declining), mussel cultivation, undersea cables, pipelines, sand and gravel extraction, and especially **tourism**. While oil reserves are insignificant, around 17,000 million cubic meters of gas are still extracted annually, and the area has considerable potential for offshore wind and tidal **energy** generation. In 2013, there were 116 offshore wind turbine installations in the North Sea and the **Baltic**, with more planned to meet an optimistic target of generating 25 gigawatt by 2030. The unique coastal landscape of mudflats (Wattenmeere) and salt marshes (located between mudflats and dunes), exposed at low tide along the chain of Frisian islands, is an ecologically complex environment that is home to around 4,000 species of animals, birds, and plants and millions of microorganisms.

With around 18 million overnight stays and 12 million daily visitors a year, the North Sea is Lower Saxony's leading center for tourism. Major attractions are the seven East Frisian (or Friesian) islands and the area directly inland (East Friesland), boasting long, sandy beaches. Similarly, the western coast of Schleswig-Holstein, with the North Frisian islands and the Wadden Sea Natural World Heritage Site—extending from the mouth of the Elbe River to the Danish border by the island of Sylt—is the largest cohesive tidal flats landscape in the world and one of the last major, comparatively undisturbed natural landscapes in Central Europe.

See also BALTIC SEA (OSTSEE); ENERGY: RENEWABLE.

O

OETTINGER, GÜNTHER (1953–). Christian Democratic Union (CDU) politician. Born in Stuttgart, Günther Oettinger studied law and economics at the University of Tübingen; passed his state law examinations in law (1978, 1982); and worked as an auditor and a consultant (1984–1988), and subsequently partner (1988–2005), for a **tax** firm. An active member of the CDU in his home state of **Baden-Württemberg**, he chaired the **Junge Union (JU)**, the party's regional youth wing (1983–1989), although disparaging comments he made about the CDU **women**'s union during this period almost ended his political career. After representing the party in various positions in Ditzingen (1977–1994) and Ludwigsburg (1979–1993), he became leader of the north Württemberg district of the main party (2001–2005) and chaired the CDU's national technical committee on **media** policy (from 1999). A member of Baden-Württemberg's regional assembly (**Landtag**) from 1984, he led the CDU parliamentary group after **Erwin Teufel** was elected **minister president** (January 1991). In April 2005, he succeeded Teufel as minister president (reelected 2006), but resigned in 2010 to take up a post as **energy** commissioner for the **European Union** (**EU**) and, from 2014, as commissioner responsible for implementing the single digital market. He also led the regional CDU from 2005 until 2010 and was succeeded as minister president by **Stefan Mappus**. Known for his conservative views, outspokenness, and technical competence, Oettinger, as minister president, introduced university tuition fees, opposed a total withdrawal from nuclear energy, and was instrumental in achieving agreement to the controversial Stuttgart 21 transport project (building work began in 2010). He attracted criticism for attempting to sell off precious medieval manuscripts held by the regional state library (2006) and for defending his predecessor, **Hans Filbinger**, who was forced to resign over his National Socialist past (2007).

OFFICE FOR THE PROTECTION OF THE CONSTITUTION (BUNDESAMT FÜR VERFASSUNGSSCHUTZ, BfV). Founded in 1950 and under Allied control until 1955, the BfV is responsible for identifying internal security threats to the Federal Republic of Germany (FRG). Its main role is to collect and evaluate intelligence on movements, groups, or individuals that endanger the democratic order as laid down in the constitution, the **Basic Law** (**BL**). Threats can emanate, for example, from violent or nonviolent, extremist left- or right-wing political groups; terrorists (e.g., al-Qaeda); and other social organizations (e.g., Scientology). The BfV further observes espionage activities by foreign intelligence services directed at German institutions, **political parties**, companies, and economic interests. Its sources range from the public **media** and the **Internet** to monitoring the postal and **telecommunications** networks. Controversy has accompanied the extension of the BfV's surveillance powers to include private computers and online searches and undertake activities in the **federal states** without their knowledge, and its control of undercover agents in extremist groups. The BfV, which is under the direct control of the interior ministry, maintains offices in each of the **federal states** and has 2,700 staff members in Cologne and Berlin (2015). It documents security threats in annual reports and publishes surveys on extremist movements and related issues. Although the president of the BfV in 2009 engaged a commission to investigate the National Socialist past of agency members in the early years, this did not begin work until November 2011. In 2013, it emerged that the BfV was regularly passing data— presumably on German citizens—to the U.S. National Security Agency (NSA) in return for information and surveillance software, although the office maintained that this was in accordance with German law on individual privacy and with the knowledge of appropriate Bundestag bodies.

See also EXTREMISM; INTELLIGENCE AGENCIES; SECURITY POLICY, INTERNAL; TERRORISM.

OFFICE OF THE FEDERAL CHANCELLOR (BUNDESKANZLE-RAMT). Created by Federal Chancellor **Konrad Adenauer** in 1949, this office coordinates the work of the government with its ministries, the **Bundestag** and **Bundesrat**, as well as the **federal states**, various interest groups, and representatives of foreign countries. Its head (**Peter Altmaier**, appointed December 2013) has the rank of cabinet minister. Six departments mirror the work of the ministries, among which many of the 600 or so staff members rotate. Based in **Berlin**, the office is also represented in Bonn (the Palais Schaumburg), with around 30 employees, and provides the chancellor with up-to-date information, plans cabinet and committee meetings, and prepares the groundwork for policy decisions. It can also undertake tasks that, for political reasons, normal ministries are unable to perform. Thus **Egon Bahr**, as **state secretary** in the Bundeskanzleramt during the SPD/**Free Democratic Party** (**FDP**) coalition after 1969, set the foundations for a new policy toward Eastern Europe (**Ostpolitik**). Similarly, **Helmut Kohl** empowered a state secretary in his office to coordinate the reconstruction of the **eastern federal states** after 1990. The **Federal Intelligence Service** (Bundesnachrichtendienst, BND) reports directly to the head of the office, as do the government representatives (Beauftragte) for culture and the **media** and for migration, refugees, and integration.

OIL. *See* ENERGY: OIL AND GAS.

OSTALGIE. Coined from the German words "Ost" (east) and "Nostalgie" (nostalgia), this word refers to a nostalgia felt by some Germans in the **eastern federal states** for the way of life in the former **German Democratic Republic (GDR)**. Based on positive memories of both everyday goods (such as particular brands) and the wider social system, Ostalgie was a response to the profound and rapid changes in east Germans' way of life that took place after reunification. As such, it appeared to call into question the lives and biographies of entire generations that had personally experienced the GDR.

Reminiscences were nurtured, among other things, by "Ostalgie shops" selling typical brands found in the former GDR (such as the sparkling wine Rotkäppchen-Sekt, as well as soft drinks, cosmetics, and chocolates); "Ostalgie parties"; and campaigns to retain the distinctive walk/halt figures on East German traffic lights (meanwhile adopted elsewhere and often—polemically—perceived as the only aspect of the GDR that survived the transformations); hotels in the pre-1990 style; **cinema**; and **literature**. The feeling of nostalgia for the east, which was observed in the **media** from the mid-1990s onward, came to a head in 2003 with the release of the internationally acclaimed film *Good Bye, Lenin*. In the same year, numerous television shows looked back at the former GDR, although they focused on (social) culture rather than politics. At the same time, a debate arose about whether it was at all appropriate to be nostalgic about a repressive regime. One obvious explanation for the emergence of Ostalgie is that, faced with record unemployment, (east) Germans were yearning for the times when jobs were still secure. Another is that the old GDR represented a period when their identity (including lifestyle, **education**, working environment, and culture) was not in doubt. Ostalgie also reflects the sense that the transition to Western culture has been too rapid.

One of the more cautious commentators on the phenomenon, the former governing mayor of **Berlin**, **Klaus Wowereit**, argued that "we really need to be careful that the GDR does not achieve cult status." Theo Mitrup, head of a support group for victims of the communist regime, maintained that "there is nothing wrong with recalling the past . . . but it is a question of balance. This nostalgia seems to ignore the oppression, the secret police, the intimidation—history somehow is being rewritten." The former premier of **Brandenburg**, **Manfred Stolpe**, pointed out that "it is a real mistake always to act as if the

GDR were just one dark concentration camp." Diverse as comments were at the time, the topic has lost its urgency a quarter of a century since the fall of the **Berlin Wall**.

Books, both fiction and nonfiction, in which Ostalgie appears as a theme include Thomas Brussig's *Am kürzeren Ende der Sonnenallee* (1999), Jana Hensel's *Zonenkinder* (2002), Susanne Fritsche's *Die Mauer ist gefallen: Eine kleine Geschichte der DDR* (2004), Daniel Wiechmann's *Immer bereit! Von einem jungen Pionier, der auszog, das Glück zu suchen* (2004), Peter Richter's *Blühende Landschaften: Eine Heimatkunde* (2004), and Martina Rellin's *Klar bin ich eine Ost-Frau! 15 Frauen erzählen aus dem richtigen Leben* (2004). The trend has also been countered by publications such as Anna Funder's *Stasiland* (2004). In the late 1990s and early 2000s, "Westalgie" emerged as a phenomenon that recognized the particularities of life in West Berlin during the Cold War. It appears, however, predominantly in literature and exhibitions, and serves to take stock of what changed in the city after 1989.

In 2014, Hester Vaizey's study *Born in the GDR: Living in the Shadow of the Wall* provided a range of case studies of people who grew up in the GDR. Highlighting the fact that post-Wall experiences remain as diverse as life itself was in the GDR, the actual period of transition in 1989/1990 is presented in sharp focus and adds perspective to sentiments such as Ostalgie. Terms such as "Wessi" and "Ossi" stressed, like Ostalgie, the challenges of the reunification process: while "Wessi" became heavily associated with arrogance and a "know-it-all" attitude, "Ossi," just as polemically loaded, stood for a presumed inability to adapt to the western way of life. As such, all three terms are indicative of the slowness of the reunification process.

OSTPOLITIK. Literally "eastern policy," the term Ostpolitik refers to the policy of rapprochement toward the Union of Soviet Socialist Republics (USSR) and Eastern European states pursued by Chancellor **Willy Brandt** between 1960 and 1974. The policy's achievements were embodied in a series of treaties with eastern bloc states: the Moscow Treaty (signed 1970), the Warsaw Treaty (1970), the Four Power Agreement on **Berlin** (1971), the Basic Treaty (1972), and the Prague Treaty (1973). Brandt's main purpose was to normalize relations between the Federal Republic of Germany (FRG) and the **German Democratic Republic (GDR)**. The policy ushered in a more pragmatic phase of links between the two states that extended beyond his chancellorship.

See also FOREIGN POLICY: 1949–1969; FOREIGN POLICY: 1970–1990.

OTTO FAMILY. Retail entrepreneurs. During the interwar period, Werner Otto (1909–2011) set up as a trader, first in Stettin (now Szczecin in Poland) and then in **Berlin**, where he leased a small cigarette shop. After World War II, he moved with his family to **Hamburg**. He invested in a shoe factory that employed 150 people (1948), but was unable to survive against competition from large manufacturers. The setback prompted Otto to move away from manufacturing into distribution by mail order, then a relatively new concept. In 1949, with 6,000 DM capital and four colleagues, he founded his mail order house, Otto Versand. Working at home, he assembled 300 16-page catalogs and presented his first "Autumn and Winter Collection" in 1950–1951. Customers were invoiced rather than paying cash on delivery and could roll up individual orders into a single one. The firm rapidly expanded, turned over 5,000 million DM in 1953, and by the 1960s dominated the German mail order market. Although Otto handed over the day-to-day running of the business to managers following a heart attack, he retained honorary chairmanship of the supervisory board and in the late 1960s embarked on a new venture: the creation of an organization to build and operate shopping malls. In 1969, he set up the Werner Otto Foundation to support medical **research** for sick or disabled children in Hamburg. His book, *Die Otto-Gruppe: Mit zwölf Unternehmerprinzipien zum Erfolg*, which outlines the foundations of his success, appeared in 1982.

Remaining members of the Otto family include the founder's son, Michael (born in 1943), and widow, Maren, and Michael's son Benjamin (born 1976). Michael trained in banking in Munich and studied economics in Hamburg and Munich, where he earned a diploma and a doctorate in business administration. He joined the board in 1971 with responsibilities for textile purchasing and, as chief executive (1981–2007), developed the company into the world's largest single retail distribution concern; in 2013, he controlled 78.5 percent of the group. The Michael Otto Foundation was founded (1993) to protect and preserve water resources, including seas, lakes, wetlands, and associated flora and fauna. Michael's son Benjamin (born in 1975), who trained in banking and graduated from the European Business School in London, founded his own company in 2002 (IHS Intelligent Solutions, an outfitter of domestic and commercial premises), before becoming chief executive of e-commerce start-ups in the Otto Group (2012), in which he holds a 12.5 percent stake. Maren, alongside her son Alexander and daughter Katharina Otto-Bernstein, founded a separate real estate empire, which includes office space in the United States and European shopping malls. The family is one of Germany's wealthiest.

The Hamburg-based Otto Group (GmbH & KG) comprises three business segments: multichannel retail (the core activity, via e-commerce, catalogs), financial services (loans and receivables management), and other services (logistics, travel, purchasing). Turnover is 12,100 million euros (2015/2016), with a workforce of more than 50,000 working in more than 30 countries.

See also DISTRIBUTION AND RETAIL.

ÖZDEMIR, CËM (1965–). Green Party politician. Born in Urach (**Baden-Württemberg**) of **immigrant** Turkish parents, Cëm Özdemir trained in child care (until 1987), before studying social pedagogy in Reutlingen and qualifying with a diploma (1994). After 1987, he also worked as a caregiver in a youth center in Reutlingen and contributed to a local newspaper and **radio** station. A German national from the age of 18, Özdemir joined the Ludwigsburg branch of the Green Party in 1981 and served on the Baden-Württemberg regional executive committee of **Alliance 90/The Greens** (1989–1994). In 1992, Özdemir cofounded an organization promoting the integration of immigrants (ImmiGrün—Das Bündnis der neuen InländerInnen). While a member of the **Bundestag** (1994–2002), he was spokesman for the Greens on internal affairs (1998–2002) and copublished a paper presenting the case for a multicultural democracy in Germany and rejecting a rigid quota system for immigration and **asylum** seekers (2000). In 2002, he resigned as party speaker and member of parliament following revelations that he had accepted a personal loan of over 80,000 DM from the lobbyist Moritz Hunzinger and used air miles acquired through official travel for private purposes. Between 2004 and 2009, Özdemir represented the Greens in the European Parliament, where he was spokesman for his parliamentary group on foreign affairs, helped investigate alleged complicity by **European Union** (**EU**) states in actions by the U.S. Central Intelligence Agency, was a member of the North Cyprus Contact Group, and supported Turkey's application for EU membership. In 2008, he was elected leader of the national Green party in Germany, and he reentered the Bundestag in 2013. His autobiography, based on his experiences as an integrated immigrant (*Ich bin InLänder: Ein anatolischer Schwabe im Bundestag*), appeared in 1997.

P

PARTY OF DEMOCRATIC SOCIALISM (PARTEI DES DEMOKRA-TISCHEN SOZIALISMUS, PDS). The PDS emerged from the disintegration of the ruling **Socialist Unity Party of Germany (SED)** in the **German Democratic Republic (GDR)** in late 1989. After adopting its new name in February 1990, it declared itself to be a different and wholly democratic party; indeed, less than 10 percent of the 2.3 million former SED members transferred to the PDS in the year of reunification. In the run-up to the elections for the **People's Chamber** (18 March 1990), the PDS, which elected the reform communist **Hans Modrow** as honorary chairman and candidate for premiership, advocated a gradual reunification with the Federal Republic of Germany (FRG) on equal terms. Aiming to attract voters on the left of the **Social Democratic Party of Germany (SPD)**, it campaigned for the right to work, an ecologically sensitive economy, and social and **human rights**. After reunification, the PDS also presented itself as a party of peace, opposing out-of-area activities by the German armed forces. In the March 1990 election, the party gained over 16 percent of the vote, and in regional elections the following October won seats in all the parliaments of the **eastern federal states**. In the all-German national election soon afterward (December 1990), it sent 17 representatives to the **Bundestag**. Drawing heavily on support in the east, where deindustrialization and high unemployment fueled discontent over reunification, the PDS increased its presence in the Bundestag to 30 seats in the 1994 national election, increasing to 36 in 1998.

In the 2002 election campaign, the PDS attempted to build on voters' disillusionment with the performance of the SPD and the **Green Party** and to extend its following to western Germany. The party argued for an end to providing financial support for the churches through **tax** revenues, a new law on **immigration**, radical changes in the **education** system, extension of the **European Union (EU)**, and a reform of European institutions. However, with no tradition and no trust in the west, the PDS failed to clear the 5 percent hurdle, winning just two direct mandates in Berlin. With its regional power base firmly in eastern Germany, it formed a grand coalition with the SPD and **Christian Democratic Union (CDU)** in **Mecklenburg-West Pom-**

erania (1998–2006), governed jointly with the SPD in **Berlin** (from 2002), and tolerated an SPD-minority government in **Saxony-Anhalt** (1998–2002). In the regional election for **Thuringia** in June 2004, the PDS consolidated its share of the vote to become the second strongest of the **political parties** behind the CDU, beating the SPD into third place. In local elections, the party also emerged as the second force in districts and town halls across eastern Germany, largely at the expense of the SPD.

Despite its successes in the eastern states, the PDS lacked the resources, organization, and members to make significant inroads in western Germany, where in 2000 it held only 109 mandates in city and regional governments, mainly in **North Rhine-Westfalia**. Marginalized by the German political establishment, the PDS continued to be regarded by the authorities as a potential danger to the constitution, largely because of its communist background and its opposition (expressed, for example, in the 1993 program manifesto) to the capitalist social order (monitoring of individual Bundestag members continued until 2014). Before the 2002 election, the PDS also came under pressure over the issue of the vast sums of money that the SED/PDS had illegally disposed of following the collapse of the GDR in 1989. The interim People's Chamber set up a commission to investigate the assets of the state-controlled parties in East Germany (May 1990). Reporting on the period between 1996 and 1998, the commission focused on the SED, whose liquid assets, amounting to 6,200 million East German marks, were inherited by the PDS in January 1990. By August 1991, these had dwindled to 200 million DM, which were handed over to the **Trust Agency** for distribution to the eastern federal states. The commission alleged that the PDS had failed to cooperate with the investigation and that illegal tactics had been used to hide the missing millions and to redirect assets back to the party in the form of private donations. From 1991, following a ruling by the party congress condemning the activities of the **Stasi**, parliamentary candidates and senior officials were obliged to register any previous activities undertaken for the organization, although a blanket ban as a result of Stasi involvement was not imposed. Party membership declined, from 200,000 in 1990 to 78,000 in 2003 (46 percent were women) and to 60,000 in 2005.

The founding leader of the PDS was **Gregor Gysi** (1989–1993), followed by **Lothar Bisky** (1993–2000) and **Gabi Zimmer** (2000–2003); Bisky was reelected in June 2003. The party suffered a major setback when Gysi, the most charismatic figure in its leadership, was forced to resign as Berlin economics senator in August 2002, although he reemerged as the PDS's lead candidate in the national election of September 2005. In July/August 2005, the PDS entered into an electoral alliance with the **Election Alternative for Labor and Social Justice (WASG)**, a breakaway group from the SPD. At the same time, the party changed its name to **The Left Party** (Linkspartei, or

Linkspartei.PDS). Campaigning nationally against the government's proposed labor reforms and benefit cuts, the new party won 8.1 percent of the vote and returned 54 deputies.
See also POLITICAL PARTIES.

PEGIDA. Founded by Lutz Bachmann in October 2014, Pegida (Patriotische Europäer gegen die Islamisierung des Abendlandes/Patriotic Europeans against the Islamization of the West) organized weekly Monday demonstrations in Dresden protesting against the alleged Islamization of Germany and the country's liberal policy on **asylum** seekers and **immigration**. The rallies, which also provoked counterdemonstrations, grew rapidly from a few hundred to around 25,000 in January 2015 and were echoed on a smaller scale in other German cities. Critics viewed the organization as encouraging racism and hostility to **foreigners**, especially through pronouncements by prominent members, although Bachmann denied links with the extreme right. Nevertheless, in January 2015 six cofounding leading members left to found a more moderate group, DDfE (Direkte Demokratie für Europa). The current leadership includes Bachmann's wife, Vicky; Thomas Tallacker, former councilor and local **Christian Democratic Union** (**CDU**) chairman in Meissen; and Siegfried Däbritz, who previously stood as a **Free Democratic Party of Germany** (**FDP**) city councilor, also in Meissen. Pegida's activities triggered counterdemonstrations, and in Cologne the cathedral responded by switching off all its nightly illumination; the same method was adopted by the **Volkswagen** plant in Dresden. Among prominent figures distancing themselves from the movement was Chancellor **Angela Merkel**, who emphasized Germany's role as a democratic country welcoming foreigners. After the peak of 2014, internal conflicts and a weakening of public support led to a marked decrease in Pegida's activity. In the first round of the June 2015 election for the governing mayor of Dresden, its candidate (Tatjana Festerling) came in third with 9.6 percent of the vote, but withdrew in favor of the FDP's nominee. After pictures emerged of Bachmann posing as Adolf Hitler in 2015, he briefly resigned from Pegida, but rejoined within a month. In the same year, he faced charges of incitement to hatred after comparing migrants with garbage.
See also EXTREMISM.

PEN. The original PEN Club (of Poets, Playwrights, Essayists, and Novelists) was founded in England in 1921, and there are now PEN branches in 145 countries. A German branch was dissolved during the Third Reich, although it continued in exile in London from 1934 onward. After World War II, at the 19th International PEN meeting in Zurich (June 1947), the author Erich Kästner handed over a declaration by the Schutzverband deut- scher

Schriftsteller, an association of German writers established the previous year (the title PEN International was adopted in 2010). The Deutsches PEN-Centrum was refounded in Göttingen (1948), but by 1952 had split into the Deutsches PEN-Zentrum West and the Deutsches PEN-Zentrum Ost (renamed the PEN-Zentrum Deutsche Demokratische Republik in 1967). After the fall of the East German regime in 1989/1990, tensions between the east and west German branches ran high. They surfaced at the annual congress in Kiel (May 1990), and the branches did not merge until 1998. A contributory factor in the dispute was that many artistic institutions of the former **German Democratic Republic (GDR)** remained intact after reunification. While some felt this was justified and avoided a simple discounting of all that had been achieved in the GDR, others, mainly former dissidents, interpreted it as justification of the regime and as backing for some of its supporters.

PEN members join by invitation and must demonstrate outstanding literary achievement. Special features of the German branch include the country's participation in PEN writers-in-exile, writers-in-prison, and writers-for-peace programs. Since 1985, the Hermann Kesten Prize has been awarded for individuals' support of persecuted writers. Current information is available at www.pen-deutschland.de/en/links.

See also LITERATURE.

PENSION SYSTEM. In 1957, the development of German pension levels was dynamically linked to national incomes, reinforcing the notion of a pension as a substitute for earnings. The 1972 pension reform helped low earners by setting rates from a minimum wage level and enabled men to apply for retirement at age 60 (since 1912, the normal retirement age had been 65). After 1969, the social **budget** assumed that pensions would be financed largely by contributions from the working population, which encompassed increasing numbers of **women**—the so-called Umlageverfahren. The standard pension was gauged to provide two-thirds of the net national average income after a 40-year working life. Since 1978, the government has presented to parliament an annual report on pensions that includes a pension adjustment figure calculated from current income levels (Rentenanpassung). Following the report of the **Rürup Commission**, the adjustment from January 2005 took into account the relationship between the number of contributors and pensioners (the so-called Nachhaltigkeitsfaktor), effectively acting as a brake on unaffordable increases. However, because the economic crisis of 2008 involved a decline in wages that would have reduced pensions, in 2009 the government introduced a "pensions guarantee," which postponed the costs of any reduction to future years. This had the effect of setting the adjustment for the western **federal states** (+0.25 percent) announced in 2013 at a much lower level than for the east (+3.29 percent). Other factors affecting pension levels include former in-payments to the insurance fund, the pension starting date and type (e.g., for widows), and its current value. Around 27 million Germans have statutory pension insurance and either pay in or are credited with contributions from their income. Separate provisions exist for civil servants, the self-employed, and war victims.

The need for changes to the German pension system emerged during the 1980s, when it became clear that pensions, which represented the largest single element of the social budget, could not be financed through the existing contributions system. After 1990, successive governments attempted to modify the system to control spending on pensions and bring expenditure in line with demographic changes. A key measure was the reform of 1989 (in force throughout the country from 1992), which reduced pensions to 67 percent of net income, set an upper limit of 22 percent on contributions, and progressively raised the compulsory retirement age to 65. The reform also promoted private pension policies to supplement the compulsory state pension. In 1997, the conservative-controlled **Bundestag** agreed to a further reform (effective from 1999), which slowed the future rate of pension increases. Although a new social democratic government of 1998 partially rescinded these changes, it faced the same problem: how to finance a pension system for people who were living longer with contributions from a shrinking workforce.

In 2000, the government finally won Bundestag approval for a watered-down pension reform. The long-term aim of the measures, which would be introduced in stages, was to stabilize the level of insurance contributions, raise the retirement age from 60 to 63 (from January 2001), and abolish the invalidity pension in its current form. In 2003, the Rürup Commission proposed progressively raising the retirement age after 2011 from 65 to 67, subject to job availability, and linking the annual pension adjustment to the numbers of contributors in order to hold contributions below 22 percent until 2030. In January 2002, the so-called Riester-pension, named after its originator, Labor and Social Policy Minister **Walter Riester**, became available. The scheme, which was part of the overall pension reform, offered Germans the option of topping up their state pension by combining it with private contributions. Under the **grand coalition** of the **Christian Democratic Union (CDU)** and **Social Democratic Party of Germany (SPD)**, elected in 2005, the Bundestag and **Bundesrat** finally agreed in 2007 that the retirement age would rise progressively from 65 to 67 between 2012 and 2029, ensuring that, in order to receive a full pension, anyone born after 1964 would normally either have to work until age 67 or accept reductions. However, somewhat in contradiction to the official policy of encouraging people to work longer, and in response to SDP pressure, a new coalition decided in 2014 to permit employees with 45 years of contributions to retire earlier than the statutory age (i.e., if they were born in 1951/1952, at age 63 instead of 65, or if born in 1964, at age 65 instead of 67) without reductions. In 2007, the maximum level of contributions was set at 20 percent until 2020 and 22 percent by 2030. Contributions actually rose to 19.9 percent in 2007, where they stayed until 2012. Starting in January 2015, the level fell from 18.9 to 18.7 percent, divided equally between employer and employee. Although approximately one in two pensions is less than 700 euros a month, actual income is generally supplemented by income from a partner and social welfare benefits, so the average joint income for a couple in the western states is more than 2,500 euros and in the east 2,000 euros (according to a government report of 2012).

See also SOCIAL SECURITY SYSTEM.

PEOPLE's CHAMBER (VOLKSKAMMER). The People's Chamber functioned as the parliamentary assembly of the **German Democratic Republic (GDR)** from October 1949 until October 1990. It emerged after World War II from the Deutscher Volksrat (German People's Council), which was set up in 1948 by nonelected delegates of the Deutscher Volkskongress (German People's Congress) in the Soviet zone of occupation. The council's main task was to draw up a constitution for the creation of an East German state in response to moves toward the establishment of the Federal Republic of Germany (FRG), which was aligned with the Western powers. From 1963 onward the 500-member chamber was dominated by members of the ruling **Socialist Unity Party of Germany (SED)**, for whose policies and decisions it provided formal votes of unanimous support. Not until the East German leader **Erich Honecker** was forced to resign in October 1989 did the assembly begin to function as a genuine forum of debate, and even then its influence was constrained by its lack of popular legitimacy until free elections were held on 18 March 1990, when the conservative **Alliance for Germany** won a majority of seats and formed an all-party government with a mandate to negotiate reunification with the FRG. Between March and October 1990, the chamber voted in a new constitution, set up the **Trust Agency** to manage the privatization of businesses, introduced legislation to establish **federal states** in eastern Germany as a precursor to acceding to the FRG, and approved the treaties on reunification. The People's Chamber ceased to exist when its 144 members joined the expanded **Bundestag** on 3 October 1990, the date of reunification. At the same time, the constitution was superseded by the **Basic Law (BL)**.

See also GERMAN DEMOCRATIC REPUBLIC (GDR): POLITICAL INSTITUTIONS; ROUND TABLE (RUNDER TISCH).

PETER, SIMONE (1965–). Green Party politician. Simone Peter studied microbiology in Saarbrücken (from 1986), graduating with a diploma (1993) before managing an environmentally oriented project on microbiological processes in the Moselle and Saar Rivers (1994–2000) and earning a doctorate (2000). Between 2004 and 2009, she worked for two agencies in the field of renewable **energy** in Bonn. A member of the **Alliance 90/The Greens** in the Saar from 1996, Peter occupied various positions in the party before entering the regional assembly (**Landtag**) of the **Saarland** (2010), where she served as regional minister for the **environment**, energy, and **transport** (2009–2012). In 2012, she also became deputy leader of the parliamentary group and business manager for the Greens, but resigned her mandate the following year when the national party elected her coleader alongside **Cem Özdemir**.

PETERS, JÜRGEN (1944–). Trade union leader. Jürgen Peters was born in Bolko/Oppeln (formerly Upper Silesia, now in Poland) into a working-class family. During World War II, the family moved to Hanover, where he later joined the engineering company Hanomag (1961) to train as a toolmaker. After attending the Akademie der Arbeit (College of Work) in Frankfurt/Main (1968–1969), Peters joined one of Germany's largest trade unions, the metalworkers' union IG Metall, as an apprentice (1961) and was active in the youth section until 1968, when he decided to pursue a full-time career in the union in preference to studying **engineering**. In 1969 he moved to Lohr (**Bavaria**), where he worked in the union's training and **education** unit. After heading IG Metall's branch office in Düsseldorf (1976–1978), where he gained firsthand experience of the steel crises in the industrial centers of the **Rhine**, Ruhr, and Saar, he returned to Hanover as local district leader.

Representing 350,000 members in **Lower Saxony** and **Saxony-Anhalt**, Peters played a key role in reaching an agreement for a 28-hour week with **Volkswagen** (VW) that averted mass dismissals (1993). Following tough negotiations, a deal to create 5,000 new jobs at VW in return for a 5,000 DM unitary wage was widely praised (2001). He also set a national precedent by negotiating groundbreaking agreements with Preussag AG on part-time work for older workers and a pilot scheme for 100 percent sickness payment over five years (1996–2001) in return for a reduction in Christmas bonuses. Between 1999 and 2001, around 1,000 workers benefited from a scheme (Verein zur Beschäftigungsförderung) established jointly between IG Metall and employers in Lower Saxony to create new jobs through voluntary agreements on part-time work.

When **Walter Riester**, deputy leader of IG Metall, became federal minister of labor and social affairs in the cabinet of **Gerhard Schröder** (1998), Peters took over his position (as second chairman) in the face of opposition from the union's leader, **Klaus Zwickel**. Peters assumed responsibility for wage policy, although differences with the traditionalist Zwickel proved damaging to the union. In April 2003, the executive board nominated Peters to succeed Zwickel, despite the latter's fierce opposition. Following a disastrous four-week campaign for a shorter (35-hour) workweek in eastern Germany, in which Zwickel openly accused Peters of mishandling negotiations (it was the union's first failed strike in decades), Zwickel stepped down prematurely (July/August 2002) in order to make way for his rival. It was agreed that Peters would cogovern the union in tandem with **Baden-Württemberg** district leader Berthold Huber until 2007, although Peters took over as first chairman in 2003, with Huber as his deputy. The 2003 round of pay negotiations with engineering employers confronted differences over wage levels, local workplace deals, and hours of work, with some doubting whether IG Metall would retain its traditional pace-setting role for national wage rates. Respected for his pragmatism and openness to new ideas, Peters was also regarded as a hard-liner who opposed aspects of Schröder's **Agenda 2010** program of economic and social reform. He resigned as union leader in 2007 and from the supervisory boards of VW (in 2010) and the steel company Salzgitter AG (in 2011).

PETERSBURG DIALOG. Following an initiative by Federal Chancellor **Gerhard Schröder** and Russian president Vladimir Putin, the Petersburg Dialog (Petersburger Dialog) was established in 2001 as a joint German–Russian discussion forum for political, economic, social, and cultural issues. The forum is held annually at alternate locations in each country and is made up of 100 delegates from each country, representing all walks of civilian, political, and business life. Financed by the two governments (in Germany by the Federal Ministry for Foreign Affairs and political foundations) and private business, the forum promotes mutual understanding and cooperation, establishes networks linking state and civilian institutions, and initiates ideas for future projects (examples include youth exchanges, medical **research**, and health-care programs). Activities are led by a steering committee, chaired jointly by a German (**Ronald Pofalla**, who succeeded **Lothar de Maizière** in 2015) and a Russian (Viktor Subkow). In 2014, the immediate future of the forum came into question when five civil organizations in Germany (including the Heinrich Böll Foundation, Greenpeace Deutschland, and Amnesty International) withdrew participation following Russia's intervention in the Ukraine and its persecution of civil rights organizations at home. Critics also accused de Maizière and German business interests of adopting an uncritical position toward the Russians.

See also FOREIGN POLICY: THE RUSSIAN FEDERATION.

PHARMACEUTICALS. Linked to the emergence of the **chemical industry** during the 19th century, the development and production of pharmaceuticals has a long tradition in Germany. In the postwar Federal Republic of Germany (FRG), the sector expanded steadily and enjoyed high annual growth rates. In 2014, the industry manufactured products worth 23,000 million euros, turning over more than 38 million euros with a workforce of at least 112,000; two-thirds of the products went for export. Although pharmaceutical products are less prone to national economic ups and downs, companies spend 13.2 percent of turnover on **research and development**, possibly the highest level in Germany. Pressure factors include the adverse effects of the expiration of patents and the state's efforts to control expenditures on its **health**-care **system**, including drugs and medicine. In particular, the health reform of 2007, coupled with cuts in external sales staff, led to a decline in the workforce during 2009–2010.

The heterogeneous pharmaceuticals industry includes medium-sized, German-owned concerns and branches of foreign multinationals alongside biotechnological companies manufacturing mainly medicines and diagnostic products. Of around 900 registered businesses (statistics are uncertain, partly because of patterns of ownership), 95 percent of these employ fewer than 500 people. Biotechnology is a major growth area and expected to be a key industry in the 21st century. Germany, with its solid research base and skilled workforce, is one the world's largest manufacturers of biotechnological products. The main challenges in the sector are seen to lie in turning fundamental research into applications, generating capital to finance new companies, and covering risk. The main clusters of pharmaceuticals/medical concerns in Germany are in the south (especially in **Baden-Württemberg** and around Munich in **Bavaria**), and the Rhein-Main region, where networks of universities, research centers, and qualified staff are grouped. Swiss-owned Novartis, with its pharma division in Nuremberg, is the largest company in Germany. Leading German-owned companies include **Bayer AG, Boehringer**, and B. Braun.

Pharmaceuticals are the biggest contributor, especially in terms of exports, to the wider health industry in Germany, which also encompasses medical and biomedical technology, spas, drugstores, and nursing care, not to mention **sports**, leisure, health foods/**tourism**, and various lifestyle products. According to the umbrella concern for drug research companies in Germany, the Wirtschaftsverband der forschenden Pharma-Unternehmen (German Association of Research-based Pharmaceutical Companies, VFA), health-related activities constitute the country's largest economic sector, employing 5.9 million people and generating 250,000 million euros of national GDP. Germany is Europe's largest market for the health industry as a whole.

See also BRAUN, LUDWIG GEORG (1943–); MERCKLE FAMILY.

PIËCH, FERDINAND (1937–). Motor industry executive. Ferdinand Piëch was born in Vienna, the son of Louise Porsche, whose father, Ferdinand (1875–1951), founded the Porsche motor company (1931), became a managing director of **Volkswagen** (1938), and created the famous "VW Beetle." After schooling in Austria, Ferdinand Piëch studied **engineering** at the

Eidgenössische Technische Hochschule (Swiss Federal Institute of Technology Zurich, ETH), graduating with a diploma (1962). He worked as a test engineer for Porsche in Stuttgart (from 1963), before becoming head of testing and development and finally technical manager (1971). He also developed a five-cylinder diesel engine for Daimler-Benz and the famous Porsche 917 racing car, but left the company after the **Porsche family** excluded its members from managerial positions. In 1972, he became head of special technical developments at NSU (the developer of the rotary Wankel engine), which had merged with Audi in 1969 to create the Audi-NSU-Auto Union AG, in which Volkswagen held a majority 59.5 percent stake. In 1988, he overcame criticism of his management style to replace Wolfgang Habbel as chairman of Audi's executive board, although unlike his predecessor, he was not at the same time appointed to the board of Volkswagen. Piëch was instrumental in developing the Audi Quattro and led the company to success at a time when Volkswagen's fortunes were declining. In 1992, he finally joined Volkswagen's executive board, succeeding Carl Hahn as chairman the following year. Although Volkswagen was in financial crisis, he refused to give in to the demands of investment bankers to fire 30,000 workers. Instead, he recruited the Spanish-born manager José Ignacio López de Arriortua from General Motors with a mandate to cut costs and improve efficiency. The move proved controversial when General Motors claimed that López had revealed commercial secrets to Volkswagen, although the dispute was resolved when López left Volkswagen (1996) and the latter paid General Motors $100 million in an out-of-court settlement (1997). In 2012, Porsche was finally merged with Volkswagen.

Considered one of Germany's top managers, Piëch proved a highly successful chief executive at Volkswagen, whose fortunes improved under his leadership. His strategy was to offer a wider range of different brands that used the same engineering technology. He also initiated a series of takeovers designed to take the company into the quality end of the market. By 2002, when he retired from the executive board to chair the supervisory board, Volkswagen was achieving record profits. Early on in his career, Piëch had developed a reputation as a demanding perfectionist, and he is reputed to have dismissed 30 subsidiary executive boards as head of Audi and Volkswagen. A long-standing, close working relationship with his chief executive, Martin Winterkorn, broke down in 2014/2015, when Piëch attempted to oust him as chief executive. After failing to win shareholders' backing for the move, Piëch and his wife quit the supervisory board. Although the Piëch family still held 43 percent of shares in Porsche SE (which in turn had a 50.7 percent stake in VW), their departure marked the end of direct patriarchal involvement in the management of Germany's largest industrial concerns.

The Technical University of Vienna (TU Wien) awarded Piëch an honorary doctorate in 1984. The Piëch/Porsche families retain extensive holdings in the company and also own Porsche Holding OHG in Salzburg, the largest trading organization in Austria, which has exclusive rights to export Volkswagen vehicles to Austria and eastern Europe.

See also AUTOMOBILE INDUSTRY.

PINKWART, ANDREAS (1960–). Free Democratic Party (FDP) politician. Andreas Pinkwart was born in Seelscheid (**North Rhine-Westfalia**). After training in banking, he studied business and economics in Münster and Bonn, graduating with a diploma (1987). While studying for a doctorate at the University of Bonn (awarded in 1991), he assisted in the Institut für Mittelstandsforschungen, an institute researching small to medium-sized businesses (the **Mittelstand**), and later worked for the parliamentary party of the FDP in the **Bundestag**. He headed the office of the parliamentary group's leader, Hermann Otto Solms (1991–1994), and was professor of business and economics at an academy for public administration in Düsseldorf (1994–1997) before taking a chair at the University of Siegen. His principal areas of research were the Mittelstand, entrepreneurship, and management. A member of the FDP from 1980, Pinkwart was district party leader in Rhein-Sieg (1989–2002), regional deputy leader (1996–2002), then leader (2002–2010). On the national executive of the FDP (from 1997), he worked on proposals for **taxation** reform and served as deputy leader of the national party (2003–2011). Elected to the Bundestag in 2002, he left in 2005 to become minister for innovation, science, **research**, and technology and deputy to the **minister president** in the regional parliament (**Landtag**) of **North Rhine-Westfalia** (until 2010), where he was instrumental in introducing university tuition fees and argued for orienting higher **education** toward economic needs. In 2011, he was appointed rector of the private Leipziger Handelshochschule (Leipzig Graduate School of Management).

See also MITTELSTAND.

PIRATES, THE (DIE PIRATEN). Inspired by the Swedish Piratpartiet, The Pirates (full name: Piratenpartei Deutschland) is a political party founded in September 2006 in **Berlin**. Initially a protest party dedicated to protecting democratic freedoms globally in a world dominated by networked digital technology, The Pirates opposed state surveillance and campaigned for free and open exchange of information on the **Internet** alongside the preservation of individual privacy. More specifically, the policy entailed unrestricted copyright, the dismantling of private monopolies, reform of patent laws, and greater transparency of state-held information and processes. The Pirates' ethos of citizens' rights in a networked society was later extended to embrace areas such as **education** (with calls for access to free education focused on the needs of the individual), the family, sexuality, the **environment**, **agriculture**, migration, **health**, drugs, youth, the protection of whistleblowers, poverty, Europe, and **foreign/security policy**. Many see The Pirates as torn between a vagueness of policy content and implementation and their clear focus on direct democracy. An innovation is their use of the "liquid democracy" software tool to sound out opinion and inform policy decisions.

The party is organized as an executive (Vorstand), which is elected annually at a party congress (Bundesparteitag). It maintains regional associations, a youth organization, and university groups. Membership soared to 20,000 when the party gained 15 seats in the Berlin city assembly election of 2011, and in the following year it gained seats in **North Rhine-Westfalia** (19), the **Saarland** (4), and **Schleswig-Holstein** (6). After falling well short of the 5 percent threshold for entry to the **Bundestag** in 2013, however, The Pirates elected a new leadership under Frankfurt-based software developer Thorsten Wirth, streamlined its organization, and pledged to focus on the key issues of data protection, the Internet, and citizens' rights. The following year, Wirth left the party and was succeeded by Stefan Körner. A prominent member is the former **Green Party** politician **Angelika Beer**.

PLATZECK, MATTHIAS (1953–). Social Democratic Party of Germany (SPD) politician. Born in Potsdam (**Brandenburg**), the son of a doctor, Matthias Platzeck served in the army of the **German Democratic Republic (GDR)** during 1972–1974 before studying biomedical cybernetics at the Technical University of Ilmenau, where he graduated with an **engineering** diploma (1979). He worked as a **research** assistant at the Institute for Air Hygiene in Karl-Marx Stadt (now Chemnitz, 1979–1980), after which he was appointed director of economics and technology at Bad Freienwalde general hospital. During this period, he also completed a postgraduate course in **environmental** hygiene at the Akademie für Ärztliche Fortbildung (Academy of Further Medical Education) in **Berlin**. In April 1988, he cofounded the AG Pfingstberg and a Potsdam-based citizens' action group, the Arbeitsgemeinschaft für Umweltschutz und Stadtgestaltung (ARGUS), to improve environmental protection and town planning in the GDR.

With the fall of the East German regime in November 1989, Platzeck cofounded and was spokesman for the Grüne Liga (Green League), a network of ecological groups, which he represented in the **Round Table** discussions between the authorities and opposition groups (December 1989–March 1990). He also served as minister without portfolio in the interim cabinet of **Hans Modrow** (February–April 1990). In the elections to the **People's Chamber** of the GDR (18 March 1990), Platzeck was returned as a **Green Party** member and was parliamentary business manager for the **Alliance 90/**

The Greens. Following regional elections in October 1990, he represented the Alliance in the Brandenburg **Landtag** (until 1992), where he served as minister for environment and planning (1990–1998), although he withdrew from the party when it merged with the west German Greens (1993). He represented Brandenburg in the **Bundesrat** (1991–1998), moving over to the SPD in 1995 after the collapse of the "traffic light coalition" of the SPD, **Free Democratic Party (FDP)**, and Greens in 1994.

When the Oder River flooded eastern Brandenburg in July/August 1997, Platzeck won national acclaim for his management of the crisis, earning the nickname "Duke of the Dike" ("Deichgraf"). His dedication and credibility also earned him the "Golden Camera" award from the **television/radio** magazine *Hörzu*—the first time this had been given to a politician. In 1998, he joined the SPD regional executive and gave up his ministerial post in Brandenburg to become (until 2002) mayor of the regional capital, Potsdam; his election prevented a threatened takeover by the **Party of Democratic Socialism (PDS)** in the wake of a corruption scandal. A member of the SPD's national executive (from December 1999), he was elected regional party chairman for Brandenburg (2000–2013) and entered the Landtag in 2004. In June 2002, Platzeck succeeded his patron, **Manfred Stolpe**, as **minister president**. The regional election of September 2004 confirmed the SPD as the strongest party, albeit with a reduced majority and dependent on continuing the coalition with the CDU. Seen as a red/green with conservative leanings, Platzeck was regarded as a rising star in the SPD. During the leadership crisis in the SPD in the wake of the party's failure in the 2005 national election, he replaced **Franz Müntefering** as chairman (leader) of the SPD (November 2005), but resigned on health grounds in April 2006 and was succeeded by **Kurt Beck**, minister president of **Rhineland-Palatinate**. Following regional elections in 2009 and the formation of a ruling coalition with **The Left Party**, Platzeck continued as minister president until 2013, when he also resigned as regional party leader. He chaired an SPD commission on drawing up a new program of basic principles (Grundsatzprogramm, 2006) and briefly chaired the supervisory board of the new Berlin-Brandenburg airport (2013). Platzeck has received various awards, mainly for **environmental** work, contributions to economic development, and services to German–Polish cooperation.

POFALLA, RONALD (1959–). Christian Democratic Union (CDU) politician. Born in Weeze/Kleve (**North Rhine-Westfalia**), Ronald Pofalla studied social pedagogy in Düsseldorf, graduating with a diploma (1981), before studying law at the University of Cologne (1981–1987). After passing his state law examinations (1987, 1991), he practiced law in Essen. A member of the CDU from 1975, he chaired the party's youth wing (**Junge Union, JU**) in North Rhine-Westfalia (1986–1992) and from 1991 occupied various positions in the local and regional party. After entering the **Bundestag** (1990), he served as legal adviser to the CDU/**Christian Social Union (CSU)** parliamentary group (2000–2004) on the legal team that defended former chancellor **Helmut Kohl** during the party donations affair. Pofalla was one of the few CDU members of parliament who maintained contact with Kohl during this period, although he fully endorsed the reform program of **Angela Merkel**. Hitherto best known at the regional level, Pofalla was abruptly projected into the national limelight when he succeeded **Volker Kauder** as general secretary of the CDU (December 2005–2009). He played an important role in the postelection negotiations with **Franz Müntefering** over the formation of a coalition government with the **Social Democratic Party of Germany (SPD**, 2005–2009) and went on to become federal minister for special tasks and head of the **Office of the Federal Chancellor** in Merkel's government of 2009–2013. A close colleague of Merkel, Pofalla withdrew from political offices in 2014 and in early 2015 joined the executive board of the rail carrier Deutsche Bahn, with responsibility for national and international relations. In the same year, he succeeded **Lothar de Maizière** as chairman of the **Petersburg Dialog**.

PÖHL, KARL OTTO (1929–2014). Banker. Born in Hanover (**Lower Saxony**), Karl Otto Pöhl studied economics at the University of Göttingen and graduated with a diploma. After working for the Ifo Economics **Research** Institute (1957–1960) and as a journalist in Bonn (1961–1967), he served briefly on the management team of the Bundesverband deutscher Banken (Federation of German **Banks**, 1968–1969), before entering the Federal Ministry for Economic Affairs and the **Office of the Federal Chancellor**. From 1973 until 1977, he was a **state secretary** in the Federal Ministry of Finance. Appointed vice president of the **German Federal Bank** (Bundesbank) in 1977 and president in 1980, he came to be regarded as one of the bank's most prominent and successful heads. Reunification, however, exposed serious policy differences between the bank and the government led by Chancellor **Helmut Kohl**, who was already distrustful of Pöhl, a member of the **Social Democratic Party of Germany (SPD)**. In particular, Pöhl strongly opposed extending the West German **currency** (DM) to the **German Democratic Republic (GDR)** before a transitional period of economic reforms. He also criticized the 1:1 exchange rate of currency union (which took place on 1 July 1990 and proved to be based on political rather than economic grounds) and the credit financing of reunification through the **German Unity Fund**. Pöhl finally announced his resignation in May 1990, amid widespread concern that the government had ignored the bank's advice and undermined its independence. Pöhl was succeeded as federal bank president by Helmut Schlesinger (1991–1993) and later by **Hans Tietmeyer**, whose appointment was widely seen as strengthening Kohl's political influence within the bank.

After leaving the federal bank, Pöhl became a partner in Sal. Oppenheim Jr. & Cie, a Frankfurt-based private bank (1991–1998). Throughout his career, he served on the boards of several international concerns and banking organizations, including the International Monetary Fund (IMF), where he was German governor (1980–1991). His academic awards include doctorates from universities in the United States, Great Britain, Israel, and Germany, and he received various honors from countries around the world (Austria, Italy, Sweden, Luxembourg, the Netherlands, and France).

POLES. *See* ETHNIC MINORITIES: POLES.

POLITICAL PARTIES. Political parties in Germany originate from the mid-19th century, when they were formed by the traditions of liberalism, conservative nationalism, Christianity, and socialism. The constitutional framework for the major parties that emerged from both these traditions and the experiences of National Socialism—the conservative **Christian Democratic Union (CDU)** and its sister party the **Christian Social Union (CSU)**, the liberal **Free Democratic Party (FDP)**, and the **Social Democratic Party of Germany (SPD)**—was laid down in the **Basic Law (BL)** of 1949 for the newly founded Federal Republic of Germany (FRG). The constitution specifies that parties shall participate in the formation of the political will of the people and may be freely established, that their internal organization must conform to democratic principles, and that they must publicly account for their assets and funding (article 21). Although the BL required the details to be worked out by parliament, disputes over funding delayed the first formal legislation (Parteiengesetz) until 1967. Nevertheless, the two big parties (CDU/CSU and SPD) commanded traditional electoral loyalties and dominated the political landscape in Germany for almost three decades after 1949. The strategy of being a "catch-all party" (Volkspartei) appealing to all sections and strata of society kept the CDU in power for well over a decade in the postwar period and also brought the SPD electoral success when the latter fully adopted it in 1959. Successful Volksparteien deemphasized ideology and resolved issues of principle internally and through compromise. Crucially, they also produced leaderships that reached out to attract voters across social boundaries, although the CDU, notably in the form of **Helmut Kohl** and **Angela Merkel**, has generally proved more effective at this than the SPD.

Since 1961, every German government has been a coalition, either between the big two parties (a so-called **grand coalition**) or between a main party and a minority one (invariably the FDP, but more recently also the **Green Party**). The German **electoral system**, a complex mix of proportional representation and first-past-the-post, arguably also favors small parties. As social values changed and more fluid voting patterns emerged during the late 1970s and 1980s, smaller protest groups gained a political foothold. Focusing on the **environment**, concerns over peace, and local issues, these groups presented an electoral challenge to the established parties (Altparteien). Coalescing as the Greens, they eventually entered the **Bundestag** in 1983.

Between the collapse of the regime in the **German Democratic Republic (GDR)** and reunification in 1990, new and reconstituted parties emerged in the east, including the **Party of Democratic Socialism (PDS)**, which, to the surprise of many, proved to be a potent political force in the new **eastern federal states**. The PDS went on to form an alliance with the **Election Alternative for Labor and Justice (WASG)** in 2005, renaming itself **The Left Party** (Die Linke) in 2007. Reunification brought a new, geographical dimension to German politics, with the former, four-party system (CDU/CSU, SPD, FDP, and the Green Party) persisting in the old western states and a three-way configuration (CDU, SPD, and PDS/The Left Party) emerging in the east. While the failure of the two main Volksparteien to attract more than 70 percent of the vote over three consecutive elections (2005, 2009, 2013) favored the formation of grand coalitions, the political landscape arguably became more unpredictable as minor parties often increased their share. Even The Left Party, despite its cooperation with the SPD in some eastern federal states, has deepened its penetration in the west, although its associations with the communist past rule it out as a coalition partner at federal level.

Broadly speaking, strongholds of the CDU are southern Germany (**Bavaria** [CSU only] and **Baden-Württemberg**), while support for the SPD is concentrated in **North Rhine-Westfalia**, northeastern Germany, and the eastern states. The traditional heartland of the FDP is Baden-Württemberg. While rural and/or Catholic areas historically support the CDU/CSU, older industrial communities tend to remain loyal to the SPD. The Greens or the FDP are more likely to find support in towns and cities with diverse or service-oriented economies.

Apart from the FDP, of the smaller parties only the Greens (first of all in 1983) and PDS/The Left (in 1990) have managed to enter the Bundestag. Parties such as the **Instead Party**, the **Schill** Party, and the **Federation of Free Citizens (BFB)** have been short-lived and of only local appeal. The recently founded **Alternative for Germany (AfD)** surprised observers by its good performance in elections in **Hessen** and for the Bundestag in 2013, falling just short of the entry threshold, while **The Pirates**, despite attracting younger voters and entering several regional parliaments, returned disappointing results in the national election.

A handful of extremist parties (left and right wing) at the edge of the political spectrum have failed to exert significant influence on mainstream politics, although their presence at the regional and local levels has caused concern, especially in the eastern states, where they have capitalized on postreunification economic failure, high unemployment (especially among young people), and resentment toward **foreigners**. Extreme right-wing parties include the **National Democratic Party of Germany (NPD)**, **The Republicans (REP)**, and (until 2012) the **German People's Union (DVU)**. While paying lip service to Germany's postwar democratic order to avoid prohibition, keynotes of their programs include **anti-Semitism**, racism, xenophobia, and vague appeals to the nationalism of the National Socialist period.

See also EXTREMISM; POLITICAL PARTIES: FUNDING.

POLITICAL PARTIES: FUNDING. In a pioneering move for European countries, the Federal Republic of Germany (FRG) introduced state funding for parties in 1959 in order to "promote political education," support democratic parties with a demonstrable following, and prevent them becoming wholly dependent on interest groups. In response to disputes over fairness and rulings by the **Federal Constitutional Court (FCC)**, the system was refined as funding was restricted to election campaign costs (1966); then extended to include smaller parties that failed to meet the 5 percent election hurdle (1983); and finally modified to provide for a mixed system combining state subsidies with members' contributions and private donations, including those from parliamentary and local council representatives (1994). Beginning in 1994, the subsidy for a party was linked to a price index (based on the party's expenditure and weighted according to national consumer prices and wage levels), the votes it received in elections (national, regional, and European), and its own resources. Since 2013, the absolute limit for the combined funding of all parties (156.7 million euros in 2014) has also been linked to the percentage increase in a typical party's expenditure from the previous year.

Historically, the **Social Democratic Party of Germany (SPD)** relied on members' contributions, while the **Christian Democratic Union (CDU)** depended more on private donations (e.g., from **industry**), although both parties now receive similar levels of both members' contributions (30 percent of income in 2013 for the SPD and 26 percent for the CDU) and public subsidy (29/32 percent). Donations, however, are relatively more substantial for the CDU (20 percent in 2013) and the FDP (17 percent in 2012) than for the SPD (9 percent in 2013). Contributions from Bundestag deputies account for between 20 and 30 percent of income. Similar figures apply to the **Greens** and **The Left Party**, although the former receive rather more in donations (over 12 percent in 2013) than the latter (9 percent). State funding varies from 40 percent (for The Left Party) to 32 percent (for the CDU). Total incomes for the two major parties in 2013 were over 151 million euros for the CDU and 165 million euros for the SPD, although the SPD registered a deficit of more than 21 million euros. All parties are obliged to declare income and expenditures and to provide an annual report (Rechenschaftsbericht) to the **president of the Bundestag**.

The complexity of party funding is a result of years of controversy over transparency and levels of subsidy. During the 1980s and 1990s, almost all the established parties lost public credibility following revelations of **tax** evasion by large donors and of illegal and undeclared donations. This also contributed to the success of the **Green Party**. Major scandals included the **Flick** affair and **Helmut Kohl**'s acceptance of anonymous donations, although the CDU in **Hessen** also partly financed its regional election campaign in February 1999 from undeclared donations, and the SPD has attracted criticism for its large holdings in **media** organizations. In 2002, legislation was introduced that criminalizes the concealment of donations and outlaws the splitting up of large donations in order to avoid declaration (the threshold figure is 10,000 euros), and for infringements the president of the Bundestag has imposed large fines on the CDU, SPD, and FDP.

POPPE, ULRIKE (1953–). Former **German Democratic Republic (GDR)** opposition leader. Ulrike Poppe (née Wick) was born in Rostock in the GDR and grew up in Hohen-Neuendorf, near **Berlin**. She began studying art pedagogy and history at Humboldt University in East Berlin in 1971, but left in 1973 to work in a home for children and young people and as a care assistant in a psychiatric clinic, before being employed as an assistant at the Museum für Deutsche Geschichte in Berlin (Berlin Museum of German History, 1976–1988). She cofounded the Frauen für den Frieden (**Women** for Peace network) and was imprisoned by the **Stasi** for six weeks under suspicion of passing information to the West (1982). **Bärbel Bohley**, another group member, was similarly accused. Poppe joined the **Initiative Peace and Human Rights** (1985) and in 1987–1988 was Berlin representative for Frieden konkret, a GDR-wide network of peace groups. She also took an active part in a group (Absage an Praxis und Prinzip der Abgrenzung) that opposed the official East German policy of delimitation (Abgrenzung) from the West (1987–1989). Awarded the Gustav Heinemann Prize for civil rights work in 2000 and a member of the board of trustees of a **research** institute on German affairs at the Institut für Deutschlandforschung (University of Bochum) since 2002, Poppe was appointed by the federal state of **Brandenburg** as a commissioner to investigate and resolve the legacy of the GDR dictatorship (2009–).

POPULATION AND PEOPLE. While the population of West Germany/ the Federal Republic of Germany (FRG) rose steadily between 1950 and 1990, from 51 to 63.7 million, the former **German Democratic Republic**

(**GDR**) faced a continual decline, from 18.4 to 16.1 million. In a first wave of **immigration** before 1949/1950, over eight million refugees and deportees flooded into the West, mainly from former German territories east of the Rivers Oder and Neiße, but also from Czechoslovakia, Poland, Yugoslavia, Hungary, and Romania; a further 3.9 million were absorbed in eastern Germany. Between 1950 and 1990, and in particular before the erection of the **Berlin Wall** in 1961, the FRG welcomed 2.4 million ethnic German immigrants (**Aussiedler**) from Poland, Romania, and the Soviet Union, and another 1.4 million German immigrants from the GDR (Übersiedler). To this influx may be added a third wave, the 2.6 million foreign "guest workers" recruited between 1955 and 1973 from Mediterranean countries, many of whom stayed and were joined by their families (until 1978). During the 1950s and 1960s, these inflows provided a vital labor reserve for the booming economy and produced a wide range of social and demographic changes: the blurring of historic religious demarcations; an explosion in urban populations alongside a decline in **agricultural** workers; a deproletarization of the workforce as industries developed more sophisticated processes and moved away from manual labor; a steep rise in the number of public service employees; the growth of a more mobile, prosperous, and more leisured consumer society; and in particular, the "leveling out" of traditional social classes toward a middle center.

Between reunification and 2002, Germany's total population grew from 79.8 to 82.5 million, at which level it has more or less remained (81.2 million in 2014). At the same time, the eastern and western federal states have developed differently, with the east in decline and the west gaining population in accordance with patterns of internal migration associated with the postreunification transition. The overall migratory balance (or net migration, i.e., the number of immigrants minus emigrants) in the FRG has fluctuated wildly since 1950, but with peaks of immigration greatly outweighing emigration occurring around 1965, 1970, 1980, and the early 1990s; since 2010 there has been a steady and continuing increase in the net balance, with 1,464,700 immigrants against 914,200 emigrants in 2014. Emigration by German nationals is not well researched, but favorite destinations are Switzerland, the United States, and Austria. The net balance for this category is, however, negative, with a moderate annual outflow of 25,000 since 2009, principally well-qualified, internationally mobile Germans seeking experience abroad who eventually return home. Citizens with a **migration background** also figure prominently as emigrants, but for different reasons: they often leave for family reasons or because they are unhappy in Germany, although they rarely return to their country of ethnic origin. Within the general category of inward migration by foreigners, Germany's demography has also been affected by refugees and **asylum** seekers, although to a much lesser extent.

The steady rise in Germany's postwar birthrate, which peaked at 1.36 million in 1964, was dramatically reversed during the late 1960s and 1970s, possibly as a result of a combination of the contraceptive pill (available from 1961) and changing social values. The rate never regained the 1964 level, remaining fairly stable at around 800,000 per year until 1997, after which it declined (down to 665,000 in 2009). Significantly, a major shift in the demographic balance has been under way since 1972, when fewer children were born than people died, with long-term consequences for **welfare** provision and the labor market in an aging society. Before 1990, birthrates in the GDR tended to exceed those in West Germany, especially after 1975, although they were offset by the outward migration of young people (notably before the erection of the Berlin Wall in 1961) and freely available birth control. A remarkable development was the sudden plummeting of childbirths in eastern Germany during the period of economic and social insecurity after reunification; recovering after 1994, they did not reach western levels until 2007, after which they remained slightly above them. Centers of population density are the city-states of **Berlin**, **Hamburg**, and **Bremen**, while the eastern states of **Mecklenburg-West Pomerania** and **Brandenburg** show the lowest concentrations.

PORSCHE FAMILY. The name Porsche came to the world's attention in 1900, when the young Austrian **automobile** engineer and test driver Ferdinand Porsche (1875–1951) presented an innovative electric motor car with wheel-hub-mounted motors. During the 1920s, he worked for Austria's largest motor manufacturer, Austro-Daimler (later Daimler-Benz AG), where he developed the Mercedes supercharged sports car, before moving in 1931 to Stuttgart, where he set up his own automobile design and construction company—the forerunner of today's firm Dr Ing. h.c. F. Porsche AG. In the same year, he sketched a prototype for a low-cost, mass-produced "people's car" (the **Volkswagen**) and, after meeting Adolf Hitler (1933), signed a contract with the government (1934) to manufacture the "Beetle." He visited the United States in order to research American methods of mass production (1936) before building the prototypes for what after World War II became Germany's most successful vehicle. During the war, the Porsche construction company moved to Austria, from where (in 1948) it negotiated exclusive rights to import Volkswagen products from Wolfsburg in Germany and to build a sports car using VW components. The Austrian concern, based in Salzburg from 1949, was managed by Ferdinand's son, Ferdinand (Ferry) Porsche (1909–1998) and his daughter Louise (1904–1999) and her husband, Anton Piëch (1894–1952), the parents of **Ferdinand Piëch**. Managing director from 1939, in 1948 Ferry began building the series of high-technology racing sports cars that was to establish Porsche's position as Germany's leading motor racing designer. In 1950, he returned to Stuttgart-Zuffenhausen to set up his own factory. A win at Le Mans (1951) secured his company's international reputation, and by 1956 Porsche had scored over 400 motor racing victories. Flagship models include the 911 series, first launched in 1963; the Boxster (from 1993); and the Cayenne (from 2002). The Porsche series 956, which appeared in 1982, was considered one of the most successful racing cars ever built.

While Ferry Porsche concentrated on the German side of the business, Louise Piëch took over management of the small Salzburg concern after her husband's death. Building up a nationwide distribution network for the highly popular "Beetle," she rapidly transformed the company into Austria's leading motor trading company, a position it holds to this day. In 1971, Louise Piëch and Ferry Porsche withdrew from operational management, although they remained the sole joint owners of both the Austrian and German branches of the company, and various family members continued to serve on supervisory boards. A share capital company from 1972, Porsche experienced a downturn during the 1990s but recovered after the appointment in 1993 of a new board chairman, Wendelin Wiedeking, who restructured the management, slashed the size of the workforce, and launched new models. By 2002, Porsche had established a network of foreign subsidiaries around the world and invested 8.2 million euros in a prestige showroom in **Berlin**. In 2005, the company announced ambitious plans to take over Volkswagen, but acquired a debt mountain in its attempt to build up a majority stake, forcing the Porsche/Piëch families to abandon the project (2009), which was also dogged by court actions. Porsche and Volkswagen eventually merged in 2012.

Ferry Porsche's son, Ferdinand Alexander (1935–2012), joined Porsche KG (1958) and became head of the design department (1962), where he worked on various racing cars, including Formula One, until he was appointed deputy managing director (1968). In 1972, he founded the independent design and **engineering** company Porsche Design in Stuttgart, which in 1974 moved to Zell am See (Austria) and in 2003 became a subsidiary of Porsche AG. From 1990 until 1992, he chaired the supervisory board of Dr. Ing. h.c. F. Porsche AG in Stuttgart. The Porsche/Piëch families have an 81 percent stake in Porsche Holding SE, established in 2007 to manage holdings in Volkswagen. The Porsche family alone comprises 34 cousins in the fourth generation. In 2015, Porsche produced more than 234,500 vehicles with more than 24,000 workers and turned over 21,530 million euros. Production is based in Stuttgart, Osnabrück (at Volkswagen AG), and Leipzig, and the principal market is the United States.

POSTAL SERVICE. *See* DEUTSCHE POST AG; TELECOMMUNICATIONS.

PRESIDENT (SPEAKER) OF THE BUNDESTAG. *See* BUNDESTAG.

PRESIDENT OF THE FEDERAL REPUBLIC (BUNDESPRÄSIDENT). The president of the Federal Republic is the titular head of state. Elected by a specially convened **Federal Assembly** for a period of five years, the president has a largely ceremonial role. The president's powers include the appointment of army officers; the dissolution of the **Bundestag** according to strict conditions laid down in the **Basic Law (BL)**; the right to propose (not appoint) a **federal chancellor** to parliament; and following proposals from the chancellor, the appointment and dismissal of government ministers. With the support of the **Bundesrat**, the president may also declare a state of legislative emergency (Gesetzgebungsnotstand) if a bill fails in the Bundestag. The president represents Germany abroad and formally concludes international treaties in the name of the **Bund**.

In practice, the president is expected to act as a neutral, balancing, and integrating force among the competing forces in parliament and beyond and to serve as a voice of democratic moral authority above narrow party political interests. A president may be reelected for a single five-year period only, although he or she may run for office again after an interruption. The president may not normally be removed from office for political reasons. Although the president is not obliged to resign from his or her political party, he or she is expected to remain above party politics, especially at election times. Thus **Joachim Gauck** came under fire in 2014 for suggesting that **The Left Party**, which was in the process of negotiating a regional coalition with the **Social Democratic Party of Germany (SPD)** in **Thuringia**, could not be trusted on account of its communist past. Many regard the office of president, alongside the **Federal Constitutional Court (FCC)**, as a guardian of the constitution: the incumbent prepares and proclaims laws passed by the Bundestag/Bundesrat and checks that, in terms of procedure and content, they conform to the requirements of the BL. Past presidents have on several occasions rejected or questioned laws on these grounds (e.g., Heinrich Lübke in 1960, **Walter Scheel** in 1976, and **Richard von Weizsäcker** in 1991). Although the president only formally appoints cabinet ministers, the extent to which he or she has a veto on the chancellor's proposals is constitutionally unclear; in practice, it is acknowledged that the president may not question an appointment on purely political grounds. Officeholders since 1969 have been **Gustav Heinemann** (1969–1974), Walter Scheel (1974–1979), **Karl Carstens** (1979–1984), Richard von Weizsäcker (1984–1994), **Roman Herzog** (1994–1999), **Johannes Rau** (1999–2004), **Horst Köhler** (2004–2010), **Christian Wulff** (2010–2012), and Joachim Gauck (2012–). Although individual presidents have all made their personal mark on the office, Richard von Weizsäcker, speaking on the 40th anniversary of the defeat of the National Socialist regime, attracted international attention by emphasizing Germany's need to take responsibility for its recent history, acting fairly toward **asylum** seekers, and by criticizing the **political parties**' preoccupation with power holding.

PRESS. In view of its special role in forming and informing public opinion, and with memories of the National Socialist regime, the general principle of press freedom in Germany is enshrined in the **Basic Law (BL**, article 5), from which specific rights, such as free access to information from most state authorities and the right of rejoinder, are derived. Nevertheless, laws about the press remain the province of the **federal states** (Länder), and the need to clarify the relationship between the latter and the executive center has led to calls for legislation at the **Bund** level. The **German Press Council** (Deutscher Presserat), set up in 1956, is the industry's self-regulatory body, which protects newspapers from unlawful interference and is responsible for maintaining ethical standards of journalism. The council handles complaints and, where appropriate, issues admonitions; following the *Spiegel* **affair** of 1962, it delivered a public warning about the danger to press freedom.

Although the distinction between print and digital media is not always clear in the available statistics, it is evident that Germans remain avid newspaper and magazine readers: around 70 percent of the population read a local or a regional newspaper every day and remain loyal to the publication of their choice. With 350 daily newspapers, many with local editions (over 1,500 in all), generating a print circulation of 16.8 million (in 2014), Germans appear spoiled for choice. To these can be added 21 weeklies (circulation 1.7 million) and 7 Sunday newspapers (2.9 million). The range of journals is even wider and includes general interest magazines (Publikumszeitschriften), with over 1,500 titles (500 fewer than in 1997), read by more than 34.7 million people at least weekly, and also specialist titles (Fachzeitschriften) for trade, industry and science, and so forth, with 3,800 titles and a circulation of 505 million (of which only 43 percent, however, is sales).

The diversity of titles, however, masks a more complex situation. Since the mid-1950s, a steady process of convergence of newspaper titles, arising partly out of mergers and takeovers and only briefly interrupted by reunification, has fueled concern over the concentration of power in a handful of multimedia organizations. In 1967, the government set up the Günther Commission to investigate press concentration, but delayed until 1976 to pass a general law aimed at restricting press mergers leading to monopolies. It is also debatable whether these measures have significantly halted the process of concentration, which has been accelerated by competition for advertising revenue from illustrated magazines and **television and radio**. Between 1954 and 2013, the total number of newspapers with independent editorial units fell from 225 to 129; the number of publishers also shrank, from 624 to 329, with the 5 largest commanding more than 43 percent of the market. The leading publisher of dailies is the **Axel Springer** concern, with 19.6 percent of market share (the Günther Commission judged a share of 20 percent or more as a danger to press freedom). Others include the Verlagsgruppe Stuttgarter Zeitung (part of Südwestdeutsche Medienholding [SWMH], with 8.6 percent), *Westdeutsche Allgemeine Zeitung* (WAZ, 5.8 percent, and part of the Funke group), DuMont Schauberg (5.5 percent), Ippen (4.2 percent), Madsack (4 percent), and *Frankfurter Allgemeine Zeitung* (FAZ, 3.1 percent).

With more than 300 print titles, local and regional dailies, supplied via subscription (Abonnement), are very popular in Germany, although individual publishers monopolize most areas and local papers, especially in the western **federal states**, taking a covering "shell" of supraregional and national news from a central, usually city-based editorial office. The number of supraregional or national dailies is small. They are the moderate left-wing *Süddeutsche Zeitung* (428,000), the liberal-conservative *Frankfurter Allgemeine Zeitung* (FAZ, 363,000), the conservative *Die Welt* (250,000), and the left-wing *Die Tageszeitung* (*taz*, 55,800) and *Frankfurter Rundschau* (130,000; declared insolvent in 2012–2013, the title was continued by FAZ). The most successful weekly newspaper is the liberal-conservative *Die Zeit* (around 500,000), followed by *Welt am Sonntag* (591,000) and *Frankfurter Allgemeine Sonntagszeitung* (347,000). The daily *Bild* (circulation 2.5 million) and its sister weekly edition, *Bild am Sonntag* (1.3 million), are the only national tabloids or "boulevard" papers, relying more on street sales from shops and kiosks than subscriptions. Both have high circulations; appeal to a popular readership through sensational stories delivered in direct, consumerist language; and produce regional editions. During the 1960s, *Bild* became notorious as a political mouthpiece of its founder, Axel Springer, and for its dubious journalistic methods. Regional competitors include the *B.Z.* (**Berlin**, 250,000), *Berliner Kurier* (Berlin, 127,000), *Express* (Cologne and Rhine area, 167,000), *tz* (Munich, 130,000), *Hamburger Morgenpost* (105,000), and *Morgenpost Sachsen* (Chemnitz and Dresden, 250,000).

After the **Socialist Unity Party of Germany** (**SED**) in the **German Democratic Republic** (**GDR**) lost power in November 1989, many new titles were founded in the east. Until 1990, the GDR had 38 dailies, of which 17 were in the hands of the SED. Only a few survived beyond 1993, as western German concerns entered into partnerships with eastern publishers and, with the approval of the **Trust Agency**, simply bought them up. While single newspaper districts in the west cover mainly towns and their environs, they encompass whole regions in the east. **Berlin** became a fierce battleground for publishers of daily newspapers: *Der Tagesspiegel* and *Berliner Morgenpost* continue to dominate the west of the city, while *Berliner Zeitung* remains popular in the east. The national daily *Neues Deutschland*, which is close to **The Left Party**, has a circulation of around 37,000, mainly in the east.

Another daily, the Marxist-oriented *Junge Welt*, formerly the youth magazine of the GDR, had a checkered history after privatization and temporarily ceased publication in 1995, but now claims a readership of 50,000. Also with origins in the former GDR, the weekly *der freitag* (founded in 1990 as *Freitag* and relaunched in 2009) is politically left/liberal and has a national circulation of around 19,500.

Aside from specialist and scientific periodicals with small readerships, the market for general interest magazines (Publikumszeitschriften) is huge. The most popular category, with over 21 percent of market share (measured in volume of circulation), is motoring; the weekly *ADAC Motorwelt* enjoys a circulation of around 13 million and reaches more than 15 million readers (it also offers various consumer services and operates as a travel agency). Motoring is closely followed by television and radio magazines (e.g., *TV14, TV Digital, TV direkt, Hör zu*, 20.4 percent of market share), titles aimed at **women** (e.g., *Brigitte, BILD der FRAU*, 16.5 percent), home and garden (e.g., *Das Haus, Wohnen*, 10.4 percent), and general interest/current affairs (7.5 percent, e.g., *Bunte* and *stern*, which is renowned for its photography). Founded after reunification in 1990, the weekly *SUPERillu* focuses on eastern Germany, where it is especially popular. Other categories include youth (*BRAVO, Mädchen*), business (*Capital, Handelsblatt*), food (*kochen & genießen*), sports (*DAV Panorama*), and lifestyle (*Playboy*). The leading publishers of magazines are the **Bauer** Media Group, Axel Springer, Burda, and **Gruner + Jahr (Bertelsmann)**.

Party political newspapers, which appear weekly or monthly, are a small and shrinking category. Examples include the *Bayernkurier* (**Christian Social Union [CSU]**, circulation 50,000) and the extreme right-wing *Deutsche National-Zeitung* (ca. 44,000); *Vorwärts* (375,000), the organ of the **Social Democratic Party of Germany (SPD)**, was reconstituted in 1989 as a monthly magazine for party members. A small but significant sector caters to **foreigners** living in Germany, in particular Russian and Turkish speakers. Turkish newspapers produced in Germany have come under increasing financial pressure and have lost popularity, especially among the younger generation.

A special category includes the weekly illustrated news magazines *Der Spiegel* (875,000) and its competitor, *Focus* (509,000), founded in 1993. *Der Spiegel* is considered a key opinion-former in Germany on account of its reputation for aggressive but well-informed reporting that is not afraid to criticize the establishment; it also maintains a strong Internet presence (SPIEGEL ONLINE). In the nonmagazine category, however, and with the exception of the internationally known *Die Zeit*, weeklies offering analysis and opinion of political, social, and cultural issues tend to have lower circulations and lead an economically fragile existence. Both the Catholic-conservative *Rheinischer Merkur/Christ* and the liberal-Protestant *Deutsches Allgemeines*

Sonntagsblatt ceased being independent papers (from 2010/2000) and now appear as supplements to other publications. Founded in 1993 as a competitor to *Die Zeit, Die Woche* was wound up in 2002; after 1997 it also incorporated *Die Wochenpost*, which originated in the former GDR, where it commanded a circulation of 1.3 million. The weekly *Das Parlament*, edited by the **Bundestag** in Berlin, is in a category of its own, aiming to document debates in the regional and national parliaments but rarely commenting on politics. "Street newspapers" (Straßenzeitungen), produced only partly by professional journalists and sold by homeless persons after the model of London's *Big Issue* in 1990, have proved popular; there are around 30 such newspapers across Germany, including *BISS* (Munich), *Hinz&Kunzt* (Hamburg), *strassenfeger*, and *motz* (Berlin). Further categories include free advertising papers (Anzeigenblätter, 1,400 locally distributed weekly titles), town-centered regional "city magazines" (Stadtmagazine, usually monthly), and "event magazines" (Eventmagazine, also monthly, directed at very small, local target readerships, such as students, music/cinema/art fans, etc.).

Of Germany's 35,000 salaried journalists, around 20,000 work for newspapers and magazines, the rest in broadcasting, agencies, and advertising. Some 12,000 are engaged in press offices of organizations. Despite online media, where about 22,000 work either as salaried or freelance, the major employers remain print based; 1,400 or so work for news agencies such as DPA (Deutsche Presse-Agentur) or Reuters.

PUBLISHING. After Great Britain and China, Germany ranks third as a producer on the international book market. Most licenses for German books go to Korea, more than all the English-speaking countries put together. At the same time, in 2000 more than 3,800 titles (70 percent of all translations) were translated from English into German. More factual books are translated than German novels, and of the latter, older authors (e.g., Bert Brecht and Hermann Hesse) predominate. Centers of book production are Munich, **Berlin**, Frankfurt/Main, Stuttgart, Cologne, and **Hamburg**. Of more than 3,000 publishers, 30 have an annual turnover of more than 50 million euros. Two annual book fairs are of particular importance. The Leipzig book fair was the first to be held after World War II (in 1946), although after 1973 it took place only once (in the spring) instead of twice a year. With 1,200 individual events, "Leipzig liest" (Leipzig reads) is Europe's biggest literary festival. The Frankfurt book fair has been held annually in October since 1964. While Frankfurt attracts the major publishing houses, Leipzig focuses on smaller companies and on readers. Since 1976, the Frankfurt fair has been based on an annual theme, oriented toward particular countries. The fair culminates in the awarding of the Peace Prize of the German Book Trade. Winners in recent years include Václac Havel, György Konrád, Friedrich Schorlemmer, **Martin Walser**, Fritz Stern, **Jürgen Habermas**, Wolf Lepenies, Saul

Friedländer, and Anselm Kiefer. "Their names," the organization states, "represent the most important currents in cultural and intellectual history of the 20th and 21st century" and are of relevance in light of the "current political situation, involvement in peace policy and historical responsibility."

Some of Germany's best-known publishing houses, some of which look back at a centuries-old tradition while others emerged after World War II, are discussed here. The Ferdinand Schöningh-Verlag, founded in 1947, is based in Paderborn, focuses on humanities and schoolbooks, and is well known for the UTB series of students' textbooks. The Kohlhammer Verlag, established in Stuttgart in 1866 and in Berlin in 1869, specializes in print and electronic **media** and is an academic publishing house. Vandenhoeck & Ruprecht, founded in Göttingen in 1735, also publishes academic books. Suhrkamp was founded in 1950. Its focus is (contemporary) German and international **literature** and the humanities. Special sections include Suhrkamp Bibliothek (1951), edition suhrkamp (1963), Suhrkamp Taschenbücher (from 1971), and Suhrkamp Taschenbücher Wissenschaft (science). Over the years the concern—like other publishing houses with an increasingly international remit—has developed partnerships with other companies (Insel Verlag, Jüdischer Verlag, and the Deutscher Klassiker Verlag). S. Fischer Verlag, which publishes fiction and poetry, is now a leader in contemporary literature. The company was split in 1936, when Gottfried Bermann Fischer was forced to emigrate to Vienna (he later moved to Stockholm), while Peter Suhrkamp tried to maintain what remained in Berlin. The split became permanent in 1950. In 1963, G. B. Fischer sold off parts of the house to Georg von **Holtzbrinck**, whose daughter, Monika Schoeller, took over the company in 2004. Rowohlt (publisher of fiction, poetry, and nonfiction) was founded by Ernst Rowohlt (1887–1960) in Leipzig (1908) and again in Berlin (1919). It was reestablished in 1945, first in Stuttgart and shortly afterward near Hamburg. Since 1982, Rowohlt has belonged to the Holtzbrinck concern. The Ernst Klett Verlag has its headquarters in Stuttgart and publishes educational/teaching books. Herder, in Freiburg (Breisgau), is one of Germany's oldest publishing houses still in family possession. The interests of the **Bertelsmann** concern currently include RTL (broadcasting), **Gruner + Jahr** (newspapers), Random House (books), and BMG (music). Hoffmann und Campe, founded in 1781 as a publisher of some of the most famous German writers and poets, was partially bought out by Kurt Ganske in 1941 and completely in 1950. Today it specializes in both established and younger authors. The Aufbau-Verlag was founded in 1945 and became a leading publisher in the **German Democratic Republic (GDR)**. It was taken over by Rütten & Loening and Bernd F. Lunkewitz (1991) and has rights to works by prewar authors such as Heinrich Mann, Anna Seghers, and Hans Fallada. In 1998, the Berlin Verlag, established in 1994 by Arnulf Conradi, took over the Siedler Verlag, which had been founded in 1980 and published authors such as Wolf Lepenies, Golo Mann, Joachim Fest, Hagen Schulze, and **Helmut Schmidt**. The Verlag der Autoren, founded in 1960, focuses on **television and radio** plays, although it also entered book publication in 1980. Unusually, it is owned by its authors and has retained its independence. Other firms responded to developments after reunification in 1990, such as Berlin Story Verlag or Das Neue Berlin; Zweitausendeins—first in Frankfurt/Main and now in Leipzig—once well-known for its reprints and select program, has had to adapt to a more commercial approach. Klaus Wagenbach founded his publishing house in 1964 and maintains a philosophy that is less focused on profit than on a literary, political, and social agenda.

See also AXEL SPRINGER SE; BAUER, HEINZ HEINRICH (1939–); BURDA FAMILY; JAHR FAMILY; KIRCH, LEO (1926–2011); MOHN, REINHARD (1921–2009); PRESS; SCHUMANN, ERICH (1930–2007); SPRINGER, AXEL (1912–1985).

Q

QUANDT FAMILY. Industrial entrepreneurs. Originally from Holland, the Quandt family settled in the province of **Brandenburg** in the 19th century. In 1883, Emil Quandt (1849–1925) established a successful textile manufacturing business, supplying the German navy with uniforms. During the interwar period (1918–1939), his son Günther (1881–1954) moved into manufacturing electrical accumulators and generating electricity. A highly successful entrepreneur, he developed close links with the National Socialist Party and was engaged in armaments production and forced labor during World War II, although he and his son Herbert (1910–1982) never divulged the extent to which they profited from them. Upon Günther's death, Herbert and his stepbrother Harald (1921–1967, whose mother was Günther's second wife, Magda, who later married Nazi propaganda chief Josef Goebbels) inherited a conglomerate of 14 concerns, including the battery producer AFA (Varta from 1962), an oil and gas company (Wintershall), a textile manufacturer (Stöhr), and shares in the **automobile** manufacturer Daimler-Benz (now part of **Daimler**). Following an approach from its employees and encouragement from **Franz Josef Strauß**, Herbert Quandt invested in an almost bankrupt **BMW** in 1959; it became not only one of Germany's most successful motor vehicle producers, but also a model of owner–workforce cooperation. In the 1970s, he restructured his holdings, distributing assets and responsibilities among heirs and family members. After Herbert's accidental death in 1982, his third wife, Johanna (born Bruhn, 1926–2015), assumed control, joining the supervisory boards of BMW and other firms in the group to become the undisputed head of the clan. Children from other marriages also retained shares in the group, although between 2003 and 2008 Johanna, once the richest woman in West Germany, gifted her stake in BMW to her offspring, Stefan (1966–) and Susanna (born in 1962 and married to Jan Klatten in 1990), thus preempting any possible inheritance disputes. At the time of her death in 2015, the family's holdings included a 46.7 percent stake in BMW as well as interests in Altana AG (specialty **chemicals** and **pharmaceuticals**), SGL Carbon (carbon fibers for the automobile industry), and Nordex (wind energy). Delton AG, a holding company for diverse activities, including pharmaceuticals and logistics, is 100 percent controlled by Herbert's son Stefan (1966–), who also has a holding in the private BHF Bank. Herbert's daughter Silvia (1937–), who originally trained as an artist, and Harald's daughter Gabriele (1952–) are actively involved in business management. Following an attempt to kidnap Johanna Quandt and her daughter (1978), the family lived in well-protected seclusion and appeared only rarely in public. With an estimated total wealth of 30,000 million euros, the Quandts have succeeded in avoiding the splits and controversies that have plagued other industrial clans.

QUELLE. *See* SCHICKEDANZ FAMILY.

R

RADICALS DECREE (RADIKALENERLASS). Also known as the resolution on extremists (Extremistenbeschluss) and, informally, as the prohibition on entering a profession (Berufsverbot), the radicals decree began life as a decision made jointly in 1972 by the government, led by **Willy Brandt** of the **Social Democratic Party of Germany** (**SPD**), and the **federal states** (Länder) to exclude political extremists and members of organizations considered hostile to the constitution (or **Basic Law, BL**) from working in public services. Adopted during a period of concern over **terrorism**, the measure was largely directed at left-wing extremists. Criticized nationally and internationally as one-sided (it was rarely used against right-wing activists and never against former National Socialists in high positions in postwar Germany) and as alienating a younger generation of peaceful reformists, it was repealed in 1979 at the government level under a new coalition led by **Helmut Schmidt** (SPD), with individual states progressively abandoning it thereafter. In 1991, **Bavaria** became the last state to no longer apply the "inquiry" (Regelanfrage), whereby candidates for public service jobs were quizzed about their constitutional loyalty, although it still required them to complete a questionnaire (Bedarfsanfrage) about membership in extremist organizations and activities in the former **German Democratic Republic** (**GDR**). Nationally, 3.5 million applicants for jobs in schoolteaching, social work, and the legal profession, not to mention the **postal** services and the railways, were subject to the "inquiry," resulting in 11,000 prohibitions, 1,250 rejections, 2,200 disciplinary procedures, and 265 dismissals. In 1986, Brandt eventually accepted that the decree was a mistake, and it was condemned by the European Court of Human Rights in 1995. The German government, however, responding to a parliamentary question from **The Left Party** in 2007, declared that the exclusion of politically suspect applicants from public service was still justified. The question of rehabilitation and compensation for its victims remains unsettled.

RADIO. *See* TELEVISION AND RADIO.

RAILWAYS. *See* TRANSPORT: RAIL.

RAMELOW, BODO (1956–). Born in Osterholz-Scharmbeck (**Lower Saxony**), Bodo Ramelow and his family moved to the Rheinhessen area of the **Rhineland-Palatinate** and then to **Hessen**, where he trained in commerce, eventually working for various retail/distribution concerns in Marburg. After serving as a **trade union** secretary in Hessen (1981–1990), Ramelow moved to the new federal state of **Thuringia** to help rebuild the trade union organization after reunification and until 1999 served as regional chair of a union representing employees in the retail trading, **banking**, and insurance sector (Gewerkschaft Handel, Banken und Versicherungen, HBV, part of ver.di since 1995). In 1997, he co-initiated a public petition signed by 40 artists, authors, intellectuals, politicians, and trade unionists calling for social justice and a new direction in German politics (the Erfurt Declaration). Ramelow joined the **Party of Democratic Socialism (PDS)** in 1999 and in the same year was elected a member of the Thuringian regional assembly (**Landtag**), where he was parliamentary group leader (from 1999), then leader (from 2001). In 2005, he played a prominent role in the merger negotiations between the PDS and the **Election Alternative for Labor and Justice (WASG)** to form what eventually became The Left Party. Between 2005 and 2009, he represented the party in the Bundestag and led its parliamentary group before returning to the Thuringian Landtag. Following regional elections in September 2014 and protracted interparty negotiations, Ramelow was elected **minister president** of a coalition of The Left Party, the **Social Democratic Party of Germany (SPD)**, and **Alliance 90/The Greens** in December. This was the first time The Left Party, the successor to the communist **Socialist Unity Party (SED)** of the former **German Democratic Republic (GDR)**, had provided a minister president at regional level. After Ramelow's election, 1,500 people staged a public protest in Erfurt, and the SPD was widely criticized for entering into the coalition. In his first parliamentary address as leader, Ramelow apologized for the injustices of the GDR regime.

RATZINGER, JOSEPH (1927–). Roman Catholic leader and pope, 2005–2013. Born in Marktl (**Bavaria**) on the Inn River, Joseph Ratzinger entered a seminary (1939) to train as a priest. Drafted into an anti-aircraft unit at age 16, he began infantry training (1944) and was interned by the Allies in 1945. After his release in 1945, he returned to the seminary and was ordained by Cardinal Faulhaber in Munich (June 1951). His doctoral dissertation, "People and the House of God in St. Augustine's Doctrine of the Church," was well received in church circles (1953), and he went on to teach Catholic theology at a number of German universities, holding chairs at

Bonn (1959–1963), Münster (1963–1966), Tübingen (1966–1969), and Regensburg (from 1969). At only age 35, he was appointed peritus (adviser, or chief theological expert) to the archbishop of Cologne, Cardinal Joseph Frings (1887–1978), during the Second Vatican Council (1962–1965). As archbishop of Cologne (1942–1969), Frings was for many years the authoritative voice of Roman Catholicism in the postwar Federal Republic of Germany (FRG). Seen initially as a progressive, independent-minded, and even antiestablishment theologian, Ratzinger became more conservative after the **students' movement** of 1968. He cofounded the theological journal *Communio* (1972), which is now published in several languages and considered an authority on Roman Catholic thought and theology. In March 1977, Pope Paul VI designated Ratzinger archbishop of Munich and Freising, and he was named a cardinal the following June. In November 1981, he was summoned to Rome, where Pope John Paul II, to whom he became a close confidant, appointed him prefect of the Congregation for the Doctrine of the Faith (formerly known as the Holy Office of the Inquisition), president of the Pontifical Biblical Commission, and president of the International Theological Commission. Ratzinger resigned from the Munich archdiocese (1982) to become cardinal-bishop of Velletri-Segni (1993), vice dean of the College of Cardinals (1998), and later dean (2002). Following the death of Pope John Paul II, Ratzinger was elected his successor as Pope Benedict XVI (2005). Seen as a conservative on questions such as ecumenical dialogue and birth control, he published extensively on religious, theological, social, and moral issues. In September 2006, he made controversial remarks about Islam during a lecture at the University of Regensburg that led to protests in the Muslim world. He retired as pope in 2013.

RAU, JOHANNES (1931–2006). Social Democratic Party of Germany (SPD) politician and **president of the Federal Republic** (1999–2004). Johannes Rau was born in Wuppertal-Barman (**North Rhine-Westfalia, NRW**), the son of a Protestant preacher. In school during the National Socialist period, he was an active member of the underground "confessing church" (Bekennende Kirche). After leaving school early (1948), he trained as a book dealer (in Wuppertal and Cologne) and combined work in **publishing** with journalism on religious affairs. In protest against German rearmament, he joined the political party Gesamtdeutsche Volkspartei (GVP), founded by **Gustav Heinemann** in 1952. When the party was dissolved, he moved to the SPD in 1957, which he represented in the state parliament (**Landtag**) for NRW (1958–1999). He was a member of the executive committee of the regional state parliamentary grouping (1962–1970) and its chairman (1967–1970). He also sat on the Wuppertal city council (1964–1978), where he led the SPD group (1964–1967), and served as city mayor (1969–1970). As minister for science and **education** for NRW (1970–1978), Rau instigated the founding of five comprehensive universities (Gesamthochschulen) in Duisburg, Essen, Paderborn, Siegen, and Wuppertal and an Open University (Fernuniversität Hagen). In 1972, Rau generated controversy by dismissing a professor of art, **Joseph Beuys**, for joining students in occupying the premises of a Düsseldorf art academy as a protest against restrictions on study places.

For much of his political career, Rau was **minister president** of NRW (1978–1999), a traditional SPD stronghold where the party gained absolute majorities in 1980, 1985, and 1990. He was also president of the **Bundesrat** (1982–1983, 1994–1995) and chaired the **Bundestag**/Bundesrat **mediation committee** (1990–1994). Rau's main challenge as minister president was to manage the decline of the region's historical coal and steel industries by negotiating a comprehensive plan for structural changes with the government (1988) and attracting businesses based on new technologies. He also introduced a plan for regenerating the **environment**, but faced criticism from opposition parties when NRW ran up a large financial deficit in the early 1990s.

At the federal level, Rau served on the executive committee of the SPD (1968–1999) and the party presidium (1978–1999), and was deputy chairman (1982–1999). In 1985, he was nominated the SPD's chancellor candidate for the 1987 national election and campaigned as a future "chancellor for all citizens." In the event, electoral support for the SPD evaporated, partly because of growing support for the **Green Party**, with which Rau refused to countenance a coalition, and partly following publicity surrounding the collapse of Neue Heimat, a housing syndicate with links to **trade unions**. The SPD also fudged the key issue of defense by pledging support for the **North Atlantic Treaty Organization (NATO)** and the United States while at the same time demanding the withdrawal of U.S. and Soviet medium-range nuclear missiles from Europe. After the election, Rau turned down the opportunity to succeed **Willy Brandt** as party chairman, although he later took over briefly between the resignation of **Björn Engholm** (May 1993) and the election of **Rudolf Scharping** (September 1993). In 1994, Rau was nominated **president of the Federal Republic**, but he was defeated by **Roman Herzog** (1994), the candidate of the **Christian Democratic Union (CDU)**.

In the 1995 regional election for NRW, the SPD gained only 46 percent of seats, losing its absolute majority and forcing it into a coalition with **Alliance 90/The Greens**. Rau later resigned as minister president (to be succeeded by **Rudolf Clement**) and as SPD regional leader (1998). When he was elected eighth president of the Federal Republic (1999), many saw him as an inappropriate choice, at age 68 representing an older generation no longer in tune with the new Germany. However, as the economy faltered, unemployment rose, and structural reforms ran aground, Rau's popularity increased. Although he did not oppose government policies (German presidents are expected to remain above party politics), he was skeptical about advances in biotechnology and argued against rapid changes in social welfare provision. Overall, Rau succeeded in reflecting the mood of an uncertain people that had become increasingly anxious about its future. In his last press interview before his departure from office, he criticized Germany's elite for their greed for power and urged citizens to be become more directly involved in political life.

A committed Christian, Rau was a leading member of the Synod of Evangelical Churches in the Rhineland (1965–1999) and of the presidium of the German Evangelical Conference (Deutscher Evangelischer Kirchentag, 1966–1974). He received numerous honors, including several from Israel, and he was the first German federal president to address—in German—the Israeli parliament (Knesset) in Jerusalem (February 2000).

RED ARMY FACTION (ROTE ARMEE FRAKTION, RAF). The RAF was a tightly organized terrorist group that emerged from the **students' movement** of the 1960s. Modeled on Marxist-Leninist lines and also known as the Baader-Meinhof Group in the early years, its leading figures included **Ulrike Meinhof**, Gudrun Ensslin, Andreas Baader, Holger Meins, Jan-Carl Raspe, and the lawyer Horst Mahler. At first the group attracted some backing from left-wing intellectuals, who identified with its opposition to the capitalist establishment and the Vietnam War, but its anarchist and violent methods, which included arson, bombings, robbery, and murder, rapidly alienated support. The acronym RAF was chosen partly in a nod to the British Royal Air Force, the logic being that, just as the latter conducted a bombing campaign against the National Socialist regime, so the terrorist group was engaged in destroying the postwar capitalist order in Germany. The group came to prominence in May 1970 when Meinhof and others used (for the first time) firearms in releasing the imprisoned Baader and Ensslin. Three people were seriously injured in the action. Following the arrest and conviction of the core members—including Meinhof, who committed suicide in prison in 1977—a second and equally ruthless generation of RAF activists emerged from radical socialist circles in Heidelberg beginning in the mid-1970s. Their activities included the murder of leading businessmen and political figures and continued into the 1980s and early 1990s. In April 1975, the German embassy in Stockholm was attacked and bombed, and the particularly violent year of 1977 saw the murders of the chief prosecutor, Siegfried Buback; the banker Jürgen Ponto; and the president of the German Employers' Association, Hanns Martin Schleyer. In a spectacular action in October 1977, a group hijacked a Lufthansa airliner en route from Majorca to Frankfurt/Main in an attempt to force the release of 11 imprisoned RAF members and two Turkish terrorists. Brigitte Mohnhaupt, a prominent leader of the new wave of terrorists and widely considered to have orchestrated many of the events of 1977, was eventually arrested in 1982 and served several life sentences before being released on parole in 2007 (completed in 2010). In March 1993, following delays in the release of convicted terrorists, a prison was bombed, while in a separate series of events some months later, Interior Minister Rudolf Seiters resigned over the fatal shooting of a police officer during an ill-managed operation in which two suspected RAF members were arrested.

The callousness of the RAF and its methods, hitherto unparalleled in the Federal Republic of Germany (FRG), provoked public revulsion, mobilized large sections of the **media**, and prompted the authorities to take vigorous countermeasures. The government expanded its internal **security** forces and introduced controversial legislation, the **radicals decree**, which excluded extremists from public employment (January 1972). Two antiterrorist laws (August 1976, February 1978) increased police powers of surveillance and investigation and in some cases restricted access to detainees' defense lawyers, who had been suspected of aiding and abetting their clients. European states also reached an agreement on sharing information and extraditing suspected terrorists (January 1977). In April 1998, in a communication to a news agency, the RAF declared itself disbanded. In all, the group had claimed around 60 victims. After reunification, it emerged that the secret service of the **German Democratic Republic (GDR)**, the **Stasi**, had actively supported the RAF and its activities since the 1970s. Several former RAF members, who had found refuge in the GDR, were convicted after reunification. The last of more than 20 jailed RAF members, Birgit Hogefeld, was released on parole in 2011.

In 1972, the author **Heinrich Böll** published an essay ("Will Ulrike Gnade oder freies Geleit?") in which he analyzed the actions and motives of the RAF and also criticized media reporting of them—in particular by **Axel Springer**'s *Bild* newspaper. His contribution unleashed a storm of protest, in which he was attacked as a sympathizer of terrorism. The RAF remains to this day a topic of debate in Germany, among other things because its members were predominantly female. Meinhof and Ensslin were leading players in the group, and in both cases the **press**, the public, and in due course academia engaged with questions relating to their actions. Exhibitions on their activities still trigger complex debates about the role of the group, of the state, and not least about the GDR's links with global **terrorism**.

See also EXTREMISM.

REICH, JENS (1939–). Civil rights activist. Jens Reich was born in Göttingen and grew up in Halberstadt (now in **Saxony-Anhalt**) in eastern Germany. After studying medicine and molecular biology at Humboldt University in East **Berlin** (1956–1962), he worked as an assistant doctor in Halberstadt and trained at the University of Jena (1961–1968), earning doctorates in medicine and science (from Humboldt, 1964 and 1976). He worked as a **research** scientist at the central institute for molecular biology at the Academy of Sciences (Akademie der Wissenschaften) in East Berlin (from 1968), undertook research visits to Moscow (1974–1975, 1979–1980), and in 1980 was appointed professor of biomathematics at the institute, specializing in computer applications in medical biology. In 1969–1970, Reich cofounded the Friday Circle (Freitagskreis), a group of around 30 dissidents who met secretly but were regularly monitored by the secret police of the **German Democratic Republic (GDR)**, the **Stasi**, during the 1980s. After refusing to break off contacts with West Germans and join one of the state-approved **political parties**, Reich was demoted (1984); he lost his professorship and was banned from visiting Western countries. Active in opposition circles during the 1980s, he published critical articles on the GDR regime under a pseudonym and in September 1989 was a coauthor and signatory to the founding manifesto (*Aufbruch 89*) of the protest group **New Forum**.

After the fall of the GDR regime in 1989, Reich sat in the **People's Chamber** (March–October 1990), where he represented the **Alliance 90/The Greens**. After a brief period in the **Bundestag** (between October and the all-German national election in December), he returned to his scientific work as a departmental head in the institute for molecular biology in Berlin. After reunification, Reich published several essays on Europe and Germany and received the Theodor Heuss Prize on behalf of the many dissidents and civil rights activists of the former GDR (1991). In 1994, he was nominated as an independent candidate for the **presidency of the Federal Republic of Germany (FRG)** and also worked as personal adviser to **Rudolf Scharping**, who was then chancellor candidate for the **Social Democratic Party of Germany (SPD)**. He is a founding member of the **Willy Brandt** Circle in Berlin, which was set up in 1997 on the initiative of the author **Günter Grass** and the politician and journalist **Egon Bahr**. In 2001, he joined the newly formed Nationaler Ethikrat (National Ethics Council), renamed Deutscher Ethikrat (German Ethics Council in 2008), and from 2004 engaged in genetic and biological **research**. He is currently ombudsman at the Max Delbrück Center for Molecular Medicine in Berlin-Buch and teaches bioethics at a private American college, also in Berlin.

RELIGION. The **Basic Law (BL)** of the Federal Republic of Germany (FRG) guarantees religious freedom (article 4) and protects Sundays and other feast days as "days of rest and spiritual elevation" (contrary to many other countries, smaller towns and villages still observe the law that shops must be closed, although there are exceptions and actual opening times are regulated by the **federal states**). However, although the BL in its preamble—in an allusion to historical Christian tradition—refers to a "responsibility before God," it precludes an established or official state church with the status, for instance, of the Anglican Church in Great Britain (article 140). Churches and religious communities may be founded without interference from the state and can apply to be recognized as public institutions in law (Körperschaften des öffentlichen Rechts) if they fulfill a public or social function within the constitutional framework of the democratic state (they do not have to be Christian). Churches with public body status include the two main Christian churches (the Evangelical Church in Germany and the Roman Catholic Church), the **Central Council of Jews in Germany**, and a number of orthodox and nonconformist churches. The term "evangelical" in Germany is widely used to refer to the belief system and churches that arose out of the Reformation in the 16th century and overlaps with the term "Protestant," which also encompasses the wider cultural and intellectual developments associated with the Reformation; branches of the evangelical church also refer to themselves as Lutheran.

Public body status gives churches a number of advantages, for example in building law, relief from **taxes** and other charges, and the right themselves to levy taxes (Kirchensteuer) on their members, although some communities choose not to derive income in this way. The amount (8 or 9 percent, depending on the federal state) is normally deducted from income and other forms of wealth by the state, which retains around 3 percent for administration before passing the rest to the church. To be exempt from tax, citizens must either be unaffiliated or leave the church altogether. This almost unique system of state taxation for the benefit of churches—recently extended to include automatic direct debits on capital gains and interest from savings accounts—has been affirmed by several rulings of the **Federal Constitutional Court** (**FCC**), although it continues to attract criticism and has ensured that Germany's main churches are among the richest in the world. At the same time, actual revenue in individual dioceses depends on the state of the economy and levels of regional prosperity, while declining church attendance and aging congregations—not to mention withdrawals as a result of extensions of the church tax—are expected to affect future income. German churches have stakes in **banks** and insurance companies and own extensive property and estates (including vineyards and breweries), as well as printing and **publishing** houses. The revelation in 2014 of the cost (over 31 million euros) of a luxury residence for the bishop of Limburg, Franz-Peter Tebartz van Elst, resulted in his transfer to the Vatican and further embarrassing disclosures about church wealth.

Germany's main churches perform a vital social welfare role, from running preschool nurseries to hospitals and old people's homes, although their costs are largely reimbursed from general state taxation. Their welfare organizations, Caritas (Roman Catholic) and Diakonisches Werk (Protestant), are among the largest employers in the country. Both churches maintain schools (more than 900 Roman Catholic and around 1,100 Protestant) and exert a considerable influence on school curricula. The BL (article 7.3) acknowledges religious **education** as a subject in the school curriculum (ordentliches Lehrfach), although many federal states allow students to opt for alternatives. Alongside social work in hospitals and prisons, the churches provide military chaplains, whose work is financed equally by the state and the churches themselves. Church representatives are also found on the supervisory councils of public broadcasters (Rundfunkräte). Relationships between church and state are regulated by formal agreements or treaties. These take the form of concordats in the case of the Vatican and, for Protestant churches, church treaties (Kirchenverträge) concluded between the state and the regional church.

Since reunification, there are roughly equal numbers of Roman Catholics and Protestants in Germany (around 24 million each, together 60 percent of the population). Strongholds of Roman Catholicism are, broadly speaking, southern and western Germany (55 percent in **Bavaria**, 64 percent in the **Saarland**), compared with just between 3 and 9 percent in the **eastern federal states**. Protestants are best represented in northern Germany, parts of the southwest, and the east (**Mecklenburg-West Pomerania**, **Thuringia**, and **Saxony**). Other Christian communities include the "free churches" (330,000 members) and orthodox/oriental (1.3 million).

The postreunification Roman Catholic Church is organized as 27 bishoprics (including 7 archbishoprics), of which the largest are Cologne (over 2 million members), Freiburg (1.95 million), Münster (1.95 million), and Rottenburg-Stuttgart (1.88 million). A national conference of German Catholicism, the Deutscher Katholikentag, has met every two or four years since 1858 and has exerted a relatively powerful influence on young people in recent years. A 72-member Conference of German Catholic Bishops, the Bischofskonferenz, meets in the spring and fall to issue church laws and decrees, set up commissions, and appoint representatives to public bodies. Formally recognized by the Vatican in 1966, the conference appoints a chairman every six years. Recent chairmen have been **Karl Lehmann** (1987–2008), Robert Zollitsch (2008–2014, archbishop of Freiburg from 2003), and Reinhard Marx (2014–, archbishop of Munich and Freising from 2008).

Since 1948, all the regional Protestant churches and their members have belonged to the Evangelische Kirche in Deutschland (Evangelical Church in Germany, EKD), an umbrella organization coordinating external relations without undermining highly prized local sovereignty. In 1991, the organization of Protestant churches in the **German Democratic Republic (GDR)**, formed in 1969, merged with the EKD. The church in East Germany, which had offered many protesters a sanctuary from the regime, played an important role during the revolution of 1989 and also in the interim government from November 1989 to March/April 1990. The Roman Catholic leadership, by contrast, despite its possibly even deeper discomfort about the regime, proved much less proactive at these critical points, partly because of Cardinal Joachim Meisner's move in early 1989 from Berlin to Cologne. The largest Protestant churches are in Hanover (2.9 million members), the Rhineland (2.8 million), Westfalia (2.5 million), Bavaria (2.5 million), and Württemberg (2.2 million); the "north church" (2.3 million) was formed in 2012 when the regional churches of the northern Elbe, Mecklenburg, and Pomerania merged. Since 1949 (biennially since 1957), German Protestants convene a national community meeting or conference, the Deutscher Evangelischer Kirchentag. The EKD is governed by a 126-member synod, which appoints a council.

Long-standing efforts to promote unity among Germany's highly fragmented Protestant community resulted in the formation in 2003 of the Union Evangelischer Kirchen (Union of Evangelical Churches, UEK), the successor to the Evangelische Kirche der Union (Evangelical Church of the Union, EKU). The UEK is also pledged to greater cooperation with the Vereinigte Evangelisch-Lutherische Kirche Deutschlands (United Evangelical-Lutheran Church of Germany, VELKD), which was founded in 1948 and represents seven independent regional Lutheran churches with 9.5 million members. While Protestant–Catholic dialogue began in the 1960s and an "ecumenical Pentecost meeting," attended by 18,000 visitors and senior church leaders, took place in Augsburg in 1971, it was not until 2003 in **Berlin** that the first large-scale congress (Kirchentag), attended by over 200,000, was held. A second congress took place in 2010 in Munich, and more were planned. The 500th anniversary of the German Reformation, scheduled for celebration in 2017, is likely to be informed by a more universal vision of church history than used to be the case.

Reunification (only around 25 percent of eastern Germans, who had lived for 40 years under an atheistic regime, were members of a church), demographic factors (an aging population and influx of **foreigners**), scandals (financial corruption and abuse of children), and changing social values (attitudes toward **women** and sexuality, secularism) have profoundly influenced membership and attendance in the main churches. A rise in incomers since 1991 (over 3,000 in 2013) and returners (nearly 7,000 in 2013) in the Roman Catholic Church has been more than offset by the number leaving (more than 178,800 in 2013 and climbing). Losses for the main Protestant churches have been even higher. Individuals appear to be viewing religious practice more as a personal activity, attaching value selectively to occasional, single rituals that are most relevant to their own lives, such as the major feasts, baptism, and marriage.

The Christian churches in Germany continue to express influential views on contemporary and social issues that are sometimes—but by no means always—out of step with politicians and the public at large. Although the

Christian churches insisted on the primacy of the traditional marriage and family, which in their view alone deserved state protection, marriage between same-sex partners was recognized by the German state in 2001, with equal status in most aspects of law and welfare provision following over the next decade or so. Both Roman Catholic and Protestant churches supported the proposals of the government on a new **immigration** law, with the EKD and the Catholic Bishops' Conference calling for a more liberal policy on allowing the children of foreigners established in Germany to join their parents. The churches and politicians were united in opposing human cloning and the destruction of human embryos and in supporting restrictions on stem cell **research**. The pope's declared opposition to the U.S.-led war against Iraq in 2003 won widespread support in Germany, as have his pronouncements against **human rights** abuses, violence, and hostility toward foreigners. The reports and practical work of charitable organizations such as Caritas have set standards informing the social policy of successive governments.

While the Roman Catholic Church removed most of its discriminatory measures against women in its canon law in 1983, it has of course yet to ordain women to the priesthood. A vote by German bishops during the 1980s to admit women to the diaconate went unanswered by the Vatican, and the issue remains a subject of debate. Women in the German Evangelical Church are organized in the EFiD (Evangelische Frauen in Deutschland), which is active in feminist theology, interfaith dialogue and ecumenism, and social policy.

The third largest religious community in Germany is Islam, with an estimated 4 million adherents. Of these, 2.5 million are of Turkish background, the long-term result of recruitment of guest workers from Turkey during the 1960s, which also explains the predominance of Muslim males in Germany and the high concentration of Muslims (one-third) in the industrial centers of **North Rhine-Westfalia**; 555,000 originate from southeastern Europe (the Balkans) and 330,000 from the Middle East. The vast majority of Muslims in Germany, of whom 45 percent have acquired citizenship, are Sunnis, followed by Shias, mainly from Iran. Less than 2 percent of Muslims, largely from central Asia and the former Soviet Union, live in the eastern federal states.

A leading organization for Muslims in the FRG is the Zentralrat der Muslime in Deutschland (Central Council of Muslims in Germany, ZMD), which was founded in its present form in 1994. Based in Cologne and financed by members' contributions, private donations, and possibly overseas sources, the ZMD is an alliance of 28 Muslim groups and 300 mosque communities. The ZMD aims to stimulate dialogue between its members and German society, represent the interests and rights of Muslims vis-à-vis the authorities, and promote religious education. Another organization, the Islamrat (Council of Islam, IR), was created in 1986, also in Cologne, and has between 40,000 and 60,000 members. In September 2006, the first German Islam Conference (Deutsche Islam Konferenz, DIK) took place in Berlin. Initiated by the then federal interior minister, **Wolfgang Schäuble**, the DIK works for the integration and welfare of Muslims in Germany and produces regular reports and analyses.

Since 1990, Jehovah's Witnesses (164,000 members) have been attempting to gain public body status in all 16 federal states (13 had recognized them by 2015). The debate centered on the question of their loyalty to the state (and the BL), although the FCC ruled in 2000 that this was irrelevant as long as they obeyed the law and remained a matter of religious belief. Scientology, on the other hand, with 7,000 members in Germany, is controversial, and doubts about its democratic credentials and status as a genuine religion have led to it being placed under observation by the **Federal Office for the Protection of the Constitution** (Bundesamt für den Verfassungsschutz, BfV) in several federal states. Other religious groups in Germany include **Jews**, Hindus (12,000 members), and Buddhists (27,000).

RENGER, ANNEMARIE (1919–2008). Social Democratic Party of Germany (SPD) politician. Annemarie Renger was born in Leipzig in a family with a strong social democratic tradition. Her father was a city councilor and edited a workers' newspaper before moving to **Berlin** (1924), where she trained for a career in commerce. After 1945, she became a close associate and friend of Kurt Schuhmacher, who reestablished the SPD in western Germany. She represented the SPD in the **Bundestag** (1953–1990), serving on numerous committees, and held various positions in the party, including membership on the national executive committee (1961–1973) and the presidium (1970–1973), as well as being parliamentary party manager (1969–1972). She was the first female SPD member to hold the position of president of the Bundestag (1972–1976) and continued as vice president until 1990. A social democrat of the old school, she campaigned against the efforts of **Willy Brandt** to create a more inclusive party in the early 1980s and demanded a return to traditional socialist values. After reunification, she withdrew from parliament. Her memoirs (*Ein politisches Leben*) appeared in 1993.

See also WOMEN.

REPUBLICANS, THE (DIE REPUBLIKANER, REP). The extreme right-wing REP was founded in November 1983 in Munich by former members of the **Christian Social Union (CSU)**, including former **Bundestag** deputies Franz Handlos and Ekkehard Voigt, together with the former SS member and journalist Franz Schönhuber (1923–2005). Handlos was elected party leader (chairman). Campaigning on an anti**foreigner** platform against a background of popular concern over the rising number of **asylum** seekers, the party made electoral gains in **Bavaria** (1986), **Berlin** (1989), and the European Parliament (1989). After it captured 2.1 percent of the vote in the 1990 national election and 10.9 percent in the 1992 regional elections in **Baden-Württemberg**, support for the REP declined. In the 1994 national election, it gained only 1.9 percent of the vote, and in the same year, following internal disputes, Schönhuber was replaced by Rolf Schlierer, who made determined efforts to change the REP's image and to portray it as a conventional, nationalist-conservative party working within the democratic system. Schlierer also consistently rebuffed offers of an electoral alliance with fellow right-wing **political parties**, the **National Democratic Party of Germany (NPD)** and **German People's Union (DVU)**. Nevertheless, membership declined from around 25,000 in 1989 and is probably now below 6,000. Since state elections in Baden-Württemberg in March 2001, the party has no representatives in German regional state parliaments, although it has some seats on local town councils, mainly in southern Germany.

The REP has branches throughout Germany, although it lacks internal unity, faces financial problems, and has a relatively weak political organization. It produces a newspaper (10 issues a year) and, like other right-wing parties, has significantly expanded its presence on the **Internet**. The REP has campaigned against **immigration**, for Germany's exit from the **European Union (EU)**, and for liberalization of the economy alongside increased social welfare provision. Since 1992, government authorities at the national and regional levels responsible for the protection of the constitution have had the party under observation, against which it has mounted a series of mainly unsuccessful legal challenges, although a Berlin court ruled in 2006 that it should no longer be included in the city's report on extremism.

See also ANTI-SEMITISM; EXTREMISM.

RESEARCH AND DEVELOPMENT (R&D). The main pillars of R&D in Germany are the publicly funded universities and research institutes, although there is a trend for research activities to move away from higher **education** burdened with high student numbers and into external institutions. Finance for R&D is derived from the state, **industry**, and private foundations (Stiftungen), to the tune of around 3 percent of GDP. The foundations, whose umbrella organization is the Stifterverband für die Deutsche Wissenschaft (with 3,000 members), are generally established by leading entrepreneurs and include well-known names such as the **Volkswagen** Foundation, the Fritz-**Thyssen** Foundation, the Robert **Bosch** Foundation, and the **Bertelsmann** Foundation. Since the 1990s, just under 70 percent of research has been funded by industry and business, mainly undertaken internally in large concerns with 500 or more employees, in the electrical, **engineering**, **chemical**, and **pharmaceuticals** sectors. Of the rest, around 18 percent is carried out by universities and 14 percent by the state, as well as registered, private, nonprofit associations (eingetragene Vereine). The **European Union (EU)** is also an important source of finance. Most publicly funded R&D is undertaken by nonprofit associations. As a rule jointly subsidized by **Bund** and **Länder**, but also through private sponsorship, these organizations have a long tradition of promoting scientific research and applications, often at universities. Prominent associations are the Max Planck Society (specializing in leading, pure research), the Fraunhofer organization (applied research), the Helmholtz Association (**energy, environment, health** care, and **transport**), the network of Leibnitz Institutes (applications-orientated basic research), and the German Research Association (Deutsche Forschungsgemeinschaft, DFG; all areas, including humanities). Directly state-funded institutions also include the Humboldt Foundation (research scholarships and the promotion of international links) and the eight regional, Länder-financed German Academies of Science in **Berlin**, Düsseldorf, Göttingen, **Hamburg**, Heidelberg, Leipzig, Mainz, and Munich; the umbrella organization for these academies is the Union of German Academies of Sciences and Humanities. The Leopoldina National Academy of Sciences (Halle) represents the German scientific community in international committees and speaks out on social and political questions. Government responsibility for promoting research lies with the Federal Ministry for Education and Research, which provides funds, coordinates with the **federal states**, and directs resources to the associations.

REXRODT, GÜNTER (1941–2004). Free Democratic Party (FDP) politician. Günter Rexrodt was born in **Berlin**. His father was a leading member of the democratically oriented Deutsche Demokratische Partei (DDP) during the Weimar Republic (1919–1933) and in 1945 in **Saxony** cofounded the Liberal-Demokratische Partei (Liberal Democratic Party, LDP), renamed the Liberal-Demokratische Partei Deutschlands (Liberal Democratic Party of Germany, LDPD) in 1952. Günter Rexrodt grew up in **Thuringia** and studied business administration at the Free University of Berlin, qualifying with a diploma (1967) and doctorate (1970). After a brief spell in a bank (1968), he worked with the Berlin branch of the German Chamber of Industry and Commerce (DIHK, 1969–1979), where he joined the senior management (1972) and later became departmental head (1979). Rexrodt was subsequently attached to the Berlin minister (senator) for economics (1979–1985) and from 1982 served as **state secretary**. From 1985 to 1989, he was minister (senator) of finance in the (West) Berlin regional assembly.

A member of the FDP from 1980, Rexrodt held various leading positions in the party, including Berlin regional chairman (1994–1996), national deputy chairman (1983–1987, 1989–1994), member of the national executive (1990–1997), party treasurer (from 2001), and member of the party presidium. An elected **Bundestag** member (from 1994), he was appointed federal minister for economic affairs in 1993, where he stayed until the national election of 1998. Other posts he held were member of the executive board of CitiBank in New York (1989–1991), board chairman of CitiBank in Frankfurt/Main (1990–1991), board member of the **Trust Agency** in Berlin (September 1991–January 1993), member of the supervisory board of Agiv AG (from 2001), and executive board member of WME Eurocom AG. Known within the FDP as "Mr. Wirtschaft" (Mr. Economy), Rexrodt was respected for his financial competence and vocal support of the **social market** economy. After reunification, he maintained a strong interest in the economic reconstruction of eastern Germany.

RHINE RIVER. The 1,230-kilometer-long Rhine River begins life at the confluence of two source rivers in the Swiss Alps (the Vorderrhein and Hinterrhein), following the border with Liechtenstein and Austria before flowing into Lake Constance (Bodensee); this section is called the Alpine Rhine (Alpenrhein, ca. 90 km). Already 130 meters wide as it leaves Lake Constance, the river in the so-called Higher Rhine (Hochrhein) then runs westward for 150 kilometers, as far as Basel, where it also forms the border with Switzerland and Germany. The following section—the Upper Rhine (Oberrhein), from Basel to Bingen—heads 350 kilometers northward across the Upper Rhine Lowland Plain and constitutes the Franco–German border before fully entering German territory; much of the original river here has been reshaped and canalized to facilitate shipping and is up to 250 meters wide. Breaking through a narrow gorge in the Rhenish Slate Mountains at Bingen, the river performs a sharp turn around the legendary Lorelei Rock before entering the Middle Rhine (Mittelrhein), which continues for 126 kilometers as far as Bonn. Part of this stretch, from Bingen to Koblenz, is a major **tourist** attraction and was designated a UNESCO world heritage site in 2002. The attractions of the "Romantic Rhine" at this point include picturesque riverside towns, steep vineyard slopes, and medieval castles, although the river valley itself also accommodates busy rail and road routes. Downstream from Bonn, the Lower Rhine section crosses **North Rhine-Westfalia** and enters the Netherlands, where it branches into a complex set of canals and rivers comprising the Rhine Delta before flowing into the **North Sea**. Between the approach to Cologne and Duisburg, the largest inland harbor in the world, the riverscape becomes increasingly industrial. The total length of the Rhine in or bordering German territory is 865 kilometers. Between Basel and Rotterdam, the river drops 260 meters. Main tributaries are the Main, Neckar, and Mosel.

Until well into the 1970s, the Rhine was used by bordering countries as a giant sewer for domestic and industrial waste, which, along with shipping traffic, made it one of Europe's most polluted rivers, killing up to 90 percent of its fish population. Since then, the water quality has been improved through a combination of waste reduction, pollution controls, and purification plants, and many species have returned. At the same time, industrial accidents remain a problem, and measures to improve the river's navigability, such as straightening it, have increased water flow rate, destroying natural habitats and breeding grounds. The International Commission for the Protection of the Rhine (ICPR) monitors the state of the river, produces technical reports, and coordinates the interests of all its users.

As part of the wider system of German waterways, the Rhine is by far the most important in terms of size and the volume of goods transported. The river is served by over 30 harbors, the largest being Duisburg and Cologne, and every year the industrial Lower Rhine carries almost 200,000 vessels (on average 500 daily), making it the busiest waterway in Europe. Some 70 percent of bulk cargo is building materials, mineral ores, gas, coal, and steel, followed by **chemical** products, although there is also a niche market for hazardous and oversized items. A single tug pulling six nonmotorized barges can move up to 17,000 tons of goods in a single voyage.

See also ENVIRONMENT: WATER; TRANSPORT: WATERWAYS.

RHINELAND-PALATINATE (RHEINLAND-PFALZ). Located on the western side of Germany, Rhineland-Palatinate (RLP) has a total area of 19,847 square kilometers and shares borders with France, Luxembourg, and Belgium. As a result, it has more European neighbors than any of the other **federal states**. The main geographical features are, in the north, the forested upland regions of the Eifel (rising to 747 m), Westerwald, Hunsrück (peak Erbeskopf, 816 m, the highest mountain in the state), and the western Taunus, and in the south, the Palatinate Forest (Pfälzer Wald). The main rivers are the **Rhine**, a major communications artery since before medieval times, and its tributaries the Mosel, Nahe, and Lahn. The mild river valleys favor the cultivation of fruit and vineyards, while cereals and sugar beets are grown on higher land. With a total **population** of nearly four million, the state's principal cities are the state capital, Mainz (201,000), Ludwigshafen (165,500), Koblenz (106,600), and Kaiserslautern (99,800). Around 50 percent of the population is Roman Catholic and 9.8 percent **foreigners** (2015).

Historically, the area was a center of Roman colonization: Trier, Germany's oldest city, was one of the three capitals of the Roman Empire (the others were Rome and Constantinople), and after the fall of Rome the land along the Rhine River became the heartland of the medieval Holy Roman Empire. The authority of the Christian church was embodied in the imperial cathedral cities of Speyer, Worms, and Mainz. Ruled by electoral prince bishops, Mainz became the greatest center of church power north of the Alps. The region was invaded by the French during the Napoleonic Wars; divided among Prussia (which controlled part of the Rhineland), **Hessen**, and **Bavaria** in 1814–1815; and used as a base to launch attacks against the French in

1870–1871, 1914–1918, and 1939–1940. After World War II, the creation of the state of RLP from four distinct regions (belonging to Prussia, Hessen, and Bavaria) was regarded as an interim arrangement, both by its people and the main **political parties**. There were no less than five petitions for a referendum on the issue in 1956, and it was not completely settled until 1975, when citizens in the administrative districts of Koblenz, Trier, Montabaur, and Rheinhessen voted to stay with RLP.

Although a largely rural, economic backwater after World War II, a wave of modernization during the 1960s and 1970s attracted new industries and created a strong, export-oriented economy in RLP. Exports, mainly to France and other countries of the **European Union** (**EU**), account for over 50 percent of the state's GDP (overall, RLP contributed 4 percent of national GDP in 2015). More than half of industrial production is devoted to **chemicals**, **automobile** production, and **engineering**, followed by rubber and synthetic items, foodstuffs (including animal feed), **pharmaceuticals**, paper products, and glass/ceramics. Leading companies in terms of turnover and employment include **BASF** (chemicals, based at Ludwigshafen), **Boehringer** Ingelheim (**pharmaceuticals**, Ingelheim), DB Schenker Rail Deutschland (railroad freight transport, Mainz), Hornbach Holding (building retailer, Neustadt an der Weinstraße), Schott (glass/ceramics, Mainz), and KSB (pumps and armatures, Frankenthal). The **Mittelstand** of small to medium-sized companies is also well represented. Numbers employed in leather goods and shoe production (Pirmasens) have dwindled since the 1960s, although gravel and stone, gemstones, ceramics, and jewelry are regionally significant (RLP has practically no raw materials or **energy** sources of its own). While no longer the main economic activity, **agriculture** is still important: 70 percent of Germany's wine comes from the region, and stock rearing and dairy farming continue in the Central Uplands. **Tourism** is based on the romantic stretches of the Rhine River downstream of Mainz and on themed routes such as the "wine route" (Weinstraße), the "volcano route" (Vulkanstraße), the "gemstone route" (Edelsteinstraße), and the "potters' route" (Kannebäckerstraße). The annual carnival marking the beginning of Lent is one of the best known throughout Germany and attracts many visitors. The state-run **television** station ZDF (Zweites Deutsches Fernsehen) is based in Mainz, as is the Rhein-Main newspaper publishing group (Verlagsgruppe Rhein Main), whose titles include the regional *Allgemeine Zeitung*. A serious blow to the regional economy was the reduction of stationed U.S. forces after the end of the Cold War. Up until then, RLP had been home to one of the largest concentrations of American military and civilian personnel in Europe, with bases in Ramstein, Kaiserslautern, and Landstuhl. Although overall unemployment (5.2 percent in 2015) is below the national average (6.4 percent), it is higher in the poorer eastern part of the state (Eifel, Hunsrück, and the western Palatinate/ Pfalz). The region has four universities (Mainz, Kaiserslautern, Trier, and Koblenz) and a number of academic and **research** institutions.

The regional constitution is strongly influenced by Roman Catholic tradition and declares from the onset that the power of the state is derived, not from the people, but from God. It has also undergone more changes and revisions than that of any other federal state (33 between 1947 and the reforms of 2000). After the **Federal Constitutional Court (FCC)** in 1972 ruled RLP's electoral system unconstitutional, this was changed from a rigid list system to one that included an element of direct voting for an individual candidate; the number of constituencies was also reduced to four of equal size, which gave small parties a bigger chance. Following two reform commissions (sitting 1991–1994 and 1996–1998), party political differences were finally overcome, and in 2000 a 34th revised constitution was passed, which included a compromise formula on the protection of the unborn child (article 3). The constitution includes a comprehensive catalog of basic and social rights (such as the right to work, equality of men and **women**, and the rights of ethnic minorities), objectives for the state (such as the promotion of European integration and **sport**, the protection of the disabled and animals, and more precise aims for **environmental** protection), and explicit provisions for constitutional appeals.

The 101-member regional assembly (**Landtag**) elects a **minister president**, who appoints a cabinet of ministers. The number of ministerial departments increased from 7 to 11 between 1981 and 1991, owing largely to an increase in functions (including responsibility for the environment and gender equality), although a reform of 1994 reduced the figure to 8. In a move since copied by other Länder, the assembly introduced in 1974 the office of ombudsman (Bürgerbeauftragte[r]), elected every eight years, who receives complaints and acts as an intermediary between citizens and officialdom. Regional elections are held every five years.

During 1951–1971 and 1987–1991, the government was in the hands of a coalition of the **Free Democratic Party (FDP)** and the **Christian Democratic Union (CDU)**. In the intervening period (1971–1987), the CDU ruled alone with an absolute majority. Minister presidents included the veteran **Peter Altmaier** (1947–1969) and his successor, **Helmut Kohl** (1971–1976), who went on to lead the CDU opposition in the **Bundestag** and become **federal chancellor**. Kohl's successor, **Bernhard Vogel**, resigned in 1988 and was replaced by Carl-Ludwig Wagner. In 1991, for the first time since 1947, the **Social Democratic Party of Germany (SPD)** gained a majority of seats and formed a coalition with the FDP, led by **Rudolf Scharping** (SPD). After Scharping moved to Bonn to become party leader, **Kurt Beck** took over (October 1994), confirming his position in regional state elections in 1996, 2001, and 2006, when his party gained an absolute majority. While both main parties have traditional bastions of support in the region, the sudden electoral shift in 1991 may be explained by a combination of the personal image of candidates, disaffection with the CDU, and the desire for change. After losing its overall majority in the 2011 regional elections, the SPD formed a governing coalition with the **Green Party**, which had first entered the state parliament in 1987. Following Beck's resignation on health grounds, **Malu Dreyer** (SPD) took over as minister president (January 2013). The coalition's main goals included supplying the region's entire electricity needs from renewable sources within 20 years, improvements in **education** (retaining small primary schools and extending all-day provision, employing more teachers and abolishing university fees), combating poverty, and cutting spending in order to meet the requirements of the debt brake. Regional elections in 2016 brought losses for the CDU (from 35.2 to 31.8 of votes) and the Greens (from 15.4 to 5.3 percent). The right-wing **Alternative for Germany (AfD)** entered parliament for the first time (12.6 percent). Dreyer continued as minister president, heading a 'traffic light' coalition of SDP, FDP and the Greens and pledging expansion for schools and digital infrastructure.

RIESTER, WALTER (1943–). Social Democratic Party of Germany (SPD) politician. Walter Riester was born in Kaufbeuren (**Bavaria**) and qualified as a tiler (1969). Between 1969 and 1970, he studied business and economics, as well as social and labor law, at the Academy of Labor (Akademie der Arbeit) in Frankfurt/Main. A member of the **trade union** IG Bau-Steine-Erde from 1957, he worked at the union's administrative center in Geislingen (1977–1978) before becoming district secretary and then district head of the **engineering** and metalworkers' union IG Metall in Stuttgart (1980–1993), rising to deputy leader (1993–1998). Riester joined the SPD in 1966 and served on a number of supervisory boards, including at **Daimler, Thyssen, Bosch,** und **Audi** (1976–1998). A **Bundestag** member (2002–2009), he served as SPD federal minister for labor and social affairs in the cabinet of Chancellor **Gerhard Schröder** (1998–2002). Riester is best known for introducing a **pension** scheme—the "Riester pension" (Riester-Rente)—that encourages citizens to take out a state-subsidized, private insurance policy in order to supplement the basic state pension. In 2010, he was awarded the **Konrad Adenauer** Foundation prize for contributions to the **social market** economy. His autobiography (*Mut zur Wirklichkeit*) appeared in 2005.

RINGSTORFF, HARALD (1939–). Social Democratic Party of Germany (SPD) politician. Harald Ringstorff was born in Wittenburg (western Mecklenburg). After his national service in the army of the former **German**

Democratic Republic (GDR, 1958–1960), he studied chemistry at the University of Rostock, where he worked as a research assistant (1965–1969) and earned a doctorate (1969) before working as a chemist in the shipbuilding industry (1969–1987) and in plants producing paint materials for seagoing vessels (1987–1990). Ringstorff entered political life following the collapse of the GDR regime in 1989 and was a founding member of the Rostock branch of the newly constituted **Social Democratic Party of Germany of the GDR** (1989). A member of the **People's Chamber** during the transition to reunification, he sat in the state parliament (**Landtag**) for **Mecklenburg-West Pomerania** (1990–2011), chaired the regional SPD (1990–2003), and led the parliamentary party group (1990–1994 and 1996–1998). Appointed regional minister for the economy and **European Union (EU)** and deputy to the **minister president** of Mecklenburg-West Pomerania in a ruling coalition of the SPD and the **Christian Democratic Union (CDU)** in 1994, he resigned in 1996 over the handling of a crisis in the shipbuilding industry. Following gains by the SPD in the November 1998 regional election, and disregarding all warnings, he entered into coalition with the **Party of Democratic Socialism (PDS)**, with himself as minister president. This was the first time that the PDS had participated in government. Despite political ups and downs (contrary to an agreement with his coalition partners, he voted in favor of government plans to reform the **pension system** in the **Bundesrat**), he strengthened his position in the regional election of 2002 and continued the coalition with the PDS. From 2006, he led a coalition with the CDU, resigning for age-related reasons in 2008. Regarded as a firm, capable leader during difficult times, he succeeded in reducing public debt and improving the state's economic outlook. From 2011, he no longer stood as a candidate for the regional assembly.

RÖSLER, PHILIPP (1973–). Free Democratic Party (FDP) politician. Born in Vietnam and adopted by a couple from **Lower Saxony** at the age of nine months, Philipp Rösler grew up from 1973 in Germany. After enlisting in the Germany navy in 1992 (his adoptive father was a professional airman), he studied medicine in Hanover (1993–1999) and also philosophy and history, finally qualifying in **Hamburg** as a practicing doctor in 2002. An FDP member from 1992 and active in the youth organization (Young Liberals), he left the **Bundeswehr** in 2002 in order to focus on party political work in Lower Saxony, but remained a reservist military doctor. He rose to become a member of the regional executive committee (1996) and general secretary (2000–2004). He also represented the party in the Hanover regional council (2001–2006), where he was deputy leader of the council's party group. He joined the FDP national presidium (2005), becoming regional party chairman (2006) and finally national chairman (May 2011). In the Lower Saxony regional assembly (**Landtag**), Rösler served as a deputy (2003–2009); leader of the parliamentary group; and, briefly, as minister for economics, labor, and transport and deputy minister president (2009). In 2009, he entered the **Bundestag** (unelected) to become federal **health** minister (2009–2011) and minister for economics and technology (2011–2013) in **Angela Merkel**'s second cabinet. His party also elected him national leader (2011), and he served as vice-chancellor (2011–2013). As health minister, Rösler led the government's health-care reform measures, which included controlling expenditure on prescribed medicines, limiting increases in doctors' fees, and promoting private health insurance. As economics and technology minister, he was closely involved in the shift from nuclear power in favor of renewable **energy**. Following the FDP's catastrophic performance in the national election of September 2013, Rösler resigned all party offices and moved to Geneva to become managing director for the World Economic Forum.

ROTH, CLAUDIA (1955–). Green Party politician. Born in Ulm (**Baden-Württemberg**), Claudia Roth studied theater arts in Munich in the early 1970s and worked as a dramaturge (dramatic adviser) at the Dortmund State Theater before managing a band (from 1982). She was press spokeswoman for the Green Party in the **Bundestag** (1985–1989) and was elected to the European Parliament (1989–1998), where she led the Green parliamentary group (from 1994). In Brussels, she campaigned for greater rights for the Kurdish minority in Turkey and presented a report (1994) that formed the basis of the **European Union** (EU)'s policy on equal rights for **homosexuals** and lesbians. In 1998 she returned to the Bundestag, where she chaired the parliamentary committee for **human rights** and humanitarian aid and contributed to new government guidelines on linking exports to sustainability and stability. At the same time, she represented Germany in the parliamentary assembly of the European Council and in the assembly of the West European Union (WEU). She was also a member of the Bundestag committee for European affairs and a deputy member on the committee investigating donations to **political parties**. In March 2001, alongside **Fritz Kuhn**, Roth was elected national leader of the **Alliance 90/The Greens**, succeeding **Renate Künast**. In December 2002, in accordance with the party's rule that an elected member of parliament could not simultaneously hold an office in the party, she and Kuhn resigned as leaders (the party failed to agree on the two-thirds majority needed to overturn the ruling, although it was finally passed the following May, ending a long period of internal debate). After serving briefly as government representative for human rights policy under Chancellor **Gerhard Schröder** (2003–2004), she returned as coleader of the Greens from 2004 until 2013, when she was elected vice president of the Bundestag. In 2015, she criticized the Turkish head of state, Recep Erdoğan, for air attacks against the Kurdish militant organization PKK (Partiya Karkerên Kurdistanê) in Iraq, while also declaring her support for action against IS

(Islamic State). Roth, who campaigns vigorously for human rights and is regarded as being on the left wing of the Green Party, coedited a book exposing myths about **asylum** seekers (*Die Asyllüge,* 1992) and was awarded the Prix Egalité (1995) and the Musa Anter Prize (1994). In 2004, she became a member of the French legion of honor.

ROUND TABLE (RUNDER TISCH). The Round Table of the **German Democratic Republic (GDR)** was a forum for dialogue between opposition groups and the interim East German government led by **Hans Modrow**. The forum, which represented 14 political parties and movements, was convened under the chairmanship of East German church leaders (7 December 1989) and saw itself as a politically neutral forum for monitoring the government during the transition to democracy. It set dates for free elections, initiated the drafting of a new constitution for the GDR, and pressed for the disbanding of the **Stasi.** Marginalized during political campaigning for the national elections (18 March 1990), the Round Table held its final meeting on 12 March 1990.

RÜHE, VOLKER (1942–). Christian Democratic Union (CDU) politician. Volker Rühe was born in **Hamburg**, where he studied English and German **language** and **literature** (1962–1968), qualified as a teacher (1968, 1970), and worked in various schools until 1976. A member of the CDU from 1963, he represented the party in the Hamburg regional assembly (1970–1976) and the **Bundestag** (1976–2005), where his posts included deputy leader of the CDU/**Christian Social Union (CSU)** parliamentary group (1982–1989, 1998–2002) with responsibility for foreign, defense, and **security policy**; membership on the CDU presidium (from 1998); general secretary of the national CDU (1989–1992); and deputy leader to **Wolfgang Schäuble** (1992–2000). As minister for defense under Chancellor **Helmut Kohl** (1992–1998), Rühe oversaw the first out-of-area operations by the **Bundeswehr** under the auspices of the **North Atlantic Treaty Organization (NATO)** and, with Kohl, argued for a rapid extension of NATO membership to include countries of eastern Europe. He stood as the CDU's candidate for **minister president** of **Schleswig-Holstein** in the regional election of 2000, but was politically weakened as the party lost seats in the wake of the scandal over Kohl's acceptance of anonymous donations, and he failed to succeed Schäuble as party leader. Appointed chairman of the Bundestag parliamentary committee on **foreign policy** affairs (2002), he visited the United States without the knowledge of Chancellor **Gerhard Schröder** in order to repair relations with the Americans, which reached a low point during the second invasion of Iraq, and was an early supporter of Turkey's admission to the **European Union (EU)**. Isolated in aspects of foreign policy, Rühe withdrew from national politics in 2005.

RÜRUP COMMISSION. Bert Rürup, an expert in finance and political economics from the University of Darmstadt, served on Germany's **Council of Experts** from 2000 to 2009, chairing it between 2005 and 2009. Soon after it was reelected in 2002, the coalition of the **Social Democratic Party of Germany (SPD)** and the **Green Party**, through Health Minister **Ulla Schmidt**, also appointed him head of a 26-member commission charged with drawing up proposals to ensure the financial sustainability of Germany's social welfare system (state **pension**, **health**-care, and social care insurance). The so-called Rürup Commission began work in November 2002 and submitted its final report in August 2003. To maintain an adequate level of state pension while holding contributions below 22 percent until 2030, the commission recommended progressively raising the retirement age to 67 between 2011 and 2035; basic pensions would also be adjusted to balance the declining number of contributors with the rising number of pensioners. For health insurance, the commission proposed two alternative models, one based on higher contributions linked to income (Bürgerversicherung) and the other on a flat-rate contribution system (Kopfpauschale). The recommendations for social care insurance aimed to retain services while stabilizing contributions and introducing an element of personal insurance. In the context of the national political debate on social policy, the **Christian Democratic Union (CDU)** produced its own proposals (the Herzog Commission, chaired by **Roman Herzog**, which reported in September 2003). The governing SPD followed up the Rürup report with a commission, chaired by **Andrea Nahles**, that opted for an income-linked contribution system for health care.

Bert Rürup was born in 1943 in Essen (**North Rhine-Westfalia**) and studied economics and political science at universities in **Hamburg** and Cologne. He worked as a research assistant in finance at the University of Cologne (1969–1974) and in the planning department of the **Office of the Federal Chancellor** (1974–1975) before taking up professorships at the University of Göttingen and the University of Essen (1975). In February 1976, he was appointed professor for economics and finance at the Technical University of Darmstadt, where he developed an international reputation as an expert in health and social security policy.

RÜTTGERS, JÜRGEN (1951–). Christian Democratic Union (CDU) politician. Born in Cologne, Jürgen Rüttgers studied law and history, qualifying as a practicing lawyer (1975, 1978) and earning a doctorate (1979). He worked as a legal adviser in local government (1978–1980) and served as a councilor for the town of Pulheim in the Rhine-Erft district of **North Rhine Westfalia** (NRW, 1980–1987). An active member of the CDU, he chaired the regional youth wing of the party (**Junge Union [JU]**, 1980–1986) and was district chairman for Erft (1985–1999). In 1993, he was elected deputy leader of the regional CDU in NRW, then in 1999, leader. He represented the CDU in the **Bundestag** (1987–2000), where he chaired a commission of inquiry evaluating the benefits and prospects of technology (1987–1989) and then served as business manager for the CDU/**Christian Social Union** (**CSU**) parliamentary group (1989–1994), before being appointed federal minister of **education**, science, **research**, and technology (1994–1998) under Chancellor **Helmut Kohl** (CDU), who called him "minister of the future." After the CDU's defeat in the 1998 national election, Rüttgers became deputy leader of the CDU/CSU parliamentary group. Elected to the NRW regional assembly (**Landtag**, 2000–2012), he chaired the CDU parliamentary group (2000–2005) there.

In the regional election of May 2005, Rüttgers led his party to a historic victory over the ruling **Social Democratic Party of Germany** (**SPD**) and its coalition partner, the **Green Party**, which had governed NRW for 10 years. The result was a severe blow to Chancellor **Gerhard Schröder** (SPD) and a major factor in his decision to force a national election the following September. In conjunction with his coalition partners, the **Free Democratic Party** (**FDP**), Rüttgers pledged that as **minister president** he would fill vacant teachers' posts, bring the region's finances under control, and invest in the economy, while not losing sight of the need to maintain a social balance in business policy.

In 2000, Rüttgers attracted controversy by suggesting that his party should promote the skills of the country's children instead of supporting the government's plan to import foreign computer specialists. In 2009, he apologized for making offensive remarks about Romanian workers and in the following year distanced himself from aggressive sponsoring activities by his regional party that encouraged businesses to buy access to politicians. Rüttgers withdrew from active politics following the CDU's defeat in the 2010 regional election, returning to private legal practice and taking up a teaching post at the University of Bonn (2011).

S

SAARLAND. Situated in the southwest corner of neighboring **Rhineland-Palatinate** and bordering France and Luxembourg, the Saarland is both on the periphery of Germany and at the geographical center of western Europe. Historically, it has been strongly influenced by French and European culture. Politically split between the Prussian Rhineland and eastern **Bavaria** after the Napoleonic Wars, the Saarland rapidly developed as an industrial center during the 19th century, forming close links with Lothringen (Lorraine), when the latter was annexed by the German Empire in 1871. **Coal** from the Saar area and iron ore from Lothringen provided the raw materials for a strong steel **industry**, which both France and Germany were eager to control (the Saarland's borders changed several times). Not until 1919, when it was detached from Germany and placed under the administration of the newly formed League of Nations, did the Saarland become a single political unit. Following an internationally supervised referendum, the region was returned to Germany in 1935. After World War II, it came under U.S. and then French occupation. Allied opposition prevented France from annexing the Saarland outright, although the French retained control of the region's coal mines and economy. A plan drawn up by French and German leaders (the so-called Saar Statute of 1954) to place the Saarland under European control—integrated economically into France and represented externally by a commissioner of the West European Union (WEU)—met with fierce resistance from the population, who rejected the proposal by a 67.7 percent majority in a referendum. Two years later, France finally agreed to return the Saarland to Germany (Treaty of Luxembourg, 1956), and in January 1957 the region officially became the 11th state of the Federal Republic of Germany (FRG), with full economic and monetary union following in July 1959. With an area of 2,570 square kilometers and around 990,000 inhabitants, the Saarland is Germany's smallest non–city-state. Most of the population, of which 63 percent is Roman Catholic, is clustered in and around the southern city of Saarbrücken, with 176,000 inhabitants. A long history of foreign domination has produced an unusual sense of regional solidarity and, since World War II, a strong commitment to western Europe.

Between 1960 and 1965, growth in the steel industry underpinned a robust economic postwar recovery, accompanied by the creation of new companies in textiles and food production, an expansion of school and higher **education**, and investment in **transport** infrastructure. The 1966–1967 recession, however, followed by a collapse in European demand for coal and steel, heralded decades of economic decline as the region became dependent on government aid; in 1985 the public deficit reached 640 million euros, and unemployment climbed to a historic 13.4 percent. The preservation of the steel industry could only be achieved by job losses, wage cuts, debt write-downs, subsidies, and state takeovers, and by 1999 the sector, along with coal, had lost its former economic importance. At the same time, the Saarland began to attract new industries, in particular **engineering**, **automobile** manufacturing, electronics, and information technology. A new technical faculty was established at the University of the Saarland, and several independent **research** institutes were created. European funding assisted in the modernization process. By the end of the 1990s, the region's deficit had begun to fall, and unemployment dropped below 10 percent, although, despite special allocations from the **federal government** and a rigorous savings program, the state government continued to manage a large deficit, preferring to incur controlled debts in order to stimulate investment and create new jobs. In 2015, unemployment (7.2 percent) was slightly above the national average (6.4 percent), and the state contributed 1 percent of national GDP. The Saarland is also a member of the Saar-Lor-Lux-Region (comprising Saarland, Lothringen, and Luxembourg), a cross-border community of European regions that coordinates infrastructural, economic, and cultural activities. **Foreigners** make up 10.6 percent of the population.

The University of the Saarland, founded in November 1948 with the support of the French government and under the auspices of the University of Nancy, has 18,100 students, 16 percent from abroad. Despite the fact that most of the French professorial staff left when the region reverted to Germany, the university has a long tradition of successful Franco–German cooperation; it awards French diplomas in certain subjects and offers degrees in French law. A Franco–German summit meeting (1998) agreed to establish a new joint university in Saarbrücken with bilateral study programs. The Saarland's second largest institution of higher education, the Hochschule für Technik und Wirtschaft (HTW Saar), has around 5,000 students specializing in technology, business, and economics. The disused iron and steelworks Alte Völklinger Hütte was the first industrial site to enter the UNESCO list of world heritage monuments.

All references to annexation by France were removed in the 1956 version of the regional constitution. In other respects, the constitution is modeled on that of Rhineland-Palatinate, and in 1992 Saarland was the first of the **federal states** to include a formal commitment to European integration. The constitution also contains provisions for state ownership of key industries and for the protection of the **environment**. A 51-member regional state parliament, elected for five years, chooses a **minister president** who, with the approval of the assembly, appoints (and dismisses) ministers. Since 1979, the minister president has enjoyed enhanced powers, in particular to decide on the responsibilities and functions of ministers. There is no fixed limit to the number of ministers, although seven is the norm. The right to petition for a plebiscite (Volksbegehren) was introduced in 1979, although no referendum (Volksabstimmung) has been held since the change.

Despite the Saarland's industrial past and current economic problems, it is not an undisputed power base of the **Social Democratic Party of Germany** **(SPD)**. Reasons for this include the region's strong Roman Catholic tradition, its lack of major industrial cities, and the historical suppression of social democracy by employers. From 1959 (when the region was fully incorporated in the FRG) until 1985, the dominant party was the **Christian Democratic Union (CDU)**, led by Minister Presidents Franz-Josef Röder (1959–1979) and Werner Zeyer (1979–1985). In 1961, Röder switched his coalition partner from the SPD to the Deutsche Partei Saar (DPS), which later became the regional branch of the **Free Democratic Party (FDP)**, thereby extending his electoral appeal to the middle classes. From 1970 until 1975, the CDU governed with an absolute majority, and thereafter in coalition with the FDP. The return of an overall SPD majority at the 1985 regional election and the loss of leading figures in the party plunged the CDU into crisis. Under Minister President **Oskar Lafontaine** (SPD), the social democrats went on to win the 1990 and 1994 elections, again with absolute majorities. When Lafontaine became federal finance minister in 1998, he was succeeded by Reinhard Klimmt. In 1999, **Peter Müller** (CDU) became minister president following a surprising electoral victory by the CDU, which gained an overall majority. The **Green Party** first entered the state parliament in 1994, and again in 2004, 2009, and 2012. After 1994, the fortunes of the FDP were mixed. The CDU's majority was confirmed in the elections of September 2004, which, in a low turnout, saw the SPD return its worst result in 44 years. Unexpected gains were registered by the right-wing extremist **National Democratic Party of Germany** **(NPD)**, which, with 4 percent of the vote, narrowly failed to pass the 5 percent hurdle for entry to the **Landtag**. The CDU lost heavily in the 2009 elections, but returned in coalition with the FDP and the Greens. After Müller resigned in 2011, he was succeeded by **Annegret Kramp-Karrenbauer** (CDU), who went on to lead a **grand coalition** with the SPD following elections in 2012. The coalition declared its priority as reducing the state's enormous debt, which had risen steadily since 2000 and reached the equivalent of over 15,000 euros per person in 2012. The reduction was to be achieved by 2020 through severe cuts in public spending.

SAXONY (SACHSEN). With over four million inhabitants, Saxony is the most populous of the east German **federal states**, although a falling birthrate and emigration have contributed to a decline in population of 15 percent since 1990. Situated in the south of eastern Germany and covering an area of 18,400 square kilometers, Saxony shares a long border with Poland and the Czech Republic and adjoins the federal states of **Brandenburg, Saxony-Anhalt, Thuringia**, and **Bavaria**. Its geography is varied and includes the low-lying area around Leipzig; to the south, a relatively hilly landscape stretching from the Thuringian border to the Elbe River; the high Ore Mountains (Erzgebirge) along the Czech border; and in the southeastern corner where the Elbe winds through the mountains, the "Saxon Switzerland" (Sächsische Schweiz), a favorite **tourism** area and destination for day-trippers from Dresden. The main cities are the state capital Dresden (530,000), Leipzig (532,000), and Chemnitz (243,000). The state is also home to the **Sorbs**, one of Germany's four constitutionally protected **ethnic minorities**.

Although Saxony is historically a Protestant state, church attendance dropped sharply during the period of the **German Democratic Republic (GDR)**. After reunification, around 24 percent of the population remained Protestant, compared to 4 percent Roman Catholic. Non-Germans make up only a small proportion of the population (4.1 percent in 2015). Around one-third of **foreigners** are from the **European Union (EU)**, followed by Russia, Ukraine, and Poland; Vietnamese who originally entered the country as workers during the GDR era constitute the largest single national group (around 10 percent) and for some years after reunification continued to experience problems of integration.

The Saxons were originally a Germanic tribe from the lower Elbe (in **Schleswig-Holstein**), whose name up until the 15th century referred to the inhabitants of the area now covered by **Lower Saxony**, Westfalia, and parts of Saxony-Anhalt (to the northwest). From 1697 to 1763, the state of Saxony was united with Poland under a common ruler but lost power and territory thereafter as, sandwiched between the more powerful states of Brandenburg-Prussia to the north and the Habsburg Empire to the south, it sided with losing parties in a series of wars (Thirty Years' War, 1618–1648; Seven Years' War, 1756–1763; Napoleonic Wars, 1803–1815; Austro-Prussian War, 1866). During the 19th century, the rise of a textile **industry** around the cities of Plauen and Chemnitz laid the foundations for industrialization. A combination of economic development and repressive policies on the part of the ruling royal family produced political tensions and a strong socialist tradition, such that Saxony came to be known as the "Red Kingdom." During World War II, the bombing of Dresden by the British Royal Air Force (February 1945) destroyed the city's baroque architecture, considered among the finest in Europe, and killed thousands of civilians and refugees. Saxony ceased to exist as a political entity in 1952, when the GDR authorities created the three administrative districts (Bezirke) of Leipzig, Dresden, and Chemnitz (called Karl-Marx-Stadt from 1953 to 1990). In October 1989, the citizens of Leipzig and Dresden led the mass demonstrations against the communist regime that resulted in its downfall, and one year later (on 3 October 1990), the "Free State of Saxony" was formally reestablished as a federal state of reunited Germany. At the request of the inhabitants, it was agreed in 1991 to transfer some small communities from southern Brandenburg to Saxony.

Saxony's constitution was the first among the new **eastern federal states** to be adopted after reunification (May/June 1992). Although the constitution was closely modeled on those of its partner states, **Baden-Württemberg** and Bavaria, its creators, mindful of the abuses of the GDR period, placed a strong emphasis on **human rights**, including data protection and the right to information on the **environment**. Former members of or collaborators with the **Stasi** can be excluded from the parliament (**Landtag**), which is elected for five years and was made up of 132 deputies in 2013. The assembly elects a **minister president**, who appoints a cabinet of ministers (nine members in 2013).

Despite Saxony's socialist traditions, regional elections after reunification were dominated by the **Christian Democratic Union** (**CDU**), many of whose leading members were active in the opposition to the GDR before 1989. This gave rise to internal conflicts between "reformers" (new members) and "blockies" (members of the former East German CDU when it belonged to the state-controlled **Democratic Block** of approved nonsocialist parties). Led by the former **North Rhine-Westfalia** politician **Kurt Biedenkopf**, the CDU won successive outright majorities in regional elections between 1990 and 2004. In 1999, the **Social Democratic Party of Germany** (**SPD**) slipped to third place after the **Party of Democratic Socialism (PDS)**, which gained 22 percent of the votes. In 1994 and 1999, the **Alliance 90/The Greens** and **Free Democratic Party** (**FDP**) failed to clear the 5 percent hurdle. The CDU was also strong at the district level, although the PDS maintained a stronghold in the coal mining town of Hoyerswerda, which the GDR had made into an industrial complex, and the SPD commanded support in Leipzig and Chemnitz. Following Biedenkopf's resignation, **Georg Milbradt** took over as minister president (April 2002). In the regional election of 19 September 2004, the CDU lose its absolute majority (41.1 percent of seats), and the SPD gained less than 10 percent of the vote (9.8 percent). Nevertheless, both parties formed a ruling **grand coalition**, and the PDS won enough votes (23.6 percent) to become the main opposition party. The FDP gained 5.9 percent of the seats, and the extreme right-wing **National Democratic Party of Germany** (**NPD**), with 9.2 percent, also entered parliament. The election was dominated less by regional issues than by protests against the government's plans to cut social welfare benefits, although the strength of the NPD vote surprised observers. The party's 12 new deputies in parliament attracted national attention in 2005 by walking out during a minute's silence observed for victims of the Holocaust, a term which they tried to appropriate for describing the Allied bombing of Dresden. Milbradt, a financial expert, resigned in 2008 against the background of the failure of the regional bank SachsenLB, in which he played a leading role. He was succeeded by **Stanislaw Tillich** (CDU), who led his party into a governing coalition with the FDP after the regional election of 2009. The 2014 election saw losses for most parties, including the FDP, which failed to clear the 5 percent hurdle. The **Alternative für Deutschland (AfD)**, by contrast, entered parliament with 14 seats. Tillich remained as minister president, in coalition with the SPD, pledging to improve nursery services and employ more police and schoolteachers. Saxony has the unfortunate distinction of being notorious for right-wing **extremism**, notably violent attacks on foreigners and asylum seekers. In 1991, regional interior minister Heinz Eggert (CDU) set up a standing special commission (Sonderkommission Rechtsxtremismus) to advise on and coordinate measures against these activities.

Before World War II, Saxony was a major industrial center. During the GDR years, it accounted for 40 percent of East Germany's industrial production. It remains the most productive of the eastern German states and has focused on developing "clusters" of new growth industries, in particular microelectronics, biotechnology, **media** and communications, **energy**, and **automobile** production. Manufacturing is concentrated on Chemnitz and Zwickau (motor vehicles, metal processing, and **engineering**), while Leipzig (with **trade** fairs and an airport) is a center of banking, communications, and commerce. Dresden is home to electronics and high-technology industries. Major companies include **Volkswagen** (which resumed production in Zwickau after the demise of the state-manufactured Trabant), **BMW** (which opened an innovative manufacturing plant in Leipzig in 2004), **Siemens**, and AMD (Globalfoundries from 2008), although the **Mittelstand** of small to medium-sized businesses is still the region's economic backbone. Textiles and paper manufacturing are also important, while Meissen remains a center of porcelain manufacturing. Many older industries either have closed down or face structural problems; examples are greatly reduced brown coal extraction in the Lausitz area, engineering in Göritz, musical instruments in the Vogtland, toy production in the Ore Mountains, and steel and tires in Riesa. Pentacon, which produced cameras in Dresden, the home of the single-lens reflex camera, closed in 1990, and uranium mining, as in eastern Thuringia, was discontinued after reunification, leaving a legacy of environmental damage. The region's main problem is unemployment, which reached around 19 percent in the late 1990s (10.2 percent in 2015) and is highest in Leipzig and the Bautzen area. During the GDR period, Saxony met 25 percent of the country's potato, cattle, and milk requirements, although farming is no longer seen as a major sector. The region contributes 2 percent of national GDP (2015).

The cities of Leipzig and Dresden are cultural centers, internationally known for their choirs and orchestras, including the Leipziger Gewandhaus orchestra, the Dresden opera house, and the Semperoper. Both cities underwent massive restoration after reunification, and Leipzig experienced a building boom. Musical events include the Johann-Sebastian Bach Competition in Leipzig, the Robert Schumann Competition in Zwickau, and the Dresden Music Festival. The Mitteldeutscher Rundfunk (MDR), with headquarters in Leipzig, broadcasts **television and radio** programs to Thuringia and Saxony-Anhalt as well as in Saxony, although private and satellite stations are very popular. Saxony has four universities, of which the largest are Leipzig (with 28,000 students and renamed Karl-Marx University during the GDR period) and the Technical University of Dresden (more than 37,000). A number of **research** establishments were reconstituted from the dismantlement of the large industrial combines of the GDR.

SAXONY-ANHALT (SACHSEN-ANHALT). Located on the western flank of the **eastern federal states** and with a total area of 20,446 square km, Saxony-Anhalt adjoins **Lower Saxony, Brandenburg, Saxony,** and **Thuringia.** The northern part of the state (the Altmark) and the area around the state capital of Magdeburg (population 232,000) are largely rural and among the most fertile in Germany. Known as the "cradle of Prussia," the Altmark is largely flat, with meadows and fields for grazing and arable crops and some swamps and lakes. Sugar beets were cultivated in the 19th century on the rich loess of the area southwest of Magdeburg, giving rise to a thriving sugar production **industry**. By 1989, the **agricultural** north contributed significantly to the food needs of the **German Democratic Republic (GDR)**, providing 20 percent of cereals, 24 percent of vegetables, and 25 percent of fruit. To the south, where most of the population of 2.2 million is concentrated, lie the cities of Halle (population 232,000) and Bitterfeld-Wolfen (41,800), forming part of an industrial region that also includes Leipzig in neighboring Saxony. Other cities include Wittenberg (135,400), Dessau-Rosslau (89,000), Stendal (41,400), and Halberstadt (41,545). The highest point in the state is the Brocken Mountain (856 m), which is located in the Harz Mountains in the southwestern corner. The main rivers are the Elbe and Ohre in the north and east and, farther south, the Saale and the Unstrut. The Saale-Unstrut region is also one of Germany's oldest and most northerly wine-producing areas. Since 1990, annual outward migration of around 25,500 to the western **federal states**, especially in the 18 to 30 age group, has steadily eroded the population, of whom only 3.7 percent are **foreigners** (2015).

The middle Elbe region was politically fragmented until the Prussian province of Saxony, which covered much of the present area of Saxony-Anhalt, was created after the Napoleonic Wars. Although the statelets of Anhalt (united in 1863) remained independent, they were economically and administratively integrated into Prussia. Rapid industrialization took place during the first half of the 19th century, with the exploitation of natural resources such as brown coal and potash (in the southern Harz) and copper (around Mansfeld). Magdeburg, which is also Germany's second largest inland harbor, became a center of **engineering**, while Halle, Merseburg, and Bitterfeld concentrated on raw materials, fertilizer, and **chemical** production. The industrial areas were heavily bombed during World War II. After 1945, the region became part of the Soviet zone of occupation under the name Province of Saxony, although this was dissolved in 1952 to make way for the administrative districts (Bezirke) of Magdeburg and Halle. Following the collapse of the GDR, it was by no means certain that a distinctive (federal) state within the **Bund** would be created at all; some argued that Saxony-Anhalt lacked a distinct identity and that its territory should be divided among the neighboring new Länder, while others proposed a separate Land for Anhalt alone. After an intense debate, the state of Saxony-Anhalt (which, in common with the other eastern German states, was established in July 1990 by an enabling law preparing for the creation of the Länder) formally joined the Federal Republic of Germany (FRG) on the date of reunification (3 October 1990). The **Landtag** voted for Magdeburg as the regional capital on 14 October.

The GDR period left a disastrous economic legacy. Most of the region's core industries, which lost their protected markets in eastern Europe after reunification, were either unable to withstand Western/global competition or shut down because of their danger to the **environment**. A drastic program of closures resulted in the highest and most persistent unemployment levels in Germany (over 21 percent in the late 1990s and at 10.2 percent in 2015, still well above the national average of 6.4 percent). The chemical industry around Halle and Bitterfeld, where 40 percent of the GDR's chemical products was made, was especially hard hit, as were copper mining (around Mansfeld) and electronics (Stassfurt), which ceased altogether. Many sectors/businesses, such as sugar production, railway carriage building, and light engineering, suffered job losses as they were restructured or taken over, and they continued to lead a precarious existence. Positive aspects include the much improved communications and **transport** infrastructure (new highways and inland waterways) and a highly qualified workforce. Following massive restructuring, the main industries in 2008 were food, chemicals, metal processing, and engineering, followed by rubber/synthetics and glass and ceramics. By 2011, investments were largely in chemicals (Dessau and Bitterfeld area), engineering (Harz), wood (Magdeburg), paper (Stendal), and services (Magdeburg). Brown coal extraction, which devastated landscapes during the GDR period, now employs around 2,100 in the Leipzig area, while former mining fields to the north of the city are being cleaned up. Despite its industrial past, Saxony-Anhalt boasts areas of outstanding natural beauty (especially in the Harz Mountains and in the north) and several historic cities (the Protestant reformer Martin Luther taught at the University of Wittenberg). The region has two universities, the historical Martin-Luther University Halle-Wittenberg (over 20,000 students) and the Otto von Guericke University, which was founded in its present form in 1993 and has around 14,000 students, studying mainly engineering and science. Saxony-Anhalt contributes 2 percent of national GDP (2015).

Despite its brevity, the regional constitution, which was adopted in July 1991, contains a comprehensive catalog of basic rights that, with the GDR years in mind, includes data protection for the individual and a guarantee of privacy in the home against "optical or acoustic surveillance." An unusual element is the detailed listing of aims in **education**. The constitution explicitly acknowledges the role of parliamentary groups and contains strong plebiscitary elements—partly informed by the peaceful revolution of 1989. The Landtag, which had 87 members in 2016, sits for four years and elects a **minister president**.

Following regional elections in October 1990, the CDU emerged as the strongest political party and formed a ruling coalition with the **Free Democratic Party (FDP)**, although the government underwent several changes of leadership during the early years. Gerd Gies (CDU), who was not a Landtag member and was elected minister president by the narrowest of majorities, was forced to resign (July 1991) on suspicion of illegally acquiring a mandate. The CDU interior minister and the FDP minister for federal and European affairs also resigned (the latter when it emerged he had been involved with the **Stasi**). Gies's successor, Werner Münch (CDU), stood down after allegations, later proved false, of receiving overpayments (1993) and was replaced by Christian Bergner (CDU). Although the CDU again emerged as the strongest party in the 1994 election, its partner, the FDP, failed to clear the 5 percent hurdle. The outcome was a minority coalition between the **Social Democratic Party of Germany (SPD)** and the **Alliance 90/The Greens** that relied on the **Party of Democratic Socialism (PDS)**, which had increased its seats to 21, for a parliamentary majority. Led by **Reinhard Höppner** (SPD) as minister president, this came to be known as the **Magdeburg model**.

The 1998 elections, in which support for the CDU collapsed, were overshadowed by the unexpected success of the extreme right-wing **German People's Union (DVU)**, which gained 12.9 percent of votes; the **Greens** failed to clear the 5 percent hurdle. The SPD continued to govern, this time alone but again tolerated by the PDS. The 2002 election returned a CDU/

FDP coalition with **Wolfgang Böhmer** (CDU) as minister president. For the 2006 state election, a historically low turnout (44.4 percent) produced losses for all parties, although the CDU emerged as the strongest (36.2 percent of votes), followed by the SPD (21.4 percent). **The Left Party** (24.1 percent) beat the FDP, which lost almost half its votes, into third place, while the DVU dropped below 5 percent. The collapse of the FDP cost the ruling coalition its majority, and the CDU and SPD, which gained fewer seats than The Left Party, agreed to a governing **grand coalition** in which Böhmer continued as premier. The coalition was reelected in the election of 2011, but with **Reiner Haseloff** as minister president; the Greens also reentered parliament. Following elections in 2016, Haseloff continued as minister president, heading a 'Kenya coalition' of CDU, SPD and the Greens—unprecedented in the FRG's history. The right-wing **Alternative for Germany (AfD)** entered the assembly after winning 24.2 percent of votes, second only to the CDU (29.8 percent).

SCHABOWSKI, GÜNTER (1929–2015). German Democratic Republic (GDR) politician. Born in Anklam (now in **Mecklenburg-West Pomerania**) to a working-class family, Günter Schabowski trained as a journalist with the **trade union** newspaper *Freie Gewerkschaft* (1945) before working for *Tribüne*, the journal of the East German organization for trade unions, the Freier Deutscher Gewerkschaftsbund (FDGB, 1948–1967; he became deputy chief editor in 1953). Schabowski qualified with a diploma in journalism at the Karl-Marx-University in Leipzig (1962) and was a member of the communist youth organization, the Freie Deutsche Jugend (Free German Youth, FDJ) from 1950 and of the **Socialist Unity Party of Germany** (**SED**) from 1953. After attending the University of the Communist Party of the Soviet Union in Moscow (1967–1968), he returned to his post as deputy editor (1968–1978) of *Tribüne* before succeeding **Joachim Herrmann** as chief editor of the SED party newspaper *Neues Deutschland* (1978–1985). He was also a member of the so-called Agitation Commission of the Politburo of the SED Central Committee, which was responsible for the dissemination of ideology and propaganda (1978–1985). His other senior positions included membership in the **People's Chamber** (1981–1990), the Central Committee (from 1984; secretary from 1986), and the Politburo (from 1986), and being head of the **Berlin** district party organization (1985–1989).

On the evening of 9 November 1989, Schabowski's announcement that East German citizens were free to leave the country promptly led to a mass crossing of the **Berlin Wall**. The circumstances of this announcement were confusing; when asked by an Italian reporter when travel restrictions would be lifted, a tired Schabowski hesitated before adding that the changes would come into effect immediately. He resigned from the Central Committee and Politburo (December 1989) and the following month was expelled from the renamed SED/**Party of Democratic Socialism (PDS)**. From 1990 until 1999, he worked as a journalist for a local newspaper in **Hessen** (the *Heimatnachrichten* in Rotenburg/Fulda). Along with other Politburo members, Schabowski was sentenced in 1997 to three years' imprisonment for his part in the shoot-to-kill policy at the Berlin Wall, although he did not begin serving his sentence until November 1999 and was granted an amnesty after nine months. Schabowski was one of the few figures in the leadership of the GDR to win respect for publicly admitting his guilt and playing a part in the process of coming to terms with the East German past. He contributed to a book on the Politburo of the former GDR (*Das Politbüro: Ende eines Mythos; Eine Befragung*, edited by F. Sieren and L. Koehne, 1990) and wrote his own account of the fall of the regime (*Der Absturz*, 1991).

SCHALCK-GOLODKOWSKI, ALEXANDER (1932–2015). German **Democratic Republic (GDR)** functionary. Alexander Schalck-Golodkowski was born in **Berlin** and trained as an engineer before studying economics and law. He joined the **Socialist Unity Party of Germany (SED**, 1955) and became an officer in the **Stasi** (1967), rising to the rank of colonel and gaining a doctorate from the Stasi's law college on the subject of generating hard (Western) **currency** (1972). From 1962 onward, he occupied various positions in the ministries for external and intra-German trade and in 1983 was closely involved in negotiations with the Federal Republic of Germany (FRG) that resulted in a 1,000 million DM trade credit for the GDR. During the negotiations he met leading West German politicians, including **Franz Josef Strauß** and **Wolfgang Schäuble**.

After **Erich Honecker** came to power (1971), Schalck-Golodkowski became one of the most important figures in the GDR. During the 1970s and 1980s, he created and managed a secret network of companies that traded with the West and brought in hard currency for the East German economy. Directly responsible to Economics Minister **Günter Mittag** (from 1974), he ran his operations as head of the so-called Department of Commercial Coordination (KoKo), which was based in the foreign trade ministry. He joined the Central Committee of the SED (1986) and during the revolution of October/November 1989 was considered as a possible successor to Mittag. In late November 1989, Schalck-Golodkowski, who also faced allegations of illegal arms and currency trading, was directed by the interim East German leader **Hans Modrow** to reveal his financial and commercial dealings. After his expulsion from the SED Central Committee (3 December 1989), he fled to West Berlin, but surrendered to the authorities three days later. He was taken into investigative detention (1992 and 1993), was charged with a number of offenses, and eventually received two suspended sentences. Schalck-Golodkowski retired to the Tegernsee Lake in the Bavarian **Alps**, worked occasionally as a business consultant, and published an autobiography (*Deutschdeutsche Erinnerungen*, 2000).

SCHARPING, RUDOLF (1947–). Social Democratic Party of Germany (SPD) politician. Born in Niederelbert/Unterwesterwald (**Rhineland-Palatinate**, RLP), Rudolf Scharping joined the SPD (1966) and studied political science, sociology, and law at the University of Bonn (1966–1974), where he graduated with a master's degree on the subject of regional election campaigns. As a student, he worked as an assistant to a member of the **Bundestag** and was briefly (1968–1969) expelled from the SPD for publishing a pamphlet that was critical of the party. An active member and regional chairman of the SPD's **Young Socialists (JUSOS)** wing in RLP (1969–1974), he rose to become deputy national leader of the movement (1974–1976). He also represented the party in the regional assembly (**Landtag**, 1974–1994), where he first managed (1979–1985) and subsequently chaired the parliamentary group (1985–1991) and headed the regional party (1985–1993). In the 1987 regional election, which was won by the **Christian Democratic Union (CDU)**, he was the SPD's candidate for **minister president**. The following year, he joined the SPD national executive. In the 1991 regional election for RLP, the SPD finally ended 44 years of CDU rule, and Scharping became minister president (1991–1994).

Following the resignation of **Björn Engholm** (1993), Scharping was elected SPD national chairman, defeating **Gerhard Schröder** (minister president of **Lower Saxony**) to become the youngest leader in the party's history. In June 1994, he was nominated to be the SPD's candidate for the chancellorship in the forthcoming national election, but was criticized for the party's heavy defeat. At the same time, he stepped down as minister president in his home state in order to concentrate on national politics. Elected to the Bundestag (1994–2005), Scharping chaired the SPD parliamentary group (1994–1998) and, together with Schröder und **Oskar Lafontaine**, formed the so-called troika of party leaders. However, differences emerged between Scharping and Schröder over economic policy, and the latter removed him as party economics spokesman (1995). In a fierce contest, Scharping also lost the party leadership to Lafontaine (November 1995).

Appointed defense minister in the first SPD/**Green Party** coalition (1998–2002) under Chancellor Schröder, Scharping pledged to review alleged links between the **Bundeswehr** and extreme right-wing elements and change the names of army barracks from those of former Wehrmacht soldiers who fought during World War II. He also presided over German forces' involvement in missions in the former Yugoslavia (1999). Although Scharping made a good start at reforming the Bundeswehr (reducing its size to 285,000 and converting it from a conscript-based army into a professional rapid reaction force), he was dogged by various scandals, which prompted Schröder to dismiss him from office two months before a national election (July 2002). In 2004, he founded and currently heads a consultancy firm (Rudolf Scharping Strategie Beratung Kommunikation GmbH, RSBK), which assists companies and institutions in strategic planning and development in China; it also advises on the public sector in Germany.

SCHÄUBLE, WOLFGANG (1942–). Christian Democratic Union **(CDU)** politician. Born in Freiburg **(Baden-Württemberg)**, Wolfgang Schäuble studied law and economics at the universities of Freiburg and **Hamburg** (from 1961) before passing his state law examinations (1966, 1970). After briefly working as a research assistant in political education at the University of Freiburg (1966–1968), he completed legal training while he was attached to a law court (1968–1970), earned a doctorate in commercial law (1971), and began work in the **taxation** department of the federal state of Baden-Württemberg. In 1978, he was admitted as a lawyer in the state court (Landgericht) in Offenburg, where he defended Renate Lutze, a secretary in the Federal Ministry of Defense who was accused of spying for the **German Democratic Republic (GDR)**. An early political activist, Schäuble joined the youth wing **(Junge Union, JU)** of the CDU (1961) before entering the main party (1965) and leading the JU in southern Baden (1969–1972).

After entering the **Bundestag** (1972), Schäuble joined the CDU regional party executive in Baden-Württemberg (1973) and served on a parliamentary committee that investigated allegations that Karl Wienand, a member of the **Social Democratic Party of Germany (SPD)**, had bribed Julius Steiner (CDU) to abstain in a constructive vote of no confidence mounted by the CDU chancellor candidate **Rainer Barzel** against **Willy Brandt** in April 1972. Schäuble was a member of the European Council Parliamentary Assembly (1975–1984), chaired a national CDU committee on **sports** (1976–1984), and led a working group on peripheral regions of the **European Union (EU,** 1979–1982). He was an early supporter of **Helmut Kohl**, CDU opposition leader in the Bundestag from 1976. In return, Kohl was instrumental in Schäuble's election to the team of party managers of the CDU/**Christian Social Union (CSU)** parliamentary group (1981). When Kohl displaced **Helmut Schmidt** as **federal chancellor** (1982), Schäuble was promoted to lead the group, rapidly becoming Kohl's closest adviser and one of the CDU's most senior politicians. He served as federal minister for special tasks (1984–1989), headed the **Office of the Federal Chancellor**, and played a major role in shaping and implementing domestic policy. As interior minister (1989–1991), he took over responsibility for new laws on **foreigners** and data protection. Schäuble also took a keen interest in links with East Germany, and his meeting with **Alexander Schalck-Golodkowski**, the East German head of "commercial coordination" (1985), marked the beginning of four years of close negotiations on intra-German relations. He also handled preparations for the state visit of **Erich Honecker** to the Federal Republic of Germany (FRG) in 1987, headed the West German team that negotiated the Treaty of Unification in the summer of 1990, and eagerly adopted the idea of the **Trust Agency** (Treuhand) to privatize industry in the new **eastern federal states**.

Shortly after joining the CDU national party executive (September 1990), Schäuble was critically injured when attacked at an election campaign meeting in Oppenau. Although the attack left him paralyzed and confined to a wheelchair, Schäuble quickly resumed his political activities. He served as chairman of the CDU/CSU parliamentary group (1991–2000) and in 1996 headed a CDU commission on tax reform. Although Helmut Kohl publicly acknowledged Schäuble as his successor in 1992, the former's decision to stand as chancellor candidate in the 1998 election kept Schäuble from highest office. When the CDU/CSU lost the election, Schäuble took over the party leadership (1998–2000) and, during the debate on future directions, proved instrumental in reaffirming the CDU's core values as a conservative party of the middle ground, leading opposition to the government's proposals to relax laws on citizenship (1999).

In 1999, Schäuble became embroiled in the scandal over illegal party donations and secret accounts. He admitted accepting a cash donation from the controversial arms lobbyist Karlheinz Schreiber in 1994, and in February 2000 resigned as chairman of the party and its parliamentary group. Nevertheless, he remained a member of the presidium and consistently denied that the leadership was corrupt, urging Kohl to reveal the names of anonymous donors. Charges were dropped in October 2001. Despite his reduced influence in the CDU, Schäuble was an active member of **Edmund Stoiber**'s campaign team in the 2002 national election and in October of the same year became deputy chairman of the CDU/CSU group in the Bundestag, responsible for security and European policy. Appointed interior minister in **Angela Merkel**'s first cabinet (2005–2009), directly after a new **immigration** law came into force (January 2005), Schäuble argued for right of residency for foreigners in Germany who could demonstrate long-term economic and social integration. He attracted controversy after suggesting that security forces should be able to use information derived from torture (2005) and was criticized for undermining the principles of **federalism** by proposing that decisions in the **Bundesrat** be reached by a relative majority, discounting abstentions (2008). In 2009, Schäuble succeeded **Peer Steinbrück** (**Social Democratic Party of Germany, SPD**) as finance minister and took a leading role in Germany's response to the **eurozone crisis**. A consistent advocate of imposing budgetary discipline on eurozone states facing financial crisis, he openly mooted the possibility of Greece's exit from the currency during negotiations for its third emergency bailout in 2015. His firm stance contrasted with that of Chancellor Merkel, for whom the political imperative lay in maintaining the continuity of the existing eurozone.

Schäuble has received several awards, including the Goethe Foundation Award, a Bambi from the German **media** industry (1991), and the Golden Microphone Award as "Speaker of Year 1991," a prize for the promotion of culture (Sonderpreis der Stiftung Kulturförderung, 1998), and several honorary doctorates. His books and publications include an account of his role in the negotiations on reunification (*Der Vertrag: Wie ich über die deutsche Einheit verhandelte*, 1991), a pamphlet arguing for a return to community values (*Und der Zukunft zugewandt*, 1994), and his perspective on the state of the CDU after its 1998 election defeat (*Mitten im Leben*, 2000).

SCHAVAN, ANNETTE (1955–). Christian Democratic Union (CDU) politician. Born in Jüchen/Neuss (**North Rhine-Westfalia**), Annette Schavan studied theology, philosophy, and pedagogical/child care sciences (1974–1980); the doctorate she received in 1980 was withdrawn in 2013 on grounds of plagiarism, a scandal that ended her later ministerial career. After working in youth **education** for Roman Catholic organizations (1980–1987), she became manager of the Cusanuswerk, a Catholic organization providing grants and other support for students (1988), and subsequently its director (1991–1995). A member of the CDU from 1973, Schavan was business manager of the party's organization for **women** (Frauen-Union, 1987–1988) and served as a local councilor in Neuss (1975–1984) before becoming minister for culture/education, youth, and **sport** in the state of **Baden-Württemberg** (1995–2005), where she also represented the party in the regional assembly (**Landtag**, 2001–2005) and sat on the regional CDU executive (1996). As education minister, she introduced greater flexibility to the start of the school year, promoted education in foreign languages at the primary level, and reformed sixth-grade education. A deputy leader of the national party (1998–2012), Schavan entered the **Bundestag** in 2005 (re-elected 2013) and served as federal minister of education and **research** under Chancellor **Angela Merkel** (2005–2013). As minister, she oversaw various initiatives to promote innovation and excellence in higher education, until she was forced to resign over the plagiarism affair. In 2014, she was appointed Germany's ambassador to the Vatican.

SCHEEL, WALTER (1919–2016). Free Democratic Party (FDP) politician and **president of the Federal Republic**, 1974–1979. Walter Scheel was born in Solingen (**North Rhine-Westfalia**); trained in banking (1938–1939); and after serving in the air force during World War II, worked as a manager in various industrial concerns (1945–1953). A member of the FDP from

1946, he represented the party at local and regional level (1948–1953) and in the **Bundestag** (1953–1974). His positions included membership in the FDP regional executive (1953–1961), the national executive (1956–1974), the assembly of the European Coal and Steel Community in Luxembourg (1955–1957, the forerunner of the European Economic Community [EEC] and **European Union [EU]**), and the European Parliament (1958–1969). He served as federal minister for economic cooperation (responsible for development aid) under **Konrad Adenauer** and **Ludwig Erhard** (1961–1966) until the FDP withdrew from the coalition with the **Christian Democratic Union (CDU)**, which led to the fall of Erhard's government. He was also vice president of the Bundestag (1967–1969).

In 1968, Scheel succeeded Erich Mende as leader of the FDP, a position he held until 1974. He was instrumental in steering the party toward the reform course embodied in the Freiburg Theses (1971) and reorienting it away from the CDU and toward the **Social Democratic Party of Germany (SPD)**. As foreign minister and deputy federal chancellor in two coalition governments led by **Willy Brandt** (SPD) from 1969 until 1974, he played a key role in developing and implementing the policy of rapprochement with the **German Democratic Republic (GDR)** and Eastern Europe. He worked particularly hard to overcome conservative-led opposition in the Bundestag to ratification of the **Ostpolitik** treaties (1972). During an official visit to Peking (1972), Scheel oversaw the assumption of diplomatic relations between China and Germany. As president of the Federal Republic (1974–1979), he supported opposition to a proposed law that would have replaced the current test for conscientious objectors with 18 months' nonmilitary service (1976), but turned down overtures from the SPD and FDP to stand for a second term of office. He was elected honorary chairman of the FDP (1979) and in 1980 joined the supervisory board of **Thyssen** AG (later Thyssen Stahl AG).

Scheel was the first German foreign minister to pay a state visit to Israel (1971) and received several awards, including the Theodor Heuss Prize (1971) and a number of honorary doctorates. He wrote prolifically on political and economic issues and published a book on the continuing division of Germany (*Wen schmerzt noch Deutschlands Teilung?* 1986).

See also FOREIGN POLICY: 1970–1990.

SCHENGEN AGREEMENT. An agreement reached in 1985 by five members of the European Economic Community (EEC), the forerunner of the **European Union (EU)**, to eliminate internal border controls and enhance cooperation in police and judicial affairs. The convention was amended in 1990 and gradually extended to include most EU member states, although it came into effect only in 1995. Its main feature is that it enables foreign visitors, including **asylum** seekers, to travel freely on a single visa within the shared borders of the signatory states (the Schengen area), although Great

Britain and Ireland, while cooperating in some aspects of the agreement, opted to maintain controls at their own frontiers. The open borders policy came under severe strain in 2015, as thousands of refugees, mainly from war-torn areas of North Africa and the Middle East, entered the EU, chiefly via Italy, Greece, and Hungary, with the intention of moving on to northern European countries, in particular Germany. In order to stem what it regarded as an overwhelming influx of asylum seekers into its territory, Germany temporarily reintroduced border checks in September 2015, while also calling for other EU states to accept quotas of refugees. The EU engaged in a difficult debate on the introduction of mandatory quotas.

SCHERF, HENNING (1938–). Lawyer and **Social Democratic Party of Germany** (**SPD**) politician. Henning Scherf was born in **Bremen**; won a scholarship to study law and social sciences at the universities of Freiburg, **Berlin**, and **Hamburg** (1958–1962); and helped manage the Evangelisches Studienwerk, an evangelical student organization (1962–1964). After passing his state law examinations, he worked in various legal capacities, including as a lawyer in Bremen, a government legal assessor in **Lower Saxony**, legal adviser to the Bremen interior minister (senator), and lawyer for the state prosecution service (1967–1971). He earned a doctorate in law in 1968.

A member of the SPD from 1963, Scherf entered the Bremen state parliament (1971) and led the local party (1972–1978). He joined the SPD national executive (1984–1999), chaired the party's One World Forum (1996–1999), and after 1978 held various ministerial posts in Bremen's governing body, the senate. These included senator for finance (1978–1979); senator for youth, social affairs, and **sport** (1979–1990); mayor and vice president (1985–1991); senator for **education**, science, and art (1991–1995); and senator for justice and the constitution (1991–2005). He was also briefly acting senator for **health** (1987). Scherf's popularity and public profile notably increased during his period as senator for social affairs. Considered a radical left-winger, especially after openly criticizing the government's support for the double-zero option proposed by the **North Atlantic Treaty Organization** (**NATO**), he demonstrated against the deployment of Pershing II missiles.

In April 1995, when the SPD had reached an electoral low point, Scherf was elected governing mayor and president of the senate. Rejecting a continuation of the troubled alliance with the **Green Party**, within two weeks he negotiated a **grand coalition** of the SPD and the **Christian Democratic Union** (**CDU**). This represented new political ground, since the SPD had hitherto governed Bremen with an overall majority (1971–1991) or in coalition with either the **Free Democratic Party** (**FDP**) or the Greens (1991–1995), who had entered the assembly in 1979 and retained a strong electoral presence there. The June 1999 regional election gave the SPD a

42.6 percent share of the vote (a gain of over 9 percent from 1995), the CDU 37.1 percent, and the Greens 9 percent (a loss of 4 percent). Nevertheless, Scherf rejected a return to a coalition with the Greens, preferring to continue the partnership with the CDU. The success of the main parties was due to Scherf's personal popularity and the coalition's perceived success in tackling Bremen's economic difficulties, in particular its high unemployment (15 percent in 1999) and **budget** deficit. In the May 2003 elections, the SPD was returned as the strongest party in the assembly (with over 42 percent of the votes). During the election campaign, it had argued for retaining the coalition with the conservatives and distanced itself from a **federal government** whose popularity had waned. In December 2003, Scherf was appointed chairman of the **mediation committee** of the **Bundestag/Bundesrat**. In September 2005, he announced his retirement from politics, citing personal reasons, and in November was succeeded as mayor in Bremen by the leader of the SPD parliamentary group, Jens Böhrnsen. An active Christian, Scherf served on the presidium of the Deutscher Evangelischer Kirchentag (Conference of German Evangelical Churches, 1997–2003).

SCHICKEDANZ FAMILY. Retail entrepreneurs. In 1923, Gustav Schickedanz (1893–1977) founded in his native city of Fürth (**Bavaria**) a wholesale company dealing in haberdashery, textiles, and woolens, which four years later became the mail order and **distribution** concern Quelle. The company, which issued its first catalog in 1928, specialized in selling high-quality goods at discount prices to customers living outside urban areas. By 1933, it was Germany's most successful mail order concern and in 1938 boasted over a million customers. Quelle's expansion was helped by the elimination and expropriation of Jewish competitors by the National Socialist regime, with which Schickedanz—a party member since 1932—cultivated a good relationship. A key figure in the company was Grete Schickedanz (1911–1994), who began as a trainee in 1927 and became Schickedanz's second wife (1942). The firm's factories and files were destroyed during World War II, and the U.S. occupation authorities closed down the business because of its owner's links with the National Socialists. After the war, Grete rebuilt the concern, opening up a small textile shop in Hersbruck near Nuremberg (1946). Quelle itself was refounded in 1948, achieving record sales within a year and opening a department store in Fürth. In the 1950s, the company experienced rapid growth, extended its product range, and established its first foreign subsidiary (in Austria, 1959). During the 1960s, branches opened in Luxembourg, France, Switzerland, and the Far East. With 10 million customers by 1974, Quelle was one of Europe's largest mail order and distribution companies. In 1985, a contract was signed for a joint German–Hungarian mail order venture and, just before reunification, with the setting up of the German–Soviet joint venture Intermoda, Quelle became the first mail order firm to operate in the former Soviet Union. After reunification, Quelle massively extended its network into the **eastern federal states**, earning Grete Schickedanz the accolade of "First Lady of the German Economy" from Federal President **Richard von Weizsäcker**. The company then expanded into eastern Europe and the **Baltic** states, also Spain (1990), Finland (1995), Denmark (1996), and Shanghai/China (1997).

During the 1980s and 1990s, Quelle broadened its product range, took over or acquired several companies, moved into life insurance, founded a restaurant company, and joined up with Touristik Union International (TUI) to set up Reise Quelle GmbH, offering international travel and holidays. Coinciding with the advent of private television in Germany, the period also saw the company launching home shopping via videotext/teletext sales (in 1987 in conjunction with Eureka TV, which later became ProSieben)—a precursor to **Internet**-based e-commerce after 1995. With Quelle Call Center GmbH in Chemnitz, the company began offering call center services to third parties. In partnership with the **energy** supply company RWE Energie, Quelle enabled private households to purchase electricity by mail order at the supplier's own rates (from 1999).

Committed to marketing ecologically friendly merchandise, Quelle's **environment** officer, Ralf Ehrhardt, received the B.A.U.M. Environment Award in 1997. In 1999, a humid biotope was inaugurated at the company's large mail order center in Leipzig.

When Gustav Schickedanz died (1977), his wife Grete continued as the driving force behind the company, assisted by her sons-in-law Hans Dedi and Wolfgang Bühler. She retired from active management in 1993 to become honorary chairwoman of the supervisory board and the executive board. Immediately after her death (1994), Dedi and Bühler sold off many of the concern's industrial and trading partners (including a paper manufacturer, a brewery, and a **bank**) to focus on the core business of mail order and services. After Bühler resigned as chairman of the holding company's executive board (1997), his successor, Ingo Riedel, masterminded a merger with Europe's largest retail department store group, Karstadt, to create Karstadt-Quelle AG, in which Quelle AG became a subsidiary and Schickedanz Holding kept a majority holding (1999). In 2009, KarstadtQuelle (later Arcandor) announced insolvency; Madeleine Schickedanz, born in 1943 and the only child of Gustav and Grete, lost much of her inherited fortune.

See also DISTRIBUTION AND RETAIL.

SCHILL PARTY. *See* SCHILL, RONALD B. (1958–).

SCHILL, RONALD B. (1958–). Politician. Born in **Hamburg**, Ronald Barnabas Schill grew up in Hamburg-Eimbüttel and studied psychology and law at the University of Hamburg (from 1979). After passing the first stage of his law degree (1988), he worked as a tutor and research assistant at the university before completing his studies (1992). Following a brief period practicing as a lawyer, he was appointed a judge for a local court (Amtsgericht, 1993), where he developed a reputation for harsh sentencing, often for minor offenses. Nicknamed "Judge Merciless" ("Richter Gnadenlos") by the *Hamburger Abendblatt* newspaper, he urged the restoration of the death penalty for especially bestial crimes and for contract killings by **foreigners**. His removal as a judge and a fine for perversion of the course of justice (1997) only enhanced his reputation as a hard-liner and prompted him to found the right-wing Partei Rechtsstaatliche Offensive (Law and Order Offensive Party, PRO), commonly known as the Schill Party (July 2000). The party attracted several hundred disaffected members from the **Christian Democratic Union (CDU)**, the **Social Democratic Party of Germany (SPD)**, and the **Instead Party (Statt Partei)**.

In local elections in September 2001, Schill's party sensationally won more than 19 percent of the vote after campaigning on a populist law-and-order platform in a city with an estimated 10,000 drug addicts, over 2,000 drug dealers, and one of the highest crime rates in Germany. The news that the terrorist attacks of 11 September 2001 had been planned by Arabs in Hamburg further fueled popular anxieties over crime and foreigners. After the election, Schill formed a coalition with the CDU and **Free Democratic Party (FDP)**, displacing the SPD, which had ruled Hamburg for 44 years (most recently in partnership with the **Green Party**). Under governing mayor **Ole von Beust** (CDU), Schill became interior minister (senator). He increased the size of the city-state's police force, created a body of less well trained officers to guard public buildings, and proposed paying African states to accept repatriated undesirables. Following its electoral success in Hamburg, Schill's party planned to establish itself in **North Rhine-Westfalia** and other **federal states**, but it failed to pass the 5 percent threshold in regional elections in **Saxony-Anhalt** (April 2002). Schill attracted widespread disapproval when he used a **Bundestag** debate on the emergency aid for the victims of flooding in eastern Germany (August 2002) to attack **asylum** seekers and to argue against accepting Poland into the **European Union (EU)**.

In August 2003, Beust fired Schill from his cabinet. The following November, Schill mounted a fierce attack on the Hamburg senate; the following month, Beust announced the end of the coalition, which had been plagued by scandals, allegations, and interparty disputes. Shortly afterward, Schill left his own party to form an independent grouping in the Hamburg senate. The election of 29 February 2004 returned the CDU with an overall majority, and

Schill's former party failed to clear the electoral hurdle. After Schill's departure, the party renamed itself Offensive D, but it faded into obscurity and was wound up in 2007. The leader after 2004 was right-wing former CDU member Markus Wagner.

Although Schill liked to remind opponents that his grandfather, Kurt Schill, was murdered as a communist in 1944 by the National Socialists in Neuengamme concentration camp, he was fiercely critical of the **students' movement** and the generation of 1968 socialists, whom he accused of having taken over key positions in German life after their proclaimed "long march through the institutions." His partner, Katrin Freund, a trained psychologist and former financial broker, assisted him closely in his political campaigns. His deputy in the party was Mario Mettbach, a former member of the Hamburg senate.

SCHILLER, KARL (1911–1994). Social Democratic Party of Germany (SPD) politician. Karl Schiller was born in Breslau (now in Poland), the son of an engineer, and grew up in Kiel. He studied economics and law at the universities of Kiel, Frankfurt/Main, **Berlin**, and Heidelberg (from 1931), graduating with a diploma in economics (1934) and a doctorate in economics and finance (1935). After heading an economics **research** institute in Kiel and qualifying as a professor at Kiel (1935–1941), he served in World War II. In 1944, he was appointed professor for economics at the University of Rostock, but the war prevented him from taking up the post. After the war, he occupied various professorial and academic posts, including guest professor at the University of Kiel (from 1946) and senior professor at the University of **Hamburg** (from 1947), where he was also rector/vice-chancellor (1956–1958).

After joining the SPD (1946), Schiller served as senator (minister) for economics and **transport** in Hamburg (1948–1953) and represented the party in the Hamburg parliament (1949–1957). An expert economist, Schiller was a strong advocate of the **social market economy**. He played a key role in the SPD's adoption of social market principles in its Godesberg Program (1959) and had special responsibility for economic policy as a member of the party's national executive (1964–1972). He served as economics senator (minister) in Berlin under Mayor **Willy Brandt** (1961–1965) and represented the SPD in the **Bundestag** (1965–1972), where he was also deputy leader of the SPD parliamentary group, party spokesman on economic affairs, and a member of the party presidium (1966–1972).

As federal minister for economic affairs during the first **grand coalition** (1966–1971), Schiller worked effectively with Finance Minister **Franz Josef Strauß** in tackling Germany's economic recession. He initiated the policy of "global control" (Globalsteuerung) and "concerted action" (konzertierte Aktion) and was largely responsible for the Stability and Growth Act

(Stabilitäts- und Wachstumsgesetz), which came into force in February 1967 and aimed to stimulate growth through credit-financed investment. At the same time, Schiller promoted dialogue among representatives of government, **industry**, and labor, although Chancellor **Kurt-Georg Kiesinger** overruled his advice to revalue the German DM upward. When Willy Brandt was elected **federal chancellor** (1969), Schiller remained in office; in May 1971, he extended his ministry to include finance following the resignation of Finance Minister Alex Möller (1903–1985) over a budgetary crisis. In July 1972, Schiller resigned as "super minister" over differences on **currency** and finance policy and was replaced by former defense minister **Helmut Schmidt** (SPD). In September, Schiller resigned from the SPD and, in the fall national election campaign, expressed support for the CDU, although he never joined the party (he rejoined the SPD in 1980). Schiller acted as a mediator in a labor dispute involving Lufthansa (1984) and joined 60 leading German economists in publishing a manifesto warning against premature introduction of a single European currency, arguing that it would harm the smooth integration of **European Union (EU)** states (1992). In 1978, he was awarded the Ludwig-Erhard Prize for services to the social market economy.

SCHILY, OTTO (1932–). **Green Party** and **Social Democratic Party of Germany** (SPD) politician. Otto Georg Schily was born in Bochum (**North Rhine-Westfalia**) and studied law at the universities of Munich and **Hamburg** and politics in **Berlin** (at the Hochschule für Politik) before passing his state law examination (1962) and founding his own legal practice (1963). During the 1960s, he was politically active and became a personal friend of **Rudi Dutschke** and Horst Mahler, leading figures in the radical students' socialist group, the **Federation of Socialist German Students (SDS)**. Schily also acted as defense lawyer for Mahler when the latter was tried as a member of the **Red Army Faction (RAF)** terrorist organization (1971) and represented Gudrun Ensslin, a convicted RAF member (1957–1977).

Schily's controversial association with the RAF dogged him for many years, although he consistently maintained that he never actively supported the group's aims or methods. After joining the Green Party (1980), he stood in West Berlin local elections (1981) and represented the Greens in the **Bundestag** (1983–1986, 1987–1989). Alongside **Petra Kelly** and Marieluise Beck-Oberdorf, Schily served on the Greens' parliamentary Sprecherrat (speakers' council, 1983–1984) before retiring in accordance with the party's policy of rotating offices. A member of the Greens' realist, as opposed to its fundamentalist, wing, Schily defended the state's exclusive right to use violence and, following the 1987 national election, argued for an alliance with the SPD. The issue of cooperation with the SPD split the party. While Kelly and other fundamentalists resisted compromises offered in return for participation in government, Schily, along with fellow realists such as **Joschka**

Fischer, was willing to work with the social democrats. In 1986, Schily initiated legal action against Chancellor **Helmut Kohl** for reportedly lying to a parliamentary commission about alleged illegal political donations (the action was abandoned for lack of evidence), although party members criticized Schily for his refusal to resign his Bundestag seat (in accordance with the Greens' rotation principle) until the proceedings against Kohl were completed. Schily was reelected to the Bundestag (1987), although disagreements in the party increased after electoral losses in **Hamburg** and **Rhineland-Palatinate** and the collapse of the coalition with the SPD in **Hessen**. Divisions came to a head at a party congress in Oldenburg (1987), when Schily suggested for the first time that he might resign from the Greens. After failing to be elected as chair of the parliamentary group or to convince the party to back a coalition with the SPD in the run-up to the 1990 national elections, he finally resigned his seat and party membership to join the SPD (1989), which he represented in the Bundestag (1990–2005).

Schily initially adopted a low profile in the Bundestag, made few speeches, and was active mainly on committees for the economy and the **environment** (which included monitoring the safety of nuclear reactors). In 1992, he defended the senior mayor (Oberbürgermeister) of Dresden, Wolfgang Berghofer (born in 1943), against charges of electoral fraud in the former **German Democratic Republic (GDR)** and chaired a parliamentary committee (1993–1994) investigating the **Trust Agency**. As deputy chairman of the SPD parliamentary group, Schily coordinated domestic and legal policy (1994–1998) and served on various committees.

When the SPD/Green Party coalition came to power, Schily became federal interior minister (Bundesinnenminister, 1998–2005). He piloted through parliament a new law on citizenship that allowed children of foreign residents to claim German nationality (1999), although he also declared that Germany had reached its limits for absorbing foreign **immigrants**, argued for the early repatriation of Albanian Kosovan refugees, and was censured (by the **federal government** representative for **foreigners**, Marieluise Beck-Oberdorf) for suggesting that 97 percent of **asylum** seekers were economic migrants. During 2002–2003, he steered a much-debated immigration law through the Bundestag and **Bundesrat**. As interior minister, he oversaw the introduction of new security measures in the aftermath of the terrorist attack on the United States (11 September 2001), including the banning of extremist Islamist organizations. He also initiated a program for modernizing government bureaucracy and was instrumental in the introduction of the biometric passport (ePass). A member of the Bundestag committee on foreign affairs, Schily has published on politics and on the financing of ecological projects.

SCHLESWIG-HOLSTEIN. Schleswig-Holstein is the northernmost of Germany's **federal states** and, with a **population** of 2.8 million, the smallest of the non-city Länder. It faces the **North Sea** to the west and the **Baltic** to the east, and shares a border with Denmark to the north. To the east lies **Mecklenburg-West Pomerania** and to the south lie **Lower Saxony** and **Hamburg**. The largest cities are the state capital, Kiel (242,000); Lübeck (211,000); Flensburg (89,000); and Neumünster (77,000). Geographically, the region, which covers 15,800 square kilometers, can be divided into three areas: the marshland along the coast (including polderland reclaimed from the sea), the sandy belt of the Geest farther inland, and hilly terrain to the east (where the nobility historically owned large estates). Schleswig-Holstein is home to two recognized ethnic minorities, Danes and North Frisians. After World War II, around one million refugees and expellees, mainly from Pomerania and East Prussia, swelled the population by 63 percent (from 1.6 million in 1939 to 2.7 million by 1949). The influx led to social tensions between natives and incomers, and the refugees' political umbrella group, the Bund der Heimatvertriebenen und Entrechteten (BHE), was discredited after it became a vehicle for former National Socialists. Because of its geography and the structure of its economy, Schleswig-Holstein currently has one of the lowest proportions of **foreigners** in the western states (6.7 percent), although 13 percent of its population has a **migration background**, with Turkish, Polish, or Russian roots. Protestants predominate, numbering 99 percent of the population until a century ago and currently around 54 percent.

Throughout most of its history, Schleswig-Holstein has been a sparsely populated rural area relying on traditional activities of farming, fishing, and shipping. Since the 1950s, however, **agriculture** has progressively declined and now accounts for only around 1 percent of the GDP and employs 3.2 percent of the workforce. The largest companies are concentrated in the more urbanized regions around Kiel, Lübeck, and the Hamburg hinterland, although traditional industries have either disappeared (textile/clothing industry around Neumünster) or shrunk (shipbuilding and repairing). While the shipyard Howaldtswerke-Deutsche Werft (now part of ThyssenKrupp Marine Systems, which also builds nuclear-powered submarines) alone employed 13,000 in 1960, only around 4,500 work directly in the sector today (2011). The biggest contributors to GDP are public services and finance/property, along with **trade**, **transport**, and **tourism**, which, attracting many visitors from **North Rhine-Westfalia**, is centered on North Friesland and eastern Holstein. At the same time, manufacturing, **energy**, and water supply account for almost 19 percent of GDP, and the sector as a whole is among the largest employers (27 percent). Leading manufacturers with an annual turnover of over 2 million euros are the oil refinery Raffinerie Heide GmbH (Brunsbüttel), whose products include diesel and aviation fuel, and the energy company E.ON. The state is a major employer, with the Schleswig-Holstein University Clinic and its 10,500 employees one of Germany's largest hospitals. Other significant employers include **Deutsche Post AG** (7,000 staff) and the retail distributer coop eG (6,900). Unemployment (6.5 percent in 2015) is close to the national average, and the region contributes 3 percent of national GDP (2015).

Schleswig-Holstein's major commercial ports are on the east coast, and since the opening up of eastern Europe both Kiel (a naval base during the 19th and early 20th centuries) and Lübeck have become important trading ports for Scandinavia and the Baltic states. The Hamburg area is also a center of economic growth, and Schleswig-Holstein's increasing cooperation with the city and Mecklenburg-West Pomerania has fueled speculation about a merger of the three states. Since the region's leaders in 1949 were convinced that the area would eventually be incorporated into the neighboring Länder, Schleswig-Holstein's constitution was regarded as provisional and accorded the lesser status of a set of statutes (Landessatzung), a classification that was not changed until 1990. In 1987, a scandal surrounding the politicians **Uwe Barschel** and **Björn Engholm** prompted Germany's first major constitutional reform and, following a parliamentary committee report in 1988, a new regional constitution was adopted in May 1990. The revised version adopted a number of objectives for the state, including equal rights for men and **women** and the explicit protection of the Danish minority and the Frisian ethnic group; a further change (1998) added the promotion of **sports** and the Low German **language**. Partly under the influence of the citizens' rights movement following the collapse of the **German Democratic Republic (GDR)**, plebiscitary elements were adopted, and the role of parliament (including the opposition) vis-à-vis the government was strengthened. The assembly, which numbered 69 (2012), is elected for five years (from 2000). A reform agreed to in 1990 abolished the mechanism whereby the **minister president** could be replaced only if he or she resigned (either voluntarily or through political pressure). As in other federal states, the post now automatically comes up for selection after regional elections. Exempted from the 5 percent electoral hurdle since 1955, the Danish minority party Südschleswigscher Wählerverband (SSW) regularly returns one or two members.

Between 1954 and 1987, Schleswig-Holstein was governed by a succession of **Christian Democratic Union (CDU)** minister presidents, with absolute majorities after 1971: Kai-Uwe von Hassel (1954–1963, in coalition with the BHE and **Free Democratic Party [FDP]** and, after 1958, with the FDP alone), Helmut Lemke (1963–1971), **Gerhard Stoltenberg** (1971–1982), and Uwe Barschel (1982–1987). Following the Barschel scandal of 1987, the political landscape shifted dramatically, and the **Social Democratic Party of Germany (SPD)**, led by Björn Engholm, won two landslide victories (1988, 1992). After Engholm resigned, **Heide Simonis** (SPD) became Germany's first female minister president (1993). With the narrowing of the electoral gap in the 1996 election, the SPD governed in coalition with the **Alliance 90/The Greens**, who finally entered parliament after five unsuccessful attempts. The red/green coalition continued in power until 2005, although 1967 and 1992 saw gains by the extreme right-wing **National Democratic Party of Germany (NPD)** and the **German People's Union (DVU)**. Following the regional election of February 2005, the SPD and CDU, which gained 29 and 30 seats respectively, formed a **grand coalition** led by **Peter Harry Carstensen** (CDU). This was succeeded in 2009 by a CDU/FDP coalition and in 2012 by a three-way coalition of the SPD, the Greens, and the SSW, with **Torsten Albig** (SPD) as minister president. Both elections were notable for being brought forward, first in 2009, following an engineered vote of no confidence after the collapse of the agreement between the coalition partners, and second in 2012, when the regional **Federal Constitutional Court (FCC)** upheld a complaint about electoral law (August 2010).

Schleswig-Holstein has three universities. Kiel is the largest, with around 24,000 students, followed by Lübeck (medical sciences, 1,500 students), and Flensburg (**education** and pedagogy, 4,800 students). Since 1990, the integrated comprehensive school type, renamed Gemeinschaftschule in 2010, has equal rank to other schools; along with the Gymnasium, it is now the only secondary school type beyond the primary level.

See also ETHNIC MINORITIES: DANES; ETHNIC MINORITIES: FRISIANS.

SCHMIDT, CHRISTIAN (1957–). Christian Social Union (CSU) politician. Born in Obernzenn (**Bavaria**), Christian Schmidt studied law in Erlangen and Lausanne (Switzerland) from 1977 to 1982, qualifying as a practicing lawyer between 1982 and 1985. After joining the CSU and its youth wing, the **Junge Union (JU)**, in 1973, Schmidt occupied various positions in the JU (1980–1992) and as a local councilor in the Obernzenn area (1984–1990) before his election to the **Bundestag** in 1990, where he specialized in European/**foreign policy** and defense. His roles included speaker on defense issues for the CSU parliamentary group (2002–2005) and **state secretary** for two federal ministers, defense (2005–2013) and economic cooperation and development (2013–2014). In 2014, he joined Chancellor **Angela Merkel**'s third coalition cabinet as federal minister for food and **agriculture**. A member of the CSU executive (1980–1993, 1999–) and elected deputy party leader in 2011, Schmidt is also an active member of the evangelical church working group of the **Christian Democratic Union (CDU)**/CSU (from 2011) and of the Gesellschaft für christlich-jüdische Zusammenarbeit, which promotes dialogue and cooperation between Christians and **Jews**. In 2006, he became president of the Deutsche Atlantische Gesellschaft (German Atlantic Association).

SCHMIDT, HELMUT (1918–2015). Social Democratic Party of Germany (SPD) politician and **federal chancellor**, 1974–1982. Helmut Schmidt was born in Hamburg-Barmbeck. After completing his school **education** (1937), he served during World War II on anti-aircraft duty in **Bremen** and later on the eastern and western fronts. After returning from British captivity (1945), he studied economics and political science in **Hamburg** (one of his tutors was the future economics minister **Karl Schiller**), graduating with a diploma (1949). Schmidt joined the SPD (1946) and was leader of the German student socialist movement, the **Federation of Socialist German Students (SDS)**. He worked in the department responsible for the economy and **transport** in the city of Hamburg (1949–1953). A member of the **Bundestag** (1953–1962, 1965–1987), he joined the executive committee of the SPD parliamentary group (1957) and the national party executive (1958). An expert on military and transport issues, Schmidt acquired a reputation as an effective parliamentary speaker, especially when attacking Defense Minister **Franz Josef Strauß**. Nevertheless, he was voted off the executive of the SPD parliamentary group while serving as an army reserve officer (he was promoted to captain in 1958).

In 1962, Schmidt resigned his Bundestag seat to concentrate on a new role as interior minister (senator) in Hamburg (1961–1965). His direction of rescue and emergency operations during the floods that hit the city in 1962 earned him a national reputation as a crisis manager. In 1964, he joined **Willy Brandt**'s shadow social democrat cabinet in the run-up to the national election the following year and was reelected to the Bundestag (1965–1987). Leader of the parliamentary group (1967–1969) and deputy party chairman (from 1969), he served in Brandt's first coalition government as defense minister (1969–1972) and succeeded Karl Schiller as economics and finance minister (July–November 1972) before becoming finance minister (December 1972). Following Brandt's resignation (May 1974), Schmidt was elected federal chancellor (reelected 1976 and 1980–1982).

Although his chancellorship was dogged by economic recession, **budget** deficits, and high unemployment, Schmidt became well known on the international stage, paying state visits to the United States, the Soviet Union, and China. Together with the French president Valéry Giscard d'Estaing, a close friend, he initiated the world economic summit of leading industrial nations (the G7/G8 group). The forum met for the first time (1975) at Ramboulliet (France) to confront global economic problems and threats to Western democracy. Backed by opposition parties, Schmidt refused to give in to **terrorist** demands during a wave of attacks in Germany, which reached their height in 1977 with the hijacking of a German airliner and the murder of employers' leader Hanns Martin Schleyer. Schmidt's support in 1979–1980 for the "dual-track decision," in which the **North Atlantic Treaty Organization (NATO)** threatened to station medium-range nuclear warheads in West Germany from 1983 unless the Soviet Union withdrew similar weapons from Europe, divided his party (he threatened to resign over the issue) and fueled a popular peace movement. In September 1982, the SPD's coalition partner, the **Free Democratic Party** (**FDP**), left the government over differences on how to handle the economic crisis. After losing a constructive vote of no confidence in the Bundestag, Schmidt was forced out of office in October and succeeded by **Helmut Kohl**, leader of the **Christian Democratic Union** (**CDU**).

In May 1983, Schmidt became coeditor of the respected weekly newspaper *Die Zeit*, for which he wrote topical commentaries and was also executive manager (1985–1989). He cofounded the InterAction Council, a forum of former heads of state (1983), and in 1986, together with Giscard d'Estaing, the Committee for European Monetary Union (he was a firm advocate of a European Central Bank). Writing in *Die Zeit* (2003), he supported the efforts of Chancellor **Gerhard Schröder** to reform Germany's rigid economic and social structures, reduce the burden of state regulations, and tackle the continuing problems of high unemployment and low productivity in the eastern **federal states**. He advocated a modest increase in credit to steer Germany through its current budget crisis and argued for abandoning national collective bargaining and returning powers to the states, which they had lost in the finance reform of 1968. Schmidt continued to comment on political and economic issues, more recently criticizing Chancellor **Angela Merkel** in 2014 for concealing the extent to which Germany would be expected to bail out states hit by the eurozone crisis.

During his career Schmidt received numerous honors, including the "Man of the Year" award by the *Financial Times* (1975); the Theodor-Heuss Prize (1977); the Goldmann Medal from the World Congress of Jews for services to peace and **human rights** (1980); and honorary citizenship of Hamburg (1983), Berlin (1989), and the state of **Schleswig-Holstein** (1998). He also wrote prolifically on defense, contemporary politics, and recent history.

SCHMIDT, RENATE (1943–). Social Democratic Party of Germany (SPD) politician. Renate Schmidt was born in Hanau, near Frankfurt/Main, trained as a computer programmer, and worked as a systems analyst for the Quelle retail and mail order concern in Fürth, where she also sat on the works council (1972–1980). She joined the SPD in 1972 and was deputy regional chairwoman of HBV, a **trade union** for employees in the **banking**, insurance, and commercial industries and later part of ver.di (1980–1988). She represented the party in the **Bundestag** (1980–1994), where she was also deputy leader of the parliamentary party group (1987–1990) and chaired a party working group on gender equality. Other offices she held include vice president of the Bundestag (1990–1994) and member of the national presidium of the SPD (from 1991). Leader of the SPD in **Bavaria** (1991–2000), she was elected to the regional assembly (**Landtag**) in 1994, where she also chaired the party's parliamentary group (until 2000). She was also deputy leader of the national SPD, with responsibility for family policy (1997–2003), served as federal minister for family, senior citizens, **women**, and youth in the second cabinet of **Gerhard Schröder** (2002–2005), and remains active in various social, welfare, and **environmental** organizations. In 2008, she was appointed ombudswoman for data protection and anticorruption at Vodafone, and subsequently also for Kabel Deutschland.

SCHMIDT, ULLA (1949–). Social Democratic Party of Germany (SPD) politician. Born in Aachen (**North Rhine-Westfalia**), Ulla Schmidt studied psychology at the Aachen University of Technology (Rheinisch-Westfälische Hochschule Aachen, 1968–1974) and trained at the Aachen Pedagogical University (Pädagogische Hochschule), graduating as a primary and secondary schoolteacher (1974). After finishing her in-service training and final state examinations for entry into the teaching profession (1974–1976), she taught pupils with learning disabilities in Stolberg (1976–1985), also studying at the University of Hagen (Westfalia) and qualifying in the rehabilitation of children with learning problems (1980–1984). She taught at a school for educational support in Aachen (1985–1990) and served on committees for special needs teachers in North Rhine-Westfalia.

After joining the SPD in 1983, she rapidly developed a career in politics, first as spokeswoman on housing for the parliamentary group on the Aachen city council (1989–1992) and from 1990 as a member of the party council, an elected body of representatives from the regions and local associations. On entering the **Bundestag** (1990), she served on the business committee of the SPD parliamentary committee (1991–2001), focusing on gender issues and family policy. She also chaired an SPD parliamentary cross-section group to promote equality between men and **women** (1991–1998), was spokeswoman for a project group on family policy (1991–1998), and organized cross-party support for legislation to make rape in marriage a criminal offense (1997).

When the SPD/**Green Party** coalition came to power, Schmidt was elected deputy chairwoman of a reformed and slimmed down SPD parliamentary group (1998–2001). She herself specialized in labor, social affairs, women, family, and senior citizens, and influenced government policy on reform of the **pension system**. She also served on the **mediation committee** of the Bundestag/**Bundesrat** and represented her party in the council of the ZDF **television** station. In January 2001, she was appointed federal minister of **health**, replacing **Andrea Fischer (Alliance 90/The Greens)**, who, together with **agriculture** minister Karl-Heinz Funke (SPD), resigned over the spread of BSE in Germany through the use of prohibited animal feed. When Schröder was reelected (October 2002), her ministry was extended to include health and social security.

A rising star in the SPD hierarchy, Schmidt began her new post with a reputation for resilience and good communication. In contrast to her predecessor, she adopted a more open attitude to modern genetic **research** and sought dialogue with the biotechnology industry and the medical establishment, although the SPD leadership was split over the issue. Schmidt became minister at a time when the government was planning a major overhaul of medical and health care. She generated controversy by restricting the right to opt out of compulsory health insurance and announcing plans to scrap the budget for medication and drugs and hand over control to doctors and the health insurance companies. At the time, she opposed the semiprivatization of health insurance (as was happening with pensions). In early 2002, the Bundestag approved two major and, for Germany, revolutionary health reform bills. The first required chemists to sell the most cost-effective drugs (Arzneimittelausgaben-Begrenzungsgesetz) and the second ensured that, by 2007, hospitals would be paid according to a patient's illness, not the number of days spent in health care (Fallpauschalengesetz). Schmidt retained her portfolio for health (but not pensions) in the SPD/**Christian Democratic Union (CDU)** coalition under Chancellor **Angela Merkel** (2005–2009). In 2010, she became deputy leader of the German delegation to the parliamentary assembly of the **North Atlantic Treaty Organization (NATO)** and in 2013 vice president of the Bundestag.

SCHOLZ, OLAF (1958–). Social Democratic Party of Germany (SPD) politician. Born in Osnabrück (**Lower Saxony**), Olaf Scholz grew up and studied law in **Hamburg** (1979–1985), where he practiced law from 1985. A member of the SPD from 1975, he was deputy leader of the **Young Socialists (JUSOS**, 1982–1988) and vice president of the International Union of Socialist Youth (1987–1989) before chairing the Hamburg-Altona branch of the main party (1994–2000) and the regional association (2000–2004). Between two spells in the **Bundestag** (1998–2001 and 2002–2011), when he worked closely with Chancellor **Gerhard Schröder** on the **Agenda 2010** reform policies, Scholz returned briefly to Hamburg as interior senator (May–October 2001). As senator, he was criticized for introducing the use of emetics to identify dealers employing body packing. In 2001, he also joined the SPD national executive and was general secretary (2002–2004) before being appointed first parliamentary party manager (2005–2007). During 2007–2009, he served as federal minister for labor and social affairs in Chancellor **Angela Merkel**'s first coalition cabinet. Elected leader of the Hamburg SPD (2009) and deputy national party leader (2009), Scholz took over from **Christoph Ahlhaus** of the **Christian Democratic Union (CDU)** in March 2011 as first mayor of the city following regional elections and was reelected in 2015.

SCHOOLS. *See* EDUCATION: SCHOOLS.

SCHRÖDER, GERHARD (1944–). Social Democratic Party of Germany (SPD) politician and **federal chancellor**, 1998–2005. Gerhard Schröder was born in Mossenberg (**Lower Saxony**). His father died serving as a soldier in Romania during World War II, and his memories of his mother keeping the family's head above water by cleaning and working in a factory were formative factors in his commitment to social democracy. He joined the SPD in 1963 and was immediately active in its youth wing (**Young Socialists, JU-SOS**) in opposing the Vietnam War. After leaving school at age 14, he completed a commercial apprenticeship in Lemgo (1958–1961) and, while working in a hardware store/metal dealer in Göttingen (1962–1964), completed his lower school certificate at evening classes. He went on to gain his higher school certificate (1966) and study law at the University of Göttingen, passing his state law examinations (1971, 1976). A trainee at the regional court (Landgericht) in Hanover (1972–1976), he later practiced law in the city (1978–1990).

In the SPD, Schröder was active at the regional executive level and nationally in the JUSOS. As the JUSOS' national chairman (1978–1980), he worked hard to unite the fragmented organization and reconcile it with the mother party. He went on to represent the main party in the **Bundestag** (1980–1986), where he was the first deputy in the history of the Federal Republic of Germany (FRG) not to wear a tie during his maiden speech (the gesture was intended to highlight the extent to which politicians had alienated themselves from young people). After visiting the United States on an exchange program (1981), he was impressed by the freedoms enjoyed by Americans but horrified by the poverty he witnessed. When the **Christian Democratic Union (CDU)** and **Free Democratic Party (FDP)** took over the government (1982), he returned to Lower Saxony, entering the state parliament (**Landtag**) in 1986. He continued his steady rise in the SPD hierarchy, chairing the local Hanover branch of the party (1983–1990) and the regional parliamentary grouping, and joining the national party executive (1986) and presidium (1989).

In June 1990, Schröder succeeded **Ernst Albrecht** (CDU) as **minister president** of Lower Saxony. Leading an alliance of the SPD and the **Green Party**, he embarked on an extensive reform of the state's administration. But despite the declared common aims of ecological reform, social justice, and multiculturalism, Schröder clashed repeatedly with his coalition partners. Although he initiated talks with **energy** companies over closing down nuclear power stations, a government ultimatum forced Lower Saxony to accept Gorleben as a storage facility for radioactive waste (1991). Schröder also came under pressure from the Greens for his willingness to compromise with the government over the introduction of a stricter **asylum** policy and his support for arms exports; both the Greens and his own party united in attacking him for backing a Taiwanese military contract for German shipyards. In a bid for the national party leadership (1993), he was defeated by **Rudolf Scharping** but joined a commission charged with drawing up a manifesto for government and also took over responsibility for energy. The following year, he became shadow cabinet minister in an SPD "super ministry" for energy, **transport**, and the economy and was regarded, along with Scharping and **Oskar Lafontaine**, as one of the troika of top party leaders.

During 1994–1998, the SPD gained enough seats in Lower Saxony to govern without the Greens. In 1994, Schröder rescued the Deutsche Aerospace Works (DASA) in Lemwerder from closure and the loss of 1,200 jobs by turning it into a company of the state of Lower Saxony. The state also became a majority shareholder of the Preussag Stahl AG, ensuring the continuation of steel production in the region (1998). Lower Saxony, however, was heavily in debt, and Schröder's insistence on a savings program that involved cuts in staff for schools and the police provoked fierce opposition from his own party. In 1995, Rudolf Scharping removed Schröder from his role as economic spokesman after he had criticized the party leadership for placing social democratic principles above the need to modernize the economy and had questioned Scharping's own leadership abilities. When Oskar Lafontaine replaced Scharping as party leader (1995), Schröder was reinstated, although he irritated the SPD's left wing by advocating changes in policies on the **environment**, stricter measures against foreign criminals, and a gradual transition to minimum national **pensions**. In 1998, he was elected chancellor candidate for the fall national election. The election brought to power an SPD/Green Party coalition with a strong parliamentary majority and Schröder as federal chancellor, the first leader of the FRG not to have personal experience with World War II. He was also elected chairman of the SPD in Lower Saxony (1998) and of the national party following Lafontaine's resignation (1999).

Schröder's government pledged to reduce unemployment, reform the social welfare and pension system, phase out nuclear energy, and levy ecological taxes on fossil fuels. While it made progress on some of these issues, unemployment remained intractable, especially in the **eastern federal states**, where Schröder made annual visits. Against strong conservative opposition, he initiated a new **immigration** law and a "green card" system to attract foreign workers in key industries. His administration was also plagued by scandals over illegal political donations (in Cologne) and by an unusually high number of ministerial resignations (or, in Scharping's case, dismissal). Under Schröder's leadership, **Bundeswehr** forces embarked on their first active military mission since World War II when they supported missions by the **North Atlantic Treaty Organization** (**NATO**) in Serbia aimed at protecting the ethnic Albanian population of Kosovo (1999).

Schröder was returned as chancellor in a closely fought electoral contest in September 2002. A flagging campaign for the SPD was helped by his firm handling of a flooding crisis in parts of eastern Germany in August and his opposition to the U.S. strategy on Iraq. The start of Schröder's period of office was marred by allegations that he had defrauded the electorate by concealing damaging news about the state of the economy and by the announcement of **taxation** increases designed to bring a spiraling domestic budget under control. Schröder staked his credibility on the success of a radical program of reform of the labor market and social welfare that attracted fierce opposition from his party's left wing. The program, **Agenda 2010**, was announced in March 2003 and was intended to lay the foundations for a restructured and economically stronger Germany by 2010. At the same time, the SPD suffered a series of defeats in regional state elections, largely due to a continuing economic downturn. Faced with popular anger over **health**-care and welfare cuts, opposition within the SPD over the reform program, an all-time low in public opinion polls, and the prospect of further defeat in local and regional elections, Schröder announced his resignation as party chairman in February 2004 (he was succeeded by **Franz Müntefering**). Following a catastrophic defeat for the SPD in regional elections in **North Rhine-Westfalia** (May 2005) and splits within the red/green coalition, Schröder controversially engineered a vote of no confidence in the Bundestag the following July in order to force national elections and win a stronger mandate for his reform program. The strategy backfired, and the election of 18 September 2005 returned a virtually hung parliament. Schröder resigned when the SPD agreed to form a national coalition with the CDU. In December 2005, shortly after signing a deal for the Russian gas company Gazprom to supply gas to Germany, he faced criticism for accepting a lucrative post as chairman of the concern's shareholders' committee, especially after it emerged that his government had guaranteed a large credit to the company; he is currently chairman of the shareholders' committee of Nord Stream AG, in which Gazprom has a majority stake.

In May 2001, Schröder argued for a federal Europe, with closer integration of economic, social, and **foreign policy**, and for a stronger European Commission and parliament. Amid signs of increasing popular support for extreme right-wing politicians in France and the Netherlands, he reaffirmed the need for the **European Union (EU)** to counteract the emergence of nationalism by integrating and strengthening its institutions. But while other German leaders since 1949 had been content to act as paymasters of the EU and follow France's political leadership, Schröder appeared for a while to be more critical of EU institutions and of what he saw as their remoteness from citizens; in particular, he regarded the technocratic language and obfuscation of EU bureaucrats and their insensitivity to the concerns of national populations as contributing to the rise of the far right and allowing it to feed on anxieties over crime, unemployment, and immigration. More ready than his predecessors to champion German national interests, Schröder also questioned the size of Germany's contribution to the EU budget. He also joined with other states (Japan, Brazil, and India) in lobbying for a permanent seat on the **United Nations (UN)** Security Council, including a right of veto (2004). Schröder's involvement with Gazprom and relationship with the Russian leader Vladimir Putin—in particular his call in 2014 for Westerners to understand Russian support for Ukrainian separatists—has led both the German government and the SPD to distance themselves from the former chancellor.

SCHUMANN, ERICH (1930–2007). Publisher. Born in Nuremberg (**Bavaria**), Erich Schumann studied law and specialized in **taxation** (1950–1956) before becoming a senior partner in a commercial law firm in Bonn. After joining the **Social Democratic Party of Germany (SPD)** as a young man, he represented party members in court and at parliamentary committees of investigation and was a close adviser to Herbert Wehner (deputy chairman of the SPD [1958–1973] and a leading modernizer in the party) and Chancellor **Willy Brandt**. Schumann's career changed abruptly in 1978 when the cofounder of the WAZ **publishing** group, Erich Brost, brought him into the family concern, appointing him an executive partner (1985) and adopting him as his son and sole heir. Schumann and his adopted mother, Anneliese Brost (born in 1921), shared equal interests in half of the concern (the rest was controlled by the Funke family) and maintained close contacts with the SPD.

Together with the conservative Jakob Funke, Brost began publishing the *Westdeutsche Allgemeine Zeitung* (WAZ), which became the group's flagship, in Essen in 1948. The Funke family's interests were represented by Günther Grotkamp, with whom Schumann, despite a difficult relationship, worked closely to expand the concern into Germany's second largest and most profitable multimedia group (after the Axel **Springer** Verlag), with holdings in both newspapers and the broadcasting **media** (WAZ sold off a stake in RTL to **Bertelsmann AG** in 2005 but retained interests in numerous local radio stations in **North Rhine-Westfalia**). Schumann remained closely involved with the group until shortly before his death (2007). In 2013, the WAZ concern was renamed Funke Media Group, with the WAZ its largest newspaper.

Throughout his career with WAZ, Schumann avoided public attention, preferring to build up the group quietly from its unpretentious Essen headquarters. In 2000, he was expelled from the SPD for making a donation to former chancellor **Helmut Kohl**, who had accepted undeclared contributions to the **Christian Democratic Union (CDU)**. He was instrumental in setting up and funding the Erich Brost Institute for Journalism in Europe at the

University of Dortmund (1991), which aims to establish a network of training facilities for journalists throughout Europe, exchange students and staff, and develop new techniques of teaching and learning. Schumann has also served on and chaired the board of trustees for the Stiftung Deutsche Sporthilfe, a foundation for the promotion of **sports** in Germany (from 1991), and was a member of the presidium of the National Olympic Committee (1991–1996).

See also PRESS; PUBLISHING.

SCHUSTER, JOSEF (1954–). Jewish community leader. Josef Schuster's parents, whose roots date back to the 16th century in Lower Franconia (Unterfranken), fled from Germany to Palestine in 1938 but returned in 1956 with their son, who was born in Haifa. Schuster qualified as a doctor in Würzburg, where he has maintained his own practice since 1988. He also performs voluntary work for the Red Cross and serves on the **Bavarian** state Commission for Bioethics (Bioethik Kommission) and on the Central Ethics Commission for the German Medical Association (Bundesärztekammer).

In 1998, Schuster followed in his father's footsteps to become leader (chairman) of the Jewish community in Würzburg and in 2002 was also elected president of the association of Jewish communities in Bavaria (Landesverband der israelitischen Kultusgemeinden in Bayern). Vice president of the national **Central Council of Jews** (from 2010), he succeeded **Dieter Graumann** as president in November 2014. Following the attacks by Islamist extremists in Paris and Copenhagen (January/February 2015), Schuster stressed that there was no need for Jews to leave Germany (Israeli minister president Benjamin Netanyahu had called for Jews to emigrate from Europe).

SCHWARZER, ALICE (1942–). Publicist and feminist. Alice Sophie Schwarzer was born in Wuppertal-Elberfeld (**North Rhine-Westfalia**). She grew up with her grandparents, attended a commercial school (Handelsschule) in Elberfeld, and trained in commerce in Wuppertal before working as a secretary in Düsseldorf and for a publisher in Munich (1960–1963). After moving to Paris, where she financed her French studies through casual work, she returned to Germany in 1966 and trained for two years with the *Düsseldorfer Nachrichten*, covering **women**'s issues. In 1969, she worked briefly for the illustrated magazine *Moderne Frau* and the satirical magazine *Pardon* in Frankfurt/Main before moving back to Paris, where she studied psychology and sociology and worked as a freelance journalist (1970–1974). During this period, Schwarzer became actively involved in the radical French feminist movement. She interviewed the philosopher Jean Paul Sartre (1970) and, for over 10 years from 1972 onward, conducted a series of interviews with the writer Simone de Beauvoir, whose essay *The Other Sex* (1949) had become a seminal text for feminists. Following the example of French feminists, Schwarzer published an article in the *stern* magazine in which 374 women, many of them well-known figures, admitted to having had an **abortion** (1971). The article marked the start of a long campaign against German abortion laws. Her first book, *Frauen gegen den Paragraphen 218*, appeared in 1971; it describes how female members of a left-wing German student group, the **Federation of Socialist German Students** (**SDS**), rebelled against male domination within the organization.

Over the following years, Schwarzer published and broadcast widely, campaigning vigorously against the exploitation of women. In *Frauenarbeit—Frauenbefreiung* (1973), she drew attention to women's pay (or lack of it) at home and work, and in *Der kleine Unterschied und seine Folgen* (1975) described in interviews how sexuality was used as an instrument to oppress women. She coedited the annual *Frauenkalender* (1975) and founded her own **publishing** house, the Alice Schwarzer Verlags-GmbH (1976), based in Cologne (later renamed Emma Frauenverlags-GmbH). She helped establish and edited the feminist magazine *Emma* (1977), which she continues to use as a platform, and in 1983 cofounded an institute for social **research** in Hamburg (Hamburger Institut für Sozialforschung) and set up and chaired a feminist archive and documentation center (Frauen/MediaTurm) in Cologne. Elected to the **PEN** Club (1984), she also taught at the University of Münster (1974–1975) and gave lecture tours. Her other books include *Eine tödliche Liebe* (1993), which analyzed the suicide of the Green politicians **Petra Kelly** and Gert Bastian; *Romy Schneider. Mythos und Leben* (1998); *Der große Unterschied: Gegen die Spaltung von Menschen in Männer und Frauen* (2000); and *Marion Dönhoff: Ein widerspenstiges Leben* (2004). During the 1980s, Schwarzer became an icon of the feminist movement and later received numerous honors for her services. In recent years, she has been vocal about the role of women in Islam and has warned against an "Islamization of Europe" with regard to women's rights. In 2015, she ignited controversy by arguing (in an article in *Emma*) that political leaders should take public support for organizations such as Pegida seriously and appreciate that the source of the refugee problem in Europe lies in Islamic fundamentalism, which she called a "a new form of fascism."

SCHWESIG, MANUELA (1974–). Social Democratic Party of Germany (**SPD**) politician. Born in Frankfurt/Oder (**Brandenburg**), Manuela Schwesig studied finance in **Berlin** and qualified with a diploma (1992–1995) before working in the finance offices of the cities of Frankfurt/Oder (1992–2000) and Schwerin (**Mecklenburg-West Pomerania**, 2000–2002); between 2002 and 2008, she worked in the regional finance ministry. After joining the SPD in 2003, she represented her party in Schwerin city and district council between 2004 and 2008, where she specialized in family affairs and modernization of the administration and also headed the SPD parliamentary group (2007–2008). In the regional parliament (**Landtag**) for MWP, to which she was elected in 2011 (resigning in 2014), she served as minister, first for social affairs and **health** (2008–2011) and then for labor, equality, and social affairs (2011–2013) under **Minister President Erwin Sellering** (SPD). In 2013, she joined chancellor candidate **Peer Steinbrück**'s election campaign team and the following year was appointed federal minister for family affairs, senior citizens, **women,** and youth in Chancellor **Angela Merkel**'s third cabinet. Her positions in the SPD also include deputy regional leader for MWP and (2013–) and member of the national executive/deputy national leader (2013–).

SDS. *See* FEDERATION OF SOCIALIST GERMAN STUDENTS (SOZIA-LISTISCHER DEUTSCHER STUDENTENBUND, SDS).

SECURITY POLICY, EXTERNAL. Germany defines its external security and defense policy primarily in terms of ensuring the safety and interests of its own citizens, promoting peace and democracy, and working in partnership with its allies. It does not have a national defense strategy as such, but rather acts according to guidelines that stress, among other things, that military missions abroad are planned and conducted in concert with allies and partners, notably the **United Nations (UN)**, the **European Union (EU)**, and the **North Atlantic Treaty Organization (NATO)**—the "multilateralism doctrine." The Federal Defense Force (**Bundeswehr**) was able to participate in out-of-area military area operations only after the **Federal Constitutional Court (FCC)** ruled in 1994 that such activities did not violate the **Basic Law (BL)**, although they were still to be undertaken as a member of a collective security system and required **Bundestag** approval. Chancellor **Helmut Kohl** approved the first combat mission in April 1993, when German forces monitored the no-fly zone over Bosnia. The first serious exchange of fire occurred between German and Serbian soldiers in June 2012 in Kosovo, where the UN Mission, which began in 1999, has been widely regarded as a success.

The institutions and mechanisms for the external security of the EU have evolved over time, creating an alphabet soup of strategies, goals, and their acronyms. Following agreement on a **foreign policy** for the newly formed EU, embodied in the Common Foreign and Security Policy (CFSP, in force with the Maastricht Treaty of 1993), the Helsinki European Council of 1999 agreed to a European Security and Defense Policy (ESDP), which provided for a defense capability comprising a rapid reaction force of 60,000 troops for crisis management, peacekeeping, and peacemaking missions (the so-called Helsinki Headline Goal, HHG). The ESDP was specifically designed to strengthen the EU's ability to act autonomously and independently of

NATO. The European Security Strategy (ESS, drawn up in 2003 and reviewed in 2008) identified a range of threats to European security (the spread of weapons of mass destruction, **terrorism**, regional conflicts, state failure, organized crime, cyber security, **energy** security, and climate change). Central to the ESS was the so-called Solana doctrine of "effective multilateralism." In 2004, the HHG was revised to enable the deployment of smaller, more flexible European battle groups delivered by single nations or groups of nations (designated the Headline Goal 2010). With the Lisbon Treaty (ratified in 2009), the ESDP was renamed the Common Security and Defense Policy (CSDP) which, while changing the mechanisms of decision making, retained the condition that deployments required the unanimous (multilateral) support of all member states. Especially during the early years, Germany fitted into this framework as a fully committed and reliable partner.

By 2013, the EU had completed 13 civilian and military missions and was engaged in a further 17. In the same year, Germany was participating in 11 missions and deploying more than 6,500 troops in the Balkans, Afghanistan, and the Horn of Africa. Military deployments could be controversial within Germany or even rejected outright. When Chancellor **Gerhard Schröder** refused to join the U.S.-led invasion of Iraq in 2003, **Angela Merkel**, then CDU opposition leader, argued that Germany should support its American allies. As the goals for German engagement (building civil society) in even the quieter area of northern Afghanistan from 2001 proved unrealistic, popular resistance to the mission increased, and Germany did not participate in missions in Libya (2011) and Mali (2013). Foreign Minister **Guido Westerwelle**, who in 2009 unsuccessfully argued for the removal of nuclear weapons from German soil and whose party opposed the Bundestag's decision in 2006 to deploy warships off the Lebanese coast, repeatedly referred to Germany's "culture of military restraint." While Germany acted in close concert with its major European partner, France, to shape EU security policy after 1993, during the following decade it distanced itself from its former closest partner and the instruments of CSDP, leaving initiatives on military involvement (in Libya and the Middle East) to France and Great Britain, who signed a 50-year mutual defense cooperation treaty in November 2010. This profound change in German policy reflected new, domestic priorities in decision making: Schröder's party was facing elections in two **federal states** in the year of the Iraq invasion, while Merkel did not wish to lose public support to the FDP (who strongly resisted Libyan involvement) in 2011. Overall, Germany felt no longer obliged to serve unconditionally the interests of its partners, especially when the supposed aims of intervention served no national gain. Disappointing as this change appeared to allies and suggesting as it did a lack of strategic direction, it contrasted sharply with Germany's leadership in the **eurozone crisis**, where its economic interests were at stake.

As the United States considers shifting its own and NATO's security focus away from Europe to Asia and the Pacific, Germany may also feel that its national interests diverge increasingly from the traditional paradigm.

See also SECURITY POLICY, INTERNAL.

SECURITY POLICY, INTERNAL. With the exception of the massacre of 11 Israeli athletes by the Palestinian Black September organization during the 1972 Munich Olympics, Germany's laws on internal security policy in the 1970s and 1980s were largely shaped in response to attacks, bombings, and kidnappings by domestic **terrorist** groups such as the **Red Army Faction**. Despite occasional challenges in the **Federal Constitutional Court** (**FCC**) and amendments, these laws, many of which are still in force, encountered little opposition from the public or the **Bundestag**. At the same time, the role and resources of the Bundeskriminalamt (federal criminal police office, BKA) were greatly expanded. Legislation provided for increased powers of surveillance and eavesdropping, restrictions on access to defense lawyers (who were suspected of collaborating with terrorists), and incommunicado detention. After members of a radical Islamist group in Germany (the "**Hamburg** Cell") were identified as involved in the 9/11 attacks of 2001, the authorities focused on foreign threats to internal security, especially from the Arab world. Measures included two security packets (Sicherheitspakete, 2001 and 2002, time-limited but renewed until 2015), which criminalized membership in and support of foreign terrorist organizations (this could now also encompass religious groups), increased powers of surveillance and data gathering (particularly of **foreigners** and **asylum** seekers), and enabled the state more easily to expel non-national suspects. Computer-based profiling or grid search techniques (Rasterfahndung), originally developed by the BKA in the 1970s for preventive identification purposes, were extended to cover over eight million people in several **federal states** (2002). In any case, the operation proved futile and was scaled down following a challenge in the FCC. Further instruments, some of which have been subject to FCC amendments, include the introduction of a biometric passport (2005); an integrated cross-agency database (Anti-Terror-Datei, ATD, 2006); and the preventive storage of telephone, mobile, and **Internet** access metadata (2008). In 2009, attending terrorist training camps abroad and financing and storing explosives for terror activities became illegal.

In a 2006 white paper, the federal defense ministry (Bundesministerium für Verteidigung) introduced the term "networked security" ("vernetzte Sicherheit," commonly known in English as the "comprehensive approach") to refer to the integration of national and foreign resources to combat security threats. A leading proponent of this approach, Germany set up two new institutions to improve on but not override the activities of existing agencies: the Gemeinsames Terrorismusabwehrzentrum (Joint Counterterrorism Center, GTAZ, established 2004) and the Gemeinsames Analyse- und Strategie-zentrum illegale Migration (Joint Center for Illegal Migration Analysis and Policy, GASIM, 2006) to combat illegal **immigration**. In 2012, the GTAZ was subsumed into the Gemeinsames Extremismus- und Terrorismusabwehr-zentrum (Joint Center for Countering Extremism and Terrorism, GETZ). These initiatives neither altered the mandates of their member institutions nor violated the German law separating police from intelligence services (the so-called Trennunsgebot). More controversial was the further expansion of the preventive security powers of the BKA, which hitherto lay with the police forces of the federal states and now required a change to the **Basic Law (BL)**. Although members of the **Christian Democratic Union (CDU)** and **Social Democratic Party of Germany (SPD)** coalition government had by 2007 both agreed on a new law in principle, the SPD, led by Justice Minister **Brigitte Zypries**, opposed proposals by Interior Minister **Wolfgang Schäuble** (CDU) to permit online searches of individuals' computers. Disputes also arose over the extent of surveillance measures. After a tortuous process involving the FCC and mediation between the Bundestag and **Bundesrat**, the new law came into effect in 2009, permitting online searches subject to judicial approval. Since 2001, security measures have been extended beyond suspected terrorists to affect activities of the civilian population as a whole. The measures have proved controversial in light of revelations that the German authorities have shared data on citizens with the U.S. National Security Agency (NSA), which also spied on heads of state, including Chancellor **Angela Merkel**. In an action reminiscent of the *Spiegel* affair (1962), the German authorities in 2015 began investigating two Berlin journalists, André Meister and Markus Beckedahl, on suspicion of treason for releasing state secrets (on the news website netzpolitik.org) about plans for setting up a new government unit to monitor the Internet and social networks. Following an outcry from politicians and the **media**, Germany's chief prosecutor, Harald Range, suspended the investigation (in July 2015) pending an internal inquiry, but he was criticized for pursuing the journalists so soon after abandoning proceedings into the NSA's activities in Germany and was eventually dismissed by the justice minister, **Heiko Maas**.

SEEHOFER, HORST (1949–). Christian Social Union (CSU) politician. Horst Seehofer was born in Ingolstadt (**Bavaria**) and qualified in management and administration at the Verwaltungs- und Wirtschaftsakademie in Munich (1979). A member of the youth wing (**Junge Union, JU**) of the CSU from 1969, he joined the main party in 1971. A deputy in the **Bundestag** (1980–2008), he was CSU spokesman on social affairs (1983–1989) and parliamentary **state secretary** to the federal minister of labor and social affairs, **Norbert Blüm** (1989–1992), before serving as federal minister of **health** in the coalition government under Chancellor **Helmut Kohl** during

1992–1998. His efforts to reform the German health-care system and control its spiraling costs met with fierce opposition from the vested interests of medical practitioners and insurance funds. As health minister, he also presided over a scandal that emerged in 1993, when blood destined for transfusions was found to be HIV-contaminated. Despite these setbacks, he retained an image as a competent modernizer and questioned the abilities of the Bavarian minister president, **Max Streibl**, who was forced to resign (May 1993) following allegations that he, along with other leading politicians, had made long-distance journeys paid for by private companies (the "Amigo-affair"). Other offices he held included vice chairman of the CSU (1994–2008) and deputy leader of the CSU parliamentary group (1998–2004). In January 2002, Seehofer fell seriously ill with a heart complaint, but he returned to active politics later in the year to support the chancellor candidate, **Edmund Stoiber**, in the national election campaign. In November 2004, he resigned as deputy leader of the CDU/CSU parliamentary group following differences with his party over health policy and a decision by the CSU to detach health from his social policy remit. As minister for **agriculture** in the first coalition cabinet of **Angela Merkel** (2005–2008), he was expected to represent the social concerns of the CSU in the new government. Succeeding Stoiber as party leader (2008), he was elected **minister president** of Bavaria the same year (reelected 2013). Adopting generally right-wing positions on political and economic issues, Seehofer opposed **immigration** from outside the **European Union (EU)**, initially opposed the withdrawal from nuclear **energy** (changing his mind after the Fukushima disaster in 2011), and argued for restrictions on wind energy installations (2013). In 2015, he criticized Merkel's opening of Germany's borders to refugees from the Middle East as "a mistake that will preoccupy us for a long time" and led his party into conflict with its governing coalition partner over **asylum policy**.

SELLERING, ERWIN (1949–). Social Democratic Party of Germany (SPD) politician. Born in Sprockhövel, near Bochum, Erwin Sellering studied law at the University of Heidelberg (from 1969). He qualified for legal practice between 1975 and 1978 and was appointed a judge (in Gelsenkirchen in 1981) and a senior judge (in Greifswald in 1994). A member of the SPD from 1994, he joined its regional executive committee in **Mecklenburg-West Pomerania** in 1997, which he chaired from 2007. During 1998–2000, he also headed the state chancellery in the regional capital, Schwerin, before becoming minister of justice (2000–2006) in the SPD/**Party of Democratic Socialism (PDS)** coalition under **Harald Ringstorff (SPD)** following the election of 1998. Sellering entered the regional assembly (**Landtag**) as a deputy in the 2006 election, which brought to power a **grand coalition** of SPD/**Christian Democratic Union (CDU)**, in which he served as social affairs and **health** minister (2006–2008). When Ringstorff resigned in 2008, Sellering took over as **minister president** and was re-elected, continuing the coalition, in 2011. In 2014, during the Ukraine crisis, he attracted controversy by visiting Russia to promote economic links for his region at the same time that the German government was officially distancing itself from President Vladimir Putin's policies.

SIEMENS AG. The story of the Siemens concern began in **Berlin** in October 1847, when Werner von Siemens, together with Johann Georg Halske, cofounded a company (the Telegraphen-Bauanstalt von Siemens & Halske) to exploit their two key inventions: a new type of telegraph and the first electric dynamo. A brilliant entrepreneur, Siemens thus laid the foundation for what is now one of the largest electrical and electronic **engineering** concerns in the world. In the 1970s, the company extended its markets in the United States, Western Europe, and Asia. In the 1990s, the company restructured divisions and shifted focus away from public clients in regulated markets in order to become globally more competitive. At the same time, Siemens simplified its portfolio through acquisitions, disinvestments, and joint ventures (including withdrawing from semiconductor production); expanded strongly in eastern Europe; and identified the Asian-Pacific region as a key future market.

Based in Munich and Berlin, Siemens AG, along with **Daimler** and **Volkswagen**, is one of Germany's largest concerns in terms of workforce (around 348,000 employees in more than 200 countries) and turnover (75,600 million euros in 2015). With an estimated 150 members, the Siemens family is the largest single shareholder in the concern (6 percent), although its direct influence on operational management has declined over the years. The company's main activities are **energy** (power generation and transmission), health care (audiology, clinical products, diagnostics and imaging, and therapy systems), **industry**, and infrastructure and cities (building technologies, low and medium voltage, mobility and logistics, **rail** and grid systems). The company's reputation was marred in 2005 by the controversial sale of its mobile phone division, which subsequently went bankrupt, and in 2007 it was fined by the commission of the **European Union (EU)** for leading a cartel that fixed the market for equipment in electricity substations. Senior executives also lost their jobs following revelations of long-standing bribes, mainly paid to foreign clients. Joe (Josef) Kaeser, appointed chief executive in 2013, undertook a further reorganization in order to bring more decision making back to the Munich headquarters. In 2014, Kaeser controversially visited President Vladimir Putin to reaffirm his company's commitment to continuing business with Russia—a move that irritated the German and other

Western governments critical of Russian support for separatists in Ukraine but also exposed the unwillingness of other German business leaders to compromise their economic interests.

SIMONIS, HEIDE (1943–). Social Democratic Party of Germany (SPD) politician. Born in Bonn, Heide Simonis (née Steinhardt) studied economics and sociology at the universities of Erlangen, Nuremberg, and Kiel, where she graduated with a diploma (1967). After teaching German for a year at the University of Lusaka (Zambia, 1967–1968), she moved to Tokyo, where she worked for the national television and radio service and taught German for the **Goethe Institute** (1970–1971) before joining Fa. Triumph International as a market researcher. Returning to Germany, she worked as a career adviser at the employment office in Kiel until 1976. A member of the SPD from 1969, Simonis served on the Kiel local executive committee (1972–1976) and the city council/assembly (1971–1976). In 1976, she entered the **Bundestag**, playing an active role in the parliamentary party group, serving on its executive committee and as a spokeswoman on budgetary affairs. A member of the SPD federal executive committee (1988–1991), she was elected to the national executive (1988–1991 and 1993–2005). Appointed regional finance minister in Schleswig-Holstein (1988), she was elected to the **Landtag** (1992) and became deputy to Minister President **Björn Engholm** (March 1993).

Following Engholm's resignation (May 1993), Simonis succeeded him as premier, the first female **minister president** in the history of the Federal Republic of Germany (FRG). She was twice reelected (1996, 2000), on both occasions forming a coalition with the **Alliance 90/The Greens**. Following a single seat difference with the opposition **Christian Democratic Union (CDU)** in the regional election of February 2005, attempts by Simonis and her party to form a coalition with the Greens were frustrated by the refusal of a mystery SPD member to support her election as minister president, and she eventually withdrew. In April, the CDU and SPD eventually agreed to a **grand coalition** with **Peter Harry Carstensen** (CDU) as premier. The disappointing result for the SPD was seen as a punishment by the electorate for the party's failure to cut unemployment (over five million nationally, and above average levels in Schleswig-Holstein); the state was also heavily in debt. After the events of 2005, Simonis withdrew from political office, but she was widely praised for her contribution to politics in Schleswig-Holstein and went on to become honorary president of UNICEF Germany (2005–2008), focusing on its Schools for Africa Project.

SINDERMANN, HORST (1915–1990). German Democratic Republic (GDR) politician. Born in Dresden (**Saxony**), Horst Sindermann joined a communist youth organization, the Kommunistischer Jugendverband Deutschlands (KJVD), while still attending school (1921–1933). During the National Socialist period (1933–1945), he was repeatedly imprisoned in concentration camps, including Sachsenhausen and Mauthausen. In 1945, he joined the Communist Party of Germany (KPD) and worked as chief editor for various party newspapers in eastern Germany. These included the *Sächsische Volkszeitung* (Dresden, 1945–1947), the *Volksstimme* (Chemnitz), and *Freiheit* (Halle, 1950–1953). He headed the agitation and propaganda department attached to the Central Committee of the **Socialist Unity Party of Germany** (**SED**, 1954–1963) and later became a member of the Central Committee (candidate from 1958 and full member in 1963) and of the Politburo (candidate in 1963 and full member from 1967). His other positions included member of the **People's Chamber** (from 1964) and deputy chairman (1971–1973), subsequently chairman (1973–1976), of the Ministerrat (Council of Ministers). He was also president of the People's Chamber and deputy chairman of the Staatsrat (Council of State, 1975–1989). During the November revolution of 1989, Sindermann was removed from all positions in the Central Committee, the Politburo, and the Council of State. He resigned as president of the People's Chamber (13 November) and was expelled from the SED (December). During January/February 1990, he was held in investigative detention, but was released shortly afterward on health grounds.

SINTI AND ROMA. *See* ETHNIC MINORITIES: SINTI AND ROMA.

SOCIAL DEMOCRATIC PARTY IN THE GDR (SOZIALDEMOKRATISCHE PARTEI IN DER DDR, SDP). After its forced merger with the Communist Party of Germany (KPD) in the Soviet-occupied zone in 1946, the historic **Social Democratic Party of Germany** (SPD) ceased to exist in eastern Germany, which became the **German Democratic Republic** (**GDR**) from October 1949. Following the collapse of the regime in October 1989, the party was formally reestablished in East **Berlin** as the Social Democratic Party in the GDR. Founding members were Angelika Barbe, Markus Meckel, Arndt Noack, Stephan Hilsberg, and **Ibrahim Böhme** (who became its leader). The party was renamed SPD (DDR) on 13 January 1990. Although it hoped to increase its membership by virtue of its historical appeal to social democracy, the SPD (DDR) relied heavily on its West German sister party for resources and personnel in the run-up to the election to the **People's Chamber** on 18 March. It merged with the SPD on 27 September 1990.

See also POLITICAL PARTIES.

SOCIAL DEMOCRATIC PARTY OF GERMANY (SOZIALDEMOK-RATISCHE PARTEI DEUTSCHLANDS, SPD). The SPD was founded in 1863 as the General German Workers' Association (Allgemeiner Deutscher Arbeiterverein). The oldest of Germany's **political parties**, the SPD was seen as an enemy of the state by Otto von Bismarck, voted in the Reichstag for money to conduct World War I (1914), played a leading role in the Weimar Republic (1919–1933), but then was banned, its members persecuted by the National Socialists. Reconstituted in 1945, the SPD opposed German rearmament and integration in the West on the grounds that such moves would hinder reunification. Although its hostility to the **social market economy** kept it in opposition for two decades, the SPD was a powerful and effective advocate of social and economic justice when **Konrad Adenauer** of the **Christian Democratic Union (CDU)** was **federal chancellor** (1949–1963). After committing itself to the postwar Western economic and political order in its Godesberg Program of 1959, the party broadened its electoral appeal. It entered the government in the Federal Republic of Germany (FRG) for the first time in 1966, forming a **grand coalition** with the CDU (1966–1969) and subsequently a majority coalition with the **Free Democratic Party (FDP,** 1969–1982).

Under Chancellors **Willy Brandt** (1969–1974) and **Helmut Schmidt** (1974–1982), the SPD pursued a policy of rapprochement with the eastern bloc states **(Ostpolitik)**, stabilized the FRG's relationship with the **German Democratic Republic (GDR)**, and embarked on far-reaching reforms in society and **education**. In 1982, the social democrats were forced back into opposition following a dispute with their coalition partners, the FDP, over economic policy. After the collapse of the GDR regime and weakened by leadership disputes, the party lost public support by advocating a slow-track approach to reunification during 1989–1990. Conflicts over **asylum** policy, the privatization of **industry** in eastern Germany, and the deployment of the **Bundeswehr** in peacekeeping operations further damaged the party's standing. In its 1989 Berlin Program, considered to be the SPD's most significant statement of basic policy values since 1959, the party stressed the importance of linking economic development with ecology, the value of equal rights for men and **women** in all areas of life, and the need to recognize unpaid work (at home, in the family, or caring for a relative); it also argued for an end to the arms race and for a fairer world order for poorer nations. The West German SPD incorporated the reconstituted **Social Democratic Party of the GDR** in September 1990.

Reelected in 1998, the SPD formed a coalition government with the **Green Party**. Led by Chancellor **Gerhard Schröder**, the coalition pledged to tackle unemployment and phase out nuclear **energy**. Reelected again in 2002, the coalition faced the problems of economic downturn, continuing unemployment, and a budgetary crisis. A decade after reunification, the social democrats had also failed to turn the **eastern federal states** into an electoral stronghold. At the end of 2003, the SPD was in ruling coalitions with the **Party of Democratic Socialism (PDS, in Mecklenburg-West Pomerania)** and the CDU (**Brandenburg**) but was in opposition in **Saxony, Saxony-Anhalt**, and **Thuringia**. In local elections (June 2004), the SPD lost heavily to the PDS, which emerged as the second political force in the eastern states. By refusing to admit former members of the **Socialist Unity Party of Germany (SED)**, the SPD had arguably excluded many reform-minded intellectuals at a time when few politicians from the east had succeeded in developing a national profile. Schröder's **Agenda 2010** reform program was also widely perceived as offering little to eastern Germans. In July 2004, an alliance of left-wing members of the party and **trade unions** was formed to resist the program. The group, led by **Oskar Lafontaine**, eventually broke away from the SPD and constituted the **Election Alternative for Labor and Justice (WASG)** to contest regional elections in partnership with the PDS. The divisions in the main party, in particular over Agenda 2010 as membership hemorrhaged, deeply unsettled both members and leaders. Although the SPD engineered a premature election in 2005 in order to reestablish party discipline and emerged as junior partner in a grand coalition with the CDU, it failed to rebuild a convincing leadership, was consistently outmaneuvered by Chancellor **Angela Merkel**, and lost heavily in the following elections; its 23 percent of the national vote in 2009 was the lowest for a major party in the history of the FRG and did not improve much in 2013/2014 (25 percent). At the same time, a new leadership under **Sigmar Gabriel** (party chairman) and **Andrea Nahles** (general secretary), promoting a left-wing policy agenda (including a minimum wage, pensions at age 63, and extended child-care benefits for parents who worked part-time), brought it political successes at the regional level and enabled it to return as coalition partner with the CDU in 2013.

In terms of members (its main source of income), the SPD has traditionally been Germany's largest party: in 1976 membership peaked at a record 1,022,191, after which it fell steadily to below 500,000 in 2011, the lowest level since 1906, and only marginally higher than the CDU. In late 2014, total membership dropped to 460,000, with many resignations in Thuringia, where the SPD agreed to become the junior partner in a coalition with the controversial **The Left Party**. Compared with the general population, the membership is dominated by males, Protestants, civil servants, public sector employees, and trade union members. Like the CDU, the SPD is well organized at the national and regional levels and has 12,000 local branches. Following reforms in 2011 designed to improve internal democracy, the party abolished its highest body, the 17-member presidium (Präsidium), slimmed down the national executive committee (Vorstand) from 45 to 35 members (elected every two years) and established a party convention (Parteikonvent). The convention's 200 delegates meet at least twice yearly and constitute the highest decision-making body, linking the national party congress (Bundesparteitag) and the regional organizations. The changes proved controversial, however, and there were moves to restore the presidium. The national congress (around 500 delegates) elects the executive committee, party leader/chairman, and general secretary. A party council (Parteirat), made up of 90 elected representatives from the regions and advisers, coordinates the work of the party across the country and provides input to the national executive. The SPD maintains a large number of working groups on social, political, and economic issues in the **Bundestag**, and it has an active youth wing, the **Young Socialists** (**JUSOS**). The Friedrich-Ebert Stiftung (Friedrich Ebert Foundation), which dates from 1925, has close links with the party and is Germany's oldest political foundation. It supports political education and young researchers and promotes international cooperation.

The SPD leaders since 1946 have been Kurt Schumacher (1946–1952), Erich Ollenhauer (1952–1963/64), Willy Brandt (1964–1987), **Hans-Jochen Vogel** (1987–1991), **Björn Engholm** (1991–1993), **Johannes Rau** (acting 1993), **Rudolf Scharping** (1993–1995), Oskar Lafontaine (1995–1999), Gerhard Schröder (1999–2004), **Franz Müntefering** (2004–2005, 2008–2009), **Matthias Platzeck** (2005–2006), **Kurt Beck** (2006–2008), **Frank-Walter Steinmeier** (2008), and Sigmar Gabriel (2009–). In 2014, Yasmin Fahimi succeeded Andrea Nahles as interim general secretary, a post created in 1999; Katerina Barley was elected to the position in December 2015. The frequent changes in leadership between 2004 and 2009 were a response to a decline in the party's electoral appeal as it struggled to retain its core supporters. It was widely seen as lacking strategic direction and as internally divided between reformists hoping to rebuild its centrist appeal and traditionalists wanting to renew links with the trade unions.

SOCIAL DEMOCRATS. *See* SOCIAL DEMOCRATIC PARTY OF GERMANY (SOZIALDEMOKRATISCHE PARTEI DEUTSCHLANDS, SPD).

SOCIAL MARKET ECONOMY (SOZIALE MARKTWIRTSCHAFT). In a social market economy, a competition-based capitalist system is subject to state interventions that are designed, on the one hand, to protect the freedoms of actors in both supplying and demanding goods and services in an open market, and on the other hand, to ensure a degree of social equity and security for the vulnerable. The model, which originated in the 1930s, was articulated most clearly after World War II by German economists such as Alfred Müller-Armack, who coined the term, and **Ludwig Erhard**, West

Germany's first economics minister. Arguing that unfettered capitalism had contributed to the wars and political upheavals of the 20th century, they promoted the social market economy as a basis for rebuilding the West German economy without reverting to state dirigisme. The term does not appear in the **Basic Law (BL)**, which does not consider the economy separately, but it was incorporated in the Treaty on Unification (1990) between the Federal Republic of Germany (FRG) and the **German Democratic Republic (GDR)** as the basis of Germany's common economic order. The model also informed the policies of the **European Union (EU)** and its precursors in attempting to provide the right conditions for developing balanced economies in member states. Although Germany is widely seen as a successful implementation of a balanced, socially benign, yet free market economy that has been described as welfare capitalism, it has faced typical problems of cyclical up- and downturns in economic performance and the dilemma of how far and in what ways the state should intervene to both promote growth and maintain standards of social welfare.

See also ECONOMIC DEVELOPMENT (FRG) 1949–1969.

SOCIAL SECURITY SYSTEM. The legal basis of Germany's system of state social security (soziale Sicherung), which includes provisions for **health** care, accident insurance, invalid care, unemployment income, and old-age **pensions**, was established by the Reichsversicherungsordnung (RVO) legislation of 1911. Conceived when industrialization had produced extremes of wealth and poverty, the RVO worked effectively to provide a social net for workers and served as a model for other countries. The framework underwent numerous revisions but survived in essence until after World War II, when calls to harmonize welfare entitlements in a single comprehensible and accessible document resulted in the publication of the social security law codex (Sozialgesetzbuch, SGB) of 1975. The first section of the codex emphasized the state's commitment to a fair, adequate, and generally available system of welfare, which included services for illness, motherhood, invalidity, and financial security in old age. It thus continued the German tradition of social partnership between the state and its people, and the model thrived as benefits rose in line with a prospering postwar **social market economy**. The "equivalence principle" (contributions and benefits are linked to income) sat alongside the "solidarity principle" (persons unable to contribute are entitled to benefits). The system traditionally comprises three pillars of service provision: statutory social insurance (gesetzliche Sozialversicherung), social support (soziale Versorgung), and welfare benefits (Sozialfürsorge).

Statutory social insurance includes health or medical insurance (Krankenversicherung, with services delivered by health insurance funds, the Krankenkassen), pension insurance (Rentenversicherung, with pensions paid out by a variety of funds depending on the nature of the employment), accident insurance (Unfallversicherung), health/nursing care insurance (Pflegeversicherung, introduced in 1994 and administered by the Krankenkassen), and unemployment insurance (Arbeitslosenversicherung). While medical care (treatment and drugs) is delivered regardless of previous payments, pension, unemployment, and sickness benefits depend on income levels, with adjustments made for dependents and family members. Apart from accident insurance (which is paid for by the employer at a rate of around 2 percent of salary), statutory social insurance is financed through annually set percentage deductions from wages and salaries (Sozialabgaben), with matched contributions from the employer. The combined joint contributions (Beitragssätze) are triggered at a minimum level of income (around 450 euros per month from 2015; below this only the employer contributes), vary for each type of insurance (ranging in 2015 from between 2 and 3 percent for nursing care and unemployment to 14.6 percent for health and 18.7 percent for pensions), and are fixed beyond a certain ceiling (the Beitragsbemessungsgrenze). The ceiling itself also varies according to insurance type and is determined each year by the central government according to average wage levels. The limit is set slightly higher than the level at which an earner may opt for private health insurance (the Versicherungspflichtgrenze) and, for some insurance types (pensions and unemployment), is currently lower for the **eastern federal states**. Total contributions for employees average 20 percent of gross income.

Social support (soziale Versorgung) is available to victims of war or violence, but it also includes child benefits (including, in some **federal states**, help for educating children, so-called Kinder- und Erziehungsgeld), subsidies for accommodation (Wohngeld), and help toward schooling and further **education** (Bundesausbildungsförderung, available partly as a subsidy and partly as a loan). Social services are financed from general **taxation**, and payments in many cases are means-tested, that is, dependent on income.

Welfare benefits (Sozialfürsorge) consist primarily of social assistance (Sozialhilfe), which is intended to provide basic and temporary financial support in times of special need (including incapacity, illness, old age, or impecunity), where other benefits are not available. Since 2005, this allowance, for those capable of work, has been combined with unemployment benefits (Arbeitslosenhilfe) and renamed "unemployment benefit II" (Arbeitslosengeld II, or simply Sozialgeld) as part of the so-called Hartz IV package of reforms initiated by the **Hartz Commission**. Where unemployment benefits from the statutory insurance scheme (Arbeitslosengeld, or Arbeitslosengeld I) fail to meet a basic level of service (Grundsicherung), which is generally the case in low-paid jobs, it is supplemented by Arbeitslosengeld II. For those on low pensions, the chronically ill, and certain categories of children, the original Sozialhilfe element continues to apply. Welfare benefits, whose levels are calculated according to the general cost of living and average wages, are continually adjusted and normally paid out by local districts and authorities. Special assistance for young people (Jugendhilfe) is administered by local youth offices and recognized welfare organizations.

The range of benefits was extended from the 1960s onward to include previously disadvantaged groups, such as adults raising children, the bereaved, and caregivers. The sharpest increases in welfare spending occurred between 1965 and 1975 and after reunification (1990–1996), with levels remaining fairly constant thereafter (around 29 percent of GDP in 2015). Within the total social budget, however, family benefits, especially for children, have risen disproportionately, while relative spending on the unemployed has fallen. In 2015, the largest single items were pensions (31 percent) and health care (25 percent); unemployment accounted for just 3 percent. In response to economic uncertainty, demographic changes (an aging population), and the rising cost of medical treatments, Germany's social security system has been subject to far-reaching structural reforms, many of which, especially in health care and pensions, involve introducing or increasing an element of private contribution ("citizens' insurance" or Bürgerversicherung).

See also AGENDA 2010; RÜRUP COMMISSION.

SOCIAL WELFARE SYSTEM. *See* SOCIAL SECURITY SYSTEM.

SOCIALIST REALISM. In contrast to the West, where writers and artists found it comparatively easy to draw on new intellectual developments, the **German Democratic Republic (GDR)** set rigid limits to artistic license. The officially approved style and direction of art, **architecture**, music, and **literature** was that of "socialist realism," which originated in a decision taken by the Communist Party of the Union of Soviet Socialist Republics (USSR) in April 1934 to lay down guidelines for artistic method and content. These required authors and artists to depict their subjects in a realistic manner and to stress the advantages of socialism and the socialist revolution in overcoming injustice or other negative features of the (capitalist) world. Their figures were workers, revolutionaries, or party members, who were presented as positive role models. The world of work and technology began to feature strongly. Socialist realism was adopted as the officially approved style in postwar eastern Germany after 1945. One of the main architectural examples in this period was the monumental Stalinallee in East Berlin (later renamed Karl-Marx Allee), showcasing an ambitious project that did, however, contribute to the unrest among the workers in 1953. Socialist realism was reinforced in the **Bitterfeld Way** and through propaganda and censorship. Not until 1964 did the ruling **Socialist Unity Party of Germany (SED)**

allow artists some leeway in adopting a more individual or personal approach that took account of new tendencies that had emerged in the work of certain painters after 1956 (such as Willi Sitte, Bernhard Heisig, Wolfgang Mattheuer, and Werner Tübke). Socialist realism should be seen in contrast to the contemporary West German "informal internationalism."

In 1971, the East German leader **Erich Honecker** encouraged artists to interpret socialist realism as a method, not as a fixed style—not least in order to gain greater international recognition for the GDR within the context of the **Ostpolitik** treaties concluded with the Federal Republic of Germany (FRG). As a result, a debate ensued about the relationship between individual aspirations and the norms of society. In the late 1970s, the old terminology of "socialist content," the "party line," and "representation of the people" once again became a focus of discussion. The early 1980s thus saw a division emerging in the GDR between official art as dictated by the state (and rewarded by exhibitions abroad) and the work of those who refused to identify with the state and preferred to retain their artistic autonomy. At the same time, some artists created their own variants of socialist realism—with influences from new objectivity, late impressionism, or even the baroque and the Renaissance. After reunification, the debate about Staatskunst (art dictated and financed by the state) in the GDR was highly polemical, but eventually, with the West German market in mind, questions were raised about the doubtful independence of art that was too closely oriented to the pressures of the market in the West.

SOCIALIST UNITY PARTY OF GERMANY (SOZIALISTISCHE EINHEITSPARTEI DEUTSCHLANDS, SED). The SED was the ruling socialist party of the former **German Democratic Republic (GDR)**. It was created through a forced merger of the **Social Democratic Party of Germany (SPD)** and the Communist Party of Germany (KPD) in the Soviet occupation zone (April 1946). The SED maintained a façade of democratic structures, including a national parliament (the **People's Chamber**) and a multiparty system, while at the same time controlling these through its own party institutions and the approval of appointments, not to mention the secret police, the **Stasi**, founded in 1950 as the party's "shield and sword" (Schild und Schwert der Partei). The first nominal party leaders were the communist Wilhelm Pieck and social democrat Otto Grotewohl (joint co-chairman from 1946 to 1954), although real power lay in the hands of **Walter Ulbricht**, general secretary of the party's central committee from 1950, retitled first secretary from 1953. When Ulbricht fell into disfavor, he was succeeded by **Erich Honecker** (first secretary 1971–1976, renamed general secretary from 1976). Final leaders in the dying days of the regime were **Egon Krenz** (general secretary 18 October–6 December 1989) and **Gregor Gysi** (chairman 9–17 December 1989).

Strictly organized in a vertical pyramidal structure, from a decision-making central committee and politburo at the top—where major policy changes were determined and usually announced at a party congress (Parteitag)—down to a "base organization" (Basisorganisation) of members at the grassroots level, the SED underwent various stages of development, notably during the Ulbricht era. After redefining itself as a Marxist-Leninist "new type" party (1950), there followed two years of purges of, among others, social democrats and veteran communists with historical links to the West. The death of the Soviet leader Josef Stalin (1953) and uncertainty over his successor unnerved the SED, eventually prompting a "new course" (Neuer Kurs) and economic concessions to the people, although the workers' uprising of 1953 triggered Soviet military intervention and a fresh wave of repression. Under the guise of "collective leadership" (kollektive Führung, 1954) and partly against the background of events in Poland and Hungary, Ulbricht finally eliminated his opponents in the leadership (1957–1961), and in 1958 he felt confident enough to declare the "completion of the building of socialism" (Vollendung des Aufbaus des Sozialismus). A period of relative internal calm and stabilization followed the erection of the **Berlin Wall** in 1961, and soon afterward the first formal party program (Parteiprogramm) was issued, outlining basic principles and objectives (1963). Ulbricht announced the commitment to creating a "socialist human community" (sozialistische Menschengemeinschaft, 1967), and a new national constitution was passed enshrining the SED's leadership role (1968). After 1971, under Honecker, continuity within the party was essentially maintained. Ideological keywords during this period were the "unity of economic and social policy" (Einheit von Wirtschafts- und Sozialpolitik) and the "main task" (Hauptaufgabe) of improving material living standards and creating an entire socialist way of life. However, from the early 1980s onward, growing disaffection with actual social and economic conditions in the country at large was increasingly reflected within the party itself. Between 1981 and 1985, 100,000 members were disciplined or expelled for "anticommunist," "social-reformist," or "opportunistic attacks," while numbers applying to leave the GDR or failing to return from approved visits abroad rose to an unprecedented level. Mass emigration as other eastern bloc states opened their borders to the West and the Soviet leader Mikhail Gorbachev's refusal to support the regime in its crackdown on protests in 1989 signaled the final death knell.

Following the revolution in the fall of 1989, the party dissolved its existing leadership structures and renamed itself Sozialistische Einheitspartei Deutschlands/Partei des Demokratischen Sozialismus (SED-PDS). The SED in the title was soon dropped (4 February 1990), resulting in the **Party of Democratic Socialism (PDS)**, which in 2005 formed an electoral alliance with the **Election Alternative for Labor and Justice (WASG)** as a precursor to merger and the creation of **The Left Party** in 2007. Although often referred to as the successor party to the SED, the PDS/The Left Party presents itself as a completely different organization.

See also GERMAN DEMOCRATIC REPUBLIC (GDR): POLITICAL INSTITUTIONS.

SOLIDARITY PACT (SOLIDARPAKT). The Solidarity Pact (or Federal Consolidation Program), proposed by Chancellor **Helmut Kohl** in September 1992 and agreed to the following March by the government, the opposition, the **federal states**, business interests, **trade unions**, and **banks**, was a package of measures designed to rejuvenate the stagnating eastern German economy. The pact envisaged annual transfers of over 100,000 million DM to the east from 1995 and additional funds for employment creation schemes. The package was financed by increases in turnover and income **tax**, with some concessions made to the **Social Democratic Party of Germany** **(SPD)**, which resisted deep cuts in social welfare. **Industry** and business undertook to increase their purchases in eastern Germany. The pact also provided for the introduction of a **solidarity surcharge** from January 1995 (7.5 percent on incomes and corporations, falling to 5.5 percent from 1998). The first version of the pact (Solidarity Pact I) ran from 1995 (when the **German Unity Fund** ceased) until 2004. The follow-up, Solidarity Pact II, agreed to in 2001 in view of continuing economic stagnation and scheduled for 2005 to 2019, provided for 105,000 million euros for infrastructure in the new Länder (Basket I) and around 51,000 million euros for the economy, **transport**, housing, **education** and **research**, **sports** facilities, and cleaning up the **environment** (Basket II). By 2010, 60 percent of the fund had been used, with **Saxony** the largest recipient. Additional transfers took place via **financial equalization**, a revised form of which had been required by the **Federal Constitutional Court** **(FCC)** in 1999.

See also AUFBAU OST; UPSWING EAST (AUFSCHWUNG OST).

SOLIDARITY SURCHARGE (SOLIDARITÄTSZUSCHLAG). Following the German government's acknowledgment that the claim made by Chancellor **Helmut Kohl** in 1990 that reunification could be financed without increasing **taxation** was no longer sustainable, a package of tax increases was announced in February 1991. The main feature was a 7.5 percent "solidarity surcharge" on incomes and corporations, initially for one year from July 1991, although the actual charge amounted to 3.75 percent, as it was levied only for six months of the year. The charge was suspended in June 1992, reintroduced in 1995 (levied monthly at up to 7.5 percent, with special provision for low earners), and reduced to 5.5 percent from 1998. The total revenue from the levy up to 2013 was estimated at around 244,000 million euros, ultimately delivering more income to the **eastern federal states** than the **Solidarity Pact**, which was being wound down. Although associated with the pact, the surcharge is a different income stream and has proved controversial. For example, in 2008 the Institut der deutschen Wirtschaft Köln (Cologne Institute for Economic Research) recommended suspending the charge in order to stimulate the general economy. As a direct tax, all proceeds go to the central government and are not tied to be used in eastern Germany. The **Federal Constitutional Court (FCC)** rejected challenges by the Bund der Steuerzahler (German Taxpayers Association) in 2006 and the finance office of **Lower Saxony** (in 2009), which argued that levying a supplementary tax, without **Bundesrat** approval and in practice for the longer term, was unconstitutional (cf. article 107 of the **Basic Law, BL**). Although the levy was introduced as a temporary expedient, Chancellor **Angela Merkel** announced before the 2013 election that her party, the **Christian Democratic Union (CDU)**, had no plans to abolish it. While the **Greens** and the social democrats argued for renaming the charge and applying it to other purposes (e.g., for **education** or highway repair), only the **Free Democratic Party (FDP)** argued for its complete removal, and by 2014 it appeared increasingly likely that it would be incorporated into the general system of **financial equalization** between **Bund** and **Länder**.

SÖLLE, DOROTHEE (1929–2003). Author and theologian. Dorothee Sölle (née Nipperdey) was born in Cologne, where from 1949 she studied philosophy and classical philology before switching to protestant theology and German **literature**. She continued her studies in Freiburg and Göttingen, earning a first doctorate (published in 1959) and a second research thesis (Habilitation) in Cologne (1971). Her work included freelance journalism and teaching German and **religion** in a girls' school in Cologne, and she was twice married (first to the painter Dietrich Sölle in 1954, later divorced). Her linking of political and theological views excluded her from an academic position in a German university, although she was a guest lecturer at a theological seminary in New York between 1972 and 1987 and was awarded an honorary professorship in **Hamburg** in 1994. In 1968, against the background of the war in Vietnam, Sölle coinitiated at a conference of German Roman Catholics in Essen the first of the "political night prayers" (Nachtgebete), which combined political discussion with prayer or meditation on a biblical text. The topics of the sessions included the military dictatorship in Greece (1969), the German **abortion** laws (1971), the **Red Army Faction** (1972), and the military putsch in Chile (1973). The tradition soon spread to Protestant churches and acted as a forerunner to the church-based Monday demonstrations in Leipzig against the regime of the **German Democratic Republic (GDR)** in 1989. A committed pacifist, Sölle played an active role in the peace movement of the 1980s, demonstrating against the stationing of missiles and other weapons in Germany by the **North Atlantic Treaty Organization (NATO)**. She also visited South America as part of her involvement in liberation theology. Sölle's extensive writings (including books and poems), public profile, and theologically based engagement in politics made her one of Germany's most influential theologians of the 20th century.

SOMMER, MICHAEL (1952–). Trade union leader. Born in Büderich, near Düsseldorf (**North Rhine-Westfalia**), Michael Sommer studied politics at the Free University of **Berlin** (1971–1980), financing himself partly by working for the post office, where he gained his first experience with trade unions. He joined the German post office workers' union, Deutsche Postgewerkschaft (DPG), in 1971. In 1980, he graduated with a diploma, which included a thesis on the privatization of the parcel post service, and took up a post as lecturer for the DPG's **education** center in Gladenbach. He went on to become secretary of the **Bremen** district executive of the DPG (1981) and head of the union's national press and publicity department (1982). Returning from a three-month study visit to the United States, he took over the basic policy unit (Abteilung Vorstands- und Grundsatzangele- genheiten) of the DPG (1988). After joining the national executive committee (October 1993), he was elected deputy leader, with responsibility for finance, assets, personnel, and publicity (1997). In March 2001, Sommer became deputy leader of the newly constituted service industry union ver.di, which incorporated the DPG, and in May 2002 he succeeded Dieter Schulte as chairman of the Deutscher Gewerkschaftsbund (German Federation of Trade Unions, DGB), a post he held until 2014. From 2010 to 2014, he was also president of the International Trade Union Federation (ITUC). As leader of the DGB, Sommer, who joined the **Social Democratic Party of Germany** (SPD) in 1981, argued consistently for **taxation** increases and an increase in the national minimum wage. In 2013, he attracted criticism from peace activists within union circles for inviting defense minister **Thomas de Maizière**, who declared that the "**Bundeswehr** is a part of the peace movement," to a dialogue at the DGB's headquarters.

SOZIALISTISCHER DEUTSCHER STUDENTENBUND (SDS). *See* FEDERATION OF SOCIALIST GERMAN STUDENTS (SOZIALISTISCHER DEUTSCHER STUDENTENBUND, SDS).

SPÄTAUSSIEDLER. *See* AUSSIEDLER/SPÄTAUSSIEDLER.

SPÄTH, LOTHAR (1937–2016). Christian Democratic Union (CDU) politician. Lothar Späth was born in Sigmaringen (**Baden-Württemberg**) and trained in public administration and finance (1953–1967) at the Staatliche Verwaltungsschule in Stuttgart. After serving as a councilor specializing in financial affairs (from 1960), he joined the CDU in 1967, was elected mayor of the town of Bietigheim-Bissingen (1968), and represented the party in Baden-Württemberg's regional parliament (**Landtag**, 1968–1991). From 1970 onward, he held executive positions in various building companies and housing associations, including Neue Heimat in Stuttgart and Hamburg, Baresel AG in Stuttgart, and Hochtief. In the Landtag, he led the CDU party group (1972–1978) and served briefly as interior minister (1977–1978) before becoming **minister president** and leader of the regional CDU (1978–1991). Other positions he held included deputy leader of the national party (1981–1989), president of the **Bundesrat** (1984–1985), and national representative for cultural affairs (1987–1990). Under his stewardship Baden-Württemberg, one of Germany's wealthiest states, developed into a hub of business and advanced technology and a focus of cultural activities. Through his mixture of commercial and political acumen, Späth became one of the most popular and admired of CDU politicians and was at one stage considered a possible successor to Chancellor **Helmut Kohl**.

Späth's political career came to an abrupt end (January 1991) when he resigned as minister president and from the Landtag following allegations of misuse of fringe benefits (he himself argued that he regarded these as benefits for the region in his function as its political representative). In the same year, he became chief executive of the optical equipment manufacturer Jenoptik GmbH (later AG) in Jena, eastern Germany. Within a few years, Späth had transformed the company, the successor of the moribund state-owned Carl Zeiss concern in the former **German Democratic Republic (GDR)**, into a highly successful business that entered the **German Stock Exchange** in 1998, employed 6,000, and turned over 3,000 million DM (2001). Although the price of success included factory closures and 16,000 layoffs (1991–1992), Späth was regarded as the savior of the company, on which around 200 smaller businesses in the region depended. Jenoptik was the largest eastern German company to be listed on the stock exchange and one of the first to buy up businesses in western Germany in a strategy to develop new markets. Späth, who had also presented a 10-point program for economic recovery in the eastern states (1992), stepped down as chief executive in June 2003 but retained close links with business and was appointed the Norwegian consul for **Thuringia** and **Saxony-Anhalt** (1992).

Späth returned to political life as adviser to Helmut Kohl in the national election campaign of 1998 and, as a member of **Edmund Stoiber**'s shadow cabinet in the election of September 2002, was expected to become economics minister in the event of a conservative victory. He wrote several books on political and economic issues (including *Countdown für Deutschland*, 1995; *Die zweite Wende*, 1998; *Die Stunde der Politik*, 1999; and *Jenseits von Brüssel*, 2001) and moderated talk shows and provided political commentaries for the **television** news channel n-tv (1998–2001, resumed in 2005). The recipient of numerous honors from universities (Karlsruhe, Pecs, and Ulm), Späth was made an honorary professor of **media** and the analysis of contemporary issues (Medien und Zeitdiagnostik) at the University of Jena. In 2000, the American Council on Germany conferred on him the J. McCloy Prize. Vice chairman of the London-based European branch of the U.S. investment bank Merrill Lynch from 2003, he became chief executive of the firm's operations in Germany and Austria in 2005.

SPATIAL PLANNING ACT (RAUMORDNUNGSGESETZ). This federal law outlines the needs and conditions that determine the design of land and space for the whole of Germany, including the need for an effective infrastructure and an avoidance of regional overdevelopment (http:// www.gesetze-im-internet.de/rog_2008/).

During the 1960s, it became obvious that German cities were undergoing major topographical changes. Although the changes gave cause for concern, no immediate action was taken. While shops and offices were taking over city centers, living and leisure time was increasingly located at the urban fringes. Other typical features of this development were the emergence of satellite towns and an ever-growing number of automobiles. Heinrich Klotz of the **Center for Art and Media Technology** has asserted that the "history of **architecture** in that decade [the 1960s] might well be the worst in the more recent history of building." The 1963 planning law (Raumordnungsgesetz) was the response by the **federal government** to the emergence of different structural forms of settlement and a rising awareness of concerns over the **environment**. In the 1970s, the call to save the cities ("Rettet die Städte") acquired a greater sense of urgency as the government attempted to tackle the problem of differences between city and country—backed by publications such as Wolf Jobst Siedler and Elisabeth Niggemeyer's *Die gemordete Stadt* (The murdered city, 1964). and **Alexander Mitscherlich**'s *Die Unwirtlichkeit unserer Städte: Anstiftung zum Unfrieden* (The inhospitality of our cities. A deliberate provocation, 1965). The 1971 law for the promotion of urban building (Städtebauförderungsgesetz) gave additional powers to local governments and municipalities (Kommunen) to enable them to target specific problems, such as the need to reduce land speculation in the larger cities.

A number of initiatives seek to further innovation and improvements, including the biennial "Bundesgartenschau," a federal horticultural show with a strong emphasis on the impact on the landscape (e.g., in 2013 in **Hamburg**, in 2014 in the Havel-region, in 2017 in **Berlin**-Mahrzahn) and international building exhibitions (IBA/Internationale Bauausstellung). The first IBA was held in Darmstadt in 1906; the next in 1957 in Berlin, subsequently between 1979 and 1987 again in Berlin, and between 1989 and 1999 in the Ruhr region (IBA Emscher Park).

SPELLING REFORM (RECHTSCHREIBREFORM). German linguists have long debated the need to reform or rationalize the orthography of written German. The main issues have been the conventions underlying the spelling of long and short vowels, the use of capitals (since Danish abandoned the custom in 1949, German is the only **language** to retain the use of initial uppercase letters for nouns), syllable/word breaks, the writing of foreign loan words, and punctuation. Fearing that the **German Democratic Republic (GDR)** would go it alone in instituting reforms, the West German government approached Austria in order to provide fresh impetus for change (1980). In 1986, representatives of the German-speaking countries (Germany, Austria, Switzerland, and Liechtenstein) set up a joint forum (known as the Viennese Discussions, or Wiener Gespräche) to agree upon and draw up reforms. In the Viennese Declaration of 1996, the forum presented its plans for a wholesale revision (Neuregelung) of the spelling conventions underlying the written standard language. Later known as the "reform of spelling" (Reform der Rechtschreibung), the changes would come into force in primary schools in 1998 and be extended to upper schools and government organizations, where it would be compulsory and, hopefully, be adopted in the **press** and **media**. To minimize the costs of the changeover, both old and new spelling conventions were permitted for an interim period (up to 2005). A commission of 12 experts was created to monitor the progress of the reforms in the German-speaking countries and advise in cases of doubt (1996).

In the fall of 1998, around 100 German authors at the Frankfurt book fair protested against the reform (the "Frankfurt declaration"), although the **education** ministers of the German **federal states** responded by restating their commitment to the changes (the "Dresden declaration"). The **Federal Constitutional Court (FCC)** had already rejected claims by parents and others that the reform violated their basic rights in their children's education and freedom of personal development (July 1998). The hostility of some intellectuals, writers, academics, and teachers to the reform reached a peak in 2000, and some newspaper and media concerns either reverted to the old spelling or announced their intention to do so. At the same time, regional education ministers pointed to the disruption for schoolchildren if the reforms were reversed and in 2004 announced plans to set up their own forum/council for monitoring and promoting the reform (Rat für deutsche Rechtschreibung). Consensus between **publishers** and education ministers was finally reached in 2006 based on recommendations of the 36-member council. Although it was unclear what the majority of Germans wished to happen, schoolchildren as a rule wanted to retain the rules, while older citizens saw no reason to adopt them.

In general, the reforms aimed to simplify the relationship between phoneme and letter (including reflecting the etymology of a form, as in *behände* [from *Hand*], formerly *behende*), separate elements of phrases (*Rad fahren* instead of *radfahren*), retain the initial uppercase in certain phrases (*in Bezug auf/im Großen und Ganzen* for *in bezug auf/im großen und ganzen*), and make punctuation usage more transparent. The idea behind the reforms was to define general, universally applicable rules that would avoid the need to consult a dictionary (such as the *Duden*) in order to identify an item among a host of idiosyncrasies. While this strategy led to greater consistency, it also introduced fresh uncertainties, especially in deciding whether to write new compound items as single words or as phrases (word combination is one of the most productive means of generating new vocabulary in German). The reform continues to be criticized, not so much for trying to introduce standard forms as such, but for its failure to provide logical and thoroughly consistent rules for the changes. To date a number of influential newspapers, magazines, and publishers have retained the old spelling, although the fact that reference books focus on the new spelling suggests that it will eventually prevail.

***SPIEGEL* AFFAIR.** *See* AUGSTEIN, RUDOLF (1923–2002).

SPIEGEL, PAUL (1937–2006). Jewish community leader. Paul Spiegel was born in Warendorf (**North Rhine-Westfalia**). A year later the family fled to Belgium to escape National Socialist persecution. When the Germans occupied Belgium during World War II, his father was arrested, his younger sister was transported to Auschwitz (where she died), and his mother was forced to give her baby son away to a Belgian family. There followed a traumatic period of hiding and moving from house to house. After 1945, his father, who survived the concentration camps, insisted on returning to Warendorf. Paul Spiegel completed his higher school certificate and trained in Düsseldorf as a journalist for the Jewish newspaper *Allgemeine Jüdische Wochenzeitung*, later becoming its editor. He subsequently worked for other newspapers and as press spokesman for a savings bank (Rheinischer Sparkassen- und Giroverband). In 1986, he established and built up a successful agency for artists (the Paul Spiegel–Internationale Künstler- und Medienagentur). After occupying senior positions in the Jewish community in Düsseldorf, Spiegel was elected one of the two vice presidents of the **Central Council of Jews in Germany** (1993). He later succeeded **Ignatz Bubis** as president (1999). Known for his tolerance, bridge-building work, and warnings about racism and **anti-Semitism**, he received an honorary doctorate from the University of Düsseldorf (2004) and died in Düsseldorf after a long illness in April 2006. His autobiography (*Wieder zu Hause? Erinnerungen*) appeared in 2001. **Charlotte Knobloch** succeeded him as council president in June 2006.

See also JEWS IN GERMANY.

SPORT AND RECREATION. In line with increased leisure time, personal wealth, and a focus on consumer culture, sport in Germany has developed into a major **industry**, with companies marketing clothes and equipment at the same time as promoting new activities, ranging from inline skating and surfing to bungee jumping. The Deutscher Olympischer Sportbund (German Olympic Sports Confederation, DOSB), the nongovernmental umbrella organization of German sport, founded in 2006 from the merger of the Deutscher Sportbund (German Sports Confederation, DSB) and the Nationales Olympisches Komitee für Deutschland (National Olympic Committee for Germany, NOK), had around 27 million members in 90,000 clubs and associations (Sportvereine) in 2015. The most popular sports in terms of club members are soccer (6.9 million), gymnastics (5 million), tennis (1.4 million), and shooting (1.4 million), followed by mountaineering (1 million), athletics (823,000), handball (767,000), horseback riding (690,000), fishing (671,000), golf (639,000), sports for the disabled (640,000), table tennis (571,000), swimming (562,000), and skiing (562,000). Significantly more males and females of all ages participate in organized sport in the western than in the **eastern federal states**, although **women** outnumber men in gymnastics and horseback riding, and a national women's soccer league (Frauen-Bundesliga) was founded in 1989 and began fielding teams in 1990–1991. Other organizations that contribute significantly to sporting life are Deutsche Sporthilfe, the Deutscher Volkssportverband (DVV), the Deutscher Alpenverein (German Alpine Association), and the **Bundeswehr**.

The main funding source for sports in Germany is the state. While the **federal states** are responsible for sports in schools and general leisure facilities, such as playing fields, stadiums, and swimming pools, the federation **(Bund)** supports national organizations, facilities, events, and top-class sportsmen and -women who represent Germany at the international level. Between 2013 and 2015, the Bund earmarked around 130 million euros annually for top-class sports, with additional resources also provided by other ministries (e.g., over 63 million euros from the defense ministry). The state also maintains dedicated sports science centers in Bonn (Bundesinstitut für Sportwissenschaft, to convert research into practice), Leipzig (Institut für Angewandte Trainingwissenschaft, for training and education), and Berlin

(Institut für Forschung und Entwicklung von Sportgeräten, to develop sports equipment). Two drug-testing laboratories at Cologne and Kreischa are accredited by the International Olympic Committee (IOC).

In the former **German Democratic Republic (GDR)**, sport for the masses was promoted at school, work, and home and enjoyed high prestige. Heavily regimented and militarized, it was closely identified with the political aims of the GDR state. Well-choreographed festivals of sport were held in Leipzig, although sports that engaged the masses or brought in Olympic medals (such as gymnastics and ice skating) were promoted at the expense of those that did not. Even leading sportsmen and -women had the status of amateurs, inasmuch as they received a wage and could not earn winnings or keep prize money. Young persons with promising talent were identified at an early stage and received special training at schools. The state also promoted the use of drugs in training and in international competitions, with several hundred victims experiencing serious physical injury and long-term feelings of guilt. After reunification, sport in eastern Germany underwent a major reorganization. Membership in sports associations plummeted as the state-sponsored organizations disappeared and were only gradually replaced by western clubs. The national sports systems of eastern and western Germany were merged and a "Golden Plan East" (Goldener Plan Ost) launched in order to raise sports facilities in the east to western standards; the plan ran from 1999 until 2009, although its results were open to question.

Following Germany's disappointing performance at the 1984 Olympic Games, the state established and financed new centers for promoting sporting excellence. Well equipped with technical, medical, training, and other resources, 20 centers (Olympiastützpunkte) aimed to produce Olympic-standard competitors, while 16 centers (Bundesleistungszentren) provided central facilities for athletes and coaches, as well as courses for sports teachers. The fruits of this investment were that Germany was ranked fifth in the 2000 Sydney Olympics (gaining 13 gold, 17 silver, and 26 bronze medals) and first in the 1998 Winter Olympics in Nagano (12 gold, 9 silver, and 8 bronze medals); in the 2010 Winter Olympics in Vancouver, Germany came in second (10 gold, 13 silver, and 7 bronze medals). Soccer is well represented in terms of sports clubs and membership, and the German Soccer Association (Deutscher Fussball-Bund, DFB) is by far the largest single sports association. Soccer matches attract the highest numbers of **television** viewers, especially where the national team is involved and in competitions such as UEFA (Union of European Football Associations) and the Champions League. The national soccer league (Bundesliga) is big business, deriving income from ticket sales, broadcasting rights, advertising, souvenir sales, and other forms of marketing. A founding figure in the formation of the league, which emerged in 1963 from a number of small amateur leagues, was the national trainer Sepp Herberger, who argued for a league of full-time, professional players on the British model. Within a few years, German teams were regularly winning the European Cup, and professional football contributes annually an estimated 5,100 million euros to national GDP, including revenues from broadcasting and corporate sponsorships. The huge sums involved, however, mask a gulf between a minority of very wealthy clubs, such as Bavaria Munich, Hamburger SV, MSV Duisburg, and Borussia Dortmund, which are able to offer enormous sums for star players, and a large number of smaller clubs, many of which are in debt. Despite these problems, soccer is still regarded as Germany's national sport, attracting millions of spectators and viewers every Saturday afternoon. Germany's hosting of the FIFA World Soccer Championships in 2006 was widely regarded as exemplary and was notable in that the portrayal of the country by the international media had moved away from the National Socialist past and the **Berlin Wall** and focused firmly on the present. Some German sporting figures have achieved international status. Examples are Steffi Graf and Boris Becker (tennis), Sebastian Vettel, and Michael Schumacher (motor racing).

SPRINGER, AXEL (1912–1985). Newspaper and magazine **publisher**. Axel Cäsar Springer was born and grew up in **Hamburg**-Altona. His father owned a printing and publishing house (Hammerich & Lesser) and published a local newspaper (*Altonaer Nachrichten*). On leaving school (1928), Springer completed an apprenticeship as a printer in his father's firm and with a paper manufacturer in Hamburg and Leipzig. After training as a journalist with a provincial newspaper (*Bergedorfer Zeitung*) and a news agency (from 1932), he joined his father's newspaper as an editor for **sports** and economics (1933). He worked as deputy chief editor for the paper (from 1934) until it was closed down by the National Socialists (1941) and used to print propaganda. Declared medically unfit for military service (1939), Springer became a partner in Hammerich & Lesser, which continued to publish books until 1944.

In 1945, Springer and his father obtained a license from the occupation authorities to resume publishing and print contributions to the radio station Norddeutscher Rundfunk and the program magazine *Hör zu* (1946). After the Axel Springer Verlag GmbH was founded (1946), Springer, with his colleague, John **Jahr** (1900–1991), obtained licenses to publish the **women**'s magazine *Constanze*, which appeared in March 1948 and went on to become one of Germany's most popular fashion magazines. He also produced the *Hamburger Abendblatt*, the first nonparty newspaper to be approved by the postwar authorities (1948). In order to handle the meteoric rise in circulation, high-rise premises in the Kaiser-Wilhelm Straße in Hamburg were built. These were completed in 1950—the year in which *Hör zu* sold one million copies—and became a city landmark. Springer launched the *Bild-Zeitung* (1952, later *BILD*), which was based on the British tabloid format; a daily and a Sunday edition followed four years later. In 1953, he purchased (from its British owners) the news titles *Die Welt*, *Welt am Sonntag*, and the popular entertainment magazine *Das Neue Blatt*. In 1956, he made his first external acquisition, a stake in the publisher Ullstein (which later produced the dailies *B.Z.* and *Berliner Morgenpost*), converting his interest into a majority holding three years later. During the 1960s, Springer acquired a number of titles (including the Düsseldorf tabloid *Mittag*); the Munich-based publisher Kindler & Schiermeyer; and special interest magazines such as *Bravo* (for youth), *twen* (teenagers), *Kicker* (soccer), and *Funk Uhr* (**television**). He also founded *Eltern*, a magazine for parents, and printed the news weekly *Der Spiegel* (from 1965).

In 1967, the premises of the new Springer concern were opened in **Berlin**. Directly overlooking the **Berlin Wall**, lit up 24 hours a day, and clearly visible from the east, the imposing 19-story building was intended as a prominent symbol of the West German economic miracle in the divided city and later became a prime target of student protests. After apparently taking little interest in politics, Springer visited Moscow in order to present to the Soviet leader, Nikita Khrushchev, proposals for reuniting Germany (1958). In 1967, he published four political principles that all his editors were obliged to observe: to support German reunification, to work for reconciliation between Germans and **Jews** (on a visit to Israel in 1965, he had donated 3.5 million DM for the building of the national Israel Museum), to reject any form of political totalitarianism, and to defend the **social market economy**. In 2001, after reunification, the principles were updated. Springer firmly opposed **Ostpolitik** and rapprochement with the east.

By the late 1960s, Springer was widely seen as having created a **press monopoly**, which he exploited to disseminate his conservative views. Calls for his disappropriation came from student protests, liberal circles, and intellectuals, including the literary group **Group 47**. In April 1968, at the height of the **students' movement**, *Bild-Zeitung* was held indirectly responsible for contributing to the attempted assassination of the student leader **Rudi Dutschke** in Berlin, and during the terrorist campaign of the early 1970s the author **Heinrich Böll** publicly rebuked Springer for whipping up public hysteria. In 1967, the **federal government** set up a commission of inquiry, the Günther Commission, which in the following year declared the Springer group a danger to press freedom. Springer subsequently sold off some of his titles.

In 1970, the group was renamed Axel Springer Verlag AG (incorporating Ullstein, Hammerich & Lesser, and Axel Springer & Sohn), with Springer as sole shareholder and chairman of the supervisory board. At the same time, Springer embarked on a further phase of controversial expansion and legal battles. In the 1970s and early 1980s, he acquired new regional titles, founded specialist magazines, and attempted (unsuccessfully, owing to a ruling by the Federal Cartel Office) to convert a stake in the Munich-based newspaper publisher Münchener Zeitungs-Verlag GmbH & Co KG into a majority holding (1976). His sixth printing plant, opened in 1973, was the largest of its kind in Europe.

Two bombs planted by the **Red Army Faction (RAF)** terrorist group in the Springer building in Hamburg injured 17 staff members (1972), and Springer-owned properties in Kampen and Gstaad were also attacked (1973). In 1977, the journalist Günther Wallraff, working undercover, revealed the inner workings of the *Bild-Zeitung* newspaper in Hanover and its questionable journalistic methods. Wallraff later won a legal action (1979–1981) following a claim in his book (*Zeuge der Anklage*) that journalists from Bild had tapped into his telephone. In 1978, the Springer concern had to pay 50,000 DM in damages to a student, Eleonore Poensgen, whom it had accused of **terrorism** after the murder of Jürgen Ponto, head of the Dresdner Bank. In 1980, scientists, writers, and artists, including members of the **PEN** Club meeting in **Bremen**, mounted a boycott of Springer, who in the same year suffered personal tragedy when his son Axel committed suicide. In 1982, the Federal Cartel Office vetoed negotiations to sell interests to the **Burda** group (Munich), which eventually acquired a 24.9 percent stake in Springer (1983). Springer offered 49 percent of his shares on the stock exchange (June 1985), enabling **Leo Kirch** to acquire his first 10 percent interest in the group. Springer died in September the same year in West Berlin. Under the terms of his will, his heirs were obliged not to sell their inheritance before 2015.

Despite the controversy that surrounded him most of his life, Springer received several honors, including awards from Israel (he was the first recipient of the Leo Baeck medal for his services to German–Jewish reconciliation [1978] and the first German to receive the title "Preserver of Jerusalem"), the United States (including the American Friendship Medal, 1977), and Germany (the **Konrad Adenauer** prize, 1981, and the Berlin Ernst Reuter medal, 1982). His publications include a collection of speeches and essays (*Von Berlin aus gesehen*, 1971) and a book (*Aus Sorge um Deutschland*, 1980). Springer was married five times (1933, 1939, 1953, 1962, 1978) and had one daughter (Barbara, born in 1933) and three sons (Axel, born in 1941, Raimund, and Nikolaus). After Springer's death, his widow Elfriede (Friede) emerged as clan leader, buying out the Burda family's stake in the concern and becoming majority shareholder. For many years, she fought Leo Kirch over control of the group, until the latter went bankrupt (2002).

See also AXEL SPRINGER SE.

STABILITY AND GROWTH PACT. Initiated by German finance minister **Theodor Waigel** in the mid-1990s and agreed to by countries that had adopted the newly established single European currency, the euro, at a **Euro-**

pean Union (EU) council meeting in Amsterdam in 1997, the pact was a framework for coordinating national fiscal policies for the common economic good. It included the stipulation of a limit on national **budget** deficits (3 percent of GDP). Germany in particular insisted on the measure, the aim of which was to regulate inflation and force member states to keep a rein on government spending as control of national interest rates passed to the European Central Bank (ECB). Ironically both Germany and France, the eurozone's largest members, hit by recession in the early 2000s, blocked application of the rule, despite warnings from the EU Commission and to the annoyance of smaller countries, which had introduced sharp spending cuts to control their own budgets. The pact was reformed in 2005 and again, notably, after its failure to ensure fiscal discipline across the EU had become all too obvious during the **eurozone crisis** in December 2011. The reform saw the addition of the "six-pack" measures (supplemented by a two pack in May 2013), which aimed to strengthen fiscal surveillance of national budgets and apply real sanctions for noncompliance. Annual monitoring of budgets was embodied in the **European Semester** program, while fiscal targets and penalties were incorporated in the binding intragovernmental **Treaty on Stability, Coordination and Governance (TSCG,** 2011).

STASI. Short for Staatssicherheit (state security), the Stasi was the secret police of the former **German Democratic Republic (GDR)**. The organization was controlled by the GDR Ministerium für Staatssicherheit (Ministry for State Security, MfS), which was run by **Erich Mielke** from 1957 until 1989. Established in 1950 as the "sword and shield" of the ruling **Socialist Unity Party of Germany (SED)**, the Stasi organized industrial and political espionage against the West (especially the Federal Republic of Germany, FRG), although its main function was to monitor the population of the GDR. By 1989, it had created a massive network of 85,000 full-time employees and an estimated 180,000 unofficial informants (Informelle Mitarbeiter, or IMs), who were recruited or pressured to spy on their fellow citizens. Despite the fact that the Stasi employed a variety of repressive mechanisms to enforce its control and accumulated a huge volume of information on the state of the country and the mood of its citizens, its reports were never adequately processed by the SED and its geriatric leadership.

The true extent of the Stasi's networks and its resources emerged after reunification. The organization's **Berlin** headquarters comprised 24 separate blocks, with 3,000 rooms and offices, and its budget swallowed up 400 million East German marks a year. It maintained more than 1,800 buildings (including **sports** and recreational facilities and holiday homes), over 18,000 apartments, and a fleet of 19,000 vehicles, and controlled an 11,000-member elite regiment of soldiers to guard SED leaders and suppress possible uprisings. The Stasi also worked out plans to arrest and imprison almost 86,000 listed East German citizens who were considered to be a threat to the state in the event of a national emergency. The service had 14 regional offices, and its total apparatus was larger than the East German regular army.

After the SED fell from power in October/November 1989, the interim premier, **Hans Modrow**, renamed the MfS the Amt für Nationale Sicherheit (Office of National Security, AfNS) in an attempt to retain the Stasi as an organization, but in early December the **Round Table** demanded that it be dissolved altogether under civilian control. When it emerged that Stasi personnel were attempting to shred and burn evidence of their activities, protesters stormed the Berlin headquarters (January 1990). Following the official disbanding of the Stasi (February 1990), the authorities were faced with the decision of what to do with its huge archives in the light of the personal information they contained and the circumstances in which this had been obtained. Under the terms of the Treaty of Unification, the archives remained in the east and were administered by a special office set up by the **Bundestag** and headed by **Joachim Gauck**. Individuals could access their personal files (e.g., for purposes of rehabilitation and compensation), and they were also available to members of parliament and officials investigating criminal charges against the SED and Stasi personnel.

After reunification, it emerged that Stasi operatives had deeply infiltrated the West German civil service, government ministries, the military, and the main **political parties**. Files containing the identities of East German spies who were active in the West, including an estimated 12,000 West Germans, ended up in the hands of the U.S. Central Intelligence Agency (CIA). The so-called Rosenholz files were finally returned to Germany in 2003. Although the unclear legal status of activities such as espionage (which, unlike treason and endangering national security, is not recognized in the German criminal code) and the 30-year period of limitations for high treason have lessened the relevance of the files, revelations have continued to be politically embarrassing. This occurred in the cases of **Lothar Bisky**, leader of the **Party of Democratic Socialism** (PDS), in July 2003, and former chancellor **Helmut Kohl**, who fought a long-running battle with the courts to prevent the release of information that the Stasi had compiled on him.

Today a number of memorials, research centers, and museums are dedicated to informing the public about the workings of the Stasi. Among the most famous is the so-called Stasi Museum in the former East Berlin headquarters. Occupied by demonstrators in 1990 who sought to stop the destruction of files, this is today one of the most important institutions in Germany to reflect a particular reality of life in the GDR. The "Runde Ecke" in Leipzig has since 1990 combined a memorial museum and the Stasi Bunker museum. The long-term trauma of the Stasi both before and after reunification has been dealt with in **literature** and **cinema** alike. Anna Funder's book *Stasiland: Stories from Behind the Berlin Wall* (2003) and Hester Vaizey's *Born* *in the GDR* (2014) exemplify the psychological (and at times physical) damage both opponents of the regime and others suffered. In 2006, Florian Henckel von Donnersmarck's film *The Lives of Others* (*Das Leben der Anderen*, 2005), dealing with a Stasi officer who falls for the person he is meant to observe and begins to see the true scale of his involvement, reached an international audience even though the critics expressed some reservations about the treatment of the topic.

See also FEDERAL COMMISSIONER FOR THE RECORDS OF THE STATE SECURITY SERVICE OF THE FORMER GERMAN DEMOCRATIC REPUBLIC; GERMAN DEMOCRATIC REPUBLIC (GDR): POLITICAL INSTITUTIONS.

STATE MINISTER (STAATSMINISTER). The title of state minister denotes a minister in the regional cabinet of certain **federal states (Bavaria, Saxony**, and **Hessen**) or the head of the state chancellery of **Saxony-Anhalt**. It can also be used for a parliamentary **state secretary** at the national (**Bund**) level, although in practice it has been used only in the **Office of the Federal Chancellor** and the Federal Ministry for Foreign Affairs.

STATE SECRETARY (STAATSSEKRETÄR). State secretaries in Germany are senior advisers to government ministers. A state secretary is second in rank to the minister and runs the ministerial department on behalf of the minister, whom he directly represents. State secretaries exist at the national level and also in some **federal states**, where they can be referred to as "ministerial directors" (Ministerialdirektoren). There are two categories of state secretary: those with civil service status (beamtete Staatssekretäre) and parliamentary state secretaries (parlamentarische Staatssekretäre). The former are appointed according to German laws on civil servants (Beamtengesetze). As a result, the length of their appointment does not depend on their minister's term of office, although they may be obliged to take temporary retirement without notification of cause (for this reason, they are sometimes called "political" state secretaries). Their role tends to be more administrative in nature. Political state secretaries may represent the minister in the cabinet, although they do not have a vote and their role there is generally advisory (an exception is **Bavaria**, where they are cabinet members). The office of parliamentary state secretary was created in April 1967 and extended to all federal ministries by 1969. Unlike political state secretaries, incumbents must be members of the **Bundestag** (although since 1999, this has not applied to the **Office of the Federal Chancellor**) and may represent the minister before parliamentary bodies (the Bundestag and **Bundesrat**), and in the cabinet. They also maintain links with the party and interest groups and may resign or be dismissed at any time. A parliamentary state secretary in the Federal Ministry for Foreign Affairs and the Federal Chancellor's Office is called a **state minister** (Staatsminister).

STEINBACH, ERIKA (1943–). Christian Democratic Union (CDU) politician. Born in Rahmel (now Rumia in Poland), Erika Steinbach fled with her mother and three-month-old sister in January 1945 from the approaching Soviet army to **Schleswig-Holstein**. From 1950 onward, she lived in Hanau. After studying music and playing the violin in orchestras, she qualified with a diploma in administration and information technology and worked in Frankfurt at the district computer center (1970–1977), where she managed a project to streamline and introduce information technology in libraries in **Hessen** (from 1974). A member of the CDU from 1974, she assisted the Frankfurt party parliamentary group, with responsibilities for youth, social and **health** policy, personnel, and housing (1977–1990).

Steinbach entered the **Bundestag** in 1990 and joined the national party executive in 2000. In parliament, she soon developed a reputation as a conservative hard-liner, opposing German recognition of the Oder-Neisse border with Poland and a joint German–Czech declaration of reconciliation. She also condemned the Wehrmacht exhibition of crimes committed by German forces during World War II and in 1997 founded a right-wing organization (Stimme der Mehrheit) that opposed the unrestricted **immigration** of **foreigners**. In 1998, she was elected president of a national association for refugees and expellees (Bund der Vertriebenen, BdV), which had emerged in 1957–1958 from regional groups of Germans who had fled or been deported from Eastern Europe (mainly Poland and Czechoslovakia) after World War II. In 2000, Steinbach became president of a foundation created to establish a center in **Berlin** dedicated to the plight of the expellees (Zentrum gegen Vertreibungen/Centre against Expulsions), in particular for their right to restitution for loss of land and property. The Polish and Czech governments refused to acknowledge such claims, and the foundation has failed to win German government support. Steinbach also publicly attacked a declaration by Chancellor **Gerhard Schröder**, made on a visit to Poland that included a commemoration of the 60th anniversary of the Warsaw uprising, that his government would not support restitution claims (2004). She was appointed to the supervisory council of the ZDF **television** service (2000), became a member of the **Goethe Institute** (in 1994), and is her party's speaker on the Bundestag committee for **human rights** and humanitarian aid (since 2005). In 2010, she announced her resignation from the national executive following disputes with the leadership over her claim that Poland had already mobilized in March 1939. In 2014, she was succeeded as president of the

Centre against Expulsions by Bernd Fabritius, who represented the **Christian Social Union (CSU)** in the Bundestag. Her book *Die Macht der Erinnerung* (2010) describes the background of her work for the German deportees.

STEINBRÜCK, PEER (1947–). **Social Democratic Party of Germany (SPD)** politician. Peer Steinbrück was born in **Hamburg** and studied economics and social sciences at the University of Kiel. He worked on land use and regional planning in the Federal Ministry for Regional Planning, Building, and Urban Development (1974–1976) before joining the planning department of the Federal Ministry for **Research** and Technology (1976–1977). Steinbrück was personal adviser to two ministers of technology, Hans Matthöfer and Volker Hauff (1977–1978), in the cabinet of Chancellor **Helmut Schmidt**. After a period in the **Office of the Federal Chancellor**, where he liaised with the Federal Ministry of Research and Technology (June 1978–February 1981), he moved to East **Berlin**, where he worked briefly in the economics section of West Germany's permanent representation (Ständige Vertretung der Bundesrepublik Deutschland in Ost Berlin). Returning to Bonn, he served again as personal adviser to the minister of technology, Andreas von Bülow (1981–1982), until the fall of the coalition of the SPD and the **Free Democratic Party (FDP)**. After this he worked on issues of the **environment** for the SPD parliamentary party (October 1983–September 1985). In October 1985, Steinbrück moved to **North Rhine-Westfalia** (NRW) as a policy adviser on environmental economic matters for the regional ministry of the environment, planning, and **agriculture** and headed the office of **Johannes Rau**, NRW's **minister president** (December 1986–May 1990). After serving briefly as **state secretary** in the ministry of nature, environment, and regional development for **Schleswig-Holstein** (May 1992–May 1993), he became the region's minister for economics, technology, and **transport** (1993–1998). He returned to NRW in October 1998 to become minister for economics, small to medium-sized enterprises, technology, and transport before taking over the finance ministry in 2000.

Elected to NRW's state parliament (**Landtag**, 2000 and 2002), Steinbrück succeeded **Wolfgang Clement** as minister president (2003), leading an SPD/**Green Party** coalition (until May 2005). As leader of Germany's most populous federal state, Steinbrück faced a number of problems, including a record level of unemployment, falling economic growth, and a high rate of business bankruptcies. Further losses of revenue and jobs accompanied the decision of the **Bundestag** to move the capital from Bonn to Berlin. Steinbrück pledged to adapt the proposals of the **Hartz Commission** to create job opportunities in the region, reduce bureaucracy, and implement reforms in **education** (including measures to promote **language** competence, expand the number of all-day primary schools, and merge two universities). At the same time, divisions emerged between the SPD and the **Greens** over transport and environmental policy, notably the building of a magnetic hover railway link, the Metrorapid, and of a gas-fired power station near Cologne. In the regional election of May 2005, the SPD suffered a severe defeat, mainly as a result of the unpopularity of the national party's **Agenda 2010** program. Following the national election of September 2005, Steinbrück took over as head of the SPD parliamentary party in the Bundestag and became deputy party leader (2005–2009). He also served as finance minister in the coalition with the **Christian Democratic Union (CDU)** led by **Angela Merkel** (2005–2013) and, until he was succeeded by **Wolfgang Schäuble** (CDU), was involved in Germany's response to the global financial crisis of 2007–2008. Steinbrück was his party's candidate for the chancellorship in the 2013 election, although this was overshadowed by revelations that he had received over 1.25 million euros in fees for extraparliamentary activities from 2009 onward. During 2015, he worked briefly for a Ukrainian-based agency for modernizing the country (Agentur zur Modernisierung der Ukraine), which included leading figures, businessmen, and politicians from the European Union.

STEINMEIER, FRANK-WALTER (1956–). **Social Democratic Party of Germany (SPD)** politician. Born in Detmold (**North Rhine-Westfalia**), Frank-Walter Steinmeier joined the SPD in 1975 and studied law and political science at the University of Gießen (1976–1982), passing his state law examinations in 1982 and 1986. After working as a research assistant on law and politics at the university (1986–1991), he became an adviser on **media** law and policy in the state chancellery of **Lower Saxony** (1991), where he went on to head the personal office of Minister President **Gerhard Schröder** (1993–1994), to whom he became a close confidant. His other positions included head of the department for policy, coordination, and planning (1994–1996) and **state secretary** and head of the Lower Saxony chancellery (1996–1998). After serving as state secretary in the **Office of the Federal Chancellor**, with responsibility for the intelligence services (1998–1999), he went on to head the office (1999–2005). During the financial scandals surrounding the **Christian Democratic Union (CDU)** from late 1999, he advised the **Bundestag** investigation committee on the missing papers related to the sale of the Leuna refinery in eastern Germany (1992). He also took part in the **security** discussions at cabinet level following the **terrorist** attacks of 11 September 2001 and mediated between Economics Minister **Wolfgang Clement** and **Environment** Minister **Jürgen Trittin** over measures to promote renewable **energy** (2003). Along with Schröder, he was also closely involved in drawing up the plans for **Agenda 2010**. As foreign minister (2005–2009) in **Angela Merkel**'s first coalition cabinet, Steinmeier, who was also vice-chancellor from 2007, almost immediately came under fire for the surrendering of terrorist suspects to the United States via German airports; the kidnapping by the Central Intelligence Agency (CIA) of Khaled al Masri, a German citizen; and the passing of intelligence to the Americans during the Iraq war. He was nominated SPD chancellor candidate for the national election in 2009, but failed to dislodge Merkel, who concluded a coalition with the **Free Democratic Party (FDP)**. Steinmeier went on to lead the opposition SPD parliamentary group (2009–2013), but was reappointed foreign minister in Merkel's third coalition in 2013. As minister he was closely involved in efforts to concluded peace agreements between the Ukrainian government and Russian-backed separatists.

See also FOREIGN POLICY AFTER 1990; FOREIGN POLICY: FRANCE; FOREIGN POLICY: THE RUSSIAN FEDERATION; FOREIGN POLICY: UNITED STATES.

STOCK EXCHANGE. *See* GERMAN STOCK EXCHANGE (DEUTSCHE BÖRSE AG).

STOIBER, EDMUND (1941–). Christian Social Union (CSU) politician. Born in the village of Oberaudorf (**Bavaria**), near the Austrian border, Edmund Stoiber grew up in a small, conservative, Roman Catholic community. His father, a businessman, worked for the National Socialist–controlled slave-labor Todt organization and after the war was not released from captivity until 1947. The family endured considerable poverty until the father established a profitable waste paper and scrap materials business, which enabled Stoiber to study law and politics at the University of Munich (1962–1967). He went on to work as a research assistant at the University of Regensburg (1967–1968), passing his state law exams (1967, 1971) and earning a doctorate in law (1971). During 1972–1974, he worked in the Bavarian Ministry of Development (Ministerium für Landesentwicklung) as the personal assistant for **Max Streibl**, the future **minister president**. An early admirer and subsequent protégé of **Franz Josef Strauß**, he entered the regional state parliament (1974–2008), served as general secretary of the CSU (1978–1983), and headed the Bavarian state chancellery (1982–1983). When Strauß died (1988), Stoiber became interior minister (1988–1993), taking a special interest in **security** issues, **foreigners, asylum** law, and right-wing **extremism**. An early opponent of the **Ostpolitik** pursued by **Willy Brandt**, he also argued for a stricter asylum law and opposed moves toward acknowledging Germany as a multicultural society.

Ambitious, hard-working, and a master of detail, Stoiber rose swiftly in the CSU hierarchy, becoming deputy party leader (1989–1993), succeeding Streibl as minister president (May 1993) and replacing **Theo Waigel** as party chairman (1999–2007). He managed the difficult task of cleaning up the CSU in the aftermath of Steibl's resignation (triggered by financial scandals) without damaging the legacy of Franz Josef Strauß and was particularly successful in promoting privatization and in encouraging high-technology **industry** to settle in Bavaria, mainly through subsidies. At the same time, he retained his profoundly conservative values and maintained strict discipline in his regional cabinet, choosing members with long-standing personal loyalties. When Jörg Haider, leader of the far-right Freedom Party, became a coalition partner in the Austrian government in 2000, Stoiber was the only mainstream German politician to congratulate him. After the German government argued that the country should be willing to admit foreigners and **immigrants** in order to meet its shortfall in skills and labor, Stoiber distanced himself from the notion of a multicultural society. In 2004, he was still criticizing the Czech government for the expulsion of Germans after World War II, and in 2006 he advocated national "citizenship tests" for would-be immigrants.

As conservative chancellor candidate for the 2002 national election, he argued for **tax** reductions for small businesses and the highest paid and for reduced or zero social welfare contributions for those lower on the pay scale; he also envisaged a greater role for private **health** insurance. Increases in ecological taxes planned by the government for 2003 would be dropped altogether. For the labor market, he proposed the creation of more lower-paid jobs, simplification of welfare benefits (including withdrawal of benefits for those unwilling to work), but no relaxation of current protection laws against dismissal. To stimulate the economy, Stoiber advocated increased state investment in infrastructure and **education**, using money derived from privatization of state concerns to develop new technologies, removing bureaucratic obstacles to businesses, and encouraging risk capital. His failure to lead the **Christian Democratic Union (CDU)** and CSU to victory in 2002 did not dampen his ambitions. Regarded as a potential member of **Andrea Merkel**'s coalition government during negotiations with the **Social Democratic Party of Germany (SPD)** after the national election of September 2005, he withdrew, however, after Merkel watered down his proposals to create a "super ministry" of economics. After this, Stoiber's personal popularity in Bavaria and the CSU declined, but he was elected honorary party chairman in 2007. During 2007–2014, he moved to Brussels to lead a **European Union (EU)** working group under industrial commissioner **Günter Verheugen** that met to consider reducing bureaucracy within the EU.

STOLPE, MANFRED (1936–). Social Democratic Party of Germany (SPD) politician. Manfred Stolpe was born in Stettin (now Szczecin in Poland). In March 1945, he fled with his family to Greifswald (eastern Germany). He began studying law in Jena (1955), but the following year the authorities of the **German Democratic Republic (GDR)** withdrew his scholarship after he became involved in a church-organized event that was critical of the

Soviet invasion of Hungary. Although he passed his state examination in law (1959), the authorities refused him permission to practice law or become a judge. Instead, he accepted an offer from the evangelical (Protestant) church of **Berlin**-Brandenburg to work as a legal adviser (Kirchenjurist).

From 1962, Stolpe represented the church in negotiations with the state, developing close relations with the leadership of the **Socialist Unity Party of Germany (SED)** while also preserving a degree of autonomy for the church. He managed the administrative office of the Konferenz der Evangelischen Kirchenleitungen in der DDR (Standing Conference of Evangelical Church Leaders in the GDR, 1962–1969) and headed the secretariat of the East German Bund der Evangelischen Kirchen in der DDR (Federation of Evangelical Churches in the GDR, 1969–1981). In 1976, he was appointed to the **human rights** commission of the World Council of Churches. His other positions included consistorial president of the eastern region of the evangelical church in Berlin-Brandenburg and member of the standing conference of evangelical church leaders (1982–1990). In his position as a representative of the evangelical churches and as a high-level go-between for state and church, Stolpe made numerous international contacts, notably with leading West German social democrats such as **Helmut Schmidt** and **Johannes Rau**.

After the fall of the GDR regime (November 1989), Stolpe joined the **Brandenburg** SPD (July 1990). He led the party to victory in three successive regional elections (1990, 1994, 1999) and was **minister president** of Brandenburg from 1990 to 2002. A member of the SPD national executive (1991–2002), he also headed a "traffic light coalition" of the SPD, **Free Democratic Party (FDP)**, and **Alliance 90/The Greens** in Brandenburg, which passed more than 200 laws and agreed on a regional constitution (1990–1994). This model of consensus politics came to be known as the "Brandenburg way." In 2002, he resigned and was succeeded by **Matthias Platzeck**. He went on to join the **Petersburg Dialog** forum for German–Russian cooperation.

Although Stolpe admitted that the **Stasi** had awarded him a service medal (1978), he consistently denied allegations by the office managing the Stasi's files that he was an informant (Informeller Mitarbeiter), a stance that was upheld by the **Federal Constitutional Court (FCC)** in 2005. An investigative committee, which was convened by the state of Brandenburg and reported in 2011, was divided on the issue. Although controversy over his links with the East German regime ultimately led to the breakup of the coalition with the FDP and the Greens, Stolpe led the SPD to an absolute majority in a second round of regional elections (1994). A proposed fusion of Brandenburg with Berlin, advocated by Stolpe and agreed to by both assemblies, was rejected by a referendum (1996). Stolpe's government also suffered from mismanagement scandals that led to the resignation of ministers responsible for building and **agriculture**. The third regional elections (1999) returned the

SPD with a reduced majority (39.3 percent of the vote), followed by the **Christian Democratic Union (CDU**, 26.5 percent) and the **Party of Democratic Socialism (PDS**, 23.3 percent); the extreme right-wing party **German People's Union (DVU)** cleared the 5 percent hurdle to gain five seats. In accordance with its policy of refusing to share power with the PDS, the SPD formed a ruling coalition with the CDU. The coalition survived Stolpe's support for the **immigration** law in the **Bundesrat**, which the conservatives opposed.

Despite the controversy over his links with the SED, not to mention Brandenburg's economic difficulties (high unemployment, bankruptcies, and delays over the projected new airport for Berlin-Brandenburg), Stolpe remained one of eastern Germany's most popular politicians. As head of a new "super ministry" for **transport**, building, and housing (Verkehr, Bau- und Wohnungswesen, 2002–2005), he was responsible for coordinating policy for the reconstruction of eastern Germany (**Aufbau Ost**) and promoting transportation links with Poland and the Czech Republic. He holds honorary doctorates from the universities of Greifswald (1989), Zurich (1991), Szczecin (1996), and Dokkyo in Japan (2001), and was awarded the Carlo Schmid Prize for contributions to democracy and European understanding (1991).

STOLTENBERG, GERHARD (1928–2001). Christian Democratic Union (CDU) politician. Gerhard Stoltenberg was born in Kiel (**Schleswig-Holstein**), the son of a Protestant pastor. While still at school, he served in an anti-aircraft battery toward the end of World War II and spent some months in British captivity. After the war, he studied history, social sciences, and philosophy at the University of Kiel, where he earned a doctorate (1954), worked as a research assistant in the history of politics (1954–1960), and qualified as a senior lecturer in modern history (1960). In 1965 and 1969–1970, he served as a director of economic policy of the **Krupp** Concern (Fried. Krupp GmbH).

After joining the CDU (1947), Stoltenberg occupied various positions in the party, including chairman of its national youth wing, the **Junge Union** (JU, 1955–1961); deputy chairman (1955–1971) and then chairman (1971–1989) of the Schleswig-Holstein party; and member of the national party presidium (from 1969). He was a long-standing member of the Schleswig-Holstein regional assembly (**Landtag**, 1954–1957 and 1971–1982) and, as **minister president** (1971–1982), led a majority CDU government that steered the mainly **agricultural** region through a period of economic change and modernization. He also sat in the **Bundestag** (1957–1971, 1983–1998) and was federal minister for science and **research** under Chancellors **Ludwig Erhard** and **Kurt Georg Kiesinger** (1965–1969). In Kiesinger's **grand coalition** (1966–1969), he was involved in preparations for university reform and took a special interest in information technology.

Elected deputy leader of the CDU/**Christian Social Union (CSU)** parliamentary group (1971), Stoltenberg became finance minister in the government of Chancellor **Helmut Kohl** (1982). Following a loss of public confidence in the wake of the financial scandal surrounding **Uwe Barschel** (1987), Stoltenberg resigned his office (1989; his successor was **Theo Waigel**) and moved to the Federal Ministry of Defense, where he stayed until 1992. As postreunification defense minister, he faced the difficult tasks of incorporating the army of the former **German Democratic Republic (GDR)** and making cuts following the dissolution of the **Warsaw Pact**. He also served on the boards of various companies and associations.

See also BUNDESWEHR.

STOPH, WILLI (1914–1999). German Democratic Republic (GDR) politician. Willi Stoph was born to a working-class family in **Berlin**, where he trained and worked as a bricklayer and building site engineer (1928–1931). He joined the communist youth organization Kommunistischer Jugendverband Deutschlands (KJVD) in 1928 and the main party (Kommunistische Partei Deutschlands, KPD) in 1931, working underground as an activist after the National Socialist takeover (1933). After his national service (1935–1937), he served in an artillery unit during World War II until he was wounded (1942). Following the war, he worked as a functionary for the KPD/**Socialist Unity Party of Germany (SED)**, specializing in rebuilding the construction and industry sector in the Soviet occupation zone and subsequently the GDR. In 1950, he became a member of the **People's Chamber** and the Central Committee of the SED; three years later, he joined the party's Politburo, where he headed the office for economic affairs.

During the early years of the GDR, Stoph occupied various key positions, including interior minister (Minister des Innern, 1952–1955) and defense minister (Minister für Nationale Verteidigung, 1956–1960). He was chairman of the Ministerrat (Council of Ministers) during 1962–1964 and, as successor to **Horst Sindermann**, from 1976 to 1989. Stoph joined the Staatsrat (Council of State) in 1963, where he served as deputy chairman (1964–1973, 1976–1989) and as chairman until 1976 (succeeding **Walter Ulbricht**), when the position was taken over by **Erich Honecker**. Stoph played a major part in rearming the GDR and building up its military forces. In 1953, he assumed responsibility for the state security service, the **Stasi**. As defense minister, he was an important figure in the **Warsaw Pact** and held the rank of army general (from 1959). In October/November 1989, Stoph was removed from all offices and in December expelled from the SED/**Party of Democratic Socialism (PDS)**. He remained in investigative detention on suspicion of misuse of office and corruption until February 1990, but was released on health grounds. He was rearrested (May 1991) in connection with the shoot-to-kill policy at the German border, although proceedings were later halted (July 1993).

STRAUSS, FRANZ JOSEF (1915–1988). Christian Social Union (CSU) politician. Born in Munich (**Bavaria**), Franz Josef Strauß studied philology, history, and economics at the University of Munich (1935–1939). He served as a soldier in World War II on the western and eastern fronts, qualifying as a schoolteacher during periods of leave. After the war, he cofounded the CSU in Schöngau (Niederbayern), steadily rising to represent the party in the regional state parliament (1946–1948) and serve on its presidium (1946–1948). He was CSU general secretary (1949–1952) and represented the party in the **Bundestag** (1949–1978), where he was elected deputy chairman of the **Christian Democratic Union (CDU)**/CSU parliamentary group (1950). In 1952, he was elected CSU deputy chairman and in 1961 chairman, a position he held until his death in 1988.

Under **Konrad Adenauer**, Strauß held a number of cabinet posts, including federal minister for special tasks (1953–1955) and minister for atomic affairs (1955–1956). As defense minister (1956–1962), he expanded the newly constituted West German army (**Bundeswehr**) to meet the demands of its role in the **North Atlantic Treaty Organization (NATO)**. He was forced to resign, however, over the *Spiegel* affair, in which he misused his office to have journalists arrested, accused of treason, and even kidnapped for publishing articles critical of defense policy. Although the affair seemed to end Strauß's ministerial career, he threw himself into transforming the Bavarian-based CSU into a party of mass appeal, using the regional newspaper *Der Bayernkurier* (founded 1950) as a vehicle for his views and policies. Returning as finance minister under the **grand coalition** of **Kurt Georg Kiesinger** (1966–1969), Strauß worked closely with the **Social Democratic Party of Germany (SPD)** economics minister **Karl Schiller** to reduce taxes and agree upon a program of recovery from Germany's first serious postwar recession.

While in opposition during the SPD/**Free Democratic Party (FDP)** coalition of 1969–1972, Strauß fiercely attacked the government's economic policy and, in particular, **Willy Brandt**'s strategy of rapprochement with the East. When the CDU eventually ratified the treaties that emerged from **Ostpolitik**, Strauß remained hostile, despite serious public disputes with the leader of the CDU parliamentary group, **Rainer Barzel**. In the national election of 1976 Strauß, who would have become deputy chancellor and finance minister in a government led by **Helmut Kohl**, conducted a virulent campaign against the "socialist" SPD. When the CDU/CSU lost the election, Strauß continued to argue for a more radical conservatism and threatened to withdraw the CSU from its partnership with the CDU in the Bundestag, drawing back only when the CDU considered campaigning directly in Bavaria.

In his various roles as government minister and as Bavarian **minister president** (1978–1988), Strauß used his influence and contacts with big business at home and abroad to attract industries to the region, transforming it from an indebted rural backwater into a hub of prosperity and new enterprise. In particular, he was instrumental in involving the **Quandt family** in the rescue of BMW in 1959, building up the aviation industry, expanding **education**, and developing the region's **transport** infrastructure. Hosting the Olympic Games in 1972 also provided the finance to enable the regional capital Munich to become a modern metropolis.

In the run-up to the 1979 national election, Strauß defeated **Ernst Albrecht**, minister president of **Lower Saxony**, in the contest to be adopted as CDU/CSU chancellor candidate. After the CDU's crushing defeat, Strauß resigned his seat in the Bundestag, although he continued to exert a vocal political influence from his Bavarian power base and as de facto leader of the conservative states in the **Bundesrat**. When the CDU/CSU eventually returned to power (1982), Strauß declined a ministerial post, preferring instead to embarrass Kohl's government by openly criticizing FDP foreign minister **Hans-Dietrich Genscher** for his policy of trying to reduce east–west tensions through advocating arms reduction.

Given his consistent hostility to Ostpolitik, Strauß astonished everyone in 1983 by arranging a 1,000 million DM credit for the GDR and making personal visits to Czechoslovakia, Poland, and East Germany, where he met **Erich Honecker**. Both Strauß and the West German government wished to prevent the GDR's attempting to solve its economic crisis by increasing its economic dependence on the Soviet Union and the eastern bloc. He had already made a surprising visit to China, meeting Mao Tse Tung and Chou En-Lai (1975). In 1987, declining to take a seat in the Bundestag for the third time (after 1980 and 1983) as a protest against the coalition partner (FDP), he continued to be critical of the government and to undertake personal political initiatives. When Strauß visited the Leipzig trade fair (1987), Honecker announced the prospect of relaxations on exit visas for East Germans and of progress in reuniting families in cases of hardship. The same year Strauß, a keen pilot, flew in his private Cessna to Moscow, where by all accounts he enjoyed congenial talks with the Soviet leader, Mikhail Gorbachev. In 1988, he died unexpectedly following a heart attack during a hunting excursion near Regensburg. He had three children; his daughter Monika was forced to resign as Bavarian cultural minister over allegations of electoral fraud (2004), while his son Max Josef was convicted of **tax** evasion (2003).

STREIBL, MAX (1932–1998). Christian Social Union (CSU) politician. Born in Oberammergau **(Bavaria)**, Max Streibl studied law and economics in Munich. A member of the CSU from 1957, he worked as a civil servant for the state of Bavaria (from 1960) and for minister presidents Hans Ehard and Alfons Goppel (from 1961). He was a cofounder and subsequently regional chairman of the party's youth wing **(Junge Union, JU, 1957)**, deputy in the Bavarian **Landtag** (1962–1994), and CSU general secretary (1966–1971). He became Germany's first minister for the **environment** when he was appointed Bavarian minister for regional development and environmental protection (Landesentwicklung und Umweltschutz, 1970). He later moved to the Federal Ministry of Finance (1997) and, as deputy to **Franz Josef Strauß**, took over as minister president following the latter's death in 1988 **(Theo Waigel** succeeded Streibl as party leader).

In May 1993, Streibl was forced to resign over the "Amigo affair" amid allegations that he, along with other leading politicians, had enjoyed services from private companies in return for political favors. Despite his fall from political grace, Streibl, a traditional conservative, was regarded as contributing to Bavaria's pioneering work in environmental protection. As finance minister, he also earned respect for his role in the region's economic regeneration through his judicious policy of combining investment with savings. He fought for the adoption of the subsidiarity principle in the Treaty of Maastricht and for recognition of the role of regions in an integrated **European Union (EU)**.

STRUCK, PETER (1943–2012). Social Democratic Party of Germany (SPD) politician. Born in Göttingen **(Lower Saxony)**, Peter Struck studied law at the universities of Göttingen and **Hamburg** (1962–1967), earning a doctorate (1971). After passing his state law examinations (1967, 1971), he joined the Hamburg city administration as a senior civil servant, working as a personal assistant to the president of the University of Hamburg and subsequently in the finance department. A member of the SPD from 1964, he was elected to the Hamburg city council (1973) and became deputy director of the city of Uelzen (Lower Saxony). In 1983, he worked as a lawyer for courts in Uelzen and Lüneburg.

A member of the public services **trade union** ÖTV and local councilor for Uelzen, Struck entered the **Bundestag** in 1980 (at about this time, he was also a member of the SPD regional executive for Lower Saxony). He worked largely in the background, specializing in **taxation**, before coming to prominence as business manager of the parliamentary party group (1990–1998). During this period, he acquired a reputation as an effective and flexible negotiator with the opposition parties on difficult issues such as the **asylum** law and the deployment of German armed forces in out-of-area operations. Due to become minister of the **Office of the Federal Chancellor** after the

SPD's election victory (1998), Struck was instead appointed chairman of the parliamentary party group, mustering internal party support for the chancellor. For the remaining 60 days of the legislative period, he replaced **Rudolf Scharping** as defense minister when the latter was dismissed in July 2002. Continuing in the post after the October 2002 national election, he was instrumental in restructuring the **Bundeswehr**, which adopted new guidelines in 2003. Known for being a formidable worker, and demonstrating touches of flamboyance, Struck formulated what came to be known as "Struck's first law": that "no law emerges from parliament in the form it was submitted." In 2004, his health deteriorated, and in the following year he was succeeded as defense minister by **Franz Josef Jung** in **Angela Merkel**'s first coalition cabinet. He also led the SPD parliamentary party group (1998–2002, 2005–2009). From 2010 until his death, he chaired the social democrat–oriented Friedrich-Ebert Stiftung (Friedrich Ebert Foundation).

STUDENTS' MOVEMENT. Also known as the "students' revolution" or the "1968 movement," the students' movement gained ground in Germany (and in other West European countries) during the 1960s and reached its peak in mass demonstrations in Paris and **Berlin** in 1968, though the unrest also manifested elsewhere in Germany. As much a cultural as a political phenomenon, the movement marks one of the most important shifts in West German contemporary history and society. Starting as a student-led demand for reforms to the university **education** system in 1965, the movement expanded into a wider protest against the U.S. war in Vietnam, Western support for authoritarian regimes in the developing world, and the materialist values of postwar capitalism. In Germany, its proponents highlighted the failure of the establishment to explore the Nazi past, took part in resistance to the national emergency laws (Notstandsgesetze, passed in May 1968), and formed the core of the **Extra-Parliamentary Opposition** (Außerparlamentarische Opposition, APO) that emerged in response to the **grand coalition** of 1966–1969. Intellectually, the movement found inspiration in the left-wing sociologists of the Frankfurt School (Theodor W. Adorno, Herbert Marcuse, and Max Horkheimer) and looked to anti-imperialist revolutionary figures such as Mao Tse Tung and Che Guevara.

Particular waves of protest in Germany were sparked by the killing of the student Benno Ohnesorg by a police officer during a demonstration against the shah of Persia in Berlin (June 1967) and the attempted murder of the student leader **Rudi Dutschke** (April 1968). After his death, it became known that the police officer had been involved with the East German **Stasi**. As extremists in the movement mounted arson attacks on perceived symbols of capitalism (in particular, the premises of the conservative newspaper publisher **Axel Springer**), the state responded with what were often perceived as overly robust security measures and efforts to exclude radicals from public service (through the **radicals decree**). While small splinter groups such as the **Red Army Faction** moved into **terrorism**, a political undercurrent, the "New Left," emerged, which eventually found institutional expression in the **Green Party**.

Students who took part in the movement set out to oppose and change traditional values as represented by their parents and national institutions. High on their agenda were new ways of living together, of education, and of individual development, although their values and aims were often denigrated as "subculture," "culture of opposition," or "alternative culture." Whatever term is used, it must be seen in opposition to the concept of a central or dominant national culture as implied by the notion of a Leitkultur (literally "model culture"), which proved controversial when it was presented by the **Christian Democratic Union** (**CDU**) and **Christian Social Union** (**CSU**) in the late 1990s in the context of a national debate on **immigration**.

While the arts had already developed "happenings" as new forms of expression, students now experimented with "go-ins," "teach-ins," "sit-ins," and "love-ins," creating a whole new vocabulary of opposition to the establishment. A new musical culture of protest emerged that mixed traditional popular songs with contemporary elements. Called "folk revival," it had echoes of "nueva canción" from Chile, music from Greece (for example, by Mikis Theodorakis), or the "nuovo canzoniere italiano" (Fausto Amodei). It drew on the popularity of American protest songs by the likes of Bob Dylan, Joan Baez, and others and led to German adaptations by the West German Drafi Deutscher. Between 1964 and 1968, the first West German Folk- and Liedermacherfestival took place in Hunsrück and launched the careers of artists such as Franz-Josef Degenhardt, Reinhard Mey, Hannes Wader, Dieter Süverkrüp, Perry Friedman, Hermann Hähnel, and Lin Jaldati.

The mood of social unrest articulated by the students' movement of the 1960s fed into the process of political reform during the 1970s and contributed to a general change of social values in the Federal Republic of Germany (FRG). The so-called Kommune 1 (Commune 1), whose most prominent spokesmen were Rainer Langhans and Fritz Teufel, achieved particular fame in that its participants tried to develop a collective way of living and combine it with political activity. Although their provocative public appearances eventually ceased, alternative kindergartens (Kinderladen) still live on, and the movement provided a starting point for the alternative life concepts that became popular in the FRG throughout the 1970s and 1980s. Changes in **theater**, **literature**, music, **cinema**, art, and the universities would not have developed as rapidly or in the same way without the impetus provided by the students' movement. Key issues that were debated included the conflicts between consumerism and individuality, career and society, self-orientation and sharing, and individualism and community spirit. The 1970s then saw the emergence of a less politically minded niche culture of so-called hippies. Known in German as Gammler, Spontis, or TUNIX, they placed a greater value on private rather than public values.

The intellectual protest movement had its critics. In 1966, the Georg Büchner Prize winner **Hans Magnus Enzensberger**, writing in the periodical *Kursbuch* (1996), referred to the "speechless intelligence" that had predominated in German society in the preceding years. In 1968, he went further, describing the left-wing intellectuals as prolific but unproductive, linked only by a belief in antifascism. Nevertheless, the immense impact of the 1968 protest culture can still be felt in Germany. From the late 1990s onward, many of the former active participants of the movement had risen to prominent positions in politics; examples include **Gerhard Schröder, Daniel Cohn-Bendit, Joschka Fischer**, and in culture, the writer Peter Schneider.

The year 1968 and its aftermath, which formed part of the "long 1960s," as Detlef Siegfried called the period from 1958 to 1973, became a cultural and political symbol of a new beginning that was in some respects paralleled by developments in the **German Democratic Republic (GDR)**. In 1972, **Willy Brandt** triumphed in the West German national election, while a year earlier **Erich Honecker** had come into power in East Germany. The emergence of these two leaders appeared to confirm the social and political change that many intellectuals and young people had hoped for, even though Honecker's restrictive politics became clear by the mid-1970s. More recently, authors such as Bernd Caillaux, who actively took part in the students' movement, contributed to the reassessment of both the time and its achievements (*Gutgeschriebene Verluste, Das Geschäftsjahr 1968/69*).

See also ALTERNATIVE MOVEMENTS (ALTERNATIVE BEWEGUNGEN).

SÜSSMUTH, RITA (1937–). Christian Democratic Union (CDU) politician. Rita Süssmuth (née Kickuth) was born in Wuppertal (**North Rhine-Westfalia**). She studied romance languages and history at the universities of Münster, Tübingen, and Paris (1956–1961) and qualified as a teacher in Münster, where she gained a doctorate in educational psychology (1964). She lectured at institutes of higher **education** in Stuttgart and Osnabrück (1963–1966) and the Pedagogical University (PU) of the Ruhr in Bochum (1966–1969) before being appointed to chairs in education (at the Ruhr University/Bochum in 1969, at the PU/Ruhr in 1971, and at the University of Dortmund in 1973). She served on an advisory council for family affairs (Wissenschaftlicher Beirat für Familienfragen) at the Federal Ministry for Youth, Family and **Health** (1971–1985) and on a commission reporting on family issues (Dritte Familienberichtskommission, 1977). An active Roman Catholic, Süssmuth was also a member of the Zentralkomitee der Deutschen

Katholiken (Central Committee of German Catholics, 1979–1991), was vice president of the Familienbund der Deutschen Katholiken (Family Federation of German Catholics, FDK, 1980–1985), and headed a Hanover-based research institute on **women** and society (Frau und Gesellschaft, 1982–1985).

After joining the CDU relatively late (1981), Süssmuth rose swiftly in the party, succeeding her mentor, Heiner Geißler, as federal minister for youth, family, and health (1985–1986), an office that later encompassed women's issues (1987–1988). As minister, she regarded health care as her central concern; stressed the role of education and counseling in preventing the spread of drug abuse and AIDS; saw family policy as extending beyond the sphere of married couples; and presided over measures to improve benefits for mothers, parents, the sick, and the old. She served as chairwoman of the national Women's Union of the CDU (1986–2001) and on the party presidium (1987–1998). Following the 1987 national elections, she won a personal (directly elected) mandate in the **Bundestag**, retaining the seat until 1998, when she reentered parliament on the regional list for **Lower Saxony**. The following year, she was elected president of the Bundestag, although she took the post reluctantly and considered herself "kicked upstairs" by Chancellor **Helmut Kohl**. At the 1989 CDU national congress in **Bremen**, she was a member of a group that included Geißler, **Kurt Biedenkopf**, and **Lothar Späth** and that privately urged replacing Kohl as party leader. She was censured for proposing a law against rape in marriage (1988) and openly criticized by the chancellor and the CDU/**Christian Social Union (CSU)** party parliamentary group for proposing a relaxation of the law on **abortion** (1991–1992).

A popular figure with the public and respected for her blend of traditional and progressive values, Süssmuth was not afraid to challenge the conservative wing of her party, which rejected her recommendation that Bundestag members forgo an increase in salaries (1992) and was critical of her support for potash miners in **Thuringia** threatened with unemployment (1993). She also drew unwelcome attention to the National Socialist past of Steffen Heitmann, the CDU contender for the position of **president of the Federal Republic**, although she voted for his candidacy (1993). In 1995, she opposed proposed cuts in sick pay, a reduction of employees' rights of protection against dismissal, and plans to raise the retirement age for women to 65. Following the collapse of communism, she championed relations with Poland and declared that critical examination of the East German past was a prerequisite for east–west reconciliation. Throughout her career, Süssmuth urged women to participate more actively in politics and in 1996 called on the CDU to introduce a quota system to encourage women to stand for party offices. She argued successfully for a reduction in the size of the Bundestag (to around 500 members) and oversaw the renovation of the Reichstag building in **Berlin**, including the assembly's move there. Increasingly mistrusted by Helmut Kohl, she finally retired as president of the Bundestag in 1998 (her successor was **Wolfgang Thierse**).

Following the reorganization of the CDU in the wake of the lost national election, Süssmuth was marginalized from the leadership. Facing fierce criticism, including calls for her to leave the CDU, she accepted an invitation from Chancellor **Gerhard Schröder** to head a government commission on **immigration** (2000–2001). Her party refused to take part in the so-called Süssmuth Commission and opposed some of its key recommendations, in particular that Germany should finally acknowledge that it had become a land of immigration.

Süssmuth received honorary doctorates from several universities and sat on numerous boards, including the experts' committee on immigration and integration (2002–2004) and the **United Nations** (**UN**) commission on international migration (2004–2005). She received the German Woman of the Year Award (1987) and was awarded the Avicenna Gold Medal by the UN Educational, Scientific, and Cultural Organization (UNESCO, 1997). After withdrawing from active politics, she continued to serve on the boards of various foundations and has published on children, women's issues, AIDS, and contemporary history. Her memoirs (*Wer nicht kämpft, hat schon verloren*, 2000) attracted attention for criticizing the Kohl system of power and patronage.

T

TAUBER, PETER (1974–). Christian Democratic Union (CDU) politician. Born in Frankfurt/Main, Peter Tauber studied history, German **literature**, and politics at the University of Frankfurt (1994–1995 and from 1996), graduating with a master's degree (2000). During 2001–2001, he worked as a research assistant at the university, and he completed a doctorate in 2007; he has also published numerous papers on historical topics, including the history of **sport**. A member of the CDU from 1992, Tauber was regional business manager (2001–2003), then leader (2003–2009), of the **Junge Union (JU)** youth organization (2001–2003) in **Hessen** and occupied various positions in the main party at regional level, including membership on the executive committee from 2008. He was also a personal assistant to the culture minister and deputy **minister president**, Karin Wolff (2003–2004), in the Hessen state parliament (**Landtag**). In 2009, he entered the **Bundestag** as a deputy and in December 2013 became general secretary of the national CDU. Although a surprise choice for this post, largely unknown outside Hessen and not considered a personal confidant of Federal Chancellor **Angela Merkel**, she selected him for his political networking skills and with a view to modernizing party organization.

TAXATION. Apart from setting the level of land purchase tax (Grunderwerbssteuer), Germany's **federal states** (Länder) have no sovereign powers in determining revenues, which are in the hands of the central government (the **Bund**). At the same time, tax income is distributed to both states and government through a revenue-sharing system (Steuerverbund) in which the **Basic Law** (**BL**, article 106) guarantees the states (and, for certain taxes, the local districts or Gemeinden) a share of the revenue from the "community taxes" (Gemeinschaftssteuern). These comprise general income tax (Einkommenssteuer), corporation tax (Körperschaftssteuer, levied largely on income from companies), and turnover or value-added tax (Umsatz-/Mehrwertsteuer, levied on sales and business transactions). They contribute 70 percent of total tax revenue, with income and turnover tax providing the most. A number of other, generally minor, taxes are allocated exclusively to the Bund (e.g.,

energy and insurance tax), Länder (inheritance, land purchase, and beer tax; wealth or asset tax [Vermögensteuer] was abolished in 1997), or districts (business and land tax).

Governments have made several attempts to reform Germany's tax system to meet often conflicting political and economic demands. A key goal has been to reduce its complexity by cutting the large number of allowances and reducing general income tax levels while also maintaining fairness, preserving revenues, and encouraging economic growth. Recommendations by the Goerdeler Commission (1990–1992) and the Bareis Commission (1994), as well as the Petersberger Proposals (1997), never reached the statute books, although partial reforms emerging from the Eberhard Commission (1971) came into force in three stages between 1972 and 1977. The **Social Democratic Party (SPD)/Green Party** coalition (1998–2005) lowered corporation tax and the top rate of general income tax, but revenues did not make up for economic downturn as the national deficit rose; ecological taxes were introduced starting in 1999. The **grand coalition** of the **Christian Democratic Union (CDU)**/SPD (2005–2009) made little progress on simplification but raised turnover tax to its highest ever level (19 percent from 2007). Although the **Free Democratic Party (FDP)** campaigned vigorously for tax cuts, it failed in coalition with the CDU (2009–2013) to enact them as Federal Chancellor **Angela Merkel** and her finance minister, Wolfgang Schäuble, focused on the **budget** deficit and the need for a debt brake. Relatively minor changes were made, notably legislation simplifying aspects of general and turnover tax (Steuervereinfachungsgesetz, in force 2012). In opposition, supporters of the SPD and the Green Party tended to advocate higher tax rates for the most wealthy.

See also AGENDA 2010; FEDERALISM; FINANCIAL EQUALIZATION (LÄNDERFINANZAUSGLEICH).

TELECOMMUNICATIONS. Following national and **European Union (EU)** initiatives during the 1980s aimed at creating a deregulated common market for telecommunications services, Germany restructured and liberalized its state-owned postal and telephone utility, the Federal German Post Office (Deutsche Bundespost), in three stages. Stage one was completed in 1989–1990, when the Post Office was split into three public enterprises: Deutsche Bundespost POSTDIENST (for postal services), Deutsche Bundespost POSTBANK (banking and giro services), and Deutsche Bundespost **TELEKOM** (phones and telecommunication). The new bodies acquired new commercial freedoms, although the state retained control over the approval of equipment specifications and the assignment and management of radio and telecommunications frequencies. Telekom lost its monopoly on landlines in 1998 and of mobile (cell) phone networks in 1991. Stage two of the reform, implemented in 1995, converted the three enterprises of Deutsche

Bundespost into share capital companies (Aktiengesellschaften) and amended the **Basic Law (BL)** by including two new articles (87f and 143b), which laid down the constitutional basis for moving the corporations and their services into private ownership. Telekom entered the **German Stock Exchange** for the first time in late 1996 (again in 2000, also with T-Online), with the **federal government** owning 43 percent of the shares (2002). The third stage of liberalization was marked by the introduction of a new regulatory framework for telecommunications, embodied in the Telecommunications Act (Telekommunikationsgesetz, effective in 1996). Designed to promote fair competition and an affordable supply of services and equipment for private and business users, the act set up a new regulatory authority, now subsumed in the Bundesnetzagentur (Federal Network Agency for Electricity, Gas, Telecommunications, Post and Railway), created in 1998.

The deregulation of telecommunications rapidly transformed the market, creating competition between telephone network providers and allowing prices for services and equipment to fall. The use of cell/mobile phones increased dramatically, and the **Internet** expanded as it was opened up to commercial applications and software companies developed more powerful browsers. After nine years of planning and development, Telekom began installing integrated services digital network (ISDN) connections, which were completed across the country by 2000; the first FTTH (fiber optics to the home) networks were rolled out in 2011. Telekom still dominates fixed-line communications, with over 80 percent of market share, although Vodafone remains a competitor in a declining subscriber market. The main cell phone companies are T-Mobile (a Telekom subsidiary), Vodafone, Telefonica Germany (O2), and E-Plus. In 2010, Telekom and Vodafone launched advanced LTE (long-term evolution) technology, providing very high speed wireless communication.

During the 1990s, Deutsche Telekom installed Germany's cable network, originally kept separate from fixed link services for voice and data traffic, in order to promote competition among **television** providers. After privatization, Telekom sold off its cable activities to various companies, of which Kabel Deutschland (created in 2003) emerged as the leader for Internet, telephone, and television services.

See also DEUTSCHE POST AG.

TELEVISION AND RADIO. In order to provide a national broadcasting service, the regionally based, state-run radio stations of the Federal Republic of Germany (FRG) joined forces in 1950 to create a single public corporation, the Arbeitsgemeinschaft öffentlich-rechtlicher Rundfunkanstalten der Bundesrepublik Deutschland (Association of Public Broadcasting Corporations in the Federal Republic of Germany, ARD). A fully national television channel, Deutsches Fernsehen, also under the auspices of the ARD, was launched in 1954. In 1961, the **Federal Constitutional Court (FCC)** confirmed the **federal states'** responsibility for broadcasting, ending attempts by Federal Chancellor **Konrad Adenauer** to create central institutions under government control. The ARD's members continue to contribute and exchange programs, share productions, and maintain a central news studio in **Berlin** alongside a global network of foreign correspondents. Following a further interstate agreement (1961), a second channel, ZDF (Zweites Deutsches Fernsehen), based in Mainz, began transmitting in 1963. A third channel (Drittes Programm), which emerged between 1964 and 1969, now takes the form of nine state-based broadcasters (e.g., Bayerisches Fernsehen, Radio Bremen TV), providing more regional programs and a relatively high proportion of cultural and educational content.

The state channels are financed by license fees—shared between the ARD and ZDF—and to a lesser extent through advertising. The charge was levied on each radio or television set until 2013, after which it normally applied to each household (it is currently around 18 euros a month). The change, which was supposed to be financially neutral, triggered a wave of protests, especially from (hitherto levy-free) **Internet** users and also some newspapers, with many arguing that the license system had been overtaken by new technologies and should be scrapped altogether.

The main state channels dominated radio and television in the FRG until the advent of private broadcasters in the 1980s. Although they compete for audiences, they also coordinate their activities via a joint directorate in Munich and do not, for example, undermine each other's political and current affairs broadcasts by simultaneously broadcasting popular entertainment. With the arrival of private broadcasters and new technologies (cable and satellite) in the 1980s, both stations expanded their services. In 1984 ZDF, in partnership with ORF (Austria) and SRG (Switzerland), introduced a national satellite channel, 3SAT; ARD joined the consortium in 1993. In 1992, ARD and ZDF began broadcasting, via satellite, a Franco-German cultural channel, ARTE, and in 1997 a children's channel (KI.KA) and PHOENIX were launched. The latter broadcasts documentaries and information on political and economic affairs. The 24-hour news channel tagesschau24 appeared in 2008.

Following mergers and reunification, the nine principal ARD radio/television stations are Bayerischer Rundfunk (BR, covering **Bavaria**), Hessischer Rundfunk (HR, **Hessen**), Mitteldeutscher Rundfunk (MDR, **Saxony, Saxony-Anhalt, Thuringia**, from 1991), Norddeutscher Rundfunk (NDR, **Lower Saxony, Schleswig-Holstein, Hamburg, Mecklenburg-West Pomerania**), Radio Bremen (**Bremen**), Rundfunk Berlin-Brandenburg (RBB, from 2003), Saarländischer Rundfunk (SR, **Saarland**), Südwestrundfunk (SWR, **Rhineland-Palatinate** and **Baden-Württemberg**), and Westdeutscher Rundfunk (WDR, **North Rhine-Westfalia**). Also in the ARD family are the national cultural and information channel Deutschlandradio (DRadio) and the multi-lingual world service **Deutsche Welle (DW)**. The structure and functions of the state-owned broadcasters are laid down in federal state laws (Landesgesetze) that require broadcasters to ensure plurality and balance in news and opinion and to meet cultural and educational needs. All state-run stations are governed by a broadcasting council (generally called Rundfunkrat, or, for the ZDF, Fernsehrat), an administrative council (Verwaltungsrat), and a director (Intendant).

Following years of criticism of the ARD-ZDF monopoly, in 1984 Germany began to develop a dual system of broadcasting, with state-run channels operating alongside and in competition with private stations financed solely by advertising revenue. In 1987, the federal states agreed to the first of a series of interstate broadcasting treaties (Rundfunkstaatsverträge), which empowered the states to license and provide the technical facilities for private broadcasters, specify the length and form of advertising, oversee media concentration, and, more recently, regulate the content of new media, including the Internet (telemedia). At the same time, private providers were not subject to the same social and cultural requirements as the ARD/ZDF, having only to meet a "basic standard" (Grundstandard) in their programming. The states also passed their own **media** laws (Landesmediengesetze) and set up media state authorities (Landesmedienanstalten) to license and regulate private broadcasting. A standing conference of media authorities' directors (Direktorenkonferenz der Landesmedienanstalten, DLM) coordinates their activities and commissions reports and analyses.

In practice, patterns of corporate ownership have proved difficult to regulate. There are no national commercial radio stations, although some operate across several states, and the service provided is highly diverse, including mainly local stations and some noncommercial community broadcasting. In television, by contrast, a gradual process of concentration has resulted in two large, national media concerns or "broadcasting families" (Senderfamilien) dominating the market: ProSiebenSat.1.Media AG, formerly owned by **Leo Kirch** (15 channels including ProSieben, Sat.1, kabel eins, sixx), and the **Bertelsmann** group (RTL, RTL II, Super RTL, VOX, n-tv). The networks ARD (12.1 percent), ARD Drittes Fernsehen (13 percent), and ZDF (12.8 percent) command the largest audience shares, followed by RTL (11.3 percent) and Sat.1 (8.2 percent).

TERRORISM. Left-wing extremist groups in the Federal Republic of Germany (FRG) emerged from the **students' movement** of the 1960s and 1970s. They condemned the social and political establishment as monopolistic and denounced capitalistic structures that exploited consumerism and manipulated the mass **media** to further their own power interests. While the radical **Federation of Socialist German Students (SDS)** was content to try to overturn these structures through largely peaceful protest and political agitation, the **Red Army Faction (RAF)** achieved notoriety from its readiness to use extreme violence in order to destabilize the establishment. A wave of kidnappings and murders reached its peak in the fall of 1977, but it was countered by firm measures from the state and continued only sporadically through the 1980s and 1990s. Other groups engaged in terrorist attacks included the Movement 2. June (Bewegung 2. Juni), Revolutionary Cells (Revolutionäre Zellen, RZ), and the feminist-oriented Rote Zora. Although purportedly left wing in orientation, they adopted anarchist methods and outlooks.

After reunification (3 October 1990), concern over terrorism shifted to physical attacks by extreme right-wing groups on **foreigners** and **asylum seekers**. These attacks increased dramatically (from around 300 recorded incidents in 1990 to more than 2,200 in 1993), with many, but not all, occurring in the **eastern federal states**. Landmark incidents were the murder of a young Angolan in Eberswalde (**Brandenburg**) in 1990; the besieging of a hostel for asylum seekers in Rostock (**Mecklenburg-West Pomerania**) in August 1992; and the deaths of an immigrant Turkish woman and two children in an arson attack in Mölln (November 1992) and of four people in a similar attack in Solingen (May 1993). In the worst racist assault in the history of the FRG, 10 immigrants and asylum seekers died in an arson attack in Lübeck (1996). This caused an outcry among the wider public, with numerous demonstrations against right-wing violence.

Overall, the incidence of right-wing-motivated violence, which had risen steadily from 1991, began to decline after 1993, to around 600 attacks each year by the end of the decade. Germans took part in mass demonstrations and processions to express their solidarity with the foreign population, and the scale of violence prompted Chancellor **Gerhard Schröder** to announce a crackdown on the extreme right that took the form of court convictions and the banning of organizations. According to figures collected by the Federal Ministry of the Interior, right-wing extremists committed more than 526 violent attacks in 2003 and were responsible for almost 7,000 offenses, including incitement to racial hatred. The total number of violent extremists was estimated at between 3,000 and 10,000, with the **eastern federal states** acting as a fertile recruiting ground. As the German security authorities made life too difficult for them, extremist groups became more mobile, meeting and organizing in secret, appearing less prominently in large cities, and relocating to rural areas and neighboring countries, including Poland, Slovenia, the Czech Republic, France, and Switzerland, from where they organized cross-border operations, often at football matches. Members of right-wing parties such as the **National Democratic Party (NPD)** were also adopting an outwardly more respectable image and stirring up hostility to foreigners and refugees under the guise of citizens' initiatives (e.g., to improve the quality of living). In the following decade, mob-driven and large-scale attacks on foreigners and their homes gave way to violent assaults on individuals, including young left-wingers, although the increase in asylum seekers and refugees in Germany (especially after Islamic State established itself within Syria in 2013) was linked to several attacks on foreigners and their accommodations, especially in eastern Germany.

Following the attack on the World Trade Center in New York (11 September 2001) and bombings in Madrid (March 2004), fears about terrorist activity in Germany focused on threats from radical Islamists. In most cases, projected attacks failed or were preempted. Groups detected include a cell in **Hamburg** (whose members were accused of involvement in the 9/11 attack); the "suitcase bombers," who targeted regional trains in Cologne (arrested in 2006; a conviction followed in 2008); and the co-called Sauerland Group, who planned to bomb U.S. institutions in Germany (arrested in 2007, convicted in 2010). Arrests prevented an attack on a Jewish center in **Berlin** by the al-Tawhid group (April 2006) and the assassination of the Iraqi prime minister, Ayad Alawi, by the Kurdish group Ansar al-Islam (2004, with convictions in 2008). Four Salafists were put on trial in 2014 for planting a bomb (which failed to detonate) in the Bonn main railway station in 2012. The shooting of two American soldiers in Frankfurt airport in March 2011 and the planned attack on American and Jewish centers by a Tunisian arrested in March 2003 involved individuals acting in isolation, as did attacks in Würzburg, Reutlingen, Munich, and Ansbach in 2016. Compared with some neighboring countries, Germany has successfully avoided attacks claiming large numbers of victims.

Concern over the need for additional internal security measures opened up differences between Germany's **political parties**. While the opposition **Christian Democratic Union (CDU)/Christian Social Union (CSU)** called for tough provisions to detain and expel suspected Islamic extremists and internment without trial for up to two years, the **Green Party** stressed the need to protect civil liberties. The **Social Democratic Party of Germany (SPD)** adopted a middle position. Although the need for international intelligence services to cooperate in sharing information about terrorist groups and individuals was widely accepted, the debate was complicated in Germany by revelations in 2013 that the U.S. National Security Agency (NSA) was spying on political leaders, and that German agencies were passing data on German citizens to their American counterparts.

See also ANTI-SEMITISM; EXTREMISM; IMMIGRATION; JEWS IN GERMANY; SECURITY POLICY, INTERNAL.

TEUFEL, ERWIN (1939–). Christian Democratic Union (CDU) politician. Born in Rottweil (**Baden-Württemberg**), Erwin Teufel developed an early interest in politics after reading stories of resistance to the National Socialist regime (1933–1945). After leaving behind early ambitions to become a **sports** reporter, he earned a diploma in administration (1961) and worked in local government in Rottweil and Trossingen (1961–1964). In 1964, aged 25, he was elected mayor of the town of Spaichingen, the youngest mayor in Germany; he held the post until 1972. A member of the CDU from 1955, he cofounded a branch of the **Junge Union (JU)** youth wing in Rottweil before entering the state parliament (**Landtag**) of Baden-Württemberg (1972), where he was **state secretary** for various regional ministries (1972–1978). He served in the regional government (1976–1978) and led the CDU parliamentary group for many years (1978–1991), declining repeated offers of a ministerial post.

In January 1991, Teufel succeeded **Lothar Späth** as **minister president** of Baden-Württemberg and in October was elected chairman of the regional CDU. As regional premier, he made a determined effort to control public spending while extending social provision in areas such as kindergartens and school-based nurseries and improving the **environment** and **transport**. He also instituted a more liberal line on **asylum policy**. Teufel led a **grand coalition** of the CDU and **Social Democratic Party of Germany (SPD**, 1992–1996) and a coalition with the liberal **Free Democratic Party (FDP)**/ DVP as junior partner after 1996. His notable achievements include the creation through mergers of a large regional bank (the Landesbank Baden-Württemberg, 1998–1999), agreement with the government on financing a major transport project (building a controversial new underground central station in Stuttgart and a high-speed ICE rail link with Ulm), and the construction of a large exhibition area at Stuttgart airport. Despite domestic opposition, the state of Baden-Württemberg also sold its holdings in the EnBW **energy** concern in order to reinvest in youth projects and set up the Landesstiftung Baden-Württemberg GmbH, a regional foundation, to promote culture, **research**, and development. Teufel was deputy leader of the national CDU (1992–1998); president of the **Bundesrat** (1996–1997); representative for Franco-German cultural affairs (1995–1998); and member, then vice president (1994–2003), of the Committee of the Regions (COR) of the **European Union (EU)**. He also represented the Bundesrat on the Convention on the Future of Europe, which was launched in February 2002.

After the conservatives lost the national election of 1998, Teufel's influence within the CDU waned as it rejuvenated its leadership. Nevertheless, he was for many years the undisputed leader of one of Germany's wealthiest states, retained very strong links with his roots, and was regarded as a highly experienced and skillful politician. He resigned as minister president in 2005 and was succeeded by **Günther Oettinger**. A member of the Central Committee of German Catholics (since 1993) and chairman of the Jerusalem Foundation Deutschland (1993–2006), Teufel has honorary positions at several universities and colleges and served on the Deutscher Ethikrat (German Ethics Council, 2008–2012).

THEATER. A distinctively political West German theater that set out to educate its audience emerged in the Federal Republic of Germany (FRG) in the 1960s. Termed "Dokumentartheater" because it used and was based on documentary evidence, its proponents saw it as essential to provide insights into historical developments and eminent personalities. In a development that fitted well into the more political atmosphere of the 1960s, theaters in Germany thus became meeting places for public debates, which, among other things, questioned the role of theaters in society in general. Important representatives of this type of theater include Rolf Hochhuth, Peter Weiss, and Heiner Kipphardt. "Regietheater" was a term used to describe the way in which plays and productions were dominated by their artistic director's interpretation, and it provoked a lively debate between progressive and more conservative forces in the 1970s. Aside from Peter Stein at the **Berlin** Schaubühne, representative directors of the time include Peter Palitzsch (who worked at Frankfurt from 1972 to 1980), Peter Zadek (Bochum, 1973–1978), Ivan Nagel (**Hamburg**, 1972–1979), and Claus Peymann (Stuttgart, 1974–1979, and Bochum, 1980–1985). The following generation of directors in the 1980s included Jürgen Flimm, Hans Neuenfels, and Luc Bondy, who extended the repertoire in new directions, such as performance, dance, and "live art" that provided no narrative or development. While theater in the FRG was characterized by experimental or political approaches, in the **German Democratic Republic (GDR)** it offered "Ersatzöffentlichkeit," a public forum that at times was able to escape the demands of a strict censorship. East German dramatists and directors such as Heiner Müller and Einar Schleef also worked in the West.

Theater in Germany is not limited to big cities; smaller towns too offer several plays at the same time ("Repertoiretheater"). The four main groups are state and city theaters, touring theaters, and private theaters. Theaters may be housed either in historical buildings dating back to the 17th to 19th centuries (such as **Bremen** or Göttingen) or in modern buildings developed after 1945 (such as the new opera in West Berlin). Large cities also boast "alternative" small stages that are often located in backyards.

With reunification, the theater landscape changed. Although to some extent the changes became a topic in itself—in both parts of the country discussion in the **media** was dominated by theater closures—the general outcome was that theaters in the **eastern federal states** soon lost their political impact. Heiner Müller's death in 1995 marked a particular turning point, since he had been one of the most eloquent figures addressing issues in both east and west. What he saw as the continuous "German misery" and the persistence of everyday fascism featured strongly in his works.

Alongside the established theater, Germany offers a very active dance and performance scene. Increasingly, the established theater was confronted in the 1990s by events aimed at attracting a wider, mass audience. Such events were often deliberately staged in unconventional locations, which was part of their philosophy. Christoph Schlingensief (1960–2010), for example, became known for his provocative, often highly political, and controversial productions, happenings, and performances in both Austria and Germany. However, recent years have witnessed a revival in the importance attached to playwrights. A leading dramatist of the 1970s and 1980s is Botho Strauss, who remains one of Germany's most frequently performed playwrights. Other established figures include Peter Weiss, Heiner Kipphardt, **Martin Walser**, Peter Hacks, Herbert Achternbusch, Peter Turrini, and Franz Xaver Kroetz. Examples of new playwrights are Marius von Mayenburg, Roland Schimmelpfennig, Katharina Gericke, Moritz Rinke, John von Düffel, Ulrich Khuon, and Albert Ostermeier.

There are about 180 theaters in Germany today, not to mention 190 private houses and 30 festival theaters. Annual festivals, such as the Berliner Theater Festival (Berliner Theatertreffen, from 1964), stage, by invitation, a range of more outstanding German-language productions. The Ruhrfestspiele in Recklinghausen, established in the late 1940s, offer a range of classical and modern works. Other prestigious events include the **Bayreuth Festival**, which first took place in 1882; directors in recent years include Werner Herzog (1987), Heiner Müller (1993), Philipp Artaud (2002), and Christoph Schlingensief (2004). Important regular publications include *Die Deutsche Bühne*, *Theater heute*, and *Theater der Zeit*. A complete list of German theaters is available under www.buehnenverein.de.

Most theater in Germany is financed from public funds (local government, the **federal states**, and the **Bund**). The system of subsidies is unique and is coming increasingly under threat, forcing theaters to close or merge. An artistic director of a theater generally holds the position for between three and five years. This was seen as counterproductive in the 1960s, when the Schauspielhaus Frankfurt and the Schaubühne Berlin, for example, moved over to a system of **codetermination**. Some of the independent theatrical groups that emerged during the 1960s focused on street theater (Straßentheater). There were about 40 such groups in the 1970s, and by the early 1990s around 300 groups and projects could be found in Berlin alone. Some of these groups have a specific focus, for example, theater for and by **women**, children/youth theaters, and cabarets.

The leading German theaters include the Bochum Schauspielhaus (which came to the public's attention from the 1970s onward under directors such as Peter Zadek, Claus Peymann, and Matthias Langhoff), the Bremer Schauspiel (which flourished in the 1960s and 1970s under a new generation of directors, including Stein and Zadek), the Deutsches Theater in Berlin (with artistic directors such as Thomas Langhoff), and the Staatsschauspiel Dresden. In the Schauspielhaus der Städtischen Bühnen Frankfurt, the opera, Kammerspiel, and Schauspielhaus share a home finished in 1963; the theater

(Schauspielhaus) thrived under directors such as Palitzsch and Bondy. The Grips Theater in Berlin, which was established in 1965, specialized in theater for children and young adults and is the home for some highly successful plays. The Deutsches Schauspielhaus Hamburg began to flourish artistically under directors such as Ivan Nagel, Claus Peymann, Wilfried Minks, and Peter Zadek, while the Thalia Theater (also in Hamburg) made its name in particular under the directorship of Jürgen Flimm. Munich boasts the Bavarian State Theater (Bayerisches Staatstheater, also called the Residenztheater) and the Kammertheater. The Schaubühne am Halleschen Ufer/Lehniner Platz in Berlin was famed for its codetermined structures under Peter Stein; a new cast in the 1970s included eminent actors such as Bruno Ganz and Jutta Lampe. The Volksbühne in Berlin is the successor to the Volksbühne East and Volksbühne West. The West Berlin Volksbühne, one of a number of prominent contemporary casualties, closed in 1992; directors in the east of the city include Benno Besson, Manfred Karge, Matthias Langhoff, and Frank Castorf. Under Castorf, the theater developed a reputation for innovation and outstanding productions from the 1990s onward. Other leading directors in more recent years include Christoph Marthaler, Claus Peymann, Michael Thalheimer, Armin Petras, Martin Kusey, and René Pollesch. Two of the leading choreographers who have contributed to Germany's reputation as a home for dance (Tanztheater) are Pina Bausch (1940–2009) and Sasha Waltz (1963–).

THIERSE, WOLFGANG (1943–). Social Democratic Party of Germany (SPD) politician. Wolfgang Thierse was born in Breslau (now in Poland). After the family were expelled at the end of World War II as the territory was incorporated into Poland, they settled in Eisfeld (southern **Thuringia**), where his father, a lawyer, became an activist in the **Christian Democratic Union (CDU)** of the **German Democratic Republic (GDR)**. Thierse trained as a typesetter with a local newspaper in Weimar and studied cultural science and German **literature** at Humboldt University in East **Berlin**, where he worked in the department of cultural theory and aesthetics (1964–1975). During his studies, he joined a Roman Catholic students' organization. He worked in the fine art department in the GDR ministry of culture, specializing in art and **architecture** (1975–1976), but was dismissed after taking part in the protest against the state's decision to deprive the singer **Wolf Biermann** of East German citizenship. Thierse then worked in the Central Institute for Literary History at the GDR Academy of Sciences (Zentralinstitut für Literaturgeschichte der Akademie der Wissenschaften, 1977–1990), where he coproduced a dictionary of aesthetics.

In October 1989, Thierse joined the protest group **New Forum**. In January 1990, he moved to the newly founded **Social Democratic Party of Germany in the GDR** in Berlin. A member of the **People's Chamber**

(March–October 1990), specializing in **media** and cultural affairs, he served as deputy leader and, from June to September 1990, as leader of the social democrats in the GDR. When the party merged with the West German SPD (September 1990), Thierse was elected national deputy chairman. At first, he backed the SPD's gradualist policy of reunification, but later advocated a swift merger. At the same time, he supported a reform of the **Basic Law** (**BL**) and called for the state to acknowledge the right to work and to protect the **environment** as an objective.

Thierse entered the **Bundestag** (October 1990) and in the all-German elections (December 1990) won a directly elected seat for a central Berlin constituency (Berlin-Mitte/Prenzlauer Berg). He served as deputy leader of the national party (1990–2005) and of the parliamentary group (1990–1998) and was also on the national executive (until 2009). Thierse strongly supported moving the government and parliament to Berlin and chaired the SPD commission on basic values (Grundwertekommission, from September 1991). From an early stage, he argued for a tribunal that would openly and objectively investigate the GDR's past. Although considered a possible successor to Walter Momper (born in 1945) following the latter's resignation as leader of the Berlin SPD in 1992, he did not stand for election, declaring that he did not wish to divide his energies between Bonn and Berlin. Soon after reunification, Thierse publicly expressed his disappointment over a process that the West Germans saw merely as an extension and continuation of their existing system without the need for reform. Reelected to the Bundestag (1994), he campaigned for equal social welfare standards in eastern and western Germany and for continuing financial transfers to the **eastern federal states** and drew attention to the dangers of uncontrolled globalization.

When the SPD/**Green Party** coalition came to power in 1998, Thierse succeeded **Rita Süssmuth** as president of the Bundestag, the first citizen of the former GDR to hold the post. While president (until 2005), he opposed a proposal for an amnesty for convicted former leaders of the GDR (1999), required the CDU to repay undisclosed assets of 41.3 million DM that the **Hessen** branch of the party had secretly moved abroad in contravention of the law on party funding (2000), and in 2000 imposed a further fine of 6.5 million DM following revelations that former chancellor **Helmut Kohl** had accepted anonymous donations to the party. From 2005 until his resignation from the Bundestag in 2013, he served as its vice president.

Thierse received the "Golden Microphone" prize for Speaker of the Year 1993 (1994) and chaired a committee of the Stiftung Denkmal für die ermordeten Juden Europas (Foundation for a Memorial to the Murdered **Jews** of Europe, 1999–2006). A committed Roman Catholic, he has authored or co-authored several writings and pamphlets on public and political issues and has contributed to and edited journals on religious and social affairs.

THURINGIA (THÜRINGEN). The smallest of the eastern **federal states** to emerge from reunification, Thuringia, with a total area of 16,171 square kilometers, lies in the geographical center of Germany and adjoins **Lower Saxony** (to the north), **Saxony-Anhalt** (northeast), **Saxony** (east), **Bavaria** (south), and **Hessen** (west). The Thuringian Forest, a wooded mountain ridge in the south, contains the region's highest peak and major tourist attraction, the 982-meter Großer Beerberg. North of this lies the fertile Thuringian Basin and in the far north a small section of the Harz Mountains. One-third of Thuringia is forested, and the major rivers are the Saale, Ilm, Werra, Unstrut, and Weiße Elster. With a total population of almost 2.2 million, the main towns are the historic city and state capital of Erfurt (206,000); followed by Jena (105,000), where precision and optical **engineering** industries have survived reunification; Gera (98,000), a former center of textile production; and Weimar (65,000), which houses national monuments to Wolfgang von Goethe and Friedrich Schiller, who established German as a major European literary **language** in the 18th century. The proportion of **foreigners** is one of the lowest, at 3.5 percent (2014).

A center of feudal power in the Middle Ages (the dukes of Thuringia, based in Wartburg near Eisenach, were leading nobles of the German Empire in the 12th and 13th centuries), Thuringia had fragmented into a patchwork of over 25 petty states by 1700. Although many of the kingdoms supported the Reformation during the 16th century (Martin Luther translated the New Testament in the Wartburg castle under the protection of the electoral prince of Saxony), the Roman Catholic archbishops of Mainz maintained footholds in Erfurt and Eichsfeld. Toward the end of the 18th century, the Grand Duchy of Saxony-Weimar established itself as a cultural center, attracting leading writers and poets. In the territorial settlement that followed the Napoleonic Wars, more than 12 statelets survived in the center and south of the region (eventually falling to 8), while the north became part of Prussia. Despite the power of the nobility and political censorship, Thuringia became a center of liberalism, culture, and social democracy during the 19th century. From the abdication of the petty princes in 1918 and elections the following year emerged the unified state of Thuringia, with Weimar as its capital. In 1944, Thuringia was enlarged to include Erfurt and other Prussian territory, although in 1952 it was once again dismembered, this time into the administrative districts (Bezirke) of Erfurt, Gera, and Suhl. After the fall of the **German Democratic Republic (GDR)**, the lack of historical continuity led to proposals for the region to merge with neighboring Hessen. Not until October 1990 was the federal state of Thuringia reestablished as part of reunited Germany, and it has taken some time for the area to develop a sense of self-identity similar to that of other eastern Länder.

Thuringia's historical sectors of **industry**, dating back to the 16th century, were glass, porcelain, and toy production (in the Thuringian Forest) and textiles (in the eastern and central area). The **Mittelstand** of small to medium-sized businesses virtually disappeared during the GDR era, but re-emerged after reunification and now employs most of the region's workforce. Large companies are concentrated in a central industrial belt stretching east–west from Eisenach to Erfurt, Jena, and Gera, and include **automobile** engineering and supplies (Opel in Eisenach), electrical engineering (**Siemens** and Bosch in Erfurt and elsewhere), precision optical engineering (Carl Zeiss and Jenoptik in Jena), and glass production (Schott in Jena). Other important sectors are retail distribution (Edeka, Metro), logistics (Deutsche Bahn and **Deutsche Post**, Erfurt), publishing (Zeitungsgruppe Thüringen, Erfurt), and medical care (Helios Kliniken, Erfurt).

With some of the best farmland in Germany, Thuringia's **agriculture** underwent major restructuring after reunification. The 660 or so large farming cooperatives of the GDR era were reconstituted under various forms of ownership. With a much reduced workforce (two-thirds of farmworkers lost their jobs) and equipped with modern machinery, they are now among the most productive and efficient in the **European Union (EU)**. **Tourism**, notably in Weimar and the Thuringian Forest, expanded rapidly, with new hotels being built and sights of cultural interest and natural beauty once again accessible. Jena is Thuringia's largest and oldest university and has close links with the Carl Zeiss and Schott concerns. Other institutions include a technical university in Ilmenau (engineering and microelectronics) and the University of Erfurt (newly founded in 1999). The region contributes 2 percent of national GDP, and unemployment (7.4 percent) is above the national average (6.4 percent in 2015).

The regional constitution lays down certain aims of the state, including rights for the disabled; protection of the **environment**, animals, and personal data; and the provision of adequate housing. The constitution has plebiscitary elements but gives considerable powers to the **minister president**. The 88-member assembly is elected for five years. Voters have two votes, and the assembly is made up in equal proportions of directly elected constituency candidates returned by simple majority and candidates allocated seats proportionally from a party list. Although the constitution refers to the "Free State" of Thuringia, the title has no legal status.

The first regional elections (October 1990) returned a coalition of the **Christian Democratic Union (CDU)** and **Free Democratic Party (FDP)**, with Josef Duhac (CDU) as minister president. When Duhac, who served in **Lothar de Maizière**'s transitional government, lost the confidence of his parliamentary party, he resigned and was succeeded by **Bernhard Vogel** (1993), formerly minister president of **Rhineland-Palatinate**. The immediate postreunification period was dogged by the prolonged debate over Duhac's leadership and by affairs surrounding two cabinet ministers who were eventually dismissed by Vogel. In the 1994 elections the CDU, despite losing seats, emerged as the strongest party and formed a coalition with the **Social Democratic Party of Germany (SPD)**. The CDU was eventually returned with an absolute majority (1999), and Vogel continued as minister president before handing over to his protégé, **Dieter Althaus** (June 2003). In successive elections, the **Party of Democratic Socialism (PDS)** was able to increase its representation (from 9 seats in 1990 to 17 in 1994 and 21 in 1999). In the June 2004 election, Althaus successful defended his overall majority, while the PDS increased its share of the vote (from 21.3 to 26.1 percent) to become the second strongest party in parliament, beating the SPD (14.5 percent) into third place. For the third time running, the FDP and the **Green Party** failed to clear the 5 percent hurdle. Following the 2009 election, in which the CDU lost its overall majority and the SDP again trailed **The Left Party**, Althaus resigned. The outcome was a CDU/SPD coalition under **Christine Lieberknecht** (CDU), with the FDP and Greens reentering the assembly. In the election of September 2014, the CDU (33.5 percent of votes) regained some seats, but after lengthy negotiations, lost power after 24 years to a red/red/green coalition of The Left Party (28.2 percent), the SPD (12.4 percent), and the Greens (5.7 percent), headed by **Bodo Ramelow** (The Left Party). This was the first time a Left Party politician had provided a regional premier, and his election was nationally controversial, with protests over his party's communist past and criticism of the coalition partners (record numbers of SPD members resigned from the regional party association). While the FDP failed to clear the 5 percent hurdle, the **Alternative for Germany** (11 percent) entered the assembly for the first time.

THYSSEN FAMILY. Industrial entrepreneurs. In 1871, August Thyssen (1842–1926) founded a steelworks in Mülheim on the Ruhr River, which during the German industrial revolution of the 19th century grew into a major coal mining and iron/steel manufacturing concern. Between the two world wars, his eldest son Fritz (1873–1951) expanded the company into Europe's largest steel manufacturer, the Vereinigte Stahlwerke AG (founded in 1926). After initially supporting the National Socialists financially (he joined the party in 1933), Thyssen distanced himself from Hitler's war-oriented policies and fled with his family via Switzerland to France (1939). Caught in France at the outbreak of World War II, he and his wife Amélie (1877–1965) were returned to Germany and imprisoned in various concentration camps. He was arrested by the Americans (1945) and fined 15 percent of his assets for his involvement with the National Socialists (1948). Two years later, the fine was revoked, and he finally moved with his wife to Buenos Aires to join his daughter, Anita (1909–1990). He died in Argentina in 1951.

After World War II, Amélie Thyssen played a leading role in the founding and reorganization of the August-Thyssen-Hütte AG (established in 1953 and later renamed Thyssen AG). In 1959, she and her daughter, Anita Zichy-Thyssen, set up the Fritz Thyssen Stiftung (Fritz Thyssen Foundation) for the advancement of the sciences and humanities. With a capital endowment of 100 million DM, this was the first major private scientific foundation in the Federal Republic of Germany (FRG) and became a model for similar institutions. In 1997, the remaining members of the Thyssen family withdrew from Thyssen AG. The family owns a castle, Schloss Landsberg, near Essen, where the ancestors are interred.

The youngest son of August Thyssen, and Fritz's brother, Heinrich Thyssen-Bornemisza (1875–1947), coinherited his father's fortune (1926) and went on to develop banking and trading interests in the Netherlands as well as numerous industrial concerns, including gas and water utilities, in Germany. Although a successful entrepreneur, Thyssen-Bornemisza was better known to the public as a collector of over 500 paintings by European masters. His fourth and youngest child, Baron Hans Heinrich von Thyssen Bornemisza (1921–2002), inherited his father's love of art and opened the collection to the public after his father's death (1947). By the early 1990s, Heinrich Thyssen had amassed around 800 paintings and owned one of the greatest private art collections in the world, which is now housed in the Thyssen-Bornemisza Museum in Madrid. He also maintained numerous business interests, sitting on the boards of about 30 companies, many of which were based on computers and technology.

THYSSENKRUPP AG. The ThyssenKrupp AG (Düsseldorf) has its origins in two steel-manufacturing family businesses, one founded by Friedrich Krupp (1787–1826) in 1811 in Essen and the other by August Thyssen (1842–1926) in 1871 in Mülheim on the Ruhr River. Both companies grew to become household names, synonymous with German heavy **industry** and associated with the families of **Thyssen** and **Krupp**.

By steadily buying up interests in coal mines, August Thyssen built up a large network of integrated plants that combined the extraction of coal and ore with the manufacture of iron and steel, also using river and **rail** links to transport both raw materials and products. Before World War I, Thyssen was an international concern employing 26,000 workers in its various mines and factories in the Ruhr. Although the company lost its foreign markets during the war, it had recovered sufficiently by 1925 to take over most of the region's iron and steel production. In 1926, the Vereinigte Stahlwerke AG was founded, which integrated over 42 percent of the Ruhr's total iron and steel manufacturing with 20 percent of its coal-mining capacity and was the largest of its kind in Europe. A pillar of the National Socialist war economy, the concern was dismantled and liquidated after World War II. However, steelmaking was resumed after a six-year interval (1951), and in the following years, the concern largely reconstituted itself as August-Thyssen-Hütte AG, steadily extending its interests to include mining and raw materials. By 1965, it was Europe's biggest and the world's fifth largest producer of crude steel. An agreement concluded in 1969 led to Mannesmann AG concentrating on tube manufacturing, while Thyssen produced rolled steel. After Thyssen acquired Rheinstahl AG (1973), it reduced its dependence on steel and began to move into broad-based manufacturing. To underline the change, Rheinstahl was renamed Thyssen Industrie AG (1976). By this time a trading company, Handelsunion AG (set up in 1960 and renamed Thyssen Handelsunion AG in 1969), was already leading a strategic diversification from steel into materials, industrial services, and project management, which were established as core businesses during the 1990s. The Thyssen family disengaged themselves from the concern in 1997.

Benefiting from railway expansion during the second half of the 19th century, the Krupp company produced cast steel, axles, springs, railway tires, and locomotives, as well as artillery for the Prussian army (from 1859). It acquired ore and coal mines, moved into plant construction and shipbuilding, and developed extensive world markets. A major weapons and munitions producer in World War I, Krupp AG diversified into general heavy manufacturing (locomotives, trucks, agricultural and building machinery) in the 1920s before resuming arms production under the National Socialists (1933–1954). Much of its plant was destroyed during World War II and either dismantled or seized by the Allies, although a divestment order was largely unfulfilled and expired in 1967. After losing most of its raw materials and steel base, the company restructured during the 1950s and 1960s, diversifying into mechanical **engineering** and merging with other concerns. Foreign markets were expanded and a plant was opened in Brazil (1961).

Between 1980 and 1983, Fried. Krupp AG became a management holding company, before amalgamating with Hoesch AG in Dortmund to form Fried. Krupp AG Hoesch-Krupp (1992). In 1983, Thyssen and Krupp concluded an alliance and coordinated their activities before combining their flat steel operations (1997); two years later, a full merger took place and a new company, ThyssenKrupp AG, was created (turnover: 36,000 million euros). In 2004, the group, which owned the shipbuilders NSWE (Deutsche Nordsee-Werke, Emden) and Blohm + Voss (Hamburg), agreed on a takeover of the HDW yard (Howaldswerke Deutsche Werft AG, Kiel), formerly owned by the U.S. financial investors OEP (One Equity Partners). The merger created the world's largest builder of non-nuclear submarines and one of the biggest manufacturers of naval frigates and corvettes. The main business areas (in 2015) were components technology, elevators, industrial solutions (including marine systems), materials services, and steel (in Europe). Turnover was 42,700 million euros, with 155,000 workers in 80 countries.

TIEFENSEE, WOLFGANG (1955–). Social Democratic Party of Germany (SPD) politician. Born in Gera **(Thuringia)** in the former **German Democratic Republic (GDR)**, Wolfgang Tiefensee worked as a **telecommunications** specialist (from 1974) and served as a soldier in a special unit after refusing to carry weapons during national service (1975). After qualifying as an industrial electrical engineer (1979), he completed a postgraduate study program in electro-energy installations (1982) while engaged as a research and development engineer in a telephony factory in Leipzig (1979–1986). He worked at the Technical University of Leipzig (1986) and obtained a diploma in electrical **engineering** (1988). After the collapse of the GDR regime, Tiefensee was politically active for the **Round Table** in Leipzig, where he was briefly a city councilor (1989–1990). After heading the department of school administration in Leipzig (1990), he served as a city councilor with responsibility for schools and **education** (1992) and as deputy mayor (1994). A member of the SPD from 1995, he was elected mayor (Oberbürgermeister) of Leipzig (1998, 2005), playing an important role in its economic regeneration and attracting new businesses to the city. Other positions he held were vice president of the association of German towns (Deutscher Städtetag, 2000) and president of Eurocities, a network of European towns and cities (2002–2004). Involved in drawing up the SPD's **Agenda 2010** reform program, he was federal minister for **transport**, building, and housing in **Angela Merkel**'s first coalition (2005–2009) and also had responsibility for the **Aufbau Ost** program. Elected to the **Bundestag** in 2009, Tiefensee was economics spokesman for the SPD parliamentary group from 2012 until 2014.

TIETMEYER, HANS (1931–). Banker. Born in Metelen **(North Rhine-Westfalia)**, Hans Tietmeyer studied Roman Catholic theology for one year (1952) before switching to economics and social sciences at universities in Münster, Bonn, and Cologne. He earned a diploma (1958) and then a doctorate (1960). Studying under Alfred Müller-Armack, Tietmeyer became a strong advocate of the doctrine of the **social market economy** as the foundation of postwar prosperity in the Federal Republic of Germany (FRG). After joining the Federal Ministry for Economic Affairs (1962), he moved steadily up the promotion ladder, eventually becoming head of the economic policy department (1973). A member of the **Christian Democratic Union (CDU)**, he joined the Federal Ministry of Finance as **state secretary** (1982), assisting the **Free Democratic Party (FDP)** economics minister Otto Graf Lambsdorff in producing a controversial paper arguing for cuts in social welfare and a growth-oriented policy, which eventually led to a change of government.

After joining the board of the **German Federal Bank** (1990), Tietmeyer became president (1993), holding the office until retirement (1999). Tietmeyer's most influential years were as state secretary and as director/president of the Federal Bank, where he worked closely with Chancellor **Helmut Kohl**. As Kohl's "sherpa," he helped prepare the chancellor for the annual G7/G8 summits of world economic leaders and took a leading role in the preparations for the monetary union between the FRG and the **German Democratic Republic (GDR)** in 1990. He also helped establish the European Central Bank (ECB), whose structures were modeled closely on the German Federal Bank and which assumed responsibility for the European **currency**, which, as the euro, entered general circulation in participating countries in January 2002. Although he avoided the political limelight, Tietmeyer was convinced that sound money was the key to economic prosperity and hence to political and social stability. During the negotiations for monetary union, Tietmeyer argued strongly for a realistic conversion rate between the strong western mark and its weak eastern counterpart, although he was overruled by Chancellor Kohl, who was under political pressure to retain the enthusiasm of East Germans for reunification. Nevertheless, Tietmeyer was instrumental in ensuring the independence of the ECB from political interference by **European Union (EU)** governments. As a committed social market economist, he expressed concerns that uncontrolled competition could threaten the potential of globalization to extend prosperity to poorer nations. After the economic crisis that affected Asia during the early 1990s, he speculated on the most appropriate rules and mechanisms for balancing the need to regulate and stimulate the world's capital markets. Tietmeyer's immediate successor as president of the German Federal Bank was Alfred Tacke.

See also BANKS.

TILLICH, STANISLAW (1959–). Christian Democratic Union (CDU) politician. Stanislaw Tillich was born in Neudörfel (**Saxony**) into a Sorbian family. He studied engineering at the Technical University of Dresden (from 1979), graduating with a diploma (1984), after which he worked for an electronics company. A member of the CDU in the former **German Democratic Republic (GDR)** since 1987, he entered the East German **People's Chamber** in the country's first free elections in 1990. From 1991 to 1994, he was an observer in the European Parliament, focusing on the integration of the **eastern federal states**. Elected to the European parliament in 1994 and 1999, he became a leading member of the executive committee of the block of Christian Democratic parties. In 1999, Tillich returned to Saxony to join the cabinet of Minister President **Kurt Biedenkopf** (CDU), becoming state minister for national and European affairs and the region's representative in the **Bund**. When Biedenkopf was succeeded by **Georg Milbradt** (2002), Tillich also took over headship of the state chancellery and in 2004 was named minister for **environment** and **agriculture**. Following the forced sell-off of Saxony's regional bank owing to a liquidity crisis, Tillich succeeded Horst Metz as finance minister in 2007. When Milbradt himself resigned in 2008, Tillich was elected **minister president**, and in the regional election of 2009 was confirmed as leader of the CDU's coalition with the **Free Democratic Party** (**FDP**). In 2008, he was also elected leader of the CDU regional party, and in 2010 joined the national presidium. After the 2014 regional elections, Tillich was confirmed as minister president, this time heading a coalition with the **Social Democratic Party of Germany** (**SPD**). Tillich proved himself a capable organizer during the catastrophic floods that affected parts of Saxony (most recently in 2010 and 2013) and pursued a policy of budget controls and investment in education and research.

TISCH, HARRY (1927–1995). German Democratic Republic (GDR) politician. Harry Tisch was born in Heinrichswalde (near Ueckermünde/ **Mecklenburg-West Pomerania**) into a working-class family. After training and working as a building-site fitter, he served in the German navy during World War II. In 1945, he joined the Communist Party of Germany (KPD), subsequently the **Socialist Unity Party of Germany** (**SED**, from 1946), and worked as a **trade union** functionary (1948–1953). Tisch studied at the Karl-Marx College of the Communist Party —attached to the Central Committee of the SED—and graduated with a diploma in history (1953–1955). His positions included membership in the SED Central Committee (from 1963), the **People's Chamber** (from 1963), the Politburo (candidate from 1971 and full member from 1975), and the State Council (from 1975). He was head of the Freier Deutscher Gewerkschaftsbund (FDGB), the trade union federation of the GDR from 1975. After the fall of the regime in October/November 1989, Tisch was succeeded as head of the FDGB by Annelies Kimmel, who after less than a month was forced to resign over her failure to regenerate the organization (it was dissolved in September 1990, shortly before reunification). Expelled from the FDGB and the SED, Tisch lost all official positions. Placed in investigative detention on suspicion of corruption and misappropriation of funds (December 1989), he was convicted and sentenced to 18 months in prison (June 1991), but was released on account of the time he had already spent in detention. As a member of the Politburo, he faced further charges of complicity in the shoot-to-kill policy at the border with West Germany (January 1995), but he died in **Berlin** the following June.

TOURISM. As a result of economic, social, and technological changes, tourism in the Federal Republic of Germany (FRG) expanded into a major **industry** during the 1950s and 1960s. It was promoted by the spread of **automobile** ownership (not least thanks to the "people's car," or **Volkswa-**

gen) and the growth of cheap mass **transport** (railways, coaches, and aviation), a rise in incomes and personal spending power, reductions in working hours, and generously paid annual holidays; an increase in leisure time made possible by labor-saving household devices was also a significant factor. Tourism boomed during the 1960s, when department stores such as Quelle and Neckermann began to offer package holidays at home and abroad. In 1968, for the first time, more Germans took a foreign vacation than one in their own country. During the 1970s, leisure activities became more differentiated, with special interest and activity vacations offered alongside more unusual destinations, although package holidays dominated the market. Popular destinations included Switzerland, Austria, and Italy.

Tourism in the **German Democratic Republic (GDR)** developed along quite different lines. In fact, the word "tourism" was rarely used in East Germany, with "recreation" or "relaxation" ("Erholung") being the preferred terms for the heavily subsidized holidays for workers organized by the state or the **trade unions**, usually spent at camping sites or in specially built compounds. Most East Germans vacationed within the GDR (the **Baltic** coast was a favorite destination), since travel to the West was normally out of the question and even opportunities to visit other socialist states, such as Poland or Czechoslovakia, were limited.

Reunification (1990) produced a boom in domestic tourism in the **eastern federal states**, although this proved short-lived as the economic situation there deteriorated. The 1996 **health** reforms, which cut subsidies for health holidays at spas and resorts in the west, resulted in a drastic decline in this sector, which began to recover, however, in 1998. Tourism in **Berlin**, which suffered a temporary downturn after the "loss" of its prime attraction, the **Berlin Wall**, has since recovered, and the city is today a major destination for international visitors. The first notable upturn was triggered by the extensive marketing of Berlin as building-work in progress between 1995 and 2000. **Theaters, cinemas,** and even restaurants cater for a predominantly English-speaking clientele. The massive increase in the number of hostels in some neighborhoods has generated discussions about "touristification"—comparable to cities such as Venice and Barcelona. Among the main marketing drives in recent years was the be.Berlin initiative.

Many Germans (almost 40 percent) vacation in their home country, the favored destinations being **Bavaria** (the Allgäu and the Alps), the Baltic and **North Sea** coasts of **Mecklenburg-West Pomerania** and **Schleswig-Holstein**, and **Baden-Württemberg** (Lake Constance). For shorter trips, the Black Forest (Schwarzwald) in Baden-Württemberg and the Rhine/Mosel regions are popular, and the annual Christmas markets—especially the one at Nuremberg—alongside wine and beer festivals are a perennial draw. In 2015, overnight visits by tourists in Germany reached a record total of 436 million, of which more than 79 million were from abroad. Germans' top destination for foreign holidays remains, by a large margin, Spain (visited by one in eight), followed by Italy, Turkey and Austria, and other European countries. While tourist interest further afield is strong (one in nine Germans travels outside Europe), it is affected by political developments (such as the Arab Spring of 2010) and economic factors (currency exchange rates); more recently, the Far East, Asia, and the Americas have attracted increased numbers. The time Germans spend away from home on vacation has fallen (from an average 18.2 days a year in 1980 to 14.8 days in 2000), although a stay of over two weeks is typical for more remote destinations.

Following mergers and takeovers, the German tourist industry was dominated by a handful of large concerns at the end of the 1990s. The main players (in 2014) were TUI (Touristik Union International) Deutschland (18 percent market share), Thomas Cook (13 percent), and DER Touristik (13 percent). Other companies include FTI (6.7 percent) and Alltours (5.7 percent), with many smaller concerns offering mainly specialist holidays. Overall the sector contributes around 4 percent of GDP and employs 2.9 million people (7 percent of the workforce). Foreign visitors to Germany account for only 13 percent of consumer expenditure.

TOWN PLANNING LAW (RAUMORDNUNGSGESETZ). *See* SPA-TIAL PLANNING ACT (RAUMORDNUNGSGESETZ).

TRADE. A striking feature of the economy of the Federal Republic of Germany (FRG) is its dependence on foreign trade. Relatively poor in raw materials, Germany relies heavily on imports, especially **energy**, while one job in four depends on exports. At the same time, since 1952 the value of exports has consistently risen faster than that of imports, resulting (with exceptions during the reunification process and the **eurozone crisis**) in ever higher annual trade surpluses: record years were 2007 (195,348 million euros) and 2014 (249,900 million euros), with the foreign trade quota (the ratio of exports to GDP) around a healthy 40 percent. The main imports, in order of value, are computers, electric and optical devices, motor vehicles and parts, oil and gas, **chemical** products, and metals. Similarly, Germany exports mainly motor vehicles and parts, machinery, chemical products, computer-related items, and electrical and optical equipment. It is also a leading exporter of arms (aircraft, warships, military vehicles, rockets, and artillery), with the United States its biggest customer in recent years. Around 58 percent of both exports and imports are traded with the **European Union** (**EU**). In 2015, Germany exported mainly to the United States, France, Great Britain, the Netherlands, and China; it imported primarily from China, the Netherlands, France, and the U.S. From the 1990s onward, trade with the EU accession states and eastern Europe (mainly the Czech Republic, Poland, and Hungary, but also Russia) expanded vigorously, as did links with China, which in 2009 took over from Germany as world export leader.

The principal trading **federal states** in the FRG are **North Rhine-Westfalia**, **Bavaria**, and **Baden-Württemberg**, which among them account for around 50 percent of both imports and exports. The role of exports in Germany's economy also has important political dimensions. Exporters have a powerful voice in policymaking, and businessmen often accompany senior politicians on visits abroad and foreign delegations. A foreign trade advisory council is located in the Federal Ministry for Economic Affairs, and Germany's overall trading position is closely monitored through monthly reports. The balance of trade forms part of the country's overall **balance of payments**.

TRADE UNIONS. Trade unions and **employers' organizations** are highly influential interest groups in the Federal Republic of Germany (FRG). They lobby government, **political parties**, and other sections of society in the interests of their members and are increasingly active both in the **European Union (EU)** and internationally. The decision by Germany's trade unions to organize at the plant or **industry** level ("one industry–one union"), and not by individual trade, was made after World War II in response to the need to prioritize reconstruction of the national economy over political and ideological differences. During the 1950s, labor and employers struck a social partnership that ensured harmonious industrial relations until the 1980s and was widely held to contribute to Germany's economic and political stability (the "German model"). The partnership, in the form of **codetermination**, gave workers in larger companies a voice in decision-making at the management level. It also underpinned the freedom for employers and employees to conclude collective wage agreements—so-called tariff autonomy (Tarifautonomie)—that were legally binding for whole sectors and regions (Flächentarif or Tarifeinheit) as well as for companies. The principle of "one industry–one union" facilitated wage negotiations and avoided damaging interunion disputes within a company. For three decades, rising prosperity in a climate of expanding **trade**, export-led growth, generous wage levels, and index-linked **pensions** encouraged German trade unions to focus on achieving a fair distribution of wealth and on widening decision-making rather than on pressing for systemic change. During the 1980s and 1990s, structural, social, and economic developments, including deregulation, globalization, and the challenges of reunification, placed the traditional notion of the social partnership under strain as the unions grappled with rising unemployment, falling memberships, and loss of income from contributions. Collective bargaining was undermined as economic pressures, especially in the **eastern federal states**, prompted businesses to negotiate at the plant rather than regional or sectoral level. In 2004, employers and unions in the engineering industry in southwest Germany agreed to loosen the rule of sector-wide wage agreements in order to accommodate individual companies (the so-called Pforzheim Agreement). Although the Federal Labor Court in 2010 finally removed the long-standing principle of tariff unity (one firm, one collective labor agreement), labor minister **Andrea Nahles**, supported by employers' organizations concerned about the growing influence of smaller unions, steered a revised law through parliament that was designed to limit the freedoms of smaller unions in tariff negotiations (2015).

The main umbrella organization for trade unions in Germany is the Deutscher Gewerkschaftsbund (Federation of German Trade Unions, DGB), with headquarters in Düsseldorf. Although not directly involved in collective bargaining or concluding pay agreements, the DGB represents the labor movement vis-à-vis governments, political parties, employers' organizations, and other groups. A sharp rise in membership after reunification as east German unions were incorporated into the DGB (membership stood at 6.1 million in 2015, compared with 10 to 11 million in 1991) was followed by an equally sudden fall, as deindustrialization in the east and privatization, restructuring, closures, and the emergence of newer, more fragmented industries (e.g., IT and renewable **energy**) took their toll; efforts to expand membership in smaller businesses met with limited success. Of the eight member organizations in the DGB, the largest are IG Metall (engineering and metalworkers, with 2.3 million members) and ver.di (mainly public sector workers, 2.1 million), representing around 70 percent of the total membership. Other members are IG Bauen Agrar-Umwelt (building and **agricultural** workers, 288,000); IG Bergbau, Chemie, Energie (mining, **chemicals**, and energy, 651,000); Gewerkschaft Erziehung und Wissenschaft (GEW, teachers and other educators, 281,000); Gewerkschaft Nahrung-Genuss-Gaststätten (food and catering, 204,000); Gewerkschaft der Polizei (police, 177,000); and for rail workers, the Eisenbahn- und Verkehrsgewerkschaft (EVG, 197,000, formed in 2010 through a merger of the Verkehrsgewerkschaft GDBA and Transnet). Unions remain strongest in the **automobile** and electrical industries and some sectors of the (privatized or part-privatized) postal services and railways. A rival to the DGB is the Deutscher Beamtenbund (German Civil Service Federation, DBB), the leading independent organization for more than 40 trade unions, representing 912,000 civil servants, who do not have the right to strike, and 370,800 other employees in public services, both state-owned and privatized. A third organization, the Christlicher Gewerkschaftsbund (Christian Trade Union Federation, CGB), with links to the **Christian Democratic Union** (CDU), has around 280,000 members in 14 individual unions. The power of the small number of nonfederated unions with professional memberships, representing, for example, journalists, doctors, pilots, and locomotive drivers, has grown in line with changes in the job market and the strength of their negotiating positions.

Unions are not formally bound to **political parties** but traditionally have close links with the **Social Democratic Party of Germany (SPD)**. Although Chancellor **Gerhard Schröder**'s second cabinet (2002–2005) strained the relationship by introducing social welfare cuts and promoting a low-wage economy, the proportion of SPD Bundestag deputies affiliated with a trade union never fell below 73 percent during 1990–2013, far above the level for any other party. German law (Arbeitszeitgesetz, 1994) stipulates an eight-hour working day over a six-day week, although exceptions are possible, and annual vacation is at least four weeks. Following a decade of union lobbying, the **Bundestag/Bundesrat** in July 2014 approved the introduction of a compulsory minimum wage (8.50 euros/hour, scheduled to rise to 8.84 euros in 2017). The right to strike is circumscribed in law and may not be exercised for issues covered during the term of a tariff agreement. The scope for supportive strikes by other unions is limited, and general or political strikes are illegal, although labor disputes involving violence or confrontations with the police are extremely rare. Historically, most strikes in Germany have been in the metal and electrical industries, but since the 1990s they have occurred more frequently in the service sectors, including **health** and **transport**. Militant positions adopted by smaller, niche unions such as the Vereinigung Cockpit (airline pilots), GDL (Gewerkschaft Deutscher Lokomotivführer, representing train drivers), and Hartmann Bund (doctors) have undermined the principle of sector-wide collective agreements and prompted discussions about limiting the right to strike in key areas.

TRANSPORT: AIR TRAFFIC. Of Germany's 16 international airports, by far the largest and busiest is Frankfurt/Main, which replaced **Berlin** as (West) Germany's national airport after World War II. In 2014, Frankfurt handled around 470,000 flights, around 60 million passengers, and 2.1 million tons of freight. Other major airports are Munich, Düsseldorf, Berlin (Tegel and Schönefeld), **Hamburg**, and Stuttgart, with Leipzig/Halle and Cologne/Bonn also important for freight. Of Germany's 13 regional airports offering scheduled and charter services, Frankfurt-Hahn leads in terms of passenger numbers, although these, alongside freight traffic, have declined in recent years (from over 4 million in 2007 to 2.6 million in 2015) as operators withdrew.

Historically, most German airports were jointly owned by the federal state (Land) or city and run as limited liability companies (GmbH), although the federal government maintained stakes in larger airports, including Berlin and (until 2007) Frankfurt. Despite the government's decision in 1982 to deregulate airport ownership, the first (partial) privatization (of Düsseldorf) did not take place until 1997. In Berlin, construction of a new privatized, international airport (full title: Flughafen Berlin Brandenburg "Willy Brandt") to replace nearby Schönefeld (formerly in the **German Democratic Republic, GDR** and after reunification used mainly by charter and budget operators such as Ryanair and EasyJet) began in 2006, but the project attracted fierce local criticism, and completion was delayed by planning errors and technical problems; by 2016 it had still not opened, despite a colossal cost overrun. Frankfurt airport entered the **German Stock Exchange** in 2001 as Fraport AG; during 2005–2007, the government sold its remaining shares, although the state of **Hessen** and Frankfurt city retained a significant holding. The state remains the main stakeholder and operator in most other larger German airports. After 2002, navigation services in German air space became the responsibility of Deutsche Flugsicherung GmbH (DFS), but plans to privatize the DFS announced in 2004 were torpedoed in 2006 by a constitutional clause that held that air traffic must be managed by a state organization. The government responded by separating the functions of supervision and implementation, handing over the former to a new body, the Bundesaufsichtsamt für Flugsicherung (BAF). At the same time, the **Basic Law (BL)** was modified to permit a European-wide union of air space, in line with the Single European Sky policy adopted by the **European Union (EU)** in 2001.

The national carrier, Deutsche Lufthansa AG, is one of the world's leading airlines in terms of passengers (more than 108 million annually), flights (one million), and cargo (1.9 million tons). Fully privatized in 1997, the Lufthansa Group, with its 540 subsidiaries and affiliates and a global workforce of 120,000, turned over 32,000 million euros in 2015, although it ran deficits in 2000, 2003, 2009, 2011, and 2014. A major restructuring program, with 3,500 job losses, was announced in 2013 as it attempted to modernize and compete with low-budget airlines by expanding through its regional subsidiary Eurowings (pilots staged numerous strikes during 2014/2015 in resistance to a loss of privileges). Other German-owned airlines, also catering for regional and holiday traffic, include Air Berlin (founded in 1978) and Condor (1956). Lufthansa became sole owner of the low-cost operator Germanwings in 2009 and in 2015 announced plans to subsume it wholly within Eurowings by 2020.

See also TRANSPORT: RAIL; TRANSPORT: ROADS; TRANSPORT: WATERWAYS.

TRANSPORT: RAIL. Germany's national rail carrier, Deutsche Bahn AG, emerged in 1994 from an amalgamation of the state-owned Deutsche Bundesbahn (Federal Republic of Germany FRG) and the Deutsche Reichsbahn (from the former **German Democratic Republic, GDR**). Although run as a commercial enterprise, the state (**Bund**) is the sole shareholder and subsidizes maintenance and infrastructure. During 2006–2008, chief executive

Hartmut Mehdorn undertook extensive restructuring to prepare for part privatization and entry into the **German Stock Exchange**. Fiercely opposed by **trade unions** and **environmental** and citizens' groups, the plans were shelved in 2008 in the wake of the global financial crisis, although DB Mobility Logistics AG, created as a wholly owned subsidiary as a management holding concern to house the privatized segments (which did not include rail, station, and **energy** infrastructure), remained alongside Deutsche Bahn AG, with the two holding companies integrating their operations. A worldwide transport and logistics concern with subsidiaries and holdings outside Germany, Deutsche Bahn/DB Mobility Logistics' core business segments now include national and regional rail and bus services (DB Bahn Fernverkehr and DB Bahn Regio), freight transport (DB Schenker), rail and station infrastructure (bundled under DB Netze), and energy management. Annual turnover is 39,720 million euros (2014), with a global workforce of around 300,000 (196,000 in Germany).

Germany's rail network comprises 33,300 kilometers of operational track (the longest in Europe), of which around 60 percent is electrified. Progressively introduced after 1991, high-speed ICE (InterCity-Express) trains traveling at speeds of up to 200–330 kph now link most major cities. Every day the track network carries more than 6.2 million passengers and 300 million tons of freight (2015); the figure for its bus and coach passenger operations is 5.6 million. Recent criticism of the state-run railways has focused on the aging and overcrowded infrastructure (leading to delays, especially for long-distance passengers) and rolling stock (exacerbated by delays in delivery and lack of competition among manufacturers); the network was also stretched by the huge influx of asylum seekers in the summer of 2015. Many smaller stations have been closed, while larger stations have been turned into "hubs" with extended shopping malls and retail outlets (Berlin's main station is one example). In order to halt the loss of passenger custom to private long-distance coach operators, Deutsche Bahn announced in 2015 an extensive modernization program, including a new railcard (Bahncard) for longer journeys, improved and extended intercity connections, better on-board Internet services, and enhanced catering services.

Private service providers have been permitted since 1994 and now number 370, mainly at the regional level, although long-distance routes include Berlin-Malmö, Berlin-Harz, and Hamburg-Cologne. The private operators usually offer different fares than Deutsche Bahn does, and competitors' tickets are not recognized. They achieved market shares of 28 percent in freight (measured in tons/km) and 25 percent in passenger transport (passengers/km) in 2012. The Transdev Group, which claims to be one of the largest private operators, owns 40 subsidiaries operating rail and bus services and focuses on regional passenger connections; it employs 5,000 people and turned over

850 million euros in 2015. Foreign operators, either private ones, such as British National Express, or state-owned concerns, such as the French SNCF, are also active.

See also TRANSPORT: AIR TRAFFIC; TRANSPORT: ROADS; TRANSPORT: WATERWAYS.

TRANSPORT: ROADS. The German transport infrastructure is one of the most modern in the world, comprising a dense network of road, rail, and air links. The total length of the high-speed highway (Bundesautobahn) network is around 12,800 kilometers, although there are significant differences in regional coverage. For reasons of geography and historical development, there is a more extensive Autobahn network in the larger western **federal states** than in the eastern Länder, despite extensive programs for infrastructural development after reunification. Other types of road, with similar regional distributions, include the national routes (Bundesstraßen, 39,700 km), regional state highways (Landesstraßen, 86,600 km), and local roads (Kreisstraßen, 91,600 km). The total network of nonminor regional roads comprises 231,000 kilometers. Overall, the building and maintenance of Germany's road network account for 56 percent of all transport investment.

Like many other Europeans, Germans have a love affair with the **automobile**, with about 45,000 million registered passenger vehicles in 2015, representing almost one for every two citizens. At the same time, individual automobile usage remained fairly constant during 2004–2010 (2 percent growth), while rail passenger traffic rose significantly (16 percent). From January 2005, a toll was levied on trucks using the Autobahnen and, from 2006, also for many national routes; in 2014 the government announced plans to increase the levy, which raised 4.5 million euros in 2011, and extend the scheme to lighter trucks and more roads. Plans to include passenger vehicles in the levy from 2016 proved controversial. Most freight is conveyed by road (3,400 million tons in 2013, followed by 365 million by rail), with 27 percent of **European Union** (**EU**) goods traffic passing through Germany. For this reason, the levy is controversial and difficult to implement, as it is largely directed at the heavy volumes of foreign road freight and may contravene EU rules. In 2013, Deutsche Bahn, the national rail carrier, lost its monopoly on long-distance scheduled bus services, opening the door to private operators. Within a year, the number of routes doubled to 3,800, with 40 companies competing in a market of over eight million passengers, although commercial losses very soon led to higher prices, closures, and consolidation, affecting especially smaller providers.

Roads remain by far the most dangerous mode of travel, accounting for about 2.4 million accidents annually between 2011 and 2014; in the same period, fatalities ranged from over 4,000 (2011) to almost 3,400 (2014), with personal injuries hovering at around 300,000. At the same time, deaths and injuries fell dramatically (from 81 percent to 32 percent) between 1970 and 2011, owing largely to measures such as speed limits on Autobahnen (from 1970), compulsory motor cycle helmets, automobile safety belts (1976), and lower limits for drunk driving.

See also TRANSPORT: AIR TRAFFIC; TRANSPORT: RAIL; TRANSPORT: WATERWAYS.

TRANSPORT: WATERWAYS. Germany is well endowed with a network of rivers, canals, and inland waterways (total length: 7,476 km, of which 623 km constitute the **Rhine** River), which carry both domestic and cross-border freight. As in Belgium and the Netherlands, waterways are well used. Although slow and subject to disruption by flooding, winter freezing, and drought, they have low operating costs and are seen as positive for the **environment**. The longest waterway system within Germany is the Rhine and its tributaries (Neckar, Main, Mosel/Saar, and Lahn, totaling 1,797 km), which connect Germany to the major ports of Antwerp, Rotterdam, and Amsterdam. This is followed by the largely canal-based network linking the Rhine and the Elbe (1,437 km). The Elbe itself (network length 1,049 km) flows into the **North Sea** at Germany's largest port, **Hamburg**, and has canal links to the **Baltic**. The Elbe-Oder network (916 km) also connects the Elbe with **Berlin** and eastern Europe, via canals to the Havel and onward to the Oder River along the Polish border; the construction of a waterway link between Hanover in western Germany and Berlin via Magdeburg was assigned a high priority after reunification. The Main River (part of the Rhine network) is linked to the Danube and eastern Europe via the Main–Danube canal. Toward its mouth the Rhine is connected via two canals to the Ems River and to the Mittellandkanal, which runs west–east across northern Germany, connecting the Rhine and the Elbe systems.

The main cargoes are raw materials for the building **industry**, solid and gas fuel, coal and iron ore (declining in line with a shrinking domestic steel industry), **chemicals**, foodstuffs, and, for finished goods, container traffic (a growing sector). Of the total tonnage (28.5 million in 2015), most is conveyed along the Rhine network. There is also a significant demand for dangerous cargo (chemicals, flammable liquids) and very large items (e.g., turbines and rotor blades for wind power). During the 1990s, the German fleet shrank in the face of a contracting economy and fierce foreign competition, especially from the Netherlands and eastern European countries; it now numbers around 2,200 vessels. Vessels are traditionally manned by families, with children attending special boarding schools (Schifferkinderheime/Schifferschulen) on land.

Alongside water for **agricultural** use, large quantities of water are extracted from the waterway and river system for industry and power generation. Most water for domestic use is derived from ground sources (over three million cubic m annually), although 650,000 cubic m are taken from rivers, lakes, and reservoirs.

See also ENERGY: COAL; TRANSPORT: AIR TRAFFIC; TRANSPORT: RAIL; TRANSPORT: ROADS.

TREATY ON STABILITY, COORDINATION AND GOVERNANCE (TSCG). Signed by 25 member states of the **European Union (EU)** and in force from December 2011 at the height of the **eurozone crisis**, the TSCG was designed as an overarching program for structural economic reform and fiscal discipline within the EU. It included an "excessive deficit procedure" that would trigger progressive fines of up to 0.5 percent of a member state's GDP if the annual government deficit rose above 3 percent and if total public debt exceeded 60 percent of GDP. Sanctions would be endorsed by "reversed qualified majority voting," meaning that a recommendation of the EU Commission would be approved unless opposed by a qualified majority of member states. Also new was the undertaking to incorporate a "debt brake" in national constitutions and the obligation of the EU Court of Justice to ensure that the rules were incorporated into the law of member states.

The changes in favor of a stricter **budget**-monitoring regime and a semi-automatic penalty system were largely driven by the German **federal chancellor, Angela Merkel**, who at a summit in Brussels (December 2011) pressed for their inclusion in a full EU treaty encompassing all member states, although this was successfully resisted by the non-eurozone members Great Britain, Hungary, and Sweden. Signatory countries outside the euro area are not subject to the treaty's provisions until they adopt the single **currency**. The fiscal, and most widely discussed, element of the TSCG is sometimes referred to as the "fiscal compact" and runs in parallel to the "six-pack" measures of the revised **Growth and Stability Pact**. Although the TSCG also covers economic governance, with provision, for instance, to identify, prevent, and correct negative macroeconomic trends, it has been criticized for setting arbitrary financial targets that do not meet the need for individual countries to develop policies for long-term economic stability.

TRITTIN, JÜRGEN (1954–). Green Party politician. Born in **Bremen**, Jürgen Trittin studied at the University of Göttingen, where he graduated with a diploma in social sciences (1973) and was active in the students' union (AStA) and president of the students' parliament. He performed community service as part of his national army service and worked as a research assistant, journalist, and press spokesman for the **media**-based **trade union**

IG Medien. After joining the Green Party (1980), he was business manager for the Alternative Greens Initiatives List (AGIL) in Göttingen (1982–1984). He represented the Greens in the **Lower Saxony** regional assembly (1985–1990, 1994–1995), where he was also press spokesman for the Greens (1984–1985), parliamentary party chairman (1985–1986, 1988–1990), and deputy chairman (1994). From 1990 until 1994, he served as regional minister for federal and European affairs (Minister für Bundes- und Europaangelegenheiten) and member of the **Bundesrat**. He worked on several committees and was spokesman for the Green Party national executive (1994–1998).

Elected to the **Bundestag** in 1998, Trittin was appointed federal minister for the **environment**, nature conservation, and nuclear safety in the **Social Democratic Party of Germany** (**SPD**)/Green Party coalition under Chancellor **Gerhard Schröder**, a post he held until November 2005. Although not at first regarded as an expert on the environment, Trittin was closely involved with key legislation in this area, some of which had been debated for years. Measures included changes in the law for the protection of nature (Naturschutzgesetz, effective April 2002), the closing down of the nuclear reactor program (Atomausstiegsgesetz, effective April 2002), and the introduction of a levy on nonrecyclable can packaging (Dosenpfandgesetz, effective January 2003). At times, Trittin appeared politically isolated, even within his own government. The chancellor publicly rebuked him for dissolving the commission on nuclear reactor safety a few weeks after the coalition had assumed office (1998), and he was sidelined in negotiations between the SPD and the Green Party over the withdrawal from atomic **energy** (these were conducted largely by the former energy executive, Werner Müller, the nonparty economics and technology minister and confidant of Schröder). Nevertheless, Trittin proved a resilient politician and tough negotiator who argued ably for a significant share of the federal budget. After 2005, he occupied various positions in the Green Party, including deputy leader (2005–2009), then leader (2009–2013), of the parliamentary party, and from 2014 served on committees for foreign and European affairs, economics, and energy.

See also ENERGY: NUCLEAR POWER/ELECTRICITY.

TRUST AGENCY (TREUHAND). The Trust Agency was set up by the outgoing government of the **German Democratic Republic** (**GDR**) between March and June 1990 to manage the privatization of the property, plants, and assets owned or controlled by the state and the former **Socialist Unity Party of Germany** (**SED**). The idea of the agency originated with the interim East German government of **Hans Modrow** as a means of enabling citizens to share in the nation's economic resources, and it was eagerly taken up by the West German team negotiating reunification and headed by the then interior minister, **Wolfgang Schäuble**. By the time the **People's Chamber** approved the legislation for it, however, speedy privatization had become its primary purpose. The aim was to set up and cofinance umbrella companies to attract west German and foreign (mainly west European) investors while keeping workforces intact. Overseen by the finance ministry and totally in West German hands, it appeared to be independent and to operate outside the government. Based in **Berlin**, the agency had outposts throughout the **eastern federal states**.

The agency's first head (president) was Rainer Gohlke, who, following differences of opinion with its administrative council, was replaced by Detlev Carsten Rohwedder in August 1990. Recruited for the agency by Chancellor **Helmut Kohl**, Rohwedder was formerly a politician in the **Social Democratic Party of Germany (SPD)**, a **state secretary** in the Federal Ministry for Economic Affairs, and manager of the steel concern Hoesch AG. When Rohwedder was murdered in April 1991 by a member of the **Red Army Faction (RAF)**, his deputy, **Birgit Breuel**, took over as head. An initial success was the transfer of a 60 percent holding of VEAG (Vereinigte Energie AG) to the west German companies RWE, Preussen-Elektra, and Bayernwerk (VEAG had emerged from the state-owned electricity plants of the GDR in August 1990). Despite expectations, however, it soon became clear that the agency, which initially owned just about every economic asset in the east, would never generate profits. While genuine assets were swiftly bought up by western interests, huge sums of money were lost in paying wages for nonviable concerns before the agency began closing down companies and laying off workers. When it was wound up (in December 1994), it had privatized or set up around 15,000 concerns in eastern Germany, closed down 3,600, secured 211,000 million DM of investment, and saved 1.5 million of 4 million jobs; its final debts exceeded 256,000 million DM. Particular controversies surrounded the liquidation of the East German airline Interflug and the sell-off of shipyards, while bribery allegations accompanied the sale of the Leuna oil refinery to the French concern Elf Aquitaine, and potash miners in Bischerode conducted a desperate campaign against closure. A limited impact was made on halting rising unemployment in eastern Germany, and the agency was criticized by the federal cartel office for backing West German over foreign capital investors, favoring large companies over small to medium-sized enterprises, and allowing businesses to dump goods on the east German market.

In 2012, a documentary film (*Goldrausch—Die Geschichte der Treuhand*) portrayed the history of the agency as one of scandal, corruption, and fraud. Since the agency became the focus of eastern Germany's economic plight, however, it helped the government retain its popularity in the west and win two further elections. After being wound up, its residual functions were moved to another agency (the Bundesanstalt für vereinigungsbedingte Sonderaufgaben, BVS), which ceased operations in 2001.

TURKS. *See* ETHNIC MINORITIES: TURKS.

U

UHSE, BEATE (-ROTHERMUND; 1919–2001). Pilot and entrepreneur. Born in Cranz (now Selenogradsk in Polen) and widowed at the end of World War II, Beate Uhse escaped from **Berlin** with her son and his nanny in an aircraft. Trying to make a living in postwar Germany, she first specialized in the provision of brochures on sexual education, which addressed a dire need at the time. She then developed the Beate-Uhse mail order business, which allowed customers to order means of birth control and erotica discreetly from their homes. In 1962, Uhse opened the first worldwide sex shop in Flensburg and in 1996 the Beate Uhse Erotic Museum in Berlin. In 1989, she received the Federal Cross of Merit. Her company was listed in 1999 on the stock exchange. Together with Oswalt Kolle (1928–2010), who contributed films and books to sexual education in Germany during the 1960s and 1970s, Uhse is today widely considered a pioneer in educating the wider public at a time when the topic was still a social taboo.

ULBRICHT, WALTER (1893–1973). German Democratic Republic of Germany (GDR) leader. Walter Ulbricht was born in Leipzig and trained as a carpenter, traveling as a journeyman in Germany and visiting Venice, Amsterdam, and Brussels (1911–1912). A committed socialist from his early years, he joined the **Social Democratic Party of Germany** (SPD, 1912) and attended the party academy in Leipzig (1913–1914). After serving during World War I (1915–1918), he took an active part in the 1918 revolution in Germany, joining workers' and soldiers' councils and the Spartacus League. A founding member of the Communist Party of Germany (KPD, 1919), he was elected to the national party leadership (1923), attended the Lenin School of the Communist International (Comintern) in Moscow (1924–1925), and worked as a party instructor in Vienna and Prague before being elected to the **Saxony** regional assembly (1926) and the Reichstag (1928–1933). In 1932, he took control of the party's secretariat and, effectively, its leadership. When the National Socialists came to power in 1933, Ulbricht worked for the party in exile in Paris, Prague, and Moscow, before returning to **Berlin** in 1945 as leader of the "Ulbricht Group" to organize the rebuilding of the KPD in postwar eastern Germany. Before the founding of the GDR in 1949, Ulbricht led the forced merger of the SPD and KPD to create the communist-controlled **Socialist Unity Party of Germany (SED,** 1946) and the purging of moderate elements, especially former social democrats (1948). During the 1950s, he eliminated further opponents after putting down a workers' uprising (1953), which he exploited to take over all key positions in the state and the party leadership. Under Ulbricht's direction, the **Berlin Wall** was erected to halt the emigration of citizens to the west (1961), and East German troops joined in the invasion of Czechoslovakia by members of the **Warsaw Pact** to suppress a reform government (1968). During 1970–1971, however, Ulbricht lost the support of Moscow by opposing economic and political moves toward normalizing relations with the Federal Republic of Germany (FRG) as part of a new West German–led **Ostpolitik,** and he was eventually marginalized from the GDR leadership, which passed to **Erich Honecker.**

UNITED LEFT (VEREINIGTE LINKE, VL). The VL was a grassroots dissident group founded in September/October 1989 in Böhlen (near Leipzig) as a "socialist opposition movement" in the former **German Democratic Republic (GDR).** Its members (300–500) came largely from disaffected members of the **Socialist Unity Party of Germany (SED)** and members of East German **trade unions.** After reunification, the group's supporters gravitated to either the **Party of Democratic Socialism (PDS)** or **Alliance 90/The Greens.**

UNITED NATIONS (UN). The postwar conflict between East and West prevented both the Federal Republic of Germany (FRG) and the **German Democratic Republic (GDR)** from joining the UN, which was founded in 1945 to promote international peace, security, and social progress. Nevertheless, both countries tried to use the organization, to achieve either reunification (in the case of the FRG) or international recognition (the GDR). At the same time, the FRG joined various UN institutions, including the World Health Organization (WHO) and the cultural and scientific organization UNESCO in 1951, and attended as an observer in 1955. The GDR formed a national UNESCO commission in 1955 but did not join UNESCO itself until 1972. Eventually, following East–West détente and the success of **Ostpolitik,** both states became full UN members in 1973. Thereafter, the FRG supported various peacekeeping missions through not only air and logistical support, but also the direct participation of **Bundeswehr** personnel. Examples include UNEF II (the Second United Nations Emergency Force, established in October 1973 to supervise the cease-fire between Egyptian and Israeli forces and operational until 1979), UNIFIL (United Nations Interim

Force in Lebanon, created by the Security Council in March 1978 to confirm Israeli withdrawal from Lebanon and restore stability to the area), and missions in El Salvador and Nicaragua.

With reunification (1990), the UN, together with the **North Atlantic Treaty Organization (NATO)**, looked to Germany to widen its international multilateral engagement. On the whole, this approach found support from subsequent federal governments, despite fierce internal debates over missions in Cambodia (UNTAC, United Nations Transitional Authority in Cambodia, 1992–1993), and Somalia (United Nations Operation in Somalia, 1993–1994). In 1994, the **Federal Constitutional Court (FCC)** approved the active deployment of Bundeswehr forces in armed peacekeeping missions mandated by the **Bundestag**, which in practice focused on NATO-led operations in the former Yugoslavia (1999) and, more controversially, Afghanistan (from 2001). In 2015, around 225 Bundeswehr personnel were engaged in various UN missions, including in Lebanon (UNIFIL) and Mali (MINUSMA). German involvement in the UN has also been reflected in the appointment of experts, diplomats, and politicians to various positions in the organization, although the FRG's campaign for permanent membership on the Security Council, supported by many states, has so far been unsuccessful; neither France nor Great Britain, for example, is willing to surrender its seat in return for a common European seat, which Germany has proposed. Since 1990, Germany has consistently ranked third in its assessed contributions to the UN budget (7.1 percent in 2013–2015), after the United States (22 percent) and Japan (10.8 percent). Criticism of Germany's role in the UN since 1990 has centered on the discrepancy between its rhetorical commitment to the organization and its reticence to engage more decisively in sanctioned military missions (e.g., with more personnel), possibly as it pursues a more pragmatic **foreign policy** based on economic interests. On the other hand, Germany views itself as a bridge builder, promoting policies for preventing crises instead of focusing on armed responses and, more generally, as giving primacy to nonmilitary aspects of the UN's charter, such as **human rights** and social development.

UNIVERSITIES. *See* EDUCATION: UNIVERSITIES AND HIGHER EDUCATION.

UPSWING EAST (AUFSCHWUNG OST). The Upswing East program (full title: Gemeinschaftswerk "Aufschwung Ost") was established in March 1991 to promote economic regeneration in the **eastern federal states**. The program contributed to the **German Unity Fund** and encompassed job creation schemes, **transport** and infrastructure (road and rail), housing, urban development, and renewal of the **environment**.

See also AUFBAU OST.

V

VAATZ, ARNOLD (1955–). Christian Democratic Union (CDU) politician. Arnold Vaatz was born in Weida, near Gera in the former GDR. After serving in the East German army (1974–1976), he studied mathematics in Dresden and graduated with a diploma (1981). He also studied theology as an external student (1976–1980) and earned a qualification that allowed him to preach. Between 1981 and 1990, he worked in various capacities as an engineer for a **chemicals** plant in Dresden (VEB Komplette Chemieanlagen Dresden), but was convicted for refusing to serve as an army reservist, spending a short period in prison (November–December 1982) and performing forced labor in a steelworks (Stahlwerk Unterwellenborn, 1982–1983). As the GDR regime collapsed, he joined the opposition group **New Forum** in Dresden (October 1989) and was press spokesman for the "Group of 20" citizens who negotiated with the authorities in the early stages of the revolution. During the period of the interim GDR government, he played an active role in the re-creation of the federal state of **Saxony** (June–November 1990), where he sat as a deputy (1990–1998) and held various offices. A member of the **Christian Democratic Union (CDU**, from February 1990), he was minister for the **environment** and regional development (Staatsminister für Umwelt und Landesentwicklung) in Saxony (1992–1998).

Vaatz entered the **Bundestag** in 1998, representing Dresden. He was a member of the CDU federal executive (1996–2000 and from November 2002) and the party presidium (1998–2000). In 2002, he became deputy leader of the CDU/**Christian Social Union (CSU)** parliamentary group, with responsibilities for economic reconstruction in eastern Germany, economic cooperation, and **human rights**. His membership on various committees and associations reflects his interests in international relations (including Poland and Cuba), culture, **cinema**, and broadcasting, and he has been a consistent critic of the withdrawal from nuclear **energy**.

VERHEUGEN, GÜNTER (1944–). Social Democratic Party of Germany (SPD) politician. Günter Verheugen was born in Bad Kreuznach (**Rhineland-Palatinate**) and trained as a journalist/editor at the *Neue Rhein-Neue*

Ruhr Zeitung (1963–1965) before studying history, sociology, and politics in Cologne and Bonn (1965–1969). He headed the public relations division in the Federal Ministry of the Interior (1969–1974) and a task force of the federal foreign ministry responsible for analysis and information (1974–1976). In 1960, he joined the **Free Democratic Party** (**FDP**) and went on to become parliamentary business manager (1977–1978) and general secretary (1978–1982). In 1982, he moved to the SPD, where he was spokesman for the national executive (1986–1987) and edited the party newspaper *Vorwärts* (1987–1989). A deputy in the **Bundestag** (1983–1999), Verheugen served on the **foreign policy** committee and was parliamentary business manager (1993–1995) and **state secretary**/minister of state for Foreign Minister **Joschka Fischer** (October 1998–September 1999). He was also deputy chairman of the SPD parliamentary group for foreign, security, and development policy (1994–1997) and was appointed chairman of the Socialist International Peace, Security, and Disarmament Council (1997).

In September 1999, Verheugen joined the Commission of the **European Union** (**EU**), with responsibility for EU enlargement. He was later appointed its vice president (2004–2010) and took over the newly created department for industrial and economic policy, with the task of overseeing the internal European market and policy on space exploration. In 2006, he came under suspicion for patronage while in office, and soon afterward responsibility for reducing bureaucracy in the EU was transferred to **Edmund Stoiber**. After withdrawing from European politics, Verheugen became honorary professor for European government at the Europa University Viadrina in Frankfurt/Oder. From 1998, he served in the **environment** and development chamber of the Evangelical Church in Germany (EKD).

VOGEL, BERNHARD (1932–). **Christian Democratic Union (CDU)** politician. Bernhard Vogel was born in Göttingen (**Lower Saxony**), younger brother to **Hans-Jochen Vogel**, who became a leading figure in the **Social Democratic Party of Germany** (**SPD**). After studying political science, history, sociology, and economics at the universities of Heidelberg and Munich (from 1953) and earning a doctorate on electoral groups in local council assemblies (1960), he lectured at the institute of political science at Heidelberg University (1961–1967) and was active in adult **education**. Despite ambitions to become a professor, he embarked on a political career, first in local politics (in Heidelberg, 1963–1965), then representing the CDU in the **Bundestag** (1965–1967) and the regional assembly (**Landtag**) of **Rhineland-Palatinate** (RLP, 1971–1988). Vogel held various positions in the local and regional CDU during 1965–1988 and joined the national executive in 1975. He became culture minister for RLP (1967–1976) under Minister President **Helmut Kohl**, whom he has known since their days as students in Heidelberg. During 1970–1976, he served as chairman and deputy chairman of the Bund-Länder-Kommission für Bildungsplanung und Forschungsförderung (BLK), a commission responsible for coordinating policy on education and **research** support at the federal and regional levels. As **minister president** of RLP (1976–1988), he chaired the Ministerpräsidentenkonferenz (National Conference of Minister Presidents); was president of the **Bundesrat** (1976–1977, 1987–1988); chaired the Rundfunkkommission der Ministerpräsidenten, a broadcasting commission of regional leaders (1976–1988); and represented Germany in Franco-German cultural affairs (1979–1982). Maintaining his interest in **media** and broadcasting, he served as chairman (from 1979), then deputy chairman (1992–2007), of the administrative council of the Mainz-based **television** channel Zweites Deutsches Fernsehen (ZDF).

In February 1992, Vogel moved to eastern Germany to become minister president of the state of **Thuringia**, to whose Landtag he was later elected (October 1994). He was also leader of the regional CDU in Thuringia (1993–2000). The first person in the history of the Federal Republic of Germany (FRG) to head two **federal states**, Vogel was a well-liked and successful figure in the east, leading the CDU to three successive electoral victories, including an absolute majority (1999). Alongside **Kurt Biedenkopf** and **Manfred Stolpe**, he was one of the "big three" popular postreunification regional leaders in eastern Germany.

Vogel developed a reputation for handling crises sensitively, notably when 70 lives were lost after two jets collided at an air force show in Rammstein (1988) and when a student shot 16 people before committing suicide at a school in Erfurt (April 2001). Known for his accessible and mediating personality, he never developed a career as a national politician. Despite his friendship with Kohl, he did not belong to the latter's inner circle of power or system of patronage, which proved an advantage when the CDU was engulfed by financial scandals in 1999. One of the few conservative politicians of the Kohl generation to emerge untainted by the affairs, Vogel was regarded as an elder statesman of the party (he was also the oldest member of its presidium) and was an early supporter of **Edmund Stoiber** in his bid for the chancellorship in the 2002 national election. In May/June 2003, Vogel announced his retirement as Thuringia's head of state and was succeeded by his protégé, **Dieter Althaus**. Vogel chaired the committee on European politics of the European Democratic Union (EDU, from 1981) and became the organization's vice president (1985). He was also closely linked with the conservative-oriented Konrad-Adenauer Stiftung (Konrad Adenauer Foundation), serving as chairman (1989–1995), then honorary chairman (from 2001).

VOGEL, HANS-JOCHEN (1926–). Social Democratic Party of Germany (SPD) politician. Hans-Jochen Vogel was born in Göttingen (**Lower Saxony**), the elder brother of **Bernhard Vogel**, who became a leading figure in the **Christian Democratic Union (CDU)**. After military service in World War II, Hans-Jochen studied law at the universities of Munich and Marburg, graduated with a doctorate in criminal law (1950), passed his state law examination (1951), and embarked on a legal career. He held various positions in the state of **Bavaria**, including as legal adviser in the Bavarian ministry of justice (1952); senior officer at the district court in Traunstein (1954); head of a working group collating Bavarian law at the state chancellery (1955); and councilor, then head, of the legal department of the city of Munich (from 1958). From 1960 to 1972, Vogel was mayor of Munich, one of the youngest in the city's history. Despite some conflicts with left-wing members of the SPD, he earned widespread praise for attracting the 1972 Olympic Games to the city.

An SPD member since 1950, Vogel joined the national executive (1970) and represented the party in the **Bundestag** (1972–1981, 1983–1994). He served as federal minister for regional planning, building, and urban development in the cabinet of Chancellor **Willy Brandt** before moving to the Federal Ministry of Justice (1974–1981) under Chancellor **Helmut Schmidt**. He was also leader of the Bavarian SPD (1972–1977). At a time of political crisis for the SPD in West **Berlin**, Vogel took over from Dietrich Stobbe as the city's governing mayor (January 1981), only to be replaced the following May by **Richard von Weizsäcker** when the SPD/**Free Democratic Party (FDP)** coalition lost the city election. After the election, Vogel led the SPD opposition in the West Berlin assembly. Following Helmut Schmidt's resignation as chancellor (1982), Vogel was nominated by his party as chancellor candidate for the national election of March 1983. When the SPD failed to regain power, Vogel returned to the Bundestag as a representative for Berlin, succeeding the veteran **Herbert Wehner** as leader of the parliamentary opposition group. For the 1987 national election, he deferred to **Johannes Rau**, **minister president** of **North Rhine-Westfalia**, as chancellor candidate in order to avoid a power struggle within the party. In the same year, Vogel also took over from Brandt as party leader.

A high point in Vogel's career was the party's adoption of the Berlin Program (1989), the most significant statement of basic policy since the Godesberg Program (1959). The program included commitments to renew **industry** along ecological lines, improve rights for **women**, introduce a 30-hour working week, and establish a new basis for **security policy**. The following years were characterized by considerable unrest within the SPD, and Vogel declared his willingness to stand down as party chairman in order to make way for a younger generation of leaders. The move was also intended to assist **Oskar Lafontaine** as chancellor candidate in the 1990 national election, although he opposed Lafontaine's cautious approach to reunification. However, following the SPD's worst electoral performance since 1957, Vogel eventually resigned as leader of both the party and the parliamentary group (May/November 1991). He was succeeded by **Björn Engholm** and **Hans-Ulrich Klose**, respectively. In 1993, he was a cofounder and chairman of a cross-party initiative (Gegen Vergessen–Für Demokratie) to preserve the memory of National Socialist war crimes and defend democracy against **extremism**, against a background of rising racial tension and right-wing violence in Germany. He was also active in a parliamentary commission for constitutional reform, where he played a role in the adoption of the protection of the **environment**, the promotion of women, and rights for disabled people as constitutionally recognized aims of the state. After 1994, he no longer presented himself for reelection to the Bundestag. In 1998, he argued for the creation of a federal foundation to compensate victims of the slave labor policies of the National Socialist regime and was honored with the Galinski Prize for promoting understanding between **Jews** and their fellow citizens. A moderate figure in the SPD, Vogel published an autobiography recounting his political experiences in Bonn and Berlin (*Nachsichten: Meine Bonner und Berliner Jahre*, 1996).

VOGEL, WOLFGANG (1925–2008). Lawyer. Wolfgang Vogel was born in Wilhelmsthal (now in Poland). After serving in the German air force during World War II, he studied law at the universities of Jena and Leipzig in East Germany, passing his state law examinations in 1949 and 1952. After working briefly in the ministry of justice (1952–1953), he practiced as a lawyer in East **Berlin** and in 1957 was also recognized by courts in West Berlin, representing Western colleagues at courts in East Berlin and elsewhere in the **German Democratic Republic (GDR)**. In 1962, the GDR authorities began using him as an intermediary to resolve humanitarian disputes with the Federal Republic of Germany (FRG), and the following year he represented the East German state in negotiating the exchange of prisoners and their release in return for Western **currency**. In 1969, he was appointed the GDR's official representative for humanitarian affairs concerning the FRG (Bevollmächtigter der DDR für humanitäre Fragen bei der Bundesregierung), a role that was extended in 1973. A member of the **Socialist Unity Party of Germany (SED**, from 1982), Vogel was appointed professor for criminal law at a law academy (Akademie für Staats- und Rechtswissenschaften, ASR) in Potsdam-Babelsberg (1985), where he had earned a doctorate (1969).

During his career, Vogel arranged the exit of over 250,000 East German citizens to the FRG and the ransoming of around 33,700. He played a part in the release of U.S. pilot Gary Powers (October 1962) and was involved in the exchange of about 150 secret agents in all, including the GDR spy **Günter**

Guillaume (October 1981). He acted as negotiator when the U.S. embassy in Berlin was occupied by citizens demanding to leave the GDR (1984) and helped organize the release to the West of several thousand people who occupied West German embassies in Budapest, Prague, and Warsaw (1989). After the fall of the regime, Vogel was briefly arrested (December 1989), but later represented the East German leader **Erich Honecker** during his trial (1990). In 1992, Vogel admitted working unofficially for the **Stasi**, and it emerged that the Bonn government had paid him 320,000 DM annually for his humanitarian activities. In January 1996, he was found guilty of extortion, perjury, and giving false evidence; fined 92,000 DM; and given a two-year suspended prison sentence for misuse of his powers during his "trade in people," although the court later acquitted him of extortion on the grounds that he was not responsible for the GDR's laws on travel and emigration.

VOLKSWAGEN AG. Volkswagen (VW) is Europe's largest **automobile** and motor vehicle manufacturer. After supplying around 60,000 vehicles to the German military during World War II, the Volkswagen GmbH resumed work in 1945, repairing British army vehicles. In 1948, company headquarters were moved from **Berlin** to Wolfsburg. In 1949, the military occupation authorities transferred control of the concern's assets to the government of the Federal Republic of Germany (FRG), which entrusted management and operation to the state of **Lower Saxony**. Taking advantage of Germany's rapid economic recovery during the 1950s and 1960s, Volkswagen soon built up a large domestic and global export market. The first models were the flagship "beetle" (remarkable for its rear-mounted, air-cooled engine with front-wheel drive), a four-seater soft top, and from 1950, the VW Transporter van. Landmark dates in Volkswagen's success were 1951, when postwar production of the beetle reached 250,000; 1953 (500,000); and 1955 (one million). By 1965, the total number of motor vehicles manufactured since the war exceeded 10 million, and by 1972 more than 15 million beetles had been built. During the 1970s, the famously functional beetle, which also inspired filmmakers, was replaced by newer models. The last beetle manufactured in Germany left the Emden factory in 1978, although production continued overseas, and official imports of the model into Germany did not cease until 1986. Volkswagen established several subsidiaries throughout the world, including, from the 1950s, plants in Mexico and Brazil, which continued producing the beetle, and also in the United States during the 1960s and 1970s. It acquired a majority interest in Audi (1969); took over the Spanish car producer SEAT (1987) and the Czech manufacturer Skoda (1990); and concluded joint ventures with China (1982), the Japanese concern Toyota (1988), and the Ching Chung Motor Co. in Taiwan (1992). After reunification Volkswagen, assisted by government grants, was one of the first to invest heavily in the **eastern federal states**, building factories in Zwickau, Chemnitz, and Dresden.

Volkswagen has a history of technical innovation and long regarded itself as a leader in electronic steering, alternative drive systems, and environmentally friendly production methods. The company's rise to preeminence in the mass motor vehicle market was presided over by Heinrich Nordhoff (1899–1968), its first managing director (1948–1968). Volkswagen was also considered a beacon for the "social partnership" between employers and **trade unions** that contributed to the economic "model Germany." The partnership enabled the company to introduce flexible working patterns and, through retraining and redeployment, to automate production processes without job losses or industrial conflict. Nordhoff's successors were Kurt Lotz (until 1975), Toni Schmücker (until 1981), Carl H. Hahn (until 1993), and **Ferdinand Piëch**, who took over at a time when Volkswagen was returning heavy losses but succeeded in turning around the company's fortunes. In 2002, Piëch moved to the supervisory board. His replacement, former BMW chairman Bernd Pischetsrieder, quit in 2006 following a power struggle on the board and was succeeded by Martin Winterkorn, head of **AUDI AG**, a division of VW. Volkswagen's image was damaged in 2005 when three senior VW executives, including personnel director Peter Hartz, resigned following allegations of corrupt practices by members of the works council. In January 2007, Hartz was fined and received a two-year suspended sentence for breach of trust and providing improper favors. The affair, alongside corruption scandals involving other leading companies, led to calls for reforms and greater transparency in German corporate governance.

In 1960, Volkswagen GmbH became a share capital company (Volkswagenwerk AG), in which 40 percent of the shares were owned by the **federal government** and the state of Lower Saxony and the rest sold to private investors. The company was renamed Volkswagen AG (1985) and restructured (1991). The Porsche family became a major shareholder in 2006. Under Piëch's and Winterkorn's leadership, VW undertook structural changes in order to develop overseas markets, with the aim of becoming the world's largest automobile manufacturer. Following a leadership battle at board level, Piëch resigned from the supervisory board in 2015, although his family, through Porsche SE, retained a shareholding stake. In September 2015, Winterkorn was forced to step down when it emerged that VW had falsified vehicle emissions tests in the United States. The scandal ruined VW's ambitions to overtake Toyota as the world's largest automobile maker and was projected to cost the company millions through clean-up costs, legal proceedings, and fines. Winterkorn was replaced by Matthias Müller, former chairman of Porsche AG. Turnover in 2015 was over 213,000 million euros, with a workforce of around 610,000, although the emission scandal produced the company's first annual loss (4,100 million euros) in 20 years.

In the late 1990s, the Commission of the **European Union (EU)** began investigating Volkswagen's ownership structure, in particular the rules that protected the company from takeover and prevented other shareholders from acquiring a stake larger than the 20 percent controlled by the state of Lower Saxony. Under EU law, this violated the principle of the free movement of capital, and the German government came under strong pressure to remove Volkswagen's special status. Following modifications by the state, the European Court of Justice ruled in 2013 to confirm Lower Saxony's holding (now the second largest after Porsche, which controls 50.7 percent); although a minority stake, it is associated with blocking rights, and the state continues to take a close interest in the company's management. The interests of the workforce are strongly represented by the **trade union** IG Metall.

In 1962, the company set up the Stiftung Volkswagen (Volkswagen Foundation). Based in Hanover, the foundation supports **research** and **educational** projects in all areas, including arts and social sciences, technology, natural sciences, and medicine. It places particular emphasis on promoting the researchers of the future and those working across national and disciplinary boundaries.

See also AUTOMOBILE INDUSTRY; PORSCHE FAMILY.

VOLLMER, ANTJE (1943–). Green Party politician. Antje Vollmer was born in Lübbecke (**North Rhine-Westfalia**); studied theology in Heidelberg, Tübingen, and Paris; and then passed her final state examinations (1968, 1971) and earned a doctorate (1973). After a period as a research assistant/ junior lecturer at a theological college, the Kirchliche Hochschule, in **Berlin** (1969–1971), she worked as a pastor in Berlin-Wedding (1971–1974) and completed a postgraduate diploma in adult education (1975) before teaching at a theological college in Bielefeld-Bethel (the Evangelische Heimvolkshochschule, 1976–1982). Although she represented the Greens in the **Bundestag** (1983–1990), leading the party's parliamentary group for three years, she did not join the party until 1985, when, in accordance with its principle of rotation, she left parliament to make room for a successor. She returned to the Bundestag in 1987–1990, again leading the parliamentary group from 1989, until the west German Greens failed to clear the entry hurdle at the 1990 national election. Reentering parliament in 1994, she was vice president of the Bundestag from 1994 until 2005. Critical of government plans to allow **homosexual** partners to adopt children (2004) and of the war in Afghanistan, she withdrew from political office in 2005. A committed peace activist and accomplished journalist, Vollmer contributed to leading newspapers and magazines, including *Der Spiegel, Die Zeit,* and *stern.* Her numerous awards include the Carl von Ossietzky Medal (1989), the CICERO Prize for rhetoric (1996), the Hannah Arendt Prize (1998), and the Heinrich Heine professorship (1999–2000). She served on the presidium of the Deutscher Evangelischer Kirchentag (Conference of German Evangelical Churches [DEK], 1988–1994) and was a member of the synod of the Evangelische Kirche in Deutschland (Evangelical Church in Germany, EKD) from 1997 to 2002.

VOSCHERAU, HENNING (1941–2016). Social Democratic Party of Germany (SPD) politician. Henning Voscherau was born in **Hamburg**, where he studied law and economics, passing his state law examinations in 1966 and 1971. He earned a doctorate in law (1969) and worked in the legal profession in Hamburg from 1971 (as a notary from 1974). In 1974, he was elected to the Hamburg state parliament and in the same year to the executive committee of the SPD parliamentary group. He chaired the interior affairs committee (1974–1982), was first deputy leader (1976–1982) and then leader of the parliamentary group (1982–1987), and served as vice president (1988–1989, 1991–1992, 1993–1994) and president (1990–1991) of the **Bundesrat**. He also chaired the joint **Bundestag**-Bundesrat committee on constitutional reform (1992–1993). In 1988, Voscherau was elected first mayor and president of the Hamburg senate (government). On the right wing of the party, he led a coalition of the SPD and **Free Democratic Party (FDP)**, ruled alone after electoral victory (1991), and entered into an alliance with the **Instead Party (Statt-Partei**, 1993). Despite pressure from the party's left wing, he refused a coalition with the Greens and attempted to present the SPD as a protector of law and order. Following disappointing results in the 1997 regional election, Voscherau resigned as mayor. In the same year, he returned to his Hamburg legal practice, then sat on the national executive of the SPD (until 2001).

WAIGEL, THEODOR (1939–). Christian Social Union (CSU) politician. Theodor (Theo) Waigel was born in Oberrohr/Krumbach (**Bavaria**), studied law and political science at the universities of Munich and Würzburg, earned a doctorate (1967), and trained as a lawyer, passing his state law examinations in 1963 and 1967. After working briefly for the state prosecution service in Munich, he became a personal assistant to the parliamentary **state secretary** in the Bavarian ministry of finance (1969–1970) and to the minister of economics and **transport** (1970–1972). He was local secretary to the **Junge Union (JU)**, the youth wing of the CSU, in Krumbach (1961–1970), before taking over leadership of the regional organization (1971–1975). Waigel rose steadily in the CSU, serving as chairman of the party commission on basic policy (1973–1988) and district leader for Schwaben (1987–1988) before joining the regional executive (1970) and the party presidium (1983). From 1988 to 1999, he was chairman of the CSU.

Elected to the **Bundestag** in 1972, Waigel focused on **education**, finance, and the **budget**. He became spokesman on economic policy for the **Christian Democratic Union (CDU)**/CSU parliamentary group (1980) and was elected leader of the CSU regional group in Bonn (1982). The following years proved trying for Waigel, as he acted as an intermediary between **Helmut Kohl** and **Franz Josef Strauß**. In April 1989, Kohl appointed him federal minister of finance, a post he held until the national election of October 1998, when he was succeeded by **Hans Eichel** of the **Social Democratic Party of Germany (SPD)**. As finance minister, Waigel played a leading role in the negotiations on reunification, including the agreement to pay the Soviet Union 15,000 million DM to withdraw its troops from German soil, but his popularity fell when he raised **taxes** after the 1990 election in order to meet the spiraling costs of reunification. One of his most important acts was to sign the Treaty of Maastricht (February 1992), which resulted in the single European **currency** and laid down the criteria for entry into the eurozone. Known as "Mr. Euro," he was instrumental in giving the currency, which up until 1995 was officially known as the ecu (European currency unit), its name. He earned the nickname "Goldfinger" when he used an upward reevaluation of the gold reserves of the **German Federal Bank** to boost the domestic budget (1997).

A personal friend of Helmut Kohl and at one point considered a rival to **Edmund Stoiber**, Waigel left the Bundestag in 2002 and withdrew from active politics. In 2009, he was elected honorary chairman of the CSU. Waigel has published an autobiographical account of his childhood and school-related experiences as a pupil, father, and politician (*Meine Erfahrungen mit der Schule als Schüler, als Vater und als Politiker*, 2000).

WALLMANN, WALTER (1932–2002). Christian Democratic Union (CDU) politician. Walter Wallmann was born in Uelzen (**Lower Saxony**) and studied law and politics at the University of Marburg, qualifying as a lawyer in Frankfurt/Main and earning a doctorate in law (1965). He worked as a judge in Kassel, Rotenburg/Fulda, and Gießen from 1965 to 1967. Wallmann joined the CDU in 1961 and was active in the party's youth wing (**Junge Union, JU**) in **Hessen**. A member of the Hessen **Landtag** (1966–1972, 1987–1991), he occupied various positions in the regional CDU, including deputy party leader (1967–1982) and leader of the parliamentary group (1968–1974). He represented the CDU in the **Bundestag** (1972–1977, January–April 1987), where he served on the executive committee of the parliamentary group (from 1973) and chaired the committee that investigated the case of **Günter Guillaume**, the East German spy and close adviser to **Willy Brandt** (1974–1975). Other positions he occupied included senior mayor (Oberbürgermeister) of the city of Frankfurt/Main (1977–1986), leader of the CDU in Hessen (1982–1991), and member of the CDU national presidium (1985–1992). In the year of the Chernobyl disaster (April 1986), he was appointed West Germany's first federal minister responsible for the **environment** (including nature conservation and nuclear safety), although he regarded a swift withdrawal from atomic **energy** as unrealistic.

In 1987, Wallmann became **minister president** of Hessen, leading a CDU/**Free Democratic Party (FDP)** coalition until 1991. As premier Wallmann was particularly active in energy and **educational** policy and was an advocate of parliamentary reform and part-time members of parliament. He also appointed Germany's first representative for the protection of animals and was instrumental in Hessen's providing a program of support for the eastern state of **Thuringia** after reunification. Wallmann, who withdrew from active politics in 1997, published several books on contemporary politics (*Der Preis des Fortschritts: Beitrag zur politischen Kultur*, 1983; *Regierungswechsel und Kontinuität im demokratischen Bundesstaat*, 1987; *Die Gegenwart der Geschichte*, 2001; *Im Licht der Paulskirche. Memoiren eines Politischen*, 2002).

WALSER, MARTIN (1927–). Writer. Born in Wasserburg/Lake Constance, Martin Walser served briefly in World War II before studying literature, philosophy, and history in Regensburg and Tübingen, earning a doctorate in 1951. After working as a reporter, producer, and writer at the Süddeutscher Rundfunk (SDR, 1949–1957), he became a full-time author, focusing on social and political issues. His novel *Halbzeit* (Half Time, 1960) established him as a major postwar German writer. The recipient of several awards, Walser, whose repertoire ranges from novels and short stories to political essays, radio plays, and drama, attracted controversy in 1998 when, in a speech given upon receiving the prestigious Peace Prize of the German Booksellers Association, he argued that it was time for Germany to stop being beaten with the "moral stick" of guilt over the Holocaust. Walser conducted a fierce debate with the Jewish community leader **Ignatz Bubis** over his 1998 speech and was accused (by *FAZ* editor Frank Schirrmacher) of using anti-Semitic clichés in his satirical novel *Tod eines Kritikers* (Death of a critic, 2002). Walser is a member of the Academy of Arts (Berlin), the Saxon Academy of Arts, the German Academy for Language and Poetry, and the German **PEN**. In 2007, the magazine *Cicero* ranked him among the 500 most influential German intellectuals.

WANKA, JOHANNA (1951–). Christian Democratic Union (CDU) politician. Johanna Wanka was born in Rosenfeld (**Saxony**) in the former **German Democratic Republic (GDR)**, studied mathematics at the University of Leipzig (1970–1974), worked as a research assistant at the technical university of Merseburg (1974–1985), and earned a doctorate in 1980. She was a cofounder of the Merseburg branch of the citizens' dissident group **New Forum** in 1990 and remained active in it until 1994. Appointed professor of mathematics at the higher technical college (Fachhochschule) in Merseburg in 1993, she served as college rector (1994–2000) and member of the regional interuniversity council in the **federal state** of **Brandenburg** (1999–2000) before becoming regional minister for science, research, and culture (2000–2009, initially nonparty). A member of the CDU from 2001 and regional party leader during 2009–2010, Wanka served as president of the Kultusministerkonferenz (Standing Conference of State Ministers of **Education**, KML) in 2005 before moving to **Lower Saxony** to become regional minister for science and culture. In 2013, she joined Chancellor **Angela Merkel**'s third cabinet as federal minister of education and **research**.

WARSAW PACT. The Warsaw Pact was a military alliance of satellite communist states of the Union of Soviet Socialist Republics (USSR), created in 1955 in response to the rearming of the newly founded Federal Republic of Germany and its joining the **North Atlantic Treaty Organization**

(**NATO**). The pact's members were Albania, Bulgaria, Czechoslovakia, Hungary, Poland, Romania, the USSR, and the **German Democratic Republic (GDR)**. Albania left the alliance in 1961, and the pact was dissolved in 1991 as the old eastern bloc under Soviet control broke up. The subsequent security vacuum led several eastern European states to seek membership in NATO.

WEBER, JÜRGEN (1941–). Airline executive. Born in Lahr (**Baden-Württemberg**), Jürgen Weber earned a diploma in aeronautics and aviation technology at the Technische Hochschule (Technical University) in Stuttgart (1965), where he also worked as a scientific assistant (until 1967). After joining the **engineering** division of the national German airline carrier Lufthansa in **Hamburg**, he moved to Frankfurt/Main as head of maintenance. Following a return to the aircraft division in Hamburg (1978) and completion of a senior management training course at the Massachusetts Institute of Technology (1980), he became general manager of the technical division (1987), where he was a protégé of the managing director, Reinhardt Abraham. Appointed deputy member of the main executive board (1989), he became a full member with responsibility for the technical division and deputy chairman (October 1990), before succeeding Heinz Ruhnau as chairman (1991).

As head of Lufthansa during the 1990s, Weber oversaw the company's total privatization, an extensive rationalization program, and the establishment of Star Alliance, a network of partnerships with other airlines offering additional routes and simplified booking facilities. In 2000, Lufthansa achieved record sales and was Europe's largest airline in terms of turnover and number of passengers carried (2002). It weathered the collapse in air traffic following the **terrorist** attacks of 11 September 2001, partly because Weber had foreseen a crisis in the early 1990s and grounded aircraft immediately after the attacks. One year later, passenger numbers had returned to their former levels of four million a month, and the airline reported a 172 percent increase in profit (790 million euros between January and September 2002), despite a drop in business travel. These developments allowed Lufthansa to steal the title of "the world's favorite airline" from its rival, British Airways. Weber was widely praised for managing Lufthansa's recovery, although worsening economic recession, war against Iraq, and the SARS virus outbreak combined to depress performance during 2003. After recording its largest ever loss in 2004 (980 million euros), the concern embarked on a major restructuring program, including shedding 8,000 jobs in its catering division, Sky Chefs. In June 2003, Wolfgang Mayrhuber succeeded Weber as chief executive of Deutsche Lufthansa AG.

See also TRANSPORT: AIR TRAFFIC.

WEHNER, HERBERT (1906–1990). Social Democratic Party of Germany (SPD) politician. Herbert Wehner was born in Dresden (**Saxony**), the son of a shoemaker. He attended evening classes in economics, literary history, and philosophy and trained in commerce (until 1924). He joined the Sozialistische Arbeiterjugend (Socialist Workers Youth) in 1923, writing articles for left-wing journals, and the Communist Party of Germany (KPD) in 1927. Wehner held various positions for the KPD and briefly represented it in the Saxony state parliament (**Landtag**, 1930–1931), until he was directed to resign by the party leadership. Active in the communist resistance against the National Socialists after 1933, he narrowly escaped arrest on several occasions before emigrating to Prague (1935), where at a party conference he was elected a candidate member of the Politburo and to the central committee of the KPD in exile (1935). Following a spell in Paris (1936), he was called to Moscow (1937) before moving to Sweden (1941) to organize the reestablishment of the party in Germany. Imprisoned by the authorities for "endangering Swedish freedom and neutrality" (1942–1944), he was expelled by the KPD on suspicion of betraying the party (June 1942).

Released from prison, Wehner worked in Sweden (1944–1946) before returning to Germany, where he joined and became active in the SPD from 1946. He worked as a journalist on foreign affairs for the SPD newspaper *Hamburger Echo* (1949–1983). Encouraged by Kurt Schumacher, the veteran SPD politician and party leader (1946–1952), Wehner entered the first **Bundestag** (1949), where he represented the SPD until he retired from active politics (1983). In the early 1950s, he worked for the return of German prisoners of war from the Union of Soviet Socialist Republics (USSR). During his postwar political career, he occupied various senior positions in the party, including as a member of the national executive and presidium (1952–1982), deputy leader (1958–1973), and leader of the parliamentary group (1969–1983). He was also federal minister for pan-German affairs in Germany's first **grand coalition** (1966–1969).

Wehner championed the Godesberg Program (1959), in which the SPD abandoned its Marxist orientation and broadened its electoral appeal. He backed Western integration and supported a coalition with the **Christian Democratic Union (CDU)** as early as 1961. Although he was a strong supporter of the **Ostpolitik** pursued by **Willy Brandt**, he disagreed with members of his party on how the policy should be implemented. His relationship with Brandt further deteriorated when the latter resigned as **federal chancellor** following the **Günter Guillaume** affair (1974). In order to promote East–West relations, Wehner visited several East European states in the early 1970s, including the **German Democratic Republic (GDR)**, where he met **Erich Honecker** for the first time (1973), and the USSR, where he publicly criticized the German government's firm line on consular representation in East **Berlin**. In 1997, the former East German spymaster **Markus Wolf** suggested that Wehner, who had died in 1990, had been in the service of the GDR, although he retracted the allegation a few months later. Wehner published his political memoirs (*Zeugnis*) in 1982.

WEIDMANN, JENS (1968–). Banker. Born in Solingen (**North Rhine-Westfalia**), Jens Weidmann studied business economics in Aix-Marseille (France) and in Bonn, completed a study visit to the Bank of France (1987), and qualified with a diploma (1993) and later a doctorate (1997). After working for the International Monetary Fund in Washington, D.C. (1997–1999), he became general secretary to Germany's **Council of Experts** on economic development (1999–2003) and head of monetary policy and analysis at the **German Federal Bank** (2003–2006), before moving to the department of economic and financial policy in the **Office of the Federal Chancellor**, where he was also Chancellor **Angela Merkel**'s personal representative at the world economic summits of G8 and G20 states. In May 2011, he was appointed president of the German Federal Bank. As a member of the European Central Bank (ECB) during the **eurozone crisis**, he strongly opposed proposals that the bank, through the purchase of government bonds, should buy up the sovereign debts of crisis-hit member states.

WEIL, STEPHAN (1958–). Social Democratic Party of Germany (SPD) politician. Stephen Weil was born in **Hamburg**, studied law at the University of Göttingen (from 1978), and qualified as a practicing lawyer (1983, 1986). In Hanover he worked as a lawyer (1987–1989), then as a judge (1989–1994) and public prosecutor (1989–1991), before becoming a senior civil servant (Ministerialrat) in the justice ministry of the state of **Lower Saxony** (1994–1997). After 1997, he was a senior councilor (Stadtkämmerer), responsible at various times for finance, legal affairs, buildings, the fire service, and public utilities. Chairman of the SPD branch of Hanover city (1991–1997) and leader of the regional SPD in Lower Saxony (from 2012), Weil served as senior mayor (Oberbürgermeister) of Hanover between 2006 and 2013. In February 2013, he was elected **minister president** of Lower Saxony, heading a coalition government of SPD and the **Green Party**. In 2013, he also joined the supervisory board of **Volkswagen AG**.

WEIMAR TRIANGLE (WEIMARER DREIECK). Launched in August 1991 in Weimar by the foreign ministers of Germany, France, and Poland as an informal trilateral discussion forum, the Weimar Triangle was instrumental in initiating the Polish application for membership in the **European Union (EU)** after the end of the Cold War in 1989. For Germany this represented, since the signing of the Élysée Treaty with France in 1963, the final stage in its reconciliation with its two largest neighbors after World War II. Following the single largest territorial enlargement of the EU in 2004 (with the accession of Cyprus, the Czech Republic, Estonia, Hungary, Latvia, Lithuania, Malta, Poland, Slovakia, and Slovenia), the Triangle gained fresh momentum when in 2009 Germany announced its intention to use the forum to deepen links among its members. The Triangle also promotes cultural links (youth exchanges) and partnerships between cities and regions ("mini-triangles").

WEIZSÄCKER, RICHARD VON (1920–2015). Christian Democratic Union (CDU) politician and **president of the Federal Republic** (1984–1994). Richard von Weizsäcker was born in Stuttgart. His father, Ernst von Weizsäcker (1882–1951), was a diplomat in the foreign ministry in **Berlin** (1938–1943). The family also lived in Copenhagen (1924–1927) and Bern (1933–1937), where the son attended school. He began studying law at the University of Oxford (Great Britain) and at Grenoble (France), returning to Germany to be drafted into the army (1938). The following year, he took part in the invasion of Poland. After World War II, he resumed his studies, this time in law and social sciences at the University of Göttingen, earning a doctorate in law (1954). Between 1947 and 1949, while still a student, he assisted the lawyer Hellmut Becker, who defended his father when he was placed on trial at the Nuremberg war trials. (Ernst von Weizsäcker was sentenced to seven years in prison in 1949 but released the following year in a general amnesty.) Weizsäcker joined the steel and tube manufacturers Mannesmann in Düsseldorf as a trainee and in 1958 took over its economic policy division. He also worked for a **bank** in Essen (1958–1962) and the **pharmaceuticals** concern C. H. **Boehringer** (1963–1976). From 1954, he worked actively for the CDU, and in 1962 became a member of the presidium of the standing conference of the Evangelische Kirche in Deutschland (Evangelical Church in Germany, EKD), on whose synod he also served (1969–1984).

Elected to the CDU national executive (1966), Weizsäcker represented the party in the **Bundestag** (1969–1981), supporting **Ostpolitik** during the fierce parliamentary debates that took place in the early 1970s. Although he failed in his first bid to become president of the Federal Republic (1974), he was elected governing mayor of West Berlin at a time when the city began to experience serious housing problems and rising unemployment (1981). In 1983, he traveled to the **German Democratic Republic (GDR)** to meet the East German leader **Erich Honecker**, the first governing mayor of Berlin to do so. The following year, he was elected federal president by a large majority, succeeding Karl Carstens, and was reelected in 1989. On the 40th anniversary of the end of World War II (1985), Weizsäcker attracted international attention by calling for Germans to acknowledge their responsibility for their National Socialist past and for injustices suffered by victims of the regime.

His speech was the first to include **homosexuals** in the list of victims of National Socialist persecution. He helped gather Western support for the reform course of the Soviet leader Mikhail Gorbachev, although he argued for a gradual reunification after the fall of the GDR regime and was criticized for proposing at an early stage that Berlin should be the capital of a united Germany.

Well known for his brilliant speeches, Weizsäcker made a determined effort to be a "president for all citizens" and proved to be one of the most popular incumbents of that position. He drew attention to the dangers of the rise of right-wing **extremism** during the 1990s and was actively involved in projects to relieve world poverty and protect the **environment**. He was succeeded as federal president by **Roman Herzog** (1994) and went on to chair a commission on the future of the German armed forces (**Bundeswehr**). Weizsäcker received many awards, especially for the promotion of peace, **human rights**, and international understanding, and honorary doctorates from universities throughout the world. His memoires (*Vier Zeiten*) appeared in 1997.

WELFARE SYSTEM. *See* SOCIAL SECURITY SYSTEM.

WESTERWELLE, GUIDO (1961–2016). Free Democratic Party (FDP) politician. Born in Bad Honnef (near Bonn), Guido Westerwelle studied law at the University of Bonn (1980–1987) and completed his state law exams in Cologne and Düsseldorf (1987, 1991), before earning a doctorate at the Comprehensive University (Gesamthochshule) of Hagen (1994). From 1991, he practiced as a lawyer and was a member of the board of trustees of the Theodor-Heuss Foundation. Westerwelle joined the FDP in 1980. A founding member of the Young Liberals, he chaired their national executive (1983–1988), transforming the organization into an active and crucial youth wing for the party, attractive to young voters. Elected chairman of the Bonn branch of the FDP (1993–2000), he joined the national executive (1988) and was party general secretary (1994–2001) before succeeding **Wolfgang Gerhardt** as national chairman (2001–2011).

Westerwelle entered the **Bundestag** in February 1996. Under his influence the FDP, after losing heavily at elections during 1994 and 1995 and virtually disappearing from the national and regional political landscape, developed a new image and attempted to present itself as a convincing alternative to the **Christian Democratic Union (CDU)** and the **Social Democratic Party of Germany (SPD)**. In 1996, the party adopted the so-called Wiesbaden Principles, which aimed to reaffirm its traditional liberal credentials by reducing the role of the state in **taxation** and **welfare**, providing incentives for small businesses, and giving achievers in German society a genuine voice. It demanded a reduction of the **solidarity surcharge** for the **eastern federal states**; an acceleration of tax reform; the abolition of conscription; and greater autonomy for schools, universities, and vocational colleges. At the same time, the FDP struggled to achieve internal coherence and began to distance itself from its coalition partners, the CDU/**Christian Social Union (CSU)**. In late 1997, the left wing of the FDP (the so-called Freiburg Group) accused the leadership of incompetence after a court found that the party had acquired 12.4 million DM of state subventions illegally (the order to refund the money was rescinded in 2000). In the run-up to the 1998 national election, Westerwelle, who was adopted by **North Rhine-Westfalia** as the state's lead candidate, controversially urged Chancellor **Helmut Kohl**, if he should win, to step down in favor of his deputy, **Wolfgang Schäuble**, and criticized the CSU's demands for stricter policies on admitting **foreigners**. During the debate on a new nationality law the following year, the FDP, in contrast to the CDU, acknowledged the merits of dual citizenship. The relationship between the two parties was not helped by the scandal surrounding Kohl's alleged acceptance of donations for political favors.

When Westerwelle, a forceful speaker, became national chairman, the party hoped that a dynamic leadership would promote a fresh image of modern liberalism and rebuild electoral appeal. Although party membership increased, the FDP performed poorly in the 2002 national election, and it attracted negative publicity during the campaign over the activities of its controversial deputy leader, **Jürgen Möllemann**, one of Westerwelle's fiercest opponents. However, following the party's best ever success in the 2009 national election, Westerwelle became foreign minister and vice-chancellor in **Angela Merkel**'s second cabinet, but was criticized for his low profile on issues such as Afghanistan and the Middle East, and he resigned in 2011. He exerted little influence on foreign policy, and his agenda of global disarmament, which he shared with U.S. president Barack Obama, lost impetus. Following the FDP's failure to enter parliament in 2013, Westerwelle also resigned as party leader and was eventually succeeded by **Christian Lindner**. In December the same year, he founded the Westerwelle Foundation for international understanding.

WIECZOREK-ZEUL, HEIDEMARIE (1942–). Social Democratic Party of Germany (SPD) politician. Heidemarie Wieczorek-Zeul was born in Frankfurt/Main, studied English and history at the University of Frankfurt (1964–1965), and worked as a schoolteacher in Rüsselsheim (1965–1974). She joined the SPD in 1965 and was elected town councilor in Rüsselsheim (1968) and local councilor for Groß-Gerau (1972). She was national leader of the **Young Socialists (JUSOS)** wing of the SPD (1974–1977) and chaired the European coordination office of international youth associations (1977–1979), before being elected to the European Parliament, where she specialized in development policy and was involved in the series of Lomé Agreements that the **European Union** (**EU**) concluded with developing countries after 1975. She was elected to the SPD national executive (1984) and the party presidium (1986).

In 1987, Wieczorek-Zeul entered the **Bundestag** (representing Wiesbaden) and was appointed parliamentary party spokeswoman for European affairs. She was also district SPD chairwoman for south **Hessen** (1988) and deputy leader of the national party (1993–2005). She opposed extending the role of the **Bundeswehr** in international peacekeeping operations and restricting Germany's **asylum** laws. Appointed federal minister for economic cooperation and development under Chancellor **Gerhard Schröder** (1998), she retained the post in the cabinet of **Angela Merkel** (November 2005). Despite the SPD/**Green Party** coalition's commitment to increasing development aid, her ministry fell victim to budgetary cuts in the government's second term. After Schröder appointed her to the Bundessicherheitsrat (Federal Security Council), she used her membership to vote consistently against arms exports. Nicknamed "red Heide" (partly for her striking red hair) since her young socialist days and a long-standing admirer of **Willy Brandt**, Wieczorek-Zeul was a leading figure in the so-called "Cologne initiative" to cancel the debt of the poorest developing countries during the 1999 G7 summit. She argued strongly for a "coalition against poverty" and for fairer structures in world trade as a response to the terrorist attacks of 11 September 2001. In 2004, she visited Namibia to commemorate the death of thousands of Africans killed by German colonial troops in an uprising in 1904–1907 and earned the disapproval of the **Central Council of Jews** for criticizing Israel's actions during the Lebanon war (2006). A committed European, she also believed in a stronger and more self-assertive EU that would act as a counterweight to the United States. Considered an able and active representative of the party's left wing, Wieczorek-Zeul remained in the Bundestag until 2013.

WISCHNEWSKI, HANS-JÜRGEN (1922–2005). Social Democratic Party of Germany (SPD) politician. Hans-Jürgen Wischnewski was born in Allenstein (formerly east Prussia), educated in **Berlin**, and served in the German armed forces during World War II, after which he became an active member of the **trade union** IG Metall, joining its staff in 1952. In 1946, he joined the SPD, representing the party in the **Bundestag** from 1957 until 1990. His positions in the party included chairman of the youth wing (1959–1961), party manager (1968–1971), deputy leader (1979–1982), deputy leader of the parliamentary group (1980–1983), and treasurer (1984–1985). In the **grand coalition** under Chancellor **Kurt Georg Kiesinger**, he was minister for economic cooperation (1966–1968), and he served as **state secretary** and junior minister in the federal foreign ministry

(1974–1976) under Chancellor **Willy Brandt**. He also worked in the **Office of the Federal Chancellor** from 1976 to 1979 and again in 1982 until **Helmut Schmidt** was forced out of office.

Nicknamed "Ben Wisch" for his personal contacts with the Arab world, Wischnewski contributed significantly to German–Arab relations. He undertook several foreign missions on behalf of the German government, including a visit to Algeria, made in 1965 at the request of **Christian Democratic Union (CDU)** foreign minister Gerhard Schröder to prevent the severance of diplomatic relations after West Germany had exchanged ambassadors with Israel. He also led negotiations for the release of hostages held by Palestinians (in Amman, 1970) and the freeing of passengers on a hijacked Lufthansa aircraft (Mogadishu, 1977). A defender of Palestinians' right to self-determination and strong advocate of peace in the Middle East, he was honored by Yassar Arafat in 1997. Wischnewski's last foreign visit was to Arafat's funeral in 2005.

WOIDKE, DIETMAR (1961–). Social Democratic Party of Germany (SPD) politician. Dietmar Woidke was born in Naundorf (**Brandenburg**) and studied **agriculture** and animal husbandry at Humboldt University in **Berlin** (1982–1987), where he graduated with a diploma. Subsequent posts that he held include research assistant at the Humboldt University in Berlin, (1987–1990), head of the scientific department in an animal feed concern (1990–1992), and head of the Spree-Neiße district office for **environment** and agriculture (1992–1994), during which time he earned a doctorate in agriculture (1993). A member of the SPD from 1993, Woidke entered the Brandenburg regional assembly (**Landtag**) the following year and was also a member of the councils of the Spree-Neiße district (1998–2004, 2008–) and the town of Forst (1998–2003, 2008–2010). In the Landtag, he led the SPD parliamentary group and served on the presidium (2009–2010). Woidke was regional minister for rural development, the environment, and consumer protection (2004–2009) and interior minister (2010–2013), where he led a reform of the police service that reduced the number of officers and merged management structures. Little known beyond Brandenburg, he succeeded **Matthias Platzeck** as minister president in 2013, leading a coalition with **The Left Party** (reelected in 2014). From 2014, he also promoted cross-border cooperation with neighboring Poland.

WOLF, CHRISTA (1929–2011). Writer. Christa Wolf was born in Landsberg (now in Poland) and fled with her family to Mecklenburg/East Germany in 1945. After earning her higher school certificate (1949), she studied German at the universities of Jena and Leipzig (1949–1953) and worked for the Schriftstellerverband der DDR, the official writers' organization of the **Ger-**

man Democratic Republic (GDR, 1953–1959). Between 1956 and 1962, she worked for publishers in **Berlin** and Halle and edited the literary journal *Neue Deutsche Literatur* (1958–1959). Wolf's writing career began in 1962 with the publication of a novel about a love affair that founders on the division of Germany (*Der geteilte Himmel*), for which she received the Heinrich Heine Prize of the East German Academy of Arts (Akademie der Künste, 1963) and which was also made into a film (1964). A member of the **Socialist Unity Party of Germany** (**SED**) from 1949, she was a candidate member of the party's Central Committee from 1963 but withdrew in 1967 following official disapproval of her defense of the author Werner Bräunig against a restrictive cultural policy.

In her later works, Wolf established herself as a leading East German author with a pan-German reputation. Her titles include *Nachdenken über Christa T.* (1968), *Kindheitsmuster* (1976), *Kein Ort: Nirgends* (1976), and *Störfall* (1987). Her themes range from the individual in society to peace and the role of **women**. *Kassandra* (1983), which is set in antiquity and deals with the position of women in a patriarchal and warlike society, was an international success.

Wolf left the SED in 1989 but argued for the continuation of a reformed GDR. She was among the intellectuals who spoke on 4 November 1989 on the Alexanderplatz at Germany's largest postwar demonstration shortly before the demise of the communist regime. Her short novel *Was bleibt* (published in 1990), which contained autobiographical elements and portrayed the activities of the GDR secret police, the **Stasi**, sparked the so-called **literary quarrel** over whether intellectuals in the GDR could have done more to resist the regime; she came under fierce attack as a "domesticated opponent" of the SED. In 1993, Wolf confessed to having spied for the Stasi between 1959 and 1962, although she herself was under surveillance between 1969 and 1989. Her later works include the novel *Medea* (1996); a collection of essays, speeches, and short stories (*Hierzulande, Andernorts*, 1999); and the semiautobiographical short novel *Leibhaftig* (2002).

Wolf was a member of the GDR Academy of Arts (from 1974) and of its West German counterpart (from 1981, with a short interruption in 1993–1994). Awarded the Georg Büchner Prize (1980) and the National Prize of the GDR (1987), she went on lecture tours in the United States and Western Europe (from 1978) and studied at the Getty Center in Santa Monica (U.S., 1992–1993). In 1990, she received an honorary doctorate from the University of Hildesheim.

WOLF, MARKUS (1923–2006). German Democratic Republic (GDR) spymaster. Markus Wolf was born in Hechingen (**Baden-Württemberg**), the son of a Jewish doctor, writer, and Marxist. When the National Socialists came to power in 1933, the family (including his younger brother) fled via

Switzerland and France to the Soviet Union (USSR). In Moscow Wolf attended school, studied aircraft construction (1940–1942), and, following evacuation from Moscow, attended the school of the Comintern (Communist International) in Kushnarenkovo (1942–1943). He joined the Communist Party of Germany (KPD) in 1942 and worked for a Soviet radio station broadcasting to Germany from 1943 until 1945. Wolf returned to Germany in May 1945 as part of the group of exiled German communists around **Walter Ulbricht**, who later became the East German leader. He began working for Radio **Berlin** (Berliner Rundfunk), reported on the Nuremberg war trials, and became head of the station's political section.

Wolf joined the **Socialist Unity Party of Germany** (**SED**) in 1946. After acting officially as adviser (with diplomatic status) to the diplomatic mission of the newly founded GDR to the USSR (1949–1951) in Moscow, Wolf was recalled to East **Berlin** and charged with building up a foreign intelligence and espionage service. He survived the political upheavals of the early years and the downfalls of the first chiefs of the service, rising to become head of foreign espionage and deputy to **Erich Mielke** in the Ministerium für Staatssicherheit (Ministry for State Security), which ran the **Stasi**. From 1953, Wolf built up a network of around 4,000 agents, many in the Federal Republic of Germany (FRG), whose task was to infiltrate Western (especially West German) society and to begin spying only when they had reached positions of influence. One of Wolf's agents was **Günter Guillaume**, whose discovery led to the resignation of Chancellor **Willy Brandt** (1974). Wolf rose to the rank of general, was decorated by the GDR and the USSR, and for many years was regarded as the "man without a face" by Western intelligence services, until he was eventually photographed on a visit to Stockholm (1978). Wolf retired from active service in 1986–1987.

When the GDR regime collapsed in 1989, Wolf admitted openly to its failings and took part in activities and demonstrations organized by the opposition; he spoke at the mass demonstration of 4 November 1989, but was booed by the crowd. After reunification (October 1990), he fled via Austria to the USSR to escape arrest by the German authorities. Returning in 1991, he was charged with and convicted of treason and corruption (1993), although the judgment was reversed in May 1995 by the **Federal Constitutional Court** (**FCC**), which ruled that agents of the defunct GDR could only to a limited degree be held accountable for their spying activities. In 1996, he appeared before a Düsseldorf court on suspicion of inflicting bodily harm and depriving persons of their freedom. The following year he received a three-year suspended sentence. In November 1997, Wolf retracted earlier impressions he had given in his published memoirs (*Spionagechef im geheimen Krieg: Erinnerungen*) that the veteran SPD politician **Herbert Wehner** had acted as an East German agent; in 1998, he spent three days in preventive detention for refusing to testify in the trial of a **Social Democratic Party of**

Germany (SPD) politician charged with espionage. Apart from his main memoirs (which appeared in 1997), his writings include a book (*Die Troika*, 1989) that recounts the story of three émigré families, one of which is clearly his own. A charismatic figure, Wolf, who died in Berlin, was regarded by many East Germans with an ambiguous mixture of pride for his espionage successes against the West and contempt for his association with a repressive regime.

WOMEN. After World War II, the traditional image of the "mother," which the National Socialist Party had promoted for the duration of its regime, was quickly overtaken by the pressing needs of postwar life; the "Trümmerfrau" (rubble woman) clearing away the debris in cities has become a lasting image. While the **German Democratic Republic (GDR)** sought to integrate women more fully into public life, by the 1970s and 1980s a high level of achievement was nevertheless not able to disguise some setbacks. In the Federal Republic of Germany (FRG) the situation was characterized until the 1970s by the tension between the often exclusive wish to either bring up children or pursue a career. By 2015, women's standing in society had dramatically improved, although men still contributed a telling 75 percent to the average household's income (compared to 78 percent in 1969 and 77 percent in 1998).

Following pressure from women's groups and public opinion, the **Basic Law (BL)** of 1949 incorporated a formal declaration of the equality of men and women (article 3). However, it was not until 1958 that women in Germany gained equal access to family property and income, with further rights in marriage (e.g., over the upbringing of children) the following year. In 1977, family law was revised to formally acknowledge the equal partnership of husband and wife with joint responsibility as parents, although conservative circles, including **political parties** and churches, continued to place the family, with the mother as housewife, at the heart of the state. Traditional role models were reinforced by the creation of a Federal Ministry of the Family (1953) and Germany's generous family benefit system, which enabled the wife/mother to stay at home while the breadwinning husband went out to work. Despite this, the proportion of women who worked outside the home rose from around 31 percent (1950) to 38 percent (1989), while the number of working mothers actually increased threefold between 1950 and 1962. Although wage discrimination was illegal after 1955, women were in practice paid less for "light work," and there was little state provision for child care (the traditional morning-only school day in Germany acted as a further obstacle to women seeking an early return to work).

Echoing developments in the United States and France, a German women's movement emerged during the 1960s and 1970s. Activists founded organizations and help centers (the first women's refuge was founded in **Berlin** in 1976), published magazines, and held conferences (the first national women's conference took place in 1972). Influential German feminist writers included **Alice Schwarzer**, Jutta Menschick, and Marie-Louise Janssen-Jureit. They rejected compromise with the male-dominated hierarchies of the establishment; specifically excluded men from their structures; and argued for loose, democratic organizations of militant activists. Their challenges and achievements have to be seen as part of the "Frauenbewegung" (women's movement) that began in the 1950s and, especially from the 1960s onward, sought to redefine the roles of women at home and at work. Reform of the **abortion** law became an important goal for German feminists and was characterized from the 1970s onward by fierce debates, changes in legislation, and interventions by the **Federal Constitutional Court (FCC)**; reform was further complicated after reunification by the need to harmonize the different practices of West Germany and the former GDR. The last major revisions to abortion legislation have been in effect since 1996.

In the 1980s, German feminism was influenced by New Age thinking (which in many respects reaffirmed the traditional notions of the mother figure) and peace movements protesting against war and nuclear confrontation. Campaigns for "wages for housework" and equal pensions were mounted, but the movement fragmented as women disagreed on issues such as pornography and the virtues of military service (although women had long been able to perform administrative, medical, and other noncombat duties in the German armed forces, it was not until 2001 that they could join combat units). Reunification also failed to unite feminists from east and west, who did not campaign effectively on abortion or on the retention of the free childcare facilities that the GDR state made available to its valued female workforce. Although East German women played a much more integral role in society than their western counterparts, the GDR's approach to women was based on its own sociopolitical ideological framework; in the 1980s, on the other hand, groups of women within churches began to consider alternative models of their role. The politics of reunification had an impact on women's employment, too: in 1992, 64 percent were without a job.

While some radical feminists, often academics and intellectuals, continued to campaign on a militant platform, a new generation of pragmatists emerged who aimed to cooperate with established structures and integrate work with family and parenthood; practical support networks for professional and other categories of women mushroomed during the 1990s. At the same time, more women entered **education**, politics, and business, although problems of underrepresentation in certain professions and an invisible glass ceiling to advancement remained, especially in business. In 1999, 57 percent of women were registered as working, engaged mainly in catering, shop floor sales, office work, and **health** care. Disparities in pay continued, due partly to the fact that men tended to occupy more senior positions, as women were disadvantaged through interruption of employment (maternity) and working only part-time.

In the 1990s, several measures were put in place designed to remove gender inequalities. Women were no longer forced to take their husbands' names (1991), could do night work (1992), and gained legal protection from marital rape (passed by the **Bundestag** in 1997). However, reports by the German Federation of Trade Unions (DGB) and the Federal Ministry for Family Affairs revealed that although the number of employable and well-trained women increased by 250,000 between 2001 and 2003, their career chances remained poorer than for men, with only 15 percent engaged in managerial positions. While the coalition of the **Social Democratic Party of Germany (SPD)** and the **Green Party** elected in 1998 had pledged to introduce a law on equality in the workplace for private **industry**, it abandoned the idea in the face of employers' opposition. In its place a voluntary code was agreed upon, and German law adopted a series of **European Union (EU)** guidelines. The Federal Ministry for Family Affairs also planned a national antidiscrimination office and closer monitoring of women's success in reaching senior positions at work. Eventually, in 2015, the **Bundestag**, with a large majority, required large concerns to open 30 percent of their seats on their supervisory boards (Aufsichtsräte) to women (effective in 2016). Medium-sized firms were also obliged to widen opportunities for women to enter leading positions (the "flexi-quota"), and provisions were made in public service companies for women to be present at decisions on wages and conditions. The measures remain controversial, however, since many argue that women would rather be employed on their merits than on the basis of a quota, while others counter that without such regulations, change remains too slow. German institutions usually have a "Frauenbeauftragte" or "Gleichstellungsbeauftragte," who observes that requirements of gender equality (including the use of politically correct terms and linguistic devices) at the workplace are observed. The highest percentage of working women in Germany is between 40 and 50 percent, which reflects the fact that many women still seem to prefer to stay at home bringing up their children. On the other hand, a significant development is that the proportion of female Bundestag members has steadily risen, from 5.8 percent in 1972 to 36.8 percent in 2015.

See also WOMEN'S LITERATURE (FRAUENLITERATUR).

WOMEN'S LITERATURE (FRAUENLITERATUR). In 1970, the first magazine for **women** appeared in **Berlin**. Called *Pelagea*, it was edited by a group of feminist activists (Aktionskreis der Befreiung der Frau). In 1976, the magazine *Courage* proved a success, although it ceased publication in 1984. In 1977 *Emma*, founded by **Alice Schwarzer**, became the world's second largest feminist magazine (in terms of circulation). In the 1970s, women established their own publishing houses, such as the Munich-based Frauenoffensive in 1976. The Berliner Autorentage, a forum for authors and publishers, coined the slogan "Write it down, woman" (schreib das auf, frau!) and demanded more writing from women, who started meeting throughout the regions to discuss the production of **literature**. In 1977, the women's literary magazine *Schreiben* was launched, and others followed (titles included *Die schwarze Botin* and *Wissenschaft und Zärtlichkeit*). More established publishing houses also set up their own sections/titles for women's literature. Fischer established *Die Frau in der Gesellschaft* (1977), Rowohlt followed suit with *neue frau* and *frauen aktuell* (1978), and Ullstein brought out *Die Frau in der Literatur* (1980).

The **Bremen**-based foundation Frauen Literatur Forschung conducts research into women's literature, provides a database of information on German female writers, and produces the series Inter-Lit. Women's networks include FrideL (Frauen in der Literaturwissenschaft, founded in 1998 in Bremen), which concentrates on literary research and gender studies, while Bücherfrauen focuses on women working in publishing, bookshops, and related areas. Women's literature has also shown marked differences between east and west. Writers from the former **German Democratic Republic (GDR)**, including Sarah Kirsch, Irmtraud Morgner, Brigitte Reimann, and **Christa Wolf**, took leading roles in debates on women's issues, but were less influenced by trends and developments in the United States and France.

WÖRNER, MANFRED (1934–1994). Christian Democratic Union (CDU) politician and **North Atlantic Treaty Organization (NATO)** general secretary. Manfred Wörner was born in Stuttgart; studied law in Heidelberg, Paris, and Munich; passed his state law examinations (1957, 1961); and earned a doctorate on the subject of the criminal liability of soldiers stationed on foreign soil (1961). A member of the CDU from 1956, he served as a parliamentary adviser in the regional assembly (**Landtag**) of **Baden-Württemberg** (1962–1964) before representing the party in the **Bundestag** (1965–1988), where he was deputy leader of the CDU/**Christian Social Union (CSU)** parliamentary group (1969–1972) and chaired the parliamentary defense committee (1978–1980). As a former **Bundeswehr** fighter pilot and reserve officer, Wörner had the ideal credentials to succeed the social democrat Hans Apel as federal defense minister when the coalition of CDU/CSU and the **Free Democratic Party (FDP)** came to power in 1982. In 1983–1984, he publicly denounced Günter Kießling, Bundeswehr general and deputy commander of NATO in Europe, as a security risk for alleged **homosexuality**. Kießling was cleared of the allegations and fully rehabilitated. Wörner, whose offer of resignation was turned down by Chancellor **Helmut Kohl**, was appointed NATO general secretary (from January 1988). The first German to hold the highest post in NATO, Wörner won universal respect in his post and since 1996, the Federal Ministry of Defense has awarded the Manfred Wörner Medal for services to peace and freedom in Europe.

WOWEREIT, KLAUS (1953–). Social Democratic Party of Germany **(SPD)** politician and governing mayor of **Berlin** (2001–2014). Born in Berlin, Klaus Wowereit studied law at the Free University of Berlin, passing his state law examinations in 1979 and 1981. Attracted by the ideas of **Willy Brandt** and **Ostpolitik**, he joined the SPD at the age of 18 and was active in the party's youth wing, the **Young Socialists (JUSOS)**. He was a senior civil servant for the senator (minister) responsible for internal affairs (1981–1984) in Berlin and represented the SPD as a district councilor for Tempelhof (1984–1995) before he was elected to the city assembly, where he served as deputy leader (from 1995), then leader (1999–2001), of the party group. In June 2001, he succeeded **Eberhard Diepgen** as governing mayor of Berlin. Following city elections (October 2001), Wowereit formed a ruling coalition with the **Party of Democratic Socialism (PDS)**. The move was seen as groundbreaking for bringing into government the successor party to the **Socialist Unity Party of Germany (SED)** of the former **German Democratic Republic (GDR)**. Little known before the election, Wowereit, who turned his **homosexuality** to advantage by portraying it as a feature of a modern, liberal Berlin, faced a number of problems, including bankruptcy, high unemployment, and a persisting cultural divide between east and west. By cutting public service jobs and temporarily withdrawing from a collective bargaining agreement with public sector **trade unions**, he succeeded, with the help of his controversial finance senator, Thilo Sarrazin, in balancing the budget by 2013. As president of the **Bundesrat** (2001–2002), Wowereit attracted controversy when, contrary to assembly rules, he interpreted a split vote by representatives of the state of **Brandenburg** on a proposed **immigration** law as an assent (2002). His decision was later declared unconstitutional by the **Federal Constitutional Court (FCC)**. Reelected mayor of Berlin in 2002, 2006, and 2011, Wowereit was a member of the supervisory board of the company set up to build Berlin's new airport (Flughafen Berlin Brandenburg GmbH) from 2003, but resigned in 2013 following repeated delays in its completion, although he survived a vote of no confidence in the city assembly and reinherited the post (from August 2013 until December 2014) when his successor, **Matthias Platzeck** (SPD), stepped down as minister president of Brandenburg. In 2014, a public referendum rejected his plans to build on the site of the former Tempelhof airport, and in the same year he quit as mayor, to be succeeded by **Michael Müller** (SPD). From 2006, while mayor, Wowereit also took over the position of minister of culture (Kultursenator) and contributed significantly to restoring Berlin's image as a cultural center; he was instrumental in rescuing the opera house (Deutsche Oper) from closure and persuaded the **Bund** to finance the Humboldt forum in the city palace. Further posts that he held include government representative responsible for cultural relations with France (2007–2010) and vice chairman of the SPD (2009–2013).

WULFF, CHRISTIAN (1959–). Christian Democratic Union (CDU) politician and **president of the Federal Republic** (2010–2012). Christian Wulff was born in Osnabrück (**Lower Saxony**) and nursed his mother when she fell ill with multiple sclerosis (he became patron of the German Multiple Sclerosis Society in 2001). He studied law at the University of Osnabrück (1980–1986), qualified in 1987, and worked as a lawyer in Osnabrück (1990). Wulff's political career began in 1978 when he joined the CDU's youth wing (**Junge Union, JU**), serving on its national executive (1979–1983) and as regional youth leader (1983–1985). In 1984, he joined the main CDU regional executive; was district chairman for Osnabrück-Emsland (1990–1994); and was elected to Osnabrück city council (1986), where he led the CDU group (1989–1994). During 1991–1994, he served on the basic policy commission (Grundsatzkommission) of the national party. In 1993, he became leader of the regional parliamentary party and was selected as the CDU's challenger to Minister President **Gerhard Schröder** in the 1994 regional election. Although Schröder and the **Social Democratic Party of Germany (SPD)** won an absolute majority, Wulff fought off a challenge to lead the parliamentary group. He replaced Josef Stock as regional chairman (June 1994) and was elected deputy leader of the national CDU under **Wolfgang Schäuble** (November 1998).

With a reputation as a dynamic and outspoken modernizer, Wulff rejuvenated and reformed the internal structures of his local party during the 1990s. Flouting the national trend of the main parties, the CDU in Lower Saxony attracted new activists and boosted membership. After 1996, he belonged to the group of reformers (others included **Roland Koch, Peter Müller**, and **Ole von Beust**) who challenged the leadership style of Chancellor **Helmut Kohl** and the national party's structures. He was also critical of Finance Minister **Theo Waigel** about family policy and **taxation** reform. After the SPD's unexpectedly decisive victory in the 1998 election in Lower Saxony, Wulff openly criticized Kohl, whom he considered to have contributed to the defeat by stifling debate and reform within the main party. In contrast to many of his colleagues in the CDU, Wulff did not oppose the principle of ecological taxes and emphasized his closeness to the **Green Party**, although he refused to rule out using Gorleben as a facility for the permanent storage of nuclear waste.

In the 2003 regional election, Wulff led his party to a sensational victory and formed a ruling coalition with the **Free Democratic Party (FDP)** as junior coalition partner. With 48.3 percent of the vote, the CDU missed gaining an overall majority by just one seat. Succeeding **Sigmar Gabriel** as **minister president**, Wulff became the region's fourth leader in under five years. Highlighting Lower Saxony's serious budget deficit (along with that of **Berlin**, the highest of all the German **federal states**), Wulff pledged a strict program of savings, cuts in subsidies, and a radical simplification of regulations and bureaucracy; at the same time, he planned to employ more teachers and reform **education**, expand the police service, and crack down on criminality.

Elected president of the Federal Republic in 2010, he resigned in 2012 after an application from the public prosecution service to remove his political immunity. Wulff had faced months of criticism and **media** attention over allegations of corruption in relation to business links while minister president; it was also alleged that he had accepted hospitality in 2007 from a film entrepreneur for public financial guarantees. Toward the end of his period of office, Wulff criticized political leaders, bankers, and the media for their role in the **eurozone crisis**, in particular for bypassing democratic institutions and entertaining the introduction of euro bonds to help indebted countries borrow more money. Honors he has received include the Leo Baeck Prize (awarded by the **Central Council of Jews**, 2011). In 2014, he opened a law firm in **Hamburg**, and in early 2015 began work as a consultant for a Swiss property company.

Y

YOUNG SOCIALISTS (JUNGSOZIALISTEN, JUSOS). During the 1960s and 1970s, the JUSOS, the youth wing of the **Social Democratic Party of Germany (SPD)**, was radicalized by neo-Marxist elements of the **students' movement**. This led to a strained relationship with the mother party, and from 1975 onward, the marginalized JUSOS attracted little public attention. Not until a reformist and more pragmatic leadership emerged from an internal power struggle in 1991 did the SPD begin to take the organization more seriously. Recognized by statutes of the main party, the JUSOS describe themselves as a youth organization in the SPD ("Jugendorganisation in der SPD"), acting beyond party limits as a working group to form a link between social democracy as represented by the SPD and elements of the wider civil society fighting for similar ideals (the "dual strategy"). Any SPD members aged under 35 are automatically enrolled in the JUSOS and account for the majority of the current 68,000 members. A further 10,000 young people are members of the JUSOS but not of the main party. A national congress elects a chairperson every two years. Johanna Uerkermann became leader in 2013.

Z

ZIMMER, GABI (1955–). Party of Democratic Socialism (PDS) politician. Gabi Zimmer was born in **Berlin** and grew up in Schleusingen (**Thuringia**) in the former **German Democratic Republic (GDR)**. She studied at the Karl-Marx University in Leipzig and graduated with a diploma in languages and linguistics (1977), before working at a factory in Suhl making motor vehicles and hunting weapons (1977–1990). A member of the ruling **Socialist Unity Party of Germany (SED**, 1981–1989), she took an active role in its successor party, the PDS, chairing the local party association in Suhl (from 1990) and the regional association for Thuringia (1990–1998). From 1990, she represented the PDS in the Thuringian state parliament (**Landtag**), where she focused on labor market and social policies, chaired a committee on equality, and led the PDS parliamentary group (1999–2000). In 1995, Zimmer joined the national party executive, rising to deputy leader (1997–2000) and leader (2000–2003), although she failed to provide the strong leadership required to unite the party, which remained split between reformers and traditionalists from the GDR era, and she was eventually succeeded by **Lothar Bisky**, former party leader (1993–2000). In 2004, she left the Bundestag to enter the European Parliament (reelected in 2009 and 2014), where she became leader of the radical left-wing GUE/NGL parliamentary grouping in 2012.

See also LEFT PARTY, THE (DIE LINKSPARTEI/DIE LINKE).

ZWICKEL, KLAUS (1939–). Trade union leader. Klaus Zwickel was born in Heilbronn (**Baden-Württemberg**) and trained as a toolmaker (1953–1956) before working for various companies in Heilbronn (1957–1965). An active member of the **engineering** and metalworkers trade union IG Metall (from 1954) and of the **Social Democratic Party of Germany (SPD**, from 1959), he performed various functions at the local and district levels before moving to union regional headquarters in Stuttgart (1984), where he became a confidant to IG Metall's leader, Franz Steinkühler. Joining the union's executive board (1986), he developed a reputation as an expert on wages policy. He played a key role in negotiating sector-wide wage deals for German metalworkers in the **eastern federal states** after reunification, when IG Metall gained around a million new members, and vigorously defended the agreements as they came under pressure from employers faced by economic recession. Industrial action in western Germany was only narrowly averted in 1992 when employers reluctantly agreed to a wage increase of over 6 percent for steelworkers. In 1993, bitter disputes erupted between IG Metall and engineering and steel **industry** employers when the latter withdrew from national wage agreements to raise eastern wage levels to those in the west. When Steinkühler was forced to stand down over allegations of share dealings, Zwickel succeeded him as leader of IG Metall (October 1993).

Assuming leadership of IG Metall at a time of economic recession and mounting unemployment, Zwickel advocated a policy of compromise and consultation while also seeking to strengthen the union through reducing its internal bureaucracy, cutting costs, and merging with other unions. Between 1998 and 2000, IG Metall amalgamated with the textile and clothing union Gewerkschaft Textil und Bekleidung (GTB) and the wood and synthetic materials workers' union Gewerkschaft Holz und Kunststoff (GHK). In 1995, as the German system of national and sector-wide wage agreements (Flächentarifvertrag) came under strain, Zwickel agreed to its partial relaxation. At the same time, he opposed weekend working, oversaw the introduction of the 35-hour week in the west German engineering and electrical industry, and continued to argue for a reduction in working hours without loss of pay, although he later moderated his stand when proposing the **Alliance for Work** in cooperation with the government led by Chancellor **Helmut Kohl**. When left-wing influence on the new SPD/**Green Party** coalition faded following the resignation of Finance Minister **Oskar Lafontaine** (March 1999), Zwickel became more critical of the government, arguing strongly for **pensions** from the age of 60 and for an employers' contribution to the proposed private top-up pension. Although agreement was reached on a phased introduction of the lower pension age (October 1999), the dispute sharpened internal divisions in the union between traditionalists and modernizers.

Zwickel served on the supervisory boards of the Mannesmann concern (from 1991), **BMW AG** (1987–1994), and **Volkswagen** (1993–2007). In 1999, IG Metall confirmed his leadership for a final four years, although his standing was marred by allegations that he had been involved in approving excessive payments to former managers at Mannesmann after the company's takeover by the cell phone company Vodafone. Following a trial for breaching shareholders' trust, Zwickel, along with a former member of Mannesmann's supervisory board, **Josef Ackermann**, and its chief executive, Klaus Esser, were acquitted (2004), although Zwickel eventually paid out 60,000 euros in a final settlement (2006). After a damaging power struggle in the union's leadership and an abortive four-week campaign of strikes in eastern Germany for a 35-hour week, Zwickel stepped down prematurely (2003). The move was an attempt to force **Jürgen Peters** to withdraw his candidacy for the leadership, whom Zwickel openly accused of mismanaging negotiations and being responsible for one of the worst defeats in the union's history.

ZYPRIES, BRIGITTE (1953–). Social Democratic Party of Germany (SPD) politician. Brigitte Zypries was born in Kassel (**Hessen**) and studied law at the University of Gießen (1972–1977). While training at the regional court in Gießen (1978–1980), she passed her state law examinations (1978, 1980), then worked as an academic assistant at Gießen University (1980–1985) before joining the Hessen state chancellery as an adviser (1985–1988). After a period at the **Federal Constitutional Court (FCC,** 1988–1990), she was appointed section head (1991) and then departmental head (1995) at the **Lower Saxony** state chancellery, where the modernizing Minister President **Gerhard Schröder** charged her with setting up an intranet. After a brief period as **state secretary** in the Lower Saxony ministry for **women**, labor, and social affairs (1997–1998), she became state secretary to federal interior minister **Otto Schily** (1998–2002). From 1999, Zypries chaired a committee of state secretaries responsible for implementing and coordinating the national program "modern state–modern government" ("Moderner Staat–Moderne Verwaltung"). The program aimed to modernize the administrative functions of government by using the **Internet** to improve efficiency and bring the state closer to the citizen. Zypries's committee managed 15 projects, including the creation of a national Internet portal for Germany (deutschland.de). Other projects included the introduction of paperfree administration and offering national services online. Zypries also represented the **federal government** on D21, an initiative of over 100 German IT companies designed to lead Germany into the 21st century by improving links between the state and business. The initiative's achievements included the introduction of computers in schools, a green card scheme to recruit foreign information technology specialists to work in Germany, and the incorporation of virus protection software in computer systems; progress was also made on introducing electronic signatures for commercial transactions.

A protégée of Gerhard Schröder, Zypries was promoted to justice minister following the resignation of **Herta Däubler-Gmelin** (2002), and she continued in that post in the first coalition cabinet of **Angela Merkel** (2005–2009). In June 2004, she announced controversial proposals to introduce equal status for marriages between same-sex couples as already existed for heterosexuals. Although gays and lesbians had been able to register relationships since 2001, the proposals, which were vigorously resisted by conservative politicians and the churches and encountered opposition from the **Bundesrat,** would give partners in same-sex marriages **taxation** benefits and rights to inherit **pensions** and property, although adoption rights were limited (these were later extended by the FCC, but remained controversial). In 2004, the Federal Ministry of Justice proposed extending the existing surveillance law (passed in 1998 and approved with some reservations by the FCC in March 2004) to encompass categories of professionals, such as priests, journalists, and doctors, who had previously been regarded as guardians of confidential information. The government's abandonment of the proposals (July 2004) was seen as a setback for Zypries. A member of the **Bundestag** from 2005, she was appointed parliamentary state secretary to the minister for economic affairs and **energy** (2013) and government coordinator for German aviation (2014).

Appendix A: Presidents of the Federal Republic of Germany

Theodor Heuss (FDP)	1949–1959
Heinrich Lübke (CDU)	1959–1969
Gustav Heinemann (SPD)	1969–1974
Walter Scheel (FDP)	1974–1979
Karl Carstens (CDU)	1979–1984
Richard von Weizsäcker (CDU)	1984–1994
Roman Herzog (CDU)	1994–1999
Johannes Rau (SPD)	1999–2004
Horst Köhler (CDU)	2004–2010
Christian Wulff (CDU)	2010–2012
Joachim Gauck	2012–

Appendix B: Federal Chancellors

Konrad Adenauer (CDU)	September 1949–October 1963
Ludwig Erhard (CDU)	October 1963–November 1966
Kurt Georg Kiesinger (CDU)	December 1966–October 1969
Willy Brandt (SPD)	October 1969–May 1974
Helmut Schmidt (SDP)	May 1974–October 1982
Helmut Kohl (CDU)	October 1982–October 1998
Gerhard Schröder (SPD)	October 1998–November 2005
Angela Merkel (CDU)	November 2005–

Bibliography

CONTENTS

INTRODUCTION

The following bibliography lists mainly books, periodicals, and Internet publications in English. Individual contributions in periodicals and German-language titles are included where they are particularly significant or where English-language material for an area is less well represented.

The bibliography is arranged in four parts. Part I ("History") covers aspects of German history since 1945, with a list of chronologies, general histories, and subsections, such as the German Democratic Republic (GDR), reunification and its aftermath (insofar as these areas are not already covered by many of the general studies), coming to terms with the past, foreign policy, and economic history. Apart from including a select bibliography of English-language works on Germany history both before and after 1945, Fulbrook (2009) offers insights into the extensive historiography of the Third Reich. Changing historical perceptions of the Holocaust is a major theme of Evans (2015), who argues that Nazi racial ideology drew from various sources, including British imperialism and the U.S. colonization of the North American plains. Also relevant is the controversial study commissioned by Foreign Minister Joschka Fischer, which reappraised the role of the German foreign ministry during the Nazi period and after 1949 (Conze et al. 2010). Readers interested in the extensive historiography of the Third Reich and the Holocaust may find useful starting points in Hiden and Fahrquharson (1989), Schiele (2000), Stone (2004), Low (1995), and Bankier and Mikhman (2008).

Accessible all-round introductions to postwar German history include Fulbrook (2000) and Kettenacker (1997), while Fulbrook (1995) and McElvoy (1992) provide thoughtful and clear analyses of the GDR and its structures; Recker (2009) presents a compact review (in German) of political developments in western Germany after 1945. Reunification and its aftermath have spawned numerous titles, although Teasdale and Bainbridge (2012) and the concise and readable account by Leiby (1999) are good starting points, while Robertson and Gellner (2003) consider the decade after reunification. Thomaneck and Niven (2001) trace German history and society from its historical roots through to reunification and the continuing division between east and west. Hans-Ulrich Wehler's study of the social histories of the FRG and GDR (2008) demonstrates how political and class power structures in each country perpetuated social inequalities over a long period. Most recently, the contributions in the voluminous *Oxford Handbook of Modern German History* (Smith 2011) examine aspects of German history, society, and culture from the early 19th century to the present day. For a systematic overview of the directions German historians have pursued in investigating developments in east and west Germany from 1945 to the present day, including an emerging historiography of the postreunification "Berlin Republic," see Schildt (2012). Significant titles include Wolfrum (2006), Wolfrum and Benz (2011), Conze (2009), and, for cultural history, Schildt and Siegried (2009). Arnold et al. (2009) examine recollections of the wartime air campaign against Nazi Germany, while Beer (2011) investigates the background, course, and consequences of the mass evacuations and expulsions of Germans at the end of World War II. For insights into research into the GDR, see Sabrow (2008) and Jessen (2010). Kleßmann (1999, 2001) and Jarausch (2004) critically assess the asymmetries and challenges posed by the parallel histories of the FRG and GDR.

For a comprehensive and readable study of West German foreign policy during the Cold War (including Ostpolitik), see Ash (1994). Among others, Duffield (1998) and Erb (2003) examine the changes since reunification. Although many of the above also cover postreunification Germany's relations with Europe, the study by Bulmer, Simon, Jeffery, and Paterson (2000) focuses on how Germany has created a "milieu" of multilateral cooperation that successfully promotes German interests within the European Union (EU), while Beichelt (2013) investigates different perspectives on Germany as an EU member state and points the reader to additional resources. Paterson (2010, 2011) reviews Chancellor Angela Merkel's conduct of foreign policy and examines the increasing role of Germany in the EU.

A section is devoted to the question of national identity and how contemporary Germany has attempted to come to terms with its past. Berger (1997) analyzes the reemergence of the notion of national identity among Germans since reunification and how this is formed by perceptions of recent history, including the Third Reich and the GDR. Other titles in this section consider the "historians' quarrel," which flared up in 1986–1987 (the anthology by Knowlton and Cates [1993] is a good starting point), while Fulbrook and Swales (2000) examine the relationship between national history and identity. A subsection on Jews in Germany contains various titles relating to the Holocaust and the reintegration of Jews into postwar Germany; the title by Michael Wolffsohn (1993) proved influential in the public debate. Readers interested in the recent development of Europe's largest economy, which has evolved from the social market model of the postwar period to one facing the twin challenges of absorbing eastern Germany and the need to adapt its structures to globalization, are referred to Smyser (1992) and Flockton (1993) in the first instance and, for a comprehensive account (in German), to Abelshauser (2004). For more recent information, the Organisation for Economic Co-operation and Development (OECD) provides updated country surveys, which are available online. An authoritative source is the German Institute for Economic Research (DIW).

Part II offers a selection of general descriptions of Germany, including titles on travel and handbooks. Given the large number of maps available, this section lists mainly publishers and their specialist areas. Of particular interest are Schäfers (1998) and *Der Fischer Atlas Deutschland: Umwelt, Politik, Wirtschaft, Kultur* (2001), which employ well-illustrated maps to introduce the reader to a wide range of topics, ranging from the natural environment to voting patterns, society, the economy, infrastructure, and the media. The website of the University of Texas at Austin lists political and physical maps online produced by the U.S. Central Intelligence Agency (CIA). As a general tourist guide, the *Lonely Planet Germany* guides are compact and balanced sources of information. Readers wanting a wide-ranging but thoughtful general introduction to Germany, with sections on history, the former GDR, politics and politicians, arts, intellectual life and education, and industry, will not be disappointed by Ardagh (1995). Other general introductory studies include Craig (1991) and Lewis (2001). The country profiles section of the CIA's *World Factbook*, updated annually and available online, covers German history, geography, politics and society, infrastructure and communications, the military, transnational issues, maps, and statistics. Websites such as *Wikipedia* and the BBC's *Country Profile: Germany* are also excellent sources of information on current topics and background issues. *A Manual on Germany/Ein Handbuch für Deutschland*, published by the Federal Government Commissioner for Migration, Refugees and Integration, provides a general guide on Germany for foreigners and immigrants.

Part III ("Topical Studies") covers various aspects of German life, culture, politics, and society. Alexandra Richie (1998) and David Clay Large (2001) provide excellent cultural-historical overviews, while Brian Ladd (1998) in dealing with Berlin's history takes the urban landscape into account. A more recent study by Rory Maclean (2014) focuses on a cast of Berliners that either represent or indeed shaped the city's development. Peter Schneider (2014) considers in a collection of essays Berlin's most recent history–where necessary in light of its past; the journal *European Urban and Regional Studies* also contains occasional articles on changes in the capital. Another excellent starting point is www.kultur-netz.de/berlin, which lists cultural events and links to local universities and references to home pages by local artists. The site www.freundeskreise-berliner-kultur.de presents a varied collection of cultural institutions, their aims, and their concerns, while www.kulturserver-berlin.de is a forum for arts and culture that mainly targets those who provide the venues. The site www.berlinergazette.de informs about statements, thoughts, and considerations by Berlin's representatives of culture. The site www.satt.org provides access to literature and reviews and lists events, while www.perlentaucher.de focuses on literature and reviews. The websites berlin.de and berlin-online, and that of the Free University of Berlin, are good sources of general information on the capital and current events.

For culture in general, Sandford (1999) is a reference work with more than 1,000 entries and short articles from over 150 contributors on leading figures, terms and institutions in postwar Germany, film, art, philosophy, literature, and music. Readers from the business world will find the German-language Internet site Deutsche Wirtschaft useful for business and market information, while Smith (1994) focuses on long-term trends in the German economy, and the journal *German Politics* contains occasional contributions and reviews on particular sectors. The *Monthly Reports* of the German Federal Bank are useful for economic and financial updates. On education, Hahn (1998) presents a long-range sociological study of the development of education in Germany during the 19th and 20th centuries, while Pritchard (1999) concentrates on developments in eastern Germany since reunification. For environmental issues, the website of the Federal Ministry of the Environment, Nature Conservation, and Nuclear Safety (BMU) contains many links to organizations, sites, and reports that provide a comprehensive picture of environmental politics in Germany. Although more than 10 years old, the volume by Jones (1994) remains one of the most detailed introductions to the human and economic geography of Germany.

For labor and employment, the English/German website of the Hans Böckler Foundation is a useful starting point. The foundation undertakes research and provides information on labor and trade union issues, corporate governance, and codetermination; it publishes an international magazine on codetermination and, through its Institute of Economic and Social Research (WSI), a monthly journal (*WSI-Mitteilungen*) aimed at the business and academic community, trade unions, and policy makers. Students of sociolinguistics developments in the modern German language will find the studies by Clyne (1995), Barbour and Stevenson (2000), and Stevenson (2002) of interest. Although the section on German law contains a number of largely self-explanatory titles on various aspects of the German legal system, the website maintained by the Library of the Institute of Advanced Legal Studies (IALS), University of London (title: *Germany. An Introduction to Legal Research in the Jurisdiction of Germany*) is the most comprehensive and up-to-date site, with links and detailed information on primary sources (codes and statutes), law reports, treatises, journals, English-language works on German law, Internet sources in English, and help with abbreviations. The site of Martina Kammer (updated 2000) remains a well-organized research aid for people involved in international legal and business transactions as well as for students, translators, and anyone else who might be interested in locating English translations of and annotations on German business and commercial laws. Turning to the media, *Media Perspektiven Basisdaten* is a compendium of basic facts, figures, and information about the German media, which is one of the largest sectors of its kind in Europe: the volume is published annually and covers broadcasting, online, print, film, theater, and public and private media concerns, as well as audiences and usage. The online media data bank of the Commission on Concentration in the Media (KEK) lists all press publishers, news titles, and broadcasters, together with their owners and stakeholders. For a general introduction to the media, see Sandford (1995), who outlines the structures and principles underpinning the press and broadcasting systems of the FRG and the GDR and traces the immediate and longer-term impacts of reunification. The media section also includes (German-language) biographies of leading figures and organizations. The lexicon by Noelle-Neumann et al. (2009) contains over 800 pages of articles (in German) on the media and an extensive bibliography.

A small section is devoted to the new federal states, although many other titles relating to this area are found under sections on history, politics, and economics. A good overview of the changes that eastern Germany faced after reunification is provided by Flockton and Kolinsky (1998).

Alongside *West European Politics*, the journal *German Politics* is one of the best sources of reviews and analyses of developments and processes in German politics as a whole, on which innumerable publications have appeared. Although dated, the volume by Paterson and Southern (1991) remains a good textbook introduction to the (West) German political system, with chapters on the origins of modern Germany, the constitution, the executive, the legislature, federalism, the political parties, the political economy, and the relationship between the FRG and the West, as well as sections on Ostpolitik and the two Germanies. For more up-to-date information, Broughton (2005) offers a comprehensive and detailed introduction written in an accessible style. The handbook by Andersen (2013, in German) contains articles and overviews on most areas of German political life. For current developments in German politics, *Developments in German Politics 3*, by Padgett, Paterson, and Smith (2003) is one of a series of volumes covering institutions, economic policy, the federal states, citizenship, welfare, and social issues. Larres (2001) looks at Germany since reunification, and Reutter (2004) examines the politics of the red/green coalition after 1998. Of the various topics in German society and social policy, major themes include the position of women (see various publications by Eva Kolinsky), immigration and migrants (Marshall 2000), welfare reform (Lee and Rosenhaft 1997), right-wing extremism (Lewis 1991, 1996), and continuing differences between east and west Germans (Cooke and Grix 2003). The journal *Local Government Studies* contains occasional articles on local government in Germany. The website Parteien-Online (www.parteien-online.de/) provides information on all German parties, including data on regional and national elections.

Part IV (References) lists printed and online (Internet) resources. Among the English-language periodicals (section 3), *Debatte*, which was founded in response to reunification, is an interdisciplinary journal covering domestic culture and society and providing documentation, debate, topical interviews, and a chronology of current trends and events. *German History* contains articles on all aspects of Germany's history, including the postwar period in the FRG and GDR. As mentioned above, *German Politics* focuses on contemporary politics (defined very broadly); it also attracts contributors from across the world and has published several special issues. *Communist and Post-Communist Studies*, which focuses on historical as well as current developments in the communist and postcommunist world, includes occasional articles on the former GDR. On security and defense issues, *European Security*, *Survival*, *Strategic Review* and *Strategic Survey* are worth monitoring for contributions relevant to Germany.

For government and official sources, the bund.de website is the Internet portal of the German government. Facts about Germany, the English-language version of the Tatsachen über Deutschland website, is maintained by the Federal Foreign Office; it provides general information, facts, and figures about Germany and its people, history, the state, the political and legal system, the role of the citizen, foreign policy, the economy, education, science and research, society, and culture. The prime source of statistical data on Germany is the German Federal Office of Statistics (Statistisches Bundesamt), which maintains a website and publishes information in book form and on CD-ROM, and issues regular updates and reports, although most information is now only available through paid subscription. Similar organizations maintained by the federal states and the EU are also listed. The section on business and finance points mainly to websites listing banks, registered business associations, and commercial services related to Germany. Among reference sources for education, the Deutsche Bildungsserver can be recommended as a German/English site providing information, statistics, and reports on most aspects of the German education system, ranging from its structures and facilities to school and higher and vocational education.

For news and current affairs, the government-supported Deutsche Auslandsschularbeit (DASAN) website includes a comprehensive list of German newspapers (local, regional, and national) and magazines (also television and radio broadcasters). Other sources of current affairs material are Deutsche Welle World Service (Germany's international broadcasting service); Expatica (for German expatriates); and the website of *The Guardian* newspaper, which offers special country reports, an archive of recent (and less recent) articles, and further links to sources of factual information. There are a number of general websites on culture and cultural affairs: Cosmopolis, Deutsche Kultur International (for cultural policy), Goethe Institute/Inter Nationes, and the Internet site of the weekly *Die Zeit* can be recommended.

I. HISTORY

A. Chronologies

Baumann, Wolf-Rüdiger, et al. *Die Fischer-Chronik Deutschland: Ereignisse, Personen, Daten.* Frankfurt/Main: Fischer TaschenbuchVerlag, 2001.

Eschenhagen, Wieland, and Matthia Judt. *Der neue Fischer-Weltalmanach— Chronik Deutschland 1949–2014: 65 Jahre deutsche Geschichte im Überblick.* Frankfurt/Main: Fischer Taschenbuch Verlag, 2014.

B. General Histories of Germany (FRG and GDR)

Ahonen, Pertti. *After the Expulsion: West Germany and Eastern Europe 1945–1990.* Oxford and New York: Oxford University Press, 2001.

Allinson, Mark. *Germany and Austria, 1814–2000.* Modern History for Modern Languages. London: Hodder Arnold, 2002.

Balfour, Michael. *West Germany: A Contemporary History.* New York: St. Martin's Press, 1982.

Bark, Dennis L., and David R. Gress. *A History of West Germany.* Vol. 1, *From Shadow to Substance 1945–1963.* Vol. 2, *Democracy and its Discontents 1963–1988.* 2nd ed. Oxford: Basil Blackwell, 1993. First published in 1989.

Berger, Stefan. *Inventing the Nation: Germany.* London: Hodder Arnold, 2004.

Calvocoressi, Peter. *Fall Out: World War II and the Shaping of Postwar Europe.* London: Longman, 1997.

Carr, William. *A History of Germany 1815–1990.* 4th ed. London: Hodder Arnold, 1991. Reprinted by Bloomsbury Academic, 2010 and 2013. First published in 1987.

Childs, David. *Germany in the Twentieth Century.* 3rd ed. New York: Icon Editions/HarperCollins, 1991.

Connor, Ian. *Refugees and Expellees in Post-war Germany.* Manchester, UK: Manchester University Press, 2007.

Conze, Eckart. *Die Suche nach Sicherheit: Eine Geschichte der Bundesrepublik Deutschland von 1949 bis in die Gegenwart.* Munich: Siedler, 2009.

Fulbrook, Mary. *A Concise History of Germany*. 2nd ed. Cambridge, UK: Cambridge University Press, 2004. First published 1991.

Fulbrook, Mary. *A History of Germany 1918–2008: The Divided Nation*. 3rd ed. Chichester, UK: Wiley-Blackwell, 2009. First published in 1991.

Fulbrook, Mary. *The Two Germanies 1945–1990: Problems of Interpretation*. 2nd ed. Basingstoke, UK: Macmillan, 2000.

Glees, Anthony. *Reinventing Germany: German Political Development since 1945*. Oxford: Berg, 1996.

Haase, Christian. *Pragmatic Peacemakers: Institutes of International Affairs and the Liberalization of West Germany, 1945–73*. Augsburg: Wissner Verlag, 2007.

Hesse, Joachim Jens, and Thomas Ellwein. 9th ed. *Das Regierungssystem der Bundesrepublik Deutschland*. 2 vols. Berlin: De Gruyter, 2004.

Hockenos, Paul. *Joschka Fischer and the Making of the Berlin Republic: An Alternative History of Postwar Germany*. Oxford: Oxford University Press, 2008.

Hofmann, Gunter. *Abschiede, Anfänge: Die Bundesrepublik, eine Anatomie*. Rev. ed. Munich: Piper, 2004.

Kettenacker, Lothar. *Germany since 1945*. Oxford: Oxford University Press, 1997.

Kirk, Tim. *Cassell's Dictionary of Modern German History*. London: Cassell, 2002.

Kitchen, Martin. *The Cambridge Illustrated History of Germany*. Cambridge, UK: Cambridge University Press, 1996.

Kleßmann, Christoph, ed. *The Divided Past: Rewriting Post-war German History*. Oxford: Berg, 2001.

Kleßmann, Christoph, Hans Misselwitz, and Günter Wichert, eds. *Deutsche Vergangenheiten: Eine gemeinsame Herausforderung; Der schwierige Umgang mit der doppelten Nachkriegsgeschichte*. Berlin: Ch. Links Verlag, 1999.

Kolinsky, Eva, ed. *The Federal Republic of Germany. The End of an Era*. Oxford: Berg, 1991.

Kraushaar, Wolfgang, ed. *Die RAF und der linke Terrorismus*. 2 vols. Hamburg: Hamburger Edition, 2006.

Merkl, Peter H. *The Federal Republic of Germany at Fifty: The End of a Century of Turmoil*. New York: New York University Press, 1999.

O'Dochartaigh, Pól. *Germany since 1945*. Basingstoke, UK: Palgrave Macmillan, 2004.

Ozment, Steven. *A Mighty Fortress: A New History of the German People*. London: Granta Publications, 2005.

Padgett, Stephen, ed. *Adenauer to Kohl: The Development of the German Chancellorship*. London: Hurst, 1994.

Recker, Marie-Luise. *Geschichte der Bundesrepublik Deutschland.* 3rd ed. Munich: C. H. Beck, 2009.

Schildt, Axel. "Zeitgeschichte der 'Berliner Republik.'" *Aus Politik und Zeitgeschichte* (blog), December 23, 2011. www.bpb.de/apuz/59780/zeitgeschichte-der-berliner-republik?p=all.

Schildt, Axel, and Detlef Siegfried. *Deutsche Kulturgeschichte: Die Bundesrepublik, 1945 bis zur Gegenwart.* Munich: Hanser, 2009.

Schulze, Hagen. *Germany: A New History.* Translated by Deborah Lucas Schneider. Cambridge, MA: Harvard University Press, 2001.

Smith, Helmut Walser, ed. *The Oxford Handbook of Modern German History.* Oxford: Oxford University Press, 2011.

Smyser, W. R. *From Yalta to Berlin: The Cold War Struggle over Germany.* New York: St. Martin's Griffin, 1999.

Sodaro, Michael J. *Moscow, Germany and the West from Khruschchev to Gorbachev.* London: I. B. Taurus, 1991.

Sperling, James, ed. *Germany at Fifty-Five: Berlin ist nicht Bonn?* Manchester, UK: Manchester University Press, 2004.

Thörmer, Heinz, and Edgar Einemann, et al. *Aufstieg und Krise der Generation Schröder: Einblicke aus vier Jahrzehnten.* Marburg: Schüren Verlag, 2007.

Tipton, Frank B. *A History of Modern Germany since 1815.* Berkeley: University of California Press, 2003.

Trentmanm, Frank, ed. *Paradoxes of Civil Society: New Perspectives on Modern German and British History.* New York: Berghahn, 2000.

Turk, Eleanor L. *The History of Germany.* Westport, CT: Greenwood, 1999.

Turk, Eleanor L. *Issues in Germany, Austria, and Switzerland.* Portsmouth, NH: Greenwood Press, 2003.

Turner, Henry Ashby, Jr. *Germany from Partition to Reunification.* New Haven, CT: Yale University Press, 1992.

Turner, Henry Ashby, Jr. *The Two Germanies since 1945.* New Haven, CT: Yale University Press, 1987.

Wehler, Hans-Ulrich. *Deutsche Gesellschaftsgeschichte: Bundesrepublik und DDR, 1949–1990.* Munich: C. H. Beck, 2008.

Wetzel, David, ed. *From the Berlin Museum to the Berlin Wall: Essays on the Cultural and Political History of Modern Germany.* Westport, CT: Greenwood, 1996.

Williamson, David G. *Germany since 1815: A Nation Forged and Renewed.* Basingstoke, UK: Palgrave Macmillan, 2005.

Wolfrum, Edgar. *Die geglückte Demokratie: Geschichte der Bundesrepublik Deut- schland von ihren Anfängen bis zur Gegenwart.* Stuttgart: Klett-Cotta Verlag, 2006.

Wolfrum, Edgar, and Wolfgang Benz, eds. *Gebhardt: Handbuch der deutschen Geschichte*. Vol. 23, *Die Bundesrepublik Deutschland: 1949–1990*. 10th, fully rev. ed. Stuttgart: Klett-Cotta Verlag, 2011.

C. The GDR 1949–1990

Ash, Timothy Garton. *The File: A Personal History*. London: Flamingo, 1997.
Barker, Peter, Marc-Dietrich Ohse, and Dennis Tate, eds. *Views from Abroad: Die DDR aus britischer Perspektive*. Bielefeld: W. Bertelsmann Verlag, 2007.
Bathrick, David. *The Powers of Speech: The Politics of Culture in the GDR*. Lincoln: University of Nebraska Press, 1996.
Bell, David S., ed. *Western European Communists and the Collapse of Communism*. Oxford: Berg, 1993.
Bentley, Ramond. *Research and Technology in the Former German Democratic Republic*. Boulder, CO: Westview, 1992.
Childs, David, and Richard Popplewell. *The Stasi: The East German Intelligence and Security Service*. Basingstoke and London: Palgrave Macmillan, 1996. Reprinted in 1999 with a new introduction.
Dale, Gareth. *Popular Protest in East Germany: 1945–1989*. London: Routledge, 2005.
Dennis, Mike. *The Rise and fall of the German Democratic Republic, 1945–1990*. Harlow, UK: Longman, 2000.
Dennis, Mike. *Social and Economic Modernisation in Eastern Germany from Honecker to Kohl*. London: Pinter, 1993.
Fulbrook, Mary. *Anatomy of a Dictatorship: Inside the GDR 1949–1989*. Oxford: Oxford University Press, 1995.
Fulbrook, Mary, and Andrew I. Port, eds. *Becoming East German: Socialist Structures and Sensibilities after Hitler*. New York: Berghahn, 2013.
Fulbrook, Mary, and Jill Stephenson, eds. "The GDR from the Perspective of United Germany." Special issue, *German History: The Journal of the German History Society* 10, no. 3 (1992).
Garland, John, ed. "The GDR's Quest for Growth and Modernization through 'Intensification.'" Special issue, *Studies in Comparative Communism* 20, no. 1 (Spring 1987).
Gedmin, Jeffrey. *The Hidden Hand: Gorbachev and the Collapse of East Germany*. Washington, DC: AEI Press, 1992.
Gerber, Margy, et al., eds. *Studies in GDR Culture and Society 9: Selected Papers from the 14th New Hampshire Symposium on the German Democratic Republic*. Lanham, MD: University Press of America, 1989.

Gerber, Margy, and Roger Woods, eds. *Changing identities in East Germany*. Selected Papers from the Nineteenth and Twentieth New Hampshire Symposia. Lanham, MD: University Press of America, 1996.

Gerber, Margy, and Roger Woods, eds. *Studies in GDR Culture and Society 11/12: The End of the GDR and the Problems of Integration.* Selected Papers from the Sixteenth and Seventeenth New Hampshire Symposia on the German Democratic Republic. Lanham, MD: University Press of America, 1993.

Gieseke, Jens. *The History of the Stasi. East Germany's Secret Police 1945–1990.* Translated from the German by David Burnett. New York: Berghahn, 2014

Glees, Anthony. *The Stasi Files: East Germany's Secret Operations against Britain.* London: Free Press, 2003.

Goeckel, Robert F. *The Lutheran Church and the East German State.* Ithaca, NY: Cornell University Press, 1990. Also published as *Die Evangelische Kirche und die DDR: Konflikte, Gespräche, Vereinbarungen unter Ulbricht und Honecker.* With Katharina Gustavs. Leipzig: Evangelische Verlagsanstalt, 1995.

Gray, William Glenn. *Germany's Cold War: The Global Campaign to Isolate East Germany, 1949–1969.* Chapel Hill/London: University of North Carolina Press, 2003.

Grieder, Peter. *The East German Leadership 1946–73.* Manchester, UK: Manchester University Press, 1999.

Grieder, Peter. *The German Democratic Republic.* London: Palgrave Macmillan, 2012.

Grix, Jonathan. *The Role of the Masses in the Collapse of the GDR.* Basingstoke, UK: Macmillan, 2000.

Gumbert, Heather. *Envisioning Socialism: Television and the Cold War in the German Democratic Republic.* Ann Arbor: University of Michigan Press, January 2014.

Hermand, Jost, and Marc Silberman. *Contentious Memories: Looking Back at the GDR.* Bern: Peter Lang, 1998.

Hoff, Henning. *Großbritannien und die DDR 1955–1973: Diplomatie auf Umwegen.* Munich: Oldenbourg, 2003.

Jäger, Manfred. *Kultur und Politik in der DDR 1945–1990.* Cologne: Verlag für Wissenschaft und Politik, 1997. First published in 1994.

Jarausch, Konrad H., ed. *Dictatorship as Experience: Towards a Socio-Cultural History of the GDR.* New York: Berghahn, 1999.

Jarausch, Konrad H. "Die Teile als Ganzes erkennen: Zur Integration der beiden deutschen Nachkriegsgeschichten." *Zeithistorische Forschungen* 1 (2004): 10–30.

Jessen, Ralph. "Alles schon erforscht? Beobachtungen zur zeithistorischen DDR-Forschung der letzten 20 Jahre." *Deutschland Archiv* 43 (2010): 1052–64.

Joppke, Christian. *East German Dissidents and the Revolution of 1989: Social Movement in a Leninist Regime.* Basingstoke: Macmillan/New York: New York University Press, 1995.

Kaiser, Paul, and Claudia Petzold, eds. *Boheme und Diktatur in der DDR: Gruppen, Konflikte, Quartiere: 1970 bis 1990.* Ausstellungskatalog. Berlin: Fannei & Walz and Deutsches Historisches Museum, 1997.

Keithly, David M. *The Collapse of East German Communism: The Year the Wall Came Down.* Westport, CT, and London: Praeger, 1992.

Koehler, John O. *Stasi: The Untold Story of the East German Secret Police.* Boulder, CO: Westview, 1999.

Kopstein, Jeffrey. *The Politics of Economic Decline in East Germany, 1945–1989.* Chapel Hill: University of North Carolina Press, 1997.

Lewis, Paul G. *Central Europe since 1945.* London: Longman, 1994.

Loth, Wilfried. *Stalin's Unwanted Child: The Soviet Union, the German Question and the Founding of the GDR.* New York: St. Martin's Press, 1998.

Maaz, Hans-Joachim. *Behind the Wall: The Inner Life of Communist Germany.* Translated by Margo Bettauer Bembo. London: W. W. Norton, 1995.

McAdams, A. James. *East Germany and Détente: Building Authority after the Wall.* Soviet and East European Studies. Cambridge, UK: Cambridge University Press, 1985.

McCauley, Martin. *Marxism-Leninism in the German Democratic Republic: The Socialist Unity Party (SED).* New York: Barnes and Noble/London: School of Slavonic and East European Studies, University of London, 1979.

McDougall, Alan. *Youth Politics in East Germany: The Free German Youth Movement 1946–1968.* Oxford and New York: Clarendon Press, 2004.

McElvoy, Anne. *The Saddled Cow: East Germany's Life and Legacy.* London: Faber and Faber, 1992.

McKay, Joanna. *The Official Concept of the Nation in the Former GDR.* Aldershot, UK: Ashgate, 1998.

Motte, Bruni de la, and John Green. *Stasi State or Socialist Paradise? The German Democratic Republic and What Became of It.* London: Artery Publications, 2015.

Müller-Enbergs, Helmut et al. *Wer war Wer in der DDR? Ein Lexikon ostdeutscher Biographien.* 10th ed. Berlin: Ch. Links Verlag, 2010. First published in 1992 as *Wer war wer-DDR: Ein biographisches Lexikon.* Edited by Jochen Černý.

Plickert, Philip. "Die große Täuschung." *Frankfurter Allgemeine Sonntagszeitung* 40, no. 5 (October 2014): 18.

Plickert, Philip. "Die unvorbereitete Wiedervereinigung." *Orientierungen zur Wirtschafts- und Gesellschaftspolitik* 115 (März 1995): 31–37.

Ritschl, Albrecht. "Aufstieg und Niedergang der Wirtschaft in der DDR. Ein Zahlenbild 1945–1989." *Jahrbuch der Wirtschaftsgechichte* 115, no. 2 (1995): 11–46.

Rock, David, ed. *Voices in Times of Change: The Role of Writers, Opposition Movements, and the Churches in the Transformation of East Germany.* New York: Berghahn, 2000.

Ross, Corey. *The East German Dictatorship: Problems and Perspectives in the Interpretation of the GDR.* London: Arnold, 2002.

Sabrow, Martin. "Die DDR in der Geschichte des 20. Jahrhunderts." *Deutschland Archiv* 41 (2008): 121–30.

Staritz, Dietrich. *Geschichte der DDR.* Rev. and ext. ed. Frankfurt/Main: Suhrkamp, 1997.

Staritz, Dietrich, Helmut Meier, and Stefan Doernberg. *Unternehmen DDR-Geschichte: Forschungsstand, Defizite, Projekte; Workshop.* Workshop aus Anlass des 15-jährigen Bestehens von "Helle Panke" und des Erscheinens der 100. Publikation der Reihe *Hefte zur DDR-Geschichte.* Berlin: Helle Panke/Gesellschaftswissenschaftliches Forum, 2006.

Steiner, André. *Von Plan zu Plan: Eine Wirtschaftsgeschichte der DDR.* Munich: Deutsche Verlags-Anstalt, 2004.

Swatos, William H., Jr., ed. *Polities and Religion in Central and Eastern Europe: Traditions and Transitions.* Westport, CT: Praeger Publishers, 1994.

Tormey, Simon. *Making Sense of Tyranny: Interpretations of Totalitarianism.* Manchester, UK: Manchester University Press, 1995.

Vaizey, Hester. *Born in the GDR: Living in the Shadow of the Wall.* Oxford: Oxford University Press, 2011.

Weber, Hermann. *Die DDR 1945–1990.* 5th rev. ed. Munich: Oldenbourg Verlag, 2012. Previous edition *DDR: Grundriss der Geschichte 1945–1990.* Hannover: Fackelträger Verlag, 1991.

Weedon, Chris, ed. *Die Frau in der DDR: An Anthology of Women's Writing from the German Democratic Republic.* Oxford: Blackwell, 1988.

Weilemann, Peter R., Georg Brunner, and Rudolph L. Tokes, eds. *Upheaval against the Plan: Eastern Europe on the Eve of the Storm.* Oxford: Berg, 1991.

Weitz, Eric D. *Creating German Communism 1890–1990: From Popular Protests to Socialist State.* Princeton, NJ: Princeton University Press, 1997.

Wharton, Janet, and William Goldsmith. *Germany 1946–1981*. Archive of Newspaper Cuttings Collected by British Military Government in Berlin with Special Reference to the German Democratic Republic. Part 1: Introductory Guide. Part 2: Index. Institute of German, Austrian and Swiss Affairs. Nottingham, UK: University of Nottingham, 1993.

Winrow, Gareth M. *The Foreign Policy of the GDR in Africa*. Cambridge, UK: Cambridge University Press, 1990.

Wolfe, Nancy Travis. *Policing a Socialist Society: The German Democratic Republic*. New York: Greenwood, 1992.

D. FRG–GDR Relations

August, Oliver. *Along the Wall and Watchtowers: A Journey Down Germany's Divide*. King's Somborne: Chalkstream, 2009. First published London: Flamingo/Harper Collins, 1999.

Berdahl, Daphne. *Where the World Ended: Re-Unification and Identity in the German Borderland*. Berkeley: University of California Press, 1999.

Dannenberg, Julia von. *The Foundations of Ostpolitik: The Making of the Moscow Treaty between West Germany and the USSR*. Oxford: Oxford University Press.

Fritsch-Bournazel, Renate. *Confronting the German Question: Germans in the East-West Divide*. Translated by Caroline Bray. Oxford: Berg, 1988.

McAdams, A. James. *Germany Divided: From the Wall to Reunification*. Princeton Studies in International History and Politics. Princeton, NJ: University Press, 1993.

Plock, Ernest D. *East-West German Relations and the Fall of the GDR*. Boulder, CO: Westview, 1993.

Schaefer, Sagi. *States of Division: Border and Boundary Formation in Cold War Rural Germany*. Oxford: Oxford University Press, 2014.

E. Reunification to the Present

Berger, Stefan. "Historians and Nation-Building in Germany after Reunification." *Past and Present: A Journal of Historical Studies*, no. 148 (1995): 187–222.

Cooke, Paul. *Representing East Germany since Unification: From Colonization to Nostalgia*. London: Berg, 2006.

Dennis, Mike, and Eva Kolinsky, eds. *United and Divided: Germany since 1990*. New York: Berghahn, 2003.

Elbe, Frank, and Richard E. Kiessler. *A Round Table with Sharp Corners: The Diplomatic Path to German Unity*. Baden-Baden: Nomos, 1996.

Fritsch-Bournazel, Renate. *Europe and German Unification*. Oxford: Berg, 1992.

Gersteenberger, Katharina, and Jana Evans Braziel, eds. *After the Berlin Wall: Germany and Beyond*. New York: Palgrave Macmillan, 2011.

Glaab, Manuela, Werner Weidenfeld, and Michael Weigl, eds. *Deutsche Kontraste 1990–2010: Politik—Wirtschaft—Gesellschaft—Kultur*. Frankfurt/Main: Campus Verlag, 2010.

Görtemaker, Manfred. *Unifying Germany, 1989–1990*. New York: St. Martin's Press/Institute for East-West Studies, 1994.

Hämäläinen, Pekka Kalevi. *Uniting Germany: Actions and Reactions*. Boulder, CO: Westview, 1994.

Hancock, M. Donald, and Helga A. Welsh, eds. *German Unification: Process and Outcomes*. Boulder, CO: Westview, 1994.

Hennecke, Hans-Jörg. *Die dritte Republik: Aufbruch und Ernüchterung*. Munich: Propyläen Verlag, 2003.

James, Harold, and Marla Stone, eds. *When the Wall Came Down: Reactions to German Unification*. New York: Routledge, 1992.

Jarausch, Konrad A. *The Rush to German Unity*. Oxford: Oxford University Press, 1994.

Jarausch, Konrad A., and Volker Gransow, eds. *Uniting Germany: Documents and Debates, 1944–1993*. New York: Berghahn, 1994.

Leiby, Richard A. *The Unification of Germany, 1989–1990*. Westport, CT: Greenwood, 1999.

Leonhard, Jörn, and Lothar Funk, eds. *Ten Years of German Unification: Transfer, Transformation, Incorporation?* Birmingham, UK: Birmingham University Press, 2002.

Maier, Charles S. *Dissolution: The Crisis of Communism and the End of East Germany*. Princeton, NJ: Princeton University Press, 1997.

McFalls, Laurence H. *Communism's Collapse, Democracy's Demise? The Cultural Context and Consequences of the East German Revolution*. London: Macmillan, 1995.

Merkl, Peter H., ed. *German Unification in the European Context*. University Park: Pennsylvania State University Press, 1993.

Miskimmon, Alister, William E. Paterson, and James Sloan, eds. *Germany's Gathering Crisis. The 2005 Federal Election and the Grand Coalition*. Basingstoke, UK: Palgrave Macmillan.

Neckermann, Peter. *The Unification of Germany or The Anatomy of a Peaceful Revolution*. New York: Columbia University Press, 1991.

Nothnagle, Alan L. *Building the East German Myth: Historical Mythology and Youth Propaganda in the German Democratic Republic, 1945–1989*. Ann Arbor: Michigan University Press, 1999.

Osmond, Jonathan, ed. *German Reunification: Reference Guide and Commentary*. Harlow, UK: Longman, 1992.

Philipsen, Dirk. *We Were the People: Voices from East Germany's Revolutionary Autumn of 1989.* Durham, NC: Duke University Press, 1993.

Pickel, Andreas. *Radical Transitions: The Survival and Revival of Entrepreneurship in the GDR.* Boulder, CO: Westview, 1992.

Pond, Elizabeth. *Beyond the Wall.* Washington, DC: Brookings, 1993.

Reutter, Werner, ed. *Germany on the Road to "Normalcy": Policies and Politics of the Red-Green Federal Government (1998–2002).* New York and Basingstoke: Palgrave Macmillan, 2004.

Robertson, John D., and Einard Gellner, eds. *The Berlin Republic: German Unification and a Decade of Changes.* Bath: Frank Cass, 2003.

Sager, Laura M. "German Reunification: Concepts of Identity, East and West." *German Quarterly* 76, no. 3 (2003): 273–88.

Schröder, Klaus. *Die veränderte Republik: Deutschland nach der Wiedervereinigung.* Munich: Verlag Ernst Vögel, 2006.

Schröder, Richard. *Die wichtigsten Irrtümer über die deutsche Einheit.* Freiburg/Breisgau: Herder, 2007.

Siefken, Sven T. *Expertenkommissionen im politischen Prozess: Eine Bilanz der rot-grünen Bundesregierung 1998–2005.* Wiesbaden: VS Verlag für Sozialwissenschaften, 2007.

Speirs, Ronald, and John Breuilly, eds. *Germany's Two Unifications: Anticipations, Experiences, Responses.* Basingstoke, UK: Palgrave Macmillan, 2005.

Szabo, Stephen. *The Diplomacy of German Unification.* New York: Macmillan, 1992.

Thomaneck, J. K. A., and Bill Niven. *Dividing and Uniting Germany.* London: Routledge, 2001.

Wallach, H. G. Peter, and Ronald A. Francisco. *United Germany: The Past, Politics, Prospects.* Westport, CT: Greenwood, 1992.

Zelikow, Philip, and Condoleezza Rice. *Germany Unified and Europe Transformed.* Cambridge, MA: Harvard University Press, 1995. Also published in German as *Sternstunde der Diplomatie: die deutsche Einheit und das Ende der Spaltung Europas.* Berlin: Propyläen, 1997.

F. Foreign Policy, Relations, and Defense

Adomeit, Hannes. *Imperial Overstretch: Germany in Soviet Policy from Stalin to Gorbachev.* Baden-Baden: Nomos, 1998.

Ash, Timothy Garton. *In Europe's Name: Germany and the Divided Continent.* London: Vintage, 1994.

Bagci, Hüseyin, Jackson Janes, and Ludger Kühnhardt, eds. *Parameters of Partnership: Germany, the US and Turkey.* Challenges for German and American Foreign Policy. Baden-Baden: Nomos, 1999.

Beichelt, Timm. "Germany: In Search of a New Balance." In *The Member States of the European Union*, 2nd ed., edited by Simon Bulmer and Christian Lesquesne. Oxford: Oxford University Press, 2013.

Bluth, Christoph. *Britain, Germany and Western Nuclear Strategy*. Oxford: Clarenden Press, 1995.

Bulmer, Simon, and Christian Lesquesne, eds. *The Member States of the European Union*. 2nd ed. Oxford: Oxford University Press, 2013.

Conversi, Daniele. *German-Bashing and the Breakup of Yugoslavia*. Seattle: University of Washington, 1998.

Craig, Gordon A. *Germany and the West: The Ambivalent Relationship*. London: German Historical Institute, 1982.

Dettke, Dieter, *Germany Says No: The Iraq War and the Future of German Foreign and Security Policy*. Washington, DC: Woodrow Wilson Center Press/Baltimore, MD: Johns Hopkins University Press, 2009.

Duffield, John S. *World Power Forsaken: Political Culture, International Institutions, and German Security Police after Unification*. Stanford, CA: Stanford University Press, 1998.

Dyson, Tom. *The Politics of German Defence and Security: Policy Leadership and Military Reform in the Post-Cold War Era*. Oxford: Berghahn Books, 2007.

Eberwein, Wolf-Dieter, and Karl Kaiser, eds. *Germany's New Foreign Policy: Decision-Making in an Interdependent World*. Basingstoke, UK: Palgrave Press, 2001.

Ehrhart, Hans-Georg, and David G. Haglund, eds. *The "New Peacekeeping"and European Security: German and Canadian Interests and Issues*. Baden-Baden: Nomos, 1995.

Erb, Scott. *German Foreign Policy*. Boulder, CO: Lynne Rienner, 2003.

Garies, Sven Bernard. *Deutschland Außen- und Sicherheitspolitik: Eine Einführung*. Opladen: Verlag Barbara Budrich, 2005.

Gatzke, Hans W. *Germany and the United States: A "Special Relationship"?* Cambridge, MA: Harvard University Press, 1980.

Geiger, Tim, Matthias Peter, and Mechthild Lindemann, eds. *Akten zur Auswärtigen Politik der Bundesrepublik Deutschland: 1983, 1 Januar bis 31. Dezember*. Munich: Oldenbourg Verlag, 2014.

Gloannec, Anne-Marie Le. *Non-State Actors in International Relations: The Case of Germany*. Manchester, UK: Manchester University Press, 2007.

Hellmann, Günther, et al. *Deutsche Außenpolitik: Eine Einführung*. Wiesbaden: VS Verlag für Sozialwissenschaften, 2006.

Gordon, Philip H. *France, Germany and the Western Alliance*. Boulder, CO: Westview, 1995.

Granieri, Ronald J. *The Ambivalent Alliance: Konrad Adenauer, the CDU/CSU, and the West 1949–1966*. New York and Oxford: Berghahn Books, 2004.

Gujer, Eric. *Schluss mit der Heuchelei: Deutschland ist eine Großmacht.* Hamburg: Edition Körber-Stiftung, 2007.

Gutjahr, Lothar. *German Foreign and Defense Policy after Unification.* London: Pinter, 1994.

Haglund, David, and Olaf Mager, eds. *Homeward Bound? Allied Forces in the New Germany.* Boulder, CO: Westview, 1992.

Harnisch, Sebastian, and Hanns W. Maull, eds. *Germany as a Civilian Power: The Foreign Policy of the Berlin Republic.* Manchester, UK: Manchester University Press, 2001.

Heuser, Beatrice. *NATO, Britain, France and the FRG: Nuclear Strategies and Forces for Europe 1949–2000.* Basingstoke, UK: Macmillan, 1997.

Hindenburg, Hannfried von. *Demonstrating Reconciliation: State and Society in West German Foreign Policy towards Israel, 1952–1965.* New York and Oxford: Berghahn.

Hodge, Carl Cavanagh, and Cathal J. Nolan, eds. *Shepherd of Democracy? America and Germany in the Twentieth Century.* Westport, CT: Greenwood, 1992.

Jäger, Thomas, Alexander Höse, and Kai Oppermann, eds. *Deutsche Außenpolitik: Sicherheit, Wohlfarht, Institutionen und Normen.* Wiesbaden: VS Verlag für Sozialwissenschaften, 2007.

Jones, Erik, et al., eds. *The Oxford Handbook of the European Union.* Oxford: Oxford University Press, 2012.

Kirchner, Emil J., and J. Sperling, eds. *The Federal Republic of Germany and NATO: 40 Years After.* Basingstoke, UK: Macmillan, 1992.

Küntzel, Matthias. *Bonn and the Bomb: German Politics and the Nuclear Option.* Translated by Helke Heino and R. Range Cloyd Jr. London: Pluto Press with the Transnational Institute, 1995.

Laird, Robbin F. *The Soviets, Germany, and the New Europe.* Boulder, CO: Westview, 1991.

Manners, Ian, and Richard G. Whitman, eds. *The Foreign Policies of European Union States.* Manchester, UK: Manchester University Press, 2000.

Maull, Hanns W. ed. *Germany's Uncertain Power: Foreign Policy of the Berlin Republic.* Basingstoke, UK: Palgrave Macmillan, 2006.

Mey, Holger H. *German Security Policy in the 21st Century: Problems, Partners and Perspectives.* New York and Oxford: Berghahn Books, 2004.

Mitchell, Otis C. *The Cold War in Germany: Overview Origins, and Intelligence Wars.* Lanham, MD: University Press of America, 2005.

Møller, Bjorn. *Resolving the Security Dilemma in Europe: The German Debate on Non-Offensive Defense.* London: Brassey's, 1991.

Murray, Andrew. *Flashpoint: World War III.* London: Pluto Press, 1997.

Newnham, Randall, E. *Deutsche Mark Diplomacy: Positive Economic Sanctions in German-Russian Relations.* University Park: Penn State University Press, 2002.

Nielsen, Anja-Dalgaard. *Germany, Pacifism and Peace Enforcement*. Manchester, UK: Manchester University Press, 2006.

Paterson, Willam E. "Foreign Policy in the Grand Coalition." *German Politics* 19, nos. 3–4 (2010): 497–514.

Paterson, Willam E. "The Reluctant Hegemon? Germany Moves Centre Stage in the European Union." Special issue, "The JCMS Annual Review of the European Union in 2010." *Journal of Common Market Studies* 49 (2011): 57–75.

Pilz, Volker. *Der Auswärtige Ausschuss des Deutschen Bundestages und die Mitwirkung des Parlaments an der auswärtigen und internationalen Politik*. Berlin: Duncker und Humblot, 2008.

Pittman, Avril. *From Ostpolitik to Reunification: West German-Soviet Relations since 1974*. Cambridge, UK: Cambridge University Press, 1992.

Rathbun, Brian C. *Partisan Inverventions: European Party Politics and Peace Enforcement in the Balkans*. New York: Cornell University Press, 2004.

Rittberger, Volker, ed. *German Foreign Policy since Unification: Theories and Case Studies*. Manchester, UK: Manchester University Press, 2001.

Rotfield, Adam B., and Walther Stützle. *Germany and Europe in Transition*. Oxford: Oxford University Press, 1991.

Rudolf, Peter, and Geoffrey Kemp. *The Iranian Dilemma: Challenges for German and American Foreign Policy*. Baltimore, MD: American Institute for Contemporary German Studies, Johns Hopkins University, 1997.

Steininger, Rolf. *Deutschland und die USA: Vom Zweiten Weltkrieg bis zur Gegenwart. Hamburg*. Reinbek/Munich: Olzog-Edition im Lau Verlag, 2014.

Stent, Angela. *From Embargo to Ostpolitik: The Political Economy of West German-Soviet Relations, 1955–1980*. Cambridge, UK: Cambridge University Press, 1981.

Szabo, Stephen F. *The Changing Politics of German Security*. London: Pinter, 1990.

Tampke, Jürgen. *Czech-German Relations and the Politics of Central Europe: From Bohemia to the EU*. Basingstoke, UK: Palgrave Macmillan, 2003.

Teasdale, Anthony, and Timothy Bainbridge. *The Penguin Companion to European Union*. 4th ed. London: Penguin Books, 2012.

Tewes, Henning, *Germany, Civilian Power and the New Europe: Enlarging NATO and the European Union*. Basingstoke, UK: Palgrave, 2001.

Wallace, Helen, William Wallace, and Mark A. Pollack, eds. 6th ed. *Policy-Making in the European Union*. Oxford: Oxford University Press, 2010.

Wyllie, James H. *European Security in the New Political Environment*. London: Longman, 1997.

G. Germany and Europe

Abse, Leo. *Wotan, My Enemy*. London: Robson Books, 1994.

Allum, Percy. *State and Society in Western Europe*. Cambridge, UK: Polity Press, 1995.

Alter, Peter. *The German Question and Europe: A History*. London: Arnold, 2000.

Arter, David. *The Politics of European Integration in the Twentieth Century*. Aldershot, UK: Dartmouth, 1993.

Balfour, Michael. *Germany: The Tides of Power*. London: Routledge, 1992.

Baranovsky, Vladimir, and Hans-Joachim Spanger, eds. *In from the Cold: Germany, Russia and the Future of Europe*. Boulder, CO: Westview, 1992.

Baring, Arnulf, ed. *Germany's New Position in Europe: Problems and Perspectives*. Oxford: Berg, 1994.

Batley, Richard, and Adrian Campbell, eds. *The Political Executive: Politicians and Management in European Local Government*. London: Frank Cass, 1992.

Behr, Timo. "The European Union's Mediterranean Policies after the Arab Spring: Can the Leopard Change Its Spots?" *Amsterdam Law Forum* 4, no. 2 (2012). http://amsterdamlawforum.org/article/view/268/0.

Bond, Martin, Julie Smith, and William Wallace, eds. *Eminent Europeans*. London: Greycoat Press, 1996.

Brechtefeld, Jörg. *Mitteleuropa and German Politics: 1948 to the Present*. Basingstoke, UK: Macmillan/New York: St Martin's Press, 1996.

Bulmer, Simon, Charlie Jeffery, and William E. Paterson. *Germany's European Diplomacy: Shaping the Regional Milieu*. Manchester, UK: Manchester University Press, 2000.

Collins, Stephen D. *German Policy-Making and Eastern Enlargement of the European Union during the Kohl Era: Managing the Agenda?* Manchester, UK: Manchester University Press, 2002.

Dinan, Desmond. *Ever Closer Union? An Introduction to the European Community*. 4th ed. Basingstoke, UK: Palgrave Macmillan, 2010/Boulder, CO: Lynne Rienner, 2011.

Duff, Andrew, John Pinder, and Roy Pryce, eds. *Maastricht and Beyond: Building the European Union*. London: Routledge, 1994.

Green, Stephen. "Reluctant Meister. How Germany's Past is Shaping its European Future." University of Chicago Press, 2014.

Görtermaker, Manfred, ed. *Britain and Germany in the 20th Century*. Oxford and New York: Berg, 2006.

Grosse, Ernst Ulrich, and Heinz-Helmut Lueger. *Understanding France in Comparison with Germany*. Bern: Peter Lang, 1994.

Haglund, D. G. *Alliance within the Alliance: Franco-German Military Cooperation and the European Pillar of Defense*. Boulder, CO: Westview, 1991.

Hayward, Jack. *The Crisis of Representation in Europe*. London: Frank Cass, 1995.

Hayward, Jack, and Edward C. Page. *Governing the New Europe*. Cambridge, UK: Polity Press, 1995.

Heinelt, Hubert, and Randall Smith, eds. *Policy Networks and European Structural Funds*. Aldershot, UK: Avebury, 1996.

Heisenberg, Wolfgang. *German Unification in European Perspective*. London: Brassey's, 1991.

Henderson, Karen, ed. *Back to Europe: Central and Eastern Europe and the European Union*. London: UCL Press (Taylor & Francis Ltd.), 1999.

Hendriks, Gisela. *Germany and European Integration: The Common Agricultural Policy—An Area of Conflict*. Oxford: Berg, 1991.

Hendriks, Gisela, and Annette Morgan. *The Franco-German Axis in European Integration*. Cheltenham, UK/Northampton, MA: Edward Elgar, 2001.

Heurlin, Bertel, ed. *Germany in Europe in the Nineties*. London: Macmillan, 1996.

Hyde-Price, Adrian. *Germany and European Order: Enlarging NATO and the EU*. Manchester, UK: Manchester University Press, 2000.

Jacquemin, Alexis, and David Wright, eds. *The European Challenges Post-1992: Shaping Factors, Shaping Actors*. Aldershot, UK: Edward Elgar, 1993.

Kulski, W. W. *Germany and Poland: From War to Peaceful Relations*. Syracuse, NY: Syracuse University Press, 1976.

Kurz, H. D., ed. *United Germany and the New Europe*. Aldershot, UK: Edward Elgar, 1993.

Lantis, Jeffrey S. *Domestic Constraints and the Breakdown of International Agreements*. Westport, CT: Praeger, 1998.

Lippert, Barbara, and Rosalind Stevens-Ströhmann. *German Unification and EC Integration: German and British Perspectives*. London: Pinter/Royal Institute of International Affairs, 1993.

Marsh, David. *Germany and Europe: The Crisis of Unity*. Rev. and updated ed. London: Mandarin Paperbacks, 1995. Originally published London: William Heinemann, 1994.

McCarthy, Patrick, ed. *France–Germany 1983–1993: The Struggle to Cooperate*. London: Macmillan, 1994.

Miall, Hugh, ed. *Redefining Europe: New Patterns of Conflict and Cooperation*. London: Pinter/Royal Institute of International Affairs, 1994.

Miskimmon, Alister. *Germany and the Common Foreign and Security Policy of the European Union: Between Europeanisation and National Adaptation.* Basingstoke, UK: Palgrave Macmillan.

Nelson, Brian, David Roberts, and Walter Veit. *The European Community in the 1990s: Economics, Politics, Defense.* New York: Berg, 1992.

Ramsden, John. *Don't Mention the War: The British and Germans since 1890.* London: Little Brown, 2006.

Rinke, Bernhard. *Die beiden großen Volksparteien und das "Friedensprojekt Europa": Weltmacht, Zivilmacht, Friedensmacht?* Baden-Baden: Nomos, 2006.

Schweiger, Christian. *Britain, Germany and the Future of the European Union.* Basingstoke, UK: Palgrave Macmillan, 2007.

Schweitzer, Carl-Christoph, and Detlev Karsten, eds. *Federal Republic of Germany and EC Membership Evaluated.* London: Pinter, 1990.

Smith, Mitchell P., ed. "From Modell Deutschland to Model Europa: Europe in Germany and Germany in Europe." Special issue, *German Politics* 14, no. 3 (September 2005).

Sperling, James, and Emil Kirchner. *Recasting the European Order: Security Architecture and Economic Cooperation.* Manchester, UK: Manchester University Press, 1997.

Story, Jonathan. *The New Europe: Politics, Government and Economy since 1945.* Oxford: Blackwell, 1993.

Tartwijk-Novey, Louise B. van. *The European House of Cards.* Basingstoke, UK: Macmillan/New York: St. Martin's Press, 1995.

Thompson, Kenneth W., ed. *Europe and Germany: Unity and Diversity.* Lanham, MD: University Press of America, 1994.

Urwin, Derek. *Dictionary of European Politics 1945–1995.* London: Longman, 1996.

Valant, Peter. "The Franco-German Couple: Potentials and Limitations." Paper presented at THESEUS Conference, Brussels, 2012. http://theseus.uni-koeln.de/fileadmin/Background_Paper_Franco-German-couple-Potential-and-limits.pdf.

Verheyen, Dirk. *The German Question: A Cultural, Historical and Geopolitical Exploration.* 2nd ed. Boulder, CO: Westview, 1999. First edition published in 1991.

Verheyen, Dirk, and Christian Søe, eds. *The Germans and Their Neighbors.* Boulder, CO: Westview, 1993.

Wurm, Clemens, ed. *Western Europe and Germany: The Beginnings of European Integration 1945–1960.* Oxford: Berg, 1995.

H. Military History

Kitchen, Martin. *A Military History of Germany: From the Eighteenth Century to the Present Day*. London: Weidenfeld and Nicholson, 1975.

Müller, Klaus-Jürgen, ed. *The Military in Politics and Society in France and Germany in the Twentieth Century*. Oxford: Berg, 1995.

Rosinski, Herbert. *The German Army*. Edited and with an introduction by Gordon A. Craig. London: Pall Mall Press, 1966.

Schönbohm, Jörg. *Two Armies and One Fatherland: The End of the Nationale Volksarmee*. New York: Berghahn, 1996.

Zabecki, David T. ed. *Germany at War. 400 Years of Military History*. Santa Barbara, CA: ABC-CLIO, 2014.

I. Coming to Terms with the Past and National Identity

Alter, Reinhard, and Peter Monteath. *Rewriting the German Past History and Identity in the New Germany*. Atlantic Highlands, NJ: Humanities Press, 1997.

Alter, Peter, ed. *Out of the Third Reich: Refugee Historians in Post-war Britain*. London: I. B. Taurus, 1998.

Arnold, Jörg, Dietmar Süß, and Malte Thiessen, eds. *Luftkrieg: Erinnerungen in Deutschland und Europa*. Göttingen: Wallstein-Verlag, 2009.

Art, David. *The Politics of the Nazi Past in Germany and Austria*. Cambridge, UK: Cambridge University Press, 2006.

Baldwin, Peter, ed. *Reworking the Past: Hitler, the Holocaust, and the Historians' Debate*. Boston: Beacon Press, 1990.

Bankier, David, and Dan Mikhman. *Holocaust Historiography in Context: Emergence, Challenges, Polemics and Achievements*. New York/Oxford: Berghahn, 2008.

Barnstone, Deborah Ascher, and Thomas O. Haakenson. *Representations of German Identity*. Bern: Peter Lang, 2013.

Beer, Matthias. *Flucht und Verbtreibung der Deutschen: Voraussetzungen, Verlauf, Folgen*. Munich: 2011.

Berger, Stefan. *The Search for Normality: National Identity and Historical Consciousness in Germany since 1800*. New York: Berghahn, 1997.

Borneman, John. *Settling Accounts: Violence, Justice and Accountability in Postsocialist Europe*. Princeton, NJ/Chichester, UK: Princeton University Press, 1997.

Costabile-Heming, Carol Anne, Rachel J. Halverson, and Kristie A. Foell. *Textual Responses to German Unification: Processing Historical and Social Change in Literature and Film*. Berlin: Walter de Gruyter, 2001.

Broszat, Martin. *Der Staat Hitlers: Grundlegung und Entwicklung seiner inneren Verfassung.* Munich: Deutscher Taschenbuch Verlag, 1969.

Buruma, Ian. *The Wages of Guilt: Memories of War in Germany and Japan.* London: Atlantic, 2009. First published in UK by Jonathan Cape, 1995.

Conze, Eckart, Norbert Frei, Peter Hayes, and Moshe Zimmermann. *Das Amt und die Vergangenheit: Deutsche Diplomaten im Dritten Reich und in der Bundesrepublik.* Munich: Karl Blessing Verlag, 2010.

Crawshaw, Steve. *Easier Fatherland: Germany in the Twenty-First Century.* London: Continuum, 2004.

Diner, Dan. "Between Aporia and Apologia: On the Limits of Historicising National Socialism." In *Reworking the Past: Hitler, the Holocaust, and the Historians' Debate,* edited by Peter Baldwin, 135–45. Boston: Beacon Press, 1990.

Evans, Richard J. *In Hitler's Shadow: West German Historians and the Attempts to Escape from the Nazi Past.* London: Tauris, 1989.

Evans, Richard J. *The Third Reich in History and Memory.* London: Little, Brown Group, 2015.

Fulbrook, Mary. *German National Identity after the Holocaust.* Cambridge, UK: Polity Press, 1999.

Fulbrook, Mary, and Martin Swales. *Representing the German Nation: History and Identity in Twentieth Century Germany.* Manchester, UK: Manchester University Press, 2000.

Gay, Caroline. "Remembering for the Future, Engaging with the Present: National Memory Management and the Dialectic of Normality in the Berlin Republic." In *Politics and Culture in Twentieth-Century Germany,* edited by William Niven and James Jordan, 201–26. Rochester, NY: Camden House, 2003.

Goldhagen, Daniel Jonah. *Hitler's Willing Executioners: Ordinary Germans and the Holocaust.* New York: Knopf/Random House, 1996.

Habermas, Jürgen. *A Berlin Republic: Writings on Germany.* Translated by Steven Rendall. Lincoln: University of Nebraska Press, 1997.

Habermas, Jürgen, et al. *The New Conservatism: Cultural Criticism and the Historians' Debate.* Cambridge, MA: The MIT Press, 1991.

Herf, Jeffrey. *Divided Memory: The Nazi Past in the Two Germanys.* Cambridge, MA/London: Harvard University Press, 1997.

Hiden, John, and John Fahrquharson. *Explaining Hitler's Germany: Historians and the Third Reich.* 2nd ed. London: Batsford, 1989.

Kershaw, Ian. *The Hitler Myth: Image and Reality in the Third Reich.* Oxford: Oxford University Press, 1987.

Knowlton, James, and Truett Cates, trans. *Forever in the Shadow of Hitler? The Dispute about the Germans' Understanding of History, Original Documents of the Historikerstreit, the Controversy Concerning the Singularity of the Holocaust.* Atlantic Highlands, NJ: Humanities Press, 1993.

Kundnani, Hans. *Utopia or Ausschwitz: Germany's 1968 Generation and the Holocaust*. London: C. Hurst & Co., 2009.

Maier, Charles S. *The Unmasterable Past: History, Holocaust, and German National Identity*. Cambridge, MA: Harvard University Press, 1997. First published in 1988.

Low, Alfred D. *The Third Reich and the Holocaust in German Historiography: Toward the Historikerstreit of the Mid-1980s*. New York: Columbia University Press, 1995.

McAdams, A. James. *Judging the Past in the Unified Germany*. Cambridge, UK: Cambridge University Press, 2001.

McGlothlin, Eric. *Second-Generation Holocaust Literature: Legacies of Survival and Perpetration*. Rochester, NY/Woodbridge: Camden House, 2006.

Niven, Bill, ed. *Germans as Victims: Remembering the Past in Contemporary Germany*. Basingstoke, UK: Palgrave Macmillan, 2006.

Niven, Bill, and Chloe Paver. *Memorialization in Germany since 1945*. Basingstoke, UK: Palgrave Macmillan, 2010.

Pearce, Caroline. *Contemporary Germany and the Nazi Legacy: Remembrance, Politics and the Dialectic of Normality*. Basingstoke, UK: Palgrave Macmillan, 2008.

Rosenfeld, Gavriel David. *Hi Hitler: How the Nazi Past Is Being Normalized in Contemporary Culture*. Cambridge, UK: Cambridge University Press, 2014.

Schiele, Ulrich. "Today's View of the Third Reich and the Second World War in German Historiographical Discourse." *The Historical Journal* 43, no. 2 (2000): 543–64.

Shirer, William. *The Rise and Fall of the Third Reich: A History of Nazi Germany*. New York: Simon and Schuster, 1960.

Stone, Dan. *The Historiography of the Holocaust*. Houndmills, Basingstoke, UK: Palgrave Macmillan, 2004.

Taberner, Stuart, and Frank Finlay. *Recasting German Identity. Culture, Politics, and Literature in the Berlin Republic*. Rochester, NY: Camden House, 2002.

Thomas, Gina, ed. *The Unresolved Past: A Debate in German History*. Weidenfield and Nicolson, 1990.

Toland, John. *Adolf Hitler*. Garden City, NY: Doubleday, 1976.

Wagner, Gottfried, and Abraham J. Peck. *Unwanted Legacies: Sharing the Burden of Post-Genocide Generations*. Lubbock, TX: Texas Tech University Press, 2014.

1. Jews in Germany

Blumenthal, Werner Michael. *The Invisible Wall: Germans and Jews; a Personal Exploration.* Washington, DC: Counterpoint, 1998.

Brenner, Michael. *After the Holocaust: Rebuilding Jewish Lives in Postwar Germany.* Translated by Barbara Harshav. Princeton, NJ: Princeton University Press, 1997.

European Monitoring Centre on Racism and Xenophobia. *Manifestations of Antisemitism in the EU 2002–2003.* Based on information by the National Focal Points of the EUMC-RAXEN Information Network. Vienna: EUMC, 2004.

European Monitoring Centre on Racism and Xenophobia. *Perceptions of Antisemitism in the European Union: Voices from Members of the European Jewish Communities.* Vienna: EUMC, 2004.

Fischer, Klaus P. *The History of an Obsession: German Judeophobia and the Holocaust.* New York: Continuum, 1998. Reprinted in 2001.

Geller, Jay Howard. *Jews in Post-Holocaust Germany 1945–1953.* Cambridge, UK: Cambridge University Press, 2004.

Gilman, Sander L. *Jews in Today's German Culture.* Bloomington: Indiana University. Press, 1995.

Herzog, Hilary Hope, Todd Herzog, and Benjamin Lapp. *Rebirth of a Culture: Jewish Identity and Jewish Writing in Germany and Austria Today.* London: Berghahn, 2008.

Hess, Jonathan M. *Germans, Jews and the Claims of Modernity.* New Haven, CT: Yale University Press, 2002.

Kahn, Charlotte. *Resurgence of Jewish Life in Germany.* Westport, CT: Praeger, 2004.

Kauders, Anthony D. *Democratization and the Jews: Munich 1945–1965.* Studies in Antisemitism Series. Lincoln: University of Nebraska Press, 2004.

Lappin, Elena, ed. *Jewish Voices, German Words: Growing up Jewish in Postwar Germany and Austria.* Translated by Krishna Winston. North Haven, CT: Catbird Press, 1994.

Laufer, Peter. *Exodus to Berlin: The Return of Jews to Germany.* Chicago: Ivan R. Dee, 2003.

Legge, Jerome S., Jr. *Jews, Turks, and Other Strangers: The Roots of Prejudice in Modern Germany.* Madison: University of Wisconsin Press, 2003.

Peck, Jeffrey M. *Being Jewish in the New Germany.* New Brunswick, NJ: Rutgers University Press, 2005.

Rabinbach, Anson, and Jack Zipes, eds. *Germans and Jews since the Holocaust: The Changing Situation in West Germany.* Teaneck, NJ: Holmes & Meier, 1986.

Rapaport, Lynn. *Jews in Germany after the Holocaust: Memory, Identity, and Jewish-German Relations*. Cambridge, UK: Cambridge University Press, 1997.

Stern, Frank. *The Whitewashing of the Yellow Badge: Antisemitism and Philosemitism in Postwar Germany*. Translated by William Templer. Oxford: Pergamon Press, 1991.

Stern, Susan, ed. *Speaking Out: Jewish Voices from a United Germany*. Chicago: Edition Q, 1995.

Timm, Angelika. *Jewish Claims against East Germany: Moral Obligations and Pragmatic Policy*. Budapest: Central European University Press, 1998.

Wittlinger, Ruth. *German National Identity in the Twenty-First Century: A Different Republic After All?* Basingstoke, UK, and New York: Palgrave Macmillan, 2010.

Wolffsohn, Michael. *Eternal Guilt? Forty Years of German-Jewish-Israeli Relations*. New York: Columbia University Press, 1993.

Zipes, Jack, and Leslie Morris. *Unlikely History: The Changing German-Jewish Symbiosis 1945–2000*. New York: Palgrave Macmillan, 2002.

J. Economic History

Abelshauser, Werner. *Deutsche Wirtschaftsgeschichte von 1945 bis zur Gegenwart*. 2nd ed. Munich: Beck, 2011.

Berghahn, Volker R. *The Americanisation of West German Industry 1945–1973*. New York: Cambridge University Press, 1986.

Berghahn, Volker R. *Quest for Economic Empire: European Strategies of German Big Business in the Twentieth Century*. New York: Berghahn, 1996.

Braun, Hans-Joachim. *The German Economy in the Twentieth Century: The German Reich and the Federal Republic*. London: Routledge, 1990. Reprinted in 2011.

Bryson, Philip J. *The Reluctant Retreat: The Soviet and East German Departure from Central Planning*. Aldershot, UK: Dartmouth, 1995.

Bryson, Philip J., and Manfred Melzer. *The End of the East German Economy: From Honecker to Reunification*. Basingstoke, UK: Macmillan, 1991.

Cobham, David, ed. *European Monetary Upheavals*. Manchester, UK: Manchester University Press, 1994.

Damsgaard Hansen, E. *European Economic History: From Mercantilism to Maastricht*. Herndon, VA: Books International/Copenhagen Business School, 2001.

D'Elia, Costanza. "Miracles and Mirages in the West German Economy: A Survey of the Literature of the 1980s." *Journal of European Economic History* 22, no. 2 (1993): 381–401.

Giersch, H., K.-H. Pacqué, and H. Schmieding. *The Fading Miracle: Four Decades of Market Economy in Germany*. Cambridge, UK: Cambridge University Press, 1992.

Gresser, Thorsten (Bochum). "Pittsburgh and the Ruhr Area: Common Patterns in the Fight against Shutdowns during the Decline of Steel." *Jahrbuch für Wirtschaftsgeschichte*, no. 2 (2001): 65–74.

Head, David. *Made in Germany: The Corporate Identity of a Nation*. London: Hodder & Stoughton, 1992.

Homburg, Heidrun. "The First Large Firms in German Retailing: The Chains of Department Stores from the 1920s to the 1970/80s: Structures, Strategies, Management." *Jahrbuch für Wirtschaftsgeschichte*, no. 1 (2001): 171–98.

Parnell, Martin F. *The German Tradition of Organized Capitalism: Self-Government in the Coal Industry*. Oxford: Clarendon Press, 1994.

Peacock, Alan T., and Hans Willgerodt. *Germany's Social Market Economy: Origins and Evolution*. London: Macmillan, 1989.

Pierenkemper, Tony. "The Standard of Living and Employment in Germany, 1850–1980: An Overview." *Journal of European Economic History* 16, no. 1 (1987): 51–73.

Reich, Simon. *The Fruits of Fascism: Postwar Prosperity in Historical Perspective*. Ithaca, NY: Cornell University Press, 1990.

Rieger, Berhard. *The People's Car: A Global History of the Volkswagen Beetle*. Cambridge, MA: Harvard University Press, 2013.

Siegel, Nicholas. *The German Marshall Fund of the United States: A Brief History*. Washington, DC: German Marshall Fund of the United States, 2012. Available at www.gmfus.org.

Smyser, W. R. *The Economy of United Germany: Colossus at the Crossroads*. London: Hurst & Co., 1992.

Sommariva, Andrea, and Giuseppe Tullio. *German Macroeconomic History 1880–1979: A Study of the Effects of Economic Policy on Inflation, Currency Depreciation and Growth*. London: Macmillan, 1987.

Steinherr, A., ed. *30 Years of European Monetary Integration: From the Werner Plan to EMU*. London: Longman, 1995.

II. GENERAL DESCRIPTIONS, TRAVEL, AND HANDBOOKS

A. Maps (Publishers, with Specializations)

ADAC (Allgeimeiner Deutscher Automobilclub): motorists.

Bacher Verlag GmbH (Stuttgart): general, regional and national, postal zones (Postleitkarte), administrative districts.

Berndtson & Berndtson (Fürstenfeldbruck): general, motor sports.

CartoTravel Verlag GmbH & Co. KG (Bad Soden/Taunus): motorists and cyclists.

Ernst Klett Verlag GmbH (Stuttgart, also incorporating the former Perthes Verlag, Gotha): school atlases, wall maps, hand maps.

Euro-Cities AG (Berlin): cities and towns.

Federal Agency for Cartography and Geodesy (Bundesamt für Kartographie und Geodäsie, BKG): digital and printed (also historical). www.bkg.bund.de.

Der Fischer Atlas Deutschland: Umwelt, Politik, Wirtschaft, Kultur. Frankfurt/Main: Fischer Verlag, 2001: politics, culture, environment, economics.

Hammond International (with Langenscheidt): *Hammond International Germany Road Atlas.*

Kompass Verlag (Rum, Austria): over 1,000 maps for ramblers, walkers, and cyclists throughout Germany.

MairDumont (including the former Mairs Geographischer Verlag, Ostfildern/Stuttgart): political, physical, and travel/road of Germany.

Michelin (Michelin Group, France): national and regional (including editions for Berlin).

Perthes-Verlag (Gotha). *See* Ernst Klett Verlag GmbH.

Polyglott Verlag: travel and tourist.

Schäfers, Bernhard, and Yvonne Bernart. *The State of Germany Atlas.* London/New York: Routledge, 1998. German edition: *Politischer Atlas Deutschland. Gesellschaft, Wirtschaft, Staat.* Bonn: J. H. W. Dietz Nachfolger, 1997.

Schroedel Verlag (part of the Westermann group, Braunschweig): atlases for school use.

University of Texas at Austin Libraries (lib.utexas.edu/maps/germany.html): political, physical, topographical, historical, and thematic online, mainly produced by the U.S. Central Intelligence Agency. Links also to other sources (tourist, city, railway, and maps of U.S. military bases in Germany).

Verlag Rheinschifffahrt (Bad Soden): national rivers and waterways.

Wasser- und Schifffahrtsdirektion Südwest: national rivers and waterways.

Westermann Schulbuchverlag (Braunschweig): atlases and wall maps.
Wolfgang Kunth Verlag (Munich): road atlases.

B. Tourist Guides

Deutsche Zentrale für Tourismus (http://www.germany-tourism.de/).
Egert-Romanowskiej, Joanna, and Malgorzata Omilanowska. *Eyewitness Travel Guide to Germany*. London: Dorling Kindersley (DK), 2014 (ebook 2010). The Eyewitness series also includes guides on Berlin, Hamburg, and Munich and the Bavarian Alps.
Eye Witness Travel Guide Series. *See under* Egert-Romanowskiej, Joanna.
Fodor's Travel Guides Series. Guides on regions and major German cities. Fodor's Travel is a division of Random House, New York.
Frommer's Germany. Hobocken, NJ: John Wiley & Sons, 2012.
German National Tourist Board. *See* Deutsche Zentrale für Tourismus.
Lonely Planet Series. Guides on Germany and Berlin. Victoria (Australia): Lonely Planet Publications.
Michelin Guides Series. General guides, restaurants, and travel maps. Michelin Travel Publications/Michelin Travel & Lifestyle.
Rough Guide Series (London). Guides on regions and major German cities.
Steves, Rick. *Rick Steves' Germany 2010*. Emeryville, CA: Avalon Travel Publishing, 2009.
Steves, Rick. *Rick Steves' Germany, Austria, and Switzerland Map: Including Berlin, Munich, Salzburg and Vienna City*. Emeryville, CA: Avalon Travel Publishing, 2007.

C. General Studies of Germany

Ardagh, John, and Katharina Ardagh. *Germany and the Germans: After Unification*. 3rd ed. London: Penguin, 1995.
Beauftragte der Bundesregierung für Migration, Flüchtlinge und Integration [Federal Government Commissioner for Migration, Refugees and Integration]. *A Manual on Germany/Ein Handbuch für Deutschland*. 2nd ed. Berlin: Author, 2005. Also available at www.integrationsbeauftragte.de and www.handbuch-deutschland.de.
Bedürftig, F. *Taschenlexikon Deutschland nach 1945*. Munich: Piper Verlag, 1998.
Buse, Dieter, and Jürgen C. Doerr, eds. *Modern Germany: An Encyclopaedia of History, People and Culture, 1871–1990*. 2 vols. New York: Garland Publishing, 1998.
Craig, Gordon A. *The Germans*. New York: G. P. Putnam's Sons, 1982. Revised in 1991.

Diem, Aubrey. *The New Germany: Land, People, Economy*. 2nd ed. Kitchener, ONT: Aljon Print-Craft, 1993.

Elias, Norbert. *The Germans: Power Struggles and the Development of Habitus in the Nineteenth and Twentieth Centuries*. Edited by Michael Schroter. Cambridge, UK: Polity Press, 1997.

Flamini, R. *Passport Germany*. San Rafael, CA: World Trade Press, 1997.

Flippo, Hyde. *When in Germany, Do as the Germans Do*. New York: McGraw-Hill, 2002.

Gros, Jürgen, and Manuela Glaab. *Faktenlexikon Deutschland: Geschichte, Gesellschaft, Politik, Wirtschaft, Kultur*. Munich: Wilhelm Heyne Verlag, 1999.

James, Peter, ed. *Modern Germany: Politics, Society and Culture*. London: Routledge, 1998.

Jeffery, Charlie, and Ruth Whittle, eds. *Germany Today*. London: Arnold, 1997.

Larres, K., and P. Panayi, eds. *The Federal Republic of Germany since 1949: Politics, Society and Economy before and after Unification*. London: Longman, 1996.

Lewis, Derek. *Contemporary Germany*. London: Arnold, 2001.

Lewis, Derek, and John R. P. McKenzie, eds. *The New Germany: Social, Political and Cultural Challenges of Unification*. Exeter, UK: Exeter University Press, 1995.

Lutzeier, Peter Rolf, ed. *German Studies: Old and New Challenges. Undergraduate Programmes in the United Kingdom and the Republic of Ireland*. Vol. 1, *German Linguistic and Cultural Studies*. Bern: Peter Lang, 1998.

Oltermann, Philip. *Keeping up with the Germans. A History of Anglo-German Encounters*. London: Faber & Faber, 2012.

Parkes, Stuart. *Understanding Contemporary Germany*. London: Routledge, 1996.

Radice, Giles. *The New Germans*. London: Michael Joseph, 1995.

Schayan, Janet. *Facts about Germany*. Frankfurt/Main: Societäts-Verlag, 2010.

Webb, Adrian. *The Longman Companion to Germany since 1945*. London: Longman, 1998.

III. TOPICAL STUDIES

A. Berlin

Altenburger, Stefan et al. *Brachland Berlin*. Zurich: Conzett und Huber, 1991.

Back, Louis, ed. *z.B. Berlin: Zehn Jahre Transformation und Modernisierung*. Berlin: Senatsverwaltung für Stadtentwicklung/Edition Foyer, 2000.

Balfour, Alan. *Berlin: The Politics of Order 1737–1989*. New York: Rizzoli, 1990.

Becker, Kathrin, and Urs Stahel, eds. *Remake Berlin*. Göttingen: Steidl Verlag, 2000.

Becker-Cantarino, Barbara, ed. *Berlin in Focus: Cultural Transformation in Germany*. London: Praeger, 1996.

Berliner Festspiele und Architektenkammer Berlin, eds. *Berlin: Offene Stadt*. Vol. 1, *Die Stadt als Ausstellung*. 4th ed., 2001. Vol. 2, *Die Erneuerung seit 1989*, 1999. Berlin: Nicolai Verlag.

Bernt, Matthias, Britta Grell and Andrej Holm, eds. *The Berlin Reader: A Compendium on Urban Cahnge and Activism*. Bielefeld: Transcript, 2013.

Bienert, Michael. *Berlin: Wege durch den Text der Stadt*. Stuttgart: Klett-Cotta, 1999.

Borneman, John. *Belonging in the Two Berlins: Kin, State, Nation*. Cambridge, UK: Cambridge University Press, 1992.

Braun, Stuart. *City of Exiles. Berlin from the Outside In*. Berlin: Noctua Press, 2016.

Brendgens, Guido, Norbert König, and Franziska Eidner. *Berlin Architektur*. Berlin: Jovis, 2003.

Broadbent, Philip, and Sabine Hake. *Berlin, Divided City, 1945–1989*. London: Berghan, 2010.

Brockmann, Stephen, ed. *Writing and Reading Berlin*. Studies in 20th and 21st Century Literature, 28. Lincoln: University of Nebraska, 2004.

Bundesministerium für Verkehr, Bau- und Wohnungswesen, ed. *Demokratie als Bauherr: Die Bauten des Bundes in Berlin 1991–2000*. Bonn: Junius, 2000.

Clement, Hans-Jörg. *Szene Berlin*. Berlin: Bostelmann & Siebenhaar, 2003.

Cobbers, Arnt. *Architecture in Berlin: The 100 Most Important Buildings and Urban Settings*. Extended and updated ed. Berlin: Jaron Verlag, 2012. Previous editions published in 1999 and 2001.

Cochrane, Allan, and Adrian Passmore. "Building a National Capital in an Age of Globalization: The Case of Berlin." *Area* 33, no. 4 (2001): 341–52.

Cullen, Michael S. *The Reichstag: German Parliament between Monarchy and Federalism*. Berlin: Bebra Verlag, 1999.

Darnton, Robert. *The Berlin Journal, 1989–1990*. New York: W. W. Norton, 1993.

Dawson, Layla. *Berlin: Modern Architecture*. London: Carlton Books, 2002.

Deutscher Bundestag, ed. *Berlin-Bonn: Die Debatte. Alle Bundestagsreden vom 20. Juni 1991*. Cologne: Kiepenheuer & Witsch, 1991.

Elkins, T. H., with B. Hofmeister. *Berlin: The Spatial Structure of a Divided City*. London: Methuen, 1988.

Feversham, Polly. *Die Berliner Mauer heute: Denkmalwert und Umgang* [*The Berlin Wall Today: Cultural Significance and Conservation Issues*]. Berlin: Verlag für Bauwesen, 1999.

Förderverein Deutsches Architekturzentrum, ed. *Neue Architektur in Berlin*: *New Architecture in Berlin 1990–2000*. Berlin: Jovis, 2000.

Funder, Anna. *Stasiland: Stories from behind the Berlin Wall*. London: Granta Books, 2003.

Gerstenberger, Katharina. *Writing the New Berlin: The German Capital in Post-Wall Literature*. Rochester, NY: Camden House, 2008.

Glass, Derek, Dietmar Rösler, and John J. White, eds. *Berlin: Literary Images of a City/Berlin: Eine Großstadt im Spiegel der Literatur*. Publications of the Institute of Germanic Studies, vol. 42. Berlin: Erich Schmidt Verlag, 1989.

Goebel, Rolf J. "Berlin's Architectural Citations: Reconstruction, Simulation, and the Problem of Historical Authenticity." *PMLA (Publications of the Modern Languages Association of America)* 118, no. 5 (October 2003): 1268–89.

Grésillon, Boris. "Berlin, Cultural Metropolis: Changes in the Cultural Geography of Berlin since Reunification." *Ecumene* 6, no. 3 (1999): 284–94.

Grübel, Nils, and Stefan Rademacher, ed. *Religion in Berlin: Ein Handbuch*. Berlin: Weissensee Verlag, 2003.

Hassemer, Volker. *Wozu Berlin? Eine Streitschrift*. Berlin: Siebenhaar, 2010.

Haubrich, Rainer, Hans Wolfgang Hoffmann, and Philipp Meuser. *Berlin— The Architecture Guide*. Berlin: Braun, 2007.

Häußermann, Hartmut. *Berlin: Von der geteilten zur gespaltenen Stadt? Sozialräumlicher Wandel seit 1990*. Wiesbaden: Springer, 2000.

Haxthausen, Charles Werner, and Heidrun Suhr, eds. *Berlin: Culture and Metropolis*. Minneapolis: University of Minnesota Press, 1990.

Hertle, Hans-Hermann. *The Berlin Wall Story. Biography of a Monument*. Berlin: Links, 2011.

Hildebrandt, Rainer. *Es geschah an der Mauer: Eine Bilddokumentation des Sperrgürtels um Berlin (West), seine Entwicklung vom 13. August 1961 bis heute mit den wichtigsten Geschehnissen/It happened at the Berlin Wall*. Berlin: Verlaghaus am Checkpoint Charlie, 1982.

Huysen, Andreas. "After the War: Berlin as Palimpsest." *Harvard Design Magazine* 10 (2000): 1–5.

Huysen, Andreas. "The Voids of Berlin." *Critical Inquiry* 24 (Autumn 1998): 57–81.

Imhof, Michael, and Leon Krempel. *Berlin: New Architecture; A Guide to New Buildings from 1989 to Today*. 10th updated ed. Petersberg: Michael Imhof Verlag, 2012.

James-Chakraborty, Kathleen. *German Architecture for a Mass Audience*. London: Routledge, 2000.

Keating, Paul. "New Urban Domains: Potsdamer Platz." *Debatte* 9, no. 1 (2001): 78–84.

Kent, F. James. *The Free University of Berlin: A Political History.* Bloomington: Indiana University Press, 1988.

Kleger, Heinz, Andreas Fiedler, and Holger Kuhle, eds. *Vom Stadtforum zum Forum der Stadt: Entwicklung und Perspektiven des Stadtforums.* Amsterdam: G+B Verlag Fakultas, 1996.

Kramer, Jane, and Eike Geisel. *Eine Amerikanerin in Berlin: Ethnologische Spaziergänge.* Berlin: Edition Tiamat, 1993.

Krüger, Thomas Michael, ed. *Architekturstadtplan Berlin.* Berlin: Verlagshaus Braun, 2001.

Ladd, Brian. "Center and Periphery in the New Berlin: Architecture, Public Art, and the Search for Identity." *Performing Arts Journal* 65 (2000): 7–21.

Ladd, Brian. *The Ghosts of Berlin: Confronting German History in the Urban Landscape.* Chicago: University of Chicago Press, 1998.

Langgut, Gerd, ed. *Berlin: Vom Brennpunkt der Teilung zur Brücke der Einheit.* Cologne: Verlag Wissenschaft und Politik, 1990.

Large, David Clay. *Berlin: A Modern History.* London: Penguin, 2001.

Le Tissier, Tony. *Berlin: Then and Now.* London: After the Battle Magazine, 1992.

MacDonogh, Giles. *Berlin.* New York: St. Martin's Press, 1998.

MacLean, Rory. *Berlin: Imagine a City.* London: Weidenfeld & Nicolson, 2014.

Nachama, Andreas, and Julius H. Schoeps. *Jews in Berlin: A Comprehensive History of Jewish Life and Jewish Culture in the German Capital up to 2013.* Berlin: Berlinica, 2013.

Peters, Günter. *Kleine Berliner Baugeschichte: Von der Stadtgründung bis zur Bundeshauptstadt.* Berlin: Stapp Verlag, 1995.

Philips, Duane. *Berlin: A Guide to Recent Architecture.* London: B. T. Batsford, 2003.

Plewnia, Ulrike, Horst Mauter, László F. Földényi, et al. *Potsdamer Platz: A History in Text and Pictures.* Berlin: Nishen, 1995.

Pugh, Emily. *Architecture, Politics, and Identity in Divided Berlin.* Pittsburgh: University of Pittsburgh Press, 2014.

Rauch, Yamin von, and Jochen Visscher, eds. *Der Potsdamer Platz: Urbane Architektur für das neue Berlin.* Berlin: Jovis, 2000.

Read, Anthony, and David Fisher. *Berlin: The Biography of a City.* London: Hutchinson, 1994.

Rebiger, Bill. *Jewish Sites in Berlin.* Berlin: Jaron Verlag, 2000.

Rebiger, Bill. *Das jüdische Berlin: Kultur, Religion und Alltag gestern und heute.* Extended ed. Berlin: Jaron Verlag, 2010. First published in 2000.

Ribbe, Wolfgang, ed. *Geschichte Berlins*. 2 vols. Berlin: Berliner Wissenschaftsverlag, 2002.

Richie, Alexandra. *Faust's Metropolis: A History of Berlin*. London: HarperCollins, 1998.

Robin, Regine. *Berlin: Gedächtnis einer Stadt*. Berlin: Transit Buchverlag, 2002.

Roth, Andrew, and Michael Frajman. *The Goldapple Guide to Jewish Berlin*. Berlin: Goldapple, 1998.

Rudolph, Hermann. *Berlin—Wiedergeburt einer Stadt: Mauerfall, Ringen um die Hauptstadt, Aufstieg zur Metropole*. Cologne: Quadriga, 2014.

Ruther, Tobias. *Heroes: David Bowie and Berlin*. London: Reaktion Books, 2014.

Scheer, Thorsten, ed. *Stadt der Architektur: Architektur der Stadt/Architecture of the City*. Berlin: Nicolai, 2000.

Schneider, Peter. *Berlin Now. The Rise of the City and the Fall of the Wall*. London: Penguin, 2014.

Schoeps, Julius H. *Berlin: Geschichte einer Stadt*. Berlin: be.bra, 2012.

Schürer, Ernst, Manfred Keune, and Philip Jenkins, eds. *The Berlin Wall: Representations and Perspectives*. Bern: Peter Lang, 1996.

Schwenk, Herbert. *Lexikon der Berliner Stadtentwicklung*. Berlin: Haude & Spener, 2002.

Siebenhaar, Klaus, ed. *Kulturhandbuch Berlin: Geschichte & Gegenwart von A–Z*. 3rd ed. Berlin: Bostelmann & Siebenhaar Verlag, 2005.

Siedler, Wolf Jobst. *Phoenix im Sand: Glanz und Elend der Hauptstadt*. Berlin: Propyläen, 1998.

Smail, Deborah, and Corey Ross. "New Berlins and New Germanies: History, Myth and the German Capital in the 1920s and 1990s." In *Representing the German Nation: History and Identity in Twentieth Century Germany*, edited by Fulbrook and Swales, 63–76. Manchester, UK: Manchester University Press, 2000.

Spiess, Volker, ed. *Berliner Biographisches Lexikon*. 2nd ed. Berlin: Haude & Spenersche Verlagsbuchhandlung, 2003.

Stewart, Janet. "Das Kunsthaus Tacheles: The Berlin Architecture Debate of the 1990s in Micro Historical Context." In *Recasting German Identity: Culture, Politics, and Literature in the Berlin Republic*, edited by Stuart Taberner and Frank Finlay, 51–66. Rochester, NY: Camden House, 2002.

Stimman, Hans, ed. *Städtebau in Berlin: Planungsatlas 1652–2030*. Berlin: Verlagshaus Braun, 2004.

Stimman, Hans, and Annegret Burg. *Berlin Mitte: Die Entstehung einer urbanen Architektur*. Basel: Birkhäuser, 1995.

Stimman, Hans, and Martin Kieren. *Die Architektur des Neuen Berlin*. Berlin: Nicolai-Verlag, 2005.

Stimman, Hans, and Philipp Meuser, eds. *Vom Plan zum Bauwerk: Bauten der Berliner Innenstadt nach 2000.* Berlin: Verlagshaus Braun, 2002.

Stöver, Bernd. *Geschichte Berlins.* Munich: Beck, 2010.

Strom, Elizabeth A. *Building the New Berlin: The Politics of Urban Development in Germany's Capital City.* Lanham, MD: Lexington Books, 2001.

Süss, Werner, and Ralf Rytlewski, eds. *Berlin: Die Hauptstadt;. Vergangenheit und Zukunft einer europäischen Metropole.* Berlin: Nicolai, 1999.

Taylor, Ronald. *Berlin and Its Culture: A Historical Portrait.* New Haven, CT: Yale University Press, 1997.

Taylor, Ronald. *The Berlin Wall: 13 August 1961–9 November 1989.* London: Bloomsbury, 2009.

Till, Karen E. *The New Berlin: Memory, Politics, Place.* Minneapolis: University of Minnesota Press, 2005.

Till, Karen E. "Staging the Past: Landscape Designs, Cultural Identity and Erinnerungspolitik at Berlin's Neue Wache." *Ecumene* 6, no. 3 (1999): 251–83.

Tusa, Ann. *The Last Division: Berlin and the Wall.* London: Hodder & Stoughton, 1996.

Uffelen, Chris V. *Berlin Architecture & Design Guide.* Architecture and Design Series. London: TeNeues Publishing UK, 2003.

Ulrich, Horst, and Uwe Prell. *Berlin Handbuch: Das Lexikon der Bundeshauptstadt.* 2nd ed. Berlin: FAB Verlag, 1993.

Ward, Janet. *Post-Wall Berlin: Borders, Space and Identity.* London: Palgrace, 2011.

Weszkalnys, Gisa. *Berlin, Alexanderplatz: Transforming Place in a Unified Germany.* Oxford: Berghahn, 2013.

Whybrow, Nicolas. *Street Scenes: Brecht, Benjamin & Berlin.* Bristol: Intellect Books, 2005.

Wise, Michael Z. *Capital Dilemma: Germany's Search for a New Architecture of Democracy.* New York: Princeton Architectural Press, 1998.

Zitzlsperger, Ulrike. "Berlin since 1989: Politics and Culture in the Capital." In *Contemporary Germany,* edited by Derek Lewis, 251–80. London: Arnold, 2001.

Zitzlsperger, Ulrike. "Filling the Blanks: Berlin as a Public Showcase." In *Recasting German Identity, Culture, Politics, and Literature in the Berlin Republic,* edited by Stuart Taberner and Frank Finlay, 37–50. Rochester, NY: Camden House, 2002.

Zitzlsperger, Ulrike. "A Worm's Eye View and a Bird's Eye View: Culture and Politics in Berlin since 1989." In *Politics and Culture in Twentieth-Century Germany,* edited by William Niven and James Jordan, 185–99. Rochester, NY: Camden House, 2003.

Zitzlsperger, Ulrike. *ZeitGeschichten: Die Berliner Übergangsjahre; Zur Verortung der Stadt nach der Mauer.* Oxford: Lang, 2007.

B. Culture

Adler, Hans, and Jost Hermand. *Concepts of Culture*. German Life and Civilization, 28. Bern: Peter Lang, 1999.

Azaryahu, Maoz. "Replacing Memory: The Reorientation of Buchenwald." *Cultural Geographies* 10 (2003): 1–20.

Blume, Eugen, et al. *Klopfzeichen: Kunst und Kultur der 80er Jahre in Deutschland; Mauersprünge*. Leipzig: Faber & Faber, 2002.

Boa, Elizabeth, and Rachel Palfreyman. *Heimat—A German Dream: Regional Loyalties and National Identity in German Culture 1890–1990*. Oxford: Oxford University Press, 2000.

Briel, Holger. *German Culture and Society: The Essential Glossary*. London: Arnold, 2002.

Bürger, Peter, and Christa Bürger. *The Institutions of Art in Modern German Culture and Literature*. Lincoln: University of Nebraska Press, 1992.

Burns, Rob, ed. *German Cultural Studies: An Introduction*. Oxford: Oxford University Press, 1995.

Cooke, Paul. *Representing East Germany since Unification: From Colonization to Nostalgia*. Oxford: Berg, 2005.

Cooper, Duncan. *Immigration and German Identity in the Federal Republic of Germany from 1945 to 2006*. Zurich: Lit Verlag, 2012.

Denham, Scott D., et al. *A User's Guide to German Cultural Studies*. Ann Arbor: University of Michigan Press, 1997.

Eshel, Amir. "Aspects of the Present: Contemporary German Culture: An Introduction." *Germanic Review* 77, no. 4 (2002): 259–63.

Glaser, Hermann. *Deutsche Kultur: Ein historischer Überblick von 1945 bis zur Gegenwart*. 3rd extended ed. Bonn: Bundeszentrale für Politische Bildung, 2003.

Glaser, Hermann. *Kleine deutsche Kulturgeschichte von 1945 bis heute*. Frankfurt/Main: Fischer, 2007.

Glaser, Hermann. *Die Mauer fiel, die Mauer steht: Ein deutsches Lesebuch 1989–1999*. Munich: Deutscher Taschenbuch Verlag, 1999.

Hahn, Hans-Joachim. *German Thought and Culture from the Holy Roman Empire to the Present Day*. Manchester, UK: Manchester University Press, 1995.

Hoffmann, Hilmar, and Heinrich Klotz, eds. *Die Kultur unseres Jahrhunderts: Die Sechziger*. Vol. 5. Düsseldorf: ECON Verlag, 1987.

Hoffmann, Hilmar, and Heinrich Klotz, eds. *Die Kultur unseres Jahrhunderts, 1970–1990*. Vol. 6. Düsseldorf: ECON Verlag, 1990.

Koepnich, Lutz P. "Negotiating Popular Culture: Wenders, Handke and the Topographies of Cultural Studies." *German Quarterly* 69, no. 4 (1996): 381–400.

Kolinsky, Eva, and Wilfred van der Will, eds. *The Cambridge Companion to Modern German Culture*. Cambridge, UK: Cambridge University Press, 1998.

Koshar, Rudy. *German Travel Cultures*. Oxford: Berg, 2000.

Niven, William, and James Jordan, eds. *Politics and Culture in Twentieth-Century Germany*. Studies in German Literature, Linguistics and Culture. Rochester, NY: Camden House, 2003.

Pape, Walter, ed. *1870/71–1989/90: German Unifications and the Change of Literary Discourse*. Berlin: Walter de Gruyter, 1993.

Parker, Stephen. "The Politics of Culture in German Unification: The Case of the Berlin Academy of Arts." In *1949/1989: Cultural Perspectives on Division and Unity in East and West*, edited by Clare Flanagan and Stuart Taberner, 101–12. Amsterdam: Rodopi, 2000.

Phipps, Alison, ed. *Contemporary German Cultural Studies*. London: Hodder Arnold, 2002.

Poiger, Uta G. *Germany Jazz, Rock, and Rebels: Cold War Politics and American Culture in a Divided Germany*. Berkeley: University of California Press, 2000.

Pommerin, Reiner, ed. *Culture in the Federal Republic of Germany 1945–1995*. Oxford: Berg, 1996.

Richter, Jana, ed. *The Tourist City Berlin—Tourism & Architecture*. Salenstein: Braun, 2010.

Riordan, Colin, ed. *Green Thought in German Culture: Historical and Contemporary Perspectives*. Cardiff: University of Wales Press, 1997.

Rösgen, Petra, and Christine Keutgen, eds. *Images of Germany: United Germany in Cartoons Abroad*. Stiftung Haus der Geschichte der Bundesrepublik Deutschland. Bielefeld: Kerber Verlag, 2003.

Sandford, John, ed. *The Encyclopedia of Contemporary German Culture*. London: Routledge, 1999.

Schlant, Ernestine. *The Language of Silence: West German Literature and the Holocaust*. London: Routledge, 1999.

Schmieding, Leonard. *Das ist unsere Party: HipHop in der DDR*. Stuttgart: Franz Steiner Verlag, 2014.

Shen, Qinna, and Martin Rosenstock, eds. *Beyond Alterity: German Encounters with Modern East Asia*. New York: Berghahn Books, 2014.

Taberner, Stuart, and Frank Finlay, eds. *Recasting German Identity: Culture, Politics and Literature in the Berlin Republic*. Rochester, NY: Camden House, 2002.

Wittmann, Reinhard. *Geschichte des deutschen Buchhandels im Überblick*. München: Beck, 1994.

Zimmermann, Olaf, ed. *Wer ist wer in der Kulturpolitik: Handbuch des Deutschen Kulturrates*. Bonn: Deutscher Kulturrat e.V., 1999.

1. Art and Architecture (FRG and Former GDR)

Almut, Otto, ed. *Das XX. Jahrhundert: Ein Jahrhundert Kunst in Deutschland.* Berlin: Nicolai, 1999.

Architektenkammer Berlin, ed. *Architektur Berlin: Baukultur in und aus der Hauptstadt.* Vols. 1–4. Salenstein: Braun 2015.

Borer, Alain, and Lothar Schirmer. *The Essential Joseph Beuys.* London: Thames and Hudson, 1996.

Feist, Günter, Eckhart Gillen, and Beatrice Vierneisel, eds. *Kunstdokumentation SBZ/DDR 1945–1990: Aufsätze Berichte Materialien.* Cologne: DuMont, 1996.

Flacke, Monika, ed. *Auftragskunst der DDR 1949–1990.* Munich: Klinkhardt und Biermann, 1995.

Gassner, Hubertus, and Eckhart Gillen. *Kultur und Kunst in der DDR seit 1970.* Lahn-Giessen: Anabas Verlag, 1977.

Gillen, Eckhart. *German Art: From Beckmann to Richter.* Cologne: DuMont, 2003.

Gillen, Eckhart, and Rainer Haarmann, eds. *Kunst in der DDR.* Cologne: Kiepenheuer & Witsch, 1990.

Hicks, Alistair, Mary Findlay, and Friedhelm Hütte, eds. *Art Works: British and German Contemporary Art 1960–2000.* London: Merrell, 2001.

Homberg, Cornelia, et al. *German Art Now.* London: Merrell, 2003.

Joachmides, Christos M., Norman Rosenthal, and Wieland Schmied, eds. *German Art in the 20th Century.* London: Weidenfeld & Nicolson, 1985.

Kaiser, Paul, and Karl-Siegbert Rehberg. *Enge und Vielfalt: Auftragskunst und Kunstförderung in der DDR.* Hamburg: Junius Verlag, 1999.

Kelly, Elaine, and Amy Wlodarski, eds. *Art Outside the Lines: New Perspectives on GDR Art Culture.* Amsterdam: Rodopi, 2011.

Kierock, Thomas. *Mauergeschichten.* Salenstein: Braun, 2009.

Klotz, Heinrich, ed. *Contemporary Art: Collection of the ZKM—Centre for Art and Media, Karlsruhe.* Munich/New York: Prestel, 1997.

Klotz, Heinrich, ed. *Kunst im 20. Jahrhundert—Moderne, Postmoderne, Zweite Moderne.* Munich: Beck, 1994.

Maclean, Rory. *Wunderkind: Portraits of 50 Contemporary Artists.* London: Wonder2wonder Press, 2016.

Muschter, Gabriele, and Rüdiger Thomas, eds. *Jenseits der Staatskultur: Traditionen autonomer Kunst in der DDR.* Munich/Vienna: Hanser Verlag, 1992.

Nationalgallerie, Staatliche Museen, Preussischer Kulturbesitz Berlin, ed. *1945–1985: Kunst in der Bundesrepublik Deutschland.* Exhibition Catalog. Berlin, 1985.

Ray, Gene. *Joseph Beuys: At the End of the Twentieth Century—Mapping the Legacy.* San Francisco: Fraenkel Gallery, 2002.

Rosenfeld, Gavriel D., and Paul B. Jaskot, eds. *Beyond Berlin: Twelve German Cities Confront the Nazi Past*. Ann Arbor: University of Michigan Press, 2015.

Schmal, Peter Cachola, Yorck Förster, and Christina Gräwe, eds. *Deutsches Architektur Jahrbuch 2015/16/German Architecture Annual 2015/16*. New York: Prestel, 2015.

Stachelhaus, Heiner. *Joseph Beuys*. Berlin: List, 2005. 1st U.S. ed., New York: Abbeville Press, 1991.

Sünner, Rüdiger. *Zeige Deine Wunde: Kunst und Spiritualität bei Joseph Beuys—Eine Spurensuche*. Zurich: Europa, 2015.

Ursprung, Philip. *Die Kunst der Gegenwart: 1960 bis heute*. Munich: C.H. Beck, 2013.

Young, James E. *At Memory's Edge: After-Images of the Holocaust in Contemporary Art and Architecture*. New Haven, CT: Yale University Press, 2000.

2. Cinema and Photography

Allan, Seán, and John Sandford, eds. *DEFA: East German Cinema, 1946–1992*. New York: Berghahn, 1999.

Bergfelder, Tim, Erica Carter, and Deniz Göktürk, eds. *The German Cinema Book*. London: BFI Publishing, 2002.

Berghahn, Daniela. *Hollywood behind the Wall: The Cinema of East Germany*. Manchester, UK: Manchester University Press, 2005.

Blaney, Martin. "The Relationship between the Film Industry and Television in the Federal Republic of Germany from 1950 to 1985." *German History* 9, no. 1 (1991): 69–70.

Corrigan, Timothy. *New German Film: The Displaced Image*. Austin: University of Texas Press, 1983.

Domröse, Ulrich, and Ludger Derenthal. *Positionen künstlerischer Photographie in Deutschland seit 1945*. Cologne: DuMont, 1997.

Elsaesser, Thomas. *German Cinema—Terror and Trauma: Cultural Memory since 1945*. London: Routledge, 2013.

Elsaesser, Thomas. *New German Cinema: A History*. New Brunswick, NJ: Rutgers University Press, 1994. First published in 1989.

Elsaesser, Thomas, and Michael Wedel, eds. *The BFI Companion to German Cinema*. London: The British Film Institute, 1999.

Eskildsen, Ute, and Esther Ruelfs. *Zeitgenössische Deutsche Fotografie*. Göttingen: Steidl, 2003.

Feinstein, Joshua. *The Triumph of the Ordinary: Depiction of Daily Life in the East German Cinema 1949–1989*. Chapel Hill: The University of North Carolina Press, 2002.

"Focus: Literature on Film." Special issue, *German Quarterly* 64, no. 1 (1991).

Franklin, James. *New German Cinema: From Oberhausen to Hamburg*. Boston: Twayne, 1983.

Ginsberg, Terry, and Kirsten Thompson, eds. *Perspectives on German Cinema*. New York: G. K. Hall, 1996.

Hake, Sabine. *German National Cinema*. London: Routledge, 2001.

Halle, Rendall, and Margaret McCarthy, eds. *Light Motives: German Popular Cinema in Perspective*. Contemporary Film and Television Series. Detroit: Wayne State University Press, 2003.

Helt, Richard C., and Marie E. Helt. *West German Cinema, 1985–1990: A Reference Handbook*. Metuchen, NJ: Scarecrow Press, 1992.

Helt, Richard C., and Marie E. Helt. *West German Cinema since 1945: A Reference Handbook*. Metuchen, NJ: Scarecrow Press, 1987.

Hughes, Helen, and Martin Brady. "German Film after the Wende." In *The New Germany: Social, Political and Cultural Challenges of Unification*, edited by Derek Lewis and John R. P. McKenzie, 276–96. Exeter: University of Exeter Press, 1995.

Jacobsen, Wolfgang, et al., in cooperation with the Berlin Film Museum/Stiftung Deutsche Kinemathek Berlin. *Geschichte des Deutschen Films*. 2nd ed. Stuttgart: Metzler, 2004. First published in 1993.

Knight, Julia. *Women and the New German Cinema*. London: Verso, 1992.

Kolker, Robert Philipp, and Peter Beicken. *The Films of Wim Wenders: Cinema as Vision and Desire*. Cambridge, UK: Cambridge University Press, 1993.

König, Ingelore, Dieter Wiedemann, and Lothar Wolf, eds. *Zwischen Bluejeans und Blauhemden: Jugendfilm in Ost und West*. Berlin: Henschel Verlag, 1995.

Murphy, Richard A., ed. "German Film." Special issue, *The Germanic Review* 66, no. 1 (1991).

Pakier, Malgorzata. *The Construction of European Holocaust Memory: German and Polish Cinema after 1989*. Oxford: Lang, 2013.

Petzke, Ingo. *Der deutsche Experimentalfilm der 60er und 70er Jahre/The German Experimental Film of the Sixties and Seventies*. Munich: Goethe Institut, 1990.

Phillips, Klaus, ed. *New German Filmmakers: From Oberhausen through the 1970s*. New York: Frederick Ungar Publishing, 1984.

Rentschler, Eric. *West German Film in the Course of Time: Reflections on the Twenty Years since Oberhausen*. Bedford Hills, NY: Redgrave, 1984.

Rentschler, Eric, ed. *West German Filmmakers on Film: Visions and Voices*. Modern German Voices. New York: Holmes & Meier Publishing, 1989.

Sandford, John. *The New German Film*. London: Wolff, 1980.

Schenk, Ralf. *Das zweite Leben der Filmstadt Babelsberg: DEFA Spielfilme 1946–1992*. Berlin: Henschel, 1994.

Wagner, Brigitta B. *DEFA after East Germany*. London: Camden House, 2014.

3. Literature

Arjouni, Jakob. *Magic Hoffmann*. Zürich: Diogenes Verlag, 1996.

Arnold, Heinz Ludwig, ed. *DDR-Literatur der neunziger Jahre*. Munich: edition text + kritik, 2000.

Beck, Wolfgang, and Manfred Brauneck, eds. *Autorenlexikon deutschsprachiger Literatur des 20. Jahrhunderts*. Reinbek bei Hamburg: Rowohlt, 1995.

Beitter, Ursula. *Schreiben im heutigen Deutschland: Die Literarische Szene nach der Wende*. Vol. 1. Bern: Peter Lang, 1997.

Beitter, Ursula. *Schreiben im heutigen Deutschland: Fragen an die Vergangenheit*. Vol. 2. Bern: Peter Lang, 1998.

Bullivant, Keith, ed. *Beyond 1989: Re-Reading German Literary History since 1945*. New York: Berghahn, 1997.

Cooke, Paul, and Andrew Plowman, eds. *German Writers and the Politics of Culture: Dealing with the Stasi*. Houndmills, Basingstoke, UK: Palgrave Macmillan, 2003.

Costabile-Heming, Carol Anne, Rachel J. Halverson, and Kristie A. Foell. *Berlin—The Symphony Continues: Orchestrating Architectural, Social and Artistic Change in Germany's New Capital*. Berlin: Walter de Gruyter, 2004.

Drews, Jörg, et al. *Kultur und Macht: Deutsche Literatur 1949–1989*. Bielefeld: Aisthesis Verlag, 1992.

Durrani, Osman, Colin Good, and Kevin Hilliard, eds. *The New Germany: Literature and Society after Unification*. Sheffield, UK: Sheffield Academic Press, 1995.

Emmerich, Wolfgang. *Kleine Literaturgeschichte der DDR*. New ed. Berlin: Aufbau Verlag, 2000. First published in 1981.

Emmerich, Wolfgang, et al., eds. *Deutsche Literaturgeschichte: Von den Anfängen bis zur Gegenwart*. Extended ed. Stuttgart: Metzler, 2013.

Eskin, Michael. "German Poetry after the Wall." *The Germanic Review* 77, no. 1 (2002).

Frenzel, H. A., and E. Frenzel. *Daten deutscher Dichtung: Chronologischer Abriss der deutschen Literaturgeschichte*. 2 vols. Munich: Deutscher Taschenbuch Verlag, 2004.

Goodbody, Axel, ed. "Geist und Macht: Writers and the State in the GDR." *German Monitor* 29 (1992).

Hallberg, Robert von, ed. *Literary Intellectuals and the Dissolution of the State: Professionalism and Conformity in the GDR*. Translated by Kenneth J. Northcott. Chicago: University of Chicago Press, 1996.

Harnisch, Antje, Anne Marie Stokes, and Friedemann Weidauer, eds. and trans. *Fringe Voices: An Anthology of Minority Writing in the Federal Republic of Germany*. Oxford: Berg, 1998.

Hermann, Elisabeth, Carrie Smith-Prei and Stuart Taberner, eds. *Transnationalism in Contemporary German Language Literature*. Rochester, NY: Camden, 2015.

Kane, Martin. *Legacies and Identity: East and West German Literary Responses to Unification*. Bern: Peter Lang, 2002.

Kane, Martin, ed. *Socialism and the Literary Imagination: Essays on East German Writers*. Oxford: Berg, 1991.

Leidig, Dorothée, and Jürgen Bacia, eds. *Handbuch deutschsprachiger Literaturzeitschriften*. Matern: Autorenverlag, 2002.

Liesegang, Torsten. "'New German Pop Literature': Difference, Identity, and the Redefinition of Pop Literature after Postmodernism." *Seminar: A Journal of Germanic Studies* 40, no. 3 (Septemebr 2004): 262–76.

Marven, Lyn, and Stuart Taberner, eds. *Emerging German-Language Novelists of the Twenty-First Century*. Rochester, NY: Camden House, 2011.

Mayer, Hans. *Die unerwünschte Literatur: Deutsche Schriftsteller und Bücher 1968–1985*. Frankfurt/Main: Suhrkamp, 1996.

Metzler Autorenlexikon. *Deutschsprachige Dichter und Schriftsteller vom Mittelalter bis zur Gegenwart*. 4th ed. Stuttgart: Metzler, 2010.

Monteath, Peter. "Kulturstreit, Streitkultur: German Literature since the Wall." *German Monitor*, no. 38 (1996).

Moser, Dietz-Rüdiger, ed. *Neues Handbuch der deutschsprachigen Gegenwartsliteratur seit 1945*. Munich: Deutscher Taschenbuch Verlag, 1993.

Oberhauser, Fred, and Nicole Henneberg. *Literarischer Führer Berlin*. Frankfurt/Main: Insel Verlag, 2003.

Owen, Ruth. "The Ex-GDR Poet and the People." *German Life and Letters* 52, no. 4 (1999): 490–505.

Palfreyman, Rachel. *Edgar Reitz's Heimat: Histories, Traditions, Fictions*. Bern: Peter Lang, 2000.

Pape, Walter, ed. *1870/71–1989/90: German Unification and the Change of Literary Discourse*. Berlin: Walter de Gruyter, 1993.

Plowman, Andrew. "Westalgie? Nostalgia for the 'Old' Federal Republic in Recent German Prose." *Seminar: A Journal of Germanic Studies* 40, no. 3 (September 2004): 249–61.

Preace, Julian, Arthur Williams, and Stuart Parkes. *German-Language Literature Today*. Oxford: Lang, 2000.

Röhnert, Jan, ed. *Die Metaphorik der Autobahn: Literatur, Kunst, Film und Architektur nach 1945*. Vienna: Böhlau, 2014.

Sagarra, Eda, and Peter Skrine. *A Companion to German Literature*. Oxford: Blackwell, 1993.

Schlant, Ernestine. *The Language of Silence: West German Literature and the Holocaust*. London: Routledge, 1999.

Schmidt-Bergmann, Hansgeorg, and Torsten Liesegang, eds. *Liter@tur: Computer—Literatur—Internet*. Bielefeld: Aisthesis, 2001.

Schmitz, Helmut, ed. *German Culture and the Uncomfortable Past: Representations of National Socialism in Contemporary Germanic Literature*. Aldershot, UK: Ashgate, 2001.

Taberner, Stuart. *Distorted Reflections: The Public and Private Uses of the Author in the Work of Uwe Johnson, Günther Grass and Martin Walser, 1965–1975*. Amsterdam: Rodopi, 1998.

Taberner, Stuart. *German Literature of the 1990s and Beyond: Normalization and the Berlin Republic*. Rochester, NY: Camden House, 2005.

Taberner, Stuart, ed. *Contemporary German Fiction Writing in the Berlin Republic*. Cambridge, UK: Cambridge University Press, 2007.

Watanabe-O'Kelly, Helen, ed. *The Cambridge History of German Literature*. Cambridge, UK: Cambridge University Press, 1997.

Wellbery, David E., et al. *A New History of German Literature*. Cambridge, MA: Harvard University Press, 2004.

Williams, Arthur, Stuart Parkes, and Julian Preece, eds. *German-Language Literature Today: International and Popular?* Bern: Peter Lang, 2000.

Zipser, Richard A. "Literary Censorship in the German-Speaking Countries: Part 2." Special issue, *The Germanic Review* 65, no. 3 (1990).

4. Theater

Daiber, H. *Deutsches Theater seit 1945*. Stuttgart: Reclam, 1976.

Englhart, Andreas. *Das Theater der Gegenwart*. Munich: Beck, 2013.

Gronemeyer, Andrea, Julia Dina Heße, and Gert Taube, eds. *Kinder- und Jugendtheater in Deutschland: Pespektiven einer Theatersparte*. Berlin: Alexander Verlag, 2009.

Haas, Birgit. *Modern German Political Drama*. Rochester, NY: Camden House, 2003.

Innes, C. *Modern German Drama: A Study in Form*. Cambridge, UK: Cambridge University Press, 1979.

Patterson, M. "The German Theatre." In *The New Germany*, edited by Lewis and McKenzie, 259–75. Exeter, UK: University of Exeter Press, 1995.

Schneider, Wolfgang. *Theater und Migration: Herausforderung für Kulturpolitik und Theaterpraxis*. Bielefeld: Transcript, 2011.

Sting, Wolfgang, Norma Köhler, et al., eds. *Irritation und Vermittlung: Theater in einer interkulturellen und multireligiösen Gesellschaft.* Münster: Lit Verlag, 2010.

Theaterverlag, ed. *Theater heute—Das Jahrbuch 2015.* Berlin: Theaterverlag, 2015.

C. Economy and Business

Allan, Matthew M. C. *The Varieties of Capitalism Paradigm. Explaining Germany's Comparative Advantage?* Basingstoke, UK: Palgrave, 2006.

Anderson, Jeffrey J. *The Territorial Imperative: Pluralism, Corporatism, and Economic Crisis.* Cambridge, UK: Cambridge University Press, 1992.

Annesley, Claire. *Postindustrial Germany: Services, Technological Transformation, and Knowledge in Unified Germany.* Manchester, UK: Manchester University Press, 2004.

Beck, Stefan, Frank Klobes, and Christoph Scherrer, eds. *Surviving Globalization? Perspectives for the German Economic Model.* Dordrecht: Springer, 2005.

Bundesanstalt für Geowissenschaften und Rohstoffe, eds. *Reserven, Ressourcen und Verfügbarkeit von Energierohstoffen 1998.* Stuttgart: E. Schweizerbart, 1998.

Bundesrepublik Deutschland: Rohstoffsituation 2001. Stuttgart: E. Schweizerbart, 2004.

Culpepper, Pepper D., and David Finegold, eds. *The German Skills Machine: Sustaining Comparative Advantage in a Global Economy.* New York: Berghahn, 1999.

Dininio, Phyllis. *The Political Economy of East German Privatisation.* Westport, CT: Praeger, 1999.

Döring, Thomas. "German Public Banks under the Pressure of the EU Subsidy Proceedings." *Intereconomics* 38, no. 2 (2003): 94–101.

Duckenfield, Mark E. *Business and the Euro: Business Groups and the Politics of EMU in Germany and the United Kingdom.* London: Macmillan, 2006.

Dyker, D. A., ed. *The National Economies of Europe.* London: Longman, 1992.

Dyson, Kenneth, ed. *The Politics of German Regulation.* Aldershot, UK: Dartmouth, 1992.

Engels, Wolfram, and Hans Pohl, eds. *German Yearbook on Business History, 1988.* Berlin: Springer Verlag, 1989.

Frowen, Stephen, and Jens Hölscher, eds. *The German Currency Union of 1990: A Critical Assessment.* London: Macmillan, 1997.

Funk, Lothar, ed. *The Economics and the Politics of the Third Way: Essays in Honour of Eric Owen Smith*. Münster: LIT Verlag, 1999.

Ghaussy, A. Ghanie, ed. *The Economics of German Unification*. London: Routledge 1993.

Graf, William D., ed. *The Internationalisation of the German Political Economy: Evolution of a Hegemonic Project*. New York: St. Martin's Press/ Basingstoke, UK: Macmillan, 1992.

Harding, Rebecca, and William E. Paterson. *The Future of the German Economy: An End to the Miracle?* Manchester, UK: Manchester University Press, 2000.

Heinrich, R. P. *Complementarities in Corporate Governance*. Berlin: Springer, 2002.

Hitchens, D. M., K. Wagner, and J. E. Birnie. *East German Productivity and the Transition to the Market Economy*. Aldershot, UK: Avebury Publishing, 1993.

Hummel, Detlev. *Innovationsfinanzierung für KMU: Besonderheiten und Chancen in den östlichen Bundesländern; Zusammenfassung zum Forschungsprojekt 2009–2012*. Potsdam: Universitätsverlag Potsdam, 2013.

Jessop, Bob et al., eds. *The Politics of Flexibility: Restructuring State and Industry in Britain, Germany and Scandinavia*. Aldershot, UK: Edward Elgar, 1991.

Kissling, Elise. *Germany's Top 500: A Handbook of Germany's Largest Corporations*. Frankfurt/Main: Frankfurter Allgemeine Zeitung, Institut für Management, Markt- und Medieninformationen, 2001.

Kitschelt, Herbert, and Wolfgang Streeck, eds. *Germany: Beyond the Stable State*. London: Frank Cass, 2004.

Knoke, David, Franz Urban Pappi, Jeffrey Broadbent, and Yutaka Tsujinaka, eds. *Comparing Policy Networks: Labor Politics in the U.S., Germany and Japan*. Cambridge, UK: Cambridge University Press, 1996.

Lange, T., and J. R. Shackleton, eds. *The Political Economy of German Unification*. New York: Berghahn, 1998.

Leaman, Jeremy. *The Political Economy of West Germany, 1945–1985*. London: Macmillan, 1988.

Minnesota Department of Trade and Economic Development. *Doing Business in the Unified Germany: Pocket Supplement to Doing Business in the European Community*. Minnesota: Faegre & Benson, 1991.

Ptak, Ralf. *Vom Ordoliberalismus zur Sozialen Marktwirtschaft: Stationen des Neoliberalismus in Deutschland*. Opladen: Leske + Budrich, 2004.

Schmidt, Hartmut, et al. *Corporate Governance in Germany*. Baden-Baden: Nomos, 1997.

Smith, Eric Owen. *The German Economy*. London: Routledge, 1994.

Stephan, Johannes. *Economic Transition in Hungary and East Germany: Graduation and Shock Therapy in Catch-up Development*. Basingstoke, UK: Macmillan, 1999.

1. Banks and Finance

Deeg, Richard. "The State, Banks, and Economic Governance in Germany." *German Politics* 2, no. 2 (August 1993): 149–76.

Deutsche Bundesbank. *Monthly Reports*. The reports are published in English by the German Federal Bank on the basis of German texts and are available online at www.bundesbank.de.

Edwards, J. S. S., and K. Fischer. *Banks, Finance and Investments in Germany*. Cambridge, UK: Cambridge University Press, 1994.

"Europe and Its Currency. A Very Short History of the Crisis." Special report, *The Economist*, 12 November 2011.

Frowen, Stephen F., and Francis P. McHugh, eds. *Financial Decision-Making and Moral Responsibility*. Basingstoke, UK: Macmillan, 1995.

Gall, Lothar, et al. *The Deutsche Bank 1870–1995*. London: Weidenfeld & Nicholson, 1995.

Hall, Peter A. "Anatomy of the Euro Crisis." *Harvard Magazine*, July–August 2013, 24–27.

Kennedy, Ellen. *The Bundesbank: Germany's Central Bank in the International Monetary System*. London: Pinter/Royal Institute of International Affairs, 1991.

Leaman, Jeremy. *The Bundesbank Myth: Towards a Critique of Central Bank Independence*. Basingstoke: Palgrave Macmillan, 2001.

Marsh, David. *The Bundesbank: The Bank That Rules Europe*. London: Heinemann, 1992.

Marsh, David. *The Most Powerful Bank: Inside Germany's Bundesbank*. New York: Times Books, 1993.

Moser, Stefan, Nicola Pesaresi, and Karl Soukup. "State Guarantees to German Public Banks: A New Step in the Enforcement of State Aid Discipline to Financial Services in the Community." *Competition Policy Newsletter*, no. 2 (2002). European Union Commission. www.ec.europa.eu/competition/publications/cpn/cpn_2002_2.html.

Scheller, Hanspeter K. *The European Central Bank: History, Role and Functions*. Frankfurt/Main: European Central Bank, 2004.

Schneider, Hannes, Hans-Jürgen Hellwig, and David J. Kingsman. *The German Banking System*. Frankfurt/Main: Knapp Verlag, 1997.

Schuster, Leo. *Banking Cultures of the World*. Frankfurt/Main: Knapp Verlag, 1996.

2. Business

Collier, Ian. *Live and Work in Germany*. Oxford: Vacation Work, 1998.

Deutsch-Amerikanische Geschäftsbeziehungen/German American Business Contacts—1996. 8th ed. Darmstadt: Verlag Hoppenstedt, 1995.

Doing Business in Germany. 8th ed. London: Price Waterhouse, 1997

Eberwein, W., and J. Tholen. *Euro-manager or Splendid Isolation? International Management, An Anglo-German Comparison*. Berlin: Walter de Gruyter, 1993.

German American Chamber of Commerce. *Subsidiaries of German Firms in the U.S. 1999/2000/ Tochtergesellschaften deutscher Unternehmen in den USA 1999/2000*. New York: German American Chambers of Commerce (GACC).

The German American Trade Magazine. Official publication of the German American Chambers of Commerce in the United States. 6 issues per year.

Hart, J. A. *U.S. Business and Today's Germany: A Guide for Corporate Executives and Attorneys*. Westport, CT: Quorum Books, 1995.

Hill, Richard. *Euromanagers and Martians: The Business Culture of Europe's Trading Nations*. Brussels: Europublications, 1994.

Kenna, P., and S. Lacy. *Business Germany: A Practical Guide to Understanding German Business Culture*. Lincolnwood, IL: Passport Books, 1994.

Lord, Richard. *Culture Shock! Succeed in Business: The Essential Guide for Business and Investment; Germany*. Portland: Times Editions/Graphic Arts Center Publishing Company, 1998.

Randlesome, C. *The Business Culture in Germany: A Portrait of a Power House*. Oxford: Butterworth-Heinemann, 1994.

Reuvid, Jonathan, and Roderick Millar, eds. *Doing Business in Germany*. 2nd ed. In Association with German-British Chamber of Industry and Commerce, Pricewaterhouse Coopers and Eversheds, Business Lawyers in Europe. London: Kogan Page, 1999. Reprinted in 2000.

Schmidt, Patrick L. *Understanding American and German Business Cultures*. 2nd ed. Montreal: Meridian World Press, 2001.

D. Education

Anweiler, Oskar, et al., eds. *Bildungspolitik in Deutschland 1945–1990: Ein historisch vergleichender Quellenband*. Opladen: Leske + Budrich, 1992.

Ash, Mitchell G., ed. *German Universities Past and Future: Crisis or Renewal?* New York: Berghahn, 1997.

Bellenberg, Gabriele, and Matthias Forell. *Schulformwechsel in Deutschland: Durchlässigkeit und Selektion in den 16 Schulsystemen der Bundesländer innerhalb der Sekundarstufe I.* Gütersloh: Bertelsmann-Stiftung, 2012.

Berg, Christa, et al. *Handbuch der deutschen Bildungsgeschichte. Band 6, 1945 bis zur Gegenwart.* Munich: C. H. Beck, 1998.

Döbert, Hans, Hans-Werner Fuchs, and Horst Weishaupt, eds. *Transformation in der ostdeutschen Bildungslandschaft: Eine Forschungsbilanz.* Opladen: Leske + Budrich, 2002.

Führ, Christoph, and Iván Tapia. *The German Education System since 1945/ Deutsches Bildungswesen seit 1945.* Bonn: Inter Nationes, 1997.

Hahn, Hans-Joachim. *Education and Society in Germany.* Oxford: Berg, 1998.

Herrmann, Dieter, and Christian Spath. *Forschungshandbuch 2006: Förderprogramme und Förderinstitutionen für Wissenschaft und Forschung.* 9th ed. Lampertheim: Alpha Informations GmbH, 2005.

Muller, Steven, ed. *Universities in the Twenty-First Century.* New York: Berghahn, 1997.

Neather, E. "Education in the New Germany." In *The New Germany*, edited by Lewis and McKenzie, 148–72. Exeter: Exeter University Press, 1995.

Onestine, Cesare. *Federalism and Länder Autonomy: The Higher Education Policy Network in the Federal Republic of Germany.* New York: Routledge and Falmer, 2002.

Pritchard, Rosalind M. O. *The End of Elitism? The Democratisation of the West German University System.* New York: Berg, 1990.

Pritchard, Rosalind M. O. *Reconstructing Education.* New York: Berghahn, 1999.

E. Environment

Blackbourn, David. *The Conquest of Nature: Water, the Landscape and the Making of Modern Germany.* London: Jonathan Cape, 2006.

Blühdorn, Ingolfur, Frank Krause, and Thomas Scharfe, eds. *The Green Agenda: Environmental Politics and Policy in Germany.* Keele: Keele University Press, 1995.

Federal Ministry of the Environment, Nature Conservation, and Nuclear Safety (BMU). www.bmu.de.

Goodbody, Axel, ed. *Umwelt-Lesebuch: Green Issues in Contemporary German Writing.* Manchester, UK: Manchester University Press, 1997.

Holl, Otmar, ed. *Environmental Cooperation in Europe.* Boulder, CO/Oxford: Westview Press, 1994.

Rucht, Dieter, and Jochen Roose. "Neither Decline Nor Sclerosis: The Organisational Structure of the German Environmental Movement." *West European Politics* 24, no. 4 (2001): 55–81.

Schreurs, Miranda A. *Environmental Politics in Japan, Germany and the United States.* Cambridge, UK: Cambridge University Press, 2002.

Speakman, Fleur, and Colin Speakman. *The Green Guide to Germany.* London: Green Print, 1992.

Tickle, Andrew, and Ian Welsh, eds. *Environment and Society in Eastern Europe.* Foreword by Václav Havel. Harlow, UK: Addison Wesley Longman, 1998.

Weale, Albert. "Vorsprung durch Technik: The Politics of German Environmental Deregulation." In *The Politics of German Regulation,* edited by Kenneth Dyson. Aldershot: Dartmouth & The Association for the Study of German Politics, 1992.

Wurzel, Rüdiger K. W. *Environmental Policy-Making in Britain, Germany and the European Union: The Europeanization of Air and Water Pollution Control.* Manchester, UK: Manchester University Press, 2002.

F. Geography

Eckart, Karl, ed. *Deutschland.* Gotha/Stuttgart: Klett-Perthes-Gotha, 2001.

Greer, Alan. *Agricultural Policy in Europe.* Manchester, UK: Manchester University Press, 2004.

Jones, Alun. *The New Germany—A Human Geography.* Chichester, UK: Eiley, 1994.

Lewis, Derek. "Geography and Regions." In *Contemporary Germany,* edited by Derek Lewis, 23–59. London: Arnold, 2001.

Rail International (International Union of Railways): http://www.uic.asso.fr/.

G. Labor and Employment

Berger, S., and D. Broughton, eds. *The Force of Labor: The Western European Labor Movement and the Working Class in the Twentieth Century.* Oxford: Berg, 1995.

Fichter, Michael. "A House Divided: German Unification and Organised Labor." *German Politics* 2, no. 1 (April 1993): 21–39.

Funk, Lothar, and Simon Green, eds. *New Aspects of Labour Policy.* Berlin: Verlag für Wissenschaft und Forschung, 2002.

Gernandt, Johannes, and Friedhelm Pfeiffer. *Wage Convergence and Inequality after Unification: (East) Germany in Transition.* Mannheim: ZEW, Zentrum für Europäische Wirtschaftsforschung, 2008.

Herbert, Ulrich. *A History of Foreign Labor in Germany 1880–1980*. Translated by William Templer. Ann Arbor: University of Michigan Press, 1990.

Jahn, Detlef. *New Politics in Trade Unions: Applying Organization Theory to the Ecological Discourse on Nuclear Energy in Sweden and Germany*. Aldershot, UK: Dartmouth, 1993.

Markovits, Andrei S. *The Politics of the West German Trade Unions: Strategies of Class and Interest Representation in Growth and Crisis*. New York: Cambridge University Press, 1986.

Pasture, Patrick, Johan Verberckmoes, and Hans de Witte, eds. *The Lost Perspective? Trade Unions between Ideology and Social Action in the New Europe*. Vol. 1, *Ideological Persistence in National Traditions*. Aldershot, UK: Avebury, 1996.

Peltzer, Martin, and Charles E. Stewart. *Labor-Management Relations*. Frankfurt/Main: Knapp Verlag, 1995.

Thelen, Kathleen. *Union of Parts: Labor Politics in Postwar Germany*. Ithaca, NY: Cornell University Press, 1991.

Turner, Lowell. *Fighting for Partnership, Labor and Politics in Unified Germany*. Ithaca, NY: Cornell University Press, 1998.

Webb, Adrian. *The PDS—A Symbol of Eastern German Identity?* Newcastle, UK: Cambridge Scholars Publishing, 2007.

H. Language and Communication

Barbour, S., and P. Stevenson. *Variation in German: A Critical Approach to German Sociolinguistics*. Cambridge, UK: Cambridge University Press, 2000.

Clyne, M. C. *The German Language in a Changing Europe*. Cambridge, UK: Cambridge University Press, 1995.

Durrell, Martin. *Using German: A Guide to Contemporary Usage*. Cambridge, UK: Cambridge University Press, 1992.

Good, Colin. *Newspaper German: A Vocabulary of Administrative and Commercial Idiom*. Cardiff: University of Wales Press, 1994.

Russ, C. V. *The German Language Today: A Linguistic Introduction*. London: Routledge, 1994.

Schmidt, Wilhelm. *Geschichte der deutschen Sprache: Ein Lehrbuch für das germanistische Studium*. 8th ed. Stuttgart: S. Hirzel Verlag, 2000.

Stevenson, Patrick, ed. *The German Language and the Real World: Sociolinguistic, Cultural, and Pragmatic Perspectives on Contemporary German*. Rev. ed. Oxford: Clarendon Press, 1997.

Stevenson, Patrick. *Language and German Disunity: A Sociolinguistic History of East and West Germany, 1945–2000*. Oxford: Oxford University Press, 2002.

Tenscher, Jens, and Helge Batt, eds. *100 Tage Schonfrist: Bundespolitik und Landtagswahlen im Schatten der Großen Koalition*. Wiesbaden: Staatliche Parteienfinanzierung, 2008.

Townson, Michael. *Mother Tongue and Fatherland*. Manchester, UK: Manchester University Press, 1992.

U.S.–German Economic Yearbook. Published annually. New York: German American Chambers of Commerce (GAAC).

I. Law

Aufenanger, Martin. *The German Trade Mark Act/Markengesetz*. English and German ed. Munich: Beck, 2006.

Beier, F.-K., G. Schricker, and W. Fikentscher. 2nd ed. *German Industrial Property, Copyright and Antitrust Laws*. Cambridge, UK: VCH, 1989.

Böcker, M. H., B. Märzheuser, M. Nusser, and K. Scheja. *Germany: Practical Commercial Law*. *European Commercial Law Series*. London: Longman, 1992.

Brooks, Jermyn P., and Dietz Mertin. *Deutsches Bilanzrecht: Deutsch-englische Textausgabe mit einführenden Erläuterungen/German Accounting Legislation: Synoptic Translation with Introduction*. 3rd ed. Düsseldorf: IDW-Verlag GmbH, 1996.

Commercial Laws of the World: West Germany. Ormond Beach, FL: Foreign Tax Law Publisher, 1989–. Updated looseleaf resource.

Dannemann, Gerhard, and British Institute of International and Comparative Law. *An Introduction to German Civil and Commercial Law*. London: British Institute of International and Comparative Law, 1993.

Dawson, John Philip. *Gifts and Promises: Continental and American Law Compared*. New Haven, CT: Yale University Press, 1980.

Debatin, Helmut, and Dieter Endres, et al. *Unternehmensbesteuerung in Deutschland*. [*Corporate Taxation in Germany*]. Düsseldorf: IDW-Verlag GmbH, 1994.

Dietl, Clara-Erika, et al. *Wörterbuch für Recht, Wirtschaft und Politik, mit erläuternden und rechtsvergleichenden Kommentaren: Einschließlich der Besonderheiten des amerikanischen Sprachgebrauchs/Dictionary of Legal, Commercial and Political Terms, with Illustrative Examples, Explanatory Notes and Commentaries on Comparative Law: Incorporating American Usage*. 6th ed. Munich: Beck, 2000–.

Drobnig, Ulrich. *American-German Private International Law*. 2nd ed. Bilateral Studies in Private International Law 4. New York: Dobbs Ferry, 1972.

Droste, Killius Triebel, ed. *German Tax and Business Law Guide*. Wiesbaden: CCH Europe, 1992–2000. Updated looseleaf resource.

European Commission Directorate-General for Regional Policy and Cohesion. *The EU Compendium of Spatial Planning Systems and Policies: Germany*. Luxembourg: OOPEC, 1999.

Fisher, Howard D. *The German Legal System and Legal Language*. 4th ed. London: Routledge Cavendish, 2009.

Foster, Nigel G. *German Legal System and Laws*. 4th ed. Oxford: Oxford University Press, 2010.

Freckmann, Anke, and Thomas Wegerich. *The German Legal System*. London: Sweet & Maxwell, 1999.

Germain, Claire M. *Germain's Transnational Law Research: A Guide for Attorneys*. Ardsley-on-Hudson, NY: Transnational Juris Publications, 1991–. Updated looseleaf resource.

Goldbach, Klara, Heike Vogelsang-Wenke, and Franz-Josef Zimmer. *Protection of Biotechnological Matter under European and German Law: A Handbook for Applicants*. Weinheim: VCH, 1997.

Hart, J. A. *U.S. Business and Today's Germany: A Guide for Corporate Executives and Attorneys*. Westport, CT: Quorum Books, 1995.

Heidenhain, Martin, et al. *German Antitrust Law*. 5th rev. ed. New York: Juris Publishing/Fritz Knapp Verlag, 1999.

Horn, Norbert, ed. *German Banking Law and Practice in International Perspective*. Berlin/New York: Walter de Gruyter, 1999.

Horn, Norbert, Hein Kötz, and Hans G. Leser. *German Private and Commercial Law: An Introduction*. Translated by Tony Weir. Oxford: Clarendon Press, 1982.

Inter Nationes. *Environmental Legislation/Umweltgesetze*. Bonn: Inter-Nationes, 1995.

Inter Nationes. *Press Laws/Presserecht*. 2nd ed. Bonn: InterNationes, 1996.

Inter Nationes. *Copyright Law/Urheberrecht*. 2nd ed. Bonn: InterNationes, 1998.

Inter Nationes. *Federal Electoral Law/Bundeswahlgesetz*. 3rd ed. Bonn: InterNationes, 1998.

Killius, Jürgen. *Business Operations in Germany*. 3rd ed. Tax Management/ Foreign Income Portfolios 962–3. Washington, DC: Bureau of National Affairs, 2007.

Lingemann. Stefan, et al. *Employment & Labor Law in Germany*. Munich: Beck, 2008.

Lodge, Martin. *On Different Tracks: Designing Railway Regulation in Britain and Germany*. Westport: CT: Praeger, 2002.

Markesinis, B. S., and Hannes Unberath. *The German Law of Torts: A Comparative Treatise*. 4th ed. Oxford: Hart, 2002. Previously published as *A Comparative Introduction to the German Law of Torts*. 2nd ed. Oxford: Clarendon, 1990.

Markovits, Inga. *Imperfect Justice: An East-West German Diary*. Oxford: Clarendon Press, 1995.

Marsh, P. D. V. *Comparative Contract Law: England, France, Germany*. Aldershot, UK: Gower, 1994.

Meister, Burkhardt W., and Martin H. Heidenhain. *The German Liability Company*. Frankfurt/Main: Fritz Knapp Verlag, 1997.

Michalowski, Sabine, and Lorna Woods. *German Constitutional Law: The Protection of Civil Liberties*. Aldershot, UK: Dartmouth/Brookfield, USA: Ashgate, 1999.

Mohr, Konrad. *German Insider and Stock Exchange Law: An Introduction to the German Law with German Text and Synoptic English Translation of the Securities Trading Act, the Stock Exchange Act, the Exchange Admissions Regulation, and the Securities Sales Prospectus Act*. Frankfurt/Main: Fritz Knapp Verlag, 1994.

Mohr, Konrad. *The Law Relating to Business Tenancies in Germany*. Frankfurt/Main: Fritz Knapp Verlag, 1985.

Pagenberg, J., and B. Geissler. *Lizenzverträge/License Agreements*. 4th ed. Cologne: Carl Heymanns Verlag, 1997.

Peltzer, Martin, and Jermyn P. Brooks. *German Banking Law: German-English Text of the Banking Law in the Version Published on July 11, 1985*. 3d ed. Cologne: Otto Schmidt, 1990.

Peltzer, Martin, et al. *German Stock Corporation Act and Co-Determination Act/Aktiengesetz und Mitbestimmungsgesetz*. Cologne: Otto Schmidt, 1999.

Peltzer, Martin, et al. *German Commercial Code/Handelsgesetzbuch*. 4th ed. Cologne: Otto Schmidt, 2000.

Peltzer, Martin, et al. *GmbH-Gesetz [German Law Pertaining to Companies with Limited Liability], Mit einer englischen Einleitung. Deutsch-englische Textausgabe*. 4th ed. Cologne: Otto Schmidt, 2002.

Peltzer, Martin, et al. *Wertpapiererwerbs- und Übernahmegesetz [German Securities, Takeover and Acquisition Act], Deutsch-englische Textausgabe*. Otto Schmidt, 2000.

Piotrowicz, Ryszard W., and Sam K. N. Blay. *The Unification of Germany in International and Domestic Law*. Amsterdam: Rodopi, 1997.

Reimann, Mathias, and Joachim Zekoll. *Introduction to German Law*. 2nd ed. The Hague: Kluwer Law International, 2005.

Reuter, Konrad. *Praxishandbuch Bundesrat: Verfassungsrechtliche Grundlagen, Kommentar zur Geschäftsordnung, Praxis des Bundesrats*. 2nd ed. Heidelberg: C. F. Müller, 2007.

Reynolds, Thomas H., and Arturo Flores. *Foreign Law: Current Sources of Codes and Basic Legislation in Jurisdictions of the World.* Littleton, CO: F. B. Rothman, 1989–2007. Looseleaf.

Schmitt, Carl. *Constitutional Theory.* Translated and edited by Jeffrey Seitzer. Durham, NC, and London: Duke University Press, 2008.

Schneider, Hannes, and Martin H. Heidenhain. *The German Stock Corporation Act.* Munich: Beck/The Hague: Kluwer Law International, 2000.

Siebel, Ulf R. *Außenwirtschaftsrecht der Bundesrepublik Deutschland* [*Foreign Trade Law of the Federal Republic of Germany*]. Frankfurt/Main: Fritz Knapp Verlag, 1989.

Siebel, Ulf R., et al. *German Capital Markets Law.* New York: Oceana Publications, 1995.

Smith, Mitchell P. *Who Are the Agents of Europeanization? EC Competition Policy and Germany's Public Law Banks.* EUI Working Papers RSC, no. 2001/39. San Domenico, Italy: European University Institute, 2001.

Stewart, Charles Evan. *Insolvency Code and Act Introducing the Insolvency Code/Insolvenzordnung mit Einführungsgesetz zur Insolvenzordnung.* Frankfurt/Main: Fritz Knapp Verlag, 1997.

Stewart, Charles Evan. *Mergers and Acquisitions in Germany.* New York: Oceana Publications, 2000.

Strobl, Killius, and Vorbrugg [Munich Law Firm]. *Business Law Guide to Germany.* 2nd ed. Bicester, UK: CCH Editions, 1988.

Tulloch, Anthony. *German Reorganization Tax Act: German-English Text Including Cross-References and an Introduction.* Cologne: Otto Schmidt, 1995.

Volhard, D., D. Weber, and W. Usinger, eds. *Real Property in Germany.* Frankfurt/Main: Fritz Knapp Verlag, 1991.

Weiss, Manfred. *Labor Law and Industrial Relations Law in Germany.* 3rd ed. The Hague: Kluwer Law International, 2000.

Wieacker, Franz. *History of Private Law in Europe, with Particular Reference to Germany.* Translated by Tony Weir. Oxford: Clarendon Press, 1995.

Wiessala, Georg. "A State in the Dock? The Legacy and Reappraisal of the GDR in German Law." *German Politics* 5, no. 1 (April 1996): 137–44.

Youngs, Raymond. *English, French and German Comparative Law.* 3rd ed. Abingdon/New York: Routledge, 2014.

Youngs, Raymond. *Sourcebook on German Law.* London: Cavendish, 1994.

Zschocke, Christian. *The German Stock Corporation Act: Introductory Act to the Stock Corporation Act in Consideration of the Law on Registered Shares and Simplified Rules for the Exercise of Voting Rights (Nastrag); A Bilingual Edition with an Introduction to the German Stock Corporation Law.* 3rd ed. Frankfurt/Main: Fritz Knapp Verlag, 2001.

Zschocke, Christian, and Stephan Schuster. *Übernahmerecht: Deutsch-Englische Ausgabe/Takeover Law: Bilingual Edition*. 2nd ed. Frankfurt/Main: Fritz Knapp Verlag, 2002.

J. Media

Boothroyd, S. "The Media Landscape." In *Modern Germany: Politics, Society and Culture*, edited by Peter James, 141–58. London: Routledge, 1998.

Clark, Thomas. *Der Filmpate: Der Fall des Leo Kirch*. Hamburg: Hoffmann & Campe, 2002.

Eilders, Christiane. "Media as Political Actors? Issue Focusing and Selective Emphasis in the German Quality Press." *German Politics* 9, no. 3 (December 2000): 181–206.

Hans-Bredow-Institut für Medienforschung an der Universität Hamburg, ed. *Internationales Handbuch Medien*. Baden-Baden: Nomos, 2003.

Hartwig, Stefan. *Deutschsprachige Medien im Ausland, fremdsprachige Medien in Deutschland*. Münster: Verlag Dr W. Hopf, 2001.

Hellack, Georg. *Presse, Hörfunk und Fernsehen in der Bundesrepublik Deutschland*. Bonn: InterNationes, 2002.

Hickethier, Knut. *Film- und Fernsehanalyse*. 5th ed. Stuttgart: Metzler, 2012.

Humphreys, Peter. *Mass Media and Policy in Western Europe*. Manchester, UK: Manchester University Press, 1996.

Humphreys, Peter, and Matthias Lang. "Regulating for Media Pluralism and the Pitfalls of Standortpolitik: The Re-Regulation of German Broadcasting Ownership Rules." *German Politics* 7, no. 2 (August 1998): 176–201.

Jürgs, Michael. *Der Verleger—Der Fall Axel Springer*. Munich: Ullstein Taschenbuchverlag, 2001.

Kain, Florian. *Das Privatfernsehen, der Axel Springer Verlag und die deutsche Presse*. Münster: LIT Verlag, 2003.

Köpf, Peter. *Die Burdas*. Paperback ed. Bergisch Gladbach: Bastei Lübbe, 2005. First published by Europa Verlag in 2001.

Media Perspektiven Basisdaten: Daten zur Mediensituation in Deutschland. Frankfurt/Main: Media Perspektiven, 1993–. Journal series.

Meyn, Hermann, and Jan Tonnemacher. *Massenmedien in Deutschland*. 4th ed. Konstanz: UVK, 2012.

Negrine, Ralph M. *Parliament and the Media: A Study of Britain, Germany and France*. London: Royal Institute of International Affairs, 1998.

Noelle-Neumann, Elisabeth, Winfried Schulz, and Jürgen Wilke, eds. *Publizistik, Massenkommunikatioin, Fischer Lexikon*. Rev. ed. Frankfurt/Main: Fischer Taschenbuch Verlag, 2009.

Posewang, Wolfgang. *Wörterbuch der Medien*. Neuwied: Luchterhand, 1996.

Riedel, Heide, ed. *Mit uns zieht die neue Zeit . . . 40 Jahre DDR-Medien: Eine Ausstellung des Deutschen Rundfunk-Museums, 25. August 1993 bis 31. Januar 1994*. Berlin: Vistas Verlag, 1994.

Sandford, J. "The German Media." In *The New Germany*, edited by Lewis and McKenzie, 199–219. Exeter, UK: Exeter University Press, 1995.

Schneider, Wolf. *Die Gruner und Jahr Story*. Munich: Piper, 2001.

Schuler, Thomas. *Die Mohns*. Updated paperback ed. Bergisch Gladbach: Bastei Lübbe, 2005.

Wacker, Katharina. *Wettbewerb und Regulierung auf dem deutschen Fernsehmarkt: Deregulierungsbedarf und Umsetzungsbedingungen*. Stuttgart: Lucius & Lucius, 2007.

Werner, Claus, and Hans Bentzien, eds. *Medien-Wende, Wende-Medien? Dokumentation des Wandels im DDR-Journalismus Oktober 89–Oktober 90*. Berlin: Vistas, 1991.

Willis, Jim, ed. *Images of Germany in the American Media*. Westport, CT: Praeger, 1999.

K. New Federal States/Eastern Germany

Ark, Bart van [Groningen]. "The Manufacturing Sector in East Germany: A Reassessment of Comparative Productivity Performance, 1950–1988." *Jahrbuch für Wirtschaftsgeschichte*, no. 2 (1995): 75–90.

Behrend, Hanna, ed. *German Unification: The Destruction of an Economy*. London: Pluto Press, 1995.

Bundesministerium des Innern/Der Beauftragte der Bundesregierung für die Neuen Länder. *Jahresbericht der Bundesregierung zum Stand der Deutschen Einheit 2013*. Berlin: Author, 2013. Available at www.bmi.de.

Cooke, Paul, and Jonathan Grix, eds. *East Germany: Continuity and Change*. Amsterdam: Rodopi, 2000.

Davidson-Schmich, Louise K. *Becoming Party Politicians: Eastern German State Legislators in the Decade following Democratization*. Notre Dame, IN: University of Notre Dame Press, 2006.

Dodds, Dinah. "Ten Years after the Wall." *European Journal of Women's Studies* 10, no. 3 (2003): 261–76.

Flockton, Chris, and Eva Kolinsky, eds. "Recasting East Germany: Social Transformation after the GDR." Special issue, *German Politics* 7, no. 3 (December 1998).

Gerling, K. *Subsidization and Structural Change in Eastern Germany*. Berlin: Springer, 2002.

Grix, Jonathan, and Paul Cooke, eds. *East German Distinctiveness in a Unified Germany*. Birmingham, UK: Birmingham University Press, 2002.

Offe, Claus. *Varieties of Transition: The East European and East German Experience*. Cambridge, UK: Polity Press, 1996.

Olk, Thomas, and Thomas Gensicke. *Stand und Entwicklung des bürgerschaftlichen Engagements in Ostdeutschland—2013*. Berlin: Bundesministerium des Innern/Der Beauftragte der Bundesregierung für die Neuen Länder. Available at www.bmi.bund.de.

Saunders, Anna. *Honecker's Children: Youth and Patriotism in East(ern) Germany, 1979–2002*. Manchester, UK: Manchester University Press, 2007.

L. Politics and Political Systems

Andersen, Uwe, and Wichard Woyke, eds. *Handwörterbuch des politischen Systems der Bundesrepublik Deutschland*. 7th ed. Wiesbaden: Springer, 2013.

Bade, Klaus J. "Germany in Transition." Special issue, *Daedalus: Journal of the American Academy of Arts and Sciences* 123, no. 1 (Winter 1994).

Baker, Kendall L., et al. *Germany Transformed: Political Culture and the New Politics*. Cambridge, MA: Harvard University Press, 1981.

Beek, Ursula J. van, ed. *Democracy under Construction: Patterns from Four Continents*. Opland: Barbara Budrich, 2005.

Berg-Schlosser, Dirk, and Ralf Rytlewski, eds. *Political Culture in Germany*. Basingstoke, UK: Macmillan, 1993.

Betz, Hans-Georg. *Postmodern Politics in Germany: The Politics of Resentment*. Basingstoke, UK: Macmillan, 1991.

Blacksell, Mark. "Germany as a European Power." In *The New Germany*, edited by Lewis and McKenzie, 77–100. Exeter, UK: Exeter University Press, 1995.

Börsch, Alexander. *Global Pressure, National System: How German Corporate Governance is Changing*. Ithaca, NY, and London: Cornell University Press, 2007.

Braunthal, Gerard. *Political Loyalty and Public Service in West Germany: The 1972 Decree against Radicals and Its Consequences*. Amherst: University of Massachusetts Press, 1990.

Brinks, Jan Herman. *Children of a New Fatherland: Germany's Post-War Right-Wing Politics*. Translated by Paul Vincent. New York: I. B. Tauris Publishers, 2000.

Bruford, W. H. "German Political, Legal and Cultural Institutions." In *Germany: A Companion to German Studies*, edited by Malcolm Pasley, 61–127. London: Methuen, 1982.

Bundeszentrale für Politische Bildung. *Das Parlament* (parliamentary affairs), *Aus Politik und Zeitgeschichte* (essays on a wide range of topical issues), and *Informationen zur politischen Bildung* (political education series).

Cerny, Karl H., ed. *Germany at the Polls: The Bundestag Elections of the 1980s*. Durham, NC: Duke University Press, 1990.

Conradt, David P., and Eric Langenbacher. *The German Polity*. 10th ed. Washington, DC: Rowman & Littlefield, 2013.

Conradt, David P., Gerald R. Kleinfeld, and Christian Søe, eds. *Power Shift in Germany: The 1998 Election and the End of the Kohl Era*. New York: Berghahn, 2000.

Craig, Gordon A. *Politics and Culture in Modern Germany. Essays from the "New York Review of Books."* Palo Alto, CA: The Society for the Promotion of Science and Scholarship, 1999.

Curtis, Michael, G., et al. *Western Europe: Government and Politics*. New York: Longman, 1997.

Daalder, Hans, ed. *Comparative European Politics*. London: Pinter, 1997.

Dalton, Russell J., ed. *Germans Divided: The 1994 Bundestag Elections and the Evolution of the German Party System*. Oxford: Berg, 1996.

Decker, Frank. *Regieren im "Parteienbundesstaat": Zur Architektur der deutschen Politik*. Wiesbaden: VS Verlag für Sozialwissenschaften, 2011.

Derbyshire, I. *Politics in Germany: From Division to Unification*. Edinburgh: Chambers, 1991.

Dettke, Dieter, ed. *The Spirit of the Berlin Republic*. Oxford and New York: Berghahn Books, 2003.

Dittberner, Jürgen. *Große Koalition, Kleine Schritte: Politische Kultur in Deutschland*. Berlin: Logos Verlag, 2006.

Döhler, Marian. "Institutional Choice and Bureaucratic Autonomy in Germany." *West European Politics* 25, no. 1 (2002): 101–24.

Feldkamp, Michael F., with Birgit Ströbel. *Datenhandbuch zur Geschichte des Deutschen Bundestages 1994 bis 2003*. Baden-Baden: Nomos, 2005.

Gabriel, Oscar W., and Everhard Holtmann, eds. *Handbuch Politisches System der Bundesrepublik Deutschland*. 3rd ed. Munich and Vienna: R. Oldenbourg Verlag, 2005.

Glaeßner, Gert-Joachim. *The Unification Process in Germany: From Dictatorship to Democracy*. London: Pinter, 1992.

Green, Simon, Dan Hough, Alister Miskimmon, and Graham Timmins. *The Politics of the New Germany*. London and New York: Routledge, 2007.

Green, Simon, and William E. Paterson, eds. *Governance in Contemporary Germany: The Semi-Sovereign State Revisited*. Cambridge, UK: Cambridge University Press, 2005.

Günnler, Manfred, et al. *Die Bundestagswahl 2002: Eine Untersuchung im Zeichen hoher politischer Dynamik*. Wiesbaden: VS Verlag für Sozialwissenschaften, 2005.

Hancock, M. Donald, David P. Conradt, B. Guy Peters, William Safran, and Ralph Zariski. *Politics in Western Europe: An Introduction to the Politics of the United Kingdom, France, Germany, Italy, Sweden and the European Community*. London: Macmillan, 1993.

Helms, Ludger. *Regierungsorganisation und politische Führung in Deutschland*. Wiesbaden: VS Verlag für Sozialwissenschaften, 2005.

Hoffmann-Lange, Ursula, ed. *Social and Political Structures in West Germany: From Authoritarianism to Postindustrial Democracy*. Boulder, CO: Westview, 1991.

Holtschneider, Rainer, and Walter Schön, eds. *Die Reform des Bundesstaates: Beiträge zur Arbeit der Kommission zur Modernisierung der bundesstaatlichen Ordnung 2003/2004 und bis zum Abschluss des Gesetzgebungsverfahrens 2006*. Baden-Baden: Nomos, 2006.

Jacoby, Wade. *Imitation and Politics: Redesigning Modern Germany*. Ithaca, NY: Cornell University Press, 2000.

James, Peter. *The German Electoral System*. Aldershot, UK: Ashgate, 2004.

Jarausch, Konrad H., ed. *After Unity: Reconfiguring German Identities*. New York: Berghahn, 1997.

Jesse, Eckhard, and Roland Sturm, eds. *Bilanz der Bundestagswahl 2005: Voraussetzungen, Ergebnisse, Folgen*. Wiesbaden: VS Verlag für Sozialwissenschaften, 2006.

Kailitz, Steffen. *Politischer Extremismus in der Bundesrepublik Deutschland: Eine Einführung*. Wiesbaden: Verlag für Sozialwissenschaften, 2004.

Katzenstein, Peter. *Policy and Politics in West Germany: The Growth of a Semisovereign State*. Philadelphia: Temple University Press, 1987.

Keating, Michael. *The Politics of Modern Europe: The State and Political Authority in the Major Democracies*. Aldershot, UK: Gower, 1993.

Kitschelk, Herbert, and Wolfgang Streeck, eds. "Beyond the Stable State." Special issue, *West European Politics* 26, no. 4 (2003).

Koopmans, Ruud. *Democracy from Below: New Social Movements and the Political System in West Germany*. Boulder, CO: Westview Press, 1995.

Korte, Karl-Rudolf, and Manuel Fröhlich. *Politik und Regieren in Deutschland: Strukturen, Prozesse, Entscheidungen*. Paderborn: Schöningh, 2004.

Lankowski, Carl, ed. *Breakdown, Breakup, Breakthrough: Germany's Difficult Passage to Modernity*. New York: Berghahn, 1999.

Larres, Klaus. *Germany since Unification: The Development of the Berlin Republic*. 2nd ed. Basingstoke, UK: Palgrave Macmillan, 2001.

Leinemann, Jürgen. *Höhenrausch: Die Wirklichkeitsleere der Welt der Politiker*. Munich: Karl Blessing Verlag, 2004.

Mény, Yves, with Andrew Knapp. *Government and Politics in Western Europe: Britain, France, Italy and Germany*. 3rd ed. Oxford: Oxford University Press, 1998.

Müller, Kay, and Franz Walter. *Graue Eminenzen der Macht: Küchenkabinette in der deutschen Kanzlerdemokratie, von Adenauer bis Schröder*. VS Verlag für Sozialwissenschaften, 2004.

Nathans, Eli. *The Politics of Citizenship in Germany: Ethnicity, Utility and Nationalism*. Oxford and New York: Berg, 2004.

Padgett, Stephen, W. E. Paterson, and G. Smith. *Developments in German Politics 3*. Basingstoke, UK: Palgrave Macmillan, 2003.

Paterson, William E., and David Southern. *Governing Germany*. Oxford: Blackwell, 1991.

Patzelt, Werner J. "German MPs and Their Roles." *Journal of Legislative Studies* 3, no. 1 (1997): 55–78.

Pulzer, Peter. *German Politics 1945–1995*. Oxford: Oxford University Press, 1995.

Reading, Brian. *The Fourth Reich*. London: Weidenfeld & Nicolson, 1995.

Reutter, Werner. *Germany on the Road to "Normalcy": Policies and Politics of the Red-Green Federal Government (1998–2002)*. New York: Palgrave Macmillan, 2004.

Rhodes, Martin, Paul Heywood, and Erik Jones. *Developments in West European Politics 2*. Basingstoke, UK/New York: Palgrave, 2002.

Rhodes, Martin, Paul Heywood, and Vincent Wright, eds. *Developments in West European Politics*. Basingstoke, UK: Macmillan, 1997.

Roberts, Geoffrey K. *German Electoral Politics*. Manchester, UK: Manchester University Press, 2006.

Schmidt, Manfred G. *Political Institutions in the Federal Republic of Germany*. Oxford: Oxford University Press, 2003.

Schweitzer, C. C., et al., eds. *Politics and Government in Germany, 1944–1994: Basic Documents*. New York: Berghahn, 1995.

Søe, Christian, and M. Hampton. *Between Bonn and Berlin: German Politics Adrift*. Oxford: Rowman & Littlefield, 1999.

Staab, Andreas. *National Identity in Eastern Germany: Inner Unification or Continued Separation?* London: Praeger, 1998.

Sturm, Roland, and Heinrich Pehle, eds. *Wege aus der Krise? Die Agenda der zweiten Großen Koalition*. Opland and Farmington Hills: VS Verlag für Sozialwissenschaften, 2006.

Thaysen, Uwe, Roger H. Davidson, and Robert Gerald Livingstone, eds. *The US Congress and the German Bundestag: Comparisons of Democratic Processes*. Boulder, CO: Westview Press for the American Institute for Contemporary German Studies, 1990.

Theen, Rolf H. W., and Frank Lee Wilson. *Comparative Politics: An Introduction to Seven Countries.* 4th ed. Upper Saddle River, NJ: Prentice-Hall, 2001.

Thornhill, Chris. *Political Theory in Modern Germany: An Introduction.* Cambridge, UK: Polity Press, 2000.

Walter, Franz. *Die ziellose Republik: Gezeitenwechsel in Gesellschaft und Politik.* Cologne: Kiepenheuer & Witsch, 2006.

Wilson, Frank Lee. *European Politics Today: The Democratic Experience.* 3rd ed. Upper Saddle River, NJ: Prentice Hall, 1999.

Wise, M. Z. *Capital Dilemma—Germany's Search for a New Architecture of Democracy.* New York: Princeton Architectural Press, 1998.

1. Basic Law (Constitution)

Benda, Ernst, Werner Maihofer, and Hans-Jochen Vogel, eds. *Handbuch des Verfassungsrechts der Bundesrepublik Deutschland.* 2nd ed. Berlin: de Gruyter, 1994.

Currie, David P. *The Constitution of the Federal Republic of Germany.* Chicago: University of Chicago Press, 1994.

Finer, S. E., Vernon Bogdanor, and Bernard Rudden. *Comparing Constitutions.* Oxford: Clarendon Press, 1995.

Hönnige, Christoph. *Verfassungsgericht, Regierung und Opposition: Die vergleichende Analyse eines Spannungsdreiecks.* Wiesbaden: VS Verlag für Sozialwissenschaften, 2007.

Kommers, Donald P. *The Constitutional Jurisprudence of the Federal Republic of Germany.* 2nd ed. Durham, NC: Duke University Press, 1997.

Limbach, Jutta. "The Effects of the Jurisdiction of the German Federal Constitutional Court." In *Distinguished Lectures of the Law Department.* EU Working Papers Law No. 99/5. Florence: University European Institute, 1999.

Quint, Peter E. *The Imperfect Union: Constitutional Structures of German Reunification.* Princeton, NJ: Princeton University Press, 1997.

Starck, Christian, ed. *New Challenges to the German Basic Law.* Third World Congress of the International Association of Constitutional Law. Baden-Baden: Nomos, 1991.

Vanberg, Georg. *The Politics of Constitutional Review in Germany.* Cambridge, UK: Cambridge University Press, 2004.

2. Federalism and Local Government

Burgess, Michael, and Alain-G. Gagnon, eds. *Comparative Federalism and Federation: Competing Traditions and Future Directions.* Hemel Hempstead, UK: Harvester Wheatsheaf, 1993.

Eckart, Karl, and Helmut Jenkis, eds. *Föderalismus in Deutschland.* Berlin: Duncker & Humblot, 2001.

Freitag, Markus, and Adrian Vatter, eds. *Die Demokratien der deutschen Bundesländer, Politische Institutionen im Vergleich.* Mit einem Vorwort von Arend Lijphart. Opladen/Farmington Hill: Verlag Barbara Budrich, 2008.

Gunlicks, Arthur B., ed. *German Public Policy and Federalism: Current Debates on Political, Legal and Social Issues.* New York: Berghahn, 2003.

Gunlicks, Arthur B. *The Länder and German Federalism.* Manchester, UK: Manchester University Press, 2003.

Hassink, Robert. "Regional Technology Policies in the Old and New Länder of Germany: Case Studies from Baden-Württemberg and Thuringia." *European Urban and Regional Studies* 3, no. 4 (1996): 287–303.

Hildebrandt, Achim. *Die finanzpolitische Handlungsfähigkeit der Bundesländer: Determinanten, institutionelle Defizite und Reformoptionen.* Wiesbaden: VS Verlag für Sozialwissenschaften, 2009.

James, Peter. *The Politics of Bavaria—An Exception to the Rule.* Aldershot, UK: Avebury, 1995.

Jeffery, Charlie, ed. *Recasting German Federalism: The Legacies of Unification.* London: Pinter, 1999.

Jeffery, Charlie, and Peter Savigear, eds. *German Federalism Today.* Leicester, UK: Leicester University Press, 1991.

Leunig, Sven. *Föderale Verhandlung: Bundesrat, Bundestag und Bundesregierung im Gesetzgebungsprozess.* Frankfurt/Main: Peter Lang, 2003.

McWhinney, Edward, Jerald Zaslove, and Werner Wolf. *Federalism-in-the-Making: Contemporary Canadian and German Constitutionalism.* National and Transnational. Dordrecht/Boston: M. Nyhoff Publishers, 1992.

Mielke, Siegfried, and Werner Reutter, eds. *Länderparlamentarismus in Deutschland.* Wiesbaden: VS Verlag für Sozialwissenschaften, 2004.

Umbach, Maiken, ed. *German Federalism: Past, Present, Future.* Houndmills, Basingstoke, UK: Palgrave Macmillan, 2002.

Wood, Gerald. "Regional Alliances in North Rhine-Westphalia: Structural Policies in the Era of Flexibility." *European Urban and Regional Studies* 4, no. 3 (1997): 262–69.

3. Political Parties and Movements

Allen, Christopher S., ed. *Transformation of the German Political Party System*. 4th ed. New York: Berghahn, 1999.

Backes, Uwe, and Eckhard Jesse. *Politischer Extremismus in der Bundesrepublik Deutschland*. Berlin: Propyläen Verlag, 1996.

Backes, Uwe, and Patrick Moreau. *Die extreme Rechte in Deutschland: Geschichte gegenwärtiger Gefahren—Ursachen—Gegenmaßnahmen*. Munich: Akademie Verlag, 1993.

Bell, D. S., ed. *Western European Communists and the Collapse of Communism*. Oxford: Berg Publishers, 1993.

Braunthal, Gerard. *The German Social Democrats since 1969*. Boulder, CO: Westview, 1994.

Bull, M. J., and P. Heywood, eds. *West European Communist Parties after the Revolution of 1989*. Basingstoke, UK: Macmillan, 1994.

Cooper, Alice Holmes. *Paradoxes of Peace: German Peace Movements since 1945*. Ann Arbor: University of Michigan Press, 1996.

Dalton, Russell J., ed. *The New Germany Votes: Unification and the Creation of a New German Party System*. Oxford: Berg, 1993.

Edward, G. E., ed. *German Political Parties: A Documentary Guide*. Cardiff: University of Wales Press, 1998.

Harnisch, Sebastian, and Hanns W. Maull, eds. *Germany as a Civilian Power: The Foreign Policy of the Berlin Republic*. Manchester, UK: Manchester University Press, 2001.

Hodge, Carl Cavanagh. *The Trammels of Tradition: Social Democracy in Britain, France and Germany*. Westport, CT: Greenwood, 1994.

Hough, Daniel. *The Fall and Rise of the PDS in Eastern Germany*. Birmingham, UK: Birmingham University Press, 2001.

Hough, Daniel, Michael Koß, and Jonathan Olsen. *The Left Party in Contemporary Politics*. Houndmills, Basingstoke, UK: Palgrave Macmillan, 2007.

Hülsberg, Werner. *The German Greens: A Social and Political Profile*. London: Verso, 1988.

Kießling, Andreas. *Die CSU, Machterhalt und Machterneuerung*. Wiesbaden: VS Verlag für Sozialwissenschaften, 2004.

Klingemann, Hans-Dieter, and Richard I. Hofferbert. *Parties, Policies and Democracy*. Boulder, CO: Westview Press, 1994.

Koelble, Thomas A. *The Left Unravelled: Social Democracy and the New Left Challenge in Britain and West Germany*. Durham, NC: Duke University Press, 1991.

Koß, Michael. *Staatliche Parteienfinanzierung und politischer Wettbewerb: Die Entwicklung der Finanzierungsregimes in Deutschland, Schweden, Großbritannien und Frankreich*. Wiesbaden: VS Verlag für Sozialwissenschaften, 2008.

Lafontaine, Oskar. *The Heart Beats on the Left*. Translated by Ronald Taylor. Cambridge, UK: Polity Press and Blackwell, 2000.

Lees, Charles. *The Red-Green Coalition in Germany: Politics, Personalities and Power*. Manchester, UK: Manchester University Press, 2001.

Lees, Charles. *Party Politics in Germany: A Comparative Politics Approach*. Basingstoke, UK, and New York: Palgrave Macmillan, 2005.

Lewis, Rand C. *A Nazi Legacy: Right Wing Extremism in Postwar Germany*. Westport, CT: Praeger, 1991.

Lewis, Rand C. *The Neo-Nazis and German Unification*. Westport, CT: Praeger, 1996.

Markovits, Andrei S., and Philip S. Gorski. *The German Left: Red, Green and Beyond*. Cambridge, UK: Polity Press, 1993.

Mayer, Margit, and John Ely, eds. *The German Greens: Paradox between Movement and Party*. Philadelphia: Temple University Press, 1998.

Miller, Susanne, and Heinrich Potthoff. *A History of German Social Democracy from 1848 to the Present*. Translated by J. A. Underwood. New York: Berg, 1986.

Milosch, Mark S. *Modernizing Bavaria: The Politics of Franz Josef Strauss and the CSU, 1949–1969*. New York and Oxford: Berghahn Books, 2006.

Müller, Kay. *Schwierige Machtverhältnisse, die CSU nach Strauß*. Wiesbaden: VS Verlag für Sozialwissenschaften, 2004.

Müller-Rommel, Ferdinand, and Thomas Poguntke, eds. *Green Parties in National Governments*. London: Frank Cass, 2002.

Padgett, Stephen, ed. *Parties and Party Systems in the New Germany*. Aldershot, UK: Dartmouth, 1993.

Padgett, Stephen. *Developments in West German Politics 3*. Basingstoke, UK: Palgrave, 2003.

Padgett, Stephen, and Tony Burkett. *Political Parties and Elections in West Germany: The Search for a New Stability*. 2nd ed. London: Hurst, 1986.

Padgett, Stephen, and Thomas Saalfeld, eds. *Bundestagswahl '98: End of an Era?* London: Frank Cass, 1999.

Padgett, Stephen, Gordon Smith, and William E. Paterson, eds. *Developments in West German Politics 2*. London: Macmillan, 1996.

Parness, Diane L. *The SPD and the Challenge of Mass Politics: The Dilemmas of the German Volkspartei*. Boulder, CO: Westview, 1991.

Poguntke, Thomas. *The German Green Party*. Edinburgh: Edinburgh University Press, 1993.

Richardson, D., and C. Rootes, eds. *The Green Challenge: The Development of Green Parties in Europe*. London: Routledge, 1995.

Roberts, Geoffrey K. *German Politics Today*. Manchester, UK: Manchester University Press, 2000.

Roberts, Geoffrey K. *Party Politics in New Germany*. London: Pinter, 1997.

Rojahn, Christoph. *Left-Wing Terrorism in Germany: The Aftermath of Ideological Violence*. Conflict Studies 313. London: Research Institute for the Study of Conflict and Terrorism (RISCT), 1998.

Scarrow, Susan E. *Parties and Their Members: Organising for Victory in Britain and Germany*. Oxford: Oxford University Press, 1995.

Scharf, Thomas. *The German Greens: Challenging the Consensus*. Oxford: Berg, 1994.

Semetko, Holli A. *Germany's "Unity Election": Voters and the Media*. Cresskill, NJ: Hampton Press, 1994.

Sloam, James. *The European Policy of the German Social Democrats*. Basingstoke, UK: Palgrave, 2005.

Spier, Tim, et al., eds. *Die Linkspartei: Zeitgemäße Idee oder Bündnis ohne Zukunft*. Wiesbaden: VS Verlag für Sozialwissenschaften, 2007.

Staud, Toralf. *Moderne Nazis: Die neuen Rechten und der Aufstieg der NPD*. Cologne: Kiepenheuer & Witsch, 2005.

Stöss, Richard. *Politics against Democracy: Right Wing Extremism in West Germany*. Translated by Lindsay Batson. Oxford: Berg, 1991.

Thompson, Peter. *The Crisis of the German Left: The PDS, Stalinism and the Global Economy*. Oxford and New York: Berghahn Books, 2005.

Veen, Hans-Joachim, Norbert Lepszy, and Peter Mnich. *The Republikaner Party in Germany: Right-Wing Menace or Protest Catchall?* Westport, CT: Praeger, with the Center for Strategic and International Studies, Washington, DC, 1993.

Waller, Michael, Bruno Coppieters, and Kris Deschouwer, eds. *Social Democracy in a Post-Communist Europe*. London: Frank Cass, 1994.

Woods, Roger. *Germany's New Right as Culture and Politics*. Basingstoke, UK: Palgrave Macmillan, 2007.

4. Interest Groups

Sebaldt, Martin, and Alexander Strassner. *Verbände in der Bundesrepublik: Eine Einführung*. Wiesbaden: VS Verlag für Sozialwissenschaften, 2004.

Staatshandbuch, Die Bundesrepublik Deutschland: Verbände; Hundbuch der Verbände, Vereinigungen und Einrichtungen des öffentlichen Rechts. Ausgabe 2004. Cologne: Carl Heymanns Verlag KG, 2004.

M. Religion and Churches

Lease, Gary. "Religion, the Churches and the German 'Revolution' of November 1990." *German Politics* 1, no. 2 (August 1992): 264–73.

Minkenberg, Michael. "The Policy Impact of Church-State Relations: Family Policy and Abortion in Britain, France, and Germany." *West European Politics* 26, no. 1 (2003): 195–217.

N. Science and Technology

Götz, Klaus H. *Intergovernmental Relations and State Discretion: The Case of Science and Technology Policy in Germany.* Baden-Baden: Nomos, 1992.

Hefeker, Carsten, and Norbert Wunner. "Promises Made, Promises Broken: A Political and Economic Perspective on German Unification." *German Politics* 12, no. 1 (April 2003): 109–34.

Prange, Heiko. "Rethinking the Impact of Globalisation on the Nation-State: The Case of Science and Technology Policies in Germany." *German Politics* 12, no. 1 (April 2003): 23–42.

O. Society and Social Policy

Anheier, Helmut K., and Wolfgang Seibel. *The Nonprofit Sector in Germany.* Manchester, UK: Manchester University Press, 2001.

Ash, Timothy Garton. *The File: A Personal History.* London: Flamingo, 1997.

Beinssen-Hesse, Silke, and Kate Rigby. *Out of the Shadows: Contemporary German Feminism.* Melbourne, Australia: Melbourne University Publishing, 1996.

Berdichevsky, Norman. "The German-Danish Border. A Successful Resolution of an Age Old Conflict or Its Redefinition?" *Boundary & Territory Briefing* 2, no. 7 (1999).

Bergmann, Werner, and Rainer Erb. *Anti-Semitism in Germany: The Post-Nazi Epoch since 1945.* New Brunswick, NJ: Transaction Publications, 1997.

Bernstein, Richard J. *Hannah Arendt and the Jewish Question.* Cambridge, UK: Polity Press, 1996.

Betts, Paul. *Within Walls: Private Life in the German Democratic Republic.* Oxford: Oxford University Press, 2013.

Bleses, Peter, and Martin Seeleib-Kaiser. *The Dual Transformation of the German Welfare State.* Basingstoke, UK: Palgrave, 2004.

Bönker, Frank, and Hellmut Wollmann. "Incrementalism and Reform Waves: The Case of Social Service Reform in the Federal Republic of Germany." *Journal of European Public Policy* 3, no. 3 (1996): 441–60.

Clasen, Jochen. *Reforming European Welfare States: Germany and the United Kingdom Compared.* Oxford: Oxford University Press, 2007.

Collier, Irwin, et al. *Welfare States in Transition: East and West.* Basingstoke, UK: Macmillan, 1999.

Compston, Hugh, ed. *The Handbook of Public Policy in Europe: Britain, France and Germany.* London: Palgrave, 2004.

Dirke, Sabine von. *All Power to the Imagination! The West German Counterculture from the Student Movement to the Greens.* Modern German Culture and Literature. Lincoln: University of Nebraska Press, 1997.

Dodds, Dinah, and Pam Allen-Thompson, eds. *The Wall in My Backyard: East German Women in Transition.* Amherst: University of Massachusetts Press, 1994.

Eigler, Friederike, and Peter C. Pfeiffer, eds. *Cultural Transformations in the New Germany: American and German Perspectives.* Columbia, SC: Camden House, 1993.

Glaeßner, Gert-Joachim, ed. *Germany after Unification: Coming to Terms with the Recent Past. German Monitor,* no. 37 (1996).

Green, Simon. *The Politics of Exclusion: Institutions and Immigration Policy in Contemporary Germany.* Manchester, UK: Manchester University Press, 2004.

Hank, Karsten. "Regional Fertility Differences in Western Germany: An Overview of the Literature and Recent Descriptive Findings." *International Journal of Population Geography* 7 (2001): 243–57.

Horrocks, David, and Eva Kolinsky, eds. *Turkish Culture in German Society Today.* New York: Berghahn, 1996.

Jones, Philip N. "Immigrants, Germans and National Identity in the New Germany: Some Policy Issues." *International Journal of Population Geography* 2, no. 1 (March 1996): 119–31.

Kolinsky, Eva, ed. *Between Hope and Fear: Everyday Life in Post-Unification East Germany, A Case Study of Leipzig.* Keele: Keele University Press, 1995.

Kolinsky, Eva. *Women in 20th-Century Germany: A Reader.* Manchester, UK: Manchester University Press, 1995.

Kolinsky, Eva. *Women in West Germany, Life, Work and Politics.* Rev. ed. Oxford: Berg, 1993.

Kolinsky, Eva, and Hildegard Maria Nickel, eds. *Reinventing Gender.* London: Frank Cass, 2003.

Kontuly, Thomas. "Political Unification and Regional Consequences of German East-West Migration." *International Journal of Population Geography* 3 (1997): 31–47.

Kurthen, Hermann, Werner Bergmann, and Rainer Erb, eds. *Antisemitism and Xenophobia in Germany after Unification.* Oxford: Oxford University Press, 1997.

Lee, W. R., and Eve Rosenhaft, eds. *State, Social Policy and Social Change in Germany 1880–1994.* Oxford: Berg, 1997.

Loehlin, Jennifer A. *From Rugs to Riches: Housework, Consumption and Modernity in Germany*. Oxford: Berg, 1999.

Marshall, Barbara. *The New Germany and Migration in Europe*. Manchester, UK: Manchester University Press, 2000.

Martin, Philip L. *Germany: Reluctant Land of Immigration*. German Issues 21. Baltimore, MD: American Institute of Contemporary German Studies, Johns Hopkins University, 1998.

McGinnity, Frances. *Welfare for the Unemployed in Britain and Germany: Who Benefits?* Cheltenham, UK: Edward Elgar, 2004.

Miller, Barbara. *Narratives of Guilt and Compliance in Unified Germany: Stasi Informers and Their Impact on Society*. London: Routledge, 2014 (e-book editions from 1999).

Mushaben, Joyce Marie. *From Post-War to Post-Wall Generations: Changing Attitudes toward the National Question and NATO in the Federal Republic of Germany*. Boulder, CO: Westview Press 1998.

Schneider, Peter. *The German Comedy: Scenes of Life after the Wall*. London: I. B. Tauris, 1992.

Seeleib-Kaiser, Martin. "A Dual Transformation of the German Welfare State?" *West European Politics* 25, no. 4 (2002): 25–48.

Seifert, Wolfgang. *Geschlossene Grenzen, offene Gesellschaften? Migrations- und Integrationsprozesse in westlichen Industrienationen*. Frankfurt: Campus Verlag, 2000.

Senocak, Zafer. *Atlas of a Tropical German: Essays on Politics and Culture, 1990–1998*. Translated and edited by Leslie A. Adelson. Lincoln: University of Nebraska Press, 2000.

Sharp, I., and D. Flinspach. "Women in Germany from Division to Unification." In *The New Germany*, edited by Lewis and McKenzie, 173–95. Exeter, UK: University of Exeter Press, 1995.

Stevenson, Patrick, and John Theobald, eds. *Relocating Germanness: Discursive Disunity in Unified Germany*. Basingstoke, UK: Palgrave Macmillan, 2000.

Turturow, Norman E., and E. L. *German Immigration into the United States*. Westport, CT: Greenwood, 2000.

Wrench, John, and John Solomos, eds. *Racism and Migration in Western Europe*. Oxford: Berg, 1993.

Young, Brigitte. *Triumph of the Fatherland—German Unification and the Marginalisation of Women*. Ann Arbor: University of Michigan Press, 1999.

Zetterholm, Staffan, ed. *National Cultures and European Integration: Exploratory Essay on Cultural Diversity and Common Policies*. Oxford: Berg, 1994.

IV. REFERENCES

A. Print

1. Bibliographies

Abbey, William, et al. *Two into One: Germany 1989–1992; A Bibliography of the Wende.* London: Institute of Germanic Studies, 1993.

Angele, Elisabeth. *Reunified Germany: A Selective Bibliography of New Books and Other Publications.* Chicago: Goethe Institute, 1993.

Cole, Helena. *The History of Women in Germany from Medieval Times to the Present: A Bibliography of English/German Language Publications.* Washington, DC: German Historical Institute, 1990.

Detwiler, Donald S., and Ilse E. Detwiler. *West Germany: The Federal Republic of Germany.* World Bibliographical Series 72. Oxford: Clio Press, 1987.

Doerr, Juergen C. *The Big Powers and the German Question, 1941–1990: A Selected Bibliographic Guide.* Canadian Review of Studies in Nationalism 9. New York: Garland, 1992.

Edgington, Peter W. *The Politics of the Two Germanies: A Guide to Sources and English-Language Materials.* Ormskirk: G. W. and A. Hesketh, 1977.

Faulhaber, Uwe K., and Penrith B. Goff. *German Literature: An Annotated Reference Guide.* New York: Garland, 1979.

Frederiksen, E. P., ed. *Women Writers of Germany, Austria, and Switzerland.* New York: Greenwood, 1989.

Frederikson, E. P., and Elizabeth G. Ametsbichler, eds. *Women Writers in German-Speaking Countries: A Bio-Bibliographical Critical Sourcebook.* Westport, CT: Greenwood, 1998.

Krewson, Margrit B. *Berlin, 750 years: A Selective Bibliography.* Washington, DC: Library of Congress, 1986.

Krewson, Margrit B. *The Economies of the German-Speaking Countries Of Europe: A Selective Bibliography.* Washington, DC: Library of Congress, 1986.

Krewson, Margrit B. *The German-Speaking Countries of Europe: A Selective Bibliography.* 2nd ed. Washington, DC: Library of Congress, 1989.

Merritt, Anna J. et al. *Politics, Economics and Society in the Two Germanies, 1945–75: A Bibliography of English-Language Works.* Urbana: University of Illinois Press, 1978.

Price, Arnold H. *The Federal Republic of Germany: A Selected Bibliography of English-Language Publications.* 2nd ed. Washington, DC: Library of Congress, Slavic and Central European Division, 1978.

Radke, Klaus, and Axel Tiemann. *German Law in English: A Select Bibliography*. 1st ed. 1987, updated by Gereon Thiele, Nikolaus Herrmann, and Gerhard Dannemann, 1993. Originally published by the German Academic Exchange Service. Now available online only at www.iuscomp.org/gla/literature/daad93/daad93index.htm.

Showalter, Dennis E. *German Military History 1648–1982: A Critical Bibliography*. Military History Bibliographies 3. New York: Garland, 1984.

Wallace, Ian. *Berlin*. World Bibliographical Series 155. Oxford: Clio Press, 1993.

Wallace, Ian, ed. *East Germany*. World Bibliographical Series 77. Oxford: Clio Press, 1987.

2. Biographies

Reinhard, Ulrike. *Who Is Who in Multimedia: Deutschland, Österreich, Schweiz*. Heidelberg: Whois, 1997.

Who Is Who in der Bundesrepublik Deutschland. Zug, Switzerland: Verlag für Personenenzyklopädien AG. Annual editions (in German) under the title *Hübners Who Is Who* since 1989.

3. Periodicals in English

Communist and Post-Communist Studies. Oxford: Butterworth-Heinemann, 1993–.

Debatte: Journal of Contemporary Central and Eastern Europe. Formerly *Debatte: A Review of Contemporary German Affairs*. Abingdon: Taylor & Francis.

Environmental Politics. London: Frank Cass.

European Security. New York: Routledge.

The European Union: Annual Review. Published by the *Journal of Common Market Studies* (JCMS). Oxford: Blackwell.

European Urban and Regional Studies. Thousand Oaks, CA: Sage Publications.

GDR Monitor. Renamed *German Monitor* from 1992. Amsterdam: Rodopi.

The German Economic Review. Published on behalf of the German Economic Association (Verein für Sozialpolitik). Hoboken, NJ: John Wiley.

German History: The Journal of the History Society. London: Hodder Arnold (formerly published by Oxford University Press).

German Institute for Economic Research (Deutsches Institut für Wirtschaftsforschung, DIW). www.diw.de/english/.

German Life: Germany, Austria Switzerland. Denville, NJ.

German Life and Letters. Oxford: Blackwell.

German Politics. London: Frank Cass.

German Politics and Society. Harvard University, Center for European Studies/Georgetown University, Center for German and European Studies/ Berkeley: University of California.

German Politics. London: Frank Cass.

The International Journal of Population Geography. Chichester, UK: John Wiley.

Journal of Common Market Studies (JCMS). Incorporating the *European Union Annual Review*. Produced under the auspices of the University Association for Contemporary European Studies (UACES) and by Blackwell (Oxford).

Journal of Contemporary History. Under the auspices of the Institute of Contemporary History and the Institute for Advanced Studies in Contemporary History. London: Weidenfeld and Nicolson/Los Angeles: SAGE Publications.

Journal of European Public Policy. London: Routledge/Taylor & Francis.

The Journal of Legislative Studies. London: Frank Cass.

Local Government Studies. Abingdon, UK: Routledge/Taylor & Francis.

Strategic Review. Boston: U.S. Strategic Institute.

Strategic Survey. London: International Institute for Strategic Studies (since 1991).

Survival. London: International Institute for Strategic Studies.

West European Politics. London: Frank Cass.

4. Periodicals in German

Archplus. Aachen: Archplus Verlag. www.archplus.net (architecture).

Aus Politik und Zeitgeschichte. Bundeszentrale für Politische Bildung.

Baukultur. Berlin: DAI Verband Deutscher Architekten- und Ingenieurvereine e.V. www.dai.org (architecture).

Baumeister. Munich: Verlag Georg D.W. Callweg. www.baumeister.de (architecture).

Bauwelt. Gütersloh: Bertelsmann Fachzeitschriften. www.bauwelt.de (architecture).

DAB: Deutsches Architektenblatt, Zeitschrift der Bundesarchitektenkammer. Stuttgart: Forum Verlag (architecture).

Das Parlament. Weekly report on German parliament. Bundestag/Bundeszentrale für Politische Bildung.

DBZ Deutsche Bauzeitschrift. Gütersloh: Bertelsmann Fachzeitschriften. www.dbz-online.de (architecture).

Der Architekt: Bund Deutscher Architekten (BDA). Darmstadt: Verlag Das Beispiel. www.bda-architekten.de (architecture).

DETAIL: Zeitschrift für Architektur und Baudetail. Munich: Institut für internationale Architektur-Dokumentation. www.detail.de (architecture).

Deutsche Bauzeitung. Stuttgart: Deutsche Verlags-Anstalt. www.db.bauzeitung.de (architecture).

Garten + Landschaft. Munich: Verlag Georg D.W. Callwey. www.topos.de (architecture).

Media Perspektiven. Frankfurt/Main: Hessischer Rundfunk/ARD-Werbung.

Media Perspektiven Basisdaten. Frankfurt/Main: Hessischer Rundfunk/ARD-Werbung.

Media Perspektiven Dokumentationen. Frankfurt/Main: Hessischer Rundfunk/ARD-Werbung.

Militärgeschichte. Zeitschrift für historische Bildung. Potsdam. Zentrum für Militärgeschichte und Sozialwissenschaften der Bundeswehr. Also appears in electronic form: http://www.zmsbw.de/html/publikationen/zeitschriften/militaergeschichte.

Stadt+Grün. Berlin and Hanover: Patzer Verlag. www.stadtundgrün.de (architecture).

Stadtbauwelt. Gütersloh: Bertelsmann Fachzeitschriften (architecture).

Structurea.de. www.structurae.de/de/people/data (architecture).

Wettbewerbe aktuell. Freiburg/Breisgau: Verlag Wettbewerbe aktuell. www.wettbewerbe-aktuell.de (architecture).

Zeitschrift für Architektur, Innenarchitektur, technischer Ausbau. Leinfelden-Echterdingen: Verlagsanstalt Alexander Koch. www.ait-online.de (architecture).

5. Statistics

Datenreport 2013. 14th ed. Statistisches Bundesamt (Destatis)/Wissenschaftszentrum Berlin für Sozialforschung (WZB)/Zentrales Datenmanagement. Bonn: Bundeszentrale für politische Bildung/bpb, 2013. The *Datenreport* is a collection of statistical data that aims to provide an overview of life and conditions in Germany. It appears generally every two years. Editions from 1999 onward are also available online.

Eurostat. The statistical office of the European Union, in Luxembourg. http://epp.eurostat.ec.europa.eu/portal/page/portal/about_eurostat/introduction.

Statistisches Jahrbuch 2014. Print ed. Wiesbaden: German Federal Office of Statistics (Statistisches Bundesamt). Also available online. *See under* References, section B., Internet.

Statistisches Jahrbuch Deutscher Gemeinden, 2013. Cologne: Deutscher Städtetag. Print edition, includes CD. Preface and index available online at www.staedtetag.de/publikationen/statistikjahrbuch/index.html.

B. Internet

1. General Descriptions

CIA World Fact Book: Germany. Produced by the U.S. Central Intelligence Agency. www.cia.gov/library/publications/the-world-factbook (follow link to Germany).

Germany: A Country Study. Washington, DC: The Library of Congress. http://lcweb2.loc.gov/frd/cs/detoc.html.

Germany Profile. BBC Monitoring. www.bbc.co.uk/news/world-europe-17299607.

The Germany Way. General information site on Germany. Published by H. Flippo & Sons/Humboldt American Express, Reno/Nevada, USA. www.german-way.com.

Just Landed. General guide to Germany on topics such as visas, housing, jobs, finance, and health. www.justlanded.com/english/Germany.

Münzinger Länderinformationen. Ravensburg: Münzinger-Archiv GmbH (subscription service). www.munzinger.de (follow link and filter by country).

Wissen.de. General knowledge search engine, with sections on social affairs and history. Produced by Konradin Medien GmbH, Leinfelden-Echterdingen. www.wissen.de.

2. Bibliographies

Bundesstiftung zur Aufarbeitung der SED-Diktatur/Bundesunmittelbare Stiftung des öffentlichen Rechts. Extensive catalog of mainly German-language publications on all aspects of the former GDR and postreunification process of confronting the consequences of the East German dictatorship. www.bundesstiftung-aufarbeitung.de.

Deutsche Nationalbibliothek (DNB.) Main catalog of the German National Library. English interface available. www.dnb.de.

DigiZeitschriften. Search engine for digital journals, arranged by subject area. Access to most journal content by institutional subscription only, although some open access periodicals are available. Includes English start page. Provided by Digizeitschriften e.V, Göttingen. http://www.digizeitschriften.de.

Fachzeitungen. A comprehensive database catalog of mainly German printed and online journals, e-books, audiobooks, and CDs/DVDs in all subject areas, arranged alphabetically and by topic. Produced by Petra Lehnert, Neuss. www.fachzeitungen.de.

H-German/H-Net Network on German History. A network of scholars and teachers, coordinating lists and providing information on resources on German history, included recent publications. Hosted by Humanities and Social Sciences Online, East Lansing, MI. https://networks.h-net.org/h-german.

Zeitschriftendatenbank (ZDB). Online catalog of printed and electronic journals held in German and Austrian libraries. Maintained by the Staatsbibliothek zu Berlin, Preußischer Kulturbesitz, and the Deutsche Nationalbibliothek. www.zeitschriftendatenbank.de.

Zahlenbilder. Text and graphic information on German current affairs, politics, economy, law, and culture (in German). Also includes a section on Europe. Aaachen: Bergmoser + Höller Verlag. www.zahlenbilder.de.

3. Biographies

Warwick German Studies Web. Links to external sites and specialist bibliographies via Warwick University library catalog, organized by theme, subject area, and period. www2.warwick.ac.uk/fac/arts/german/resources.

Wer war Wer in der DDR. Online search engine for biographies of leading figures in the former GDR. Based on Müller-Enbergs (2010). Also includes leading communists from before the GDR. Based on Hermann Weber and Andreas Herbst, *Deutsche Kommunisten: Biographisches Handbuch 1918–1945*, 2nd ed. (Berlin: K. Dietz, 2008) and produced by the Bundesstiftung zur Aufarbeitung der SED-Diktatur/Bundesunmittelbare Stiftung des öffentlichen Rechts (www.bundesstiftung-aufarbeitung.de; follow links to Recherche, then Bibliographische Datenbanken).

Deutsches Historisches Museum/Lebendiges Museum Online (LEMO). Online biographies accessible alphabetically and by period. www.dhm.de/lemo/bestand (follow link to Biografien).

Münzinger Biografien. Ravensburg: Münzinger-Archiv GmbH. Subscription service. www.munzinger.de (follow link).

4. Chronologies

Deusche Geschichten. Extensively annotated chronology of events from 1890 to 2005. A coproduction by Cine Plus Leipzig GmbH and the Bundeszentrale für politsche Bildung (bpb), with the support of Mitteldeutsche Medienförderung (MDM) and hosted by the Deutsches Historisches Museum. German language. www.deutschegeschichten.de.

Deutsches Historisches Museum/Lebendiges Museum Online (LEMO). Annotated chronology of events from 1815 to the present, arranged by timeline and with links to themes, resources, and witness accounts. www.hdg.de/lemo/kapitel.html or www.dhm.de/lemo/.

Münzinger Chronik. Ravensburg: Münzinger-Archiv GmbH (subscription service). www.munzinger.de (follow link).

Post und Telekommunikation: Chronik der Entwicklung der Kurier-, Express- und Postdienste und der Telekommunikation in Deutschland nach der Postreform 1989. Chronology of telecommunications and postal reforms since 1989 (in German). Produced by Günter Schott, Würzburg. www.post-und-telekommunikation.de.

Sechzig Jahre Deutschland. Review of main events in German history from 1949 to 2009. Produced by Sascha Plischke as part of a diploma in online journalism in Darmstadt. www.60-jahre-deutschland.de/index.php.

5. Government and Official Sources (Including European Union)

Bund.de. Gateway to public administrative services and agencies. The German version focuses on frequently used services (e.g., job offerings in the public sector, lists of public tenders). The English version (www.bund.de/Service/english-.6118.htm) provides more general information about public facilities and e-government services available through the Internet.

Bundesagentur für Arbeit (Federal Employment Agency). The largest provider of labor market services in Germany, with a national network of over 700 agencies and branch offices. Online information on job and training placement, career counseling, and welfare benefits. The Familienkasse (Family Benefits Office), which provides child benefit, is part of the agency. www.arbeitsagentur.de.

Bundesamt für Migration und Flüchtlinge (Federal Office for Migration and Refugees). Also in English. Based in Nuremberg. www.bamf.de.

Bundesamt für Seeschifffahrt und Hydrographie (BSH). Information (also in English) on maritime affairs. Hamburg. www.bsh.de.

Bundesanstalt für Geowissenschaften und Rohstoffe (Federal Institute for Geosciences and Natural Resources, BGR), Hanover. The central geoscientific authority providing advice to the federal government on all geo-relevant questions and subordinate to the Federal Ministry for Economic Affairs and Energy (BMWi). Also in English. www.bgr.bund.de.

Bundesrat (regional assembly of federal states). Information on the role and composition of the assembly, with links to basic data on the states. www.bundesrat.de.

Bundesregierung (German federal government). Includes links to all ministries, the role of the federal chancellor, topical themes, the press office, and a media archive. www.bundesregierung.de.

Bundesverfassungsschutz (Federal Office for the Protection of the Constitution). Information on the agency's tasks, powers, and fields of work, along with the latest publications, reports, exhibition dates, press releases, and job offers. www.verfassungsschutz.de.

Bundesverwaltungsamt, BVA (Federal Office of Administration). The Cologne-based central service agency of the federal German government (introductory pages in English). Also links to its subdivisions, including the Zentralstelle für das Auslandsschulwesen (ZfA), which oversees German schools abroad (www.auslandsschulwesen.de), and the Bundesstelle für Informationstechnik (BIT), which provides integrated IT services for the BVA (www.bit.bund.de). www.bva.bund.de.

Bundeswehr. www.bundeswehr.de.

Common Agricultural Policy of the European Union (CAP). www.cap2020.ieep.eu.

Das Deutschland-Portal. Presse- und Informationsamt der Bundesregierung (Press and Information Office of the Federal Government of Germany). www.deutschland.de.

Deutsche Bundesbank (German Federal Bank). Also in English. www.bundesbank.de.

Deutsche Gesellschaft für die Vereinten Nationen, DGVN (United Nations Association of Germany, UNA-Germany).

Deutsche Vertretungen in den USA/German Missions in the United States. Information on the German embassy and its consulates in the United States. Further links to the German Information Center USA and the Deutschlandzentrum USA, providing public policy and general information on German affairs. www.germany.info.

Die Beauftragte der Bundesregierung für Migration, Flüchtlinge und Integration (Federal Government Commissioner for Migration, Refugees and Integration). www.integrationsbeauftragte.de and www.handbuch-deutschland.de.

Euractiv.com. European Union news and policy debates. Brussels: International Press Center. www.euractiv.com.

Europaministerkonferenz, EMK (Conference of European Ministers). Standing conference of German regional state ministers responsible for European affairs. The conference (and its Internet presence) is hosted in rotation by a federal state, e.g., Hamburg in 2014. www.hamburg.de/europaministerkonferenz.

European Parliament. www.europarl.europa.eu.

European Union. Index to all topics and publications. www.europa.eu/index_en.htm.

Facts about Germany. www.auswaertiges-amt.de.

German Federal Government. *See* Bundesregierung.

Goethe Institute. Information on the language and culture of Germany, as well as courses and materials for students and teachers. www.goethe.de/en/index.html.

Institute of International and European Affairs. Ireland-based think tank on European and International affairs. www.iiea.com.

Migration und Bevölkerung. An information portal for immigrants, including an online newsletter. www.migration-info.de/. A joint project of Network Migration in Europe (www.network-migration.org) and the Bundeszentrale für politische Bildung (www.bpb.de).

Petersburger Dialog (Petersburg Dialog). Berlin. www.petersburger-dialog.de.

Robert Schumann Foundation. An independent but state-approved foundation for policy research on the European Union, founded in 1991 after the fall of the Berlin Wall. www.robert-schuman.eu.

Sachverständigenrat für Umweltfragen (German Advisory Council on the Environment). Also in English. Berlin: Sachverständigenrat für Umweltfragen. www.umweltrat.de.

Sachverständigenrat zur Begutachtung der gesamtwirtschaftlichen Entwicklung (Council of Economic Experts). Wiesbaden. www.sachverständigenrat-wirtschaft.de.

a) Ministries   Links to the following ministries are available from the Bundesregierung/German federal government at www.bundesregierung.de/Webs/Breg/DE/Bundesregierung/Bundesministerien/bundesministerien.html.

Auswärtiges Amt, AA (Federal Foreign Office).

Bundesministerium der Finanzen, BMF (Federal Ministry of Finance).

Bundesministerium der Justiz und Verbraucherschutz, BMJV (Federal Ministry of Justice and Consumer Protection).

Bundesministerium der Verteidigung, BMVg (Federal Ministry of Defense).

Bundesministerium des Innern, BMI (Federal Ministry of the Interior).

Bundesministerium für Arbeit und Soziales, BMAS (Federal Ministry for Employment and Social Affairs).

Bundesministerium für Bildung und Forschung, BMBF (Federal Ministry of Education and Research).

Bundesministerium für Ernährung und Landwirtschaft, BMEL (federal Ministry of Food and Agriculture).

Bundesministerium für Familie, Senioren, Frauen, und Jugend, BMFSFJ (Federal Ministry for Family Affairs, Senior Citizens, Women, and Youth).

Bundesministerium für Gesundheit, BfG (Federal Ministry for Health).

Bundesministerium für Umwelt, Naturschutz, Bau und Reaktorsicherheit, BMUB (Federal Ministry for the Environment, Nature Conservation, Building and Nuclear Safety).

Bundesministerium für Verkehr und digitale Infrastruktur, BMVI (Federal Ministry of Transport and Digital Infrastructure).

Bundesministerium für Wirtschaft und Energie, BMWi (Federal Ministry for Economic Affairs and Energie).

Bundesministerium für wirtschaftliche Zusammenarbeit und Entwicklung, BMZ (Federal Ministry for Economic Cooperation and Development).

b) The Federal States   Baden-Württemberg. www.baden-wuerttemberg.de (English version available).

Bavaria. www.bayern.de.

Berlin. www.berlin.de (English version available).

Brandenburg. www.brandeburg.de.

Bremen. www.bremen.de.

Hamburg. www.hamburg.de (English version available).

Hessen. www.hessen.de.

Mecklenburg-West Pomerania. www.mecklenburg-vorpommern.de (English version available).

Lower Saxony. www.niedersachsen.de/portal (English version available).

North Rhine-Westphalia. www.nrw.de (English version available).

Rhineland-Palatinate. www.rlp.de/.

Saarland. www.saarland.de.

Saxony. www.sachsen.de (English version available).

Saxony-Anhalt. www.sachsen-anhalt.de (English version available).

Schleswig-Holstein. www.schleswig-holstein.de (English version available).

Thuringia. www.thueringen.de (English version available).

6. History, Politics, and Political Systems

Bundeszentrale für politische Bildung. Center for Political Education. A comprehensive site with links to information and articles on all aspects of German (and international) politics and society. Editions of the printed series Informationen zur politischen Bildung from 2000 onward are also available at www.bpb.de.

Election.de. Database of local/district, regional, national and European election results since at least 1949 (German language). Also includes election-related news items and results of surveys. Based in Hamburg. www.election.de.

Governments on the WWW: Germany. Produced by Gunnar Anzinger. In English. Last updated 2002. www.gksoft.com/govt/en/de.html.

Lernen aus der Geschichte (Learning from History). Also in English. Berlin: Agentur für Bildung—Geschichte. Politik und Medien e.V. http://lernen-aus-der-geschichte.de/

Penguin Companion to the European Union. London: Penguin/Random House. http://penguincompaniontoeu.com.

Political Resources. Links to parties, organizations, government and media. www.politicalresources.net (follow country link to Germany).

Politik Digital. Berlin. www.politik-digital.de.

Wahlrecht.de. Database of election-related information, including regional and national results since at least 1949, documentation on electoral law, descriptions and analyses of electoral systems, an online lexicon of electoral terms, and a discussion forum. Some sections also in English. www.wahlrecht.de.

a) Political Parties and Organizations Alliance 90/The Greens (Bündnis 90/Die Grünen). www.gruene.de.

Alternative for Germany (Alternative für Deutschland, AfD). www.alternativefuer.de.

Christian Democratic Union (Christlich Demokratische Union, CDU). www.cdu.de.

Christian Social Union (Christlich Soziale Union, CSU). www.csu.de.

Free Democratic Party (Freie Demokratische Partei,, FDP). www.fdp-de.

German Communist Party (Deutsche Kommunistische Partei, DKP), www.dkp.de.

The German People's Union (Deutsche Volksunion, DVU). *See* National Democratic Party of Germany.

Junge Union Deutschlands (JU). www.junge-union.de.

Konrad-Adenauer-Stiftung. Berlin. www.kas.de.

The Left Party (Die Linke). www.die-linke.de.

National Democratic Party of Germany (Nationaldemokratische Partei Deutschlands, NPD). www.npd.de.

Parteien-Online. www.parteien-online.de (information up until 2009).

Party of Democratic Socialism (PDS). www.pds.de.

The Pirate Party (Die Piratenpartei), www.piratenpartei.de.

The Republicans (Die Republikaner). www.rep.de.

Social Democratic Party of Germany (Sozialdemokratische Partei Deutschlands, SPD). www.spd.de.

Young Socialists (Jungsozialisten, JUSOS). www.jusos.de.

7. Statistics

Datenreport 2013. 14th ed. *See under* 5. Statistics, above.

Handelsdaten.de. Statistics on trade and retail compiled by the EHI Retail Institute in Cologne (www.ehi.org) and Statista in Hamburg (de.statista.com).

Statistical Office of the European Communities (Eurostat). http://epp.eurostat.ec.europa.eu/.

Statistical Offices of the Federation and the Federal States (Statistische Ämter des Bundes und der Länder). www.statistikportal.de/Statistik-Portal/.

Statistisches Jahrbuch Deutscher Gemeinden, 2013. Cologne: Deutscher Städtetag. Print ed. also with CD. Preface and index available online. See also www.staedtetag.de/publikationen/statistikjahrbuch/index.html.

Statistisches Jahrbuch 2014. Print ed., also available online. Wiesbaden: German Federal Office of Statistics (Statistisches Bundesamt). Some services are subscription-based. See also https://www.destatis.de/EN/Homepage.html (English), and https://www.destatis.de/DE/Startseite.html (German).

8. Economy (Including Business, Finance, Industry, and Labor)

Arbeitsgemeinschaft Energiebilanzen. Publishes reports and data (also in English) on energy provision and usage in Germany. Issued by the Deutsches Institut für Wirtschaftsforschung (German Institute for Economic Research, DIW) in Berlin (www.diw.de) and the Deutscher Braunkohlen-Industrie-Verein (DEBRIV) in Cologne (www.braunkohle.de). www.ag-energiebilanzen.de.

Bundesarbeitgeberverband Chemie (BAVC). Chemicals and pharmaceuticals industry umbrella organization, Wiesbaden. www.bavc.de.

Bundesverband der deutschen Industrie (BDI). Also in English. Berlin. www.bdi.eu.

Bundesverband Großhandel, Außenhandel, Dienstleistungen (Federation of German Wholesale, Foreign Trade and Services, BGA). Berlin. Also in English. www.bga.de.

Bundesverband WindEnergie (BWI). Umbrella organization for wind energy. Also in English. www.wind-energie.de.

Deutscher Gewerkschaftsbund (Confederation of German Trade Unions, DGB). Berlin. Also in English. www.dgb.de.

Deutsches Institut für Wirtschaftsforschung (German Institute for Economic Research, DIW). Berlin. www.diw.de.

Deutsches Verbaende-Forum. Database and archive for more than 14,000, mainly registered, associations. www.verbaende.com.

ECONSTOR. Online publications on economic affairs. Includes search engine for Germany and regions. English interface, publications in German and English. Published by ZBW, the German National Library of Economics, Leibniz Information Centre for Economics, Kiel. www.econstor.eu.

Euromonitor International. London, Chicago, etc. www.euromonitor.com.

European Association for Coal and Lignite/EUROCOAL. Brussels. www.euracoal.org.

Gabler Wirtschaftslexikon. Online economics and business lexicon (in German). Berlin: Springer. www.wirtschaftslexikon.gabler.de/.

German Corner. A "German-American Homeport" for a variety of U.S.-based services with German interests. www.germancorner.com/.

Germany Trade & Invest. The economic development agency of the Federal Republic of Germany. www.gtai.de.

Gesamtverband Deutscher Holzhandel/GD Holz (German Timber Trade Federation). Partly in English. Berlin. www.holzhandel.de.

Handelswissen. Information (in German) on all aspects of Germany's trade and retail industry. Includes an almanac and an online lexicon (Handelslexikon) of terms and concepts. Maintained by IFH Retail Consultants, Cologne. www.handelswissen.de/data/handelslexikon.

Hans-Böckler Stiftung (Hans Böckler Foundation). Information on codetermination and research on vocational education on behalf of the Deutscher Gewerkschaftsbund (Confederation of German Trade Unions, DGB). Based in Düsseldorf. Interface and some publications also in English. www.boeckler.de.

Haushaltssteuerung.de. Information (in German), including an online lexicon on the German taxation system (regional and national). Provided by Andreas Burth, Darmstadt. www.haushaltssteuerung.de.

Ifo Business Climate Index. An monthly early indicator for economic development in Germany, published by the ifo Institute, Munich. Detailed results are published in the printed (German language) journals *ifo Konjunkturperspektiven* and *ifo Schnelldienst* (follow links). www.cesifo-group.de/ifoHome/facts/Survey-Results/Business-Climate.html.

Institut der deutschen Wirtschaft. Reports and analysis on the German economy. Also in English. Cologne. www.iwkoeln.de.

Institut für Arbeitsmarkt- und Berufsforschung (Institute for Employment Research, IAB). Also in English. General information on the labor market. Nuremberg. www.iab.de.

Institut für Mittelstandsforschung (IfM) Bonn. Research institute with reports, statistics, and analysis of small and medium-sized businesses. Also in English. http://en.ifm-bonn.org.

International Monetary Fund (IMF). Follow links to publications, country reports, Germany. www.imf.org.

IWK-Business Studio. Follow links to online lexicon of economic and business terms (in German). Maintained by Institut für Wirtschaftskybernetik und Computer & Web Based Training, Dresden. www.business-studio.de.

Jugend und Finanzen. Financial and banking education site (in German) provided for schools and young people by the Bundesverband der DeutschenVolksbanken und Raiffeisenbanken, Berlin. www.jugend-und-finanzen.de.

Kernengergie.de. Information on nuclear energy. Also in English. Berlin: INFORUM Verlags- und Verwaltungsgesellschaft mbH/Informationskreis Kernenergie. www.kernenergie.de.

Organisation for Economic Co-operation and Development (OECD). Based in Paris, the OECD provides updated country surveys and forecasts. www.oecd.org/germany.

Ost-Ausschuss der Deutschen Wirtschaft (Committee on Eastern European Economic Relations). Berlin: Haus der Deutschen Wirtschaft. Partly in English. www.ost-ausschuss.de.

U.S. Commercial Service Germany. Provides services and programs to help American companies export goods and services to Germany. Includes market research information and country reports. www.export.gov/germany.

Verband der deutschen Banken (Association of German Banks). Links to private banks and member associations. www.germanbanks.bankenverband.de.

Verband der Elektroelektronik, Elektronik und Informationstechnik (Association for Electrical, Electronic, and Information Technologies, VDE). Umbrella organization for the IT industry. Frankfurt/Main. Also in English. www.vde.com.

Verband Deutscher Maschinen- und Anlagenbau (VDMA). Umbrella organization for engineering companies. Also in English. Frankfurt/Main. www.vdma.org.

Verband Forschender Arzneimittelhersteller (or Wirtschaftsverband der forschenden Pharma-Unternehmen, Association of Research-Based Pharmaceutical Companies, VFA). Also in English. www.vfa.de.

Wirtschaftslexikon24. Online lexicon (in German) of economic and business terms, maintained by Gudrun Stiller in Managua, Nicaragua. www.wirtschaftslexikon24.com.

Zentralverband Elektrotechnik- und Elektronikindustrie (German Electrical and Electronic Manufacturers' Association, ZVEI). Umbrella organization for the electrical industry. Partly in English. Frankfurt/Main. www.zvei.org.

9. Education

Academics.de Includes information (in German) on academic life, appointments, and higher education institutions. Hamburg: Academics GmbH. www.academics.de.

Allgemeine Hochschulreife. Information (in German) mainly on the higher school-leaving certificate (Abitur) and its variations, but also sections on other school-leaving qualifications and pathways into vocational training. Produced by OAK-Online Akademie, Cologne. www.allgemeine-hochschulreife.com.

Ausbildung.de. Information (in German) on vocational education. Bochum: Employour GmbH. www.ausbildung.de.

Bachelor Studium. Information portal (in German) on studying for the bachelor's degree in Germany. Cologne: OAK—Online Akademie. www.bachelor-studium.net.

Bildungsbericht 2014. Report (in German) on the state of all areas of German education. Produced by the Deutsches Institut für Internationale Pädagogische Forschung (DIPF, German Institute for International Educational Research) in Frankfurt, and supported by the Kultusministerkonferenz (KMK) und dem Bundesministeriums für Bildung und Forschung (BMBF). Previous editions for 2006, 2008, 2010, 2012. Available online at www.bildungsbericht.de.

Deutscher Adakemischer Austauschdienst (German Academic Exchange Service, DAAD). Includes information for non-Germans on studying in Germany, for Germans planning to study abroad, and the organization's role in promoting German studies. Also in English. www.daad.de.

Deutscher Bildungsserver. The German Education Server. Information on all aspects of the German education system. A joint Bund-Länder project coordinated by the Deutsches Institut für Internationale Pädagogische Forschung (DIPF, German Institute for International Educational Research) in Frankfurt. *See also* Eduserver, which is theEnglish-language version. www.bildungsserver.de.

Eduserver. The English-language version of the German Education Server; provides access and background information regarding the German education system and its international context. www.eduserver.de.

Fachportal Pädagogik. Portal to printed and electronic resources for all aspects of educational practice and research. Hosted by the Deutsches Institut für Internationale Pädagogische Forschung (DIPF, German Institute for International Educational Research) in Frankfurt. Includes English interface. www.fachportal-paedagogik.de.

German Institute for Vocational Education (Bundesinstitut für Berufsbildung, BIBB). www.bibb.de/de/index.htm.

Gewerkschaft Erziehung und Wissenschaft. Site of German trade union for education and science (in German), based in Frankfurt/Main. www.gew.de.

Hochschulrektorenkonferenz, HRK (German Rectors' Conference). Standing conference of university heads. Information on current developments in higher education, entry requirements, student grants, and international links. www.hrk.de.

Konferenz der Kultusminister, KMK (Standing Conference of Regional Cultural Ministers). Includes press releases and information on historical and current developments in general school education and types of qualification. www.kmk.org/.

PISA: The OECD Programme for International Student Assessment. www.oecd.org/pisa/. For access to PISA reports on Germany see www.oecd.org/berlin/presse/pisa-2012-deutschland.htm.

Privatschulberatung. Register of private/boarding schools in Germany. Also offers consultation. Published by BP Internet GmbH, Munich. www.privatschulberatung.de.

Schulabschluss abholen. www.schulabschluss-nachholen.net. Information on school-leaving certificates, including types of Abitur and pathways for their completion.

Studienwahl.de. Information on degrees, courses of further study, lists of institutions, and links to other sites. Partly in English. Provided by the federal state of Hessen (Hessisches Ministerium für Wissenschaft und Kunst) and the Federal Employment Agency (Bundesagentur für Arbeit, Nuremberg). www.studienwahl.de.

UNICUM. Internet site of German student news publication of the same name. Includes general information on studying in Germany and a glossary (in German). Bochum: UNICUM GmbH. www.unicum.de.

Uni-pur.de. Information portal (in German) for students in Germany. Maintained by Ulf Dingler, Buxtehude. www.uni-pur.de.

Verband Deutscher Privatschulverbände, VDP. Umbrella association for private school associations. Berlin. www.privatschulen.de.

10. Geography (Including Maps) and Environment

Agrar heute.com. All aspects of agriculture (in German). Hanover: Deutscher Landwirtschaftsverlag (www.dlv.de). www.agrarheute.com.

Alpine Convention. Information (in English) on the Alpine region. Based in Innsbruck and Bozen/Bolzano. www.alpconv.org.

Bund Freunde der Erde (Friends of the Earth Germany). www.bund.net.

Bundesamt für Naturschutz (German Federal Agency for Nature Conservation, BfN). Bonn. Also in English. www.bfn.de.

Deutsche Bundesstiftung Umwelt (German Federal Environmental Foundation, DBU). Also in English. Osnabrück. www.dbu.de.

Deutscher Forstwirtschaftsrat. Information (in German) on forestry. Berlin: Deutscher Forstwirtschaftsrat. www.dfwr.de.

Die Nordsee. Information (in German) on the North Sea coast. Münster: DreiZeitenVerlag UG. www.die-ganze-nordsee.de.

Eco-Management and Audit Scheme (EMAS). Partly in English. www.emas.de/ueber-emas.

Für Mensch und Umwelt. Dessau-Roßlau: Umweltbundesamt/ Präsidialbereich. www.fuer-mensch-und-umwelt.de.

Gentechnikfreie Regionen. Current and background information on non-GMO farming in Germany. Berlin: Bund für Umwelt und Naturschutz (BUND). www.gentechnikfreie-regionen.de.

Geographie Infothek: Deutschland. Information mainy on the geography of Germany, but also sections on history, politics, and the economy. http://www2.klett.de/sixcms/list.php?page=geo_infothek&node=Deutschland.

German Environmental Information Network: PortalU. www.portalu.de/.

Integriertes Küstenzonenmanagement, IKZM (Integrated Coastal Management Zone). Includes a guide to coastal management in the Baltic Sea Region. Also in English. Warnemünde: EUCC Die Küsten Union Deutschland/Institut für Ostseeforschung Warnemünde (IOW). www.ikzm-d.de.

Internationale Kommission zum Schutz des Rheins/International Commission for the Protection of the Rhine. IKSR/ICPR. Also in English. Koblenz. http://www.iksr.org.

Landkartenindex Deutschland. Index of mainly tourist maps. www.landkartenindex.de/deutschland.

Lexikon der Nachhaltigkeit. Lexicon (in German) on environmental sustainability. Aachen: Aachener Stiftung Kathy Beys. www.nachhaltigkeit.info.

Meine Landwirtschaft. Focuses on political campaigning on farming issues. Berlin: Kampagne Meine Landwirtschaft. www.meine-landwirtschaft.de.

Nationale Naturlandschaften. Portal (in German) for national parks, biosphere reserves, and nature parks in Germany. Berlin: EUROPARC Deutschland. www.nationale-naturlandschaften.de.

Naturschutzbund Deutschland (NABU). Nature and Biodiversity Conservation Union. Also in English. Berlin. www.nabu.de.

Naturwälder.de. Information (in German) on forest and woodland reserves. Bonn: Bundesministerium für Landwirtschaft und Ernährung. www.naturwaelder.de.

Perry-Castañeda Library Map Collection (Germany), University Library, Texas. Online digitized maps (country, thematic, historical, and topographic). www.lib.utexas.edu/maps/germany.html.

Recycling für Deutschland. Information (in German) provided by participants in Germany's dual system of waste recycling. www.recycling-fuer-deutschland.de.

Stiftung Unternehmen Wald. Information (in German) on a foundation for forestry and related issues. Hamburg. www.wald.de.

Trinkwasser Wissen. Information (in Geman) on drinking water provision in Germany. Frankfurt/Main: Verband Deutscher Maschinen- und Anlagenbau (VDMA). www.trinkwasser-wissen.net/de.

Umweltinstitut München (Munich Environmental Institute). Partly in English. www.umweltinstitut.org.

Wald-in-Not. Information (in German) about the project Wald in Not ("endangered forest"). Bonn: DBU Naturerbe GmbH. www.wald-in-not.de.

11. Law

Anwaltzentral.de. Directory of lawyers alongside information (in German) on aspects of law. Lohne: cemore GmbH. www.anwaltzentrale.de.

Bundesgerichtshof (Federal Court of Justice). Also in English. Karlsruhe. www.bundesgerichtshof.de.

Bundesverfassungsgericht (Federal Constitutional Court). Also in English. Karlsruhe. www.bundesverfassungsgericht.de.

Deutsche Justiz.de. Information (in German) on types, functions, and locations of German courts. Produced by Wolf Poppensieker, Bad Iburg. www.deutschejustiz.de.

European Court of Human Rights. Follow links to country profiles, Germany. Strassburg: European Council/European Court of Human Rights. http://echr.coe.int.

German Business and Commercial Laws: Guide to Translations into English and Select Auxiliary Sources. Published by GlobaLex/Hauser Global Law School Program at NYU School of Law. www.nyulawglobal.org/globalex/Germany_Business1.htm.

German Business and Commercial Laws: Guide to Translations into English and Select Auxiliary Sources. Produced by Martina Kammer and published by Law and Technology Resources for Legal Professionals (LLRX), 2000. (Possibly an older version of the site with the same name listed above). www.llrx.com/features/german.htm.

Germany. An Introduction to Legal Research in the Jurisdiction of Germany. A comprehensive and up-to-date site with links and detailed information on primary sources (codes and statutes), law reports, treatises, journals, English-language works on German law, Internet sources in English, and help with abbreviations. Produced by the Library of the Institute of Advanced Legal Studies (IALS), University of London. http://libguides.ials.sas.ac.uk/germany.

Guide to Law Online: Germany. Washington, DC: Library of Congress. www.loc.gov/law/help/guide/nations/germany.php.

Jusline. Portal (in German) for lawyers and jurists. www.jusline.de.

Rechtsanwalt-Wissen.de. General information (in German) on law and the legal profession. Cologne: Greven Medien. http://rechtsanwalt-wissen.de.

Rechtslexikon Online. General legal lexicon (in German). Unterschleißheim: Valuenet GmbH. www.rechtslexikon-online.de.

Statutes. German legal statutes (in translation). Produced by Gerhard Dannemann. www.iuscomp.org/gla/statutes/statutes.htm.

World Legal Information Institute (World LII). A single search facility for German law databases. Maintained by UTS Faculty of Law, NSW, Australia. www.worldlii.org/de/

12. News and Current Affairs

Carnegie Europe. Analysis and reports on European foreign policy, with special reference to the European Union. Based in Brussels. http://carnegieeurope.eu.

Deutsche Welle. English language service. www.dw.de.

Expatica. Provides mainly information on Germany for expatriates from other countries. www.expatica.com/de/main.html.

Geheimdienste.org. Information (in German) compiled by journalist Kalle Selchert (Celle) on the the secret services of the world, including Germany's. www.geheimdienste.org.

RP-Online. Online news and e-paper (in German). www.rp-online.de.

13. Media

Bundesverband Deutscher Zeitungsverleger, BDZV (Federation of German Newspaper Publishers). Facts, figures, and reports (also in English) on the newspaper publishing industry. www.bdzv.de.

Deutsche Presserat (German Press Council). Berlin. www.presserat.de/presserat/.

Deutsches Rundfundarchiv. Archive of German radio, incorporating former GDR state television and radio. Frankfurt/Main and Potsdam-Babelsberg: Internetpräsenz der Stiftung Deutsches Rundfunkarchiv. www.dra.de.

Informationsgemeinschaft zur Feststellung der Verbreitung von Werbeträgern e.V., IVW (German Circulation Research Organization). Berlin. www.ivw.de.

Institut "Deutsche Presseforschung" (Institute for German Press Research). Bremen. www.presseforschung.uni-bremen.de

Institut für Medien- und Kommunikationspolitik GmbH (IfM). Also in English. Database of media providers, dossiers, and forums. Berlin. www.mediadb.eu.

Institut für Zeitungsforschung (Institute for Newspaper Research). Dortmund. www.dortmund.de/de/leben_in_dortmund/bildungwissenschaft/institut_fuer_zeitungsforschung/start_zi/index.html www.zeitungsforschung.de.

Internationale Medienhilfe (International Media Help). Also in English. Includes information on foreign language media in Germany. Berlin. www.imh-deutschland.de.

Kommission zur Ermittlung der Konzentration im Medienbereich, KEK. (Commission on Concentration in the Media). Berlin. www.kek-online.de.

Media Tribune. News, topical and policy reports, and a history section relating to German media (in German). Hamburg: Media Tribune. www.mediatribune.de.

   a) News Titles   *Bild*. (daily). www.bild.de.

Bild am Sonntag. (weekly). www.bams.de/ (links directly to *Bild, see below*).

Bild-Zeitung. Hamburg/Berlin (daily). www.bild.t-online.de/.

Der Spiegel. Hamburg (weekly). www.spiegel.de.

Der Tagesspiegel. Berlin (daily). www.tagesspiegel.de.

Die Welt. Hamburg (daily). www.welt.de.

Die Zeit. Hamburg (weekly). www.zeit.de.

Focus. Munich (weekly). www.focus.de.

Frankfurter Allgemeine Zeitung (FAZ). Frankfurt/Main (daily). www.faz.de.

Frankfurter Rundschau. Frankfurt/Main (daily). http://www.fr-online.de.

Google News Deutschland. Internet only. www.news.google.de.

The Guardian (English-language daily newspaper, with online current and archived news about Germany). www.theguardian.com/world/germany.

Münzinger Presse. Ravensburg: Münzinger-Archiv GmbH. (Subcription service to archives of several national news titles. www.munzinger.de; follow link).

Manager Magazin. Hamburg (monthly). www.manager-magazin.de.

Neues Deutschland. Berlin (daily). www.neues-deutschland.de.

Süddeutsche Zeitung. Munich (daily, with weekend edition). www.sueddeutsche.de.

taz. Berlin. (daily). www.taz.de.

T-Online. www.t-online.de/nachrichten/deutschland/.

Welt am Sonntag. www.epaper.apps.welt.de/wams/.

Westdeutsche Allgemeine Zeitung (WAZ). Essen (daily). www.derwesten.de.

Wirtschaftsdienst/Interconomics: Review of European Economic Policy. Kiel/Hamburg (monthly). www.wirtschaftsdienst.eu.

Wirtschaftswoche. Düsseldorf (weekly). www.wiwo.de.

b) Online Listings of Publishers Verlage und Buchhandlungen. www.chemie.fu-berlin.de/outerspace/verlage.html/

14. East Germany/Former GDR

Chronik der Mauer. A chronology of the Berlin Wall, including its physical scope and construction, a register of its victims, and further documentation and audiovisual/digital material. A joint project by the Zentrum für Zeithistorische Forschung, Potsdam, the Bundeszentrale für politische Bildung, and Deutschlandradio. www.chronik-der-mauer.de.DDR-Suche. German-language search engine, also with links to most aspects of life and culture in the former GDR. www.ddr-suche.de.

DDR-im-Web. A German-language site still under construction, with some links to various aspects of the former GDR. Produced by Marko Busch (Nuremberg). www.ddr-im-web.de.

Der Bundesbeauftragte für die Unterlagen des Staatssicherheitsdienstes der ehemaligen Deutschen Demokratischen Republik (BStU, The Federal Commissioner for the Records of the State Security Service of the former GDR). Information (also in English) on access to the archives, contact details for shorter publications by the BStU itself, and links to publishers of longer works. A "Biografische Quellen" (Biographical sources) series is available from the publishers, Verlag Edition Temmen (vols. 1 and 2) and Verlag Vandenhoeck & Ruprecht (vol. 3). www.bstu.bund.de.

Germany Propaganda Archive. A section on the GDR includes speeches by leaders, visual material (wall posters), types of propaganda, and links to related sites. Produced by Randall Bytwerk, Calvin College (USA). http://research.calvin.edu/german-propaganda-archive/.

15. Culture

Akademie der Künste in Berlin, Adk (Academy of Arts in Berlin). Also in English. www.adk.de.

Akademie der Wissenschaften und der Literatur Mainz. www.adwmainz.de.

Arbeitskreis selbständiger Kultur-Institute. Bonn. www.aski.org.

Bayerische Akademie der Schönen Künste (Bavarian Academy of Fine Arts). Also in English. www.badsk.de.

Berlin-Brandenburgische Akademie der Wissenschaften (Berlin-Brandenburg Academy of Sciences and Humanities). Also in English. www.bbaw.de.

Cosmopolis (online magazine for culture, history, and politics; articles also in English). www.cosmopolis.ch.

Cultural Portal of the City of Frankfurt (Kultur in Frankfurt). kultur.inm.de/prs/WebObjects/portal.woa.

Deutsche Kultur International. www.deutsche-kultur-international.de/home/index.html.

Germany Today! www.cs.umb.edu/~alilley/german.html.

Goethe Institute/Inter Nationes. www.goethe.de/enindex.htm.

Germany on the WWW/Deutschland im Internet. www.goethe.de/r/dservlis.htm.

Grove Art Online. www.groveart.com.

Institut für Auslandsbeziehungen (IFA). cms.ifa.de.

Kulturnetz. www.kultur-netz.de.

Kulturportal Deutschland. www.kulturportal-deutschland.de.

Kulturrat (German Cultural Council). www.kulturrat.de.

Open-berlin. www.open-berlin.de.

Sächsische Akademie der Künste (Saxon Academy of Arts). Partly in English. www.sadk.de.

Union der deutschen Akademien der Wissenschaften (Union of the German Academies of Sciences and Humanities). Also in English. Mainz and Berlin. www.akademienunion.de.

a) Literature Deutsche Akademie für Sprache und Dichtung. www.deutscheakademie.de.

Litrix.de. www.litrix.de.

Lyrikline.org. www.lyrikline.org/.

b) Theater Deutscher Buehnenverein. Bundesverband Deutscher Theater. www.buehnenverein.de.

Die Deutsche Bühne. www.die-deutsche-buehne.de.

German Theater Museum (Munich). http://www.stmwfk.bayern.de/kunst/museen/theatermuseum.html.

Theater der Zeit. www.theaterderzeit.de.

Theater, Film and Performing Arts. WESSWEB (Web service of the Western European Studies Section, Association of College and Research Libraries, German Studies Web). www.dartmouth.edu/~wess/wessthea.html.

c) Museums and Galleries German Galleries. www.germangalleries.com/index_Berlin.html.

German Historical Museum (Deutsches Historisches Museum). www.dhm.de/lemo.

Virtual Library Museen. http://www.historisches-centrum.de/index.php?id=272.

WebMuseen. www.webmuseen.de/Museen.html.

d) Language BBC German Language Courses. www.bbc.co.uk/languages/german/index.shtm.

Deutsche Sprachwelt. www.deutsche-sprachwelt.de.

German Dialects. www.webgerman.com/german/dialects/index.html. (last updated in 2007).

German Language Society (Gesellschaft für deutsche Sprache, GfdS). www.gfds.de.

Institute for German Language (Institut für deutsche Sprache, IDS). www.ids-mannheim.de.

Spelling Reform. www.neue-rechtschreibung.de.

Spracharchiv. www.sprachrat.de.

Web German. webgerman.com.

e) Art and Architecture   AIT (Architektur, Innenarchitektur, technischer Ausbau). www.ait-online.de.

Arbeitsgemeinschaft Leseranalyse Architekten und planende Bauingenieure agla a+b. Gütersloh: Bauverlag BV GmbH. www.agla-ab.de.

Archinform: International Architecture Database. www.archinform.net.

Artnet: www.artnet.com/library.

Bau.net: www.bau.net/lexikon.htm.

Cicero Rednerpreis. Bonn: Verlag für die Deutsche Wirtschaft. www.cicero-rednerpreis.de.

Federation of German Landscape Architects (BDLA/Bund Deutscher Landschaftsarchitekten). Hamburg: A+I Verlag. www.bdla.de.

Greatbuildings.com. www.greatbuildings.com/architects.

Structurea.de. www.structurae.de/de/people/data.

Vereinigung für Stadt-, Regional- und Landesplanung (SRL). www.srl.de.

f) Berlin   Art in Berlin. www.art-in-berlin.de.

Berliner Gazette. www.berlinergazette.de.

Berliner Salon. www.berlinerzimmer.de.

Cultural institutions. Freundeskreise. www.freundeskreise-berliner-kultur.de.

Cultural network. www.kultur-netz.de/berlin.

Culture server. www.kulturserver-berlin.de.

Film and cinema. Jump Cut Magazine. www.jump-cut.de.

Literature. Satt.org. www.satt.org.

Literature and art. www.perlentaucher.de.

16. Society

Interfriesischer Rat (Interfrisian Council). Partly also in English. Bredstedt. www.interfriesischerrat.de.

Krankenkassen.de. Information (in German) on health-care funds and their function. Berlin: Euro-Informationen (GbR). www.krankenkassen.de.

Mediendienst Integration. Information (in German) on migration, integration, and asylum in Germany. Berlin. www.mediendienst-integration.de.

Minderheitensekretariat. Information (in German) on officially recognized minorities in Germany. Berlin: Bundesministerium des Innern. www.minderheitensekretariat.de.

Mut gegen Gewalt. Campaigning organization that also documents acts of right-wing extremism. Berlin: Amadeu Antonio Stiftung. www.mut-gegen-rechte-gewalt.de.

Nordfriisk Instituut (North Frisian Institute). Partly also in English. Bredstedt. www.nordfriiskinstituut.de.

Rat für Migration. A council of academics and researchers aiming to provide a solid information basis for political dialogue on migration issues. www.rat-fuer-migration.de. Also operates a media service at www.mediendienst-integration.de.

Rentenversicherung.de. Portal (also in English) on pension provision. Berlin: Deutsche Rentenversicherung Bund. www.deutsche-rentenversicherung.de.

Sozialpolitik-aktuell.de. Reports, documentation, analysis, and data on Germany's social security system (in German). Maintained by Prof. Gerhard Bäcker of the University of Duisburg-Essen. www.sozialpolitik-aktuell.de.

Stiftung für das sorbische Volk. In German. Bauzen. http://stiftung.sorben.com.

Verein für soziales Leben. Online guide to welfare benefits (in German). Lüdinghausen. www.sozialhilfe24.de.

Wollheim Memorial. Named after the concentration camp survivor Norbert Wollheim, the site provides information and documentation (in German and English) on Nazi forced labor policies and the campaign for compensation. Frankurt/Main: Wollheim Commission of the Goethe University and the Fritz Bauer Institute. www.wollheim-memorial.de.

Zentralmoschee Köln (Cental Mosque Cologne). In German. www.zentralmoschee-koeln.de.

Zentralrat Deutscher Sinti und Roma. In German. Heidelberg. http://zentralrat.sintiundroma.de.

Zentrum gegen Vertreibungen (Centre against Expulsions). Also in English. Troisdorf: www.zentrum-gegen-vertreibungen.de.

17. Religion and Churches

Deutsche Islam Konferenz (DIK). Also in German. Nuremberg: Bundesamt für Migration und Flüchtlinge (BAMF). www.deutsche-islam-konferenz.de.

Evangelical Church in Germany. Hanover. www.ekd.de/english/.

Islam.de. Information (in German) on Islam, produced in conjunction with the Zentralrat der Muslime in Deutschland, Cologne. www.islam.de. See also www.zentralrat.de.

Katholische Kirche in Deutschland. Official information portal of the Roman Catholic Church in Germany (in German). Bonn. www.katholisch.de.

The Hierarchy of the Catholic Church: Current and Historical Information about Its Bishops and Dioceses. Independent, unofficial site in English maintained by David M. Cheney. Follow country link to Germany. www.catholic-hierarchy.org.

Religionswissenschaftlicher Medien- und Informantionsdienst, REMID (Religious Studies Media and Information Service). Marburg. www.remid.de.

a) *Jewish* *and* *Related* *Organizations* Antisemitism. www.antisemitismus.de.

Central Archives for Research on the History of Jews in Germany. www.uni-heidelberg.de/institute/sonst/aj/.

Central Council of Jews in Germany. www.zentralratjuden.de.

haGalil. www.hagalil.de.

Salomon Ludwig Steinheim-Institut. www.steinheim-institut.de.

Zentrum für Antisemitismusforschung. German-language site (center for research into anti-Semitism maintained by Technische Universität Berlin). www.tu-berlin.de/fakultaet_i/zentrum_fuer_antisemitismusforschung.

About the Authors

Dr. Derek Lewis lectured at the University of Dundee (Scotland) and the University of Exeter (England). As senior lecturer in German and director of the Foreign Language Centre at the University of Exeter until July 2005, he was engaged in providing campus-wide language services to the university and business and was responsible for postgraduate studies in applied translation. But his interests reach much further than language, with an emphasis on what is known as country studies, and some of his lecturing and writing is devoted to explaining to his students and the broader public current trends in Germany. His publications include *The New Germany: The Social, Economic and Cultural Challenge of Unification* (1995) and *Contemporary Germany. A Handbook* (2001). For many years, he was also a visiting lecturer at the University of Würzburg, and he has published in the area of linguistic studies, machine-aided translation, and historical lexicography.

Key material in this book on cultural aspects of Germany was written by his colleague, Professor Ulrike Zitzlsperger, who is a lecturer at the University of Exeter and has published widely on cultural topics, such as the role of coffeehouses, train stations, and hotels in literature, and on Berlin in the 19th and 20th centuries. She is part of a collaborative project on department stores as focal points of cultural and critical engagement with modernity and consumer culture.